Birds of Peru

MUSEO DE HISTORIA NATURAL
UNIVERSIDAD NACIONAL
MAYOR DE SAN MARCOS

The Field Museum

LOUISIANA STATE UNIVERSITY
MUSEUM OF NATURAL HISTORY

Princeton Field Guides

For additional titles in this series, visit *www.birds.princeton.edu*

Birds of Peru

Thomas S. Schulenberg, Douglas F. Stotz,
Daniel F. Lane, John P. O'Neill,
and Theodore A. Parker III

Foreword by Dr. Antonio Brack Egg

Principal Illustrators
Dale Dyer, Daniel F. Lane, Lawrence B. McQueen,
John P. O'Neill, and N. John Schmitt

Additional Color Plates by
David Beadle, F. P. Bennett, Peter S. Burke,
Hilary Burn, Diane Pierce, H. Douglas Pratt,
Barry Van Dusen, and Sophie Webb

Princeton University Press
Princeton and Oxford

Library of Congress Cataloging-in-Publication Data
Birds of Peru/Thomas S. Schulenberg ... [et al.] ; principal illustrations, Dale Dyer ... [et al.].
    p. cm.—(Princeton field guides)
  Includes bibliographical references and index.
  ISBN-13: 978-0-691-04915-1 (cloth : alk. paper)
    1. Birds—Peru—Identification. I. Schulenberg, Thomas S.
QL689.P5B57 2007
598.0985—dc22   2006052700

British Library Cataloging-in-Publication Data is available

This book has been composed in Goudy and Futura

Introduction illustration credits
Introduction maps (Figures 1–4 and 6): Sergio Rabiela and Jonathan Markel
Line drawings (Figures 5A, 5B, bird topography): Daniel F. Lane

Printed on acid-free paper.

nathist.press.princeton.edu

Designed by D & N Publishing, Hungerford, Berkshire, UK

Printed in Italy by EuroGrafica

10 9 8 7 6 5 4 3 2 1

CONTENTS

FOREWORD

After an arduous effort of 45 years of study, *Birds of Peru* is being published. This book had its beginnings in fieldwork initiated by John P. O'Neill in 1961, during which time he and his colleagues conducted ornithological explorations and collected bird specimens in some of the remotest parts of Peru. When O'Neill began his work in Peru there were only 1,542 species known from the country; today, the number exceeds 1,800.

I first met John O'Neill in 1974 when I held the post of subdirector of Fauna Silvestre in the Ministry of Agriculture. Many times we talked about unexplored areas and where it might be possible to find new species of birds. Each of the technical reports on his fieldwork that came to me with information on newly discovered species evoked a special emotion. Through the years, I have been able to record the advancement of investigations benefiting the knowledge of the diversity of Peru's avifauna, one of the richest of any country on the planet.

O'Neill, together with his colleagues at the Louisiana State University Museum of Natural Science, as well as colleagues and students from the Museo de Historia Natural de San Marcos in Lima, directed decades of exploration to the Cordillera del Cóndor, Huancabamba and Cerro Chinguela, Yanachaga-Chemillén National Park, Cordillera Azul National Park, Quillabamba, Ampay, Río Yavarí, Río Napo, Paracas, Tumbes dry forests, Pampas del Heath, and many other areas of Peru to learn about and understand the avifauna and to collect data firsthand on the species inhabiting these areas.

This volume, with more than 300 color plates showing all of the species of birds known from Peru through 2004, presents descriptions, distribution maps, and information on the vocalizations of almost all species. Nevertheless, this extremely important work is not the end of exploration and investigation on the birds of Peru, because there still exist many unexplored and unknown areas in a country that is complex and full of surprises.

This volume is a collaborative product combining the efforts of John P. O'Neill, Thomas S. Schulenberg, Douglas F. Stotz, Daniel F. Lane, Larry B. McQueen, and the late Theodore A. Parker III. The detailed color plates are the work of various artists, and in them one sees the artistic influence of John O'Neill, who provided the basis for many directly from his fieldwork.

Birds of Peru is one of the best bird books that has been published for any region of the world and is an invaluable contribution to avian conservation (especially of rare and endemic species), to ecotourism, to bird tourism, and to the pleasure of those who appreciate observing these marvelous feathered creatures. It will be an inspiration for dozens of Peruvian ornithologists who are participating in the conservation of biodiversity and in the development of new directions for ecotourism in Peru. The authors, and especially John O'Neill, deserve the recognition of all Peruvians for putting such a valuable volume into our hands.

Antonio Brack Egg
Member, Board of Directors, National Council of the Environment
Member, National Council of Education
Vice President, Peruvian Amazon Institute of Research
Lima

PREFACE

Conceptually this book originated in 1974. At that time John O'Neill was a seasoned veteran with over a decade of experience in ornithological research and exploration in Peru. Ted Parker was a greenhorn, an undergraduate invited by O'Neill to participate on a months-long expedition to Peru. Although this was Ted's first visit to South America, he arrived prepared, having already committed to memory the distribution and characters of most of the birds of the continent. Before that expedition was over, O'Neill and Parker were planning a collaboration to produce a book on the birds of Peru.

This book on the birds of Peru passed from idle chatter round a campfire to something approaching reality by 1981, when Larry McQueen initiated the artwork and Ted began writing species accounts. Work proceeded in stops and starts until Ted's tragic and untimely death in a plane accident in 1993 in Ecuador.

Ted was an extraordinary field biologist, gifted with remarkable talents of observation, memory, and synthesis. He quickly established himself as one of the premier ornithologists working in South America. Ted also had boundless enthusiasm for his work, coupled with great personal charisma. Directly or indirectly, he influenced several generations of ornithologists working in Peru, including all of the coauthors of this guide.

This book we now offer up is our updated version of the book that John and Ted first conceived so long ago, and one that incorporates many of Ted's original contributions. We trust that Ted would be satisfied with our efforts, but we know that he also would take great pleasure in catching our mistakes.

We learned more than we ever would have imagined about the birds of Peru during the past few years of work. We hope that this field guide will be equally informative and useful for those who use it, and that it serves to educate Peruvians and visitors alike about the spectacular diversity of Peru's birds, supports the efforts of Peruvian and international ornithologists and birders, and serves as a tool for the conservation of Peru's natural resources.

ACKNOWLEDGMENTS

Authors' Acknowledgments

During many years of fieldwork, research, writing, and illustrating, we have received an extraordinary amount of assistance from countless friends and colleagues.

Avecita Chicchón (John D. and Catherine T. MacArthur Foundation) kept this project alive during an early critical phase; we are extremely grateful for her timely support. We also owe deep gratitude for the generous support of the Gordon and Betty Moore Foundation, which saw this project through to the end. Other financial support for the artwork, for the writing, or for the facilitation of our fieldwork in Peru came from Dick and Danie Barrow, John Barton, Kay Benedict,* John P. Ver Bockel, Kathleen E. Carbonara, Winnie Carter,* Jane Church, Taylor Clark, George* and Jane Clayton, Mr. and Mrs. Paul F. Cruikshank, Robert B. Debellevue, David M. Demaree,* Salome "Bix" Demaree, Paul Dickson, Victor Emanuel, Mrs. Joseph N. Field,* Dielle Fleischman, Ann Forster, the Marshall B. Front Family Charitable Foundation, Anne Gaylord, Anne Geier, Fred* and Esther* Goldman, James and Ruth* Kessler (who gave the first, important donation for the artwork), George P. Mitchell, Barbara Moulton,* Lawrence O'Meallie, Kate* and Haylett* O'Neill, George Perbix, Mr. and Mrs. Frank A. Reichelderfer, Steve and Ruth Russell, H. Irving and Pete Schweppe, Laura R. Schweppe,* Sally and Kenyon Stebbins, Jesse A. Stewart, Edward Thayer,* and donors who wish to remain anonymous.

Manuel Plenge provided unstinting support and advice for decades. His detailed and extensive knowledge of the literature on Peruvian ornithology provided the backbone of our field guide; our project would have taken much longer, and been much less successful, were we not able, time and time again, to turn to Manuel for advice and information.

Museums have been an essential part of this work, which would not have been possible without the collections housed by natural history museums. This project began in the Museum of Natural Science, Louisiana State University. Staff at the museum, especially J. V. Remsen, Jr., and Steven W. Cardiff, were extremely generous with access to the collection (both for artists and for authors) and tolerated a seemingly never ending stream of questions about the specimens under their care.

Similarly, The Field Museum provided invaluable support during the writing of this book. We are grateful to John Bates and Shannon Hackett (Division of Birds, Department of Zoology) for office space and access to the collection, and to Dave Willard and Mary Hennen for their help with specimen loans and other assistance. Also at The Field Museum, Debby Moskovits and Corine Vriesendorp (Environmental and Conservation Programs) supervised this project and guided it to completion; we never would have been able to finish this book without their support and encouragement.

In Lima, the Museo de Historia Natural de la Universidad Nacional Mayor de San Marcos provided a "home away from home" for us all and has been a collaborating partner since the beginning of our work in Peru in 1961. We are deeply grateful to the scientific staff of the museum, particularly María Koepcke,* Hernando de Macedo R., and Irma Franke J., for their support during this time. We are very appreciative of the many courtesies extended by Dra. Franke in particular during the recent years we have labored to complete this guide.

We are grateful to the following additional natural history museums for information on Peruvian collections. We would like to express our deepest gratitude to Leo Joseph and Nate Rice (Academy of Natural Sciences, Philadelphia); Sievert Rohwer and Rob Faucett (Burke Museum, University of Washington); Paul Sweet and Thomas Trombone (American Museum of Natural History); Robert Prŷs-Jones and Michael Walters ([British] Natural History Museum); Douglas J. Long (California Academy of Sciences); Bradley Livezey and Robin Panza (Carnegie Museum of Natural History); Kevin McGowan and Charles Dardia (Cornell University Museum of Vertebrates); Gene Hess (Delaware Museum of Natural History); Andrew Kratter (Florida Museum of Natural History, University of Florida); Tony Parker (Liverpool Museum); Mauricio Ugarte-Lewis (Museo de Historia Natural de la Universidad Nacional de San Agustín de Arequipa); Constantino Aucca (Museo de la Universidad Nacional San Antonio Abad del Cusco); Tomasz D. Mazgajski (Museum and Institute of Zoology, Polish Academy of Sciences); Eric Pasquet (Muséum National d'Histoire Naturelle); Douglas Causey and Jeremiah Trimble (Museum of Comparative Zoology, Harvard University); Carla Cicero and Ned Johnson* (Museum of Vertebrate Zoology, University of California, Berkeley); Kimball Garrett and Christina Couroux (Natural History Museum of Los Angeles County); Janet Hinshaw and Tom Dietsch (University of Michigan Museum of Zoology); Gary Graves and Craig Ludwig (United States National Museum of Natural History); Town Peterson and Mark Robbins (University of Kansas Natural History Museum); Per Ericson (Swedish Museum of Natural

---

* deceased

History); Jon Barlow and Brad Millen (Royal Ontario Museum); René Corado (Western Foundation of Vertebrate Zoology); Kristof Zyskowski (Yale Peabody Museum); Armando Valdés-Velásquez and Bernd Freymann (Zoologisches Forschungsinstitut und Museum Alexander Koenig); and Jon Fjeldså and Niels Krabbe (Zoology Museum, University of Copenhagen).

We also are grateful to Jeremy Flanagan and Rob Williams for sharing information on the Markl collection at the Naturhistorisches Museum, Basel. Todd Mark compiled the data on the material at the Muséum National d'Histoire Naturelle (Paris), a remarkable task for which we long will be in debt. R. Haven Wiley supplied much supplemental information on the Olalla collections at the American Museum of Natural History. Shannon Kenney supplied very useful digital photographs of specimens of some of the rarer species in the American Museum of Natural History. In addition, we thank the many people who checked specimens on our behalf at natural history collections far and wide: Todd Mark, José "Pepe" Tello, Paul Sweet, Peter Capainolo, Sara Bertelli, and Ana Luz Porzecanski (American Museum of Natural History); Robert Prŷs-Jones, Michael Walters, Paul Salaman, Pamela Rasmussen, and Dan Davison ([British] Natural History Museum); and Miguel Lentino and Robin Restall (Colección Ornitológica Phelps). We thank Micha Skakuj and Jan Lontkowksi for their assistance in putting us in contact with the staff at the Museum and Institute of Zoology, Polish Academy of Sciences.

We were fortunate that several seabird enthusiasts shared their expertise with us. Lisa Ballance and Robert Pitman (National Marine Fisheries Service) generously shared their seabird observations off the coast of Peru. Noam Shany provided a great deal of additional information on seabirds. Luke Cole and Larry Spear* supplied useful literature on seabird distribution.

We are grateful for the indispensable technical support from The Field Museum. Pete Cruikshank labored for years, entirely as a volunteer, to help develop the database of Peruvian bird records that underlies all of our distribution maps; there is no way that we can thank him properly for this monumental effort. Ryan Peters, Sergio Rabiela, and Peter Lowther provided technical advice on digitizing images and kept our (sometimes temperamental) computers in good working order. Many others at The Field Museum, too numerous to mention, helped in a myriad of ways; we are grateful to them all. Two additional Field Museum volunteers played vital roles: Helga Karsten helped us organize our growing collection of Peru plate digital images, and Leslie Majors translated much of the early literature on Peruvian ornithology from French to English. Marga and Charles Lane also helped with a German to English translation. Brian O'Shea and Michi Schulenberg compiled much useful data from museum specimen labels. Robin B. Foster provided helpful comments on our discussion of the topography and habitats of Peru.

We used a digital version of an ornithological gazetteer of Peru, based on Stephens and Traylor (1983), to georeference Peruvian localities. The gazetteer was compiled by Lorna Anderberg and was given to us by Mort and Phyllis Isler. Mary LeCroy (American Museum of Natural History) provided important documents that helped us to pinpoint some historical AMNH localities in Peru.

Josh Engel prepared our initial map of Peru and also initiated the long process of georeferencing our distribution database. Patty Ruback and Sean Bober extended the mapping process. Final editions of all raw species distribution maps were prepared by Laura Rico and converted to field guide format by Sergio Rabiela.

There is a long list of birders and field ornithologists who shared their field observations, made comments on our maps or text, or patiently answered our many questions. Inadvertently we may have overlooked some who provided important information, and we apologize to anyone whose name we have forgotten. Barry Walker has been an invaluable source of information on all aspects of the birds of Peru, drawing on his many years of birding and exploration throughout Peru. Terry Chesser was on the receiving end of a great many questions regarding austral migration in Peru; we appreciate his insight and patience. José "Pepe" Alvarez Alonso provided a wealth of information on bird distribution in Loreto. Paul Donahue shared freely from his decades of observation and experiences. Others who supplied important observations, comments, or reviews are Roger Ahlman, Christian Albujar, Peter Alden, Michael Andersen, Fernando Angulo Pratolongo, César Arana, Jim Armacost, Thomas Arndt, John Arvin, Constantino Aucca, Liliana Ayala, Katya Balta, Juan Mazar Barnett, Alfredo Begazo, Oscar Beingolea, Don Brightsmith, Dan Brooks, Colin Bushell, Clive Byers, Angelo Capparella, Juan Chalco, Zac Cheviron, Jim Clements,* Paul Coopmans,* Daniel Cristian, Tristan Davis, Alvaro del Campo, Rob Dover, Karen Eckhardt, Gunnar Engblom, Craig Farquhar, Rob Faucett, Mirko Fernandez, Judith Figueroa, Jon Fjeldså, Jeremy Flanagan, Michael Force, Ignacio García-Godos, Nathaniel Gerhart, Michael Gochfeld, Oscar González, Devon Graham, James Graham, Paul Greenfield, Ben Haase, Jürgen Haffer, Wim tem Have, Bennett Hennessey, Sebastian Herzog, Steve Hilty, Christoph Hinkelmann, Peter Hocking, Tor Egil Høgsås, Peter Hosner, Mort Isler, Phyllis Isler, Jaime Jahncke, Ottavio Janni, Alvaro Jaramillo, Leo Joseph, Barb Knapton, Guillermo Knell, Niels Krabbe, Andy Kratter, Frank Lambert, Dan Lebbin, Huw Lloyd, Lawrence Lopez, Tom Love, Ernesto Málaga, Curtis Marantz, Todd Mark, Jean Mattos, Sjoerd Mayer, Carlos Mendoza, Matthew Miller, Tim Moermond, Bertram Murray, Jonas Nilsson, Eduardo Nycander, Pat O'Donnell, Enrique Ortiz, Rosana Paredes Vela, Mark

ACKNOWLEDGMENTS

Pearman, Dave Pearson, Tatiana Pequeño, Mikko Pyhälä, Van Remsen, David Ricalde, Bob Ridgely, Mark Robbins, Don Roberson, Scott Robinson, José-Ignacio "Pepe" Rojas, Gary Rosenberg, Ken Rosenberg, John Rowlett, Rose Ann Rowlett, Edwin Salazar, Letty Salinas, Fabrice Schmitt, Derek Scott, Nathan Senner, Grace Servat, Noam Shany, José Maria Cardoso da Silva, Barbara Sleeper, Mark Sokol, John Sterling, Dan Tallman, John Terborgh, Joe Tobias, Mauricio Ugarte-Lewis, Joaquín Ugarte-Núñez, Armando Valdés-Velásquez, Thomas Valqui, Paul Van Gasse, Willem-Pier Vellinga, Richard Webster, Doug Wechsler, André Weller, John Weske, Rob Westerduijn, Clayton White, Bret Whitney, Andy Whittaker, Bud Widdowson, Margaret Widdowson, Rob Williams, Chris Witt, Ramiro Yabar, Virgilio Yabar, Carlos Zavalaga, Renzo Zeppilli, and Kevin Zimmer.

The voice descriptions in our species accounts were taken, in the vast majority of cases, from field recordings, not paraphrased from other publications; these include our own recordings, those published on various compact disks and cassettes (see Vocal References), and field recordings sent to us by other parties. Many of our original field recordings (and all of those by Parker) are archived at the Macaulay Library, Cornell Laboratory of Ornithology. We are very grateful to the staff there, especially Greg Budney, Robert Grotke, Jim Gulledge,* and Andrea Priori, for welcoming us during our many visits to the lab, for their long-term support of our sound recording activities in Peru, and for allowing us access to their sound collections. Many thanks to the many additional recordists who generously allowed us access to their unpublished field recordings: José Alvarez A., John Arvin, Alfredo Begazo, Benjamin Clock, Mario Cohn-Haft, Paul Coopmans,* Paul Donahue, Gunnar Engblom, A. Bennett Hennessey, Mort Isler, Phyllis Isler, Niels Krabbe, Huw Lloyd, Todd Mark, Sjoerd Mayer, Jonas Nilsson, Thomas Valqui, Barry Walker, Bret Whitney, and Kevin Zimmer (see Vocal Credits). Sjoerd Mayer was particularly helpful in allowing us the use of an unpublished, updated version of his Bolivia, Peru, and Paraguay DVD-ROM of bird sounds. We also thank Phyllis and Mort Isler for allowing us access to their sound collections. Bret Whitney, Mort Isler, and Phyllis Isler provided helpful comments on the voice descriptions.

This book has been shaped by our research experiences in Peru, conducted by generous permission of the Instituto Nacional de Recursos Naturales (INRENA), and by its predecessor, the Dirección General Forestal y de Fauna of the Ministerio de Agricultura. We are grateful to all of the staff from these ministries who supported our work, including Rosario Acero V., Luís Alfaro L., César Álvarez F., Antonio Brack E., Richard Bustamante M., Eric Cardich B., Marc Dourojeanni R., Susan Moller H., Antonio Morizaki T., Armando Pimentel B., Carlos Ponce del Prado, Matías Prieto C., José Purisaca P., Victor Pulido C., Marco Romero, and Gustavo Suárez de Freitas.

Much of our work in Peru over the past 40 years took place under the auspices of the Museum of Natural Science at Louisiana State University, with the generous support of John S. McIlhenny,* Babette M. Odom,* Robert B. Wallace,* and the National Geographic Society. We also benefited over the years from the support of our work from the directors of the LSU museum: J. Michael Fitzsimons, Mark S. Hafner, George H. Lowery, Jr.,* J. V. Remsen, Douglas A. Rossman, and Fred S. Sheldon. The museum continues to function only through the hard work of the support staff, including Mary M. Burnett,* Alice J. Fogg, Jynx Hunter,* Gwen Mahon, Peggy Sims, and Musette M. Richard*. O'Neill also is grateful to George M. Sutton* for initially suggesting what became a decades-long association with LSU, and to Kenneth M. Kensinger, who introduced him to the Cashinahua people and the village of Balta on the Río Curanja. In Peru, field expeditions were successful in large part due to our many field assistants, especially Reyes Rivera A., Manuel Villar, Manuel Sánchez, Marta Chávez de Sánchez, and Abraham Urbay T.; and to our many field companions, especially those who were fellow students or the students and colleagues from the museum in Lima. We also greatly appreciate the assistance from our many friends in Lima, especially Margarita and Alfred Campbell; the Koenig family (Arturo, Helen, Larry, Richard, Kathy, and Caroline); Ruth* and Germán* Larrabure; the Plenge family (Manuel, Isabel, John, and Eddie); José "Pepe" and Goya Parodi; and Gustavo del Solar R. Beatrice Berger of Panorama Viajes/Turismo and her office colleagues extended us many courtesies and provided valuable assistance with logistics. We also benefited from work based at The Field Museum's Departments of Zoology and of Environmental and Conservation Programs, and at Conservation International. Additional experiences in Peru were provided through birding tours that we led, especially under the auspices of the Massachusetts Audubon Society, Cincinnati Nature Center, Victor Emanuel Nature Tours, Bird Bonanzas, and Wings.

We are most grateful to Max Günther (Explorer's Inn), Peter Jenson (Explorama lodges), José Koechlin von Stein (Cuzco Amazonico Lodge, Machu Picchu Pueblo Inn), and Eduardo Nycander and Kurt Holle of Rainforest Expeditions (Tambopata Research Center) for the access that they provided to us, sometimes for extended periods, for the study of Peruvian birds at their tourist lodges, and for their promotion of ecotourism in Peru.

Additional interest in O'Neill's field programs and encouragement for our research came from Brent and Eloise Ann Berlin, James Boster, Antonio and Cecilia Brack, Kenneth M. Kensinger, José and Denise Koechlin von Stein, Hans-Wilhelm Koepcke,* Juliane Koepcke Diller, Maria Koepcke,* Mikko and Pia Pyhälä, Peter Raven (Missouri Botanical Garden), and John W. Terborgh; and from O'Neill's many friends at the Instituto Lingüístico de Verano, but especially Jeanne Grover and Mildred Larson.

We also are indebted to everyone at Princeton University Press, who have been helpful, encouraging, and patient, during the long development of this book. Sam Elworthy and Robert Kirk committed themselves to this guide, without really knowing what they were getting into. Ellen Foos ably managed the final production process. Dimitri Karetnikov brought great skill and attention to detail to all aspects of every map, figure, and illustration. Anita O'Brien, our copy editor, brought order and stylistic consistency to our text. The challenge of designing the final product was taken on with great skill by David and Namrita Price-Goodfellow of D & N Publishing.

Finally, we are grateful to our wives and families for tolerating our long absences while in the field: Michi, Sarah, and Sam (Schulenberg); Francie (Stotz); Leticia A. Alamía (O'Neill); and Elga (McQueen). They also learned to live with far too many working weekends, and to tiptoe around us when we continued working at home late into the evening.

Artists' Acknowledgments

Photographs, especially of poorly known species, were essential in helping us to understand the details of shape and color of unfamiliar birds. We gratefully acknowledge photographs loaned by Peter Alden, José Alvarez A., Bob Behrstock, Oscar Beingolea, William Belton, Daniel Brooks, Shallin Busch, Steven W. Cardiff, Terry Chesser, William S. Clark, Benjamin Clock, Mario Cohn-Hoft, Tristan Davis, Paul Donahue, Thomas Donegan, Victor Emanuel, Gunnar Engblom, Anne Faust, Jake Faust, John W. Fitzpatrick, Kimball Garrett, John Gerwin, Ben Haase, Jon Hornbuckle, Steve Howell, Mort Isler, Phyllis Isler, Shannon Kenney (American Museum of Natural History), Niels Krabbe, Dan Lane, Huw Lloyd, Susan Lohr, Rosemary Low, Ross MacLeod, Curtis Marantz, Manuel Marín, Todd Mark, Sjoerd Mayer, Larry McQueen, Allan Mee, George Nixon, John O'Neill, José Antonio Otero, Ted Parker,* Ian Powell, Martin Reid, Van Remsen, Robin Restall, Bob Ridgely, Mark Robbins, Clemencia Rodner, Gary Rosenberg, Ken Rosenberg, Tom Schulenberg, Nigel Simpson, John Sterling, Doug Stotz, Guy Tudor, Thomas Valqui H., John Wall, Doug Wechsler (VIREO, Academy of Natural Sciences of Philadelphia), Mark Whiffin, Bret Whitney, Bud Widdowson, Kevin Zimmer, Dale Zimmerman, and Kristof Zyskowski.

We are grateful to Robert Kirk, David Beadle, and Peter Burke for permission to use some of the illustrations from Alvaro Jaramillo's *Birds of Chile* (Princeton University Press).

The illustrations for our guide could not have been completed without access to museum specimens. We are exceedingly grateful to the natural history museums that loaned material to the artists, and to relevant curators and staff who approved and processed these loans. The bulk of these specimens came from the Museum of Natural Science, Louisiana State University (Van Remsen, Steven W. Cardiff, and Donna L. Dittmann), supplemented by The Field Museum (Shannon J. Hackett, John Bates, David L. Willard, Mary Hennen, Melvin A. Traylor, Jr., and Emmet R. Blake*). We also borrowed material from the American Museum of Natural History (François Vuilleumier, George Barrowclough, Joel Cracraft, Mary LeCroy, Paul Sweet, Peter Capainolo, and Christine Blake), the Academy of Natural Sciences of Philadelphia (Leo Joseph, Nate Rice), and the Museo de Historia Natural in Lima (Irma Franke). Peter Burke primarily used specimens from the Royal Ontario Museum (Mark Peck, Glen Murphy); Hilary Burn relied on material at the (British) Museum of Natural History (Robert Prŷs-Jones, Mark Adams); and John Schmitt is indebted to the Western Foundation of Vertebrate Zoology (Linnea S. Hall, René Corado). We again thank these institutions and their staffs.

John O'Neill critiqued all of the plates by the other artists, and in later stages of the project Dan Lane also provided many helpful reviews. William S. Clark provided helpful reviews of the raptor plates. Not only did Larry McQueen provide the largest number of illustrations for the book, but he also was a careful and diligent reviewer of almost all of the rest of the illustrations. We all owe a large debt to Larry for his careful and helpful comments.

INTRODUCTION

Peru is one of the richest countries in the world for birds, with 1,800 species. This book is a guide to the field identification of all birds recorded in Peru and in offshore waters within 200 nautical miles of the Peruvian coast.

A field guide can take many forms. We have endeavored to "stick to the basics" and include only information directly relevant to identification. Our intention was to produce a guide that was complete and accurate, yet sufficiently small and portable to be carried close at hand during long days afield. Consequently we have had to jettison, often with great reluctance, much additional information on the distribution and natural history of each species. Additional material on the birds of Peru that did not fit within the covers of this field guide will be incorporated into future publications.

This book includes all species reported from Peru through May 2004, based on specimens in natural history museums, literature records, and unpublished sight records, tape recordings, and photographs. We exclude a few species, often attributed in the literature to Peru, for which we have been unable to confirm a valid record for the country. We have been relatively generous in including species reported from Peru only from sight records, including some species on the basis of records that have not been published previously. We encourage anyone who observes a species not previously known from Peru, or known from Peru only on the basis of sight records, to document such records as thoroughly as possible with specimens (with Peruvian governmental authorization), or with photographs, tape recordings, and field sketches and notes, and to publish these records and the supporting evidence.

The classification and nomenclature of birds is under constant review. This affects how many species to recognize for Peru (in other words, whether to "split" or to "lump" geographic varieties into more or fewer species, respectively), the families to which various genera belong, and the sequence of families. We largely follow the classification and nomenclature of the South American Classification Committee (SACC) of the American Ornithologists' Union (http://www.museum.lsu.edu/~Remsen/SACCBaseline.html).

HOW TO USE THIS BOOK

For each species, we present color figures, species accounts, and with few exceptions a distribution map. We include brief introductions to many (but not all) families, and to some genera or species groups. We use these short accounts to introduce species-rich families, or to summarize information that is similar across a group of related species. It often may be helpful to peruse this material, when present, as an aid to field identification.

Species Accounts

Each species account begins with English and scientific names of the species. A name is enclosed in brackets ([ ]) if the species is known in Peru only from sight records, tape recordings, or photographs, but not from a specimen from Peru.

LENGTH The length of each species is given in centimeters and in inches. These measurements, representing the length from the tip of the bill to the tip of the tail, are taken from museum specimens and therefore are only an approximation of the size of a live bird. Nonetheless, they provide a useful index to the size of each species and are useful especially for comparing species that are similar in appearance but differ in size. Note that the length will be influenced both by bill length and by tail length; two species can be of similar length but differ in mass (for example, if much of the length measurement of one species is taken up by lightweight feathers from a particularly long tail). For some species we provide additional measurements, such as wingspan (ws) estimates of species more frequently observed in flight (seabirds, raptors) or bill length in hummingbirds.

GEOGRAPHIC VARIATION An asterisk (*) identifies polytypic species, that is, species with recognized geographic variation (two or more subspecies, across the entire distribution of the species). We do not discuss geographic variation in any detail in this guide, except for instances when subspecies are sufficiently different in appearance or in voice that they might be recognizable in the field.

SPECIES ACCOUNT The bulk of each species account is taken up with notes on the relative abundance, habitat, elevational range, and behavior of each species, and with a description of its voice. Unless noted otherwise, all of our comments refer specifically to that species in Peru. Due to the constraints of the plate-facing format, the text often is terse. We employ a small number of abbreviations:

ca.   for "approximately"
cf.   for "compare to"
sec   for "seconds"
ws   for "wingspan"

We also abbreviate the names of months. For some species, especially those with distinctive plumages, we say little or nothing about the bird's appearance. In other cases, we comment on particular features ("field marks") that may be important for identification. We may call attention to similar species, with notes on how these differ or a suggestion to read the account of that species. We usually do not repeat distinguishing characters; these will be discussed under one species or the other, but not under both.

A familiarity with standard ornithological terminology for the parts of a bird is helpful in understanding the species accounts. Please consult the diagrams in figure 5 and accompanying glossary of bird topography.

RELATIVE ABUNDANCE Relative abundance is a subjective assessment and can vary geographically, but we have tried to present an "average" assessment. Our assessments are based on our experiences with average encounter rates of free-flying birds, within the species-appropriate habitat, elevation, and range. Relative abundances of some species may differ, for a variety of factors, based on other methods of sampling (such as with mist-net capture rates). We use the following terms in ranking relative abundance:

Common: Encountered daily, or almost daily, in moderate numbers.
Fairly common: Encountered daily or nearly daily in small numbers.
Uncommon: Easily can be missed at a site, even during several days of observation, but should be encountered during longer stays of a week or more.
Rare: Residents that are present in such low numbers, or, in the case of migrants, present at such irregular intervals, that they can be missed even in a stay of multiple weeks.
Vagrant: Nonresident; has been recorded once or on only a few occasions beyond the "normal" range; might be expected to occur again, but not with regularity.

Statements such as "poorly known" or "rare and local" should be interpreted as referring specifically to the status in Peru. The species may be better known, or more common, elsewhere in its distribution.

HABITATS Habitat often is an important clue in bird identification. Most species are restricted to a particular habitat or a suite of similar habitats and are not expected to be encountered in other situations. We use relatively few specialized terms to describe habitats; these are described in the section Habitats of Peru.

BEHAVIOR Our notes on behavior are focused on field identification. We pay particular attention to the foraging level in the habitat (ground, understory, midstory, canopy), since such behavior often is "fixed" within a species (although some species may forage at one level but sing or nest at another). We may comment on foraging behavior, especially where differences in such behavior may help to distinguish between species of similar appearance.

ELEVATIONAL DISTRIBUTION Our notes on the elevational distribution of each species reflect both museum specimens and sight observations within Peru. Elevational distributions may vary locally, depending upon a variety of factors, and so occasional deviations may be encountered from the elevational data that we present. Generally, however, the elevational distribution of a species is an important aspect of its biology; learn to pay attention to elevation when in the field.

VOICE Many more birds are heard than are seen. Additionally, there are many instances of birds with similar appearance that are identified more easily by differences in their vocalizations. The way to learn bird vocalizations is through hearing them in the field, or through study of the increasing library of tropical bird song collections (on cassette tapes, compact disks, or DVDs). Our descriptions of the vocalizations of Peruvian birds are "the next best thing."

The vocal descriptions presented here, almost all of which were prepared by Lane, are intended to cover the most frequently heard vocalizations produced by each species. Voices are described using qualitative modifiers and,

13

when possible, phonetic descriptions (based on contemporary American English usage). In the phonetic descriptions, stressed syllables are written in capital letters (e.g., "*CHEW*"). Notes that are very stressed or abruptly given are followed by an exclamation point ("!"). Sounds that resemble a question in human speech are followed by a question mark ("?"). The relative length of pauses between notes or phrases is indicated as follows: notes that are produced with almost no discernable pause are run together (e.g., "*tututu*"); a very short pause is marked by an apostrophe (e.g., "*tu'tu'tu*"); short pauses are denoted with a hyphen (e.g., "*tu-tu-tu*"); moderate pauses are indicated with a space (e.g., "*tu tu tu* "); and the longest pauses are denoted by "…" The same punctuation ("…") also is used at the end of a phonetic description if the voice continues in a similar manner for an extended period. Usually we describe the song first, followed by the call; but we reverse this order in some cases, when calls are heard much more frequently or are more characteristic of the species. We use the terms "song" and "call" frequently, although there are many species for which it is difficult to label a particular vocalization as one or the other. Generally, we classify vocalizations that are produced in territorial defense, mate attraction, and pair bond maintenance as "songs." In some cases, the "song" of a bird is not vocal at all, but rather is produced mechanically: guans rattle wing quills during short predawn flights, for example, and woodpeckers drum on resonant substrates. Some species also combine mechanical sounds with vocal sounds in elaborate displays (especially among the cotingas and manakins, as well as other groups). "Calls," on the other hand, are a class of vocalizations containing sounds with many different functions, such as to maintain contact among members of a pair, family, or flock; to warn others of danger; to mob predators; and sometimes in territorial defense. Most species have a wide repertoire of calls, many of which are seldom used.

Some species typically sing in duets. Duets are of two types, antiphonal and asynchronous. An antiphonal duet is one in which the members of the pair produce their respective vocalization in a very orderly manner, many times one answering the other with perfect timing. Often the duetted song sounds like only one individual is singing (particularly with wood-quail and *Thryothorus* wrens). In contrast, in an asynchronous duet (such as are given by wood-rails, many furnariids, and a few other species) the members of a pair sing in a haphazard fashion, with their vocalizations overlapping in a manner seemingly without order.

Voices frequently vary, due to such factors as geographic variation, dialects, individual variation (differences between individuals present at any given site), repertoires (variation between the songs of any particular individual), age- and sex-related differences in song, and the emotional state of the individual bird. Generally, calls are less stereotyped than are songs; and the vocalizations of nonpasserines and of suboscines are more stereotyped than are those of oscines. We often describe discernable geographic variation, although much remains to be learned about variation in the vocalizations of the birds of Peru.

The majority of our vocal descriptions are taken directly from field recordings; only very rarely do we rely on a literature source for a vocal description. We have preferred to use recordings made in or near Peru; we provide brief locality data for recordings that were made outside of Peru and if these voices differ from those of Peruvian populations of that species. The majority of these descriptions are based on recordings by the authors, supplemented by published sound recordings (see Vocal References). Unpublished vocalizations from other recordists are credited in Vocal Credits.

REGIONAL DISTRIBUTION Each species account ends with a note as to whether that species is entirely restricted to Peru ("**ENDEMIC**") or is known from any of the countries that border Peru (**Co**, Colombia; **E**, Ecuador; **Br**, Brazil; **Bo**, Bolivia; and **Ch**, Chile).

Distribution Maps

We map the distribution of the majority of the species reported from Peru. Species whose distributions are not mapped include those reported only from far off the coast, vagrants known from only a few records, and some extremely local species. For widespread species we show all of Peru, including the 24 political departments (fig. 1) and the major rivers (see also fig. 2). Some species are restricted to only a small portion of Peru; when possible we use larger-scale regional maps to show these distributions in greater detail.

We use shading to connect areas within which we expect a species will be found, even if there are some apparent gaps in the distribution. The maps are color coded to reflect the seasonal status of each species in Peru (fig. 3). Because some species may contain populations that are both resident and migratory, this can lead to some complicated distribution maps. Although migration is an important part of the life history of many of Peru's birds, migration in Peru has not been well studied. Questions remain about the seasonality of some species. In some cases the seasonal pattern of occurrence for a species was unclear, and there is the possibility that some of our assessments may be shown to be incorrect, as Peru's avifauna becomes better known.

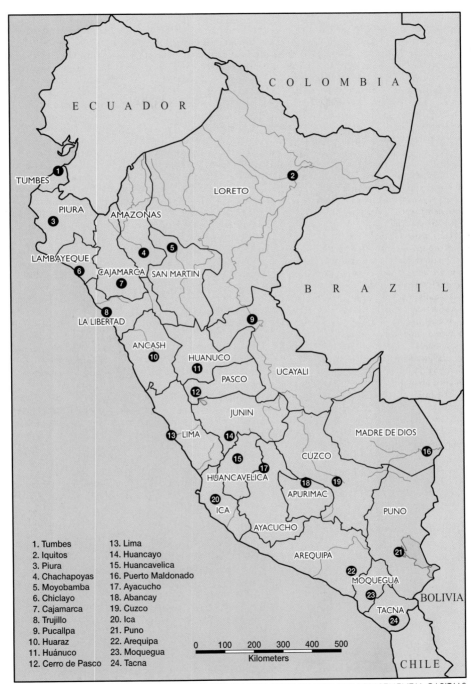

ECUADOR

COLOMBIA

TUMBES

LORETO

PIURA

AMAZONAS

LAMBAYEQUE

CAJAMARCA SAN MARTIN

BRAZIL

LA LIBERTAD

ANCASH

HUANUCO

PASCO UCAYALI

JUNIN

LIMA

MADRE DE DIOS

CUZCO

HUANCAVELICA

APURIMAC

ICA

PUNO

AYACUCHO

AREQUIPA

MOQUEGUA

BOLIVIA

TACNA

CHILE

1. Tumbes	13. Lima
2. Iquitos	14. Huancayo
3. Piura	15. Huancavelica
4. Chachapoyas	16. Puerto Maldonado
5. Moyobamba	17. Ayacucho
6. Chiclayo	18. Abancay
7. Cajamarca	19. Cuzco
8. Trujillo	20. Ica
9. Pucallpa	21. Puno
10. Huaraz	22. Arequipa
11. Huánuco	23. Moquegua
12. Cerro de Pasco	24. Tacna

0   100   200   300   400   500
Kilometers

FIG. 1. POLITICAL MAP OF PERU, SHOWING THE 24 DEPARTMENTS AND THE DEPARTMENTAL CAPITALS

15

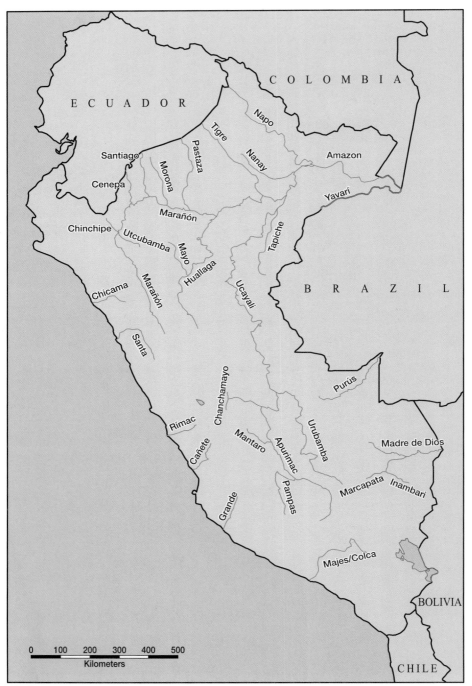

FIG. 2. MAJOR RIVERS OF PERU

The vast majority of birds in Peru are *permanent residents*, in part of or all of Peru. In such cases a species remains throughout the year in the same areas where it breeds (although there may be very local movements in the nonbreeding season). Areas where a species is resident are shown in *light blue*.

A handful of species are *breeding residents*. They breed in Peru but then depart, either leaving Peru completely (Gray-capped Cuckoo, Snowy-throated Kingbird) or vacating the breeding area and migrating to another part of Peru (White-crested Elaenia in part, Slaty Thrush, Black-and-white Tanager). The areas where these species are breeding-season residents are shown in *dark blue*. The movements away from the breeding grounds represent intratropical migrations, which are discussed below.

Austral migrants are species that breed in temperate latitudes in the Southern Hemisphere from December to February and migrate north during the austral winter. Most such species spend the entire austral winter in Peru, roughly March–October. Arrival and departure periods vary among species and are poorly documented for most species (especially among landbirds). A small number of species (such as Slaty Elaenia) migrate through Peru en route to wintering areas farther north and so are present only for a few weeks each year. There also are species that are known to occur in Peru as austral migrants, but we do not yet know whether they remain through the nonbreeding season or occur only during migration. Species that occur in Peru strictly as austral migrants are mapped in *red*. We also show in red areas of Peru that are occupied by an austral migrant population, although the same species may be resident elsewhere in the country (e.g., Swainson's Flycatcher, Bran-colored Flycatcher, Tropical Pewee).

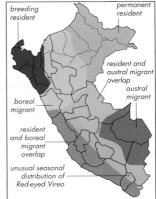

FIG. 3. KEY TO SEASONAL STATUS COLORS ON THE SPECIES DISTRIBUTION MAPS

In a few cases, such as Tropical Kingbird and Southern Rough-winged Swallow, a resident population is augmented by migrants from farther south. If these migrants are similar (or identical) to the resident population, then migrants can be impossible to recognize as such in the field (except during those rare occasions when a flock is seen clearly in the act of migrating). Therefore, since migrants usually cannot be distinguished from residents, we do not indicate on the map where these austral migrants occur.

We also count as austral migrants some seabirds that breed in southern South America or near Australia and New Zealand. Many of the austral breeding seabirds may occur in Peru year round, in part because many of the individuals that occur in Peru are nonbreeding immatures; however, numbers may noticeably increase during the austral winter.

Overlap of residents and austral migrants becomes more interesting in cases in which the resident and migrant populations belong to different subspecies and can be identified as such in the field. An example of this is White-winged Becard in southeastern Peru, where resident males are black and males of a migrant subspecies are largely gray, facilitating recognition in the field. *Areas of overlap* between identifiably different *resident and austral migrant* populations are mapped in *pink*.

Boreal or northern migrants are species that breed in North America and migrate to Peru during the nonbreeding season. Most boreal migrants are present September–April, although some may arrive earlier or depart later. The majority of species spend the entire northern winter in Peru, but a few (e.g., Swainson's Hawk) may occur primarily as passage migrants that winter farther south. Boreal migrants are mapped in *ochre*. Very rarely (Red-eyed Vireo) there is *seasonal overlap* between *resident and boreal migrant* populations that can be distinguished in the field; this overlap is mapped in *green*.

Finally, there is an unusual situation in one species (Red-eyed Vireo) where much of Peru is occupied by two different migratory populations: boreal migrants from North America and austral migrants from southern South America. So, although the species may be present year round, it does not breed in most of this region. This unusual seasonal pattern is mapped in *orange*.

Certain species engage in *intratropical migrations*. These may be movements east/west across the Andes (e.g., the *modesta* subspecies of White-crested Elaenia), elevational movements (e.g., Black-and-white Seedeater), migrations from one region of the tropics into another (e.g., the movements into Peru, from northeastern South America, of Lesson's Seedeater), or postbreeding dispersal by seabirds southward (e.g., Waved Albatross, Galapagos Petrel) or northward (e.g., Peruvian Booby, South American Tern) from breeding areas at tropical latitudes. We map most of these nonbreeding distributions with *red* (the same color as is used for austral migrants) because the basic timing of these movements resembles that of the austral migrants. The few seabirds (including some coastal gulls and terns) that visit Peru from breeding areas to the north are mapped as northern migrants (with *ochre*). These birds are typically in Peru mostly during the period September to April.

Plates

We endeavored to illustrate all plumages that can be identified in the field, including examples of recognizable geographic variation, seasonal plumages, sexual dimorphism, and various subadult plumages. Inevitably we fell just short of our goal, but nonetheless the vast majority of the plumages shown by birds in Peru are represented. Typically all figures on a given plate are to the same scale, although the scale may vary from one plate to the next. In some cases we employ supplemental figures, at smaller scales, to illustrate additional features (such as the appearance of the bird in flight). We assume that the smaller scale used for such images is evident as such.

Abbreviations used on the plates include:

ad.	adult	juv.	juvenile	s-c	south central
alt.	alternate	nonbr.	nonbreeding	se	southeast
Amaz.	Amazonia	n	north	subad.	subadult
br.	breeding	ne	northeast	subsp.	subspecies
e	east	nw	northwest	var.	variation
imm.	immature	pops.	populations	w	west
intermed.	intermediate	s	south		

TOPOGRAPHY OF PERU

The topography of Peru is very complex, resulting in a delightful variety of habitats and bird species (fig. 4). A dominant feature of Peru is the Andean cordillera, which runs north/south down the length of country. The Andes interrupt the westward flow of air across the Amazon Basin of South America. As a result the east-facing slopes of the Andes, and Amazonian lowlands to the east, are very humid. Typically the Amazon Basin and the humid forests of the east slopes of the Andes are covered in humid evergreen forest, rich in species. Local soil differences, perhaps coupled with a history of fire, can produce less diverse forests or even scrub and savanna.

Most of Amazonian Peru is flat and low. Much of eastern Peru is little more than 300 m above sea level, despite being some 2500 km from the Atlantic Ocean. The large floodplains of the Amazon and its major tributaries (including the Napo, Marañón, Huallaga, Ucayali, Yavarí, and Madre de Dios) are wide and flat. Within these floodplains the rivers are constantly scouring out new channels, periodically leaving behind detached old bends (oxbow lakes) and forming or consuming islands. The action of the rivers contributes a variety of additional habitats that are important for birds, such as different types of river-edge forest and scrub, marshes at the edges of oxbow lakes, and the secondary vegetation that develops as older oxbow lakes slowly fill in with sediment and are reclaimed. The largest Amazonian rivers often are important barriers to bird species distribution; frequently the edge of a species' range will coincide with one bank of a river, and there is no sign of that species on the opposite bank only a short distance away.

Portions of the Amazon Basin, although still quite low in elevation, have somewhat greater relief, with series of very low hills or ridges, even far from the Andes (such as along the upper Río Purús). Areas with substantial relief are quite rare in eastern Amazonian Peru, the most notable exception being the Sierra del Divisor on the Brazilian border in central Peru, but ridges become more frequent, and increasingly higher, near the base of the Andes. The tops of these *outlying ridges* often harbor bird species that are not found in adjacent lower elevations, and that are scarce or absent at comparable elevations farther west on main slopes of the Andes.

The eastern slope of the Andes is especially humid and often exceedingly steep. Landslides are frequent. In contrast to the relatively lazy, looping courses of rivers and streams in the Amazon, Andean streams and rivers typically flow very fast. These east-facing slopes typically are forested up to 3000+ m, eventually giving way to shrub zones and grasslands, the most humid of which are termed "paramo" or "jalca." Treeline varies across Peru from about 3200 m to 3600 m. Above treeline isolated groves of *Polylepis* trees can be found, growing up to about 4500 m.

Intermontane valleys of the Andes are drier than the eastern slopes, due to rainshadow effects. The upper portions of these valleys, although less humid than east-facing slopes, still may be wet enough to support evergreen forest. Often the lower elevations in these valleys are much more arid and can be covered in deciduous forest, dry scrub, and columnar cacti. The larger dry intermontane valleys, such as the broad valley of the Río Marañón, often are barriers to the distributions of birds in humid forest. The majority of the human population of the Andes lives in intermontane valleys, however, and now much of the original vegetation in these regions is degraded or lost completely.

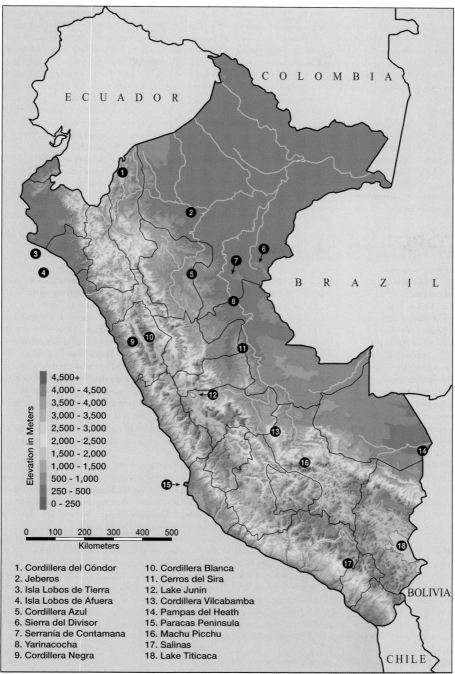

Elevation in Meters

4,500+
4,000 - 4,500
3,500 - 4,000
3,000 - 3,500
2,500 - 3,000
2,000 - 2,500
1,500 - 2,000
1,000 - 1,500
500 - 1,000
250 - 500
0 - 250

0   100   200   300   400   500
Kilometers

1. Cordillera del Cóndor
2. Jeberos
3. Isla Lobos de Tierra
4. Isla Lobos de Afuera
5. Cordillera Azul
6. Sierra del Divisor
7. Serranía de Contamana
8. Yarinacocha
9. Cordillera Negra
10. Cordillera Blanca
11. Cerros del Sira
12. Lake Junín
13. Cordillera Vilcabamba
14. Pampas del Heath
15. Paracas Peninsula
16. Machu Picchu
17. Salinas
18. Lake Titicaca

FIG. 4. RELIEF MAP OF PERU, ALSO SHOWING THE LOCATIONS OF IMPORTANT SITES MENTIONED IN THE TEXT

The highest parts of the Andes, the puna, are above treeline and are covered in dry grassland up to about 5000 m, variably laced with wet meadows, bogs, lakes, and streams. Above 5000 m, most land is unvegetated rock and snow.

The western (Pacific) coast of Peru is very dry. Most of the coast of central and southern Peru is bare desert, with little or no vegetation other than on *lomas* and in river valleys. Lomas are hills near the coast that are high enough to intercept the low clouds coming in off the cold ocean and to capture, seasonally, sufficient humidity to support more vegetation than the lower, surrounding desert. Originally rivers crossing the coast would have supported riparian forest. The coastal valleys now are heavily populated, however, and are dominated by agriculture and by cities and towns. The north coast of Peru is more humid than are the central and southern sectors. Remnant deciduous forest is found at lower elevations along the coast and in the Andean foothills, south to Lambayeque; at higher elevations humid montane forest, similar to that found on the east slopes of the Andes, occurs patchily south to Cajamarca. These forested areas on the western slope always were patchy distributed, but habitat destruction has reduced their extent dramatically, and little intact forest remains.

East of the Andes there is a pronounced dry season (variable, but typically May–October) in central and southern Peru. Seasonality is much reduced in the northern portion of the Peruvian Amazon. On the coast, the winter months (May–October) are cool, and skies often are overcast; however, typically there is little or no rain in central and southern Peru, although fog may "mist" the ground (especially on lomas). Rainfall is more frequent in the northwest and tends to occur December–March.

HABITATS OF PERU

More detailed descriptions of bird habitats can be found elsewhere. Many of our habitat descriptions are based on Stotz et al. (1996); habitat names presented here in italics correspond to terms used by that source.

FOREST As used here, "forest" refers to humid lowland forests, including both *tropical lowland evergreen forests* and *flooded tropical evergreen forests*. Most of the Amazon Basin is covered by these two tropical evergreen forests. These forests typically are tall (25–40 m, with scattered emergents that can reach 50–60 m). Forests may be found on upland terraces that never flood (*terra firme*) or occupy low-lying areas that are flooded for at least a portion of the year. These seasonally flooded forests include *varzea*, transitional forests, and swamp forests, depending upon the duration of flooding. In the species accounts we refer to these habitats as "forest," with the understanding that, in the context of a species with an Amazonian distribution, the habitat will include the full spectrum of tropical evergreen forests. We use terms such as "terra firme" or "varzea" for species that are restricted to, or particularly associated with, these types of forest.

Tropical lowland evergreen forests of much lower stature are found locally in extreme northwestern Peru, in Tumbes and perhaps in northernmost Piura.

RIVER-EDGE FOREST Amazonian rivers are bordered by a variety of lower-stature, successional vegetation, which may include grasses and other herbs or a mix of herbs and tall shrubs, such as cane (*Gynerium*), willow (*Salix*), and *Tessaria*, and low-stature forests (10–25 m tall) that form a narrow band between the river and taller forest in the interior. These forests often grow in even-aged stands and are dominated by genera such as *Cecropia* and *Ochroma*. The understory of these river-edge forests often is quite dense. Similar habitats are found on islands in the larger Amazonian rivers, especially in northern and central Amazonian Peru.

MONTANE FOREST We use *montane evergreen forest*, or humid montane forest, for the forests that cover the eastern slopes of the Andes and outlying ridges from about 500 m up to treeline. It is lower in stature than tropical evergreen forests, rarely exceeding 30 m in height; forest stature also tends to decrease with increasing elevation or steepness of terrain. The canopy often is broken, and branches and trunks of many trees are covered in moss, bromeliads, orchids, ferns, and other epiphytes. Tree species composition of montane evergreen forests usually changes significantly above 1500–1800 m, above which point epiphytes, including bryophytes, and lichens also become more prevalent. Below this elevation the montane forest contains significant elements of the lowland flora and is transitional between lowland terra firme forest and true montane forest.

ELFIN FOREST At the highest elevations (and locally much lower, depending upon soil and wind conditions), forests are particularly low and dense. These forests, which usually are on ridgetops or at treeline, sometimes are referred to as *elfin forests*.

POLYLEPIS FOREST *Polylepis* (Rosaceae) is a genus of low trees with rugged scaly bark. They grow in more or less open groves at high elevations, typically well above other forest, and so usually are surrounded by scrub or grass. A small set of bird species is restricted to these unique woodlands.

DRY FOREST Dry forests, or *tropical deciduous forests*, are of variable stature, but rarely exceed 20–25 m in height. Most species lose all of their leaves during the dry season, which usually is pronounced where dry forests are found, but these forests may contain some evergreen species, especially along river courses or at higher elevations. Transitions to more humid forests are referred to as semideciduous forests. In Peru dry forests primarily are found on the west slope in northwestern Peru, from Tumbes south to Cajamarca or to La Libertad, and in dry intermontane valleys (such as the Chinchipe, Marañón, Huallaga, Pampas, and Urubamba valleys).

WHITE-SAND FOREST Very locally in Amazonian Peru there are sites dominated by pure white sands, or a white-sand mixture. Forests growing on such substrates typically have reduced species richness (although they are rich in endemic or habitat-specific species) and often are low in stature as well. Some of these habitats have specific local names, such as *varillal* (a lower-stature forest type that occurs on sandy soil) and *chamizal* (the most stunted white-sand forests, located on sites with poor drainage or occasional natural fires). A related forest type, *irapayal* (an open-canopy forest on poor soils with a palm-dominated understory), may occur on very weathered clays or on soils with a sandy mixture. Streams that drain white-sand areas carry heavy tannin loads, and the water often is the color of dark tea; these are referred to as *blackwater streams*. Blackwater streams also form downstream from forested swamps, including palm swamps and *Ficus* swamps. Forests influenced by sandy soil are found in northern and central Amazonian Peru on both banks of the Amazon. White sands are most developed, however, on the north bank of the Amazon, especially in the drainages of the Río Tigre, Río Nanay (including the Zona Reservada Allpahuayo-Mishana), and the lower Río Morona. White-sand sites south of the Amazon are fewer but are located at Jeberos (between the lower ríos Marañón and Huallaga); on the east bank of the lower Río Ucayali; and on both sides of the Río Blanco (a tributary of the Río Tapiche). There is a set of bird species associated with these habitats that is most diverse in forests on pure white sands, but some portion of which also occurs in other nutrient-poor habitats.

MANGROVE FOREST Mangroves are salt-tolerant trees that form low, dense forests in warm-water coastal lagoons. In Peru they are restricted to Tumbes and to northwestern Piura.

SECOND GROWTH Second growth refers to regenerating forest. Most second growth is the result of human disturbance, but second growth also is a feature of naturally disturbed habitats, such as landslides. Second-growth forests differ in species composition from adjacent undisturbed forests and are dominated by a small number of rapidly growing species. We treat the successional habitats created by river dynamics as a separate habitat.

SCRUB Scrub is a variety of plant communities that are dominated by shrubs, scattered low trees, and, in some areas, cactus or terrestrial bromeliads. Dry scrub (*arid lowland scrub*) is widespread in northwestern Peru, and dry or semihumid scrub (*arid montane scrubs* and *semihumd/humid montane scrubs*) also is characteristic of the west slopes of the Andes and of intermontane valleys. In some areas in the Andes, semihumid or humid scrub may persist in areas where the soil and climate would support montane forest in the absence of human disturbance (for example, around Cuzco).

Scrub is present very locally in Amazonia as well. The largest such site is at Jeberos, in northern Amazonia between the lower ríos Marañón and Huallaga, where habitats are a mosaic of small patches of grassland bordered by a semidry scrub, varillal forest, and taller terra firme forest. This habitat may be maintained in part by human activity. Similar scrub is found along the upper Río Mayo, a tributary of the Huallaga.

SAVANNA Savanna in Peru is found only on the Pampas del Heath, an open grassland with scattered patches of trees, shrubs, or groves of *Mauritia* palms, and penetrated along streams by tongues (*gallery forest*) of the surrounding evergreen forest. These pampas are the terminal extension of a much more extensive savanna found in adjoining Bolivia. They are maintained by fire, including fires set by humans.

PUNA Dry or semidry grasslands often cover high elevations in the Andes and are known as puna. Also characteristic of many puna sites are cushion plants, which may form broad mats. Woody vegetation is scarce in puna, apart from (local) patches of *Polylepis* (see discussion above).

PARAMO Paramos, also known in Peru as *jalcas*, are humid montane grasslands. We use this term for humid grasslands that occupy a narrow strip along the crest of the east slope of the Andes, at and just above treeline. Paramo often consists of a mosaic of grasslands with scattered shrubs and small patches of trees.

MARSH Marshes are areas with standing or very slow-moving water, filled with aquatic vegetation such as grasses, sedges, and cattails. Marshes may be freshwater or brackish. They are most common in coastal lagoons, at high elevations in the Andes, and along the edges of oxbow lakes and river channels in Amazonia.

BEACH Coastal beaches and mudflats are an important habitat for waterbirds, especially for boreal migrants from North America. Sandy beaches predominate along the coast south to central Peru, but in southern Peru rocky beaches become more common. Sandbars and the sandy margins of rivers are similar habitats in Amazonia.

LAKES AND PONDS Freshwater lakes and ponds may be found throughout Peru, including oxbow lakes in Amazonia, and lakes (sometimes quite large, such as lakes Junín and Titicaca) in the Andes. Natural lakes and ponds are scarce in western Peru, although reservoirs approximate this habitat.

ALKALINE LAKES Locally in the southern Andes are shallow (seasonally dry), brackish lakes. The most important such site in Peru is Salinas, in Arequipa.

BOGS Bogs are poorly drained, perpetually damp sites that in Peru are found only in the high Andes.

In addition to the major habitats, several "microhabitats" are mentioned in the species accounts:

BAMBOO Several bird species are largely or entirely restricted to bamboo, which is found locally in the understory of humid montane and tropical evergreen forests or (less commonly) forms large, dominant stands. Bamboo typically goes to seed at long intervals (from several years to up to 20 or so years), after which the bamboo dies (and may or may not be replaced by a new generation). Consequently at least some birds associated with bamboo are nomadic. Bamboo (primarily *Chusquea*) is widespread in montane forest along the entire length of the Andes, especially at disturbed sites, although it may be absent from some localities. Tall *Guadua* bamboo is relatively common in southern Amazonian Peru, but is very rare in central and northern Peru.

TREEFALL GAPS Treefalls in continuous forest create gaps in the forest canopy; these small forest openings facilitate the growth of dense, low vegetation, often including many vines.

ARMY ANTS Army ants (primarily *Eciton burchellii* and *Labidus praedator*) form large swarms on the floor and lower vegetation of tropical forests. Several species of birds are "professional" or "obligate" army ant followers: these birds follow columns of army ants and capture arthropods and small vertebrates that attempt to flee the ants. Many other species of birds display similar foraging behavior opportunistically but do not follow army ants on a regular basis. Other species of ants, including some that occur in the Andes, also swarm, but species other than *Eciton burchellii* and *Labidus praedator* are smaller-bodied, form smaller swarms, or are active at night, and usually do not attract ant-following birds.

GLOSSARY OF BIRD TOPOGRAPHY

Alula: Small group of feathers attached to the "thumb."
Auricular: The feather tract covering the ear opening (a contrasting color pattern on the auriculars sometimes is called an "ear patch"). On owls and harriers, see "facial disk."
Axillars: Feathers at the base of the underside of the wing; normally lie in the wing's "armpit" and usually are concealed when the wing is closed.
Carpal: Refers to the "wrist" portion of the wing.
Cere: Fleshy, exposed skin surrounding the nares or the bill base, or connecting the bill to the eye.
Covert: A group of feathers that cover the bases of flight feathers (remiges and rectrices).
Culmen: The central (dorsal) ridge along the length of the maxilla.
Facial disk: The flat, semicircular auriculars of most owls and harriers.

Gorget: A contrasting, usually iridescent, patch of feathers on the throat of some hummingbirds.

Graduated tail: A tail that has progressively shorter rectrices from the central pair outward. Thus, the tip of the spread tail is wedge-shaped.

Interscapular: A contrasting patch of plumage on the mantle between the scapulars. Usually composed of the bases of mantle feathers, the interscapular patch may be concealed or flashed at will by a bird. Most frequently exhibited by understory antbirds.

Lores: The region immediately between the eye and the rictus.

Malar: A feather tract starting at the base of the mandible and separating the auricular and throat feather tracts.

Mandible: The "lower mandible" of the bill.

Mantle: The center of the back between the scapulars (loosely used, may include the scapulars as well).

Maxilla: The "upper mandible" of the bill.

Moustache: A stripe along the border of the auricular and malar feather tract, leading back from the rictus.

Nares: A bird's nostrils.

Orbit: The ring of feathers or skin immediately around the eye. Orbital feathers may contrast with other face plumage as an eyering or orbital ring (when forming a complete circle) or as eye crescents or broken eyering (when only broken portions of the orbit contrast). Orbital skin also may be brightly or contrastingly colored.

Patagium/patagial: The portion of the wing between the "wrist" and the "elbow" (the latter is usually hidden by body plumage). Usually used in reference to the underside of the leading edge of the wing.

Primary/primaries: The remiges that originate at the "hand" portion of the wing. The inner primaries abut the secondaries; the outer primaries are those at the leading edge of the wing when open. Most birds have ten primaries, but some oscine passerines have only nine.

Primary extension: When the wing is closed, the portion of the primaries that extends beyond the end of the tertials. Short primary extension often translates to a rounded wing when opened. Long primary extension often translates to a pointed wing when opened.

Rectrix/rectrices: The feathers that compose the tail. The "outer rectrices" are those farthest from the center of the tail when open and are usually the rectrices visible from below when the tail is folded. The "inner" or "central rectrices" are those at the center of the tail when open and usually are those most easily visible from above when the tail is folded. Most birds have 10 or 12 rectrices (depending on the species).

Remex/remiges: The flight feathers of the wing. These strictly include the primaries, secondaries, and tertials, but not the wing coverts.

Rictal bristles: Hairlike feathers that originate by the rictus. Most prominent in insectivores.

Rictus: The corner of the mouth; may be fleshy and/or contrastingly colored (especially in young fledglings).

Secondary/secondaries: The remiges that originate from the "arm" of the wing, more basal than the primaries. The inner secondaries are those closest to the body when the wing is open; the outer secondaries are those closest to the primaries when the wing is open.

Shaft: A feather's main support structure. Most streaked plumage comprises contrasting pigments along the shaft, and adjacent portions, of feathers.

Speculum: A contrastingly colored patch (often pale or iridescent) on the wing. Many passerines have a primary speculum, a contrasting color patch at the base of the primaries visible even when the wing is closed. Many ducks have a colored (often iridescent) speculum crossing their secondaries.

Superciliary: Linear feather tract from base of the bill over the eye to rear of the head; often contrastingly colored.

Tarsus: Lower portion of the "leg" (anatomically, composed of fused foot bones), bearing the toes.

Tertial/tertials: The innermost secondaries, often slightly different from the remaining secondaries in shape, in color pattern, or in both. Most bird species have only three tertials.

Vent: The feathering around the cloaca (loosely used, may also include the undertail coverts and/or the lower belly). Also called "crissum."

Web: The broad, flat portions of a feather that grow from the feather shaft. On many remiges and rectrices, the outer web is narrower than the inner; the outermost remex and rectrix are the most asymmetric.

Wing bars: Contrasting tips to the wing coverts (most often the greater and median secondary coverts) that line up as a bar across the wings.

Wing coverts: The feathers along the leading edge of the wings that cover the remiges. Unless "primary coverts" is used, it is implied that we are referring to the secondary wing coverts.

Lesser coverts: The coverts closest to the leading edge of the wing.

Median coverts: The coverts between the lesser and greater coverts.

Greater coverts: The coverts farthest from the leading edge of the wing, and touching the remiges.

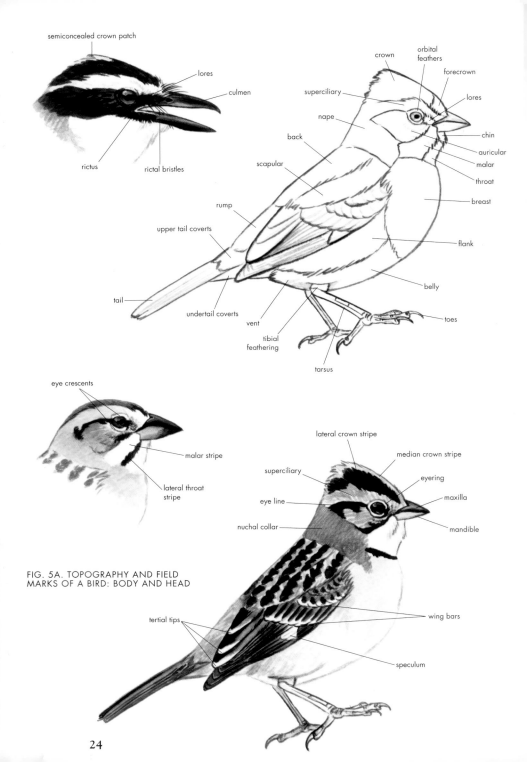

semiconcealed crown patch

lores

culmen

rictus

rictal bristles

crown

orbital feathers

forecrown

superciliary

lores

nape

chin

back

auricular

scapular

malar

throat

breast

rump

upper tail coverts

flank

tail

belly

undertail coverts

toes

vent

tibial feathering

tarsus

eye crescents

malar stripe

lateral throat stripe

lateral crown stripe

median crown stripe

superciliary

eyering

eye line

maxilla

nuchal collar

mandible

FIG. 5A. TOPOGRAPHY AND FIELD
MARKS OF A BIRD: BODY AND HEAD

tertial tips

wing bars

speculum

24

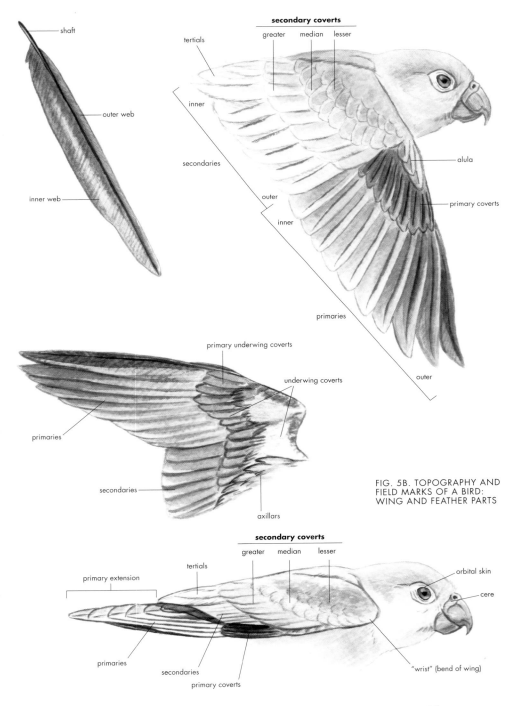

shaft

outer web

inner web

tertials

secondary coverts

greater   median   lesser

inner

secondaries

outer

inner

alula

primary coverts

primaries

outer

primary underwing coverts

underwing coverts

primaries

secondaries

axillars

FIG. 5B. TOPOGRAPHY AND
FIELD MARKS OF A BIRD:
WING AND FEATHER PARTS

secondary coverts

greater   median   lesser

tertials

primary extension

orbital skin

cere

primaries

secondaries

primary coverts

"wrist" (bend of wing)

25

MOLTS AND PLUMAGES

Birds undergo a series of molts throughout their lives. In most species all feathers are replaced once a year; in many species, there also is a second, incomplete molt in which part of the plumage (typically that of the body) is replaced again. Consequently, in many species there is a period (immediately following a complete molt) when all feathers of the body are fresh; feathers in fresh condition typically are at their brightest colors and are more intact, and the plumage overall will look "even." Note that because, in many species, some feathers may be molted twice a year (body) and others only once per year (wing and tail feathers), many birds wear two (or more) "generations" of feathers at any given time for at least part of the year.

The pattern and schedules of molts vary considerably, however. In large-bodied, long-lived species (e.g., larger seabirds and raptors), molt is more continuous. The color and pattern of the plumage of many species does not change throughout the year, at least once a bird has become an adult. In other species, however, the appearance of a bird may change significantly during the course of a year, either because the color or patterns of the plumage may change as a result of a molt, or because older feathers (i.e., those that have been worn a long time since the last molt) may become increasingly worn and faded, which sometimes can be noticeable in the field.

Plumages can be named based, in part, on the molt by which that plumage is attained. For adult birds such distinctions may be useful for species that have distinct plumages at different times of the year. This situation does not apply to the vast majority of resident birds of Peru, for which the plumage color and pattern changes little, if at all, once the bird reaches maturity. For many boreal migrants, however, and for some resident species (e.g., Black-and-white Seedeater), the plumages of adults vary throughout the year. The two fundamental plumages are the *basic plumage*, which usually is attained by a complete prebasic molt, and the *alternate plumage*, which usually is acquired during a partial prealternate molt. Molt is energetically very "costly" to a bird. Usually molting does not occur at the same time as other energetically "costly" activities, such as breeding or migrating. Typically the prebasic molt occurs following breeding; in some long-distance migrants this molt may be delayed, at least in part, until arrival on the wintering grounds. The prealternate molt typically precedes breeding. The timing of molts in resident birds at tropical latitudes is not well known, but in at least some species (or some individuals within these species?), there may be at least limited overlap of molt and breeding.

The first plumage that a bird acquires, after the short-lived downy stage, is the *juvenile plumage*; properly, the term "juvenile" refers to a bird that wears this first set of feathers, which may be retained, in whole or in part, for some time.

The molt schedules of most Peruvian birds have not been studied. In many cases we are not certain whether a particular plumage represents the juvenile plumage or instead is a distinct plumage acquired by a subsequent molt. Therefore, we frequently refer to birds as "immatures," which is a generalized term for a bird that is not fully adult. Also, be aware that some species take several years to attain a full adult (*definitive*) plumage. This is particularly true of large-bodied species, but some small birds (e.g., some *Sporophila* seedeaters) also may take two or more years, and several molt cycles, before reaching a definitive plumage. In at least some such species, however, birds may breed before obtaining the definitive plumages. In such cases we may refer to "subadult" plumages, which is a generalized term for birds that are older than one year old but are not fully adult.

A bird in molt may show a confusing mosaic of plumages. We rarely illustrate such intermediate plumages; but for some examples of them, see the figures of Scarlet, Summer, and Hepatic tanagers.

We realize that our terminology for the plumages of many species is imprecise, but in many cases, again, this is because the understanding of the molts and plumages of Peruvian birds is incomplete. We encourage field workers and museum scientists to pay more attention to molts and plumages of Peruvian birds, and to help advance our understanding of this important aspect of bird biology.

CAUTIONARY NOTE REGARDING SEABIRD IDENTIFICATION

Knowledge of the distribution and seasonal occurrence of seabirds in Peru is very incomplete. A number of species not yet reported from Peru, most of which are not discussed in this volume, may well occur, especially far at sea near the limits of Peru's territorial waters. Be aware that the identification of many seabirds is difficult, due both to the nature of seabird plumages (typically dull in color, with relatively few strong identifying features) and to the challenging nature of seabird observation (the birds often are distant and obscured by waves, and, if they are viewed from a boat, the observer is in constant motion as well). Finally, identification criteria for many seabirds still are being developed. Identification of seabirds, especially those that typically occur far at sea, best is attempted only by experienced observers, in consultation with specialized seabird literature, and with a healthy willingness to let some birds pass unidentified.

CONSERVATION

Humans and birds have coexisted in Peru, the site of several great pre-Columbian civilizations, for millennia; throughout that time humans have been modifying the landscape to better suit their needs. In modern times, however, the natural habitats of Peru, and the birds and other species that depend upon them, face unprecedented levels of threat.

These threats primarily stem from habitat destruction, but direct persecution also poses grave risks to some species. Habitat destruction is driven not only by expanding urbanization and agriculture, such as that along rivers in the lowlands and along roads throughout Peru, but also by extractive industries such as logging, mining, and fishing. Habitat loss is a particular threat for the many species in Peru that have geographically restricted distributions and so are most vulnerable to habitat degradation or loss. We recognize 101 species as endemic to Peru, for example, and there are many others whose distributions are centered on Peru but that also narrowly spill over into adjacent countries. Many of these species, such as those found in Andean intermontane valleys, long have survived human-mediated habitat modifications, but these may become threatened if future trends of habitat loss continue unabated.

Hunting is a threat primarily to select groups of birds that are favored for food, such as waterfowl, guans, and curassows. A depressingly large variety of birds are captured and sold for the pet trade in Peru, but parrots bear the brunt of the pressure from the captive bird trade, and populations of some species now are greatly reduced from what they were only a few years ago.

We are aware of only a single species, Southern Pochard, that has been extirpated (or nearly so) from Peru during the modern era; this species, fortunately, is more widely distributed elsewhere in South America (although it is in decline throughout the continent) and in Africa. Apparently the White-faced Whistling-Duck, if it truly occurred in Peru, also has disappeared. Currently the Wattled Curassow is particularly vulnerable to extirpation within Peru, and the Orinoco Goose also is in sharp decline. Two species endemic to Peru are particularly vulnerable: the White-winged Guan, long thought to have been extinct, was rediscovered in the late 1970s, but the total population of this Peruvian endemic remains very small and threatened; and the Junín Grebe, restricted entirely to Lake Junín, has suffered drastic declines in recent decades. Many of the breeding seabirds of Peru, including Humboldt Penguin and Peruvian Diving-Petrel, also have experienced serious population declines. The populations of many other species, too numerous to list here, also show signs of decline, or at least are potentially vulnerable and bear monitoring. Further information on the conservation status of birds in Peru may be found in the following sources:

Collar, N. J., L. P. Gonzaga, N. Krabbe, A. Madroño Nieto, L. G. Naranjo, T. A. Parker III, and D. Wege. 1992. *Threatened birds of the Americas. The ICBP/IUCN Red Data book.* 3d ed., part 2. Cambridge: International Council for Bird Preservation.

Stotz, D. F., J. W. Fitzpatrick, T. A. Parker III, and D. K. Moskovits. 1996. *Neotropical birds: ecology and conservation.* Chicago: University of Chicago Press.

http://www.birdlife.org/datazone/index.html

CONSERVATION

The government of Peru has a protected areas program that administers a nationwide system that encompasses a variety of units, including national parks (*parques nacionales*), sanctuaries (*santuarios*), reserved zones (*zonas reservadas*), and national reserves (*reservas nacionales*). The more important, for birds, of these protected areas are shown in figure 6.

Key to Fig 6.
1. Zona Reservada Güeppí
2. Zona Reservada Pucacuro
3. Zona Reservada Santiago-Comaina
4. Santuario Nacional Manglares de Tumbes
5. Parque Nacional Cerros de Amotape, Reserva Nacional Tumbes
6. Reserva Nacional Allpahuayo-Mishana
7. Reserva Nacional Pacaya-Samiria
8. Santuario Nacional Tabaconas-Namballe
9. Zona Reservada Cordillera de Colán
10. Bosque de Protección Alto Mayo
11. Refugio de Vida Silvestre Laquipampa
12. Bosque de Protección Pagaibamba (w), Parque Nacional Cutervo (n), Zona Reservada Chancaybaños (s)
13. Zona Reservada Sierra del Divisor
14. Parque Nacional Cordillera Azul
15. Parque Nacional Río Abiseo
16. Bosque de Protección Puquio Santa Rosa
17. Santuario Nacional Calipuy (n), Reserva Nacional Calipuy (s)
18. Parque Nacional Huascarán
19. Parque Nacional Tingo María
20. Reserva Comunal El Sira
21. Parque Nacional Yanachaga-Chemillén, Reserva Comunal Yanesha
22. Reserva Comunal Alto Purús
23. Parque Nacional Alto Purús
24. Zona Reservada Cordillera Huayhuash
25. Bosque de Protección San Matías-San Carlos
26. Reserva Nacional de Lachay
27. Santuario Nacional Huayllay
28. Reserva Nacional Junín
29. Zona Reservada Pampa Hermosa
30. Refugio de Vida Silvestre Pantanos de Villa
31. Bosque de Protección Pui Pui
32. Parque Nacional Otishi, Reserva Comunal Ashaninka, Reserva Comunal Machiguenga
33. Santuario Nacional Megantoni
34. Parque Nacional Manu
35. Reserva Comunal Amarakaeri
36. Reserva Nacional Tambopata
37. Parque Nacional Bahuaja-Sonene
38. Bosque de Protección A.B. Canal Nuevo Imperial
39. Reserva Nacional de Paracas
40. Santuario Nacional de Ampay
41. Reserva Nacional Pampa Galeras Barbara D'Achille
42. Reserva Nacional Titicaca
43. Reserva Nacional Salinas y Aguada Blanca
44. Santuario Nacional Lagunas de Mejía
45. Zona Reservada Aymara Lupaca

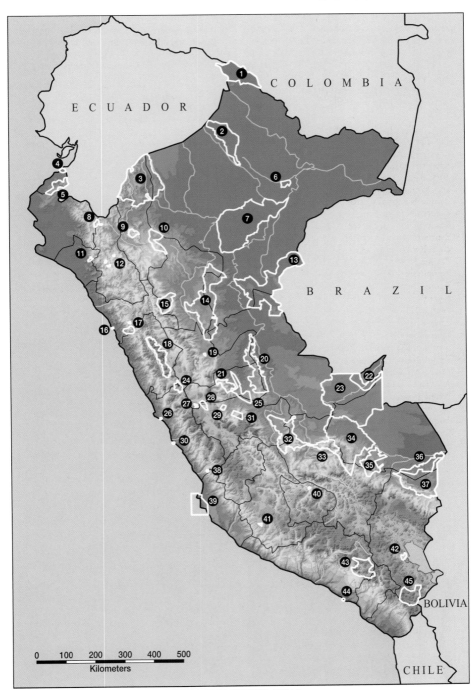

FIG. 6. THE PERUVIAN NATIONAL SYSTEM OF PROTECTED AREAS

PLATE
1

LARGE FOREST TINAMOUS

Tinamous are terrestrial and cryptically colored. Superficially resemble tailless quail but usually forage singly or as adult (male) with 1 or 2 juveniles. Heard much more often than are seen. Prefer to escape on foot; when flushed, explosively rocket away before dropping quickly into cover. Tinamus roost in trees, all other species on the ground. Forest species primarily eat fallen fruit. Nest on the ground; eggs are glazed and usually some shade of blue, olive, or purplish brown. All species on plate are large tinamous of humid forest interior.

1 BLACK TINAMOU *Tinamus osgoodi* * 40–46 cm (15¼–18 in)

Poorly known. Rare to locally fairly common in humid montane forest, 900–1400 m (locally to 2100 m), on east slope of southern Andes. Large, very dark; note restricted distribution. Gray Tinamou is larger and paler with white freckling on sides of head and throat; elevation range of Gray also does not extend as high. **VOICE** Song, generally crepuscular, a descending deep whistle, similar to first note of song of White-throated Tinamou. **Co, E**

2 GRAY TINAMOU *Tinamus tao* * 43–46 cm (17–18 in)

Uncommon but widespread, mainly in humid montane forest along east slope of Andes up to 1400 m; locally in terra firme of Amazonia in southeast, especially in hilly terrain. Distinctive combination of large size, blackish head with white freckling behind eyes and on throat, and grayish overall plumage. In south cf. Black Tinamou. **VOICE** Song, generally crepuscular and given at long intervals, is a low, even "*whoo.*" Also a single quavering whistle similar to that of Great Tinamou, but not in a series. **Co, E, Br, Bo**

3 GREAT TINAMOU *Tinamus major* * 38–43 cm (15–17 in)

Fairly common throughout Amazonia and (perhaps in the absence of other *Tinamus*) locally in foothills to 800 m; the most widespread large forest tinamou. Primarily in low-lying, seasonally flooded forest (including varzea in north); also in tall second growth. Note large size, distinctly rufescent head, and unspotted upperparts. Replaced by White-throated Tinamou in terra firme. **VOICE** Song, generally crepuscular, a series of rising then falling, quavering whistles, normally in series of 4. Has "sawing" rhythm. **Co, E, Br, Bo**

4 WHITE-THROATED TINAMOU *Tinamus guttatus* 33–36 cm (13–14 in)

Fairly common and widespread in eastern lowlands, also locally to 1100 m; the characteristic large tinamou of terra firme, which it shares with the smaller Variegated Tinamou. Less numerous along edges of seasonally flooded forest. Distinguished from other lowland tinamous by large size and conspicuous buff spotting on back and wing coverts. **VOICE** Song is 2 notes with about a 1- to 2-sec pause between: "*whooooooo… hoo,*" the first note often dipping in pitch, the second barely rising. **Co, E, Br, Bo**

5 HIGHLAND TINAMOU *Nothocercus bonapartei* * 35.5–38 cm (14–15 in)

Rare to uncommon, in humid montane forest, 1800–2100 m, on east slope of Andes north and west of the Marañón. Overlaps with few other species: Tawny-breasted Tinamou is found at higher elevations; also note differences in crown and throat color. **VOICE** Song, usually given in the morning, is a series of rising yelps: "*B'yirr!*" **Co, E**

6 TAWNY-BREASTED TINAMOU *Nothocercus julius* 35.5–38 cm (14–15 in)

Poorly known and perhaps local (or overlooked?). Found in humid montane forest on east slope of Andes at 2500–3000 m; the only forest tinamou of these elevations. Also note reddish crown and white throat. **VOICE** Song a long series of burry, slightly descending "*brreew*" notes, closely spaced. **Co, E**

7 HOODED TINAMOU *Nothocercus nigrocapillus* * 33 cm (13 in)

Fairly common in humid montane forest along east slope of Andes, 1300–2500 m (locally to 3200 m), south of range of Highland Tinamou. May concentrate in areas where bamboo (*Chusquea*) is seeding, when may become quite vocal. Northern *cadwaladeri* (Amazonas and San Martín) more reddish than central and southern *nigrocapillus*. Similar to Tawny-breasted Tinamou of higher elevations, but note differences in crown and throat color. Cf. other terrestrial forest species (Brown Tinamou, Rufous-breasted and Stripe-faced Wood-Quail, and White-throated Quail-Dove), all of which are smaller. **VOICE** Song a series of burry, rising-falling "*brreew*" or "*bwow*" notes, averaging about 1 note per 10 sec. **Bo**

BLACK TINAMOU

GRAY TINAMOU

GREAT TINAMOU

HIGHLAND TINAMOU

WHITE-THROATED
TINAMOU

cadwaladeri

HOODED TINAMOU

TAWNY-BREASTED TINAMOU

nigrocapillus

PLATE
2

WIDESPREAD *CRYPTURELLUS* TINAMOUS

Crypturellus are small to medium-sized tinamous; species on this plate occupy humid forest or forest edges in eastern Peru.

1 CINEREOUS TINAMOU *Crypturellus cinereus* 30–30.5 cm (11¾–12 in)

Common and widespread, locally up to 1000 m, in dense understory of low-lying forest, such as seasonally flooded forest and edges of swampy forest; also seasonally on larger river islands in north. Darkest, most uniformly colored medium-sized tinamou of Amazonia. **VOICE** Song an even, clear whistle, repeated at regular intervals of 5 sec or more. Easily imitated; characteristic sound of riverine Amazonia. **Co, E, Br, Bo**

2 LITTLE TINAMOU *Crypturellus soui* * 21.5–23 cm (8½–9 in)

Fairly common and widespread in east, up to 1350 m, in forest (especially near rivers and streams) and tall second growth; prefers dense undergrowth. Also rare in evergreen forest in Tumbes below 750 m. Plumage variable. Females generally brighter than males. Most richly colored are female *nigriceps* (north of the Amazon, also south of Marañón in San Martín). Male *nigriceps*, and both sexes of *inconspicuus* (rest of Amazonia) and *harterti* (Tumbes), are drabber. Note small size, unpatterned upperparts. **VOICE** Song, generally crepuscular, a series of quavering whistles raising in pitch and accelerating in pace. Daytime call a single quavering note rising and then quickly dropping in pitch: "*heeEE'E'u'u'u'u'u.*" Reminiscent of Great Tinamou but slightly higher pitched, and song phrases never in pairs. Also a clear rising whistle. **Co, E, Br, Bo**

3 BROWN TINAMOU *Crypturellus obsoletus* * 25.5 cm (10 in)

Fairly common in humid montane forest along east slope of Andes, 900–2500 m, usually in dense understory. Also very local at lower elevations in central and southern Peru, especially in hilly terrain. Geographic variation and taxonomy not well understood. Andean populations generally darker, more richly colored; populations at lower elevations paler and buffier. Similar to Little Tinamou, but primarily Andean (not Amazonian); also larger with gray throat. See also Hooded Tinamou. **VOICE** Song a long series of ringing phrases rising in pitch and accelerating in pace until near the end, when voice "cracks" and notes become cleaner whistles: "*Prr… prr… prr prr prr, prr, prr-prr-prr-prr'prr'pi'pi'pi?*" Daytime call, similar in quality to song, is a shorter phrase of rising notes: "*Prrrr, prr-prree?*" Voice in San Martín clearer, less strident. **Co, E, Br, Bo**

4 UNDULATED TINAMOU *Crypturellus undulatus* * 25.5–26.5 cm (10–10½ in)

Common in floodplain forest (including edges of varzea); also regularly in second growth and forest edge with dense understory near low-lying forest, and seasonally (mainly Aug–Mar) on river islands in north. Geographically variable: relatively plain in northern and central Peru (*yapura*) but regularly barred in southeast (*undulatus*). **VOICE** Song, often given throughout day, is 3 or 4 deep, whistled notes, the last rising: "*whooo… whoo-whoo?*" (or "*com-pra pan?*"). Characteristic sound of riverine Amazonia. **Co, E, Br, Bo**

5 VARIEGATED TINAMOU *Crypturellus variegatus* 25.5–26.5 cm (10–10½ in)

Fairly common and widespread, locally up to 950 m. The characteristic small tinamou of terra firme (compare to larger White-throated Tinamou). Richly colored, with strongly barred upperparts. Distinguished from brighter examples of Bartlett's Tinamou by black crown and sides of head, stronger barring, slightly larger size, and longer bill. Bartlett's also is more prevalent in low-lying forest. **VOICE** Song, often given throughout day, but most often at dusk, long, clear whistle followed by a long pause, then a rising and accelerating series of quavering whistles: "*whooooo….. whoo wrrr-wrrr-wrrr-wrrr-wrr-wrr-wrr-wi?*" **Co, E, Br, Bo**

6 BARTLETT'S TINAMOU *Crypturellus bartletti* 23–24 cm (9–9½ in)

Fairly common and widespread in eastern lowlands. Most common in seasonally flooded forest, less commonly found along streams in terra firme. Highly variable in color, even within a single population; some birds relatively dull and brown, whereas others relatively bright tawny color. Always barred on back and wing coverts. Cf. Variegated Tinamou. **VOICE** Song, given most often at night, dawn, and dusk, an accelerating, rising series of pure, fairly flat whistles, occasionally changing pace and pitch more variably. Similar to Cinereous Tinamou but rarely maintains an even pace for long, and often pauses between bouts. At times introductory notes of song quaver and fall a little in pitch, reminiscent of Little Tinamou, but usually accelerate into typical song. **E, Br, Bo**

CINEREOUS TINAMOU

♀ nigriceps

♂

LITTLE TINAMOU

Andean

lowland

BROWN TINAMOU

yapura

undulatus

UNDULATED TINAMOU

VARIEGATED TINAMOU

BARTLETT'S TINAMOU

PLATE
3

RANGE-RESTRICTED *CRYPTURELLUS* TINAMOUS

Species on this plate are Crypturellus *that are geographically restricted, rare, or both.*

1 GRAY-LEGGED TINAMOU *Crypturellus duidae* 28.5–31 cm (11–12¼ in)

Uncommon to locally fairly common, but restricted to varillal forests north of Amazon. Female more strongly barred than male, especially on wing coverts. Very richly colored. Superficially similar to Variegated Tinamou, but note rufous-brown (not blackish) crown and sides of head; upperparts also not as uniformly barred as in Variegated. **VOICE** Song a single rising, slightly quavering whistle lasting about 3 sec: *"whoo'ooo'ooee?"* **Co, Br**

2 BLACK-CAPPED TINAMOU *Crypturellus atrocapillus* * 28–31 cm (11–12¼ in)

Locally common in dense second growth and in riverine and disturbed forests, in south up to 1000 m in Andean foothills. Sexually dimorphic; female more prominently barred above, especially on lower back and wing coverts. Superficially similar to Variegated Tinamou, but note contrast between cinnamon throat and belly, and dark gray chest; also different habitat. **VOICE** Song, often given throughout the day, is an explosive *"QUEEWAH!"* **Br, Bo**

3 BARRED TINAMOU *Crypturellus casiquiare* 25.5–27 cm (10–10½ in)

Poorly known. Local and apparently rare in varillal forests on Río Tigre and possibly also on upper Río Nanay. Note small size, rufous crown and sides of the head, and contrast between gray breast and belly and brown, boldly barred upperparts. **VOICE** Song an accelerating-decelerating series of clear whistles, the fastest notes also the highest pitched, averaging about 1 note/sec for most of song. **Co, Br**

4 BRAZILIAN TINAMOU *Crypturellus strigulosus* 27–29 cm (10½–11½ in)

Poorly known. Reported from several sites in eastern and southeastern Amazonia, but probably more widespread; largely restricted to terra firme (especially on sandy or nutrient-poor soils). Female more strongly barred than male on lower back, wing coverts, and tail. Otherwise note relatively plain appearance and contrast between reddish brown head and gray-brown body. **VOICE** Song, generally crepuscular, a long (> 5 sec) whistle that rises slightly, sometimes becoming quavering near the end; sounds more like an insect than a bird. **Br, Bo**

5 PALE-BROWED TINAMOU *Crypturellus transfasciatus* 25.5 cm (10 in)

Locally fairly common in dry forest of northwest, below 800 m. Occurs in forest with light undergrowth but probably prefers thicker vegetation. Female more strongly barred than male on lower back and wing coverts. Cf. Andean Tinamou, with which it locally overlaps. **VOICE** Song an explosive, piercing, rising *"cuuEEE?"* **E**

6 SMALL-BILLED TINAMOU *Crypturellus parvirostris* 20–25 cm (7¾–9¾ in)

Fairly common but very local. Recorded from dry upper Urubamba Valley at ca. 1000 m, near Puerto Maldonado (where probably spreading following widespread forest clearing), and Pampas del Heath. Found in dense, scrubby second growth of recently cleared areas, and tall grass with scattered bushes. Very small and plain. Similar to Paint-billed Crake but browner and with narrower, uniformly red bill. Also very similar to Tataupa Tinamou, but the two are not known to overlap; paler brown than Tataupa, with more brightly colored tarsi (reddish rather than purplish or gray of Tataupa), and has brown wash on crown and breast (purer gray in Tataupa). **VOICE** Song, often given throughout day, but particularly in the morning, is an accelerating series of notes with a ringing quality, the song rising in pitch, then dropping sharply into churring phrases: *"tu... tu... tu tu, tu, tu-tu-ti'ti'ti'ti'tur-chur-chur-chur-chur."* Daytime call is 2 or 3 ringing, quavering notes that rise, then drop in pitch, usually ending in a churr: *"prjrjr-prjrr'jrrrrrrr."* **Br, Bo**

7 TATAUPA TINAMOU *Crypturellus tataupa* * 23 cm (9 in)

Uncommon to locally common in dry northern and central intermontane valleys (Marañón, Huallaga, Chanchamayo, and Apurímac), 200–1300 m. Found in riparian thickets, undergrowth of dry forest, and (in central Peru) at edge of humid forest. Cf. Small-billed Tinamou and Paint-billed Crake (which is paler brown and has a thicker, bicolored bill). **VOICE** Song, most often given in the morning, is a gruff series, accelerating in pace and descending in pitch, ending in low chatter. Call, given throughout the day, is an explosive series of notes, also with quickening pace: *"Brrree, brree-bre-br-br."* Quality of all vocalizations brings to mind a police whistle. **E, Br, Bo**

BLACK-CAPPED TINAMOU

GRAY-LEGGED
TINAMOU

BRAZILIAN TINAMOU

BARRED TINAMOU

PALE-BROWED TINAMOU

TATAUPA TINAMOU

SMALL-BILLED
TINAMOU

PLATE
4

OPEN-HABITAT TINAMOUS

These all are tinamous of grasslands and other open habitats. Bills decurved and relatively long (Rhynchotus, Nothoprocta) or relatively stubby (Nothura, Tinamotis).

1 DARWIN'S NOTHURA *Nothura darwinii* * 26 cm (10¼ in)

Fairly common in dry grassland above 3800 m in Titicaca Basin. Locally found at similar elevations north to central Peru; also an isolated population at ca. 1000 m in dry middle Urubamba Valley. Note very small size and strongly marked breast. **VOICE** Song (Bolivia, Argentina) is a rapid, incessant series of short piping whistles. **Bo**

2 ORNATE TINAMOU *Nothoprocta ornata* * 35 cm (13¾ in)

Uncommon to locally fairly common in grassland at 3300–4400 m. Typically in dry sites with scattered bushes; may prefer sloping, rocky areas with a mixture of shrubs, bunch grasses, cushion plants, and cactus. Also found in open *Polylepis* scrub. Geographically variable. Southern *ornata* (Puno, Arequipa) is larger, paler, and browner above and has a buffier belly than *branickii* of central and northern Peru. Northwestern populations (La Libertad) may average more reddish brown (less gray). The most widespread grassland tinamou above 3500 m, where may overlap with the much larger Puna Tinamou. Smaller Andean Tinamou is found at lower elevations, lacks spotting on sides of head, and has a spotted breast. **VOICE** Call when flushed a high, plaintive, ringing "*wee'up*" in a series. Also may give (Bolivia) low clucks. **Bo, Ch**

3 TACZANOWSKI'S TINAMOU *Nothoprocta taczanowskii* 36 cm (14¼ in)

Little known and apparently rare or uncommon. Found in wet grassland, often near treeline, along east slope of Andes, 2800–4000 m; also locally in mosaics of scrubby woods, remnant grassy areas, and fields in upper portions of intermontane valleys. Note large size, largely gray appearance, and long curved bill. **VOICE** Song (?) a high, rising-falling, piercing whistle: "*TU'EEEEEEeer.*" **Bo**

4 ANDEAN TINAMOU *Nothoprocta pentlandii* * 28 cm (11 in)

Widespread and often fairly common on western slopes of Andes and in intermontane valleys, 2000–3600 m, where found in montane scrub, including edges of *Polylepis*, and grassland. Also locally in scrub and in open undergrowth of dry forest in Andean foothills and on lomas, 200–900 m. Plumage variable. Brownest birds, with tawny underparts and longitudinal whitish streaks on upperparts, occur in lowlands of northwest (*ambigua*). Other populations (including those of coast farther south) more gray breasted; also may have longitudinal whitish streaks on upperparts, although some (primarily males?; not illustrated) are blacker above, with pale gray longitudinal stripes on upperparts. The most frequently encountered small tinamou on arid and semiarid slopes of Andes, below 3500 m. Cf. Ornate Tinamou (high Andes) and Pale-browed Tinamou (northwest). **VOICE** Song an explosive, rising thin whistle: "*tuEEE!*" or "*tu-tuEEE!*" **E, Bo, Ch**

5 CURVE-BILLED TINAMOU *Nothoprocta curvirostris* * 28 cm (11 in)

Uncommon and local in humid grassland with scattered shrubs at 2800–3600 m on east slope of Andes in northern and central Peru. Found in both short and tall grasses, near treeline, and on upper slopes of intermontane valleys, where occurs in a mosaic of grazed grassland, fields, and montane scrub. The most common high-elevation grassland tinamou in its range. May overlap locally with Andean Tinamou in some intermontane valleys but is slighter larger, blacker above, and tawnier and more heavily marked on breast; also note rufous on inner remiges. **E**

6 RED-WINGED TINAMOU *Rhynchotus rufescens* * 39–42.5 cm (15¼–16¼ in)

Fairly common but restricted to savannas of Pampas del Heath, where it is the only large tinamou. Frequently heard, but usually concealed by tall grass. Rufous primaries readily seen in flight. **VOICE** Song, given even in heat of day, is a mournful yet pleasing series of clear whistles, the first note longest and rising-falling, followed by 3 stuttered, falling notes: "*whooEEoo, hee'hee-hoo.*" **Br, Bo**

7 PUNA TINAMOU *Tinamotis pentlandii* 42 cm (16½ in)

Uncommon in dry puna above 3900 m, especially in brushy or rocky areas. More often seen in small groups than are most tinamous. Readily identified by very large size, boldly striped head, and rufous vent. **VOICE** Song, usually given in chorus, is a series of musical notes, somewhat reminiscent of a wood-quail: "*cuDU cuDU cuDU...*" **Bo, Ch**

DARWIN'S
NOTHURA

branickii

ornata

ORNATE TINAMOU

TACZANOWSKI'S TINAMOU

nw

CURVE-BILLED TINAMOU

ambigua

ANDEAN TINAMOU

RED-WINGED TINAMOU

PUNA TINAMOU

PLATE
5

RHEA, STORKS, AND FLAMINGOS

This plate is an assemblage of large, long-necked, long-legged birds. Rheas are flightless birds of dry open country. Storks are wading birds with long, heavy bills. They carry the neck outstretched in flight, with legs trailing behind; unlike other wading birds, they frequently soar and can ascend to great heights. Flamingos are wading birds with particularly long, graceful necks and long legs; most notable for distinctive "kinked" bill. All three species are highly gregarious, with preference for brackish or saline water. They feed by wading in water with head held low, bill upside down and immersed; use bill to filter tiny organisms from water. Juveniles (not illustrated) of all species are brownish, with duller color to base of bill.

1 LESSER RHEA *Pterocnemia pennata* * 92–100 cm (36–39 in)
Rare and local (and populations probably declining) above 4300 m in southwest. Preferred habitat is flat open terrain with some bogs or wetlands. Usually found in small groups. Takes several years to reach maturity. Immatures lack white feather tips of adults. **Bo, Ch**

[MAGUARI STORK *Ciconia maguari*] 110 cm (43 in)
Very rare vagrant to southeast; reported, as singles or pairs, both in lowlands of Madre de Dios and (photographed) at 3650 m in Andes. Found in open country, usually near marshes or wet grasslands. Similar to Wood Stork, but note feathered (not bare) neck and head, reddish tarsi, and more colorful facial skin; also has more extensive black on wing coverts and lower back (more visible on ground than in flight). **Co, Br, Bo**

2 WOOD STORK *Mycteria americana* 89–101.5 cm (35–40 in)
Most widespread stork. Uncommon in Amazonia, where found in marshes and along rivers; also rare in similar habitats in southern Amazonia. Rare vagrant (primarily juveniles) to Andes and central and southern coast. Often gregarious and may form small flocks. Readily recognized by large size, bare head and neck, and white body with contrasting black remiges. Bill of juvenile is yellow or yellowish, and head may be partially feathered. **Co, E, Br, Bo, Ch**

3 JABIRU *Jabiru mycteria* 127–150 cm (50–59 in)
Rare but widespread in central and southern Amazonia; very scarce or absent from north. Also a very rare vagrant to Andes and coast. Immense, essentially all-white bird with bare black head; at close range, note bare reddish lower neck. Juvenile is brownish gray, with duller skin colors; head and neck also may be feathered. Plumage progressively whiter with age. May be seen as singles or pairs on banks of large rivers, but perhaps most often detected when soaring high overhead. **Co, E, Br, Bo**

4 JAMES'S FLAMINGO *Phoenicoparrus jamesi* 90 cm (35 in)
Nonbreeding visitor to south, congregating at Salinas (4300 m); very rare vagrant to coast and to Amazonia. Smallest flamingo, with least amount of black on bill. Tarsi of adult entirely red. Immature much duller but identifiable by size, reduced black on bill, and yellowish base to bill (shared with Andean). **VOICE** Calls higher and more screechy than calls of Chilean Flamingo. **Bo, Ch**

5 ANDEAN FLAMINGO *Phoenicoparrus andinus* 110 cm (43 in)
Rarest of the three flamingos. Nonbreeding visitor to southwest, where congregates at Salinas (4300 m); up to several hundred may be present, but typically outnumbered by the two other species. Adult readily recognized by yellow tarsi, more prominently black rear body, and more black on wings (extending onto tertials); also has more extensively black bill than James's. Immature similar to Chilean; at close range, note yellowish (not pink) base to bill and dark (not pale) iris. **Br, Bo, Ch**

6 CHILEAN FLAMINGO *Phoenicopterus chilensis* 95–105 cm (37–41 in)
The most widespread flamingo. Breeds very locally in Andes. More widespread as nonbreeding visitor in Andes at 3200–4600 m and on coast; often found on freshwater lakes (unlike other flamingos). Adult readily recognized by reddish "knees" contrasting with blue-gray tarsi, and pinkish base to bill. Long pink plumes often cover black in wing when at rest. Immature lacks pink or red; see Andean and James's flamingos. **VOICE** Calls low grunts and gravelly, multisyllabic honks. **E, Br, Bo, Ch**

imm.

LESSER RHEA

ad.

JABIRU

ad.

WOOD STORK

MAGUARI STORK

juv.

ad.

juv.

JAMES'S
FLAMINGO

ad.

imm.

ad.

imm.

ANDEAN
FLAMINGO

ad.

CHILEAN
FLAMINGO

imm.

PLATE
6

LARGE WATERFOWL

This plate covers the larger species of Peruvian waterfowl; otherwise most of these species are very different from one another. The three whistling-ducks, however, are similar in structure and behavior. They have notably long necks and tarsi; stand with a more upright posture; are found in marshes, usually in flocks; call frequently in flight; and often are active at night, when easily detected by their loud whistling calls.

WHITE-FACED WHISTLING-DUCK *Dendrocygna viduata* 43–48 cm (17–19 in)

Probably extirpated from Peru. Known only from 19th-century records, from Lima (this report perhaps in error?) and the Río Ucayali. Adult unmistakable. Juvenile much duller; cf. juvenile Black-bellied Whistling-Duck (which has bold white wing stripe). **VOICE** Call a reedy whistled series: *"wheew hi-hi-hew."* **Co, Br, Bo, Ch**

1 BLACK-BELLIED WHISTLING-DUCK *Dendrocygna autumnalis* * 48–53 cm (19–21 in)

Perhaps the most common whistling-duck. Apparently resident and fairly common in mangroves in Tumbes. Rare and local in Amazonia, where mostly found in north; rare vagrant elsewhere. Perches freely in trees (especially on dead branches), unlike the two other whistling-ducks, and often nests in tree cavities. Juvenile duller overall than adult. **VOICE** Calls a reedy whistle, followed by rising, stuttered second phrase: *"pi-CHEE hee'hee'hee'hee."* **Co, E, Br, Bo**

2 FULVOUS WHISTLING-DUCK *Dendrocygna bicolor* 45–53 cm (18–21 in)

Poorly known. Apparently an uncommon resident in mangroves in Tumbes; rare and local in Amazonia, where mostly reported from north (especially along the Amazon and in the Pacaya-Saimiria region). Rare vagrant elsewhere, including to the central coast, Lake Junín, and southern Amazonia. Readily recognized by characteristic whistling-duck shape and by buffy body (contrasting with blackish wings); in south cf. Orinoco Goose. **VOICE** Calls a reedy whistle: *"whi'SEW."* **Co, E, Br, Bo, Ch**

3 ANDEAN GOOSE *Chloephaga melanoptera* 75–80 cm (29–32 cm)

Fairly common and widespread in high Andes, 3700–4600 m; very rare vagrant to the coast (only during austral winter?). Found at edges of Andean bogs (only rarely or locally in marshes). Usually in pairs but may form small flocks when not breeding. Male noticeably larger than female. **VOICE** Calls soft, ringing honks, quiet peeps, and low whining sounds. **Bo, Ch**

4 ORINOCO GOOSE *Neochen jubata* 56–63.5 cm (22–25 in)

Probably once widespread in Amazonia; now rare and apparently restricted to more remote portions of Madre de Dios drainage. Usually seen as singles or pairs on riverbanks and sandbars. A brown, long-legged goose with a thick neck. Note 2-toned appearance (pale buff foreparts contrast with rufous-brown rear) and small white patch on secondaries (visible in flight). **VOICE** Calls rising fluty whistles and low barking quacks. **Co, E, Br, Bo**

5 MUSCOVY DUCK *Cairina moschata* male 76–84 cm (30–33 in), female 71–76 cm (28–30 in)

Uncommon but widespread in Amazonia; increasingly is confined to more remote areas (although common in captivity; domesticated Muscovy, often with white-blotched plumage, commonly seen in or near villages). Found on oxbow lakes and rivers in forest (not in open marshes), as singles or pairs; does not associate with other waterfowl. Frequently perches in trees and nests in tree cavities. Wary. Male significantly larger than female, with fleshy caruncles on face and at base of bill. Adults show prominent white on wings in flight. Compare all-dark juvenile to Neotropic Cormorant and Anhinga. **VOICE** Generally quiet. Calls include whistled peeps. **Co, E, Br, Bo, Ch**

6 COMB DUCK *Sarkidiornis melanotos* * male 68.5–71 cm (27–28 in), female 53.5–56 cm (21–22 in)

Poorly known; rare and local. Perhaps most common along middle Río Huallaga (and also in adjacent lowlands?). May also be resident in middle Marañón Valley. Very rare vagrant to coast and Andes. Found along rivers and in rice fields; usually seen only in small numbers but may form large flocks. Male much larger than female, with large "comb" over base of bill (larger when breeding). Easily identified by large size, black and white freckled neck and sides of face, and white underparts, but take care not to confuse with domesticated Muscovy Duck, which may be partially white below. **VOICE** Calls growled honks. **Co, E, Br, Bo**

juv.

ad.

WHITE-FACED
WHISTLING-DUCK

juv.

ad.

BLACK-BELLIED
WHISTLING-DUCK

FULVOUS
WHISTLING-DUCK

ANDEAN GOOSE

ORINOCO GOOSE

♂

♀

MUSCOVY DUCK

♂

COMB DUCK

♀

juv.

ad.

PLATE
7

DABBLING DUCKS

Dabbling ducks (Anas) are familiar aquatic birds. They forage primarily in water, often tipping forward to feed on submerged vegetation. Often in flocks. Can take flight by springing directly into the air from the water's surface. Sexes similar in most species, but males of Cinnamon and Blue-winged Teal and Red Shoveler have distinctive basic plumage; short-lived alternate (or "eclipse") plumage is dull, similar to female's. These three also share a common wing pattern, with a conspicuous blue-gray panel on forewing.

1 YELLOW-BILLED PINTAIL *Anas georgica* * 48–56 cm (19–22 in)
Fairly common but local in Andes, 3200–4400 m; also resident locally on southern coast, and rare vagrant to central and northern coast. Primarily on lakes and marshes, often in small flocks. Note long slender neck and relatively long, pointed tail. Easily identified by shape, pale head, and yellow bill; but cf. Speckled Teal. **VOICE** Calls include a bell-like chirp (male) and rough growling quack (female). **Co, E, Br, Bo, Ch**

2 PUNA TEAL *Anas puna* 45–49 cm (17½–19 in)
Common and widespread in Andes, 3000–4600 m, on lakes and marshes; rare vagrant to coast. Gregarious. Note bright blue bill, dark cap, and white cheeks and throat. **VOICE** Call a plaintive, drawn out quack. **Bo, Ch**

3 WHITE-CHEEKED PINTAIL *Anas bahamensis* * 44–47 cm (17¼–18½ in)
Common and widespread on coast, in both fresh and brackish water marshes, lagoons, and bay shores. Present very locally in Andes (Amazonas, 2000 m). Very gregarious. Easily identifiable by white cheeks and throat; also note prominent red base to bill. **VOICE** Calls include whistles (males) and gruff quacks (females). **Co, E, Br, Bo, Ch**

4 SPECKLED TEAL *Anas flavirostris* * 40.5–43 cm (16–17 in)
Common, widespread duck of the Andes, 2800–4800 m, on lakes, rivers and in marshes; also rare vagrant to coast. Small, compact, grayish brown. Bill dark north and west of the Marañón (*andium*); note differences in head and wing pattern from female Blue-winged Teal. More widespread *oxyptera* has yellow bill; smaller, grayer than Yellow-billed Pintail, with head darker (not paler) than body and with plain (not spotted) flanks. **VOICE** Calls include rising, clear whistle (male) and quacks (female). **Co, E, Br, Bo, Ch**

5 BLUE-WINGED TEAL *Anas discors* 37–41 cm (14½–16 in)
Uncommon boreal migrant; primarily present Oct–Apr, but a few may persist through austral winter. Most regular on coast, but also in small numbers in eastern lowlands and, locally, in Andes. May flock with Cinnamon Teal. Alternate male has distinctive white crescent on dark head; also note white patch on lower flanks. Drab brown female similar to female Cinnamon, but grayer, less reddish, brown; also has small white spot or crescent near bill base and narrow white eyering. Bill also smaller and narrower, especially at tip. Cf. also Speckled Teal. **VOICE** Calls whistles (males) and popping quacks (female). **Co, E, Br, Bo, Ch**

6 RED SHOVELER *Anas platalea* 46–51 cm (18–20 in)
Rare; mainly on altiplano, 3200–4200 m, but also very rare vagrant to coast. Perhaps primarily a rare austral migrant but has bred. Very similar to Cinnamon Teal and should be identified with great care. Bill relatively long and broad, especially at tip; often carries head tipped forward, with bill held low over water. Alternate male paler than Cinnamon, with whitish head and neck, whitish iris, densely spotted flanks, and small white patch on lower flanks (cf. subadult male Cinnamon). Female similar to female teal, but larger, paler, with plainer face pattern (lacking suggestion of pale superciliary) and longer tail. **Br, Bo, Ch**

7 CINNAMON TEAL *Anas cyanoptera* * 38–48 cm (15–19 in)
Locally common in coastal marshes, north at least to Lambayeque. Also common on lakes and marshes in southern Andes, 3200–4400 m, but only a rare visitor to Lake Junín. Medium sized. Chestnut male in alternate plumage unmistakable; some have sparse back spotting on flanks. Female is most common black-billed, reddish brown duck; "eclipse" male similar but more rufescent, with red iris. Subadult males intermediate, paler than adult males and extensively marked with black spots and bars. **Co, E** (where now extirpated?), **Br, Bo, Ch**

YELLOW-BILLED PINTAIL

PUNA TEAL

WHITE-CHEEKED PINTAIL

oxyptera

andium

SPECKLED TEAL

♂
♀
BLUE-WINGED TEAL

♀
♂
RED SHOVELER

♀
♂
♀

subad. ♂

CINNAMON TEAL

PLATE
8

DUCKS, POCHARDS, AND SUNGREBE

Ruddy and Masked ducks are "stiff-tailed ducks," with long dark tails (often cocked up in Ruddy Duck). Crested Duck is similar to a dabbling duck but larger. The distinctive Torrent Duck is associated with swift Andean rivers. Pochards are very rare in Peru. Sungrebe, an Amazonian aquatic bird, is not a duck (or a grebe). Pochards, stiff-tailed ducks, and sungrebe all must run along the water's surface, flapping the wings, to gain enough airspeed for flight.

1 MASKED DUCK *Nomonyx dominicus* 32–33 cm (13 in)
Widespread in Amazonia, but uncommon and rarely seen; primarily below 500 m, rarely up to 1500 m. Very rare vagrant (formerly resident?) to northern and central coast. Secretive; usually close to cover in still water with dense grassy vegetation. Often in small flocks (family groups?). Male similar to Ruddy Duck but smaller, with less extensive black on head and densely spotted body. Females and immatures very buffy, densely barred with distinctive heavily striped face. In all plumages note small white patch on wing in flight (although usually retreats into aquatic vegetation rather than taking flight). **Co, E, Br, Bo**

2 RUDDY DUCK *Oxyura jamaicensis* * 42–48 cm (17–19 in)
Fairly common in Andes, 2800–4500 m; also fairly common, but local, on coast. Found on lakes and marshes. Has relatively stout, thick-necked shape. Male is only common, widespread duck with bright blue bill and black head. Female very drab; best identified by characteristic body shape. **VOICE** Usually silent. Male's call in display is a puttering series ending in a quack. **Co, E, Bo, Ch**

3 CRESTED DUCK *Lophonetta specularioides* * 50–60 cm (19–24 in)
Uncommon to fairly common in Andes, 3500–4800 m, on lakes and on rivers, usually as singles or pairs (not in flocks). Large, drab brown, with characteristic dusky mask surrounding eye. Rarely appears crested, but longer feathers on rear crown give a large, block-headed appearance. Note extensive white speculum in flight. **VOICE** Calls include whistles and quiet quacks. **Bo, Ch**

4 TORRENT DUCK *Merganetta armata* * 38–42 cm (15–16½ in)
Fairly common on east slope of Andes, 900–3500 m; very local on Pacific slope. Characteristic bird of clear, fast-moving, boulder-strewn rivers and streams, in both open and forested regions. Singles or pairs often seen standing, with very upright posture, on rocks at water's edge. Agile when swimming, even in turbulent water. Sexes differ but always readily identifiable. Males generally paler overall and whiter below in north; more heavily streaked and darker overall (sometimes almost black-chested) in south. Juvenile very pale. **Co, E, Bo, Ch**

5 SUNGREBE *Heliornis fulica* * 28–31 cm (11–12¼ in)
Uncommon but widespread in Amazonia. Highly aquatic; usually seen swimming, low in water, close to shore on oxbow lakes and other sluggish water bodies, under overhanging vegetation. Usually solitary. Small brown body and boldly striped head unmistakable. Flies low over water with long brown tail protruding behind body. Sexes similar, but female has cinnamon color on side of neck. **VOICE** Largely silent. Calls (song?) include loud cooing bark: "*coo coo COO-AH*" or "*cuAH cuAH cuAH*" and similar notes. Also raspy "*coooah.*" **Co, E, Br, Bo**

SOUTHERN POCHARD *Netta erythrophthalma* * 48–51 cm (19–20 in)
Apparently now almost extirpated from Peru. Formerly reported from coastal marshes; the few recent reports are from high Andean lakes. Due to its current rarity, should be identified with great care. Male is very dark chestnut with blue or blue-gray bill with white subterminal band and reddish iris. Female paler with bold pattern of white stripes and patches. Note large white speculum in flight. **Co, E, Br, Ch**

[ROSY-BILLED POCHARD *Netta peposaca*] 53–57 cm (21–23 in)
Very rare vagrant; photographed in lowlands of Madre de Dios. In flight note broad white stripe on wing (more extensive than in Southern Pochard). Adult male, with bright red bill (including enlarged knob at base of bill) and overall dark body with contrasting pale flanks and vent, is unmistakable (cf. male Muscovy Duck). Immature male (not illustrated) similar but duller. Female similar to female Southern Pochard but has less apparent face pattern and more white on vent. **Br, Bo, Ch**

MASKED DUCK

RUDDY DUCK

CRESTED DUCK

♀

♂ n

juv.

♂ s

TORRENT DUCK

SUNGREBE

♀

♂

SOUTHERN POCHARD

♂

♀

ROSY-BILLED POCHARD

♂

♀

PLATE
9

CHACHALACAS AND WOOD-QUAIL

Chachalacas are small arboreal cracids (see plate 10). Usually in small flocks that often remain concealed in vegetation but reveal their presence with loud vocalizations. The song often is performed at dawn or dusk as a duet or chorus. Wood-quail are terrestrial birds of humid forest in eastern Peru. Typically forage in pairs or small flocks (coveys). Heard far more often than seen. More compact than tinamous, with short bushy crests and a short thick bill; unlike tinamous, also frequently call when alarmed.

1 RUFOUS-HEADED CHACHALACA *Ortalis erythroptera* 56–61 cm (22–24 in)
Restricted to semideciduous and evergreen forests in Tumbes below 900 m, where uncommon (and apparently hunted for food); only chachalaca in northwest. Note plain appearance and rusty-colored head and, in flight, rufous primaries and outer rectrices. **VOICE** Song (in duet or chorus) a raucous 3-note chatter: "*ra-DUK-quaw!*" Other calls include various rattles, purrs, whines, and other sounds. **E**

2 SPECKLED CHACHALACA *Ortalis guttata* * 49.5–52 cm (19½–20½ in)
Widespread and fairly common in eastern Peru, to 1700 m. Originally a bird of river-edge forest that has successfully colonized second growth and forest edge; often persists close to towns and villages if not hunted heavily. Much smaller than *Penelope* guans, with drabber plumage, and a reduced dewlap. **VOICE** Song (in duet or chorus) a raucous 4-note chatter: "*rah-KA'DUK-kah!*" or "*cha-cha'LAH-kah!*" Other calls include cackles, rattles, purrs, whines, and other sounds. **Co, E, Br, Bo**

3 RUFOUS-BREASTED WOOD-QUAIL *Odontophorus speciosus* * 24–26.5 cm (9½–10½ in)
Uncommon in humid montane forest along east slope of Andes and on outlying ridges, 900–2600 m. Usually in pairs. The most widespread montane wood-quail (but in south cf. Stripe-faced Wood-Quail). Sexually dimorphic; geographically variable. Female of northern *speciosus* (south to Ayacucho) has gray belly. Male of southern *loricatus* has reduced whitish superciliary (especially behind the eye), and belly of female not gray but (variably) washed with brown (contrasting less with rufous breast). **VOICE** Song duet is a musical caroling: "*DUEE-do,*" a second bird responding "*CHEER-a-lo.*" At very close range, a quiet "*ro-coco*" introductory phrase may be audible. Voice higher pitched than the two lowland wood-quail; more syllables than Stripe-faced Wood-Quail. Calls a series of fussing peeps when alarmed; also loud chirping. **E, Bo**

4 MARBLED WOOD-QUAIL *Odontophorus gujanensis* * 25.5–28 cm (10–11 in)
Widespread and uncommon to fairly common in northern and central Amazonia. Sexes similar; a drab, grayish brown wood-quail with dull brown crest. Cf. Starred Wood-Quail, which has more ornate plumage pattern. Northern *buckleyi* (north of the Amazon) is duller and grayer; populations south of the Amazon browner, with rufous wash on the face and throat (especially in *rufogularis* of eastern Peru; less so in *pachyrhynchus* [not illustrated] closer to foothills). **VOICE** Song duet a mellow caroling, the second note higher: "*quoo-coo,*" a second individual answering with a rising bisyllabic "*hoo-Li?*" Very similar to (not safely distinguishable from?) Starred Wood-Quail, but more bubbly, less quavering, slightly faster paced. **Co, E, Br, Bo**

5 STRIPE-FACED WOOD-QUAIL *Odontophorus balliviani* 26 cm (10¼ in)
Uncommon to locally fairly common, in humid montane forest on east slope of Andes of southern Peru, 1800–3300 m, occasionally down to 800 m. Readily recognized by rufous crown and boldly black- and buff-striped face pattern. **VOICE** Song duet, a mellow whistled chattering series: "*cur-REE,*" a second individual answering with "*BEE-tur.*" Higher pitched than the two lowland wood-quail, fewer syllables than Rufous-breasted Wood-Quail. Calls popping chirps. **Bo**

6 STARRED WOOD-QUAIL *Odontophorus stellatus* 24–26.5 cm (9½–10½ in)
Widespread and fairly common in much of Amazonian Peru up to 1000 m, although scarce or absent from northeastern Peru. Crown rufous in male, browner in female, but in both sexes shows contrast with plain gray sides of the face and nape; also note prominently spotted body plumage. **VOICE** Song duet a mellow caroling, the second note higher and quavering: "*whoo-COO'O'O'O'O,*" a second individual answering with a rising "*crui*" ("*whoHEE*") between phrases. Very similar to (not safely distinguishable from?) Marbled Wood-Quail, but slightly more rolling and slower paced. **E, Br, Bo**

RUFOUS-HEADED CHACHALACA

SPECKLED CHACHALACA

speciosus
♂

♀

RUFOUS-BREASTED
WOOD-QUAIL

buckleyi

MARBLED
WOOD-QUAIL

loricatus
♂

♀

rufogularis

STRIPE-FACED
WOOD-QUAIL

STARRED WOOD-QUAIL

♀

♂

PLATE
10

BROWNISH GUANS

Cracids (chachalacas, guans and curassows) are large, long-tailed, and long-necked birds resembling pheasants or turkeys. Primarily eat fruit, including fruit that has fallen to the ground. Most are heavily hunted for food; populations of many species have declined significantly, and several are critically endangered. Some genera (Penelope, Pipile, Chamaepetes, Aburria) have a characteristic predawn display: as the male sails from one tree to another, air rushing through the narrow outer primaries produces a whirring or rattling sound. Guans on this plate (Penelope, Chamaepetes) are largely brown, primarily arboreal, and usually encountered as singles or pairs.

1 WHITE-WINGED GUAN *Penelope albipennis* 70 cm (27½ in)

Very rare; confined to dry forests of northwest, in small isolated populations in valleys at base of Andes, 300–1200 m (but formerly occurred into lowlands). Greatly threatened, primarily by habitat destruction, but now the focus of a captive breeding and release program. No known overlap with other guans (but see Crested Guan). Readily recognized by the large white area on the primaries (although white on closed wing may be almost concealed when at rest). The blackest *Penelope* guan (enhancing contrast to white wings), and only one with two-toned bill. **VOICE** Predawn display interspersed with loud yelps. Calls grunting barks and yelps. **ENDEMIC**

2 SICKLE-WINGED GUAN *Chamaepetes goudotii* * 61–63.5 cm (24–25 in)

Uncommon and local in humid montane forest along east slope of Andes and on outlying ridges; primarily 900–2200 m, but in Puno only at much higher elevations (3000 m). Readily recognized by prominent blue facial skin and rufous underparts. Geographically variable; northern *tschudii* has a more extensive rufous breast than does southern *rufiventris*, but the two subspecies intergrade in central Peru. **VOICE** Song, usually given predawn, is a series of thin, high-pitched, rising whistles: "*weeee weeEE WEEEEE WEEEEE?*" accompanied by wing-quill rattling when changing singing perches. Alarm calls a quiet rising "*wee?*" and more popping "*wee-op*" calls in series. **Co, E, Bo**

3 BEARDED GUAN *Penelope barbata* 56–61 cm (22–24 in)

Uncommon and geographically restricted to humid montane forest in northwest, 1700–2950 m, on both slopes of western cordillera. Similar to Andean Guan, which it replaces north and west of Marañón (no geographic overlap); note Bearded's rufous band at tip of tail and more heavily streaked underparts and crown. **VOICE** Predawn display occasionally interspersed with popping yelps. Calls popping yelps and barks. **E**

4 ANDEAN GUAN *Penelope montagnii* * 53.5–58.5 cm (21–23 in)

The widespread guan of humid montane forest of east slope of Andes, 1700–3450 m, locally down to 900 m. Occasionally encountered in small flocks (family groups?). Much smaller and browner than Sickle-winged Guan and does not have a blue face. More similar to Spix's Guan, which replaces Andean in lowlands, but is smaller and has less extensive red wattle, less pronounced crest, and more white "grizzling" on face and upper neck. **VOICE** Predawn display occasionally interspersed with yelps or screams (similar to those of woolly monkey). Calls include yelps and barks. **Co, E, Bo**

5 [CRESTED GUAN *Penelope purpurascens*] * 84–91.5 cm (33–36 in)

Apparently rare, and restricted to evergreen forests at ca. 800 m in Tumbes. No overlap with similar Spix's Guan of Amazonia. Much browner overall (especially on lower belly) than White-winged Guan, and wings are entirely dark (but white of White-winged can be largely concealed at rest). Also more heavily streaked on breast. Facial skin is slate (not purplish), gular flap redder (less orange), and tarsi and feet are red (not pinkish flesh). **VOICE** Predawn display interspersed with loud yelps. Calls include barks and popping yelps. **Co, E**

6 SPIX'S GUAN *Penelope jacquacu* * 76–84 cm (30–33 in)

Widespread and fairly common in Amazonia, up to 1500 m. Partially arboreal, but also frequently forages on or near ground. When alarmed, takes flight with loud calls, often accompanied by crashing sounds as it takes refuge in trees. The only large brown cracid in most of Amazonia. **VOICE** Predawn display occasionally interspersed with yelps or barks. Calls varied and loud and include a honking or yelping "*peeyuk*," becoming harsh barks when flushed. **Co, E, Br, Bo**

WHITE-WINGED GUAN

tschudii

rufiventris

SICKLE-WINGED GUAN

BEARDED GUAN

ANDEAN GUAN

CRESTED GUAN

SPIX'S GUAN

PLATE
11
BLACKISH GUANS AND CURASSOWS

Piping-Guan and Wattled Guan are primarily arboreal. Curassows are the most terrestrial cracids.

1 BLUE-THROATED PIPING-GUAN *Pipile cumanensis* * 68.5–73.5 cm (27–29 in)
Widespread, locally fairly common in Amazonia, up to 700 m, locally to 1100 m. Often in river-edge forest, also in terra firme. Typically as singles or pairs, less frequently in small groups. Crosses large open spaces (such as rivers) in long glide on flat wings. **VOICE** Song, usually predawn, is a series of thin, high pitched, rising whistles: "*weeee weeEE WEEEEE WEEEEE?*" accompanied by wing-quill rattling when changing singing perches. Call a popping squeak: "*Pqueeew.*" **Co, E, Br, Bo**

2 WATTLED GUAN *Aburria aburri* 73.5–81.5 cm (29–32 in)
Rare to uncommon in humid montane forest on east slope of Andes and on outlying ridges, 650–2200 m; formerly also local on west slope in Cajamarca (where now extirpated?). Often concealed within dense vegetation; easily overlooked except by voice. Very dark, with contrasting blue bill, small orange and yellow gular wattle, and short yellow tarsi. **VOICE** Song, usually at night and predawn, is a reedy, unbirdlike growl, rising and falling in pitch: "*grrrrREEEEEERRRrrrrrrr.*" Calls high whistled notes. **Co, E**

3 SALVIN'S CURASSOW *Mitu salvini* 84–89 cm (33–35 in)
Rare and local in humid forest in northern Amazonia. Heavily hunted; scarce near human settlements. Behavior like that of Razor-billed Curassow; the two species may meet (or overlap?) very locally north of the Amazon, near the Colombian border. Salvin's has white (not chestnut) lower belly and undertail coverts; bill relatively small. **VOICE** Song, mostly at dawn, a series of deep booming notes similar in pattern to Razor-billed Curassow, but final 2 notes not as emphasized: "*mmm mmmMMMM… BMM'mmmm-mmmm.*" Calls rising whistles and popping notes. **Co, E**

4 RAZOR-BILLED CURASSOW *Mitu tuberosum* 83–89 cm (32¼–35 in)
Heavily hunted; extirpated or rare in much of its range. Even so, remains the most commonly seen curassow in Amazonia, up to 1350 m. Widespread south of the Amazon; also locally on the north bank of the Amazon near the Colombian border (where cf. Salvin's Curassow). Usually seen as singles or pairs, on ground in humid forest, but may fly up to low perch when alarmed. Bright red bill laterally compressed, variable in size; bill size overlaps between sexes (although largest-billed birds probably are males). **VOICE** Song, mostly at dawn, is a series of deep booming notes, the first 3 rising, the last 2 even at a slightly higher pitch: "*BMMM mmMMMM… mmMMM'BMMM-BMMM,*" sometimes followed after pause by sharp "*BMM!*" Calls rising whistles and popping notes. **Co, Br, Bo**

5 NOCTURNAL CURASSOW *Nothocrax urumutum* 66–71 cm (26–28 in)
Widespread and fairly common in terra firme, up to 600 m, in north; reported south to west bank of lower Río Ucayali (but no recent records from there). Very rarely observed, habits not well known; presumably forages on ground. Much more rufescent and uniformly colored than Spix's Guan, with no gular patch. **VOICE** Sings from well above ground, at night (primarily in first few hours after dusk, less commonly before dawn). Song a series of deep, booming notes: "*mmmm mmmm-mmmmm mmmm-MMUUU-MMUUU!*" Sometimes followed after pause by sharp "*BMM!*" **Co, E, Br**

6 HORNED CURASSOW *Pauxi unicornis* * 85–95 cm (33½–37½ in)
Very local and rare in humid forest. Found on the outlying Cerros del Sira in east central Peru, possibly also on outlying ridges in Puno; 900–1200 m. Note prominent blue casque or "horn" at base of bill, and white (not chestnut) lower belly and undertail coverts; red bill is smaller than that of Razor-billed Curassow. **VOICE** Song (Bolivia), mostly at dawn, is a series of deep booming notes: "*mmmmMM mmmMMM-MMM mmMM mmMM-MMM… BMM!*" Call a sharp, popping "*pseet!*" **Bo**

WATTLED CURASSOW *Crax globulosa* 84–89 cm (33–35 in)
Formerly widespread in Amazonia; now almost extirpated, restricted to small, isolated populations in remote northern areas. Restricted to varzea and to tall forest on larger river islands. Poorly known; apparently more arboreal than other curassows. Tip of tail black. Also note bushy crest and black bill, with colorful wattle at base. Bill wattle red, belly and undertail coverts white in male; wattle yellow and lower underparts brown in female. **VOICE** Song (?) is a long, descending whistle, somewhat like a falling bomb: "*Pseeeew.*" Calls similar to song as well as popping sounds. **Co, E, Br, Bo**

BLUE-THROATED PIPING-GUAN

SALVIN'S CURASSOW

WATTLED GUAN

RAZOR-BILLED
CURASSOW

NOCTURNAL
CURASSOW

HORNED CURASSOW

♂

♀

WATTLED CURASSOW

PLATE
12

GREBES

Grebes are highly aquatic; typically never found on dry land (nest is a floating mat of aquatic vegetation). Very adept swimmers (riding high on the water) and divers; also may sink below the water, exposing only the head. Tarsi are placed well to the rear of the body, and toes are lobed (not webbed). Rarely seen in flight (two species are flightless). Superficially similar to ducks but have much finer bills and appear nearly tail-less.

1 TITICACA GREBE *Rollandia microptera* 40 cm (15¾ in)
Large flightless grebe, restricted to Titicaca Basin, 3600–3900 m; formerly fairly common, but populations have declined significantly in recent years, in part because they often become tangled and drown in fishing nets. Note large size, large yellowish bill, rufous wash on neck and breast, and contrast between dark crown and white throat. **Bo**

2 WHITE-TUFTED GREBE *Rollandia rolland* * 26 cm (10¼ in)
Fairly common and widespread both in coastal marshes and on Andean lakes and marshes, above 3200 m. Adults have pale sides of face that contrast with rest of head and neck; this pattern is particularly pronounced in alternate-plumaged birds but visible in all plumages. Immature similar to basic-plumaged adult. Juveniles lack whitish cheek tufts and have black-and-white stripes on sides of face. Cf. Least and Pied-billed grebes. **VOICE** Apparent song (rarely heard) is a series of groans. **Br, Bo, Ch**

3 SILVERY GREBE *Podiceps occipitalis* * 29–30.5 cm (11½–12 in)
Widespread and fairly common in Andes, 3200–4700 m; very rare vagrant to coast and Amazonia. Found on lakes and marshes. Primarily light gray and white (and appearing largely white from any distance). Similar in size to White-tufted Grebe, but readily identified by gray (not brown) flanks and white (not brown) neck. **VOICE** Call a high, bell-like "*tink*" note. **Co, E, Bo, Ch**

4 JUNIN GREBE *Podiceps taczanowskii* 35 cm (14 in)
Endemic to Lake Junín (4080 m); formerly common, but populations have declined drastically (largely from water pollution), and now is local and endangered. Flightless. Breeds (Feb–Mar) in reeds close to shore but otherwise remains in open water far out in lake, typically in small flocks. Very similar to Silvery Grebe, which also is common on Lake Junín, but is slightly larger and appears "lankier" with slimmer neck, longer bill, and paler flanks. At close range, bill is light gray (black in Silvery). **ENDEMIC**

5 LEAST GREBE *Tachybaptus dominicus* * 21.5–23 cm (8½–9 in)
Widespread but scarce, both in central and southern Amazonia and in northwest. Prefers ponds and oxbow lakes in forested areas. Mostly in lowlands, but occasional to at least 3000 m. Smallest grebe in Peru. Adult in alternate plumage very dark, with contrasting yellow iris and black crown and throat. In immatures and adults in basic plumage, throat is white, neck and head are browner, and crown is less contrasting (especially so in immatures?). Juvenile (not illustrated) even browner, with white and dusky stripes on sides of face. Cf. Pied-billed and White-tufted grebes. **VOICE** Song, rarely heard, a reedy chattering trill. Also a nasal honking "*chew.*" **Co, E, Br, Bo**

6 PIED-BILLED GREBE *Podilymbus podiceps* * 28–33 cm (11–13 in)
Uncommon to locally fairly common in coastal marshes; very rare in Andes, also a vagrant to Amazonia. A very brown grebe with characteristic stout, pale bill. Adults in alternate plumage have striking white bill, crossed with black ring, and gray-and-black head pattern. Basic-plumaged adults and immatures are more uniformly colored, and bill lacks black ring. **VOICE** Song is a series of puttering hoots. **Co, E, Br, Bo, Ch**

7 GREAT GREBE *Podiceps major* * 70–78 cm (27–31 in)
Uncommon to locally fairly common on coast. Breeds locally in marshes, but nonbreeding birds often found on ocean, especially on protected bays, where may congregate in flocks. Large, with distinctive long slender neck and long daggerlike bill. Alternate plumage unmistakable. Basic plumage much drabber; typically retain some rufous on neck but can look largely gray at a distance. **VOICE** Calls weak, nasal honks, also thin whistles. **Br, Ch**

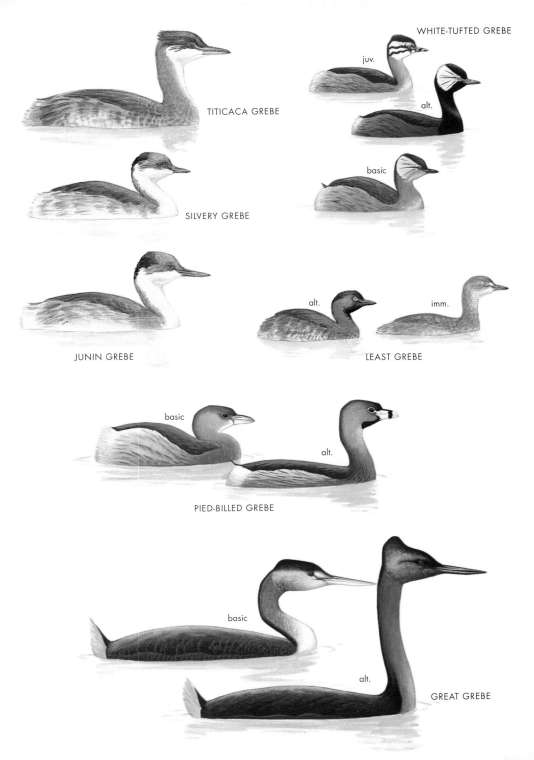

WHITE-TUFTED GREBE

juv.

alt.

basic

TITICACA GREBE

SILVERY GREBE

JUNIN GREBE

alt.

imm.

LEAST GREBE

basic

alt.

PIED-BILLED GREBE

basic

alt.

GREAT GREBE

PLATE
13

WAVED ALBATROSS, GIANT-PETRELS, AND PELICANS

This plate combines several very large, largely brown seabirds that are superficially similar but otherwise not related. All also take several years to reach maturity. Albatrosses and giant-petrels are highly pelagic seabirds that forage entirely at sea. Pelicans also are large and brown and occur in coastal waters (though, unlike albatrosses and petrels, are very common in inshore waters). Pelicans have very long bills with large gular pouches. Frequently seen in flocks flying over water in long lines. Dive into water, from the air, sometimes in spectacular fashion, to catch fish underwater. Molts of pelicans are complicated and poorly understood; in Brown (and probably also Peruvian), these include supplemental molts on head and neck during breeding season. Birds in a flock may show wide range of plumages. Soft part colors also vary seasonally.

1 WAVED ALBATROSS *Phoebastria irrorata* 85–93 cm (33½–37 in); ws 230–240 cm (90–94 in)
Breeds on the Galapagos Islands and Isla de la Plata (Ecuador). Fairly common nonbreeding visitor, throughout the year, south to Ica; much rarer farther south. Relatively long-necked, long-billed, and long-tailed, with whitish head that contrasts with gray-brown body. Not similar to any other Peruvian albatross; more similar to giant-petrels, but even larger, with much longer and distinctly yellow bill. **Co, E, Ch**

2 SOUTHERN GIANT-PETREL *Macronectes giganteus* 86–99 cm (34–39 in); ws 185–205 cm (72–81 in)
Rare to uncommon; primarily present May–Oct but may occur in small numbers throughout year. Regular north to central Peru; rarely north to Tumbes. The expected species of giant-petrel in Peru. Most records are of dark-morph juveniles and immatures, but some adults may occur; white morph also occurs but much less frequently. Superficially similar to albatrosses (especially to Waved) but smaller with broader wings and shorter bill; also note (close range) long nasal tube along culmen. Juveniles very dusky; plumage gradually lightens as bird matures, over several years time. At close range note light greenish tip to yellowish or pinkish bill. **Br, Ch**

[NORTHERN GIANT-PETREL *Macronectes halli*] 81–94 cm (32–37 in); ws 180–200 cm (71–79 in)
Status not clear. Apparently a very rare nonbreeding migrant; photographed off Lima coast. Plumage very similar to that of Southern Giant-Petrel; distinguishable only with great care. In all age classes, has red or reddish tip to the bill (tip green in Southern Giant-Petrel). Juveniles of the two otherwise identical. Adult lacks white morph. Also, white usually restricted to face and upper throat (more extensive on head of Southern). Typically has dark leading edge to wing (this area pale in adult Southern). Adult very unlikely to occur in Peru. **Ch**

3 PERUVIAN PELICAN *Pelecanus thagus* 152 cm (60 in); ws 228 cm (90 in)
Common resident on coast, breeding on offshore islands from Piura south to Chile. Primarily a bird of cold Peruvian Current but disperses in small numbers north to Ecuador. Neck of adult may be largely white or brown; may breed in either plumage, and in white-bellied "immature" plumage as well. Note enormous size and distinctive pelican shape, with long wings, long bill and large gular pouch, and short tail. The most abundant and widespread pelican. Cf. smaller Brown Pelican; also Waved Albatross. **E, Ch**

4 BROWN PELICAN *Pelecanus occidentalis* * 117–132 cm (46–52 in); ws 203 cm (80 in)
Fairly common (and increasing?) nonbreeding visitor to northern coast. Regularly in warm waters off Tumbes and Piura; less common farther south, but during El Niño episodes ranges at least to Ica (and perhaps farther south). Always smaller than more widespread Peruvian Pelican; size is very helpful when both are together but can be difficult to use otherwise. Upperwings always dark (cf. older plumages of Peruvian). Plumages of immature Brown and Peruvian pelicans more similar, but Brown always paler, less chocolaty brown. Bills of immature Brown remain dark; pale yellow or yellow-orange color to bill tip of Peruvian usually develops relatively early. Also note gray gular pouch, rather than paler, often yellowish gular pouch of immature Peruvian. **Co, E, Br, Ch**

WAVED ALBATROSS

WAVED ALBATROSS

NORTHERN
GIANT-PETREL

juv.

ad.

SOUTHERN
GIANT-PETREL

SOUTHERN
GIANT-PETREL

juv.

ad.

ad.

juv.

juv.

ad.

white
morph

SOUTHERN
GIANT-PETREL

juv.

ad. "br."

ad.
"nonbr."

imm.

PERUVIAN
PELICAN

ad.

imm.

ad.

juv.

ad.
"early br."

BROWN PELICAN

ad.

ad. "late br."

ad. "nonbr."

imm.

juv.

ad.

imm.

juv.

PLATE
14

ALBATROSSES (MOLLYMAWKS)

Albatrosses are very large, long-winged, highly pelagic seabirds that soar low over the water on stiff wings, with infrequent wingbeats. The species shown on this plate, collectively known as "mollymawks," breed on subantarctic islands and occur in Peruvian waters as nonbreeding visitors. Mollymawks have white rumps and underparts, and extensively white underwings. Identification is based on bill pattern, presence or absence of a gray hood, and extent and pattern of white on the underwing. Immatures may differ from adults in these same features. In many species nonbreeding juveniles and immatures may be more frequent off of Peru than are full adults. Identification, especially under challenging field conditions at sea, can be difficult if albatrosses are not viewed at close range. Also note that another black-and-white albatross, **Royal Albatross** *(Diomedea epomophora), is not confirmed for Peru but has been reported off northern Chile. Royal is very similar to another species also reported from Chile,* **Wandering Albatross** *(Diomedea exulans). Seabird enthusiasts are encouraged to consult specialized literature on identification of all these species.*

1 BULLER'S ALBATROSS *Thalassarche bulleri* * 80 cm (30 in); ws 210 cm (83 in)
Rare nonbreeding visitor. Black leading edge of underwing is broader than in Shy Albatross; but narrower and more even (rear border generally parallel to shape of wing itself) than in Gray-headed. Gray hood is relatively pale, and white cap contrasts more than in Gray-headed. Bill relatively slender, with broad yellow stripes; yellow stripe on mandible comes closer to tip of bill. Juvenile has pale bill with dark tip; similar to Shy (especially to widespread *salvini*) but has broader black leading edge to underwing coverts. **Ch**

2 SHY ALBATROSS *Thalassarche cauta* * 95 cm (37 in); ws 250 cm (98 in)
Two recognizably different subspecies visit Peru: *salvini* ("Salvin's" Albatross) is the most common mollymawk in Peru, whereas *eremita* ("Chatham" Albatross) is rare. These also may segregate at sea to some extent, with *eremita* more highly pelagic (most common in waters > 3000 m deep) than *salvini*. Both are distinguished from other mollymawks by very narrow black leading edge to underwing coverts. Also note small black "thumbmark" where underside of wing joins body. Bill of *salvini* always is pale with dark tip, although bill of juvenile is darker than in adult; always has light gray hood with white cap. Rare *eremita* has darker gray hood with less of a white cap, and bill is somewhat shorter and thicker. Adult readily identifiable by bright yellow bill. Immature with duller bill less easily separable from *salvini*, although head and neck are darker gray. **Br, Ch**

3 GRAY-HEADED ALBATROSS *Thalassarche chrysostoma* 81 cm (32 in); ws 220 cm (87 in)
Rare nonbreeding visitor. Black leading edge of underwing is broad and uneven; head and neck always gray. Cf. adults of Black-browed and Buller's albatrosses. Bill of adult is black with narrow yellow stripe down culmen, and another (which does not reach tip) on lower mandible. Juvenile has dusky underwings and bill; cf. juvenile Black-browed Albatross. **Br, Ch**

4 BLACK-BROWED ALBATROSS *Thalassarche melanophris* * 88 cm (35 in); ws 220 cm (87 in)
Uncommon nonbreeding visitor, although probably more common in southern waters. Resembles immensely overgrown Kelp Gull. Black leading edge of underwing very broad and "ragged," as in Gray-headed Albatross; but Black-browed differs by white head (the only white-headed mollymawk) and, in adult, by bright yellow bill with orange tip. Juvenile has very dusky underwing coverts and dusky bill; head is white, but often shows a light gray collar on neck and breast. Juvenile is very similar to juvenile Gray-headed Albatross, but Gray-headed has a gray head (often with paler "cheeks") and bill that is more uniformly dark, lacking Black-browed's pale base to bill. **E, Br, Ch**

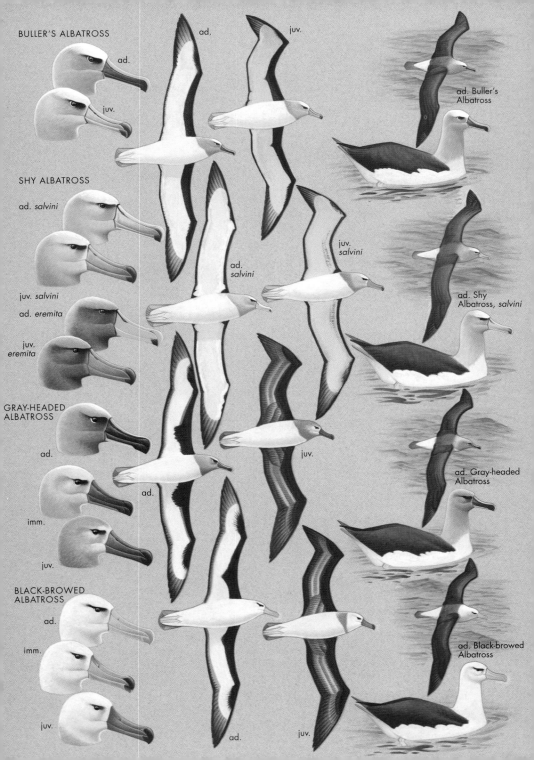

BULLER'S ALBATROSS

ad.

juv.

ad.

juv.

ad. Buller's
Albatross

SHY ALBATROSS

ad. *salvini*

juv. *salvini*

ad. *eremita*

juv.
eremita

ad.
salvini

juv.
salvini

ad. Shy
Albatross, *salvini*

GRAY-HEADED
ALBATROSS

ad.

imm.

juv.

ad.

juv.

ad. Gray-headed
Albatross

BLACK-BROWED
ALBATROSS

ad.

imm.

juv.

ad.

juv.

ad. Black-browed
Albatross

PLATE
15

GADFLY PETRELS (*PTERODROMA*)

Gadfly petrels (Pterodroma) *are highly pelagic and rarely are encountered within 50 km or so of shore. None breed in Peru. Some are reported only from westernmost fringes of Peruvian waters. Several other species of central Pacific, not yet reported from Peru, also may occur in this region, at least occasionally; consult seabird literature for more discussion of these species.* Pterodroma *have a distinctive flight style, often soaring high above water before dropping down again. Plumage differences between species can be subtle; be prepared to leave some individuals unidentified. "Cookilaria" group (Cook's, Masatierra, and Stejneger's petrels) are relatively small, short-tailed, and short-winged compared to other* Pterodroma.

1 **[JUAN FERNANDEZ PETREL** *Pterodroma externa*] 43 cm (17 in); ws 95 cm (37 in)
Status not well known; reported only from sight records, primarily Apr–May (following breeding off coast of Chile, Dec–Mar), but presumably occurs again in southbound passage (Oct–Nov?). Significantly larger and long-winged than "*Cookilaria*" petrels with stronger, more buoyant flight. Tail all dark, and often shows narrow white band on rump. Some have variably pale collars on nape, separating blackish crown from gray back. Bill heavy; underwings extensively white. **Ch**

2 **[KERMADEC PETREL** *Pterodroma neglecta*] * 38 cm (15 in); ws 92 cm (36 in)
Status not well known, but apparently is regular far out at sea, Mar–Nov; only reported from sight records. Polymorphic; dark morphs are most frequent in Peru, although intermediate morph also has been reported. Dark plumage, white flash at base of primaries and strong flight lend superficial similarity to jaegers. White bases of primaries are particularly prominent from below. Rarely dark-morph individuals may lack white feather bases but always show white feather shafts. **Br, Ch**

3 **MASATIERRA (De Filippi's) PETREL** *Pterodroma defilippiana* 26 cm (10¼ in); ws 66 cm (26 in)
Status, distribution, and seasonality not well known, due in part to confusion with very similar Cook's Petrel; recorded Apr–Oct. Slightly larger than Cook's with thicker bill (only apparent at close range). Note more extensive gray partial collar on sides of breast, which sets off intrusion of white below and behind eye smudge (a feature lacking in Cook's). Dark eye smudge also larger than in Cook's. Tip of tail usually pale (always dark in Cook's, but also may be dark in some Masatierra). May appear broader-winged than Cook's. Sometimes (especially when worn?) may appear to have dusky crown and nape; cf. Stejneger's Petrel. Adults may begin wing molt Oct–Nov; Cook's primarily molts Mar–Aug. **Ch**

4 **COOK'S PETREL** *Pterodroma cookii* 26 cm (10¼ in); ws 66 cm (26 in)
Primarily present June–Oct, but status, distribution, and seasonality poorly known due to great similarity to Masatierra Petrel. Both are small *Pterodroma*, light gray above with distinct "M"-shaped pattern across mantle, and have light gray crowns, with black smudge around eyes. Cook's lacks gray neck collar of Masatierra; black eye smudge is smaller; and bill is thinner, more delicate. Cook's may look thinner-winged and shorter-tailed. Always has narrow dark tip to tail (tail of Masatierra may be tipped black but usually all gray). Little or no overlap in timing of wing molt. Sometimes (especially when worn?) may appear to have dusky crown and nape; cf. Stejneger's Petrel. **Ch**

[STEJNEGER'S PETREL *Pterodroma longirostris*] 26 cm (10¼ in); ws 66 cm (26 in)
No confirmed record, but may be expected (breeds Dec–Mar on Masatierra Island off Chile). Similar to Cook's and Masatierra petrels, but white forehead contrasts with dusky crown. Worn Cook's and Masatierra may appear black-crowned; carefully note forehead pattern. Partial collar to sides of breast is darker, but less extensive, than half-collar of Masatierra. Dorsal surface of primaries of Stejneger's also is blacker. Bill thinner, longer than bill of Masatierra. Cf. also Juan Fernandez Petrel, which is larger with longer wings and often has narrow white rump. **Ch**

5 **GALAPAGOS PETREL** *Pterodroma phaeopygia* 43 cm (17 in); ws 91 cm (36 in)
Regular nonbreeding migrant (Sept–Feb) to northern waters. Relatively large, long-winged petrel. Note blackish crown and sides of face, dark upperparts, and white forehead. Superficially similar to Stejneger's and Juan Fernandez petrels but lacks prominent "M" pattern on mantle. Black crown and nape form an extensive "shawl" from head to upper breast (with no white intrusion behind auriculars), and has more extensive carpal bar on underwings. Also, bill heavy, and tail relatively long. **Co, E**

JUAN FERNANDEZ
PETREL

rump pattern
var.

pale
morph

intermed.
morph

KERMADEC PETREL

pale
morph

dark
morph

MASATIERRA PETREL

COOK'S PETREL

Masatierra
tail var.

STEJNEGER'S PETREL

GALAPAGOS
PETREL

PLATE
16

WHITE-BELLIED SHEARWATERS AND DIVING-PETREL

Shearwaters are pelagic seabirds that glide low over the water, with wings held stiffly outstretched; none breed in Peru. Species on this plate are small to medium-sized, with white underparts; rarely seen from shore. The diving-petrel is a small seabird of inshore waters.

[**WEDGE-TAILED SHEARWATER** *Puffinus pacificus*] 41–46 cm (16–18 in); ws 97–104 cm (38–41 in)
Rare; known only from a few sight records far off of Piura. Polymorphic; all records are of light morph, but dark morph (not illustrated) also exists. Wedge shape to tail difficult to notice (except when tail is fanned) but contributes to long-tailed appearance. Light morph similar to Pink-footed Shearwater, but Wedge-tailed has more extensively white underwings, flanks, and throat; more slender build (accentuated by long tail); and thinner, dingy-colored bill. Dark morph is entirely dark; resembles Flesh-footed Shearwater but is more slender and longer-tailed, and has slim, dingy-colored bill. **Co, E**

1 SOUTHERN FULMAR *Fulmarus glacialoides* 46–50 cm (18–20 in); ws 114–120 cm (45–47 in)
Rare to uncommon visitor; abundance may vary from year to year, and probably more regular in south. Primarily present Jul–Oct. Medium-sized, with stocky neck and relatively broad, blunt wings. Very pale gray above and white below. Superficially similar to a large gull but has typical stiff-winged shearwater flight profile. Note dark-tipped pink bill and white bases to primaries on upper surface of wing. **E, Br, Ch**

2 BULLER'S SHEARWATER *Puffinus bulleri* 46 cm (18 in); ws 97 cm (38 in)
Uncommon; probably primarily present Nov–May. Long tail and narrow wings impart a slender appearance. Readily identifiable by white underparts, extensively white underwing coverts, and prominent black "M" pattern across wings and back. Superficially similar to some *Pterodroma* petrels (such as Juan Fernandez Petrel), but does not have well-defined white forecrown, and underwings lack dark carpal mark. **E, Ch**

3 PINK-FOOTED SHEARWATER *Puffinus creatopus* 48 cm (19 in); ws 109 cm (43 in)
Fairly common migrant, primarily Mar–Nov; the most numerous white-bellied shearwater. Large, relatively stout with short broad tail. Bill light pink with dark tip. Underwing coverts often white; but variably clouded and may be largely dark. Throat and sides of neck freckled with brown, and flanks are variably mottled brown (other white-bellied shearwaters have clean white throats and white flanks). **Co, E, Ch**

GRAY PETREL *Procellaria cinerea* 48 cm (19 in); ws 117–127 cm (46–50 in)
Status unclear. A few undocumented sight records and 2 skulls found on beaches (reportedly of this species; identifications should be confirmed); possibly does not occur (rare in Chile, where only reported from far south). Long, narrow wings may impart similarity in flight to much larger albatrosses. Note generally dark upperparts, and dark underwings that contrast with white underparts (other large white-bellied shearwaters have largely white underwings). Bill also is yellowish. **Br, Ch**

[**AUDUBON'S SHEARWATER** *Puffinus lherminieri*] * 29–30.5 cm (11½–12 in); ws 69 cm (27 in)
Status not clear; a few undocumented sight records off northern and central Peru. Associated with warm water. Very similar to Little and Manx shearwaters, but undertail coverts black (not white). Also browner (less blackish) above, with broader dark margins to underwings. Bill longer than bill of Little; tarsi typically pinkish. Sightings should be extensively documented. **Co, E**

[**LITTLE SHEARWATER** *Puffinus assimilis*] * 25–30 cm (10–12 in); ws 58–67 cm (23–26 in)
Status unclear; a few undocumented sight records off central and southern coast (May–Aug). Associated with cold water. Very small black-and-white shearwater, with relatively short, blunt-tipped wings. Flight characterized by rapid wingbeats with little gliding. Often shows narrow pale panel on greater wing coverts. [**Manx Shearwater** (*Puffinus puffinus*; not illustrated), not known from Peru, is potential vagrant to south. Very similar to Little, and also has all-white undertail coverts; but slightly larger with pinkish tarsi and toes (typically light blue or bluish gray in Little). Also, wings are less rounded, underwing coverts more clouded, and upperparts more uniformly dark.] Sightings of Little or Manx should be extensively documented. Cf. also Audubon's Shearwater. **Br, Ch**

4 PERUVIAN DIVING-PETREL *Pelecanoides garnotii* 20–24 cm (8–9½ in)
Rare and seriously declining resident. Small, chunky, gray and white seabird. Often seen as singles or small groups resting on water, or flying away with very rapid, whirring wingbeats; does not soar or glide. **Ch**

WEDGE-TAILED
SHEARWATER

SOUTHERN
FULMAR

BULLER'S SHEARWATER

GRAY PETREL

PINK-FOOTED SHEARWATER

AUDUBON'S
SHEARWATER

LITTLE SHEARWATER

PERUVIAN DIVING-PETREL

PLATE
17
DARK SHEARWATERS AND PETRELS

Cape Petrel has a very distinctive black-and-white pattern. The other species on this plate are large, dark-bellied shearwaters. Procellaria are stockier than Puffinus shearwaters and have a deeper-chested appearance. They also have larger heads, stouter bills, and tails are relatively short, and slightly graduated; the toes may extend beyond the tail tip in flight.

1 CAPE PETREL *Daption capense* * 38–40 cm (15–16 in); ws 81–91 cm (32–36 in)

Fairly common off southern and central Peru, less common in far north. May occur throughout year, but probably most numerous June–Sept. Medium-sized and built somewhat like Southern Fulmar: rather stout, with thick neck and broad wings. Distinctive dark throat and "pied" pattern on upperparts. White bases to primaries, and white patch on inner wing, are prominent on upper surface. Also note broad white tail with dark terminal band. Underparts largely white, contrasting with dark head and throat. **Co, E, Br, Ch**

[FLESH-FOOTED SHEARWATER *Puffinus carneipes*] 41–45 cm (16–18 in); ws 99–106 cm (39–42 in)

Status not certain, but perhaps a very rare visitor; known only from a few undocumented sight records off northern and central Peru. Larger and broader-winged than Sooty Shearwater, with dark underwing coverts. Pink bill (with small dark tip) often visible at a distance; tarsi also pink but difficult to see under most field conditions. Cf. also dark morph of Wedge-tailed Shearwater (not yet reported from Peru). Most *Procellaria* petrels are larger and bulkier, with relatively shorter wings and tails, dark tarsi, and deeper, yellower bills; but cf. Parkinson's, which is close to Flesh-footed in size. **Ch**

2 SOOTY SHEARWATER *Puffinus griseus* 40–46 cm (16–18 in); ws 94–104 cm (37–41 in)

Perhaps the most abundant shearwater in Peru, and one of the species most likely to be seen from shore. Often seen in large flocks. Found throughout the year, but most numerous May–Oct. Medium-sized, with narrow wings and rapid wingbeats. Largely sooty brown; underwing coverts silvery white, but this sometimes is difficult to see in the field (depending on distance and light conditions). Bill black. **Co, E, Br, Ch**

3 WHITE-CHINNED PETREL *Procellaria aequinoctialis* 51–58 cm (20–23 in); ws 134–147 cm (53–58 in)

Uncommon, but the most widespread *Procellaria* in Peru; probably found throughout the year. Superficially similar to Sooty Shearwater but larger, broader-winged, and with dark underwing coverts. Also note heavier bill, which is yellowish (narrowly etched with dusky) with pale tip. Usually has white chin, although rarely visible in the field, and in some individuals (subadults?) may be represented by no more than a few white feathers. **E, Br, Ch**

[WESTLAND PETREL *Procellaria westlandica*] 51 cm (20 in); ws 137 cm (54 in)

Status not certain (and confirmation of occurrence in Peru highly desirable). Known only from a few sight records from off Piura, but probably also occurs (more regularly?) off southern Peru (apparently occurs regularly off coast of Chile). Usually distinguished from White-chinned Petrel by dark tip to bill, and more extensively dusky on nasal tube; chin also all dark. Apparently a small minority (ca. 1♀?) of White-chinneds have some dusky on the tip of the bill; carefully check details of bill pattern and chin color. Typically undergoes molt during austral spring and summer (Oct–Mar); little overlap in timing of wing molt with White-chinned (Feb–Aug). Larger than Parkinson's Petrel, with relatively larger head and neck, and shorter, broader wings. **Ch**

4 PARKINSON'S (Black) PETREL *Procellaria parkinsoni* 46–47 cm; ws 115 cm (45 in)

Primarily known from northern waters, but distribution not well known and may occur farther south. Very similar to White-chinned Petrel, but smaller and looks less "heavy" in flight; also has relatively longer, narrower wings. Primarily differs by yellow bill with dark tip. Lacks white throat spot. Cf. also larger Westland Petrel; Parkinson's is less stocky, with relatively smaller, more rounded head and has longer, narrower wings. At rest, wings project farther beyond tail tip. Often associates with cetaceans and may follow pods of small whales for long distances. **E**

FLESH-FOOTED
SHEARWATER

CAPE PETREL

Flesh-footed

Sooty

SOOTY
SHEARWATER

WESTLAND PETREL

WHITE-CHINNED
PETREL

White-chinned

Westland

PARKINSON'S
PETREL

PLATE
18

PRIONS AND STORM-PETRELS

Prions (Pachyptila) are very small shearwaters that fly low over the water. Note small size, pale color and narrow "M" pattern across upperparts. Species are very similar to one another; best distinguished in the hand by bill size and shape, features that are difficult to determine accurately in the field. Storm-Petrels are very small pelagic seabirds that fly low over the water. Plumage differences often are subtle. Other than Ringed, species on this plate are rare or geographically restricted, nonbreeding visitors.

1 DOVE (Antarctic) PRION *Pachyptila desolata* 27 cm (10½ in); ws 61 cm (24 in)

Status poorly known; most records are of carcasses found dead on beach, Jun–Aug, but presumably occurs at sea as well. Can be difficult to distinguish from Slender-billed Prion. Bill deeper and broader than in Slender-billed, but this is difficult to gauge in the field. Dove has duskier face with narrower white superciliary, more prominent black band at tip of tail, and blacker "M" pattern across back and wings. Flight also is less acrobatic. **Br, Ch**

2 SLENDER-BILLED (Thin-billed) PRION *Pachyptila belcheri* 26 cm (10¼ in); ws 56 cm (22 in)

Uncommon, primarily present Jun–Aug, but abundance variable from year to year. Most widespread and usually most common prion. Has thin, narrow bill, but this rarely is helpful in the field. Distinguish with care from Dove Prion by broader white superciliary, less contrasting dark "M" across wings and back, and (on average) less extensive black on tip of tail (black often not reaching outer rectrices). **Br, Ch**

BROAD-BILLED PRION *Pachyptila vittata* 25–30 cm (10–12 in); ws 57–66 cm (22½–26 in)

Known from a single beached carcass (Arequipa); not regularly found in waters off Pacific coast of South America, and so not expected to recur. Relatively large prion with very large, blackish bill. Head dark, with no strong face pattern. Also may show gray partial collar on sides of breast. **Br**

3 RINGED (Hornby's) STORM-PETREL *Oceanodroma hornbyi* 21–23 cm (8–9 in)

Resident and presumably breeds, but nest remains unknown. Occasionally found well inland, far from the ocean, prompting speculation that breeding sites are in coastal deserts or hills (and not on islands, where most other storm-petrels breed). Relatively large with distinctive plumage. Tail is long and deeply notched. Wingbeats slow, interspersed with glides. **Co, E, Ch**

[WHITE-BELLIED STORM-PETREL *Fregetta grallaria*] * 20 cm (8 in); ws 46 cm (18 in)

Reported only from undocumented sight records; probably more regular in occurrence far at sea (outside of Peruvian waters?), especially in south. Medium-sized, relatively robust storm-petrel. This and Black-bellied Storm-Petrel are only white-rumped species with white belly and underwing coverts; other species with white rumps are entirely dark below. Both fly very low, dangling legs and hitting the water with breast, then bouncing clear. They are extremely similar to one another and difficult to distinguish in the field. Belly of White-bellied is entirely white; Black-bellied has narrow dark stripe down center of belly (which can be difficult to see). Also, White-bellied has shorter tarsi (do not project beyond the tail in flight) and paler upperparts, with more prominent pale bar on greater coverts. Underwing coverts of White-bellied also whiter, and border to dark hood straighter. **Br, Ch**

BLACK-BELLIED STORM-PETREL *Fregetta tropica* * 20 cm (8 in); ws 46 cm (18 in)

Known from a single specimen off central Peru. Cf. extremely similar White-bellied Storm-Petrel (also rare in Peru). **Br, Ch**

4 WHITE-FACED STORM-PETREL *Pelagodroma marina* * 18–21 cm (7–8 in); ws 42–43 cm (16–17 in)

Status not clear, but perhaps a regular but uncommon visitor far off coast. A large, gray-and-white storm-petrel with very long tarsi (extend beyond the tail in flight). Note distinctive dark mask and broad white superciliary. Cf. Ringed Storm-Petrel. **E, Br, Ch**

5 LEAST STORM-PETREL *Oceanodroma microsoma* 14–15 cm (5½–6 in); ws 32 cm (12½ in)

Rare off the northern coast (Nov–Mar). Very small, with relatively short tail. All dark, except for pale bar along upperwing surface. Due to dark color and short tail, can resemble a small bat flying low and direct over water. Much smaller than Markham's and Black storm-petrels, with wedge-shaped (not forked) tail. **Co, E**

prions at sea

DOVE PRION

DOVE PRION

SLENDER-BILLED PRION

SLENDER-BILLED PRION

BROAD-BILLED PRION

RINGED STORM-PETREL

WHITE-BELLIED STORM-PETREL

foot skidding

BLACK-BELLIED STORM-PETREL

WHITE-FACED STORM-PETREL

LEAST STORM-PETREL

PLATE
19

TYPICAL STORM-PETRELS

Species on this plate are dark-bellied storm-petrels, most of which also have white rumps. Plumage differences often are subtle; identification also depends upon overall structure and on flight behavior.

1 WILSON'S STORM-PETREL *Oceanites oceanicus* * 15–19 cm (6–8 in); ws 38–42 cm (15–16½ in)

This and the similar White-vented are the most common and widespread storm-petrels. Probably present throughout year, but most numerous during austral winter. Associated with cold water. Forages while "pattering" over water, dangling feet; otherwise flight is low and rapid but relatively direct. Both *Oceanites* species hold wing relatively straight; cf. more strongly arced profiles of *Oceanodroma* species. In *Oceanites* toes may extend beyond tail in flight; no *Oceanodroma* shows this. Webbing between toes in Wilson's is yellow; diagnostic but rarely seen (webbing dark in similar species). Cf. other white-rumped storm-petrels (especially White-vented). **E, Br, Ch**

2 WHITE-VENTED (Elliot's) STORM-PETREL *Oceanites gracilis* * 15–16 cm (6–6½ in); ws 40 cm (16 in)

Very similar to Wilson's Storm-Petrel, and with similar association with cold waters, but is fairly common resident (though very few breeding sites are known). Slightly smaller than Wilson's. Small white patch on lower belly diagnostic but difficult to see. Also has pale area on underwings (lacking in Wilson's), and white rump is slightly narrower. Flight similar to Wilson's, but perhaps somewhat more erratic. **Co, E, Ch**

3 WEDGE-RUMPED STORM-PETREL *Oceanodroma tethys* * 18–20 cm (7–8 in); ws 45 cm (18 in)

Fairly common resident and local breeder, but highly pelagic and rarely seen close to shore. Small, with white rump and lower flanks. Very long white uppertail coverts almost completely cover tail, forming much larger white rump patch than in other species. Also note that front edge of rump patch is very straight, rather than gently curved as in Wilson's and White-vented storm-petrels. In the hand, note narrow dark shafts to white feathers of rump. **Co, E, Ch**

[BAND-RUMPED STORM-PETREL *Oceanodroma castro*] 20–21.5 cm (8–8½ in)

Known only from a few sight records, far off northern coast, where may be regular visitor. Large, dark, with white rump and lower flanks. Flies with deep, quick wingbeats, often interspersed with glides; usually quite unlike the erratic, bounding flight of Leach's Storm-Petrel. Also differs from Leach's by uninterrupted white rump band and extension of white onto flanks. Further distinguished with care from *Oceanites* species by shorter tarsi, wing shape, and flight behavior. In the hand, note blackish tips to feathers of white rump band. **Co, E**

4 [LEACH'S STORM-PETREL *Oceanodroma leucorhoa*] * 19–22 cm (7½–8½ in); ws 45–48 cm (18–19 in)

A regular nonbreeding visitor to waters far off coast of northern and central Peru. Variable, with both dark- and white-rumped populations; all Peru records are of white-rumped individuals. Large, dark, with deep wingbeats, bounding, erratic flight, and large, prominent pale bar on upperwing surface. Little or no extension of white rump onto lower flanks. Tail is more deeply notched than in other white-rumped storm-petrels, and the white rump band is narrowly divided in middle (often visible in the field). **E**

5 MARKHAM'S STORM-PETREL *Oceanodroma markhami* 23 cm (9 in); ws 50 cm (19 in)

Resident and local breeder. Large, dark, with prominent pale bars on upper surface of wing and long, notched tail. Flies with deep wingbeats, interrupted by relatively long glides. Much larger than the geographically restricted Least Storm-Petrel. See Black Storm-Petrel for distinctions from that species. **Co, E, Ch**

6 BLACK STORM-PETREL *Oceanodroma melania* 21.5–23 cm (8½–9 in); ws 46–51 cm (18–20 in)

Regular migrant to waters off northern and central Peru, primarily Sep–Apr. Large, all-dark, very similar to Markham's Storm-Petrel, and difficult to distinguish by observers not very familiar with one or both species. Compared to Markham's, has narrower and less prominent pale bar on upper surface of wing and slightly shallower notch to the tail, and is overall blacker (less sooty brown). Flight is deliberate with deep wingbeats interspersed with short glides. **Co, E**

WILSON'S
STORM-PETREL

WHITE-VENTED
STORM-PETREL

WEDGE-RUMPED
STORM-PETREL

BAND-RUMPED
STORM-PETREL

LEACH'S
STORM-PETREL

MARKHAM'S
STORM-PETREL

BLACK
STORM-PETREL

foraging
postures of
Oceanites

PLATE
20

WARM-WATER BOOBIES

Boobies and gannets are large seabirds with characteristic long, pointed, thick-based bills and long wedge-shaped tails. Flight is strong and direct but often interspersed with glides. Some species often form large flocks. Capture prey with spectacular plunge-dives. Take several years to reach maturity; plumages intermediate between juvenile and adult frequently are encountered. Species on this plate are rare to uncommon in Peru, and are associated with warm ocean waters.

NAZCA BOOBY *Sula granti* 81–92 cm (32–36 in); ws 152 cm (60 in)

Breeds in small (but increasing?) numbers on Islas Lobos de Tierra and Lobos de Afuera; rare but probably regular elsewhere at sea off northwest coast. Very similar to Masked Booby in all plumages, but usually can be distinguished by bill color; see Masked for distinguishing field characters. **Co, E**

1 MASKED BOOBY *Sula dactylatra* * 81–92 cm (32–36 in); ws 152 cm (60 in)

Status in Peru not clear, due to confusion with similar Nazca Booby; apparently a rare but regular visitor to Peruvian waters, far offshore, north at least to Lambayeque. Peruvian birds presumably originate from Chilean breeding colonies. Adults of both Masked and Nazca strikingly white with black remiges (including tertials) and rectrices; some Nazca have white central rectrices, but tail always all-black in Masked. Both species proceed through a complex series of plumages. With good views, bill color separates the two species except as juveniles (when both have all-gray bills). Bill color brightens as bird matures; color at base of bill is most important for identification. Bill of adult and subadult Masked is yellow (tip may be orange); bill of Nazca is bright orange to pink (tip may be yellow). Juveniles of both species have brown upperparts and hood; this plumage superficially is similar to that of adult female Brown Booby, but hood is less extensive (white of belly extends farther forward up neck in Masked and Nazca) and usually is not cut straight across breast (instead, white intrudes up the throat in inverted "V" rather than being confined to lower breast and belly); also, juvenile Masked and Nazca have dark bills (relatively pale in adult female Brown). See also juvenile Blue-footed Booby. Juveniles of Masked and Nazca very similar to one another; distinguishing features still being researched. Young Masked usually show white collar across hindneck; this collar typically lacking in Nazca. **Co, E, Br, Ch**

[BROWN BOOBY *Sula leucogaster*] * 64–74 cm (25–29 in); ws 132–150 cm (52–59 in)

Vagrant to Peruvian coastal and offshore waters, known only from sight records (some photographed). Adult recognized by solid brown upperparts and hood that contrast sharply with white belly. Similar to juvenile Masked and Nazca boobies. Juvenile Masked has white collar on hindneck; most Nazca lack the collar, more closely resembling Brown, but also lack the crisp straight-across demarcation between dark breast and white belly of Brown. Adult male has light gray face, and blue-gray bill; head of female all dark, bill yellow. Juvenile is similar in pattern to adult, but white belly is replaced by light brown. Cf. juvenile Red-footed Booby. **Co, E, Br, Ch**

[RED-FOOTED BOOBY *Sula sula*] * 66–77 cm (26–30 in); ws 91–101 cm (36–40 in)

Vagrant to Peru; known from a few sight records (some photographed) at sea. Small, slender, and polymorphic. Bright red tarsi of adults diagnostic. White-morph adult similar to Masked and Nazca boobies, but smaller and has white tertials; tail usually white but may be black. Also has black carpal mark on white underwing coverts. Typical dark morph uniformly brown, but intermediate plumages also occur (e.g., body brown with white tail). Dark-morph adult distinguished from juvenile Brown Booby by smaller size and more slender build, lighter brown plumage with no demarcation between breast and belly, darker underwing, pinkish face, and red tarsi. Juvenile similar to larger juvenile Brown, but lacks sharp demarcation between dark breast and paler belly of Brown; also underwing coverts of Red-footed often are darker and belly is paler. Some young Red-footeds are very similar to Brown in plumage pattern, however, and can be difficult to identify when size and shape differences cannot be compared directly. **Co, E, Br, Ch**

NAZCA BOOBY

ad.

ad.

juv.

MASKED BOOBY

ad.

BROWN BOOBY

juv.

ad. ♀

ad. ♀

white morph

brown
morph

white morph

RED-FOOTED BOOBY

juv.

PLATE
21

PENGUIN, BOOBIES, GANNET, AND TROPICBIRDS

Penguins are familiar flightless seabirds; they swim well, but on land they stand with a distinctive upright posture and have a peculiar waddling gait. Peruvian and Blue-footed boobies are the most abundant boobies in Peruvian waters; flocks of Peruvian Boobies, in long lines, are a frequent sight along the coast. Cape Gannet is the largest booby reported from Peru, where it is only a vagrant. Tropicbirds are highly pelagic, rare nonbreeding visitors to Peru. Typically seen as single individuals, not in flocks. Fly high over the water with rapid wingbeats; less commonly observed resting on the ocean surface. Capture prey by plunge diving.

1 HUMBOLDT PENGUIN *Spheniscus humboldti* 65–70 cm (25½–27½ in)
Scarce and declining in numbers. Breeds locally on offshore islands; occurs more widely at sea. Usually seen as single individuals or in very small groups. Swims well, but body rests very low in water, with only head and neck projecting much above surface. Young birds are much paler and less patterned, gradually acquiring darker colors and adult pattern as they age. **E, Ch**

2 PERUVIAN BOOBY *Sula variegata* 71–76 cm (28–30 in); ws 150 cm (59 in)
Very common in cold waters. Northernmost breeding site is Isla Lobos de Tierra; some individuals wander north, especially during El Niño events, but in most years is rare to uncommon in northwest. All ages have brown wings with coverts that are narrowly tipped white, producing scaled effect. Cf. Blue-footed Booby, which predominates in northwest but usually is much less common than Peruvian farther south. **VOICE** Calls at colonies include a coughing chatter and whistles. **Co, E, Ch**

3 BLUE-FOOTED BOOBY *Sula nebouxii* * 76–84 cm (30–33 in); ws 152 cm (60 in)
Breeds in large numbers on northern islands (Islas Lobos de Tierra and Lobos de Afuera), and ranges south regularly to central Peru; rare in south, where associated with El Niño episodes. Adult has diagnostic bright blue feet (rarely visible in flight). Adult also differs from Peruvian by extensive narrow brown streaking on head and neck. In all plumages differs from Peruvian by browner wings (with no white speckling or bars above) and white rump. Browner juvenile is hooded, with white belly and flanks; can be confused with juveniles of Masked and Nazca, but juvenile Blue-footed distinguished by white on rump, base of tail, and nape (note that white nape of Blue-footed is discrete patch, not white collar as in juvenile Masked). **Co, E, Ch**

[CAPE GANNET *Morus capensis*] 85–94 cm (33½–37 in); ws 171–185 cm (67–73 in)
Reported from a single sight record (photographed) of an adult off the northern coast. Breeds primarily in southern Africa; not expected to occur again, although breeds in small numbers in Australia and New Zealand and so range may be expanding. Much larger than boobies. Adult also differs from Masked and Nazca boobies by less black on secondaries, by white tertials, and by buffy yellow nape (difficult to see at a distance). Other species of gannets, although equally unexpected, perhaps also could occur in Peru, so note such details as amount and distribution of black on tail and inner wing, and extent of gular patch (if visible). Juvenile is gray-brown, heavily speckled with white. Takes several years to mature; plumage increasingly white as ages.

[RED-TAILED TROPICBIRD *Phaethon rubricauda*] * 78 cm (31 in); ws 107 cm (42 in)
Very rare vagrant; known only from single sight record from coastal waters of Tacna. Very white adult, with unmistakable long red tail streamers. Subadults have short, often pinkish to whitish tail streamers, but still have extensively white wings of adults. Juvenile more similar to Red-billed Tropicbird but has dusky bill (becoming yellower as bird ages) and little black on outer portion of wing. **Ch**

4 RED-BILLED TROPICBIRD *Phaethon aethereus* * 98 cm (39 in); ws 105 cm (41 in)
Highly pelagic; rare nonbreeding visitor to Peruvian waters far from shore. Adult readily recognized by long white tail streamers, red bill, black mask, and barred upperparts. Immature lacks tail streamers, and bill is yellowish; note that black on outer wing includes not only primaries but also primary coverts. **Co, E, Br, Ch**

HUMBOLDT PENGUIN

ad.

ad.

juv.

imm.

ad.

PERUVIAN BOOBY

ad.

juv.

ad.

CAPE GANNET

juv.

ad.

BLUE-FOOTED BOOBY

juv.

ad.

ad.

RED-TAILED TROPICBIRD

ad.

juv.

ad.

RED-BILLED TROPICBIRD

ad.

juv.

PLATE
22

FRIGATEBIRDS, CORMORANTS, AND ANHINGA

Frigatebirds readily are identifiable as such by large size, very long slender wings, and long, deeply forked tail. Soar gracefully and often high above the water; do not swim. Pluck food in flight from surface of the water or pursue other seabirds and force them to disgorge. In display, breeding male enlarges the gular pouch like a large red balloon. Identification to species can be challenging; plumages are similar between species, and the plumage sequence also is complicated. Cormorants and Anhinga are aquatic birds with long necks and long slender bodies. Swim with the body low in the water; dive underwater to catch fish. Frequently seen perched with the wings spread, drying the plumage. Fly well but have difficulty taking flight, running across surface of water flapping wings before becoming airborne. Most species breed colonially; colonies of Guanay Cormorants can be especially large, numbering into the hundreds of thousands.

1 MAGNIFICENT FRIGATEBIRD *Fregata magnificens* 96.5–106.5 cm (38–42 in); ws 217–244 cm (85½–96 in)
The regularly occurring species of frigatebird; fairly common in warm waters of northwest. Very rarely wanders to southern Peru. Adult male all dark. Breast and flanks of female white; remainder of plumage (including throat) dark. Entire head and breast of juvenile white. Adult females and most immature plumages also show some narrow white barring in the axillars. Cf. Great Frigatebird. **Co, E, Br**

[GREAT FRIGATEBIRD *Fregata minor* * 89–96.5 cm (35–38 in); ws 206–230 cm (81–90½ in)
Status not clear; known from a few sight records from far northwest. Similar in all plumages to Magnificent Frigatebird, and to be identified with great care. Adult male extremely similar to male Magnificent, but toes pink or pinkish red (gray in male Magnificent) and has light brown panel on upperwing surface (lacking in Magnificent). Often shows pale gray scaling on axillars. Female similar to female Magnificent, but throat white (not black); Great also has red (not blue) orbital ring. Head of juvenile buffy (variable in extent and saturation), not white. **Co, E, Br, Ch**

2 NEOTROPIC CORMORANT *Phalacrocorax brasilianus* * 58–73 cm (23–29 in)
Fairly common throughout Peru below 1000 m; also present locally on altiplano at 3200–4200 m in southern Peru. Formerly regular at Lake Junín but no longer resident there. The only freshwater cormorant; also forages in ocean, but only close to shore. Adult black; in alternate plumage has narrow white border to the orange gular patch, and for a short period (when breeding) also has white plumes on side of neck. Juvenile and immature dull brown, buffier below. **VOICE** Calls a rarely heard low grunting, and barks that recall a sea lion. **Co, E, Br, Bo, Ch**

3 GUANAY CORMORANT *Phalacrocorax bougainvillii* 76 cm (30 in)
Common to abundant in central and southern Peru, breeding north to Isla Lobos de Tierra; disperses farther north, but only in small numbers, and is irregular in Tumbes. Large, with prominent white belly (variably extending to breast and lower neck) and reddish face. Immature patterned similarly but duller: browner above with yellowish face. Usually seen in large flocks. Forages from shore to well out to sea. **Co, E, Ch**

4 RED-LEGGED CORMORANT *Phalacrocorax gaimardi* 76 cm (30 in)
Rare to uncommon in inshore waters near islands and rocky headlands. Usually seen as singles or in small numbers. Readily recognized by light gray plumage, white neck patch, and bright soft part colors. **Ch**

5 ANHINGA *Anhinga anhinga* * 82.5–89 cm (32½–35 in)
Uncommon but widespread in eastern Peru below 500 m. Very rare vagrant up to 3100 m in Andes. Superficially similar to Neotropic Cormorant (and, like cormorants, spreads wings to dry), but larger with longer tail, extensive white spotting on upperwing coverts, and sharply pointed (not hooked) bill. Also is much less social than cormorants, and often seen only as single individuals. Can lower the body while swimming such that only head and neck are above water. Unlike cormorants, also soars, sometimes high above ground; may be mistaken for a raptor, but note long thin neck and bill. Male is largely black. Head, neck, and breast of female are buffy. Immature similar to female, but white of wing coverts reduced. **Co, E, Br, Bo**

MAGNIFICENT FRIGATEBIRD

♀

♂

juv.

♀

♂

GREAT FRIGATEBIRD

♂

juv.

♀

♀

♂

imm.

basic

NEOTROPIC CORMORANT

alt.

imm.

GUANAY
CORMORANT

ANHINGA

♀

soaring

ad.

RED-LEGGED
CORMORANT

imm.

ad.

♂

♀

PLATE
23

LARGE DARK OR PATTERNED HERONS AND SPOONBILL

Herons and egrets are long-necked, long-legged birds with long, daggerlike bills; fly with neck retracted and long tarsi protruding beyond tail. Most forage by wading slowly in water, capturing animal prey with sudden lunges of neck and bill. Some species nest in colonies that may contain several species of herons and ibis. In many species soft parts become more intensely colored for a short period in breeding season, at which time some also acquire long plumes on neck or lower back. The spoonbill is superficially similar but is related to ibis; note its peculiar bill shape.

1 COCOI HERON *Ardea cocoi* 104–127 cm (41–50 in)
Fairly common and widespread in Amazonia. Locally present but rare on coast; very rare vagrant to Andes. Found in marshes, lakes, and other wetlands. Largest heron in Peru. Readily recognized by large size, gray color, and black cap. Colors of bare facial skin duller when not breeding. Neck of adult strikingly white; neck of juvenile typically much dingier, and in some (second year?), center of crown also may be gray (not black). **VOICE** Calls, often given in flight, include various hoarse croaks, sometimes given in a descending series: "*REH raaahh ruhhhhhh.*" **Co, E, Br, Bo, Ch**

2 BARE-THROATED TIGER-HERON *Tigrisoma mexicanum* 71–81 cm (28–32 in)
Rare resident of mangroves in Tumbes, where is the only expected tiger-heron. Adult readily recognized by gray sides to head, black crown, and bare skin of upper throat. Juvenile also has completely bare throat (although note that throat feathering can be sparse on other tiger-herons). **Co, E**

3 FASCIATED TIGER-HERON *Tigrisoma fasciatum* * 61–66 cm (24–26 in)
Uncommon along fast-flowing, rocky streams and rivers in forest along east slope of Andes, 350–2000 m. Typically found at higher elevations than Rufescent Tiger-Heron, but the two may overlap at base of Andes. Adult unmistakable. Compare juvenile to very similar juvenile Rufescent Tiger-Heron. **Co, E, Br, Bo**

4 RUFESCENT TIGER-HERON *Tigrisoma lineatum* * 66–76 cm (26–30 in)
Uncommon but widespread in Amazonia, locally up to 900 m, along forested streams and at margins of oxbow lakes; stays within cover. Solitary. Stands motionless for long periods at water's edge. Rufous neck of adult distinctive. Juvenile banded, not streaked as is Black-crowned Night-Heron. Juvenile extremely similar to juvenile Fasciated Tiger-Heron (not safely separable?), but bill is longer and heavier (bill shape differences less apparent in youngest juveniles, however); also has more heavily barred flanks and darker, more heavily barred underwing coverts (difficult to see in the field). **VOICE** Calls a muffled mooing and quiet barks and honks upon flushing. **Co, E, Br, Bo**

5 AGAMI HERON *Agamia agami* 63.5–71 cm (25–28 in)
Scarce and inconspicuous, but widely distributed in Amazonia. Solitary heron that remains within cover of canopy, along streams and edges of oxbow lakes and in swamps. Stands still or slowly wades through water, often up to its belly. Ornate plumage of adult unmistakable. Juvenile duller, but similarly distinctive; note the particularly long, thin bill. **Co, E, Br, Bo**

[PINNATED BITTERN *Botaurus pinnatus*] * 63.5–76 cm (25–30 in)
Very rare vagrant; a single sight record from grassy margin of a forested oxbow lake in Madre de Dios. Usually remains concealed within wet grasses, with neck retracted. Very similar to immature tiger-herons, but those species are more regularly barred on upperparts and wing coverts and have black tails narrowly barred white. Immature night-herons are heavily streaked below. **VOICE** Probably largely silent in Peru. Song is a series of pumping notes ending with a deep booming: "*p'clk, p'clk, p'clk-BMM.*" **Co, E, Br, Bo**

6 ROSEATE SPOONBILL *Platalea ajaja* 71–79 cm (28–31 in)
Rare. Local in Amazonia, where seen along rivers; also in small numbers in far northwest, where found in mangroves and adjacent mudflats. Very rare vagrant farther south along coast. Forages in small flocks by wading in water with tip of bill submerged, swinging head from side to side. Pink plumage recalls flamingos, but spoonbill is much smaller with long flat bill and shorter neck, and lacks black in wings. Immature much paler, with feathered head and yellowish bill. Flies with neck outstretched (as do ibis). **Co, E, Br, Bo, Ch**

COCOI HERON

juv.

ad. br.

pale-crowned imm.

FASCIATED
TIGER-HERON

ad.

juv.

juv.

ad.

BARE-THROATED
TIGER-HERON

RUFESCENT TIGER-HERON

ad.

juv.

ad.

AGAMI HERON

juv.

PINNATED BITTERN

imm.

ad.

ROSEATE SPOONBILL

PLATE
24
WHITE HERONS, NIGHT HERONS, AND LIMPKIN

Compare the juvenile night-herons with juvenile tiger-herons (preceding plate), and the white species on this plate with other largely white egrets (following plate). Limpkin is not a heron but superficially is similar. Note that Limpkin flies with neck outstretched (not retracted).

1 CATTLE EGRET *Bubulcus ibis* * 47–52 cm (18½–20½ in)

Common. Perhaps most abundant on coast, where found in pastures and recently plowed fields. Often follows cattle or other livestock, in search of flushed insects. Less common, but widespread, throughout Amazonia, locally in clearings to 2000 m; primarily near livestock but also on grassy sandbars and other open habitats. Fairly common but local in altiplano, at 3000–4400 m. Readily recognized by habitat, small size, stocky build, and combination of yellow bill and yellow or grayish tarsi. **VOICE** Usually quiet. Calls include raspy barks and throaty gulping sounds. **Co, E, Br, Bo, Ch**

2 GREAT EGRET *Ardea alba* * 91.5–99 cm (36–39 in)

Uncommon to fairly common on coast and in Amazonia; very local in Andes. Most numerous in marshes, irrigated agricultural land, river edges, mudflats, and mangroves along coast; in Amazonia prefers lake margins and marshes and is much scarcer along rivers. Usually outnumbered by Snowy and Cattle egrets, but sometimes seen in large aggregations. Large, long-necked white heron with yellow bill and black tarsi and toes. Breeding birds have long white plumes on lower back, and lores become brighter green. **VOICE** Calls, often given in flight, a series of hoarse groaning notes. **Co, E, Br, Bo, Ch**

3 LIMPKIN *Aramus guarauna* * 66–71 cm (26–28 in)

Rare but widespread in central and southern lowlands; scarce or absent from north. Large wading bird of grassy margins of oxbow lakes and other wetlands; feeds primarily on large aquatic snails. Flies with characteristic stiff upward jerk of wings. Resembles an ibis but note thicker, straight bill; cf. also juvenile night-heron. **VOICE** Call loud guttural screams and yaps that carry for long distances, also lower growled chatters. **Co, E, Br, Bo**

4 BOAT-BILLED HERON *Cochlearius cochlearius* * 48–53.5 cm (19–21 in)

Widespread in Amazonia, but local and rare. Highly nocturnal; roosts inside cover by day, feeds by night at edges of oxbow lakes, rivers, and streams. Similar to adult Black-crowned Night-Heron, but note very broad, flat ("boat"-shaped) bill, largely gray upperparts, brownish belly, and black flanks; also, black underwing coverts. Juvenile brown above and buff below. Forages by wading in shallow water or standing at water's edge, then plunging head and neck out to capture prey; but also uses broad bill as a "scoop." **VOICE** Call a series of muffled hooting barks: "*poo poo pah poo.*" **Co, E, Br, Bo**

5 CAPPED HERON *Pilherodius pileatus* 53.5–58.5 cm (21–23 in)

Fairly common and widespread in Amazonia, along forested rivers and lakes. Solitary, or in pairs or trios. Flies stiffly, with wings strongly bowed and scarcely raised above horizontal. A beautiful heron, readily recognized by striking blue face and base to bill and the black cap; also note light buff wash on foreparts. **VOICE** Usually quiet. Calls are muffled hoots. **Co, E, Br, Bo**

6 YELLOW-CROWNED NIGHT-HERON *Nyctanassa violacea* * 56–61 cm (22–24 in)

Restricted to mangroves of northwest; very rare vagrant south to Lima. Similar in behavior to Black-crowned Night-Heron. Adult unmistakable. Juvenile distinguished from juvenile Black-crowned by all-black bill (mandible of Black-crowned is mostly yellow) and longer tarsi that project farther beyond tail in flight. Also grayer (less brown) with smaller white spots and streaks. **VOICE** Call, often given in flight, higher pitched and less emphatic than call of Black-crowned. **Co, E, Br**

7 BLACK-CROWNED NIGHT-HERON *Nycticorax nycticorax* * 56–61cm (22–24 in)

Uncommon to fairly common on coast and in Andes (3100–4700 m). Also widespread, but rare, in Amazonia, up to 750 m. Found in marshes, at lake edges, and along relatively open rivers. Less nocturnal than Boat-billed Heron, but typically rests during day and begins feeding in evening. Squat, relatively short-legged. Adult readily identified by black crown and back, contrasting with gray wings; underparts may be white or smoky gray. Juvenile largely brown, heavily streaked. Successive plumages (not illustrated) more similar to adult, but browner above, and (in second year) retain some streaking on underparts. **VOICE** Call, often given in flight, a sharp "*pok!*" **Co, E, Br, Bo, Ch**

CATTLE EGRET

alt.

basic

GREAT EGRET

alt.

basic

LIMPKIN

ad.

ad.

juv.

BOAT-BILLED
HERON

juv.

ad.

CAPPED HERON

ad.

juv.

YELLOW-
CROWNED
NIGHT-HERON

juv.

ad.

juv.

ad.

BLACK-CROWNED
NIGHT-HERON

PLATE
25

EGRETTA HERONS AND SMALL HERONS

Compare the Egretta *herons on this plate with other white egrets (plate 24). Striated Heron is the most widespread and commonly seen small heron; Zigzag Heron and Least Bittern are much less common, and Stripe-backed Bittern is only a vagrant to Peru.*

1 SNOWY EGRET *Egretta thula* * 53.5–63.5 cm (21–25 in)

Widely distributed. Most common along coast, in marshes and irrigated fields, along rivers and mudflats, and (less commonly) on beaches and tidal pools. Less common but widespread in Amazonia. Locally fairly common at Andean lakes and marshes. Medium-sized, uniformly white, with black bill and legs and yellow feet. Juvenile (not illustrated) similar to basic-plumaged adult, but rear of tarsi may be greenish, not black. **VOICE** Calls, often given in flight, a series of rasping barks and complaining sounds. **Co, E, Br, Bo, Ch**

2 LITTLE BLUE HERON *Egretta caerulea* 56–66 cm (22–26 in)

Uncommon but widespread resident (increasing in abundance?) along coast, in marshes, mangroves, and rice fields. Rare in Amazonia (boreal migrant?). In all ages note relatively thick, bicolored bill. Adult is stockier than Tricolored Heron and is uniformly dark (including belly). Juvenile all white, with bicolored bill, grayish green tarsi and toes, and dusky tips to primaries; cf. Snowy Egret. Second-year immature has large irregular patches of blue-gray scattered throughout white plumage. **VOICE** Calls, often given in flight, a series of rasping barks and complaining sounds. **Co, E, Br, Bo, Ch**

3 TRICOLORED HERON *Egretta tricolor* * 58.5–68.5 cm (23–27 in)

Resident on coast. Fairly common in northwest; local and uncommon (but increasing?) breeder south to Arequipa, but may wander farther south. Usually alone, in shallow water in or near marsh vegetation. Medium-sized, long-necked heron. Note white throat and belly, and relatively long, slender bill; cf. adult Little Blue Heron. **VOICE** Calls, often given in flight, include a series of rasping barks and complaining sounds. **Co, E, Br**

4 STRIATED HERON *Butorides striata* * 38–43 cm (15–17 in)

Uncommon to fairly common in lowlands of coast and Amazonia (where occurs locally to 800 m); found in marshes and along margins of lakes and rivers. Typically waits motionless at water's edge. Note small size, dark color, and brightly colored tarsi. Adult has plain neck, which is pale gray but often washed with reddish brown, and sometimes appearing largely that color. Juvenile is more streaked, especially on neck and wing coverts. **VOICE** Call, often given in flight, is a sharp "*scalp!*" sometimes followed by a chattered series. Rarely heard song a gulping sound, usually uttered from deep within vegetation. **Co, E, Br, Bo, Ch**

[STRIPE-BACKED BITTERN *Ixobrychus involucris*] 32–34 cm (12½–13½ in)

Apparently a rare austral migrant to southeastern Peru, where known only from a few sight records at grassy margins of oxbow lakes (a habitat shared with Least Bittern). Similar to female Least, but neck buffier, upperparts pale buff or ochraceous with conspicuous black streaking on back and scapulars, remiges tipped rufous, and has a narrower black coronal stripe. **Co, E, Br, Bo, Ch**

5 LEAST BITTERN *Ixobrychus exilis* * 28–30.5 cm (11–12 in)

Locally fairly common in coastal marshes. Less common (or overlooked?) and presumed to be resident along rivers in northern Amazonia, in marshes of tall grasses (such as on large river islands); less commonly at edges of oxbow lakes. Also scarce resident or rare austral migrant to southeastern Amazonia. Usually remains hidden low in thick vegetation, where can move agilely and quickly through dense growth. Most easily seen and heard at dawn or dusk, in low flight or perching high in reeds, grasses, or sedges. Note small size, tawny color of neck and wing coverts, and contrasting dark crown, back, and remiges. **VOICE** Song (Amazonia) a single muffled coo, rising in pitch: "*G'woOO.*" Calls a series of coughing notes. Also a sharp "*scap!*" in flight, similar to calls of Striated Heron. **Co, E, Br, Bo**

6 ZIGZAG HERON *Zebrilus undulatus* 30.5–33 cm (12–13 in)

Poorly known and rare. Solitary, quiet heron, easily overlooked, of shaded forest pools, swamps, and streams. Forages from low branches, logs, or emergent tree roots close to water; often remains motionless for long periods, then lunges at aquatic prey, greatly extending neck. Distinctive small size, closely barred plumage, and overall dark appearance. Juvenile is more brightly colored, especially on sides of face. **VOICE** Song, given at dawn and dusk, is a hollow, descending coo: "*COOool.*" **Co, E, Br, Bo**

SNOWY EGRET

basic

alt.

ad.

LITTLE BLUE HERON

juv.

2nd year imm.

ad.

TRICOLORED HERON

juv.

ad.

ad.

ad.

juv.

STRIATED HERON

LEAST BITTERN

♀

♂

STRIPE-BACKED BITTERN

juv.

ZIGZAG HERON

ad.

PLATE
26

SCREAMERS AND IBIS

Screamers are large, heavy-bodied, peculiar birds of marshes and rivers. They are related to ducks and geese. Ibis are similar to herons and egrets but have strongly curved bills; also fly with neck outstretched. Forage with probe-and-grab motions.

[SOUTHERN SCREAMER *Chauna torquata*] 83–95 cm (32½–37½ in)
Vagrant (only during austral winter?); a few sight records of singles, on sandbars in Madre de Dios. Paler in color than Horned Screamer, with distinctive banded pattern on neck, and red facial skin and tarsi. **VOICE** Probably largely silent in Peru. Song, usually given as a duet, is a loud series of high yelping honks. Not confusable with Horned Screamer. Voice carries for long distances. **Br, Bo**

1 HORNED SCREAMER *Anhima cornuta* 84–91.5 cm (33–36 in)
Widespread and fairly common in Amazonia. An enormous, ungainly bird of rivers and marshes; usually seen as singles or pairs on river banks and sandbars, or perched in low bushes or trees at margins of oxbow lakes or marshes. Seems to have difficulty taking flight, but once airborne flight is sure and steady; may even soar. Grazes on aquatic vegetation. At close range note long white "horn" (modified feather) on forehead, and "spurs" at bend of wing. **VOICE** Unmistakable song, usually a duet, is a loud, reedy, honking series of multisyllabic notes, some rising, others falling. Carries for long distances. **Co, E, Br, Bo**

2 WHITE IBIS *Eudocimus albus* 56–61 cm (22–24 in)
Fairly common in mangroves of northwest; feeds on mudflats and in shallow water. Gregarious, often in loose flocks. In all plumages note reddish bill, facial skin, and tarsi. White adult (with narrow black primary tips) distinctive (but beware of rare albinistic individuals of other species). Juvenile largely brown with white belly and rump; plumage becomes progressively whiter with age. **VOICE** Usually quiet. Calls gruff honks. **Co, E**

3 PUNA IBIS *Plegadis ridgwayi* 60–61 cm (23½–24 in)
Common in Andes, 3200–4500 m, locally down to 2200 m. Local breeder on coast, and also may be expanding range to north. Very rare vagrant to southern Amazonia. Found in marshes, lake edges, and wet fields; often in flocks. Only widespread dark ibis of open wetlands. Alternate adult has reddish bill and relatively glossy plumage. Colors of bill and plumage duller in juvenile and adult in basic plumage, and head and neck may be narrowly streaked with buff. **VOICE** A reedy, coughing series: "kvek kvek kvek," usually given in flight. **Bo, Ch**

[WHITE-FACED IBIS *Plegadis chihi*] 57 cm (22½ in)
One unconfirmed sight record from coast (Arequipa). Adult in alternate plumage has red facial skin, narrowly rimmed with white feathers; distinctive. Basic adult (not illustrated) very similar to basic Puna, but bill never red, and overall is slightly smaller, with relatively longer tarsi; in flight, lower portion of tarsi extend beyond tail (only toes extend past tail in Puna). Also, belly brown (black in Puna), and usually overall greener (less purplish gloss to plumage); face reddish but duller than when breeding. Juvenile similar to juvenile Puna, but belly sooty (not as black as in Puna). [In north, **Glossy Ibis** (*Plegadis falcinellus*; not illustrated, no record for Peru) also is potential vagrant; reports of either species require careful documentation.] **Br, Bo, Ch**

4 BLACK-FACED IBIS *Theristicus melanopis* * 74–75 cm (29 in)
Striking ibis of dry upland habitats. Ranges in small flocks. Andean *branickii* is widespread but uncommon at 3700–4600 m, locally down to 3000 m; open grasslands, often near rocky outcrops, where roosts and nests. Coastal *melanopis* formerly was widespread but now is almost extirpated; most recent records are from northwest, where found in agricultural fields. Differs from *branickii* by often showing a black throat wattle (lacking in *branickii*); paler (sometimes almost white) wing coverts, more extensive black on belly, and generally darker buff lower breast and belly. **VOICE** A tinny honking, either as single notes or in a series. **E, Bo, Ch**

5 GREEN IBIS *Mesembrinibis cayennensis* 56–58.5 cm (22–23 in)
Widespread but uncommon in Amazonia, in forested wetlands: lake margins, rivers, and swamps. Forages singly or in pairs (not in flocks) and primarily is active at night. Frequently perches in trees. Only Amazonian ibis. Also is shorter-legged than other dark ibis. **VOICE** Barks that, when alarmed, accelerate and become eerie hollow hooting. **Co, E, Br, Bo**

SOUTHERN
SCREAMER

HORNED
SCREAMER

ad.

juv.

PUNA IBIS

alt.

basic

alt.

WHITE IBIS

ad.

melanopis

melanopis

branickii

branickii

alt.

WHITE-FACED IBIS

BLACK-FACED IBIS

GREEN IBIS

PLATE
27

VULTURES

New World vultures are familiar carrion feeders, with bare, unfeathered skin on the head and neck. Most often seen in soaring flight. Black Vulture locates food sources entirely by sight, but all Cathartes have well-developed sense of smell and can detect carrion that is hidden in vegetation. The largest and most impressive vultures, King Vulture and Andean Condor, are on plate 28. The flight profile of Zone-tailed Hawk closely mimics Cathartes vultures; see account on plate 40.

1 BLACK VULTURE *Coragyps atratus* 60–65 cm (23½–26 in); ws 133–160 cm (52–63 in)

Common and widespread below 1200 m, locally up to 2900 m. Frequently seen in towns, cities, pastures, and other open country, and along rivers; not found in closed-canopy forest. Formerly present in southwest, but largely disappeared from that region in early 1960s; now may be staging a slow recovery there. Soars with wings held flat (in same plane as body), alternating with short bouts of relatively rapid ("choppy") wingbeats; also, body does not rock from side to side while soaring. May soar to great heights, and often congregates in large groups while soaring or at roosts. Bare skin of neck slightly less extensive in juvenile. Black Vulture stands more upright than other vultures and is more agile on its feet; occasionally overtakes and kills small animals (such as lizards or nestlings). Despite smaller body size, may dominate Turkey Vultures at carrion. Often seen at relatively large carcasses, as well as in garbage dumps, where may congregate in large numbers. Shorter wings and tail and flat wing posture lend a different flight profile from long-winged and longer-tailed *Cathartes* vultures. Immature King Vulture is larger, always has some white in plumage, especially on underwing coverts, and lacks white near wing tips. Dark hawks have feathered (not bare) heads, different plumage patterns. **Co, E, Br, Bo, Ch**

2 TURKEY VULTURE *Cathartes aura* * 60–70 cm (23½–27½ in); ws 160–182 cm (63–72 in)

Widespread and common in coastal lowlands, interior valleys, and Amazonia, up to 2200 m; only a vagrant to the high Andes. One of the characteristic vultures of open habitats, such as beaches (along seacoasts and rivers), fields, and pastures; but less common than Black Vulture around cities. Usually seen in flight, singly or in small groups. Flight profile distinctive, with wings held notably above horizontal in a "dihedral"; also often "rocks" from side to side as it soars. Flaps wings infrequently, with rather slow, deep strokes. Bare skin of head and neck of adult red (coast and Andes), or red with contrasting whitish band across the nape (Amazonia; sometimes also on northern and central coast). Head of juvenile dark, gradually lightening during first year. In Amazonia, cf. yellow-headed vultures. **Co, E, Br, Bo, Ch**

3 LESSER YELLOW-HEADED VULTURE *Cathartes burrovianus* 55–60 cm (21½–23½ in); ws 150–165 cm (59–65 in)

Uncommon and local in Amazonia. More widespread in north; in south probably once was confined to Pampas del Heath, but now may be spreading as more areas are deforested. Found in open habitats, usually marshes on margins of large rivers and lakes, also (Pampas del Heath) over drier grasslands. Forages singly or in small groups, usually gliding low over marshes and grasslands; rarely soars high, unlike Turkey and Greater Yellow-headed vultures. "Rocks" from side to side as it soars, as does Turkey Vulture. Distinguished from Turkey Vulture by yellow head of adult (visible only at close range), white shafts on dorsal surface of outer primaries, blacker plumage, and by differences in foraging behavior; cf. also forest-based Greater Yellow-headed Vulture. **Co, E, Br, Bo**

4 GREATER YELLOW-HEADED VULTURE *Cathartes melambrotus* 68–75 cm (26¾–29½ in); ws 166–178 cm (65–70 in)

Widespread and common in forested areas of Amazonia, up to 1300 m; largely replaces Turkey Vulture in continuous forest. Flight steadier than Turkey Vulture's, and wings are broader and held flatter, not as high above horizontal as in that species. Undersides of inner primaries are dusky, contrasting with pale secondaries and outer primaries (all remiges are pale in Turkey and Lesser Yellow-headed vultures). Also has white shafts on dorsal surface of outer primaries, and plumage is blacker than Turkey Vulture. Yellow head of adult visible only at close range. **Co, E, Br, Bo**

BLACK VULTURE

GREATER YELLOW-HEADED VULTURE

LESSER YELLOW-HEADED VULTURE

TURKEY VULTURE

ad.

juv.

BLACK VULTURE

GREATER YELLOW-HEADED VULTURE

BLACK VULTURE

LESSER YELLOW-HEADED VULTURE

TURKEY VULTURE

ad. Amaz.

juv.

TURKEY VULTURE

ad.

ad.

juv.

LESSER YELLOW-HEADED VULTURE

ad.

juv.

GREATER YELLOW-HEADED VULTURE

PLATE
28

KING VULTURE AND ANDEAN CONDOR

King Vulture and Andean Condor are the largest New World vultures; indeed, the Condor is the largest flying bird in Peru (and one of the largest in the world).

1 KING VULTURE *Sarcoramphus papa* 70–75 cm (27½–29½ in); ws 170–200 cm (67–79 in)
Uncommon but widespread in humid forested areas in Amazonia, locally up to 1300 m. Also rare in northwest up to 800 m. Rarely seen perched, except near carrion, where may perch in forest canopy; typically does not perch in the open, unlike smaller vultures. Dominant over Black and Turkey vultures at carcasses. Usually seen singly or in pairs soaring over forest. Soaring flight is steady, with no "rocking" from side to side and little flapping. Adult distinctive: no white-bodied hawk or eagle has as much black in wings (but cf. Wood Stork). At close range, also note white or whitish iris, multicolored bare skin of neck and head, and fleshy wattle at base of bill. Juvenile largely dark-bodied, with duller soft part colors, but always shows at least some white mottling on underwings; cf. smaller Black Vulture. Amount of white in plumage and brightness of head and neck colors increase with age, but note the entire underparts are white (aside from the dusky neck ruff) before any white appears on the upperparts. May take 5 or 6 years to reach full adult plumage. **Co, E, Br, Bo**

2 ANDEAN CONDOR *Vultur gryphus* 100–122 cm (39–48 in); ws 274–310 cm (108–122 in)
Uncommon and declining; increasingly, this spectacular bird is confined to more remote parts of Peru. Occurs from coast to highest parts of Andes. Most common on west slope of Andes, but also ranges over uppermost elevations (down to ca. 3000 m) on more humid eastern Andean slopes; appears to be very scarce or absent, however, from east side of Andes in central Peru. Usually found in relatively open habitats, especially near high cliffs (where roosts and nests). Usually seen singly or in small groups. Often soars at great heights, but occasionally drops to low over the ground or beaches (where feeds on carcasses of sea lions and whales). Soars on long, broad, rectangular wings, held horizontal to body or in a slight dihedral. Outer primaries usually are well separated when soaring, and tips may bend upward. An immense raptor, larger than other vultures and all hawks and eagles (although the great size may be difficult to appreciate at a distance). Adult is entirely dark from below, other than distinctive large white neck ruff, but upperwings are extensively white on wing coverts and on inner remiges. Male has large comb over bill and on forehead; female lacks the comb and has duller facial skin (grayer, less pink or pinkish orange). Juvenile is mostly smoky brown, with paler wing coverts (particularly contrasting on upper surface). Takes several years to attain adult plumage; note size, shape, and flight behavior. **Co, E, Br, Bo, Ch**

KING VULTURE

ad.

ad.

subad.

imm.

ad.

imm.

ad. ♀ ANDEAN CONDOR

ad. ♂

juv.

ANDEAN CONDOR

ad. ♀

juv.

juv. ♂

ad. ♂

imm. ♂

PLATE
29

KITES AND BLACK-AND-WHITE HAWK-EAGLE

Kites, hawks, and eagles are familiar raptors, with short, hooked beaks and strong claws. Strong in flight, and prey on vertebrates or larger invertebrates. Female hawks and eagles are larger than males. Species on this plate are mostly white.

1 SWALLOW-TAILED KITE *Elanoides forficatus* * 52–62 cm (20½–24½ in); ws 119–136 cm (47–53½ in)

Widespread and fairly common in humid forest in eastern Peru, up to 2450 m in the Andes. Also in moist deciduous forest in Tumbes. Immature similar to adult, but tail shorter; in youngest birds, head and breast may be washed with brown. Primarily feeds on insects, snatched in flight from air or forest canopy, and on small vertebrates. Usually seen in graceful, effortless soaring flight, often in small groups. Also perches inside forest canopy, where rarely noticed. Resident population probably augmented by boreal (and austral?) migrants, but these cannot be identified as such in the field. **VOICE** Call high, chirping whistles. **Co, E, Br, Bo**

2 GRAY-HEADED KITE *Leptodon cayanensis* * 43–49 cm (17–19½ in); ws 90–110 cm (35½–43 in)

Widespread but uncommon in forested areas in Amazonia, up to 600 m. Perches in forest canopy, usually in more or less concealed location but may perch in the open, especially in early morning or late afternoon. Also regularly soars, especially in mid- to late morning, although usually does not stay in air for long periods; typically holds wings bowed slightly downward. Has a display flight in which wings are held upward and the kite strokes the air with rapid shallow wingbeats. Gray head of adult distinctive, as is underwing pattern. Cf. Black-and-white Hawk-Eagle (similar to light-morph juvenile Gray-headed Kite). Cf. also Hook-billed Kite (which has shorter tail and more projecting head and neck). Dark-morph juvenile, with heavily streaked underparts and entirely brown head, apparently is much less common; cf. juvenile of much smaller Double-toothed Kite. **VOICE** Song is a loud mewing note, *"reeaOW!"* often followed by a series of *"cak"* notes. **Co, E, Br, Bo**

3 BLACK-AND-WHITE HAWK-EAGLE *Spizastur melanoleucus* 54–60 cm (21–23½ in); ws 110–135 cm (43–53 in)

Rare in eastern lowlands, up to 1400 m, occasionally to 2800 m; widespread in central and southern Peru, but very scarce or absent in northeast. Usually seen soaring over humid forest; also perches within canopy. Easily confused with several other large black-and-white raptors. Similar to light-morph juvenile Gray-headed Kite, but cere of the hawk-eagle is orange (yellow in the kite), lores black (pale in the kite), tarsi are feathered (bare in the kite), barring on the underside of the primaries is less prominent, the upperparts are blacker, and the hawk-eagle is larger; also, the hawk-eagle has white along the leading edge of the wing, usually visible in flight. Distinguished from juvenile Ornate Hawk-Eagle by black "mask" that contrasts with reddish orange cere (Ornate has pale lores, and yellower cere), the white blaze along fore edge of wing, and unbarred flanks and tibial feathers. **VOICE** Calls rising piercing whistled *"WHEElew"* notes and lower whistled notes. **Co, E, Br, Bo**

4 [WHITE-TAILED KITE *Elanus leucurus*] * 35–43 cm (14–17 in); ws 88–102 cm (35–40 in)

Recently has colonized Peru, where found in cleared areas in Madre de Dios; may continue to spread. Also should be looked for in northwest. Often perches in an exposed site in open country (pastures, fields). Light and graceful in flight, with wings held above horizontal; frequently hovers low over prey, then drops suddenly to make the capture. Adult readily recognized by largely white plumage offset by black wing coverts (cf. smaller Pearl Kite). Juvenile similar but foreparts washed with brown, and upperparts may be scaled or streaked. **Co, E, Br, Bo, Ch**

5 PEARL KITE *Gampsonyx swainsonii* * 20–25 cm (8–10 in); ws 45–55 cm (18–21½ in)

Uncommon in northwest, in arid scrub, fields, and other open habitats with scattered perches. Rare and local (but perhaps overlooked, and so more widespread?) in Amazonia, where found at river edges (and perhaps will spread into cleared areas). Typically seen perched on exposed branch or wire, from which drops to ground to catch prey. Small and very white below, especially in coastal *magnus*; Amazonian *swainsonii* has rufous sides and flanks. **VOICE** Call a series of peeps, sometimes quavering. Reminiscent of some shorebirds. **Co, E, Br, Bo**

SWALLOW-TAILED KITE

GRAY-HEADED KITE

ad.

juv. light
morph

juv. dark
morph

ad.

juv.

BLACK-AND-WHITE
HAWK-EAGLE

ad.

GRAY-HEADED
KITE

juv. light
morph

WHITE-TAILED KITE

ad.

juv.

PEARL KITE

swainsonii

magnus

ad.

juv.

PLATE
30

DARK KITES AND CRANE HAWK

Species on this plate are medium-sized hawks of open country or forest edge; the plumages of most are largely gray.

1 CRANE HAWK *Geranospiza caerulescens* * *caerulescens* 42–46 cm (16½–18 in); *balzarensis* 46–50 cm (18–19¾ in); ws 92–105 cm (36–41 in)

Uncommon in dry forest of northwestern Peru, below 700 m (*balzarensis*); rare but widespread in Amazonia, where primarily found in river-edge forest (*caerulescens*). A medium-sized, slender, gray hawk with notably long reddish tarsi, relatively long tail, and small-headed appearance; also note dull-colored cere. Often forages by reaching into cavities and crevices with its long tarsi, sometimes while flapping the wings for balance. May soar, but usually only for a short distance, and not at great heights. Superficially similar species, such as Slate-colored Hawk, are much stouter and have brightly colored cere. In flight, note distinctive white crescent on underwing surface; also has relatively broad, blunt wings and relatively long tail, usually kept closed and narrow. Belly and tibial feathers sometimes narrowly barred white, especially in *balzarensis*. Juvenile is paler below, white or tawny streaked with gray; has characteristic Crane Hawk structure, and pattern of tail and underwing resemble that of adult. **VOICE** Call is a loud, descending, whistled "*keer*," sometimes in a series. **Co, E, Br, Bo**

2 SNAIL KITE *Rostrhamus sociabilis* * 39–46 cm (15½–18 in); ws 99–115 cm (39–45 in)

Rare and local in Amazonia. Found in marshes and wet grassy river margins; preys heavily on large aquatic snails. Social, and often seen in small groups; less commonly seen in large concentrations (migrants?). Perches low over water, or flies low over marshes. May be partially migratory or nomadic. Bill notably hooked. In all plumages note broad rounded wings and extensive white at base of tail and on undertail coverts, as well as narrower white tail tip. Adult male otherwise slaty gray, with red iris and bright red cere. Female browner, with an indistinct whitish superciliary; the underparts are heavily streaked with dusky brown (streaks often merging into blotchy brown mass). Cere yellow or orange. Juveniles are paler below, whiter and more obviously streaked below, and typically with a whiter, more well-developed superciliary. Cf. superficially similar Slender-billed Kite; Snail Kite always has a dark iris and white base to the tail, and is found over open marshes (Slender-billed occurs at forest edge). **VOICE** Call a thin creaking series: "*cr-cre-cree-cree-creee*." **Co, E, Br, Bo**

[MISSISSIPPI KITE *Ictinia mississippiensis*] 35.5–38 cm (14–15 in); ws 84–94 cm (33–37 in)

Rare boreal migrant, perhaps only during the southbound passage. Known only from very few sight records, all from Oct and Nov, in Madre de Dios (but has been reported from eastern Ecuador in Apr). Very similar to widespread and common Plumbeous Kite; distinguish from that species with great care. Typically migrates in flocks that often soar very high. Relatively longer tailed than Plumbeous Kite. Adult has pale secondaries (visible both when perched and, from above, in flight) and yellow (not orange) tarsi. May have rufous on inner webs of primaries, but rufous in wings rarely as extensive or as prominent as in Plumbeous. Tail of adult unbanded. Juveniles very similar to Plumbeous of same age, but are streaked below with rufous (not gray-brown). Birds in first basic plumage (not illustrated; might be seen during northbound migration), which have largely gray bodies, retain tail bands of juvenile; birds in this plumage also have brown underwing coverts. **Co, E, Br, Bo**

3 PLUMBEOUS KITE *Ictinia plumbea* 34.5–37 cm (13½–14½ in); ws 84–94 cm (33–37 in)

Fairly common and widespread in Amazonia up to 1500 m; also uncommon and local in Tumbes. Found in humid forest and at forest edge. Often perches in high exposed snags. Effortlessly glides and soars over canopy, alone or in small flocks, capturing insects in flight or snatching them from the canopy. Occurs in Peru throughout the year, but species is partially migratory, and presumably migrants (boreal, austral, or both) also reach Peru. When perched, note very long wings and short tarsi. Rufous bases to primaries prominent in flight; tail also banded. Juvenile has similar shape but is streaked below, largely brown. **VOICE** Song, a weak descending series of twittered notes: "*TI ti-ti-ti-ti, TI ti-ti-ti, TI ti-ti-ti*." **Co, E, Br, Bo**

ad. *caerulescens*

juv.

ad. *balzarensis*

CRANE HAWK

ad. *caerulescens*

CRANE HAWK

juv.

ad.

MISSISSIPPI KITE

ad.

MISSISSIPPI KITE

ad.

juv.

juv.

ad.

♂

SNAIL KITE

♂

♀

juv.

juv.

PLUMBEOUS KITE

juv.

PLUMBEOUS KITE

ad.

ad.

ad.

juv.

PLATE
31

ACCIPITER HAWKS

Accipiter are small to medium-sized hawks of forest interior. Some species may soar over the forest canopy, but hunting (primarily for smaller birds) is by ambush as the hawk weaves rapidly through vegetation. Females significantly larger than males. Wings relatively broad and short, tails relatively long, and Accipiter often have a small-headed look.

1 TINY HAWK *Accipiter superciliosus* * male 22–24 cm (8½–9½ in), female 28–29 cm (11–11½ in); ws 38–48 cm (15–19 in)

Widespread but rare in Amazonia, locally up to 1350 m. Very small forest *Accipiter*, gray or brown with narrowly barred underparts. Adult males largely gray above, barred white and gray below. Adult females and brown-morph juveniles similar, but browner. Rufous morph is less common; primarily a juvenile plumage, but possibly retained as adult in some individuals. Note very small size and narrowly barred underparts; adults also have red or orange iris. Readily identifiable in its lowland habitat. **VOICE** Call a series of descending peeps. **Co, E, Br, Bo**

2 SEMICOLLARED HAWK *Accipiter collaris* male 23–24 cm (9–9½ in), female 29–30 cm (11½–11¾ in); ws 43–53 cm (17–21 in)

Rare hawk of humid montane forest of east slope of Andes, 1500–2500 m. Most records are from south, but also occurs (only locally?) in north. Similar to Tiny Hawk, which is found at lower elevations. Semicollared is larger and browner, with more coarsely barred underparts, a pale collar on sides of neck, and pale auriculars. Iris also apparently always yellow (never red or orange, as in adult Tiny). **VOICE** Call a series of descending "*kee*" notes. Similar to (not safely distinguishable from?) voice of Sharp-shinned Hawk. **Co, E**

3 SHARP-SHINNED HAWK *Accipiter striatus* * male 27–29 cm (10½–11½ in), female 32–34 cm (12½–13½ in); ws 51–63.5 cm (20–25 in)

Fairly common and widespread in humid montane forest along east slope of Andes, 900–3500 m; also found above 750 m on west slope of Andes south at least to southern Cajamarca, and on both slopes of Marañón Valley. Adult highly variable in color of underparts, from largely white below (with rufous tibial feathering) to almost solid rufous. Juveniles brown above, variably streaked below. Cf. Semicollared and Bicolored hawks. Most similar to Double-toothed Kite, with which there may be overlap on lower slopes of Andes; but kite has prominent fluffy white undertail coverts, dark line down throat, and greenish cere. **VOICE** Call a series of reedy yelps: "*kew kew kew kew kew.*" Also thin peeps and whistles. **Co, E, Br, Bo**

GRAY-BELLIED HAWK *Accipiter poliogaster* male 40 cm (15¾ in), female 45–47 cm (17¾–18½ in); ws 69–84 cm (27–33 in)

Rare but widespread in Amazonia, up to 600 m. Status not clear; most records are from austral winter, so perhaps is only a scarce migrant to Peru, but has been reported from Ecuador during austral summer. Adult is a large 2-toned *Accipiter*, gray above and white below; similar in size and proportions to more common Bicolored Hawk, but paler below (white rather than pale gray), with white or pale gray (not rufous) tibial feathering and blacker cap. Cheeks black or gray; cheek color may be individually variable or perhaps represents sexual dimorphism (gray cheeks may occur only in males?). Also similar to Slaty-backed Forest-Falcon, but has blacker cap, yellow or yellow-orange iris, and shorter tarsi, and often has more extensively dark cheeks. Plumage pattern of juvenile strikingly similar to adult Ornate Hawk-Eagle, but juvenile is much smaller, has bare (not feathered) tarsi, and lacks a crest. **VOICE** Call a high, rising whistle given singly: "*wee?*" **Co, E, Br, Bo**

4 BICOLORED HAWK *Accipiter bicolor* * male 36–37 cm (14–14½ in), female 42–46 cm (16½–18 in); ws 58–83 cm (22¾–32¾ in)

Rare in forests (humid and dry) of lowland Peru; widespread in Amazonia, but on west slope of Andes confined to north. Primarily below 900 m, but locally ascends to 1800 m. Adult largely gray, paler below (light gray to whitish gray), with darker cap and rufous tibial feathering. Juveniles variable; buffy below, but may be pale buff, sometimes almost white, below, or much more richly colored. Adult readily recognized (but cf. adult Gray-bellied Hawk). Juvenile may be confused with Collared or Buckley's forest-falcons, but forest-falcons have dark irides, greenish ceres, pale cheeks framed by dusky crescent, and graduated tails. **VOICE** Call a hollow yapping: "*keh keh keh keh keh....*" **Co, E, Br, Bo, Ch**

ad.

ad.

ad.

SHARP-SHINNED HAWK

juv.
brown
morph

juv.
rufous
morph

TINY HAWK

ad.

ad.

juv.

ad.

juv.

SHARP-SHINNED HAWK

juv.
rufous
morph

juv. brown
morph

SEMICOLLARED
HAWK

ad.

ad.

ad.

BICOLORED HAWK

ad.

BICOLORED
HAWK

GRAY-BELLIED HAWK

juv.

ad. gray-cheeked

juv.
white-
breasted
morph

juv. buffy-
breasted morph

PLATE
32

LAUGHING FALCON, KITE, AND SMALL FOREST-FALCONS

The kite and forest-falcons superficially are similar to Accipiter hawks (preceding plate). Forest-falcons (see also plate 33) are long-tailed falcons of forest interior; hunt by ambush within cover of vegetation. Do not soar. Iris dark in most species (yellow or orange in Accipiter), and long tails are graduated (usually more square-tipped in Accipiter). Forest-falcons are rarely seen but often vocal, especially predawn and at dusk. Structurally similar Laughing Falcon is more lethargic and is a bird of forest edges, not interior.

1 LAUGHING FALCON *Herpetotheres cachinnans* * 43–52 cm (17–20½ in); ws 75–91 cm (29½–36 in)

Heard far more frequently than is seen. Uncommon but widespread in Amazonia, up to 1000 m; rare and local in northwest up to 800 m. Sluggish hawk of forest borders. Perches, often in relatively high open sites, for extended periods watching for prey (primarily reptiles). Does not soar. Flies low with shallow, choppy wingbeats and short glides on slightly bowed wings; swings up to perch. Characteristically looks large-headed. Adult Yellow-headed Caracara has very different behavior and much narrower dark line through eyes. **VOICE** Song, usually given at dawn and dusk and sometimes in duet, a long series (often lasting over 5 min) of yelps eventually changing to couplets, the first rising and the second falling: "*ya, ya, ya, ya ya, ya ya, yeh-yaw, yeh-yaw,*" etc. Sometimes, couplets are given without the introductory series. Also may give a loud series of accelerating "*aw*" notes, similar to Slaty-backed Forest-Falcon. Call chuckling notes. **Co, E, Br, Bo**

2 DOUBLE-TOOTHED KITE *Harpagus bidentatus* * 29–35 cm (11½–14 in); ws 60–72 cm (23½–28 in)

Uncommon but widespread in humid forest of eastern lowlands, up to 1300 m. Has shape of an *Accipiter* and may be especially similar in soaring flight. Perches quietly in midlevels of forest. Frequently follows troops of monkeys to capture insects and other prey that they disturb in moving through forest. In all plumages, throat white with narrow, dark central stripe and has fluffy, white undertail coverts (prominent in soaring flight, when tail often held closed). Pattern of underparts of adults variable; may be solid rufous below or variably barred below, sometimes with pronounced gray wash on breast (predominantly males). Breast and belly of juvenile typically white, streaked dusky, but extent of streaking variable and some individuals almost unmarked below. **VOICE** Song thin, chirping notes interspersed with rising whistles: "*ti, ti, weee-weh ti-weee-weh.*" **Co, E, Br, Bo**

3 LINED FOREST-FALCON *Micrastur gilvicollis* 32–38 cm (12½–15 in); ws 51–60 cm (20–23½ in)

Widespread but rare, up to 1000 m. Cf. Barred Forest-Falcon (adults readily separated; juveniles extremely similar). **VOICE** Primary song, usually given predawn and at dusk, a repeated series of 2 notes, the second emphasized and higher in pitch: "*kur KYEER.*" Occasionally a single, repeated "*caw,*" similar to Collared Forest-Falcon, but usually with shorter intervals. Aggressive song similar to primary song but 3 notes, the middle note highest: "*KEER kee-wur,*" or the latter notes on same pitch "*ko COW-COW;*" also may give "*cu... kyew KYEW-whew*" vocalization very similar to that of Barred, but slightly mellower and lower pitched; and a rapid series of clucking notes rising in pitch, ending usually with 2 notes slightly lower: "*kuh-kuh-kuh-kuh-KUH-KUH-WAY-wuh.*" Quality of voice similar to Slaty-backed Forest-Falcon, but note different pattern. **Co, E, Br, Bo**

4 BARRED FOREST-FALCON *Micrastur ruficollis* * 31–38 cm (12–15 in); ws 46–60 cm (18–23½ in)

Most common and widespread forest-falcon in Peru; found throughout eastern lowlands and up to 2000 m on east slope of Andes, also rare in semideciduous forest in Tumbes up to 800 m. Small. Adult distinguished from similar (but often less common) Lined Forest-Falcon by brown iris, yellower (less orange) cere and facial skin, more heavily barred belly, and more white tail bands (typically 3–4 in Barred, 1–2 in Lined). Cf. also much smaller Tiny Hawk. Juvenile white or buff below, with variable barring; very similar to juvenile Lined, but browner (less gray) above, with more white tail bands. Also usually has small white spots on uppertail coverts (visible in hand, not in field); these spots lacking in Lined. **VOICE** Primary song, usually given predawn and at dusk, a repeated monosyllabic bark, descending in pitch: "*kyew!*" Aggressive song a series of 3 or 4 notes of similar quality, the penultimate highest in pitch and most emphasized: "*kyew KYEW-whew!*" or "*cu... kyew KYEW-whew*"; usually higher and more ringing in quality than that of Lined. Call when alarmed a series of hollow, reedy barks. **Co, E, Br, Bo**

LAUGHING
FALCON

DOUBLE-TOOTHED KITE

juv.

ad.

ad.

DOUBLE-TOOTHED KITE

ad.

juv.

BARRED FOREST-FALCON

LINED
FOREST-FALCON

ad.

juv.

ad.

juv.
buffy-breasted

juv.
white-breasted

PLATE
33

HOOK-BILLED KITE AND LARGER FOREST-FALCONS

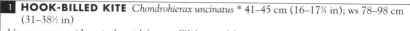

The forest-falcons on this plate are similar in behavior and structure to those on the preceding plate, but are larger. These forest-falcons are furtive, and rarely seen; primarily feed on smaller birds. Hook-billed Kite is remarkable for the wide range of plumages shown by the various color morphs and different sex and age classes.

1 HOOK-BILLED KITE *Chondrohierax uncinatus* * 41–45 cm (16–17¼ in); ws 78–98 cm (31–38½ in)

Uncommon resident in humid forests. Widespread but scarce in Amazonia and on east slope of Andes, up to 2100 m, locally to 3000 m; also found on west slope, up to 1700 m. Perhaps most common in dry forests in central Marañón and Huallaga valleys. Quiet and inconspicuous; spends much time perched in forest canopy. Primarily feeds on land snails. Frequently soars, often relatively low over forest, but not for long periods. Broad wings, constricted at base, recall shape of much larger Black Hawk-Eagle; the kite usually has more prominent tail bands and a less rounded shape to the tail than do hawk-eagles. Plumage notably variable. Always has strongly curved bill and bare yellowish crescent before the eye; these features may be especially important in identifying dark-morph individuals. Light-morph adults more distinctive, but cf. Roadside and Broad-winged hawks. Male light-morph adult is primarily gray, barred below with white. Light-morph female brown above, with broad rufous nuchal color and rufous barring on pale underparts. Dark crown and broad pale nuchal color of light-morph juvenile also distinctive (but see Collared Forest-Falcon). **VOICE** Song a cackle, rising and falling in pitch. **Co, E, Br, Bo**

2 COLLARED FOREST-FALCON *Micrastur semitorquatus* * 51–58.5 cm (20–23 in); ws 76–94 cm (30–37 in)

Rare but widespread; found throughout eastern lowlands, and foothills to 800 m, also less commonly in Tumbes below 800 m. The largest forest-falcon. Light- and buffy-morph adults recognized by pale nuchal collar and dark crescent on sides of face; cf. juveniles of Bicolored Hawk and Hook-billed Kite. Rare dark morph (not illustrated) is entirely sooty; has not been reported from Peru. Juveniles have similar head and neck pattern but variably are coarsely barred below. Cf. smaller Buckley's Forest-Falcon. **VOICE** Primary song, usually given at dawn and dusk, is a series of nearly human "AW" notes, sometimes doubled, with second note higher in pitch: "*aw, AW.*" Aggressive song is a more rapid, rising series of clucking notes ending with two longer notes lower in pitch: "*aw-aw-aw-Aw-AW-AW WOW... ow.*" **Co, E, Br, Bo**

3 BUCKLEY'S FOREST-FALCON *Micrastur buckleyi* 41–46 cm (16–18 in); ws 61–72 cm (24–28 in)

Poorly known; apparently rare but widespread in eastern lowlands, locally to 1350 m. A small version of Collared Forest-Falcon. Female may show white spots on scapulars and inner secondaries (lacking on Collared). Otherwise identified, with care, by smaller size (including proportionately shorter tarsi). Juvenile also is more slaty above than juvenile Collared. Most readily identified by **VOICE** Primary song, usually given at dawn and dusk, is a series of 3 notes, the last separated by a pause and much lower and quieter: "*ah-ow OW.... aw.*" **Co, E, Br**

4 SLATY-BACKED FOREST-FALCON *Micrastur mirandollei* 40–44 cm (16–17¼ in); ws 65–71 cm (25½–28 in)

Rare to uncommon forest-falcon of eastern lowlands. Adult most similar to adult Gray-bellied Hawk, but forest-falcon's crown and back are more uniformly colored, forest-falcon also has more extensive yellow facial skin and a dark iris. Juvenile is larger than juvenile Barred and Lined forest-falcons, lacks the white rim to the face, is grayer above, and usually is more coarsely scaled below. **VOICE** Primary song, usually given predawn and at dusk, is a series of descending "*awwr*" notes. Also a rollicking series of cries with a human quality, the penultimate more drawn out and rising in pitch: "*aw-aw-aw AAaawwah? awah*"; similar to Collared Forest-Falcon but slightly higher and faster. May give a loud series of accelerating "*aw*" notes, similar to Laughing Falcon. **Co, E, Br, Bo**

HOOK-BILLED KITE

dark morph

♂

♀

dark morph

HOOK-BILLED
KITE

juv.

juv.

ad. light
morph

ad. buffy
morph

COLLARED
FOREST-FALCON

juv.
light morph

juv. dark
morph

ad. ♂

juv.

juv.

ad.

SLATY-BACKED
FOREST-FALCON

BUCKLEY'S FOREST-FALCON

PLATE
34

LEUCOPTERNIS HAWKS

Leucopternis are large hawks of the forest with very broad wings and tails. Some species regularly soar over the canopy; other species apparently never do so.

1 [**GRAY-BACKED HAWK** *Leucopternis occidentalis*] 45–52 cm (18–20½ in); ws 104–116 cm (41–45½ in)

Geographically restricted: known only from 600 to 800 m in semideciduous forest in Tumbes, where rare to uncommon. Seen singly or in pairs, usually soaring low over forest. Superficially similar to Variable Hawk, but note extensive streaking on crown and nape of Gray-backed Hawk; crown of Variable is unstreaked gray. Variable not as broad-winged in flight and is found in more open habitats, not in forest. **VOICE** Call a series of 2 or 3 rasping screams, each rising in the middle: "*keEEEeer*." **E**

2 **WHITE HAWK** *Leucopternis albicollis* * 47–50 cm (18½–19¾ in); ws 98–117 cm (38½–46 in)

Uncommon but widespread in humid forest of Amazonia. Most frequent in hilly terrain near base of Andes, on outlying ridges and in hill forest to 1500 m; also found (disjunctly?) in northeastern Loreto. Frequently soars (unlike other white Amazonian *Leucopternis*). Juvenile (not illustrated) similar to adult, but head lightly streaked. Larger than Black-faced and White-browed hawks, with different tail pattern. **VOICE** Call a series of rising whistles: "*rhee rhee rhee*." **Co, E, Br, Bo**

3 **BLACK-FACED HAWK** *Leucopternis melanops* 36–39 cm (14–15½ in); ws 65–78 cm (25½–30¾ in)

Rare to uncommon; apparently restricted to the north bank of the Amazon. A medium-sized black-and-white hawk with largely white head and prominent black "mask" and orange cere. Juvenile similar to adult, but tail is crossed with 2 (not 1) white bands. Does not soar. Usually remains within forest cover, but may perch at forest edge, especially early in morning. Cf. larger White Hawk. **VOICE** Call a descending, thin, piping whistle: "*KEEler*" or "*KEEyer*," sometimes given in a series. **Co, E, Br**

4 **WHITE-BROWED HAWK** *Leucopternis kuhli* 34–39 cm (13½–15½ in); ws 65–76 cm (25½–30 in)

Rare to uncommon; replaces Black-faced Hawk south of the Amazon. Occurs locally up to 1100 m. Much smaller than White Hawk, and with head and nape largely gray (not white); cere orange (not gray). Also has different tail pattern: tail of White-browed is black with a narrow white median band and a very narrow white tip; tail of White is black with white base and broad white tip. Similar in structure and behavior to Black-faced; head of Black-faced is mostly white, with small black "mask," rather than mostly gray with narrow white superciliary as in White-browed. **VOICE** Call a descending, thin, piping whistle: "*KEEler*" or "*KEEyer*," sometimes given in a series. **Br, Bo**

5 [**SEMIPLUMBEOUS HAWK** *Leucopternis semiplumbeus*] 31–34 cm (12–13½ in); ws 51–64 cm (20–25 in)

Status in Peru not clear. Hawks matching description of this species have been reported from a few sites in Amazonia, on both banks of the Amazon downstream from mouth of the Río Ucayali; may be associated with forests on white-sand soils. A small hawk of forest interior with sharp contrast between slate upperparts and white underparts; also note orange cere and tarsi. Juvenile similar but paler and lightly streaked. In South America this hawk otherwise is known only from west of the Andes in Colombia and Ecuador; it is not expected in Amazonian Peru, and confirmation of its occurrence there is highly desirable. **VOICE** Call (western Ecuador) a series of thin, rising whistles with voice cracking: "*reeEELEW reeEELEW reeEELEW*." **Co, E**

6 [**BARRED HAWK** *Leucopternis princeps*] 51–57 cm (20–22½ in); ws 112–124 cm (44–49 in)

Rare and perhaps local; reported from a few sites in humid montane forest on east slope of Andes in Amazonas and San Martín, 1150–1800 m. Usually seen in soaring flight over forest. Readily identified by large size and contrast between dark chest and pale lower breast and belly (barring often not noticeable at any distance); but cf. Black-chested Buzzard-Eagle of higher elevations. Juvenile (not illustrated) similar to adult, but upperparts narrowly edged white. **VOICE** Call a descending whistle with voice cracking: "*KEEleeuu*," sometimes given in a series that accelerates into a rapid series of piping notes. **Co, E**

GRAY-BACKED HAWK

WHITE HAWK

ad.

ad.

WHITE-
BROWED
HAWK

juv.

BLACK-FACED HAWK

juv.

SEMIPLUMBEOUS HAWK

BARRED HAWK

juv.

ad.

PLATE
35

DARK HAWKS AND EAGLES

Black-and-chestnut Eagle and Black Hawk-Eagle are large to very large, dark forest eagles. Slate-colored Hawk is a blackish Leucopternis (see white-breasted species on plate 34) of Amazonian forest. Slender-billed Kite is a much smaller species that superficially is similar to Slate-colored Hawk and is found in similar habitats.

1 BLACK-AND-CHESTNUT EAGLE *Oroaetus isidori* 63–74 cm (25–29 in); ws 147–166 cm (58–65 in)

Rare and local on east slope of Andes, 1700–3500 m, occasionally down to 1000 m. Usually seen soaring over humid montane forest; note very broad wings, often thrust forward, and relatively short tail. Little elevational overlap with most other forest eagles. Adult identifiable by large size, dark plumage, and (in flight) contrasting pale base to primaries and tail; chestnut underparts and wing coverts often not visible at a distance. Juvenile has similar structure, but plumage primarily is pale brown; even in this plumage, bases of outer primaries are pale. Also note the very pale, almost whitish, coverts on upper wing. Cf. much smaller Black-and-white and juvenile Ornate hawk-eagles, and Black-chested Buzzard-Eagle. **VOICE** Call a clear gull-like "*KEEeeww*" and a whistled series of "*pew-EEEWW*" notes. **Co, E, Bo**

2 BLACK HAWK-EAGLE *Spizaetus tyrannus* * 60–66 cm (23½–26 in); ws 115–148 cm (45–58 in)

Widespread but uncommon in eastern lowlands (up to 1800 m); also local in Tumbes up to 750 m. Found in humid forest and forest edge. Ambushes prey from perch, but frequently soars, especially at mid-day and often to great heights, when much more often seen (or heard). Note large size, long tail, black body, and (in flight) relatively short broad wings that are constricted at the base and have conspicuously barred outer primaries. Juvenile much browner; note prominent whitish superciliary and white throat. **VOICE** Call, usually given in flight, a whistled yelp, highest in middle: "*hewLEEew*," sometimes preceded with lower "*pup pup pup*" notes. **Co, E, Br, Bo**

3 SLENDER-BILLED KITE *Rostrhamus hamatus* 35–38 cm (13¾–15 in); ws 80–90 cm (31½–35½ in)

Rare and local in Amazonia. Similar to Snail Kite, which it replaces in more forested areas (swamps, lake margins, and varzea); like that species, primarily feeds on large snails. Sexes similar; note short tail that lacks white, strongly hooked bill, and striking pale iris. Regularly soars low over forest canopy, often in pairs. Shape in flight similar to much larger Slate-colored Hawk. Juvenile is browner than adult and narrowly barred white; also has narrow white tail bands. Immatures may be slate gray, like the adult, but retain the barred tail of juvenile. **VOICE** Call, a reedy "*weeeooh.*" Sometimes a series of reedy chatters. **Co, E, Br, Bo**

4 SLATE-COLORED HAWK *Leucopternis schistaceus* 45–48 cm (17¾–19 in); ws 85–96 cm (33½–38 in)

Widespread but uncommon in Amazonia. Closely associated with water; usually seen perched at margins of oxbow lakes, forest streams, swamps, and other wetlands in forest. Large, chunky, dark hawk with relatively short tail. Juvenile similar, but belly and the tibial feathers often are narrowly barred white, and underwing coverts and bases of primaries barred gray and white; tail also may show additional white tail band, narrow and close to base of tail. In all plumages note combination of slate gray plumage, relatively short black tail with white band, and reddish orange cere and tarsi. Cf. Slender-billed Kite (much smaller, with more strongly curved bill, pale iris, and no white in tail), Snail Kite (which has an extensive white base to tail, not a black tail with white band), Crane Hawk (more slender, with dark cere), and Great Black-Hawk (much larger, with a yellow cere and legs). **VOICE** Call a descending, mellow, whistled scream: "*keeleeuu.*" Also, a rapid series of ringing "*kak*" notes. **Co, E, Br, Bo**

BLACK HAWK-EAGLE

BLACK-AND-CHESTNUT EAGLE

BLACK-AND-CHESTNUT EAGLE

ad.

juv.

ad.

juv.

ad.

ad.

juv.

SLENDER-BILLED KITE

juv.

ad.

juv.

SNAIL KITE
(for comparison)

ad.

SLATE-COLORED HAWK

SLATE-COLORED HAWK

ad.

juv.

juv.

ad.

PLATE
36

SOLITARY EAGLE, BLACK-HAWKS, AND BLACK-COLLARED HAWK

The two species of black-hawks are large blackish hawks of the lowlands. Solitary Eagle superficially is very similar, especially to Great Black-Hawk, but primarily occurs at higher elevations. Black-collared Hawk is a large, rufous-brown hawk of the lowlands of eastern Peru.

1 SOLITARY EAGLE *Harpyhaliaetus solitarius* * 66–75 cm (26–29½ in); ws 157–180 cm (62–71 in)

Rare black hawk of montane areas. Found in humid montane forest along east slope of Andes and on outlying ridges, 700–2100 m; also locally in deciduous forests of northwest. In all plumages very similar to more common Great Black-Hawk, but usually is found at higher elevations. The eagle is larger and has a shorter tail; tail barely reaches wing tips when bird is perched, and tail scarcely extends beyond trailing edge of wing in flight; tail of the black-hawk is much longer. The Solitary Eagle also has a different tail pattern (black crossed with single white band, rather than black with broad white base). The eagle also is slightly paler (slate gray rather than black), may show a very short crest, and the tarsi are shorter and thicker; these features rarely are apparent in the field, however. The juvenile eagle is more easily confused with juvenile Great Black-Hawk but is larger, has somewhat shorter tail (although not as proportionally short as in adult), and tail is less banded. The juvenile eagle also is more heavily marked with black below, always showing dusky tibial feathering and dark markings on sides of breast; but beware that older immature Great Black-Hawks can acquire similar markings. The tarsi of the eagle also are relatively shorter and stouter. **VOICE** Call a long, rising whistled note and a series of rising piping whistles. **Co, E, Bo**

2 GREAT BLACK-HAWK *Buteogallus urubitinga* * 55–63 cm (21½–25 in); ws 113–136 cm (44½–53½ in)

Widespread and fairly common in eastern lowlands, up to 800 m; rare and local in northwest below 400 m. Usually found near water in forested areas, such as along rivers and streams; in Amazonia often seen perched on muddy riverbanks or on branches low over water. Widespread, and adult is perhaps the most frequently seen blackish hawk in Peru, at least in Amazonia. Frequently soars. Note the broad white base to the tail, relatively long yellow tarsi, and dull yellow cere; cf. Slate-colored Hawk. Juvenile a large, long-legged, brown and buff hawk, with a broad pale superciliary and often with buff streaks on the nape. The underparts are buff, coarsely streaked with dusky; streaking often particularly heavy on the sides of the breast. Tail buff or light brown, narrowly barred dusky; tibial feathers buffy, often barred. Cf. Solitary Eagle and (northwest) Mangrove Black-Hawk. **VOICE** Call a piercing, whistled scream, usually rising. **Co, E, Br, Bo**

3 MANGROVE BLACK-HAWK *Buteogallus subtilis* * 45–49 cm (17¼–19¼ in); ws 96–106 cm (38–42 in)

Uncommon in northwest, where confined to mangrove forests. Smaller and duskier than Great Black-Hawk, which occurs in northwest Peru but does not enter mangrove forests; in this region Great Black-Hawk occurs in semideciduous forests, and so the two species should not overlap. Mangrove Black-Hawk has relatively shorter tail and tarsi (note that wing tips almost reach tip of tail when perched), extensive rufous on secondaries, and black tail with single white band (rather than a broad white base to the tail). Juvenile brown with largely pale face, and contrasting dusky line through eye. Similar to juvenile Great Black-Hawk, and best identified by habitat; but also is slightly smaller, with relatively shorter tail and tarsi, and usually has dark streaking on the malars (this "moustache" typically lacking in juvenile Great). **VOICE** Call a series of rising, mewing whistles. **Co, E**

4 BLACK-COLLARED HAWK *Busarellus nigricollis* * 46–52 cm (18–20½ in); ws 115–143 cm (45–56 in)

Uncommon but widely distributed in Amazonia. Closely associated with water; always found along rivers or at edges of marshes and lakes. Often perches low over the water; drops down to capture prey. Also may soar. A very attractive hawk. Juveniles much browner than adults, but Black-collared readily is recognized in all plumages by pale head, blackish chest band, and short tail. Cf. Savanna Hawk, which also is largely rufous but is not currently known from eastern Peru; Savanna lacks the pale head and black chest band, and is a hawk of open habitats. **VOICE** Call a deep growl that trails off: "*G'hehrrrrrr.*" Young give whistled screams. **Co, E, Br, Bo**

SOLITARY EAGLE

juv.

ad.

GREAT BLACK-HAWK

juv.

ad.

ad.

SOLITARY EAGLE

ad.

juv.

GREAT BLACK-HAWK

MANGROVE
BLACK-HAWK

ad.

juv.

ad.

ad.

juv.

MANGROVE
BLACK-HAWK

juv.

BLACK-COLLARED
HAWK

ad.

juv.

PLATE
37

SMALL *BUTEO* HAWKS

Buteo are medium-sized hawks with relatively broad, rounded wings and relatively short, broad tails. Many frequently soar (indeed, some rarely are observed except when soaring). Characteristic of open habitats, light woodland, and forest edge, not forest interior. Species on this plate are small, pale Buteo; see also plates 38, 39, and 40.

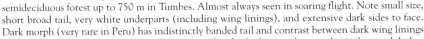

1 WHITE-THROATED HAWK *Buteo albigula* 40–43 cm (15¾–17 in); ws 84–102 cm (33–40 in)

Rare on east slope of Andes at 1500–3700 m; very rare on west slope. Possibly only an austral migrant. Almost always seen in soaring flight over broken-canopy humid montane forest. Note small size and lack of strong banding on tail. Superficially similar to juveniles of other small *Buteo*, but distinguished by coarse streaking and dark blotches on flanks and sides of breast; adult also has hooded appearance (lacking pale streaking on head). Proportions in flight lankier than other small *Buteo*. **VOICE** Call a reedy, descending "*keeEEeh*." **Co, E, Bo, Ch**

2 SHORT-TAILED HAWK *Buteo brachyurus* * 37–41 cm (14½–16 in); ws 83–103 cm (32½–40½ in)

Uncommon but widespread in east up to 1100 m, at humid forest edge. Also uncommon in semideciduous forest up to 750 m in Tumbes. Almost always seen in soaring flight. Note small size, short broad tail, very white underparts (including wing linings), and extensive dark sides to face. Dark morph (very rare in Peru) has indistinctly banded tail and contrast between dark wing linings and paler remiges; cf. Zone-tailed and Swainson's hawks. Light-morph juvenile similar to adult, but lightly streaked on crown and sides of face; cf. White-throated Hawk, which has dark flanks and sides to breast, and longer tail. **VOICE** Call a high, piercing "*peeeyer*." **Co, E, Br, Bo**

3 BROAD-WINGED HAWK *Buteo platypterus* * 37–42 cm (14½–16½ in); ws 82–92 cm (32–36 in)

Uncommon boreal migrant (primarily Oct–Mar) to east, occasionally up to 3000 m; rare migrant to coast. Found in humid forest and at forest edge. Regularly soars; in all plumages note pale wing linings. Slightly larger than Roadside Hawk, with dark iris, dull cere, and no rufous remiges. Juvenile much less heavily marked below than Roadside, especially on breast, and shows broad dusky malar; cf. juvenile Gray Hawk. Rare dark morph (not illustrated) not reported from Peru. **VOICE** Call a high, thin whistle, the second note rising at end: "*pit-seEEEE*." **Co, E, Br, Bo**

4 ROADSIDE HAWK *Buteo magnirostris* * 34–40 cm (13½–15¾ in); ws 68–92 cm (27–36 in)

Common in forest- and river-edge; rapidly colonizes open habitats (such as along roads). Widespread in east (up to 1600 m, locally to 2600 m), uncommon in northwest. Learn Roadside well, as basis of comparison for rarer species. Frequently perches low. Generally does not soar, but flies from one perch to another, flight interspersed with short glides; often shakes tail from side to side after alighting. Note pale iris, yellow cere, and rufous primaries of adult; upperparts may be gray or brown. Some individuals in southeast (*saturatus*-like; not illustrated) have brown upperparts and hood, more orange belly barring, and rufous tail bars. Juvenile browner and drabber; note contrast between streaked breast and coarsely barred belly. Cf. Gray and Broad-winged hawks. **VOICE** Vocal. Frequent call a clear, descending, nasal "*Kiyerrrr!*" with complaining quality: also a slow series of rising, nasal notes "*kree kree kree kree...*" and a rapid series of rising, reedy notes, recalling a woodpecker and often uttered in flight: "*ree kree-keekikikikikikikikiki*." **Co, E, Br, Bo**

5 GRAY HAWK *Buteo nitidus* * 41–43 cm (16–17 in); ws 75–94 cm (29½–37 in)

Rare in east, at edge of humid forest and in river-edge forest. Often perches higher than Roadside Hawk, and more likely to soar (although rarely very high). Pure gray above, lightly barred gray below; also note dark iris, lack of rufous in primaries, and white wing linings (with less prominent dusky tips to remiges than in Broad-winged Hawk). Juvenile much browner. Superficially similar to juvenile Broad-winged, but head is paler and buffier, and often shows a narrow dark line through the eye; underparts are buffier, with broader, more irregular, more blackish spotting below; and upperparts are blacker. Also may show pale panel at base of primaries on upper surface of wing, and a narrow white band across upper tail coverts. **VOICE** Calls a descending, slightly raspy whistled scream: "*peeyler!*" and a series of bisyllabic whistles: "*leer, hooLEER hooLEER hooLEER*." **Co, E, Br, Bo**

WHITE-THROATED
HAWK

juv.

ad.

SHORT-TAILED HAWK

juv. light morph

ad. dark
morph

ad. light morph

WHITE-THROATED HAWK

ad.

juv.

dark morph

SHORT-TAILED HAWK

light morph

juv.

ad.

ad.

juv.

ROADSIDE HAWK

ad.

BROAD-WINGED HAWK

ad.

juv.

ad.

GRAY HAWK

juv.

juv.

ad.

PLATE
38

VARIABLE HAWK AND BLACK-CHESTED BUZZARD-EAGLE

Variable Hawk is the common large Buteo of Peru; also is notable for its great plumage diversity. Variable Hawk includes the widespread "Red-backed" Hawk, and "Puna" Hawk, restricted to the high Andes, which formerly were regarded as separate species. The buzzard-eagle is a large, heavy-bodied hawk; primarily found in the Andes but locally descends to the coast; may be mistaken at a distance for Andean Condor.

1 VARIABLE HAWK *Buteo polyosoma* * 47–59 cm (18½–23¼ in); ws 113–151 cm (44½–59½ in)

One of the most common and widespread large hawks of coast and Andes, found in a variety of open habitats from sea level to 4600 m; but more common on west slope of Andes and in intermontane valleys, rare on more humid east slope (where down only to 2000 m). Frequently soars. Large, long-winged. Plumages highly variable. In adults of all plumages the tail is mostly white, with black band near tip; tail typically is barred narrowly with gray but sometimes is more extensively pale gray ("whitish" rather than white). The most frequent adult plumage is the light morph, in which the underparts and underwing coverts are white. The upperparts of males are uniformly gray, and the belly often is pure white, or nearly so. The back of light-morph females often is reddish brown, and the belly of females more frequently is narrowly barred with gray. Dark morphs are less common, especially at lower elevations, and apparently are particularly rare on the northwest coast. Dark morphs occur in many different color combinations, primarily due to varying patterns of distribution of rufous in body plumage. The least common dark morph is an all-gray plumage (not illustrated). Juvenile has similar body structure, but the tail is longer, gray, narrowly barred. Light-morph juveniles show pale superciliary and dusky malar, and vary in the amount of streaking on the breast; belly is variably barred. Cf. immature Black-chested Buzzard-Eagle (which is larger, has broader but less round-tipped wings, and often has a dark belly) and White-throated Hawk (smaller; more heavily marked on sides of breast and flanks). Dark-morph juveniles, which are much less common, can be very heavily marked below. Older immatures may show a rufous back, and some rufous on the wing coverts; birds in this plumage could be confused with juvenile Harris's Hawk, but juvenile Harris's is more heavily and more extensively streaked below, has more extensive rufous on the wing coverts but none on the center of the back, has white upper tail coverts, and a white tip to the tail. **VOICE** Call a raspy series of screams: "*eeeew kywa kywa kywa.*" Also rasping "*kyew*" and squeaky cackles. **Co, E, Br, Bo, Ch**

2 BLACK-CHESTED BUZZARD-EAGLE *Geranoaetus melanoleucus* * 60–76 cm (23½–30 in); ws 149–184 cm (59–72 in)

Uncommon but widespread eagle of open habitats; primarily found above 1600 m, but locally descends to coast. Most often found in relatively dry, open areas, such as intermontane valleys, puna, and on west slope of Andes, often near rocky cliffs; scarce on humid east slope of Andes. Adult readily recognized by large size, very short and triangular tail, wings that are very broad at the base but with noticeably narrower wing tips, dark chest contrasting with pale belly (gray barring on belly usually not visible at any distance), and pale upper wing coverts. Immatures drab brown, with a longer tail, and much less distinctive. Plumages also can be confusingly variable; some (younger?) immatures often show distinctive contrast between buffy breast and dusky belly, whereas others are more densely and extensively spotted or blotched with dusky on underparts. Much larger than and has broader, less rounded wings than juvenile Variable Hawk, and typically has a dark belly (belly pale in most juvenile Variable Hawks). Cf. also Black-and-chestnut Eagle (but with which there is only limited overlap). **VOICE** Call squeaky yelps and a reedy series "*keh-keh-keh-keh-keh.*" **Co, E, Br, Bo, Ch**

ad. dark morph

VARIABLE HAWK

ad. ♀ light
morph

ad. dark morph

ad. ♂
light morph

ad. light morph

juv. light
morph

VARIABLE HAWK

juv. light
morph

juv. dark
morph

ad. dark
morph

ad.
dark
morph

VARIABLE HAWK

BLACK-CHESTED
BUZZARD-EAGLE

ad.

juv. light morph

imm.

imm.

imm.

ad.

BLACK-CHESTED
BUZZARD-EAGLE

PLATE
39

LARGE RARE *BUTEO* HAWKS

Species on this plate are large Buteo that are rare or geographically restricted in Peru. White-tailed Hawk superficially is similar to Variable Hawk (plate 38) but barely enters Peru, and the two do not overlap geographically. Swainson's Hawk is only a migrant and rarely is seen; it shows tremendous plumage diversity.

1 [**WHITE-TAILED HAWK** *Buteo albicaudatus*] * 44–50 cm (17¼–19¾ in); ws 118–143 cm (46½–56 in)

Known only from the Pampas del Heath, where a rare resident on savanna grasslands with scattered shrubs and woodlots. Frequently soars. Light-morph adult superficially similar to typical female light-morph Variable Hawk of Andes and coast, but there is no geographic overlap between these two species. Rufous on upperparts of White-tailed Hawk is confined to the wing coverts; in rufous-backed individuals of Variable, rufous is located on center of back and does not extend onto wing coverts. Wings of White-tailed also are broader, and tail is shorter. Upper throat of White-tailed often is dark (throat always is white in light-morph Variable), and sides of face are more uniformly colored (sides of face of Variable often narrowly streaked with white). Poorly known (and apparently very rare or local) dark morph has not been reported from Peru. Juvenile is a stout, blackish hawk with pale upper tail coverts and narrowly banded tail; also may show irregular white patch on breast, and some whitish marks on head. Subadults may be similar in pattern to adult, but blacker above and more heavily marked below. **VOICE** Calls similar to those of Variable. **Co, Br, Bo**

2 **SWAINSON'S HAWK** *Buteo swainsoni* 50–55 cm (19¾–21½ in); ws 117–137 cm (46–54 in)

Apparently a regular boreal migrant (both in southbound and northbound passage) through northeastern Amazonia. There are very few observers in this region; currently Swainson's presence is known mainly from satellite-tracking studies, which suggest that it may be seasonally common (presumably Mar–Apr and Oct–Nov) but primarily confined to a narrow migration corridor in northeastern Amazonia, near the Colombian border. Much less common elsewhere in Amazonia, although reported south to Madre de Dios; very rare in Andes (to 3800 m) and on coast. Usually migrates in large flocks, although most records away from northeastern Peru are of single individuals. Plumage highly variable. In all plumages note long slender wings and tail, lack of strong tail barring, and typical dihedral wing shape in soaring flight. Light morph is the most common plumage. Adult light morph has strong contrast between dark remiges and whitish underwing coverts; dark breast band contrasts with white throat and with lighter belly. Cf. Short-tailed Hawk, which is widespread in eastern Peru and also can show contrast on the underwings between white wing coverts and darker remiges. Light-morph Swainson's is much larger than Short-tailed, with different flight profile; also has darker remiges (contrasting more with white underwing coverts), the remiges are more evenly colored (Short-tailed has paler bases to outer primaries), and has a prominent dark band on the upper breast (underparts of Short-tailed are entirely white). Rufous morph is variably rufous below, with rufous or whitish wing coverts; intermediates also occur between "typical" light- and rufous-morph plumages. Dark-morph birds are least common and can be confusing, but note structure and flight profile. Dark-morph adults are more or less uniformly dark brown but always have white undertail coverts; underwing coverts mottled with rufous and sometimes with whitish. Juveniles (other than dark morph) are buffy-headed with a light superciliary, heavy dark moustachial streak, and white or buffy underparts, streaked with dusky. Underwing pattern of light-morph juveniles is similar to that of adults, but less contrasting. Dark-morph juveniles are more heavily marked below, especially on the breast and underwing coverts. Often more easily identified by shape and flight behavior. **Co, E, Br, Bo**

WHITE-TAILED HAWK

ad. dark morph

ad. light morph

subad.

subad.

juv.

WHITE-TAILED
HAWK

juv.

ad. light
morph

SWAINSON'S HAWK

ad. light morph

SWAINSON'S HAWK

ad. light morph

ad. dark morph

juv. light
morph

ad. rufous morph

juv. dark
morph

juv. light morph

SWAINSON'S HAWK

juv. dark morph

PLATE
40

MEDIUM-SIZED DARK HAWKS AND SAVANNA HAWK

Harris's Hawk is a large, dark-bodied hawk of dry open habitats, superficially similar to a Buteo. Zone-tailed and White-rumped are two small to medium-sized, dark-bodied Buteo. Both are relatively easy to identify, but cf. other blackish hawks (plate 36); also note that in flight Zone-tailed Hawk easily can be passed over as a Cathartes vulture.

1 ZONE-TAILED HAWK *Buteo albonotatus* 47–50 cm (18½–19¾ in); ws 117–140 cm (46–55 in)

Rare; found in lowlands of northwest to 800 m, in middle Marañón Valley 900–2600 m, and locally in Amazonia, over dry and humid forests. Rarely seen perched. Usually observed in soaring flight, with long wings held in a dihedral, and tilting from side to side. Flight style and 2-toned pattern to underwing (paler remiges contrasting with darker underwing coverts) cause the Zone-tailed Hawk greatly to resemble a Turkey Vulture in flight; but the hawk has a feathered head and banded tail. At close range also note the yellow cere and iris. Body plumage of juvenile often lightly spotted with white, and tail is narrowly barred gray and black. **VOICE** Call a rasping, descending scream. **Co, E, Br, Bo**

2 HARRIS'S HAWK *Parabuteo unicinctus* * 48–54 cm (19–21 in); ws 92–121 cm (36–47½ in)

Uncommon in northwest, rare farther south along the coast. Also present locally in dry intermontane valleys (Marañón, Pampas, and Urubamba). Primarily below 1200 m. Found in open dry forest, scrub and fields; locally also in urban areas. The size of a large *Buteo* and superficially similar, but has broader wings, a relatively longer tail, and a heavier build. In all plumages has white upper tail coverts and whitish bases to primaries (visible from below in flight). Adult readily recognized by black-and-rufous plumage, contrasting white upper- and undertail coverts, and black tail with broad white tip. Juvenile much browner, with heavily streaked underparts, but has same structure as adult. Juvenile has rufous on upper wing coverts, which usually is prominent, but the amount of rufous may be reduced in some (younger?) individuals. Juvenile also has white upper tail coverts. **VOICE** Usually quiet. Call a gravelly bark: *"PAHH!"* **Co, E, Br, Bo, Ch**

3 WHITE-RUMPED HAWK *Buteo leucorrhous* 33–40 cm (13–15¾ in); ws 67–79 cm (26¼–31 in)

Rare to uncommon but widespread in humid montane forest along east slope of Andes, 1650–3300 m; also on west slope of Andes south to southern Cajamarca. Usually seen in low soaring flight over broken-canopy forest. Adult readily recognized by small size, dark body plumage and contrasting white wing linings; also note white rump and undertail coverts. Juvenile variably streaked or mottled with rufous; but note pale wing linings and black tail broadly banded white. **VOICE** Call a high, squeaking whistle, the second note descending: *"pi'SEEW,"* sometimes a rising whistle, quavering in quality. **Co, E, Br, Bo**

4 SAVANNA HAWK *Buteogallus meridionalis* 47–52 cm (18½–20½ in); ws 121–140 cm (47½–55 in)

Uncommon to fairly common below 700 m in northwest and in dry middle Marañón Valley. A large hawk of open habitats, such as dry scrub and fields. Often seen perched low or standing on the ground. Note the relatively long tarsi. Adult readily identified by large size and extensively rufescent plumage. Streaked juvenile is much duller and is more easily confused with similar plumages of black-hawks, but usually shows rufous on wings (especially remiges) from an early age; also note preference for more open habitats. Not yet reported from Amazonia, but may spread into this region as more forests are cleared; most likely to occur in southeastern Peru, as it occurs in adjacent northwestern Bolivia; cf. Black-collared Hawk. **VOICE** Call a descending whistled scream: *"pyeerh."* **Co, E, Br, Bo**

HARRIS'S HAWK

ad.

ad.

juv.

ZONE-TAILED HAWK

juv.

ad.

juv.

ad.

ZONE-TAILED HAWK

ad.

HARRIS'S HAWK

juv.

TURKEY VULTURE
(for comparison)

ad.

juv.

juv.

ad.

WHITE-RUMPED
HAWK

ad.

juv.

juv.

SAVANNA HAWK

ad.

PLATE
41
OSPREY AND LARGE FOREST EAGLES

Species on this plate are large to very large, mostly white or gray-bodied hawks and eagles. Osprey is found only near water, both on the coast and inland, and preys entirely on fish. Eagles and hawk-eagles are birds of humid forest; the immense Crested and Harpy eagles are among the largest and most spectacular eagles in the world.

1 OSPREY *Pandion haliaetus* * 50–66 cm (19½–26 in); ws 127–174 cm (50–68½ in)

A fairly common boreal migrant; perhaps most common Oct–Apr, but a few may remain throughout the year. Over-summering birds occasionally engage in nest building, but there are no confirmed breeding records for Peru. Most common along coast, but also widespread in Amazonia, mostly below 800 m. Rare visitor to Andes. Usually seen singly. A large, long-winged hawk, with distinctive foraging behavior, wing posture, and head pattern. Always found near water. Feeds exclusively on fish, captured with spectacular dives. After catching a fish, carries it, head first, to a perch to consume it. In flight, wings held in distinctive "kinked" posture, with carpal area ("wrist") pointed forward; distinctive flight profile a shallow "M." **VOICE** Most frequent call, usually given in flight, is a rising series of peeping whistles: "*too teoo tee ti whooeee?*" Also gives various chirps and whistles. **Co, E, Br, Bo**

2 ORNATE HAWK-EAGLE *Spizaetus ornatus* * 56–62 cm (22–24½ in); ws 107–127 cm (42–50 in)

Widespread but uncommon in eastern lowlands up to 800 m; formerly also in Tumbes, but no records there since 19th century. Behavior similar to Black Hawk-Eagle; usually hunts within canopy of forest but may soar over forest, although rarely as high as Black. Striking adult almost unmistakable (but cf. juvenile Gray-bellied Hawk, which is much smaller and has bare tarsi). Whiter juvenile has feathered tarsi, with barred tibial feathers; cf. Black-and-white Hawk-Eagle and juvenile Gray-headed Kite. **VOICE** Call, usually given in flight, a rising-falling series of pure whistles, often with the last given as a rapid couplet: "*whew WHEW WHEW-ew.*" Also a series of yelping whistles. **Co, E, Br, Bo**

3 CRESTED EAGLE *Morphnus guianensis* 79–89 cm (31–35 in); ws 138–154 cm (54–60½ in)

A rare eagle of humid forest of eastern lowlands, locally up to 1100 m. May soar briefly over forest canopy, and soars more frequently than does Harpy Eagle; but typically perches in canopy or subcanopy and hunts for small to medium-sized mammals within cover of vegetation. Very large, surpassed only by similar but even larger Harpy; Crested also has relatively longer tail and smaller bill than Harpy, and relatively longer, thinner tarsi. Spiky crest has a single point (crest of Harpy is bifurcated). Light-morph adult variably barred rufous or gray below; lacks dark breast band of adult Harpy. Also has unmarked underwing coverts. Dark morph is rare (but readily identifiable). Juveniles are very white, gradually becoming darker (over several years) with age. Juveniles can be very difficult to distinguish from juvenile Harpy other than by body structure and (in good view) crest shape; possibly also has blacker lores than juvenile Harpy. Also compare later immature stages (and even light-morph adult), with gray breast, to similar gray-breasted immature plumages of Harpy; aside from size, structure, and crest shape, note that with age Harpy gradually acquires some black in breast band and on underwing coverts. **VOICE** Call a series of high, descending pure whistles. **Co, E, Br, Bo**

4 HARPY EAGLE *Harpia harpyja* 89–102 cm (35–40 in); ws 176–201 cm (69–79 in)

Rare in humid forest of eastern lowlands. Rarely soars. Hunts within vegetation; waits from perch in canopy or subcanopy, then weaves through foliage to capture large mammal prey or to move to new perch. Largest and bulkiest eagle in Peru; larger and relatively shorter tailed than Crested Eagle, with heavier bill and shorter but massively thick tarsi and toes. Crest usually bifurcated (also juvenile can be bushy-headed, with no distinct points). Adult and late-stage immatures more readily recognized by size and black or dusky breast band; also note black underwing coverts. Juveniles and younger immatures are paler and much more easily confused with Crested Eagle; see that species for distinctions between the two. **VOICE** Call a long, descending, mewing whistle, lower pitched than other large raptors: "*HEEleww.*" **Co, E, Br, Bo**

OSPREY

ad.

juv.

ad.

ORNATE
HAWK-EAGLE

juv.

CRESTED EAGLE   ad. light
                        morph

ad. light morph

ad. dark
morph

ad. dark
morph

CRESTED EAGLE

juv.

juv.

juv.

subad.   ad. light morph

subad.

ad.

HARPY EAGLE

juv.

HARPY EAGLE

ad.

juv.

PLATE
42

CARACARAS

Caracaras are related to falcons and forest-falcons but are larger and have long wings and tails. Other than Red-throated, most species are found in open habitats and are scavengers or omnivorous.

1 RED-THROATED CARACARA *Ibycter americanus* 50–52 cm (19¾–20½ in); ws 97–115 cm (38–45 in)

Uncommon but widespread in Amazonia, up to 1500 m. Very social, and usually travels in pairs or in small noisy parties in the canopy of humid forest or at forest edge. Feeds largely on nests of bees and wasps; also eats some fruit. May follow and mob intruders. Readily identified by voice and behavior, white belly, and (cf. Black Caracara) dull reddish facial color. **VOICE** Loud, complaining screeches, screams, and caterwauls, often in chorus, some notes monosyllabic, "*kyeeer*," others multisyllabic: "*Ki-ki-KAAAWWW*" (the source of a vernacular name, *tatatáo*). At a distance, can be reminiscent of large macaws. **Co, E, Br, Bo**

2 BLACK CARACARA *Daptrius ater* 41–43 cm (16–17 in); ws 91–100 cm (36–39 in)

Fairly common and widespread in eastern lowlands, up to 750 m. A caracara of forest edge, frequently seen in flight along rivers or standing on riverbanks, as singles or in loose parties of several individuals. Does not soar. Slender, with long wings and tail. Readily recognized by black plumage, white rump, and bright facial skin. Face duller in juvenile, and base of tail barred white. **VOICE** Call a rasping scream, falling in pitch: "*kyeeeer*." Also a series of shorter raspy "*chuck*" notes when interacting. **Co, E, Br, Bo**

3 MOUNTAIN CARACARA *Phalcoboenus megalopterus* 50–55 cm (19¾–21½ in); ws 111–124 cm (44–49 in)

Uncommon to common in open habitats of Andes, mostly 3200–4700 m, down to 2000 m in Marañón Valley and arid parts of northern mountains. Found in fields, puna, and paramo. Frequently seen walking on the ground (especially in recently plowed fields), as singles or pairs, rarely in larger congregations. Flies with strong shallow wingbeats, and aided by wind may glide for some distance. Note long wings and tail. Adult readily recognized by striking black-and-white pattern (appearing largely black from above but white from below in flight) and reddish face. Juvenile similar in shape and pattern, but is largely brown; in flight, note conspicuous whitish bases to primaries and pale base to tail. **VOICE** Call grating barks. **Bo, Ch**

4 YELLOW-HEADED CARACARA *Milvago chimachima* * 43–46 cm (17–18 in); ws 81–95 cm (32–37½ in)

Fairly common and widespread in northern and central Amazonia; rare and local in southeast. Small caracara of open habitats, probably originally a bird of rivers but now colonizing pastures. Frequently interrupts flapping flight with glides. Adult readily identified by small size, buff coloration, and prominent buffy bases to primaries (but cf. Laughing Falcon). Juvenile is browner and heavily streaked; may recall an immature *Buteo*, but note slender, long-winged caracara shape and pale bases to primaries. **VOICE** Call a loud descending whistle, sometimes raspy: "*peeyer*" or "*peeyah*." Also rasping clucks and screams. **Co, E, Br, Bo**

5 SOUTHERN CARACARA *Caracara plancus* 50–55 cm (19–21¼ in); ws 107–133 cm (45–52 in)

Rare in southeastern lowlands, where primarily found on savannas of Pampas del Heath; very rarely wanders farther north. Formerly also a rare resident on southern coast, where perhaps now extirpated; the few recent records may be vagrants from Chile. Very similar in all plumages to Crested Caracara, but more extensively barred, especially in center of back. **VOICE** Rarely heard; occasional cackles and rasping chatters in aggressive interactions. **Br, Bo, Ch**

6 CRESTED CARACARA *Caracara cheriway* 49–54 cm (19¼–21¼ in); ws 107–133 cm (42–52 in)

Fairly common on coastal plain of northwest; possibly also a rare resident (or merely an occasional visitor?) in dry middle Marañón Valley, up to 900 m. A caracara of open country, found in dry forest and scrub. Frequently perches conspicuously atop low trees or shrubs, as singles or pairs. Often forages on the ground and joins vultures at carrion. Flight steady, with strong deep wingbeats; also note lanky shape and pale neck, bases to primaries, and base to tail. Juvenile similar in pattern to adult, but black is replaced with brown. In south cf. Southern Caracara. **VOICE** Rarely heard; occasional cackles and rasping chatters in aggressive interactions. **Co, E, Br**

RED-THROATED
CARACARA

ad.

juv.

BLACK CARACARA

ad.

juv.

ad.

MOUNTAIN
CARACARA

ad.

juv.

MOUNTAIN
CARACARA

ad.

YELLOW-HEADED
CARACARA

ad.

ad.

juv.

juv.

YELLOW-HEADED
CARACARA

SOUTHERN CARACARA

juv.

ad.

ad.

ad.

CRESTED CARACARA

juv.

PLATE
43

HARRIERS AND SMALL FALCONS

Harriers are long-winged, long-tailed hawks of open country. Typically show a narrow white band on the upper tail coverts. Harrier flight is distinctive, a mixture of frequent flapping interspersed with short glides and sudden tilting motions; wings often are held noticeably above the plane of the body. Harriers forage by flying low over the ground, often passing back and forth over an area, then dropping down suddenly on prey. Cinereous is the only expected harrier in Peru. Merlin and American Kestrel are the two smallest species of falcon found in Peru; see also plate 44.

[LONG-WINGED HARRIER *Circus buffoni*] 48–55 cm (19–21¼ in); ws 119–155 cm (47–61 in)

Very rare visitor to southeastern lowlands (only during austral winter?); reported only from a few sight records from Madre de Dios. Plumages highly variable. In all plumages shows gray primaries, tipped and barred with black (visible in flight), and dark, solid-colored upperparts. Adult light-morph birds also are much whiter below than Cinereous Harrier and have a whitish face. Birds in the rare dark morph are mostly blackish (belly sometimes dark rufous-brown), with little or no white band on rump; can be identified by structure, flight profile, and habitat. Cinereous never as dark as dark-morph Long-winged. Juveniles are similar to adult female but (light morph) scaled above and more heavily streaked below or (dark morph) very dusky above and heavily streaked below. **VOICE** Call musical cackles. **Co, Br, Bo, Ch**

1 CINEREOUS HARRIER *Circus cinereus* 39–48 cm (15½–19 in); ws 90–115 cm (35–45 in)
Locally fairly common in Andes, 2700–4200 m; rare but widespread along coast. Prefers marshes and moist grasslands and fields; less commonly found over dry fields and puna. Typically shows a narrow white band across upper tail coverts. Male is noticeably gray on breast and upperparts; female is browner. Juveniles are brown above, like adult female, but broadly streaked below. **VOICE** Call a rasping "*kah*." **Co, E, Br, Bo, Ch**

MERLIN *Falco columbarius* * male 26.5–27.5 cm (10½–10¾ in), female 30–32 cm (11¾–12½ in); ws 53–73 cm

Rare boreal migrant, but may be regular in northwest, on coastal plain (although has been reported up to 3000 m in Ecuador); very rare south to Lima. Probably present Oct–Mar. Slightly larger than kestrel, but with a heavier build, and much stronger and more direct flight, often low near the ground. Does not hover. Always brown or gray (not rufous) above, and more heavily marked below. Much smaller than Peregrine Falcon, with narrower wings and very plain face pattern. Also cf. Sharp-shinned Hawk (especially juvenile). Sharp-shinned is found only in the Andes; little or no overlap of these two species would be expected in Peru. Also, Sharp-shinned has a yellow (not brown) iris, rufous tibial feathers, more rounded wings, and more solidly colored upperparts. **Co, E, Br**

2 AMERICAN KESTREL *Falco sparverius* * 27–30 cm (10½–11¾ in); ws 52–61 cm
Smallest and most frequently seen falcon in Peru. Common and widespread on coast and in Andes, up to 4700 m; but scarce or absent on humid east slope, and not in Amazonia. Found in a wide variety of dry open habitats, including fields, scrub, and grasslands. Perches conspicuously on wires, fences, and trees; nests in cavities. Frequently hovers. In all plumages note rufous tail and ornate facial pattern, with gray crown and narrow black lines on face. Male has blue-gray wings, rufous back (variably barred with black; barring often sparse), and rufous tail with broad black subterminal band; underparts are pale buff, variably spotted. Wings, back, and tail of female are rufous brown, barred with black. Juveniles are similar to respective adult plumages. **VOICE** Common call a series of shrill "*killy-killy-killy-killy*" notes. Interactions often accompanied by trills and whining "*cree*" notes. **Co, E, Br, Bo, Ch**

ad. ♀ light morph

LONG-WINGED HARRIER

ad. ♀

ad. ♂

CINEREOUS HARRIER

ad. ♂

ad. ♀

ad. ♂ dark morph

ad. ♀
light morph

juv. dark morph

juv.

CINEREOUS HARRIER

juv. light morph

ad. ♂ dark morph

juv. light morph

ad. ♂ light morph

LONG-WINGED HARRIER

♂

AMERICAN KESTREL

♂

♀

♀

MERLIN

♀

♂

♂

♀

AMERICAN KESTREL

PLATE
44

FALCONS

Falcons have long, tapered wings, long tails, and strong flight. Iris always dark (cf. Accipiter). Females significantly larger than male. Usually solitary except when breeding.

1 ORANGE-BREASTED FALCON *Falco deiroleucus* male 33.5–35 cm (13–13¾ in), female 38–40 cm (15–15¼ in); ws 69–85 cm (27–33½ in)

Rare in east, primarily below 800 m but locally to 2000 m. In southern Peru primarily restricted to hilly terrain near the base of the Andes, but in northern (and central?) Peru may occur well into Amazonia. Superficially similar to much more common Bat Falcon, but larger (although small male is not much larger than female Bat Falcon). Orange-breasted also is a bulkier bird than Bat Falcon, often recalling a Peregrine Falcon in structure rather than the more delicate Bat Falcon, compared to which Orange-breasted has a proportionately larger head (more projecting in flight), shorter tail, and shorter, broader wings; also has heavier tarsi, toes, and bill (although these features may be difficult to use in field without extensive experience with Bat Falcon). Orange-breasted also is more coarsely barred black-and-white below; the black "vest" is less extensive on breast; and has contrast between white throat and orange-rufous sides of neck and lower breast (these regions more uniformly white or buff on Bat Falcon). Juvenile browner than adult and more streaked below. The undertail coverts and tibial feathers are buffy brown, not rufous, and the tibial feathers are heavily barred or spotted black, unlike any plumage of Bat Falcon. **VOICE** Call a whining *"reee reee reee reee,"* also various chattering and chirping notes. **Co, E, Br, Bo**

2 BAT FALCON *Falco rufigularis* * male 26–28.5 cm (10¼–11¼ in), female 29–31 cm (11½–12¼ in); ws 53–73 cm (21–29 in)

Fairly common and widespread in Amazonia up to 1500 m; rare and local in northwest. Usually seen at forest edge. Makes sorties for flying insects, birds, or bats from high exposed perch; often most active at dusk. Flight very swift and agile. Very little overlap with Aplomado Falcon, which is larger, longer tailed, and has prominent pale superciliary. Female significantly larger than male, approaching size of male Orange-breasted Falcon. Juvenile similar to adult but "bib" is buffy and undertail coverts are barred (Orange-breasted also has barred undertail coverts). **VOICE** Call a series of high, slightly raspy *"cree"* notes or descending *"kew"* notes, shorter and more forceful than other notes of small falcons. **Co, E, Br, Bo**

3 PEREGRINE FALCON *Falco peregrinus* * male 38–42 cm (15–16½ in), female 43–46 cm (17–18 in); ws 95–117 cm (37–46 in)

Rare resident (*cassini*) in Andes and foothills, primarily 1800–4300 m, but probably locally on coast as well. Boreal migrant throughout, but probably scarce above 900 m; in Amazonia primarily winters along large rivers. Flight very powerful. Primarily preys on birds, captured in flight, often after long steep dive or fast aerial pursuit. Nest is on ledge of rock wall. Common boreal migrant *anatum* (not illustrated) is similar to *cassini*. Note large size, broad wings, and prominent "moustachial" streak on side of face. Adults of *cassini* and *anatum* are blue-gray above, with buffy or whitish underparts, barred on the belly and undertail coverts. Adult (not illustrated) of boreal migrant *tundrius* is paler than other Peregrines, with a narrower moustachial streak. Juvenile Peregrines are brown above, with streaked underparts. Juvenile *cassini* and *anatum* are similar to one another; juvenile *tundrius* typically is paler, with a narrower moustachial streak, and also often has pale superciliary (cf. Aplomado Falcon). **VOICE** Call a rasping *"kreee"* in slow series. **Co, E, Br, Bo, Ch**

4 APLOMADO FALCON *Falco femoralis* * male 37–40 cm (14½–15¾ in), female 41–42 cm (16–16½ in); ws 76–102 cm (30–40 in)

Uncommon but widespread in open habitats of Andes, 2400–4300 m. Rare on coast, where perhaps in part only a visitor from Andes; but probably is resident in northwest. Perches with upright posture on or near ground, or pursues prey in very low, rapid flight. Easily identified by lanky shape (long tail and narrow wings) and by broad pale superciliary and extensive white throat and breast, contrasting with black or dusky belly. **VOICE** Call a series of thin, high *"cree"* notes, similar to some calls of kestrel. **Co, E, Br, Bo, Ch**

ad. ♂

ORANGE-BREASTED FALCON

juv. ♀

ad. ♂

ad. ♂

juv. ♀

BAT FALCON

ad. ♀

ORANGE-BREASTED FALCON

juv. ♀

ad. ♂
cassini

ad. ♂

APLOMADO FALCON

juv. ♀

PEREGRINE FALCON

juv. ♀
cassini

ad. ♀
cassini

juv. ♀

PEREGRINE FALCON

juv. ♂
cassini

ad. ♂

APLOMADO FALCON

juv. ♂
tundrius

PLATE
45

SUNBITTERN, TRUMPETERS, AND WOOD-RAILS

Sunbittern is a peculiar rail-like bird of stream and river margins in eastern Peru. Trumpeters are found in the interior of humid forest, where they roam the floor of upland forest in small flocks while foraging for fallen fruit and insects. Trumpeters have a characteristic hunched posture. Their deep booming voices may carry for long distances. When alarmed, they usually retreat on foot uttering loud "kak!" calls, but will fly awkwardly if hard pressed. Roost communally on low perches. Trumpeters frequently are kept as pets in Amazonia. Rails, crakes, coots, and gallinules are found in a variety of habitats but usually are associated with wetlands, marshes, or swamps. Often flick the tail when walking or swimming. Many species, especially crakes and rails, are very secretive, remaining concealed with vegetation and difficult to observe. Wood-Rails are large rails of forest with heavy, stout bills; reddish tarsi; unstreaked plumage; reddish remiges; and black or gray lower belly and flanks, and black tail.

1 SUNBITTERN *Eurypyga helias* * 43–48 cm (17–19 in)
Uncommon but widespread in eastern lowlands (*helias*; buffier and more heavily barred); rare in foothills and lower slopes of Andes (*meridionalis*; darker, grayer, less barred, perhaps also with brighter bill and tarsus?), up to 1800 m. Found along streams, rivers, and edges of forest lakes, both on fast-moving, rock-lined streams and sluggish or still water, including pools in forest interior. Singles or pairs walk sedately along shore (only rarely wading in water), occasionally lunging after prey. Flies with distinctive shallow wingbeats interspersed with short glides, showing off ornate wing pattern; open wings also used in threat display. **VOICE** Song a melancholy whistle with a "voice crack" near the end, rising in pitch slightly: "*hooooEEEE.*" Call a decelerating series of growled notes, becoming more hooted toward end. **Co, E, Br, Bo**

2 PALE-WINGED TRUMPETER *Psophia leucoptera* * 45–52 cm (17¾–20½ in)
Replaces Gray-winged Trumpeter south of the Amazon. Found in humid forest up to 1050 m. Now relatively rare except in less disturbed forest. Easily identified by prominent whitish "rump." **VOICE** Song, usually given by several individuals, is a deep booming series of rolling and puttering notes. Calls include a harsh "*kak!*" and deeper puttering sounds. **Br, Bo**

3 GRAY-WINGED TRUMPETER *Psophia crepitans* * 46–52 cm (18–20½ in)
Rare in humid lowland forest, and confined to the north side of the Amazon. Note gray inner remiges and plumes, forming prominent gray "rump" patch. **VOICE** Song, usually given by several individuals, is a deep booming series of rolling and puttering notes. Calls include a harsh "*kak!*" and deeper puttering sounds. **Co, E, Br**

4 [RUFOUS-NECKED WOOD-RAIL *Aramides axillaris*] 29.5–31 cm (11½–12¼ in)
Found only in extreme northwest, where primarily occurs in mangrove but (less commonly and very locally?) also in evergreen forest up to 900 m. The only wood-rail in northwest. Adult easily recognized by extensively rufous body (with pale gray nape). Immature much browner and duller, but retains reddish remiges and a dull gray nape. **VOICE** Song duet a strident series of musical notes, the notes of the pair overlapping haphazardly: "*CHI burr... CHI burr... CHI burr....*" **Co, E**

5 GRAY-NECKED WOOD-RAIL *Aramides cajanea* * 33–38 cm (13–15 in)
Widespread and fairly common in eastern lowlands, up to 1400 m; found in flooded and swampy forest and along forest streams. Less timid than most other rails. Easily identified by contrast between gray head and neck (forming a "hood") and brown lower breast and belly. Immature paler, with buffy brown belly (but retains black undertail coverts and tail). **VOICE** Song, often given in asynchronous duet, a series of musical barks and hoots: "*pidunk-HOOIT pidunk-HOOIT pidunk-HOOIT POO POO POO.*" Also, deep booming notes, various cackles, and barks. **Co, E, Br, Bo**

6 RED-WINGED WOOD-RAIL *Aramides calopterus* 32–35 cm (12½–13¾ in)
Very poorly known, and apparently rare and local. Reported from scattered locations in lowland eastern Peru, many (but not all) of which are associated with hilly terrain. Either very quiet (unusual for a wood-rail) or the voice has not yet been identified. Note prominent gray throat and breast, contrasting with rufous sides of neck; cf. more common and widespread Gray-necked Wood-Rail. **E, Br**

SUNBITTERN

meridionalis

helias

PALE-WINGED TRUMPETER

GRAY-WINGED TRUMPETER

imm.

RUFOUS-NECKED WOOD-RAIL

GRAY-NECKED WOOD-RAIL

ad.

RED-WINGED
WOOD-RAIL

PLATE
46

CRAKES AND RAILS I

Blackish, Plumbeous, and Spotted rails are long-billed rails of marshes. Uniform and Chestnut-headed crakes are rarely seen, short-billed rails found in dense understory in Amazonia.

1 BLACKISH RAIL *Pardirallus nigricans* * 27.5–29.5 cm (10¾–11½ in)

Rare and local in marshes, lake edges, and wet grasslands, primarily at 400–1050 m along base of Andes; also locally into Amazonia in southeast. As the name suggests, a dark-colored rail (brown and slate gray) with a long, entirely yellow bill. Does not overlap with Plumbeous Rail (which is very similar but has blue and red spots on base of bill and lacks white on throat). Juvenile similar to juvenile Plumbeous. **VOICE** Song duet is a series of pumping drums that end in squeals, "*pm pm pm grrrrrr-WEEE? grrrr-WEEE?*" punctuated by occasional descending chatters. Call a chirping "*tidik.*" Also, a loud cry very like that of Roadside Hawk. **Co, E, Br, Bo**

2 PLUMBEOUS RAIL *Pardirallus sanguinolentus* * 28–30 cm (11–11¾ in)

Common and widespread in marshes and lake edges, both along coast of Peru (*simonsi*) and in Andes (*tschudii*) at 2000–4400 m. Adult readily identified by gray and brown plumage and long, colorful bill; the two subspecies are not distinguishable in the field as adults. No overlap with Blackish Rail. Juvenile *tschudii* more uniformly drab brown. Usually develops some color on bill from an early age; no other long-billed rail is expected in Andean marshes (but see Bogota Rail). Juvenile *simonsi* apparently are gray-breasted, similar to adult but paler. **VOICE** Song duet is a rollicking series of screeching notes, "*urr ti-gree, ti-gree, CHI-reh, CHI-reh, CHI-reh trrrrrr,*" mixed with trills and pumping sounds (the latter audible only at close distance). Also gives an accelerating series of deep pumping sounds: "*pm pm pmPMPMPM.*" Calls include a sharp "*peet!*" note. **E, Br, Bo, Ch**

3 SPOTTED RAIL *Pardirallus maculatus* * 25.5–27 cm (10–10½ in)

Uncommon to locally fairly common in northwest and in middle Marañón Valley, where found in marshes and wet rice fields; mainly in lowlands but occasionally as high as 2200 m. Very rare vagrant to southeastern Amazonia. Adult readily recognized by bold black-and-white plumage and long yellow bill. Immature much drabber (some may lack barring), but older immatures have pattern of the adult. **VOICE** Song (?) is a deep accelerating drumming series: "*pmm pmm pmm-pmmPMMPMMPMM.*" Agitated song is a loud, decelerating-accelerating coughing: "*pJEW-pJEW pJEEEW pJEEEW pJEEW-pJEW.*" Calls include a deep thumping sound, almost low enough that one feels it more than hears it. Also a series of reedy chatters: "*tchi-di-dert,*" similar to the bisyllabic chirp of Blackish Rail. **Co, E, Br, Bo, Ch**

4 UNIFORM CRAKE *Amaurolimnas concolor* * 20.5–21.5 cm (8–8½ in)

Rare and local, but widespread, in eastern lowlands, locally up to 1200 m. Found in swampy forest, the margins of oxbow lakes, and wet dense second growth. Similar to Chestnut-headed Crake, but duller and browner, less chestnut with no contrast between head and back. The bill also is slightly longer than bill of Chestnut-headed and is all yellow; and breast and belly are same color. Tarsus red (but note that the population of Chestnut-headed in northeastern Amazonia also has red tarsi). **VOICE** Song a series of 7–15 clear, rising whistled "*weee?*" notes at a variable, but fairly leisurely, pace. **Co, E, Br, Bo**

5 CHESTNUT-HEADED CRAKE *Anurolimnas castaneiceps* * 20.5–21.5 cm (8–8½ in)

Uncommon in eastern lowlands; primarily found in dense humid understory, especially in *Heliconia* thickets, of second growth and at forest edge, sometimes far from water. Often in pairs or family groups. Note chestnut-brown head and neck and somewhat bicolored bill. In most of Peru the tarsi are olive or brown (*castaneiceps*), but in northeastern Amazonian Peru (primarily north of the Amazon and east of the Río Napo) the tarsi are bright reddish or pinkish (*coccineipes;* not illustrated). Cf. Uniform and Black-banded crakes. **VOICE** Song, usually given in duet, is a long (lasting up to 5 min) series of tri- or bisyllabic whistles: "*wee-hoohoo wee-hoohoo wee-hoohoo....*" Aggressive calls may include a quiet puttering sound. **Co, E, Br, Bo**

PLUMBEOUS RAIL

ad.

BLACKISH RAIL

juv. *tschudii*

ad.

imm.

SPOTTED RAIL

castaneiceps

UNIFORM CRAKE

CHESTNUT-HEADED CRAKE

PLATE
47

RAILS AND CRAKES II

Most of the species shown on this plate are rare in Peru or are geographically restricted. Two species shown here, Virginia Rail and Paint-billed Crake, are more widespread, but even these two species rarely are seen.

BOGOTA RAIL *Rallus semiplumbeus* * ca. 21–22 cm (8¼–8½ in)

Known only from a single 19th-century specimen of unknown origin; possibly a rare (or now extirpated in Peru?) resident of Andean marshes. Similar to Virginia Rail, but slightly larger; also more olive above and much grayer below, with no contrast between gray sides of face and buffy brown throat and breast as in Virginia. Any modern report would require extensive documentation. **Co**

1 VIRGINIA RAIL *Rallus limicola* * 20–21 cm (7¾–8¼ in)

A rare, local, and secretive resident of coastal marshes of central and southern Peru. Much smaller and buffier than Plumbeous Rail; no known overlap with Clapper Rail, and primarily reported from freshwater marshes (although also may occur in brackish water?). Probably has been overlooked at many sites where it might occur; on the other hand, may be becoming increasingly rare with ongoing human destruction of or disturbance to coastal marshes. **VOICE** Aggressive song is a rapid, descending series of high nasal oinks. Song (North American forms) is a series of ticks, usually paired. Calls include a series of harsh notes ending in a long rasp: "*tche-tche-tche DJZZSH*." **Co, E**

2 CLAPPER RAIL *Rallus longirostris* * 33–37 cm (13–14½ in)

Rare in Peru, and confined to extreme northwest, where forages on mudflats in mangrove forests. Rufous-necked Wood-Rail, the only other rail in this habitat, is larger with a shorter, heavier bill, deeper rufous and olive coloration, and black belly and flanks. No overlap known with much smaller Virginia Rail. **VOICE** Aggressive song is a loud series of pumping coughs, accelerating in pace: "*CHUFF CHuff-chuff-chuff chuff chuff*." Other calls include grating cackles and coughing notes. Song (North America) is an accelerating series of ticking notes. **Co, E, Br**

3 PAINT-BILLED CRAKE *Neocrex erythrops* * 18–18.5 cm (7–7¼ in)

Rare but widespread on coast and in Marañón Valley, where found in marshes, tall wet grasses, and rice paddies. Rare and local (but overlooked?) in eastern lowlands, where presumably found in grassy lake margins and wet fields. Very rare vagrant to altiplano. Small and gray-breasted, with prominent red-and-yellow bill and indistinctly barred flanks. Unmistakable if seen well (but cf. Small-billed and Tataupa tinamous). **Co, E, Br, Bo**

4 ASH-THROATED CRAKE *Porzana albicollis* * 21–24 cm (8¼–9½ in)

Very local in Peru; reported only from damp grasslands and edges of marshes near Jeberos (where rare) and on Pampas del Heath (fairly common). A dull brown-and-gray rail with short bill and black-streaked upperparts. Much larger than Gray-breasted and Paint-billed crakes; also lacks colorful bill of the latter. **VOICE** Song, a duet, involves one individual giving a cackling series while the other gives a longer gurgled trill that rises and falls in pitch. **Co, Br, Bo**

SORA *Porzana carolina* 20–23 cm (7¾–9 in)

Rare boreal migrant (Oct–Mar) to the coast. Few recent records; may have declined in abundance as migrant to Peru or is overlooked. Probably regular (at least formerly) south to Lima, irregular farther south. Found in marshes, at lake edges, and perhaps in damp grasslands. Note black face and throat of adult, contrasting with gray sides of face and yellowish bill; also note greenish tarsi. Juvenile brown and drabber; larger than Paint-billed Crake, buffier, with more boldly barred flanks and duller tarsi. **VOICE** Calls include an explosive "*keek!*" and a reeling, descending whinny. **Co, E**

5 OCELLATED CRAKE *Micropygia schomburgkii* * 14–15 cm (5½–6 in)

Rare. Confined to Pampas del Heath, where found in savanna with scattered shrubs; presumably is resident there but perhaps occurs only as a nonbreeding migrant (also has been reported once from Andes of Cuzco). Very difficult to observe; usually seen only as it flushes from close underfoot, flying weakly a short distance before dropping down again into grass. Note the small size and buffy color; at close range the small white spots on back and wings may be seen. **VOICE** Song is a weak trill that becomes a raspy chatter. **Co, Br, Bo**

BOGOTA RAIL

VIRGINIA RAIL

CLAPPER RAIL

PAINT-BILLED CRAKE

ASH-THROATED CRAKE

ad.

SORA

juv.

OCELLATED CRAKE

PLATE
48

LATERALLUS CRAKES

Laterallus are very small crakes and rails (the smallest species are about the size of a sparrow). They are very secretive and can be difficult to observe; they are most readily detected by voice. All have short but relatively stout bills and often carry the tail cocked upright. Most also have prominent barring on the flanks. Most species have a chattering song that is similar across species, but the song of Black Rail is very different.

1 BLACK-BANDED CRAKE *Laterallus fasciatus* 17–18 cm (6¾–7 in)
Rare (especially in southeast) but widespread crake of Amazonian lowlands, locally up to 1200 m. Found in dense undergrowth of wet forest edge thickets and wet grassy areas, including on river islands. Reddish brown, with obscurely banded flanks and dusky bill. Smaller Rufous-sided Crake is paler, has whitish center to throat and breast, black-and-white barred flanks, and yellowish bill. Uniform and Chestnut-headed crakes have yellowish bills and no barring on flanks. **VOICE** Chatter is a rubbery, musical trill, deeper and more bubbly than that of other *Laterallus* crakes, and not as ringing as that of Russet-crowned Crake. **Co, E, Br**

2 RUFOUS-SIDED CRAKE *Laterallus melanophaius* * 14–16 cm (5½–6¼ in)
Fairly common and widespread in eastern lowlands, locally to 1050 m. More closely associated with water than other *Laterallus*, this is the most common crake at grassy margins of lakes and in marshes and wet grasslands. Readily identified by small size, habitat, and rusty color; also note barred flanks. Forehead cinnamon in most of Peru (*oenops*), but birds in southeastern Peru may be similar to nominate *melanophaius* (found in Pando, Bolivia), which has a dusky forehead. **VOICE** Chatter more musical than that of Gray-breasted and Russet-crowned crakes, perhaps slower-paced than the former. Calls include a harsh, descending "*djreer.*" **Co, E, Br, Bo**

3 BLACK RAIL *Laterallus jamaicensis* * 13–15 cm (5–6 in)
Rare and local in Peru, but perhaps also overlooked: one of the most secretive and difficult to observe rails in Peru. *Murivagans* a rare resident in coastal marshes. Sexes similar, but female is paler than male. Also resident at Lake Junín (4080 m), where endemic subspecies (*tuerosi*) is more prominently barred above. The only *Laterallus* that is found on the coast or in high Andes; but take care to avoid confusion with black downy chicks of Plumbeous Rail. **VOICE** Song (*tuerosi*), given nocturnally, is a rapid "*ki'ki'ki'ki-brrr.*" Voice of *murivagans* is unknown but presumably is like that of *tuerosi*. **Ch**

4 RUSSET-CROWNED CRAKE *Laterallus viridis* * 15.5–16 cm (6–6¼ in)
Rare to uncommon and local in eastern lowlands, locally up to 1000 m. Found in dense secondary thickets and grasslands; usually in drier situations than other *Laterallus* crakes. A small rufescent crake. Note contrast between rusty cap and gray sides to face; also note rufous underparts with plain (unbarred) flanks. **VOICE** Chirp call a musical whinny, sometimes reminiscent of a raptor. Chatter is a mechanical, ringing, puttering series. Calls include a deep "*churrt.*" **Co, E, Br, Bo**

5 GRAY-BREASTED CRAKE *Laterallus exilis* 13–14 cm (5–5½ in)
Widespread in eastern lowlands, but uncommon and local (or often overlooked). Found in grassy margins of oxbow lakes, marshes, and wet grasslands. Very small. Gray-breasted with contrasting rusty nape. Does not overlap with Black Rail (which also is barred above). **VOICE** Chirp call is a high, ringing, clear series: "*ti pi pi pi pi pi,*" the first note highest. Chatter drier, faster, and less musical than Rufous-sided and Russet-crowned crakes. Calls include a sharp series of reedy, piping "*pi-pi-pi-pi*" phrases. **Co, E, Br, Bo**

BLACK-BANDED
CRAKE

melanophaius

RUFOUS-SIDED
CRAKE

oenops

♂ *tuerosi*

BLACK RAIL

♀ *murivagans*

♂ *murivagans*

BLACK RAIL

RUSSET-CROWNED
CRAKE

GRAY-BREASTED
CRAKE

PLATE
49
GALLINULES, MOORHEN, AND COOTS

Gallinules, moorhen, and coots are large, heavy-bodied, short-billed rails of marshes. Moorhen, coots, and Spot-flanked Gallinule often are seen swimming in marshes and in lakes near dense aquatic vegetation; may be mistaken for ducks by the casual observer (but coots, like grebes, have lobed toes; very different from webbed toes of ducks). Toes of moorhen and gallinules are long, unwebbed.

1 AZURE GALLINULE *Porphyrio flavirostris* 23–25 cm (9–10 in)

Rare, and apparently only a nonbreeding visitor. Reported from lower Río Napo and the Amazon in northern Peru, Jan–Jun; and (less commonly?) in Madre de Dios in Dec–Jan (but where perhaps is present through Mar or Apr). Similar to Purple Gallinule, but smaller. Adult light blue with yellow bill. Juvenile similar to Purple, but smaller, more mottled above, wings are more extensively light blue, and rump and upper tail coverts are blacker. **VOICE** Calls plaintive, reedy, whining notes. **Co, E, Br, Bo**

2 PURPLE GALLINULE *Porphyrio martinica* 28–32 cm (11–12½ in)

Fairly common in eastern lowlands, in marshes and grassy margins of lakes. Somewhat nomadic and a rare visitor to coast and Andes (typically as juveniles). Usually does not swim; forages among aquatic vegetation. Ornate adult unmistakable; even in poor light, when bright plumage may not be apparent, fluffy white undertail coverts distinguish it from moorhen. Juvenile very different: a buffy brown, chickenlike bird with dusky yellowish bill, long yellowish tarsi and toes, and prominent white undertail coverts. Cf. Azure Gallinule. **VOICE** Calls ticks, sharp clucking, and complaining sounds. **Co, E, Br, Bo, Ch**

SPOT-FLANKED GALLINULE *Gallinula melanops* * 25–30 cm (10–12 in)

No certain record; one early 19th-century report, from an unspecified location (may be based on specimen from another country?). Small; recognized by relatively light gray head and breast and prominent white spotting on flanks; also note small yellow bill. Juvenile is paler and browner. **Co, Br, Bo, Ch**

3 COMMON MOORHEN *Gallinula chloropus* * *pauxilla* 29–33 cm (11½–13 in); *garmani* 35–37 cm (13¾–14½ in)

Common in marshes of coast and in Andes, 2200–4400 m, although very local in Andes north of Lake Junín. Also very local in Amazonia. Often feeds while swimming, picking food from water's surface; also feeds on shore near marsh vegetation. Superficially similar to a small coot, but more lightly built, and when swimming carries tail higher than body. At all ages note white line along side of body. Andean *garmani* is much larger and darker than coastal *pauxilla*. **VOICE** Song a harsh cackle, decelerating and descending in pitch. Calls a sharp "*PEEK!*" and a low, hoarse "*ka-gah?*" **Co, E, Br, Bo, Ch**

4 RED-FRONTED COOT *Fulica rufifrons* 36–43 cm (14–17 in)

Rare resident, restricted to coastal lagoons in Arequipa. Always close to cover; does not enter open water, as do other coots. Similar to Common Moorhen, which is common in same marshes. Often carries tail cocked up, exposing extensive white on undertail; also has gray (not olive-brown) upperparts and lacks white flank stripe of moorhen. Bill is extensively yellow (rather than red with yellow tip). Cf. also Andean Coot. **VOICE** Calls muffled, hooting chuckles. **Br, Ch**

5 GIANT COOT *Fulica gigantea* 48–64 cm (19–25 in)

Locally fairly common on Andean lakes, 3900–4600 m. Massive adults reportedly are flightless, although is a very rare vagrant to southern coast. May graze on land or by picking surface of water while swimming. Note size, red tarsi, ornate bill pattern, and bulbous shape to forehead (at close range, narrow frontal shield is bordered to each side by a feathered knob). **VOICE** Calls low growls, rising cries, and muffled chuckles. **Bo, Ch**

6 ANDEAN COOT *Fulica ardesiaca* * 40–46 cm (15¾–18 in)

The widespread, common coot; occurs on much of coast and in Andes, 2500–4600 m, in marshes and on lakes. Often congregates in flocks. Note sooty gray plumage, with little or no white visible on undertail coverts, and overall size. Bill and shield color variable, although often one bill/shield color combination dominates at any single site. Most commonly seen are birds with chestnut shield and yellow bill, which predominates on coast and in southern Andes; or birds with white shield and bill, which is most common on lakes of central Andes. Birds with yellow shields and white bills also occur. Juvenile pale gray, with dull bill. **VOICE** Calls dry ticking, hoarse barking series, and squeaky popping notes. **Co, E, Bo, Ch**

AZURE GALLINULE

ad.

juv.

PURPLE GALLINULE

juv.

ad.

juv.

ad.

SPOT-FLANKED GALLINULE

RED-FRONTED COOT

juv.

COMMON MOORHEN

ad.

GIANT COOT

ANDEAN COOT

juv.

GIANT COOT

ANDEAN
COOT

RED-FRONTED COOT

pauxilla

COMMON MOORHEN

garmani

PLATE
50

LARGE PATTERNED SHOREBIRDS

Oystercatchers are large, stocky shorebirds, with long, thick red bills. Generally occur as singles or pairs on the immediate coast, where they forage for bivalves. Jacanas are a frequent sight at margins of marshes and oxbow lakes. Notable for long tarsi and the very long toes, which help support their weight on floating aquatic vegetation, and the small carpal spur. Lapwings are large plovers, with a small carpal spur, broad rounded wings, and bold plumage patterns, including a broad, contrasting white band on the open wing; Andean and Southern are notable for their loud calls. Stilts and avocets have very long, slender tarsi and long, delicate bills.

1 AMERICAN OYSTERCATCHER *Haematopus palliatus* * 40–44 cm (15¾–17 in)

Fairly common resident along coast, mainly on sandy beaches. Other large shorebirds with obvious black-and-white wing pattern (e.g., Willet, Hudsonian Godwit) are not boldly black and white on their bodies and do not have blood-red bills. **VOICE** Song, given in duet, an excited chatter of piping whistles. Calls include piping whistles "*pip*" and "*peeeeyeee.*" **Co, E, Br, Ch**

2 BLACKISH OYSTERCATCHER *Haematopus ater* 43–45 cm (17–17½ in)

Fairly common resident on coast, almost exclusively in rocky areas. Entirely blackish plumage distinguishes this from American Oystercatcher. **VOICE** Similar to American Oystercatcher. **Ch**

3 WATTLED JACANA *Jacana jacana* * 20–24 cm (8–9½ in)

Common resident in marshes in Amazonian lowlands (*peruviana*); also rare in far northwest (*scapularis*). Nearly unmistakable. Note yellow-green remiges and very long yellow legs and toes. Plumage of *scapularis* is paler overall, with black scapulars. **VOICE** Calls reedy barking and coughing notes. Another vocalization (song?) is a series of yaps that accelerate into a dry chatter. **Co, E, Br, Bo, Ch**

4 ANDEAN LAPWING *Vanellus resplendens* 33–36 cm (13–14 in)

Fairly common and conspicuous resident at 3000–4600 m (locally down to 2000 m in Amazonas) in open grassy marshes, edges of lakes and bogs, and dry fields. Rare vagrant to coast; very rare vagrant to southern Amazonia. Identified by pale gray head and breast (contrasting with white belly), pinkish red tarsi and base to bill, bold wing pattern, and loud **VOICE** Calls cackles and yapping barks; similar to Black-necked Stilt, but more grating, particularly when mobbing intruders. **Co, E, Br, Ch**

5 PIED LAPWING *Hoploxypterus cayanus* 21–24 cm (8¾–9½ in)

Fairly common resident on sandy beaches throughout Amazonian lowlands, locally up to 1000 m. Usually seen as singles or in pairs. Note bold black-and-white head pattern, black breast band, and long red tarsi. **VOICE** Calls a mechanical whistled "*hoot-toot*" and a rapid series of mechanical, whistled notes when flushed. **Co, E, Br, Bo**

SOUTHERN LAPWING *Vanellus chilensis* * 33–38 cm (13–15 in)

Recently found near large rivers in northern Loreto, where probably spreading into region with deforestation; also one record from Madre de Dios. Substantially larger than Pied Lapwing, which lacks crest and has bolder black-and-white pattern. Andean Lapwing, very rare in lowlands, lacks crest, has pearly gray head and breast. **VOICE** Calls cackles and yapping barks; similar to Black-necked Stilt, but usually more grating, particularly when mobbing intruders. **Co, E, Br, Bo, Ch**

6 ANDEAN AVOCET *Recurvirostra andina* 43–46 cm (17–18 in)

Uncommon resident at shallow, usually saline lakes in altiplano at 3900–4600 m; very rare vagrant to central and southern coast. Note all white head and strongly upturned bill; unmistakable. **VOICE** Calls reedy yips and low grunts. **Bo, Ch**

7 BLACK-NECKED STILT *Himantopus mexicanus* * 36–41 cm (14–16 in)

Fairly common on coast; uncommon and local in altiplano at 3200–4300 m, and in Amazonian lowlands below 800 m. Unmistakable, largely black above, white below, with extremely long bright pink legs and a fine black bill. In Andes, cf. Andean Avocet. Adult *melanurus* has white crown and white collar across upper back. Juvenile *melanurus* has gray crown and white collar obscured by dark tips; may be confused with *mexicanus*, which has black crown and lacks neck collar. Intermediates also occur. Distribution, particularly when breeding, of two subspecies not yet clear. *Mexicanus* occurs along entire coast (breeding south at least to central coast) and is reported from central altiplano; also occasionally in northern Amazonia. *Melanurus* occurs throughout Amazonia (breeding at least in central Amazonia, presumably elsewhere); also occurs (and breeds?) on altiplano, and breeds on southern coast (north at least to Lima, where may intergrade with *mexicanus*). **VOICE** Calls sharp yips and barking notes. Voice of *mexicanus* sharper and higher than that of *melanurus*. **Co, E, Br, Bo, Ch**

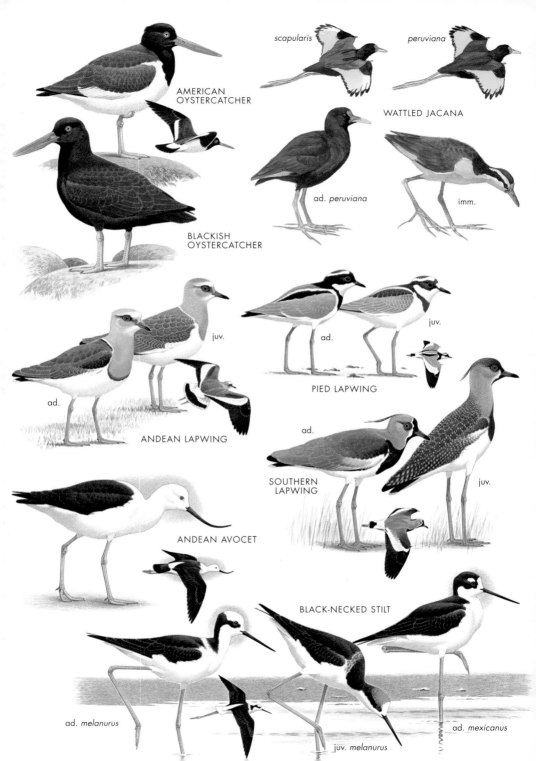

AMERICAN
OYSTERCATCHER

scapularis

peruviana

WATTLED JACANA

ad. *peruviana*

imm.

BLACKISH
OYSTERCATCHER

juv.

ad.

ad.

juv.

PIED LAPWING

ANDEAN LAPWING

ad.

SOUTHERN
LAPWING

juv.

ANDEAN AVOCET

BLACK-NECKED STILT

ad. *melanurus*

juv. *melanurus*

ad. *mexicanus*

PLATE
51

PLOVERS, THICK-KNEE, AND SEEDSNIPE

The Thick-knee is a large, long-legged shorebird of upland areas; primarily nocturnal, with notably large eyes. Plovers are shorebirds with relatively short, stout bills. Often have distinctive "stop-and-start" foraging behavior, running forward a short distance, then stopping abruptly, sometimes reaching down to pluck food from ground or surface of mudflats. Seedsnipe are peculiar, short-legged, short-billed birds, cryptically colored and difficult to spot on the ground; they have long tapered wings and strong flight. Often found in flocks.

1 PERUVIAN THICK-KNEE *Burhinus superciliaris* 39–42 cm (15½–16½ in)

Uncommon resident in desert scrub and agricultural lands of coastal lowlands; but sometimes encountered in large groups. Mostly nocturnal. Unmistakable strong eyeline and large yellow eye; also has distinctive wing pattern in flight. **VOICE** Display calls, usually given in nocturnal flight displays, are a loud series of "KAK" notes, reminiscent of Black-necked Stilt. When flushed, gives a stuttered series: "*ka'ka'ka'ka-KAH!*" Common vernacular name, *huerequeque*, stems from the loud vocalizations. In mild alarm, may give very quiet puttering sound. **E, Ch**

2 TAWNY-THROATED DOTTEREL *Oreopholus ruficollis* * 25–28 cm (10–11 in)

Uncommon resident in agricultural areas and desert scrub in lowlands of northwest (*pallidus*) and in puna near Lake Titicaca at 3500–4500 m (*ruficollis*); *ruficollis* also uncommon as austral migrant along coast north to Lima and more widely in puna of southern Peru, and at least occasionally breeds on west slope north to Lima. Very slim; posture often more upright than other plovers. Fairly distinctive; cf. American Golden-Plover (in flight), which has less prominent wing stripe and light gray (not white) underwing linings. **VOICE** Call a musical descending trill: "*pi'r'r'r*" sometimes mixed with a rising whistled "*pir'ree?*" **E, Br, Bo, Ch**

3 AMERICAN GOLDEN-PLOVER *Pluvialis dominica* 24–27 cm (9½–10½ in)

Uncommon boreal migrant in fields, marshes, and sandy beaches, mostly Aug–Nov and Mar–Apr. Occasionally birds overwinter or oversummer. Most common in Amazonian lowlands and on altiplano; rare elsewhere. On coast cf. Black-bellied Plover. **VOICE** Call, often given in flight, similar to that of Black-bellied, but shorter, descends more, and not so emphasized at end: "*cleeru.*" **Co, E, Br, Bo, Ch**

4 BLACK-BELLIED PLOVER *Pluvialis squatarola* 27–30 cm (10½–12 in)

Common boreal migrant (Sep–Apr) to beaches and mudflats along coast; very rare elsewhere. Occasional nonbreeders (mostly immatures?) oversummer. More characteristic of beaches and mudflats than is Golden-Plover, which is similar in all plumages. Black-bellied is larger with a larger bill. In flight, note black axillars, obvious white wing stripe, and white rump; Golden-Plover lacks the white rump and prominent wing stripe, and has pale axillars (except when in the black-bellied alternate plumage). Basic plumage and juveniles of Black-bellied also are much grayer than comparable plumages of Golden-Plover, with weaker superciliary; underparts of juveniles also appearing streaked, not mottled or barred as in juvenile Golden-Plover. Alternate plumage (rarely seen fully developed in Peru) is gray (not golden) above, with white vent and undertail coverts. **VOICE** Call, often given in flight, a pleasing clear, rising whistle: "*cleerEE.*" **Co, E, Br, Bo, Ch**

5 RUFOUS-BELLIED SEEDSNIPE *Attagis gayi* * 29–31 cm (11½–12 in)

Fairly common resident in open puna at high elevation, 4400–5000 m. Largest seedsnipe; distinctive within its elevational range. Note extensive rufous underparts; underparts white in female of smaller Gray-breasted Seedsnipe. **VOICE** Call a rising, ringing, popping "*cuee*" or "*cuEEP.*" Also, a piping chatter, usually given in flight. **E, Bo, Ch**

6 GRAY-BREASTED SEEDSNIPE *Thinocorus orbignyianus* * 22–24 cm (8½–9½ in)

Common resident in open puna at 3000–4600 m. In flight, note black underwing linings. Cf. Least Seedsnipe (which is found at lower elevations). **VOICE** Song, given in a flight display, is a mellow whistled series "*cu-HOO cu-HOO cu-HOO....*" Calls in flight a quiet churring series. **Bo, Ch**

7 LEAST SEEDSNIPE *Thinocorus rumicivorus* * 16–18 cm (6½–7 in)

Common resident in open, barren desert scrub below 400 m. Female very similar to female Gray-breasted Seedsnipe, but much smaller (scarcely larger than a sparrow); no overlap in elevation. Foreparts of male have black line from throat down to broad black border at lower edge of gray breast; on Gray-breasted, black is limited to narrow borders to throat and breast. **VOICE** Song, often given in a flight display, is a hollow series of popping hoots: "*pu-HOOP pu-HOOP pu-HOOP...*" or "*pu-pu-HU'U'UUP pu-pu-HU'U'UUP pu-pu-HU'U'UUP...,*" sometimes preceded by a raspy series of barks or a short chatter. Call a quiet, shorebirdlike "*tuk-tuk*" or "*cut-tuk,*" often in a series. **E, Bo, Ch**

TAWNY-THROATED
DOTTEREL

pallidus

ruficollis

PERUVIAN
THICK-KNEE

alt.

basic

BLACK-BELLIED PLOVER

alt.

basic

AMERICAN
GOLDEN-PLOVER

alt.

alt.

juv.

juv.

basic

RUFOUS-BELLIED
SEEDSNIPE

GRAY-BREASTED
SEEDSNIPE

♀

♀

♂

♂

LEAST SEEDSNIPE

PLATE
52

SMALL PLOVERS

Species on this plate are small, plump plovers, most of which have a partial dark breast band across white underparts. Species can be distinguished by features such as bill and tarsus color, presence or absence of a white collar across hindneck, and details of breast band and facial patterns.

1 COLLARED PLOVER *Charadrius collaris* 14–16 cm (5½–6½ in)

Common resident on Amazonian beaches; uncommon on northwest coastal beaches and rivers. The only expected small Amazonian plover. Other coastal small plovers have white band across hindneck. Also, Snowy Plover is paler and grayer above, has grayish legs, and lacks a complete black breast band. Semipalmated is darker above and has orangish legs and a shorter, stubby bill. **VOICE** Calls a peeping "*peet*" and a musical chatter given in territorial interactions. **Co, E, Br, Bo, Ch**

2 SNOWY PLOVER *Charadrius alexandrinus* * 15–17 cm (6–6½ in)

Fairly common resident on sandy beaches along coast, where is the most common and widespread resident small plover. Note pale upperparts, incomplete breast band (always restricted to sides of breast), gray tarsi, and slender, all-dark bill. Often has a cinnamon wash on crown and sides of head. Cf. darker Semipalmated and larger, darker Wilson's plovers. See also Collared and Puna plovers. **VOICE** Calls a deep, throaty "*churt*" or "*pip*," also a rising "*cheweet?*" **Co, E, Ch**

3 PUNA PLOVER *Charadrius alticola* 16.5–18 cm (6½–7 in)

Fairly common resident along shores of high-elevation lakes, 3800–4500 m, occasionally lower in altiplano; rare nonbreeding visitor (May–Aug) to coast from Lima south. The only expected small plover on altiplano. In all plumages, note brown band across lower breast. On coast, cf. Snowy Plover, which has slightly paler upperparts, less black on face, whitish collar on hindneck, and lacks rufous on crown. Juvenile (not illustrated) is duller; has pattern of adult but lacks rufous and black in plumage. [**Two-banded Plover** (*Charadrius falklandicus*; not illustrated) is not known from Peru but could occur on southern coast in austral winter; winters along Chilean coast north to Antofagasta. Basic plumage resembles juvenile Puna, but Two-banded is larger and typically shows more extensive, partial brown band on upper breast.] **VOICE** Call a peeping "*pit*" note. **Bo, Ch**

4 SEMIPALMATED PLOVER *Charadrius semipalmatus* 17–19 cm (6½–7½ in)

Locally common boreal migrant (Jul–Apr, a few oversummering) on mudflats and beaches along coast; very rare vagrant to lakes in altiplano. Distinguished from Snowy Plover by darker brown upperparts, complete (or nearly complete) breast band, yellow tarsi, and yellow at base of bill (reduced in nonbreeding plumages). Breast band and forecrown black (alternate) or brown (basic and juvenile). **VOICE** Call, often given in flight, a pleasing piping "*kewEET*" or "*keeuk*," also a shorter "*keet*." In aggressive interactions, a rapid puttering series that accelerates, then slows: "*keet keetkit'i'i'i'i'i'i'u'u'u-uut.*" **Co, E, Br, Bo, Ch**

5 WILSON'S PLOVER *Charadrius wilsonia* * 18–20 cm (7–8 in)

Fairly common resident on sandy northwest beaches, with a few records south along coast to Arequipa; has bred in Lima. Smaller than Killdeer, with only a single black breast band, and lacks orange-rufous rump. Larger than Snowy Plover, with darker back and complete breast band; larger than Semipalmated, with pinkish tarsi and heavier, all-black bill. **VOICE** Calls a musical rattle, a sharp "*PEEP!*" and piping "*pip*" and "*pi-dip*" notes. **Co, E, Br**

RUFOUS-CHESTED DOTTEREL *Charadrius modestus* 19–22 cm (7½–8½ in)

Very rare vagrant in austral winter (May, Jun) to coast (north to Lima). Not likely to occur in Peru in distinctive alternate plumage. Duller birds in basic plumage could be confused with the shorter-legged Ruddy Turnstone, but turnstone has more variegated dark areas, has orange tarsi, and in flight shows an ornate wing pattern. **VOICE** Calls a descending whinny: "*PEE'ee'ew*" and a rising "*wee?*" **Br, Ch**

6 KILLDEER *Charadrius vociferus* * 24–26 cm (9½–10½ in)

Common resident along coast in agricultural areas, marshes, estuaries, and occasionally beaches. Only plover with double black breast band; also larger than other collared plovers, and has contrasting orange-rufous rump. **VOICE** Vocal. In alarm and display, gives a loud series of rolling "*kill-deer*" notes, often in flight. Calls a rising "*deee?*" or "*kidee?*" and piping "*dee dee dee*" notes. **Co, E, Ch**

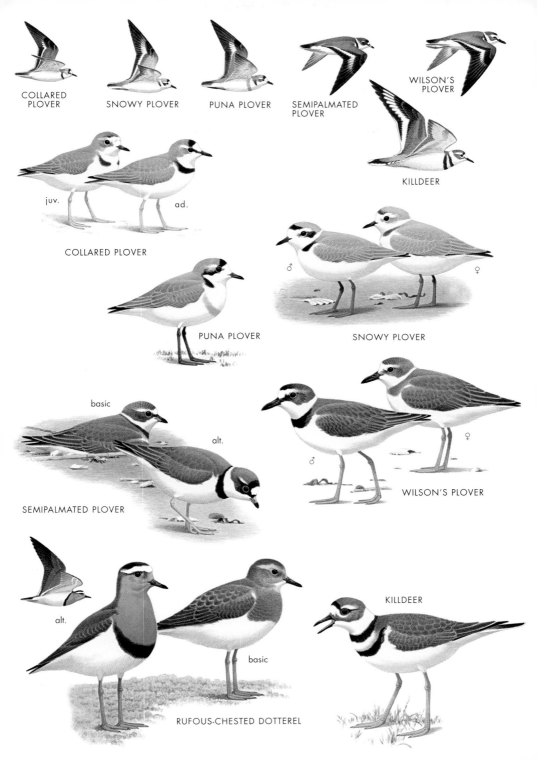

COLLARED
PLOVER

SNOWY PLOVER

PUNA PLOVER

SEMIPALMATED
PLOVER

WILSON'S
PLOVER

KILLDEER

juv.

ad.

COLLARED PLOVER

♂

♀

PUNA PLOVER

SNOWY PLOVER

basic

alt.

♂

♀

SEMIPALMATED PLOVER

WILSON'S PLOVER

alt.

basic

KILLDEER

RUFOUS-CHESTED DOTTEREL

PLATE
53 | SNIPE AND DIADEMED PLOVER

Snipe are moderate-sized, heavy-bodied shorebirds with long, thick, straight bills and short legs. All have heavily marked, brown plumage that makes them difficult to see as they sit in heavy vegetation, until they suddenly erupt at close range in a whirring, direct flight. In the twilight of dusk and dawn, snipes have characteristic aerial displays with distinctive calls, and they often also produce mechanical sounds by air passing rapidly through their wing and tail feathers. Diademed Plover is a peculiar plover of the high Andes.

1 PUNA SNIPE *Gallinago andina* 22.5–25 cm (9–10 in)
Fairly common resident in bogs, in marshes, and at edges of lakes at 3000–4600 m. More of a puna species (although in wet areas) than other snipes. Compared to Andean Snipe is smaller, paler with unmarked whitish abdomen, has white trailing edge to wing (visible in flight), and shows fairly obvious pale stripes on back. **VOICE** Flight calls include a dry "*che'che'che.*" Flight display is a harsh rattled sound produced by spread tail feathers: "*tch'ch'ch'ch'ch.*" Song is a series of mellow notes: "*cut cut cut cut....*" **E, Bo, Ch**

2 SOUTH AMERICAN SNIPE *Gallinago paraguaiae* * 26–29 cm (10–11½ in)
Status poorly known. Apparently rare resident in open, wet, grassy habitats in northeastern Amazonia; scattered records from elsewhere in Amazonia, south to Madre de Dios, and near base of Andes. The only Amazonian snipe. There also is at least one sight record of a snipe from the northwest coast, which could be a wandering South American Snipe or a vagrant of the boreal migrant **Wilson's Snipe** *Gallinago delicata* (which is not reported from Peru, and is very similar to South American; field identification of Wilson's would be very difficult). **VOICE** Call, usually given when flushed, is a deep, almost rasping, "*chup*" or "*chut-up.*" **Co, E, Br, Bo, Ch**

3 ANDEAN SNIPE *Gallinago jamesoni* 29–30 cm (11½–12 in)
Fairly common resident in boggy paramo and grassland-forest ecotone at treeline (2800–3600 m). Large and dark; much larger than Puna Snipe. Otherwise, in many respects intermediate between paler (and geographically restricted) Noble Snipe and darker, more rufescent (and rare and local) Imperial Snipe. **VOICE** Flight call a dry "*whi-whi*" when flushed, sometimes in a longer series. Song, given in flight usually at night, is a roaring sound (produced mechanically) followed by a series of woodpecker-like "*wee-kew*" notes. Calls include a strident "*whi'whi'whi'whi'whi'whi*" (female in response to male display?). **Co, E, Bo**

4 IMPERIAL SNIPE *Gallinago imperialis* 29–31 cm (11½–12½ in)
Rare and local resident in elfin forest at 2750–3500 m. Difficult to see well; mainly crepuscular, staying hidden in dense vegetation during day. Much darker and more rufescent above, more heavily banded on underparts than other snipes. **VOICE** Song, given in flight and usually predawn, is a series of grating quacks: "*keke-keh keke-keh kah-kah kuh kuhh kuhh,*" followed by a roaring sound (mechanically produced), the latter only audible at close distance. Calls include a series of rasping barks. **Co, E**

5 [NOBLE SNIPE *Gallinago nobilis*] 30–32 cm (12–12½ in)
Rare resident in bogs around treeline, ca. 3100 m in extreme north (north and west of the Marañón Valley). Most likely to be confused with Andean Snipe, with which it is broadly sympatric. Noble is slightly larger and longer billed; is paler and less rufescent above, with more apparent pale stripes on back. Center of abdomen is whitish and unmarked; in Andean, the abdomen is barred. **VOICE** Flight call is a series of reedy "*keekeekee*" notes. Flight display is a hollow, reedy sound produced mechanically, rising in pitch: "*cor-cor-cur-cur-keh-keh.*" Song is a series of musical barks: "*kyuck-kyuck-kyuck-kyuck-kyuck.*" **Co, E**

6 DIADEMED PLOVER (Diademed Sandpiper-Plover) *Phegornis mitchellii* 17–19 cm (6½–7½ in)
Rare resident in bogs and at edges of streams and small lakes at high elevations (4100–5000 m) in altiplano. Very local, and seemingly absent from some sites with suitable habitat; but also can be cryptically colored and surprisingly difficult to spot (despite ornate plumage pattern). Unmistakable. Note stocky build, lack of wing stripe, and narrow barring in all plumages. Bill long and thin, more like a sandpiper's than a plover's. **VOICE** Calls include a descending whistled "*peee.*" **Bo, Ch**

PUNA SNIPE

SOUTH AMERICAN SNIPE

ANDEAN SNIPE

IMPERIAL SNIPE

juv.

DIADEMED
PLOVER

ad.

NOBLE SNIPE

PLATE
54

LARGE, LONG-BILLED SHOREBIRDS

Dowitchers, Willet, godwits, and Whimbrel all are large, long-billed sandpipers. All also are boreal migrants, primarily present during the northern winter, although small numbers of nonbreeding individuals may remain in Peru during the northern summer. Dowitchers and godwits feed by probing with long bills, often while wading in shallow water; dowitchers in particular often have a "hump-backed" posture while foraging and feed in tightly packed flocks. Whimbrel and Willet pluck prey from the surface or with shallow probes.

1 SHORT-BILLED DOWITCHER *Limnodromus griseus* * 25–29 cm (10–11½ in)

Common boreal migrant (Sep–Apr; a few individuals present year-round) on mudflats and in marshes along coast; very rare at altiplano lakes and in Amazonian lowlands. Very long, straight bill (recalling a snipe) and "sewing-machine" foraging behavior, usually while wading in shallow water, distinguish dowitchers from other shorebirds; Short-billed is only dowitcher expected to occur in Peru. In basic plumage resembles basic-plumaged Stilt Sandpiper, but white stripe up lower back is distinctive in all plumages. Also dowitcher has longer, straighter, bill. Cf. also larger, less common Hudsonian Godwit and Red Knot. **VOICE** Call, often given in flight, is a clear, liquid, peeping "*tu-tu-tu*," usually more staccato than Long-billed Dowitcher, and almost always in triplets. Song (sometimes heard in northbound passage) is a musical, but grating, "*ti-ti-ZAYburr ti-ti-ZAYburr ti-ti-ZAYburr-burr.*" **Co, E, Br**

LONG-BILLED DOWITCHER *Limnodromus scolopaceus* 27–30 cm (10½–12 in)

Very rare vagrant (boreal migrant) to coast. Easy to overlook due to great similarity to Short-billed Dowitcher (best distinguished by voice), but known to winter regularly south only to Costa Rica (thus not expected in Peru). Alternate plumage is more chestnut (not orangey) below than Short-billed's, with heavier barring on sides of breast and flanks, and with chestnut extending to undertail coverts. Juvenile Long-billed typically much less colorful than Short-billed, with little or no buff on neck, and little or no pattern on tertials and scapulars. Not readily separable from Short-billed in basic plumage; Long-billed has darker centers to back feathers, giving a more mottled look, black bars on rectrices wider than white (usually reversed in Short-billed), and shorter primary projection. Bill lengths overlap. Any report of Long-billed from South America requires extensive documentation. **VOICE** Call, often given in flight, is a clear "*peep*" or "*peet!*"

2 WILLET *Catoptrophorus semipalmatus* * 35–39 cm (13¾–15½ in)

Uncommon boreal migrant (Sep–Apr; occasional individuals remain through summer) on coastal mudflats and beaches. Large shorebird with stout, straight bill. In flight, note distinctive bold black-and-white wing pattern. At rest, larger and plainer than Greater Yellowlegs, with gray or olive legs. Cf. also much less common Hudsonian Godwit. **VOICE** Calls, often given in flight, include an almost gull-like "*gaa-ahh*" and some more rolling notes. Song, unlikely to be heard in Peru, is a rollicking series of rolling whistles: "*pill-will-WILLIT.*" **Co, E, Br, Ch**

3 HUDSONIAN GODWIT *Limosa haemastica* 38–41 cm (15–16 in)

Uncommon boreal migrant (Sep–Apr) to coastal marshes and mudflats; very rare vagrant to altiplano lakes. A few remain in summer. Compare basic-plumaged godwit to Willet; godwit has longer, thinner, upturned bill with pink base (bill of Willet is shorter, thicker, and straighter, never pinkish at base); less extensive white wing stripe; and broad dark tip to tail. **VOICE** Calls, often given in flight, include a high, reedy "*weet*" or "*weet-eet.*" **Co, E, Br, Bo, Ch**

4 MARBLED GODWIT *Limosa fedoa* * 42–48 cm (16½–19 in)

Rare boreal migrant (primarily Aug–Dec) on mudflats in northwest; scattered records farther south along coast. Relatively plain brownish buff underparts, cinnamon underwing linings and slightly upturned bill with pinkish base distinguish this species from other large shorebirds. Alternate plumage of Hudsonian Godwit more bicolored (chestnut below, gray above), with strong black-and-white wing pattern; Hudsonian much grayer in basic plumage. **VOICE** Calls, often given in flight, include high, reedy "*weed-wi*," more forceful than Hudsonian. **Co, E, Br, Ch**

5 WHIMBREL *Numenius phaeopus* * 40–45 cm (14–17½ in)

Fairly common boreal migrant (Sep–Apr; a few individuals may oversummer) along coast on mudflats and beaches; very rare vagrant to altiplano lakes. Large, but rather slim-bodied. Long, slender, deeply downcurved bill makes this species unmistakable. Note relatively strong head pattern. **VOICE** Calls, often given in flight, include a musical peeping "*pipipi-pi.*" **Co, E, Br, Bo, Ch**

SHORT-BILLED DOWITCHER

alt.

basic

juv.

SHORT-BILLED
DOWITCHER

dowitcher

LONG-BILLED
DOWITCHER

basic

juv.

LONG-BILLED
DOWITCHER

alt.

WILLET

alt.

basic

HUDSONIAN GODWIT

basic

alt.

WHIMBREL

MARBLED
GODWIT

PLATE
55

MEDIUM-SIZED SANDPIPERS

Species on this plate are medium to large sandpipers, most of which also are long-legged.

1 LESSER YELLOWLEGS *Tringa flavipes* 24–27 cm (9½–10½ in)

Common boreal migrant (Aug–May; a few may oversummer) throughout on mudflats, in marshes, and at edges of lakes and rivers; most common on coast. Yellowlegs are easily recognized by long, bright yellow legs, mottled gray upperparts, plain wings, and white rump. Active forager, picking at water surface with long bill; also frequently bobs forward. Cf. Greater Yellowlegs, Stilt and Solitary sandpipers, and Wilson's Phalarope. **VOICE** Call, often given in flight, single descending *"tew"* notes, sometimes given in pairs or longer series, particularly when alarmed. Primary call lacks plaintive quality of Greater Yellowlegs, and occurs rarely in triplets. **Co, E, Br, Bo, Ch**

2 GREATER YELLOWLEGS *Tringa melanoleuca* 30–33 cm (12–13 in)

Fairly common boreal migrant (Aug–May; a few may oversummer) throughout on mudflats, in marshes, and at edges of lakes and rivers; most common on coast. Larger than similar Lesser Yellowlegs. Greater has proportionally longer bill (longer than head), with thicker base and slight upturn at tip. Also, flanks of Greater more heavily barred in alternate plumage. Note different calls. **VOICE** Calls, often given in flight, a series (usually 3 or 4) of rising, plaintive notes, the last note usually lower: *"klee-klee-kle,"* sometimes in a longer series. When alarmed, a series of descending *"tu"* notes, usually deeper and fuller than those of Lesser Yellowlegs. **Co, E, Br, Bo, Ch**

3 STILT SANDPIPER *Calidris himantopus* 20–23 cm (8–9 in)

Fairly common boreal migrant (Aug–Apr; a few may oversummer) along coast on mudflats and in marshes; uncommon along rivers in Amazonia and at altiplano lakes. Long-legged; recalls a small yellowlegs. Foraging behavior similar to that of dowitchers. Alternate plumage readily identifiable by heavily barred underparts, and reddish ear patch and crown. Basic plumage paler above and below than dowitchers', with shorter bill; less patterned than Lesser Yellowlegs, with longer bill, and different foraging behavior. Wilson's Phalarope is paler, especially below, with fine, needlelike bill. **VOICE** Calls, often given in flight, single *"tew"* notes; very similar to those of Lesser Yellowlegs, but somewhat less forceful. **Co, E, Br, Bo, Ch**

[RUFF *Philomachus pugnax*] male 27–32 cm (10½–12½ in); female 22–25 cm (8½–10 in)

Very rare boreal migrant to coast; also a record from altiplano. Reported only from sight records. Alternate male (not illustrated) unlikely in Peru; has broad ruff on breast, with highly variable color pattern. Female, male in basic plumage, and juvenile have short bill (usually with a pale base in adults) and small head, often with white on face at base of bill; upperparts typically scaly (not streaked); and tarsi often yellowish or orange. Often has a "hump-backed" appearance. Juveniles also unmarked buff below. Smaller Pectoral Sandpiper has strongly streaked breast contrasting with plain abdomen. Buff-breasted Sandpiper resembles juvenile but is smaller, more compact, with plainer face. In flight, Ruff has white ovals on sides of rump (forming U-shaped pattern); tail of Buff-breasted all dark. **Co, Br**

4 SOLITARY SANDPIPER *Tringa solitaria* * 19–21 cm (7½–8½ in)

Uncommon boreal migrant to Amazonia. Rare migrant elsewhere (Aug–Apr) south to Ica and Cuzco; very rarely farther south. Occurs along rivers, at edges of lakes, and in marshes, but seldom on open mudflats. Smaller, darker, more brownish above, and with shorter, more olive legs, than Lesser Yellowlegs. Also note narrow, white eyering and dark rump with black bars across white outer rectrices. Smaller Spotted Sandpiper is plain above (not spotted with white) and has different breast pattern, white wing stripe, and distinctive flight stroke. **VOICE** Calls, often given in flight, a sweet series of rising notes: *"ti'weet-weet."* Notes shorter and have a purer quality than those of Spotted Sandpiper. **Co, E, Br, Bo, Ch**

5 SPOTTED SANDPIPER *Actitis macularius* 18–20 cm (7–8 in)

Fairly common boreal migrant (Aug–Apr) below 1500 m on both east and west slopes, along rivers, on coastline, marshes, and lake edges; rare at altiplano lakes to 4100 m. Teeters constantly when on ground; typically flies low over water with shallow, stiff-winged wingbeats. Also note strongly spotted underparts in alternate plumage. In basic plumage, note plain upperparts, whitish underparts, and brown "thumbmark" at side of breast. **VOICE** Call, often given in flight, is a high peeping: *"pee'wee-weet."* **Co, E, Br, Bo, Ch**

GREATER YELLOWLEGS

basic

alt.

LESSER YELLOWLEGS

alt.

basic

LESSER YELLOWLEGS

GREATER YELLOWLEGS

alt.

basic

STILT SANDPIPER

juv.

basic

SOLITARY SANDPIPER

RUFF

basic

alt.

SPOTTED SANDPIPER

basic

alt.

PLATE
56

"PEEPS" (SMALL *CALIDRIS* SANDPIPERS)

"Peeps" or "stints" (the small Calidris) *are boreal migrants. Smaller than other sandpipers, and confusingly similar, each with a complex array of plumages. Varying molt patterns complicate identification among species. Juveniles of some species (particularly Baird's and Pectoral sandpipers) may arrive with much of the juvenile plumage retained; in others, juveniles may arrive showing a mixture of juvenile and basic plumages. For identification note size, tarsus color, bill length and thickness, wing extension, rump and tail pattern, and details of underparts pattern.*

1 LEAST SANDPIPER *Calidris minutilla* 13–15 cm (5–6 in)
Common boreal migrant (Sep–Mar; a few may oversummer) along coast in marshes and on mudflats and beaches; rare along Amazonian rivers and at lakes in altiplano. Smallest sandpiper, but close in size to Semipalmated and Western. Much smaller than Pectoral and other yellow-legged sandpipers. Note yellowish or greenish tarsi (beware of birds with muddy legs, appearing unnaturally dark) and generally richer, brown plumage on back and breast. Breast concolor with back, not paler as in Semipalmated and Western. Bill short, like Semipalmated's, but not as thick. **VOICE** Call, often given in flight, a slightly trilled, rising "*breEET.*" Unlike other sandpipers. **Co, E, Br, Bo, Ch**

2 SEMIPALMATED SANDPIPER *Calidris pusilla* 13–15 cm (5–6 in)
Common boreal migrant (Aug–Apr; small numbers oversummer) along coast on mudflats and beaches; very rare at altiplano lakes. Smaller than most other sandpipers, except Western and yellowish-legged Least. Very similar to Western. Bill of Semipalmated averages shorter and thicker than bill of Western; but bill of female Semipalmated longer, and may overlap bill length of male Western. Semipalmated lacks distinct droop to bill tip (often shown by Western, especially females). Alternate plumaged Semipalmated is grayer and plainer above, lacking rufous in back and crown; underparts less strongly patterned with markings more restricted to breast. Juvenile duller and grayer, lacking rufous scapulars of Western (although some Semipalmated may be decidedly buffy; also beware of fading and feather wear). In basic plumage is virtually identical to Western; some (males and some females) may be distinguished by shorter bill. **VOICE** Calls, often given in flight, a short, rough "*djirt*" and a whining "*whi-whi-whi-whi*" in aggressive interactions. **Co, E, Br, Ch**

3 WESTERN SANDPIPER *Calidris mauri* 14–16 cm (5½–6½ in)
Common boreal migrant (Aug–May; small numbers oversummer) along coast on mudflats and beaches. Small, dark legged "peep." Cf. Semipalmated; also cf. Least Sandpiper. **VOICE** Call, often given in flight, a sharp "*whit.*" **Co, E, Ch**

4 WHITE-RUMPED SANDPIPER *Calidris fuscicollis* 16–18 cm (6½–7 in)
Uncommon boreal migrant (mainly as passage migrant Oct–Nov, Mar–May) in Amazonia along rivers and in marshes; rare on coast and at lakes on altiplano. A large peep; like Baird's has long wings, primaries projecting past end of tail. In flight, fully white rump distinguishes this from all peeps except vagrant Curlew Sandpiper. Breeding and juvenile plumages resemble smaller Western Sandpiper, but longer wings give different shape; also has less rufous and a stronger superciliary. In basic plumage resembles Baird's, but is grayer (Baird's relatively buffy), with a stronger superciliary and streaked flanks. **VOICE** Calls, often given in flight, thin, ringing chirps: "*tsirt.*" **Co, E, Br, Bo, Ch**

5 BAIRD'S SANDPIPER *Calidris bairdii* 15–18 cm (6–7 in)
Common boreal migrant (Aug–May; a few may oversummer) at lakes on altiplano (3200–4600 m); uncommon along coast on mudflats and in marshes, rare in Amazonia. Decidedly buffy brown coloration combined with dark legs and relatively long bill distinguish Baird's from most other small sandpipers; cf. White-rumped Sandpiper, which is of similar size and bill length. Note long wings, projecting past end of tail. Juveniles are the most strongly buffy and are scaled above rather than streaked. **VOICE** Call, often given in flight, a scratchy, trilled "*tchirr.*" Similar to Pectoral Sandpiper's, but higher-pitched and drier. **Co, E, Br, Bo, Ch**

6 PECTORAL SANDPIPER *Calidris melanotos* 19–23 cm (7½–9 in)
Common boreal migrant (Aug–May; a few may oversummer) throughout on mudflats and beaches, at lake edges, and in marshes. Large peep with yellow or olive legs. Note generally brown plumage, strongly streaked breast with sharp demarcation from white belly, and erect posture. Cf. much smaller Least Sandpiper and (vagrant) Ruff. **VOICE** Call, often given in flight, a gruff, descending "*tchirr.*" **Co, E, Br, Bo, Ch**

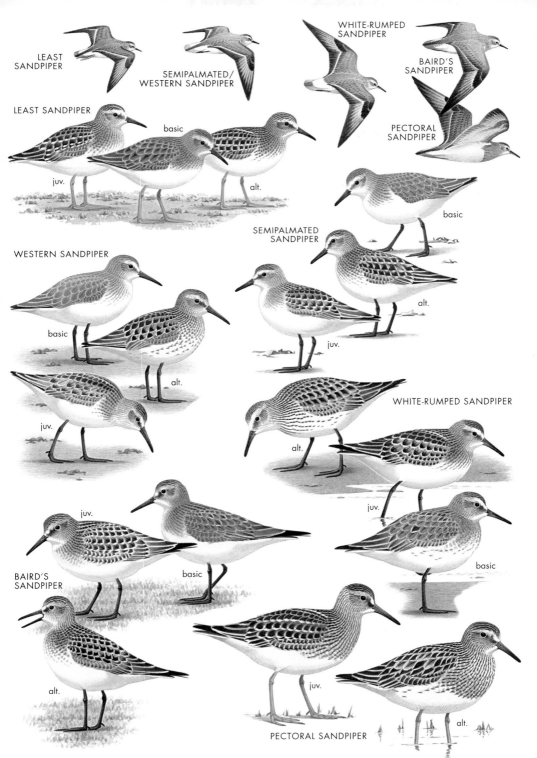

LEAST
SANDPIPER

SEMIPALMATED/
WESTERN SANDPIPER

WHITE-RUMPED
SANDPIPER

BAIRD'S
SANDPIPER

PECTORAL
SANDPIPER

LEAST SANDPIPER

basic

juv.

alt.

SEMIPALMATED
SANDPIPER

basic

alt.

juv.

WESTERN SANDPIPER

basic

alt.

juv.

WHITE-RUMPED SANDPIPER

alt.

juv.

juv.

basic

BAIRD'S
SANDPIPER

juv.

basic

alt.

juv.

alt.

PECTORAL SANDPIPER

PLATE
57

LARGE *CALIDRIS* AND GRASSLAND SANDPIPERS

Upland and Buff-breasted sandpipers are birds of fields and pastures, not mudflats. Sanderling is an abundant, relatively large Calidris; sometimes confused with the smaller species, especially by inexperienced observers. Red-necked Stint, Dunlin, and Curlew Sandpiper are only vagrants. Red Knot is a very large, heavy-bodied Calidris.

1 UPLAND SANDPIPER *Bartramia longicauda* 29–32 cm (11½–12½ in)

Uncommon boreal migrant (mainly as passage migrant Sep–Nov, Feb–Apr) in fields, grasslands, and river islands in Amazonia; rare on coast, in open areas on east slope of Andes, and in altiplano to 3800 m. Usually not associated with water. Long, thin neck, large eye, and upright posture give it a different look from other shorebirds. Cf. smaller Buff-breasted Sandpiper. **VOICE** Calls, often given in flight, a liquid, warbled "*whi-wi-wi-wi-wi-wi.*" **Co, E, Br, Bo, Ch**

2 BUFF-BREASTED SANDPIPER *Tryngites subruficollis* 18–20 cm (7–8 in)

Uncommon boreal migrant (primarily a passage migrant, Aug–Oct) in Amazonia along rivers and in fields; rare on coastal mudflats and in marshes, and at lakes on altiplano, but not closely associated with water. Readily identified by small size and strongly buff underparts; also note yellow tarsi and (in flight) white underwings. Cf. juvenile Baird's Sandpiper. **VOICE** Calls, often given in flight, reedy "*keet*" notes. **Co, E, Br, Bo, Ch**

3 SANDERLING *Calidris alba* * 19–21 cm (7½–8½ in)

Common boreal migrant (Aug–Apr; occasional birds remain in summer) on sandy beaches and mudflats along coast; rare on altiplano lakes and along Amazonian rivers. Characteristic along sandy beaches at water line where large flocks scurry back and forth as waves move in and out. In basic plumage is very pale; not strong white wing stripe and black lesser wing coverts, which can be visible even at rest. Juvenile similar, but upperparts heavily spangled with black (even so, appears very pale). In alternate plumage, upperparts and breast much more richly rufous than other small shorebirds. **VOICE** Calls, often given in flight, a sharp, dry "*kit*" and a quiet, squeaky "*kiyuck-yuck-yuck.*" **Co, E, Br, Ch**

[RED-NECKED STINT *Calidris ruficollis*] 14–16 cm (5½–6½ in)

Very rare vagrant on coast; known only from sight records. Orange-red unstreaked throat and upper breast of breeding plumage distinctive, but beware of brightly colored alternate-plumaged Sanderlings, which also can be very rufous on foreparts. Sanderling is larger, streaked across breast, and more extensively bright, and lacks a hind toe. In other plumages, difficult to identify; most similar to Semipalmated Sandpiper, which it resembles in proportions, although bill is finer. At extremely close range, note that stint lacks Semipalmated's partial webbing between toes. The similar **Little Stint** *Calidris minuta* is not reported from Peru but also could occur; reports of either stint would require extensive documentation. **VOICE** Call, often given in flight, a dry, gravelly "*djit.*"

4 RED KNOT *Calidris canutus* * 24–27 cm (9½–10½ in)

Uncommon boreal migrant (Sep–May; a few may oversummer) on coastal mudflats and in marshes. In alternate plumage, combination of bright rufous underparts and largely gray back distinctive; cf. longer-billed Short-billed Dowitcher. In basic plumage, note stocky build and pale gray, relatively unpatterned plumage. Basic-plumaged dowitchers and Stilt Sandpiper have longer bills and contrasting white rump or lower back. **VOICE** Calls, often given in flight, quiet, mewed, descending "*kew*" notes. **Co, E, Br, Bo, Ch**

[DUNLIN *Calidris alpina*] * 18–21 cm (7–8½ in)

Very rare vagrant (boreal migrant) on coastal mudflats. Bill relatively long, with drooped tip. Alternate plumage distinctive. Very plain in basic plumage; larger, darker (especially on breast), longer-billed than the very common Western Sandpiper. **VOICE** Call, often given in flight, a rasping "*tcheerr*" more ringing than that of Baird's or Pectoral sandpipers. **E**

CURLEW SANDPIPER *Calidris ferruginea* 19–21 cm (7½–8½ in)

Very rare vagrant to coast. Only peep with strongly decurved bill (although bills of Dunlin and Western Sandpiper droop at tip); note also white rump. In alternate plumage, deep chestnut underparts and mottled chestnut on back distinctive (but cf. Red Knot). In basic plumage, most resembles Dunlin (also very rare), but Dunlin has different bill shape, is darker above, lacks white rump, and has less of a superciliary. Also cf. Stilt Sandpiper. **E**

UPLAND SANDPIPER

BUFF-BREASTED
SANDPIPER

juv.

ad.

RED-NECKED STINT

juv.

basic

alt.

SANDERLING

DUNLIN

RED KNOT

alt.

alt.

basic

basic

CURLEW SANDPIPER

CURLEW SANDPIPER

alt.

basic

juv.

PLATE
58

"ROCK" SANDPIPERS AND PHALAROPES

Wandering Tattler and Surfbird are characteristic of rocky shorelines. Surfbird is fairly common in Peru, but the Tattler is rare. Ruddy Turnstone is a distinctive species that forages both on rocky or sandy beaches. Phalaropes are small shorebirds that commonly forage by swimming. Individuals spin in tight circles, forming a whirlpool that brings food to the surface, where they pluck it. Females are larger than males and more colorful when in alternate plumage, which is rarely seen in Peru. Two species are almost entirely pelagic during the nonbreeding season. Wilson's is found on lakes and in marshes, where it may be confused with other pale, long-billed sandpipers (such as Stilt Sandpiper or Lesser Yellowlegs).

1 RUDDY TURNSTONE *Arenaria interpres* * 21–24 cm (8–9½ in)

Common boreal migrant (Sep–Apr; a few may oversummer) on coastal beaches and rocks; rare in Amazonia, and very rare at altiplano lakes. Plump and short-legged. Alternate plumage is unmistakable, as are birds in flight in all plumages. Basic plumage much duller, but retains distinctive variegated pattern. Also note orange tarsi, irregular white throat patch, and short, ploverlike bill (often slightly upturned at tip). **VOICE** Calls a puttering "*pit'it'ur*" and a longer grating, puttering series that rises and falls in pitch. **Co, E, Br, Ch**

2 SURFBIRD *Aphriza virgata* 23–25.5 cm (9–10 in)

Fairly common boreal migrant (Aug–Apr; a few may oversummer) on coast, especially in rocky areas. Dumpy and ploverlike, largely dark gray in nonbreeding plumage. Larger than Turnstone, with different wing and tail pattern in flight. Nonbreeding Red Knot similarly shaped but paler, especially on breast, and has duller legs and dark bill. **Co, E, Ch**

3 WANDERING TATTLER *Heteroscelus incanus* 26–28 cm (10–11 in)

Rare boreal migrant along coast, mainly in rocky areas. Plumage overall is very gray (especially in basic plumage), with relatively short, yellow tarsi and a moderately long bill. The other rock sandpipers, Surfbird and Ruddy Turnstone, have strong wing patterns and shorter bills. Tattlers also bob or teeter like Spotted Sandpiper (unlike Surfbird and Turnstone). Spotted Sandpiper is smaller, paler below (in basic plumage), with white wing stripe, and distinctive flight. **VOICE** Call, often given in flight, a pleasing, ringing trill "*tree'e'e.*" **Co, E, Ch**

4 RED-NECKED PHALAROPE *Phalaropus lobatus* 18–19 cm (7–7½ in)

Uncommon boreal migrant (Sep–Apr) at sea, mostly out of sight of land but within 30 km of coast. Occasionally found in coastal lakes or harbors. This and Red Phalarope almost always are seen on the water, where they form flocks, or in flight; only rarely seen standing on land. In flight, resemble Sanderlings (which are not expected far at sea). Shorter billed than Wilson's Phalarope; in basic plumage also has dark marks and crown and sides of head, and back shows indistinct whitish streaks. Cf. similar basic Red Phalarope. First-year birds may arrive retaining some juvenile plumage (not illustrated); upperparts of juveniles blackish, with contrasting pale streaks. **VOICE** Call, often given in flight, dry "*kip*" notes. **Co, E, Ch**

5 RED PHALAROPE *Phalaropus fulicarius* 20–22 cm (8–8½ in)

Fairly common boreal migrant (Sep–Apr) at sea, mostly out of sight of land. Much more likely than Red-necked to be far at sea (more than 50 km offshore). Occasionally found in coastal lakes or harbors. Alternate plumage unmistakable (but seldom seen in Peru). In basic plumage resembles Red-necked Phalarope but is bulkier, with thicker neck; has thicker, shorter bill (often with a pale base) and unmarked pearly gray back; and center of crown often is whiter. **VOICE** Call, often given in flight, rising whistles: "*rhee.*" **Co, E, Br, Ch**

6 WILSON'S PHALAROPE *Phalaropus tricolor* 22–24 cm (8½–9½ in)

Fairly common boreal migrant (Aug–May; a few may oversummer) in coastal marshes and at Andean lakes; rare in Amazonia. Ornate alternate plumage distinctive. Otherwise identifiable by distinctive phalarope spinning behavior; but frequently forages with other shorebirds on mudflats and in marshes, where plucks prey from ground and is more readily confused with other species (especially in basic plumage, when tarsi are yellowish). Cf. Lesser Yellowlegs and Stilt Sandpiper; Wilson's is paler and more uniform above than either, and is unmarked below. **VOICE** Call, often given in flight, deep, hollow "*pook*" notes. **Co, E, Br, Bo, Ch**

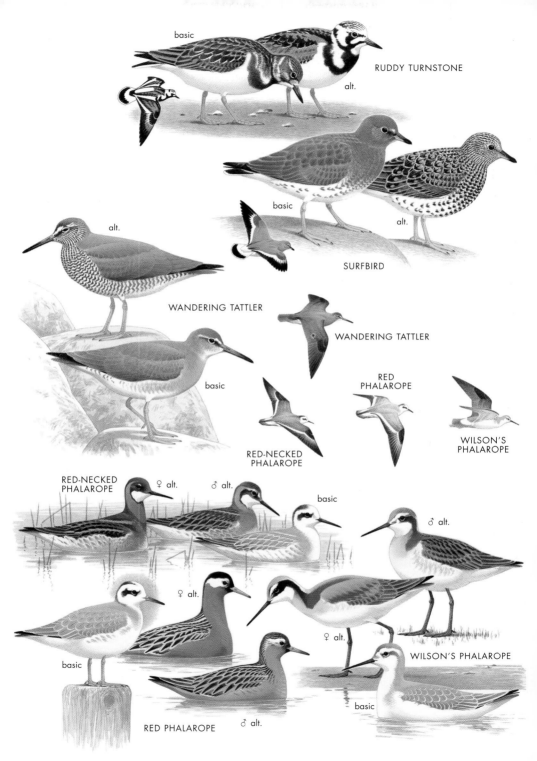

basic

RUDDY TURNSTONE

alt.

SURFBIRD

basic

alt.

alt.

WANDERING TATTLER

WANDERING TATTLER

basic

RED-NECKED
PHALAROPE

RED
PHALAROPE

WILSON'S
PHALAROPE

RED-NECKED
PHALAROPE

♀ alt.

♂ alt.

basic

♂ alt.

basic

♀ alt.

♀ alt.

WILSON'S PHALAROPE

basic

RED PHALAROPE

♂ alt.

PLATE
59

JAEGERS AND SKUAS

Jaegers and skuas occur only as nonbreeding visitors, usually far out at sea. Characteristically chase other seabirds, forcing them to give up prey items. All show a pale underwing primary flash. Heavier-bodied skuas resemble large immature gulls; jaegers are smaller, although Pomarine is intermediate in size. Identification often difficult. Parasitic and Pomarine jaegers are polymorphic, with light, dark, and intermediate morphs. Jaegers mature over several years. Adults have dark underwing coverts (barred in immatures and juveniles); alternate plumage, with fully developed projecting central rectrices, rarely seen in Peru. Basic plumages of adult jaegers more similar to immatures (central rectrices less projecting, and plumage more barred, especially on rump and undertail coverts), but retain dark underwing coverts. Juveniles have narrowly barred upperparts, including wing coverts and scapulars; juveniles and early immature plumages also lack dark cap of older immatures and adults.

1 PARASITIC JAEGER *Stercorarius parasiticus* 41–45 cm (16–18 in) plus 8–14 cm (3–6 in) tail streamers

Uncommon boreal migrant (Oct–May), pelagic but primarily within 80 km of shore; occasionally in harbors or bays. Intermediate between other jaegers in size and flight characteristics. Bill thinner than Pomarine's, but longer than Long-tailed's. Central rectrices pointed; extent of projection variable, but never as long as in Long-tailed, and may be scarcely longer than other rectrices in immatures and basic adults. Upper wing shows 3–6 outer primaries with white shafts (intermediate between Pomarine and Long-tailed). Black cap of light-morph adult typically fades before touching gape. Often lacks breast band. Juvenile is the most cinnamon-colored juvenile jaeger; nape often pale and rump relatively unbarred (appearing relatively dark), and projecting central rectrices are pointed. Cf. larger, broader-winged Pomarine and smaller, more lightly built Long-tailed. **Co, E, Br, Ch**

2 LONG-TAILED JAEGER *Stercorarius longicaudus* * 38–41 cm (15–16 in) plus 15–25 cm (6–10 in) tail streamers

Rare boreal migrant (Oct–May), pelagic, but within 80 km of shore; very rare close to shore, however. Smallest jaeger with ternlike flight; bill short, and in juveniles only basal half is pale. Adult paler, grayer above than other jaegers, with contrasting darker remiges. Upper wing shows only 2 or 3 white primary shafts (least of any jaeger). Black cap reaches gape. Alternate adult lacks breast band and has very long thin central rectrices. Juveniles grayer than other jaegers (never cinnamon-toned like Parasitic), and projecting central rectrices are blunt-tipped. Light-morph juvenile (not illustrated) most distinctive, with pale head and belly. **Co, E, Br, Ch**

3 POMARINE JAEGER *Stercorarius pomarinus* 43–51 cm (17–20 in) plus 17–20 cm (6½–8 in) tail streamers

Fairly common boreal migrant (Oct–May), mostly within 80 km of shore; occasionally in harbors or bays. Largest jaeger; barrel-chested, with broad wings and direct gull-like flight. Polymorphic, but dark morph rare in adults. Tips of central rectrices broad; projecting and twisted in alternate plumage, but much shorter, less projecting in immatures and adults in basic plumage. Upper wing shows 5 or more outer primaries with white shafts (most of any jaeger). Black cap of light-morph adults extends onto malar region, and contrasts with heavy, bicolored bill. Extent of dark breast band variable (often broader in females). Juveniles (not illustrated), which usually are dark or intermediate in color, lack cinnamon tone of juvenile Parasitic. Underwing of juveniles and immatures also shows pale primary coverts, in addition to whitish bases of primaries, creating a double pale crescent. **Co, E, Br, Ch**

4 SOUTH POLAR SKUA *Stercorarius maccormicki* 50–55 cm (19½–21½ in)

Status uncertain; apparently rare austral migrant, usually far from shore. Recorded May–Jan, but primarily in May and Oct–Nov. Polymorphic, but never shows dark cap or cinnamon tone of Chilean Skua. Lighter individuals have pale hindneck and often show small, pale patch on face at base of bill; underwing coverts blackish, contrasting with rest of underwing. Dark morph more uniformly dark brown. **E, Br, Ch**

5 CHILEAN SKUA *Stercorarius chilensis* 53–58 cm (21–23 in)

Uncommon austral migrant; present throughout year, but probably more common Mar–Sep. Distinguished from rarer South Polar Skua by dark cap, and usually has cinnamon tone to body plumage, especially to underparts and underwing coverts (cf. contrastingly dark underwing coverts of South Polar). Bill often bicolored, gray with black tip. **E, Br, Ch**

PARASITIC JAEGER

juv.

dark morph alt.

POMARINE JAEGER

imm.

SOUTH POLAR SKUA

dark morph

CHILEAN SKUA

juv.

ad. alt.

LONG-TAILED JAEGER

light morph alt.

PARASITIC JAEGER

light morph alt.

POMARINE JAEGER

dark morph alt.

light morph

PLATE
60

LARGE GULLS, PELAGIC GULLS, AND INCA TERN

Gulls are familiar aquatic birds. Many are omnivorous and feed in part by scavenging. Most take several years to reach maturity, with a number of intermediate plumages. Most species on this plate are restricted to inshore waters or the immediate vicinity of the coast, but also shown here are two highly pelagic species, rarely seen from shore when not breeding.

[HERRING GULL *Larus argentatus*] * 54–63 cm (21½–25 in)

Very rare vagrant to coast (photographed once in Lima); rare south of Mexico. Similar in size to Kelp Gull, but with smaller, less heavy bill. Adult pale gray on back with black wing tips and pink legs. First-year birds typically show pale inner primaries contrasting with darker outer primaries and secondaries; these feathers more evenly colored in first-year Kelp. Similar to several other Northern Hemisphere gulls that also could occur as vagrants to Peru; any suspected extralimital gull should be extensively documented. **Co, E**

1 KELP GULL *Larus dominicanus* * 56–64 cm (22–25 in)

Common resident along coast, breeding on offshore islands. Bulky; largest gull in Peru. Adult has white head and tail, greenish tarsi, and small white spots at tips of primaries. First-year plumage largely brown above, with a contrastingly paler head and white rump and base to tail. Compare all plumages to smaller Belcher's Gull. **VOICE** Calls a deep "*keeYOW*" and weaker "*keew*" calls, also a quiet chuckle "*gah-gah-gah.*" Also various higher squeaks, whistles, and cries. Laugh series starts with longer notes and accelerates: "*skreeee skreee kya-kya-kya-kya-kya.*" **E, Br, Ch**

2 BELCHER'S (Band-tailed) GULL *Larus belcheri* 51–54 cm (20–21½ in)

Fairly common resident in nearshore waters along coast. Mainly breeds on offshore islands north to Lambayeque, also locally on mainland. A large gull, but slightly smaller than Kelp Gull. White-headed alternate adult distinguished from Kelp by black band on tail, brighter yellow (less greenish) tarsi, entirely dark wing tips, and red tip to bill (red not restricted to a spot on mandible). Dark-headed basic adults unmistakable. First-year birds also dark-headed, unlike first-year Kelp. **VOICE** Calls a clear, short "*yap*" and "*yeow.*" Laugh series is of clear notes that accelerate: "*yaaaah yaaaah-yah-yah-yah-yah-yah,*" sometimes without the introductory notes. **Co, E, Ch**

3 GRAY GULL *Larus modestus* 45–46 cm (17½–18 in)

Common austral migrant (present year-round, although less common Nov–Feb) along sandy coastal beaches and nearshore waters. Largely gray with pale head in alternate plumage. In other plumages is all dark: uniformly gray in adult basic plumage, browner in first basic plumage. Usually easily recognized. At a distance, especially in flight, can be confused with Inca Tern (which is smaller and longer tailed, and has odd, fluttering, erratic flight on rather stiff wings). **VOICE** Calls a yelping "*kyow*" and a growled, rising "*grrrrraaaah,*" also a low moan and shrill cries. Laugh series ending with a longer note than Laughing Gull: "*he'he'he'he'heeaaaaaaoowww.*" **Co, E, Ch**

4 INCA TERN *Larosterna inca* 40–43 cm (15¾–17 in)

Common resident on coast north to La Libertad, breeding on rocky cliffs both on mainland and on offshore islands. Nonbreeding birds disperse in nearshore waters north to Piura. Inca Tern easily identified by sooty plumage, long dark tail, and erratic flight with stiff-winged look. Adult also has spectacular white tufts and red bill (although these may be difficult to see at a distance and are lacking on immatures). Cf. much larger Gray Gull. **Co, E, Ch**

5 SWALLOW-TAILED GULL *Creagrus furcatus* 54–59 cm (21½–23 in)

Fairly common nonbreeding migrant from Galapagos Islands; primarily present Sep–May, but occasional birds remain through the austral winter. Pelagic. Almost unmistakable. Much larger than Sabine's Gull, with less black on the primaries, forked tail and paler upperparts. In most plumages also has whiter head than Sabine's. **Co, E, Ch**

6 SABINE'S GULL *Xema sabini* 33–35 cm (13–14 in)

Uncommon boreal migrant (Oct–May); pelagic, only rarely seen close to shore. Small gull with distinctive wing pattern (note black outer primaries and white inner remiges) in all plumages. Juvenile similar in pattern but is browner above, barred dusky, and tip of tail is black. Cf. larger Swallow-tailed Gull. **Co, E, Ch**

ad. basic

ad. alt.

1st basic

HERRING GULL

HERRING GULL

ad.

KELP GULL

1st basic

2nd alt.

BELCHER'S GULL

1st basic

ad. alt.

ad. basic

2nd alt.

ad. alt.

ad.
basic

ad. alt.

1st basic

ad. alt.

GRAY GULL

INCA TERN

ad. alt.

juv.

1st basic

ad. alt.

SWALLOW-TAILED GULL

ad. basic

ad. basic

ad. alt.

juv.

ad. basic

SABINE'S GULL

PLATE
61

HOODED GULLS AND KITTIWAKE

Species shown on this plate are small or medium-sized gulls. Four of them (including the very rare vagrant Brown-hooded Gull) have a dark hood in alternate plumage, although several of these are migrant species and rarely show a complete hood when present in Peru. Gray-hooded Gull is similar to the dark-hooded gulls but has only a pale gray hood in alternate plumage. Black-legged Kittiwake is highly pelagic when not breeding and is only a very rare vagrant (usually occurs only in Northern Hemisphere).

1 LAUGHING GULL *Larus atricilla* * 39–43 cm (15½–17 in)

Fairly common boreal migrant (Oct–Apr) to northwest coast, south regularly to Lima, rarely to Arequipa; very rare vagrant to Amazonia. Wing tips lack white (other than short-lived, narrow white tips to primaries in freshly molted plumage), the dark gray mantle shading into black primaries; and undersides of primaries also are dark. Cf. smaller Franklin's Gull's. Other dark-hooded gulls have stronger wing patterns with white flashes on outer primaries. **VOICE** Call a plaintive *"kyeow."* Laughing series is maniacal as it accelerates and decelerates: *"ha ha-ha-hahaha haw haaw haaaaw."* **Co, E, Br**

2 FRANKLIN'S GULL *Larus pipixcan* 35–39 cm (14–15½ in)

Locally abundant boreal migrant (Oct–May) in coastal marshes, nearshore waters, and irrigated agricultural lands along coast; rare visitor to altiplano lakes and to Amazonia. Adults distinguished from larger Laughing Gull by shorter bill, paler mantle that contrasts with black-and-white wing tips, and (all nonbreeding plumages) more extensive black hood with contrasting white eye crescents. Second-year Franklin's (not illustrated) lack white band across wing tip; distinguished from Laughing by paler mantle and by hood. In first winter plumage also note incomplete black tail band (outermost rectrices are white); all rectrices tipped black in comparable Laughing. **VOICE** Calls a mellow yelp and piping calls. Laugh series is weaker and higher pitched than Laughing. **Co, E, Br, Bo, Ch**

[BLACK-LEGGED KITTIWAKE *Rissa tridactyla*] 40–46 cm (15¼–18 in)

Very rare vagrant to coast (photographed near Lima). Highly pelagic; rarely seen close to shore. Relatively small, graceful gull. Adult has unmarked yellow bill, black tarsi, and small black tips to pale gray wings; in basic plumage has dark smudge on sides of head. Immature shows broad black bar forming dark "W" pattern across upperparts, and black collar across nape. Compare with Sabine's and larger Swallow-tailed gulls, both of which have whiter wedge on inner remiges and more strongly notched or forked tails.

3 GRAY-HOODED GULL *Larus cirrocephalus* * 41–43 cm (16–17 in)

Fairly common resident along coast in marshes and nearshore waters. Most common coastal gull with white primary flash (present in all plumages, although reduced in immature). Medium gray hood of alternate adult distinctive. Also, in all plumages has more black on outer primaries than do Andean or Brown-hooded gulls. **VOICE** Call a deep, descending, grating caw: *"graaaaa."* Also shorter *"kek"* notes. **E, Br**

[BROWN-HOODED GULL *Larus maculipennis*] 36–38 cm (14–15 in)

Very rare vagrant to coast from southern South America; photographed in Lima. Most similar at all ages to comparable plumages of larger Andean Gull, but bill and tarsi are brighter red. Dark hood of alternate plumage is brown (not black or gray as in other "hooded" gulls). Upper surface of wing of adults almost entirely gray, with white outer primaries; black confined to tips of inner primaries. In first-year plumage the black band along trailing edge of inner primaries is broader than in immature Andean, and there is more white visible on outer portion of wing's upper surface (in particular, less black on primary coverts and a pale carpal area or "bend" of wing). **Br, Ch**

4 ANDEAN GULL *Larus serranus* 46–48 cm (18–19 in)

Common resident around high-elevation (3000–4400 m) lakes and rivers. Rare visitor to coast (mostly in austral winter) north to Lima; very rare vagrant to Amazonia. Only gull that occurs regularly in altiplano, but overlaps with similar species along coast. Larger than other hooded gulls, except for very different nonbreeding Belcher's Gull. Cf. Gray-hooded and (very rare) Brown-hooded gulls. **VOICE** Calls shrill cries, some with a somewhat trilled quality: *"gah!"* and *"grrreeeuh,"* higher than most other Peruvian gulls' voices. Also a chuckling series. **E, Bo, Ch**

ad. basic

ad. alt.

ad. basic

ad. alt.

1st basic

LAUGHING GULL

ad. basic

ad. alt.

ad. basic

FRANKLIN'S GULL

1st basic

1st basic

1st basic

ad. alt.

BLACK-LEGGED
KITTIWAKE

ad. basic

ad. alt.

ad. basic

ad. alt.

GRAY-HOODED GULL

1st basic

ad. basic

ad. alt.

ad. alt.

1st basic

BROWN-HOODED
GULL

ad. basic

ad. alt.

ad. alt.

1st basic

ANDEAN GULL

PLATE
62

SMALL TERNS, LARGE TERNS, AND SKIMMER

Terns are smaller than gulls, with longer, thinner bills and often with long forked tails. Terns are lighter and more graceful in flight and typically capture prey with shallow dives; do not scavenge. The largest and the smallest species are shown here; see also plate 63. The skimmer resembles a large tern but has distinctive bill and foraging behavior.

LEAST TERN *Sternula antillarum* * 21–23 cm (8¼–9 in)

Status not clear, but apparently a rare boreal migrant along coast; presumably more common in north, but reported south to Arequipa. Rarely may oversummer. Size and behavior similar to Peruvian Tern. Least Tern is paler gray above and always white below; Peruvian is darker overall, with darker gray upperparts and usually light gray underparts. Bill bright yellow with black tip (breeding plumage) or all black; bill of Peruvian is duller yellow with a dusky culmen and tip. Black cap of nonbreeding Least Tern also is more restricted than in similar plumages of Peruvian. **VOICE** Calls high pitched "*kee-DJEET*" and rising "*arreet*" notes. **Co, E, Br**

1 YELLOW-BILLED TERN *Sternula superciliaris* 23–25 cm (9–10 in)

Fairly common resident along Amazonian rivers and oxbow lakes. The only small, yellow-billed tern in Amazonia. Similar in size to Peruvian Tern of coast, and has similar rapid wingbeats. Cf. much larger Large-billed Tern, with which it often occurs. **VOICE** Calls raspy "*kree*" and "*kew*" notes, often in a series. **Co, E, Br, Bo**

2 PERUVIAN TERN *Sternula lorata* 23–24 cm (9–9½ in)

Local, uncommon, and declining along coast. Breeds in small colonies on sandy beaches. Very small, with fast ("snappy") wingbeats. Underparts of adult light gray (other small terns are white below). **VOICE** Calls squeaky "*kik*," rough "*gree*," and descending, quavering "*kee'ee'eer*" notes. **E, Ch**

3 LARGE-BILLED TERN *Phaetusa simplex* * 37–40 cm (14½–15¾ in)

Fairly common resident along Amazonian rivers. Unmistakable within its range: note striking wing pattern (recalling pattern of pelagic Sabine's and Swallow-tailed gulls) and large, heavy, yellow bill. Alternate plumage of adult has solid black crown. Juvenile heavily barred brown above. **VOICE** Calls gull-like "*keeeah*" and "*keeyaw*" notes. **Co, E, Br, Bo**

4 ROYAL TERN *Thalasseus maximus* * 46–52 cm (18–20½ in)

Fairly common boreal migrant (Aug–May) along sandy beaches of coast and in nearshore waters. Often seen with slightly smaller Elegant Tern. Royal has stouter, less curved bill; less black on the sides of the face (black barely extends to eye, rather than surrounding the eye as in Elegant); and crest is shorter. **VOICE** Calls grating "*kiREH*" and short laughing series: "*ke reereereereeree.*" Harsher and deeper than Elegant. **Co, E, Br**

5 ELEGANT TERN *Thalasseus elegans* 40–43 cm (15½–17 in)

Common boreal migrant (Aug–May; occasionally may remain into northern summer) along sandy beaches of coast and in nearshore waters. Most common and widespread orange-billed tern in Peru. Cf. similar Royal Tern. In Peru both species are seen most commonly in basic plumage, with white forecrown; birds in alternate plumage also may show light pink breasts, and in fresh plumage have paler outer primaries. **VOICE** Calls high grinding "*keeREEH*" and short laughing series: "*kree jeejeejeejeejee.*" Higher and thinner than Royal. **Co, E, Ch**

6 SANDWICH TERN *Thalasseus sandvicensis* * 38–41 cm (15–16 in)

Uncommon boreal migrant (Oct–May; occasionally may remain into northern summer) along sandy beaches of coast and in nearshore waters. Often seen with structurally similar Elegant and Royal terns, but is smaller, with bill mostly black. Cf. smaller terns, especially Common and Gull-billed terns. **VOICE** Calls grating "*kree*" and "*kirrik.*" **Co, E, Br, Ch**

7 BLACK SKIMMER *Rynchops niger* * 41–48 cm (16–19 in)

Fairly common resident along Amazonian rivers. Also can be fairly common on sandy beaches of coast. Not known to breed on coast; may be present there year-round, but perhaps most common Sep–Apr. Very rare vagrant to altiplano. Social; often seen in flocks. Bill laterally compressed, and mandible obviously longer than maxilla. Flies low over water; when feeding, slices shallow waters with elongated mandible to locate and capture fish. Black-and-white plumage and unusual bill and foraging behavior make it unmistakable. **VOICE** Calls dull yaps and barks: "*yup*" and "*kew.*" **Co, E, Br, Bo, Ch**

YELLOW-BILLED TERN

ad. alt.

ad. basic

juv.

LEAST TERN

alt.

basic

ad. basic

1st alt.

juv.

ad. alt.

PERUVIAN TERN

juv.

ad. basic

ad. alt.

ad. alt.

LARGE-BILLED TERN

ad. alt.

alt.

basic

juv.

ROYAL TERN

alt.

end of molt
(Nov–Dec)

fresh
(Jan–Feb)

alt.

basic

1st basic

ELEGANT TERN

1st basic

end of molt
(Nov–Dec)

fresh
(Jan–Feb)

SANDWICH TERN

juv.

alt.

basic

BLACK SKIMMER

ad.

PLATE
63

MEDIUM-SIZED TERNS

South American, Arctic, and Common are regular, and confusingly similar. Other small to medium-sized species on this plate are much less common, at least near shore.

1 GULL-BILLED TERN *Gelochelidon nilotica* * 34–39 cm (13½–15½ in)
Rare boreal migrant (Aug–May; occasionally may remain into northern summer) on sandy beaches and marshes. Very pale, whitish, with notably stout black bill and relatively short tail with only a shallow fork. Sandwich Tern is larger; more crested; has longer slender bill; and more deeply forked tail. In basic plumage Sandwich also has black rear crown. Similar to basic plumaged Snowy-crowned, which has longer, thinner bill with pale tip. Cf. also Common, South American, and Arctic terns. **VOICE** Call mellow "*geh-rep*," reminiscent of Black Skimmer, but bisyllabic. **Co, E, Br**

2 SOUTH AMERICAN TERN *Sterna hirundinacea* 40–44 cm (15¾–17½ in)
Fairly common resident along Pacific coast north to Ica, breeding (or formerly bred?) locally on offshore islands. Nonbreeders occur north along coast, and in coastal waters within 80 km of shore. Resembles Common and Arctic terns in all plumages, but larger, with heavier bill; bill of adult also always red. Never shows dark carpal bar. Trailing edge to primaries relatively crisp but broad. Rear border to black cap in immatures and basic-plumaged adults is smoother than in Common or Arctic; also, black cap extends below the eye, usually offset by a white crescent. Juvenile strongly barred dusky above. Barred tertials retained into first basic plumage; tertials of immature Common/Arctic never are barred. Older immatures are more similar to Common/Arctic of comparable age; identify by larger size, heavier bill, head pattern, and less apparent carpal bar. **E, Br, Ch**

[SNOWY-CROWNED TERN *Sterna trudeaui*] 28–35 cm (11–14 in)
Rare vagrant during austral winter to coast, reported north to Ica (photographed). Very pale with very little black in wing tip. Always lacks a black crown (black restricted to narrow patch on side of face), and tip of long slender bill always is pale; base of bill may be red in alternate plumage, otherwise is dark. Cf. Gull-billed Tern. **VOICE** Calls a short, grating "*jeer*," and a rapid series of "*je-je-je-je...*" notes. **Br, Ch**

3 ARCTIC TERN *Sterna paradisaea* 33–38 cm (13–15 in)
Fairly common boreal passage migrant (Aug–Nov, Apr–May, but a few may remain through northern summer). More pelagic than other *Sterna*, and least likely to be seen near shore. Very rare vagrant to Amazonia. Bill and tarsi relatively short. Dark trailing edge to primaries narrow and crisp, and remiges more translucent than in other *Sterna*. Also relatively short-necked compared to South American and Common terns. Carpal bar not as strong as in Common. Immature also has pale secondaries (cf. Common). **Co, E, Br, Bo, Ch**

4 COMMON TERN *Sterna hirundo* * 33–38 cm (13–15 in)
A common boreal migrant (Aug–May) along coastal sandy beaches, and in marshes and nearshore waters; rare vagrant to altiplano lakes and Amazonia. Cf. similar Arctic and South American terns. Smaller than South American, with more slender bill, but similarly long-legged. Dark trailing edge to primaries relatively broad, and less crisply defined. In basic plumage adult distinguished from South American by black bill and dark carpal bar; also may show dark "wedge" on outer primaries. Immature similar to basic adult, but has darker primaries and secondaries (secondaries of South American and Arctic terns paler). **Co, E, Br, Bo, Ch**

[SOOTY TERN *Onychoprion fuscatus*] * 41–45 cm (16–17½ in)
Highly pelagic; status not certain, known from only a few sight records, but perhaps regular far out at sea. Black-and-white adult plumage distinctive; subadults are all-dark with white undertail coverts. **Co, E, Br, Ch** [Similar **Bridled Tern** *Onychoprion anaethetus*, unreported for Peru, is potential vagrant, especially off northwest coast. Adult is dark gray above with black cap, narrow whitish collar on nape, slightly longer white superciliary, and gray (not black) undersides to remiges. Immature like adult but scaled or barred whitish above, and forecrown is pale.]

5 BLACK TERN *Chlidonias niger* * 22–25 cm (8½–10 in)
Uncommon boreal migrant (Oct–Apr), primarily at sea; also rarely in coastal marshes. Very rare vagrant to altiplano lakes and Amazonia. In Peru rarely seen in mostly black alternate plumage (with light gray underwings and white vent). In other plumages note relatively small size, short dark bill, relatively short broad wings, and dark gray upperparts and shoulder spur. **Co, E, Br, Ch**

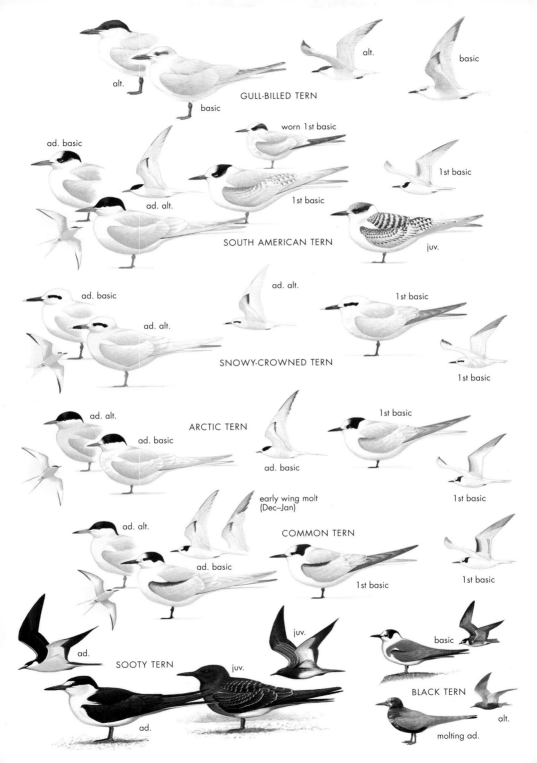

GULL-BILLED TERN

alt.

basic

alt.

basic

ad. basic

worn 1st basic

ad. alt.

1st basic

1st basic

SOUTH AMERICAN TERN

juv.

ad. basic

ad. alt.

ad. alt.

1st basic

SNOWY-CROWNED TERN

1st basic

ad. alt.

ARCTIC TERN

1st basic

ad. basic

ad. basic

1st basic

early wing molt
(Dec–Jan)

COMMON TERN

ad. alt.

ad. basic

1st basic

1st basic

ad.

SOOTY TERN

juv.

juv.

basic

BLACK TERN

ad.

alt.

molting ad.

PLATE
64

FOREST PIGEONS

These are large, primarily arboreal pigeons of forest and forest edge.

1 PLUMBEOUS PIGEON *Patagioenas plumbea* * 29.5–32 cm (11½–12½ in)

Fairly common and widespread in eastern lowlands, regular but somewhat less common up to 2300 m on east slope of Andes (*pallescens, bogotensis*). Also rare in evergreen forest in Tumbes up to 800 m (*chapmani*). Plumbeous and Ruddy are pigeons of forest interiors. Both forage in subcanopy and canopy of humid forest, and only rarely fly above canopy. Typically seen as singles or as pairs, not in flocks, although may congregate in small groups at fruiting trees. Distinguished from other pigeons by habitat, behavior, uniformly drab plumage, and proportionally longer tails; but difficult to distinguish from each other by sight. Plumbeous averages slightly larger. Also is paler and grayer (plumage less suffused with reddish tones). Iris often pale (whitish); Ruddy always has dark (reddish) iris. **VOICE** Song in most of eastern Peru (*pallescens*) a variable series of 3 coos, middle of which may be bisyllabic. First note rises, second usually quavers, and final note rises then falls: "*woo whOOoOO whoOOoo*"; occasionally, last note is not included. Song of *bogotensis* (north of Amazon/east of Napo) may have a shorter descending middle note: "*woo HOO whoOOoo.*" Song of *chapmani* more forceful "*whee whi-whi-HEEOOO.*" Very similar to song of Ruddy, but usually deeper, and note different pattern. Call a rising growl: "*grrooOOW.*" **Co, E, Br, Bo**

2 RUDDY PIGEON *Patagioenas subvinacea* * 28–30.5 cm (11–12 in)

Fairly common and widespread in eastern lowlands, regular but somewhat less common up to 1900 m on east slope of Andes. Also rare in evergreen forest in Tumbes up to 800 m. Cf. Plumbeous Pigeon. **VOICE** Song a series of 4 coos, somewhat variable in delivery. First note rises, and last falls; internal notes variable: "*WOOP ah-WOOP oo*" ("hit the foul pole") or "*woop OOY-woop woo.*" Cf. Plumbeous. Growl call like that of Plumbeous. **Co, E, Br, Bo**

3 BAND-TAILED PIGEON *Patagioenas fasciata* * 35.5–37 cm (14–14½ in)

Fairly common and widespread in humid montane forest along east slope of Andes, 1000–3600 m; also in similar habitats on west slope, south locally to Lima. Usually in flocks (up to 30 individuals, occasionally more) that often remain within cover. Only arboreal pigeon of high altitudes; cf. Plumbeous and Ruddy of lower elevations. **VOICE** Song, quieter than most pigeons, a low coo with introductory note rising, but other long notes falling: "*WOO uh-wooh uh-wooh.*" **Co, E, Br, Bo**

4 SCALED PIGEON *Patagioenas speciosa* 33–35.5 cm (13–14 in)

Uncommon and local in eastern lowlands, at humid forest edge or along rivers, locally up to 1500 m; also rare (and perhaps seasonal) in semideciduous forest in Tumbes up to 800 m. Usually seen as singles or small groups, although may congregate in fruiting trees. Often perches conspicuously in bare branches of tall dead trees. Unmistakable when seen well, but cf. Pale-vented Pigeon (often found in same habitats). **VOICE** Song, deeper than other pigeons, a low cooing with the long notes rising: "*booOOO oo-booOO oo-booOO.*" **Co, E, Br, Bo**

5 PERUVIAN PIGEON *Patagioenas oenops* 30.5–33 cm (12–13 in)

Uncommon to locally fairly common, but entirely restricted to arid middle and upper Marañón Valley, 200–2400 m, where primarily found in riparian forest. Similar in behavior and appearance to Pale-vented Pigeon, but with limited geographic overlap; Peruvian is darker, undertail coverts are same color as belly (not paler), has solid-colored tail (no pale terminal band) and, at close range, bluish gray bill with red base. **VOICE** Song a mellow cooing: "*wooo wu-HOOoo wu-HOOoo wu-HOOoo wu-HOOoo*" or "*wooo wu-hoo-HOO wu-hoo-HOO....*" **E**

6 PALE-VENTED PIGEON *Patagioenas cayennensis* * 28–30.5 cm (11–12 in)

Common and widespread throughout most of eastern lowlands, locally up to 1600 m. A pigeon of forest edge and lake and river margins, where often congregates in flocks. Frequently seen in flight overhead, or perched in open on bare snags. Note gray wing coverts and rump, and pale belly and tail band. Very local in dry Chinchipe Valley, where may overlap with similar Peruvian Pigeon. **VOICE** Song a strident cooing: "*whooOOOoo up-up-whooOOoo up-up-whooOOoo.*" Call a rising, hoarse, hissing growl, not as loud or punctuated as Plumbeous and Ruddy pigeons: "*rrhhhAHH.*" **Co, E, Br, Bo**

PLUMBEOUS PIGEON

RUDDY PIGEON

BAND-TAILED PIGEON

SCALED PIGEON

PERUVIAN PIGEON

PALE-VENTED PIGEON

PLATE
65

ANDEAN AND PACIFIC-SLOPE PIGEONS
AND DOVES

Pigeons and doves on this plate are medium-sized to large species found on the coast or in more arid and open habitats of the Andes. Pigeons and doves characteristically bob the head while walking. Sexes usually are similar, although many species also have some iridescence on the sides of the neck, which typically is stronger in males. Flight usually is strong and direct.

1 SPOT-WINGED PIGEON *Patagioenas maculosa* * 33–34 cm (13–13½ in)
Locally fairly common in southern Andes, 2500–4100 m, locally down to 1200 m on west slope; rare as far north as Lima. Found in light woods and scrub in river valleys on west slope of Andes, and in intermontane valleys; not present on more humid east slope of Andes. Usually in small flocks. Often feeds on ground. Note large size, pale color, scaled upperparts, and white wing band (particularly visible in flight). **VOICE** Song (Argentina) a gruff "*rrrrrow grr-g'RRRR grr-g'RRRR grr-g'RRRR.*" Call a short growl. **Br, Bo**

2 BARE-FACED GROUND-DOVE *Metriopelia ceciliae* * 17–18 cm (6½–7 in)
Fairly common and widespread on west slope of Andes and in intermontane valleys at 1700–4100 m. also present locally at 500–1000 m on west slope of southern Andes and in Marañón Valley. Found in montane scrub, usually in semiarid areas, and often in villages; not present on more humid east slope of Andes. Social, often in small flocks. Note short tail, heavily spotted upperparts, conspicuous yellow-orange skin surrounding eye, and pale tips to outer rectrices. Wings produce a rattling or ringing whistle when flushed. **Bo, Ch**

3 EARED DOVE *Zenaida auriculata* * 25.5–26 cm (10–10¼ in)
Common and widespread on coast, west slope of Andes, and in intermontane valleys, up to 4000 m. Usually very rare on east slope of Andes, although locally fairly common in dry Huallaga Valley; very rare vagrant to Amazonia. Typically found in open, semiarid areas, in fields and scrub, and in towns. Social, often found in flocks. Note slender shape, long tail, and black spotting on wings and neck. Larger and longer tailed than ground-doves (but in Andes, cf. Black-winged Ground-Dove). Also cf. White-tipped Dove. **VOICE** Song a gruff series of deep descending coos, last notes inaudible at a distance: "*hooWHOO hoo-hoo-hoo.*" Wings whistle when flushed. **Co, E, Br, Bo, Ch**

4 WEST PERUVIAN DOVE *Zenaida meloda* 28.5–31 cm (11¼–12 in)
Common to abundant on coast and west slope of Andes, locally up to 1000 m. Found in fields, gardens, and open woodland; where not disturbed can be a conspicuous member of the urban avifauna (and is the common pigeon of Lima). Social, and often seen in flocks flying high overhead. Large and stocky (almost pigeon-sized), with prominent white patch on wing coverts (especially visible in flight). Also note blue facial skin. **VOICE** 2 song patterns, both composed of very deep notes. In one song (source of local name "*cuculí*"), first notes are even in pitch, followed by louder and higher final note: "*oo... oo-LOO.*" Second song type a longer series of deep coos: "*oo-LOO HOO oo-LOO HOO oo-LOO.*" Familiar sound in coastal cities. Wings whistle when flushed. **Co, E, Ch**

5 GOLDEN-SPOTTED GROUND-DOVE *Metriopelia aymara* 18–19 cm (7–7½ in)
Fairly common in arid puna grassland, fields, and villages in southern Andes, 3100–4500 m; less common and local north to central Peru in similar habitats. Has short-tailed, compact build of Bare-faced Ground-Dove but color is superficially similar to Black-winged. Also lacks bare facial skin and white wing marks of Black-winged; at close range, note small gold spots on wing coverts (more prominent on male). Also, bases of primaries rufous, especially on undersurface (but this rarely visible in field). Wings produce a ringing rattle when flushed. **Bo, Ch**

6 BLACK-WINGED GROUND-DOVE *Metriopelia melanoptera* * 21–23 cm (8–9 in)
Fairly common and widespread in semiarid high Andes, 2600–4500 m; very rare vagrant to coast. Found in montane scrub, including *Polylepis*, and puna grasslands; sometimes present in towns and villages. Usually encountered as singles, pairs, or small groups. Note drab plumage, relatively long dark tail (no white), small area of bare skin below eye, and small whitish area on fore edge of wing (innermost lesser wing coverts). **VOICE** Quiet. Song a peculiar, ringing "*p'churreeeu.*" Wings whistle when flushed. **Co, E, Bo, Ch**

SPOT-WINGED PIGEON

EARED DOVE

BARE-FACED GROUND-DOVE

GOLDEN-SPOTTED GROUND-DOVE

WEST PERUVIAN DOVE

BLACK-WINGED
GROUND-DOVE

PLATE
66

ROCK PIGEON AND *COLUMBINA* GROUND-DOVES

Rock Pigeon is a familiar bird of urban environments worldwide. Ground-doves (Columbina, Claravis, and Metriopelia) are small doves that feed on the ground; most are found in open habitats, but a few occupy forest or forest edge. Most ground-doves are sexually dimorphic in plumage, although only in Claravis are the differences pronounced.

ROCK PIGEON (Rock Dove) *Columba livia* 33–35.5 cm (13–14 in)

Not native to Peru; a common human commensal, familiar to any city-dweller, expected almost anywhere in towns and cities but rarely away from human settlements. "Wild" type is largely gray with dark hood, dark bars on wing coverts and remiges, and white rump, but feral populations show stunning variety of plumages. Highly gregarious. **VOICE** Song, remarkably quiet for a pigeon, is a muffled, pulsing, cooing series, the first 2 notes rising and modulated, followed by a falling note: "*o'o'o'o-o'o'o'oop COOoo.*" The song is usually given while the male parades around a female with his neck inflated. Nestlings give a rasping call when begging. **Co, E, Br, Bo, Ch**

1 PICUI GROUND-DOVE *Columbina picui* * 18–19 cm (7–7½ in)

Uncommon to fairly common austral migrant to southern Amazonia (north to southern Ucayali); much less common north to northern Ucayali. Occurs up to 600 m. Present at least Jun–Sep (but probably arrives as early as Apr or May, and remains until Oct). Behavior and habitat similar to that of Ruddy Ground-Dove: singles, pairs, or small groups forage on ground in open areas such as pastures and gardens. Note drab plumage with little or no spotting, relatively long tail, and white greater wing coverts (particularly prominent in flight). **VOICE** Perhaps does not sing in Peru. Song (Bolivia) is a rapid series of bisyllabic coos: "*cuLOO-cuLOO-cuLOO....*" **Co, Br, Bo, Ch**

2 ECUADORIAN GROUND-DOVE *Columbina buckleyi* * 16.5–18 cm (6½–7 in)

Fairly common in open forest and scrub in arid middle and upper Marañón Valley, 200–1000 m (*dorsti*); also uncommon in similar habitats in Tumbes and northern Piura below 600 m (*buckleyi*). A pale version of Ruddy Ground-Dove. *Buckleyi* (not illustrated) is particularly gray, *dorsti* is rosier. Larger, longer tailed, and more heavily spotted than Plain-breasted Ground-Dove and has black (not rufous) remiges and underwing coverts. **VOICE** Songs of both subspecies similar, a series of bisyllabic coos: "*hi-WHOOP hi-WHOOP hi-WHOOP....*" Probably indistinguishable from song of Ruddy. **E**

3 RUDDY GROUND-DOVE *Columbina talpacoti* * 16.5–18 cm (6½–7 in)

Fairly common and widespread in eastern lowlands up to 800 m, in pastures, towns, forest edge, and river margins. Usually seen as pairs or small flocks foraging on ground in open areas. Most widespread ground-dove in Amazonia. Male unmistakable. Female usually sufficiently reddish to be readily identifiable, but cf. Plain-breasted and female Blue ground-doves. **VOICE** Song is a series of (usually) bisyllabic coos: "*cu-WHOOP cu-WHOOP cu-WHOOP cu-WHOOP....*" Probably indistinguishable from song of Ecuadorian Ground-Dove. **Co, E, Br, Bo, Ch**

4 PLAIN-BREASTED GROUND-DOVE *Columbina minuta* * 15.5–16 cm (6–6¼ in)

Uncommon and local; patchily distributed on coast of northern Peru and in intermontane valleys up to 2300 m, and very locally in scrubby areas in northern Amazonia. Typically found as singles or pairs in very open habitats, often with bare soil exposed and little ground vegetation. Very small, drab, and relatively short-tailed; more lightly spotted above than Ruddy or Ecuadorian ground-doves, and with no rufescent tones to body plumage. Inner webs of remiges rufous, visible in flight; underwing coverts also rufous (black in other *Columbina*). **VOICE** Song a series of soft, rising monosyllabic coos: "*whooOOP... whooOOP... whooOOP....*" **Co, E, Br, Bo**

5 CROAKING GROUND-DOVE *Columbina cruziana* 16.5–18 cm (6½–7 in)

Common and conspicuous in western Peru, up to 2800 m on west slope of Andes, and locally in dry intermontane valleys (Marañón, upper Huallaga, Mantaro, and Pampas). Found in a wide variety of open habitats, including gardens, parks, fields, and scrub. Often social and seen in small flocks. Both sexes readily identifiable by conspicuous yellow-orange fleshy base to bill and by dark bar (chestnut, in good light) on scapulars. **VOICE** Song a very undovelike series of flatulent notes, descending slightly in pitch: "*gWOW gwow gwo.*" Sometimes only single notes given. Apparent aggressive call a quiet dry growl. **E, Ch**

color var.

"wild" type

ROCK PIGEON

PICUI GROUND-DOVE

♀

♂

ECUADORIAN
GROUND-DOVE

♀

♂

RUDDY GROUND-DOVE

♀

♂

PLAIN-BREASTED GROUND-DOVE

♀

♂

CROAKING GROUND-DOVE

PLATE
67

CLARAVIS GROUND-DOVES AND LEPTOTILA DOVES

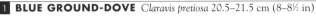

Claravis are the most sexually dimorphic doves; less social and conspicuous than other ground-doves. Leptotila are large, heavy-bodied doves of forest and edge; usually are solitary and feed on ground inside cover. All are drab and brown, with rufous or chestnut underwings (often obvious in flight) and relatively long, broad tails with white tips to outer rectrices.

1 BLUE GROUND-DOVE *Claravis pretiosa* 20.5–21.5 cm (8–8½ in)
Widespread in eastern Peru below 1300 m, but uncommon. Also uncommon in Tumbes and Piura below 600 m. Singles or pairs forage on ground at edge of humid forest, in second-growth or river-edge forest; never far from cover. Light powder-blue male unmistakable. Duller female less distinctive; larger than *Columbina* ground-doves, with unspotted plumage, and redder tail contrasting with brown body. Wing coverts spotted with chestnut (not black). Cf. female Maroon-chested. **VOICE** Song a series of loud coos, usually in pairs, second note slightly lower than first: "POOP POOP... POOP POOP...." **Co, E, Br, Bo**

2 MAROON-CHESTED GROUND-DOVE *Claravis mondetoura* * 21.5–23 cm (8½–9 in)
Rare and local in humid montane forest, 1700–3000 m; primarily occurs on east slope of Andes, but also very local on west slope in Piura. Apparently nomadic. Usually found near seeding bamboo; very rarely encountered in forest interior away from bamboo. Usually solitary or in pairs. Male unmistakable. Female similar to female Blue Ground-Dove of lowlands but has buffy face, is browner below (especially on flanks and belly), has broader purplish (not chestnut) bars on wing coverts and white tips to outer rectrices. **VOICE** Song a series of bisyllabic rising coos: "pa'WOO...pa'WOO...pa'WOO." **Co, E, Bo**

3 [PALLID DOVE *Leptotila pallida*] 26–27.5 cm (10¼–10¾ in)
Only in evergreen forests in Tumbes up to 900 m, where fairly common. More restricted to forest interior and to more humid forests than White-tipped. Compared to White-tipped, note more rufous upperparts, gray nape and crown, and contrast between gray crown and pale forehead; head and neck of White-tipped are more uniformly colored and lack strong contrast. Cf. also Ochre-bellied. **VOICE** Song a nearly monotone coo, swelling, then dying at a pace of about a note every 3–5 sec: "oooOOOOooo." **Co, E**

4 WHITE-TIPPED DOVE *Leptotila verreauxi* * 26.5–28 cm (10½–11 in)
Fairly common in woods and forests on west slope of northern Andes, and in dry middle and upper Marañón Valley (*decolor*), up to 2700 m. Fairly common on east slope of Andes, 600–2000 m, locally down to lowlands; also enters some drier intermontane valleys (*decipiens*). In east primarily found at forest edge; in northeastern Loreto largely restricted to river islands. Relatively pale *Leptotila* with no strong facial pattern. Bare orbital skin reddish in *decolor*, bluish in *decipiens*. **VOICE** Song (*decolor*) a monotone pair of coos: "HOO-HOO"; at close range preceded with short "pup" note. Song of *decipiens* more leisurely, second note more drawn out and falling then rising: "oo hooOOOoo." Sometimes omits first note. Similar to Gray-fronted Dove, but delivery is slower, with a note every 10 sec or longer. **Co, E, Br, Bo**

5 GRAY-FRONTED DOVE *Leptotila rufaxilla* * 26–27.5 cm (10¼–10¾ in)
Fairly common and widespread in eastern lowlands, up to 1200 m, locally to 1700 m. Primarily at edge of humid forest, in river-edge forest, and on river-islands; also enters forest interior, especially along streams. Overlaps with similar White-tipped Dove, but is more widespread in Amazonia. Also is more richly colored, with buffy (not light grayish brown) sides to face and greater contrast between gray crown and white forehead. At close range, orbital skin is reddish (blue in Amazonian White-tipped). **VOICE** Song is a series of descending coos, normally delivered at about a note every 5 sec: "whooOOOoo." In Amazonia song of White-tipped similar, but delivery slower and usually with 2 notes. **Co, E, Br, Bo**

6 OCHRE-BELLIED DOVE *Leptotila ochraceiventris* 26–27.5 cm (10¼–10¾ in)
Locally fairly common in evergreen and semideciduous forest in Tumbes and northern Piura, above 600 m. Also found (locally?) up to 2600 m south along slopes of Andes to eastern Piura, where much rarer. Compared to Pallid and White-tipped doves, is much buffier and more uniformly colored. **VOICE** Song is a gruff, descending note: "WHOOoo." At a distance, may be confused with first note of Eared Dove song. **E**

BLUE GROUND-DOVE

♀

♂

PALLID DOVE

♀

♂

MAROON-CHESTED GROUND-DOVE

WHITE-TIPPED DOVE

decipiens

decolor

OCHRE-BELLIED DOVE

GRAY-FRONTED DOVE

PLATE
68

QUAIL-DOVES AND RED-FAN PARROT

Quail-doves are solitary terrestrial doves of forest interior. They are relatively large, with heavy bodies and short tails. Often not seen until they flush off a forest trail, like a small tinamou. Usually sing from a low concealed perch. Parrots are familiar social birds that feed on seeds and fruit. They are found throughout Peru but are most common and most diverse in forested areas of Amazonia. All species nest in cavities. Highly gregarious, but usually travel in single-species flocks. Several species may congregate in fruiting trees, however, or at clay licks (colpas), where parrots descend to the ground, sometimes in large numbers, to eat soil. Many species commonly are kept in captivity, much to the detriment of wild populations; the larger species in particular have declined or disappeared from much of their former range. Red-fan Parrot is unusual, with a very restricted distribution in Peru.

VIOLACEOUS QUAIL-DOVE *Geotrygon violacea* * 21.5–24 cm (8½–9½ in)
Very poorly known in Peru; apparently very local and patchily distributed in central and southern Amazonia, but perhaps more widespread there in hilly terrain. Found in interior of humid forest. Does not show a malar stripe; also is much paler below than Ruddy Ground-Dove and has whitish forehead and throat. Superficially may resemble a *Leptotila* dove, but the shorter tail lacks white tips to outer rectrices, and has short, reddish bill (bills of *Leptotila* are black). Also, in duller female, note contrast between brown wing coverts and back, and reddish brown remiges and tail. **VOICE** Song (eastern Brazil) a high hollow coo, descending, then rising slightly at the very end: "*heeOOOe.*" **Co, E, Br, Bo**

1 RUDDY QUAIL-DOVE *Geotrygon montana* * 21.5–24 cm (8½–9½ in)
Uncommon to fairly common in eastern lowlands, up to 1750 m; the most widespread quail-dove in Amazonian Peru. Found in interior of humid forest. Male readily recognized by overall reddish brown color and striped sides to face. Female is much duller and browner; facial pattern usually is apparent, but shape and dull brown color alone are sufficient for identification. **VOICE** Song is a deep, even-pitched or descending coo, dying away at the end at a pace of about a note every 3 sec: "*wooOOOoooo.*" **Co, E, Br, Bo**

2 SAPPHIRE QUAIL-DOVE *Geotrygon saphirina* * 23–24 cm (9–9½ in)
Uncommon and patchily distributed in eastern lowlands, up to 1000 m. Found in terra firme, usually in hilly terrain or on lower slopes of Andes; may favor stream margins. Lovely iridescent colors of upperparts may be difficult to discern in dim light, but note whitish face and underparts, and consequently more contrasting facial pattern. **VOICE** Song is a high, 2-note coo, the second descending slightly: "*hu HEEOOO.*" Reminiscent of songs of Ochre-striped and Elusive antpittas. **Co, E, Br**

3 WHITE-THROATED QUAIL-DOVE *Geotrygon frenata* * 29.5–32 cm (11½–12½ in)
Uncommon but widespread in humid montane forest along east slope of Andes, 1000–3300 m; also present in similar habitats on west slope of the Andes, south at least to southern Lambayeque. Found at higher elevations than other quail-doves. Note large size, dull gray-brown plumage, narrow black malar stripe, and gray crown. **VOICE** Song is a deep, slightly descending coo at a pace of about a note every 3–5 sec: "*HOOoo.*" Similar to other quail-doves, but notes shorter. **Co, E, Bo**

4 RED-FAN PARROT *Deroptyus accipitrinus* * 33–35 cm (13–14 in)
Rare and local in Peru, where restricted to sandy-soil, blackwater areas of upper Río Pastaza and middle Río Yavarí. Very long-tailed. Plumage dark, with dull white forecrown. Long nape feathers usually held flat, but may be raised in a frill. Usually seen in pairs or small flocks. Flight not high but very distinctive, a mix of shallow wingbeats interrupted with short glides; flight style and long-tailed appearance recall an *Accipiter* hawk in flight. **VOICE** Flight calls include high, rising, ringing "*keeeut*" or "*chut*" notes and piercing whistles; also various conversational vocalizations. **Co, E, Br**

VIOLACEOUS QUAIL-DOVE

♀

♂

RUDDY
QUAIL-DOVE

♂

♀

SAPPHIRE QUAIL-DOVE

RED-FAN PARROT

WHITE-THROATED
QUAIL-DOVE

PLATE
69
MACAWS

Macaws are the largest Peruvian parrots, although smaller species are scarcely larger than some Aratinga *parakeets (plate 70). Tail long; face largely bare (except for Blue-headed Macaw). Flight strong and direct. Largest species have notably loud, harsh calls; most of the smaller species have much quieter voices. All also have quieter, "conversational" vocalizations.*

1 BLUE-AND-YELLOW MACAW *Ara ararauna* 81.5–86.5 cm (32–34 in)
Widespread in Amazonia up to 800 m, but increasingly scarce; locally remains fairly common in more remote areas, especially in Madre de Dios. Typically found in low-lying forest, including varzea, swamp forest, and especially *Mauritia* palm swamps (*aguajales*). Occasionally seen flying high over cleared areas and major rivers; probably nomadic. Usually found in small flocks, but occasionally in large groups. Unmistakable. **VOICE** Flight call a loud rasping screech, loudest and often with a stuttering effect at the end "g'RAA'A'AH!"; also a loud braying. Somewhat fuller and more nasal than voices of Scarlet and Red-and-green. **Co, E, Br, Bo**

2 RED-BELLIED MACAW *Orthopsittaca manilata* 46–48 cm (18–19 in)
Locally common throughout Amazonia up to 650 m. Associated with swamps and flooded forests, particularly *Mauritia* palm swamps. Often in flocks of up to 30 individuals (occasionally more). Small, with bare yellowish face and yellowish underwings; red belly difficult to see. **VOICE** Flight call a distinctive high-pitched, weak, almost pleasant, rolling "*greeeah*"; also a more braying series. **Co, E, Br, Bo**

3 SCARLET MACAW *Ara macao* * 84–91.5 cm (33–36 in)
Formerly widespread throughout Amazonia, up to 850 m; now scarce and declining, although locally uncommon in more remote areas (especially in Madre de Dios). Not very gregarious; usually in pairs or small groups of 4–6. Paler than similar Red-and-green, and face whiter (not crossed by distinct feathered lines), with yellow coverts on upper side of wing. Tail also slightly longer; tip may wobble up and down in flight. **VOICE** Flight call a loud rasping screech "*RAAAH!*"; loudest near middle and descending at end. Also braying vocalizations. Similar to other large macaws, but with particularly unpleasant screeching quality. **Co, E, Br, Bo**

4 MILITARY MACAW *Ara militaris* * 66–71 cm (26–28 in)
Locally fairly common, but largely restricted to east slope of Andes and outlying ridges, 600–1500 m; occasionally wanders higher or lower. Formerly local on west slope in northwest (only a seasonal visitor?), but apparently no longer occurs there. Associated with cliffs on steep ridges, usually in humid montane forest but locally in drier valleys. Little overlap with much smaller Chestnut-fronted, which also has red underwings. **VOICE** Flight call a loud screeching "*RAAH!*"; similar to other large macaws, but perhaps a little thinner, rising at end. **Co, E, Bo**

5 CHESTNUT-FRONTED MACAW *Ara severus* * 48–50 cm (19–19½ in)
Widespread and fairly common in east, up to 1000 m, primarily in forest bordering rivers, oxbow lakes, and clearings. Usually in pairs, occasionally in small flocks (up to 10 individuals); larger numbers (20–40) may congregate in feeding areas and roosts. Often found in isolated trees in small clearings, usually not far from rivers. Note reddish underwings. Larger than *Aratinga* parakeets; cf. Military and Red-bellied macaws. **VOICE** Flight calls rasping screeches, higher pitched, faster, and more braying than other macaws. Also a characteristic gobbling conversational vocalization. **Co, E, Br, Bo**

6 RED-AND-GREEN MACAW *Ara chloropterus* 89–96.5 cm (35–38 in)
Widespread in central and southern Peru below 1000 m. Populations declining, especially near populated areas; uncommon or absent from much of north. Typically in terra firme; less common than other macaws along large rivers. Usually in pairs or small groups. Cf. Scarlet Macaw. **VOICE** Flight call a loud rasping screech "*RAAAH!*" Very similar to Scarlet Macaw, but perhaps more nasal and not as unpleasant; also braying vocalizations. **Co, E, Br, Bo**

7 BLUE-HEADED MACAW *Primolius couloni* 44–47 cm (17¼–18½ in)
Uncommon to locally fairly common below 1500 m; largely restricted to Peru. Perhaps most common in forested hilly terrain and on outlying ridges. Possibly partly nomadic. Typically in pairs or small flocks (3–8). Small; may be confused at a distance with Red-bellied (or perhaps Chestnut-fronted), but head is dark and entirely feathered, with contrasting white iris; bill paler. Also note different **VOICE** Flight call a distinctive, fairly mellow, rolling "*graaaaa*," often in series, but not braying. **Br, Bo**

BLUE-AND-YELLOW MACAW

RED-BELLIED MACAW

MILITARY MACAW

SCARLET MACAW

CHESTNUT-FRONTED MACAW

RED-AND-GREEN MACAW

BLUE-HEADED MACAW

PLATE
70

RED-SHOULDERED MACAW AND *ARATINGA* PARAKEETS

Red-shouldered Macaw is similar to Aratinga *but has extensive bare facial skin.* Aratinga *have long graduated tails but are smaller than macaws, with only a narrow ring of bare skin surrounding eye. Most are more gregarious than macaws. Flight direct and rapid, and usually well above canopy. Most have conversational notes in addition to flight calls.*

1 RED-SHOULDERED MACAW *Diopsittaca nobilis* * 33–34 cm (13–13½ in)

Uncommon on Pampas del Heath, in forest bordering savanna; also reported from sites to north and west, and may be spreading. Gregarious, often in noisy flocks of 20–30 birds. Smallest macaw; distinguished from White-eyed Parakeet by slightly larger size, bare face, red carpal mark, and lack of yellow on underwings. **VOICE** Flight calls distinctive: short, rolling barks, often in series "*greh greh greh....*" **Br, Bo**

2 WHITE-EYED PARAKEET *Aratinga leucophthalma* * 31–33 cm (12¼–13 in)

Fairly common and widespread throughout Amazonia; locally (or seasonally?) also up to 1700 m in Andes. Mainly in river-edge forest and forest edges; rarely forages in terra firme but often heard flying over it. Typically in small flocks, occasionally in pairs. Green, with small and variable amount of red flecking on sides of head and neck; bend of wing and lesser underwing coverts red, greater underwing coverts bright yellow. Immature mostly green, with little or no red and yellow on underwings. **VOICE** Flight calls rolling screeches "*curee'ee'ee*" and short braying series. **Co, E, Br, Bo**

3 MITRED PARAKEET *Aratinga mitrata* * 34–38 cm (13–15 in)

Very similar to Scarlet-fronted Parakeet in appearance and behavior, but more associated with humid forests on east slope of Andes, 1600–3400 m; also enters more humid portions of intermontane valleys, and locally approaches or overlaps Scarlet-fronted. There is a possible difference in orbital ring color: yellowish or creamy in Scarlet-fronted, white in Mitred. Lacks red in wing. In south (north at least to Cuzco) often has extensive red frontal patch, with ragged border, and scattered red feathers on sides of neck and breast. Red restricted to forecrown on other individuals, especially in northern and central Peru, and on immatures; much more similar to Scarlet-fronted, but lacks red in wing, and some individuals lack red tibial feathering. **VOICE** Flight call a high ringing "*kerEET*" or "*krEET*"; also some braying phrases. **Bo**

4 RED-MASKED PARAKEET *Aratinga erythrogenys* 29–31 cm (11½–12¼ in)

Fairly common but declining in northwest, below 700 m; locally up to 1700 m. Also a feral population in Lima, where occurs up to 2400 m. Found in dry and riparian forests; also attracted to orchards and cornfields. Slightly smaller than Scarlet-fronted Parakeet, with more extensive red on head (red extending below eye, and often behind eye as well), and entirely red underwing coverts. Immature has little or no red on head, and green underwing coverts; identify by accompanying adults. **VOICE** Flight calls rolling "*jeer*" screams and low braying phrases. **E**

5 SCARLET-FRONTED PARAKEET *Aratinga wagleri* * 36–40 cm (14–15¾ in)

Locally fairly common but patchily distributed, below 3000 m. Widespread in Marañón Valley; local on west slope of Andes and in dry Pampas Valley. Also a feral population in Lima. Found in dry and semihumid forest; visits fields (especially corn) and orchards. Red forecrown restricted to relatively narrow band. Adult has narrow band of red on fore edge of underwing coverts (visible in flight, and also often visible on closed wing), often has red on lesser wing coverts, and has red tibial feathers. Immature has less red on head and may lack red on wings and legs. Usually found at higher elevations than Red-masked Parakeet; compare carefully to Mitred Parakeet. **VOICE** Flight calls short, nasal "*keh-keh*" notes. **Co, E**

6 DUSKY-HEADED PARAKEET *Aratinga weddellii* 23.5–27 cm (9¼–10½ in)

Common and widespread in eastern lowlands, below 700 m, in river-edge forest, varzea, forest edge, and second growth; rarely more than a few hundred meters from a river. Usually in small, noisy flocks of 6–10 individuals (uncommonly larger groups of 20–30); typically twists from side to side in flight. Also attracted to seeding bamboo thickets, where large numbers may gather. Much smaller than White-eyed Parakeet, usually in smaller flocks and flying lower over the forest. **VOICE** Flight calls thin rusty notes "*kree-kree*" and rasping brays. Higher pitched and more annoying than White-eyed. **Co, E, Br, Bo**

RED-SHOULDERED
MACAW

imm.

ad.

WHITE-EYED PARAKEET

imm.

ad.

MITRED PARAKEET

imm.

ad.

RED-MASKED
PARAKEET

imm.

ad.

SCARLET-FRONTED PARAKEET

DUSKY-HEADED
PARAKEET

PLATE
71

PYRRHURA PARAKEETS AND PEACH-FRONTED PARAKEET

Peach-fronted Parakeet is an Aratinga *that barely enters Peru.* Pyrrhura *are green parakeets with long, graduated tails. Smaller than most* Aratinga, *with reddish or purplish undersides to tail. Unlike other parakeets, fly rapidly in small, close flocks through the canopy or subcanopy, coming into open only at forest edge or when darting across a small river. Usually only a single species occurs at a site, although locally 2 species may overlap.*

1 WAVY-BREASTED PARAKEET *Pyrrhura peruviana* 22 cm (8½ in)

Very poorly known. Reported from two disjunct areas: foothills of Andes in northwest Amazonia, south to south bank of the Marañón; and in upper Apurímac Valley. Found below 1650 m. Approaches or may meet Painted Parakeet on lower Huallaga. Very similar to Painted, with dark brown crown and pale buffy brown sides to head; but lacks any red on forecrown, which is washed with light blue (would be very difficult to see in field, however). Also, pale tips to breast feathers are broader. **E**

2 ROSE-FRONTED PARAKEET *Pyrrhura roseifrons* 21–23 cm (8¼–9 in)

Fairly common and widespread below 1500 m in eastern lowlands and foothills south of Marañón and Amazon, although local in south (where perhaps more confined to near base of Andes). Extent of red on head variable, but typically very extensive; always light orange- or pinkish red in tone. Locally overlaps with Rock Parakeet in south. **VOICE** Flight call rolling bursts "*prrrt prrrt*"; also screeches and other conversational vocalizations. **Br, Bo**

3 PAINTED PARAKEET *Pyrrhura picta* * 22 cm (8½ in)

Very poorly known; distribution and taxonomic status not settled. Probably not conspecific with nominate Painted Parakeet of the Guianas. Very local on south bank of the Amazon, and from lower Río Huallaga southeast to lower Río Ucayali. Identified by dark crown, paler sides to face, and narrow scarlet red forecrown. Cf. very similar Wavy-breasted Parakeet. Rose-fronted has more extensive red on head, and red is orangish or pinkish, not scarlet. **Co, E, Br**

4 MAROON-TAILED PARAKEET *Pyrrhura melanura* * 23–24 cm (9–9½ in)

Uncommon in humid forests of eastern lowlands north of the Amazon, locally crossing to south bank of the Amazon along both banks of lower Huallaga; up to 1350 m in foothills of Andes. Note red fore edge of wing, green belly and sides of face, and dull crown (mixed green and black). Extent of pale scaling on breast variable, reaching greatest extent in birds of upper Huallaga Valley (*berlepschi*). Immature mostly green (lacks red in wing). No overlap with similar Rock Parakeet. **VOICE** Flight calls (nominate?) descending grating screeches. *Berlepschi* has short, more mellow "*pew*" and "*grr*" notes, not as screechy in quality. **Co, E, Br**

5 WHITE-NECKED PARAKEET *Pyrrhura albipectus* 24–25.5 cm (9½–10 in)

Barely enters Peru; known only from a few sites in the Cordillera del Cóndor at ca. 1800 m (in Ecuador, known from 900 to 1800 m). Found in humid montane forest. Wing and tail pattern similar to Maroon-tailed, and beware of light-breasted examples of that species; but note White-necked Parakeet's orangey yellow sides to face. **VOICE** Flight calls mellow, rolling "*jeer*," often doubled; also conversational screeches. **E**

6 ROCK (Black-capped) PARAKEET *Pyrrhura rupicola* * 23.5–25 cm (9¼–9¾ in)

Uncommon to locally fairly common in lowlands and Andean foothills of central and southern Peru, up to 2000 m. Similar to Maroon-tailed Parakeet of north (no overlap), but crown more uniformly dusky and upper side of tail entirely green; also may have some red feathering on belly. Extent of scaling on breast is variable; breast may appear dusky heavily scaled off-white, or (especially in Andes) breast is almost entirely buffy (broader pale feather tips). **VOICE** Flight call thin, rolling, rising screeches "*jiree*"; also thin rusty creaks. Montane birds sound similar. **Br, Bo**

7 PEACH-FRONTED PARAKEET *Aratinga aurea* 23–28 cm (9–11 in)

Only known from the Pampas del Heath, where fairly common in open savanna with clumps of bushes and short trees. Often seen in pairs or small flocks (4–8). Generally forages in tall weeds, bushes, and short trees, occasionally on ground; also in canopy of woodland bordering grassland. Similar to Dusky-headed Parakeet, with which it occurs, but smaller; orange on crown diagnostic. **VOICE** Flight call rolling nasal "*curr'r'r-curr'r'r*" series. Deeper than other Amazonian *Aratinga* calls, more like small macaws. **Br, Bo**

ROSE-FRONTED PARAKEET

ROSE-FRONTED PARAKEET

WAVY-BREASTED PARAKEET

imm.

ad.

PAINTED PARAKEET

MAROON-TAILED PARAKEET

imm.

ad.

MAROON-TAILED PARAKEET

ad. *berlepschi*

WHITE-NECKED PARAKEET

ROCK PARAKEET

PEACH-FRONTED PARAKEET

PLATE
72

ANDEAN AND PACIFIC-SLOPE PARAKEETS AND PARROTLETS

All species on this plate are small to very small parrots. Gray-cheeked Parakeet is a coastal representative of Brotogeris, *which also is represented in Peru by 3 Amazonian species (plate 73). Andean, Mountain, and Barred parakeets are Andean. Pacific and Yellow-faced parrotlets occur on coast and in Marañón Valley; two other species of* Forpus *parrotlets occur in Amazonia (plate 73).*

1 **GRAY-CHEEKED PARAKEET** *Brotogeris pyrrhoptera* 19.5–21 cm (7½–8¼ in)

Locally fairly common, but declining, in semideciduous forest below 900 m in Tumbes, and, less commonly, in northern Piura. Usually seen in pairs and small flocks. Feeds on flowers and seeds of large trees. Orange underwing coverts are prominent in flight. **VOICE** Flight calls include a low rolling *"jurt"* as well as a series of scratchy calls; also conversational vocalizations including calls given in rapid duet between members of a pair. **E**

2 **PACIFIC PARROTLET** *Forpus coelestis* 12–13 cm (4–5 in)

Common in northwest and in middle Marañón Valley, up to 2100 m. Found in arid scrub, forest edge, and fields; also may be found in towns and villages. Feral population also now established in Lima. The only parrotlet in its range (but see Yellow-faced Parrotlet in Marañón Valley). Green of plumage is washed with light gray, especially on upperparts; also note powder-blue nape of male. **VOICE** Flight calls include high, ringing *"tchit"* notes, rapidly delivered. **E**

3 **YELLOW-FACED PARROTLET** *Forpus xanthops* 13–14 cm (5–5½ in)

Locally fairly common, but perhaps declining, in upper Marañón Valley, 600–2000 m, where is the only parrotlet present; ranges of Pacific and Yellow-faced parrotlets presumably meet somewhere in Marañón Valley, but such contact has not yet been discovered. Similar to Pacific Parrotlet, but head is yellower (rather than yellowish green as in Pacific), and underparts are greener (less washed with gray, as in Pacific). Also, rump of female is blue (bluish green in female Pacific); blue of wings and rump of male Yellow-faced is brighter than in male Pacific, but blue behind eye is paler and less conspicuous. **VOICE** Flight calls include high, ringing *"tjeet"* notes, rapidly delivered. **ENDEMIC**

4 **BARRED PARAKEET** *Bolborhynchus lineola* * 16–17 cm (6¼–7 in)

Rare to uncommon in humid montane forest on east slope of Andes, 900–3300 m; recorded from few localities, but easily overlooked and also may be at least partly nomadic. May be associated with seeding bamboo. Difficult to see (especially perched); usually observed in small flocks in flight high above canopy. Note small size and relatively short, graduated tail; does not undulate in flight. **VOICE** Flight call a characteristic low, mellow, rolling *"juree."* **Co, E**

5 **ANDEAN PARAKEET** *Bolborhynchus orbygnesius* 17–18 cm (6¼–7 in)

Uncommon to locally fairly common in Andes, 2400–3900 m. Found in montane scrub in intermontane valleys, and, locally, on east slope of Andes. Usually occupies sites that are more humid than those in which Mountain Parakeet is found; only rarely do the two species overlap. Usually in small flocks; does not undulate in flight. Superficially similar to Mountain, but heavier bodied, with shorter, blunter tail, little blue in wings, and grayish bill. **VOICE** Flight calls include a rapid fussy chatter: *"jit jit jit..."* or *"jujuju"*; also a squeaky *"kyu kyu."* **Bo**

6 **MOUNTAIN PARAKEET** *Psilopsiagon aurifrons* * 17–19 cm (7–8 in)

Widespread and locally fairly common in Andes, up to 3100 m; in montane scrub and open habitats, primarily on west slope of Andes and in intermontane valleys, also in Titicaca Basin at 3450–4200 m. May feed on ground. Social, usually in small flocks. Flight undulating. Note small size and relatively long graduated tail; bill typically pale (but may be gray or grayish in females, especially of *margaritae*). Male plumage varies geographically. Male has yellow face and upper throat in Marañón Valley (*robertsi*); variably but often extensively yellow below on west slope of Andes (*aurifrons*), where amount of yellow is greatest in northern areas but is reduced in extent (mostly limited to face) in south; and is mostly green in Titicaca Basin (*margaritae*). Female mostly green in all subspecies. **VOICE** Flight calls include high, squeaky, House Sparrow-like chirps: *"jirt."* Occasionally interspersed with low squeaky notes. **Bo, Ch**

GRAY-CHEEKED
PARAKEET

PACIFIC
PARROTLET

♂

♀

♂

♀

YELLOW-FACED
PARROTLET

BARRED PARAKEET

ANDEAN
PARAKEET

♂ *robertsi*

♂ *aurifrons*

♂ *margaritae*

♀

MOUNTAIN PARAKEET

PLATE
73

SMALL AMAZONIAN PARAKEETS AND PARROTLETS

All species on this plate are small to medium-sized Amazonian parrots. Forpus parrotlets are very small, very short-tailed parrots, and are sexually dimorphic: males have blue in the wings and on the rump, whereas females are much greener. Amazonian Parrotlet (Nannopsittaca) is similar, but is slightly larger, and the sexes are similar. Brotogeris parakeets are highly social parakeets of low elevations, with moderately long, graduated tails. Brotogeris and Forpus often seen in flight in tight flocks; periodically tuck in the wings while flying, thus undulating up and down.

1 WHITE-WINGED (Canary-winged) PARAKEET *Brotogeris versicolurus* 21.5–22.5 cm (8½–9 in)
Fairly common in northern and central Amazonian Peru, primarily along the Amazon and major Amazonian tributaries. Also a feral population in Lima. Characteristic of river-edge forests and second growth. Easily recognized by striking yellow wing coverts and white inner remiges. **VOICE** Flight calls include mellow rolling "*chuur*" notes mixed with scratchy chatters; also conversational vocalizations including calls given in rapid duet between members of a pair. **Co, E, Br**

2 COBALT-WINGED PARAKEET *Brotogeris cyanoptera* * 19–20.5 cm (7½–8 in)
The most widespread *Brotogeris* parakeet in Peru; fairly common throughout eastern lowlands, locally up to 1350 m. Found in humid forests and adjacent forest edge. May form large flocks. Largely green, with prominent blue remiges and wing coverts; tail much shorter than in White-winged Parakeet. In upper Huallaga Valley, *gustavi* tends to have yellow primary coverts (underwing coverts entirely yellow in immatures) and bluer crown. **VOICE** Flight calls include high, ringing "*jeet*" notes mixed with scratchy chatters; also conversational vocalizations including calls given in rapid duet between members of a pair. Similar to White-winged Parakeet, but higher and less musical. **Co, E, Br, Bo**

3 TUI PARAKEET *Brotogeris sanctithomae* * 18–19 cm (7–7½ in)
Fairly common in eastern lowlands, especially in northern Peru; less common in south. Similar in behavior to Cobalt-winged Parakeet, and may join that species in fruiting trees, but is restricted to river-edge forests. Usually has more extensive yellow forecrown and overall is purer, grass green (Cobalt-winged is more olive-green); also bill is dusky, iris is pale, tail is completely green (centers of upper surfaces of rectrices of Cobalt-winged are blue), and wings are largely green (although there may be a blue tinge to greater primary coverts). **VOICE** Flight calls nearly indistinguishable from those of Cobalt-winged Parakeet, but slightly thinner and more ringing; also conversational vocalizations including calls given in rapid duet between members of a pair. **Co, E, Br, Bo**

4 AMAZONIAN PARROTLET *Nannopsittaca dachilleae* 14 cm (5½ in)
Uncommon to locally fairly common (but frequently overlooked?) in eastern lowlands, locally up to 1000 m in bamboo. Poorly known and possibly nomadic. Found in river-edge forest and at forest edge; in southeastern Peru often associated with bamboo. Usually seen as pairs or in small flocks. Slightly larger than a *Forpus* parrotlet, and with blunter tail; also lacks blue in wings or on rump (but so does female *Forpus*). Also note the light blue crown. **VOICE** Flight calls include a high, ringing "*tcheereet*"; conversational calls include various chirps. Similar to Dusky-billed Parrotlet. **Br, Bo**

5 BLUE-WINGED PARROTLET *Forpus xanthopterygius* * 12–12.5 cm (4¾–5 in)
Fairly common in eastern lowlands of northern and central Peru up to 1050 m; southern distributional limit not well known in Peru, but apparently occurs south (patchily?) to the upper Apurímac Valley. Found in river-edge forest (including on river islands) and in second growth and forest edge. Cf. Dusky-billed and Amazonian parrotlets. **VOICE** Flight calls include high ringing "*tcheet*" notes, rapidly delivered. **Co, E, Br, Bo**

6 DUSKY-BILLED PARROTLET *Forpus sclateri* * 12.5–13.5 cm (5–5¼ in)
Widespread in eastern lowlands below 600 m, but uncommon. Found in humid forest and at forest edge; more closely associated with forest than is Blue-winged Parrotlet. Maxilla is dusky (bill of Blue-winged is all pale). Male is more deeply colored than Blue-winged, the blues and greens being darker. In contrast, female Dusky-billed tends to be paler and yellower on face and breast than female Blue-winged. Best identified by **VOICE** Flight calls include a high, rising "*tcheeng*," more metallic than call of Blue-winged; also more liquid conversational vocalizations. **Co, E, Br, Bo**

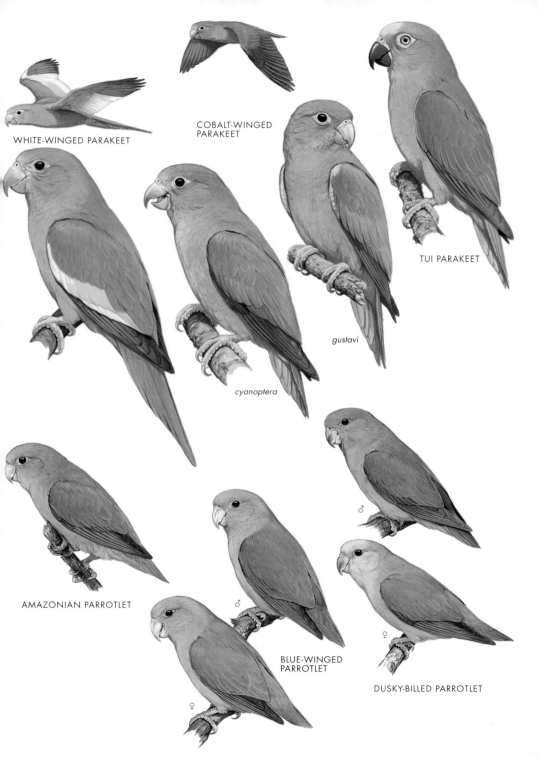

WHITE-WINGED PARAKEET

COBALT-WINGED
PARAKEET

TUI PARAKEET

gustavi

cyanoptera

AMAZONIAN PARROTLET

♂

♂

♀

BLUE-WINGED
PARROTLET

♀

DUSKY-BILLED PARROTLET

PLATE
74

SMALL PARROTS AND *TOUIT* PARROTLETS

Species on this plate are small to medium-sized parrots of Amazonia and the east slope of the Andes with relatively square-tipped tails. Pionites are medium-sized parrots with chunky bodies and pale bellies. They are found in small flocks (10 or fewer individuals) in humid forest. Rarely perch in the open but call frequently when feeding. Flight, typically low over the canopy, is rapid and direct. Pionopsitta is larger than Pionites, with a green belly and distinctive pattern on head and underwing coverts. Touit parrotlets are small, with long upper tail coverts. Sexually dimorphic. Uncommon. Forage quietly, well concealed within treetops, and difficult to see when perched; usually noted (by call or by sight) in flight. Flight is rapid and direct, and often over the canopy.

1 BLACK-HEADED PARROT *Pionites melanocephalus* * 21–22.5 cm (8¼–8¾ in)
Fairly common in eastern lowlands, north of Amazon and west of Río Ucayali. The only white-bellied parrot in its range; does not overlap with White-bellied Parrot. Adult has distinct black crown. Immature is similar in pattern to adult, but plumage is duller, and underparts are dirty buff or yellowish. **VOICE** Vocalizations varied, but characteristically punctuated by a sharp, metallic "*zhin*" and high, thin screeches. A common vocalization, usually given just before flight, is a screeching "*seeeee skzz skzz skzz.*" **Co, E, Br**

2 WHITE-BELLIED PARROT *Pionites leucogaster* * 21–22.5 cm (8¼–8¾ in)
Fairly common in eastern lowlands, south of the Amazon and east of Río Ucayali. The only white-bellied parrot in its range; does not overlap with Black-headed Parrot. Head of adult is yellow and orange; may contain a few scattered black feathers. Crown of immature more extensively mixed with black but never is completely black-crowned, and underparts are dingier. **VOICE** Vocalizations very like those of Black-headed. **Br, Bo**

3 SPOT-WINGED PARROTLET *Touit stictopterus* 16–17 cm (6¼–6¾ in)
Rare to uncommon in humid montane forest on lower slopes of Andes and on outlying ridges in north, 1100–2200 m. Usually in pairs or flocks of only a few individuals. Flight usually low over canopy. Note *Touit* structure and small size; otherwise largely green with dull yellowish face. Wing coverts of male dusky with small white spots and small orange patch on outermost greater primary coverts. Wing coverts of female green with dusky spotting; no orange. **VOICE** Flight call a low, rolling "*kurt,*" sometimes doubled; also quiet conversational vocalizations. **Co, E**

4 SCARLET-SHOULDERED PARROTLET *Touit huetii* 15–16.5 cm (6–6½ in)
Rare to uncommon but widespread in humid forest throughout eastern lowlands, up to 1000 m, locally to 1300 m. Usually seen in small flocks, but may occur in groups as large as 50 or so. Most often seen in flight overhead (often high overhead), when bright red underwing coverts usually are conspicuous. At rest note pale eyering and blue outer wing coverts. Tail mostly purplish red in male, mostly green in female. **VOICE** Flight call a low, mellow, rising "*tchu-it.*" **Co, E, Br, Bo**

5 [SAPPHIRE-RUMPED PARROTLET *Touit purpuratus* * 16.5–18 cm (6½–7 in)
Rare to uncommon, in humid forest in northeastern Amazonian Peru (but reported only from sight records and sound recordings). Less likely to form large flocks than Scarlet-shouldered, and usually flies low over canopy. In flight, note *Touit* shape and green underwing coverts; blue rump visible when seen from above. At rest, has brown band on scapulars; otherwise largely green, lacking blue on wings or bare eyering. Female similar to male, but tail has green subterminal band. **VOICE** Flight call a remarkably low-pitched (for the bird's size), mellow "*ke-ah.*" **Co, E, Br**

6 ORANGE-CHEEKED PARROT *Pionopsitta barrabandi* 24–25.5 cm (9½–10 in)
Fairly common and widespread in humid forest of eastern lowlands. Rarely perches in the open; forages quietly concealed within crowns of trees. Usually in pairs or in small groups. Flies low over or through canopy, rapidly and with deep wingbeats; in flight also often rolls from side to side. Note medium size, red underwing coverts, yellow "headlights" on bend of wing, square tail, and contrasting head pattern. **VOICE** Flight call a rising "*cueet*" similar to call of Blue-headed Parrot, but lower, more musical; also "*kak*" notes and conversational vocalizations. **Co, E, Br, Bo**

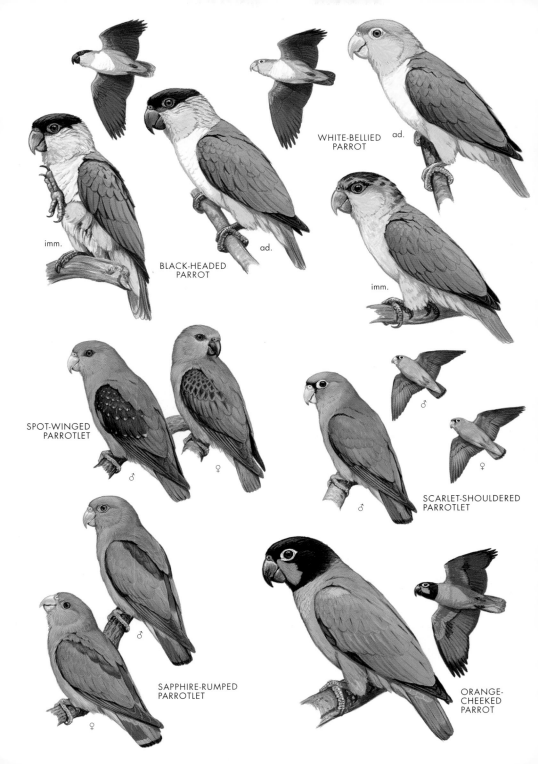

WHITE-BELLIED
PARROT

ad.

imm.

BLACK-HEADED
PARROT

ad.

imm.

SPOT-WINGED
PARROTLET

♂

♀

SCARLET-SHOULDERED
PARROTLET

♂

♀

♂

SAPPHIRE-RUMPED
PARROTLET

♂

♀

ORANGE-
CHEEKED
PARROT

PLATE
75

PIONUS PARROTS AND HIGH ANDEAN PARROTS

Hapalopsittaca are two rare parrots of the Andes. Pionus are medium-sized, chunky parrots with square-tipped tails and contrasting red undertail coverts. Conspicuous, often perching in the open or flying high overhead. May form flocks, of varying size, but also often seen as singles or widely separated pairs. Flight pattern is distinctive: flight is steady, with very deep wingbeats, and the wings seem not to rise above the plane of the body. Golden-plumed Parakeet is a large, long-tailed parrot of the high Andes, built like a small macaw or large Aratinga.

1 BLUE-HEADED PARROT Pionus menstruus * 24.5–27 cm (9½–10½ in)
Widespread and common in eastern lowlands, up to 1300 m, locally to 2000 m. Found in humid forest and forest edges; has higher tolerance for disturbed forests than do most other large parrots. The only Pionus in Amazonia, easily recognized by blue head, red undertail coverts, and distinctive Pionus flight profile. Immature much duller, with little or no blue on head or red undertail coverts. **VOICE** Flight calls a high, rising "cueet," similar to Orange-cheeked Parrot, but higher, more ringing; also various barks and conversational vocalizations. **Co, E, Br, Bo**

2 SPECKLE-FACED PARROT Pionus tumultuosus * 26–28 cm (10–11 in)
Uncommon, in humid montane forest on east slope of Andes, 1400–3300 m; also found on west slope south to southern Cajamarca. Geographically variable, but in all populations bill is pale and head and breast are dark. In widespread tumultuosus (Huánuco south), head and breast are strongly washed with rose, and belly is green; northern seniloides (west of the Marañón, and south in eastern Andes at least to La Libertad) has less rose color on the white-speckled head, and belly is more reddish. **VOICE** Flight calls low, harsh "craah" and "cuit" calls; also various conversational vocalizations. **Co, E, Bo**

3 BRONZE-WINGED PARROT Pionus chalcopterus 27–28 cm (10½–11 in)
Uncommon, and geographically restricted in Peru, found only in humid and semideciduous forest in Tumbes up to 800 m. Very dark. The only square-tailed parrot in its range. Unmistakable. **VOICE** Flight call thin rolling "jeer" calls; also conversational vocalizations. **Co, E**

4 RED-BILLED PARROT Pionus sordidus * 27–30 cm (10½–11¼ in)
Uncommon to fairly common in humid montane forest at 1200–2500 m on east slope of Andes in northern Peru. Similar to Blue-headed Parrot, which it largely replaces at higher elevations. Bill is completely red (not black and red), and head largely is green with blue confined to forecrown and breast. **VOICE** Flight calls rising "cree" and a rolling "chah"; also conversational vocalizations. **Co, E, Bo**

5 GOLDEN-PLUMED PARAKEET Leptosittaca branickii 35.5–38 cm (14–15 in)
Uncommon, local, and perhaps nomadic, in humid montane forest along east slope of Andes, 2700–3350 m. Usually found much higher in elevation than other long-tailed parrots. Presence may be associated with fruiting of a few species of trees, especially Podocarpus. Usually in small, tightly knit flocks, rapidly flying low over forest or woodland and grassland at treeline. Flocks descend on Podocarpus, where they often perch conspicuously and spend hours feeding on the cones. Note reddish underside of tail, golden plumes on side of face. **VOICE** Flight calls raspy shrieks: "keeah." **Co, E**

6 BLACK-WINGED (Black-eared) PARROT Hapalopsittaca melanotis * 22.5–24 cm (8¾–9½ in)
Uncommon and local in humid montane forest on the east slope of the Andes, 1950–3100 m. Forages quietly concealed within crowns of trees; usually seen as pairs or small flocks in flight over forest. Flight is rapid and direct; note relatively long, graduated tail. Structure and flight pattern very different from other Andean parrots (Aratinga, Pionus, Amazona); plumage pattern also distinctive. **VOICE** (Bolivia) Soft "churt" notes and conversational squeals; flight call a squeaky "ka'reet" or rising "chuit." **Bo**

7 RED-FACED PARROT Hapalopsittaca pyrrhops 21.5–23 cm (8½–9 in)
Rare to uncommon and local in humid montane forest on east slope of Andes, north and west of Río Marañón, 2550–3000 m. Behavior similar to that of Black-winged Parrot. Forages quietly concealed within crowns of trees; usually seen as pairs or small flocks in flight over forest. Flight is rapid and direct; note relatively long, graduated tail. Unmistakable. **VOICE** Flight calls low "churt" notes; also short conversational notes. **E**

ad.

BLUE-HEADED PARROT

imm.

tumultuosus

SPECKLE-FACED PARROT

seniloides

RED-BILLED
PARROT

BRONZE-WINGED
PARROT

GOLDEN-PLUMED
PARAKEET

RED-FACED
PARROT

BLACK-WINGED
PARROT

PLATE
76

AMAZONA PARROTS AND SHORT-TAILED PARROT

Parrots on this plate are large, with relatively short, square-tipped tails; cf. Pionus parrots (plate 75). Short-tailed Parrot is a green parrot of riverine forests in northern Amazonia; superficially similar to Amazona parrots, but wings are entirely green and flies with deep wingbeats. Amazona parrots are large green parrots of humid forest. Most show a red or orange speculum on wing, visible in flight. May be seen as pairs, or flocks of varying size. Often fly high overhead. Readily identified to genus in flight by rapid but very shallow wingbeats and square-tipped tail. Very vocal. Each species has a characteristic flight call by which it may be identified, but all also give varied, complex, and less distinctive "conversational" vocalizations. Frequently are kept in captivity.

1 SHORT-TAILED PARROT *Graydidascalus brachyurus* 21.5–23 cm (8½–9 in)

Fairly common in lowlands of northern Peru. Found in humid forest along large rivers and on river islands. Usually in small flocks. Largely green, with relatively large head and very short tail. Bases of outer rectrices red (but usually concealed), also may show small, dark red spot on sides of breast under wing. Has narrow, dark orbital ring that extends to bill (forming a narrow dark line on lores). Flies with rapid, deep wingbeats. *Amazona* parrots are larger and longer-tailed, and have much shallower wingbeats. **VOICE** Flight call a rapid series of rising, ringing notes "*kree ki-ki*"; also various conversational vocalizations. **Co, E, Br**

2 FESTIVE PARROT *Amazona festiva* * 31–33 cm (12¼–13 in)

Locally fairly common in northern lowlands. Always found near water, in forest along large rivers, oxbows, and other lakes. The only *Amazona* that does not show a red wing speculum. Also has red band through eye (may appear at a distance as a dark mask). Adult has bright red rump (difficult to see when perched, but usually conspicuous in flight). **VOICE** Flight calls low, gruff notes ending with a ringing component: "*waghh't.*" **Co, E, Br, Bo**

3 YELLOW-CROWNED PARROT *Amazona ochrocephala* * 33–36 cm (13–14 in)

Uncommon to fairly common and widespread in humid forest of eastern lowlands below 800 m. Frequently occurs with, but typically outnumbered by, the larger Mealy Parrot. Extent of yellow on crown variable, but always conspicuous in the field. Smaller than Mealy, with greener plumage, narrower orbital ring of bare skin and different voice. Cf. also Orange-winged Parrot. **VOICE** Flight call a characteristic, mellow, rolling "*urGWOW*" (or "*bow wow*"), distinctive among Amazonian parrots. **Co, E, Br, Bo**

4 ORANGE-WINGED PARROT *Amazona amazonica* 31–33 cm (12¼–13 in)

Uncommon to locally fairly common in lowlands of northeastern Peru. Found in river-edge forest and at forest edge. The smallest *Amazona* in Peru. Wing speculum is orange (not red), and typically shows extensive yellow or yellow-orange on crown and on sides of face, with blue band across forecrown and over eyes. **VOICE** Flight calls high, ringing "*tcheeurt*" and rising "*joit*" calls, distinctive among Amazonian parrots. **Co, E, Br, Bo**

5 SCALY-NAPED PARROT *Amazona mercenaria* * 31–33 cm (12¼–13 in)

Fairly common in humid montane forest along east slope of Andes, 1100–3400 m. The only high-elevation *Amazona*, but locally may overlap with Mealy Parrot on lower slopes of Andes. Much smaller than Mealy (although size difference is difficult to appreciate when the two are not together). Also plumage is heavily scaled with dusky, especially on crown, nape, and upper breast; and plumage overall is a brighter, greener color (Mealy is a paler, bluer shade of green). **VOICE** Flight calls mellow, rolling "*jeeurt*" and "*jet-jet*" calls. **Co, E, Bo**

6 MEALY PARROT *Amazona farinosa* * 38–41 cm (15–16 in)

Fairly common and widespread in eastern lowlands and lower Andean foothills to 1200 m; most common *Amazona* in terra firme in eastern Peru, but also occurs in river-edge forests. Largely a washed-out green (often looks grayer than other *Amazona*), with no yellow on face, but may show some yellow on center of crown. Orbital ring of bare skin pale, and broader than in other *Amazona*. Often more easily recognized by distinctive vocalizations. **VOICE** Flight call a loud, rolling "*TCHOP*," often doubled, distinctive among Amazonian parrots. **Co, E, Br, Bo**

SHORT-TAILED PARROT

FESTIVE PARROT

ad.

imm.

ORANGE-WINGED PARROT

YELLOW-CROWNED
PARROT

SCALY-NAPED
PARROT

MEALY PARROT

PLATE
77

SMALLER CUCKOOS

Cuckoos, anis, and ground-cuckoos are a diverse family of insectivores. Feet zygodactyl (2 toes facing forward, 2 toes facing back) and tails long; otherwise vary considerably in size, shape, and behavior. Coccyzus cuckoos are very slender birds with long tails and slightly curved bills. Quiet and inconspicuous, in mid- and upper story of forest; may join mixed-species flocks but often forage apart. Striped Cuckoo has a similar long-tailed shape but is found on open habitats and has a ragged crest.

1 [ASH-COLORED CUCKOO *Coccyzus cinereus*] 22–24 cm (8½–9½ in)

Rare austral migrant to lowlands of southeast; very rare north to north bank of the Amazon. Reported only from sight records. The smallest *Coccyzus* cuckoo, and tail is not strongly graduated (unlike other *Coccyzus*). Relatively gray above (not brown); light gray-brown wash on throat and breast contrasts with whiter belly. The few records primarily are Jul–Sep, but presumably arrives earlier in the year. **VOICE** Probably largely silent in Peru. **Co, Br, Bo**

2 BLACK-BILLED CUCKOO *Coccyzus erythropthalmus* 28–29 cm (11–11½ in)

Rare boreal migrant to Peru, where found in northwest, and on lower slopes of east side of Andes, adjacent lowlands, and in Marañón Valley, up to 2400 m. Recorded Sep–May, but apparently most common Feb–Apr. Found in dry and humid forests and forest edge. Largely white below, although throat usually washed with pale buff, and breast and belly washed with light gray. Note brown upperparts, all dark bill, small grayish white spots on long graduated tail, and narrow red orbital ring. **VOICE** Probably largely silent in Peru. **Co, E, Br, Bo**

3 YELLOW-BILLED CUCKOO *Coccyzus americanus* 26–29 cm (10¼–11½ in)

Rare boreal migrant (Oct–May) to eastern Peru below 1200 m, where found in humid forest and at forest edge; very rare vagrant to northwest. Readily recognized by white underparts, conspicuous yellow base to mandible, and large white tips to rectrices. Inner webs of remiges largely rufous, prominent in flight; only a small amount of rufous visible on closed wing. **VOICE** Probably largely silent in Peru. **Co, E, Br, Bo** [**Pearly-breasted Cuckoo** (*Coccyzus euleri*; not illustrated) is a potential vagrant (reported from Ecuador), presumably as very rare austral migrant. Extremely similar to Yellow-billed Cuckoo, but lacks rufous in wings and is slightly smaller. Any report would require extensive documentation.]

4 GRAY-CAPPED CUCKOO *Coccyzus lansbergi* 27–28 cm (10½–11 in)

Rare and poorly known. Apparently breeds (Jan–Apr or May) in northwest below 800 m, but then departs; presumably migrates north, but very rarely recorded (Aug and Sep) on coast south to Arequipa. Rufous, paler below, with contrasting slate gray crown. Much more richly colored than Dark-billed Cuckoo, with distinctly capped appearance and no dusky "mask." **VOICE** Song a soft rolling series of hollow cooing notes, descending in pitch: *"CL'oo-coo-coo-coo-coo-coo-oh."* **Co, E**

5 DARK-BILLED CUCKOO *Coccyzus melacoryphus* 27–28 cm (10½–11 in)

Uncommon austral migrant (Mar–Oct) to east, where found at forest edge and in river-edge forest. Mostly in lowlands, but occasionally to 3600 m. Also recorded from western Peru, where status is not certain; probably a rare (and local?) resident, south to Arequipa. Relatively small, with buffy underparts, dusky "mask" on side of face, and prominent white tail spots. Intensity of color on underparts variable, but always buff (not rufous), and upperparts always brown, not rufous; cf. Gray-capped Cuckoo. **VOICE** Call a low rattle. **Co, E, Br, Bo, Ch**

6 STRIPED CUCKOO *Tapera naevia* * 28–30 cm (11–12 in)

Fairly common in eastern lowlands; uncommon in northwest and in dry Marañón Valley. Solitary; found in thickets in open country and in pastures. Mostly found below 1000 m, but to 2450 m in Marañón. Sings from top of a bush or post, but when not vocalizing; heard far more often than seen. Brown, long-tailed, with loose ragged crest (usually flat but may be raised when calling). Juvenile similar to adult, but wing coverts and crest feathers tipped with round golden buff spots; and breast lightly scaled dusky. Brood parasite; lays eggs in nests of other species (especially birds that build domed nests). **VOICE** Song, a rising series of high whistles, the last note often slightly lower: *"hew hew hew HUI-hee?"* Call, a 2-note whistle, the second higher in pitch *"hew-HEE,"* often given incessantly throughout day. **Co, E, Br, Bo**

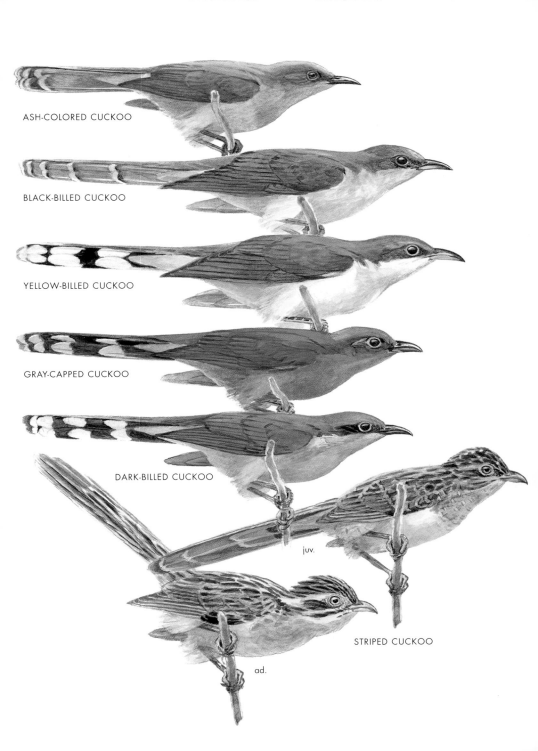

ASH-COLORED CUCKOO

BLACK-BILLED CUCKOO

YELLOW-BILLED CUCKOO

GRAY-CAPPED CUCKOO

DARK-BILLED CUCKOO

juv.

STRIPED CUCKOO

ad.

PLATE
78

LARGER CUCKOOS AND ANIS

Piaya are rufous cuckoos with long to very long, strongly graduated tails and short, curved, red or yellow bills. Anis are black, long-tailed cuckoos with tall, laterally compressed bills. Social; always forage in flocks, and nest communally, several individuals incubating eggs and feeding nestlings.

1 BLACK-BELLIED CUCKOO *Piaya melanogaster* * 38–40.5 cm (15–16 in)

Uncommon but widespread in Amazonia up to 900 m. Largely restricted to canopy of terra firme. Darker overall than Squirrel Cuckoo, with black belly (but note that Squirrel Cuckoo has black undertail coverts), red bill, blue-and-yellow orbital ring, and distinct gray cap. **VOICE** Calls less emphatic: a lazy, hoarse, sneezing "*rhi'kid'CHOO'oo*" and a dry throaty rattle. Flight call a series of sharp "*kleh!*" notes. Song a hoarse, mechanical-sounding series: "*cooEE-pah cooEE-pah cooEE-pah...*" (very unlike Squirrel Cuckoo). **Co, E, Br, Bo**

2 SQUIRREL CUCKOO *Piaya cayana* * 40.5–46 cm (16–18 in)

Most common and widespread *Piaya*. Found in humid and semihumid forest throughout eastern Peru (up to 2800 m), and in northwest, below 2400 m. Singles or loose pairs forage in mid- and upper-story of forest; frequently joins mixed-species flocks. Note yellow bill, rufous head, and gray belly. Orbital ring greenish yellow west of Andes (*nigricrissa*); red in Marañón Valley and in east (*mesura, boliviana*). Despite size, not always conspicuous; often first detected by loud (but infrequent) calls, or gliding from one tree to another. **VOICE** Calls varied: a sneezing "*rhi-KID'd'oo*"; an explosive "*KEEK! wahh*" (source of vernacular name "*chiqua*"); and a dry throaty rattle. Flight call a series of sharp "*kleh!*" notes. Song (?) a series of sharp, rising whistled "*whik*" or "*wheep*" notes. **Co, E, Br, Bo**

3 LITTLE CUCKOO *Piaya minuta* * 25.5–28 cm (10–11 in)

Uncommon but widespread in Amazonia; found locally up to 1050 m. Singles or loose pairs forage low, primarily in river- and lake-edge forest and thickets, but locally in forest edge away from water. Typically does not associate with mixed-species flocks. Much smaller, more uniformly colored than other *Piaya*. **VOICE** Song (?) a descending "*kewl*," given in slow series. Calls a somewhat gruff, rising, mewing chuckle: "*meeeeeeh he-hehehehehe*"; also descending "*tou*," and a sharp "*kik!*" sometimes followed by a rising growled "*rahhh.*" **Co, E, Br, Bo**

4 GREATER ANI *Crotophaga major* 46–48 cm (18–19 in)

Fairly common in Amazonia, but restricted to thickets over water along rivers and at edge of lakes. Often in flocks of up to 20 individuals, foraging within cover of vegetation. In some regions seems to disappear from some sites for months at a time (partially nomadic or migratory?). Easily identified by very large size, conspicuous pale iris, glossy blue plumage, and casqued bill. **VOICE** Calls gruff grunts, hisses, groans, and sometimes a sharper bark: "*pok.*" Also an exited series of hollow hoots or gobbles; these may be given by several individuals in chorus that accelerates into a low sound reminiscent of a bubbling cauldron. **Co, E, Br, Bo**

5 SMOOTH-BILLED ANI *Crotophaga ani* 33–35.5 cm (13–14 in)

Fairly common in eastern Peru, up to 2100 m. Found low or on ground, at forest edge, in pastures and fields, and other open habitats. Much smaller than Greater Ani. Very limited overlap with Groove-billed Ani in middle Marañón Valley. Most easily distinguished from Groove-billed by voice, but also is slightly larger, is more common in humid habitats (Groove-billed prefers drier habitats in area of overlap), and bill is smooth with a different shape: deeper, with distinct "hump" along culmen. **VOICE** Call a questioning: "*cuLEE?*" Also dull grunts. Begging juveniles may give a quiet series of warbled notes, remarkably musical. **Co, E, Br, Bo**

6 GROOVE-BILLED ANI *Crotophaga sulcirostris* * 28–30 cm (11–12 in)

Fairly common on west slope and in dry Marañón Valley, up to 2750 m; only very limited overlap with Smooth-billed Ani in middle Marañón. Found in fields, pastures, and at forest edge. Bill has a more continuous curve than bill of Smooth-billed, with no distinct "hump." Bill also has several lateral grooves (which may be reduced or absent in juveniles). **VOICE** Call a sharp 2-note phrase, the first note much higher than the second: "*PEEK-olek.*" Sometimes gives just sharp "*PEEK*" notes. Also dull grunts. **Co, E**

BLACK-BELLIED
CUCKOO

SQUIRREL
CUCKOO

w   e

LITTLE CUCKOO

GREATER ANI

SMOOTH-BILLED
ANI

GROOVE-BILLED
ANI

PLATE
79

HOATZIN, *DROMOCOCCYX* CUCKOOS, AND GROUND-CUCKOOS

Hoatzin is a very peculiar, large, prehistoric-appearing bird of Amazonian rivers and lakes. An arboreal cow: feeds on leaves, which are digested in a specialized crop and foregut. Nest is a stick platform over water. Wings of nestlings have claws (lost later in life); drop into the water when threatened, then use the claws to climb back to nest. The two species of Dromococcyx cuckoo superficially are similar to Striped Cuckoo (plate 77) but are found in humid forest, not in open habitats. Solitary and secretive, heard far more often than are seen. Found low in dense undergrowth or even on the ground. Brood parasites, laying eggs in nests of other species. Ground-cuckoos are very large terrestrial cuckoos of humid forest. Largely solitary, although sometimes encountered in pairs or apparent family groups. Frequently associated with army ant swarms; also may follow herds of White-lipped Peccaries. Can be very furtive and difficult to observe (despite large size). Tail often carried cocked. Also note the generally brown plumage, black breast band, and ragged crest.

1 HOATZIN *Opisthocomus hoazin* 61–68.5 cm (24–27 in)

Common and widespread in eastern lowlands. Always found over water, usually encountered perched low over still or slow-moving water such as oxbow lakes or sluggish rivers (but may venture deeper into forest when foraging at night). Social; almost always in groups. Note large size, long ragged crest, very broad wings, blue skin on face, buff-streaked upperparts, and rufous-chestnut primaries and belly. Sluggish, ungainly, and clumsy. When perched, often holds wings partially outstretched (especially after landing), as if for balance. Flies with apparent difficulty and only for short distances, deep wingbeats interspersed with short glides. Can be very tame, allowing a close approach, but then clumsily and noisily retreating into cover with short crashing flights or hops and much calling. **VOICE** Common calls include hoarse coughing and grunting sounds, also loud hisses. **Co, E, Br, Bo**

2 PAVONINE CUCKOO *Dromococcyx pavoninus* 28–30 cm (11–12 in)

Rare in lowland forests of eastern Peru, primarily south of the Amazon, locally up to 900 m. In southern Peru often associated with bamboo thickets. Cf. larger Pheasant Cuckoo. **VOICE** Song, most often heard at night, is higher pitched than Pheasant Cuckoo and never ends in a trill, the final 2 notes on the same pitch: "*too TEE too-TEE-TEE.*" **Co, E, Br, Bo**

3 PHEASANT CUCKOO *Dromococcyx phasianellus* 37–41 cm (14½–16 in)

Rare (and rarely seen) but widespread in eastern Peru, locally up to 1000 m. Large; tail often held broadly fanned. In flight, may resemble a chachalaca in shape and flight style. Larger than Pavonine Cuckoo, and browner, less buffy overall, with pale buff or whitish base to heavily marked breast, and whitish or pale buff line behind eye. Pavonine has deeper buff, unmarked breast and throat, and deeper buff line behind eye. **VOICE** Song, most often heard at night, has 2 longer introductory whistles followed by a quavering trill, "*tew TEE tr-r-r,*" or less often, a raising series of notes: "*tew TEE tu-tee-tee-tee?*" **Co, E, Br, Bo**

4 RED-BILLED GROUND-CUCKOO *Neomorphus pucheranii* * 46–51 cm (18–20 in)

Rare in eastern Amazonian Peru. Similar to Rufous-vented Ground-Cuckoo, but has red bill and orbital skin, solid back crown, and cinnamon-buff belly; undertail coverts dusky brown (not rufous). Not known to overlap with Rufous-vented, but distributions of the two are incompletely known; presumably they meet somewhere in central and perhaps in northern Peru. **VOICE** Song, rarely heard, is a very deep, rising, muffled "*whoop*" in a slow series. Presumably claps bill, as do other ground-cuckoos. **Co, E, Br**

5 RUFOUS-VENTED GROUND-CUCKOO *Neomorphus geoffroyi* * 46–51 cm (18–20 in)

Rare in eastern Peru. Range is disjunct, with one population in northern Amazonia, and another in southern Peru, where found up to 1600 m. Not reported in Peru from east bank of Río Napo, but distribution in Ecuador suggests that it may occur there. Distinguished from Red-billed Ground-Cuckoo by greenish yellow (not red) bill, bluish orbital skin, and narrow brown scaling on forecrown. Belly also is duller, less cinnamon-buff, brown, contrasting with rufous-brown undertail coverts. **VOICE** Song, rarely heard, a deep booming hoot. Occasionally claps bill loudly. **Co, E, Br, Bo**

HOATZIN

PAVONINE CUCKOO

PHEASANT CUCKOO

RED-BILLED GROUND-CUCKOO

RUFOUS-VENTED GROUND-CUCKOO

PLATE
80

SMALL OWLS

Owls are predatory birds with strongly hooked bills and sharp claws. Species on this plate are small; see also plate 81.

1 KOEPCKE'S SCREECH-OWL *Megascops koepckeae* 24 cm (9½ in)

Very poorly known, probably often overlooked. Locally on west slope of Andes and in dry intermontane valleys (Utcubamba and Apurímac), where found in woods (including *Polylepis*) and at forest edge. Very similar to Peruvian Screech-Owl, but found at higher elevations (2200–4000 m); nape concolor with crown and lacks white nape band. Not known to overlap with very similar Tropical Screech-Owl. Underparts more coarsely patterned than Peruvian or Tropical. Population in Apurímac Valley (not illustrated) very gray. **VOICE** Primary song a loud, staccato series of notes with slowing pace and rising volume: "*ko-ko-ko-ko ka ka KA KAH!*" Aggressive song a series of quieter short hoots rising and falling in pitch, similar to Tropical. May duet, one individual answering mate's primary song with a similar song or a hiss (female only?). **ENDEMIC**

2 PERUVIAN SCREECH-OWL *Megascops roboratus* * *pacificus* 19.5–20 cm (7½–8 in); *roboratus* 22.5–23 cm (8¾–9 in)

Uncommon in dry forests of northwest (*pacificus*) and in dry middle Marañón Valley (*roboratus*), mostly below 900 m, but locally up to 2100 m (Ancash). Very similar to Tropical Screech-Owl (especially the larger *roboratus*), although no known overlap. In Peruvian (but especially in *roboratus*) crown noticeably darker than back, and bordered behind with narrow white ring; cf. Tropical and Koepcke's. In the hand, inner webs of primaries (especially outer primaries) are dark with little or no mottling (both webs equally mottled in Tropical and Koepcke's). **VOICE** Primary song (both subspecies) a quiet, fairly rapid trill, often rising and falling in pitch. Aggressive song similar, but more stuttered, usually rising in pitch. Also may give mewing or yapping notes (female only?). **E**

3 WHITE-THROATED SCREECH-OWL *Megascops albogularis* * 25.5–26.5 cm (10–10½ in)

Uncommon to fairly common in humid montane forest on east slope of Andes, 2500–3700 m, locally as low as 1800 m; also at similar elevations on west slope of Andes south to southern Cajamarca. Found at higher elevations than other screech-owls. Puffy-headed, with prominent white throat, but no "ear" tufts. **VOICE** Primary song a mellow series of hoots descending slightly in pitch, sometimes doubled (particularly when duetting). Aggressive song of birds north of Marañón a staccato series of notes rising in pitch, ending with couplets "*pu pu pu pu pu PU PU-PU PU-PU PU-PU PU!*" Aggressive song south of Marañón a loud series of single hoots descending in pitch. **Co, E, Bo**

4 LONG-WHISKERED OWLET *Xenoglaux loweryi* 13–14 cm (5–5½ in)

Rare, local, and very poorly known; reported from only a few localities in humid montane forest in Amazonas and San Martín, 1900–2400 m. Very small and short-tailed. Largely brown with whitish belly, finely vermiculated with dusky, and with very long, delicate facial plumes. **VOICE** Primary song (?) a single, slightly hoarse, hoot, rising then falling slightly in pitch: "*whoOOo.*" Apparently given in a series of 4–6 notes/min. **ENDEMIC**

5 BUFF-FRONTED OWL *Aegolius harrisii* * 19–20 cm (7½–8 in)

Rare and local (but often overlooked?) in humid and semihumid montane forest, 1500–2900 m; most records from east slope of Andes, but also found on west slope in Piura. Readily identified by distinctive facial pattern and unmarked buff underparts. **VOICE** Song a very rapid series of toots, about 13 notes/sec, often slightly uneven in pitch by rising and falling in an irregular manner. **Co, E, Br, Bo**

6 BURROWING OWL *Athene cunicularia* * coastal 21–24 cm (8¾–9½ in); Andean 28–30 cm (11–12 in)

Fairly common and widespread on coast and lower western slopes of Andes, in dry Marañón Valley, and in high Andes, up to 4600 m. Found in open country, such as fields and grasslands. Highly terrestrial (rarely perches far above ground) and partially diurnal. Nests in burrows underground, and often seen in small groups standing at or near entrance to burrows. When flushed, often flies in a semicircle around intruder; characteristic flight is very undulating. Note long legs and brown, spotted plumage. Andean populations are larger than coastal birds. Juvenile similar in structure but buffy below and less spotted. **VOICE** Call, often given in flight, a cackling "*djee-JEEE-jeee-jee*"" or "*DJEE ji-ji-ji-ji.*" Song (elsewhere in range), rarely heard (?), is a 2-note hoot, the second slightly higher pitched: "*hoo HOO.*" **Co, E, Br, Bo, Ch**

KOEPCKE'S
SCREECH-OWL

pacificus

red morph

gray morph
PERUVIAN SCREECH-OWL

roboratus

gray morph

red morph
PERUVIAN
SCREECH-OWL

WHITE-THROATED
SCREECH-OWL

LONG-WHISKERED OWLET

BUFF-FRONTED
OWL

juv.

BURROWING OWL

ad. coastal

ad. Andean

PLATE
81

HUMID-FOREST SCREECH-OWLS

Screech-owls (Megascops) are small nocturnal owls of forest and woods. Have large-headed appearance; many have "ear" tufts (a small tuft of feathers on either side of face), although these rarely are visible when bird is active. Plumage usually an intricate mixture of streaks and bars; background color highly variable, and many species have "gray," "red," and intermediate morphs. For identification consider voice (often the best guide), habitat and elevation, iris color, and relative prominence of a black rim to facial disk. See also plate 80.

1 TAWNY-BELLIED SCREECH-OWL *Megascops watsonii* * 23–25 cm (9–9¾ in)

Fairly common and widespread in eastern Peru, below 700 m; the common screech-owl of interior of humid forest in Amazonia. Iris typically brown, but rarely is amber. Plumage highly variable; but "eyebrows" never as whitish as in Tropical Screech-Owl; facial disk is darker; has white band across rear crown; and upperparts are darker (less noticeably streaked). **VOICE** Primary song a long series of low hoots, about 2 notes/sec, swelling in volume, then dying away. East of Napo/north of the Amazon, song pace is faster, about 3–4 notes/sec. Aggressive song starts at a slow pace and abruptly shifts to a faster pace: "*woo woo woo woo woo wu-wu-wu.*" Call a descending mew "*woah!*" (female only?). **Co, E, Br, Bo**

2 TROPICAL SCREECH-OWL *Megascops choliba* * 21–23 cm (8¼–9 in)

Common and widespread in eastern lowlands; locally ascends to 2400 m. Found at edge of humid forest, in river-edge forest and in tall second growth. Iris always yellow. Underparts heavily streaked and black rims to facial disk prominent. Also note prominent whitish "eyebrow" lines and reduced or absent white border to rear crown. Not known to enter arid Marañón Valley; no known overlap with very similar Peruvian or Koepcke's screech-owls. **VOICE** Primary song a slow, rolling trill usually ending with a longer, punctuated note (occasionally doubled): "*pu-pu-pu-pu-pu-pu POO.*" Aggressive song a series of short hoots rising and falling in pitch. Also a variety of cackles and longer hooting notes, particularly when agitated. **Co, E, Br, Bo**

3 CINNAMON SCREECH-OWL *Megascops petersoni* 23–24 cm (9–9½ in)

Uncommon, in humid montane forest on east slope of Andes in north, 1700–2450 m; poorly known, and possibly occurs farther south than currently reported. Very similar to Rufescent Screech-Owl, but smaller and even more rufescent, completely lacking white in plumage. Usually at higher elevations than Rufescent, but there is overlap; may prefer more stunted forest. Best identified by **VOICE** Primary song similar to that of Rufescent, but faster, about 7 notes/sec. Aggressive song starts with fast pace, then abruptly shifts to slower pace and rises in pitch: "*pu-pu-pu-pu-pu pu pu pu pu pu.*" Also whining notes when aggravated (female only?). **E**

4 VERMICULATED SCREECH-OWL *Megascops guatemalae* * 20.5–21 cm (8–8¼ in)

Uncommon in humid montane forest on lower slopes of Andes and on outlying ridges, 600–1700 m. Small, with yellow or amber iris, no black border to facial disks, and relatively narrowly streaked underparts. Little or no white band on rear crown. **VOICE** Primary song a rapid trill, about 10–15 notes/sec, swelling and slowing pace slightly toward the end, similar to song of Scaled Antpitta. Also may give mewing call when aggravated (female only?). **Co, E, Br, Bo**

5 CLOUD-FOREST SCREECH-OWL *Megascops marshalli* 20–23 cm (7¾–9 in)

Poorly known; apparently uncommon in humid montane forest, 1650–2250 m, but recorded from very few sites (overlooked?). May replace Cinnamon Screech-Owl in central Peru. Small, with dark iris, distinct black rim to reddish facial disks, and prominent white scapulars and white spotting on underparts. **VOICE** Song similar to that of Cinnamon, lower-pitched than Rufescent with pace of about 5 notes/sec. **Bo**

6 RUFESCENT SCREECH-OWL *Megascops ingens* * 25–28 cm (10–11 in)

Uncommon but widespread, in humid montane forest along east slope of Andes and on outlying ridges, 1000–2200 m. Rather large, with brown iris and no black rim to facial disks. Typically light rufescent brown; red morph less common. **VOICE** Primary song a series of hoots, about 6 notes/sec, usually at a flat pitch although sometimes rising. Aggressive song starts at a slow pace and abruptly shifts to a faster pace, descending in pitch at the end: "*poo poo poo poo pu-pu-pu-pu-pu.*" Also whining notes when aggravated (female only?). **Co, E, Bo**

brown morph

TAWNY-BELLIED SCREECH-OWL

red morph

brown morph

gray morph

gray morph

red morph

TROPICAL SCREECH-OWL

brown morph

red morph

CINNAMON SCREECH-OWL

red morph

gray morph

VERMICULATED SCREECH-OWL

RUFESCENT SCREECH-OWL

CLOUD-FOREST SCREECH-OWL

brown morph

red morph

PLATE
82

LARGE HUMID-FOREST OWLS

Large owls of humid forest. Crested Owl has very long "ear" tufts. All other species shown here are round-headed. The two Pulsatrix *have prominent white markings on face, including large white "eyebrows," and dark chests contrasting with paler bellies. The four* Ciccaba *are smaller and more varied in plumage pattern but are notable for having a wide variety of calls (in addition to more stereotyped songs).*

1 CRESTED OWL *Lophostrix cristata* * 40–42 cm (15¼–16½ in)

Uncommon but widespread in humid forest of eastern lowlands below 700 m. May roost within a few meters of ground, but hunts at night from subcanopy or canopy. When disturbed white plumes may be erected nearly vertically, otherwise plumes are more relaxed. Plumage variable; is finely vermiculated but not streaked. Juvenile largely white, with reddish facial disks; dark iris. **VOICE** Primary song a deep booming growl, usually with a stuttered introduction not audible at a distance: "*b-b-b-b GRRR.*" **Co, E, Br, Bo**

2 SPECTACLED OWL *Pulsatrix perspicillata* * 43–48 cm (17–19 in)

Fairly common and widespread in humid forest of eastern lowlands, locally to 1150 m; uncommon and local in northwest, in semideciduous and riparian forest below 900 m. Adult unmistakable: note distinctive face pattern and sharp contrast between brown breast and buffy belly. Juvenile largely white, with dusky facial disks and upper throat. **VOICE** Primary song is a muffled series of rapid hoots, swelling then dying away. Quality of the song is similar to wobbling a thin piece of sheet metal. Call a breathy descending rasp. **Co, E, Br, Bo**

3 BAND-BELLIED OWL *Pulsatrix melanota* * 35.5–38 cm (14–15 in)

Uncommon to fairly common in humid montane forest along east slope of Andes and on outlying ridges, 650–2200 m. Similar to larger Spectacled Owl, which it replaces at higher elevations, but iris brown (not yellow); also white (not buff) belly extensively banded with rufous brown. Juvenile golden buff with dusky facial disks and upper throat. **VOICE** Primary song similar to that of Spectacled, but usually higher-pitched, faster-paced, and more bubbly. Usually given in a duet, with one bird singing, the second answering, and the first singing again. Also may give mewing cries. **Co, E, Bo**

4 BLACK-AND-WHITE OWL *Ciccaba nigrolineata* 38–39.5 cm (15–15½ in)

Rare and local in semideciduous and humid forest in Tumbes and Piura below 800 m. Only black-and-white barred owl west of Andes. **VOICE** Primary song a rising series of short hoots followed by a pause, then a louder hoot: "*h-hu-hu-hu.. HOO!*" Aggressive song is a series of evenly spaced, rising hoots "*hooOO? hooOO? hooOO?*" Frequently also single mewing "*hooOOOoo*" notes and other vocalizations. Vocalizations probably all indistinguishable from Black-banded Owl (with which there is no overlap). **Co, E**

5 BLACK-BANDED OWL *Ciccaba huhula* * 38–39.5 cm (15–15½ in)

Uncommon but widespread in humid forest of eastern lowlands, below 1800 m. Only black-and-white barred owl east of Andes. **VOICE** Primary song a rising series of short hoots followed by a pause, then a louder hoot: "*h-hu-hu-hu.. HOO!*" Aggressive song is a series of evenly spaced, rising hoots "*hooOO? hooOO? hooOO?*" Frequently gives single mewing "*hooOOOoo*" or shorter "*huo*" notes. Also rising screams, and other vocalizations. **Co, E, Br, Bo**

6 RUFOUS-BANDED OWL *Ciccaba albitarsis* * 35.5–38 cm (14–15 in)

Fairly common in humid montane forest on east slope of Andes, 1900–3500 m; also in similar habitats on west slope south to Cajamarca. Richly colored. Barred rufous and brown above; more marked with white below. No overlap with Mottled Owl of lowlands; cf. also larger Band-bellied. **VOICE** Primary song a rising series of short, hoarse hoots followed by a pause, then a louder hoot: "*h-hu-hu-hu.. HOOo!*" Call a series of "*whoOOo*" notes, clear or gruff in quality. **Co, E, Bo**

7 MOTTLED OWL *Ciccaba virgata* * 30.5–34.5 cm (12–13½ in)

Uncommon but widespread in humid forest in eastern lowlands, below 1000 m. A nondescript medium-sized brown owl, with large rounded head and dark iris. Also note whitish "eyebrows" and rim of facial disks, and streaked underparts. **VOICE** Primary song a low series of muffled hoots, rising slightly in pitch and volume in the middle. Probably also has a single, mewing hoot (as do other *Ciccaba*). **Co, E, Br, Bo**

juv.

ad.

CRESTED OWL

rufous morph

SPECTACLED
OWL

brown morph

ad.

juv.

juv.

BAND-BELLIED
OWL

BLACK-AND-
WHITE OWL

BLACK-BANDED
OWL

RUFOUS-
BANDED
OWL

MOTTLED
OWL

PLATE
83

LARGE OPEN-HABITAT OWLS

Five large to very large species of owl, which are found in open or lightly forested habitats. Great Horned Owl is the largest owl in Peru, with broad, prominent "ear" tufts. The two Asio are heavily streaked, and both have "ear" tufts; these tufts are conspicuous on Stygian Owl but small and inconspicuous on Short-eared Owl. Striped Owl superficially is similar to a long-tufted Asio. Barn Owl is long-legged and has a very well-defined, pale facial disk with a prominent dark border.

1 GREAT HORNED OWL *Bubo virginianus* * 48–56 cm (19–22 in)

Uncommon but widespread in the Andes, 2600–4400 m; locally as low as 450 m on Pacific slope, and also very local in lowlands of southeast. Found in a variety of woodlands (including *Polylepis*) and at forest edges; not found in forest interior. Very large, with prominent "ear" tufts, white throat, and heavily barred underparts. Geographic variation in plumage and voice poorly understood. Blackest north and west of the Marañón (*nigrescens*); browner and more finely barred in central and southern Peru, but these may intergrade with *nigrescens* in northern Peru. **VOICE** Song variable, but geographic patterns in voice (and correlations with subspecies) not well documented. In the northern Andes and Amazonia song is a deep, 2- to 4-note boom: "*hoo HOO-hu*" (longer in females?). Another widespread Andean song is 2 notes followed by a low chatter: "*hoo HOO-hr'r'r'r'r.*" Apparently, individuals in Piura give both song types. Calls include screeches and hisses. **Co, E, Br, Bo, Ch**

2 STRIPED OWL *Pseudoscops clamator* * 35.5–38 cm (14–15 in)

Uncommon but widespread in eastern lowlands, locally to 1700 m; possibly spreading, following deforestation. Also present on the coast, where status not clear; uncommon to locally common in northwest, found locally south to Arequipa. Also a 19th-century report from upper Marañón Valley (where now extirpated? or overlooked?). Occurs in open woods, fields, pastures, and (Amazonia) shrubs on river islands. Note heavily streaked plumage, dark iris, and very white facial disks; long "ear" tufts often held folded back. **VOICE** Primary song a decelerating series of cackling barks: "*ka-ka-ka-kah KAH KAHW KAAHW.*" Calls include muffled barking, screeches, hoots, a high, descending whine, and whines. When protecting nest, may give a deep hissing growl similar to a quiet Great Potoo, also snaps bill audibly. **Co, E, Br, Bo**

3 SHORT-EARED OWL *Asio flammeus* * 38–40 cm (15–15¼ in)

Rare and local on the coast, where found in marshes. Also rare to uncommon at 4100 m on Junín plateau. Hunts in characteristic loose, floppy flight over marshes and grasslands, and may be active at dusk. Note overall brown, streaked plumage, yellow iris, and short (rarely even visible) "ear" tufts. In flight, also note buffy bases to primaries. **VOICE** Calls include rising, reedy barks and hisses. Song (Dominican Republic) is a series of low hoots; in flight display (North America), claps wings together. **Co, E, Br, Bo, Ch**

4 STYGIAN OWL *Asio stygius* * 41–43 cm (16–17 in)

Status not clear; rare or local (or overlooked?) in open woods or forest edge at 2200–2900 m, north and west of Río Marañón. Very blackish, with coarse "herringbone" pattern on underparts, long dark "ear" tufts, and white "eyebrows." Cf. Great Horned and Short-eared owls. **VOICE** Song is a muffled hoot given singly: "*boo.*" Calls include a higher whistle. **Co, E, Br, Bo**

5 BARN OWL *Tyto alba* * 35.5–40.5 cm (14–16 in)

Uncommon but widespread in western Peru, on coast and in Andes, up to 4300 m; rare on humid east slope of Andes, more widespread in drier intermontane valleys. Status in Amazonia not clear, but is reported from scattered localities. Found in towns and in agricultural areas. Forages in flight, capturing prey (primarily small rodents) detected while flying back and forth over fields and other open habitats. A large owl with dark iris and well-defined, "heart"-shaped facial disk, with distinct dark rim. Generally pale, largely white (male) or buffy (female) below and on face. **VOICE** Typical call a loud hiss or screech; also a variety of unbirdlike clicking notes. **Co, E, Br, Bo, Ch**

GREAT HORNED OWL

nigrescens

STRIPED OWL

GREAT HORNED OWL

SHORT-EARED OWL

BARN OWL

STYGIAN OWL

♀

♂

PLATE
84

PYGMY-OWLS

Pygmy-Owls (Glaucidium) are very small owls. They have large rounded heads and a pair of prominent black marks (false "eye spots") on the nape. Often active by day. Plumage is variable within a species, both because of different color morphs within a species (in many, but not all, species), and also age-related differences in white markings on the crown; but plumages often are very similar between species. Pygmy-Owls usually are best identified by voice, but also note habitat and elevation.

1 SUBTROPICAL PYGMY-OWL *Glaucidium parkeri* 14.5 cm (5¾ in)

Poorly known; reported from few localities, but possibly overlooked and more widespread. Uncommon in humid montane forest on east slope of Andes and on outlying ridges, 950–1600 m. Often perches very high. Cf. Andean Pygmy-Owl (which usually is found at higher elevations); Subtropical has shorter tail with only 2 visible white bars, fewer markings on the mantle, and more prominent white spots on scapulars and barring on secondaries. Uncommon rufous morph very difficult to separate in field from longer-tailed rufous-morph Andean, other than by voice. Very similar also to Amazonian Pygmy-Owl of lowlands, but has a more boldly spotted crown, more white spotting on scapulars, and prominent white barring on secondaries. **VOICE** Song is a series of 3 whistled notes: "*toot toot toot.*" Occasionally may have a longer pause before the third note is delivered. **E, Bo**

2 AMAZONIAN PYGMY-OWL *Glaucidium hardyi* 14–15 cm (5½–6 in)

Locally fairly common in central and southern Amazonia up to 1150 m; found to the north bank of the Amazon, but not known to reach Ecuador border. Found in humid forest interior. Often perches in the subcanopy or canopy. Not known to have a rufous morph. Crown finely spotted. Ferruginous Pygmy-Owl usually is found at forest edge, usually is rufous, typically has a streaked crown, is longer-tailed, and apparently never has white tail bands in Peru. **VOICE** Song is a slightly descending, melancholy, rapid series of whistled notes: "*tutututututututututo*" (about 10 notes/sec). **Br, Bo**

3 ANDEAN PYGMY-OWL *Glaucidium jardinii* * 17–18 cm (6¾–7 in)

Uncommon to locally fairly common in humid montane forest on east slope of Andes, 1500–3600 m; also on west slope of Andes south to Cajamarca. Crown of adult usually spotted; crown narrowly streaked in immatures and unmarked in juveniles. Found at higher elevations than other humid forest pygmy-owls. **VOICE** Song includes a series of rapid piping notes followed by a series of "*poop*" notes, given at about 3 notes/sec in northern *jardinii* (north of Río Marañón), about 2 notes/sec in southern *bolivianum* (south of Marañón): "*HU'u'u'u'u HU'u'u'u'u POOP POOP POOP POOP POOP.*" Also gives a longer series of "*poop*" notes without the introductory phrases. Calls include thin chirps and warbling notes. **Co, E, Bo**

4 PERUVIAN PYGMY-OWL *Glaucidium peruanum* 16.5–18 cm (6½–7 in)

Replaces Ferruginous Pygmy-Owl on west slope of Andes and in dry intermontane valleys, up to 3300 m. Fairly common to common in dry woods, riparian forest, scrub, and gardens. Brown or gray morphs are frequent (in contrast to Ferruginous Pygmy-Owl, which usually is very rufous), especially in Andes. Best identified by range, habitat, and voice. Also similar to Andean Pygmy-Owl, but found in drier woods. Typically a colder, grayer shade of brown, and with whiter spots on scapulars and barring on remiges. **VOICE** Song on Pacific slope is a rapid (about 4 notes/sec or faster) of rising hoots: "*poop'poop'poop'poop....*" Song in Marañón Valley similar. Calls include chirping and thin warbling notes. **E, Ch**

5 FERRUGINOUS PYGMY-OWL *Glaucidium brasilianum* * 16–18 cm (6¼–7 in)

Fairly common and widespread in Amazonia, locally up to 2000 m. Found in river-edge forest, at forest edge (especially of varzea forest) and in second growth. Typically very rufous; brown morph less common. Crown has narrow streaks or is unmarked. Tail relatively long, rufous banded with black or (less commonly, in brown morphs) with buffy (not white) bands. **VOICE** Song a fairly slow (about 2 notes/sec) series of rising hoots: "*poop poop poop poop....*" Sometimes starts song with thin chirping notes that descend in pitch to "normal" song. Calls include chirps and thin warbling notes. **Co, E, Br, Bo**

gray morph

gray morph

rufous morph

SUBTROPICAL PYGMY-OWL

AMAZONIAN
PYGMY-OWL

ANDEAN PYGMY-OWL

buffy-brown morph

brown morph

imm.

rufous morph

juv.

ANDEAN PYGMY-OWL

FERRUGINOUS
PYGMY-OWL

juv.

rufous morph

PERUVIAN PYGMY-OWL

brown morph

brown morph

juv.

rufous morph

FERRUGINOUS PYGMY-OWL

PLATE
85

POTOOS AND OILBIRD

Potoos are large nocturnal insectivores. Perch vertically, and in most species high above ground. Rely on cryptic coloration during day (resembling a dead branch, enhanced by posture) for concealment. When feeding, sally forth to capture prey in flight. Bill short but very wide. Eyes highly reflective of light. Notches in eyelid permit potoos to see even when eyes are closed (as when in defensive posture). Are most vocal on moonlit nights, especially around the full moon, and at twilight. Oilbirds nest and roost in colonies in caves, from which they venture out at night to feed on fruit (especially of palms and Lauraceae) that are plucked while in flight. Oilbirds navigate with echolocation.

1 COMMON POTOO Nyctibius griseus * 35.5–40.5 cm (14–16 in)
Most common and widespread potoo. Fairly common in eastern lowlands, up to 1400 m, locally to 2200 m; also rare and local in northwest. Primarily a bird of forest edge. Usually predominately gray (less frequently brownish), with lightly streaked underparts and a double "necklace" of black spots on breast. Lacks obvious white on wing coverts. **VOICE** Song a forlorn series of whistled notes, the first the longest, descending in pitch: "*Waaoo, woo-woo-wooh-wuuh.*" May sing on the wing. Song occasionally hoarse in quality. **Co, E, Br, Bo**

2 ANDEAN POTOO Nyctibius maculosus 38–40.5 cm (15–16 in)
Rare and local (but also possibly overlooked?) in humid montane forest on east slope of Andes, 1400–2600 m. Typically found at higher elevations than Common Potoo. Has characteristic white lesser wing coverts. Plumage also more densely mottled than Common Potoo, lacking strong contrast of a cluster of dark spots on light gray breast. **VOICE** Song a loud human-sounding cry: "*raaAAH!*" Call, often given in flight or just upon landing, a quieter "*bu bu bu.*" **Co, E, Bo**

3 LONG-TAILED POTOO Nyctibius aethereus * 48–53.5 cm (19–21 in)
Rare but widespread in Amazonia, below 1000 m, locally to 1500 m. Found in the under- and midstory of humid forest. Tail very long, extending well beyond closed wing tips. Also usually shows white or buffy wing coverts and overall tawny plumage. **VOICE** Song a somewhat human-sounding cry "*rahOOL!*" given repeatedly about 1 note per 7 sec. Usually starts a singing bout with more muffled notes at a faster pace: "*ow ow aOW raOW rahOOL....*" Call, often given in flight or just upon landing, a series of quieter "*woof*" notes. At dawn, sometimes a harsh clucking series. **Co, E, Br, Bo**

4 GREAT POTOO Nyctibius grandis * 48–53.5 cm (19–21 in)
Widespread but uncommon in Amazonia, below 1000 m. Found in canopy of humid forest, including river-edge forest. Readily recognized by very large size and pale gray, unstreaked plumage. Juvenile (not illustrated) is particularly "ghostly" white. Iris brown (yellow in other potoos). **VOICE** Song is an explosive, fearsome growl, fit for a large mammal: "*BAAWWWrrr.*" Call, often given in flight or on landing, muffled "*gwaw*" notes. **Co, E, Br, Bo**

5 WHITE-WINGED POTOO Nyctibius leucopterus 24–29 cm (9½–11½ in)
Rare and local; in Peru known only from stunted white-sand forests on north bank of the Amazon, but should be looked for elsewhere in similar habitats. Smaller than Common and Long-tailed potoos, with extensively white wing coverts. **VOICE** Song a long, clear, descending whistle, dying away at end. Call a short "*bweep*" note. **Br**

6 RUFOUS POTOO Nyctibius bracteatus 25–26 cm (9¾–10¼ in)
Rare and poorly known in Peru (but also overlooked?). Most records are from sites on white-sand forests, but also known from some localities with no apparent white-sands associations. Found in forest understory, perching within a few meters of ground. Much smaller than Oilbird, with upright posture, different behavior, yellow iris, and more heavily spotted rufous plumage. Cf. also nightjars. **VOICE** Song, similar to a screech-owl in quality, is a fairly rapid descending series of notes: "*PAHpahpahpahpah.*" Call a short "*wup*" note. **Co, E, Br**

7 OILBIRD Steatornis caripensis 43–47 cm (17–18½ in)
Local but widespread along east slope of Andes, 500–2200 m. Patchily distributed. May fly long distances in search of food; very rarely is reported from coast or from eastern Amazonia, far from any known roost cave. Note large size, hooked bill, long tail, and white-spotted, reddish brown plumage; unmistakable. **VOICE** At caves, colonies produce a deafening cacophony of screeches, growls, and clicks. When foraging, individuals also may give grating growls. **Co, E, Br, Bo**

COMMON POTOO
gray morph   brown morph

ANDEAN POTOO

LONG-TAILED
POTOO

GREAT POTOO

WHITE-WINGED
POTOO

RUFOUS POTOO

OILBIRD

COMMON POTOO

PLATE
86
NIGHTHAWKS

Nighthawks are cryptically colored. Roost during day on the ground or lengthwise along branches, and capture insects, usually at dusk or night, during extended bouts of flight. Eggs laid directly on ground or (Lurocalis) on branch.

1 RUFOUS-BELLIED NIGHTHAWK *Lurocalis rufiventris* 23 cm (9 in)

Uncommon but widespread in humid montane forest on east slope of Andes, 1500–3450 m. Similar to Short-tailed Nighthawk; distinguished by elevation, voice, larger size, and unbarred, rufous belly. **VOICE** Song, in flight and when perched, a descending series of hoarse rising whistles, recalling Common Potoo: "*WEEE weeee weeuu.*" Calls a muffled "*pow*," a series of muffled rising coos, and a low growl. **Co, E, Bo**

2 SHORT-TAILED NIGHTHAWK *Lurocalis semitorquatus* * *semitorquatus* 19 cm (7½ in); *nattereri* 21.5–22.5 cm (8½–8¾ in)

Uncommon but widespread in Amazonia. Forages over humid forest. Remarkably batlike flight enhanced by short tail. Two subspecies: *nattereri* (more richly colored, underparts only lightly barred; austral migrant) and *semitorquatus* (smaller, more heavily barred below; resident?). **VOICE** Song (*semitorquatus*), in flight and when perched, a liquid whistle "*tuip*" interspersed with a series, often rising, of more gruff barks: "*pah pah pah.*" Song (*nattereri*) a more drawn out whistled "*toooeeet*" and a muffled "*bah.*" **Co, E, Br, Bo**

3 SAND-COLORED NIGHTHAWK *Chordeiles rupestris* * 20.5–21.5 cm (8–8½ in)

Fairly common and widespread in Amazonia below 600 m. Colonial (colonies sometimes large) on sandy river margins and sandbars (shares habitat with Ladder-tailed Nightjar). In flight note striking black-and-white wing pattern and largely white underparts. Female has more extensive mottling on breast; tip of tail brown (not black). **VOICE** Song, usually given from ground, a gurgling purr, similar to Lesser Nighthawk, interspersed with quiet throat-clearing sound and loud "*grawh*" notes. Calls a series of loud "*grawh*" notes, quiet "*pup*" notes, and (when performing chase flights) a grating trill interspersed with a "*gaw-gaw-gaw,*" reminiscent of a truck down-shifting on a hill. **Co, E, Br, Bo**

4 COMMON NIGHTHAWK *Chordeiles minor* * 23–24 cm (9–9½ in)

Uncommon but widespread boreal migrant to eastern lowlands, present at least Oct–Apr; also very rare vagrant to coast. Sometimes seen in loose flocks. Structure like Lesser Nighthawk, but larger, and wings more sharply pointed. Flies with deep, pounding wingstrokes (wingbeats of Lesser usually are faster and shallower). Wing band always white (never buff), and closer to base of primaries; also lacks buffy spots on remiges. Female has buff throat (not white), lacks white in tail. **VOICE** Usually silent in Peru. May give a deep, buzzy "*BEEurt.*" **Co, E, Br, Bo**

5 NACUNDA NIGHTHAWK *Podager nacunda* * 27–30 cm (10–11¾ in)

Rare to uncommon austral migrant to eastern lowlands. Most records northern Amazonia, but also on savanna on Pampas del Heath (resident?). Found in open habitats, including river islands. Often rests on ground in open, and frequently seen flying in daylight. Usually as singles or pairs, but sometimes in flocks (especially when migrating?). Readily identified by very large size, contrast between dusky breast and white belly, and large white wing band on broad, round-tipped wings. Female (not illustrated) lacks white in tail. **VOICE** Usually silent. May give a deep, booming "*bmmm-HOOP.*" **Co, E, Br, Bo**

6 BAND-TAILED NIGHTHAWK *Nyctiprogne leucopyga* * 18–19 cm (7–7½ in)

Uncommon and local in northern Amazonia. Forages with erratic flight low over water, usually blackwater streams or lakes, and often in small groups. Typically perches vertically; most other nightjars usually perch horizontally. Note dark plumage, long tail, and all-dark wings; white at base of tail also diagnostic but can be difficult to see (and sometimes may be lacking: immature plumage?). **VOICE** Song, usually from concealed perch, a mellow "*chew, CHEEwunk-WHEEoo.*" **Co, E, Br, Bo**

7 LESSER NIGHTHAWK *Chordeiles acutipennis* * 20.5–21.5 cm (8–8½ in)

Fairly common on coast and in dry Marañón Valley up to 950 m; not recorded from Amazonian Peru, although there are a few records from eastern Ecuador (migrants from North America?). Found in open habitats, including fields and dry scrub. Flight erratic, with frequent glides on slightly raised wings. Note long tapered wings with white (male) or buff (female) band, and long tail; cf. Common Nighthawk. **VOICE** Song, usually given from ground, a gurgling purr interspersed with a snorting sound. Call a goatlike bleat or whinny. **Co, E, Br, Bo, Ch**

SHORT-TAILED NIGHTHAWK

nattereri

semitorquatus

COMMON NIGHTHAWK

♀

RUFOUS-BELLIED NIGHTHAWK

SAND-COLORED NIGHTHAWK

♂

COMMON NIGHTHAWK

♂

♀

NACUNDA NIGHTHAWK

♂

♀

♂

♂

NACUNDA NIGHTHAWK

♂

BAND-TAILED NIGHTHAWK

BAND-TAILED NIGHTHAWK

LESSER NIGHTHAWK

♂

BAND-TAILED NIGHTHAWK

COMMON NIGHTHAWK

RUFOUS-BELLIED NIGHTHAWK

SAND-COLORED NIGHTHAWK

♀

NACUNDA NIGHTHAWK

♂

♀

LESSER NIGHTHAWK

PLATE
87

LONG-TAILED NIGHTJARS AND POORWILL

Nightjars are cryptically colored and nocturnal. Sally after flying insects. Often most easily detected, and identified, by voice. Note amount and distribution of white on wings and tail; males also often show more white than do females. See also plate 88.

1 **LYRE-TAILED NIGHTJAR** *Uropsalis lyra* * male up to 100 cm (39½ in) including tail streamers, female 23.5–25.5 cm (9¼–10 in)
Uncommon and local, at edge of humid montane forest on east slope of Andes, 1300–2100 m; prefers areas around cliffs or rock cuts. Larger than Swallow-tailed, with prominent rufous collar. Tail streamers of male much broader, longer, and tipped white; for most of length outer webs are dark (not white). **VOICE** Song, usually only in a short period after sunset and before sunrise, a rollicking series of whistles, rising in pitch and volume: "*wipple-weeoo wipple-WEEooo WIPPLE-WEEOOO.*" **Co, E, Bo**

2 **COMMON PAURAQUE** *Nyctidromus albicollis* * 26.5–28 cm (10½–11 in)
Fairly common, widespread in eastern lowlands, below 1200 m; also uncommon in Marañón Valley and in northwest, up to 2400 m in forest edge and second growth. Note long tail, boldly spotted scapulars, and rufous sides of face (less contrasting in rare rufous morph). Immatures more heavily marked; white on throat and wings reduced or lacking. In flight shows conspicuous pale band on primaries (reduced in females); buff in immatures); male has long white stripes on side of tail (white very reduced in female). **VOICE** Song "*pah-whEEER*" or "*gwEEEO.*" When agitated, may give quiet "*wup*" notes and a hoarse "*gaw.*" **Co, E, Br, Bo**

3 **LADDER-TAILED NIGHTJAR** *Hydropsalis climacocerca* * male 25–26 cm (9¾–10¼ in), female 22.5–23.5 cm (8¼–9¼ in)
Fairly common, widespread in eastern lowlands; primarily below 600 m but locally enters intermontane valleys to 2600 m. Found in river edge forest, beaches, and lake margins; sometimes forms loose flocks. Tail long; central and outermost rectrices longer than others, forming peculiar double notch. Male has large white throat and belly and extensive white in tail. Both sexes have band on primaries (reduced, and sometimes buff, in female). **VOICE** Song, in flight, a rasping "*kweek*" note, interspersed with a ringing whistled rattle (mechanical?). May give "*kweek*" when perched; also a chirping "*chip.*" **Co, E, Br, Bo**

4 **OCELLATED POORWILL** *Nyctiphrynus ocellatus* * 21–22.5 cm (8¼–8¾ in)
Uncommon, in eastern lowlands below 1300 m, widespread, except scarce or absent from northeast. Humid forest interior. Dark; sooty- (male) or rufous- (female) brown with white throat, black spots on scapulars and white spots on belly. Outer rectrices narrowly tipped white; no white on upper surface of wings. Blackish Nightjar superficially similar but smaller, barred below, densely spotted buff above, and wing tips nearly reach tail tip when perched. **VOICE** Song a hollow, purred note with a similar effect to plucking a taut string: "*qurr'u'u.*" Call a rough, short "*pjur pjur pjur.*" **Co, E, Br, Bo**

5 **SWALLOW-TAILED NIGHTJAR** *Uropsalis segmentata* * male up to 75 cm (29½ in) including tail streamers, female 21–23 cm (8¼–9 in)
Uncommon to locally fairly common in humid montane forest and treeline shrub zones on east slope of Andes, 2000–3600 m; also local on west slope (Cajamarca). Found at higher elevations than Lyre-tailed. Male has very long, relatively narrow outer rectrices, with white outer webs. Female dusky, densely spotted with buff. Smaller than female Lyre-tailed, with buff spots on crown and less prominent rufous collar. Cf. also female Scissor-tailed (no elevational overlap). **VOICE** Song a rough growl, rising in pitch and volume, then abruptly falling: "*wuuurrrRRRREEEEEEEERrrrrrr.*" Call a liquid, rising "*pwip,*" and a musical mellow stuttered whistle when agitated. **Co, E, Bo**

6 **SCISSOR-TAILED NIGHTJAR** *Hydropsalis torquata* * male up to 66 cm (26 in) including tail streamers, female 25–30 cm (9¾–11¼ in)
Rare to uncommon resident locally in dry intermontane valleys and scattered sites in Amazonia with open habitats, up to 1700 m; also apparent rare austral migrant to southern Amazonia, in pastures, grasslands, and forest edge. Male has very long outer rectrices with white inner webs; cf. *Uropsalis* nightjars of higher elevations, more humid habitats. Female similar to female Ladder-tailed, but differs in habitat; also is larger, darker, with more obvious rufous collar, and lacks pale wing band. **VOICE** Song a thin, peeping "*ti,*" apparently accompanies a low raspy "*rhi rhi-grrr*" (mechanical?). **Br, Bo**

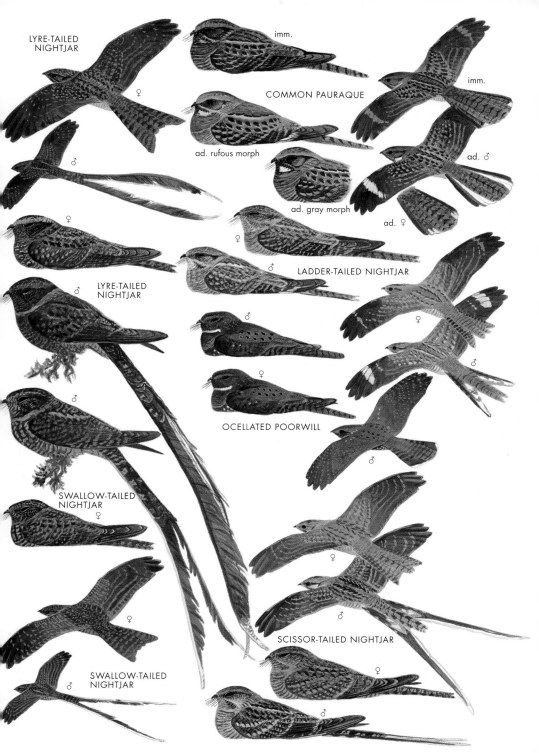

LYRE-TAILED
NIGHTJAR

♀

imm.

♂

COMMON PAURAQUE

ad. rufous morph

imm.

ad. ♂

♀

ad. gray morph

ad. ♀

LYRE-TAILED
NIGHTJAR

♂

♀

LADDER-TAILED NIGHTJAR

♂

♀

♂

♂

♀

SWALLOW-TAILED
NIGHTJAR

♀

OCELLATED POORWILL

♂

♂

♀

♂

SCISSOR-TAILED NIGHTJAR

♀

♀

SWALLOW-TAILED
NIGHTJAR

♂

♂

PLATE
88

CAPRIMULGUS NIGHTJARS

Species shown here vary in size but never have long tail streamers. Cf. also the species on plate 87.

1 **BLACKISH NIGHTJAR** *Caprimulgus nigrescens* 19.5–21 cm (7¾–8¼ in)

Rare and local. Found at forest edge, especially in rocky or gravelly sites, and in stunted forest, primarily 600–1350 m along east slope of Andes; descends to lowlands, especially along rivers and in stunted forest on white sands in northern and central Amazonia. Small, very dark nightjar with white throat. Wings and tail have very little (male) or no (female) white. When perched, wings reach nearly to tail tip. **VOICE** Song a quiet purred series of "*wurt*" notes. Also a louder, more Pauraque-like "*quEEo.*" Call a liquid "*pip*" note. **Co, E, Br, Bo**

2 **BAND-WINGED NIGHTJAR** *Caprimulgus longirostris* * 22–23 cm (8½–9 in); *decussatus* 20–21 cm (7¾–8¼ in)

Fairly common in dry scrub and fields on west slope of Andes, below 1300 m. Also in open habitats and at forest edge of Andes, 1950–4400 m. Varies in size and color (probably includes more than one species). Always has rufous collar, white or buff primary band, and white tips to outer rectrices (much broader in male). Coastal *decussatus* is small and pale. *Ruficervix* of Andes north and west of Marañón is darker than more widespread Andean *atripunctatus*. **VOICE** Song (both montane subspecies) a series of high, thin slurred whistles: "*teeeEEEEuu.*" In flight 3 wing snaps accompany a "*teee*" note. Call a peeping "*chi.*" Song of *decussatus* quite different, a loud series of "*cueeo*" notes, reminiscent of Pauraque and Scrub Nightjar, but more monosyllabic. **Co, E, Br, Bo, Ch**

3 **RUFOUS NIGHTJAR** *Caprimulgus rufus* 25.5–28 cm (10–11 in)

Uncommon and local. Primarily in dry intermontane valleys, 300–1650 m, but also at some more humid sites. Large, rufescent nightjar with some white spots on center of breast, but no wing markings; usually appears dark overall. Inner webs of outer rectrices of male extensively white (not visible on closed tail); outer rectrices of female tipped buff. Separated from most species by size, overall color, plain wings, and nearly complete rufous collar; cf. Silky-tailed. **VOICE** Song a loud, staccato "*chup, whi-whi-RIoh*" or "*chuck whip-his-WIDdow,*" repeated fairly rapidly. When agitated, a series of quiet "*gaw*" notes. **Co, E, Br, Bo**

4 **SILKY-TAILED NIGHTJAR** *Caprimulgus sericocaudatus* * 24–30 cm (9½–11¾ in)

Status and distribution not clear; apparently rare, local resident in lowlands near base of Andes, locally to 1900 m. Found in humid forest. Similar to Rufous, but sootier, less rufescent, and with white spotting on belly as well as breast. Also note different tail pattern: outer webs of outer rectrices tipped white (male) or narrowly tipped buff (female); and has whiter throat and grayer mottling on crown. **VOICE** Song a musical "*a'chewEEoo,*" rising in middle. **Br, Bo**

5 **LITTLE NIGHTJAR** *Caprimulgus parvulus* 19–21 cm (7½–8¼ in)

Status not clear; perhaps primarily an austral migrant, but also has bred, at least locally. Rare and local in eastern lowlands. Presumably found primarily at forest edge. Small, with a rufous collar and white (male) or buffy (female) throat. In flight male has broad white band on primaries and small white tips to outer rectrices; wings and tail of female lack white. **VOICE** Song a peculiar popping and gurgling "*jerEEdjeedle-eedle-eedle.*" **Co, Br, Bo**

6 **SPOT-TAILED NIGHTJAR** *Caprimulgus maculicaudus* 19–20.5 cm (7½–8 in)

Uncommon and very local. Very small nightjar found in grasslands and other open habitats in eastern lowlands and dry intermontane valleys, up to 1350 m. Very buffy with a rufous collar; also note contrast between dusky crown and irregular buffy superciliary. Primaries have several narrow buffy bands but no single obvious band. Tail of male has small white spots on corners; tail of female unmarked. **VOICE** Song a high lisping "*tip-SEEEUUEEET.*" **Co, E, Br, Bo**

7 **SCRUB NIGHTJAR** *Caprimulgus anthonyi* 18.5–19 cm (7¼–7½ in)

Uncommon in dry scrub of northwest and of middle Marañón Valley below 800 m. At rest similar to Little (but no overlap); darker and more heavily mottled than *decussatus* Band-winged (which might overlap locally). In flight both sexes have white band on primaries and white stripes on outer rectrices (white reduced in female). Cf. also larger, longer-tailed Pauraque. **VOICE** Song a clear "*keeLEEoo*" somewhat similar to songs of Pauraque or *decussatus* Band-winged Nightjar. **E**

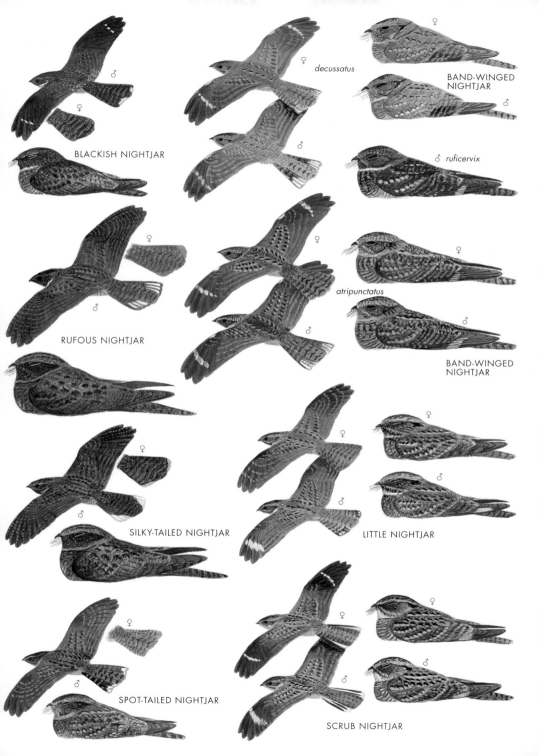

BLACKISH NIGHTJAR

decussatus

BAND-WINGED
NIGHTJAR

♂ ruficervix

RUFOUS NIGHTJAR

atripunctatus

BAND-WINGED
NIGHTJAR

SILKY-TAILED NIGHTJAR

LITTLE NIGHTJAR

SPOT-TAILED NIGHTJAR

SCRUB NIGHTJAR

PLATE
89

LARGE SWIFTS

Swifts feed entirely in flight but roost and nest in cavities in trees or on cliff ledges. Wingbeats rapid and shallow, with frequent glides; flight looks "twinkling." Often forage in flocks, which may contain several species. Field identification often very difficult and should be attempted only with excellent light and close scrutiny. Status of many species poorly known; also, additional migratory species may occur in Peru (but are not yet documented). Shape often a good clue to identification but may vary when a bird is gliding, "stalling out," or preening. White-collared Swift is very large. Cypseloides and Aeronautes are medium-sized; usually in montane areas but may descend to lowlands. Nest and roost under waterfalls (Cypseloides) or on cliffs and ledges (Aeronautes).

1 WHITE-CHINNED SWIFT *Cypseloides cryptus* 15 cm (6 in)
Rare (but also often overlooked?), on east slope of Andes and adjacent lowlands, up to 2000 m. Similar to Chestnut-collared but has larger, more bulbous head extending farther ahead of wings, no notch in tail, and straighter wings (less bowed). In good light, white markings on face may be visible. Immatures may have extensive white mottling on lower belly. **VOICE** Call a dry, buzzy, accelerating rattling; less electric in quality than calls of Chestnut-collared. Also single dry "*tick*" notes. **Co, E, Br**

2 WHITE-COLLARED SWIFT *Streptoprocne zonaris* * 20.5–21.5 cm (8–8½ in)
Fairly common in mountainous regions, except altiplano; regularly up to treeline at 3500 m, occasionally to 4300 m. Also sometimes in Amazonian lowlands well away from foothills. Largest swift (although size not always apparent, especially when flying high above ground). Note long wings and characteristic slow, floppy, rowing wingbeat. White collar of adult visible at long distances. Collar on immature less pronounced; in good light, extensive whitish scaling may be visible. Note size, wing shape, and flight style; also note deeply notched tail. **VOICE** Calls, often given in chorus from large groups, include shrill "*sheeat*" notes, usually accelerating excitedly. Also quiet peeps. **Co, E, Br, Bo**

[WHITE-CHESTED SWIFT *Cypseloides lemosi*] 14 cm (5½ in)
Rare (but also often overlooked?), on east slope of Andes in north, 350–1600 m. Also rare visitor east to Río Yavarí and south to Cuzco. May be only a nonbreeding migrant. Adults have white blaze on chest (on some may look like a collar); usually lower on breast than collar of White-collared Swift, also note proportionately shorter wings and less notched tail. Immatures may lack white; very difficult to separate from White-chinned Swift in field. **VOICE** Calls a rapid, piping "*pi'pi'pi-pee pee*" and single "*tip*" and "*pee*" notes. **Co, E, Br, Bo**

3 ANDEAN SWIFT *Aeronautes andecolus* * 12–12.5 cm (4¾–5 in)
Uncommon to common over arid and semihumid vegetation along west slope from Cajamarca south, occasionally descending to sea level, also locally in arid upper Marañón Valley (*parvulus*). Also (*peruvianus*) in arid intermontane valleys (Mantaro, Apurímac, and Urubamba), 2000–4500 m. Medium-sized swift with deeply notched tail. Regularly overlaps only White-collared Swift over most of range. Note white band on rump, white collar, and extensive white underparts. Interior *peruvianus* whiter below than more widespread *parvulus*, but darker undertail coverts; sexual dimorphism may play a role in plumage variation. **VOICE** Calls a dry, grating chatter similar to that of White-tipped, but higher pitched and drier: "*ti ti tzzeeee'tz'tz'tzeee'tz'tz'tzeee.*" **Bo, Ch**

4 WHITE-TIPPED SWIFT *Aeronautes montivagus* * 12 cm (4¾ in)
Uncommon to fairly common, over humid montane forest on east slope of Andes; local in arid middle Marañón Valley and in northwest. Mostly 1200–2400 m, but locally up to 3000 m and down to 750 m. Medium-sized, with notched tail and bold patches of white. White vent strap always present, usually easy to see. Plumage variation poorly understood. Males appear to be more boldly marked, with white throat and blaze extending down breast; white tips to rectrices may be visible against dark background. Females apparently darker; may have dull brownish throats and lack white on tail tip. Lesser Swallow-tailed Swift has longer, more pointed, tail; and white on flanks does not meet across vent. Andean occurs in more arid habitats, has white on rump and on belly. **VOICE** Calls a ringing, grating chatter: "*bzz-zz'zzz'zzz'zeee'tur'tur.*" **Co, E, Br, Bo**

WHITE-CHINNED
SWIFT

juv.

ad.

WHITE-COLLARED
SWIFT

ad.

ad.

juv.

WHITE-CHESTED SWIFT

juv.

ad.

ANDEAN SWIFT

WHITE-TIPPED SWIFT

parvulus

♂

peruvianus

♀

PLATE
90
CHESTNUT-COLLARED SWIFT AND *CHAETURA* SWIFTS

Chaetura are small to medium-sized swifts. Fairly common over lowlands and foothills. Most species nest and roost in hollow trees. Often vocal. Plumage differences very subtle and can be difficult to determine in field; for example, dark rumps can appear light when reflecting strong sunlight, and light rumps can appear dark when backlit. Cf. also immature Chestnut-collared Swift (which has notched tail and smaller-headed appearance).

1 CHESTNUT-COLLARED SWIFT *Streptoprocne rutila* * 13–13.5 cm (5–5¼ in)

Uncommon to locally common on east side of Andes, from lowlands to 3000 m. Also in northwest at 1900–3000 m. Medium sized, with small head that does not project very far in front of bowed wings; tail has shallow notch. Adults have rufous collar (restricted to nape on some females). Some immatures (females?) are uniform in color, but in good light still appear paler brown than *Cypseloides*. Larger size, broad-winged shape and notched tail help separate from *Chaetura*. **VOICE** Calls buzzy, sound like electric crackles or static, occasionally strung into a chatter: "*bzzzz'tzz'tzz'tzz zz zzzz zzzzz zzzz.*" **Co, E, Bo**

2 PALE-RUMPED SWIFT *Chaetura egregia* 13.5 cm (5¼ in)

Rare to locally uncommon over humid forest in eastern lowlands, up to 1100 m. Pale rump appears (in good light) whitish and very contrasting. Throat paler than breast (but can be very difficult to see in field). Other *Chaetura* have gray or brownish gray rumps. **VOICE** Calls a rapid insectlike chippering: "*ti-ti-trr'r'r'r'r'r.*" Very similar to voice of Gray-rumped Swift, but thinner, higher, sweeter. Also single descending "*tip*" and "*tew*" notes. **E, Br, Bo**

3 GRAY-RUMPED SWIFT *Chaetura cinereiventris* * 10.5–12 cm (4–4¼ in)

Uncommon to fairly common over humid forest in eastern lowlands, up to 1500 m (*sclateri*); and over deciduous forest in Tumbes (*occidentalis*) to at least 500 m. Perhaps most widespread and common *Chaetura* away from large rivers. Relatively small, with the most consistently fast wingbeats of any *Chaetura*. Similar to larger Pale-rumped but, in good light, rump not contrastingly whitish; also, throat not noticeably paler than breast. Rump of *occidentalis* hardly paler than back. Rumps of other *Chaetura* are browner. **VOICE** Call a rapid insect-like chippering: "*tir-tchree'ree'rr.*" Very similar to voice of Pale-rumped, but slightly lower pitch and harsher, not so tinkling. Also gives single "*tew*" notes. **Co, E, Br, Bo**

4 SHORT-TAILED SWIFT *Chaetura brachyura* * 11 cm (4¼ in)

Fairly common over river-edge forest and forest edge in Amazonia below 1100 m (*cinereocauda*); rare to uncommon over deciduous forest in northwest, up to 1900 m (*ocypetes*). Small or medium sized, with characteristic short-tailed shape, exaggerated by broad wings with bulge along trailing edge of primaries. Rump and undertail coverts pale gray, contrasting with body. *Ocypetes* smaller with shorter wings; may show paler chin. **VOICE** Calls (both subspecies) single chip notes and rapid chippering phrases: "*pi-di'di'chip,*" variable in delivery. More tinkling, not quite as buzzy as most other *Chaetura* swifts. **Co, E, Br, Bo**

5 CHIMNEY SWIFT *Chaetura pelagica* 13 cm (5 in)

Boreal migrant (Oct–Apr). Rare (or overlooked?) in Amazonia below 500 m. Rare to uncommon along coast; very rare on passage in highlands on west slope and on altiplano, 2300–4500 m. The only swift regularly encountered on coast south of Lambayeque, where may be common in cities during austral summer. Large *Chaetura* swift with throat noticeably paler than breast; rump barely paler than back. Very similar to Amazonian, which has paler rump, and throat nearly concolor with breast (good light necessary). Other *Chaetura* smaller, more slender-winged. **VOICE** Call a chatter of loose, chippering twitters; also single "*tip*" notes. **Co, E, Br, Bo, Ch** [Sick's Swift (*Chaetura meridionalis*), an austral migrant (May–Sep) to central Amazonia, is possible in eastern lowlands. Nearly identical to Chimney but has paler, more contrasting brownish gray rump. Limited seasonal overlap with Chimney; voice different, drier, not as musical. Any report should be extensively documented.]

6 AMAZONIAN SWIFT *Chaetura viridipennis* 13–14 cm (5–5½ in)

Rare over humid forest in eastern lowlands; only a few records (but overlooked?). Large, dark *Chaetura*. Brownish gray rump contrasts with back; throat concolor with breast. Cf. very similar Chimney and smaller Gray-rumped swifts. **VOICE** Calls single "*tcheep*" and "*tchip*" notes, often in slow series; not as dry or trilled as other *Chaetura*. **Co, E, Br, Bo**

CHESTNUT-COLLARED
SWIFT

♂

CHESTNUT-
COLLARED
SWIFT

imm.

♀

Chestnut-collared and Gray-
rumped swifts, "stalled" with
flared tail and wings

GRAY-RUMPED
SWIFT

occidentalis

SHORT-TAILED
SWIFT

sclateri

GRAY-RUMPED
SWIFT

SHORT-TAILED
SWIFT

PALE-RUMPED SWIFT

cinereocauda

ocypetes

AMAZONIAN SWIFT

SICK'S SWIFT

CHIMNEY
SWIFT

PLATE
91

LONG-TAILED SWIFTS AND LARGE ANDEAN HUMMINGBIRDS

The swallow-tailed swift and palm-swift are two small, very long-tailed swifts of the lowlands. Hummingbirds are a diverse family of small, hyperactive birds. All have long bills, short tarsi, very rapid wingbeats, and the ability to hover, even to fly backwards. Hummingbirds primarily are nectarivorous, although they also regularly eat tiny arthropods. Some species vigorously defend a patch of flowers, but others visit flowers scattered at various sites following a regular route (a feeding strategy known as "traplining"). Most are solitary, although may congregate at large clusters of flowers (such as flowering Inga trees). Many have iridescent plumage that can shift from blindingly brilliant to black depending upon light conditions. Nests usually are small and cup-shaped, often fastened with cobwebs, attached to small limbs; but some attach nest to underside of a large leaf (hermits) or to rock faces (some high-elevation species, such as hillstars). One measurement is provided for total length and one for bill length. Shown here are the 3 largest hummingbird species.

1 LESSER SWALLOW-TAILED SWIFT *Panyptila cayennensis* * 13.5 cm (5¼ in)
Rare to uncommon over humid forest in eastern lowlands up to 800 m. Also rare in northwest, along base of Andes. Usually found singly or in pairs, but will join mixed swift congregations. Nests are socklike structures attached under a horizontal surface, such as a tree branch; not colonial. Medium sized with long, pointed tail (rarely spread to show fork). White collar and flank patch fairly distinctive; cf. White-tipped Swift of Andes. Larger, heavier body and more boldly patterned than Fork-tailed Palm-Swift. **VOICE** Call a ringing buzzy chatter similar to Andean Swift: "*dzzee d'd'dzeee-dzeee-zzeer.*" **Co, E, Br, Bo**

2 FORK-TAILED PALM-SWIFT *Tachornis squamata* * 13 cm (5 in)
Fairly common over riverine forest in Amazonia up to 800 m, particularly near stands of *Mauritia* palms. Often in small groups, occasionally joined by other swift species. Smallest Peruvian swift, with distinctive shape: narrow wings and tail, the latter usually held closed, rarely showing forked shape. Often flies low over trees. Nests within dangling dead *Mauritia* palm fronds. Compared to Lesser Swallow-tailed Swift, note Palm-Swift's distinctive slender shape and lack of bold white collar or flank patches. **VOICE** Call a thin buzz: "*bzzzzzzz bzz bzzzzzzz.*" Not as harsh as other swifts. **Co, E, Br, Bo**

3 SWORD-BILLED HUMMINGBIRD *Ensifera ensifera* 19.5–22 cm (7¾–8¾ in), bill 7.8–10 cm (3–4 in)
Uncommon in humid montane forest along east slope of Andes, 2400–3600 m; widespread, but somewhat local, especially in south. Rare and local in similar habitats on west slope of Andes in Piura and Cajamarca. Unmistakable, even when seen in rapid flight over forest canopy (when looks like a flying sewing needle). Holds the bill sharply upright when perched; often perches within cover, but sometimes chooses a surprisingly open site. Feeds on a variety of flowers with long corollas, but particularly partial to *Datura*. **VOICE** Call a sharp "*tchip.*" **Co, E, Bo**

4 GIANT HUMMINGBIRD *Patagona gigas* * 20–21 cm (8–8¼ in), bill 3.7–4.1 cm (1½ in)
Widespread and fairly common on west slope of Andes and in intermontane valleys, 2000–4300 m. Occupies open, relatively arid habitats: montane scrub, hedgerows, and open woods (including *Polylepis*). The largest hummingbird, and easily recognized by large size. Wingbeats noticeably slow; may be mistaken for Andean Swift (due to pale rump and wingbeat). Dull, with no gorget or brilliant colors but contrasting pale rump. Underparts variable, dull rufous or light rufous scaled with grayish brown. **VOICE** Call a squeaky, loud "*heee.*" **Co, E, Bo, Ch**

5 GREAT SAPPHIREWING *Pterophanes cyanopterus* * 17–18 cm (6 in), bill 3 cm (1⅛ in)
Fairly common and widespread on east slope of Andes, 2600–3700 m; also locally on west slope of Andes south at least to Cajamarca. Found in elfin forest, shrubby paramo, and at forest edge. Very large, usually identifiable by size alone. When hovering, wingbeats are noticeably slow. Deep blue of wings very apparent in flight; covers most of wing in male, but restricted to wing coverts in female. Male otherwise glittering green; females rich buff below, with pale outer web to outer rectrix. Immature males variably green and dusky brown below. **VOICE** Call a high, thin, liquid chatter. **Co, E, Bo**

LESSER SWALLOW-TAILED
SWIFT

SWORD-BILLED
HUMMINGBIRD

FORK-TAILED PALM-SWIFT

GREAT
SAPPHIREWING

GIANT HUMMINGBIRD

PLATE
92

SICKLEBILLS, HERMITS, AND BARBTHROAT

Sicklebills easily recognized by highly curved bill and streaked plumage. Rufous-breasted Hermit and barbthroat have curved bills, like Phaethornis *hermits (see also pates 90–91), but tails are rounded. All species on this plate forage by traplining in humid forest understory.*

1 WHITE-TIPPED SICKLEBILL *Eutoxeres aquila* * 13.5 cm (5¼ in), bill 3 cm (1¼ in)

Uncommon in humid forest on east slope of northern Andes, 750–2000 m; continues farther south on outlying ridges. Quiet, inconspicuous. Often clings to flowering plants (especially *Heliconia*), probing corollas with remarkable bill. Locally overlaps with Buff-tipped Sicklebill; where both occur, White-tipped may be more common at higher elevations. Rectrices tipped pure white (with no buff or pale rufous); underparts streaked black and white (not dusky and buff). **VOICE** Song a complex series of thin, whiny squeaks followed by some strident, high, "*tseep*" notes. **Co, E**

2 BUFF-TAILED SICKLEBILL *Eutoxeres condamini* * 12–13 cm (4¾–5 in), bill 3 cm (1¼ in)

Uncommon in humid forest along east slope of Andes and outlying ridges, up to 2800 m; locally into lowland forest at base of foothills. Behavior similar to White-tipped Sicklebill's. Tips of rectrices white, but base always buff or pale rufous. Also has shiny patch of blue-green on sides of neck (lacking in White-tipped). **VOICE** Song an incessantly repeated series of ringing notes "*pling! seet-sweet.*" **Co, E, Bo**

3 RUFOUS-BREASTED HERMIT *Glaucis hirsutus* * 11–12 cm (4–4¾ in), bill 2.8–3 cm (1⅛ in)

Fairly common and widespread in Amazonia, up to 1000 m. Usually in seasonally flooded forests and in second growth; most common in *Heliconia* thickets near water. Sexes similar; males slightly duskier on throat and grayer on belly. Long curved bill and face pattern recalls *Phaethornis* hermits, but note extensive rufous in broad, rounded tail. **VOICE** Call a series of descending thin notes: "*tsee tsee tsip-tsit-tsu*"; also an upslurred "*sweet.*" **Co, E, Br, Bo**

4 PALE-TAILED BARBTHROAT *Threnetes leucurus* * 11–12 cm (4¼–4¾ in), bill 3.2 cm (1¼ in)

Uncommon, local in eastern lowlands, up to 1200 m; locally to 1800 m. Understory of humid forest, at forest edge and in second growth; prefers dense thickets, such as along streams, forest borders, or at treefall gaps inside forest. Sexes similar, but female duller than male. Note ornate throat pattern and mostly pale tail. Rectrices primarily light buff in north (crossing to south bank of the Amazon: *cervinicauda*), but white or whitish buff in south (north to San Martín: *rufigastra*); locally both tail colors can be present in same population. **VOICE** Song a series of very high lisping notes: "*tsu-ee-see SI SI SI SI.*" Call in flight a short "*tsi*" note. **Co, E, Br, Bo**

5 PLANALTO HERMIT *Phaethornis pretrei* 14.5–15.5 cm (5¾–6 in), bill 3.1 cm (1¼ in)

Locally common but only in lower Mayo Valley and adjacent portions of Huallaga Valley at 200–600 m. Understory and edge of dry forest. Note large size, very rufous rump (contrasting with green back), buffy underparts, and white-tipped outer rectrices. Occurs at lower elevations and in drier habitats than Koepcke's Hermit (which also has buff-tipped outer rectrices) but overlaps with Long-tailed. **VOICE** Song (E Bolivia) a series of 3-note chips: "*CHU tsi-tsi… CHU tsi-tsi....*" Call in flight a ringing "*seep.*" **Br, Bo**

6 LONG-BILLED HERMIT *Phaethornis longirostris* * 16 cm (6¼ in), bill 4 cm (1½ in)

Fairly common in understory of semideciduous forest in Tumbes and northern Piura, up to 400 m. Large, dull-colored, with dusky "whiskers" framing buff central throat stripe. The only other hermit in northwest, Gray-chinned Hermit (*porcullae*), is much smaller with yellow (not red) mandible and plain, unpatterned throat. **VOICE** Song a somewhat metallic "*tuchee*" repeated incessantly. Call in flight a thin "*seep.*" **Co, E**

7 GREEN HERMIT *Phaethornis guy* * 14.5–15.5 cm (5¾–6 in), bill 3.8–4 cm (1½ in)

Fairly common to common in understory of humid montane forest at 500–1800 m along east slope of Andes and on outlying ridges. Males sing at leks in dense thickets. Both sexes relatively large and dark; females have longer, slightly broader white tips to central rectrices and are slightly paler below, often with buffier throat and belly. **VOICE** Song a tinny "*enkt*" repeated incessantly. Call in flight a loud, rising "*sweet*"; also a descending series of high "*seet*" notes. **Co, E**

WHITE-TIPPED
SICKLEBILL

BUFF-TAILED
SICKLEBILL

PALE-TAILED
BARBTHROAT

rufigastra

cervinicauda,
underside of tail

RUFOUS-BREASTED HERMIT

PLANALTO
HERMIT

LONG-BILLED
HERMIT

GREEN HERMIT

PLATE
93

SMALL HERMITS

Phaethornis are small to medium-sized, dull-colored hummingbirds. Notable for very long bills, often slightly curved, and for long, graduated tails that have elongated central rectrices. Forage by traplining. Males of some species sing at communal sites (leks); singing is accompanied by tail wagging. Inquisitive; may hover briefly in front of a person before zipping away, often with a quick call. Smaller species shown here; see also plates 89, 91.

1 WHITE-BROWED HERMIT *Phaethornis stuarti* * 9.5–10.5 cm (3¾–4 in), bill 2.3 cm (⅞ in)
Uncommon to locally fairly common in Andean foothills and adjacent lowlands of central and southern Peru, 350–1400 m, where replaces Reddish. Rectrices margined with buff in widespread *longipennis* but may be white in southern Cuzco and Puno (*stuarti*). Sexes similar; males usually show narrow black breast band and may be slightly more rufous (less buff) below. Also central rectrices of males are rounded with very narrow pale tips; notably longer, more pointed, and with broader pale tips in females. Larger, buffier below than widespread *nigricinctus* subspecies of Reddish. In south, doubtfully distinguishable from *ruber* subspecies of Reddish (even in the hand). White-browed may be slightly larger; paler below; with greener (less bronzy) rectrices; and longer, more projecting central rectrices in female. Further research required on identification, taxonomic status of hermits in this region. **VOICE** Song a very high, descending, accelerating series of notes: "*TSEE-TSEE-tsee-tsi'ti'tu'tu'tu*" interspersed with quiet "*tewp*" notes. **Bo**

2 REDDISH HERMIT *Phaethornis ruber* * *nigricinctus* 8.5 cm (3¼ in), bill 2 cm (¾ in); *ruber* 9 cm (3½ in), bill 2.3 cm (⅞ in)
The smallest, and most widespread, small hermit in east. Fairly common in understory of humid forest. Richly colored below. Sexes similar, but males usually show narrow black breast band and may be slightly more rufous (less buff) below. Central rectrices never are white or projecting as in other small hermits: rounded with very narrow pale tips (male) or slightly longer, more pointed, and with broader pale (whitish or buff) tips (females). Widespread *nigricinctus* is particularly small; nominate *ruber* (not illustrated; southeast) is slightly larger (cf. White-browed). Also see Gray-chinned (northern Peru). **VOICE** Song a series of high, descending, wiry notes occasionally interrupted by a quickened series of notes: "*tsee tseew tsew tsip, tsee tseew tsew tsip, tseetseutseutseu, tsee tseew tsew tsip....*" **Co, E, Br, Bo**

3 BLACK-THROATED HERMIT *Phaethornis atrimentalis* * 10.5–11.5 cm (4⅛–4½ in), bill 2.3–2.6 cm (⅞–1 in)
Locally fairly common in northern Amazonia, up to 1100 m. Not recorded east of Río Napo, but may occur there as well. Found in dense understory, usually at edge of humid forest. Sexes similar. Central rectrices may be projecting (as illustrated) or rounded (only slightly longer than adjacent pair). Note dusky throat and relatively dull-colored belly. Also is much larger than Reddish Hermit; in Andean foothills cf. Gray-chinned. **VOICE** Song a monotonous series of high wiry notes: "*see sew tsee tsew see sew tsee tsew....*" Calls a sharp, descending "*psew*" and a descending series of falling notes: "*psee psee-psew-psew-psu.*" **Co, E**

4 GRAY-CHINNED HERMIT *Phaethornis griseogularis* * 10 cm (4 in), bill 2 cm (¾ in); *porcullae* 10.5 cm (4 in), bill 2.3 cm (⅞ in)
Small, brightly colored eastern subspecies (*griseogularis, zonura*) are uncommon and local in understory of humid and semihumid montane forest in Marañón Valley and along east slope of northern Andes, 650–2200 m. Larger paler *porcullae* is fairly common in understory of dry and semideciduous forest in northwest, 400–1600 m. Sexes similar; central rectrices of males usually rounded but longer and more projecting in females. Also, some males may show narrow black breast band. Chin is whitish or washed with pale gray, but not extensively dusky as in Black-throated Hermit. May approach Reddish Hermit in foothills, but the two are not known to overlap. Differs from Reddish by pale gray (not white or buff) chin, yellow base to the mandible (usually orange-red in Reddish), and longer tail with more prominent pale tips to rectrices. In the hand, has a distinct gray band on central rectrices, separating white tip from dusky green base. In most of northwest, larger *porcullae* is the only hermit, but overlaps locally with much larger Long-billed. **VOICE** Song (*griseogularis, zonura*) a series of high wiry notes, occasionally interrupted by a quickened section of notes: "*sew-tsew-seew sew-tsew-seew si-si-tsi'tsi-seeew sew-tsew-seew....*" Call a sharp, rising "*sweet*." **Co, E, Br**

longipennis

♂ ♀

WHITE-BROWED HERMIT

nigricinctus

♂ ♀

REDDISH HERMIT

♀

♂, underside
of tail

stuarti

e

porcullae

BLACK-THROATED HERMIT

GRAY-CHINNED HERMIT

PLATE
94

LARGE HERMITS

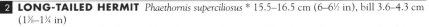

Species on this plate are larger, longer-tailed species of Phaethornis; *see also plates 92, 93.*

1 WHITE-BEARDED HERMIT *Phaethornis hispidus* 13.5–14.5 cm (5¼–5¾ in), bill 3.0–3.4 cm (1¼ in)

Fairly common and widespread in Amazonia, up to 850 m, locally to 1400 m. Found in understory of varzea and seasonally flooded forest, and at forest edge, especially near dense thickets. Sexes similar. Very gray below, with well-defined narrow white stripe down center of throat, and with gray rump and upper tail coverts. Base of mandible yellow. **VOICE** Song a thin, high, downslurred "*tsit*" repeated incessantly. Call a rising "*pseet*" given in flight. **Co, E, Br, Bo**

2 LONG-TAILED HERMIT *Phaethornis superciliosus* * 15.5–16.5 cm (6–6½ in), bill 3.6–4.3 cm (1⅜–1¾ in)

The most common and widespread large hermit in Amazonia. Found in understory of lowland forest, especially terra firme, up to 1300 m. Geographically variable. All populations have long, curved bill with red or orange-red mandible, dusky cheeks framed above and below with pale stripes, and cinnamon scaling on rump and uppertail coverts. Subspecies north of the Amazon (*moorei*) is dull grayish buff below, and chin often dusky (pale throat stripe reduced or lacking); also has relatively little cinnamon on rump. All populations south of the Amazon somewhat brighter, especially on underparts, with more extensive cinnamon on rump. Population south of the Amazon, east of the lower Río Ucayali (*ochraceiventris*) is tawny-buff below and is the most richly colored subspecies. Birds of south-central and southeastern Peru (*bolivianus*; not illustrated) are duller buff below than *ochraceiventris*. Bill length varies; longest in *ochraceiventris* (4.0–4.3 cm; 1¾ in), shortest in *bolivianus* (3.6–3.8 cm; 1⅜–1½ in); other populations intermediate. **VOICE** Song a musical, squeaky "*suilee*" repeated incessantly. Call a thin "*seep*" given in flight. **Co, E, Br, Bo**

3 TAWNY-BELLIED HERMIT *Phaethornis syrmatophorus* * 16–16.5 cm (6¼–6½ in), bill 4 cm (1½ in)

Fairly common in understory of humid montane forest along east slope of Andes of northern Peru, 1200–2200 m. Sexes similar. Very buffy, with rufous-buff rump, whitish throat, and curved bill. Occurs much higher than Koepcke's Hermit, which has straighter bill and much weaker face pattern. **VOICE** Song (eastern Ecuador) a simple, high "*tsing tsang*" repeated incessantly. **Co, E**

4 STRAIGHT-BILLED HERMIT *Phaethornis bourcieri* * 13–14 cm (5–5½ in), bill 3 cm (1⅛ in)

Fairly common in terra firme in lowlands of northern Peru. Crosses the Amazon, on both banks of the Río Ucayali, and is found south to southern Ucayali. Not known to overlap with Needle-billed Hermit, although the two species may meet in central Peru. Note dull tones and straight bill, with yellow base to mandible. Sexes similar. **VOICE** Song a descending series of high, thin notes ending with a high chip repeated incessantly: "*tsii'ti'ti'tsii-ti tip tsii'ti'ti'tsii-ti tip-tip tsii'ti'ti'tsii-ti tip...*" occasionally interrupted with a lower warbled sound. Calls a descending series of high "*seet*" notes, a dull "*chep*," and a rising "*sweet*." **Co, E, Br**

5 KOEPCKE'S HERMIT *Phaethornis koepckeae* 14–15 cm (5½–6 in), bill 3.5 cm (1⅜ in)

Common, but very patchily distributed; primarily restricted to outlying ridges near base of east slope of Andes, 450–1300 m, in understory of humid montane forest. Sexes similar. Note long straight bill, tawny underparts, and whitish throat with dull gray "whiskers"; Needle-billed Hermit is similar but largely found at lower elevations and has tawny throat and no "whiskers." In Mayo Valley see Planalto Hermit. **VOICE** Song a ringing, buzzy series of short notes: "*b'zee b'zee b'zee....*" Calls a ringing, rising "*tchwee*" or "*tchwing*," also a descending, accelerating series of high notes. **ENDEMIC**

6 NEEDLE-BILLED HERMIT *Phaethornis philippii* 14–15 cm (5½–6 in), bill 3.0–3.3 cm (1¼ in)

Fairly common in eastern Amazonia, south of the Amazon, below 500 m. Status in east central Peru (east of Río Ucayali) not certain, but appears to be absent on east bank of middle Ucayali (although present on south bank of the Amazon and in the upper Ucayali). Understory of humid forest, primarily in terra firme. Note the buffy underparts, whitish throat, and straight bill. Sexes similar. Apparently does not lek. **VOICE** Song a monotonous series of high even-pitched or slightly rising "*pseet*" notes. Call a rising "*tsweet?*" **Br, Bo**

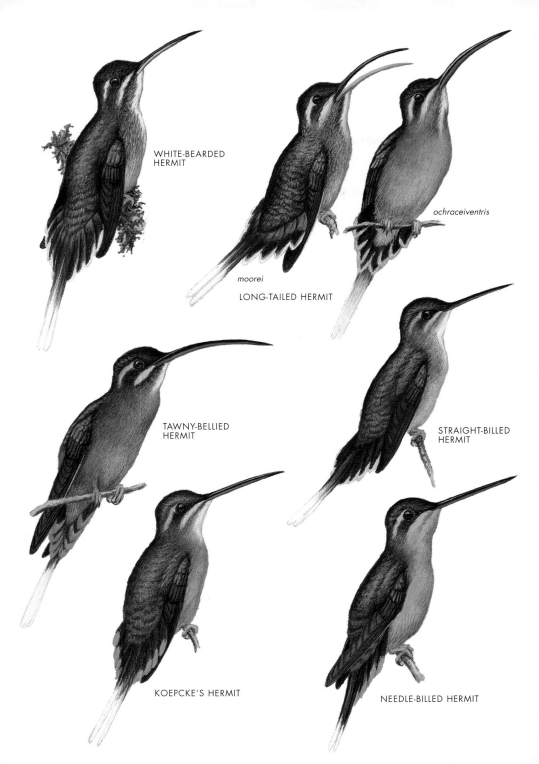

WHITE-BEARDED
HERMIT

ochraceiventris

moorei

LONG-TAILED HERMIT

TAWNY-BELLIED
HERMIT

STRAIGHT-BILLED
HERMIT

KOEPCKE'S HERMIT

NEEDLE-BILLED HERMIT

PLATE
95

SABREWINGS, JACOBIN, HILLSTAR, AND MANGOS

Species on this plate are large to medium sized. Sabrewings have relatively thick bills; males have thickened, curved shafts to outer primaries. Swallow-tailed Hummingbird is notable for the very long, forked tail. Jacobin and hillstar are hummingbirds of humid forest with ample white in tail. Mangos have relatively thick, slightly decurved bills.

1 NAPO SABREWING *Campylopterus villaviscensio* 13.0–13.5 cm (5–5¼ in), bill 2.5 cm (1 in)
Rare to uncommon in understory of humid montane forest in northern Andes, 1050–1400 m, primarily on outlying ridges. Note overall dark color of male, glittering green crown, and contrast between blue throat, breast, and dusky belly. Female similar to very large, dark female woodnymph; darker gray below than Gray-breasted Sabrewing, and with much smaller white tail spots. **VOICE** Song a bisyllabic repeated series: "*trip-SEEP trip-SEEP trip-SEEP....*" Call a rich "*tchup*" or "*tchit*," sometimes doubled. **E**

2 GRAY-BREASTED SABREWING *Campylopterus largipennis* * 13.5–14.5 cm (5¼–5¾ in), bill 2.7–3 cm (1–1⅛ in)
Uncommon but widespread in Amazonia, where is one the largest hummingbirds; up to 1300 m. Found in humid forest, usually at forest edges or margins of streams, oxbow lakes, and other forest openings. Forages at all heights, but most often in under- and midstory. Mandible may be red or black. Undersides of rectrices broadly tipped white. Superficially similar to female Fork-tailed Woodnymph, but is much larger, has larger white tail spots, and a more prominent white postocular spot. **VOICE** Call single "*tchip*" notes. Song like call, but in more regular series. **Co, E, Br, Bo**

3 WHITE-TAILED HILLSTAR *Urochroa bougueri* * 12–13 cm (4¾–5 in), bill 3 cm (1⅛ in)
Rare and local in humid montane forest, 800–1500 m, in northern Andes. Found in midstory and canopy, especially near mountain streams. Medium-sized drab hummingbird with long straight bill. Other than central rectrices, tail is mostly white (particularly prominent from below). Throat and breast glittering purplish blue, contrasting with dingy grayish brown belly. Sexes similar, but female somewhat duller. Distinctive; but cf. male Napo Sabrewing (which lacks white in tail). **VOICE** Song an incessant series of descending "*tsew*" or "*tsing*" notes. **Co, E**

4 SWALLOW-TAILED HUMMINGBIRD *Eupetomena macroura* * male 17–17.5 cm (6¾ in), female 14.5 cm (5¾ in), bill 2.2 cm (⅞ in)
Uncommon to locally fairly common, but found only in dry upper Río Urubamba at 1000–1500 m and on Pampas del Heath. Found at forest edge, in gallery forest, and in woodlots on savanna. A large dark hummingbird with long, deeply forked tail; largely green with blue throat and breast, and blue rectrices. Sexes similar, but tail streamers longer on male. **VOICE** Call a rich "*tchup*." **Br, Bo**

5 WHITE-NECKED JACOBIN *Florisuga mellivora* * 10.5–11.5 cm (4–4½ in), bill 2 cm (¾ in)
Uncommon but widespread in Amazonia, up to 1200 m. Found in humid forest; forages primarily in canopy, but may be lower at forest edges. Spectacular male is unmistakable. Some females also attain this plumage. Immature males (and some immature females) similar to adult male, but breast is duller, with conspicuous buff border to throat or to throat and breast. "Standard" female plumage has largely dark tail; heavily scaled below, especially on throat. **VOICE** Song (Surinam) a high, thin, descending "*tseew*." Call a high, thin "*tsip*" note repeated about twice per sec. **Co, E, Br, Bo**

6 GREEN-BREASTED MANGO *Anthracothorax prevostii* * 11.5–12 cm (4½–4¾ in), bill 2.5 cm (1 in)
Rare to uncommon, at borders of humid forest in Tumbes. No overlap with very similar Black-throated Mango. Note relatively heavy, distinctly curved bill. Male also very dark, with glittering purplish tail. Female readily identifiable by long black stripe down white throat, breast, and belly. Juvenile similar, but sides of throat and breast variably cinnamon. **Co, E**

7 BLACK-THROATED MANGO *Anthracothorax nigricollis* 11.5–12 cm (4½–4¾ in), bill 2.5 cm (1 in)
Uncommon in eastern lowlands, below 800 m; apparently scarce or absent in northwestern Amazonia. Found at forest edge and in river-edge forest. No overlap with extremely similar Green-breasted Mango. Note relatively heavy, distinctly curved bill. Male also very dark, with glittering purplish tail. Female readily identifiable by long black stripe down white throat, breast, and belly. Juvenile does not show cinnamon on sides of breast (unlike juvenile Green-breasted Mango). **VOICE** Call a rising "*pseep*." Also gives a rich "*tchup*." **Co, E, Br, Bo**

NAPO
SABREWING

GRAY-BREASTED
SABREWING

WHITE-TAILED
HILLSTAR

SWALLOW-TAILED
HUMMINGBIRD

ad.   imm. ♂   ♀ ("standard")

WHITE-NECKED JACOBIN

GREEN-BREASTED
MANGO

♂

juv.

BLACK-THROATED
MANGO

PLATE
96

EMERALD, WOODNYMPHS, PLUMELETEER, JEWELFRONT

Blue-tailed Emerald is a widespread species of edge habitats in Amazonia. Woodnymphs are common hummingbirds of humid forest. Forage primarily in the under- and midstory. Males are colorful with forked, deep blue tails; females are light gray below, with noticeable white tips to the rectrices of a rounded tail. Violet-bellied Hummingbird resembles a small woodnymph; both it and White-vented Plumeleteer occur in Peru only in Tumbes. Gould's Jewelfront is an Amazonian representative of the mostly Andean genus Heliodoxa (plate 99).

1 GREEN-CROWNED WOODNYMPH *Thalurania fannyi* * 9.5–10 cm (3¾–4 in), bill 2 cm (¾ in)

Uncommon in humid forest in Tumbes up to 950 m; no overlap with Fork-tailed Woodnymph of eastern Peru. Male is largely glittering green, including crown, with deep glittering blue lesser wing coverts and sides of back. Cf. smaller Violet-bellied Hummingbird (the only similar species with which it overlaps). Female uniformly whitish gray or light gray below, with all-dark bill. **VOICE** Call a series of sweet "*tew*" notes. **Co, E**

2 FORK-TAILED WOODNYMPH *Thalurania furcata* * 9.5–10.5 cm (3¾–4 in), bill 2 cm (¾ in)

Fairly common and widespread in the interior and canopy of humid forest of eastern Peru, up to 1400 m; one of the most frequently seen hummingbirds in Amazonian forests. Male readily recognized by dark plumage, deep blue or purplish blue belly, and forked tail. There is slight (and continuous?) geographic variation; in particular, green gorget more extensive in northern Peru, sometimes also with distinct black border; but gorget is reduced in size, and usually not bordered with black, in south. Female, with uniformly light gray underparts, superficially resembles Gray-breasted Sabrewing but is much smaller with smaller white tips to rectrices. **VOICE** Song an incessant series of bisyllabic, thin, wiry notes: "*see-tseet see-tseet see-tseet….*" Calls a rich "*tchup*," sometimes given in a long series, and a dry trill. **Co, E, Br, Bo**

3 VIOLET-BELLIED HUMMINGBIRD *Damophila julie* * 8.5–9 cm (3¼–3½ in), bill 1.4 cm (½ in)

Fairly common in the understory of humid forest, and forest edges, in Tumbes below 750 m. Green throat and blue belly of male lend superficial similarity to Fork-tailed Woodnymph of Amazonia (no overlap); distinguished from male Green-crowned Woodnymph by smaller size, blue (not green) belly, reddish mandible, and notched (less deeply forked) tail. Female similar to female woodnymph, but is smaller and with reddish base to mandible; throat also usually lightly spotted (plain gray in woodnymphs). **VOICE** Song is a repeated thin, nasal note: "*eee-eh.*" **Co, E**

4 BLUE-TAILED EMERALD *Chlorostilbon mellisugus* * 7.5–8 cm (3 in), bill 1.5 cm (⅝ in)

Widespread and fairly common in eastern lowlands; less common at higher elevations up to 1200 m, locally ascending to 2000 m. A small hummingbird of forest edge and second growth. Male identified by small size, entirely black bill, uniformly green plumage, and slight fork to deep blue tail; cf. Blue-chinned Sapphire. Female has distinctive masked appearance and all-dark bill. Cf. female of larger Fork-tailed Woodnymph. **VOICE** Song is a series of wheezy, electric "*chew*" notes. Calls dry "*pit*" and "*sip*" notes. **Co, E, Br, Bo**

5 WHITE-VENTED PLUMELETEER *Chalybura buffonii* * 11–11.5 cm (4¼–4½ in), bill 2.3 cm (⅞ in)

Uncommon in understory of humid forest in Tumbes up to 800 m. Both sexes have prominent white, fluffy undertail coverts. Female otherwise similar to female Green-crowned Woodnymph, but woodnymph is uniformly gray below (not contrasting white undertail coverts), and plumeleteer is larger, with longer, slightly curved bill. **VOICE** Calls a descending electric whinny, and harsh chatters. **Co, E**

6 GOULD'S JEWELFRONT *Heliodoxa aurescens* 11–11.5 cm (4¼–4½ in), bill 2 cm (¾ in)

Uncommon but widely distributed in humid forest of eastern Peru, below 1400 m. Largely confined to forest interior, where usually seen in under- or midstory, especially at light gaps and stream edges. Largely green, with prominent contrasting rufous breast band; tail also rufous. Narrow glittering purplish blue forecrown of male difficult to see; also has black chin. Female similar in pattern but duller; blue on crown reduced or absent, chin buff or green. No similar species in Amazonia. **VOICE** Song a series of high, thin "*tseet*" notes. Call a high, descending "*tsee tee tee tuu.*" **Co, E, Br, Bo**

FORK-TAILED WOODNYMPH

GREEN-CROWNED WOODNYMPH

♀

♂ n   ♂ se

BLUE-TAILED
EMERALD

♂

♀

VIOLET-BELLIED
HUMMINGBIRD

WHITE-VENTED
PLUMELETEER

♂

♀

juv.

GOULD'S
JEWELFRONT

PLATE
97
VIOLETEARS, TOPAZ, AND GOLDENTHROATS

Violetears are three Andean hummingbirds; all have a violet patch on side of face. Fiery Topaz is a distinctive Amazonian species. Goldenthroats are very local, on Amazonian savannas and other open scrubby habitats.

1 GREEN-TAILED GOLDENTHROAT *Polytmus theresiae* * 9.5 cm (3¾ in), bill 1.8 cm (¾ in)
Fairly common but very patchily distributed. In western Loreto (Jeberos) and at Pampas del Heath on open grassland with scattered shrubs; habitat along Río Pastaza not known. Small, glittering green, with slightly curved bill (with pink base to mandible), small white spots by eye, and all-green tail. Female similar but variably speckled white below. On Pampas del Heath, cf. White-tailed Goldenthroat (note differences in tail pattern). **VOICE** Song, from perch atop a bush, a decelerating and descending series of thin, nasal notes: "*dididdee dee deh deh.*" **Co, E, Br, Bo**

2 FIERY TOPAZ *Topaza pyra* * male 19–19.5 cm (7½–7¾ in), female 13–13.5 cm (5–5¼ in), bill 2.3 cm (⅞ in)
Rare and local in northern Amazonia. Primarily associated with blackwater streams on white-sand and other nutrient-poor soils. Usually seen flycatching over streams, or perched over water; also visits flowering canopy trees. Spectacular male unmistakable. Note large size of female, also pale tarsi and toes (often conspicuous), glittering orange-red throat, and rufous underwing coverts. **VOICE** Song a rich chatter decelerating into a series of "*tchip*" notes followed by high wiry "*pseet-seet*" notes. Sings from perch near canopy; occasionally flies out laterally in a loop, then returns to song perch. **Co, E, Br**

3 WHITE-TAILED GOLDENTHROAT *Polytmus guainumbi* * 10.5–11 cm (4–4¼ in), bill 2.3 cm (⅞ in)
Restricted to Pampas del Heath; fairly common on savanna with scattered shrubs. Medium-sized, green, with noticeably curved bill and white crescents above and below eye. Tail with prominent white tips and outer webs of bases of outer rectrices. Male light glittering green below; female buffy, throat and breast speckled green. **VOICE** Song a series of high thin nasal chatters. Calls thin "*wsst*" and "*psit*" notes. **Co, Br, Bo**

4 BROWN VIOLETEAR *Colibri delphinae* 11–12 cm (4¼–4¾ in), bill 1.5–1.8 cm (⅝–¾ in)
Rare to uncommon, and patchy, along east slope of Andes, 700–1700 m. Canopy of humid montane forest and forest edge. Medium-sized, very drab. Note broad dark patch (iridescent purple) on sides of head and neck, and pale stripe between brown side of face and narrow gular patch. Gular patch largely glittering green, but lower border may be blue (more frequently in females?). Undertail coverts cinnamon-buff. Underside of tail appears largely dusky, with broad paler tips. Cf. the equally dull, but longer-billed and much more common, Brown Inca. **VOICE** Song variable, but generally a long repeated series of bisyllabic high metallic chips: "*p'tip p'tip p'tip….*" Calls liquid chatters and chuckling, also "*tick*" notes. **Co, E, Br, Bo**

5 SPARKLING VIOLETEAR *Colibri coruscans* * 13.5–14 cm (5¼–5½ in), bill 2.5 cm (1 in)
Most widely distributed violetear. More common in drier intermontane valleys and on west slope, but may occur almost anywhere. Elevational range very broad, 400–4500 m, but apparently wanders widely; probably only breeds at higher elevations, above ca. 2500 m. Found in open areas, including agricultural fields, with scattered shrubs, at forest edge, and in eucalyptus groves. Cf. smaller Green Violetear. **VOICE** Very vocal. Song variable, but generally a long repeated series of monosyllabic metallic chips: "*djiit djiit djiit….*" Also an aerial display: flies up from a song perch, circling, and returning, while giving rapid chatters and liquid, almost warbling, phrases. Calls include a dry rattle. **Co, E, Br, Bo, Ch**

6 GREEN VIOLETEAR *Colibri thalassinus* * 10.5–11.5 cm (4–4½ in), bill 2 cm (¾ in)
Uncommon to fairly common, and widespread, along east slope of Andes, mostly 1300–2800 m, locally 1000–3300 m; also on west slope in northwest at 1500–2400 m. Found at edge of humid montane forest, shrubby areas near forest, and forest canopy (especially at gaps). Dull green, with distinctly curved bill, glittering purple auricular patch, and broad dark band across glittering bluish green tail. Smaller than Sparkling Violetear, has no purplish blue on chin or belly, is duller green, and often has buffy undertail coverts. **VOICE** Very vocal. Song variable, but generally a long repeated series of multisyllabic high metallic chips and buzzes: "*piti-CHIP piti-CHIP piti-CHIP…*" or "*zzz-TIP zzz-TIP zzz-TIP….*" Call a dry rattle. **Co, E, Bo**

GREEN-TAILED GOLDENTHROAT

FIERY TOPAZ

WHITE-TAILED
GOLDENTHROAT

SPARKLING VIOLETEAR

BROWN VIOLETEAR

GREEN VIOLETEAR

PLATE
98

VIOLET-HEADED HUMMINGBIRD, COQUETTES, THORNTAILS

These species all are very small. Violet-headed Hummingbird is relatively plain. Male coquettes and thorntails are elaborately ornamented; some have spectacular crests, held flat when foraging but often erect when bird is perched. Both sexes have a white band on rump; thorntails also have large white flank spots. Coquettes and thorntails have a slow, weaving flight (like a heavy-bodied bee). Usually seen in canopy of humid forest, especially at forest edge, visiting flowering trees.

1 BLACK-BELLIED THORNTAIL *Discosura langsdorffi* * male 2 cm (4¼ in), female 7 cm (2¾ in), bill 1 cm (⅜ in)

Rare but widespread in eastern lowlands, in canopy of humid forest and at forest edge. Little overlap with similar Wire-crested Thorntail. Male lacks crest; green gorget is more extensive (extending lower onto belly), and bordered at lower end by small band of glittering coppery red (often difficult to see). Rectrices narrower than in Wire-crested, but with broader shafts; undersides of shafts white (as in Wire-crested), but bluish gray webs (webs deeper, purplish blue in Wire-crested). Female similar to female Wire-crested, but throat and breast green or white flecked with green, not blackish; and upper tail coverts green, not deep blue. Cf. also female Festive Coquette. **Co, E, Br, Bo**

2 WIRE-CRESTED THORNTAIL *Discosura popelairii* male 11.5 cm (4½ in), female 6.5–7 cm (2½–2¾ in), bill 1.2 cm (½ in)

Rare in canopy of humid montane forest and at forest edge, along east slope of Andes, 500–1500 m. Male has very long, deeply forked tail; undersurface of feather shafts of rectrices white. Crest long but very narrow and wispy. Underparts blackish, although in good light throat shows glittering green gorget. Female lacks ornamentation; blackish below, with white malar and flank patches. Cf. female Festive Coquette and Black-bellied Thorntail (although Wire-crested usually occurs at higher elevations than does either of those two species). **VOICE** Call a quiet, liquid "*tew.*" **Co, E, Bo**

3 FESTIVE COQUETTE *Lophornis chalybeus* * 7.5–8 cm (3 in), bill 1.3 cm (½ in)

Rare in eastern lowlands; widely distributed, but scarce or absent from northwestern Amazonia. Male very dark, save for white rump, but has long wispy green crest (usually carried down against the nape) and green gorget with elongated lateral feathers speckled with white. Female lacks ornamentation but has broad white or whitish malar stripes (separated by dusky green center to throat). Female similar to female thorntails but lacks white flank patches (prominent in thorntails); also is dusky brown below, especially on belly, not black or blackish as in female thorntails. **Co, E, Br, Bo**

4 VIOLET-HEADED HUMMINGBIRD *Klais guimeti* * 8.5–9 cm (3¼–3½ in), bill 1.3 cm (½ in)

Uncommon along east slope of Andes and on outlying ridges at 500–1550 m. Found at edge of humid montane forest. Often forages low near ground, but also may visit crowns of flowering trees. Note small size, conspicuous white postocular spot, short square-tipped tail, and black bill. Male has purplish blue crown and throat; crown of female a duller light bluish green. **VOICE** Song a rapid series of thin "*ee'sip*" notes. **Co, E, Bo**

5 SPANGLED COQUETTE *Lophornis stictolophus* 6.8 cm (2¾ in), bill 1 cm (⅜ in)

Known only from a few sites in valleys of Marañón and its tributaries. Not known to overlap with very similar Rufous-crested Coquette, but distributions of these scarce hummingbirds not well known. Male very similar to male Rufous-crested Coquette; dark spots on crown are larger and more extensive, appearing from center of crown back to tip. On present knowledge, female indistinguishable from female Rufous-crested. **Co, E**

6 RUFOUS-CRESTED COQUETTE *Lophornis delattrei* * 7.5–7.8 cm (2¾–3 in), bill 1–1.2 cm (⅜–½ in)

Uncommon to locally fairly common, 500–1400 m, occasionally to 1900 m, along east slope of Andes, south of Marañón; reported from few localities. Male has long rufous crest; tiny dark feather tips confined to crest's rear edge. Glittering green gorget extends laterally onto sides of face. Female lacks crest. Typically shows rufous throat and crown; occasionally throat may be buff, flecked with rufous. Some individuals (immature males?; not illustrated) are very dark below with blackish throats and rufous crown. Plumages and molts of females and immatures poorly known; female may be indistinguishable from female Spangled Coquette. **Co, E, Bo**

BLACK-BELLIED
THORNTAIL

♂

♀

WIRE-CRESTED
THORNTAIL

♀

♂

FESTIVE
COQUETTE

♂

♀

SPANGLED COQUETTE

♂

RUFOUS-CRESTED COQUETTE

VIOLET-HEADED
HUMMINGBIRD

♀

♂

♀

♀, buff-throated

♀

♂

PLATE
99

SAPPHIRES AND EMERALDS

Medium-sized hummingbirds of Amazonian forest and forest edge. All have bills that are partially pink or red; bills of male Hylocharis sapphires are particularly brightly colored.

1 GLITTERING-THROATED EMERALD *Amazilia fimbriata* * 9.5–10 cm (3¾–4 in), bill 1.8 cm (¾ in)

Uncommon to fairly common in northern Amazonia. Found at forest edge, in river-edge forest, and in second growth. Little overlap with Sapphire-spangled Emerald, which occupies similar habitats, but both occur in lower Mayo Valley and on central Río Ucayali. Throat and breast glittering light green or bluish green; green flanks divided by conspicuous white ventral stripe. Throat may show blue tints but never is deep blue. Female (not illustrated) may be duller, throat and breast flecked with white or gray. **VOICE** Song is a repetitive series of short, high, squeaky notes in a random sequence: "*tseet tchew tchip tchew tseet....*" Calls rich chatters and a sweet "*tsee*," the latter sometimes in descending series. **Co, E, Br, Bo**

2 SAPPHIRE-SPANGLED EMERALD *Amazilia lactea* * 9.5–10 cm (3¾–4 in), bill 1.8 cm (¾ in)

Fairly common in lowlands and foothills of central and southern Peru, up to at least 1400 m. Found at forest edge, in river-edge forest, and in second growth. Locally may overlap Glittering-throated; similar to that species, and also with contrasting white ventral stripe, but throat and breast are glittering purplish blue (not green). Female (not illustrated) similar but duller; throat and breast flecked with white or gray. **VOICE** Song (eastern Brazil) a series of harsh, spitting, descending chatters. Calls a rich chatter and "*tchip.*" **E, Br, Bo**

3 BLUE-CHINNED SAPPHIRE *Chlorestes notata* * 8.5–9 cm (3¼–3½ in), bill 1.8 cm (¾ in)

Widespread and locally fairly common in northern and central Peru; status in southern Peru not clear, but reported south to Cuzco. Usually forages low near ground, at or near humid forest edge, below 800 m. Note deep blue, square-tipped tail, and largely pinkish red mandible. Male glittering green, with slight bluish cast to underparts. Cf. male Blue-tailed Emerald (which is smaller, with black bill and notched tail). Female whiter below; superficially similar to larger Glittering-throated Emerald, but has whiter underparts (lacking contrast between white ventral stripe and green flanks) and dark undertail coverts (white on emerald). **Co, E, Br**

4 GOLDEN-TAILED SAPPHIRE *Chrysuronia oenone* * 9.5–10 cm (3¾–4 in), bill 2 cm (¾ in)

Uncommon but widespread in eastern lowlands, up to 1700 m. Found at edge of humid forest and in second growth. Both sexes have glittering coppery upper tail coverts and golden-coppery rectrices; bill black, with pink base to mandible. Male of widespread *josephinae* has blue crown and glittering green underparts; blue-headed *oenone* reported locally from near Ecuadorian border. Female less distinctive, but note tail and rump color. **VOICE** Song an individually variable, somewhat complex, repetitive series of hollow electric-sounding "*zing*" and "*tchup*" notes, and thin chatters. Calls a hollow "*tsuck*" and a liquid chatter. **Co, E, Br, Bo**

5 RUFOUS-THROATED SAPPHIRE *Hylocharis sapphirina* 9 cm (3½ in), bill 2 cm (¾ in)

Poorly known. Locally fairly common in humid forest in northern Amazonia; very scarce and local in central Peru (south possibly to Madre de Dios). Both sexes have small but prominent rufous upper throat. Also note coppery (male) or bronzy (female) tail. Compare to White-chinned and Golden-tailed sapphires. **VOICE** Song (Brazil) a series of rapidly repeated high lisping whistles and chips. Calls high, rich "*tchp*" notes, often given in rapid series. **Co, E, Br, Bo**

6 WHITE-CHINNED SAPPHIRE *Hylocharis cyanus* * 9 cm (3½ in), bill 1.8–2 cm (¾ in)

Uncommon but widespread in central and southern Amazonia below 600 m; reaches north bank of the Amazon, but generally very scarce or absent from most of northern Amazonia. Found in interior of transitional forest. Note coppery rump and deep blue tail; underside of rectrices of female may show pale tips. Male readily recognized by bright red bill, blue head and throat; small white chin not always apparent. Little or no overlap with blue-headed subspecies (*oenone*) of Golden-tailed Sapphire; note differences in bill and tail color, and in habitat. Female more nondescript, but note pale mandible and rump color. **VOICE** Song, from a perch in midstory, highly individually variable, a rapidly given series of high, ringing, electric lisps and chips. Calls a thin, liquid "*tsit*" and "*tip.*" **Co, E, Br, Bo**

GLITTERING-THROATED
EMERALD

♂

SAPPHIRE-SPANGLED
EMERALD

♂

♂ *josephinae*

BLUE-CHINNED
SAPPHIRE

♀

♂

GOLDEN-TAILED
SAPPHIRE

♀

♂ *oenone*

RUFOUS-THROATED
SAPPHIRE

♂

♀

♀

♂

WHITE-CHINNED
SAPPHIRE

PLATE
100

AMAZILIA AND LEUCIPPUS HUMMINGBIRDS

Species on this plate are medium-sized hummingbirds with green upperparts, and underparts that are largely white or pale gray. All found at forest edge or in open habitats.

1 GREEN-AND-WHITE HUMMINGBIRD *Amazilia viridicauda* 10–11 cm (4–4¼ in), bill 2 cm (¾ in)

Locally fairly common but patchily distributed on east slope of Andes, 1000–2750 m. Found in canopy of humid forest and at forest edge; more closely associated with forest than very similar White-bellied Hummingbird. Where the two overlap, reportedly is found in more humid sites, with White-bellied locally restricted to drier habitats. Underside of tail uniformly dull bronzy green. Pale undersurface of tail of White-bellied usually visible, with a good view, but may be pale gray (not strikingly white). **VOICE** Song perhaps not distinguishable from White-bellied. Call also similar, a rich musical chatter, second note highest: "*tsit TSEET tsew-tsew-tsew.*" **ENDEMIC**

2 WHITE-BELLIED HUMMINGBIRD *Amazilia chionogaster* * 10–11 cm (4–4¼ in), bill 2.2 cm (⅞ in)

Fairly common along east slope of Andes, south of Marañón, and in upper, more humid portions of intermontane valleys. Widespread in Utcubamba Valley but replaced in drier Marañón by similar Andean Emerald. Primarily 1200–3500 m, occasionally as low as 350 m. Found at forest edge, in towns and gardens, and in shrubby areas near forest. Very plain: green above, white below with light green spotting on sides of breast. Undersides of inner webs of outer rectrices variably whitish; white may occupy entire web or be reduced to whitish gray base to rectrices (see Green-and-white Hummingbird). **VOICE** Song in most of Peru (south at least to Cuzco) a series of high, ringing squeaks and screeches in random order: "*tseet tchew tchip tchew tseet tchip....*" Song (Bolivia; perhaps also Puno) a series of ringing descending notes "*pseek*" occasionally interspersed with faster "*si si si si si*" notes. Call a rich, buzzy chatter, sometimes in a descending series. **Br, Bo**

3 ANDEAN EMERALD *Amazilia franciae* * 10 cm (4 in), bill 2 cm (¾ in)

Fairly common, but restricted to dry middle and upper Marañón, 400–2750 m. Found in dry scrub and at edge of woodlots. Cf. similar White-bellied Hummingbird (no known overlap). Whiter below than White-bellied (often strikingly white). Crown, nape, and sides of neck of male glittering light blue (often duller on forecrown). Female duller but usually shows light greenish blue wash to nape or light blue sides of breast. Tail may show indistinct dark transverse bar near tip; underside of rectrices lacks white. **VOICE** Song a loud, ringing series of liquid whistles "*TEE TEW TEW.*" **Co, E**

4 SPOT-THROATED HUMMINGBIRD *Leucippus taczanowskii* 11.5–12.5 cm (4½ in), bill 2.3 cm (⅞ in)

Fairly common in arid scrub on west slope of Andes, primarily 900–1900 m; and in dry middle and upper Río Marañón Valley, 350–2800 m. Usually at higher elevations than Tumbes Hummingbird, but locally (southernmost Lambayeque) as low as 200 m. Larger than Tumbes, and throat conspicuously spotted with green; flanks variably washed green. Tail uniformly bronzy green, with no white tips to undersides of outer rectrices and no dark transverse bar (although tips of upper surfaces of rectrices may be more bronzy, less green, than rest of tail). **VOICE** Song a complex series of chips and wheezing electric warbles. Calls a dry chatter and "*tip*" notes. **ENDEMIC**

5 OLIVE-SPOTTED HUMMINGBIRD *Leucippus chlorocercus* 10–11 cm (4–4¼ in), bill 1.8 cm (¾ in)

Rare to uncommon along large rivers in northern Amazonia. In shrubby open vegetation on river islands, and locally in pastures and other open habitats on adjacent "mainland." Plumage drab, with lightly spotted throat. Much less heavily marked below than other similarly sized hummingbirds (e.g., Glittering-throated Emerald or female Blue-chinned Sapphire), and tail largely green (not blue). **VOICE** Song a monotonous series of ringing, multisyllabic notes: "*cliCHEW cliCHEW cliCHEW....*" Calls a sharp "*seek,*" wiry "*seeuee,*" a rich chatter, and a hard "*tcht.*" **Co, E, Br**

6 TUMBES HUMMINGBIRD *Leucippus baeri* 11 cm (4¼ in), bill 1.9 cm (¾ in)

Fairly common in arid scrub and at edge of dry forest in northwest, below 800 m. Very drab; similar to larger Spot-throated Hummingbird, but usually lower elevations. Also note plain (unspotted) throat. Has dark band across end of tail; undersides of outer rectrices pale at base, with whitish spots at tip (cf. tail of Spot-throated). **VOICE** Song a complex series of chips and wheezing electric warbles. Call a gruff "*dzee*" and chips. **E**

GREEN-AND-WHITE
HUMMINGBIRD

WHITE-BELLIED
HUMMINGBIRD

ANDEAN EMERALD

♀ ♂

SPOT-THROATED
HUMMINGBIRD

OLIVE-SPOTTED
HUMMINGBIRD

TUMBES
HUMMINGBIRD

PLATE
101

UNDERSTORY HUMMINGBIRDS

Hummingbirds of the understory of humid montane forest and forest edges of the Andes.

1 BLUE-FRONTED LANCEBILL *Doryfera johannae* * 9–10 cm (3½–4 in), bill 3 cm (1⅛ in)
Uncommon in humid montane forest along east slope of Andes and on outlying ridges of northern and central Peru. Elevational range (500–1400 m) averages lower than Green-fronted Lancebill. Small dark male readily recognized. Duller female similar to larger Green-fronted, but forecrown is bluer; also, center of crown greener (contrasting more with coppery rear crown), upper tail coverts grayer, and tail bluer (less dusky green). **VOICE** Calls scratchy "*churt*" notes. **Co, E, Br**

2 GREEN-FRONTED LANCEBILL *Doryfera ludovicae* * 11.5–12 cm (4½–4¾ in), bill 3.2–3.4 cm (1¼ in)
Uncommon to locally fairly common in humid montane forest along east slope of Andes and on outlying ridges, 1000–2500 m; locally up to 2850 m, down to 800 m in south. Sexes similar, but some females lack green forecrown. Note dull colors and very long, straight bill. Traplines in under- and midstory; favors flowers with relatively long, hanging corollas. Cf. Blue-fronted Lancebill. **VOICE** Calls thin "*tip*" notes, sometimes in chattered series, also occasional high "*tsee*" notes. **Co, E, Bo**

3 MARVELOUS SPATULETAIL *Loddigesia mirabilis* male 14 cm (5½ in), not including long rackets; female 9–10 cm (3½–4 in), bill 1.4 cm (½ in)
Small, spectacular, restricted to Utcubamba Valley, 2000–2900 m. Forages low at edge of humid forest, in second growth, and in dense shrubbery. Extraordinary tail of male reduced to only 2 pairs of rectrices: a long straight central pair, and a very long, racket-tipped outer pair that bob independently of body movement. Note glittering blue crown and green gorget. Female white below, speckled with green; note long, largely white outer rectrices (with relatively broad tips). Cf. Booted Racket-tail. **VOICE** Call a thin, sweet, rising note "*wsst*," often given in series. **ENDEMIC**

4 WEDGE-BILLED HUMMINGBIRD *Schistes geoffroyi* * 9–10 cm (3½–4 in), bill 1.5 cm (½ in)
Uncommon but widespread in humid montane forest on east slope of Andes, 800–2300 m. Inconspicuous. Forages in understory, in forest interior. Small, with ornate face and breast pattern, and a coppery rump. Glittering throat and sides of neck sometimes difficult to discern, but note prominent white patches on side of breast and white postocular stripe in widespread *geoffroyi* (white reduced or lacking in *chapmani*, of southern Cuzco and Puno). Throat white in female; has masked appearance (cf. much browner Speckled Hummingbird). In the hand, tip of bill is very narrow and sharply pointed. **VOICE** Song a rapid series of "*ti*" notes. **Co, E, Bo**

5 ECUADORIAN PIEDTAIL *Phlogophilus hemileucurus* 8.5 cm (3¼ in), bill 1.8 cm (¾ in)
Fairly common but local in humid montane forest on east slope of Andes, 800–1200 m, primarily on low outlying ridges. Inconspicuous, foraging very low in forest interior. Easily identified by white flashes in tail and broad white breast band. **VOICE** Song a high shrill screeching: "*ssiiiii-SSSIIII-suuuu ti'ti'ti*." Reminiscent of Chestnut-capped Brush-Finch, but shriller and usually song longer, more continuous. Several may sing in loose association. Call a characteristic thin, shrill series of notes, each lower in pitch than the previous: "*SIIII siii suuu*." **Co, E**

6 PERUVIAN PIEDTAIL *Phlogophilus harterti* 8.5 cm (3¼ in), bill 1.5 cm (⅝ in)
Locally fairly common, but patchily distributed in humid montane forest in central and southern Peru, primarily on low outlying ridges at 750–1500 m. Inconspicuous; forages near ground in forest interior. Small and cinnamon-buff or whitish buff below. White or light buff in tail conspicuous, especially when tail is fanned. **VOICE** Call similar to that of Ecuadorian Piedtail. **ENDEMIC**

7 SPECKLED HUMMINGBIRD *Adelomyia melanogenys* * 9–9.5 cm (3½–3¾ in), bill 1.5 cm (⅝ in)
Fairly common and widespread in humid montane forest along east slope of Andes, 1000–2900 m; also on west slope of Andes, south to La Libertad (*maculata*). Forages low, in forest interior or at forest edge. Readily identifiable by small size, brown plumage, and distinct face pattern. Throat speckled with light green (most of Peru) or light purplish blue near Bolivian border (*inornata*). Inner webs of rectrices of *maculata* (not illustrated) whitish; *maculata* also relatively large and pale. **VOICE** Song a long series of high, metallic "*ti*" notes. Calls a thin "*seek*" given in flight, a harsh chatter in alarm, and a thin, ringing chatter rising and falling in pitch as it decelerates: "*ti-tititi-si-si-see-see-seee*." **Co, E, Bo**

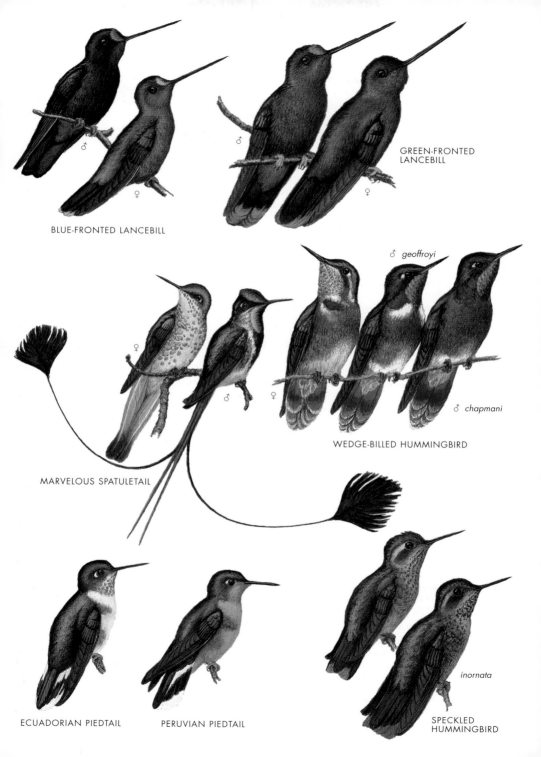

BLUE-FRONTED LANCEBILL

GREEN-FRONTED
LANCEBILL

♂ geoffroyi

♂ chapmani

MARVELOUS SPATULETAIL

WEDGE-BILLED HUMMINGBIRD

ECUADORIAN PIEDTAIL

PERUVIAN PIEDTAIL

inornata

SPECKLED
HUMMINGBIRD

PLATE
102

BRILLIANTS AND MANY-SPOTTED HUMMINGBIRD

Brilliants are medium to large, with robust bills. Feathering of crown extends onto base of maxilla, and head often has flat-topped appearance. Females of most species have white or whitish malar. Juveniles have buffy cheeks. Found in forest interior. Many-spotted Hummingbird resembles a female brilliant.

1 MANY-SPOTTED HUMMINGBIRD *Taphrospilus hypostictus* 11.5–12 cm (4½–4¾ in), bill 2.3 cm (⅞ in)

Rare and patchily distributed in humid montane forest and forest edge along east slope of Andes; 750–1500 m, but occasionally up to 2800 m in upper Apurímac Valley (isolated resident population, or seasonal wanderers?). Poorly known. Large. Very similar to female Violet-fronted Brilliant, but brilliant always shows short white malar stripe and usually has buffy belly (belly usually white in Many-spotted); also, in northern Peru female brilliant has bluish crown. In the hand, note feathering stops at base of bill (brilliants have more extensive feathering). **VOICE** Song a quiet series of wheezy, electric warbles and gravelly chatters. Calls a thin "*tchit*" and a wheezy "*dew dew dew.*" **E, Bo**

2 VIOLET-FRONTED BRILLIANT *Heliodoxa leadbeateri* * male 14 cm (5½ in), female 12 cm (4¾ in), bill 2.5 cm (1 in)

Fairly common and widespread in humid montane forest along east slope of Andes, 900–2300 m. Large, with relatively long, notched, greenish or bluish tail. Male green with glittering green throat and breast, and glittering purplish blue crown. Female white below, heavily spotted with green; belly usually buffy, flecked with green. Also note short but distinct white malar. Crown of female glittering light blue in *leadbeateri* (south to Pasco) or green (*otero*, southern Peru; not illustrated). Upper throat of juvenile may be rufous (in addition to rufous cheeks). **VOICE** Song a series of sweet "*tchew*" notes. Call a squeaky, descending chatter: "*dee-dih-doo,*" similar to Booted Racket-tail, but more stuttering, squeakier. **Co, E, Bo**

3 BLACK-THROATED BRILLIANT *Heliodoxa schreibersii* * *schreibersii* male 12.5–13 cm (5 in), female 11.5–12 cm (4½–4¾ in); *whitelyana* 13–14 cm (5–5½ in), bill 2.8 cm (1⅛ in)

Uncommon and patchily distributed in humid montane forest, 600–1250 m, on east slope of Andes and on outlying ridges. Also rare in humid forest interior of northern Amazonia. Large, very dark. Throat black, with glittering purple gorget on lower throat; gorget difficult to see, and may be smaller on female. Northern *schreibersii* (south to San Martín) is smaller, and tail of female shorter than male's; also lower breast green and belly dusky; underparts extensively blackish in *whitelyana* of central and southern Peru, and sexes of similar size. **VOICE** Song a long, thin, very rapid descending trill: "*see'e'e'e'e'e'e'u'u.*" Calls a rich "*tchup*" and a rising series of ringing notes: "*tsu tse tsi tsee.*" **Co, E, Br**

4 FAWN-BREASTED BRILLIANT *Heliodoxa rubinoides* * 12–12.5 cm (4¾–5 in), bill 2.5 cm (1 in)

Uncommon in humid montane forest along east slope of Andes, 1500–2500 m. Forages primarily in under- and midstory of forest interior. Buffy or buffy brown below, variably speckled with green and with small glittering pink gorget on lower throat. Sexes similar, although gorget greatly reduced in some females. Gorget of juvenile reduced or absent, and crown and nape scaled with rufous-brown. **VOICE** Song a rich "*tchew*" in long series. Call a rich "*tchew.*" **Co, E, Bo**

5 PINK-THROATED BRILLIANT *Heliodoxa gularis* 11.5–12 cm (4½–4¾ in), bill 2.6 cm (1 in)

Rare, poorly known; a few records from outlying ridges, 400–1050 m, in understory of humid montane forest or at forest edge. Smallest brilliant, with white undertail coverts and bronzy green tail. Male glittering green below with small glittering pink gorget; female similar but duller, and variably flecked with white below. Not known to overlap with Rufous-webbed Brilliant; note differences in tail and wing color. Also compare female to female Rufous-vented Whitetip. **Co, E**

6 RUFOUS-WEBBED BRILLIANT *Heliodoxa branickii* 11–11.5 cm (4¼–4½ in), bill 2.5 cm (1 in)

Uncommon to fairly common in humid montane forest mainly on outlying ridges, but also locally on main Andean slopes in central Peru, 650–1700 m. Forages in forest understory and at forest edge. Small brilliant with prominent white undertail coverts and deep blue tail. Bases of inner webs of secondaries and inner primaries rufous-brown; conspicuous in flight. Male has narrow glittering green stripe down central crown, and glittering pink gorget. Female duller, variably speckled with white below. **VOICE** Call a sweet, descending "*tew.*" **Bo**

MANY-SPOTTED
HUMMINGBIRD

♀ *leadbeateri*

juv.

♂

VIOLET-FRONTED BRILLIANT

♂ *whitelyana*

BLACK-THROATED
BRILLIANT

FAWN-
BREASTED
BRILLIANT

♂ *schreibersii*

juv.

♀

dull ♀

PINK-THROATED
BRILLIANT

♂

♀

♂

♀

RUFOUS-WEBBED BRILLIANT

PLATE
103

SUNBEAMS AND HILLSTARS

Shown on this plate are two genera typical of the high Andes. Sunbeams are medium-sized hummingbirds of humid montane scrub, hedgerows, humid forest edge, Polylepis woods, and eucalyptus groves. Throats are dull, with no glittering gorget, but all sunbeams have a tuft of white or rufous feathers on the breast, and the rump usually is some shade of iridescent purple. Sexes are similar, but the iridescent rump is much reduced in females. Bills are medium length. Hillstars are large hummingbirds of puna and upper elevation montane scrub in the Andes. The bill is moderately long and slightly curved; tail is broad and relatively long, and in most plumages it shows considerable white. Primarily forages on Chuquiragua, a shrub with bright orange flowers.

1 WHITE-TUFTED SUNBEAM *Aglaeactis castelnaudii* * 11–12 cm (4¼–4¾ in), bill 1.8–2 cm (¾ in)

Locally fairly common but patchily distributed; primarily found in more humid areas of upper portions of intermontane valleys, 2600–4100 m. Overlaps with Shining Sunbeam at many localities; not known whether both species breed at these sites, or whether overlap is due to postbreeding movements (but hybrids between the two have been reported). Always has prominent white pectoral tufts. In central Peru has rufous lower throat, belly, and tail (*regalis*); darker in southern *castelnaudii*, with only a small amount of rufous on throat and belly, and duller tail. **VOICE** Calls rapid jumbled squeaks, also a very high, descending "*seeeee.*" **ENDEMIC**

2 SHINING SUNBEAM *Aglaeactis cupripennis* * 11–12 cm (4¼–4¾ in), bill 1.5–1.9 cm (½–¾ in)

Fairly common and widespread on the Andes, 2500–4600 m, locally down to 2200 m. The most widespread sunbeam in Peru, and the only species found on west slope of Andes. Also widespread in intermontane valleys, including on both slopes of Marañón Valley, and less commonly on humid east-facing slopes of eastern Andes. Plain, with no white in the plumage. Populations on both slopes of western Andes south to La Libertad and on the east side of Marañón Valley are relatively pale and rufous; elsewhere are darker above with dusky chin and belly, and more contrasting light rufous pectoral tufts (*caumatonota*). **VOICE** Song a series of high, springy notes: "*chew tree tsip chew sweet tree chew….*" Calls a characteristic loud, jerky, squeaking series: "*wee-SEET chew-chew-chew wee-SEET chew-chew-chew….*" **Co, E**

3 PURPLE-BACKED SUNBEAM *Aglaeactis aliciae* 11.5–12 cm (4½–4¾ in), bill 1.5 cm (⅝ in)

Uncommon and very local. Occupies very small area on slopes facing west bank of Río Marañón in La Libertad at 3000–3400 m. Little or no overlap with Shining Sunbeam, which it replaces geographically. Dark sooty brown (no rufous in plumage), with distinctive white face, lower throat, and pectoral tufts; bases of rectrices also pale. **VOICE** Call a characteristic loud, jerky, squeaking series similar to that of Shining Sunbeam: "*wee-SEET chew-chew-chew wee-SEET chew-chew-chew….*" **ENDEMIC**

4 ANDEAN HILLSTAR *Oreotrochilus estella* * 11–12 cm (4¼–4¾ in), bill 1.7–1.9 cm (¾ in)

Widespread and usually fairly common in puna at 3400–4600 m, locally down to 3000 m; rare north and west of Marañón Valley. Geographically variable, in disjunct populations (which may represent several different species; note that its distribution is interrupted in central Peru by Black-breasted Hillstar). Male always readily recognized by white belly with dark ventral stripe, and large glittering gorget; tail also largely white. Throat green; ventral stripe black in northern Peru (*stolzmanni*) but brown in southern Peru (*estella*). Female is much duller; note the extensive white in tail (bases and tips of all but central pair of rectrices), lightly spotted throat, and gently curved bill. Cf. female Black-breasted Hillstar. **VOICE** Calls include a rising "*swit*" or "*spit.*" **E, Bo, Ch**

5 BLACK-BREASTED HILLSTAR *Oreotrochilus melanogaster* 12–12.5 cm (4¼–5 in), bill 1.6–1.8 cm (⅝–¾ in)

Fairly common in puna in central Peru, 3500–4800 m. Narrowly sympatric with *stolzmanni* subspecies of Andean Hillstar; contact also is possible with *estella*, but distributions of both species in south-central Peru not well documented. Otherwise the only hillstar in most of its range. Male readily recognized by contrast between glittering green gorget and black breast and belly; no white in tail. Female very similar to female Andean Hillstar, but bases of rectrices are dark, with white confined to the tips. **ENDEMIC**

WHITE-TUFTED SUNBEAM

castelnaudii

regalis

caumatonota

nw

SHINING SUNBEAM

PURPLE-BACKED
SUNBEAM

♀

♂

ANDEAN HILLSTAR

♂ *stolzmanni*

♀ *stolzmanni*

♂ *estella*

BLACK-
BREASTED
HILLSTAR

♀

♂

♀ *estella*

PLATE
104

INCAS, STARFRONTLETS, AND CORONET

Incas and starfrontlets (Coeligena) are medium-sized hummingbirds with notably long straight bills. Species replace one another elevationally, with overlap. Lower-elevation incas primarily in under- and midstory of humid montane forest interior; higher-elevation starfrontlets venture into adjacent shrub zones near treeline, also often seen in rapid flight above forest canopy or crossing forest openings. Chestnut-breasted Coronet resembles a starfrontlet but has a much shorter bill.

1 CHESTNUT-BREASTED CORONET *Boissonneaua matthewsii* 11.5–12 cm (4½–4¾ in), bill 1.8 cm (¾ in)

Uncommon to common in humid montane forest on east slope of Andes, 1500–3300 m; also on west slope in similar habitats south to Cajamarca. Forages primarily in midstory and canopy of forest. Often holds wings briefly extended above body after landing. Bill relatively short (cf. starfrontlets). Readily recognized by rufous-chestnut lower breast, belly, and tail, contrasting with glittering green throat. **VOICE** Calls a high, thin, liquid "*tip*," a rapid, sweet trill, and various squeaky notes. **Co, E**

2 BRONZY INCA *Coeligena coeligena* * 12.5–13 cm (5 in), bill 3.3 cm (1¼ in)

Fairly common in humid montane forest along east slope of Andes, 1000–2200 m, locally to 2600 m. Drab brown; throat whitish, speckled with brown, but entirely lacks iridescent colors. Readily recognized by very drabness and long straight bill. **VOICE** Song a series of sweet "*tsuEE*" notes. Calls include a "*tsweet*" or "*tsee*" given in flight. **Co, E, Bo**

3 RAINBOW STARFRONTLET *Coeligena iris* * 13.5–14 cm (5¼–5½ in), bill 2.9 cm (1⅛ in)

Fairly common, at edge of humid montane forest and adjacent shrubby areas, 1500–3300 m. Recognizable by extensive rufous color, large size, and long bill. Color and pattern of crown of male highly variable. Forecrown glittering green, with blue spot on crown, in *iris* (west slope of Andes in Piura) and *fulgidiceps* (not illustrated; Amazonas). Birds farther south on west slope similar but nape and upper back coppery, with no black on nape (*flagrans*). In Marañón drainage of northern Cajamarca, crown all green, and upper throat blue (*aurora*). Crown has central blue stripe in *eva* of Marañón drainage of southern Cajamarca. Females similar to males but duller; throat sometimes mixed with buffy. **VOICE** Calls include a thin "*tip*" and a high, wiry, squealing chatter that rises and falls in pitch, the latter often while engaged in high aerial chases well above the canopy. **E**

4 COLLARED INCA *Coeligena torquata* * 13.5–14 cm (5¼–5½ in), bill 3–3.5 cm (1¼–1⅜ in)

Fairly common in humid montane forest along east slope of the Andes, 1800–3000 m. Much geographic variation, but tail always mostly white and has a broad breast band, which is white in most of Peru, rufous in southeast (*omissa*, "Gould's" Inca). Male *torquata* (north and west of Marañón) has dark belly with blue crown. In all populations south of Marañón, belly is green; crown of males is green and blue from central Amazonas south to Pasco (*margaretae*), green in other subspecies: *insectivora* (Pasco to Ayacucho), *eisenmanni* (Cordillera Vilcabamba and lower Urubamba Valley), and *omissa* (eastern Cuzco south). Also, *eisenmanni* has coppery upper tail coverts (both sexes) and blackish sides to head (male). Females of all populations duller; throat white and rectrices tipped green (like males) in northern and central Peru but throat buffy and rectrices white to tip in *eisenmanni* and *omissa*. **VOICE** Calls a high, jerky, wiry chatter. **Co, E, Bo**

5 BUFF-WINGED STARFRONTLET *Coeligena lutetiae* 13.5–14 cm (5¼–5½ in), bill 3–3.5 cm (1¼ in)

Restricted to east slope of Andes, north and west of Marañón Valley, 2600–2950 m, where fairly common. Forages in forest interior, elfin forest, and adjacent shrub zones. Large, dark; note conspicuous buff secondaries. Replaced south of Marañón by Violet-throated Starfrontlet. **VOICE** Calls a dull "*unk*" and a high, wiry chatter, the latter often while engaged in high aerial chases well above canopy. **Co, E**

6 VIOLET-THROATED STARFRONTLET *Coeligena violifer* * 14–14.5 cm (5½–5¾ in), bill 3–3.5 cm (1¼ in)

Fairly common along east slope of Andes, south and east of Marañón Valley at 2500–3900 m, occasionally down to 1900 m. Forages in interior of humid and elfin forest, and in adjacent shrub zones. Note buffy belly and coppery wing coverts. Tail buffy in *dichroura* (Amazonas to Junín) and in *osculans* (eastern Cuzco south), but white or whitish buff in Apurímac drainage (*albicaudata*). Male has violet center of throat and glittering forecrown, green (*dichroura*), blue (*albicaudata*) or blue-green (*osculans*). Females lack glittering forecrown; throat buffy, flecked with green. **VOICE** Calls a rich "*tchweep*" and a single "*tchip*," also a rapid chatter ending with a squeaky "*tsee-tsi-tser*." **Bo**

CHESTNUT-BREASTED CORONET

BRONZY INCA

♂ torquata

♂ margaretae

♀ margaretae

♀ iris

♂ iris

RAINBOW STARFRONTLET

♂ omissa

♀ omissa

COLLARED INCA

♂ eisenmanni

COLLARED INCA

♀ eisenmanni

♂ insectivora

♂ aurora

♂ flagrans

♂ eva

♂ albicaudata

VIOLET-THROATED STARFRONTLET

♂

♀

BUFF-WINGED STARFRONTLET

♂ dichroura

♀ dichroura

♂ osculans

PLATE
105

SUNANGELS, VELVETBREAST, AND SYLPH

Sunangels are medium-sized, relatively short-billed Andean hummingbirds. Several species have a distinct, broad white pectoral collar. Throat of females usually duller than males, but females of some species may show a partial or almost complete iridescent gorget. Found in humid montane forest and forest borders. The velvetbreast is a distinctive Andean species. Long-tailed Sylph is the only small, long-tailed hummingbird of humid montane forest (cf. trainbearers, of open habitats: plate 104).

1 MOUNTAIN VELVETBREAST *Lafresnaya lafresnayi* * 11–12 cm (4¼–4¾ in), bill 2.2–2.5 cm (⅞–1 in)

Widespread but uncommon and local on east slope of Andes, 1800–3200 m; also on west slope in Piura. Found at edge of humid forest and in adjacent humid shrub zones and low second growth. Both sexes readily recognized by extensively white tail and gently curved bill; central pair of rectrices are green, so folded tail when viewed from rear can appear dark, but white readily apparent from below or when tail is fanned. Male glittering green below with black belly; female white below, densely spotted with green, throat washed buffy. **VOICE** Call a high series of chipping notes and a high, thin, descending "*pseew.*" Also, a thin rattle. **Co, E**

2 LONG-TAILED SYLPH *Aglaiocercus kingi* * male 15–18 cm (6–7 in), female 10 cm (4 in), bill 1.3 cm (½ in)

Fairly common and widespread on east slope of Andes, 1200–2500 m, locally to 2800 m. Forages in canopy and midstory of humid montane forest, and at forest edge. Male may bob the tail when perched. Male is superficially similar to male trainbearers, but note different habitat; also upper surface of tail is more uniformly glittering, rectrices are wider, and gorget is glittering blue (not green). Crown also glittering bluish green. Female readily recognized by long forked tail and extensively tawny belly. **VOICE** Call a dry, scratchy "*tchit*" or "*tchit-it.*" **Co, E, Bo**

3 LITTLE SUNANGEL *Heliangelus micraster* * male 11 cm (4¼ in), female 9.5–10 cm (3¾–4 in), bill 1.5 cm (⅝ in)

Fairly common at 2200–3000 m, but restricted to Andes north and west of Río Marañón. Overlaps Amethyst-throated Sunangel but ranges higher in elevation. Note conspicuous white undertail coverts. Male has fiery orange-red gorget; female similar, but gorget less fully developed and throat often shows a mix of white, green, and orange. **VOICE** Call a dry "*djit.*" **E**

4 AMETHYST-THROATED SUNANGEL *Heliangelus amethysticollis* * 10.5–11.5 cm (4–4½ in), bill 1.5–1.8 cm (⅝–¾ in)

Fairly common; the most widespread sunangel, found along entire east slope of Andes, 1950–3700 m, but only up to 2500 m north and west of Río Marañón. Forages primarily in understory of humid forest and at forest edge. Always shows a broad white or buffy collar. Gorget of male glittering purplish blue; forecrown glittering blue-green (*laticlavius*; north and west of Marañón Valley) or green (elsewhere in Peru: *decolor, amethysticollis*). Throat of female typically dull rufous-brown, but iridescent gorget can be well developed, especially in *laticlavius*. **VOICE** Call a dry, ringing trill. **Co, E, Bo**

5 ROYAL SUNANGEL *Heliangelus regalis* 10–10.5 cm (4 in), bill 1.4 cm (½ in)

Fairly common but patchily distributed. Restricted to stunted humid forest and shrub zones, usually on sandy soils or on sandstone on outlying ridges, 1350–2200 m. Forages low at forest edge and in shrubs. Male readily identifiable by uniform blue plumage, with long, deeply forked tail; most populations dull blackish blue, but undescribed subspecies of Cordillera Azul is brighter steely blue. Female very different; tail blue and forked, although shorter than in male, but note buffy brown underparts and whitish buff collar. **VOICE** In aerial display, male makes large circles in air while producing a high "*teep*" note. Call a rich "*tchip,*" often given in a series. **ENDEMIC**

6 PURPLE-THROATED SUNANGEL *Heliangelus viola* male 12.5–13 cm (5 in), female 11.5 cm (4½ in), bill 1.4 cm (½ in)

Fairly common on west slope of Andes in Piura and Cajamarca; also in Marañón Valley in Cajamarca and Utcubamba Valley in Amazonas. Found at edge of forest, and in adjacent second growth and shrubby areas at 1800–3200 m. Sexes similar, but female has shorter tail. Readily identifiable by long, deeply forked tail and dark green plumage. Not known to overlap with smaller blue Royal Sunangel. **VOICE** Song (?) is a series of scratchy and electric, wheezy phrases. Calls a rich, popping chatter. **E**

MOUNTAIN
VELVETBREAST

♀

♂

LONG-TAILED
SYLPH

♀

♂

LITTLE
SUNANGEL

♂

♀

AMETHYST-
THROATED
SUNANGEL

♂ *decolor*

♀ *decolor*

♀ *laticlavius*

AMETHYST-
THROATED
SUNANGEL

♂ *laticlavius*

♀

♂

ROYAL
SUNANGEL

♂ Cordillera
Azul

♂

♀

PURPLE-THROATED SUNANGEL

PLATE
106

PUFFLEGS, WHITETIP, AND RACKET-TAIL

Pufflegs are medium-sized to small hummingbirds with white, fluffy tarsal tufts. Occupy humid habitats in the Andes; Haplophaedia is found in forest interior, but Eriocnemis are more characteristic of forest edge, elfin forest, and adjacent humid shrub zones. Rufous-vented Whitetip and Booted Racket-tail are two small, distinctive Andean hummingbirds.

1 GLOWING PUFFLEG *Eriocnemis vestita* * 10.5–11 cm (4–4¼ in), bill 1.8 cm (¾ in)
Fairly common in humid montane forest and forest edge at 2450–3200 m, but restricted to Andes north and west of Río Marañón. Small glittering puffleg with blue, forked tail. Note gorget of male; Sapphire-vented Puffleg is larger, paler green, and has an entirely green throat. Female duller than male, although usually retains some blue in throat; note extensive rufous or buff flecking on underparts (other pufflegs are more uniformly green, lacking brown or buff). **VOICE** Call a metallic *"tink."* **Co, E**

2 SAPPHIRE-VENTED PUFFLEG *Eriocnemis luciani* * 11.5–12 cm (4½–4¾ in), bill 2 cm (¾ in)
Largest and most widely distributed puffleg; fairly common, along east slope of Andes, south and east of Marañón Valley; not reported from Peru north of Marañón, but might occur there. Found in elfin forest, humid montane forest (especially at openings in forest), and forest edge at 2400–3500 m. Glittering green with purplish blue undertail coverts and a long blue forked tail; belly of male washed with blue in *catharina* (Amazonas to La Libertad), green in widespread *sapphiropygia*. Female similar but duller, variably flecked with white below. **Co, E**

3 EMERALD-BELLIED PUFFLEG *Eriocnemis alinae* * 8.5–9 cm (3¼–3½ in), bill 1.5–1.9 cm (⅝–¾ in)
Uncommon, along east slope of Andes at 1650–2400 m. Unlike other *Eriocnemis*, regularly found in interior of humid montane forest, where forages in dense understory. Small and glittering green, with a green, notched tail. In addition to prominent white tarsal tufts, has prominent but irregularly shaped patch of white in center of breast. Female similar, or slightly duller. **VOICE** Calls a thin *"tsit."* **Co, E**

4 GREENISH PUFFLEG *Haplophaedia aureliae* * 10–10.5 cm (4 in), bill 1.8 cm (¾ in)
Uncommon to locally fairly common, but patchily distributed, along east slope of Andes, 1500–2450 m. Found in under- and midstory of humid montane forest. A dull green hummingbird with white tarsal tufts (less conspicuous than in *Eriocnemis* pufflegs) and long, deep-blue tail. Female similar but duller. Superficially similar to lancebills (*Doryfera*), but bill is shorter, tail is bluer, and note puffed legs. **VOICE** Calls a dry rattle and a scratchy *"tskut."* **Co, E, Bo**

5 RUFOUS-VENTED WHITETIP *Urosticte ruficrissa* 10–10.5 cm (4 in), bill 2 cm (¾ in)
Uncommon and local in understory of humid montane forest on east slope of Andes and on outlying ridges, 1350–2200 m. Usually forages in under- or midstory. Medium-sized. Male green with glittering green gorget and large distinctive white spots on upper surface of central rectrices; tail forked. Rare variant with purplish blue spot on throat reported from southern Amazonas (*"intermedia"*). Female very different: largely white below, heavily spotted with green. Tail forked, bronzy green, outer rectrices tipped white. Similar to female Booted Racket-tail, but larger and longer-billed, tail greener (not blue or bluish green), and usually throat is more heavily spotted with green and has less obvious, paler buff on undertail coverts; also more likely to be seen in understory rather than canopy. Also cf. female of much larger Violet-fronted Brilliant. **VOICE** Calls a dry chatter and a rising squeaky, jerky series of notes. **Co, E**

6 BOOTED RACKET-TAIL *Ocreatus underwoodii* * male 11.5–12 cm (4½–4¾ in), female 9 cm (3½ in), bill 1.6 cm (⅝ in)
Uncommon but widespread in humid montane forest on east slope of Andes, 1000–2400 m. Primarily forages in canopy, although at rest may perch lower. Male unmistakable. Racketed outer rectrices straighter in *peruanus* (south to central Peru), more curved and often crossed in *annae* (Pasco south). Female white below, spotted with green, and undertail coverts usually buffy. Most other small forest hummingbirds not as white below; in northern Peru cf. female Rufous-vented Whitetip. **VOICE** Call a rapid, musical, springy *"dee'i'i'i'u'u-dee'i'i'i'u'u-dee'i'i'i'u'u,"* similar to a call of Violet-fronted Brilliant, but less jerky and stuttered. Also shorter *"du-du"* notes of similar quality to the longer vocalization. **Co, E, Bo**

GLOWING PUFFLEG

♂   ♀

♂ catharina

♂ sapphiropygia

♀ sapphiropygia

SAPPHIRE-VENTED PUFFLEG

EMERALD-BELLIED PUFFLEG

GREENISH PUFFLEG

♂ annae

♂ peruanus

♂ "intermedia"

♂

♀

RUFOUS-VENTED WHITETIP

♀

BOOTED RACKET-TAIL

PLATE
107
TRAINBEARERS, MOUNTAINEER, AND COMETS

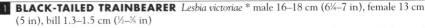

Species on this plate are long-tailed, and occupy scrub and other open habitats in the Andes. Trainbearers (Lesbia) are small hummingbirds of open shrub zones and forest edge of the Andes. The tail is extremely elongated, especially in males. Cf. Long-tailed Sylph, which is found in humid forest (not in open habitats). Bearded Mountaineer is a very distinctive species of the southern Andes. Bronze-tailed and Gray-bellied comets are much drabber; Gray-bellied Comet also is inexplicably rare and very local.

1 BLACK-TAILED TRAINBEARER *Lesbia victoriae* * male 16–18 cm (6¼–7 in), female 13 cm (5 in), bill 1.3–1.5 cm (½–⅝ in)

Locally present on west slope of Andes south to northern Lima, both slopes of Marañón Valley, and in intermontane valleys, very locally crossing to upper east-facing slopes of Andes, at 2700–4100 m. Found in montane scrub, forest edge, gardens, and other open shrubby habitats. Tail largely black; only tips of rectrices are glittering, bluish green. Cf. Green-tailed Trainbearer; Black-tailed usually is larger, longer billed, and with less visible color in tail, but in southern Peru the two species are more similar. **VOICE** Song a gravelly chatter. In display, produces a snapping sound with tail. Calls a sweet, descending whinny ending in a dry chatter: "*seet si-si-si-si-sutititi*"; also a sharp "*tseek.*" **Co, E**

2 GREEN-TAILED TRAINBEARER *Lesbia nuna* * male 16–19 cm (6¼–7½ in), female 10–12.5 cm (4–5 in), bill 1 cm (⅜ in), bill (*nuna*) 1.3–1.5 cm (½–⅝ in)

Locally present on west slope of Andes south to northern Lima, both slopes of Marañón Valley, and in intermontane valleys at 1700–3800 m. Overlaps with Black-tailed Trainbearer and found in similar habitats; but more common in drier habitats, and is less common on east-facing slopes of Andes. Similar to Black-tailed, but shorter rectrices are extensively glittering green (iridescence of Black-tailed is bluish green, and limited to tips of all rectrices), the underparts of the male are greener, and gorget is rounded (gorget of Black-tailed is more pointed and contrasts more against duller green belly). In most of Peru, bill of Green-tailed is very short, and upper surface of all but the longest rectrices is mostly green; but in south (*nuna*; north to Huancavelica, one record from Junín), bill is longer (almost same length as bill of Black-tailed), and in some lights the iridescence of next-to-longest rectrices is restricted to tips (as in Black-tailed). **VOICE** Song is a repetitive, gravelly chatter. In display, produces a snapping sound with tail. Calls include a sweet, descending whinny "*seet si-si-si-si-su*" and gravelly rattles "*dzzzt dzzzt.*" **Co, E, Bo**

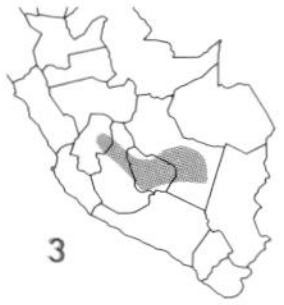

3 BEARDED MOUNTAINEER *Oreonympha nobilis* * 15.5–16.5 cm (6–6½ in); bill 2.4 cm (1 in)

Uncommon in dry montane scrub in intermontane valleys of south-central Andes, 2700–3900 m. Often seen at tree tobacco, *Nicotiana*, an exotic plant found along road edges. Large size, long forked black-and-white tail, and white underparts render it unmistakable. Male has narrow green and purple gorget. Crown bordered with whitish line, speckled with green, in *albolimbata* (Huancavelica), or with deep glittering blue (more widespread *nobilis*). **VOICE** Call a descending, squeaky series followed by a rich chatter: "*swee swee chew-chew-chew.*" Also a dry "*dzzrt.*" **ENDEMIC**

4 GRAY-BELLIED COMET *Taphrolesbia griseiventris* male 16–17 cm (6½–6¾ in), female 14 cm (5½ in), bill 2 cm (¾ in)

Inexplicably rare and local. Known only from a few sites on west side of Marañón Valley, 2750–3200 m. Found in montane scrub. A large hummingbird with a long, deeply forked tail, the upper surface of which is green to bluish green, with steely blue under surface. Underparts light gray (male) or whitish buff (female); juveniles (not illustrated) similar to female but perhaps ever buffier. Gorget of male pale blue. Compare carefully to more common and widespread Bronze-tailed Comet. Gray-bellied is significantly larger; tail is bluish green or blue (not bronzy red); males have different gorget colors; and female is less heavily speckled below and does not show white on outer webs of outer rectrices. **ENDEMIC**

5 BRONZE-TAILED COMET *Polyonymus caroli* male 12.5 cm (5 in), female 11 cm (4¼ in), bill 1.8–2.0 cm (¾ in)

Uncommon but widespread on west slope of Andes, and locally in intermontane valleys (Marañón and Mantaro), 2100–3400 m. Found in montane scrub and forest edge, often in dry areas. A dingy hummingbird with a long, forked tail (shorter in female); upper surface of tail mainly purplish red or bronzy red (outer 3 rectrices) or green (central rectrices), with white or whitish gray outer vane to outer pair of rectrices. Gorget of male is rosy red. Female is duller than male, grayish white below heavily speckled with·green, but usually shows some rosy red speckles on throat, sometimes coalescing into small throat patch. **VOICE** Call a dry, rapid chatter: "*tcht*" or "*tchtcht.*" **ENDEMIC**

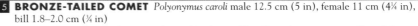

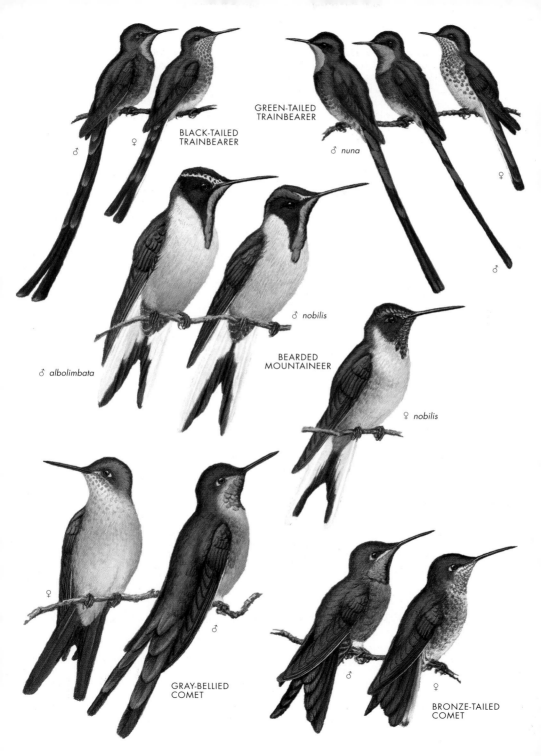

BLACK-TAILED
TRAINBEARER

♂ ♀

GREEN-TAILED
TRAINBEARER

♂ *nuna*

♀

♂

♂ *albolimbata*

♂ *nobilis*

BEARDED
MOUNTAINEER

♀ *nobilis*

GRAY-BELLIED
COMET

♀ ♂

♂ ♀

BRONZE-TAILED
COMET

PLATE
108

METALTAILS AND AVOCETBILL

Metaltails are small, short-billed hummingbirds of the high Andes. Metaltails are so named after the metallic sheen to the tail, which is glittering green, purplish, or coppery. Most are found in humid montane shrub zones. Neblina, Coppery, Scaled, and Fire-throated are a series of species that geographically replace one another, near treeline and in shrubby paramo. Tyrian Metaltail (plate 106) overlaps with each of these species and also ventures into humid forest. Cf. also Rufous-capped Thornbill (plate 106). Black Metaltail is found in drier habitats. Mountain Avocetbill is an uncommon hummingbird of the understory of humid montane forest in the northern Andes.

1 NEBLINA METALTAIL *Metallura odomae* 10–10.5 cm (4 in), bill 1.4 cm (½ in)
Fairly common, at the edge of elfin forest and shrubby paramo, on east slope of Andes north and west of Marañón Valley, 2600–3000 m. Glittering bronzy green with glittering green tail and rosy red gorget; female similar but duller. No geographic overlap with similar Fire-throated Metaltail of central Peru. **VOICE** Calls include a jerky, wiry chatter similar to Tyrian Metaltail, but perhaps lower, less emphatic, buzzier notes; also scratchy chatters. **E**

2 COPPERY METALTAIL *Metallura theresiae* * 10–10.5 cm (4 in), bill 1.3 cm (½ in)
Fairly common, at edge of elfin forest and shrubby paramo, on east slope of Andes between Marañón and upper Huallaga valleys, 2800–3550 m. Very dark, reddish coppery with a narrow, glittering green gorget. Crown of widespread *theresiae* is glittering reddish coppery; underside of tail dark bronzy green. Female similar, but duller. Underside of tail is paler and greener, and crown duller, in Amazonas (*parkeri*). **VOICE** Calls include a jerky, wiry chatter similar to Tyrian Metaltail, but perhaps lower, less emphatic, with buzzier notes. **ENDEMIC**

3 FIRE-THROATED METALTAIL *Metallura eupogon* 10–10.5 cm (4 in), bill 1.2 cm (½ in)
Fairly common, at edge of elfin forest and shrubby paramo, on east slope of Andes in central Peru, 3100–3800 m. Green metaltail with orange-red gorget. Similar to Neblina Metaltail of northern Andes, but no geographic overlap; equally brilliant in color, but the gorget is more orange, less pinkish red. **VOICE** Calls include a descending series of high wiry notes ending in a lower, gravelly chatter. **ENDEMIC**

4 SCALED METALTAIL *Metallura aeneocauda* * 11 cm (4¼ in), bill 1.8 cm (¾ in)
Uncommon, at edge of elfin forest and shrubby paramo on east slope of Andes in southern Peru, 2750–3600 m. A dull green metaltail with a glittering green gorget and bronzy green tail. Female (not illustrated) duller; throat usually buff or whitish, flecked with green. Female not as deep or richly buffy as female Tyrian Metaltail and has green (not purplish blue) tail and longer bill. **VOICE** Calls include a jerky, wiry chatter similar to Tyrian Metaltail, but perhaps lower, less emphatic, buzzier notes; also scratchy chatters. **Bo**

5 MOUNTAIN AVOCETBILL *Opisthoprora euryptera* 11 cm (4¼ in), bill 1.3 cm (½ in)
Uncommon and apparently local, in understory of humid montane forest on east slope of Andes in northern Peru, 2700–3200 m. May be more common at openings in forest (rather than forest interior). Nondescript medium-sized hummingbird with a long tail. Note distinctive bill shape: tip of bill is sharply curved upward. Underparts appear streaked with green (not spotted). **VOICE** Calls include a series of descending thin whistles, reminiscent of a piculet: *"wsee wsee wsee wsee."* **Co, E**

6 BLACK METALTAIL *Metallura phoebe* 11.5–12.5 cm (4½–5 in), bill 1.5–1.7 cm (⅝–¾ in)
Fairly common along west slope of Andes south to Arequipa; very uncommon farther south, but occurs south to Tacna. Also fairly common on both slopes of Marañón Valley, and locally in intermontane valleys in Pasco and Junín. Found in montane scrub and open woods, including *Polylepis*, at 2700–4300 m. Larger and much darker than other metaltails. Overlaps, very locally, with Tyrian Metaltail; no overlap with other species of metaltail. Almost black (male) or dark smoky gray (female; not illustrated), with long coppery red tail. Narrow gorget is greenish blue; size of gorget of female is reduced. **VOICE** Calls include a low, dry chatter. **ENDEMIC**

NEBLINA METALTAIL

♀ *theresiae*

♂ *theresiae*

COPPERY METALTAIL

♂ *parkeri*

♀

♂

FIRE-THROATED METALTAIL

♂

SCALED METALTAIL

MOUNTAIN
AVOCETBILL

♂

BLACK METALTAIL

PLATE
109

THORNBILLS AND TYRIAN METALTAIL

Tyrian Metaltail is more widespread, geographically and ecologically, than are other species of metaltails (plate 108). Purple-backed Thornbill is a small hummingbird of humid montane forest, with only a very short bill. Chalcostigma thornbills are Andean hummingbirds that also are similar to metaltails, but the bill is shorter (although not as short as in Purple-backed Thornbill), and the gorgets of males are narrower and more elongated. Most Chalcostigma also have longer tails than do metaltails.

1 PURPLE-BACKED THORNBILL *Ramphomicron microrhynchum* * male 10 cm (4 in), female 8.5 cm (3¼ in), bill 0.6 cm (¼ in)

Rare and local. Found on both slopes of Andes in Cajamarca, and along east slope of Andes in central Peru, 2500–3600 m. Usually found at edge of humid montane forest or in humid shrub zones adjacent to forest, less commonly inside humid forest. Small, long-tailed hummingbird with extremely short bill. Male unmistakable. Female also should be identifiable by extremely short bill; but plumage is similar to that of female Tyrian Metaltail, and the two can be confused. Note whiter throat, and coppery upper tail coverts. Be aware it is easier to mistake a female metaltail for a female thornbill than to misidentify in the opposite direction. **VOICE** Song is a quiet scratchy, mechanical series of notes. Call a short, ringing trill "*tj'i'it.*" **Co, E, Bo**

2 TYRIAN METALTAIL *Metallura tyrianthina* * 9.5–10 cm (3¾–4 in), bill 1–1.2 cm (⅜–½ in)

Common; the most widely distributed metaltail. Found on west slope of Andes south locally to Lima, in Marañón Valley and locally in humid upper reaches of other intermontane valleys, and along east slope of Andes, 2400–4200 m, occasionally to 1900 m. Found in humid montane forest (especially at forest openings), elfin forest, forest edge, and woods. Small hummingbird with glittering tail and small glittering green gorget (male) or buff throat speckled with green (female). Tail coppery red in Piura (*tyrianthina*); purplish blue elsewhere in Peru. Underparts paler in Marañón and on west slope south of Piura (*septentrionalis*), darker on east slope of eastern Andes (*smaragdinicollis*). Compare female to female Purple-backed and Rufous-capped thornbills. **VOICE** Call a jerky, wiry chatter repeated excitedly: "*tu-tu-ti-wseetoochew-wseetoochew-wseetoochew…,*" also a rich rattle and a single "*pit*" note. **Co, E, Bo**

3 RAINBOW-BEARDED THORNBILL *Chalcostigma herrani* * 10.5–11 cm (4–4¼ in), bill 1 cm (⅜ in)

Uncommon on east slope of Andes, north and west of Marañón Valley at 2450–3100 m. Found in shrubby paramo near treeline. Dark hummingbird; underparts lack the buff color of the smaller Rufous-capped Thornbill. Tail long, prominently tipped white. Crown rufous; narrow gorget glittering green and red. Upper tail coverts coppery, contrasting with purplish blue tail and green back. Female similar but duller. **VOICE** Call a descending squeaky chatter. **Co, E**

4 RUFOUS-CAPPED THORNBILL *Chalcostigma ruficeps* 9.5–10 cm (3¾–4 in), bill 1.2 cm (½ in)

Uncommon but widely distributed on east slope of Andes, 1800–2800 m, locally to 3600 m. Primarily found at edge of humid montane forest, or at openings in forest. Small, but has relatively long tail, notched and bronzy green. Male readily recognized by bright rufous crown and narrow, glittering green gorget. Female much duller: more or less buffy below, speckled with bronzy green; easily can be confused with female Tyrian Metaltail, but has a green (not purplish) tail, and usually is more extensively buffy below (belly of metaltail usually is greener than throat). **VOICE** Call a rich chatter. **E, Bo**

5 OLIVACEOUS THORNBILL *Chalcostigma olivaceum* * 14–15 cm (5½–6 in), bill 1.4 cm (½ in)

Rare to uncommon and patchily distributed in high Andes, 3500–4700 m. Found in humid puna grassland or among cushion plants, less commonly in montane scrub. Often walks on ground of very short grasslands, feeding on small flowers. Distinguished by large size, dull sooty gray or sooty brown plumage, and long dull-colored tail (concolor with back). Cf. Blue-mantled Thornbill. **Bo**

6 BLUE-MANTLED THORNBILL *Chalcostigma stanleyi* * 11.5–12 cm (4½–4¾ in), bill 1 cm (⅜ in)

Fairly common in paramo grasslands and humid *Polylepis* woods, 2800–4500 m. Found in the Cordillera Blanca in western Andes, and on both slopes of eastern Andes. Primarily feeds at foliage, but sometimes may walk on the ground (as does Olivaceous Thornbill). Plumage dark, but note long dark blue tail. Upperparts of male also deep purplish blue. Narrow gorget green and purple; reduced or absent in female. **VOICE** Call a descending squeaky chatter. **E, Bo**

PURPLE-BACKED
THORNBILL

♂

♀

TYRIAN
METALTAIL

♂ *tyrianthina*

♂ *septentrionalis*

TYRIAN
METALTAIL

♂ *smaragdinicollis*

♀ *smaragdinicollis*

RAINBOW-
BEARDED
THORNBILL

♀

♂

RUFOUS-CAPPED
THORNBILL

♀

♂

OLIVACEOUS
THORNBILL

♀

♂

BLUE-MANTLED
THORNBILL

♂

♀

PLATE
110

FAIRY, STARTHROAT, AND WOODSTARS

Black-eared Fairy is a beautiful hummingbird of humid forests in eastern Peru. The long bill of Long-billed Starthroat is accentuated by a relatively short tail. Woodstars are very small, short-tailed hummingbirds of humid forest edge in both lowlands and Andes. Woodstars have noticeably slow and direct flight, resembling a large, heavy-bodied bee. All show a white spot on the lower flanks (may be concealed when at rest, but visible in flight). May forage at all heights, but often sit on a high, exposed perch. Tails of the males are forked, and rectrices also often are very narrow. Identification of woodstars, especially of females, can be difficult.

1 BLACK-EARED FAIRY *Heliothryx auritus* * 13 cm (5 in); bill 1.8 cm (¾ in)
Uncommon but widespread in eastern Peru, up to 1300 m. Found in humid forest, especially in the canopy, and at forest edge. A long-tailed hummingbird, with strikingly white belly and long, mostly white tail. Chin and sides of male's throat usually glittering green (*auriculatus*), but may be white in northern Amazonia near Ecuador border (*auritus*). Throat of female lightly and variably spotted light gray. **VOICE** Call a rich "*tchip.*" **Co, E, Br, Bo**

2 LONG-BILLED STARTHROAT *Heliomaster longirostris* * 11–11.5 cm (4¼–4½ in), bill 3.3–3.6 cm (1¼–1⅜ in)
Uncommon at forest edge and in second growth in eastern lowlands, up to 1000 m; widespread, but apparently scarce or absent from northwestern Amazonia (*longirostris*). Also uncommon in dry forest in northwestern Peru (*albicrissa*) up to 700 m. Forages at all heights; often seen perched in a high open site. Note the very long, very straight bill. Crown light blue and gorget reddish purple; gorget often appears dark in the field, but note prominent, contrasting white border to dark throat. Has a semiconcealed white stripe on lower back and rump. Female duller, with reduced gorget and little or no blue on crown. Undertail coverts whiter in *albicrissa*. **VOICE** Call a rich, descending "*tchew.*" **Co, E, Br, Bo**

3 WHITE-BELLIED WOODSTAR *Chaetocercus mulsant* male 8–8.5 cm (3–3¼ in), female 7.5 cm (3 in), bill 1.7 cm (¾ in)
Uncommon to locally fairly common in humid areas of Andes, 800–3100 m, especially at forest edge. Found on east slope of Andes, and locally on west slope to Cajamarca and west slope of Marañón Valley, south locally to La Libertad. Male small and with a short spiky tail; similar to male Amethyst Woodstar of lowlands but tail shorter; outermost rectrices extremely narrow; white breast band broader; white postocular stripe more prominent; center of belly white, and chin usually white. Female has white flank patches and a dark mask framed by white postocular. Cf. female Amethyst and Little woodstars. **VOICE** Call a low "*djurt*" call. Male's wings produce a ringing in flight. **Co, E, Bo**

4 LITTLE WOODSTAR *Chaetocercus bombus* 6.5 cm (2½ in); bill 1.2 cm (½ in)
Rare, but probably also easily overlooked due to close similarity to more common and widespread White-bellied Woodstar. Most records are from middle Marañón Valley (and tributaries), but sparingly reported from west slope of Andes in Piura, and from intermontane valleys south to the Huallaga. Found in semideciduous and humid forest and forest edge at 600–2700 m. Smaller than White-bellied Woodstar (but size difference probably rarely apparent in the field). Rectrices of male extremely narrow; most also very short, with the next-to-central pair elongated (spiky). Gorget pinker, less purplish, than White-bellied Woodstar; and white of underparts and superciliary replaced by tawny buff. Superciliary and underparts of female uniformly tawny buff. **VOICE** Call a rich "*tchip.*" **Co, E**

5 AMETHYST WOODSTAR *Calliphlox amethystina* male 8.5 cm (3¼ in), female 7.5 cm (3 in), bill 1.4 cm (½ in)
Uncommon but widespread in eastern Peru, up to 1250 m. Found in canopy and at edge of humid forest. Male a tiny hummingbird with long, deeply forked tail. Gorget purplish or pinkish, bordered below by white breast band. Remaining underparts mostly dull grayish, variably speckled with green flecks (especially immediately below white breast band, and on flanks). Female is largely buffy or tawny below; throat whitish, lightly speckled. Very similar to female White-bellied Woodstar of Andes (with which there is only slight elevational overlap). Female Amethyst has more extensively tawny underparts (white center of belly reduced or lacking); and possibly narrower pale tips to rectrices. **Co, E, Br, Bo**

♂ auriculatus

♀

♂ auritus

BLACK-EARED FAIRY

♀ longirostris   ♂ longirostris

LONG-BILLED
STARTHROAT

♂ albicrissa

WHITE-BELLIED
WOODSTAR

♂

♀

LITTLE
WOODSTAR

♀

♂

AMETHYST
WOODSTAR

♂

♀

PLATE
111

PACIFIC-SLOPE HUMMINGBIRDS AND WOODSTARS

Species on this plate all are found in relatively arid, open habitats of the coast; Purple-collared Woodstar also enters the arid Marañón Valley.

1 OASIS HUMMINGBIRD *Rhodopis vesper* * male 12.5–13.5 cm (5–5¼ in), female 11–11.5 cm (4¼–4¾ in), bill 3 cm (1¼ in)
Uncommon but widespread west of Andes, up to 3800 m. Found in scrub, forest edge, agricultural areas, and gardens. Medium-sized, plain-colored hummingbird with long curved bill; male also with long narrow tail. Rump tawny. Northern populations smaller, whiter below with less prominent pale rump (*koepckeae*). **VOICE** Call a rapid, thin liquid chatter and a rich "*chew*" note. **Ch**

2 AMAZILIA HUMMINGBIRD *Amazilia amazilia* * 9–10 cm (3½–4 in), bill 1.8–2.1 cm (¾ in)
Common and conspicuous, mostly below 1000 m, locally up to 2400 m; in dry forest, scrub, towns, and gardens. Bill red, with dark tip. Amount of rufous in plumage geographically variable. Northern *dumerilii* (Tumbes; tail largely green) and *leucophoea* (south to northern Lima; tail largely rufous) have extensively white throats and breasts. Throat of *amazilia* is glittering green; tail rufous and green. In southern Ica *caeruleigularis* is similar, but throat is glittering blue. Females duller than males, with less red on bill. **VOICE** Song a quiet series of wheezy chatters and warbles. Call (*amazilia*) a rich chatter and a drawn out, descending "*seeet seeeuuuu*"; call of *leucophoea* similar, but usually more notes: "*seet see sew su so.*" Calls of *dumerilii* short "*jert*" and rattles, as well as sweet "*tsip*" notes. **E**

3 SHORT-TAILED WOODSTAR *Myrmia micrura* 6 cm (2¼ in), bill 1.3 cm (½ in)
Uncommon to fairly common in desert scrub of northwest, locally up to 1200 m. Very tiny hummingbird with ridiculously short tail; wing tips extend beyond tail when perched. Male has brilliant purple gorget; female buffy white below. **VOICE** Song, performed in a flight display, is a sweet, high series of "*tititi*" notes interspersed with a high "*sweee.*" Call thin "*tchi-tchi-tchi*" phrases. **E**

4 PURPLE-COLLARED WOODSTAR *Myrtis fanny* * male 9–9.5 cm (3½–3¾ in), female 8–8.5 cm (3–3¼ in), bill 1.7 cm (¾ in)
Fairly common in montane scrub on west slope of Andes and in Marañón Valley, although rare south of Arequipa. Most commonly at 700–3200 m, but locally (or seasonally?) down to sea level. Found in montane scrub, forest edge, and agricultural areas. Bill moderately long, distinctly curved. Male has long, slender, dark tail, gorget glittering bluish green, bordered below by narrow purple band and broad white collar. Female tawny below, with white-tipped tail; cf. female Peruvian Sheartail. **VOICE** In display male flies in a large, arching "U" over female. At upper ends of the "U" the male gives a series of thin "*ti-ti-ti*" notes; at bottom of "U" mechanically produces a thin, hollow "*aah aah aah.*" Call a series of thin "*ti-ti-ti*" notes. **E**

[CHILEAN WOODSTAR *Eulidia yarrellii*] 7.2–7.5 cm (3 in), bill 1.5 cm (⅝ in)
A few sight records at gardens in Tacna; presumably a very rare nonbreeding visitor. Endangered. Similar to Peruvian Sheartail; identify only with great care. On male note purple gorget; all dark, forked tail; and inward curvature to outer rectrices (may cross when perched). Female very similar to female sheartail, but tawny or buff usually deepest on flanks or belly, with whiter throat (female sheartail more likely to show tawny throat and whiter belly). Woodstar carries tail slightly cocked when foraging but does not regularly pump tail; sheartail carries tail held down but consistently pumps tail up and down. In the hand, has buff bases to outer rectrices (not apparent in the field). **VOICE** Call slight raspy "*tsick*" notes; less musical than louder, chipping calls of Peruvian Sheartail. **Ch**

5 PERUVIAN SHEARTAIL *Thaumastura cora* male 13–15 cm (5–6 in), female 7–7.5 cm (2¾–3 in), bill 1.2 cm (½ in)
Fairly common (except in north) and widespread west of Andes, up to 2800 m. Found in scrub, forest edge, agricultural areas, and gardens. Small. Long white train of male (consisting of the pair of rectrices next to central pair) is distinctive, although these feathers often broken. Female similar to female Purple-collared Woodstar but has shorter, straight bill. **VOICE** Song, from an exposed perch, a rapid, jumbled series of rich "*tchip*" notes, electric buzzes, and squeaky warbles. Call a rich "*tchip*," sometimes given in a rapid series. **E, Ch**

♀

♂

♂ *koepckeae*

OASIS
HUMMINGBIRD

amazilia

caeruleigularis

AMAZILIA HUMMINGBIRD

♂

SHORT-TAILED
WOODSTAR

♀

dumerilii

leucophoea

closed tail
of male

♂

♀

imm. ♂

♂

♀, white-
throated

PURPLE-COLLARED
WOODSTAR

♂

♀

CHILEAN
WOODSTAR

♀, buff-
throated

PERUVIAN SHEARTAIL

PLATE
112

TROGONS

Trogons are colorful, lethargic birds of forest midstory and canopy. Quickly raise then slowly lower their tails when nervous, while quietly calling. Frugivorous, but also eat arthropods. Do not join mixed species flocks. Nest in tree cavities.

1 MASKED TROGON *Trogon personatus* * 25–26 cm (9¾–10¼ in)

Uncommon to fairly common in humid montane forest along east slope of Andes, also local on west slope in Piura, 1100–3300 m. May overlap Collared Trogon (compare) at lowest elevations. Male has more finely barred undertail and wing coverts; orbital ring red. Female has black mask and entirely yellow bill. **VOICE** Song variable, one version a series of "*whew*" notes, usually quickening toward end; also a faster song, more like Collared Trogon, but usually lacking the initial stutter: "*kew whew-whew-whew.*" Calls descending musical chattered "*teegr'r'r'r'r,*" and descending quiet mewing whistles. **Co, E, Br, Bo**

2 COLLARED TROGON *Trogon collaris* * 24–25.5 cm (9½–10 in)

Uncommon in humid forest up to 1200 m (locally to 1700 m on outlying ridges). Male has finely barred undertail and green foreparts; orbital ring usually dull and inconspicuous. Female brown with broken white eyering, and black culmen on yellow bill; cf. female Black-throated and Masked trogons. **VOICE** Song a series of mellow whistled notes, usually with a stuttered introductory note: "*whi'whi whew-whew-whew.*" Calls a rising, quiet mew and a descending rattle: "*teer'r'r'r'r'r.*" **Co, E, Br, Bo**

3 BLACK-TAILED TROGON *Trogon melanurus* * 30.5–32 cm (12–12½ in)

Uncommon to locally common in humid forests up to 1000 m (*eumorphus*); rare to fairly common in humid and semideciduous forest in northwest, 400–1250 m (*mesurus*). Large red-bellied trogon, with no white in tail; *mesurus* has pale iris and (male) yellow bill. **VOICE** Song (*eumorphus*) a series of deep mewing whistles: "*cow cow cow cow cow cow*"; also a more muffled hooting "*woo woo woo woo woo....*" Deeper, more mewing than songs of other trogons. Song (*mesurus*) similar, perhaps slightly faster paced. Call of both a rapid series of churring notes: "*crra crra crra crra.*" **Co, E, Br, Bo**

4 WHITE-TAILED TROGON *Trogon viridis* * 28–29 cm (11–11½ in)

Uncommon to fairly common in humid forest, up to 750 m, locally to 1350 m. Largest yellow-bellied trogon. Orbital ring blue and complete in both sexes. Undertail of male broadly white. Compare female to Violaceous and Blue-crowned trogons (females of which have broken white orbital rings; Blue-crowned also has red belly, blacker tail). **VOICE** Song a series of hollow, mellow whistles, usually accelerating and rising in pitch slightly: "*cowl cowl cowl cowl cowl,*" sometimes becoming more mewing in quality. Call a deep chucking, often in slow series: "*cuk cuk cuk.*" **Co, E, Br, Bo**

5 BLUE-CROWNED TROGON *Trogon curucui* * 24–25.5 cm (9½–10 in)

Uncommon to fairly common in humid forest (most common in varzea), up to 1500 m; often near edges and second growth. Male has yellow or orange orbital ring and bluish foreparts. Female only red-bellied trogon with slate head and upperparts and gray bill. **VOICE** Song a series of mewing whistles: "*whew-whew-whew-whew-whew.*" Very similar to Violaceous, but perhaps a little faster paced; generally faster than White-tailed. Call a rapid rattle: "*tr'r'r'r'r'r.*" **Co, E, Br, Bo**

6 BLACK-THROATED TROGON *Trogon rufus* * 25–26 cm (9¾–10¼ in)

Uncommon but widespread in northern and central Amazonia in humid forest, up to 650 m; also reported from southeast, where status not clear. Male has yellow bill and green head. Female only yellow-bellied trogon with brown foreparts. **VOICE** Song similar to Collared Trogon, but usually slower in delivery and with fewer notes: "*whi'whi whew whew*"; sometimes lacks introductory stutter. **Co, E, Br, Bo**

7 VIOLACEOUS TROGON *Trogon violaceus* * 22.5–23 cm (8¾–9 in)

Rare to uncommon in humid forest, up to 800 m; also rare below 400 m in Tumbes (*concinnus*). Male has yellow orbital ring, barred tail, and bluish foreparts. Note broken white orbital ring and gray foreparts of female; tail also more finely barred than female White-tailed Trogon's. **VOICE** Song (Amazonia) a fairly rapid series of mewing whistles: "*whew whew whew whew whew,*" sometimes sounding bisyllabic: "*whi-ew whi-ew....*" Cf. Blue-crowned Trogon. Song (*concinnus*) a descending series of mewing notes: "*PEW Pew pew pew pew pew pew.*" Call a rapid rattle: "*tr'r'r'r'r.*" **Co, E, Br, Bo**

MASKED
TROGON

♀

♂

COLLARED TROGON

♀

♂

BLACK-TAILED
TROGON

♀

*eumor-
phus*

♀

WHITE-TAILED
TROGON

BLUE-CROWNED
TROGON

♀

♂

♂

*eumor-
phus*

♀

♂

BLACK-TAILED
TROGON
♂
*mesu-
rus*

♀

♂

BLACK-THROATED
TROGON

♂

♀

VIOLACEOUS
TROGON

PLATE
113

MOTMOTS AND QUETZALS

Motmots sit quietly and motionless in forest under- and midstory; can be difficult to spot. Usually solitary or in pairs; do not join mixed-species flocks. Often switch tail side-to-side like pendulum, particularly when nervous. Nest in burrows in ground.

1 BLUE-CROWNED MOTMOT *Momotus momota* * 39–41 cm (15½–16 in)
Uncommon to fairly common in humid forest and forest edge in Amazonia, up to 750 m. Also fairly common in humid and semideciduous forests in northwest to 900 m (*argenticinctus*). Note black-and-blue pattern on face and crown. Amazonian birds usually rufescent below, but may be greenish. *Argenticinctus* variably buffy below with bright greenish throat. Upper surface of rackets tipped black. Cf. Highland Motmot (no known elevational overlap). **VOICE** Song (Amazonia) a bubbling "*whOOP-oop*"; first note rises (unlike Rufous Motmot). In duet, one individual usually responds with slower "*whoop whoop*" or single "*whoop?*" Also rolling series of hoots in duet. Song of *argenticinctus* a single "*whoop*." Call a gruff "*kak*," sometimes several such notes strung together in a jumbled, excited series. **Co, E, Br, Bo**

2 HIGHLAND MOTMOT *Momotus aequatorialis* * 46–48 cm (18–19 in)
Rare to uncommon in humid montane forests along east slope of Andes, 1000–2400 m. Usually near streams. Similar to Blue-crowned, but larger, greener below (only occasionally shows tawny on breast), rear tip of black mask cut off by blue streak, and upper surface of rackets entirely blue. **VOICE** Song a monotone "*boop-oop*," very similar to Rufous Motmot. Also a monosyllabic "*whoop?*" Duetting birds give a rolling series of hoots. **Co, E, Bo**

3 BROAD-BILLED MOTMOT *Electron platyrhynchum* * 33–35.5 cm (13–14 in)
Uncommon to fairly common in humid forest, up to 1200 m; usually perches in midstory, often fairly high off ground. Similar to much larger Rufous, but note green chin, more extensive green on belly. From underneath, broader-based bill is easily seen. **VOICE** Song a hoarse series of "*gaw*" notes, sometimes in a more rapid series; also sometimes as a duet. Call a quiet series of "*tuk*" notes, sometimes becoming a soft rattle. Vocalizes more regularly during daylight than other motmots. **Co, E, Br, Bo**

4 RUFOUS MOTMOT *Baryphthengus martii* * 43–46 cm (17–18 in)
Uncommon in terra firme below 1300 m, locally up to 1600 m; not as closely tied to treefalls and edges as Blue-crowned Motmot. Largest lowland motmot. Cf. smaller Broad-billed Motmot. **VOICE** Song a rapid, monotone "*boop-oop*"; very similar to Blue-crowned but does not change pitch. In duet a rolling series of hoots (very similar to *Momotus*). **Co, E, Br, Bo**

5 CRESTED QUETZAL *Pharomachrus antisianus* 33–34 cm (13–13½ in)
Rare to uncommon in subcanopy of humid montane forest of east slope of Andes and outlying ridges, 1000–2300 m. Generally at lower elevations than Golden-headed Quetzal, and rarely as numerous. Male distinctive. Female very similar to Golden-headed, but iris redder; also note narrow white bars on outer edges of rectrices, and less extensive red on underparts. **VOICE** Song a slow, mellow series of 2 notes, second somewhat higher: "*weeoweee-WEEoo*." Calls a musical series of down-slurred mews and louder cackles: "*keeew keh-HEEAH keh-HEEAH*." **Co, E, Bo**

6 PAVONINE QUETZAL *Pharomachrus pavoninus* 33–34 cm (13–13½ in)
Rare to locally uncommon in subcanopy of terra firme, up to 1100 m. Underside of tail all dark (male) or with small amount of pale barring (female). Male has red bill and poorly developed crest. Bill of female dull reddish. **VOICE** Song descending mewing whistle followed by a quiet "*chuck*," often given in a series: "*WHEEEW chuck WHEEEW chuck WHEEEW chuck….*" Also, a loud, excited cackle, often given in agitation or just before flight. Call a quiet mewing "*weeo*." **Co, E, Br, Bo**

7 GOLDEN-HEADED QUETZAL *Pharomachrus auriceps* * 33.5–35.5 cm (13¼–13¾ in)
Uncommon to locally fairly common in humid montane forest on east slope of Andes; locally on west slope south to Cajamarca, 1200–3000 m. Generally more common than Crested and at higher elevations, but with broad elevational overlap. Underside of tail always dark; iris brown. Note reduced crest of male; golden iridescence of head not always visible. Compare female to female Crested. No elevational overlap with similar Pavonine Quetzal. **VOICE** Song a series of long, quavering, mellow whistles "*weeoWEEEEw*." Call a rapid, descending musical chatter: "*keh-kehkahkahkahkaka*." **Co, E, Bo**

BLUE-CROWNED
MOTMOT

nw

HIGHLAND MOTMOT

BLUE-CROWNED MOTMOT

Amaz.

BROAD-
BILLED
MOTMOT

RUFOUS
MOTMOT

♀

♀

♂

♀

♂

GOLDEN-
HEADED
QUETZAL

♂

CRESTED QUETZAL

PAVONINE
QUETZAL

♂

PLATE
114

KINGFISHERS

Kingfishers are closely tied to water. Forage mostly on fish captured by diving into water; the smaller species also take aquatic arthropods. Usually prey is spotted from a perch over the water, but sometimes the kingfisher may hover momentarily over water looking for prey. Preferred perching height is directly correlated to the size of the species, with Ringed Kingfisher often sitting high over rivers and lakes, but smallest species sitting only centimeters above the water's surface. Nest in burrows in riverbanks.

1 AMAZON KINGFISHER *Chloroceryle amazona* 28–29 cm (11–11½ in)

Uncommon to fairly common along rivers and over marshes and lakes in Amazonia, locally up to 1300 m. Large with a very heavy, thick-based bill that merges with forehead producing rather "flat-headed" profile. Similar to smaller Green Kingfisher, but Amazon has heavier bill, lacks white bands in wing and base of outer rectrices, and flanks broadly streaked (not barred) with green. When seen in flight, underwing less heavily marked. Male has broad chestnut breast band; breast of female has narrower green breast band, often broken in center of breast, and white underparts are not washed with buff. **VOICE** Song (?) a descending and decelerating squeaky series of notes: "*titi-twi-twi-twe twe too.*" Call a dull "*kek.*" **Co, E, Br, Bo**

2 RINGED KINGFISHER *Megaceryle torquata* * 30.5–32 cm (12–12½ in)

Uncommon but widespread over larger rivers, lakes, and marshes in Amazonia and the northwest, locally up to 1000 m; formerly found along coast south to Lima, but no recent reports south of Lambayeque. Large size, blue-gray head and upperparts, and large, ragged crest are distinctive. Underparts of male extensively rufous; female has broad blue and narrow white bands on breast. In flight, note large white patch at base of primaries. **VOICE** Call, usually given in flight, a loud "*CLACK*" sometimes strung into a loose chatter: "*KEK'KEK'KEK'KEK'KEK'KEK....*" **Co, E, Br, Bo, Ch**

3 GREEN KINGFISHER *Chloroceryle americana* * 18.5–20.5 cm (7¼–8 in)

Uncommon to fairly common along rivers, streams, marshes, and lakes on east side of Andes; the only small kingfisher along coast, where fairly rare, and in upper Río Marañón; up to 1400 m, and locally up to 2400 m. Smallest of the "white-collared" kingfishers; cf. larger Amazon Kingfisher. When seen in flight, underwing is more heavily marked. Male has broad chestnut breast band. Breast band of female is narrower, green; often there is a second band across belly. Collar and underparts also usually washed with buff. **VOICE** Song (?) a descending series of squeaky notes: "*tsi-tsi-tswee-tswee-tsew.*" Call a quiet "*tick,*" sometimes given in a series of rattling ticks. Also an electric "*dzew.*" **Co, E, Br, Bo, Ch**

4 AMERICAN PYGMY KINGFISHER *Chloroceryle aenea* * 13 cm (5 in)

Rare (but difficult to detect, and often overlooked?) but widespread along forest streams with closed canopy, swamps and at bushy edges of lakes in Amazonia, locally up to 700 m. Rarely perches in open; almost always under cover of overhanging vegetation, and low near the water. Tiny (very much the smallest kingfisher). Collar tawny-rufous, underparts mostly rufous with white center to belly. Breast of male rufous. Female has green breast band flecked with white Cf. larger Green-and-rufous Kingfisher. **VOICE** Song (?) a descending series of high, thin squeaks "*ti-ti-tew-tew-tew.*" Call a quiet rattling series of ticks. **Co, E, Br, Bo**

5 GREEN-AND-RUFOUS KINGFISHER *Chloroceryle inda* 21.5–23 cm (8½–9 in)

Rare to uncommon, and difficult to detect, along forest streams with closed canopy, swamps, and at bushy edges of lakes in Amazonia, locally up to 750 m. Rarely perches away from cover; usually seen in flight along watercourses between favored feeding perches. Similar in size to Green Kingfisher, but entirely rufous below and on collar (female has green breast band flecked with white); smaller American Pygmy Kingfisher has white center to belly and vent. **VOICE** Song (?) a descending series similar to that of Amazon Kingfisher, but slower and squeakier, and ending with some nasal chatter: "*swee squeet squeet squeet squeet chuh chuh chuchuchu*"; also a squeaky "*swee-tsee.*" Calls a buzzy "*dzzew*" and a series of ticks. **Co, E, Br, Bo**

AMAZON KINGFISHER

♂

♀

GREEN KINGFISHER

♀

♂

RINGED
KINGFISHER

♂

♀

GREEN-AND-RUFOUS KINGFISHER

♀

AMERICAN PYGMY
KINGFISHER

♀

♂

♂

PLATE
115

JACAMARS

Jacamars are long-billed birds that sally for flying insects (particularly moths and butterflies), usually returning to their initial perches, upon which they beat their prey before consuming it. Some species also may take small vertebrates. Nest in burrows. The two Galbalcyrhynchus are chunky, short-tailed, dark jacamars with thick reddish bills. Brachygalba are small jacamars that are restricted to varzea and river-edge forest; also may occur at the edges of nearby gaps and clearings. Often several individuals perch in close proximity on exposed branches overhanging water. Paradise Jacamar is notably slender and long-tailed. Great Jacamar is the largest species, with a particularly heavy bill.

1 PARADISE JACAMAR *Galbula dea* * 25.5–34 cm (10–13¼ in)

Rare to locally uncommon in the canopy of terra firme, usually around gaps; also around edges of savannas where may be more common (or at least easier to see). Usually seen perched on dead branches above or just within canopy. Shape diagnostic, with long, pointed graduated tail. Overall glossy blackish with white throat and tan crown; appears very dark at a distance. Cf. Purplish Jacamar. **VOICE** Song a long, descending series of rich whistles: *"KEEYEW… keew.. keew keew-keew-kew…."* Calls a rapid series of *"pew"* or squeakier *"kyew"* notes, sometimes as an introduction to a song. **Co, E, Br, Bo**

2 GREAT JACAMAR *Jacamerops aureus* * 29.5–30.5 cm (11½–12 in)

Rare to uncommon in midstory and subcanopy of terra firme, primarily in lowlands, but locally as high as 1200 m. The largest jacamar. Both sexes have iridescent green upperparts and rufous underparts; undertail blackish. Female lacks white throat. Bill more curved than those of other jacamars, and also heavier than in most others (except for the pink-billed *Galbalcyrhynchus* species). Not likely to be confused. **VOICE** Song a long, melancholy whistle that usually changes to a lower pitch fairly abruptly: *"heeeeee'ooooooooo."* Calls a very different, almost mammalian-sounding whining and groaning. **Co, E, Br, Bo**

3 BROWN JACAMAR *Brachygalba lugubris* * 16–17 cm (6¼–6¾ in)

Rare in canopy and midstory of varzea, and in edges and second growth along rivers; usually perches on exposed branches overhanging water or gaps. Replaces White-throated Jacamar in northern Amazonia (but crosses to south bank of Río Marañón in Amazonas). A small, all-brown jacamar with paler buffy brown belly. Not likely to be confused. **VOICE** Song a high, thin series of whistles that accelerates, then ends with several longer rising notes: *"pee-pipi-peeee tewee tewee tewee."* Call a high, thin whistle *"pee-yer."* Very similar to voice of White-throated Jacamar, but lower pitched. **Co, E, Br, Bo**

4 WHITE-THROATED JACAMAR *Brachygalba albogularis* 15–16 cm (6–6¼ in)

Rare to locally uncommon below 600 m in canopy and midstory of varzea and river-edge forest and their edges; usually perches on exposed branches overhanging water or gaps. Replaces Brown Jacamar in central and southern Amazonia. A small, dull brownish jacamar with whitish face, pale bill, and chestnut center to belly. **VOICE** Song a high, thin series of whistles that accelerates, then ends with several longer rising notes: *"pee-pipi-peeee tewee tewee tewee."* Call a high, thin whistle *"tee-wer."* Very similar to voice of Brown, but higher pitched. **Br, Bo**

5 WHITE-EARED JACAMAR *Galbalcyrhynchus leucotis* 19–20 cm (7½–8 in)

Rare to uncommon in open swampy forest, edges to rivers and oxbow lakes, and young river islands; replaces Purus Jacamar in northern Amazonia. Usually found in small groups in exposed branches. Very similar to Purus but has prominent white ear patch. Not likely to be confused with any other species. **VOICE** Song, usually given as a duet or chorus, is a rising and falling chatter somewhat reminiscent of Plain Softtail, but richer, with the pitch changes accelerating: *"trrreeeeeeeerrrr-reeeerrr-reeerr-reerreerr…."* Call a rich whistled *"pew!"* sometimes in a series. Voice probably indistinguishable from Purus. **Co, E, Br**

6 PURUS JACAMAR *Galbalcyrhynchus purusianus* 20 cm (8 in)

Rare to uncommon in open swampy forest, edges to rivers and oxbow lakes, and young river islands. Replaces White-eared Jacamar in central and southeastern Amazonia; the two species are not known to meet, but their distributions approach one another along the central Río Ucayali. Similar in appearance and behavior to White-eared but lacks the white cheek patch. **VOICE** Effectively indistinguishable from White-eared. **Br, Bo**

PARADISE JACAMAR

BROWN JACAMAR

GREAT JACAMAR

♂

♀

WHITE-EARED
JACAMAR

PURUS JACAMAR

WHITE-THROATED JACAMAR

PLATE
116

GALBULA JACAMARS

Galbula are medium-sized jacamars. Most species forage in the understory of humid forest, but Paradise (plate 115) and Purplish jacamars typically are in the subcanopy or canopy. Often perch in relatively open sites. The plumage is mostly glittering or iridescent green or bronze. Two pairs of species geographically replace one another, with no known overlap: the yellow-billed Blue-cheeked and Yellow-billed jacamars, and the black-billed Bluish-fronted and White-chinned jacamars.

1 PURPLISH JACAMAR *Galbula chalcothorax* 23.5 cm (9¼ in)

Rare to locally uncommon in midstory of varzea and transitional forest; widespread in northern Amazonia, very local in west central Amazonian Peru. No rufous in plumage. Dark overall (may appear bluish or bronzy depending on light), with large white (male) or buffy (female) throat patch. Cf. Paradise Jacamar. **VOICE** Song a characteristic rising series of mellow, rising whistles, each followed by a grinding note: "*weee-jurt wee-jurt wee-jurt wee-jurt....*" Also a descending dry chatter similar to other *Galbula*. Call a descending, mellow whistle "*whew,*" nearly identical to a common call of Dusky-capped Flycatcher, but usually repeated at a more rapid pace. **Co, E, Br**

2 BLUE-CHEEKED JACAMAR *Galbula cyanicollis* 19–22 cm (7½–8 in)

Rare to uncommon in under- and midstory around treefalls in terra firme south of the Amazon and east of Ucayali (although found west of lower Ucayali, near its mouth). Female tawny buff below; averages paler and buffier (less rufous) than other green jacamars. Male very similar to female Yellow-billed Jacamar. Blue-cheeked has blue iridescence on rear crown and along border of throat (often difficult to see in the field); identify by distribution, and by accompanying female. **VOICE** Effectively indistinguishable from Yellow-billed. **Br, Bo**

3 YELLOW-BILLED JACAMAR *Galbula albirostris* * 19 cm (7½ in)

Rare to uncommon in under- and midstory around treefalls in terra firme below 800 m north of the Amazon and west of central and southern Río Ucayali; replaced on west bank of lower Ucayali, and everywhere on east bank, by Blue-cheeked Jacamar. Yellow bill and lack of green below distinguish it from most jacamars. Male has white throat. Compare female to very similar Blue-cheeked. **VOICE** Song a series of mellow rising whistles that often accelerates into a chatter: "*weeet weeet weeeet weeeweeweeewi-tr'r'r'r'r'r'r.*" Call a series of rich "*tew*" notes. Voice probably indistinguishable from that of Blue-cheeked. **Co, E, Br**

4 [COPPERY-CHESTED JACAMAR] *Galbula pastazae* 23 cm (9 in)

Rare to uncommon on east slope of Andes north of Río Marañón; currently known from sight records (tape recorded) from a single site in Peru, but elevational range 750–1500 m in Ecuador. Found at treefall gaps, landslides, and at forest edge. Note bright yellowish orbital skin and greenish iridescent crown. Female has distinctive rufous throat and green breast. **VOICE** Song a rising series of "*wee*" notes, sometimes ending in a descending rattle, also a "*weet*" note, singly or in a series. Very similar to vocalizations of White-chinned and Bluish-fronted jacamars. **Co, E**

5 WHITE-CHINNED JACAMAR *Galbula tombacea* * 23.5 cm (9¼ in)

Uncommon to locally common north of Marañón and the Amazon. Found in vine tangles, treefall gaps, and edges of varzea and transitional forest, locally up to 1200 m. Very similar to Bluish-fronted Jacamar (no known overlap), but forehead and crown of White-chinned is a dull grayish brown. Belly of female is washed-out buffy rufous. Black bill, dark orbital skin, and green throat and breast separate it from other jacamars within range. **VOICE** Song an accelerating and rising series of mewing, somewhat squeaky whistles, sometimes ending in a descending rattle: "*whew whew we-we-wewiwiwiwi-kee'e'rrrrr.*" Calls a "*weet*" note, either single or in a series, and a rapid dry rattle. Probably indistinguishable from Bluish-fronted. **Co, E, Br**

6 BLUISH-FRONTED JACAMAR *Galbula cyanescens* 20–23 cm (7¼–9¼ in)

Common and widespread in Peru south of Marañón and the Amazon, where it replaces White-chinned Jacamar. Found in vine tangles, treefall gaps, and edges of varzea, transitional forest, and river islands, also around *Guadua* bamboo and landslides in foothills, locally up to 1400 m. Very similar to White-chinned, but crown iridescent blue-green; no known geographic overlap. Belly of female a more washed-out buffy rufous. Some individuals in southeast may show white chin. **VOICE** Effectively indistinguishable from White-chinned. **Br, Bo**

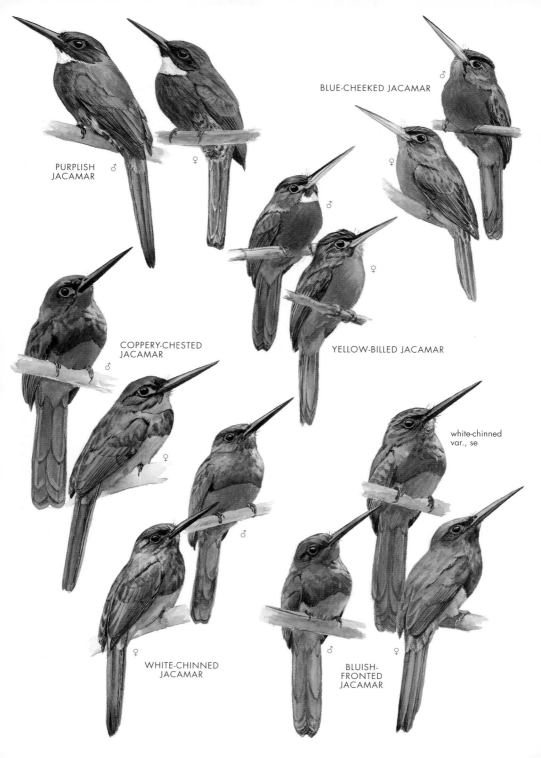

PURPLISH
JACAMAR ♂ ♀

BLUE-CHEEKED JACAMAR ♂ ♀

COPPERY-CHESTED
JACAMAR ♂ ♀

YELLOW-BILLED JACAMAR ♂ ♀

white-chinned
var., se

WHITE-CHINNED
JACAMAR ♂ ♀

BLUISH-
FRONTED
JACAMAR ♂ ♀

PLATE
117

BAND-BREASTED PUFFBIRDS

Puffbirds have heavy, hook-tipped bills. Lethargic and easily overlooked; sit motionless for long periods, then sally to capture prey (large arthropods and small vertebrates). Usually in pairs or family groups; most species do not join mixed species flocks. Nest in burrows or cavities. Most species vocalize only occasionally, most often in the predawn; vocalizations of many species also seem ventriloquial.

1 PIED PUFFBIRD *Notharchus tectus* * 14.5–17 cm (5¾–6¾ in)

Rare to uncommon in canopy of forest and forest edge in Amazonia. A fairly small, black-and-white puffbird most likely to be confused with the much larger White-necked Puffbird; Pied also has smaller bill, white spotting on crown, white scapulars, and large white spots on tail. Also cf. Brown-banded Puffbird. **VOICE** Song, sometimes given in duet, a series of high whistles that accelerates, then descends and decelerates with rising whistles: *"pipipi whi whi whi WHEE-WHEE-whee whee whee,"* sometimes preceded by a series of monosyllabic whistles. Calls a mewing *"tewww"* and *"teee-ew,"* as well as a harsh *"djer."* **Co, E, Br, Bo**

2 WHITE-NECKED PUFFBIRD *Notharchus hyperrhynchus* * 25–25.5 cm (9¾–10 in)

Rare to uncommon in canopy and midstory of forest in eastern lowlands, particularly in terra firme (up to 700 m). Large, boldly patterned black-and-white puffbird. Heavy bill, white forehead, broad white collar, and black breast band should distinguish it easily; cf. smaller Pied and Brown-banded puffbirds. **VOICE** Song, often in duet, a long trill of musical notes; occasionally ends with a descending series of mewing whistles: *"br'r'r'r'r'r'r'r'r'r'r'r'r'r'r'r wi-wi-wi wur-wi wur-wi wur-wi."* Similar to song of Cinnamon-throated Woodcreeper, but ends abruptly without dying away, and without terminal churr. Calls a descending whistled *"wheeew"* and a quiet growl. **Co, E, Br, Bo**

3 BROWN-BANDED PUFFBIRD *Notharchus ordii* 19 cm (7¼ in)

Rare and local in canopy and midstory in eastern lowlands. Most frequent in forests on sand substrates. Patchily distributed in central and northern Peru; also a few records from southeast. Large, mostly black-and-white puffbird. Intermediate in size between White-necked and Pied puffbirds, but lower part of breast band is brown, has no white superciliary, and white forecrown is very narrow. **VOICE** Song, often given in duet, an accelerating whistled chatter followed by decelerating, weak, descending series of whistled notes: *"whi-WIWIWIWIWI-WUR-WI wur wi-wi wur wi-wi wur wi-wi wur wi-wi."* **Co, Br, Bo**

4 COLLARED PUFFBIRD *Bucco capensis* * 18.5–19 cm (7¼–7½ in)

Rare to uncommon in subcanopy and midstory of terra firme; widespread in northern Peru, seemingly less common or more local in southeast. A large, blocky puffbird with large reddish bill and bold black collar; largely rufescent brown above with fine black vermiculations, buffy below. Unlikely to be confused within its habitat. **VOICE** Song, usually given predawn, often as a duet, is a series of wheezy, mechanical mewing notes: *"awww awwAWW-chaw awwAWW-chaw awwAWW-chaw."* Also (Ecuador) a more musical, mewing series *"weeWAH weeWAH weeWAH."* **Co, E, Br, Bo**

5 CHESTNUT-CAPPED PUFFBIRD *Bucco macrodactylus* 16–16.5 cm (6¼–6½ in)

Uncommon in the midstory and edge of varzea and second-growth forest and around treefalls and large vine tangles in terra firme up to 1000 m. A small, boldly patterned puffbird with black collar and mask, chestnut crown, brown upperparts, and buffy underparts lightly barred. Adults have reddish eyes, juveniles have dark brown eyes. Cf. Spotted Puffbird (more heavily marked with black below, lacks defined, complete collar). **VOICE** Call a series of rising-falling whistles *"wheEEEeeu,"* similar to common call of Dusky-capped Flycatcher, but usually shorter notes and given at faster pace. **Co, E, Br, Bo**

6 SPOTTED PUFFBIRD *Bucco tamatia* * 18–18.5 cm (7–7¼ in)

Rare to locally uncommon in the under- and midstory of varzea and swamp forest, often near streams. More frequently encountered in northern Amazonia than southern. A medium-sized, boldly marked puffbird with black scaling below, heavy black mark on sides of neck, and narrow white collar; upperparts brown with blackish barring. Cf. Chestnut-capped Puffbird. **VOICE** Song, usually given predawn, often in duet, is a long series of rising mellow whistles: *"tuEE tuEE tuEE tuEE tuEE tuEE…."* Call a quiet series of mellow, whistled *"whe"* notes. **Co, E, Br, Bo**

PIED PUFFBIRD

BROWN-BANDED
PUFFBIRD

WHITE-NECKED PUFFBIRD

COLLARED PUFFBIRD

CHESTNUT-
CAPPED
PUFFBIRD

SPOTTED PUFFBIRD

PLATE
118

STREAKY PUFFBIRDS

Striolated Puffbird is found in the subcanopy and canopy, where it is easy to overlook until the voice is learned. The four species of Malacoptila *are medium-sized puffbirds of forest understory. Often in pairs. Quiet and inconspicuous; sometimes first noticed by the pendulum-like, side-to-side twitching of the tail. All species have a white or buff chest patch, which usually is concealed unless the bird is excited. Lanceolated Monklet is a small, inconspicuous puffbird.*

1 STRIOLATED PUFFBIRD *Nystalus striolatus* * 20–21 cm (7¾–8¼ in)

Rare to uncommon in canopy and midstory of terra firme up to 1200 m. Widespread in foothills and southern Amazonia; scarce or absent from much of northern Peru, where appears to be mostly confined to Andean foothills. A medium-sized, cryptically patterned puffbird with dull greenish bill and tan-colored eyes. Plumage is largely buffy with blackish streaks, back is browner and mottled. Cf. *Malacoptila* puffbirds (which are restricted to understory, have dark eyes and smaller bills). Usually first detected by its intermittent song. **VOICE** Song, usually in duet or chorus, is a series of slow, quiet whistles often with a pause between the first (rising) and second (falling) phrases; mournful quality: "*whi-whi'wheeeee? whi'woooooo.*" **E, Br, Bo**

2 RUFOUS-NECKED PUFFBIRD *Malacoptila rufa* * 18 cm (7 in)

Rare to uncommon in northern Amazonia. Usually in understory of humid forest. Apparently restricted to varzea and transitional forest where it overlaps with White-chested Puffbird, but otherwise can be found in terra firme; not known whether Rufous-necked replaces Semicollared Puffbird, or whether these two species also overlap. Not likely to be confused, but cf. Chestnut-capped Puffbird and nunlets. **VOICE** Song a long, descending musical trill, indistinguishable from songs of White-chested and Semicollared puffbirds. Call an agitated harsh rasping series: "*trr'r'r'r'r-SHEEAH trr'r'r'r'r-SHEEAH trr'r'r'r'r-SHEEAH....*" **Br, Bo**

3 BLACK-STREAKED PUFFBIRD *Malacoptila fulvogularis* * 18.5–19 cm (7¼–7½ in)

Rare to uncommon (difficult to detect) in understory of humid montane forest from 900–1900 m. A medium-sized puffbird, heavily streaked. Overlaps at lower edge of elevational range with Semicollared and White-chested puffbirds. Note all dark bill, buffy throat, and extensive black-and-white streaking on underparts. May overlap in elevation with Striolated Puffbird, but unlikely to be confused; also cf. Lanceolated Monklet. Buffy chest patch often concealed. **VOICE** Song is a series of high, rising whistles: "*sueeee?*" Similar to voices of some fruiteaters, but usually shorter. Calls include a thin "*whi-whee?*" and a rapid, ringing, descending chatter followed by rising notes: "*ti-trrrrrrr swee-swee-swee-swee.*" **Co, E, Bo**

4 LANCEOLATED MONKLET *Micromonacha lanceolata* 13.5 cm (5¼ in)

Rare and difficult to detect, from understory to subcanopy of humid montane forest in foothills, 500–1500 m; also rare and local in terra firme in northeastern Amazonia. Sometimes associates with mixed species flocks. A small, attractive puffbird with white lores bordered with black, black streaks on white underparts, and rich brown upperparts with black vermiculations on back and wings. Unlikely to be confused, but cf. larger *Malacoptila* puffbirds. **VOICE** Song an accelerating series of rising, high, mewing whistles: "*sewee.. sewee sewee-sewee-sewee'swee'swee*"; easily overlooked. **Co, E, Br, Bo**

5 WHITE-CHESTED PUFFBIRD *Malacoptila fusca* * 18–18.5 cm (7–7¼ in)

Uncommon but widespread in humid forests below 1500 m, north of the Amazon and west of central and upper Río Ucayali. Locally overlaps very different Rufous-necked Puffbird; where both species occur, White-chested is mostly restricted to terra firme (and Rufous-necked occurs in varzea). South of the Amazon cf. similar Semicollared Puffbird. **VOICE** Song a long, descending musical trill: "*tree'e'e'e'e'e'e'ew.*" Calls a descending, high, mewing whistle "*peeww*" and a descending, high, trill: "*seeewww.*" **Co, E, Br**

6 SEMICOLLARED PUFFBIRD *Malacoptila semicincta* 18–19 cm (7–7½ in)

Uncommon but widespread in humid forests up to 1250 m, east of Río Ucayali and in southeastern Peru. Geographically replaces White-chested Puffbird; there is no known contact or overlap between these two similar species. Differs from White-chested Puffbird by the prominent chestnut collar across nape. **VOICE** Vocalizations indistinguishable from those of White-chested. **Br, Bo**

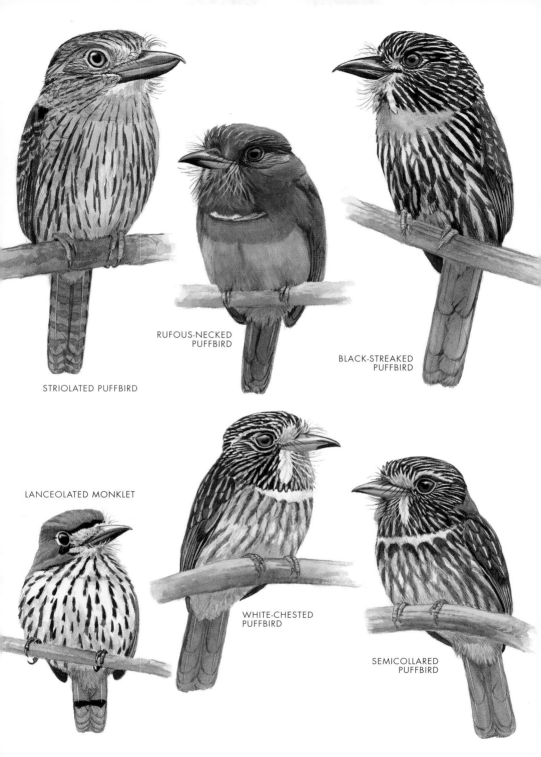

STRIOLATED PUFFBIRD

RUFOUS-NECKED
PUFFBIRD

BLACK-STREAKED
PUFFBIRD

LANCEOLATED MONKLET

WHITE-CHESTED
PUFFBIRD

SEMICOLLARED
PUFFBIRD

PLATE
119

WHITE-EARED PUFFBIRD, SWALLOW-WING, AND NUNBIRDS

White-eared Puffbird is unusual: restricted to disjunct populations in dry or scrubby forest in Amazonia. Swallow-wing is a peculiar puffbird that captures prey in long aerial sallies over forest or forest edge. White-faced Nunbird is a rare puffbird of humid montane forest. The three Monasa nunbirds are large puffbirds, often in boisterous groups of 4–7 individuals, notable for loud cacophonies of long chatters. During such performances, several birds may perch side-by-side and wave their tails up and sideways excitedly. They often are curious and inspect intruders to their territories, frequently putting up an alarm. As they move through the midstory, nunbirds typically glide on slightly bowed, forward-thrust wings, then sharply swing up onto a new perch.

1 WHITE-EARED PUFFBIRD *Nystalus chacuru* * 21–22 cm (8¼–8½ in)

Rare to uncommon in open, semideciduous or dry forest and scrub edge in Apurímac and Urubamba valleys, 1000–2200 m; reported from Mayo Valley (but no recent records?). Also at borders of savannas on Pampas del Heath. Frequently sits on exposed perches such as dead crowns of small trees and telephone wires; usually in pairs. Boldly marked puffbird with large red bill and black "muttonchops" contrasting with largely white face and underparts. **VOICE** Song (Bolivia), usually in antiphonal duet, a pleasant descending, low, whistled series of "*co-lo*" phrases answered by a higher "*de-le*," thus "*co-lo'de-le co-lo'de-le co-lo'de-le….*" **Br, Bo**

2 SWALLOW-WING *Chelidoptera tenebrosa* * 16.5 cm (6 in)

Common and highly visible; perch on exposed limbs in canopy and gaps along large rivers, in clearings, and in savannas below 800 m. Usually in pairs, but locally may congregate in large numbers (seasonal movements?). Highly aerobatic as they sally far above perches to capture flying insects, flashing the white rump and underwing coverts. Note characteristic short-tailed, broad-winged shape. Large headed, short-tailed with slightly decurved, fairly short bill; dark slate overall (appearing blackish at a distance) when perched. Cf. similarly shaped, but much smaller, White-browed Purpletuft; Swallow-wing also is much blacker, and lacks purpletuft's distinctive face pattern. **VOICE** Calls high voice-cracking notes, often in a series rising and falling in pitch excitedly: "*peet*" and "*wee wee weet*." Recalls chatter of Tropical Kingbird, but clearer. **Co, E, Br, Bo**

3 WHITE-FACED NUNBIRD *Hapaloptila castanea* 23–24 cm (9–9½ in)

Rare in subcanopy and midstory of tall humid montane forest, 1800–2600 m. Large puffbird with white face, rusty underparts, gray crown, and olive-brown upperparts. Unlikely to be confused. **VOICE** Song a series (about a note every 2 sec) of mellow rising, falling, or even-pitch whistles: "*puee?*" or "*peeo*"; may be interspersed with a raspier note. Call a gruff, accelerating then decelerating series of barks: "*pah pah-pahpahpapapapa-pah pah-grr?*" **Co, E**

4 BLACK-FRONTED NUNBIRD *Monasa nigrifrons* * 26–27.5 cm (10¼–10¾ in)

Common and widespread in varzea and transitional forests throughout Amazonia below 750 m; usually at forest edge or openings, and often forages lower than other nunbirds. Often tame. Bright coral-red bill of adult contrasts strongly with blackish head and slate-gray body. Juveniles browner overall; bill may be pale orange or even yellow. Usually accompanied by parents when in this plumage. Cf. Yellow-billed Nunbird. **VOICE** Song, usually in chorus, an endless, rapid, rolling, musical chatter: a repeated "*kew CHU-garrooo.*" Very similar to White-fronted Nunbird, but perhaps a little lower, slower in pace. Calls a musical "*churl-url-url*," mellow descending whistles, and quiet mewing. **Co, E, Br, Bo**

5 YELLOW-BILLED NUNBIRD *Monasa flavirostris* 24–25.5 cm (9½–10 in)

Rare to uncommon in midstory of viny terra firme, ridgetop forest, and in association with *Guadua* bamboo, up to 1250 m. Smaller, quieter, and less conspicuous than other nunbirds. Plumage blacker, contrasting strongly with yellow bill; bill thinner, more curved than bills of other nunbirds. Cf. juvenile Black-fronted Nunbird. Diagnostic white at bend of wing often concealed by body plumage. **VOICE** Song, usually in chorus, a rapid musical chatter, somewhat parakeet-like. Also a descending series of whistles that ends in a chattering phrase. Less rolling and musical than other nunbirds. **Co, E, Br, Bo**

6 WHITE-FRONTED NUNBIRD *Monasa morphoeus* * 25–26 cm (9¾–10¼ in)

Uncommon in midstory and subcanopy of terra firme and foothill forest up to 1000 m. Typically not as noisy as slightly larger Black-fronted Nunbird. Note white facial patches of adults. Juvenile duller; face patches tawny. **VOICE** Song very similar to Black-fronted, but perhaps a little higher, more rapid, and is more often introduced with whistled notes. Call a quiet "*pew*," sometimes followed by a rapid puttering. **Co, E, Br, Bo**

WHITE-EARED
PUFFBIRD

SWALLOW-WING

BLACK-FRONTED
NUNBIRD

juv.

ad.

WHITE-FACED
NUNBIRD

YELLOW-BILLED
NUNBIRD

ad.

WHITE-FRONTED
NUNBIRD

juv.

PLATE
120

NUNLETS AND BARBETS

Nunlets (Nonnula) are a group of small puffbirds that are found in dense understory and vine tangles of forest and edge. Nunlets are easily overlooked (even their soft vocalizations can be difficult to notice) but can be surprisingly tame and may allow a very close approach. Usually seen singly or in pairs. Usually are not associated with mixed-species flocks. Nunlets often pounce to the ground for their prey. Most species are local and restricted in distribution in Peru, and geographically replace one another; only Rufous-capped Nunlet is more widespread, and may overlap with other species of nunlet. Barbets are colorful, stout-billed birds of the midstory and canopy of humid forests, in both lowlands and Andes of eastern Peru. Often in pairs, and regularly join mixed-species flocks. Eat fruit and invertebrates; often search dead leaf clusters and bromeliads for prey. Nest in cavities. See also plate 121.

1 BROWN NUNLET *Nonnula brunnea* 14 cm (5½ in)

Rare in northwestern Amazonia: occupies the north bank of the Amazon west of Río Napo, and also crosses to south bank of Marañón, west of Río Ucayali. Found in terra firme. Uniformly fulvous brown below, slightly more olive-brown above; note reddish orbital skin. Other nunlets have paler vents. **VOICE** Song a weak series of thin, mewing whistles: *"wee weep weep weep weep weep…."* Similar to Rufous-capped Nunlet, but perhaps slower. **Co, E**

2 RUSTY-BREASTED NUNLET *Nonnula rubecula* * 14 cm (5½ in)

Rare; found on both banks of the Amazon in northern Peru, east of Río Napo and lower Río Ucayali. Usually found in terra firme. Fairly dull brown overall with strongly contrasting white eyering. Also note paler lower belly. All other nunlets have red orbital skin. **VOICE** Song (Ecuador) a series, increasing in volume, of rising mewing notes: *"whew whew whew whew…."* **Co, E, Br**

3 RUFOUS-CAPPED NUNLET *Nonnula ruficapilla* * 13.5–14 cm (5¼–5½ in)

Rare to uncommon but rather widespread, up to 1250 m. Most often found in varzea and river-edge forest; locally also may occur in second growth in upland areas, and even in semidry forests (in middle Huallaga Valley). Gray face and sides of breast contrast with rufous crown, throat, and breast. Also note paler belly, red orbital skin, and olivaceous brown back. Cf. other nunlets (Rufous-capped's face pattern unique). Where overlaps with other species, Rufous-capped is found in varzea or floodplain forest, and the second nunlet species occurs in terra firme. **VOICE** Song is a weak series of thin, mewing whistles: *"wee weep weep weep weep weep…."* **Br, Bo**

4 FULVOUS-CHINNED NUNLET *Nonnula sclateri* 14–15.5 cm (5½–6 in)

Rare and local in southern Amazonia, where usually found in terra firme. Overall a dull fulvous brown with slightly grayer side of face, red orbital skin, and paler lower belly. Cf. Rusty-breasted Nunlet; the two species are not known to occur together in Peru, but distributions may overlap in southern Loreto or northeastern Ucayali. Otherwise is most similar to Brown Nunlet (with which there is no known overlap). **VOICE** Song a weak series of thin, mewing whistles: *"wee weep weep weep weep weep…."* Similar to Rufous-capped Nunlet, but perhaps slower. **Br, Bo**

5 SCARLET-CROWNED BARBET *Capito aurovirens* 18–19 cm (7–7½ in)

Uncommon in varzea and older river-island forest along larger rivers in northern Peru, south to upper Río Ucayali. A large barbet with orange, unstreaked breast; unstreaked olive flanks and upperparts; and a fairly long tail. Crown whitish in female, largely red in male. **VOICE** Song a series, descending slightly in pitch, of loud, ringing, purring notes: *"grrr grrr grrr grrr grrr."* Slower, louder, and more ringing than Lemon-throated Barbet. Calls include various grunts and snarls. **Co, E, Br**

6 SCARLET-BANDED BARBET *Capito wallacei* 19.5 cm (7¾ in)

Locally fairly common in humid montane forest in northeastern Cordillera Azul, 1300–1550 m. Boldly patterned; note contrasting white throat and superciliary, red breast band and crown, and yellow flanks and upper belly. Female differs from male in having golden edges to scapulars and pale spots on tertials. Note highly restricted distribution. Unmistakable. **VOICE** Song a quiet, rapid purr of very deep notes, reminiscent of a distant woodpecker drumming: *"b'b'b'b'b'b'b'b'b'b'b'b'b'b."* Calls include various grunts and snarls. **ENDEMIC**

1

2

3

4

5

6

RUSTY-BREASTED
NUNLET

RUFOUS-CAPPED
NUNLET

BROWN NUNLET

FULVOUS-CHINNED
NUNLET

♀ ♂

SCARLET-CROWNED BARBET

SCARLET-BANDED BARBET

♂

♀

PLATE
121

BARBETS

Gilded Barbet is the most widespread species of Capito *barbet in Peru (see also plate 120).* Eubucco *are smaller than* Capito, *with greenish or yellowish bills. Scarlet-hooded and Red-headed barbets are geographically restricted. Versicolored and Lemon-throated barbets, in contrast, are widespread in the Andes and in Amazonia, respectively. Both of these species, and the larger Gilded Barbet, are highly variable geographically.*

1 GILDED BARBET *Capito auratus* * 17–18 cm (6¾–7 in)

Uncommon to fairly common in midstory and canopy of terra firme in eastern lowlands and foothills up to 1350 m. A large barbet, bright yellow below with orange or (*auratus*; east of Río Napo and locally along both banks of the Amazon) scarlet throat. Females are more heavily streaked on back, auriculars, and underparts. Throat of female spotted or streaked in population west of Ríos Napo and Ucayali (*punctatus*); elsewhere throat of female unmarked, and scarlet (*auratus*) or, south of the Amazon and east of Ucayali, orange (*insperatus, orosae*). Colorful and boldly marked plumage not likely to be confused. **VOICE** Song a series of coupled hoots, accelerating in pace and descending in pitch: "*boop-boop, boop-boop boopboop-booboop-bubup.*" Calls include various grunts and snarls. **Co, E, Br, Bo**

2 VERSICOLORED BARBET *Eubucco versicolor* * 16 cm (6¼ in)

Rare to uncommon in canopy of humid montane forest on east slope of Andes, 750–2100 m. Male always has red crown, chin, and lower breast, but otherwise is geographically variable. Throat and malar yellow (*steerii*, southern Amazonas south to Huánuco); malar yellow and throat broadly blue (*glaucogularis*, Pasco south to Ayacucho); or malar blue and throat narrowly blue (*versicolor*, western Cuzco east to Bolivia). Males near Ayacucho/Cuzco border intermediate in malar and throat color. Females have extensively blue face and throat with red crescent on upper breast; unique within range. Compare male *steeri* to male *aurantiicollis* Lemon-throated Barbet. **VOICE** Song a musical purred series of notes, usually with a punctuated introductory note: "*PA-brrrrrrrrrrrr,*" very similar to Red-headed Barbet. Calls include various grunts and snarls. **Bo**

3 SCARLET-HOODED BARBET *Eubucco tucinkae* 17 cm (6¼ in)

Rare to uncommon in transitional forest, canopy over *Guadua* bamboo stands, and edges of rivers and lakes in southeast, locally up to 900 m. Note relatively large size and gray sides of breast. Female remarkably similar to male *aurantiicollis* Lemon-throated Barbet, but Scarlet-hooded is more olive above, has no red on lower breast, and has gray patch on sides of breast. Not known to overlap Scarlet-crowned Barbet, which also is larger, is masked, has no streaking, and has gray or blackish bill. **VOICE** Song a series of bubbling hoots: "*whu-whu-whu-whu-whu-whu.*" Calls include various grunts and snarls. **Br, Bo**

4 LEMON-THROATED BARBET *Eubucco richardsoni* * 14.5–15 cm (5¾–6 in)

Uncommon in midstory and canopy of humid forest of eastern lowlands up to 1000 m. Male highly variable geographically: crown crimson and nape blue-gray north of Marañón (*richardsoni*); crown blackish and nape blue-gray east of Napo (*nigriceps*); and crown crimson and nape yellow south of Marañón and the Amazon (*aurantiicollis*). In all forms, males have diffuse reddish band separating breast from belly; cf. female Scarlet-hooded Barbet and male *steeri* Versicolored Barbet (which is montane, and has a blue nape). Females masked, with grayish throat and forehead, and yellowish breast band (more orange in *aurantiicollis*). **VOICE** Song a series of purred notes, the pace reminiscent of a galloping horse: "*prrp-prrp-prrrp-prrp-prrp-prrp,*" more quietly and rapidly delivered than Scarlet-crowned Barbet. Calls include various grunts and snarls. **Co, E, Br, Bo**

5 RED-HEADED BARBET *Eubucco bourcierii* * 15.5–16 cm (6–6¼ in)

Rare to uncommon in canopy of humid montane forest on east slope of Andes north and west of Río Marañón, 1200–1900 m, where replaces Versicolored Barbet. Male distinctive within range. Female similar to female Lemon-throated Barbet of lowlands, but Red-headed has face blue with no strong auricular mask. **VOICE** Song a musical purred series of notes, usually with a punctuated introductory note: "*PA-brrrrrrrrrrrr,*" very similar to Versicolored. Calls include various grunts and snarls. **Co, E**

♂ auratus

♂ insperatus/orosae

♂ punctatus

♀ insperatus/orosae

♀ auratus

♀ punctatus

GILDED BARBET

♂ glaucogularis

♂ glaucogularis × versicolor

♂ versicolor

♀

VERSICOLORED BARBET

♂ steerii

♀

♂

SCARLET-HOODED BARBET

♂ nigriceps

LEMON-THROATED BARBET

♀ aurantiicollis

RED-HEADED BARBET

♂ aurantiicollis

♀

♂ richardsoni

♀

♂

PLATE
122

ARACARIS

Toucans are large, colorful birds, well-known for their large and often gaudily patterned bills, that are found in the canopy and midstory of humid forest. Usually in pairs or small flocks; may join other species at fruiting trees but do not follow mixed-species flocks, and different species of toucans do not flock together. Omnivorous. Nest in cavities. In most species bill of male is longer than female's; sexes otherwise usually similar in most species, but in a few species plumages are sexually dimorphic. Bills are highly patterned, and the edge of the maxilla is serrated. Skin around eye is bare and in many species is brightly colored. Aracaris are small to medium-sized, slender toucans with plumage that is predominately brown or olive above, with yellow underparts and a red rump.

1 LETTERED ARACARI *Pteroglossus inscriptus* * 33–35.5 cm (13–14 in)
Rare to uncommon in humid forest of eastern lowlands, locally up to 900 m. Small. Name derives from distinctive dark "lettering" along cutting edge of maxilla. Yellow underparts not divided by any distinct bands (at best, a brownish smudge may be visible on belly). Head black (males) or brown (females). **VOICE** Calls include a series of electric grunts: "*jrnk jrnk jrnk....*" **Co, E, Br, Bo**

2 IVORY-BILLED ARACARI *Pteroglossus azara* * 33–35.5 cm (13–14 in)
Uncommon in humid forests of eastern lowlands up to 1200 m. Small. Note combination of rich brown head; red-and-black breast-bands that are contiguous with the dark head and neck, with yellow restricted to belly; and crimson mantle. Bill generally pale, especially the maxilla. Mandible mostly cream, although often with longitudinal smudge of brown, in *flavirostris* (north of Marañón and the Amazon); also, *flavirostris* may show a short brown streak along nares. Brown smudge on mandible is much broader in southern *mariae* (south of Marañón and the Amazon); maxilla of *mariae* lacks the brown mark at nares. There is variation in mandible color within both subspecies; for example, birds with *flavirostris*-like bills have been reported south to middle Río Ucayali (although bills of most individuals there have typical *mariae* patterns). Cf. female Golden-collared Toucanet. **VOICE** Calls include a low, grinding grunt, sometimes in series: "*rrk.*" Also a clearer, rising cry: "*cureee?*" **Co, E, Br, Bo**

3 CURL-CRESTED ARACARI *Pteroglossus beauharnaesii* 42–46 cm (16½–17¼ in)
Rare to uncommon in forest, south of Marañón and the Amazon up to about 900 m. A fairly large aracari, with unique combination of whitish throat with dark speckles and yellow underparts with red "belt." At close range, feathers of crown curled, with fused barbs and plastic-like texture. **VOICE** Calls include a series of clear, rising yaps: "*REEEyuk REEEyuk....*" Also electric grunts, either singly or in a series: "*jrnk jrnk jrnk....*" **Br, Bo**

4 CHESTNUT-EARED ARACARI *Pteroglossus castanotis* * 43–45.5 cm (17–18 in)
Common and widespread in forest and second growth of eastern lowlands, up to 1000 m. Rarely in terra firme. One of the most common toucans in Peru, and perhaps most easily seen. A large aracari. Chestnut on sides of head difficult to see in field (usually looks as dark as crown). Best distinguished from similar species by single red band across yellow underparts. Dark base of maxilla contrast more with pale serrations along cutting edge than on bill of Many-banded Aracari. **VOICE** Calls include a high, rusty whistle: "*teee-sik.*" **Co, E, Br, Bo**

5 [PALE-MANDIBLED ARACARI *Pteroglossus erythropygius*] 40.5–43 cm (16–17 in)
Rare in humid forest in Tumbes up to 800 m, where reported only from sight records. Somewhat similar to Many-banded Aracari, but mandible is largely pale, skin around eye is red (not blue), and has a large black spot on center of the breast (rather than a band across the breast). The only toucan in northwest. **VOICE** Call a high, rusty whistle: "*teee-sik.*" **E**

6 MANY-BANDED ARACARI *Pteroglossus pluricinctus* 40.5–43 cm (16–17 in)
Rare to uncommon in forest of northern Amazonia; primarily found north of Marañón and the Amazon, but locally crosses to south bank. Large aracari. Similar to Chestnut-eared Aracari, but note the 2 bands across underparts: upper is blackish, lower black and red. **VOICE** Call is a high, rusty whistle: "*teesik*"; this call is shorter or more quickly uttered than call of other, similar-voiced aracaris. **Co, E, Br**

LETTERED ARACARI

♂

♀

IVORY-BILLED ARACARI

mariae

flavirostris

CHESTNUT-EARED ARACARI

CURL-CRESTED ARACARI

PALE-MANDIBLED ARACARI

MANY-BANDED ARACARI

PLATE
123

GREEN TOUCANETS AND MOUNTAIN-TOUCANS

Aulacorhynchus toucanets are small to medium-sized, green toucans; mostly Andean, but Emerald Toucanet also occurs into central and southern Amazonia. Mountain-Toucans are large, mostly gray toucans of humid montane forests.

1 EMERALD TOUCANET *Aulacorhynchus prasinus* * 29.5–31.5 cm (11½–12½ in)

Rare to uncommon in humid montane forest and, rarely, in lowlands. Always has chestnut undertail coverts and tips to rectrices, and some yellow on bill. Northern *cyanolaemus* (south to San Martín), generally at higher elevations (1200–2500 m), has blue throat and less yellow on bill. Southern populations (*atrogularis, dimidiatus*) generally occur lower (350–1650 m) and have black throats. Similar Chestnut-tipped Toucanet has all-dark bill, white throat, and green undertail coverts. **VOICE** Call a long series of grinding grunts *"grra grra grra…"* or barking yaps *"yak yak yak yak yak."* Notes shorter and sharper than those of Chestnut-tipped, less unpleasant than those of Blue-banded Toucanet. **Co, E, Br, Bo**

2 YELLOW-BROWED TOUCANET *Aulacorhynchus huallagae* 38–44 cm (15–17¼ in)

Rare and local in tall humid montane forest on east slope of Andes in north central Peru, 2000–2600 m. Geographically replaces the similar Blue-banded Toucanet; Yellow-browed differs by prominent white base to mandible; yellow undertail coverts; and indistinct yellowish superciliary. Chestnut-tipped Toucanet of lower elevations has all-dark bill, no red on rump, and green undertail coverts. **VOICE** Call a series of harsh grunts: *"rehh rehh rehh…."* **ENDEMIC**

3 BLUE-BANDED TOUCANET *Aulacorhynchus coeruleicinctis* 38–43 cm (15–17 in)

Fairly common in humid montane forest on east slope of Andes of central and southern Peru, 1300–2500 m, locally up to 3100 m. Gray bill has creamy tip and lacks white border at base; also note red rump band, pale blue breast band (not easily seen in field), and greenish undertail coverts. Iris usually pale, but sometimes (or always?) dark in south central Peru (Ayacucho and Cuzco). Cf. Chestnut-tipped Toucanet. **VOICE** Call a series of harsh, rattled barks: *"grra grra grra grra…."* Generally more harsh and unpleasant-sounding than the voices of other green toucanets. **Bo**

4 CHESTNUT-TIPPED TOUCANET *Aulacorhynchus derbianus* * 37–43 cm (14½–17 in)

Rare to uncommon in humid montane forest in foothills and outlying ridges along east slope, 800–2100 m. Bill dark crimson at base and black for most of length; undertail coverts and rump green, and longest rectrices tipped chestnut (rest green); throat white. Cf. other green toucanets. **VOICE** Call a series of rising yaps with slightly harsh quality: *"rah? rah? rah?"* Generally softer and less harsh than the voices of other green toucanets, with longer notes. **Co, E, Br, Bo**

5 HOODED MOUNTAIN-TOUCAN *Andigena cucullata* 41–44 cm (16–17¼ in)

Rare in humid montane forest in southern Andes, 3000–3350 m. Similar to Gray-breasted Mountain-Toucan, but bill is mostly green with dark tip and well-defined black spot at base of mandible; has blue facial skin and lacks chestnut tail-tip. No distributional overlap with other mountain-toucans. **VOICE** Calls include shorter barking yaps *"yak,"* sometimes in a series, and a long, mewing, rising cry: *"cuuuueeee?"* Very similar to voice of Gray-breasted. Also rattles tongue loudly in bill: *"trrrrr."* **Bo**

6 BLACK-BILLED MOUNTAIN-TOUCAN *Andigena nigrirostris* * 42–44.5 cm (16½–17½ in)

Rare in humid montane forest on east slope of Andes north of Río Marañón, 2200–2400 m. Found at lower elevations than Gray-breasted Mountain-Toucan. Black-billed is fairly distinctive: powder blue below with white throat and largely black bill. Unlikely to be confused. **VOICE** Calls shorter barking yaps *"yak,"* sometimes in a series, and a long, mewing, rising cry: *"cuuuueeee?"* Lower pitched than Gray-breasted. Also rattles tongue loudly in bill: *"trrrrr."* **Co, E**

7 GRAY-BREASTED MOUNTAIN-TOUCAN *Andigena hypoglauca* * 41–44 cm (16–17¼ in)

Uncommon in humid montane forest on east slope of Andes, 2300–3500 m, occasionally down to 1500 m. A rather ornate toucan with bold red, black, and yellow bill, gray-blue underparts, bronzy green upperparts; yellow rump and red undertail coverts flash in flight. Most individuals north of the Marañón have dark iris. Cf. Hooded Mountain-Toucan (no overlap). **VOICE** Call shorter barking yaps *"yak,"* sometimes in a series, and a long, mewing, rising cry: *"cuuuueeee?"* Also rattles tongue loudly in bill: *"trrrrr."* **Co, E**

cyanolaemus

atrogularis

dimidiatus

EMERALD TOUCANET

s-c Peru

CHESTNUT-TIPPED
TOUCANET

YELLOW-BROWED TOUCANET

BLUE-BANDED TOUCANET

HOODED MOUNTAIN-TOUCAN

BLACK-BILLED
MOUNTAIN-TOUCAN

n

GRAY-BREASTED
MOUNTAIN-TOUCAN

PLATE
124

GOLDEN-COLLARED TOUCANET AND
LARGE TOUCANS

Golden-collared Toucanet is a distinctive, medium-sized toucan, notable for the pronounced sexual dimorphism in plumage; golden tufts on the side of the head of the male; relatively short (for a toucan) bill; and peculiar growling song. Ramphastos are the largest toucans, easily recognizable by the black plumage with a prominent white or yellow "bib," and the very large bills. Their far-carrying voices are often the first evidence of their presence. Ramphastos sing from the canopy, when they usually perch on an open branch or just within canopy leaf cover. As they sing, they usually move their large, colorful bills with exaggerated up-and-down motions.

1 GOLDEN-COLLARED TOUCANET *Selenidera reinwardtii* * 30.5–32 cm (12–12½ in)
Uncommon in humid forest in Amazonia and into foothills up to 1000 m. Small toucan, usually found in pairs. Strongly sexually dimorphic: males are glossy black below and have extensive yellow auricular tufts; females are rich brown, with little or no yellow auriculars. Both sexes have prominent yellow collar across upper back. Base of bill red in *reinwardtii* of northern Amazonia, green in *langsdorffii* (south of the Amazon); the two subspecies intergrade south of the Amazon in San Martín. Unmistakable. **VOICE** Song, usually in duet, is a series of throaty growls with a steady rhythm: "*grrow grraw grrow grraw....*" The singer lowers its bill and raises its tail when delivering the "*grrow*" phrase, then lowers its tail and raises its bill on the "*grraw*" phrase, the entire process looking rather exhausting. **Co, E, Br, Bo**

2 BLACK-MANDIBLED TOUCAN *Ramphastos ambiguus* * 53.5–56 cm (21–22 in)
Rare to uncommon in humid montane forest along east slope of Andes in northern and central Peru, 900–1850 m. Like other *Ramphastos* toucans in general behavior, but appears to be less vocal. Unlikely to be confused within range and habitat; other Peruvian *Ramphastos* have white throats and generally are found at lower elevations. **VOICE** Song, usually given from an exposed perch in the canopy, often in duet, is a loud yelping: "*KEEU de-deh de-deh,*" hence the local name "*Dios te de.*" Faster than White-throated Toucan. **Co, E**

3 WHITE-THROATED TOUCAN *Ramphastos tucanus* * 53.5–57 cm (21–22½ in)
Common in forest in lowland Amazonia, locally into foothills (mostly below 800 m, locally up to 1100 m). Cf. nearly identical, but smaller, shorter-billed Channel-billed Toucan. Best distinguished by **VOICE** Song, usually given from an exposed perch in the canopy, sometimes in duet, is a loud yelping: "*KEE-yu REEP REEP,*" sometimes just the latter 2 notes. A second bird (the female?) often overlaps these notes with a similar rising "*YAP YAP*", sometimes preceded by a low growl. The sound can carry for great distances and is a characteristic sound of Amazonian forest. **Co, E, Br, Bo**

4 CHANNEL-BILLED TOUCAN *Ramphastos vitellinus* * 43–46 cm (17–18 in)
Fairly common and widespread in lowland forest in Amazonia, locally into foothills (mostly below 600 m, locally up to 1350 m). Almost indistinguishable from White-throated Toucan in plumage, but slightly smaller, with relatively shorter bill. Within each species, however, bill length longer in males than in females; male Channel-billed approaches female White-throated in bill length. In the hand, maxilla has lateral groove (or "channel") along each side of culmen. South to central Peru, bill patterns match those of White-throated exactly; in southeast, Channel-billed differs by having a short yellow streak along base of cutting edge of mandible. Best distinguished by **VOICE** Song, usually given from an exposed perch in the canopy, is a series of descending croaks: "*keer keer keer....*" The sound can carry for great distances. **Co, E, Br, Bo**

5 [TOCO TOUCAN *Ramphastos toco*] * 55–61 cm (21½–24 in)
Rare and restricted to Pampas del Heath. Found in gallery forest in savanna and forest edge. Largest toucan. Bill pattern distinctive: orange with black tip. **VOICE** Song is a low, grinding grunt or croak, rising slightly: "*krrk krrk krrk....*" **Br, Bo**

GOLDEN-COLLARED TOUCANET

langsdorfii

reinwardtii

BLACK-MANDIBLED
TOUCAN

WHITE-THROATED
TOUCAN

CHANNEL-BILLED TOUCAN

TOCO TOUCAN

PLATE
125

PICULETS

Woodpeckers are notable for their distinctive foraging behavior: most species cling to tree trunks and limbs, bracing their bodies with their stiff tails and using their strong bills to chisel into bark or to probe crevices. Nests are placed in cavities. Flight is strong but undulating. Primarily insectivorous, although some species also eat some fruit. Most species "drum" rather than sing. Piculets are tiny woodpeckers that creep actively along slender branches (often near the tips) and vines, in the manner of a xenops; see also plate 126. Unlike larger woodpeckers, piculets do not have stiffened rectrices and do not use their tails as a brace against the trunk. Most often encountered as singles or pairs, often associated with mixed-species flocks.

1 LAFRESNAYE'S PICULET *Picumnus lafresnayi* * 9 cm (3½ in)

Fairly common in canopy of lowland forest in western Amazonia, up to 1200 m; replaced in eastern Amazonia (south of the Amazon) by Bar-breasted Piculet. Yellowish green above. Both sexes are evenly barred below (lacking belly streaks of Bar-breasted); underparts also are paler (less yellow) than in Bar-breasted. Forehead of male speckled red (northern Peru; *lafresnayi*, not illustrated) or golden yellow (Huánuco south; *punctifrons*). **VOICE** Song is a slow, descending series of high, lisping even-pitched notes (generally 3): "*seeep seeep seep.*" Very similar to calls of Orange-fronted Plushcrown. **Co, E, Br**

2 BAR-BREASTED PICULET *Picumnus aurifrons* * 9 cm (3½ in)

Uncommon in the canopy of lowland forest, occasionally in adjacent second growth, up to 1250 m. Primarily found south of the Amazon and east of Río Ucayali, but apparently crosses to west bank of Urubamba Valley. A yellowish green piculet with a barred breast but a streaked belly. Forehead of male speckled orange-yellow. Little or no overlap with Lafresnaye's Piculet, which also differs in having a barred (not streaked) belly. Cf. also Fine-barred Piculet. **VOICE** Song is a slow, descending series of high, lisping even-pitched notes (generally 3): "*seeep seeep seep.*" Very similar to calls of Orange-fronted Plushcrown. **Br, Bo**

3 PLAIN-BREASTED PICULET *Picumnus castelnau* 9–10 cm (3½–4 in)

Fairly common along large rivers in Amazonia. Mainly found in canopy of *Cecropia*-dominated young forest of river islands and in riparian forest; locally occurs in secondary forest away from rivers. Occasionally forages close to ground in shrubbery along edges of gardens and pastures. A very drab piculet; entirely off-white below with no streaks or bars at all. Forecrown of male spotted red; crown of female entirely black. **VOICE** Song a high-pitched, rapid, falling trill: "*tree'e'e'e'e'e'e.*" **Co**

4 FINE-BARRED PICULET *Picumnus subtilis* 9–10 cm (3½–4 in)

Fairly common but geographically restricted. Found 450–1100 m in southern Peru close to base of Andes, in river-edge forests. May meet Plain-breasted Piculet in upper Ucayali drainage (where a possible hybrid has been reported). Fine-barred differs from Plain-breasted by presence of white spots on nape (and, in female, on crown), yellower underparts, narrow gray barring on breast, and indistinct barring on back. Also similar to sympatric Bar-breasted Piculet, which is much more heavily barred on breast, is strongly striped on belly, and is more associated with terra firme. **VOICE** Song a medium speed, descending series of sharp, high notes (generally about 7): "*SEE see see see see see see.*" **ENDEMIC**

5 SPECKLE-CHESTED PICULET *Picumnus steindachneri* 9–10 cm (3½–4 in)

Uncommon and geographically restricted. Found in humid montane forest and forest edge at 1100–2100 m, in central Huallaga Valley and also very locally in upper Río Utcubamba Valley. A gray-and-white piculet, very heavily marked below with white spots on black breast and heavy barring on belly; very different in pattern from Lafresnaye's Piculet of lower elevations. Not known to contact Ocellated Piculet of central Peru, which has different breast pattern. **VOICE** Song a high-pitched, rapid, falling trill: "*tree'e'e'e'e'e.*" **ENDEMIC**

6 OCELLATED PICULET *Picumnus dorbignyanus* * 9–10 cm (3½–4 in)

Uncommon, in humid montane forest and forest edge at 800–2400 m along east slope of Andes in central Peru. Habitat and elevational distribution similar to that of Speckle-chested Piculet, with which there is no known geographic overlap. Upperparts gray or grayish brown; white or buffy white below, scaled or sparsely spotted with black. Much browner above and whiter below than Lafresnaye's Piculet, which is found at lower elevations. **VOICE** Song a high-pitched, rapid, falling trill: "*tree'e'e'e'e'e.*" **Bo**

♀

♂ *punctifrons*

LAFRESNAYE'S
PICULET

♀

♂

BAR-BREASTED
PICULET

♀

♂

PLAIN-BREASTED
PICULET

♀

♂

FINE-BARRED
PICULET

♂

♀

OCELLATED PICULET

♀

♂

SPECKLE-CHESTED PICULET

PLATE
126

PICULETS AND SMALL WOODPECKERS

Rufous-breasted Piculet is widely distributed; Ecuadorian and Olivaceous piculets, in contrast, are restricted to the northwest. Veniliornis are small, plain-colored woodpeckers that often forage inconspicuously as pairs; most species frequently associate with mixed-species flocks. They are distributed in wooded habitats throughout much of Peru; see also plate 127.

1 **[OLIVACEOUS PICULET** *Picumnus olivaceus]* * 9–10 cm (3½–4 in)

In Peru found only in evergreen forest in Tumbes, 400–900 m, where rare to uncommon; reported only from sight records. Geographically overlaps Ecuadorian Piculet but is restricted to more humid sites and does not venture into dry forest. Much more olive (less gray) than Ecuadorian, and is not barred below. **VOICE** Song a rapid descending trill of very high notes. Call a descending pair of longer notes: "*SEEEW seeeew.*" **Co, E**

2 **ECUADORIAN PICULET** *Picumnus sclateri* * 9–10 cm (3½–4 in)

Uncommon in dry and semideciduous forests of northwestern Peru up to 1800 m. Brownish gray above; heavily barred black and white below. Cf. Olivaceous Piculet, with which there is overlap in Tumbes. **VOICE** Song is a slow, descending series of notes (generally 3, sometimes up to 7): "*swee swee swee.*" Calls include single rising "*sweet*" notes and a quick, stuttering series when changing perches: "*tititi-swee.*" **E**

3 **RUFOUS-BREASTED PICULET** *Picumnus rufiventris* * 11 cm (4¼ in)

Uncommon and local, but widely distributed in Amazonia, up to 1250 m. Primarily occurs in undergrowth of river-edge forest (particularly in thickets of *Gynerium* cane or *Guadua* bamboo mixed with small, vine-covered trees) and in dense second growth, especially near rivers. Inconspicuous. A relatively large piculet with rufous-chestnut sides to face and underparts, and unmarked, yellow-olive back. Immature (not illustrated) is duller; crown is brown, with narrow buff scaling on forecrown. **VOICE** Song is a slow, descending series of high, lisping notes (generally 2): "*seep seep.*" Calls include single quick "*seep*" notes or a rapid "*tsit tsit*" in flight. **Co, E, Br, Bo**

4 **SCARLET-BACKED WOODPECKER** *Veniliornis callonotus* * 14 cm (5½ in)

Fairly common on Pacific slope of northwest, and uncommon in dry Marañón Valley. Found in dry and semideciduous forest, desert scrub, and taller forest along rivers up to 1600 m. Forages at all heights, often in pairs. Bright red back and wings contrast strikingly with off-white underparts and sides to neck; very distinctive (no overlap with Crimson-mantled Woodpecker). Also note pale bill and iris. **VOICE** Song a rapid rattle: "*keer'r'r'r'r'r'r'r'r,*" similar to Golden-olive Woodpecker, but higher pitched, more strident. Call single "*kik*" notes. **Co, E**

5 **SMOKY-BROWN WOODPECKER** *Veniliornis fumigatus* * 15.5–16 cm (6–6¼ in)

Uncommon to fairly common in humid montane forest, 1200–2900 m. Occurs along west slope of Andes in northern Peru, on both slopes of Marañón Valley, and on east slope of Andes and outlying ridges in northern and southernmost Peru. Remarkably drab and very brown; note contrasting pale sides to face. **VOICE** Song is a low harsh chatter: "*djedjedjedjedje-r.*" Call single gravelly "*kik*" notes. **Co, E, Bo**

6 **RED-RUMPED WOODPECKER** *Veniliornis kirkii* * 15–16.5 cm (6–6¼ in)

In Peru restricted to evergreen forests of Tumbes at 600–900 m, where it is fairly common, and the only small olive woodpecker. Both sexes possess a red rump. **VOICE** Song is a slow series of descending "*klee*" notes. Call "*klee!*" notes. Also a variety of excited squeaky calls in interaction with mate, similar to calls of Red-stained and Little woodpeckers. **Co, E, Br**

7 **YELLOW-VENTED WOODPECKER** *Veniliornis dignus* * 17 cm (6½ in)

Uncommon, in canopy and subcanopy of humid montane forest along east slope of Andes, 1500–2100 m. No records between Amazonas and central Huánuco. Yellow-green above, male with red crown and nape (crown of female dusky, with red restricted to nape). Note contrasting face pattern and narrow pale streaks on wing coverts; otherwise similar to Bar-bellied Woodpecker, which replaces it at higher elevations. Also cf. much larger Golden-olive Woodpecker. **VOICE** Song (Ecuador) is a rapid rattle: "*keer'r'r'r'r'r'r'r'r'r,*" higher than that of Golden-olive or Crimson-mantled woodpeckers. **Co, E**

OLIVACEOUS PICULET

♂

♀

RUFOUS-BREASTED PICULET

♀

♂

ECUADORIAN PICULET

♀

♂

SCARLET-BACKED
WOODPECKER

♀

♂

SMOKY-BROWN
WOODPECKER

♀

♂

RED-RUMPED WOODPECKER

♀

♂

YELLOW-VENTED WOODPECKER

♀

♂

PLATE
127

SMALL AND MEDIUM-SIZED WOODPECKERS

Species shown on this plate are medium-sized woodpeckers. Yellow-tufted and White woodpeckers are the only Peruvian representatives of the widespread genus Melanerpes; *Yellow-tufted is a common, frequently encountered species in eastern Peru, whereas White Woodpecker barely enters Peru. Crimson-mantled Woodpecker is an Andean species of* Piculus; *lowland* Piculus *are shown on plate 128. Red-stained, Little, and Bar-bellied woodpeckers are widespread species of* Veniliornis *(see plate 126).*

1 **[WHITE WOODPECKER** *Melanerpes candidus*] 24–26 cm (9½–10 in)

In Peru known only from sight records from Pampas del Heath, where found in scattered trees and woodlots on savanna. Social; usually encountered in pairs or small groups; often seen crossing openings with characteristic floppy wingbeats. Striking black-and-white plumage distinctive. Lower belly of both sexes pale yellow; male also has yellow patch on breast and a yellow nape. **VOICE** Call mellow, a descending, slightly grinding "*geer.*" **Br, Bo**

2 **YELLOW-TUFTED WOODPECKER** *Melanerpes cruentatus* * 19 cm (7½ in)

Widespread, common, and conspicuous in Amazonia, up to 1200 m. Forages in forest canopy, especially at forest edge and at clearings inside continuous forest. Often perches on exposed snags and trunks. Social; usually encountered in small noisy groups. Omnivorous, regularly consuming small fruit. Gaudy plumage unmistakable; note the white rump (may be visible at great distance). **VOICE** Song a rolling, churring descending chatter: "*cheer-eer-err.*" Also a rising rattle: "*churr'ee'ee.*" Pairs give a "*wik-up wik-up*" series during interactions. **Co, E, Br, Bo**

3 **RED-STAINED WOODPECKER** *Veniliornis affinis* * 17.5–18 cm (7 in)

Uncommon but widespread in eastern Peru, up to 1400 m. More typical of forest interior than is Little Woodpecker. Forages in canopy and subcanopy. Superficially similar to Little, but is larger, and sides of face are plain (lacking weak facial stripes of Little). Also, nape always is yellow, and wing coverts of both sexes are variably spotted with red. **VOICE** Song is a fairly rapid series of clear notes: "*ki kir-keer-keer-keer-keer-keer-keek!*" Very *Accipiter*-like in quality. Also a series of squeaky "*kee-wick*" notes. **Co, E, Br, Bo**

4 **LITTLE WOODPECKER** *Veniliornis passerinus* * 16–17.5 cm (6¼–7 in)

Fairly common in eastern Peru, below 1000 m. Found in river-edge forest and adjacent second growth. Often forages as singles or pairs apart from mixed-species flocks. A small yellowish green woodpecker with indistinct, pale yellowish or whitish lines above and below auriculars. Wings olive green, with small pale tips to wing coverts. Nape red (male) or gray (female). **VOICE** Song is a strident, slightly rising series of reedy notes: "*keer ki-ki-ki-ki-ki-ki-ki.*" Call a single "*kik*" note. **Co, E, Br, Bo**

5 **CRIMSON-MANTLED WOODPECKER** *Piculus rivolii* * 23–25 cm (9–10 in)

Fairly common, but quiet and inconspicuous. Found in humid montane forest along east slope of Andes, 1900–3500 m, locally down to 1500 m; also in similar habitats on west slope of Andes in Piura, and on west side of central Marañón Valley. Widespread subspecies (*brevirostris*) is replaced in Cuzco and Puno by *atriceps*, which has less red on crown, wings, throat, and breast. Regularly associates with mixed-species flocks. **VOICE** Song (?) of widespread *brevirostris* is a series of fairly monotone, rapid metallic notes, more stuttering than the rattle of Golden-olive Woodpecker: "*kee'r'r-ker'r-ke'r'r.*" Also a rising "*REE?*" Song of southern race *atriceps* is descending low churr, quite different from that of *brevirostris*: "*grr'r'r'l.*" **Co, E, Bo**

6 **BAR-BELLIED WOODPECKER** *Veniliornis nigriceps* * 16.5–18 cm (6½–7 in)

Uncommon but widespread in humid montane forest along east slope of Andes, 2400–3500 m; ranges up to treeline. Forages low near the ground where vegetation is stunted, otherwise primarily in canopy or subcanopy. Both sexes of *equifasciatus* (not illustrated; south to central Amazonas, south of Río Marañón) have broader, whiter pale bars on underside; pale bars are narrower and more greenish in most of Peru. Crown of females is dusky in northern and central Peru (*equifasciatus*, *pectoralis*) or blackish in southern Peru (*nigriceps*). **VOICE** Song is a series of rising *Accipiter*-like notes: "*kree kree kree kree kree....*" Aggressive song includes a rapid series of ringing chatters: "*djeerdjeerdjeerdjeer.*" Also more quiet smacking "*tuip-tuip-tuip*" notes. **Co, E, Bo**

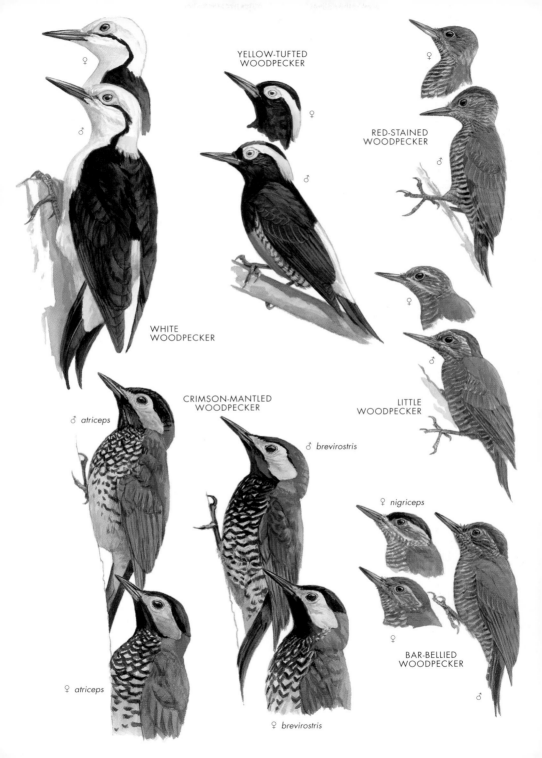

YELLOW-TUFTED
WOODPECKER

♀

♀

♂

RED-STAINED
WOODPECKER

♂

♀

WHITE
WOODPECKER

♀

♂

LITTLE
WOODPECKER

CRIMSON-MANTLED
WOODPECKER

♂ atriceps

♂ brevirostris

♀ nigriceps

♀

♀ atriceps

BAR-BELLIED
WOODPECKER

♂

♀ brevirostris

PLATE
128

MEDIUM-SIZED WOODPECKERS (*PICULUS, COLAPTES*)

Piculus are medium-sized woodpeckers of the midstory and canopy. The 4 species shown here are mostly olive in color; see also Crimson-mantled Woodpecker (plate 127). Spot-breasted Woodpecker is superficially similar but has very different vocalizations. Black-necked Woodpecker is an endemic species, found in drier forests in the western Andes and in intermontane valleys. Cf. Andean Flicker (plate 129).

1 BLACK-NECKED WOODPECKER *Colaptes atricollis* * 23–25 cm (9–10 in)
Uncommon; particularly rare and local in south. Found on west slope of Andes, 600–2800 m, and in arid Marañón Valley, 900–3100 m. In wooded river valleys and adjacent scrub, especially with columnar cacti. Inconspicuous. Forages both on trunks and branches and on the ground. Note the barred upperparts, black throat and breast, and prominent pale cheeks. Little or no overlap with Golden-olive Woodpecker. **VOICE** Song a series of notes similar to those of Crimson-mantled and Golden-olive woodpeckers: "*ki'ki'ki'ki'ki'ki'ki'ki'ki'ki'ki'ki'ki*." Call is a single descending "*keer!*" Also gives "*whi-cop whi-cop*" series during interactions. **ENDEMIC**

2 SPOT-BREASTED WOODPECKER *Colaptes punctigula* * 22 cm (8½ in)
Widespread and fairly common throughout eastern lowlands, up to 1150 m. Primarily in river-edge forest and second growth. May follow mixed-species flocks, but often found apart. Often forages for ants in *Cecropia*; also eats fruit. Note the striking white sides of face, red rear crown, and barred back; little overlap with Golden-olive Woodpecker of the Andes. **VOICE** Song a weak, slow series of unwoodpecker-like (more raptor-like) mewing notes: "*wee-wee-wee-wee-wee-wee*." Calls a mewing "*toowee*" and quiet "*wi'kop wi'kop*" notes. **Co, E, Br, Bo**

3 GOLDEN-OLIVE WOODPECKER *Piculus rubiginosus* * 20–23 cm (8–9 in)
Fairly common. Found in dry and riparian forests in northwest, up to 800 m (*rubripileus*; crown more extensively red, underparts paler). Other subspecies (with gray forecrowns, yellower underparts) occupy humid montane forest on east slope of Andes and outlying ridges, 750–2400 m. Often with mixed-species flocks. Easily identified by plain green upperparts and prominent white sides to face; little or no overlap with Black-necked Woodpecker (which also has black breast). **VOICE** Song in east a series of rapid notes: "*kee'r'r'r'r'r'r'r'r'r'r'r.*" Call a rising "*REE?*" All vocalizations similar to those of Crimson-mantled Woodpecker. Call of *rubripileus* different, a harsh series: "*djee djee djee djee.*" **Co, E, Br, Bo**

4 YELLOW-THROATED WOODPECKER *Piculus flavigula* * 20–21 cm (8 in)
Rare to uncommon in northeastern Amazonia. Forages in canopy and midstory of forest, especially in terra firme; usually with mixed-species flocks. Readily identified by bright yellow throat and sides to face; some males have a red whisker. Cf. White-throated Woodpecker. **VOICE** Call a single, rising-falling raspy gasp: "*psheeeah.*" Similar to calls of White-throated and Golden-green woodpeckers. **Co, E, Br, Bo**

5 WHITE-THROATED WOODPECKER *Piculus leucolaemus* 20 cm (8 in)
Uncommon to fairly common in Amazonia, up to 850 m, but absent from northeast. Inconspicuous. Singles or pairs forage in the canopy of forest interior. Often associates with mixed-species flocks. Locally overlaps with Yellow-throated Woodpecker, from which distinguished by green sides to face, whitish throat, and streaked upper breast. Cf. also Golden-green Woodpecker; White-throated has whitish throat, streaked, and greenish yellow cheeks. Also, male White-throated has red (in addition to yellow) facial stripe; female has red nape, and yellow facial stripe is less well defined. **VOICE** Call a single, descending raspy gasp: "*psheeeah*"; also a series of rising rasps: "*rahh rahh rahh.*" Perhaps indistinguishable from Yellow-throated and Golden-green, but may be higher pitched, thinner. **Co, E, Br, Bo**

6 GOLDEN-GREEN WOODPECKER *Piculus chrysochloros* * 21 cm (8½ in)
Uncommon to fairly common in eastern lowlands, up to 1100 m. Forages in midstory and canopy of forest, primarily in terra firme; rare in varzea. Joins mixed-species flocks, but forages apart from flocks more frequently than do the smaller White- and Yellow-throated woodpeckers. Note prominent yellow facial stripe and evenly barred (not spotted) underparts. Female has green nape. Some males have red stripe below yellow "whisker." **VOICE** Call a single, descending raspy gasp: "*psheeeah*"; also a series of rising rasps: "*rahh rahh rahh,*" and a somewhat squeaky "*wicka wicka wicka*" when agitated or in interaction with another *Piculus*. Similar to calls of Yellow-throated and White-throated. **Co, E, Br, Bo**

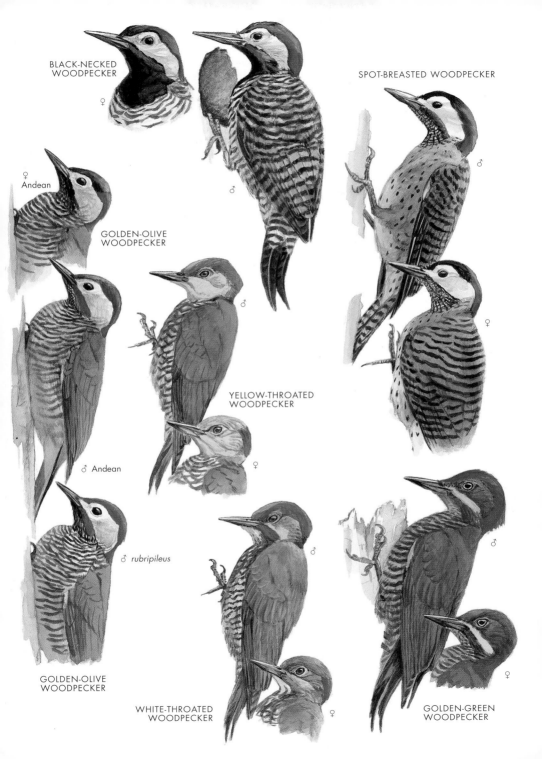

BLACK-NECKED
WOODPECKER

♀

SPOT-BREASTED WOODPECKER

♂

♀

♀
Andean

GOLDEN-OLIVE
WOODPECKER

♂

YELLOW-THROATED
WOODPECKER

♀

♂ Andean

♂ rubripileus

♂

♂

GOLDEN-OLIVE
WOODPECKER

WHITE-THROATED
WOODPECKER

♀

♀

GOLDEN-GREEN
WOODPECKER

PLATE
129

ANDEAN FLICKER AND *CELEUS* WOODPECKERS

Andean Flicker is a large, primarily terrestrial woodpecker of the high Andes; superficially similar to Black-necked Woodpecker (plate 128) but occurs at higher elevations, with little or no overlap. Celeus are large, rufous or buff-colored woodpeckers; in most species bill is pale. Found in lowland forest, and most species are quiet and inconspicuous. Feed primarily on ants and termites gleaned from bark and at nests, and to a lesser extent on fruit. Celeus occasionally join mixed-species flocks.

1 ANDEAN FLICKER *Colaptes rupicola* * 30 cm (12 in)

Fairly common in puna and paramo grasslands, 2700–4500 m; often found where there are no trees, although may enter *Eucalyptus* stands or edges of humid woods. Particularly common near rocky outcrops, although when feeding will occur well out in open. Forages on ground, often by walking (not hopping). Nests in cavities in rocks, in old buildings, or in holes excavated in earthen banks. Northern *cinereicapillus* (more richly colored on underparts and sides of face, breast barred, male lacks red on nape) and southern *puna* (paler, breast spotted, male has red nape) meet in a narrow hybrid zone in central Peru (north of Lake Junín). **VOICE** Song a series of loud chattered notes: *"ki'ki'ki'ki'ki'ki'ki'ki'ki."* Also a single *"kik"* note and a rising *"ooEET,"* sometimes in a series in flight. **E, Bo, Ch**

2 CHESTNUT WOODPECKER *Celeus elegans* * 28 cm (11 in)

Fairly common and widespread in Amazonia, up to 600 m. Forages in midstory and canopy of forest. Singles or pairs forage along trunks or limbs, gleaning from bark and probing in termite nests. Often associates with mixed-species flocks. Regularly eats fruit. Generally dark brown, with yellowish buff flanks and rump. Larger and darker than Scale-breasted Woodpecker, and has no barring at all. **VOICE** Call a mewing series of muffled barks: *"rrrEW CHWEE-CHWEE-CHWEE."* **Co, E, Br, Bo**

3 RINGED WOODPECKER *Celeus torquatus* * 28–29 cm (11–11½ in)

Rare but widespread in Amazonia. Singles or (less commonly) pairs forage in midstory and canopy. Primarily found in terra firme, often near forest edge, but also may occur in transitional forest or varzea. Picks ants from bark on trunks and vines, and visits termite nests; also eats some fruit. Cf. Rufous-headed Woodpecker. **VOICE** Song a loud, ringing series of slightly rising whistles: *"pur PEE PEE PEE."* Unlike any other *Celeus* in Peru. **Co, E, Br, Bo**

4 SCALE-BREASTED WOODPECKER *Celeus grammicus* * 22–23 cm (8¾–9 in)

Fairly common and widespread in Amazonia, up to 1200 m. Forages in midstory and canopy of forest, primarily in terra firme. Frequently follows mixed-species flocks. Plumage variable, both within a subspecies and across Peru. Generally rufous- or chestnut-brown; upperparts usually barred, but barring sometimes sparse in north. Typically paler overall south of Amazon; brightest birds, with cinnamon head and throat, in southeast (*latifasciatus*). Usually has prominent yellowish buff flanks and rump, but rump, flanks, or both sometimes mostly brown north of the Amazon. Cf. larger Chestnut Woodpecker. **VOICE** Call a rising, then falling nasal phrase: *"wuRIK-hoo."* **Co, E, Br, Bo**

5 RUFOUS-HEADED WOODPECKER *Celeus spectabilis* * 29 cm (11½ in)

Rare and local; perhaps more common in southeast, but nowhere common. In south is associated with large thickets of spiny bamboo (*Guadua*) up to 700 m. Habitat preferences in north not well known, but presumably occurs in riverine or disturbed forest. Singles forage within a few meters of the ground, on bamboo or on tree trunks. Superficially similar to Ringed Woodpecker, but note pale wing coverts and back, unmarked remiges, and darker head; also forages lower to ground. **VOICE** Call a muffled, mewing chuckle: *"wur'HEE hrr-hrr-hrr-hrr."* **E, Br, Bo**

6 CREAM-COLORED WOODPECKER *Celeus flavus* * 26 cm (10 in)

Uncommon to fairly common and widespread in Amazonia, below 600 m. Usually found near water, in varzea forest, tall woods on larger river islands, younger river-edge forest, and forest edge, and at margins to oxbow lakes. Primarily feeds on ants and termites, along trunks and limbs. Social; often in pairs or small noisy groups. Plumage variable from creamy buff to bright yellow-buff (not illustrated); wing coverts usually scaled with buff or yellow-buff but sometimes plain; and remiges vary from mostly dusky to mostly rufous. Always recognizable by overall pale body contrasting with darker wings. **VOICE** Calls a series of descending wheezing whistles: *"PEE PEE PEE pur."* **Co, E, Br, Bo**

♀ *puna*

♂ *puna*

♂ *cinereicapillus*

ANDEAN FLICKER

CHESTNUT
WOODPECKER

♀

♂

♂

♀

RINGED
WOODPECKER

SCALE-BREASTED
WOODPECKER

♂ n

♂ n

♂ *latifasciatus*

♀ *latifasciatus*

♂

♀

RUFOUS-HEADED
WOODPECKER

♂

♀

CREAM-COLORED
WOODPECKER

PLATE
130

LARGE WOODPECKERS

Lineated Woodpecker (Dryocopus) and the 5 species of Campephilus are very large, strong-billed, crested woodpeckers. They chisel and pry at bark and drill wood for insects; Lineated Woodpecker also may eat some fruit. The flight of all is particularly strong, but undulating. The distribution of red, black, and white on the sides of the face can be important for identification. Although Lineated Woodpecker superficially is similar to some Campephilus, note that it has very different vocalizations and a different pattern of white striping on the upperparts.

1 POWERFUL WOODPECKER *Campephilus pollens* * 34–35 cm (13½–14 in)
Rare, in humid montane forest along east slope of Andes, 2100–3100 m. Often forages in pairs or in small (family?) groups. Little contact with other large woodpeckers, other than limited elevational overlap with Crimson-bellied Woodpecker. **VOICE** Calls include a squeaky, descending whine: *"P'seew."* Also a rapid series: *"kek-kek-kek-kek."* Drum is heavy, 4 or 5 strikes. **Co, E**

2 CRIMSON-BELLIED WOODPECKER *Campephilus haematogaster* * 34–35 cm (13½–14 in)
Rare, in humid montane forest along east slope of Andes, 900–2300 m; usually occurs at lower elevations than Powerful Woodpecker. Cf. also Red-necked Woodpecker of Amazonia (with which there may be limited elevational overlap). Immatures similar to adults, but may be blacker below, and facial stripes may be whiter (less buff). **VOICE** Calls a high, squeaky *"psit!"* and a longer squeaky rattle: *"psit-trr'r'r'r'."* Drum is heavy, 2–4 strikes. **Co, E**

3 RED-NECKED WOODPECKER *Campephilus rubricollis* * 33–34 cm (13–13½ in)
Fairly common and widespread in Amazonia, up to 950 m, locally up to 1600 m. Singles or loosely associated pairs forage on large trees in forest interior, primarily in terra firme. Note extensive rufous at base of remiges, particularly visible in flight. **VOICE** Calls a squeaky, drawn out *"P'tuum."* Drum is heavy, 2 strikes. **Co, E, Br, Bo**

4 GUAYAQUIL WOODPECKER *Campephilus gayaquilensis* 34 cm (13½ in)
Uncommon in dry and semideciduous forest in northwestern Peru up to 1700 m. Overlaps with Lineated Woodpecker (but not with any other *Campephilus*); compared to Lineated, note different face pattern with much less black on sides of face, black rather than white throat, more extensively red head, and white stripes that converge on back. **VOICE** Call like that of Crimson-crested Woodpecker. Drum is heavy, dying away at end, 4–7 strikes. **Co, E**

5 LINEATED WOODPECKER *Dryocopus lineatus* * 34–35 cm (13½–14 in)
Fairly common and widespread in eastern Peru, up to 1500 m, where found in river-edge forest, forest edge, and tall second growth (subspecies *lineatus*). Subspecies *fuscipennis* (not illustrated) is uncommon in dry and semideciduous forest in northwest, up to at least 800 m; very similar to *lineatus* but is browner, less glossy black. Singles or pairs forage on trunks and large limbs of tall trees; frequently conspicuous, and may visit isolated tall dead trees in pastures relatively far from forest. Overlaps broadly (in distribution and habitat) with Crimson-crested Woodpecker; compared to that species, note narrower white stripes and more extensive black and gray on sides of face, paler throat, and white dorsal stripes that do not meet. In northwest, the same features distinguish Lineated from Guayaquil Woodpecker. **VOICE** Call a loud series of rising yelps: *"REE REE REE REE REE REE REE ruh."* Also a sharp note followed by a throaty rattle: *"KEEP grr'rr'r'r'r,"* sometimes only *"KEEP."* Drum is heavy, a fairly long series, accelerating slightly. **Co, E, Br, Bo**

6 CRIMSON-CRESTED WOODPECKER *Campephilus melanoleucos* * 34–35 cm (13½–14 in)
Fairly common and widespread in eastern lowlands, up to 1400 m. A large woodpecker of river-edge forest, forest edge, and tall second growth, where singles and pairs forage on large trunks. Cf. Lineated Woodpecker, although Crimson-crested is more closely associated with continuous forest. **VOICE** Call a hollow, popping series of notes, sometimes delivered in a rapid chatter: *"tkep-tkep-tkep."* Drum is heavy, 3–5 strikes. **Co, E, Br, Bo**

CRIMSON-BELLIED
WOODPECKER

imm. ♂

RED-NECKED
WOODPECKER

POWERFUL
WOODPECKER

CRIMSON-CRESTED
WOODPECKER

GUAYAQUIL
WOODPECKER

LINEATED
WOODPECKER

PLATE
131

SMALL AND ANT-FOLLOWING WOODCREEPERS

Woodcreepers forage by hitching up woody trunks and branches, supported in part by stiffened tips to the tail feathers. Plumages are drab and can be confusingly similar. Note bill size and shape (which often helps place a woodcreeper to genus) in addition to subtle plumage characters, as well as voice and habitat. Nest in cavities in trees.

1 LONG-TAILED WOODCREEPER *Deconychura longicauda* * male 21–22 cm (8¼–8¾ in), female 19 cm (7½ in)

Uncommon in Amazonia and Andean foothills, up to 1100 m, locally to 1750 m. Slender, long-tailed; looks small-headed but with a somewhat shaggy crown. Also note plain back, lightly marked breast and sides of head, and narrow superciliary. Cf. smaller Spot-throated Woodcreeper and larger *Xiphorhynchus* (which lack the superciliary). Also may be confused with Plain-brown Woodcreeper (especially in southeast), but proportionally longer-tailed, with breast and sides of head more heavily streaked, and lacks gray on cheeks and lores. Males larger than females, especially in southern Peru. Breast marks are narrow streaks throughout most of Peru, but in undescribed foothills population (900–1750 m; not illustrated) in northern and central Peru marks are broader, more diamond-shaped. Usually in the mid- or understory; may follow mixed species flocks. **VOICE** Song (Amazonia) an even-paced, melancholy, descending series of shrill whistles: "*heee heer heeu hoo hoor hur.*" Easily imitated. Song of foothills birds very different, a higher, more rapid, rising-falling series of bisyllabic notes reminiscent of song of Strong-billed Woodcreeper, but not as loud or ringing: "*psi psi-psiLEE-psiLEE-peeLEE-peeLEE-peeLEE-peeLEE.*" Call a long series of stuttered, chirping "*tchi-tchi-tchi*" notes. **Co, E, Br, Bo**

2 SPOT-THROATED WOODCREEPER *Deconychura stictolaema* * male 18.5–19 cm (7¼–7½ in), female 15.5–16 cm (6–6¼ in)

Rare to uncommon, in northern and central Amazonia below 750 m. Sexually dimorphic in size; always smaller than Long-tailed Woodcreeper, with females almost as small as Wedge-billed Woodcreeper. Has shorter bill than Long-tailed, and has less obvious superciliary, fewer streaks on crown, and lightly spotted throat; also rump is more extensively rufous. Cf. Wedge-billed Woodcreeper; Spot-throated is larger with longer, more normal-shaped bill, and lacks buffy wing stripe. Forages in understory, generally lower than Long-tailed. Usually with mixed-species flocks. **VOICE** Song (Ecuador, Brazil) a short, rising, dry trill: "*drrrrrrreee.*" Call a rapid series of short chatters. **Co, E, Br**

3 WEDGE-BILLED WOODCREEPER *Glyphorynchus spirurus* * 13.5–14 cm (5¼–5½ in)

One of the most widespread and ubiquitous birds of humid forest in Amazonia, up to 1400 m. Forages singly or in pairs, often with mixed species flocks but also apart, on vertical trunks relatively near ground. Small; bill very short with upturned tip to the mandible. Inner webs of most remiges partially buff, forming a buff wing stripe, visible in flight. Throat rufous-buff in most of Peru (*castelnaudii*), but white in *albigularis* (not illustrated) of Madre de Dios and Puno. **VOICE** Song an inconspicuous rising series of twittery notes: "*tu-tu-tew-twi-twi.*" Call a sharp, sneezing "*tchi,*" often in short series. **Co, E, Br, Bo**

4 PLAIN-BROWN WOODCREEPER *Dendrocincla fuliginosa* * 20.5–22.5 cm (8–9 in)

Uncommon to fairly common in humid forest in Amazonia, up to 1200 m, locally to 1500 m. Rare in semideciduous forest in Tumbes (*ridgwayi*). Usually over army ant swarms; also forages in understory away from ants, but rarely with mixed species flocks. Drab; note paler, grayish lores and cheeks, and dusky moustachial streak. In southeast (*atrirostris*) may have faint narrow streaks on crown and breast. **VOICE** Song (Amazonia) a long (up to 1 min), reeling chatter similar to that of Chestnut-winged Hookbill, but richer in quality and usually given from nearer ground. Also gives a short, descending rattle. Calls a sharp "*psh'AH!*" with a squeaky and raspy quality and a raspy, whining "*eeeww.*" Song of *ridgwayi* different, a long series of machine-gun bursts of notes. Call a piercing "*TOOEET.*" **Co, E, Br, Bo**

5 WHITE-CHINNED WOODCREEPER *Dendrocincla merula* * 20.5 cm (8 in)

Uncommon in humid forest in Amazonia, below 500 m. Usually forages lower in forest than Plain-brown Woodcreeper, and almost always over army ant swarms. Plain brown, unstreaked, with a contrasting narrow white throat, a plain face and bluish gray iris. **VOICE** Calls, often heard around army ant swarms, include a short, staccato rattle "*pit-it-it*" and a rich "*chew.*" Song is a rising or rising-falling series of rich piping notes at an even pace: "*pit-it-ti-ti-TI*" or "*pit-it-TI-ti-ter.*" **Co, E, Br, Bo**

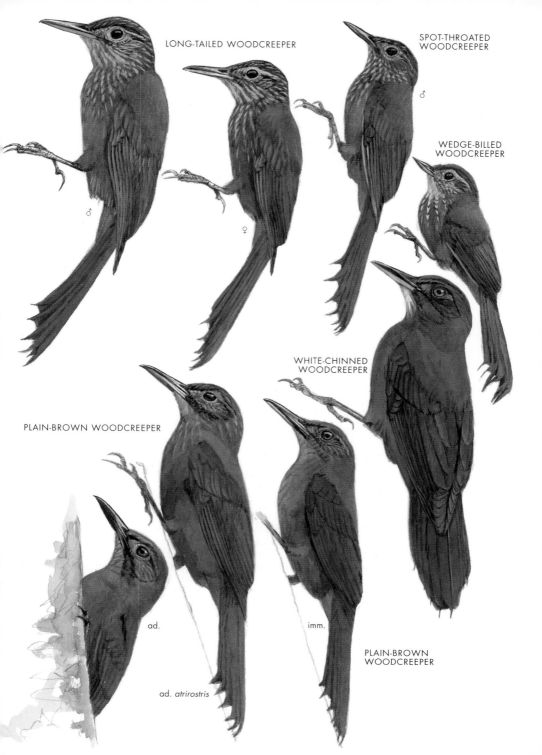

LONG-TAILED WOODCREEPER

SPOT-THROATED
WOODCREEPER

♂

WEDGE-BILLED
WOODCREEPER

♂

♀

WHITE-CHINNED
WOODCREEPER

PLAIN-BROWN WOODCREEPER

ad.

imm.

ad. *atrirostris*

PLAIN-BROWN
WOODCREEPER

PLATE
132

LARGE WOODCREEPERS

These are 5 large, large-billed woodcreepers. Buff-throated by far is the most common species and should be learned well as a basis for comparison to others on this plate; also see the smaller species on plate 133.

1 STRONG-BILLED WOODCREEPER *Xiphocolaptes promeropirhynchus* * 30 cm (12 in)
Widespread, but usually rare; largest woodcreeper in most of Peru. Andean group in humid montane forest of Andes, 1000–3100 m; also (*crassirostris*) in semideciduous forest in Tumbes at 400 m. Amazonian group in lowland forest, up to ca. 750 m, but apparently absent from northwestern Amazonia. All have large, stout, slightly curved bill, and a streaked breast; forage as singles or pairs in under- and midstory. Andean populations are more olive, with whitish superciliary, dusky moustachial stripe, and narrow dark edges to pale ventral streaks. Amazonian birds are more rufescent with blacker crowns, a weaker facial pattern, and the ventral streaks lack dark margins. Cf. smaller Buff-throated Woodcreeper. **VOICE** Variation poorly understood. Andean song (*compressirostris*; south at least to southern Amazonas) a long, descending, slightly accelerating series of ringing, bisyllabic notes, with the second syllable higher than the first: "*wlee-chewLEEchewLEEchewLEEchewLEEchewLEE.*" Pace slower and with more noticeable acceleration in central and southern Andean birds; song also often starts with a longer whine. Call a nasal, whiny "*wheeeeeu.*" In northwest (*crassirostris*) similar to highland birds, but pace is slow, voice thinner. Song (Amazonia) a descending series similar to that of *compressirostris*, but with first syllable higher than second (variable?): "*CHEElew-CHEElew-CHEElew-CHEElew-CHEElew-CHEElew-CHEElew-CHEElew.*" Calls a rising "*chew-LEEip*"; also a coughing, whiny "*ch'aaw.*" **Co, E, Br, Bo**

2 BUFF-THROATED WOODCREEPER *Xiphorhynchus guttatus* * 26 cm (10½ in)
Common and widespread in Amazonia, up to 700 m, locally to 900 m. Forages from understory to canopy, but most often relatively high. Regularly (and noisily) investigates dead leaf clusters and palm fronds; occasionally forages over army ant swarms. Large, rufescent, with buffy throat and strong, relatively long bill. **VOICE** Very vocal. Song, most often heard at dawn and dusk, loud, decelerating, rising-falling series of rich, descending notes: "*chu-chu-CHU CHEW chew chew chew chew.*" Calls a loud, rich, descending "*TEW!*" often heard in duet at dusk. Also a short, descending series, often periodically through the day: "*hewLEE hewLEE hew-hew-hew*"; sometimes gives only the introductory notes. **Co, E, Br, Bo**

3 BAR-BELLIED WOODCREEPER *Hylexetastes stresemanni* * 30 cm (12 in)
Poorly known; apparently rare in eastern Amazonia, below 450 m. Found in terra firme; probably forages in midstory, either over ant swarms or with mixed species flocks. Very large with stout, reddish bill. Similar to Amazonian Barred-Woodcreeper, which is slightly smaller with longer, straighter, narrower bill and barred breast and upperparts. Cf. also Black-banded Woodcreeper (which has streaked head, back, and breast, and dusky bill). **VOICE** Song, usually at dawn and dusk, a loud, musical, slightly descending series of falling-rising whistles: "*chewLEE chewLEE chewLEE chewLEE.*" Similar to Strong-billed Woodcreeper, but slower-paced, has fewer notes, and each note rises and falls. Call a rising, nasal sneeze: "*ewwww-IH!*" **Br, Bo**

4 BLACK-BANDED WOODCREEPER *Dendrocolaptes picumnus* * 29 cm (11¼ in)
Uncommon in Amazonia, up to 1350 m. Behavior similar to Amazonian Barred-Woodcreeper, but more closely associated with army ant swarms, and seldom with mixed-species flocks. Note large size; long, straight bill; and combination of streaked breast and barred belly. **VOICE** Song similar to Amazonian Barred-Woodcreeper, but normally not as steeply descending, more staccato, and without chirping terminal notes. Call a low, wheezy, whining "*aaah.*" **Co, E, Br, Bo**

5 AMAZONIAN BARRED-WOODCREEPER *Dendrocolaptes certhia* * 28 cm (11 in)
Uncommon in Amazonia, below 800 m. Found in under- and midstory of forest. Often forages over army ant swarms; may join mixed-species flocks. Note long, straight bill, which may be reddish brown (but is dusky in immatures); large size; and plumage narrowly barred above and below. **VOICE** Song a musical, relatively evenly paced, obviously descending series of mewing whistles, sometimes ending with short accelerating series of more liquid, chirping notes: "*whi-whi-whi-whe-whe-wha-wha-wu tir'u'u*"; delivery can be quite variable. Similar to Black-banded Woodcreeper. Call a descending wheezy, mewing "*gaaaah.*" **Co, E, Br, Bo**

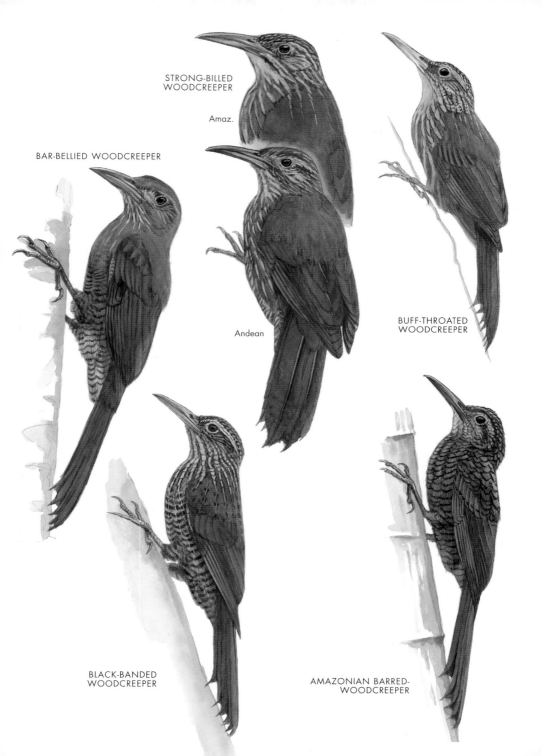

STRONG-BILLED
WOODCREEPER

Amaz.

BAR-BELLIED WOODCREEPER

Andean

BUFF-THROATED
WOODCREEPER

BLACK-BANDED
WOODCREEPER

AMAZONIAN BARRED-
WOODCREEPER

PLATE
133

SMALLER *XIPHORHYNCHUS* WOODCREEPERS

These Xiphorhynchus *are medium-sized to large Amazonian woodcreepers. Forage in under- and midstory, usually with mixed-species flocks. Bill slightly curved (except Straight-billed and Zimmer's woodcreepers); cf. longer, straighter bills of* Dendrocolaptes *and slender, curved bills of* Lepidocolaptes. *Largest Amazonian species (Buff-throated Woodcreeper) is on plate 132.*

1 ZIMMER'S WOODCREEPER *Xiphorhynchus kienerii* 22–24 cm (8½–9½ in)
Very similar to Straight-billed Woodcreeper, and easily overlooked; status and distribution poorly known. Overlaps with Straight-billed in varzea and river islands, but perhaps more confined to forest interior. Less rufescent than Straight-billed, with brown (not rufous) lesser wing coverts; pale breast markings more elongated (streaky, less scaled); belly slightly tawnier; and tail longer. Best distinguished by **VOICE** Song faster than fast song of Straight-billed, and evenly paced throughout, with steady descent, no rising component: "*br'r'r'r'e'e'e'e'e'u'u'u*." **Br**

2 STRAIGHT-BILLED WOODCREEPER *Xiphorhynchus picus* * 22.5 cm (8¾ in)
Fairly common in varzea, on wooded river islands, in river-edge forest, and in second growth, below 500 m, locally to 1100 m. Note pale, rather pointed bill, whitish throat, striped breast, and overall rufescent plumage. Striped Woodcreeper is similar but is more olivaceous, has striped back and pinkish buff throat. Cf. Zimmer's Woodcreeper. **VOICE** Song a rapid, accelerating, and descending trill: "*bi-bi-bi-b'r'r'r'r'r'r'r'r'r'u*." Second song type a more musical descending trill that accelerates, then decelerates: "*chew-ew-ew'ew'ew'ew'ew-ew ew ew*." Call a sharp "*kip*." **Co, E, Br, Bo**

3 STRIPED WOODCREEPER *Xiphorhynchus obsoletus* * 21.5 cm (8½ in)
Uncommon, in under- and midstory of varzea and swampy forest below 350 m, locally to 500 m; relatively widespread in north, but local in south. Striped both above and below, with relatively pale, short bill and pinkish buff throat. Cf. Straight-billed and Lineated woodcreepers. **VOICE** Song a rapid, ringing, evenly paced, rising trill, starting and ending abruptly: "*tr'r'r'r'ee'ee'ee'ee'ee*." **Co, E, Br, Bo**

4 OCELLATED WOODCREEPER *Xiphorhynchus ocellatus* * 20–21cm (8–8¼ in)
Uncommon in under- and midstory of humid forest interior in northern Amazonia below 250 m (*ocellatus* group, not illustrated; upperparts with only a few, very narrow buff streaks). Fairly common in humid montane forest along east slope of Andes and outlying ridges, 800–1700 m; local in lowlands of south (*chunchotambo* group, probably a separate species, "Tschudi's" Woodcreeper). Often sympatric in lowlands with very similar Elegant Woodcreeper. Ocellated is more streaked (less spotted) on breast and belly than Elegant. In the hand, streaks of Ocellated have plain margins; streaks and spots of Elegant narrowly tipped with dusky. North of Amazon *ocellatus* group also differ from sympatric Elegant (*ornatus*) by narrower, almost nonexistent dorsal streaking. South of the Amazon, Ocellated even more similar to Elegant (*insignis, juruanus*). Perplexus (*ocellatus* group; northern Peru, south of Amazon) more rufescent than Elegant, especially on throat; breast more streaked, less spotted. In southern Amazonia, *chunchotambo* group more streaked above than Elegant (*juruanus*), and breast markings are much larger. In Andes also cf. Olive-backed and Montane woodcreepers. **VOICE** Song of *ocellatus* group, north of Amazon, a quiet, accelerating series of rapid whistled notes ending in a stuttered or quavering series: "*hee-ee-ee-i'i'i'i'i chee'ee'ee tree'ee'ee tree'ee'ee*." Sometimes gives only stuttered series. Call a clear, descending whistled "*teeew*" or "*heew*." South of the Amazon (*perplexus*) call multinote (typically 4 notes, but up to 6), first note louder, slightly higher-pitched, then a short pause and 3 closely spaced notes: "*PEW tu-tu-tu*." *Chunchotambo* group: Song a staccato, descending, evenly paced series of notes: "*PEE-ti-ti-ti-ti-ti*." Calls a short, descending, whistled "*tew*" or more quavering, liquid, descending "*tre'e'ew*"; also a dry rattle. **Co, E, Br, Bo**

5 ELEGANT WOODCREEPER *Xiphorhynchus elegans* * 20–22 cm (8–8½ in)
Common in understory of Amazonian forest, up to 700 m. Breast spotted; spots are larger and buffier in populations north of the Amazon (*ornatus*), smaller and drabber in populations east of Río Ucayali (*juruanus*); and intermediate in size and color in west central Amazonian Peru (*insignis*; not illustrated). Cf. much larger Buff-throated Woodcreeper and Ocellated Woodcreeper. **VOICE** Song a loud, descending series of rich, ringing, evenly paced notes, sometimes ending in a single or doubled whine: "*ti ti TCHI TCHI TCHE TCHEW TCHU TCHU TCHU wheew-wheew*." Calls: sharp series of smacking notes often followed by a descending whine: "*CHEW-CHEW-CHEW wheeew*." Also a long series of quiet "*chew*" notes. **Co, E, Br, Bo**

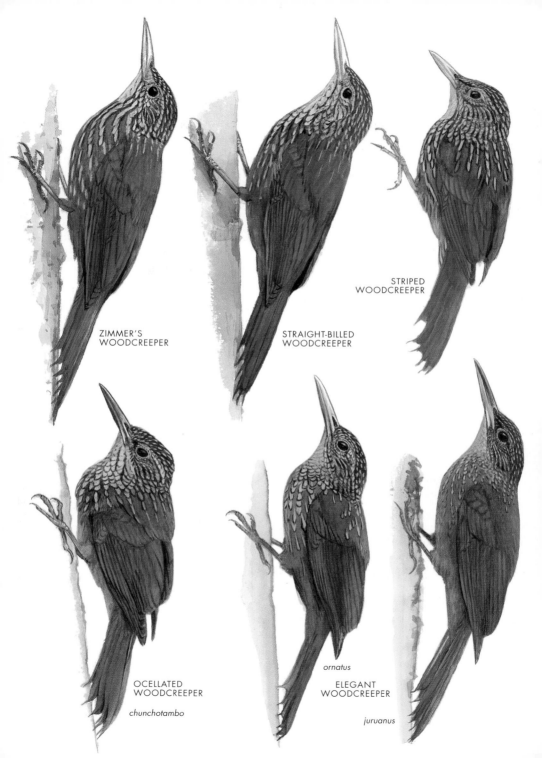

ZIMMER'S
WOODCREEPER

STRAIGHT-BILLED
WOODCREEPER

STRIPED
WOODCREEPER

OCELLATED
WOODCREEPER

chunchotambo

ornatus

ELEGANT
WOODCREEPER

juruanus

PLATE
134

WOODCREEPERS

Tyrannine is a large Andean woodcreeper with a straight, dark bill. Olive-backed is the only Andean Xiphorhynchus (see plate 133). Olivaceous Woodcreeper is a small, short-billed, plain species. The three species of Lepidocolaptes are similar in size to the smaller species of Xiphorhynchus but have thin, distinctly decurved bills. All are heavily streaked below. Regular members of mixed-species flocks.

1 TYRANNINE WOODCREEPER *Dendrocincla tyrannina* * 25.5 cm (10 in)

Rare in humid montane forest along east slope of Andes, 1850–3150 m. Forages primarily in the midstory, especially on relatively bare trunks and branches. Usually solitary, rarely associated with mixed flocks. Relatively large and plain; other montane woodcreepers more prominently spotted or streaked. **VOICE** Song, lasting perhaps 15 sec, is a rapid series of musical notes that accelerates and rises in pitch until abruptly decelerating and dropping in pitch near end: *"tu tu-tu-tu'tu'tututetetetetetetiti-tu-tu tu."* Call a loud, ringing chatter, often given in bursts: *"CHEE-CHEE-CHEE-CHEE-CHER!"* **Co, E, Bo**

2 OLIVE-BACKED WOODCREEPER *Xiphorhynchus triangularis* * 21–23.5 cm (8¼–9¼ in)

Fairly common in humid montane forest along east slope of Andes, 1000–2400 m. Drab olive in color, lightly spotted below, with back largely or entirely plain. **VOICE** Song in northern Peru a mellow, decelerating, descending series of musical whistled notes: *"whi'we-we-we-we we we wur."* Call a descending, mewing *"ewEEW"* or *"whew."* Subspecies *bangsi* (Pasco south) has an additional song, a wiry, insistent, rising-falling series of nasal whines: *"WHEEEW whi-WHI-WHI-whi-whi-whi."* Calls are nasal whines: *"wheew-whi."* **Co, E, Bo**

3 OLIVACEOUS WOODCREEPER *Sittasomus griseicapillus* * 16–17 cm (6¼–6½ in)

Fairly common in humid forest in Amazonia, up to 1700 m; also locally fairly common in semideciduous forest below 1000 m in northwest. Most often in under- and midstory; often with mixed-species flocks. Captures prey with short sallies or by gleaning. Unstreaked and 2-toned: rufous wings and tail contrast with gray (Amazonia; *amazonus*) or buffy olive (northwest Peru; *aequatorialis*) head, back, and underparts. **VOICE** Song (Amazonia) a loud, musical rising series of squeaky whistles, falling at very end: *"oo tur tee teeu teeu tew."* Calls a quiet rolling chatter (similar to Plain-brown Woodcreeper song). Song of *aequatorialis* a rich, rising-falling trill: *"wur'r'r'e'e'e'r'r'r,"* which may be short or drawn out in a loose series. Calls a high, twittery *"tee-tee-tee-tee-ter."* **Co, E, Br, Bo**

4 STREAK-HEADED WOODCREEPER *Lepidocolaptes souleyetii* * 21 cm (8¼ in)

Fairly common in dry and semideciduous forests and riparian thickets in northwestern Peru, up to 800 m. The only woodcreeper that is widespread in northwest (limited overlap only with very different Strong-billed and Olivaceous woodcreepers). Note also relatively long bill and light cinnamon throat. **VOICE** Song a loud, ringing, rapid, descending series of puttering notes: *"pee'i'i'i'i'i'i'i'i'i'i'i'i'i'i'i'ew."* Call a loud, rapidly quavering, descending *"pee'i'i'u."* **Co, E, Br**

5 MONTANE WOODCREEPER *Lepidocolaptes lacrymiger* * 22 cm (8¼ in)

Fairly common in humid montane forest on east slope of Andes at 1300–3200 m, mostly 2000–2900 m; also on west slope in northwest. Primarily forages in canopy. Rufescent, and heavily streaked below; back at most only lightly streaked. Cf. Olive-backed Woodcreeper. **VOICE** Song a high, accelerating, twittering series of clear, descending whistles: *"tititi ti-tseew ti-tseew-tseew."* Delivery of song variable, may have more notes and a terminal descending chatter; sometimes only a portion given. **Co, E, Bo**

6 LINEATED WOODCREEPER *Lepidocolaptes albolineatus* * 21 cm (8¼ in)

Widespread in Amazonia up to 600 m, locally to 1200 m, but uncommon and easily overlooked. Forages in forest canopy, usually with mixed-species flocks. Heavily streaked below; largely plain above, including crown. **VOICE** Song a rapid, accelerating, descending series of sharp notes, sounding rather antwrenlike: *"tee-teeteeteetitititititititu'u'u."* **Co, E, Br, Bo**

TYRANNINE
WOODCREEPER

amazonus

OLIVACEOUS
WOODCREEPER

aequatorialis

OLIVE-BACKED
WOODCREEPER

STREAK-HEADED
WOODCREEPER

MONTANE
WOODCREEPER

LINEATED
WOODCREEPER

PLATE
135

SCYTHEBILLS AND LARGE AMAZONIAN WOODCREEPERS

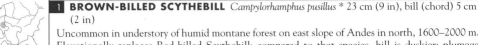

Scythebills readily are recognized by the long, extraordinarily curved bill. Long-billed and Cinnamon-throated woodcreepers are two distinctive Amazonian woodcreepers.

1 BROWN-BILLED SCYTHEBILL *Campylorhamphus pusillus* * 23 cm (9 in), bill (chord) 5 cm (2 in)

Uncommon in understory of humid montane forest on east slope of Andes in north, 1600–2000 m. Elevationally replaces Red-billed Scythebill; compared to that species, bill is duskier; plumage overall is darker, less rufescent, brown; throat and breast streaks are buffier; streaks above and below are narrower, less clearly defined (lack narrow dark borders). **VOICE** Song a rising-falling series of stuttering, whining notes: "*d'd'day-d'd'dee-d'd'dee-d'd'dee-d'd'day-d'd'ur.*" Calls a mewing "*eww*" and a staccato "*tsew-tsew-tsew,*" the latter similar to Red-billed chatter, perhaps slower-paced. **Co, E**

2 LONG-BILLED WOODCREEPER *Nasica longirostris* 34 cm (13½ in)

Forages in midstory and canopy of varzea in Amazonia; fairly common in north, less common in south. Probes epiphytes and crevices with its extraordinarily long bill. Solitary or in pairs, generally not with mixed-species flocks. **VOICE** Song a haunting series of 3–7 long, hollow, rising-falling whistles: "*hoooo hooOOoo hooOOoo hooOOoo.*" Easily imitated. Agitated song has more notes and becomes a rapid series that first accelerates then falls in pitch and decelerates. Call a low, quiet "*pk'ung,*" similar to Red-necked Woodpecker calls, but softer and less squeaky. **Co, E, Br, Bo**

3 RED-BILLED SCYTHEBILL *Campylorhamphus trochilirostris* * 24 cm (9½ in), bill (chord) 5.5–6.5 cm (2¼–2½ in); *zarumillanus* 29 cm (11 in), bill (chord) 8 cm (3 in)

The most widespread scythebill. Rare to uncommon in humid forest understory in Amazonia; typically below 800 m, especially in north, but locally to 1700 m farther south. Also locally in semideciduous forest in Tumbes up to 600 m (*zarumillanus*: larger with an even longer bill). Most prevalent in varzea or seasonally flooded forests; in southern Peru often found in bamboo thickets in river floodplains. Note reddish tone to bill and streaks on upper back. **VOICE** Song (northern Amazonia, Tumbes) a decelerating and descending series of notes that ends with more rising notes: "*tititi-ti-tee-tee-tee tui TUI TUI TUI.*" Song in southeastern Peru a melancholy, descending series of mellow, whistles: "*DWEE dwee dwee dwee dweer*"; faster, accelerating, and rising when agitated. Call a sharp chatter: "*tsi'tsi'tsee!*" **Co, E, Br, Bo**

4 GREATER SCYTHEBILL *Campylorhamphus pucherani* 28 cm (11 in), bill (chord) 6 cm (2½ in)

Rare, in humid montane forest at 2100–3200 m. Poorly known. Usually encountered as single individuals, alone or with mixed-species flocks, in forest midstory. Note large size and dark cheek framed by whitish superciliary and whitish malar stripe. **VOICE** Call a rising whining note and a descending series of rising whines sometimes ending in a sharper, rising note: "*eek-eek p'ee-eek p'ee-eew RWEE.*" **Co, E**

5 CURVE-BILLED SCYTHEBILL *Campylorhamphus procurvoides* * 22 cm (8¾ in), bill (chord) 5.5 cm (2¼ in)

Poorly known in Peru, where reported from few localities. Very similar to Red-billed Scythebill, but bill is slightly shorter, and back is less streaked. Not known to overlap in Peru with Red-billed, but contact is possible east of Río Napo (especially near Ecuador border?). **VOICE** Song (northeast Amazonian Brazil) an accelerating, slightly rising series of musical notes strongly recalling White-chinned Jacamar: "*whew whew-whew-whi'i'i'i'i'i'i.*" Call a descending series of mellow whistles: "*WEEEE wee-wee-wee-wi-wi.*" **Co, E, Br**

6 CINNAMON-THROATED WOODCREEPER *Dendrexetastes rufigula* * 25 cm (9¾ in)

Uncommon to fairly common in Amazonia, primarily at humid forest edge, up to 700 m (to 1100 m in south). Singles or pairs forage in midstory and canopy, seldom with mixed-species flocks. Bill stout and pale. Large, tawny-buff, relatively unmarked save for cinnamon-buff throat and blaze of short narrow white streaks on breast. **VOICE** Song, primarily heard at dawn and dusk, a loud, explosive rich, purring rattle that accelerates slightly, then ends with an abruptly decelerating churr: "*wur-r'r'r'r'r'r'r'r'r'r'r'r-rrrll.*" Similar to White-necked Puffbird's song, which does not accelerate or have the terminal churr. Call a squeaky bark: "*ch-ooee?*" **Co, E, Br, Bo**

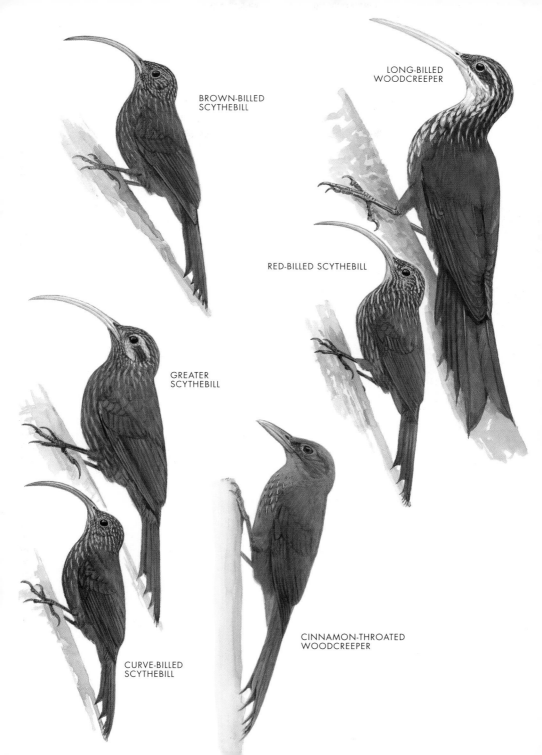

BROWN-BILLED
SCYTHEBILL

LONG-BILLED
WOODCREEPER

RED-BILLED SCYTHEBILL

GREATER
SCYTHEBILL

CURVE-BILLED
SCYTHEBILL

CINNAMON-THROATED
WOODCREEPER

PLATE
136

SMALL MINERS

Ovenbirds (plates 136–156) are a large family with diverse life styles; found throughout Peru, in both forest and open habitats. Sexes are alike, and in most species plumage is largely brown. Largely insectivorous. Behavior variable; many species regularly flock, and in any habitat a mixed-species flock of insectivorous birds is sure to include one or more species of ovenbird. Nest site and structure also variable: some species nest in burrows or in cavities, others build enclosed nests (some quite large) of sticks or mud. Miners (Geositta) are terrestrial ovenbirds found in open habitats, from the coast to the altiplano. Most are drab, relatively short-tailed, short-billed birds; important identification characters are wing and tail patterns, presence or absence of breast streaking, overall size, and bill length. Smaller species are shown here; see also plate 137.

1 COASTAL MINER *Geositta peruviana* * 14–14.5 cm (5½–5¾ in)

Common on coastal plain, below 700 m. Often in sandy open areas, sometimes with little or no vegetation. Usually solitary or in pairs (not in flocks, unlike Grayish Miner). Sandy buff, with short bill and plain breast; bases of remiges pale rufous, forming a wing stripe in flight, and outer tail feathers extensively creamy white. Subspecies *peruviana* of central Peru (Ancash to Lima) browner above, with dull wing bar and browner outer rectrices. No documented overlap with Common Miner; cf. Grayish. **VOICE** Song, given while hovering at apex of flight display, an unmusical "*pjee-aww.*" Call a squeaky "*cueet.*" **ENDEMIC**

2 GRAYISH MINER *Geositta maritima* 12.5–13 cm (5 in)

Uncommon to locally fairly common; often in flocks. Not found on coastal plain, but in hills and lower slopes of Andes, up to 2450 m (rarely to 3500 m). Usually in sandy or rocky areas with little vegetation. Gray above, with short bill and plain breast; flanks buffy. Tail black (with narrow white border to outer pair of rectrices). Wings lack rufous. Overlaps with Coastal Miner, but typically at higher elevations; lacks wing stripe and pale bases to outer rectrices. **VOICE** Song a quick, unmusical rattle. Call, often given in flight, a short, somewhat squeaky "*kew*" note. **Ch**

3 DARK-WINGED MINER *Geositta saxicolina* 16.5 cm (6½ in)

Locally fairly common to common on altiplano of central Peru (4000–4900 m) in stony puna; may occur more on sloping terrain than Common Miner. Solitary, in pairs, or (less often) in small groups. Note pinkish buff face and breast, and pinkish buff rump patch. Wings plain (no rufous wing bar), outer rectrices creamy at base. Cf. Common Miner. **VOICE** Song an accelerating series of "*peep*" notes that rises and falls. **ENDEMIC**

4 PUNA MINER *Geositta punensis* 15.5 cm (6 in)

Locally fairly common in puna grasslands of high Andes (3900–4200 m) of extreme southwestern Peru, especially in bunch grass; scattered shrubs may be present. Similar to Common Miner, which it overlaps, but slightly smaller, with shorter bill and plain breast; also, upper tail coverts and bases to outer rectrices are pale rufous (not whitish buff). **VOICE** Song (Argentina), given in low flight, a series of reedy whistles: "*wheeu wheeu wheeu wheeu….*" Call a squeaky "*peew.*" **Bo, Ch**

5 COMMON MINER *Geositta cunicularia* * 15–16 cm (6–6¼ in)

The most widespread highland miner. Common in open areas with short grass on altiplano (3100–4800 m), local on arid Pacific slope of southwestern Peru (above 2300 m) presumably south to Tacna. Disjunct coastal population is locally common on lomas in southern Peru below 900 m. Andean birds have moderately long, slightly curved bill, mottled breast, rufous wing stripe (in flight), creamy or buff upper tail coverts, and creamy white bases to outer rectrices. Coastal birds duller, breast more distinctly streaked, rump only slightly paler than back, and outer rectrices basally rufous. **VOICE** Call of highland birds a clear "*peep.*" Calls of coastal subspecies a short rattle and a series of rich "*chew*" notes. **Bo, Br, Ch**

COASTAL MINER

peruviana

GRAYISH MINER

DARK-WINGED MINER

PUNA MINER

coastal

COMMON MINER

Andean

PLATE
137

LARGE MINERS AND EARTHCREEPERS

The two larger miners are shown on this plate; see also plate 136. Earthcreepers are large terrestrial ovenbirds, found in open habitats or lightly wooded areas in the Andes. All are long-billed and have a long tail, which often is partially cocked. Usually solitary, sometimes in pairs. Probe in loose dirt or gravel. Often difficult to approach, and may fly long distances when disturbed. All are relatively drab but vary in bill shape (straight vs. curved) and color patterns of breast, wings, and tail.

1 THICK-BILLED MINER *Geositta crassirostris* * 18.5–19 cm (7¼–7½ in)
Uncommon to locally fairly common in coastal lomas at 300–800 m, and on Andean slopes, 1875–3500 m. Occurs as singles or pairs on arid boulder-strewn slopes, with scattered shrubs and columnar cacti; frequently perches on rocks. Largest miner with long, stout bill and rufous band on open wing. The size of an earthcreeper, but distinguished by shorter tail and whitish tarsi. **VOICE** Song a forceful, accelerating series of "*cueew*" notes often becoming a harsh, grating series of "*djeer-djeer-djeer-djeer…*" notes. Call a rising then falling mewing "*reew.*" **ENDEMIC**

2 SLENDER-BILLED MINER *Geositta tenuirostris* * 17.5–18 cm (7 in)
Fairly common in high Andes, 2650–4600 m. Occurs on puna and in high intermontane valleys. Frequently found in bare and short-grass fields and rock outcroppings. Often near water or damp areas, although not restricted to them. Usually solitary or in pairs. Note long slender, slightly curved bill, light mottling on breast, dark rump, and (in flight) extensively rufous wings. Cf. longer-tailed earthcreepers. **VOICE** Song, usually given in low flight, a series of clear "*pew*" or "*pip*" notes that accelerate and decelerate. Call a squeaky, mewing "*wheew.*" **E, Bo, Ch**

3 SCALE-THROATED EARTHCREEPER *Upucerthia dumetaria* * 22 cm (8¾ in)
Very poorly known; recorded only from western shore of Lake Titicaca (3800–3900 m). Presumably found on shrubby slopes. Large earthcreeper with strongly scalloped breast pattern. Distinguished from Plain-breasted Earthcreeper by scaled throat and breast, and by tawny tips to outer tail feathers. **VOICE** Calls (Argentina) include a sharp "*pyuk.*" **Bo, Ch**

4 STRIATED EARTHCREEPER *Upucerthia serrana* * 19.5–20.5 cm (7¾–8 in)
Fairly common in arid montane areas at 3000–4600 m, locally down to 2300 m. Usually prefers areas with a greater density of shrubs than do other earthcreepers; also found in *Polylepis* woodland. A dark-colored, relatively straight-billed earthcreeper; note heavily streaked underparts and extensive rufous color in wings. **VOICE** Song a dry accelerating-decelerating trill: "*tp tp tp trr'r'r'r'r'e'e'e'e'r'r.*" Call a scratchy "*djer-djer-djer-djer-djree.*" **ENDEMIC**

5 STRAIGHT-BILLED EARTHCREEPER *Upucerthia ruficaudus* * 16–16.5 cm (6¼–6½ in)
Fairly common to common in montane scrub (including *Polylepis*) at 3500–4500 m. Secretive, keeping close to cover. Tail often cocked at a high angle. Compared to other earthcreepers, has a very straight bill. Also distinguished by very white throat and breast, and relatively bright rufous upperparts. Larger and longer billed than canasteros. **VOICE** Song a descending series of squeaking notes, "*tip tip pseep-pseep-pseep-pseep-pseep-pseep.*" Calls include a scratchy, squeaky series of peeping notes, grinding chatters, and a plaintive "*peeyee.*" **Bo, Ch**

6 PLAIN-BREASTED EARTHCREEPER *Upucerthia jelskii* * 18–20 cm (7–7¾ in)
The most widely distributed earthcreeper, common at 3400–4800 m in open habitats, such as grassland or slopes with scattered rocks and shrubs. Nondescript, with long, curved bill and long tail but no "field marks." In flight, wings mostly dull rufous. Cf. Slender-billed Miner. **VOICE** Song, sometimes given in flight, a musical, rising-falling, rapid puttering rattle. **Bo, Ch**

7 WHITE-THROATED EARTHCREEPER *Upucerthia albigula* 19.5 cm (7½ in)
Rare to uncommon in a narrow elevational band (2700–3500 m) in southwest. Found in rocky, steep-walled washes and adjacent desert with a mixture of scattered bushes and clumps of columnar cacti; also occurs where this habitat meets irrigated farmland. Closely resembles Plain-breasted Earthcreeper (although generally at lower elevations). White-throated has a stouter, somewhat shorter bill, more rufescent wing coverts, entirely rufous outer webs of secondaries (narrowly edged sooty in Plain-breasted); stronger superciliary; and more contrast between tawny flanks and paler brown belly. **VOICE** Song an accelerating, rising-falling series of liquid chipping notes: "*tup tup chi-chi-chi-chi-chi.*" **Ch**

THICK-BILLED MINER

SLENDER-BILLED MINER

SCALE-THROATED
EARTHCREEPER

STRIATED EARTHCREEPER

PLAIN-BREASTED
EARTHCREEPER

STRAIGHT-BILLED
EARTHCREEPER

WHITE-THROATED EARTHCREEPER

PLATE
138

CINCLODES AND WREN-LIKE RUSHBIRD

Cinclodes are large terrestrial ovenbirds of open country; most species also are closely associated with water. Most are Andean; one is strictly coastal. All have prominent white or rufous wing stripes and usually have pale tips to moderately long tails. Often droop the wings and carry the tail slightly cocked, like a thrush. Usually solitary or in pairs. Most, if not all, species have a characteristic display in which they wave the wings over the body while giving a trilled song. Wren-like Rushbird is a small ovenbird restricted to marshes.

1 SURF CINCLODES *Cinclodes taczanowskii* 21 cm (8¼ in)
Always found in the immediate vicinity of the coast, foraging at or near the water's edge, picking at the surface of rocks or of sandy beaches. Fairly common on rocky headlands. Note overall dark color and long tail. This is the only passerine that regularly forages on rocks at the surf's edge. **VOICE** Song a trill. Call an abrupt "*chec.*" **ENDEMIC**

2 WREN-LIKE RUSHBIRD *Phleocryptes melanops* * 13.5–14 cm (5¼–5½ in)
Common locally along Peruvian coast, and on altiplano (3200–4300 m). Confined to beds of tall to moderately tall reeds (especially *Scirpus*) in both fresh and brackish water. Usually solitary or in pairs, largely concealed within reed beds, but easily seen as it moves between patches of reeds with weak, buzzy flight. **VOICE** Song a remarkably insectlike series of dry "*tick*" notes, reminiscent of tapping 2 pebbles together, often rising and falling slightly in pitch, interspersed with a more rapid series of notes as if "rewinding tape" (this component possibly lacking on coast): "*tick-tick-tick-tick ZZZZIPP tick-tick-tick....*" Sometimes interrupts song with a squeaky, descending whinnying phrase. Calls a squeaky "*teek*" or "*peek*" and a short, buzzy "*zit.*" **Br, Bo, Ch**

3 ROYAL CINCLODES *Cinclodes aricomae* 20 cm (7¾ in)
Rare and local, known only from a few isolated, humid *Polylepis* groves at 3700–4600 m. Threatened, in part due to cutting of *Polylepis* woodlands for fuel. Hops on lichen- and moss-covered rocks, probing moss and flaking off pieces of moss in dirt; also probes at base of *Polylepis* trees. Larger than Bar-winged Cinclodes, with thicker, longer, more curved bill; underparts heavily mottled with brown; wing markings rufous, not whitish buff. **VOICE** Song a trill. **Bo**

4 BAR-WINGED CINCLODES *Cinclodes fuscus* * 17.5–18 cm (7 in)
The most abundant and widespread cinclodes in open country throughout the Andes, 2750–4800 m. Found in puna and paramo grasslands, usually near water such as along streams, in bogs, or at margins of lakes. Often somewhat confiding, foraging near human habitations, and even nesting in crevices in houses. Often flies long distances, low to the ground. North and west of Marañón Valley, wing stripe is rufous, not white (*albidiventris*). The "standard" Andean cinclodes; cf. White-winged Cinclodes. **VOICE** Song a high, rising, twittery trill: "*trrreee'i'i'i'i'i.*" Song of northern *albidiventris* slightly different, a monotone twittery trill: "*trrrrrrrrr.*" Call high twittering notes. **E, Br, Bo, Ch**

5 WHITE-BELLIED CINCLODES *Cinclodes palliatus* 23–25 cm (9–9¾ in)
Rare and local. Only at extremely high elevations (4400–5000 m) in west central Peru. Largely restricted to bogs with cushion plants (*Distichia*) and rocky outcroppings. Solitary, in pairs or small groups of 3 or 4 individuals (family groups?). Much larger than other cinclodes, and gleaming white below. Large size and long tail gives this bird more the appearance of a large, brown-and-white mockingbird than of a cinclodes. **VOICE** Song a rapid puttering, chatter "*pipipipipi pi pi*" that sometimes accelerates into a higher, piping series: "*WEE-WEE-WEE-WEE-WEE....*" **ENDEMIC**

6 WHITE-WINGED CINCLODES *Cinclodes atacamensis* * 20.5–21.5 (8–8½ in)
Fairly common in high Andes, 2800–4600 m. Very rare vagrant to coast in south. Rarely found away from fast-flowing, clear streams. Less confiding than Bar-winged Cinclodes. Compared to Bar-winged is larger and the white wing markings are gleaming white and extensive, even on closed wing. Also is more rufescent brown above and has a whiter superciliary and whiter tips to outer tail feathers. **VOICE** Song a trill. Calls a loud "*queet*" and a whistle followed by a chatter. **Bo, Ch**

SURF CINCLODES

WREN-LIKE
RUSHBIRD

BAR-WINGED
CINCLODES

albidiventris

ROYAL CINCLODES

WHITE-BELLIED
CINCLODES

WHITE-WINGED
CINCLODES

PLATE
139

TIT-SPINETAILS

Tit-spinetails are found in shrubby areas and open woodlands of the high Andes, with one species also found near the coast in south. They are small bodied, but with very long, graduated tails; rectrices also are narrow and pointed. Active and acrobatic, they often use their tail as a brace. They glean leaves, twigs, and flowers of bushes and small trees for insects. Travel in pairs or small flocks (family groups?), often with other species.

1 WHITE-BROWED TIT-SPINETAIL *Leptasthenura xenothorax* 16 cm (6¼ in)
Local and patchy in *Polylepis* woods and adjacent *Gynoxys* thickets at 3800–4500 m in south-central Peru. Habitat threatened by increasing demand for firewood and building materials. Very like rufous-crowned subspecies of Rusty-crowned Tit-Spinetail, but there is no geographic overlap. Note the rufous crown, heavily spotted throat (contrasting with unstreaked lower breast and belly), and prominent white superciliary. **VOICE** Song a rather rapid, dry, descending chipping trill: "*ti ti trrrrrreeeeeeeeuuu.*" Call single metallic "*tip*" or "*tchit*" notes. **ENDEMIC**

2 TAWNY TIT-SPINETAIL *Leptasthenura yanacensis* 17–17.5 cm (6¾–7 in)
Rare to uncommon, and patchy. Restricted to uppermost patches of *Polylepis* woodland and adjacent shrubbery (especially *Gynoxys* and *Senecio*), usually surrounded by grassland or talus, from 3950 to 4600 m. Records are from Cordillera Blanca (Ancash) and northern Lima; and from scattered sites in Apurímac, Cuzco, and Puno. The only bright cinnamon, long-tailed bird in *Polylepis* (but cf. juvenile Azara's Spinetail). **VOICE** Song a series of rapid, loud, sharp chips that accelerate into a chatter of variable length and delivery: "*tchp tchp tchp-tchi'tchi'tchi'tchi'tchi'tchi-tchp.*" Calls include quiet, liquid "*tchp*" notes. **Bo**

3 RUSTY-CROWNED TIT-SPINETAIL *Leptasthenura pileata* * 16.5–17 cm (6½–6 in)
Fairly common in high-elevation shrub (2900–4200 m, locally down to 2000 m) and relict woodland zone. Found along west slope of Andes from La Libertad south to Arequipa; and in Marañón and upper Huallaga valleys. Primarily in *Polylepis*, *Gynoxys*, and *Buddleia* woodlands and adjacent shrubbery; in south more wide-ranging in shrub zone. Elevational range intermediate between Streaked (lower) and Andean (higher) tit-spinetails. Crown plain rufous (*pileata*, Lima; *latistriata*, west slope in south, not illustrated) or streaked with black (*cajabambae*; west slope north of Lima, and intermontane valleys). **VOICE** Call a sharp, high "*tchit.*" **ENDEMIC**

4 STREAKED TIT-SPINETAIL *Leptasthenura striata* * 15.5–16 cm (6–6¼ in)
Uncommon to fairly common on arid, sparsely vegetated slopes of western Andes (*superciliaris*, *striata*); also in dry, intermontane valleys in south central Peru (*albigularis*). Primarily 2000–4200 m, locally down to 900 m. Throat of *albigularis* whiter than other subspecies, and unspotted. Streaked is much like Rusty-crowned Tit-Spinetail, but shows more rufous or tawny on the closed wing, is whiter, nearly unmarked below, crown is tawnier (less rufous), and where the two overlap usually is found at lower elevations. Cf. also Andean Tit-Spinetail, with which Streaked overlaps in *Polylepis* scrub in southwest. **VOICE** Song a melancholy, but musical, descending series of high, ringing whistles: "*tchee-LEEa'LEEa'LEEa'LEEa'LEEa'LEEa'LEE.*" Calls a sharper chattered series of less musical "*tcht*" and "*tsit*" notes; also a lower, gruff "*tchut.*" **Ch**

5 PLAIN-MANTLED TIT-SPINETAIL *Leptasthenura aegithaloides* * 16–17 cm (6¼–6¾ in)
Locally fairly common along coast and foothills in southern Peru (*grisescens*), from 50 to 2000 m. Also in the southern Titicaca Basin (*berlepschi*), 4000 m. *Grisescens* occurs in thickets, often in hedgerows bordering agricultural land or pastures, and in lomas with cacti and scattered small trees. *Berlepschi* is poorly known in Peru; in adjacent Chile found in puna grasslands with scattered shrubs and in villages. Much like Streaked Tit-Spinetail, but upperparts uniformly gray, unmarked. **VOICE** Song (*berlepschi*) a rapid, slightly descending tinkling trill, "*ti ti-trreeeeeeeee.*" Calls a lower, less musical "*tre'ee'ee*" and scratchy chatters. Call of *grisescens* a high, metallic "*tchee-tchee-tchee*"; also a dry "*tchit.*" **Bo, Ch**

6 ANDEAN TIT-SPINETAIL *Leptasthenura andicola* * 16 cm (6¼ in)
Uncommon and local in high-elevation shrubbery and *Polylepis* woodland, 3500–4200 m. Large, dark colored tit-spinetail of very high elevations. Broadly overlaps with Rusty-crowned Tit-Spinetail in the west central Andes and Streaked Tit-Spinetail in southwest, but less common than either. Note prominent whitish superciliary and heavily streaked back, breast, and rufous crown. **VOICE** Call a ringing, high, tinkling series of "*trrree*" notes. **Co, E, Bo**

WHITE-BROWED
TIT-SPINETAIL

albigularis

pileata

cajabambae

RUSTY-CROWNED
TIT-SPINETAIL

STREAKED
TIT-SPINETAIL

TAWNY
TIT-SPINETAIL

berlepschi

grisescens

PLAIN-MANTLED
TIT-SPINETAIL

ANDEAN TIT-SPINETAIL

PLATE
140
THISTLETAILS AND STREAKED SPINETAILS

Thistletails are small, long-tailed ovenbirds found near treeline in the humid Andes. Tail is strongly graduated; rectrices, especially central pair, thin and "wispy." Solitary or in pairs, sometimes with mixed-species flocks. Forage within a few meters of ground, gleaning arthropods from leaves and stems. Often partially cock the tail and frequently flick the wings. Species are similar vocally and replace one another geographically. Cf. also dull-colored juveniles of Azara's and Rufous spinetails, and Rusty-fronted Canastero. Necklaced and Great spinetails are two streak breasted ovenbirds of dry scrub in northern Peru.

1 EYE-RINGED THISTLETAIL *Schizoeaca palpebralis* 19 cm (7–7½ in)
Known only from a small area along east slope of Andes in Junín, at 3000–3700 m. Note rusty brown upperparts, prominent white eyering, and large rusty chin spot. **VOICE** Like other thistletails. **ENDEMIC**

2 MOUSE-COLORED THISTLETAIL *Schizoeaca griseomurina* 19–21 cm (7½–8 in)
Fairly common, although secretive, at 2900–3300 m; locally as low as 2000 m. Plain, although usually with a fairly obvious white eyering. Only thistletail north and west of Marañón. **VOICE** Song like other thistletails. Call a descending "*pseeu.*" **E**

3 WHITE-CHINNED THISTLETAIL *Schizoeaca fuliginosa* * 19–19.5 cm (7½–7¾ in)
Fairly common along east slope of Andes, south of Marañón, to central Peru, at 2800–3300 m. May meet Eye-ringed Thistletail in southern Pasco or northern Junín (but contact is not yet known). Distinguished from other thistletails by more rufescent tone to upperparts and by prominent olive-gray (*peruviana*; Amazonas) or white (*plengei*; San Martín to Huánuco) superciliary. Chin white; upper throat of *plengei* also narrowly streaked white. **VOICE** Primary song a long, slightly accelerating, dry trill, rising until end when often falls abruptly: "*ti-ti-tri'i'i'i'i'i'i'i'i'u.*" Calls a rising, whiny "*wee*" and "*pee.*" **Co, E**

4 PUNA THISTLETAIL *Schizoeaca helleri* 17.5–18.5 cm (6¾–7¼ in)
Fairly common in southern Andes, at 2700–3700 m; occurs below treeline more than other thistletails. In Cuzco chin white, or rufous narrowly streaked with white. In Puno (undescribed subspecies? not illustrated) chin spot usually well-developed and rufous or orange-brown; also more olive on upperparts (can be very similar to *ayacuchensis* subspecies of Vilcabamba Thistletail but smaller and has pale lores; also no overlap). Cf. Rusty-fronted Canastero (found on drier slopes; brighter above, with a rusty tail and buffy underparts). **VOICE** Like other thistletails, but primary song often doubled. **Bo**

5 VILCABAMBA THISTLETAIL *Schizoeaca vilcabambae* * 18–19 cm (7¼–7½ in)
Fairly common in humid elfin forest and forest edge on both sides of Apurímac Valley, 2800–3600 m. Two subspecies: *ayacuchensis* (west of Río Apurímac), and *vilcabambae* (northern Cordillera Vilcabamba, east of Apurímac). Relatively dull, unpatterned thistletail; note rusty chin spot and vague mottling or scaling on gray breast. **VOICE** Like other thistletails. **ENDEMIC**

6 GREAT SPINETAIL *Siptornopsis hypochondriaca* 18.5 cm (7¼ in)
Uncommon, restricted to dry upper Marañón Valley, in arid montane scrub and low dry forest, 2150–2800 m. Singles or pairs forage in crowns of small trees and shrubs; also descends to ground. Similar in plumage to Necklaced Spinetail (no geographic overlap), but much larger. **VOICE** Song, usually in duet, a reeling, sputtering chatter of rich "*thk*" notes that rises and falls, accelerates and decelerates excitedly, with interspersed nasal "*dew*" notes. Calls a metallic "*TCHEE-TCHEE*" and "*tchep.*" Also a longer "*tu-ter-CHEE-CHEE-CHEE.*" **ENDEMIC**

7 NECKLACED SPINETAIL *Synallaxis stictothorax* * 12–13 cm (4¾–5 in)
Common in arid scrub on coastal plain in northwest, up to 300 m (*maculata*) and at 400–600 m in the middle Marañón and Chinchipe drainages (*chinchipensis*). Usually in pairs, often in mixed-species flocks. Breast streaking reduced or absent in southernmost coastal birds (undescribed subspecies). *Chinchipensis* has longer bill and is spotted, not streaked, on underparts. **VOICE** Song (*maculata*) an accelerating chatter, nearly always in duet: a squeaky "*kweet kweet kik-kik-kuit'kuit'kuit*" answered by a descending, dry rattle. Calls a single "*kweet*" and a squeaky "*di'vot.*" Song of undescribed subspecies a dry, rising-falling rattle in duet, usually introduced by several sharp "*tsweet*" notes. Calls "*tsweet*" or "*tswit-tswit*" and a dry "*tik.*" Song of *chinchipensis*, usually in duet, a rising trill followed by a loud squeak and a stuttered monotone trill: "*tr'r'r'r'up-KSEEP'tra'a'a.*" May be answered with the same song or a descending rattle. Calls include shortened song phrases, "*KSEEP-KSEEP'tra'a'a,*" and dry rattles. **E**

EYE-RINGED THISTLETAIL

MOUSE-COLORED
THISTLETAIL

peruviana

WHITE-CHINNED
THISTLETAIL

plengei

PUNA THISTLETAIL

vilcabambae

VILCABAMBA
THISTLETAIL

ayacuchensis

NECKLACED
SPINETAIL

maculata

GREAT SPINETAIL

chinchipensis

NECKLACED
SPINETAIL

undescribed
subsp.

PLATE
141

ANDEAN SPINETAILS AND SOFTTAIL

Synallaxis *spinetails usually forage in dense cover, close to ground, where difficult to observe. Seldom with mixed-species flocks. Species shown here are Andean; see also plates 142–143. Also shown on this plate are two uncommon Andean ovenbirds, Russet-mantled Softtail and White-browed Spinetail, that resemble* Synallaxis *spinetails.*

1 APURIMAC SPINETAIL *Synallaxis courseni* 19–20 cm (7½–8 in)
Fairly common to common at humid montane forest edge in upper Apurímac Valley, 2500–3500 m. Geographically replaces very similar Azara's Spinetail; slightly darker gray, and tail averages longer, but only significant difference is tail color: rufous in Azara's, blackish in Apurimac. Rectrices of many individuals of Apurimac, however, have rufous on inner webs. **VOICE** Not distinguishable from typical voice of Azara's. **ENDEMIC**

2 AZARA'S SPINETAIL *Synallaxis azarae* * 16.5–17.5 cm (6½–7 in)
Most common and widespread spinetail of Andes, 1250–3100 m; also locally down to 600 m in Tumbes. Primarily at humid cloud forest edge; also inhabits scrub in intermontane valleys, hedgerows, and *Polylepis* woods. *Elegantior* group of northwest (both slopes of western Andes) browner above and whiter below; *azarae* group of eastern Andes from Amazonas south is darker and grayer. Birds similar to both groups occur on east side of Marañón Valley. All populations have rufous crown and mostly rufous wings; tail usually entirely rufous (but occasionally blackish in Cuzco). Juveniles are plain brown above (including tail), buffy below. **VOICE** Song a high, plaintive "*pip-squeak*" or "*pip-puee?*," second note rising slightly. Often one (female?) answers with a low chatter. In Mantaro Valley, song a more modulated "*keek-gureh*," second note lower. Calls a quiet growl or "*tchurrt*," mewing "*weee?*" notes, single "*pip*," and a series of rising notes, "*weet-weet-weet-weet-weet....*" Cf. song of Rufous Spinetail. **Co, E, Bo**

3 RUSSET-BELLIED SPINETAIL *Synallaxis zimmeri* 16.5 cm (6½ in)
Fairly common but very local along west slope of Andes, 2100–2900 m. Singly or in pairs, in arid montane scrub; sometimes in adjacent denser forest or riparian thickets. Note gray and brown upperparts, buffy underparts, and rufous-chestnut wing coverts; no similar species occurs with it. **VOICE** Song a mewing chatter: "*p'kuit-kuit*," the number of "*kuit*'s" variable. Resembles song of *maculata* Necklaced Spinetail. Calls a nasal, wheezy "*tu-vit*" or squeakier "*djewit?*"; also a dry rattle. **ENDEMIC**

4 RUFOUS SPINETAIL *Synallaxis unirufa* * 17–18 cm (6¾–7 in)
Fairly common in humid montane forest and at forest edge along east slope of Andes, 1700–3300 m. Forages in understory, usually within 1–2 m of ground. Adult rufous and long-tailed; cf. larger Rufous Wren and Russet-mantled Softtail. Juvenile dusky brown; much darker than juvenile Azara's Spinetail. **VOICE** Song north and west of Río Marañón (*unirufa*) 2 rising notes, second slightly higher than first: "*weet-weet*." Song of *ochrogaster* (south of Marañón) a repeated rising, mewing note: "*dwee? dwee? dwee?....*" Call a sharp, dry "*keet!*" or "*ki-it!*" **Co, E**

5 RUSSET-MANTLED SOFTTAIL *Thripophaga berlepschi* 18 cm (7 in)
Cranioleuca-like in size, behavior, and voice; found in humid montane forest along east slope of northern Andes, 3050–3400 m, locally down to 2500 m. Rare to uncommon; usually with mixed-species flocks. White-browed Spinetail is smaller, shorter tailed, and has white throat and superciliary. Rufous Spinetail superficially similar, but lacks whitish or grayish forecrown, is more confined to understory, and rarely with mixed-species flocks. Also cf. Sharpe's and Peruvian wrens. **VOICE** Primary song a short, descending, high-pitched chatter: "*tchee tchee-tchi-tchi'trrr*." Very similar to Marcapata Spinetail (no range overlap). **ENDEMIC**

6 WHITE-BROWED SPINETAIL *Hellmayrea gularis* * 13–13.5 cm (5–5¼ in)
Uncommon in forest on east slope of Andes, 2900–3700 m. Singles and pairs forage in dense bamboo thickets and other tangled vegetation within 3 m of ground. Creeps along branches, probing bark, clumps of mosses, and internodes of bamboo stalks. Note short spiky tail, white throat. South of Río Marañón bright rufous-brown (*ochrogaster*); north and west of Marañón paler and buffier below (*gularis*; not illustrated). Juvenile duller, partially scaled on breast. Rufous Spinetail is larger with a long tail, rufous throat. **VOICE** Song (*gularis*) an accelerating and descending chatter of high, piercing notes becoming a lower trill: "*psee psi-psi-psi'tr'r'r'r'r'r*," often answered by a dry chatter from the mate (female?). Call a high, descending "*pseeu*." **Co, E**

APURIMAC SPINETAIL

juv.

AZARA'S
SPINETAIL
azarae group

ad.

RUSSET-BELLIED SPINETAIL

juv.

AZARA'S SPINETAIL
elegantior group

ad.

juv.

RUFOUS SPINETAIL

RUSSET-MANTLED
SOFTTAIL

ad.

juv.

ad.

WHITE-BROWED SPINETAIL

PLATE
142

LOWLAND SPINETAILS I

Spinetails on this plate all are in the lowlands of eastern Peru. These species occupy a variety of habitats, including forest edge and grasslands with scattered trees and shrubs.

1 MARAÑON SPINETAIL *Synallaxis maranonica* 14.5–15 cm (5¾–6 in)
Restricted to dry portions of middle Marañón Valley and tributaries. 450–1800 m. Locally fairly common in understory of deciduous forest, in second growth, and in riparian thickets. Very similar to Plain-crowned Spinetail (no geographic overlap), but has grayish (not whitish) throat, gray underparts, reddish-tinged back, and rounded tail feathers (pointed in Plain-crowned). **VOICE** Song, sometimes in duet, a whining, squeaky *"whEEu pi'EEEW,"* first note rising and falling, second falling. Call a descending, mewed *"peeeu."* **E**

2 PLAIN-CROWNED SPINETAIL *Synallaxis gujanensis* * 16–16.5 cm (6¼–6½ in)
Fairly common in Amazonia. Below 500 m in north; mostly below 1000 m in south, locally to 1300 m. Most widespread dull-crowned *Synallaxis*, found in undergrowth of forest-edge and riverine woodland; in north also on wooded river islands. No black on throat; throat usually white, but pale throat is less obvious in darker, grayer undescribed subspecies (not illustrated) from semiarid Huallaga Valley. Cf. White-bellied and Marañon spinetails. **VOICE** Song in northeast (Amazon, Yavarí, and Napo drainages) 2-noted with a noticeable pause between notes: *"KEEK way"* or *"KEEK'uh way,"* first note sharper and higher, second rising. Song in rest of Peru 3-noted: *"pew pit-weet?"* first note descending and last rising. Calls a rising *"puee?,"* a short rattle, and a stuttered *"p'pit weet?"* **Co, E, Br, Bo**

3 CINEREOUS-BREASTED SPINETAIL *Synallaxis hypospodia* 16 cm (6¼ in)
Very local, in dry valleys (Mayo, 1000–1400 m; Urubamba, 1050 m), and Pampas del Heath (300 m). Fairly common in grassland with scattered shrubs and woodlots. Very similar to Dark-breasted Spinetail, but with different voice and blackish (not olive-brown) tail (less useful in south, where Dark-breasted is darker overall). Also note more rounded tips to rectrices and more extensive rufous of wings (confined to wing coverts in Dark-breasted). **VOICE** Song similar to Dark-breasted, but longer, more notes, rising before falling in pitch: *"pit pi-pi-PI-PI'PI'pi'pi'pi'pi'pi'pi-chew."* Calls a low growl; a rising-falling chatter of musical notes *"trrrr wee'wee'wee'wee'wee'wee...";* and a shorter *"weet-wi-wi."* **Br, Bo**

4 DARK-BREASTED SPINETAIL *Synallaxis albigularis* * 15–16 cm (6–6¼ in)
Widespread and fairly common in Amazonia, although scarce or local in southeast; up to 1050 m, locally to 1800 m in San Martín. Occurs in early successional vegetation, including on river islands. Most common and widespread rufous-crowned Amazonian *Synallaxis*. Differs from Cabanis's and Dusky spinetails (foothills) by brighter orange-rufous crown with grayish forecrown, olive-brown (not chestnut) tail, less extensive rufous on wings, and pale gray (not gray-brown) breast. Cf. also Cinereous-breasted Spinetail, local in savanna. Juvenile buffy brown (lacks rufous on crown or wings); cf. Plain-crowned Spinetail. Similar Azara's Spinetail occurs above 1200 m, has a rufous tail, and different song. **VOICE** Song a musical descending series: *"deet dee-dee-dee,"* occasionally ending with a quiet, descending trill: *"deet dee-dee-dee-trrru."* Often answered with a rising series: *"dwee-dwee-dwee."* Calls a short *"djurt,"* often in chattered phrases; also a longer series of *"dwee-dwee-dwee-dwee..."* notes. **Co, E, Br, Bo**

5 PALE-BREASTED SPINETAIL *Synallaxis albescens* * 14.5 cm (5¼ in)
Barely reaches eastern Peru. Possibly only a seasonal visitor to southeast, where recorded from shrubby savanna (Pampas del Heath) and, very locally, tall grass in river-edge scrub. Also possible on river islands along Amazon, as is known from adjacent Colombia. Small, pale spinetail with rufous crown; note small size, pale throat and underparts, brown tail, and voice. **VOICE** Song (Bolivia) *"weet-jeer,"* first note rising, second burry and descending. Sounds remarkably like a tyrant flycatcher. Call a descending, sneezy *"pseeu!"* **Co, Br, Bo**

6 WHITE-BELLIED SPINETAIL *Synallaxis propinqua* 14.5–15 cm (5¼–6 in)
Locally common on islands in large Amazonian rivers, in grassy places with scattered bushes and short trees. During periods of high water may occur in more varied vegetation remaining above water on high ground. Plain, with no rufous on crown, and relatively long bill. Most like Plain-crowned Spinetail, but has dark throat patch and occurs in open areas, not woodland undergrowth or tall forest-edge second growth. Shares shrubby thickets on islands with Dark-breasted Spinetail. **VOICE** Song a harsh, grating chatter: *"djr djr-djr'djr'djr'djr'djr'djr'djr'djr'djr-djr."* Calls a low, drawn out, raspy snarl *"rrhhhhh";* a dry, scratchy *"gri-grrreh";* and a longer, descending series of growls: *"ri-gri-gri-gri-grreh."* Also a rapid chatter of ticking notes. **Co, E, Br, Bo**

MARAÑON SPINETAIL

juv.

ad.

PLAIN-CROWNED
SPINETAIL

CINEREOUS-BREASTED
SPINETAIL

DARK-BREASTED
SPINETAIL

juv.

ad.

PALE-BREASTED SPINETAIL

WHITE-BELLIED SPINETAIL

PLATE
143

LOWLAND SPINETAILS II

Cabanis's Spinetail is widespread in Andean foothills and adjacent lowlands in central and southern Peru. Ruddy Spinetail is the only widely distributed species that is found in the interior of humid forest in eastern Peru. The four other species on this plate have restricted distributions in Peru (Dusky, Blackish-headed, and Slaty spinetails) or are very patchily distributed (Chestnut-throated Spinetail).

1 DUSKY SPINETAIL *Synallaxis moesta* * 16 cm (6¼ in)

Uncommon and perhaps local in foothills on east slope of Andes and adjacent lowlands, up to 1250 m. Found in second growth at edge of humid forest. Similar in pattern to Azara's and Dark-breasted Spinetails, but darker, with chestnut (not rufous) wings and chestnut tail. **VOICE** Song a deep, rich stuttering machine-gun-like chatter: "*grr'r'r'r'r'r'r'r'r'r.*" Call a rich "*djik*" or "*di-djik,*" sometimes given in chattered series. **Co, E**

2 CABANIS'S SPINETAIL *Synallaxis cabanisi* * 15.5 cm (6 in)

Uncommon to locally fairly common below 1400 m along east slope of Andes and in adjacent lowlands. Found in successional habitats such as bamboo thickets (especially in southern Peru), river-edge thickets (*Gynerium*), and second growth. Note the chestnut (not rufous) wings and tail, whitish malar, and olive-brown (not gray) underparts. Crown duller in immature. No overlap with Dusky Spinetail, which is gray (not olive-brown) on the underparts. **VOICE** Song a quiet, deliberate series of nasal "*nyip*" or "*nyip-nyip*" notes, sometimes extended into a more excited-sounding chatter, rising slightly in pitch, "*RR-nyip RR-nyipnyip RRnyipnyipnyipnyip-nyip.*" Call a dry, descending rattle: "*ti-trrrrrrr.*" **Br, Bo**

3 CHESTNUT-THROATED SPINETAIL *Synallaxis cherriei* * 13–14 cm (5–5½ in)

Very local in Amazonia, primarily near base of Andes, 500–1100 m. Habitat requirements not well understood (and may vary geographically?); has been found in early second growth (San Martín), understory of mature humid forest (Apurímac Valley), and a mosaic of young second growth and young bamboo on a river terrace (Cuzco). Very similar to Ruddy Spinetail. Chin is chestnut or rufous (not black; Ruddy's black chin can be difficult to see in the field) and belly is gray, contrasting more strongly with rufous breast. Juvenile brown, not rufous, with gray belly and black tail. **VOICE** Song a trilled note followed by a rising, musical note: "*prrrrrt-pree?*" Calls a dry "*tck*" or "*trt*"; also a descending rattle: "*tuee-tee-ti-ti'trrrrrrrr,*" very like a call of Cabanis's Spinetail (limited overlap). **E, Br, Bo**

4 RUDDY SPINETAIL *Synallaxis rutilans* * 14–15 cm (5½–6 in)

Widespread but uncommon to locally fairly common in Amazonia. In contrast to most *Synallaxis*, occupies the interior of humid tropical forest, where it occurs in the understory, especially in dense vegetation at treefalls and other interior forest light gaps. Extensively chestnut with small black throat patch and blackish tail. The only widespread chestnut-brown spinetail in the lowlands. Juvenile duller. **VOICE** Song a sharp note followed by a rising, mewing note: "*pit-kuee?*" or "*keet-kuu'it?*" Call a dry, descending rattle: "*trrrrrr.*" **Co, E, Br, Bo**

5 BLACKISH-HEADED SPINETAIL *Synallaxis tithys* 14.5 cm (5¼ in)

In Peru only in semideciduous forests in Tumbes, 400– 750 m, where fairly common. Overlaps with Azara's and Slaty spinetails; differs from both by blackish face and lack of rufous crown patch. Also separated from Azara's by blackish, not rufous, tail; and from Slaty by brighter color to wing coverts and paler underparts. Juvenile duller, but plumage pattern similar. **VOICE** Song a rising, slightly decelerating chatter: "*tu'tu'tu'tu'te-ti?*" Calls a loud, nasal rising series, "*geer-geer geer-geer geer-geer!*"; a ringing "*pee-pee-pee,*" a short, descending "*pew*"; and a dry "*tick.*" **E**

6 SLATY SPINETAIL *Synallaxis brachyura* * 16–16.5 cm (6¼–6½ in)

In Peru only in humid evergreen forests at 750 m in Tumbes, where primarily in thickets at forest edge. Overlaps with two other species, Azara's and Blackish-headed spinetails. Slaty Spinetail is much darker, both above and below, than the local population of Azara's, and has a dusky, not rufous, tail. See Blackish-headed. **VOICE** Song a low, gruff, descending, accelerating churred chatter: "*tjik-tje'tjr'r'r'r.*" Call a low, squeaky "*kyuk*" or "*ku-tik.*" **Co, E**

DUSKY SPINETAIL

ad.

juv.

CABANIS'S SPINETAIL

CHESTNUT-
THROATED
SPINETAIL

ad.

ad.

juv.

ad.

RUDDY SPINETAIL

juv.

BLACKISH-HEADED
SPINETAIL

juv.

ad.

SLATY SPINETAIL

juv.

ad.

PLATE
144

RIVERINE SPINETAILS, SOFTTAIL, AND PLUSHCROWN

Certhiaxis spinetails are found along rivers in Amazonia, where individuals or widely spaced pairs forage in marsh grasses, bushes, and other vegetation low over water at oxbow lakes, or in marshes on river islands. Rusty-backed and Parker's spinetails are two Amazonian Cranioleuca (see plate 145), superficially similar to Certhiaxis. Plain Softtail and Orange-fronted Plushcrown are two peculiar Amazonian ovenbirds.

1 **[YELLOW-CHINNED SPINETAIL** Certhiaxis cinnamomeus] * 14–14.5 cm (5½–5¾ in)

Status unclear. Apparently local along eastern Amazon; perhaps more widespread. Also a sight record from Madre de Dios. May have greater preference for floating vegetation than does very similar Red-and-white Spinetail. Distinguished by pale yellow chin or upper throat, grayish lores, and pale superciliary; but some of these features, especially color of throat and lores, can be difficult to see in the field. **VOICE** Song (Bolivia) a low, gravelly, rising-falling rattle: "*p-p-p'rrrrRRRRrrrrrrrr.*" Very similar to Red-and-white, but accelerates more noticeably. Call a rich "*tchew.*" **Co, Br, Bo**

2 **RED-AND-WHITE SPINETAIL** Certhiaxis mustelinus 14 cm (5½ in)

Fairly common in marsh habitats in northern and central Amazonia along larger rivers. Two-toned, red above and white below; whiter below than other lowland spinetails (such as Parker's and Rusty-backed spinetails), with relatively long but very slender, all-black bill. **VOICE** Song a low, gravelly, rising-falling rattle reminiscent of the whinny of several *Laterallus* crakes: "*p'p'p'rrrrRRRRrrrrrrr.*" Sometimes given in duet, the mate responding with a slow series of "*dew*" notes. Calls "*dew,*" given singly, doubled, or in a series; also a drier "*pi'pit.*" **Co, Br**

RUSTY-BACKED SPINETAIL Cranioleuca vulpina * 14–14.5 cm (5½–5¾ in)

Status unclear. Known from a few sites in Amazonia (lower Río Yavarí; Yarinacocha), but probably more widespread. Forages singly, in pairs, or in small groups within a few meters of ground in flooded forests and at lake margins. Very similar to Parker's Spinetail, which primarily is on river islands, but duskier below with more sharply defined white superciliary, and smaller bill; best distinguished by voice. Cf. also Red-and-white Spinetail. **VOICE** Song (Brazil) a descending series of squeaky notes ending in a low churred chatter: "*tree tleep-tleep-tleep-tleep'tuk'tk'tk.*" Call a rising "*tu'leep?*" **Co, Br, Bo**

3 **PARKER'S SPINETAIL** Cranioleuca vulpecula 15–16 cm (6–6¼ in)

Uncommon to fairly common on recently formed river islands and along banks of large rivers, in shrubby *Tessaria* thickets and small trees. Locally in old pastures with a mixture of tall grasses, bushes, and small trees. Arboreal, usually in pairs that forage at all heights. Cf. Red-and-white Spinetail and Lesser Hornero; see also Rusty-backed Spinetail. **VOICE** Song an accelerating, rising-falling chatter of nasal notes: "*teer teew-tew'tu'tutrrr.*" Calls "*tew*" or "*tu-tu*"; also a longer, descending chatter: "*tchew-tew'tu'tu.*" **Co, E, Br, Bo**

4 **PLAIN SOFTTAIL** Thripophaga fusciceps * 15–16 cm (6–6¼ in)

Uncommon and local in Amazonia, below 650 m. Found in midstory in vine tangles, forest edge, and advanced second growth, along rivers and streams and in seasonally flooded forest. Usually encountered as pairs or small groups, seldom with mixed-species flocks. Nondescript; smaller than foliage-gleaners. The small size, almost total lack of pattern to the brown plumage, and habitat are the best clues to identifying this scarce species. Also may be seen attending hanging, sacklike nest (similar foliage-gleaners nest in holes). **VOICE** Song an accelerating chatter becoming a long (may be over 30 sec), fairly low, reeling, churring rattle: "*tchee-tchee-tchi-tchi'tchrrr'r'r'r'r'r'r'tchrrr'r'r'r' rtchrrr'r'r'r'r.*" Call low bursts of chatters: "*tchrr'r'rt.*" **Co, E, Br, Bo**

5 **ORANGE-FRONTED PLUSHCROWN** Metopothrix aurantiaca 11.5 cm (4½ in)

Uncommon to locally fairly common in Amazonia, but scarce or absent at many localities. Primarily in river floodplains in canopy of advanced second growth, borders of forest, and river-edge forest; in south also occurs in foothills up to 1100 m. Encountered as singles, pairs, or small groups; sometimes associates with mixed-species flocks, but often forages apart. Not easily confused with any other ovenbird. Orange tarsi of plushcrown are distinctive, but compare (especially immature) to small tanagers such as Orange-headed Tanager, or to female Yellow Warbler. **VOICE** Song (?) a series of 2–5 high "*pseet*" notes. Calls very high "*ti*" and "*psee*" notes. Voice very reminiscent of some piculets. **Co, E, Br, Bo**

YELLOW-CHINNED
SPINETAIL

RED-AND-WHITE
SPINETAIL

PARKER'S SPINETAIL

ad.

PLAIN
SOFTTAIL

RUSTY-BACKED SPINETAIL

juv.

ad.

ORANGE-FRONTED
PLUSHCROWN

juv.

PLATE
145

CRANIOLEUCA SPINETAILS

Cranioleuca *spinetails are small to medium-sized ovenbirds with relatively long, graduated rufous tails. More arboreal than* Synallaxis *spinetails, and more frequently associated with mixed-species flocks. See also plate 144.*

1 ASH-BROWED SPINETAIL *Cranioleuca curtata* * 15 cm (6 in)

Uncommon, inconspicuous bird of humid montane forest, 800–2000 m, along east slope of Andes. Pairs or small family groups usually seen with mixed-species flocks in canopy or midstory. Like other *Cranioleuca*, forages by creeping and hopping along moss-covered limbs, pausing to probe epiphytic growth. Chestnut crown and shoulders, plain underparts, and small size separate it from other montane ovenbirds. Ochraceous juveniles are much smaller, and smaller billed, than other tawny montane ovenbirds, such as Rufous-rumped and Buff-fronted foliage-gleaners. **VOICE** Primary song an accelerating, descending series of high, peeping, metallic notes: "*pee pee-pee'pi'pi'pi'pipitrrrr.*" Call a high, metallic "*teep.*" **Co, E, Bo**

2 SPECKLED SPINETAIL *Cranioleuca gutturata* 14.5–15.5 cm (5¾–6 in)

Widespread, but local and uncommon in Amazonia, up to 850 m, locally to 1100 m. Found in vine tangles in midstory of low-lying and seasonally flooded forest; less common in terra firme. Usually in pairs with mixed-species flocks. Searches curled, dead leaves, also clumps of epiphytes. Only small spinetail with rufous crown, wings, and tail of midstory in Amazonia; also note speckled breast and flanks. Iris often pale, yellow or whitish. Juvenile has gray crown and paler breast speckles. Much smaller than foliage-gleaners. **VOICE** Primary song a high, slow, evenly paced series of piercing whistles, the first lowest: "*tsew tsee tsee tsee tsee.*" Call thin, high "*tsew*" notes. **Co, E, Br, Bo**

3 MARCAPATA SPINETAIL *Cranioleuca marcapatae* * 16 cm (6¼ in)

Two populations: white-crested *weskei* in Cordillera Vilcabamba and rufous-crested *marcapatae* of eastern Cuzco. Uncommon to fairly common in *Chusquea* bamboo thickets and in humid forest understory, 2400 to 3350 m. *Weskei* very like Light-crowned Spinetail, but no overlap; also has buff wash on malars and pale superciliary. Nominate *marcapatae* similar to Ash-browed Spinetail of lower elevations (below 2000 m) but is less arboreal and has a more prominent superciliary and whiter throat. **VOICE** Primary song (*marcapatae*) a thin, descending, accelerating series of high, liquid notes: "*tew ti-ti-ti'ti'titititi.*" Calls a high, liquid "*tew-tik*" and "*tewp.*" **ENDEMIC**

4 CREAMY-CRESTED SPINETAIL *Cranioleuca albicapilla* * 17 cm (6¼ in)

Locally fairly common in central and southern Andes, 2500–3800 m. Inhabits semihumid shrubland with scattered trees and remnant woodlands (including *Polylepis*) on upper slopes of intermontane valleys. Also locally in cloud forest and alder (*Alnus*) thickets, especially along streams. Birds in Junín (nominate *albicapilla*) have paler crowns, duller underparts, and more rufous in wings than birds farther south (*albigula*). **VOICE** Primary song a squeaky, accelerating, descending series: "*tee tleep-tlee-tee'ti'trr.*" Calls a rising, squeaky "*tlee'lee*"; "*dew*"; and a rapidly chattered series of "*tleep*" notes. Vocalizations very similar to those of Line-cheeked Spinetail. **ENDEMIC**

5 LIGHT-CROWNED SPINETAIL *Cranioleuca albiceps* * 14 cm (5½ in)

Fairly common, but only in high elevation (2750–3200 m) montane humid forest in Puno. Habitat and behavior much like that of Marcapata Spinetail. Crown usually dull white but may be buffy (at least in Bolivia); no overlap with the white-crested subspecies of Marcapata. **VOICE** Primary song (Bolivia) a descending, accelerating chatter of high, piping notes: "*PEE pee-pi'pi'pipipi.*" Call a chattered series of "*twee*" notes. **Bo**

6 LINE-CHEEKED SPINETAIL *Cranioleuca antisiensis* * *antisiensis* group 14.5–15.5 cm (5¾–6¼ in); *baroni* group 17.5–19 cm (6¼ –7½ in)

Widespread and locally common in Andes of northern and central Peru, at 2000–4400 m (locally down to 850 m on west slope in north). Found in semihumid forest, cloud forest, *Polylepis* and alder (*Alnus*) woods, epiphyte-laden thorn forest, and hedgerows. Geographically variable. Northern birds are browner and smaller (*antisiensis* group), southern populations generally grayer and larger (*baroni* group; "Baron's" Spinetail), but variation is complex (and requires further study); some populations seem intermediate, in other regions adjacent populations may differ strikingly in size but not in plumage, or in plumage but not in size. All populations have rufous crown, wings, and tail; Azara's Spinetail also has rufous crown and tail but is less arboreal and lacks prominent white superciliary. **VOICE** Primary song a squeaky, accelerating, descending series: "*tee tseep-tsee-tee'ti'trr.*" Calls a rising, squeaky "*tlee'lee*" and a rapidly chattered series of "*dree*" notes. **E**

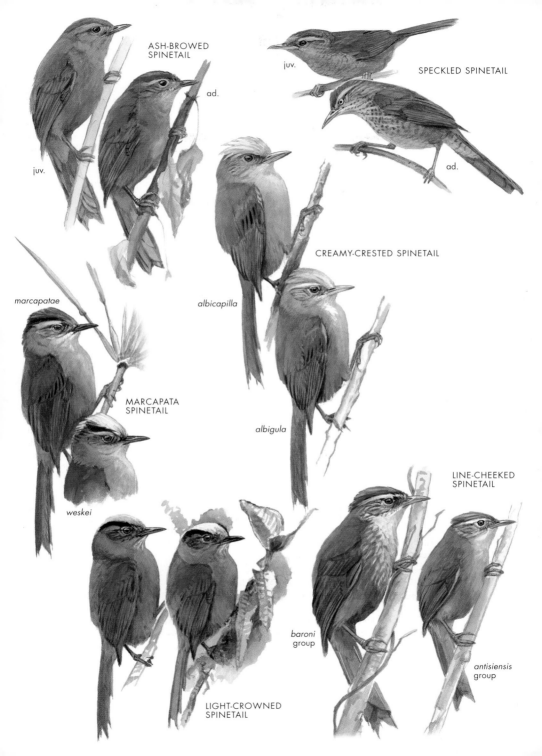

ASH-BROWED
SPINETAIL

juv.

ad.

SPECKLED SPINETAIL

juv.

ad.

CREAMY-CRESTED SPINETAIL

marcapatae

albicapilla

MARCAPATA
SPINETAIL

albigula

weskei

LINE-CHEEKED
SPINETAIL

baroni
group

antisiensis
group

LIGHT-CROWNED
SPINETAIL

PLATE
146

CANASTEROS

Canasteros are a large group of Andean ovenbirds found in open habitats, usually at high elevations. They are dull colored with long, graduated tails. Details of the throat pattern, habitat and distribution, and tail pattern are important for identification. Many species have similar songs, a dry accelerating trill. See also plates 147 and 148.

1 CACTUS CANASTERO *Asthenes cactorum* * 14.5 cm (5¾ in)
Uncommon or locally common on western slopes of the Andes. Found at 100–450 m in lomas of Lima and Arequipa; also on lower slopes of Andes, 800–2400, from Lima south to Arequipa. Found at low densities, as single individuals or in pairs. Forages on the ground, also investigates the arms of columnar cacti and boulders. Similar in overall pattern to Cordilleran Canastero, but they do not overlap in elevation; Cactus also has a much longer bill. Cactus is much paler than the two other west slope canasteros, Creamy-breasted and Canyon; cf. also House Wren. **VOICE** Song (?) a short, rapid, dry trill: "*trrrrr.*" **ENDEMIC**

2 CORDILLERAN CANASTERO *Asthenes modesta* * 14.5–15 cm (5¾–6 in)
Common in puna at 3600–4600 m. Most often in arid areas with relatively short grass. Highly terrestrial. Usually encountered as solitary individuals, running quickly across the ground or hopping onto rocks. Frequently cocks its tail. A drab, unpatterned canastero. Paler overall than Streak-throated Canastero, with a plain back (but back markings of Streak-throated can be obscure), fairly plain throat and breast, and more rufous in the tail (relatively broad margins or tips on outer 3–4 pairs of rectrices). **VOICE** Song (Puno) a rapid, rising-falling, twittering chatter: "*tur-turturtetetete-ter-tur.*" Call a quiet, piping "*pi,*" sometimes in series. **Bo, Ch**

3 STREAK-THROATED CANASTERO *Asthenes humilis* * 15–16.5 cm (6–6½ in)
Common in high elevation grasslands at 3700–4800 m, locally to 3100 m in north. Prefers rocky, short-grass areas devoid of bushes. Usually encountered as solitary individuals, or less often in pairs. Forages on ground among grasses, or on bare ground between grass tussocks. Most similar to Cordilleran Canastero, but note dusky streaks on the back (sometimes difficult to see). Streak-throated also has a more prominently streaked throat, breast, and sides of the face, and shows little or no rufous in the tail. **VOICE** Primary song a stuttering series of high, ringing trills: "*tree'e'e-tree'e'e-tree'e'e.*" Call a series of piping "*pi*" notes. **Bo**

4 RUSTY-FRONTED CANASTERO *Asthenes ottonis* 18 cm (7 in)
Locally fairly common in dense shrubbery and shrub/cactus mosaics in dry intermontane valleys in central Peru, 2900–4000 m; much rarer in *Polylepis* forest. Generally secretive, staying hidden within bushes. Active, moves constantly, occasionally runs on ground. The only small brown bird in its habitat with a very long reddish tail. Cf. Streak-fronted Thornbird and House Wren. **VOICE** Song a dry, accelerating, descending trill: "*tzree-tzree-tzi'ti'ti'ti'ti'tu.*" Calls a scraping "*dzzzz,*" a descending, mewing "*peew,*" and a sharp, descending "*tsee.*" **ENDEMIC**

5 CANYON CANASTERO *Asthenes pudibunda* * 17 cm (6¾ in)
Fairly common on western slope of Andes, at 2450–4000 m on shrubby, often rock-strewn, slopes or in arid forest (including *Polylepis*). Largely arboreal, but occasionally forages on ground. Encountered singly or in pairs, working through shrubs and trees. Frequently cocks its tail. A drab-colored, long-tailed bird; note the rusty chin spot and long reddish brown tail. No geographic overlap with Rusty-fronted Canastero of interior valleys. Cf. House Wren. **VOICE** Song an accelerating, rising-falling, chatter of ringing notes: "*tur-turturtetititititi-ter.*" Call a series of sharp "*pit*" notes. **Ch**

6 LINE-FRONTED CANASTERO *Asthenes urubambensis* * 16–17 cm (6¼–6¾ in)
Uncommon in treeline forest and *Polylepis* forest along crest of eastern slope of Andes, 3100–3800 m. Two disjunct populations: northern, plain-backed *huallagae*, and southern, streaked-backed *urubambensis*. Primarily arboreal (unlike other canasteros). Hops along lower limbs of *Polylepis* and other trees and shrubs, probing mosses, bark, and leaf clusters. Less frequently encountered on ground, foraging underneath dense cover. Other streaked canasteros are in open grasslands, lack the narrow white superciliary, and have more obvious rufous or reddish wing edgings. **VOICE** Song a dry, accelerating, descending trill that may have a stuttering quality: "*tree'ti-treeti-treeti'titrrrrrrrrrru.*" Call a descending, clear "*teew.*" **Bo**

CORDILLERAN CANASTERO

CACTUS CANASTERO

STREAK-THROATED CANASTERO

RUSTY-FRONTED CANASTERO

urubambensis

CANYON CANASTERO

ad.

LINE-FRONTED CANASTERO

huallagae

juv.

PLATE
147

GRASSLAND CANASTEROS

The canasteros shown here occupy shrublands or dry grasslands. They fall into two groups of geographically replacing species. Streak-backed and Puna canasteros are buffy brown, with unstreaked breasts but brown upperparts streaked with black or dusky; Streak-backed is widespread (although patchily distributed), whereas Puna is geographically restricted. Many-striped, Junin, and Scribble-tailed canasteros, in contrast, are darker above, streaked with buff or whitish; breasts may be plain or streaked with dusky. Cf. Line-fronted Canastero (plate 146) and Sedge Wren. Many-striped is the most widely distributed of the three and apparently does not overlap with the other two. Junin and Scribble-tailed both are more geographically restricted but also overlap one another very locally.

1 STREAK-BACKED CANASTERO *Asthenes wyatti* * 16–18 cm (6¼–7 in)
Locally common, but patchily distributed in high-elevation grasslands in the Andes, 3500–4600 m, locally down to 3000 m. Found in open expanses of bunch grass, or in grasslands with scattered shrubs. Largely terrestrial. Usually encountered as single individuals, or in well-spaced pairs, that run furtively along the ground between clumps of grass. A long-tailed, conspicuously buffy-colored canastero; the upper parts are brown with black streaks, not dark with pale streaks as in Junin, Many-striped, and Scribble-tailed canasteros. In the Titicaca Basin, see Puna Canastero. **VOICE** Song a rapid, dry, accelerating trill: "*tur-turtrtrtrtrtrtrtri'i'i'i'ew.*" Calls a mewing "*pi,*" sometimes in series; also a descending, metallic series of "*tink*" notes. **Co, E, Bo**

2 PUNA CANASTERO *Asthenes sclateri* * 18–19 cm (7–7½ in)
Replaces Streak-backed Canastero in western and southern Titicaca Basin (Puno); note that Streak-backed is found on north side of Titicaca Basin. Fairly common at 3800–4150 m in open expanses of bunch grass, especially where the grass is tall. Very similar to Streak-backed, but the 3 outer rectrices are dusky, tipped with tawny or rufous (rather than entirely rufous as in Streak-backed). **VOICE** Song a rapid, accelerating, descending trill, becoming drier at end: "*tur-turtrtrtrtrtrtrtri'i'i'i'ew.*" Calls a quiet, piping "*pi,*" also a twittering "*teep,*" sometimes in series. **Bo**

3 JUNIN CANASTERO *Asthenes virgata* 18 cm (7 in)
Uncommon to locally fairly common in high-elevation grasslands of central and southern Peru, 3300–4600. Found in tall bunch grass, sometimes in areas with scattered bushes near edge of *Polylepis* forest. Forages on ground among bunch grass; when flushed, may fly toward and drop into cover at base of a bush. In early morning sings from tops of bushes. Very similar to Many-striped Canastero (*taczanowskii*), but no known overlap; differs by orange-buff or pale rufous chin spot (lacking in *taczanowskii*), remiges are browner with reduced rufous wing edging, and streaking on underparts is paler, more olive brown. Cf. Scribble-tailed Canastero, with which it overlaps locally in south. **VOICE** Song a dry, accelerating, descending trill sometimes with a stuttering quality: "*tzree-tzree-tzree'ti'ti'ti'ti'ti-ti'ti'ti-ti'ti'tu.*" **ENDEMIC**

4 MANY-STRIPED CANASTERO *Asthenes flammulata* * 16.5–18 cm (6½–7 in)
Fairly common in paramo and puna grasslands at 2900–4400 m, south to central Peru. Darker subspecies *flammulata*, with more prominent rusty chin spot, occurs near Ecuadorian border; *taczanowskii*, paler, less streaked on breast, and with chin spot reduced, occurs from central Cajamarca south. Usually found in grassland with scattered shrubs. A widely distributed "streaked" canastero of high-elevation grasslands; overlaps extensively with Streak-backed Canastero, but that species is brown above streaked dusky (not dark brown streaked with buff). Replaced in central and southern Peru by Junin Canastero. **VOICE** Song a dry, accelerating, descending trill: "*tzree-tzree-tzree'ti'ti'ti'ti'ti'ti'ti'ti'ti'ti'tu.*" Calls a low, descending mewed "*eew*"; a longer rising-falling "*weeeew*"; and a buzzy "*trzzew.*" **Co, E**

5 SCRIBBLE-TAILED CANASTERO *Asthenes maculicauda* 17–18 cm (6¼–7)
Fairly common, but very local; known from a few high-elevation (3000–3950 m) grasslands in Cuzco and Puno. Occurs in relatively lush, tall bunch grass, sometimes with scattered small bushes; where it overlaps with Junin Canastero, prefers more humid paramo with taller grasses. Has an unstreaked rufous forecrown and a plain throat, and the central rectrices are extensively "scribbled" with rufous and black ("scribbles" reduced or lacking in Junin). **VOICE** Song a dry, accelerating, descending trill sometimes with a stuttering quality: "*tzree-tzree-tzree'ti'ti'ti'ti-ti'ti'ti-ti'ti'ti-ti'ti'tu.*" Calls a clear, rising whistled "*hooeet?*" and a buzzy "*dzzrt.*" **Bo**

STREAK-BACKED CANASTERO

PUNA CANASTERO

JUNIN CANASTERO

MANY-STRIPED CANASTERO

flammulata

SCRIBBLE-TAILED
CANASTERO

taczanowskii

PLATE
148

THORNBIRDS AND CREAMY-BREASTED CANASTERO

Thornbirds are medium-sized ovenbirds of dry, open scrub habitats in the Andes and in intermontane valleys. All have relatively plain plumage with white or pale underparts. Thornbirds build large enclosed stick nests, often placed conspicuously in trees or shrubs. They have restricted, nonoverlapping distributions. The more broadly distributed Creamy-breasted Canastero is classified as an Asthenes but behaviorally is similar to thornbirds.

1 RUFOUS-FRONTED THORNBIRD *Phacellodomus rufifrons* * 16.5 cm (6½ in)

Common but restricted to open dry forests and scrub of Río Marañón and tributaries, and locally in Mayo and Huallaga drainages; 350–1400 m. Active and noisy in pairs and small groups. Sometimes forage on ground, but primarily arboreal. Builds elongated, immense (up to 2 m long) stick nests that often hang vertically from ends of branches; often particularly conspicuous in the vicinity of nests. Plumage very plain. **VOICE** Primary song a short, rising-falling, fairly even-paced series of reedy, nasal notes: "*chiff-CHEEF-cheef-chiff-chiff-chu.*" Aggressive song, usually sung in duet, similar, but longer (up to 20 sec), often starting with a short rattle: "*tu-tu-tu-tu chiff-chiff-CHEEF-CHEEF-cheef-cheef-cheef-chiff-chiff-chiff….*" Call a high, sharp, metallic "*tsi.*" **Co, E, Br, Bo**

2 CREAMY-BREASTED CANASTERO *Asthenes dorbignyi* * 14.5–16.5 cm (5¾–6½ in)

Highly variable geographically. The most widespread subspecies, *arequipae*, is fairly common and widespread along west slope of Andes in southern Peru (from Arequipa south) in arid montane scrub and *Polylepis* forest, 2450–4200 m. Note pale underparts, dark breast, largely black tail, and rusty flanks and rump. From Lima south to Ayacucho, also on the west slope, is a very dark undescribed subspecies that is similar to *arequipae* (and occupies similar habitats) but can be identified by a pale iris, duller rump, and even less rufous in tail. Three disjunct populations, found in dry scrub and cacti in arid intermontane valleys, are paler and have outer rectrices extensively rufous or pale ("Pale-tailed" Canastero, possibly one or more separate species). Such birds occur in the Santa Valley in Ancash, where there is a undescribed subspecies (not illustrated), 2450–3000 m, with rufous outer rectrices and rump. Another population is in the Mantaro drainage (*huancavelicae*), at 3350–3700 m; characterized by light rufous or cinnamon outer rectrices, and light rufous rump. The third such population is in the Pampas and upper Apurímac drainages (*usheri*; not illustrated), at 2150–3800 m; the palest subspecies, with outer rectrices light rufous or whitish buff, and a brown rump. **VOICE** Song (*arequipae*) a rapid, descending, buzzy trill: "*tzee-tzee-ti-trrreerrreerrrrr.*" Calls a high, thin "*tsit,*" often in series; also various squeaks and chatters. Song of *usheri* a thin even-paced trill that rises and falls: "*ti' ti' ti' ti' TI' TI' TI' ti' ti' ti.*" **Bo, Ch**

3 CHESTNUT-BACKED THORNBIRD *Phacellodomus dorsalis* 19.5 cm (7¾ in)

Large and uncommon thornbird, with very restricted distribution in Marañón Valley. Found in arid montane scrub with scattered trees (*Prosopis*) and in hedgerows, at 2000–3100 m. Primarily arboreal, and usually encountered in pairs or as single individuals. Note large size, long tail, and rufous upper parts: unmistakable. **VOICE** Primary song an accelerating, descending series of rich notes: "*kew KYEW kyew kew-kew.*" Aggressive song, usually sung in duet, a similar but longer, rising-falling, accelerating series of notes, often initiated with a rattle: "*trrrt kyew-KYEW-KYEW-kyew-kyew-kew-kew-kew'kew'kew'kew….*" Calls a sharp, metallic, squeaky "*TSEEK!*" or "*ti,*" often in series; also a low rattle: "*trrt.*" **ENDEMIC**

4 STREAK-FRONTED THORNBIRD *Phacellodomus striaticeps* * 17 cm (6¾ in)

Local and uncommon in thorny arid scrub, hedgerows, and other bushy vegetation in intermontane valleys in central and southern Peru, 2900–4150 m. Forages in pairs or small groups in low shrubs or on ground. May carry tail partially cocked. Might be confused with some canasteros, but note larger size, white chin and throat (usually rufous in canasteros, such as Rusty-fronted) and rather bright ochraceous flanks. Cf. also Creamy-breasted Canastero. **VOICE** Primary song a short, rising-falling series of loud, yelping notes: "*pyuh pyuh pyuh pyuh PYEE PYEE PYEE pyuh pyuh.*" Aggressive song, usually sung in duet, a longer, more rapid, descending series of mono or bisyllabic notes (bisyllabic notes in only one sex?), usually initiated by calls: "*ti ti ti TSEEK'R-TSEEK'R-tseek'r-tsik'r-tsik'r-tr'r'r.*" Calls a high, squeaky "*ti*" and a series of metallic ticking notes. **Bo**

arequipae

huancavelicae

undescribed
subsp.,
Ayacucho

RUFOUS-FRONTED THORNBIRD

CHESTNUT-BACKED THORNBIRD

CREAMY-BREASTED CANASTERO

STREAK-FRONTED THORNBIRD

PLATE
149

BARBTAILS, TREERUNNER, AND ANDEAN FOLIAGE-GLEANERS

Several ovenbirds of humid montane forests. Barbtails and treerunner are somewhat similar to one another. Compare the three foliage-gleaners shown here to each other, and to treehunters (plate 153).

1 SPOTTED BARBTAIL *Premnoplex brunnescens* * 13.5 cm (5¼ in)
Uncommon to fairly common along eastern slope of Andes and outlying ridges, 850–2500 m (occasionally to 3000 m) in humid montane forest understory, especially where moss and epiphytes are thick. Solitary or pairs; sometimes join mixed-species flocks. Hitches along branches and trunks, within 1–2 m of ground; does not use tail for support. Reclusive. Note overall dark color and tawny throat. Rusty-winged Barbtail paler, with longer rufous tail and paler throat and superciliary. **VOICE** Primary song a high, rapid, rising-falling, sputtering trill: "*trrEEEEeeerrr.*" Call a series of descending "*pseew*" notes. **Co, E, Bo**

2 RUSTY-WINGED BARBTAIL *Premnornis guttuligera* * 14.5 cm (5¼ in)
Uncommon to locally fairly common, but inconspicuous, in humid montane forest understory on east slope of Andes, 1300–2500 m. Singles or pairs join mixed-species flocks. Does not creep along branches as do Spotted Barbtail and Pearled Treerunner. General appearance like a foliage-gleaner (such as Buff-browed), but much smaller. **VOICE** Rather quiet. Song (Ecuador) an accelerating, rising series of high chippering notes: "*ti ti ti-ti'ti'ti'ti.*" Call high "*tsi*" notes. **Co, E, Bo**

3 PEARLED TREERUNNER *Margarornis squamiger* * 15 cm (6 in)
Common along east slope of Andes, 2100–3700 m; locally down to 1525 m. Also fairly common on west slope in northwest. Inhabits humid montane and elfin forests. Forages in small groups in mixed-species flocks, creeping along slender branches, probing moss and bromeliads; may use tail as brace. Very distinctive; note bright rufous upperparts and heavily spotted underparts. In Puno (*squamiger*) underparts tinged yellow. **VOICE** Song inconspicuous, very high lisping series of chips that accelerates and decelerates: "*ti ti ti-ti-ti'ti'ti'ti-ti ti.*" Calls very high "*ti*" notes and a slightly descending trill: "*tiiiiiirr.*" **Co, E, Bo**

4 MONTANE FOLIAGE-GLEANER *Anabacerthia striaticollis* * 16 cm (6¼ in)
Fairly common in canopy and subcanopy of humid montane forest at 750–2100 m along east slope of Andes. Singles or pairs are regular in mixed-species flocks. Actively hops on branches or through tangles, investigating branches and foliage (including clumps of dead leaves). Drab; note buff eyering, short buff superciliary, lightly spotted upper breast, and lack of streaking. In north cf. Rufous-rumped Foliage-gleaner (*subfulvum*), which has bolder superciliary, tawnier (less olive) underparts, and unspotted throat and upper breast. **VOICE** Song an accelerating-decelerating series of thin, metallic notes; sometimes on an even pitch, but often it falls before rising: "*chip chip chip-chip-chip'tip'tip'tiptiptipt'tip'tip'chip-chip chip.*" Reminiscent of song of Marble-faced Bristle-Tyrant in pattern, but differs in note quality. Call a quick, rising metallic "*psik,*" singly or in a loose series. **Co, E, Bo**

5 LINEATED FOLIAGE-GLEANER *Syndactyla subalaris* * 18–18.5 cm (7–7¼ in)
Uncommon in humid forest understory along east slope of Andes, at 1050–2100 m, south to Apurímac Valley. Also in taller second growth at forest edge. Typically seen singly or in pairs, usually with mixed-species flocks. Forages actively along limbs and through tangles. Similar to Buff-browed Foliage-gleaner, but crown and back are streaked, and lacks buff superciliary. Resembles treehunters, but smaller with a smaller, slightly upturned bill. **VOICE** Song a dry, accelerating, slightly rising or rising-falling series of dry, nasal ticking notes: "*djk djk djk-djk-djk'djkdjkdjkdjk.*" Similar to Buff-browed, but lower-pitched, slightly richer. Call a low, dry, sneezing "*djk*" or "*djow.*" **Co, E**

6 BUFF-BROWED FOLIAGE-GLEANER *Syndactyla rufosuperciliata* * 18 cm (7 in)
Uncommon to fairly common in humid montane forest understory on east slope of Andes, 1000–2750 m, locally down to 700 or up to 3300 m. Also at forest edge in taller second growth. Cf. behaviorally similar Lineated Foliage-gleaner. In northwest may overlap locally with Rufous-necked Foliage-gleaner, which is more brightly colored on sides of face and neck, and less streaked below. Cf. also treehunters and Rusty-winged Barbtail. **VOICE** Primary song an accelerating, rising or falling series of dry ticking notes: "*djt djt djt-djt-djt-djt'djt'djt'djt'djt'djt.*" Cf. song of Lineated. Calls a sharp, descending, squeaky "*tchew*" and a nasal "*enk.*" **E, Br, Bo**

SPOTTED BARBTAIL

RUSTY-WINGED
BARBTAIL

squamiger

PEARLED
TREERUNNER

MONTANE
FOLIAGE-GLEANER

LINEATED
FOLIAGE-GLEANER

BUFF-BROWED
FOLIAGE-GLEANER

PLATE
150
PHILYDOR FOLIAGE-GLEANERS AND HOOKBILL

Philydor are medium-sized ovenbirds of Amazonia and the east slope of the Andes. Most forage in midstory or canopy (although Cinnamon-rumped is in understory), usually with mixed-species flocks. Most regularly investigate dead-leaf clusters using acrobatic movements, often using tail as a prop as they hang down or probe for arthropods. Philydor are smaller, more slender than Automolus foliage-gleaners (plate 152), with slighter bills, and are less vocal; most species forage at greater heights. Hookbill is superficially similar to Philydor.

1 CHESTNUT-WINGED FOLIAGE-GLEANER *Philydor erythropterum* * 18.5 cm (7¼ in)
Widespread but uncommon in canopy and midstory of Amazonian forest, up to 900 m. Often forages in foliage near ends of slender branches in canopy. Probes curled leaves, but not as strongly tied to dead leaves as are many other foliage-gleaners. Note reddish wings and bright tawny-ochraceous lores and tawny-buff throat contrasting with grayish buff underparts; cf. Chestnut-winged Hookbill with similar wing pattern. **VOICE** Song an even-paced, slightly descending trill: "*treeeeeeeeeeeerrrrrrrr.*" Call a screeching "*gree-greeh.*" **Co, E, Br, Bo**

2 CHESTNUT-WINGED HOOKBILL *Ancistrops strigilatus* 17–18 cm (6¾–7 in)
Uncommon in midstory and canopy of terra firme, up to 1100 m. Almost always in mixed-species flocks. Rather sluggishly hops through vine tangles, peering about, searching foliage; also scans and probes dead leaves and other debris. Similar to Chestnut-winged Foliage-gleaner but has uniformly pale yellowish, lightly streaked underparts (with no contrast between throat and breast) and buff-streaked crown and back. **VOICE** Primary song a short (3 sec), rising, rapid ringing trill: "*trrrrrrrrrreeeeeeeeeeeep*"; aggressive song may be up to 30 sec long. **Co, E, Br, Bo**

3 RUFOUS-RUMPED FOLIAGE-GLEANER *Philydor erythrocercum* * 16–17 cm (6¼–6¾ in)
Geographically variable. Browner lowland subspecies *subfulvum* (north of the Amazon, also south of Marañón/west of Ucayali) and *lyra* (rest of Amazonia) are uncommon to fairly common in terra firme, up to 900 m. Forage singly or in pairs, usually with understory mixed-species flocks; very similar to Rufous-tailed Foliage-gleaner. Juveniles of Amazonian subspecies are buffier, similar to adults of montane *ochrogaster*, which is in canopy with mixed-species flocks in foothills and low mountain ridges (900 to 1700 m) from central Peru south. Overlaps locally with Buff-fronted Foliage-gleaner but is smaller; has browner (less gray) crown, with darker auriculars; wings browner, less reddish; and bill shorter. Also cf. Russet Antshrike, which has a heavier, hooked bill. **VOICE** Song of *subfulvum* and *lyra* a rising-falling series of rusty notes: "*tre-TREE-TREE-TRE-tre*," pace somewhat variable. Calls a rapid series of antbirdlike "*pit-pit-pit*" or "*pur-pit*" notes, also a single rusty "*treet.*" Song of *ochrogaster* similar, notes sharper, higher pitched. **Co, E, Br, Bo**

4 BUFF-FRONTED FOLIAGE-GLEANER *Philydor rufum* * 18.5–19 cm (7¼–7½ in)
Uncommon in midstory and canopy of humid forest on east slope of Andes and outlying ridges, 1000–1700 m; in southeast also local in river-edge forest below 500 m. Singles or pairs join mixed-species flocks. Investigates dead leaf clusters less often than most other *Philydor*. A slim, long-tailed foliage-gleaner with ochraceous buff underparts. Cf. montane *ochrogaster* subspecies of Rufous-rumped Foliage-gleaner, with which it overlaps in central Peru. Cf. also Russet Antshrike, which is smaller with a heavier, hooked bill. **VOICE** Song a descending, accelerating series of high metallic notes: "*TEE-TEE-teh-teh-te-te-te-te.*" Calls a very high, descending "*tsew*" and a lower, metallic "*tchenk*" or buzzier "*tzenk.*" **Co, E, Br, Bo**

5 RUFOUS-TAILED FOLIAGE-GLEANER *Philydor ruficaudatum* * 16.5–18 cm (6½–7 in)
Uncommon and local in midstory and canopy of Amazonian forest, up to 1050 m. Very scarce or absent from northwestern Loreto and Ucayali floodplain. Broadly overlaps with similar lowland races of Rufous-rumped Foliage-gleaner. Rufous-tailed is more yellowish (not buffy) below and olive above, is vaguely streaked or mottled on breast, and throat and superciliary are more yellowish. Rump is concolor with back (but this rarely visible in field). Rufous-tailed usually accompanies canopy flocks, while Rufous-rumped usually with understory flocks. Also have different vocalizations. **VOICE** Dawn song a low, inconspicuous 2-part series of fussing notes, the first part slower, the second a more rapid low-pitched, descending trill: "*purp-purp-purp-purp-trrrrrrrrr.*" Daytime song a 2-part series of notes, the first part higher pitched and slower paced than second: "*keet keet keet keet put-put-put-put-put*"; the second part may become an even faster trill. Call a series of "*keet*" notes that may accelerate and decelerate. **Co, E, Br, Bo**

CHESTNUT-WINGED
FOLIAGE-GLEANER

CHESTNUT-WINGED
HOOKBILL

subfulvum

ochrogaster

RUFOUS-RUMPED
FOLIAGE-GLEANER

lyra

BUFF-FRONTED
FOLIAGE-GLEANER

RUFOUS-TAILED
FOLIAGE-GLEANER

PLATE
151

PALMCREEPER, WOODHAUNTER, AND
FOLIAGE-GLEANERS

Palmcreeper is a seldom seen, Amazonian ovenbird. Striped Woodhaunter and Peruvian Recurvebill are Amazonian foliage-gleaners; cf. species on plates 150 and 152. Cinnamon-rumped Foliage-gleaner is the only understory Philydor. Rufous-necked and Henna-hooded foliage-gleaners are restricted to the northwest.

1 POINT-TAILED PALMCREEPER *Berlepschia rikeri* 21.5 cm (8½ in)

Restricted to stands of moriche palm (*Mauritia*) in flooded areas in forest or wet grassland in Amazonia, below 600 m (locally to 800 m). Apparently local, even within this habitat, but probably more widespread than the few records indicate. Adept at remaining concealed; often difficult to detect except by song. Creeps among green palm fronds, often hanging nearly upside down, using tail as a brace. Probes curled blades of palm fronds; less frequently searches dead fronds near trunk. Unmistakable. **VOICE** Vocalizes very sporadically. Primary song, loud and far-carrying, a slightly accelerating, rising series of piping notes: "*tu tu-tu-tu-tu-tu-TI-TI-TI-TI-TI.*" **Co, E, Br, Bo**

2 STRIPED WOODHAUNTER *Hyloctistes subulatus* * 17 cm (6¾ in)

Uncommon but widespread inhabitant of terra firme throughout Amazonia, up to 1400 m. Associates with mixed-species flocks. Difficult to observe as it quietly forages in vine tangles and epiphytes on trunks and large limbs; probes dead leaves and bromeliads. A dull, brownish foliage-gleaner of midheights. Browner and more streaked than *Philydor* foliage-gleaners; browner, more uniform-looking, less obviously streaked than Chestnut-winged Hookbill. Also note the bill, relatively longer and more pointed than in other foliage-gleaners; often looks "flat-headed," a profile accentuated by bill shape. In foothills cf. *Syndactyla*. **VOICE** Song, usually given at dawn and dusk, 2 whistles, the second higher and falling: "*hee-HEER*"; often followed by a low, dry trill when agitated: "*hee-HEER trrrrrr.*" Occasionally trill given alone. Call a quick, descending, rough "*djr.*" **Co, E, Br, Bo**

3 RUFOUS-NECKED FOLIAGE-GLEANER *Syndactyla ruficollis* 18 cm (7 in)

Uncommon in dense to moderately open montane humid forest understory (especially bamboo) and midstory, on west slope of Andes, 600–2650 m. Singles or in pairs, usually with mixed-species flocks. Probes arboreal bromeliads, ferns, and mosses on limbs, and hops through dense tangles in bamboo. Overlaps with few other foliage-gleaner species; see Buff-browed Foliage-gleaner. The overall rufous color and conspicuous cinnamon- or orange-rufous superciliary and sides of neck are distinctive. **VOICE** Song very like those of Lineated and Buff-browed foliage-gleaners. Calls include a sharp, scratchy "*tchp.*" **E**

4 CINNAMON-RUMPED FOLIAGE-GLEANER *Philydor pyrrhodes* 17 cm (6¾ in)

Uncommon but widespread in understory of humid forest below 500 m. Primarily forages as singles or pairs, usually apart but sometimes with mixed-species flocks, in low, dense cover, especially understory palms and thickets with *Heliconia*. Note bright ochraceous underparts, rump and tail that contrast with brown back and blackish wings; unmistakable. **VOICE** Primary song a rapid-paced, strongly rising trill of ringing musical notes: "*trrrrUUUEEEEEEEEEEEE,*" descending again when highly agitated. Calls a long phrase of chatters, and a sharp "*pit-it.*" **Co, E, Br, Bo**

5 HENNA-HOODED FOLIAGE-GLEANER *Hylocryptus erythrocephalus* * 21 cm (8¼ in)

Uncommon to locally fairly common in deciduous forests in northwest, 400–1500 m. Forages near or on ground, as singles or pairs, often with mixed-species flocks. Hops along ground, tossing dead leaves aside and probing leaf litter; during dry season the rustling noises made when foraging in leaf litter may be conspicuous. Note the brownish olive body contrasting with orange-rufous head and neck, wings, and tail; unmistakable. **VOICE** Song a series of semimusical, decelerating rattles: "*tr'r'r'r'r'r.*" Call a sharp, high "*tchiff!*" **E**

6 PERUVIAN RECURVEBILL *Simoxenops ucayalae* 20 cm (8 in)

Rare to uncommon, in patches (usually large) of *Guadua* bamboo in lowlands of southeast, up to 1300 m. Singles or pairs sometimes associate with mixed-species flocks, but often forage apart. Primarily in the understory. Uses large, chisel-shaped bill to hammer and pry at bamboo stalks, especially small cavities. Bill shape is distinctive. No other foliage-gleaner is as uniformly rufous, but cf. also Brown-rumped, Ruddy, and Chestnut-crowned foliage-gleaners. **VOICE** Song a rising (often the last note falling in pitch) dry rattle of variable pace, often of even-pace, sometime accelerating or decelerating or both: "*tr-tr-tr-tr-tr-TR-TR-TR-TR-TR.*" Call a sharp, scratchy "*tchik.*" **Br, Bo**

POINT-TAILED
PALMCREEPER

STRIPED
WOODHAUNTER

RUFOUS-NECKED
FOLIAGE-GLEANER

CINNAMON-
RUMPED FOLIAGE-
GLEANER

PERUVIAN
RECURVEBILL

HENNA-HOODED
FOLIAGE-GLEANER

PLATE
152

LARGE AMAZONIAN FOLIAGE-GLEANERS

Automolus are foliage-gleaners of Amazonia and lower slopes of the Andes. Often keep to deep cover but are vocal, especially at dawn or dusk. Forage as singles or in pairs, sometimes in mixed-species flocks but often apart. Cf. smaller Philydor *foliage-gleaners. Dusky-cheeked Foliage-gleaner is similar in behavior, but differs vocally.*

1 RUDDY FOLIAGE-GLEANER *Automolus rubiginosus* * 19.5–20 cm (7½–8 in), northeast Amazonia 18 cm (7 in)

Uncommon and local in Amazonian forest, up to 1400 m in dense undergrowth. Regularly forages on ground. Dark brown with cinnamon throat, and rufescent wash on sides to neck. In northeastern Amazonia, is smaller and darker; crown reddish brown (rather than chestnut). Resembles Brown-rumped Foliage-gleaner, which lacks rufescence on sides of neck and usually has a paler iris. Cf. also Buff-throated and Chestnut-crowned foliage-gleaners, and Peruvian Recurvebill. **VOICE** Song in central and southern Peru (*watkinsi*) a mellow, nasal 2-note phrase, with second note higher than first and rising: "*kew-TUR*" or "*kew-TOOEE?*" Song in northeast a faster "*t'KOOEE?*" **Co, E, Br, Bo**

2 CHESTNUT-CROWNED FOLIAGE-GLEANER *Automolus rufipileatus* * 18–19 cm (7–7½ in)

Widespread and fairly common throughout Amazonia, up to 700 m (locally to 1050 m), primarily in understory of seasonally flooded and river-edge forest. Usually in dense tangles and thickets. Relatively large. Crown more rufescent than back. Lacks the buff eyering and throat of Buff-throated Foliage-gleaner. Differs from Ruddy Foliage-gleaner by drab throat and sides of neck, and yellow or orange iris. Brown-rumped Foliage-gleaner has crown concolor with back, redder iris, and contrasting tawny malar. **VOICE** Song an even-paced, descending musical rattle: "*t'rrrrrrrrrrrrrrr.*" Similar to Olive-backed Foliage-gleaner's song, but higher pitched, and usually introductory hiccup less distinct. Call a low, rasping "*tjow.*" **Co, E, Br, Bo**

3 BROWN-RUMPED FOLIAGE-GLEANER *Automolus melanopezus* 19 cm (7½ in)

Locally uncommon in southeast; rare and very local in north, primarily below 450 m, locally to 800 m. Inhabits low-lying transitional and seasonally flooded forest undergrowth, especially bamboo thickets. Distinguished from other foliage-gleaners by lack of strong pattern, tawny-buff throat with brighter, tawny-ochraceous malars, and by paler (usually reddish orange) iris. Cf. Ruddy, Buff-throated, and Chestnut-crowned foliage-gleaners. **VOICE** Primary song begins with rising whistles, followed by an accelerating chatter that rises and falls, ending in a low rattle: "*WHEEP! WHEEP! Chur-chur-CHEER-CHI-CHURRrrrrrrrr.*" **Co, E, Br, Bo**

4 BUFF-THROATED FOLIAGE-GLEANER *Automolus ochrolaemus* * 19–20 cm (7½–7¾ in)

The most common and widespread foliage-gleaner in Peru; learn well as a benchmark for comparisons. Up to 1400 m (locally to 1550 m) in foothills. Occurs in both seasonally flooded and terra firme, and in taller second growth. Drab brown; note buff or ochraceous eyering and throat, and indistinct flammulations on breast. Chestnut-crowned and Brown-rumped foliage-gleaners are more uniform, lacking distinctive face pattern of Buff-throated. **VOICE** Song a descending series of whiny notes usually ending in a low churr: "*WEE-WEE-wee-wee-wur'trrrr.*" Call a dry, snarling "*t'jahh.*" **Co, E, Br, Bo**

5 DUSKY-CHEEKED FOLIAGE-GLEANER *Anabazenops dorsalis* 18.5 cm (7¼ in)

Uncommon and local in bamboo and cane thickets of humid forest and tall second growth on lower slopes of Andes, up to 1350 m. Less common in southeast lowlands; very local in northeast Amazonia. Usually in pairs following mixed-species flocks through bamboo crowns. Probes internodes of bamboo stalks. Also searches dead leaves in vine tangles and dense foliage. Much like Olive-backed Foliage-gleaner, but reddish brown above with pale buffy superciliary and grayish underparts. Much larger than *Philydor* foliage-gleaners. **VOICE** Two common vocalizations are a long, rising, dry rattle and a slower series of 5–15 "*kleet*" or "*clock*" notes, the latter sometimes given alone. Also a sneezing, descending "*tchrk.*" **Co, E, Br, Bo**

6 OLIVE-BACKED FOLIAGE-GLEANER *Automolus infuscatus* * 18–19 cm (7–7½ in)

Widespread and fairly common in undergrowth of terra firme throughout Amazonia, up to 600 m; less common in transitional and seasonally flooded forest. Often with understory mixed-species flocks. Uniform and brown with prominent whitish throat. Cf. Dusky-cheeked Foliage-gleaner. **VOICE** Song an even-paced, musical rattle that begins with a hiccupping higher note: "*ti'churr-RRRrrrrrrrrr.*" Cf. Chestnut-crowned Foliage-gleaner. Call a bisyllabic, squeaky hiccupping phrase: "*PEEK'up.*" **Co, E, Br, Bo**

ne Amaz.

RUDDY
FOLIAGE-GLEANER

CHESTNUT-CROWNED
FOLIAGE-GLEANER

BROWN-RUMPED
FOLIAGE-GLEANER

BUFF-THROATED
FOLIAGE-GLEANER

DUSKY-CHEEKED
FOLIAGE-GLEANER

OLIVE-BACKED
FOLIAGE-GLEANER

PLATE
153

TUFTEDCHEEK AND TREEHUNTERS

Streaked Tuftedcheek is a distinctive slender, long-tailed ovenbird of humid montane forests, readily recognized by the conspicuous white tufts on the side of the head and neck. Treehunters are large, long-tailed foliage-gleaners of the understory of montane forests of the Andes; often difficult to see as they forage in dense vegetation. Occasionally join mixed-species flocks, but mostly forage apart as singles or pairs. Treehunters are heavily streaked, especially on the upper parts. Up to 3 species may occur in the same area at different, but partially overlapping, elevations. Cf. Lineated and Buff-browed foliage-gleaners; treehunters are larger and have longer, heavier, slightly hooked bills.

1 STREAKED TUFTEDCHEEK *Pseudocolaptes boissonneautii* * 21–21.5 cm (8¼–8½ in)

Common in canopy and subcanopy of humid montane forest at 1700–3450 m, along east slope of Andes and on west slope in northwest. Encountered as single individuals or in pairs, most often with mixed-species flocks. Uses its bill to probe arboreal epiphytes, especially bromeliads, and also moss and lichen on limbs and trunks. Bill of females longer than bill of males in north; bill of female shorter in central and southern Peru, with little or no sexual dimorphism in bill length. Note prominent white cheek tufts, long tail; unmistakable. Juvenile darker than adult, with black crown, scaly throat, and short bill. **VOICE** Song a 3-part series, the first section of ticking notes, the second (the loudest and farthest-carrying) a rising trill of high, ringing, chippering notes, and the third a dry rattle: "*tink-tink-tink tee'tee'tee' TEE'TEE'TEE'TEE'TEE'TEE-trrrrrrrrr.*" Calls a nasal "*rehnk*" and a metallic "*ptik.*" **Co, E, Bo**

2 BLACK-BILLED TREEHUNTER *Thripadectes melanorhynchus* * 20.5 cm (8 in)

Uncommon to locally fairly common along east slope of Andes, 850–1750 m. Elevational distribution generally lower than Striped Treehunter's, but some overlap. More ochraceous, less olive below than Striped; in particular the throat is tawny, scaled with dusky, and breast is much less streaked. **VOICE** Song a slow-paced (2–3 notes/sec) slightly decelerating, slightly rising-falling series of high, nasal notes, the final note usually distinctly lower-pitched: "*KEEK-keek-keek-keek keek kheek.*" Call a sharp, rich, doubled note: "*t'tchp.*" **Co, E**

3 STRIPED TREEHUNTER *Thripadectes holostictus* * 21 cm (8¼ in)

Uncommon to locally fairly common in humid forest understory along east slope of Andes, 1500–2400 m, where typically in dense cover within 1 or 2 m of the ground. Frequently searches for arthropod prey in tangles of dead leaves suspended in vegetation. May overlap in elevational distribution at lower end with Black-billed Treehunter, and at upper end with Buff-throated Treehunter. **VOICE** Song a rather fast-paced, rising-falling, series of semimusical notes: "*tr'r'r'R'E'E'E'E'E'R'r'r'r'.*" Calls a slow series of "*keep*" notes and a rising chattered series of high notes: "*tutiti?*" **Co, E, Bo**

4 BUFF-THROATED TREEHUNTER *Thripadectes scrutator* 24 cm (9½ in)

A large, dark, streaked foliage-gleaner that is rare in understory of humid montane forest along east slope of Andes, 2100–3500 m. Furtive. May overlap with Striped Treehunter, although usually occurs at higher elevations. Buff-throated is larger, more heavily streaked on underparts, less heavily streaked on back and rump, and back, rump, and wings are more rufescent. **VOICE** Song an accelerating-decelerating, rising-falling rapid series of semimusical notes: "*tchu-tchu-tchu'tchu'TCHI'TCHI'-TCHI'TCHI'TCHI'tchu'tchu-tchu-tchu-tchu.*" Call a sharp, loud "*TCHK!*" **Bo**

5 FLAMMULATED TREEHUNTER *Thripadectes flammulatus* * 24 cm (9½ in)

Rare to uncommon in humid forest understory at 2100–2950 m, north and west of Marañón Valley (where it replaces similar Buff-throated Treehunter). Inconspicuous, foraging for arthropods usually within 2 m of the ground, in tangles of bamboo and other foliage, and in thickets at forest edge. Large. Largely blackish with prominent buff stripes, on crown, upper parts, and breast; generally at higher elevations than Striped Treehunter, and much more boldly patterned. **VOICE** Song an accelerating-decelerating, rising-falling rapid series of semimusical notes: "*tchu-tchu-tchu'tchu'TCHI'TCHI'-TCHI'TCHI'TCHI'tchu'tchu-tchu-tchu-tchu.*" Calls include a sharp, doubled note: "*T'TCHK!*" **Co, E**

BLACK-BILLED
TREEHUNTER

juv.

ad. c, s

STREAKED
TUFTEDCHEEK

BUFF-THROATED
TREEHUNTER

STRIPED
TREEHUNTER

FLAMMULATED
TREEHUNTER

PLATE
154
LEAFTOSSERS AND STREAMCREEPER

Leaftossers are short-tailed terrestrial ovenbirds with dark dull plumage and relatively short legs and tail. They occur in humid forests of Amazonia and the lower slopes on the east side of the Andes, where they are difficult to observe as they shuffle or hop along the ground; easiest to detect when they vocalize (mostly at dawn and dusk). Probe leaf litter with their long thin bills. Do not associate with mixed-species flocks. Bill length and the pattern of throat and breast are important for identification. Sharp-tailed Streamcreeper is similar in structure to leaftossers but is restricted to fast-flowing streams in humid forest in the Andes.

1 GRAY-THROATED LEAFTOSSER *Sclerurus albigularis* * 18 cm (7 in)

Rare but widespread, at lower elevations on east slope of Andes (up to 1700 m). Also very local in southeastern Amazonia, primarily in hill forest. A large leaftosser with a relatively contrasting throat and chest pattern. Bill long (2 cm; ¾ in), straight. White or pale gray throat, contrasting with rufous breast band, is distinctive, although not always easy to see (cf. Black-tailed Leaftosser). **VOICE** Primary song a rising series of rising notes ending in a lower trill (trill sometimes not given): *"wur-weer-wee-WEET-WHIT-WHIT'trrrrrrr."* Calls a sharp, high *"tsiff!,"* and a chattering series of *"tcheet"* notes. **Co, E, Br, Bo**

2 BLACK-TAILED LEAFTOSSER *Sclerurus caudacutus* * 17 cm (6¾ in)

Widespread but uncommon in Amazonia; rarely up to 1000 m. Primarily found in terra firme. A large, dark leaftosser with a straight bill of medium length (1.8 cm; ¾ in); due to larger body size, does not appear as long-billed as does Tawny-throated Leaftosser. Dull-colored chest and white chin also separate this species from Tawny-throated and Short-billed leaftossers but are difficult to see. **VOICE** Primary song a descending, even-paced series of ringing piping notes: *"PEE-pee-pee-pee-pee."* Call a sharp, high *"tcheep!"* **Co, E, Br, Bo**

3 SHORT-BILLED LEAFTOSSER *Sclerurus rufigularis* * 15 cm (6 in)

Uncommon in northern Amazonia, also locally in Andean foothills to 800 m. A small leaftosser with a relatively short bill and tawny throat. Similar to Tawny-throated Leaftosser, but bill is significantly shorter (1.5 cm; ½ in). Black-tailed Leaftosser also has a relatively short bill but is larger, duller in color, and has a white chin and throat. Brightest is *rufigularis* (south of the Amazon and east of the Ucayali); *brunnescens* (not illustrated; north of the Amazon, and south of Marañón west of Ucayali) is similar but darker, less rufescent, especially on underparts. **VOICE** Primary song (*brunnescens*) a falling-rising, decelerating-accelerating series of high whistles: *"TEE-tee-ti tu tu-ti-tee."* Calls a sharp, very high *"tseep!"* and a high, purring, descending *"tseerrrr!"* **Co, E, Br, Bo**

4 TAWNY-THROATED LEAFTOSSER *Sclerurus mexicanus* * 16.5–17 cm (6½–6¾ in)

Uncommon on east slope of Andes and in adjacent lowlands (below 1100 m, rarely up to 1900 m). Also very local in Amazonia, primarily in northern Peru; perhaps most often in areas with hill forest. A leaftosser with a relatively brightly colored throat and chest, and long slender bill. Similar in color pattern to Short-billed Leaftosser, but has a longer bill (2 cm; ¾ in), and averages larger in overall body size; despite geographic overlap, the two only rarely occur together. **VOICE** Primary song a rising-falling series of piping, ringing whistles: *"pi-pee-PEE-TU-tu-tu-tu-tu-tu."* Call a sharp, metallic *"tchit!"* **Co, E, Br, Bo**

5 SHARP-TAILED STREAMCREEPER *Lochmias nematura* * 15–16 cm (6–6¼ in)

Widespread but usually rare or uncommon; distributed along east slope of Andes (500–2300 m, occasionally to 2800 m). Almost always found along forested mountain streams with mossy boulders. Singles or pairs forage close to water, usually in dense cover. Hops along stream margins or rocks in streams, where it forages somewhat like a leaftosser: pecking at or probing the substrate with its bill, or using bill to flick through leaf litter. Leaftossers are not spotted below. Spotted Barbtail is superficially similar but is smaller, is not terrestrial, and has a tawny throat. **VOICE** Song a rising-falling musical chatter: *"tur-tr-tr-tr-tr-ti-TI-TI-TI-TI-tr-tr."* Call a buzzy or sputtering rattle: *"tzz'z'z'z"* or *"ti'ti'ti'ti"*; also a rising whistled *"weep?"* **Co, E, Br, Bo**

GRAY-THROATED LEAFTOSSER

BLACK-TAILED LEAFTOSSER

SHORT-BILLED LEAFTOSSER

TAWNY-THROATED LEAFTOSSER

SHARP-TAILED STREAMCREEPER

PLATE
155

XENOPS, PRICKLETAIL, AND GRAYTAIL

Xenops are small ovenbirds that forage like piculets: hop or hitch along slender bare branches or vines, gleaning for arthropods. Frequent members of mixed-species flocks. Tail rufous; dusky wings crossed centrally by a rufous band. Most have laterally compressed bills upturned at end of mandible and noticeable white malar mark. The pricketail and graytail are two small, uncommon ovenbirds of humid montane forest in northern Peru. The pricketail superficially resembles a xenops, whereas the graytail is unlike any other ovenbird.

1 SLENDER-BILLED XENOPS *Xenops tenuirostris* * 10–10.5 cm (4–4¼ in)

Rare and apparently local in Amazonia, where found in canopy of river-edge and seasonally flooded forest below 500 m. Very similar to Streaked Xenops, but there is limited geographic overlap. Where they co-occur in southeast, Slender-billed more likely in river-edge forest or in second growth, whereas Streaked is in forest interior. Slender-billed slightly smaller, with more slender and pointed bill, less noticeably upturned at end. The bases of the inner primaries and secondaries are brighter rufous than in Streaked, providing more "contrast" on closed wing. Also, tail is shorter and has black extending onto both inner and outer webs of some rectrices (black confined to inner webs in Streaked), although this difficult to see in field. **VOICE** Song (?) a high, rising-falling, chirping series of descending notes: "*tseep tseep tseep tseep tseep.*" **Co, E, Br, Bo**

2 PLAIN XENOPS *Xenops minutus* * 11.5–12.5 cm (4½–5 in)

Widespread and fairly common in Amazonia in understory and midstory of both terra firme and seasonally flooded forests, up to 1400 m; also in semideciduous forest in Tumbes. Often with mixed flocks, but also forages apart. The only xenops with an unstreaked back. Distinguished from Wedge-billed Woodcreeper by behavior, shorter tail, and white malar streak. **VOICE** Song a slightly descending, slightly accelerating, series of high, lisping, rising notes, usually a pause before the last note: "*wisst wisst-wisst-wisst-wisst wisst.*" Probably indistinguishable from Streaked Xenops. Call high "*spi!*" notes, singly or in series. **Co, E, Br, Bo**

3 SPECTACLED PRICKLETAIL *Siptornis striaticollis* * 12 cm (4¾ in)

Uncommon, on east slope of Andes north and west of Río Marañón in subcanopy of humid montane forest, 1600–2000 m. Usually with mixed-species flocks. Creeps along branches, probing clumps of moss, dead leaves, lichens, and crevices in bark; often braces tail against bark when probing deep crevices. Resembles Streaked Xenops, but lacks conspicuous white malar stripe and sharply upturned mandible; also is smaller, more chestnut (less rufous), and not streaked on upperparts. Cf. also Rusty-winged Barbtail and Pearled Treerunner. **Co, E**

4 STREAKED XENOPS *Xenops rutilans* * 11.5–12.5 cm (4½–5 in)

Fairly common in humid montane forest along east slope of Andes, 600–2100 m; also found locally in lowland forest in southeast and in semideciduous forest in Tumbes and the dry Marañón Valley. Usually in canopy and subcanopy of tall forest; generally forages higher above ground than does Plain Xenops. Cf. less common Slender-billed Xenops and also Spectacled Pricketail. **VOICE** Song a descending series, accelerating and then decelerating, of high, lisping, rising notes: "*tsst tsst-tsst-tsst-tsit tsit.*" Call high, single or double "*tsit.*" **Co, E, Br, Bo**

5 EQUATORIAL GRAYTAIL *Xenerpestes singularis* 11.5 cm (4½ in)

Uncommon in tall humid montane forest and forest edge, 1050–1700 m. Inconspicuous as pairs or small groups in mixed-species flocks in canopy and subcanopy. Foraging behavior reminiscent of a greenlet; gleans from small leaves at or near ends of limbs. Occasionally hangs from undersides of leaves and probes their bases. Cf. Gray-mantled Wren (which has barred tail, no streaks below); in poor light, could be confused with a warbler or greenlet. **VOICE** Song a very high, sputtering, reeling series of chippering notes: "*ti ti trrEErrEErrEErrEErrEErr,*" like sound of a hand-cranked eggbeater. Calls high, lisping "*tseet*" and "*ti-ti-ti*" notes. **E**

6 RUFOUS-TAILED XENOPS *Xenops milleri* 11 cm (4¼ in)

Rare to uncommon in eastern Amazonia. Restricted to canopy of tall humid forest (both terra firme and seasonally flooded). Note small size, streaking, and characteristic creeping foraging behavior. Distinguished from other xenops by lack of white malar stripe, and pointed, less chisel-shaped bill. The tail is entirely rufous. Cf. also piculets. **VOICE** Song a rich, rising-falling chatter: "*tchi-tchi-tchrrrEEEEEeeer.*" **Co, E, Br, Bo**

SLENDER-BILLED XENOPS

PLAIN XENOPS

SPECTACLED PRICKLETAIL

STREAKED XENOPS

EQUATORIAL GRAYTAIL

RUFOUS-TAILED XENOPS

PLATE
156

HORNEROS AND ANTSHRIKES

Horneros are chunky, largely terrestrial ovenbirds of the lowlands of eastern and northwestern Peru. Usually alone or in pairs. They walk slowly on the ground, with chest held out, head bobbing, and tail held down toward the ground. Name "hornero" comes from the large, domed mud nests resembling an oven ("horno"); nests typically are placed on stout horizontal tree limbs (also on telephone poles) a few meters above ground. Black-crested and Great antshrikes are members of the large antbird family; see family introduction on plate 157.

1 PALE-BILLED HORNERO *Furnarius torridus* 18 cm (7 in)

Uncommon to fairly common. Primarily on seasonally flooded, wooded river islands, especially with dense understory; also locally in mainland varzea forest. Shy, not found near human habitation, unlike Pale-legged Hornero. Slightly larger than Pale-legged with dark chestnut upperparts (less contrast with dusky crown) and dark brown breast. Lesser Hornero is paler and much smaller. **VOICE** Most songs and calls probably not safely distinguished from Pale-legged (*tricolor*). Agitated call a series of piping notes: "*pep'pep'pep'pep'pep....*" **Co, E, Br**

2 LESSER HORNERO *Furnarius minor* 15–15.5 cm (6 in)

Locally common on recently formed islands in large rivers of northern Amazonia. Prefers open, seasonally flooded areas of scrub. Usually in pairs or small groups, but congregates when water levels high. Miniature version of Pale-legged Hornero. In the hand, vent is whitish buff; bases of vent feathers black or dusky in Pale-legged. Also prefers more open river-island habitats than the two larger species. Cf. also Rusty-backed and Red-and-white spinetails. **VOICE** Song, often given in asynchronous duet, a descending series, sometimes accelerating at very end, of loud, reedy whistles, often preceded by a rapid puttering: "*p'p'p'p'p... pi-pi-PI-PI-PI-PI-PI-PI-pipipipih.*" Similar to Pale-legged's song, but less musical, drier, and does not obviously decelerate. Calls a low, gruff "*chut*" and a quiet puttering chatter. **Co, E, Br**

3 PALE-LEGGED HORNERO *Furnarius leucopus * tricolor* 17–18 cm (6¼–7 in); *cinnamomeus* 19–19.5 cm (7½–7¾ in)

Common and widespread. Larger paler *cinnamomeus*, found on coast and in dry Marañón Valley, below 2100 m, is a characteristic bird of riparian woods, orchards, and farmlands; frequently around houses. Amazonian *tricolor* (to 800 m, rarely to 1700 m) occurs in river-edge forest and scrub. Prefers well-shaded, damp to muddy ground. Iris whitish (*cinnamomeus*) or chestnut (*tricolor*). In eastern Peru, cf. Pale-billed and Lesser horneros. **VOICE** Songs often given in asynchronous duet from low branches of a tree. Song (*cinnamomeus*) a descending, decelerating series of loud, reedy whistles: "*PEE-PEE-pee-pee-pee-pee-pee pee pee pee*," often preceded by a raspy chattered series. Call a loud, reedy "*CHIFF!*" Song (*tricolor*) similar, but faster-paced, particularly at start: "*PIPIPI'PI'pi'pi-pi-pi-pi-pi pee pee pu.*" Call a rich, reedy "*CHEW!*" **Co, E, Br, Bo**

4 BLACK-CRESTED ANTSHRIKE *Sakesphorus canadensis * 16 cm (6¼ in)

Fairly common but local in northern Amazonia in low permanently or frequently flooded riparian scrub, along edges of rivers or lakes; perhaps more prevalent in blackwater areas. Typically forage in pairs. Both sexes crested. Male is only antbird in Amazonian Peru with clearly defined black hood. Combination of rufous crest and streaked breast distinguishes female from other brown antshrikes within its range. **VOICE** Song a rising and accelerating series of downslurred musical notes ending on a higher doubled note: "*turl turl-turl-url-url-url'url'urlurlee'ee.*" Calls quiet "*purp*" notes and a chuckled "*wee-rl'rl.*" **Co, Br**

5 GREAT ANTSHRIKE *Taraba major * 19–20 cm (7½–8 in)

Fairly common and widespread in Amazonia, where found in understory of second growth, forest edge, river-edge forest, and on river islands (up to 1500 m). Rare in Tumbes in semideciduous and humid forest below 800 m. Singles or pairs typically forage apart from mixed-species flocks. Strikingly bicolored, black (male) or reddish brown (female) above and white below. Compare male to smaller Black-and-white Antbird and female to White-lined Antbird female. **VOICE** Song a long (often 10 sec or more), accelerating series of deep "*chew*" notes ending in a snarl (not audible at a distance): "*wah chew chew chew-chew-chew-chew'chew'chu'chu'chu'chuchuchu waahhhh.*" Calls a mewing "*ewweh*"; a decelerating deep, musical churr "*TCHRLU'u'u-u-u-chu-chu chu*"; and a drier rattled churr. **Co, E, Br, Bo**

PALE-BILLED
HORNERO

LESSER HORNERO

cinnamomeus

tricolor

PALE-LEGGED HORNERO

BLACK-CRESTED ANTSHRIKE

GREAT ANTSHRIKE

PLATE
157

BARRED ANTSHRIKES

Antbirds are mostly insectivorous. Most have a hooked bill tip. Many have concealed white in plumage, especially bases of back feathers (interscapular patch), which may be exposed when agitated. Both sexes sing, often in duet; usually female's song shorter and higher pitched than male's. Antshrikes are larger antbirds; males of species on this plate are barred black and white.

1 BAMBOO ANTSHRIKE *Cymbilaimus sanctaemariae* 16–17 cm (6¼–6¾ in)
Very similar to slightly larger Fasciated Antshrike, and may occur with it. Usually in large patches of bamboo, but sometimes in viny tangles in floodplain forest; up to 1450 m. Compared to Fasciated, has longer crown feathers (forming a crest, often flat, but raised in agitation), less heavy bill, and iris brown (not red). Underside of tail of male more conspicuously barred. Female has black rear crown, is deeper buff below than female Fasciated, and breast less heavily marked with black, usually barred only on sides and flanks. **VOICE** Song a loud, slightly descending series of 8–15 ringing metallic "*tchink*" notes. Calls a sharp "*tchew!*" note, often given in chattered series; a thin, dry rattle; and a whining "*ewwee?*" **Br, Bo**

2 FASCIATED ANTSHRIKE *Cymbilaimus lineatus* * 18 cm (7 in)
Fairly common in Amazonia, up to 1000 m, locally to 1500 m. Frequently heard, but often concealed within cover in midstory and canopy of humid forest and tall second growth. Solitary or in pairs, only occasionally with mixed-species flocks. Only widespread, barred antshrike of forest interior. Similar Barred and Lined antshrikes use forest edge and have less heavy bills. In southeast cf. Bamboo Antshrike. **VOICE** Song 3–7 mellow, rising-falling mewing whistles: "*weeo wEEo wEEo weeo.*" Call a querulous mewing followed by a harsh "*tchack!*," often extended to a chatter: "*tch-tch-tch-tch-tch!*" and a descending mewed "*eww.*" **Co, E, Br, Bo**

3 CHAPMAN'S ANTSHRIKE *Thamnophilus zarumae* * 15 cm (6 in)
Uncommon in semideciduous forest and forest edge, 600–2100 m, locally to 2600 m. Regularly forages inside forest, often in dense tangles in the under- and midstory. Forages as singles or pairs, sometimes with mixed-species flocks. No geographic overlap with Barred Antshrike. Iris color variable: whitish or yellow to gray-brown or brown. **VOICE** Song a high, nasal accelerating and rising-falling series of notes followed by an abrupt shorter, higher series ending in a rattle: "*pew pew-pew-pew'pu'puPEWpee pew-trr'eh.*" Call a high, descending, mewing whistle: "*peew.*" **E**

4 BARRED ANTSHRIKE *Thamnophilus doliatus* * 15–16 cm (6–6¼ in)
Fairly common near ground in dense second growth and forest edge, up to 1400 m; in northeastern Amazonia largely restricted to river islands. Usually in pairs, not in mixed-species flocks. Compare male to Lined and Fasciated antshrike males. Buffy female is distinctive (but cf. female White-lined Tanager). **VOICE** Song an accelerating, rising-falling series of mellow notes ending with a higher bark: "*kyuh kya-kya-kya-kya'ko'kokoWAH!*" Similar to Lined and Chestnut-backed antshrikes, but usually has fewer notes, pace less accelerating, and terminal bark more obvious. Calls a nasal "*AW*" and a mewing whistled "*wheeu.*" **Co, E, Br, Bo**

5 LINED ANTSHRIKE *Thamnophilus tenuepunctaus* * 16 cm (6 in)
Fairly common along east slope of northern Andes, 700 to 1700 m, locally down to 200 m in Marañón Valley. Found at edge of humid forest and in second growth. Forages in pairs; rarely with mixed-species flocks. Iris color variable: gray, whitish, or pale yellow to reddish brown. Male similar to Barred, but usually at higher elevations; also more narrowly barred (appearing blacker). Female indistinguishable from female Chestnut-backed Antshrike (no known overlap). **VOICE** Similar to Chestnut-backed. **Co, E**

6 CHESTNUT-BACKED ANTSHRIKE *Thamnophilus palliatus* * 16–17 cm (6¼–6¾ in)
Fairly common along east slope of Andes in central and southern Peru, 400 to 1700 m. Found at edges of humid forest, inside humid forest at openings (such as landslides or large treefall gaps), and in second growth; in south also found in bamboo. Forages in pairs, sometimes with mixed-species flocks. Combination of chestnut upperparts and black-and-white barred underparts distinctive within range. Iris color variable: usually whitish or pale yellow but may be light brown. **VOICE** Song an accelerating falling, or slightly rising before falling, series of mellow notes ending in a lower bark: "*kah kah-kah-kah-ka'ka'ka'kaka'pah.*" Cf. Barred Antshrike song. Call a sharp bark "*awr!*" and a mewing whistled "*wheeu.*" **Br, Bo**

BAMBOO ANTSHRIKE

♂

♀

♂

CHAPMAN'S ANTSHRIKE

♂

♀

FASCIATED ANTSHRIKE

♀

♀

BARRED ANTSHRIKE

♂

♂

CHESTNUT-BACKED
ANTSHRIKE

♀

LINED ANTSHRIKE

♂

LINED/CHESTNUT-
BACKED ANTSHRIKE

PLATE
158

PERCNOSTOLA ANTBIRDS AND ANTSHRIKES

The long crest of White-lined Antbird (especially of the male) recalls antshrikes, but the three Percnostola *antbirds on this plate have more slender bills. Undulated is a large antshrike with a very heavy bill. Collared Antshrike is one of the few antbirds in dry forest and scrub of northwest.*

1 BLACK-HEADED ANTBIRD *Percnostola rufifrons* * 13–14 cm (5¼–5½ in)
Very local and poorly known in northeast, where found in dense forest understory, such as treefall gaps and forest borders, including in stunted forest on sandy soils. Forages, in pairs or as solitary individuals, on or very close to ground; in Brazil often follows army ants. No geographic overlap with similar Allpahuayo Antbird. Note black throat and crown and white wing bars of male (reminiscent of smaller Black-chinned Antbird of water-edge habitats). Compare female to Slate-colored and Spot-winged antbirds. **VOICE** Song a moderate-paced series of monotone whistles with a stuttered, higher-pitched introductory whistle: *"hee'hee hew hew hew hew."* **Co, Br**

2 WHITE-LINED ANTBIRD *Percnostola lophotes* 14.5 cm (5¾ in)
Locally fairly common in southeast up to 1350 m. Primarily in tall (nearly pure) stands of spiny bamboo (*Guadua* sp.) in river-edge forest or along edges of gardens or roads. Scarce away from bamboo, in tall thickets of *Heliconia* or similar plants in riverine forest. Resembles antshrikes in behavior and calls. Both sexes raise conspicuous crest feathers when excited, and routinely pump down and slowly raise (and fan) their tails. Pairs forage on or near ground. Compare female to Great Antshrike female. **VOICE** Song a descending, accelerating series of hollow whistles, with a noticeably long space between first note and rest of the song: *"TEW tew-tew-tew'tew'tew'tu'tutu."* Call a hollow, musical *"chew"* note, often followed by a growled *"reeh."* **Br, Bo**

3 ALLPAHUAYO ANTBIRD *Percnostola arenarum* 13–14 cm (5¼–5½ in)
Very local in northern Amazonia in understory of poor-soil habitats, especially varillales and irapayales. Behavior similar to Black-headed Antbird. Male is like Black-headed, but crown gray. Female is grayer above and has white belly and center to throat (eastern population); underparts more uniformly tawny in population on Río Morona (undescribed subspecies? not illustrated). **VOICE** Song a moderately paced, slightly decelerating series of monotone whistles usually with a stuttered, higher-pitched introductory note: *"hi'hi hew-hew-hew-hew-hew-hew-hew."* Faster paced than song of Black-headed. Calls a descending whine or whistle, a harsher *"tchah,"* a rising, melodic *"k'lee?"* and a musical, rising-falling sputtering rattle: *"pur'E'E'E'e'e'rr."* **ENDEMIC**

4 COLLARED ANTSHRIKE *Sakesphorus bernardi* * 18 cm (7 in)
Fairly common to common in dry forest and desert scrub in northwest below 1200 m and to 1950 in dry Marañón Valley. Typically in pairs, sometimes joins mixed-species flocks. Both sexes have bushy crest and broad white (male) or buffy or buffy white (female) collar. Male *shumbae* (lower Marañón in and near Chinchipe Valley; not illustrated) has more white on face, darker upperparts, and reduced black throat patch; female is paler overall (nearly white below), with brighter rufous crown. "Coastal" forms and *shumbae* approach one another in Marañón drainage in north central Cajamarca. **VOICE** Song (coast and western Marañón) a slow, accelerating, monotone series of deep barking notes: *"WUR-wur-wur-wur-wur-wur-WURL!"* Song (*shumbae*) much faster with distinct introductory and terminal notes: *"WURKtr'r'r'r'r'r'r'r'r'r'r'r'rWURK!"* Call a series of complaining or mewing caws: *"AWW aww aww awr."* Also mewing whines, and a bark-rattle, the rattle rising in pitch: *"PERK! gr'r'r'r'r'r'r"*; sometimes only the bark is given. **E**

5 UNDULATED ANTSHRIKE *Frederickena unduligera* * 22–24 cm (8½–9½ in)
Rare to uncommon in dense forest understory, primarily in terra firme, and in advanced second growth, locally up to 1050 m. Male blackish, narrowly barred white; much more narrowly barred than other barred antshrikes (plate 157). Female plumage geographically variable; browner subspecies *fulva* with barred breast is north of the Amazon, and buffier, less barred subspecies *diversa* south of the Amazon. Note large size and crest; often jerks tail from side to side when foraging. **VOICE** Song a rising series of rising notes: *"wur we wee wee WEE WEE,"* faster in southern *diversa* than northern *fulva*. Call a loud, bisyllabic, descending, metallic snarl: *"TCHEErrrl"* or *"DJEErrrl."* **Co, E, Br, Bo**

BLACK-HEADED
ANTBIRD

♀

♂

WHITE-LINED
ANTBIRD

♂

♀

ALLPAHUAYO
ANTBIRD

♀

♂

COLLARED
ANTSHRIKE

♂

♀

♀ *fulva*

UNDULATED
ANTSHRIKE

♂

♀ *diversa*

PLATE
159

LOWLAND BLACK AND GRAY ANTSHRIKES

Amazonian antshrikes in which male is black or gray, and usually with little or no patterning on the wings; see plate 161.

1 MOUSE-COLORED ANTSHRIKE *Thamnophilus murinus* * 14 cm (5½ in)
Uncommon to locally fairly common in understory of humid forest in northern Amazonia below 1200 m. More confined to terra firme than Plain-winged Antshrike. Also slightly smaller, with more slender bill, and grayish (not red or brown) iris. Male paler than Plain-winged, especially below, with narrow white tips to wing coverts. Wings gray. Female paler than female Plain-winged, especially below, with duller rufous crown (less contrast); small pale tips to wing coverts can be difficult to see. **VOICE** Song a fairly slow-paced, accelerating series of nasal notes, ending in a bisyllabic rising-falling terminal note: "*arr arr arr-arr wee'AWR.*" Usually slower-paced than Plain-winged, with fewer notes, and terminal note more distinctively bisyllabic; but songs of these two species sometimes indistinguishable. Calls a high whiny "*weeu,*" a quiet rising growl, and a short, unmodulated "*aw*" (shorter than Plain-winged). **Co, E, Br, Bo**

2 PLAIN-WINGED ANTSHRIKE *Thamnophilus schistaceus* * 14 cm (5½ in)
Most common and widely distributed *Thamnophilus* of Amazonian humid forest, up to 1300 m. Often associates with mixed-species flocks in under- and midstory. Iris reddish. Male gray, with unspotted wings; crown black north of the Amazon, well east of Andes (*capitalis*), dusky or gray elsewhere. Rufous crown of female contrasts with grayish face and dull brown body. Cf. Mouse-colored Antshrike. **VOICE** Song a fairly fast-paced, accelerating series of nasal notes, ending in a descending terminal note: "*rah rah-rah-rah-ra'ra'rara'aw*"; cf. Mouse-colored. Calls a quick "*kyuk,*" and a fairly drawn-out modulated, descending caw: "*aahhhrr.*" **Co, E, Br, Bo**

3 WHITE-SHOULDERED ANTSHRIKE *Thamnophilus aethiops* * 16 cm (6¼ in)
Uncommon, in humid forest understory in eastern lowlands, below 1500 m (*kapouni*). Forages in pairs, usually not with mixed-species flocks. Male dark gray (may appear black in poor light) with a few white spots on wing coverts. Female chestnut-brown, tawnier below. Darker *aethiops*, which more often joins mixed-species flocks, is rare in Andean foothills north of Río Marañón; male black with white spotting on upper wing coverts, female dark reddish brown. Cf. Bicolored and White-streaked antvireos. **VOICE** Song a slow, monotone series of 4–7 down-slurred notes: "*aww aww aww aww aww.*" Resembles forest-falcon or trogon, particularly at a distance. Calls a descending, slightly growled caw "*graaah,*" a clearer "*aww,*" and a higher "*kyuk.*" **Co, E, Br, Bo**

4 [ACRE ANTSHRIKE *Thamnophilus divisorius*] ca. 16 cm (6¼ in)
Restricted to the Sierra del Divisor (photographed and tape recordings), where fairly common but confined to low-stature forest with dense understory on low ridges (ca. 500 m). Difficult to observe. Forages in pairs, apart from mixed-species flocks. Two-toned female unmistakable. Male similar to male White-shouldered but lacks white spots on wing coverts, is a bluer shade of gray, and head is darker than body, creating a "hooded" appearance. **VOICE** Song an accelerating, descending series of rich notes with a distinctive, higher pitched, bisyllabic terminal bark: "*kuk kuk-kuk-kuk-ku-ku-ku-ku'wah'AH.*" Calls cawed "*aw*" and a longer, descending "*awwr.*" **Br**

[COCHA ANTSHRIKE *Thamnophilus praecox*] 16 cm (6¼ in)
No record, but occurs in Napo drainage in immediately adjacent Ecuador. Restricted to forest understory along blackwater streams and lakes. Forages in pairs, rarely with mixed-species flocks. Cf. uncannily similar but larger White-shouldered Antbird, which has prominent pale orbital skin. Male antbird also has white "shoulders"; female antbird less deeply colored than female antshrike. **VOICE** Song a slightly accelerating, slightly descending series of rich, hooting notes: "*choo-choo-choo-choo-choo-choo.*" Calls a deep, rich cooing note, usually doubled: "*pu pu*"; also a deep, rising or rising-falling, modulated, rattle: "*awrrr*" or "*wa'RRRRrrr.*" **E**

5 CASTELNAU'S ANTSHRIKE *Thamnophilus cryptoleucus* 17–18 cm (6¾–7 in)
Uncommon to locally fairly common in dense undergrowth of *Cecropia*-dominated river islands; locally also in similar habitats on mainland. Forages in singles or pairs, usually apart from mixed-species flocks. Black with semiconcealed white interscapular patch; male has prominent white tips to wing coverts. **VOICE** Song an accelerating, descending series of downslurred notes: "*kyuk kyuk-kyew-kew-kew'ku'ku'kukuku.*" Call a cawing "*raow*"; a similar bark-rattle, the rattle rising in pitch: "*raow-brrrrrrrr*"; and a down-slurred mewing "*aww,*" often doubled. **Co, E, Br**

MOUSE-COLORED
ANTSHRIKE

♀

♂

PLAIN-WINGED
ANTSHRIKE

♀

♂ *capitalis*

♂ *kapouni*

♀ *aethiops*

WHITE-SHOULDERED
ANTSHRIKE

♀ *kapouni*

♂ *aethiops*

WHITE-SHOULDERED ANTSHRIKE

ACRE ANTSHRIKE

♂

♀

COCHA ANTSHRIKE

♂

♀

♂

♀

CASTELNAU'S
ANTSHRIKE

PLATE
160
ANTVIREOS AND ANDEAN ANTSHRIKES

Antvireos are similar to antshrikes but are smaller, with more slender bills.

1 WHITE-STREAKED ANTVIREO *Dysithamnus leucostictus* * 12.5 cm (5 in)

Uncommon and local in humid montane forest understory, 1350–1850 m, on east slope of northern Andes. Pairs usually with mixed-species flocks. Black breast of male darker than gray belly; cf. male Bicolored Antvireo and (*aethiops*) White-shouldered Antshrike. Female easily recognized by rufous crown, and gray-and-white streaked underparts. **VOICE** Song a descending, fairly even-paced series of whistles; introductory note lower than the next: "*wee WEE wee wee wee whew.*" Less accelerating than San Martín song of Bicolored. Call a quiet "*pu.*" **Co, E**

2 PLAIN ANTVIREO *Dysithamnus mentalis* * 11.5 cm (4½ in)

Fairly common in humid montane forest understory on east slope of Andes and outlying ridges, 600–2100 m. Also fairly common in semideciduous forest in Tumbes at 400–800 m. Frequently in pairs, often with mixed-species flocks. Small and plain, with relatively large head and short tail. Male paler below than other plain gray antbirds, antshrikes, and antvireos; dusky cheek usually evident. Compare female to smaller Tawny-crowned Greenlet (which has white iris and is more yellowish). **VOICE** Song an accelerating, descending series of whistled notes, the introductory note lower than the next: "*whew WHEW whew-whew-whew-whew-wew'wew'wew'wew'tutu.*" Call a down-slurred, mewing "*pew,*" sometimes a doubled "*chew-ew.*" Also a gruff "*grr*" and a musical rising series of quiet mewing or whining notes: "*pew ew-ew-ew?*" **Co, E, Br, Bo**

3 BICOLORED ANTVIREO *Dysithamnus occidentalis* * 13.5 cm (5½ in)

Rare, local, poorly known; in humid montane forest understory on east slope of Andes at 2000–2500 m. Apparently prefers dense understory at forest light gaps (treefalls, landslides). Singly or in pairs, not with mixed-species flocks. Dark, 2-tone female unmistakable. Male very similar to slightly smaller White-streaked Antvireo, but more uniformly colored below. Cf. also male of White-shouldered Antshrike (*aethiops*). **VOICE** Song (San Martín) an accelerating, descending series of clear, rising whistles: "*WEE wee-wee-wee-whe'he'huhu.*" Call a deep chattered growl: "*prr'r'r'r.*" Also a rising series of mewing or whining notes: "*dew-dew dwi-dwee-dwee?*" Only known vocalization of Ecuadorian (and north Peruvian?) *punctitectus* a louder, slower version of this chatter: "*djer-der-der.*" In Ecuador, also a descending, clear, mewed "*dew.*" **Co, E**

4 RUFOUS-CAPPED ANTSHRIKE *Thamnophilus ruficapillus* * 16 cm (6¼ in)

Rare to uncommon, in 2 disjunct populations in Andes at 1800–3000 m, at low to middle heights at edges of semihumid montane forest and in second growth. Compare male to Lined and Chestnut-backed antshrikes; note unstreaked sides of head and the gray back. Crown and wings of female reddish; cf. females of Variable, Upland, and Uniform antshrikes. Northern *jaczewskii* paler than southern *marcapatae*. **VOICE** Song an accelerating, rising-falling series of high, nasal notes ending in a lower bark: "*wah nyah nyah-nyah-nya-nya-nya'nya-arr.*" Call a low, rasping snarl "*aarrrr*"; also (Bolivia) a rising whine. **Br, Bo**

5 UPLAND ANTSHRIKE *Thamnophilus aroyae* 14.5–15 cm (5½–6 in)

Poorly known. Recorded only on low ridges, 800–1000 m (to 1700 m in Bolivia). Forages in pairs, usually not with mixed-species flocks, in dense undergrowth at humid montane forest edge. Male grayer than Variable Antshrike of higher elevations. Cf. White-shouldered Antshrike (lower elevations, less white in wing and tail) and Black Antbird. Female similar to female Plain-winged Antshrike, but tawnier below. **VOICE** Song a fast-paced, accelerating series of nasal notes, ending in a down-slurred terminal note poorly defined from the penultimate note: "*wur wur-wur-wur-wur'rrrr.*" Calls high whines; a drawn-out, modulated, throaty, descending caw "*aarrrr*"; and a mewing "*awww,*" similar to Variable Antshrike. **Bo**

6 UNIFORM ANTSHRIKE *Thamnophilus unicolor* * 15.5–16 cm (6–6¼ in)

Uncommon to fairly common in humid montane forest understory on east slope of Andes, 1250–2300 m. Pairs often forage apart from mixed-species flocks. Male uniformly dark gray, sometimes with small white tips to rectrices; iris gray or grayish white. Gray sides of head of female contrast with reddish brown crown and tawny-brown breast. **VOICE** Song a slightly accelerating and rising, slow series of 4–8 high, descending notes "*NYAH NYAH-nyah-nyah.*" Song in Cuzco similar but much higher pitched. Calls a gruff bark-rattle: "*trr-grr'r'r,*" sometimes the bark is given alone; also a descending whine and a slightly modulated, throaty, descending caw: "*raahhh.*" **Co, E**

WHITE-STREAKED ANTVIREO

PLAIN ANTVIREO

♂

♀

♀

BICOLORED ANTVIREO

♀

♂

♀ *marcapatae*

RUFOUS-CAPPED
ANTSHRIKE

♀ *jaczewskii*

♂ *jaczewskii*

♂ *marcapatae*

UPLAND ANTSHRIKE

♂

♀

♂

♀

♀

UNIFORM ANTSHRIKE

PLATE
161

PATTERN-WINGED ANTSHRIKES

Antshrikes in which the males have patterned wings. Most are Amazonian, but Variable Antshrike is Andean, and the two slaty-antshrikes occur in drier forests in Tumbes or in low, semiarid valleys.

1 PEARLY ANTSHRIKE *Megastictus margaritatus* 13 cm (5¼ in)
Rare to uncommon, in forest understory in northern Amazonia, also very locally in south-central Peru; perhaps most common in terra firme. Forages in pairs, seldom with mixed-species flocks. Typically sallies or hover-gleans for prey, to air or to vegetation; sallies may be several meters long, rivaling sallies of *Thamnomanes* antshrikes. Frequently flicks or twitches tail side to side. Note light gray iris and very large, pale spots on wing coverts and tertials of both sexes. Plumage in both sexes resembles that of much smaller Plain-throated Antwren. **VOICE** Song a series of clear, rising whistles followed abruptly by some lower grating notes: "*wheeu wheeu wheeu'djrrr-djrrr-djrrr.*" Call a rising, squeaky "*kweet-kweet-kweet,*" also a short rattle. **Co, E, Br**

2 SPOT-WINGED ANTSHRIKE *Pygiptila stellaris* * 13.5 cm (5¼ in)
Fairly common and widespread in Amazonia, below 600 m. Pairs forage in midstory and canopy of forest and in vine tangles, usually accompanying mixed-species flocks. Frequently forages among dead-leaf clusters. Foraging position and distinctive shape—chunky body, large head and bill, accentuated by very short tail, often twitched from side to side—often are best clues to identification. Female similar to female Gray Antwren, but much larger with larger, heavier bill. **VOICE** Song a stuttered musical, ringing trill followed by a descending whistle: "*p'p'p'p'p'p'p'REEER.*" Call a sharp, metallic note usually followed by a descending rasp or whistle: "*tchip! jeer.*" **Co, E, Br, Bo**

3 NORTHERN SLATY-ANTSHRIKE *Thamnophilus punctatus* * 14 cm (5½ in)
Locally fairly common in heavily fragmented dry forests in north: in Chinchipe and Marañón valleys up to 1200 m (*leucogaster*; belly whitish in both sexes); and along a short stretch of Río Huallaga (*huallagae*). Males similar to male Amazonian Antshrike, but no reported geographic overlap; also note different habitats. Brown females very different from female Amazonian. **VOICE** Song an accelerating, rising or rising-falling series of rich nasal notes with no obvious terminal note: "*kah kah kah-kah-kah'ka'ka'ka'ka'kr.*" Calls a short bark "*aw*"; a drawn-out monotone rattle of variable pace, "*churr'r'r'r'r'r,*" similar to that of Great Antshrike; a descending 1–3-note whiny caw: "*ahh-ahhr*"; and a series of hollow "*kuk*" notes. **Co, E, Br**

4 VARIABLE ANTSHRIKE *Thamnophilus caerulescens* * 14.5 cm (5¾ in)
Fairly common and widespread along east slope of Andes at 1000–2400 m, locally down to 600 m and up to 3000 m. Found in humid montane forest understory, especially at edge, in second growth, and in openings (such as treefalls and landslides). Forages in pairs, often with mixed-species flocks. Male mostly black; belly varies from black to mottled white. Cf. Black Antbird. Female readily identified by contrast between tawny belly and gray head and breast; also note blackish cap. **VOICE** Song a short, even-paced, even-pitch series of 4–8 nasal, descending notes: "*nyah nyah nyah nyah.*" Recalls Uniform Antshrike, but more rapid and even-paced, and series is monotone. Calls a descending "*aww,*" often doubled "*aww-aww*"; also a low, growled bark: "*grrr.*" **Br, Bo**

5 [WESTERN SLATY-ANTSHRIKE *Thamnophilus atrinucha*] * 14.5–15 cm (5¾–6 in)
Locally fairly common in understory of semideciduous forest in Tumbes, 400–800 m; reported only from sight records. Cf. smaller Plain Antvireo. Male only large, gray antshrike in northwest. Brown female with white wing bars unlikely to be confused with other species in range. **VOICE** Song an accelerating series of nasal notes ending with 1 or 2 higher notes: "*wur wur wur-wur-wur-wur'wur'wur'wur'wur'AH.*" Calls a 1–4-note (usually 2) caw "*arr-arr*" and a bark-rattle: "*arr-grr'r'r'r*"; sometimes only the bark is given. **Co, E**

6 AMAZONIAN ANTSHRIKE *Thamnophilus amazonicus* * 14 cm (5½ in)
Uncommon and local in river-edge forest in Amazonia, including stream margins and seasonally flooded forests. Singles or pairs forage a few meters above ground; sometimes with mixed-species flocks. Male much more heavily marked with black and white than other gray Amazonian antshrikes (no overlap with slaty-antshrikes). Bright orange-brown foreparts of female are unmistakable. **VOICE** Song a rapid, accelerating, rising then abruptly falling, series of musical notes "*kur kur kur-kur-kur-kur-kur'ke'ke'ke'ke'kahkahkah.*" Calls high whines and a descending whining "*aww.*" **Co, E, Br, Bo**

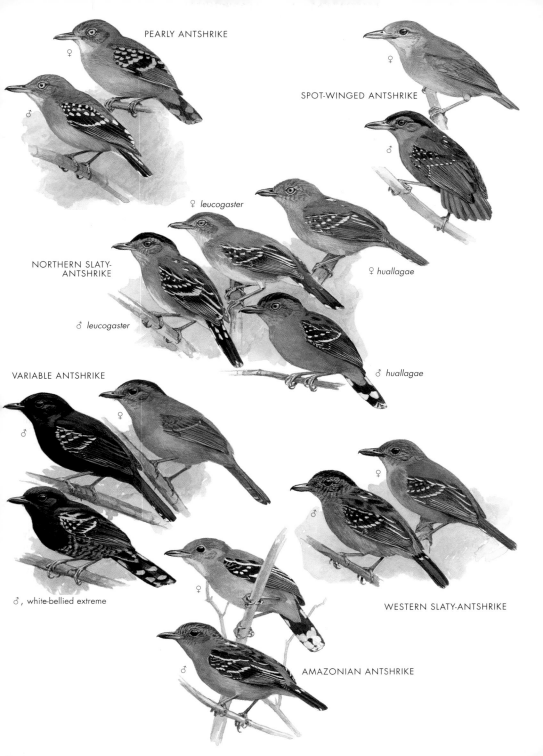

PEARLY ANTSHRIKE

♀

♂

SPOT-WINGED ANTSHRIKE

♀

♂

♀ leucogaster

NORTHERN SLATY-
ANTSHRIKE

♀ huallagae

♂ leucogaster

♂ huallagae

VARIABLE ANTSHRIKE

♂

♀

♀

♂

♂, white-bellied extreme

WESTERN SLATY-ANTSHRIKE

♀

AMAZONIAN ANTSHRIKE

♂

PLATE
162

THAMNOMANES AND RUSSET ANTSHRIKES
AND FIRE-EYE

Russet Antshrike resembles a foliage-gleaner (see plate 150). Thamnomanes *antshrikes perch with a vertical, flycatcher-like posture and forage with long sallies. Also attract attention with frequent sharp calls. Characteristic birds of humid Amazonian forests, where they are "leaders" of understory mixed-species flocks. Typically flocks contain two species of* Thamnomanes *that occupy slightly different strata: Cinereous or Bluish-slate forages in midstory, and Saturnine or Dusky-throated in understory. Fire-eye is a large, long-tailed understory antbird.*

1 CINEREOUS ANTSHRIKE *Thamnomanes caesius* * 14.5 cm (5¾ in)

Common in northern Amazonia, up to 500 m. No known overlap with Bluish-slate Antshrike, which it approaches (or meets?) on west bank of lower Río Ucayali; males almost indistinguishable. Otherwise all-gray male identified by posture, voice, and relatively long tail; cf. Dusky-throated Antshrike. Female drab brown with a rich tawny belly; more brightly colored and longer-tailed than female Dusky-throated. **VOICE** Song an accelerating, rising-falling series of clear, rising whistles that become a rapid, falling chatter: "*drEE-drEE-drEE-dri'dri'i'i'i'i'i'i'irrrrrrrrr.*" Call a series of rising mewing notes followed by a metallic chatter, the mewing notes sometimes omitted: "*dwer dwer-TEW'TEW'TEW.*" Also a mewing "*eewooee*" and a series of loud, rising whistles: "*WHEE WHEE WHEE.*" **Co, E, Br, Bo**

2 BLUISH-SLATE ANTSHRIKE *Thamnomanes schistogynus* 14.5 cm (5¾ in)

Replaces very similar Cinereous Antshrike in most of eastern Peru south of the Amazon, up to 1400 m. Cf. also male Dusky-throated Antshrike. Contrast between gray breast and tawny-rufous belly of female is unmistakable. **VOICE** Vocalizations probably not safely distinguished from Cinereous; song possibly has slightly longer and more widely spaced introductory whistles. **Br, Bo**

3 SATURNINE ANTSHRIKE *Thamnomanes saturninus* * 14.5 cm (5¾ in)

Locally replaces Dusky-throated Antshrike in limited area of east-central Peru south of the Amazon. Slightly larger than Dusky-throated with a longer tail; male is a darker, more plumbeous shade of gray; has larger, better-defined black throat and a white interscapular patch (lacking or very small in Dusky-throated), which rarely is visible in field. Throat of female white, showing more contrast against drab olive-brown breast than does female Dusky-throated. **VOICE** Very similar to Dusky-throated, and most vocalizations not safely distinguished. Song possibly has more notes in the rising series. **Br, Bo**

4 DUSKY-THROATED ANTSHRIKE *Thamnomanes ardesiacus* * 14 cm (5½ in)

Most widely distributed *Thamnomanes*; uncommon to fairly common in most of Amazonia up to 1000 m. Male often has small ragged black throat patch; separated from Cinereous or Bluish-slate antshrikes by voice, black throat (when present), less upright posture and shorter tail (may show very narrow white tips). Female dull brown with tawny belly and drab throat; best identified by behavior and voice. See Saturnine Antshrike. **VOICE** Song a rising, accelerating series of grinding notes, usually ending with a rising, grating terminal note: "*grrr girr-geer-geer'gree'gri'ti'ti djurrreee.*" Calls a grinding, down-slurred "*geer*"; a sharp, squeaky, descending "*TSEW!*" and a rising, hoarse "*djreet?*" **Co, E, Br, Bo**

5 RUSSET ANTSHRIKE *Thamnistes anabatinus* * 16 cm (6¼ in)

Uncommon but widespread in humid montane forest on east slope of Andes, at 600–1600 m. Forages in canopy mixed-species flocks that often include similarly plumaged foliage-gleaners (especially Rufous-rumped and larger Buff-fronted). Sexes similar; male has semiconcealed orange-rufous patch on lower back. Bill stouter, more hooked than in foliage-gleaners; also note fine pale streaks on upperparts. **VOICE** Song (south at least to Cuzco) a high, slightly accelerating, rising series of thin down-slurred whistles: "*tseeeu-tsew-tsew-tsew-tsew.*" Call a high "*swee-tip*" or simply "*swee.*" Also (Puno) a short, descending "*tsew.*" **Co, E, Bo**

6 WHITE-BACKED FIRE-EYE *Pyriglena leuconota* * 17.5–18 cm (6¾–7 in)

Fairly common on east slope of Andes, 500–2100 m, in understory of humid montane forest with broken canopy, at forest edge and in second growth. Also in humid evergreen forest in Tumbes at 400–800 m (*pacifica*). Forages near ground in pairs or family groups. Often attends army ants, but not with mixed flocks. Iris bright red; long black tail frequently "pounded" down. Females geographically variable. *Castanoptera* (Cajamarca, southern Amazonas) intergrades with *picea* (found south to western Cuzco). Very different *marcapatensis* in southern Cuzco and Puno. **VOICE** Song (all subspecies), a descending series of fairly evenly paced, piping whistled notes: "*PEE-PEE-pee-pee-pee-pi-pi.*" Calls a quiet, puttering "*pit'cht'cht*" and a low "*prrt*"; also a ringing, chattered "*tutututututu,*" a sharp "*pick*" and a mewed, descending "*eeww-eww.*" **Co, E, Br, Bo**

CINEREOUS ANTSHRIKE

BLUISH-SLATE ANTSHRIKE

SATURNINE ANTSHRIKE

♂, black-throated extreme

♀

RUSSET ANTSHRIKE

♂

DUSKY-THROATED ANTSHRIKE

♀ *castanoptera*

♀ *marcapatensis*

♂

♀ *pacifica*

♀ *picea*

WHITE-BACKED FIRE-EYE

PLATE
163

"CHECKER-THROATED" ANTWRENS

"Checker-throated" antwrens are mostly brown; males gray below in most species with the throat more or less "checkered" with black and white. All characteristically search for arthropod prey in curled dead leaves trapped in foliage in forest understory, and almost always forage in understory mixed-species flocks. One to three species are found at most Amazonian sites or in Andean foothills.

1 RUFOUS-TAILED ANTWREN *Myrmotherula erythrura* * 10–11.5 cm (4–4½ in)
Uncommon and local in Amazonia; in south confined to Andean foothills (up to 1000 m). Usually forages higher than other checker-throated species. Throat of male has little or no black-and-white stippling. Otherwise note reddish back and tail in both sexes. No strong geographic variation in plumage; minor variation in **VOICE** Song (*erythrura*; south to Amazonas) a slow, even-paced series of high whistles: "*wsew-wsew-wsew-wsew-wsew.*" Song of southern *septentrionalis* similar but notes may rise more. Calls a high, sputtering rattle and high "*tsip*" notes, also a descending, mewed "*eeyew.*" **Co, E, Br**

2 ORNATE ANTWREN *Myrmotherula ornata* * 10–11 cm (4–4¼ in)
Rare to uncommon. Local in north; more widespread in south, up to 1500 m, where largely restricted to bamboo thickets. Throat of male solid black. Center of back reddish brown north of Amazon (*saturata*); back color gray or gray-brown in central (*atrogularis*; not illustrated) and southern (*meridionalis*) Peru, but rarely individuals show some red. Females readily recognized by checkered throat pattern, contrasting with buff underparts. Female *meridionalis* are bright buff below; underparts grayish buff in other subspecies. **VOICE** Song (*meridionalis*) a rapid, but variably paced, descending, slightly decelerating series of high, thin ringing notes, usually with a distinct (higher-pitched or longer) introductory note: "*TSEE'tsee'tsee'tsee-tsee-tsee-tsee-tsee-tsu.*" Song of *saturata* similar, but usually slower-paced. Call a thin, squeaky series of high notes: "*p'tee tsee-tsee-tsee-tsee-tsee.*" Also a sharp "*p'tsee.*" **Co, E, Br, Bo**

3 FOOTHILL ANTWREN *Myrmotherula spodionota* * 10–11 cm (4–4¼ in)
Uncommon to fairly common in foothills on east slope of Andes, 750 to 1500 m. Similar to Stipple-throated Antwren, but generally darker and back brown. Male distinguished from White-eyed Antwren (which it replaces elevationally) by darker gray breast, darker brown back, and smaller pale (sometimes white) tips on wing coverts. Female generally darker than female White-eyed, with smaller, more spotted wing markings. **VOICE** Song a rapid, even-paced, rising-falling series of thin, high ringing whistles: "*ti'ti'TI'TI'ti'ti'ti'ti'ti'ti'ti.*" Calls a sharp "*pseet!*"; high thin "*tseet-tseet-tseet*" notes; and a thin, lisping "*tss-tss-tss*" as a scold (Cuzco). Also (southern Ecuador) a high, sputtering rattle. **Co, E**

4 WHITE-EYED ANTWREN *Myrmotherula leucophthalma* * 11 cm (4¼ in)
Fairly common and widespread in central and southeastern Peru below 800 m, locally to 1050 m. Also disjunct population along Río Morona. Relatively pale "checker-throated" antwren. Both sexes distinguished by plain brown (not reddish brown or red) back and tail and by largely cinnamon or buff (not white) wing bars. Cf. Stipple-throated Antwren, with which White-eyed locally overlaps in southern Peru. **VOICE** Song a descending, accelerating series of high, thin whistles: "*teeyu teeyu teeu-teeu'tew'tew.*" Calls a high, thin, ringing, descending rattle; thin peeping notes; and a high, rising, mewed "*ts'wee.*" **Br, Bo**

5 BROWN-BACKED ANTWREN *Myrmotherula fjeldsaai* 11 cm (4¼ in)
Poorly known; reported only from north of the Amazon and west of the upper Napo, mostly in forests on nutrient-poor soils. Very locally overlaps with Stipple-throated Antwren. Both sexes differ from Stipple-throated, Rufous-tailed, and northern populations of Ornate antwrens by brown upperparts. Closely resembles White-eyed Antwren, but male generally darker, and pale tips on median and lesser wing coverts usually whiter. Female distinguished by whitish throat, lightly streaked with black. **VOICE** Nearly identical to Stipple-throated. **E**

6 STIPPLE-THROATED ANTWREN *Myrmotherula haematonota* * 11 cm (4¼ in)
Uncommon to fairly common in humid forest; widespread in northern Amazonia but local farther south. Both sexes differ from White-eyed, Brown-backed, and Foothill antwrens by red or reddish brown back; from Rufous-tailed Antwren by brown tail, and (male) more strongly marked throat; and from *saturata* Ornate Antwren by "checkered" (not black) throat (male), and by buff throat, at best obscurely streaked with black (not clearly streaked black and white) in female. **VOICE** Song a fairly rapid but even-paced, descending series of very high, thin whistles: "*ti-TI-TI-ti-ti-ti-ti.*" Calls a high, thin, sputtering rattle and single high, thin "*tspi*" notes. **Co, E, Br, Bo**

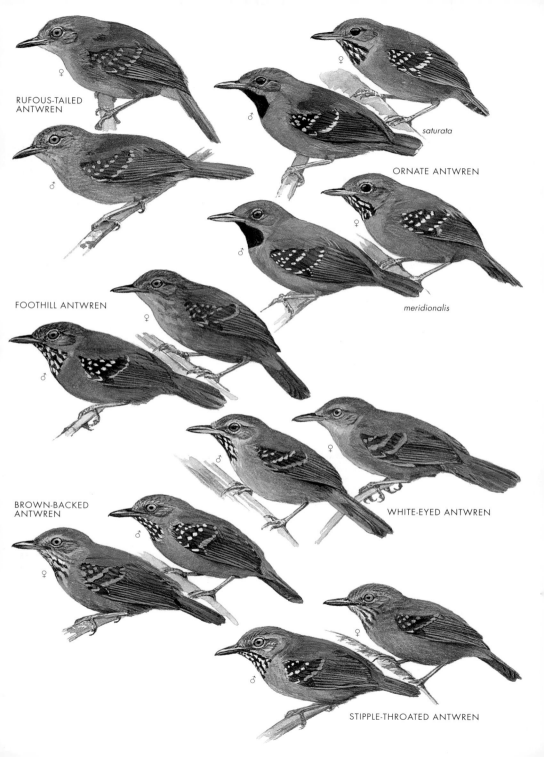

RUFOUS-TAILED
ANTWREN

♀

♂

ORNATE ANTWREN

♀

♂

saturata

♀

♂

meridionalis

FOOTHILL ANTWREN

♀

♂

WHITE-EYED ANTWREN

♂

♀

BROWN-BACKED
ANTWREN

♂

♀

♀

♂

STIPPLE-THROATED ANTWREN

PLATE
164

STREAKED *MYRMOTHERULA* ANTWRENS

Species on this plate are very small, yellow or white antwrens streaked with black and white.

1 MOUSTACHED ANTWREN *Myrmotherula ignota* * 8 cm (3–3¼ in)

Locally common in northern and central Amazonia, up to 1000 m, in forest canopy, sometimes foraging lower at forest edge; particularly found at "breaks" in forest such as along streams or treefall edges. Often occurs with similar Pygmy Antwren, but more widespread in forest interior. Moustached is blacker above, especially on crown, with broader, more prominent black lateral throat streak; female also more extensively buffy than female Pygmy. Also differs in **VOICE** Song an accelerating, descending, moderately paced, musical trill: "*tyip tyip-tyip-tip-tip-tip-tip-tip-tip.*" Calls include a rich "*tchip*" and descending "*tew.*" **Co, E, Br**

2 PYGMY ANTWREN *Myrmotherula brachyura* 8 cm (3–3¼ in)

Most common and widespread yellow-breasted *Myrmotherula* in Amazonia, up to 1000 m, especially at forest edge (including along forest streams) and in second growth. Pairs forage in canopy, especially in vine tangles, sometimes with mixed-species flocks. Cf. Moustached and Sclater's antwrens. Most easily identified by **VOICE** Song an accelerating, rising-falling, rapid, musical trill: "*tur ti ti-ti-ti'ti'te'te'te'te'tur'tur'tur'tur.*" Similar to song of Moustached, but faster, and accelerates more at end. Calls include a rapid, quiet, descending rattle: "*tree'e'e'r.*" Also rich "*tchirp*" notes. **Co, E, Br, Bo**

3 STRIPE-CHESTED ANTWREN *Myrmotherula longicauda* * 10–11 cm (4–4¼ in)

Fairly common along east slope of Andes, 500 to 1550 m. Found in under- and midstory at edge of humid and semihumid forest, in second growth, and in bamboo. Also a disjunct population in Río Samiria Basin, in a stunted, permanently flooded forest associated with blackwater lakes. Usually in pairs, occasionally with mixed-species flocks. Male less heavily streaked than male Amazonian Streaked-Antwren, especially on throat and belly, lacks semiconcealed white interscapular patch, and is longer-tailed. Ventral streaking all but lacking in female, which also has buff (not bright ochraceous) head. **VOICE** Song a slow, even-paced, monotone series of musical couplets: "*tee-tip tee-tip tee-tip tee-tip tee-tip.*" Calls a descending "*tew,*" quiet "*sick-sick*" notes, and a ringing, harsh rattle. **Co, E, Bo**

4 SCLATER'S ANTWREN *Myrmotherula sclateri* 8.5 cm (3¼ in)

Fairly common in humid forest canopy, up to 700 m. Inconspicuous member of mixed flocks, in canopy vine tangles and dense foliage. Differs from Pygmy and Moustached antwrens by yellow throat (both sexes); center of breast of female also narrowly streaked, and head more washed with ochre-buff. More confined to forest interior than are Pygmy and Moustached. **VOICE** Song an even-paced, slow series of mewing rising-falling whistles: "*wheew wheew wheew wheew wheew.*" Similar to Fasciated Antshrike but higher-pitched and quieter. Calls a rising whistled "*huree-huree?*" and a quiet "*pip,*" sometimes in series. **Br, Bo**

5 CHERRIE'S ANTWREN *Myrmotherula cherriei* 10 cm (4 in)

Fairly common, but very local along ríos Tigre and Nanay. Found in stunted forest that is flooded for all or much of year, usually in association with very sandy soils, at edges of streams or lakes. Male very similar to male Amazonian Streaked-Antwren, but black ventral streaks broader; bill entirely black (mandible gray in Streaked); and lacks semiconcealed white interscapular patch. Female more evenly colored than female Streaked: belly same color as breast, and head buff (not bright ochraceous). **VOICE** Song a rapid, even-paced, monotone or rising, dry rattling trill: "*trr'e'e'e'e'e'e'e'e'e'r,*" similar to Amazonian Streaked-Antwren. Call a mewing "*kyew.*" **Co, Br**

6 AMAZONIAN STREAKED-ANTWREN *Myrmotherula multostriata* 9.5 cm (3¾ in)

Fairly common in Amazonia (below 500 m) in under- and midstory tangles at edges of oxbow lakes and forest streams; never far from water. Forages in pairs, usually apart from other species, but may join mixed-species flocks. Most widespread black-and-white striped Amazonian antwren. Male more heavily streaked below than similar Stripe-chested Antwren of foothills, and has a semiconcealed white interscapular patch. Female readily recognized by bright ochraceous head, and streaked, buffy breast contrasting with a whitish belly. **VOICE** Song a rapid, even-paced, monotone or rising, musical trill (male only): "*tree'e'e'e'e'e'e'e'r,*" often answered by female by a rising-falling series of squeaky whistles "*pew pew PEE PEE peh.*" Latter vocalization may be given alone by either sex. Call a mewing "*eew,*" often doubled to "*ee-ew*" or in short series. **Co, E, Br, Bo**

MOUSTACHED ANTWREN ♀

♂

PYGMY ANTWREN

♂

♀

STRIPE-CHESTED ANTWREN ♀

♂

SCLATER'S ANTWREN

♂

♀

CHERRIE'S ANTWREN ♂

♀

♂

AMAZONIAN STREAKED-ANTWREN

PLATE
165

GRAY MYRMOTHERULA ANTWRENS

Confusingly similar; learn the common species (Slaty, Long-winged, and Gray antwrens) well as a basis for comparison to rarer or geographically restricted species.

1 LEADEN ANTWREN Myrmotherula assimilis * 10 cm (4 in)

Uncommon, in under- and midstory of wooded river islands; also locally on mainland along margins of streams or oxbow lakes. Forages in pairs; less closely associated with flocks than other gray *Myrmotherula*. Frequently twitches wings and tail. Male similar to male Gray Antwren (*pallida*), but little overlap in habitat or foraging strata. Also has semiconcealed white interscapular patch (lacking in Gray), and wing coverts gray tipped white (black or black and gray tipped white in Gray). Note wing bars on female. **VOICE** Song an accelerating, descending trill: "*tew tew-tew-tew'tew'tew'-tew'tu'tu'teerrrrrrru.*" Calls a descending, buzzy "*pzeeru*" and a rich "*tchew.*" **Co, Br, Bo**

2 GRAY ANTWREN Myrmotherula menetriesii * 9.5–10 cm (3¾–4 in)

Fairly common and widespread in mid-story and lower canopy of humid forest of Amazonia, up to 1100 m. Singles or pairs forage with mixed-species flocks; usually higher in canopy than other antwrens but overlaps with Long-winged. Twitches short tail much like Ihering's. Male paler gray than Long-winged; throat entirely gray (north of Amazon; *pallida*) or with less extensive black throat patch, limited to center of throat and breast (south of Amazon; *menetriesii*). Female very similar to *garbei* female Long-winged, but purer gray above, and deeper buff below. **VOICE** Song an even-paced or slightly accelerating, slow, rising series of whistled notes: "*wur wur whew whew-whew-whew-whe-whe-wee-wee-wee-wee.*" Calls a series of musical "*pew-pew'pwee*" or "*tu-tu'pip*" phrases, last note highest. Also quiet "*pi-chee*"; a quiet "*pew*" or "*psew*"; and a chatter: "*chuichuichuichuichui.*" **Co, E, Br, Bo**

3 IHERING'S ANTWREN Myrmotherula iheringi * 9.5–10 cm (3¾–4 in)

Local and uncommon in southern Amazonia, below 650 m. Singles or pairs forage mostly at dead leaves and twigs in forest understory; usually with mixed-species flocks. Often restricted to bamboo, where bamboo is present. Wags tail from side to side. Male similar to male Long-winged, but darker gray, with more extensive black throat patch (extending onto malars), and underwing coverts white (not gray or gray and white). Note bold black-and-white wing markings of female. **VOICE** Song a slow, slightly accelerating series: "*pu pew pew pew pew pew pew pew.*" Calls short "*pi*" and "*pwi*" notes, sometimes as a quiet chatter. Also a higher, squeaky "*pwi'ee.*" **Br, Bo**

4 LONG-WINGED ANTWREN Myrmotherula longipennis * 10–11 cm (4–4¼ in)

Fairly common in under- and midstory of humid forest, up to 900 m. Singles or pairs are regular in mixed-species flocks. Frequently flicks wings (but does not wag tail). Black throat of male extensive, often with irregular border; cf. Gray Antwren. Narrow white scapulars diagnostic, but difficult to see. Female geographically variable. Brown-backed, pale-bellied *longipennis* north of Amazon/east of Napo. Elsewhere upperparts grayish olive; underparts buff (*zimmeri*, west of Napo) or light buff (*garbei*, south of Amazon; cf. very similar female Gray Antwren). **VOICE** Song a rising series: "*durooee duree duree deree dreee.*" Calls a squeaky, mewed "*eew-ew*" (sometimes in rapid series of several notes) and a mewing, whistled "*whew-whew,*" very similar to White-flanked Antwren. **Co, E, Br, Bo**

5 RIO SUNO ANTWREN Myrmotherula sunensis * 8.5–9 cm (3¼–3½ in)

Very local, in foothills of central Peru, 300–700 m (*yessupi*); also possibly along lower Río Yavarí (*sunensis?*). Singles and pairs forage in under- and midstory of humid forest, usually with mixed-species flocks. Similar to Slaty Antwren, but at lower elevations; note shorter tail. Female more brown above and paler below than female Slaty; more richly colored than female Long-winged and Gray antwrens. **VOICE** Song (*sunensis*) a short, descending series of rising whistles "*p'see sui-sui.*" Calls a quiet, mewing "*rhee?*" and a descending trill. Also a rapid chattered "*p'ti-chu-chu.*" **Co, E, Br**

6 SLATY ANTWREN Myrmotherula schisticolor * 10–11 cm (4–4¼ in)

Fairly common on east slope of Andes and outlying ridges, 1100 to 2000 m, locally down to 800 m. Singles or pairs forage in humid montane forest understory, usually with mixed-species flocks. Male very dark. Female 2-toned (gray or gray-brown back contrasts with deep buff underparts). Little or no elevational overlap with Amazonian species. **VOICE** Song a short series of rising whistles: "*heeip heeip heeip.*" Call a quiet, whiny mewed "*eew.*" **Co, E, Bo**

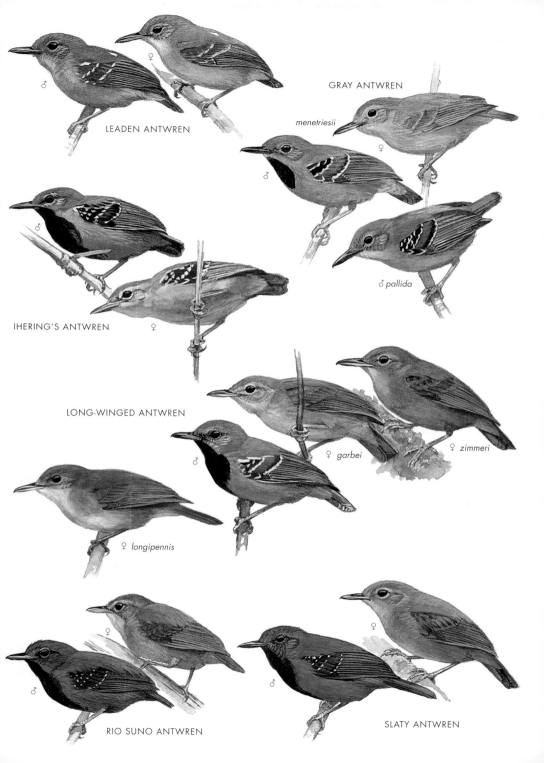

LEADEN ANTWREN

GRAY ANTWREN

menetriesii

♂

♀

♂ *pallida*

IHERING'S ANTWREN

♂

♀

LONG-WINGED ANTWREN

♀ *garbei*

♀ *zimmeri*

♂

♀ *longipennis*

RIO SUNO ANTWREN

♀

♂

SLATY ANTWREN

♀

♂

PLATE
166

TERENURA, FORMICIVORA, AND WHITE-FLANKED ANTWREN

White-flanked Antwren is a widespread, distinctive Myrmotherula (cf. species on plate 165). Terenura are very small, long-tailed canopy antwrens. They almost always associate with mixed-species flocks, foraging near ends of slender branches and in vine tangles. Very active, gleaning leaves and twigs, frequently hanging upside down or lunging after prey. The four species replace one another geographically or elevationally. Cf. also greenlets (plate 240), which lack wing bars.

1 RUSTY-BACKED ANTWREN *Formicivora rufa* * 14 cm (5½ in)

Three disjunct populations: in dry middle Huallaga and Urubamba valleys and on the Pampas del Heath. Found in open scrubby habitats: pastures, field edges, and savannas with scattered shrubs. Pairs forage actively in dense growth near ground. Note long tail, white superciliary, brown upperparts, and extensive black breast (male) or heavily streaked underparts (female). **VOICE** Song a series of rich notes in long stuttering bursts (up to 10 sec): "trr're'e trr're'e trr're'e trr're'e." Occasionally a longer, more uniform rattle. Calls a descending, mewed "dew," often in loose series, or a much more rapid chattered series: "dew'di'di'di'di'di'di'di." Also a rich note followed by a longer, breathy note: "tchip-heeet." **Br, Bo**

2 WHITE-FLANKED ANTWREN *Myrmotherula axillaris* * 10–11 cm (4–4¼ in)

One of the most common and widespread antwrens in Amazonia, up to 1050 m. Forages in forest understory, including second growth. Usually in pairs; often joins mixed-species flocks, but occurs away from flocks more often than most *Myrmotherula*. Frequently flicks wings, exposing long whitish flank plumes. Male very dark, especially in northern Peru (*melaena*); males in central and southern Peru usually (but not always) have gray sides to breast (*heterozyga, fresnayana*). Females less variable, usually buffy below with paler flanks; females of semideciduous forests along middle Río Huallaga more richly colored below with contrasting gray crown (not illustrated; undescribed subspecies?). **VOICE** Song (*melaena*) a slow, even-paced, descending series of mewing whistles: "pee pew-pew-pew-pew-pew." Song (*heterozyga, fresnayana*) a rapid, accelerating series of rich notes: "chew chu-chu-chu'chu'chu'chuchuchu." Calls a loud, squeaky "ee-ew" or "eew!" and a mewed, rising "duee?" often in series; also a rapid sputtered chatter, and a series of "tche" notes. **Co, E, Br, Bo**

3 ASH-WINGED ANTWREN *Terenura spodioptila* * 10 cm (4 in)

Restricted to northeastern Amazonia, where uncommon in canopy of terra firme. Cf. Chestnut-shouldered Antwren (which perhaps occurs locally on north bank of the Amazon). Male Ash-winged easily distinguished by white underparts and extensively reddish brown upperparts. Females more similar, although female Chestnut-shouldered is pale yellow on belly and has greener upperparts. **VOICE** Probably indistinguishable from other *Terenura*. **Co, E, Br**

4 CHESTNUT-SHOULDERED ANTWREN *Terenura humeralis* * 10 cm (4 in)

Uncommon in canopy of humid forest in Amazonia below 650 m. Distribution in northeastern Loreto not clear; apparently found near north bank of Amazon, east of Río Napo, but replaced farther north and east by Ash-winged Antwren. In south most common in transitional forest along upper edge of floodplain. Upper back usually olive, but may be rufous (like rump). Much like Rufous-rumped Antwren of Andes, but male has chestnut "shoulders." Cf. also Ash-winged Antwren. **VOICE** Probably indistinguishable from other *Terenura*. **E, Br, Bo**

5 YELLOW-RUMPED ANTWREN *Terenura sharpei* 11 cm (4¼ in)

Uncommon in canopy of humid montane forest, 1000–1700 m. Where it overlaps (Cuzco) with Rufous-rumped Antwren, Yellow-rumped at higher elevations. Both sexes much like Rufous-rumped, but rump yellow, not rufous. Also, feathers of middle and lower back bright yellow bordered by black; underparts grayer; sides and belly duller, more olive. **VOICE** Probably indistinguishable from other *Terenura*. **Bo**

6 RUFOUS-RUMPED ANTWREN *Terenura callinota* * 11 cm (4¼ in)

Uncommon in canopy of humid montane forest, 1050–2000 m, south to central Peru; also in Cuzco at 750–1000 m. Both sexes have yellowish bellies and rufous rump; male also has yellow "shoulders" (often concealed). Rump yellow or yellowish olive in similar Yellow-rumped. Little or no overlap with lowland Chestnut-shouldered Antwren; male Chestnut-shouldered has rufous "shoulder," but females are very similar. **VOICE** Song an accelerating, rising series of high, thin notes ending in a falling, chippering trill: "tew tew-tew-ti-ti-ti't't't't't'ti." May be answered by slower but similar song (female?). Calls high "tsi" and "ti" notes. **Co, E**

RUSTY-BACKED ANTWREN

WHITE-FLANKED ANTWREN

♂ *melaena*

♀

♂ s

ASH-WINGED
ANTWREN

CHESTNUT-SHOULDERED
ANTWREN

YELLOW-RUMPED
ANTWREN

RUFOUS-RUMPED ANTWREN

PLATE
167

HERPSILOCHMUS ANTWRENS

Herpsilochmus are small-bodied antwrens of the canopy and subcanopy of humid forests in eastern Peru. All species have wing bars, broad white tips to tail feathers, and a pale superciliary; in most species the tail also is long. Cf. other light-bellied, long-tailed canopy birds, such as Gray-mantled Wren (Andes; plate 247) and Polioptila gnatcatchers (plate 251).

1 CREAMY-BELLIED ANTWREN *Herpsilochmus motacilloides* 12 cm (4¾ in)

Uncommon to locally fairly common, in humid montane forest and forest borders at 900–2100 m. Frequently joins mixed-species flocks, although also forages apart. Light cream-colored wash on breast not easily noticed in field; most similar to Ash-throated and Dugand's antwrens (but no overlap with either). Rufous-winged Antwren has a prominent rufous wing panel, is more strongly yellow below, and female has a rufous crown. Yellow-breasted Antwren is even deeper yellow below and greenish above. **VOICE** Song a rapid, accelerating, slightly rising then falling series of rich notes, with 2 or 3 distinct introductory notes, the louder 2 are even-pitched and higher than rest of song: *"chew-PEE-PEE kree'e'E'E'e'e'e'e'rr."* Calls include a rich *"tchew."* **ENDEMIC**

2 DUGAND'S ANTWREN *Herpsilochmus dugandi* 10 cm (4 in)

Rare to uncommon, and local, in northern Amazon. Found in canopy of tall terra firme, where pairs associate with mixed-species flocks. Relatively short-tailed. The only white-breasted *Herpsilochmus* of Amazonia. Ash-winged Antwren does not have a prominent superciliary or white-tipped rectrices. **VOICE** Song a fairly rapid, accelerating series of rich notes, rather like dropping a table tennis ball: *"tchew-chew-tew-tew'tu'tu'tu'tutututututu."* Call a quiet *"tchew."* **Co, E**

3 ASH-THROATED ANTWREN *Herpsilochmus parkeri* 12 cm (4¾ in)

Locally fairly common, in Andean foothills in San Martín at 1250–1450 m, in Río Mayo drainage. Found in humid montane forest, especially at sites with sandy substrate. Most similar to Creamy-bellied Antwren, but no known overlap. Slightly larger, male grayer on throat, breast, and flanks; female has distinctive buff superciliary, throat, and breast. **VOICE** Song a rapid, accelerating-decelerating, rising-falling series of rich notes, with a rising series of 2 or 3 introductory notes: *"pew-PEW-PEW-pee'e'E'E'E'e'e-e-e-u."* Call a rich, short *"tchew,"* often doubled or tripled. **ENDEMIC**

4 RUFOUS-WINGED ANTWREN *Herpsilochmus rufimarginatus* * 11.5 cm (4½ in)

Locally fairly common, in canopy of tall humid and semihumid forest and at forest borders along lower slope of east slope of Andes and in adjacent lowlands up to 1150 m. Also occurs on low outlying ridges, including locally on east bank of Río Ucayali. The rufous outer webs to primaries and secondaries form a prominent wing "panel" that sets it apart from other *Herpsilochmus* (but in northern Peru cf. Rufous-winged Tyrannulet). **VOICE** Song a fairly rapid, accelerating-decelerating, rising-falling series ending with a lower bark: *"ke-ker'er'er'r'r'r'r'E'E'E'r'r-bur."* Unlikely to be confused with any other species. Calls a harsh bark: *"raahh"* or *"arr."* Also gives a descending cackle and a quiet, liquid *"tew."* **Co, E, Br, Bo**

5 ANCIENT ANTWREN *Herpsilochmus gentryi* 11.5 cm (4½ in)

Locally fairly common in northern Amazonian Peru, but restricted to sandy or poor soil forests such as varillales and irapayales. Occurs in pairs in forest canopy, often in association with mixed-species flocks. Dugand's Antwren is smaller and is white-breasted. No overlap with Andean Yellow-breasted Antwren. **VOICE** Song a rapid but decelerating series of low rich notes: *"pi'pi'pi-PEE-PEE-pe-peh-puh."* Calls bell-like, liquid *"tew"* and *"pi."* **E**

6 YELLOW-BREASTED ANTWREN *Herpsilochmus axillaris* * 12 cm (4¾ in)

Rare to uncommon, in subcanopy of humid montane forest and forest edge along lower east slope of Andes at 750–1900 m; but note gap in south-central Peru. Often in vine tangles. Usually forages as pairs with mixed-species flocks. Rufous-winged Antwren paler yellow below, has white throat, and has prominent rufous "panel" on closed wing. **VOICE** Song in north and central Peru a rapid, accelerating, rising-falling series of thin notes: *"tee-tee-TI-TI-ti-ti'ti'titititititititer."* Song in Cuzco is slower, with longer introductory notes giving it a somewhat more musical quality and greater acceleration: *"chew tew-tew-TEE-TEE-ti-ti'ti'ti'tititi."* Calls quiet *"tew"* and *"tchew"* notes. **Co, E**

CREAMY-BELLIED ANTWREN

DUGAND'S ANTWREN

ASH-THROATED ANTWREN

RUFOUS-WINGED ANTWREN

ANCIENT ANTWREN

YELLOW-BREASTED ANTWREN

PLATE
168
STREAKED ANTBIRDS AND DOT-WINGED
ANTWREN

Small antbirds of humid forest understory. The two Hypocnemis *may overlap one another; one species,
Warbling Antbird, also has interesting geographic variation. In contrast, the two long-tailed* Drymophila
are separated by elevation. Dot-winged Antwren is a distinctive, geographically variable species.

1 YELLOW-BROWED ANTBIRD *Hypocnemis hypoxantha* * 12 cm (4¾ in)

Uncommon to fairly common, but inconspicuous in under- and midstory of terra firme and old
second-growth forest; generally more common north of the Amazon than south. Usually in pairs,
only occasionally with mixed-species flocks. Little or no overlap with yellow subspecies of Warbling
Antbird. Also note yellow superciliary, blacker breast streaking and bill, and olive flanks. See also
Ancient Antwren (which is only in canopy). **VOICE** Song an evenly and slow-paced, descending
series of modulated whistles: "DCHEET djeet djeer djeer djeer djeer djer." Notes more hesitant than
song of Warbling, and lacks rasping terminal notes. Calls a whistled, whiny series of descending
notes: "*pwee-pwee-pwee*" and burry "*grr-grr.*" **Co, E, Br**

2 WARBLING ANTBIRD *Hypocnemis cantator* * 12 cm (4¾ in)

Uncommon to fairly common, and widespread, throughout Amazonia below 1100 m, locally up to
1600 m. Two distinct plumage types (which locally overlap; probably are separate species): yellow-
breasted *subflava* and *collinsi* found at base of Andes from Huánuco south, also locally in lowlands of
southeast. More widespread white-breasted *saturata* and *peruviana* occupy remaining area. In forest
understory, primarily at treefall gaps, forest borders, in advanced second growth, and along streams;
in southern Peru, yellow-breasted birds also commonly in bamboo. Typically in pairs; may join mixed-
species flocks, but not regularly. **VOICE** Song (white-breasted) a moderately paced series of modulated
notes ending with 2 or 3 rasping notes: "*DJEE-djeh-DJEER-djeer-djer-djer-DJRZZ-DJRZZ.*" Calls a
mellow, whistled "*hur HEER*" or "*hur HEER-HEER*" and low "*che-chet*" notes. Song of yellow-
breasted birds similar, but with more noticeable spaces between notes, and often not having the harsh
terminal notes: "*chee cher-CHEER-cheer-cher-chrrr.*" Calls a low, raspy "*hrjzz hrjzzesh.*" **Co, E, Br, Bo**

3 LONG-TAILED ANTBIRD *Drymophila caudata* * 15 cm (6 in)

Uncommon in humid montane forest along east slope of Andes, 1600–2500 m. Occurs primarily in
extensive thickets of *Chusquea* bamboo. Behavior similar to that of Striated Antbird, but typically
closer to ground in lower, outer parts of bamboo thickets and tangled second growth along edges. Note
long tail, streaked appearance, and bamboo habitat. **VOICE** Song (male) a loud "*tchip! tchip! djzzew-
djzzew-djzzew-djzzew,*" often answered by female's descending, less buzzy "*tchip tchip tew-tew-tew.*" Calls
a sharp, ringing "*pi-pit!*" and a paired series of descending mewing whistles: "*dew-dew.*" **Co, E, Bo**

4 STRIATED ANTBIRD *Drymophila devillei* * 14 cm (5½ in)

Locally fairly common in lowlands of southern Amazonia, where restricted to bamboo; up to
1300 m. Occurs both in river-edge forest and in terra firme. Pairs forage in crowns of thickets;
regularly with mixed-species flocks, but often forage apart. Very like Long-tailed Antbird of Andes,
but less streaked below, flanks usually paler (more tawny, less rufous), and lacks rufous
tinge on upperparts. Male superficially like white-breasted Warbling Antbird, but note long tail.
VOICE Song 2-parted, first several harsh, buzzing notes followed by an accelerating series of peeping
whistles: "*chewDJZZ-DJZZ-DJZZ tew-tew-ti-ti-titutututututu.*" Call a paired series of descending
mewing whistles: "*pew-pew.*" **Co, E, Br, Bo**

5 DOT-WINGED ANTWREN *Microrhopias quixensis* * 11.5–12.5 cm (4½–5 in)

Uncommon to locally fairly common in eastern lowlands, primarily in river-edge or second-growth
forest; in south usually in bamboo. Mostly below 700 m, but in bamboo up to 1400 m. Everywhere
prefers vine tangles and other dense vegetation in midstory, often along edges. Usually in pairs with
mixed-species flocks. Females highly variable geographically: *quixensis* (throat black, underparts
rufous) north of the Amazon; *nigriventris* (throat and belly black, breast rufous-chestnut) in Andean
foothills (south to Urubamba Valley); *intercedens* and *albicauda* (underparts rufous) in Amazonia
south of the Amazon, including southern foothills. Forages actively; perches horizontally, frequently
flicking tail from side to side, often flashing it open slightly. Unmistakable. **VOICE** Song an
accelerating series of high, sweet notes: "*tew tew-tew'tew'tee'tee'ti'titi.*" Call repertoire wide, including
a descending note, often given in pairs or short series: "*PEEyu PEEyu.*" Also a softer "*pew,*" a much
higher "*psEEu,*" "*peet-peet,*" and a rising "*swee*" note and rising, harsh "*djuree*"; also a sharp, rising
"*swee*" and quiet "*tew.*" **Co, E, Br, Bo**

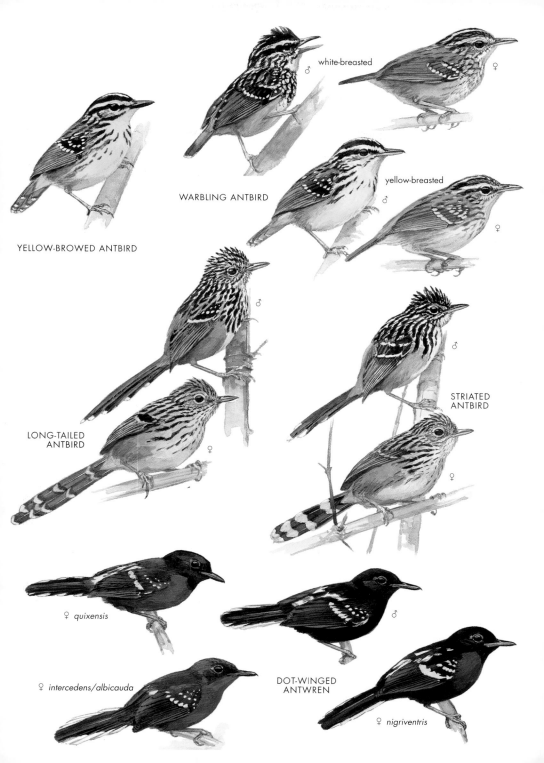

white-breasted ♂

♀

WARBLING ANTBIRD

yellow-breasted ♂

♀

YELLOW-BROWED ANTBIRD

♂

STRIATED ANTBIRD

♂

LONG-TAILED ANTBIRD

♀

♀

♀ quixensis

♂

♀ intercedens/albicauda

DOT-WINGED ANTWREN

♀ nigriventris

PLATE
169

CERCOMACRA AND GRAY-HEADED ANTBIRDS

Cercomacra are medium-sized antbirds with long tails and long slender bills. Most forage in pairs in the understory or middle story at forest edge or in dense tangled vegetation and do not regularly associate with mixed-species flocks. Gray-headed Antbird is superficially similar; restricted to northwest.

1 MANU ANTBIRD *Cercomacra manu* 15 cm (6 in)

Uncommon to fairly common in south. Restricted to nearly pure, usually tall stands of spiny bamboo (*Guadua* sp.) only partially shaded by forest, along river edges and landslides, and along man-made clearings and roads up to 1350 m. Both sexes have white spots on underside of rectrices. Forages lower than Gray Antbird. Male much blacker than male Gray; female distinctively gray below and light brown above. **VOICE** Song a slow series of deep, rich note pairs: "*pook-CHA pook-CHA pook-CHA pook-CHA.*" Female may respond with, or both pair members may give in duet, a series of "*kl'du*" notes similar to call of Gray, but much deeper in pitch. Call a descending chortling series of musical, hooting whistles: "*t'hee-hoo-lu'lu'lu'lu'lu.*" **Br, Bo**

2 GRAY ANTBIRD *Cercomacra cinerascens* * 15 cm (6 in)

Common and widespread, in midstory and canopy of humid forest, forest borders, and tall second growth below 1150 m. Forages higher than other *Cercomacra*. Usually in vine tangles and other dense thickets where difficult to see (although easily located by calls). Note long, white-tipped tail and small white spots on wing coverts in both sexes. Male mostly gray; female dull buffy-brown below. **VOICE** Song a slow to moderate-paced series of mechanical-sounding note-pairs. The first note has a harsh quality; the second is higher-pitched (although order sometimes reversed): "*djjj-HUR djjj-HUR djjj-HUR.*" Calls a harsh "*djrr*" bark and a series of hollow "*clew*" or "*cl'chu*" notes. **Co, E, Br, Bo**

3 BLACKISH ANTBIRD *Cercomacra nigrescens* * 15 cm (6 in)

Widespread in eastern Peru. Two vocally distinct populations. Amazonian *fuscicauda* is uncommon and local in undergrowth of river-edge forest and second growth below 600 m; in north nearly restricted to river islands. Andean *aequatorialis* and *notata* are fairly common at humid forest borders and in bamboo, at 700–2100 m, south to Cuzco. All males similar, although *fuscicauda* usually has smaller white spots on wing coverts. Females differ in tail color: gray (*fuscicauda*) or reddish brown (*aequatorialis, notata*). Compare both sexes to Black Antbird. Male Blackish uniformly gray (Black is black or dark gray with a blacker throat); forecrown of female Blackish more extensively rufous, and with less contrast between crown and cheek. Most easily identified by **VOICE** Andean subspecies sing an antiphonal duet; song of male a short introductory note followed by a rapid, descending chatter, "*twa CHEE-EE-ee-ee-eer*," answered by female's slower-paced rising, mewed series of whistles: "*tew TEW TEW TEW.*" Duet of *fuscicauda* similar, but second phrase of male song a rapid, descending buzz, with no individual notes distinguishable: "*ber BEEEER.*" Call of both forms a hoarse, descending "*bjzzeeer*" or "*br'ahhhh*"; also a quiet "*purp-urp.*" **Co, E, Br, Bo**

4 BLACK ANTBIRD *Cercomacra serva* * 15 cm (6 in)

Uncommon but widespread in Amazonia and on outlying ridges, to 1100 m, locally to 1500 m. Primarily in overgrown treefalls in terra firme, but also in dense second growth, and locally bamboo understory of upland forest. Similar behavior as Blackish Antbird: pairs forage in dense thickets, usually within 2 m of ground. Cf. Blackish. Best distinguished by **VOICE** Song, usually given in antiphonal duet, begins with male's fairly evenly paced, rising series of rich whistles: "*pew-pew-pew-pew-pew-pew-peer*," answered by female's more accelerating, more steeply rising series of slightly more metallic notes: "*churt chirt-cheet-cheet'chee?*" Sometimes one or both terminate duet with quiet falling chatter "*tu-tu-tu*," or this vocalization may be given separately. Call a rapid series of bursts of deep, harsh churrs: "*JEER-jrr-jrr-jrr-jrr-jrr.*" **Co, E, Br, Bo**

5 GRAY-HEADED ANTBIRD *Myrmeciza griseiceps* 13–13.5 cm (5–5¼ in)

Rare to uncommon, in understory of humid montane forest at 700–2900 m in northwest. Often associated with bamboo, although not restricted to it. Pairs and family groups actively forage in understory (but not on ground) in vine tangles and other dense thickets. Sometimes with mixed-species flocks. Note relatively long white-tipped tail and gray head. Breast and lower throat black (male) or mostly gray (female). **VOICE** Song a short, rapid, descending series of churred notes: "*CHEER'R'r'r'r'r'ew.*" Call a harsh, whining "*rheer-rhurr.*" **E**

MANU ANTBIRD

♀

♂

GRAY ANTBIRD

♀

♂

BLACKISH ANTBIRD

♀ *aequatorialis/notata*

♀ *fuscicauda*

♂

BLACK ANTBIRD

♀

♂

GRAY-HEADED ANTBIRD

♀

♂

PLATE
170

SHORT-TAILED ANTBIRDS (*MYRMOBORUS,*
DICHROZONA)

Myrmoborus are 4 species of plump, short-tailed antbirds found in the understory of Amazonia. Forage on or near the ground, often in pairs but only rarely with mixed-species flocks. Black-faced and White-browed antbirds may attend army ant swarms, although when they do so they are subordinate to "professional" ant followers. Often 2 or more Myrmoborus species may be found at a site, although there is some segregation by habitat. Banded Antbird is a delicately-built, distinctive terrestrial antbird.

1 ASH-BREASTED ANTBIRD *Myrmoborus lugubris* * 13.5 cm (5¼ in)

Common, but largely restricted to islands in larger rivers of north. Occurs in dense undergrowth in even-aged forest 10–30 m tall. Very rare, if ever resident, in structurally similar habitats along mainland riverbanks. Unmistakable in river-island undergrowth. May occur in varzea near Colombia/Brazil border where Black-faced Antbird inhabits terra firme; male Black-faced has noticeable white wing bars and whitish superciliary, and female is cinnamon-buff below. **VOICE** Song a moderate and even-paced (about 5 notes/sec), descending series of slightly hoarse notes: "*JEE-JEE-jee-jee-jee-jee-jee-jee-jee-jer.*" Calls a rapid, descending, metallic, sputtering chatter: "*pt'rr'rr'rr*" and a quiet "*pew*" note, sometimes doubled. **Co, E, Br**

2 BLACK-FACED ANTBIRD *Myrmoborus myotherinus* * 13.5 cm (5¼ in)

One of the most common and widespread Amazonian antbirds. Found in understory of terra firme below 1250 m. Note the black face and throat and white wing markings of male; and black mask, white throat, and buff underparts of female. **VOICE** Song north of the Amazon and west of the Ucayali is a fairly slow-paced (<4 notes/sec), slightly decelerating, rising-falling series of burry whistles: "*djzeer DJZEER-djzeer djzeer djzeer djzeer.*" Song south of the Amazon and east of the Ucayali is similar, but clearly whistled with little or no modulation. Calls a harsh, descending "*jeer,*" very similar to call of White-browed Antbird, and a sharp, descending "*tchew!*" **Co, E, Br, Bo**

3 BLACK-TAILED ANTBIRD *Myrmoborus melanurus* 12 cm (4½ in)

Rare to uncommon, in seasonally flooded forest along larger rivers in northern and central Peru, especially at sites with low, dense, viny thickets near water. Male is very dark, with slight crest, reddish iris, and prominent white wing markings. Female has similar wing pattern; note white underparts with buff wash on breast. **VOICE** Song a moderately paced (4–10 notes/sec), obviously accelerating, descending series of slightly burry notes: "*djee DJEE-djee-djee-djee-djee'dje'dje'djedjedjr.*" Call a sharp "*tchew*" note, sometimes doubled. **Br**

4 WHITE-BROWED ANTBIRD *Myrmoborus leucophrys* * 13.5 cm (5¼ in)

Common in Amazonia, up to 1400 m, although absent from much of northern and central Peru. Found in understory of transitional forest, successional river-edge forests, and advanced second growth. Males are gray with bold white forecrown and superciliary; there is a tendency in birds from the Río Huallaga Valley for white to cover entire crown (*koenigorum*). Note the striking head pattern of white-breasted females. **VOICE** Song a fairly long (about 5 sec), rapid (about 10 notes/sec), even-paced descending series of hoarse notes: "*CHI'CHI'chi'chi'chir'chir'jir'jir'jir'jir'jir'jir'jir'jir'jrr.*" Similar to songs of other *Myrmoborus* and *Hypocnemis* antbirds, but faster paced. Calls a burry, descending "*jeer,*" a rapid, springy, sputtering chatter, and a rising "*chueet?*" **Co, E, Br, Bo**

5 BANDED ANTBIRD *Dichrozona cincta* * 10 cm (4 in)

Rare to uncommon, but widespread in Amazonia, locally up to 900 m. Terrestrial, in humid terra firme; may favor sites with relatively open understory. Does not associate with mixed-species flocks; singles or pairs walk along forest floor, bobbing head and occasionally flicking wings and fanning tail. Note the long legs, very short tail with white outer rectrices, white band on rump, broad buff wing bars and streaked breast. Unlikely to be confused with any other species (but cf. Ringed Antpipit, plate 206). **VOICE** Song a long (>10 sec) slightly rising and slightly accelerating series of long (note length about 1 sec), rising whistles: "*reeEE reeEE reeEE reeEE reeEE-reeEE-reeEE-reeEE.*" Calls a quiet, descending, puttering chatter. Also a thin, whistled, rising-falling-rising "*wee'i'wip!*" **Co, E, Br, Bo**

ASH-BREASTED ANTBIRD

BLACK-FACED ANTBIRD

BLACK-TAILED ANTBIRD

BANDED ANTBIRD

koenigorum

leucophrys

WHITE-BROWED ANTBIRD

PLATE
171

MEDIUM-SIZED ANTBIRDS (*MYRMECIZA, PERCNOSTOLA*)

Species shown on this plate are medium-sized antbirds that forage on or very close to the ground in humid forest. Males are very dark, and females are more or less rusty brown. Forage as singles or in pairs, apart from mixed-species flocks.

1 SLATE-COLORED ANTBIRD *Percnostola schistacea* 14.5 cm (5¾ in)
Uncommon in northern Amazonia, in dense terra firme understory. Male extremely similar to male Spot-winged Antbird; best identified by voice or by female. Otherwise, iris gray (not brown); mandible black (usually gray in Spot-winged); and spots on wing coverts smaller. Note pale orange-rufous (not gray or brown) crown and sides of head of female, and faint pale streaks on mantle. **VOICE** Song a slow, accelerating, rising series of clear whistles: "*heew hew-hew-hew-hew,*" rarely with a buzzy terminal note. Calls a dry "*chit-it,*" a rapid, ringing sputtered chatter, also a mewed, whistled "*whee-u,*" and a descending "*tew.*" **Co, E, Br**

2 SPOT-WINGED ANTBIRD *Percnostola leucostigma* * 15 cm (6 in)
Widespread, but geographically variable in voice, plumage, and soft part colors (may represent more than one species). Understory of terra firme, especially along streams and in damp spots. Uncommon to fairly common in northern Amazonia (*subplumbea*). Also in foothills (up to 1650 m) south to Apurímac Valley (*intensa*, not illustrated; crown of female blackish), replaced farther south by *brunneiceps* (crown and sides of head of female dark brown). Local in southeastern Amazonia (*humaythae*, not illustrated; tarsi pale, female with brown crown, male paler gray). Cf. Slate-colored Antbird; where ranges overlap, may occur at the same sites. **VOICE** Song (*subplumbea, intensa*) a rapid, fairly even-paced series of ringing notes: "*pi'i'i'i'i'i'I'I'I'i'i'i'i'i'i'i.*" Song of *brunneiceps* a rapid, accelerating, series of high ringing notes: "*tee tee-ti-ti'ti'ti'i'i'I'I'I'i'i'i'i'ew.*" Song of *humaythae* similar to northern birds but tends to be lower-pitched, rising for most of its length with little falling at end. Calls a dry, sputtering chatter often interspersed with a mewed, descending "*eew,*" sometimes given in series, also a dry "*chit-it.*" **Co, E, Br, Bo**

3 ZIMMER'S ANTBIRD *Myrmeciza castanea* * 12 cm (4¾ in)
Uncommon and local, in northern Amazonia up to 1350 m; narrowly overlaps with Chestnut-tailed Antbird in Mayo Valley. Primarily found in forests, often somewhat stunted, on sandy or nutrient-poor soils. Difficult to distinguish from Chestnut-tailed except by distribution and voice. Zimmer's has little or no pale tips to the inner tertials; inner tertials of Chestnut-tailed usually have small but distinct white or buff tips. Female Zimmer's also has entirely black bill (mandible pale in Chestnut-tailed) and whiter belly with slightly greater breast/belly contrast. **VOICE** Song a slow but accelerating, rising series of loud whistled notes: "*TEW TEW-tew-tu'ti'ti'ti'ter'tu*"; occasionally last 1 or 2 notes are lower in pitch. Call a quiet, descending, throaty churred rattle. Also a dry "*tchit*" or "*tchit-it,*" often in short series. **Co, E**

4 CHESTNUT-TAILED ANTBIRD *Myrmeciza hemimelaena* * 12 cm (4¾ in)
One of the most common and widespread antbirds of Amazonian forest understory south of the Amazon, up to 1500 m. Note reddish brown tail (both sexes); also black throat and white belly of male, buffy throat and chest of female. Saturation of body plumage variable in both sexes. Cf. very similar Zimmer's Antbird. **VOICE** Song a slow but accelerating, descending series of loud, chiming notes, usually ending with a quiet churred phrase: "*TEE TEE-tee-ti-tidjrdjr,*" sometimes answered by female's fairly even-paced, descending series of rising whistles: "*WEE-wee-wee-wee-wee-djr-djr.*" Calls a single, sharp "*pik,*" sometimes in short series, and a quiet, descending, thin rattle. **Br, Bo**

5 BLACK-THROATED ANTBIRD *Myrmeciza atrothorax* * 14 cm (5½ in)
Widespread in Amazonia, up to at least 1000 m, in dense understory at humid forest edge, at forest openings, and in second growth. Note long black tail, frequently dipped slowly and then quickly flicked upward. Male dark; *tenebrosa* (north of Amazon) more extensively black below, and covert spots are smaller. **VOICE** Song a slow and slightly decelerating, rising series of high, plaintive notes introduced by a higher-pitched couplet: "*ti-ti tew-tew-tee-teep,*" often answered by female's similar song. Calls a high, sneezy "*t'seep*" and thin chip notes, usually in pairs, often interspersed with a rising whistle: "*thp-thp wee.*" **Co, E, Br, Bo**

SLATE-COLORED
ANTBIRD

♀

♂

SPOT-WINGED ANTBIRD

♀ *subplumbea*

♀ *brunneiceps*

♂

CHESTNUT-TAILED ANTBIRD

♀

light morph

♂

♂

♀

ZIMMER'S ANTBIRD

♂

dark morph

CHESTNUT-TAILED ANTBIRD

♀

♂

BLACK-
THROATED
ANTBIRD

♀

♂

tenebrosa

PLATE
172
LARGE *MYRMECIZA* ANTBIRDS AND BARE-EYES

All species on this plate are large, relatively short-tailed antbirds of humid forest understory. The four species of large Myrmeciza *typically forage in pairs, apart from mixed-species flocks. The two species of bare-eyes are obligate or "professional" ant followers (see plate 173).*

1 SOOTY ANTBIRD *Myrmeciza fortis* * 18.5 cm (7¼ in)
Uncommon to fairly common in Amazonia, to 1300 m. Found in understory of terra firme. Pairs forage on or near the ground and regularly attend army ant swarms. Rufous crown and gray face of female are distinctive. Dark male is similar to Goeldi's Antbird but is grayer, lacks a white interscapular patch, and has a brown (not red) iris; male White-shouldered Antbird is blacker and has white "shoulders" (often concealed). **VOICE** Song a slowly and even-paced, rising series of ringing, descending whistled notes: "*pew pew PEW PEW PEW PEW PEW PEW.*" Distantly recalls song of Undulated Antshrike, but that species has rising notes. Calls a loud, musical, puttering rattle, also a descending, mewed "*aaww*" and a hollow, musical chatter: "*PEW'kur'kur'kur'kur'kur.*" **Co, E, Br, Bo**

2 PLUMBEOUS ANTBIRD *Myrmeciza hyperythra* 17–18 cm (6¾–7 in)
Fairly common to common, and widespread in Amazonia, below 500 m, locally to 800 m. Found in understory of seasonally flooded forest and along stream margins, on or close to the ground. May follow army ant swarms. Large, plump antbird with prominent light blue skin around eye. Male largely gray (with white-spotted wing coverts); female distinctly bicolored. Cf. the smaller Black-headed, Allpahuayo, Slate-colored, and Spot-winged antbirds. **VOICE** Song a rapid, slightly accelerating, rising series of notes: "*wur-wur-wurwrwrwe'e'e'e'ip.*" Calls a characteristic, hollow "*perp-erp,*" also a low churring or puttering chatter. **Co, E, Br, Bo**

3 GOELDI'S ANTBIRD *Myrmeciza goeldii* 18 cm (7 in)
Fairly common in southeast. Understory of seasonally flooded forests, in second-growth forest, and in bamboo, mostly below 500 m, but locally to 800 m. Closely approaches range of similar White-shouldered Antbird on lower Río Urubamba. Male black, with concealed white interscapular patch and white lesser wing coverts (also concealed). Cf. male Sooty Antbird. Female largely rufous with gray face and white throat. Iris red in both sexes. **VOICE** Song a slow series of mellow whistled notes, first a stuttered pair, then several falling notes: "*her-her hEEr hEEr hEEr hEEr.*" Easily imitated. More strident than White-shouldered. Call a slow, electric chatter "*cher'che'che'che'che'che,*" reminiscent of calls of White-chinned Jacamar. **Br, Bo**

4 WHITE-SHOULDERED ANTBIRD *Myrmeciza melanoceps* 18.5 cm (7¼ in)
Fairly common and widespread south to mouth of Río Urubamba; replaced in southeast by Goeldi's Antbird. Forages close to the ground in varzea and seasonally flooded forest; also at forest edge, but primarily associated with water. Female very distinctive. Male similar to male Goeldi's, but wing coverts are more extensively white and lacks white interscapular patch. Male Sooty Antbird is grayer (less black), has more extensive pale skin around eye, and brown (not reddish) iris. **VOICE** Song a slow series of mellow whistled notes, first a stuttered pair, then several falling notes: "*her-her hEEr hEEr hEEr hEEr.*" Easily imitated. Calls a thrushlike, clucked "*querk*" note, sometimes doubled, and an unbirdlike musical chatter: "*quer'ru'ru'ru'ru'ru'ru.*" **Co, E, Br**

5 REDDISH-WINGED BARE-EYE *Phlegopsis erythroptera* * 18.5 cm (7¼ in)
Rare to uncommon in northern and eastern Amazonia, primarily in terra firme. Ornate plumage unmistakable. **VOICE** Song a slow, decelerating, series of rasping whistles: "*rrr RHEEEW-rheeew rheew rhew rhhw.*" Call a distinctive, loud series of harsh, rising-falling notes: "*RHEEW-RHEW-RHEW-RHEW-RHEW!*" "Chirr" is a fairly loud, grinding, descending note with a distinctly metallic start: "*T'djeeerw.*" **Co, E, Br, Bo**

6 BLACK-SPOTTED BARE-EYE *Phlegopsis nigromaculata* * 18.5 cm (7¼ in)
Widespread, uncommon to fairly common in Amazonia (but apparently absent from northwest) below 800 m. Occurs in understory of humid forest, regularly in transitional forests and less commonly in terra firme. Bright red orbital skin (gray in juvenile); back is brown, prominently spotted with black. Sexes similar. **VOICE** Song a slow, descending, 2- or 3-note series of slightly burry whistles; first note is longest, loudest, and least burry: "*HEEEW heeer heer.*" Calls a quiet series of burry whines and "*pew*" notes. "Chirr" is a thin, descending "*djeeer.*" **Co, E, Br, Bo**

SOOTY ANTBIRD

PLUMBEOUS ANTBIRD

WHITE-SHOULDERED ANTBIRD

GOELDI'S ANTBIRD

BLACK-SPOTTED BARE-EYE

REDDISH-WINGED BARE-EYE

PLATE
173

ANT-FOLLOWING ANTBIRDS

All species on this plate are "professional" or "obligate" army ant followers (see also bare-eyes, plate 172). Rarely seen away from army ants, except when "cruising" through forest in search of ant swarms. Forage low to ground over ant swarms; do not eat ants, but capture arthropods and small vertebrates flushed by the swarm. Large swarms may attract several species, and often multiple individuals of each species. Generally, larger species are dominant to smaller ones, which may be restricted to periphery of the swarm. All species have some version of a growling "chirr" call.

1 BICOLORED ANTBIRD *Gymnopithys leucaspis* * 14–14.5 cm (5½–5¾ in)

Fairly common in northern Amazonia below 750 m. Found in understory of humid terra firme. Subordinate to most other "obligate" ant followers. Simple color pattern is distinctive. Female (but not male) has semiconcealed tawny-buff interscapular patch. **VOICE** Song an accelerating-decelerating, rising-falling series of rising mewed whistles becoming more raspy toward the end: "*TUEE TUEE-TUEE-tui-ti'ti'ti'ter-tjer-tjyer-tjyer.*" Calls a sharp "*tcheet!*" and "*chit'it!*" and a rising series of complaining, somewhat raspy "*rhee-rhee-rhee-rhee…*" notes. "Chirr" is a medium-pitched, descending "*djeeerw*" and "*grrrl.*" **Co, E, Br**

2 HAIRY-CRESTED ANTBIRD *Rhegmatorhina melanosticta* * 15 cm (6 in)

Widespread, but typically rare to uncommon, in Amazonia, below 1350 m. Found in understory of humid forest, primarily in terra firme. Crest light gray in most of Peru, light brown or orange-brown in birds of foothills from Marañón south to Apurímac Valley (*brunneiceps*). Back spotted black in females. Juveniles (both sexes) have spotted backs and a sooty crown. **VOICE** Song a slow, slightly accelerating then decelerating, rising-falling series of mewed whistles that become raspy once the series begins falling: "*heew heee-heee-heer herjzz hrjzzzz.*" Calls include a rich "*tchip*" or "*tchip-ip.*" "Chirr" a low, descending "*grrrl,*" "*djrrrl,*" or with a sharp intro: "*tchi'rrrl.*" **Co, E, Br, Bo**

3 LUNULATED ANTBIRD *Gymnopithys lunulatus* 14.5 cm (5¾ in)

Rare to uncommon in northern and western portions of Amazonia. Occurs in understory of humid forest. Male similar to male White-throated Antbird, but no geographic overlap (also note difference in tail pattern). Compare female to Scale-backed Antbird. **VOICE** Song a distinct introductory note followed by a fairly rapid, decelerating, rising-falling series of popping notes becoming rising mellow whistles: "*PEW pipi'pi'pwee-pwee-pwee-peeerr.*" Aggressive song ends in drawn-out rasps. Calls include a sharp "*tchip.*" "Chirr" is a throaty, descending snarl with a somewhat liquid start: "*djeerrrrl.*" **E**

4 WHITE-MASKED ANTBIRD *Pithys castaneus* 14 cm (5½ in)

Very local in northern Amazonia, where found in understory of varillales. Larger than White-plumed Antbird, with white "mask" (but no plumes), largely rufous body, and black head. Juvenile (not illustrated) has sooty gray face and duller brown underparts. **VOICE** Song a rising, whiny whistled "*huuuuuureee?*" with short, quiet, chiming "*tur'e'e*" notes often interspersed between whistles. Calls a quiet, descending, mewed "*whew,*" also a harsh, descending "*t'char*" and sharp "*tchip!*" "Chirr" is a low, barely descending, harsh "*grrah,*" lower pitched overall than other sympatric professional ant followers' calls. **ENDEMIC**

5 WHITE-THROATED ANTBIRD *Gymnopithys salvini* * 14.5 cm (5¾ in)

Widespread but generally uncommon in Amazonia south of Amazon up to 800 m. Primarily in terra firme, less frequently in seasonally flooded forests. No overlap with similar Lunulated Antbird (also note difference in tail pattern). Compare female to Musician Wren. **VOICE** Song a slow, even-paced, descending series of rising, slightly burry, whistles: "*RHEEE?-rheee?-rheee?-rheee?-rhrrr.*" Aggressive song may have more notes, the final notes becoming distinctly raspy. Calls a puttering, descending rattle and a rich "*tchup.*" "Chirr" a throaty, descending snarl with a somewhat liquid start: "*djeerrrrl.*" **Br, Bo**

6 WHITE-PLUMED ANTBIRD *Pithys albifrons* * 12 cm (4¾ in)

Fairly common in northern and western Amazonia, up to 1350 m. Found in understory of humid terra firme. Often one of the most numerous species at an ant swarm. Gaudy adults are unmistakable. Juveniles much duller, lacking the white facial plumes, but still are largely reddish brown below. **VOICE** Song (?) is a thin, descending, mewing whistle: "*peeu.*" Call a quiet, rising series of peeping notes. "Chirr" a fairly high-pitched, descending snarl: "*tjerrrrah,*" fairly drawn out for a professional ant follower's chirr. **Co, E, Br**

HAIRY-CRESTED ANTBIRD

♀

♂

brunneiceps

♀

♂

BICOLORED ANTBIRD

LUNULATED ANTBIRD

♀

♂

WHITE-PLUMED ANTBIRD

ad.

WHITE-MASKED ANTBIRD

WHITE-THROATED ANTBIRD

♂

♀

juv.

PLATE
174

BUSHBIRD AND RIVERINE ANTBIRDS

Black Bushbird is notable for the sharp upturn at the tip of the bill. Hypocnemoides are a pair of medium-sized, short-tailed antbirds closely associated with water. More active than the larger Silvered Antbird, which shares the same habitats, and which overlaps with both Hypocnemoides. Black-and-white Antbird is a small, bicolored antbird found on Amazonian river islands.

1 SILVERED ANTBIRD *Sclateria naevia* * 14–14.5 cm (5½–5¾ in)
Fairly common throughout Amazonia, up to 600 m. Found at water's edge, along edges of streams (white- and blackwater), oxbow lakes, and *Mauritia* swamps (*aguajales*). Almost always under continuous cover of overhanging vegetation. Pairs hop on damp ground, lightly probing and flicking leaves. Easily recognized; note long pinkish legs, 2-toned appearance, and close association with water. Cf. Black-chinned and Band-tailed antbirds. **VOICE** Song a single, long, rising whistle followed by a rapid-paced (6–10 notes/sec), rising-falling series of musical notes that abruptly becomes a rapid, descending, quiet chatter: "WHEE! *whi-whi-whi-whi-WHEE-WHEE-trrrr*." Calls a quiet "*pwip*," like dripping water, also a rapid, dry chatter. **Co, E, Br, Bo**

2 BLACK BUSHBIRD *Neoctantes niger* 16 cm (6¼ in)
Widespread but uncommon in northern Amazonia; very locally present also in south, up to 750 m. Forages near ground in dense forest understory, along forest streams, at treefalls, and in dense second-growth forest. Solitary or in pairs, usually apart from mixed-species flocks. Gleans vines or leaves, or uses bill (laterally compressed, with an upturned mandible) to hammer woody substrates or to flake off dead bark. **VOICE** Song a long, slow-paced series of whistled "*weeo*" notes with little variation within. Easily imitated. Call a slow-paced, musical rattle of squeaky, puttering notes: "CHI'r'r'r'r'r'r'r"; also a bisyllabic, squeaky phrase, the first syllable higher: "CHI'bu." **Co, E, Br**

3 BAND-TAILED ANTBIRD *Hypocnemoides maculicauda* * 12 cm (4¾ in)
Widespread and fairly common in central and southern Amazonia. Very similar to Black-chinned Antbird, but the two species mostly or entirely replace one another geographically. Both forage in understorey, usually in vegetation overhanging water (typically forest streams, also lake margins and backwater areas). Hop on the ground or on logs at water's edge, picking at leaves and debris. Tail often bobbed; in low light movement of white tip to tail may give away the bird's presence. Band-tailed has broader white band at tip of tail (ca. 3–4 mm wide vs. ca. 1 mm) and a white interscapular patch (usually concealed). **VOICE** Song an accelerating series of rising, modulated whistles followed by an abruptly decelerating series of rising burry notes: "*hew hew-hu-hu'huHU'DJZE'DJZEE-djzwee djzwee djzwee?*" Somewhat like song of Warbling Antbird, but the latter does not accelerate. Calls quiet whiny and chuckling notes, also a descending, slightly hoarse "*hew*" and a sneezy "*tzew*." **Br, Bo**

4 BLACK-CHINNED ANTBIRD *Hypocnemoides melanopogon* * 11.5 cm (4½ in)
Fairly common in northern Amazonia. Note male's black throat, prominent wing bars, and short tail with very narrow white tip; lacks a white interscapular patch. Female largely white below, more or less scaled with gray, and often with buff tinge to breast and belly. Cf. Band-tailed Antbird. Similar Scale-backed and larger Black-headed antbirds occur in terra firme. **VOICE** Song an accelerating, rising series of modulated, rising whistles that descends slightly at the end with much more buzzy notes: "*whee wee-wee'wee'wi'wi'wiwiwidz'dz'dzee*." Calls a sneezy "*tzeew*" and a descending, whistled "*hew*." **Co, E, Br**

5 BLACK-AND-WHITE ANTBIRD *Myrmochanes hemileucus* 11.5 cm (4½ in)
Locally fairly common on young to medium-aged river islands along larger rivers in northern Amazonia. Pairs occupy low, dense thickets of vine-covered trees, shrubs, and tall grasses, as well as edges of woods. Stays on flooded portions of islands during flood season. Only small, black-and-white antbird on river islands; looks like a miniature Great Antshrike (also see similarly patterned *Sporophila* seedeaters). Female has white lores. **VOICE** Song an accelerating, descending series of hollow, piping notes: "PU-pu-pu'pu'puprrrrr." Often given in duet (female usually with a higher-pitched voice) in rapid succession. Calls a series of hollow piping notes "*pu pu pu*," also a more rapid musical rattle (similar to end of song), sometimes in series, also a single "*pew*" and a bisyllabic "*tuk-et*." **Co, E, Br, Bo**

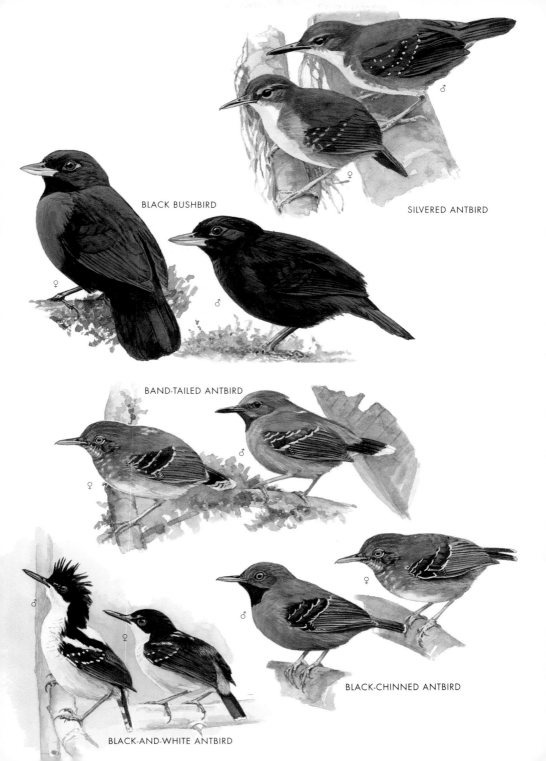

SILVERED ANTBIRD

BLACK BUSHBIRD

BAND-TAILED ANTBIRD

BLACK-CHINNED ANTBIRD

BLACK-AND-WHITE ANTBIRD

PLATE
175

PATTERNED UNDERSTORY ANTBIRDS

Species on this plate forage on or near the ground; do not associate with mixed-species flocks, or do so only rarely. Some may attend army ant swarms, however.

1 DOT-BACKED ANTBIRD *Hylophylax punctulatus* * 11 cm (4¼ in)

Rare to uncommon in northeastern Amazonia, also very local in southeast. Primarily in seasonally flooded forests, especially along streams and lake edges with dense ground cover. Similar to more common and widespread Spot-backed Antbird but has darker (gray) tarsi; pale gray cheeks and lores; and black tail. Spots on back extend onto rump; these spots usually white, but may be buff in some females. **VOICE** Song paired notes given at an irregular pace, first note rising and second higher and falling: "*wee-HEEew.*" Sometimes an evenly and slow-paced (about 2 note-pairs/sec) descending series of 4–6 paired notes. Calls a somewhat harsh, descending "*tjeer*" and a sharp "*sweet-sweet-sweet,*" also quiet mewing notes. **Co, E, Br, Bo**

2 SPOT-BACKED ANTBIRD *Hylophylax naevius* * 11.5 cm (4½ in)

Widespread, uncommon to fairly common in Amazonia. Found in understory of humid forest, up to 1200 m. Most often found at sites with relatively dense understory, such as at treefalls and other light gaps, and along streams. Tail color variable. Generally, tail olive-gray or brown in lowland populations, and in foothills; tail reddish in foothills of central Peru (south at least to Pasco), as well as in some individuals in Amazonia east of Río Napo. Note pinkish tarsi and dark cheeks in all populations (cf. Dot-backed Antbird). **VOICE** Song a rising-falling series of paired notes: "*hew tee'tu- tee'tu-TEE'TU-TEE'TU-tee'tu-tee'tu ti.*" Pace of song variable. Some populations, especially in foothills and locally in northern Amazonia, have slow-paced songs; faster-paced songs more widespread in Amazonia. Calls a quiet, descending "*tew,*" a rising "*tuit,*" and a high, ringing, sputtered rattle. Also a characteristic, thin, high "*spit-spit-spit,*" "*swit-swit-swit,*" or "*weet-weet-weet.*" **Co, E, Br, Bo**

3 SCALE-BACKED ANTBIRD *Hylophylax poecilinotus* * 13 cm (5 in)

Widespread and common throughout Amazonia. Understory of humid forests, up to 900 m, locally to 1350 m. Regularly attends army ant swarms, where subordinate to "obligate" ant followers, but frequently found apart from ants as well. Both sexes geographically variable. Widespread male pattern is gray body with black-and-white "scaled" back; subspecies *gutturalis* (south of the Amazon/east of lower Río Ucayali) also has black throat. Otherwise throat gray. Female *lepidonotus* (north of the Amazon, also west of Río Ucayali south to Apurímac Valley) is brown below with tawny face and black–and-white "scaled" back; female *gutturalis* similar but duller below. Very different female *griseiventris* (east of central Río Ucayali, south to southeastern Peru) lacks "scaling" above; gray below with white throat. **VOICE** Song a slow, even-paced or slightly accelerating, rising series of rising whistles: "*hew hui hui hui? hui? hui? hui? hui? hui?*" Calls a slightly descending sputtered rattle, a drier, descending rattle-chirr, and a sharp "*tchip!*" sometimes doubled. **Co, E, Br, Bo**

4 WING-BANDED ANTBIRD *Myrmornis torquata* * 15 cm (6 in)

Poorly known; reported from only a few sites. Found in understory of terra firme, perhaps especially in areas with low hills. Singles or pairs forage on ground. Inconspicuous. Superficially resembles a *Formicarius* antthrush, but shorter legged, and hops rather than walks; note squat body, short tail, long bill, and harlequin pattern. **VOICE** Song a slow, rising series of even whistled notes: "*whew whew whew whew WHEW WHEW WHEW WHEW.*" Call a musical, modulated, descending, whistled "*wuu'r'r'r'r*"; reminiscent of call of Thrush-like Antpitta, but louder, and perhaps higher pitched. **Co, E, Br**

5 PLAIN-THROATED ANTWREN *Myrmotherula hauxwelli* * 9.5 cm (3¾ in)

Uncommon to fairly common and widespread in Amazonia, locally up to 700 m. Forages close to the ground in forest understory, clinging to sides of slender vertical stems. Solitary or in pairs; rarely associates with mixed-species flocks, but may attend army ant swarms. Note the small size, very short tail, and prominent pale spots on tertials and tip of tail in both sexes. Cf. much larger Scale-backed Antbird and Pearly Antshrike. **VOICE** Song an accelerating series of raspy, rising whistles: "*huree hurizz-hurizz-heriz-hrz-hrz-hrz'rz'rz'rz'rz'rz.*" Calls a metallic, dry note, often in series: "*tdj tdj tdj…*" and a faster, descending, sputtering rattle. Also a descending series of squeaky notes. **Co, E, Br, Bo**

DOT-BACKED ANTBIRD

♀

♂

gray-tailed ♂

♀

SPOT-BACKED ANTBIRD

reddish-tailed ♂

♀

♀

gutturalis ♂

♂

SCALE-BACKED ANTBIRD

PLAIN-THROATED ANTWREN

♀

♀ griseiventris

♂

♂

WING-BANDED ANTBIRD

♀

PLATE
176

ANTTHRUSHES

Antthrushes are large, long-legged, secretive antbirds that walk deliberately across the forest floor. Chamaeza are larger and heavier bodied. Formicarius walk with an erect posture, typically with tail cocked, rail-like. All antthrushes are much more often heard than seen.

1 STRIATED ANTTHRUSH *Chamaeza nobilis* * 22.5 cm (8¾ in)

Widespread but generally rare in Amazonia, where primarily found in terra firme. Cf. Short-tailed Antthrush, although elevational range of Striated (below 450 m) is lower. **VOICE** Song a long, accelerating (from 3–17 notes/sec), descending series of hollow, hooting whistles that abruptly becomes a much slower-paced descending series of rising hoots (which can be hard to hear at a distance): "*poop poop-pu-pu-pu'pu'pu'pu'pupupupupupupupupupupup-WOOP WOOP woop woop woop.*" Call a popping, liquid, rising "*quock.*" **Co, E, Br, Bo**

2 SHORT-TAILED ANTTHRUSH *Chamaeza campanisona* * 19 cm (7½ in)

Rare to uncommon in humid montane forest on lower slopes of Andes, and on outlying ridges, 900–1700 m. Brown above; underparts streaked or scalloped black, but background color geographically variable. Northern *punctigula* (south to San Martín, possibly to Huánuco) is white below. Underparts of southern subspecies deep ochraceous buff (*olivacea*; central Peru) or buffy (*berlepschi*; eastern Cuzco south). Short-tailed superficially similar to Striated Antthrush, but no elevational overlap. Striated also is larger, more rufescent above and whiter below, especially on throat and belly. Cf. also Barred Antthrush. **VOICE** Song (*punctigula*) a moderate-paced, slightly accelerating, rising series of hollow, hooted whistles that abruptly become a descending, decelerating series of descending popping notes: "*pup u-pu-pu-pu'PU'PU'PUPUPU'WAH-wah-wah-wah.*" Song of *olivacea* (and probably *berlepschi*) faster-paced. Calls a liquid, rising "*quork*" note, sometimes in a series, particularly in flight. **Co, E, Br, Bo**

3 BARRED ANTTHRUSH *Chamaeza mollissima* * 20.5 cm (8 in)

Rare to uncommon in humid montane forests with dense undergrowth on east slope of Andes, 1800–3100 m. Discontinuously distributed; no records from central Peru. Plumage dark: brown above, densely barred black and buff or white below. **VOICE** Song a long (up to 50 sec), rapid, slightly decelerating, rising series of hollow whistled notes: "*pupupupupupupupupupupupupupupuPUPUPUPUPU'PU'PU'PU'PU.*" Call a series of mellow, rising whistles: "*whee-whee-whee*" or "*whip-whip.*" **Co, E, Bo**

4 RUFOUS-BREASTED ANTTHRUSH *Formicarius rufipectus* * 19 cm (7½ in)

Rare to uncommon in humid montane forest on east slope of Andes, 1100–1850 m. Found at higher elevations than other *Formicarius*. Plumage very dark, with black face and throat and dark rufous breast. **VOICE** Song a pair of piping whistled notes, the second usually slightly higher: "*PEW PEEW*"; at a distance may sound like a *Grallaria* antpitta. Easily imitated. Call a sharp, doubled note: "*TU'TCHOOP,*" often in series in flight. **Co, E**

5 RUFOUS-CAPPED ANTTHRUSH *Formicarius colma* * 18 cm (7 in)

Widespread but uncommon in Amazonia; primarily found in terra firme below 500 m. Note the rufous crown, extensively black underparts, and gray vent. Sexes similar; but young birds have white lores and white throat, spotted with black. **VOICE** Song a rapid, even-paced, falling-rising series of bell-like piping whistles: "*TEE-ti'ti'tu'tu'tu'tu'tu'te'te'te'te'ti'ti'ti'ti.*" Call a sharp, descending "*PEW!*" or "*CHEW!*" often in a short series in flight. **Co, E, Br, Bo**

6 RUFOUS-FRONTED ANTTHRUSH *Formicarius rufifrons* 18 cm (7 in)

Rare and local in southeast. Restricted to low-lying areas on river floodplains with dense understory, such as bamboo (*Guadua*) stands or edges of *Heliconia* thickets. Brown crown contrasts with small but prominent rufous-brown forecrown; throat gray, not black. Orbital skin pale gray. **VOICE** Song a series of piping notes; pitch of song rises in middle before falling to slightly below the original pitch: "*hu-hu-hu-HWEE-HWEE-HWEE-hew-hu-hu-hu-hu-hu-hu.*" Easily imitated. Call a loud, ringing "*TCHEW!*" similar to Rufous-capped Antthrush. **Br, Bo**

7 BLACK-FACED ANTTHRUSH *Formicarius analis* * 18 cm (7 in)

Most common and widespread Amazonian antthrush. Primarily found in seasonally flooded and transitional forests at lower elevations, but also up to 1150 m in foothills. Crown plain brown, breast gray, vent rusty; also has pale orbital skin (gray or light blue). **VOICE** Song introduced by a single note, then a space, then a rapid descending series of piping whistles: "*HUR HEE'HEE'hee'hee'hee-hee-heer-heer her her.*" Easily imitated. Often breaks long periods of silence with a very long rising-falling version of song. Call a sharp, doubled note: "*TU'TCHOOP,*" often in series in flight. **Co, E, Br, Bo**

STRIATED ANTTHRUSH

berlepschi

punctigula

SHORT-TAILED
ANTTHRUSH

BARRED
ANTTHRUSH

RUFOUS-
BREASTED
ANTTHRUSH

olivacea

juv.

ad.

RUFOUS-CAPPED ANTTHRUSH

RUFOUS-FRONTED
ANTTHRUSH

BLACK-FACED ANTTHRUSH

PLATE
177

GRALLARIA ANTPITTAS I

Antpittas are antbirds with plump bodies, short tails, and notably long tarsi. Grallaria, Hylopezus and Myrmothera antpittas (plates 177–180) primarily are terrestrial, running or hopping along the ground, although they may sing from an elevated perch. Most are secretive, heard far more often than are seen. Most species on this plate are Amazonian or occur on the lower slopes of the Andes, although Undulated Antpitta occupies humid montane forests at high elevations.

1 OCHRE-STRIPED ANTPITTA Grallaria dignissima 19 cm (7½ in)

Rare, in northern Amazonia (where it replaces Elusive Antpitta). Found in understory of terra firme, usually in dense tangles bordering treefall gaps. Large, with deep ochraceous breast and heavily streaked flanks. **VOICE** Song a pair of low whistled notes, the second sliding down in pitch: "*hoo HEEeeoo.*" Easily imitated. Nearly identical to song of Elusive. Call a descending, rolling, musical trill; similar to mewing call of Collared Trogon, but starts with a pure whistle, then becomes more trilled: "*heeuu'r'r'r'r.*" **Co, E**

2 UNDULATED ANTPITTA Grallaria squamigera * 21.5 cm (8½ in)

Widespread but often uncommon in humid montane forests, and forest edge, at 2250–3500 along east slope of Andes; also locally on west slope in Piura. Usually inside cover of forest but sometimes ventures onto forest trails early in the morning. Often sings from elevated perch. The largest Andean antpitta. Gray above, buffy or rufescent below; pattern and density of black barring or spotting on underparts variable. **VOICE** Song a 4–6 sec rapid, even-paced, rising then slightly falling, series of purred notes: "*pr'r'r'r'r'r'r'r'r'r'R'R'R'R'R'R'ew.*" Reminiscent of some screech-owls of lower elevations (e.g., Vermiculated Screech-Owl), although no high elevation screech-owl has this song pattern. Call a quiet, short, falling-rising purr. **Co, E, Bo**

3 ELUSIVE ANTPITTA Grallaria eludens 19 cm (7½ in)

Rare and poorly known; replaces Ochre-striped Antpitta in eastern Amazonia south of the Amazon. Similar to Ochre-striped in behavior, habitat, and appearance, but breast is paler, washed with buff (rather than deep ochraceous). **VOICE** Song a pair of low whistled notes, the second sliding down in pitch: "*hoo HEEeeoo.*" Easily imitated. Nearly identical to song of Ochre-striped, but no distributional overlap. Call much like that of Ochre-striped. **Br**

4 PLAIN-BACKED ANTPITTA Grallaria haplonota * 16 cm (6¼ in)

Poorly known; apparently rare and local in humid montane forest on east slope of northern Andes, at 1150–1500 m. Generally dull brown, almost unpatterned, but paler on lores and throat. **VOICE** Song a fairly slow, slightly decelerating, rising-falling, loudest at the highest pitch, series of hooted notes: "*hu-hu-hu-hu-HOO-HOO-HOO-hu-hu.*" Similar to song of Thrush-like Antpitta, but contains more notes. **Co, E**

5 VARIEGATED ANTPITTA Grallaria varia * 18 cm (7 in)

Poorly known; reported from a few localities in northeastern Amazonia, where found in terra firme. Gray-crowned, with variegated breast pattern and whitish malar and breast spots. Similar to Scaled Antpitta (no known overlap) but larger, with smaller white breast patch, and with breast and flanks streaked or spotted (flanks are unmarked in Scaled). **VOICE** Song a slow (about 5 notes/sec), decelerating-accelerating, monotone series of hoots, becoming loudest in the middle (the loudest notes audible at a distance): "*pu'pu-pu-poo POO POO poo-pu'pu.*" **Br**

6 SCALED ANTPITTA Grallaria guatimalensis * 16 cm (6¼ in)

Rare to uncommon in humid montane forest on east slope of Andes and on outlying ridges at 650–1750 m. Also local on west slope south to Cajamarca. Very local in northern Amazonia, near Ecuador border. Generally buffy brown with gray crown; note the prominent white or buff malar stripe and crescent on breast, and uniform buffy brown breast. **VOICE** Song (*regulus*; south to Cuzco) a rapid (12 notes/sec at maximum), decelerating-accelerating series of hooted notes; notes about two-thirds through the song are the longest, loudest, and highest-pitched: "*pupupu'pu'pu'pu'pu-pu-POO-POO-pu'pu'pu.*" Similar to Undulated Antpitta, but shorter, and noticeably decelerates. Song of *sororia* (Cuzco south) a slower-paced (6 notes/sec maximum) series of hooted notes that accelerates-decelerates at the loudest and highest-pitched notes, then accelerates again slightly: "*poo-poo-pu-pu'pu'pu-pu-POO-POO-POO-pu'pu.*" Reminiscent of song of Variegated Antpitta (no overlap). **Co, E, Bo**

OCHRE-STRIPED
ANTPITTA

UNDULATED ANTPITTA

ELUSIVE
ANTPITTA

VARIEGATED
ANTPITTA

PLAIN-BACKED
ANTPITTA

SCALED ANTPITTA

PLATE
178

GRALLARIA ANTPITTAS II

Small to medium-sized antpittas of the Andes.

1 STRIPE-HEADED ANTPITTA *Grallaria andicolus* * 16–16.5 cm (6¼–6½ in)

Locally fairly common. Primarily a bird of drier habitats and higher elevations than other antpittas. Typically found in *Polylepis-Gynoxys* woodlands at 3500–4600 m, locally down to 3000 m. Occasionally ventures into boulder-strewn grassland. Relatively small, brown, heavily streaked. Widespread *andicolus* streaked above (although back streaking sometimes reduced). In Puno, *punensis* has plain back, buffier face, and blacker crown. **VOICE** Song a low, grinding, froglike trill that rises and falls, often with an introductory stutter: "*gr-grrrEEEEErrrr.*" Also a thin, mewed "*p'yuk.*" **Bo**

2 TAWNY ANTPITTA *Grallaria quitensis* * 16 cm (6¼ in)

Fairly common on both slopes of Andes north and west of Marañón Valley (*quitensis*), and on east slope of Andes south of Marañón (*atuensis*). Found in treeline forest (including *Polylepis*); also adjacent grasslands with scattered shrubs, at 2850–3400 m, where relatively easy to observe. Buffy, especially *quitensis*; *atuensis* mottled white below. **VOICE** Song (*quitensis*) a 3-note, hollow whistle, the first note higher, second 2 monotone: "*WHEEP tu-tu.*" Easily imitated. Call a squeaky "*ts'EEW!*" Last note rises in song of *atuensis*: "*WHEEP tu-TUEE?*" Call a harsh, rolling screech: "*TCHEE'ew.*" **Co, E**

3 WATKINS'S ANTPITTA *Grallaria watkinsi* 18 cm (7 in)

Locally fairly common, but restricted to northwest, in semideciduous forests, 400–900 m. No geographic overlap with Chestnut-crowned Antpitta; also note smaller size, pinkish tarsi, paler colors, more extensive white on sides of face, and narrow streaks on upperparts. Also differs in **VOICE** Song an accelerating series of descending hollow notes ending with a longer rising note: "*CLEW clew-clew'clew'clew cu-HOOEE?*" Call a doubled hollow whistle, rising at end: "*clew-clewEE?*" **E**

4 CHESTNUT-CROWNED ANTPITTA *Grallaria ruficapilla* * 18.5 cm (7¼ in)

Fairly common in northern Andes; found on west slope, both sides of Marañón Valley, and in upper Utcubamba Valley, in humid and semihumid montane forest, at forest edge, and in tall second growth, 1200–3100 m. Often persists in fragmented or degraded forests, unlike many other *Grallaria*. Note chestnut crown, and boldly striped underparts; cf. Watkins's Antpitta. **VOICE** Song 3-note low whistle, first note usually highest, second lowest, and third loudest: "*hee hoo-HEW.*" Easily imitated. Call a hollow, plaintive whistled "*clew.*" **Co, E**

5 CHESTNUT ANTPITTA *Grallaria blakei* 14.5 cm (5¾ in)

Locally fairly common in humid montane forest on east slope of Andes, at 1700–2500 m, locally to 3100 m. Cf. larger Bay Antpitta. Typically at lower elevations than similar rufous populations of Rufous Antpitta. Chestnut averages redder, lacks eyering, and center of belly is barred (barring sometimes indistinct, especially at southern end of range). Also differs in **VOICE** Song a rapid, monotone, slightly accelerating series of chiming notes: "*chew'chu'u'u'u'u'u'u'u'u'u'u'u.*" Call single "*clew*" or short series of notes. Birds from Pasco appear to sing a single chiming note: "*clew.*" Call a series of songlike notes. **ENDEMIC**

6 RUFOUS ANTPITTA *Grallaria rufula* * 14.5 cm (5¾ in)

One of most common antpittas in humid montane forest, especially near thickets of *Chusquea* bamboo. Primarily at 2400–3700 m, locally in southern Peru down to 2000 m. Found on east slope of Andes, also on west slope south to Cajamarca. Relatively small, uniformly colored, usually shows a pale eyering. Geographically variable; generally, populations are more rufous on east slope of Andes near Ecuador border (*rufula*) and in northern Peru south of the Marañón (undescribed subspecies?); birds on west slope (*cajamarcae*) and in central and southern Peru (*obscura, occabambae*) are tawnier. **VOICE** Song (*rufula*) a short, chiming series, last note becoming a short, musical rattle: "*chew chew'ew'r'r'r.*" Calls a quiet, descending, plaintive "*pe'ew,*" also a long series of songlike phrases. Song of *cajamarcae* a series, sometimes slightly accelerating, of descending chiming notes with an initial stutter: "*chew'chew-chew-chew.*" Call a long series of songlike phrases. Song of *obscura* (central Peru) a slightly gravelly, rolling, rising-falling series with a stuttered intro: "*kik'krreeeeerr.*" Call a long series of songlike churrs, rising at end. Song of *occabambae* (southern Peru, north at least to Cordillera Vilcabamba) 2-note, chiming, the second note descending: "*hee-hew.*" Call a descending series of "*hew*" notes and single notes. **Co, E, Bo**

STRIPE-HEADED ANTPITTA

andicolus

punensis

TAWNY
ANTPITTA

quitensis

atuensis

WATKINS'S
ANTPITTA

CHESTNUT-CROWNED
ANTPITTA

CHESTNUT
ANTPITTA

rufous pops.

tawny
pops.

RUFOUS ANTPITTA

PLATE
179

GRALLARIA ANTPITTAS III

Medium-sized to large antpittas of humid montane forest. White-bellied, Rusty-tinged, Bay, and Red-and-white antpittas are a set of similarly sized species that geographically replace one another at middle elevations in the Andes. White-throated Antpitta resembles some members of this group but overlaps with Red-and-white Antpitta. Chestnut-headed and Pale-billed antpittas are large antpittas with gray underparts and that replace one another across the Marañón Valley.

1 WHITE-BELLIED ANTPITTA *Grallaria hypoleuca* * 16–16 cm (6¼–6¼ in)

Fairly common, but limited to east slope of Andes north and west of Río Marañón at 1700–2100 m. Occurs in dense secondary forest, primarily along edges of natural landslides, trails, and man-made clearings, as well as in adjacent humid montane forest (especially where bamboo is present). Replaced south of Río Marañón by Rusty-tinged Antpitta. **VOICE** Song a 3-note hollow whistle, with the first note lower, the second 2 usually monotone: "*hu HEW-HEW.*" Easily imitated. Call a series of rising whistled "*clew'ee?*" notes. **Co, E**

2 RUSTY-TINGED ANTPITTA *Grallaria przewalskii* 16–17 cm (6¼–6¼ in)

Fairly common in humid montane forest on east side of Andes in north-central Peru at 1700–2750 m. Similar to White-bellied Antpitta (no geographic overlap), but gray of breast is paler, throat is creamy or "dirty" (not pure) white, crown usually is duskier, and sides of the breast are rufous. Replaced in central Peru by Bay Antpitta. **VOICE** Song very similar to that of Chestnut-capped Antpitta, a 3-note song with the middle note lowest and the final note highest and loudest: "*hip hew-HEE.*" Easily imitated. Call a series of rising, plaintive, hollow "*clew?*" notes. **ENDEMIC**

3 BAY ANTPITTA *Grallaria capitalis* 16–17 cm (6¼–6¼ in)

Fairly common in humid montane forest at 1800–3000 m, locally down to 1500 m, in central Peru. A medium-sized, largely chestnut antpitta. Overlaps geographically with the smaller Chestnut and Rufous antpittas; elevational overlap is broad with Chestnut but only very limited with Rufous. Bay has blue-gray bill, blackish crown, and white unbarred belly. Bay also usually is redder (less brown) overall than Chestnut; all populations of Rufous that overlap with Bay are much paler, tawnier brown. **VOICE** Song a 4-note (occasionally 5) hollow whistle: "*HEEP hew-hew-hew.*" Easily imitated. Call a mellow, descending whistle: "*heeww.*" **ENDEMIC**

4 WHITE-THROATED ANTPITTA *Grallaria albigula* 18.5 cm (7¼ in)

Fairly common in humid montane forest in southern Andes at 1150–2100 m. Large, with rufous crown and nape, white throat, and light gray underparts. **VOICE** Song a 2-note hollow whistle, the second note slightly higher: "*hee-KEE*"; similar to song of Rufous-breasted Antthrush, but more obviously on 2 pitches. Easily imitated. Call a descending, hollow note: "*clew.*" **Bo**

5 RED-AND-WHITE ANTPITTA *Grallaria erythroleuca* 17.5 cm (7 in)

Uncommon to fairly common in humid forest, forest borders, and tall secondary forest on east slope of Andes in south central Peru, at 2100–3000 m. Cf. White-throated Antpitta, with which there is limited overlap in Cuzco (but which primarily is found at lower elevations). Population in Cordillera Vilcabamba (undescribed subspecies?) is pale yellow (not white) below. **VOICE** Song a 3-note hollow whistle with the first note highest, the second 2 monotone: "*HEE hew-hew.*" In Cordillera Vilcabamba song is 4 notes: "*heep hew-hew-hew.*" Easily imitated. Calls include a series of plaintive, descending "*clew*" notes. **ENDEMIC**

6 CHESTNUT-NAPED ANTPITTA *Grallaria nuchalis* * 20–21 cm (8–8¼ in)

Fairly common, but restricted to humid montane forests on east side of northern Andes, north and west of Río Marañón, 2200–2950 m. Found in bamboo thickets and adjacent forest undergrowth on steep slopes and in stream ravines. Large; note rufous-brown crown, blackish face, and gray underparts. **VOICE** Song a steeply accelerating, series of hollow whistles, rising at end, usually with a quiet introductory note or stutter: "*clew TUR TUR TUR-TUR'TUR't't't't'r'ee'ee?*" Call a series of high, metallic "*teek*" notes. **Co, E**

7 PALE-BILLED ANTPITTA *Grallaria carrikeri* 20–21 cm (8–8¼ in)

Uncommon, in humid montane forest on east side of northern Andes (south of Río Marañón), at 2350–2900 m. Partial to bamboo (*Chusquea*) thickets. Large, with distinctive ivory-colored bill, blackish face, red or reddish brown iris, and gray underparts. **VOICE** Song a series of low hoots, first a higher note, then a stuttered series of lower notes: "*WHEE wur'KUK-KUK-KUK-KUK KUK.*" Call a series of high, metallic "*teet*" notes. **ENDEMIC**

WHITE-BELLIED
ANTPITTA

RUSTY-TINGED
ANTPITTA

BAY
ANTPITTA

WHITE-THROATED
ANTPITTA

RED-AND-WHITE
ANTPITTA

CHESTNUT-NAPED
ANTPITTA

PALE-BILLED
ANTPITTA

PLATE
180

GRALLARICULA AND THRUSH-LIKE ANTPITTAS

Grallaricula *are very small Andean antpittas, found mostly in low dense vegetation (such as treefall gaps, stream edges, and bamboo thickets). May forage on the ground but more often forage in understory within 2 m of the ground. Regularly make sallies to foliage and small branches to capture prey. Thrush-like Antpitta is a drab, terrestrial antpitta (similar to* Grallaria*).*

1 OCHRE-FRONTED ANTPITTA *Grallaricula ochraceifrons* 11.5–12 cm (4½–4¾ in)
Uncommon (and local?), in understory of humid forest of east slope of northern Andes south of Río Marañón at 1850–2400 m. Male has distinctive ochraceous forecrown and sides of face. Female has olive crown, boldly streaked underparts; similar to Ochre-breasted Antpitta, but is larger, darker above, whiter below, and lacks a buff loral spot. **VOICE** Song (?) a single whistled note, given every 6–15 sec: a rising-falling *"wheeu?"* Compare to song of Ochre-breasted. Apparently females are more aggressive singers (more likely to respond aggressively to playback) and sing more loudly than males. Call a chatter when responding aggressively. **ENDEMIC**

2 OCHRE-BREASTED ANTPITTA *Grallaricula flavirostris* * 10 cm (4 in)
Uncommon to fairly common in humid montane forest at 1300–2300 m, locally down to 800 m, along east slope of Andes. Not recorded north of the Marañón, but may occur there (is known from adjacent Ecuador). Breast typically extensively scalloped, washed with buff; intensity of buff variable, and scalloping reduced in some individuals. Cf. Peruvian and Ochre-fronted antpittas. **VOICE** Song (?) a single whistled note given about every 10–20 sec, occasionally faster. Somewhat variable, some birds give a descending *"tew"* or an even longer *"teew,"* others give a rising-falling *"wheew."* Similar to songs of Ochre-fronted and Peruvian antpittas, but most notes shorter, hollower, and often more descending. **Co, E, Bo**

3 PERUVIAN ANTPITTA *Grallaricula peruviana* 10.5 cm (4¼ in)
Very poorly known; presumably secretive and rare, in understory of humid forest of east slope of Andes north of Río Marañón, at 1700–2100 m. Male boldly black-and-white below, with rufous crown and nape. Duller female has olive crown; similar to Ochre-fronted Antpitta (no geographic overlap), but has bolder face pattern. **VOICE** Song (?) a single whistled note, given every 4–15 sec: a rising-falling *"wheeu?"* Compare to song of Ochre-breasted Antpitta. **E**

4 RUSTY-BREASTED ANTPITTA *Grallaricula ferrugineipectus* * 11 cm (4¼ in)
Widespread in humid montane forest of east slope of Andes, south of Río Marañón, at 2000–3250 m. Fairly common in northern Peru; more local and less common in south. Also local and uncommon on west slope in Piura at 1750–2450 m. Mainly at higher elevations than Ochre-breasted Antpitta; more extensively buffy or rufous below, with no dusky scalloping. No overlap with Slate-crowned Antpitta. **VOICE** Song a moderate to fast-paced (6–9 notes/sec), even-pitched or slightly rising-falling, pure-toned series of whistled notes: *"hee-hee-hee-hee-hee-hee-hee-hee."* Calls a descending *"tew"* and *"tew tip"* (the number of *"tip"* notes variable), as well as a moderately paced (3–5 notes/sec) slightly descending series of hollow, descending whistles: *"chew-chew-chew-chew-chew."* **Co, E, Bo**

5 SLATE-CROWNED ANTPITTA *Grallaricula nana* * 11 cm (4¼ in)
Fairly common in humid montane forest on east slope of Andes, north and west of Río Marañón, from 2200 to 2900 m; replaces similar Rusty-breasted Antpitta in areas close to Ecuador border. Note the buffy, unmarked breast and gray crown. **VOICE** Song a moderately paced (about 7 notes/sec), rising-falling series of plaintive whistled notes: *"pee-pee-PEE-pee-pee-pee-pee-pee."* Call a descending *"tew"* note. **Co, E**

6 THRUSH-LIKE ANTPITTA *Myrmothera campanisona* * 14.5 cm (5¾ in)
Widespread and fairly common in Amazonia, to 1000 m, locally to 1500 m. Primarily in terra firme, particularly near dense understory such as at treefalls, areas with wet forest floor, and along streams. Very plain; breast streaking "soft" in comparison to Amazonian *Grallaria* and to *Hylopezus*, and there is no buff or rufous in plumage. **VOICE** Song (south of the Amazon; minor) a series, rising and falling in pitch and amplitude, of 4–7 low hoots: *"hoo HOO HOO hoo hoo."* Song of *signata* (north of the Amazon) higher-pitched, usually more monotone. Easily imitated. Call a quiet, musical chortle. **Co, E, Br, Bo**

OCHRE-FRONTED
ANTPITTA

♂

♀

OCHRE-BREASTED
ANTPITTA

PERUVIAN ANTPITTA

♀

♂

RUSTY-BREASTED
ANTPITTA

SLATE-CROWNED
ANTPITTA

THRUSH-LIKE
ANTPITTA

PLATE
181

GNATEATERS AND *HYLOPEZUS* ANTPITTAS

Gnateaters are small, with very short tails, relatively long tarsi, and an overall plump appearance. Forage on or very close to the ground, as singles or in pairs; do not associate with mixed-species flocks. Most distinctive feature is a prominent long white or silvery postocular stripe (somewhat reduced in females), which may be largely concealed, or flared laterally, especially when agitated. Hylopezus are drab, mostly terrestrial Amazonian antpittas.

1 CHESTNUT-BELTED GNATEATER *Conopophaga aurita* * 11.5–12 cm (4½–4¾ in)
Uncommon in eastern Amazonia; perhaps more common and widespread north of Amazon. Understory of terra firme; south of Amazon may have greater preferences for areas of blackwater drainage than does Ash-throated Gnateater. Male distinctive. Compare female to Ash-throated Gnateater female. **VOICE** Song a thin, puttering, metallic rattle, rising slightly in pitch: "*ptr'tr'tr'tr'-tr'tr'tr'tr'tr.*" Calls a low, coughing "*tchk*" or "*tchew*," also a weak "*pit-tu.*" **Co, E, Br**

2 ASH-THROATED GNATEATER *Conopophaga peruviana* 11.5–12 cm (4½–4¾ in)
Most widespread Amazonian gnateater, although uncommon; absent completely from north bank of the Amazon east of the Napo. Primarily found in understory of terra firme below 1000 m. Male distinctive. Female similar to female Chestnut-belted Gnateater, but note prominent buffy tips to wing coverts; also back more scalloped. **VOICE** Song an unmusical, often bisyllabic, sneezing sound, first syllable louder and rising, second lower pitched: "*shrEE'dit.*" May be repeated frequently. Call a low, coughing "*tchk*" very similar to Chestnut-belted. **E, Br, Bo**

3 CHESTNUT-CROWNED GNATEATER *Conopophaga castaneiceps* * 13–13.5 cm (5–5¼ in)
Widespread but uncommon, in humid montane forest at 1000–2200 m south to Cuzco; scarce and local at southern end of the range. Male of northern *chapmani* has gray throat and breast and rufous-brown crown, brighter on forecrown. Male from Huánuco south (*brunneinucha*; not illustrated) has blackish throat and duller crown; distinguished from female Slaty Gnateater by much darker throat and breast. **VOICE** Vocalizes most often predawn and at dusk. Song a slightly rising, grinding phrase in a series, stuttering at start and end: "*grrrew-grr'grr'grr'grr'grr'gree-grew.*" In display, will give a mechanical rattle (produced in part by the wings) introduced by a "*PSEW!*" Call a sharp "*PSEW!*" similar to Slaty and leaftossers. Also a quiet, gravelly "*grew.*" **Co, E**

4 SLATY GNATEATER *Conopophaga ardesiaca* * 13–13.5 cm (5–5¼ in)
Uncommon, in humid montane forest at 850–2000 m, locally to 2450 m. Typically found in dense undergrowth, such as at treefalls. Little or no elevational overlap with Ash-throated Gnateater; overlaps very locally in Cuzco with Chestnut-crowned Gnateater, where Slaty is mainly at lower elevations. Note plain dark brown back and gray throat and breast in both sexes; female has light rufous lores and forecrown. **VOICE** Vocalizes most often predawn and at dusk. Song a rising, grinding phrase in a series: "*djree? djree? djree?*" In display, will give a mechanical rattle (produced in part by the wings) introduced by a "*PSEEK!*" Call a sharp "*PSEEK!*" similar to Chestnut-crowned and leaftossers. **Bo**

5 WHITE-LORED ANTPITTA *Hylopezus fulviventris* * 14 cm (5½ in)
Uncommon and local in low, damp river-edge forest and thickets bordering man-made clearings, in Amazonia north of the Marañón and Amazon. Note gray crown and nape, contrasting with white lores and postocular spot. Cf. Spotted Antpitta. **VOICE** Song a series of 3–5 deep, hollow hoots: "*coop coop coop,*" about 2 notes/sec. **Co, E**

6 SPOTTED ANTPITTA *Hylopezus macularius* * 14 cm (5½ in)
Poorly known. Occurs locally in eastern Amazonia, primarily north of the Amazon but apparently also south of it in Pacaya-Samiria. Note gray crown and prominent buff eyering. Cf. White-lored Antpitta. **VOICE** Song a 6-note, hooted whistle, second and fourth notes rising: "*who-WHEE who-WHEE-who-who.*" Easily imitated. Call (Brazil) a series of deep hoots: "*COO-cu-cu-cu-cu.*" **Co, E, Br, Bo**

7 AMAZONIAN ANTPITTA *Hylopezus berlepschi* * 14.5 cm (5¾ in)
Rare to uncommon in central and southern Amazonia, in dense undergrowth of riverine forest, at forest edge and in advanced second growth, locally up to 700 m. Relatively plain, with no strong face pattern (unlike Spotted or White-lored antpittas); also usually more extensively buffy below. **VOICE** Song a series of 3–5 deep, hollow hoots: "*coop coop coop.*" Similar to White-lored Antpitta, but slower paced (about 1 note/sec). Call a rapid series of hooting notes: "*KEW'hoo'hoo'hoo'hoo.*" **Br, Bo**

CHESTNUT-BELTED
GNATEATER

♂

♀

ASH-THROATED
GNATEATER

♀

♂

♂ *chapmani*

CHESTNUT-
CROWNED
GNATEATER

SLATY GNATEATER

♀

WHITE-LORED
ANTPITTA

♂

SPOTTED ANTPITTA

AMAZONIAN
ANTPITTA

PLATE
182
TAPACULOS AND CRESCENTCHESTS

Tapaculos are terrestrial insectivores with weak flight; often secretive and difficult to observe. All have an operculum that covers the nostrils. Forage singly or in pairs, and do not join mixed-species flocks. Nests are domed and placed on or near the ground or in small cavities. Identification, especially among the many species of Scytalopus (plates 183–185) can be difficult or impossible. Myornis is an Andean tapaculo, superficially very similar to a Scytalopus. Rusty-belted Tapaculo is the only Amazonian tapaculo. The two crescentchests are also found in the lowlands, but in arid scrub of the northwest and in the Marañón Valley. The very distinctive Ocellated Tapaculo is the largest tapaculo; rare and local in humid montane forests.

1 ASH-COLORED TAPACULO *Myornis senilis* 14–16 cm (5½–6¼ in)
Uncommon; on east slope of Andes, also on west slope in Piura. 2600–3450 m. Usually found in *Chusquea* bamboo thickets. Similar in appearance and behavior to a *Scytalopus*, but larger than most; also note long tail. Generally gray; birds south of the Marañón are darker (undescribed subspecies?). Juvenile light brown, paler below, only lightly barred. **VOICE** Song a long (over 30 sec) series of notes in 3 parts: a series of rich "*tchup*" notes that accelerates into couplets then into a rising-falling chatter, ending with stuttered bursts of descending chatters: "*tchup... tchup... tchup...tch'chup tch'chup tchu'tchirrrrrrrrrr trrup trrup trrup trrup....*" Calls a long, musical rattle "*grrrrrrrrrrr...*" and a drier, rattled "*trrrrrr.*" **Co, E**

2 RUSTY-BELTED TAPACULO *Liosceles thoracicus* * 19–19.5 cm (7½–7¾ in)
Widespread in Amazonia, where uncommon to fairly common in understory of terra firme, up to 1100 m; less common, or more local, in southern Amazonia. Primarily found at sites with dense understory, such as near treefalls. Terrestrial, walking on the ground or on fallen logs. Secretive, heard far more easily than seen. Dark brown above, with long tail. White breast (not always easily seen in dark of forest interior) is crossed by band of dark rufous, or rufous and pale yellow. Cf. Ringed Antpipit, antthrushes. **VOICE** Song a slightly accelerating, descending series of hollow whistles: "*toot toot-toot-toot'toot'toot'toot.*" Easily imitated. Calls a liquid "*dewp,*" a hollow "*tchop,*" and a slightly buzzy "*dzzp.*" Also a higher "*kyip-kyip.*" **Co, E, Br, Bo**

3 MARAÑON CRESCENTCHEST *Melanopareia maranonica* 16 cm (6¼ in)
Similar to Elegant Crescentchest in appearance, behavior, and habitat, but no geographic overlap: replaces Elegant in the dry portions of the middle Marañón Valley at 200–700 m. Larger and longer-tailed than Elegant; wings lack chestnut but are broadly edged with white, and underparts are more deeply colored. Crown of female is sooty, only slightly paler than in male; female also lacks chestnut lower border to black breast band. **VOICE** Song a slightly accelerating, moderate-paced, series of rich notes: "*tu tu-tu-tu'tu'tu'tu'tu'tu'tu.*" Calls a yelping, often squeaky "*yip*" or "*yek,*" sometimes delivered with more modulation: "*djer,*" often in short series. Also a metallic "*tik!*" **E**

4 ELEGANT CRESCENTCHEST *Melanopareia elegans* * 14.5 cm (5¾ in)
Fairly common in deciduous forests and scrub of northwest, below 2000 m. Largely terrestrial, always found on or very near the ground. Relatively tolerant of habitat disturbance, but requires relatively dense ground cover. Frequently cocks the long tail. Ornate plumage pattern is distinctive. Male has black crown, nape, and "mask," also a chestnut breast band; female similar but black of head replaced by olive, and lacks chestnut on underparts. **VOICE** Song a rapid series of rich, musical notes lasting about 1.5 sec: "*tutututututututututututu.*" Calls deep, rich, clicking "*tuk*" and "*tu-tik*" notes, churrs, and short rattles. **E**

5 OCELLATED TAPACULO *Acropternis orthonyx* * 21.5–22 cm (8½–8¾ in)
Rare (and local?) in dense humid forest undergrowth along east slope of Andes in northern Peru, 2300–2950 m. Secretive, rarely seen. Walks on forest floor in the manner of a rail, and hops deliberately through dense vegetation (especially bamboo) within 1 m of the ground. Note the large size and unmistakable plumage pattern. **VOICE** Song a loud, far-carrying, descending or rising-falling, piercing whistle: "*PEEWW,*" often doubled, the second note slightly higher-pitched. Calls include a nasal mewing "*week.*" **Co, E**

RUSTY-BELTED TAPACULO

ASH-COLORED
TAPACULO

n

juv.

s

ELEGANT
CRESCENTCHEST

♂

♀

MARAÑON
CRESCENTCHEST

♀

♂

OCELLATED
TAPACULO

PLATE
183

SCYTALOPUS TAPACULOS I

Scytalopus (plates 183–185) and Ash-colored Tapaculo (plate 182) all are very similar small, furtive birds of humid montane forests and shrubby paramos. Forage as singles or pairs on or very close to ground; do not join mixed-species flocks. Two or three species may occur at a single site. Drab; differences in color between species can be subtle or nonexistent and often are less than differences between sexes within a species. Females typically paler than males, with more of a brown wash on upperparts, and browner flanks. Juveniles and immatures, frequently encountered, largely brown, often barred dusky. Taxonomy of tapaculos and distributions of some species not well known. For identification rely on voice, supplemented by distribution (geographic and elevational), but recognize that identification to species is not always possible on the basis of current knowledge. Four species on this plate are so similar that we use figures of a single male and female to represent the plumages of all four species.

1 BLACKISH TAPACULO Scytalopus latrans * 11.5–12 cm (4½–4¾ in)

Fairly common in humid and semihumid forest of northern Andes at 1500–3200 m. Male sooty gray. Females (not illustrated) of east slope of Andes north (latrans) and south (intermedius) of Marañón similar, but with brown wash on flanks. Females of west slope of Andes (subcinereus) paler gray, with light brown flanks, often faintly barred. **VOICE** Song (latrans) a moderately rapid series of "toop" notes, either in bursts, or in a longer series. Calls a plaintive, mewing "wurp?" often doubled. Song of subcinereus short series of "purp" notes (less muffled than latrans). Call a single or paired, plaintive "wurp?" Song of intermedius a moderately paced series of muffled "purp" notes, either in short bursts (usually rising and falling in pitch) or long series (>15 sec). Calls quiet peeps. Also rapid, rising-falling musical rattled phrases, similar to song notes, but much faster paced. **Co, E**

2 UNICOLORED TAPACULO Scytalopus unicolor 12 cm (4¾ in)

Poorly known. Occurs in Marañón drainage of western Andes at 2400–3400 m; presence on Pacific slope possible but requires confirmation. Very similar to subcinereus Blackish Tapaculo, but male is paler gray. **VOICE** Song an accelerating, slightly descending series of mewing notes, notes shortening over the course of the phrase, these phrases given in a rapid series: "kew-ki-du'u'u kew-ki-du'u'u kew-ki-du'u'u...." Call a fairly sharp "keep." Also a buzzy "bzzu." **ENDEMIC**

3 TRILLING TAPACULO Scytalopus parvirostris 11–12 cm (4¼–4¾ in)

Fairly common along east slope of Andes south of Marañón. Elevational range 2100–3200 m in northern and central Peru, but broader (2100–3600) in south. Small gray tapaculo, sometimes with brown wash on flanks (especially in south). Females paler, with more obvious brown flanks. Virtually identical to Tschudi's Tapaculo, with which broadly sympatric, but found at lower elevations where the two overlap. **VOICE** Song an extremely fast trill (of up to 20 sec), even or slightly falling-rising in pitch, but usually with a slightly higher introduction: "TEE'rrrrrrrrrrrrrrrrrrr...." Call a short, descending, rapid rising-falling chatter: "pteerrrrr." Female gives a moderate-paced short series of falling notes: "pee-ti'ti'tu pee-ti'ti'tu pee-ti'ti'tu...." **Bo**

4 TSCHUDI'S TAPACULO Scytalopus acutirostris 11–12 cm (4¼–4¾ in)

Virtually identical to sympatric Trilling Tapaculo, but the two usually show some elevational segregation; in humid montane forest at 2500–3700 m (higher than Trilling) on east slope of Andes. **VOICE** Primary song a short, accelerating, descending burst, usually in a series at a pace of 1 phrase/sec: "chew-chew'd'drr chew-chew'd'drr chew-chew'd'drr...." Aggressive song (?) a slightly simpler series of descending "cheer'r'r" phrases. Call a descending "tew." **ENDEMIC**

5 LARGE-FOOTED TAPACULO Scytalopus macropus 14–15 cm (5½–6 in)

Rare. Particularly associated with dense undergrowth near montane streams, 2400–3500 m. The largest Scytalopus. Adult uniform blackish gray. Juvenile (not illustrated) paler, washed with brown on upperparts; underparts narrowly barred buff or white. **VOICE** Song a long (up to 3 min), slightly accelerating, series of low, rising, mellow "wurp" notes (about 3/sec at maximum). Call a short series of rising, mellow notes given at a more rapid pace (about 4 notes/sec): "purp-purp-purp-purp." Similar to voice of intermedius Blackish Tapaculo, but pace slower. A recording from eastern Junín thought to be of this species is a rapid, rising chatter: "chrr'ti'ti'ti?" **ENDEMIC**

JUV. *SCYTALOPUS*

BLACKISH/UNICOLORED/TRILLING/
TSCHUDI'S TAPACULOS

BLACKISH/UNICOLORED/TRILLING/
TSCHUDI'S TAPACULOS

♂

♀

LARGE-FOOTED TAPACULO

PLATE
184

SCYTALOPUS TAPACULOS II

Relatively large tapaculos of humid montane forest. Includes 2 sets of geographically replacing, similar species: Long-tailed and Rufous-vented tapaculos, and White-crowned and Bolivian tapaculos.

1 LONG-TAILED TAPACULO *Scytalopus micropterus* 14–14.5 cm (5½–5¾ in)

Fairly common, but restricted to east slope of Andes north and west of the Marañón, at 1500–2000 m. Large tapaculo with a notably long tail. Dark gray, with brown flanks, barred black. Very similar to Rufous-vented Tapaculo, but longer-tailed; no distributional overlap. Chusquea Tapaculo has shorter tail, occurs at higher elevations. **VOICE** Song a slow, slightly accelerating series of notes beginning with a single note, but quickly becoming couplets: "*tchew tchew'r tchew'ew tchew-chew tchew-CHEW tchew-CHEW tchew-CHEW….*" Female gives a slow-paced short, descending series of notes in bursts: "*tchee-chu-chu-chup tchee-chu-chu-chup….*" Call a rising plaintive "*wurp?*" sometimes in short series of 2–4 notes. **Co, E**

2 RUFOUS-VENTED TAPACULO *Scytalopus femoralis* 13 cm (5 in)

Fairly common in humid montane forest on east slope of Andes south of the Marañón, at 1000–2600 m; south at least to Junín, and probably to Ayacucho. Large dark tapaculo with brown flanks, barred black. Similar to White-crowned Tapaculo, but largely found at higher elevations, is less blackish, and crown always gray. **VOICE** Song a slow, slightly accelerating series of notes: "*purp… purp. purp purp purp-purp-purp….*" Female gives a slow-paced, short, descending series of notes in bursts: "*TCHEE-tu-tu TCHEE-tu-tu TCHEE-tu-tu….*" Call single plaintive "*purp?*" notes, often in long, loose series. **ENDEMIC**

3 CHUSQUEA TAPACULO *Scytalopus parkeri* 12–13 cm (4¾–5 in)

Relatively common in high-elevation forest on east slope of Andes, north and west of Marañón Valley, at 2200–2900 m. Usually found in bamboo. Medium-sized tapaculo with tawny flanks, moderately barred with black. Similar to Long-tailed Tapaculo, but tail shorter; found at higher elevations. **VOICE** Song a rapid, even-paced, descending then leveling out, series of sharp notes lasting up to 10 sec: "*tchi'i'i'e'e'e'e'e'e'e'r'r'r'r'r'r'r'r'r'r'r'r'r'r'r'r'r'r.*" Aggressive song similar, but usually in choppy bursts. Calls a rapid, stuttering chatter given in bursts: "*chitter-itter-itter-itter…,*" also a buzzy "*bzzewk.*" **E**

4 BOLIVIAN TAPACULO *Scytalopus bolivianus* 11–12 cm (4¼–4¾ in)

Apparently restricted to Puno, known at 1800–2000 m (in Bolivia, 1000–2300 m). Medium-sized, relatively short-tailed, blackish tapaculo with white crown spot and dark brown, barred flanks. **VOICE** Primary song similar to that of central and southern Peruvian forms of White-crowned Tapaculo, but faster paced (15–18 notes/sec), often starting with higher-pitched, accelerating notes falling in pitch, then slowly rising slightly over course of song, a single song may last up to 40 sec: "*TWEE-twi-twi trr'r'r'r'r'r'r'r'r'r'r'r'r'r'r'r'r'r'r'e'e'e'e'e'e'e.*" Aggressive song slower-paced (5–8 notes/sec), more similar to song of southern Peruvian forms of White-crowned, in bursts of 4–30 notes. Call a buzzy "*bzzew.*" **Bo**

5 WHITE-CROWNED TAPACULO *Scytalopus atratus* * 12–13 cm (4¾–5 in)

Fairly common in humid montane forest on east slope of Andes at 1000–2000 m, locally to 2400 m, and on outlying ridges, south to Cuzco. Blackish tapaculo with dark brown, barred flanks, and usually with a white spot on forecrown; size of white crown spot is variable, however, and in some populations is reduced or lacking. Feathers of center of belly often tipped white. Overlaps with Rufous-vented Tapaculo, but generally found at lower elevations. **VOICE** Geographically variable. North of Marañón song a rapid series of bursts of notes: "*wur'wur'wurWEE wur'wur'wurWEE…*" (there is within-individual variation in pitch of phrases, sometimes phrases rise-fall or fall-rise); occasionally, songs may be longer series. South of the Marañón, song more similar to that of Rufous-vented, but notes more staccato and pace is different. Primary song in San Martín and La Libertad a slow (about 4 notes/sec) series, lasting up to 30 sec, of plaintive "*kyuk*" notes. Aggressive song often a long series (often up to 1 min) of "*kyuk*" notes, often in stuttered bursts (of 2–5 notes, usually in couplets or triplets) at a similar pace to primary song, each burst with a higher introductory note. Song in Cordillera Azul and Cuzco (and intervening populations?) are similar, but generally faster-paced (6–9 notes/sec in Cordillera Azul, 4–6 notes/sec in Cuzco), and seem to lack the couplet and triplet bursts, usually giving longer bursts (5–15 notes) and long, unbroken series (up to 90 sec), probably the latter as primary song. Calls include a buzzy "*bzzk*" or "*bzzew*" (lacking in Cordillera Azul and north of Marañón populations?). **Co, E**

LONG-TAILED TAPACULO

RUFOUS-VENTED TAPACULO

♂

CHUSQUEA TAPACULO

♂

♂

WHITE-CROWNED
TAPACULO

♂

dark crowned

WHITE-CROWNED
TAPACULO

♂

BOLIVIAN TAPACULO

♀

PLATE
185

SCYTALOPUS TAPACULOS III

Illustrated on this plate are the smallest species of tapaculos. These species are found in high-elevation humid montane forest, often all the way to treeline. They are very similar to one another in plumage and also have similar vocalizations; but most of these species geographically replace one another, facilitating identification. Note, however, that Diademed Tapaculo overlaps with Puna Tapaculo in southern Peru. In addition to the species shown here, there are similar, undescribed species of tapaculo from comparable habitats in the Andes of central Peru (Pasco and Junín) and in south-central Peru (Apurímac). Most species on this plate also overlap (geographically and, narrowly, in elevation) with Trilling Tapaculo (plate 183).

1 PARAMO TAPACULO *Scytalopus canus* * 10 cm (4 in)

Fairly common, in treeline forest and adjacent shrubby paramos on east face of Andes in far northern Peru, north of Río Marañón, 2900–3300 m. A small tapaculo, medium gray with light brown, barred flanks. Typically at higher elevations than other species, but may have limited overlap with Ash-colored and Chusquea tapaculos. **VOICE** Primary song a series of bursts of rising-falling churred phrases at a pace of about 1 every 2 sec (each phrase about 1 sec long): "*treEEerr… treEEerr… treEEerr….*" Aggressive song a longer, dry rattle lasting up to about 15 sec: "*trrrrrrrrrrrrr.*" Call short bursts similar to song, but less regularly paced. **Co, E**

2 NEBLINA TAPACULO *Scytalopus altirostris* 11–12 cm (4¼–4¾ in)

A small gray tapaculo with light brown, barred flanks; very similar to Ancash and Puna tapaculos, but does not overlap with either. Found at or near treeline (2900–3700 m) in humid montane forest and adjacent shrubby paramos, along east slope of Andes from Amazonas south to Junín. **VOICE** Primary song a rapid series (about 4/sec) of descending, dry churring phrases: "*djrr djrr djrr djrr djrr djrr.*" Aggressive song a series of bursts of short (<2 sec), rapid (about 12 notes/sec), squeaky rattles: "*tee'i'i'i'i'i… tee'i'i'i'i'i'i….*" **ENDEMIC**

3 ANCASH TAPACULO *Scytalopus affinis* 10.5–11.5 cm (4–4½ in)

A small, pale gray tapaculo with tawny-brown, barred flanks. Known with certainty from the Cordillera Blanca in Ancash, where found in open woodland (often *Polylepis*) with grass tussocks and scattered boulders, at 3000–4600 m. Reported to occur north to Cajamarca, but presence there requires confirmation, due to potential confusion with female of Blackish Tapaculo (*subcinereus*). Best distinguished from Blackish by different **VOICE** Primary song a series of rising churred phrases (about 3 phrases/sec): "*chree chree-chree-chree-chree-chree?*" Aggressive song a series of bursts of short (about 1 sec), very rapid (about 20 notes/sec), dry rattles: "*trrrrr… trrrrr… trrrrr….*" **ENDEMIC**

4 DIADEMED TAPACULO *Scytalopus schulenbergi* 11–11.5 cm (4¼–4½ in)

A small dark tapaculo with a silvery forecrown (reduced in females), found in undergrowth of humid forest near treeline (2750–3400 m) in Cuzco and Puno. Sympatric with Puna Tapaculo, which is found from treeline out into adjacent grasslands (and has different voice). Puna also has only a pale gray superciliary (not a white forecrown) and more distinctly barred flanks and tail. **VOICE** Song (Bolivia) a stuttering series of dry churred notes that accelerates and descends in pitch before becoming a continuous chatter and fading away: "*djrr-djrr'djrr'rr'rr'rr'rr'rr'rr'r'r'r'r'r'r'r'r'r'r'r'r'r'r'r'r'-r'r'r.*" Female's song an accelerating series "*psew psew-chew psew-chew-chew-chew'chew'ew'ew.*" Call (Cuzco) a rising-falling chatter over 1 sec long, usually in an uneven series: "*djreEEer… djreEEer….*" Also (in Bolivia) a dry sneezing "*tchrr.*" **Bo**

5 PUNA TAPACULO *Scytalopus simonsi* 11–12 cm (4¼–4¾ in)

Small tapaculo, often with short, indistinct pale gray superciliary; flanks ochraceous brown, barred black. Restricted to high elevations (2900–4300 m) in south; occurs from edge of humid treeline forest into adjacent grasslands with scattered bushes, also in *Polylepis* forest. Cf. Diademed Tapaculo. **VOICE** Primary song a series of descending churred phrases (about 1–2 phrases/sec): "*tcherr tcherr tcherr tcherr….*" Call a descending whinny: "*djee-ee-ee-eer.*" Also a 2-note "*er-er.*" **Bo**

6 VILCABAMBA TAPACULO *Scytalopus urubambae* 11–12 cm (4¼–4¾ in)

A small gray tapaculo with contrasting ochraceous buff flanks. Very poorly known. Apparently restricted to upper Urubamba Valley in Cuzco, where found in high-elevation (3500–4200 m) humid forest, reportedly especially in sites with moss and boulders. **VOICE** Primary song a series of rising churred phrases (about 2–3 phrases/sec): "*chree-chree-chree-chree.*" **ENDEMIC**

PARAMO TAPACULO

subad. ♂

♂

NEBLINA/ANCASH TAPACULOS

♂

DIADEMED TAPACULO

♂

PUNA TAPACULO

♂

VILCABAMBA TAPACULO

♂

PLATE
186

PHYLLOMYIAS AND BUFF-BANDED TYRANNULETS

Phyllomyias *tyrannulets and Buff-banded Tyrannulet (a* Mecocerculus*) are small with short, stubby bills; most species also have conspicuous wing bars (except for Sooty-headed Tyrannulet). Often in the canopy, and difficult to see well in taller forest. Usually seen as singles or in pairs; most species also join mixed-species flocks. Compare birds on this plate to other genera of small flycatchers, particularly* Zimmerius*,* Phylloscartes*, and other* Mecocerculus.

1 ROUGH-LEGGED TYRANNULET *Phyllomyias burmeisteri* * 11.5 cm (4½ in)

Poorly known. Forages in canopy or midstory of humid montane forest, 750–1600 m. A relatively sluggish tyrannulet. Forages with sallies, hover-gleans, and perch-gleans; takes both insects and some fruit. Note the gray crown, narrow white forehead, pale base to mandible, and unmarked auriculars. Cf. in particular Plumbeous-crowned Tyrannulet and Ecuadorian Bristle-Tyrant, both of which lack white forecrown and pale mandible; Plumbeous-crowned also has a dark mark on auriculars. **VOICE** Song a high, squeaky "*wseeu*," sometimes in a rapid series. Also a similar, but longer, descending "*pseeuuuu.*" **Co, E, Br, Bo**

2 BLACK-CAPPED TYRANNULET *Phyllomyias nigrocapillus* * 11 cm (4¼ in)

Uncommon but widespread along east slope of Andes (1700–3100 m); also rare on west slope in Piura and Cajamarca. Found in humid montane forest, including elfin forest, and forest borders, usually in canopy or midstory. Posture horizontal, behavior active. Readily identified by small size, blackish crown, and strong wing bars. **VOICE** Daytime song a rapidly repeated phrase, a sharp, high note followed by an even-pitched springy trill: "*seek-si'i'i'i'i seek-si'i'i'i'i seek-si'i'i'i'i,*" sometimes followed by a series of "*seek*" notes. Dawn song a single song phrase with longer pauses between phrases. Call a wheezy, mewed "*eeeee.*" **Co, E**

3 SOOTY-HEADED TYRANNULET *Phyllomyias griseiceps* * 10 cm (4 in)

Poorly known. Recorded at few locations, all in foothills or near base of Andes, below 1200 m. Found in canopy or upper strata of humid forest, forest borders, and taller second-growth forest. Usually apart from mixed-species flocks. Forage for insects and small fruits with hover- and perch-gleans. Very plain; easily overlooked (except by voice). Note the small stubby bill, lack of distinct face pattern, and unpatterned wings; most other tyrannulets have wing bars or (*Zimmerius*) have extensive, pale margins to secondaries and wing coverts. **VOICE** Song nearly always given in duet, with 1 individual giving a rising, growled "*gree*" or a longer "*djee! grr-grr-grree*" answered by "*CHEE wordEE-RIP!*" Cf. duet of Yellow Tyrannulet. **Co, E, Br**

4 SCLATER'S TYRANNULET *Phyllomyias sclateri* * 12 cm (4¼ in)

Rare to uncommon along east slope of southern Andes, 1500–2000 m. Found in canopy of humid montane forest, and at forest edge. Posture horizontal, with relatively long tail. Active and restless, often flicking wings. Insectivorous; perch-gleans and hover-gleans. Cf. other small tyrannulets, in particular Buff-banded and Mottle-cheeked (which is much yellower below, with yellower wing bars, and auriculars more or less grizzled with dusky). **VOICE** Song (?) a deep, gruff churring: "*djeer djeer djeer djeer*" interspersed with sharper "*tchik tchik tchik*" notes. **Bo**

5 BUFF-BANDED TYRANNULET *Mecocerculus hellmayri* 11 cm (4¼ in)

Poorly known; presumably a rare resident, but possibly a rare austral migrant. In midstory and canopy of humid montane forest; in Bolivia at 1100–2600 m. Forages with short sallies. Note small size, gray crown, narrow white superciliary, and buff wing bars; upper tail coverts slightly tawny. Similar to Tawny-rumped Tyrannulet, but Buff-banded is more olive (less brown) above, has gray crown, and no tawny rump. Also cf. the slightly larger Sclater's Tyrannulet, which has browner crown, yellower wing bars, and longer tail. **VOICE** Call a plaintive, slightly falling "*pseee*" or "*psee-psee-psee*" (2–5 notes), similar to White-tailed Tyrannulet (no overlap). Also thin chatters. **Bo**

6 TAWNY-RUMPED TYRANNULET *Phyllomyias uropygialis* 11.5 cm (4½ in)

Uncommon to locally fairly common on east slope of Andes, at edge of humid montane forest or in adjacent shrubby areas, 2500–3600 m, locally down to 1800 m. Also on west slope in Piura and Cajamarca; once each in Lima and Arequipa. Active. Easily identified by small size, brown tones to upperparts, tawny-buff wing bars and prominent tawny rump. **VOICE** Song a high, rising whistle followed by thin, bisyllabic (occasionally seems monosyllabic) whistle, consecutive phrases rarely closer than 3 sec: "*squee squeeze-it.*" Call high chips. **Co, E, Bo**

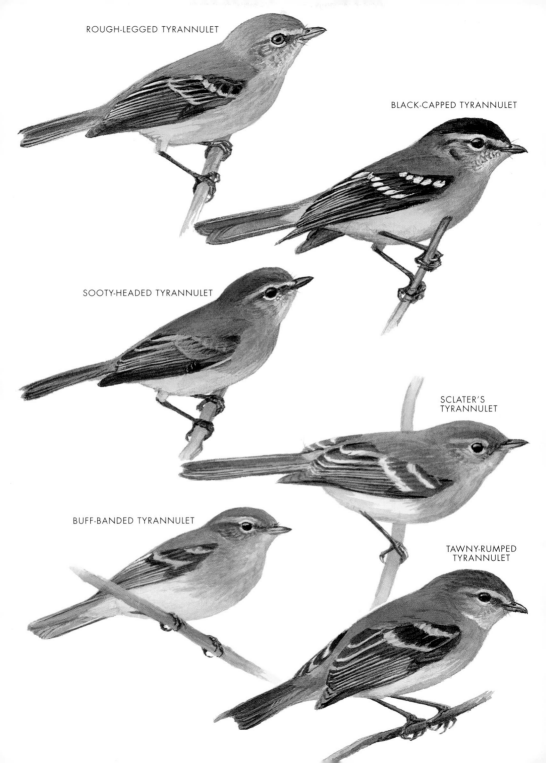

ROUGH-LEGGED TYRANNULET

BLACK-CAPPED TYRANNULET

SOOTY-HEADED TYRANNULET

SCLATER'S
TYRANNULET

BUFF-BANDED TYRANNULET

TAWNY-RUMPED
TYRANNULET

PLATE
187

TYRANNULETS AND BRISTLE-TYRANTS

See plate 186 for notes on Phyllomyias. Phylloscartes *are small, slender flycatchers with a slender bill, long tail, and wing bars. Found in humid forest; insectivorous and typically associate with mixed-species flocks. Frequently "flick" one wing open over the back. Species differ in posture: many have a warblerlike, horizontal stance, whereas others (sometimes placed in* Pogonotriccus) *perch vertically.*

1 ASHY-HEADED TYRANNULET *Phyllomyias cinereiceps* 11 cm (4¼ in)
Rare to uncommon along east slope of Andes, 1300–2450 m. In canopy and subcanopy of humid montane forest, and forest borders. Posture vertical. Behavior relatively sluggish. Note the clear blue-gray crown, black auricular spot, and short stubby bill; also, wing bars contrast strongly to dark wing coverts (lacking narrow pale margins). Similar to several other tyrannulets; cf. Plumbeous-crowned (which has less prominent auricular mark, paler throat) and Marble-faced Bristle-Tyrant (which has larger bill; duskier crown; and wing coverts have narrow pale margins as well as yellowish wing bars). **VOICE** Song a high, sharp note followed by a descending springy trill: "*PSEE-ti'i'i'i'ew.*" Similar to song of Black-capped Tyrannulet, but rarely given in a series. Call a gruff "*pit-tuck.*" **Co, E**

2 PLUMBEOUS-CROWNED TYRANNULET *Phyllomyias plumbeiceps* 11.5 cm (4½ in)
Poorly known. On east slope of Andes, where rare to uncommon but probably often overlooked; locally may be fairly common. In canopy and subcanopy of humid montane forest, 1200–1900 m. Relatively sluggish, often remaining stationary for long periods. Cf. Ashy-headed and Rough-legged tyrannulets and Ecuadorian Bristle-Tyrant. Also note surprisingly loud **VOICE** Song a slightly accelerating, rising or rising-falling series of sharp, moderate-pitched notes: "*pip-pip-PIP-PIP-PIP-pip,*" sometimes ending with a lower trill: "*pip-pip-PIP-PIPtrr.*" Similar to Sulphur-bellied and Rufous-winged tyrannulets, but more staccato in pattern. Call a rich, rising-falling chatter: "*drr'r'l'l'l'r'r'r.*" **Co, E**

3 VARIEGATED BRISTLE-TYRANT *Phylloscartes poecilotis* * 11.5 cm (4½ in)
Uncommon, and perhaps local, on east slope of the Andes, 1400–2300 m. In under- and midstory of humid montane forest. Perches vertically, foraging with short sallies. Note gray crown, black auricular mark, rufous wing bars, and bright orangey mandible. Most similar to Slaty-capped Flycatcher, which is slightly larger and has an all-black bill and less bold wing bars. Sulphur-bellied Tyrannulet has different posture and face pattern. Cf. also Marble-faced Bristle-Tyrant. **VOICE** Song a high, sharp note followed by a rising chippering trill: "*tsew! tsi-tree'tee'tee'ti'ti'ti.*" Call a high "*tsew.*" Also a high "*tsee-tsee*" and "*tsi'wit.*" **Co, E**

4 MARBLE-FACED BRISTLE-TYRANT *Phylloscartes ophthalmicus* * 11.5 cm (4½ in)
Fairly common but local on east slope of Andes. Under- and midstory of humid montane forest, 750–1800 m. Perches vertically, forages with short sallies. Mandible usually gray, but can be black. Northern *ophthalmicus* (south to Junín or Ayacucho) is deeper yellow below; slightly larger *ottonis* (Cuzco south) is paler, with light gray chest and very pale yellow belly. Cf. Slaty-capped Flycatcher (larger; bill longer, all black); Yellow-olive Flycatcher (broader bill; larger size; canopy); Plumbeous-crowned Tyrannulet (stubbier all-black bill; less prominent face pattern; canopy); and Ashy-headed Tyrannulet. **VOICE** Song an accelerating and falling, then decelerating and rising, series of weak, chippering notes: "*pit-it-it'it'tu'tu'tu'ti'ti-ti twit twit.*" Reminiscent of song of Montane Foliage-gleaner, but different note quality. Call a high "*t'tcheep*" or "*tu'tchip.*" **Co, E, Bo**

5 ECUADORIAN TYRANNULET *Phylloscartes gualaquizae* 11.5 cm (4½ in)
Known only from upper Mayo Valley, in canopy of humid montane forest at 800–1500 m. Posture horizontal, sometimes partially cocking the tail. Note light gray crown, relatively faint auricular mark, and yellow wing bars. Cf. Rough-legged Tyrannulet; also Plumbeous-crowned Tyrannulet, which has shorter bill, bolder auricular mark, and different **VOICE** Song a sputtering, descending, quavering trill: "*dzEEeerrrrEEerrrrr.*" Calls short songlike phrases and high "*teep*" and "*ptip*" notes. **Co, E**

6 SPECTACLED BRISTLE-TYRANT *Phylloscartes orbitalis* 11 cm (4¼ in)
Uncommon to locally fairly common on east slope of Andes at 500–1400 m. Found in understory and midstory of humid montane forest. Upright posture; sallies for insects. Note gray crown, well-defined yellow wing bars, narrow yellow eyering, yellow underparts (including throat), and pink mandible. **VOICE** Song (?) a rising series of high notes: "*pit-ti TU-TI-TEE.*" Call thin "*pit-tew*" notes, also a thin, high, dry, descending trill, rising slightly at end: "'*ti'tiiiiiiiir.*" **Co, E, Bo**

ASHY-HEADED TYRANNULET

PLUMBEOUS-CROWNED TYRANNULET

VARIEGATED BRISTLE-TYRANT

ophthalmicus

MARBLE-FACED BRISTLE-TYRANT

ottonis

ECUADORIAN TYRANNULET

SPECTACLED BRISTLE-TYRANT

PLATE
188

LEPTOPOGON FLYCATCHERS AND *PHYLLOSCARTES* TYRANNULETS

These three Phylloscartes *typically perch horizontally, with the tail cocked, and forage in the canopy and midstory of humid montane forest.* Leptopogon *are small insectivorous flycatchers of under- and midstory of humid forest; forage as singles or in pairs, often with mixed-species flocks. All have a relatively long, slender black bill, wing bars, and a gray face grizzled with white; some species also have a conspicuous dark mark on the auriculars. Superficially similar to some* Phylloscartes, *which are slightly smaller and have shorter bills with pale mandibles.* Leptopogon *perch with an upright posture, and forage with quick sallies. They frequently "wing lift" (rapidly opening 1 wing over the back and then retracting it).*

1 SLATY-CAPPED FLYCATCHER *Leptopogon superciliaris* * 13.5 cm (5¼ in)

Fairly common along east slope of Andes and on outlying ridges, at 600–2000 m. Widespread *superciliaris* (south to Ayacucho) has rufous wing bars and deep yellow belly; southern *albidiventer* is paler with buff or yellowish wing bars. Cf. Sepia-capped and Inca flycatchers, and Marble-faced and Variegated bristle-tyrants. **VOICE** Song (*superciliaris*) a squeaky "*ur-too ur-too,*" with occasional "*kuk*" notes interspersed between song phrases. Call a sharp, squeaky toylike "*sKEEKurr,*" usually in a series. Also a quiet "*kuk.*" Song (*albidiventer*) a squeaky chattered "*t'tchew-seek-quay? t'tchew-seek-quay?*" Call a squeaky series of stuttered "*t'tchew-tchew-tchew*" notes and a quiet "*pik.*" Also various chatters and loose trills. **Co, E, Bo**

2 SEPIA-CAPPED FLYCATCHER *Leptopogon amaurocephalus* * 13.5 cm (5¼ in)

Widespread in Amazonia, below 1300 m. Uncommon to fairly common in central and southern Peru; rare and local north of the Amazon and absent from northeast. No other Amazonian flycatcher shares the *Leptopogon* face pattern (but cf. large *Ramphotrigon* flatbills). Replaced in the Andes by Slaty-capped Flycatcher, which has a gray (not brown) crown. **VOICE** Song an abrupt, loud, slightly falling, semimusical chatter: "*ski'i'i'i'i'i'i'eew.*" Call a quiet "*tuk.*" **Co, E, Br, Bo**

3 RUFOUS-BREASTED FLYCATCHER *Leptopogon rufipectus* * 13.5 cm (5¼ in)

Fairly common in humid forest on east slope of Andes north and west of the Marañón, 1650–2150 m. Easily identifiable by tawny-rufous breast and mottled face. Handsome Flycatcher is much smaller, with shorter bill, pale mandible, and more conspicuous wing bars. No overlap with Inca Flycatcher. **VOICE** Calls a high squeaky "*skweew,*" usually given in a loose series, also sharp "*pik*" notes. **Co, E**

4 INCA FLYCATCHER *Leptopogon taczanowskii* 13.5 cm (5¼ in)

Fairly common on east slope of Andes, 1700–2700 m. Similar in behavior to Slaty-capped Flycatcher, which it generally replaces at higher elevations. Note tawny wash to breast, lack of prominent auricular mark, and olive-gray (not slate-gray) crown. **VOICE** Song a squeaky "*skleew-di-wurdee?*" Calls a series of 1–5 "*skleew*" notes, also sharp "*pik*" notes. **ENDEMIC**

5 [RUFOUS-BROWED TYRANNULET] *Phylloscartes superciliaris* * 11.5 cm (4½ in)

Locally fairly common, but in Peru only known from Cordillera del Cóndor, 1400–1800 m. Long-tailed, white-breasted tyrannulet with short, narrow rufous superciliary (may be difficult to see in the field) and auriculars clearly outlined with black. **VOICE** Song a high, springy, laughing chatter that quavers: "*chi chi tchrrEE'EE'ee'EE'EE'eew*" or shorter "*tchwee tchwee ti-titititew.*" Call a high "*tchwee.*" **Co, E**

6 MOTTLE-CHEEKED TYRANNULET *Phylloscartes ventralis* * 12 cm (4¾ in)

Fairly common and widespread on east side of Andes, 1000–2400 m. Very active. Dark mark on auriculars is not prominent. Identify by shape and posture, well-defined yellow wing bars, relatively long dark bill, and olive crown. Cf. smaller, stubby-billed *Phyllomyias* tyrannulets. **VOICE** Song a descending, accelerating rattle "*tchep tik tik-teer'r'r'r'.*" Call weak, sneezy, metallic "*tchee*" or "*tchep*" notes. Wings produce an audible rattle in flight (and display?). **Br, Bo**

7 CINNAMON-FACED TYRANNULET *Phylloscartes parkeri* 11.5 cm (4½ in)

Locally fairly common along east slope of Andes and on outlying ridges, at 650–1550 m. Very active, foraging with short sallies. Usually in pairs, apart or with mixed-species flocks. Note the yellow underparts, yellow wing bars, and distinctive rufous "face" (lores and eyering). **VOICE** Song a high, springy, laughing chatter that quavers, rising slightly: "*chi chi tchrrEEEEeeeEEEEEew.*" Reminiscent of the common call of Lemon-browed Flycatcher, but weaker, higher pitched. Call a high "*tchew.*" **Bo**

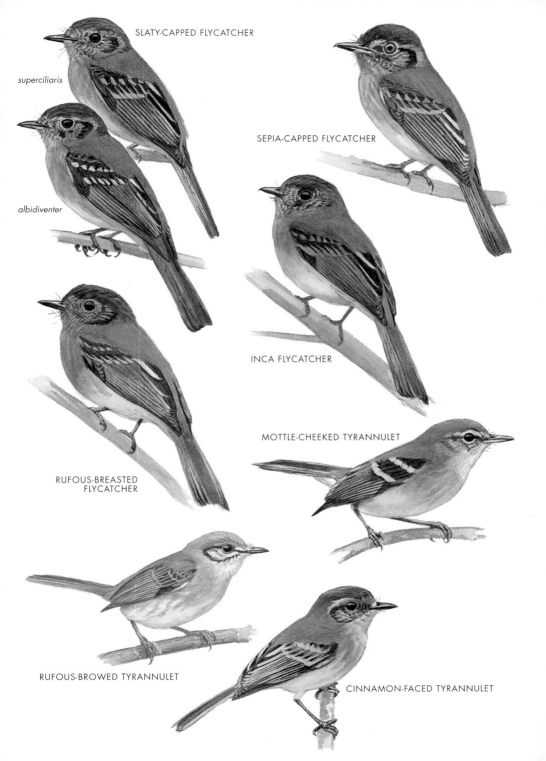

SLATY-CAPPED FLYCATCHER

superciliaris

albidiventer

SEPIA-CAPPED FLYCATCHER

INCA FLYCATCHER

RUFOUS-BREASTED
FLYCATCHER

MOTTLE-CHEEKED TYRANNULET

RUFOUS-BROWED TYRANNULET

CINNAMON-FACED TYRANNULET

PLATE
189

ZIMMERIUS AND YELLOW TYRANNULETS

Zimmerius are small, stubby-billed flycatchers. Lack wing bars, although wing coverts and some remiges are edged with yellow-green. Primarily frugivorous, particularly feeding on mistletoe berries; many species often associate with mixed-species flocks. Usually in forest canopy or at edge. Yellow Tyrannulet is superficially similar to Phylloscartes.

1 BOLIVIAN TYRANNULET *Zimmerius bolivianus* * 12 cm (4¾ in)

Fairly common on east slope of southern Andes, 1000–2600 m. Similar to Slender-footed Tyrannulet, but found at higher elevations. Also has a plain face, more olive crown, less contrasting wing markings, and grayer breast that contrasts more with whiter throat. Only limited overlap with Red-billed Tyrannulet, which has pale mandible, yellower (less greenish) wing markings, grayer crown, and is deeper yellow below. **VOICE** Dawn song a rising, plaintive series of whistles: "*hee-hee-heEEew.*" Call a mellow descending "*teew.*" **Bo**

2 GOLDEN-FACED TYRANNULET *Zimmerius viridiflavus* * 11 cm (4¼ in)

Common and widespread in humid montane and (Tumbes) semideciduous forest. All subspecies have yellowish lores and eyering, and dark iris. White-bellied in Tumbes, 500–750 m, and on west side of Andes in Piura, 1200–2600 m (*flavidifrons*; not illustrated); and on east slope of northern Andes at 1000–2450 m (*chrysops*). Yellow-bellied *viridiflavus* occurs in central Peru. Cf. Slender-footed and Bolivian tyrannulets. **VOICE** Dawn song of *chrysops* (north of the Marañón) a slightly rising, accelerating, laughing series of notes: "*tee-hee'hee'hee'hee.*" Calls a descending, melancholy "*teww,*" occasionally also a chuckled "*whee-hee-hee-hew.*" Dawn song of *chrysops* (south of Marañón) and of *viridiflavus* a rising, musical, chiming series "*tew-tew-tee.*" Call a 1–4-note upslurred "*hooooeet?*" or "*hu-hu-hu'eeet?*" Dawn song (*flavidifrons*) a slow, descending "*peet peet purt.*" Call like *viridiflavus*, but typically (always?) monosyllabic. **Co, E**

3 RED-BILLED TYRANNULET *Zimmerius cinereicapilla* 12 cm (4¾ in)

Uncommon (but often overlooked?) on east slope of Andes and in foothills, 550–1300 m. Note pale mandible, pale iris, and prominent pale margins to wings. In Mayo Valley may overlap with smaller Mishana Tyrannulet, which has olive crown, yellower throat, and different voice. Cf. also Slender-footed and (in south) Bolivian tyrannulets. **VOICE** Song rising "*chi-wheet*" interspersed with a rich, chuckling "*pi'CHEE'CHEE'CHEE'CHEE.*" Calls a rich "*pi'chew*" or "*pi'chew-chew-chew.*" **E**

4 SLENDER-FOOTED TYRANNULET *Zimmerius gracilipes* * 10.5–11 cm (4–4¼ in)

Fairly common and widespread in Amazonia (up to 1000 m), but often overlooked except by voice. Note the gray crown with indistinct superciliary, pale iris, and dark bill. Cf. other *Zimmerius*; other small Amazonian tyrannulets (Yellow-crowned, White-lored) have wing bars and dark iris. **VOICE** Dawn song of *gracilipes* (northeast) a rising musical chatter: "*tew-tui'i'i tew-tui'i'i.*" Call a mewing, rising "*huee?*" also a chatter followed by several rising "*huit?*" notes. Dawn song of *gilvus* (central and southern Peru) an accelerating, monotone series of musical notes "*chew-chu-chi'chi.*" Call a liquid "*duit.*" **Co, E, Br, Bo**

5 MISHANA TYRANNULET *Zimmerius villarejoi* 9.5 cm (3¾ in)

Fairly common but very local; known only from stunted white-sand forests near the Río Nanay, and in semidry forests and second growth of Mayo Valley, up to 1100 m. Note very small size, pinkish mandible, and pale iris. Slender-footed Tyrannulet is larger and has an all-dark mandible and grayish crown with short white superciliary. In Río Mayo area cf. Red-billed. **VOICE** Dawn song 2–4 whining, rising whistles: "*tooeet tueet tuit.*" Calls a rising "*tueet,*" singly or in a series of 2–4 notes. Similar to call of Forest Elaenia, which is louder and more run-together. Also a quiet, descending, chuckled "*heeu-heu'hi'hu*" and a series of rising whistles: "*hueet hueet hueet.*" **ENDEMIC**

6 YELLOW TYRANNULET *Capsiempis flaveola* * 11.5 cm (4½ in)

Patchy distribution in Amazonia and on lower eastern slope of Andes, up to 1150 m. Found in successional habitats: river-island forest and stream edges (northern Amazonia); forest edge and hedgerows (Huallaga drainage); and bamboo (in south). In pairs or groups, usually not with mixed-species flocks. Posture often upright. No other small flycatcher is so yellow; but cf. Yellow-breasted Flycatcher and *Phylloscartes*. **VOICE** Song, usually a duet, a rhythmic chatter: "*tchippy'per-tchippy'per-tchippy'per….*" Call a low, purred trill "*trrrrrrr,*" often interspersed between song bouts. Recalls duet of Sooty-headed Tyrannulet, but is less varied and includes trills. **Co, E, Br, Bo**

BOLIVIAN TYRANNULET

chrysops

GOLDEN-FACED TYRANNULET

viridiflavus

RED-BILLED TYRANNULET

SLENDER-FOOTED TYRANNULET

MISHANA TYRANNULET

YELLOW TYRANNULET

PLATE
190

ELAENIAS (*MYIOPAGIS*)

Myiopagis have semiconcealed white or yellow crown patches; smaller than Elaenia, and otherwise more closely resemble tyrannulets. Cf. also Tolmomyias (which have much broader bills) and to Slender-footed and Yellow-crowned tyrannulets (both much smaller).

1 GREENISH ELAENIA *Myiopagis viridicata* * 13.5 cm (5¼ in)

Fairly common austral migrant to southeast, up to 1000 m, in forest understory; primarily in varzea (*viridicata*). May be resident in dry middle Huallaga Valley. Also resident in Tumbes, in semideciduous forest at 400–800 m (*implacens*). Usually encountered as singles, not associated with mixed-species flocks. Note lack of wing bars and of a strong face pattern. Cf. Sulphur-bellied Tyrant-Manakin. **VOICE** Dawn song (*implacens*) thin, fairly high notes "*heeee*" notes interspersed with an occasional "*tsew-er.*" Reminiscent of song of Black Phoebe. Day songs a high, quavering rising-falling "*tseeEE-yew*" or a descending "*tzeew.*" Vocalizations of *viridicata* burrier. Dawn song a trisyllabic, rising-falling, burry "*cheery'ZEEyew*" interspersed with occasional "*pee'chew*" notes. Day song a falling-rising, burry "*bjeerEEP,*" a sharp, falling "*skeep!,*" and a chattered "*chZEE-chZEE-chew.*" Calls quiet chuckles. **Co, E, Br, Bo**

2 PACIFIC ELAENIA *Myiopagis subplacens* 14 cm (5½ in)

Fairly common in northwest, in dry forest and tall scrub up to 1800 m. Typically not with mixed-species flocks. Posture upright. Relatively sluggish. Few similar flycatchers within its range; note lack of wing bars, the blurry streaks on breast, and ill-defined whitish superciliary. Greenish Elaenia (very limited overlap in Tumbes) is smaller, yellower below, and has a plainer face. **VOICE** Call a gruff "*pjrt*" and similar notes. Dawn song a series of low, gruff "*djer*" notes occasionally interspersed with a rising "*p'chewree?*" Day song a sharp, burry "*PJIT! djurrrree,*" the second note rising. **E**

3 YELLOW-CROWNED ELAENIA *Myiopagis flavivertex* 13 cm (5 in)

Fairly common in northern Amazonia, in the under- and midstory of varzea. Singly or in pairs, usually not associated with mixed-species flocks. Posture upright; behavior otherwise probably similar to Forest Elaenia. Relatively dingy in appearance, browner above than Forest Elaenia with olive wash on breast and even less well-defined wing bars. Crown yellow (not whitish). Also note the loud distinctive **VOICE** Song a low, gruff "*per-DJEER-DJEER-djer,*" with variable numbers of "*djeer*" notes, these occasionally accelerating into a descending chatter. Also a stuttering, decelerating gruff chatter: "*DJEER t'DJI'dje'djewr.*" **E, Br**

4 GRAY ELAENIA *Myiopagis caniceps* * 12–12.5 cm (4¾–5 in)

Uncommon but widespread, in Amazonia below 700 m. Canopy of humid forest, often in pairs associated with mixed-species flocks. Behavior much like that of Forest Elaenia, but posture frequently horizontal. Gray-and-white male distinctive (cf. larger, broader-billed becards). Yellow-bellied female more difficult to identify (except by association with male). Similar to Forest, but shorter tailed, with plain breast (not lightly mottled), green (not grayish) sides to crown, and more well-defined wing bars. Yellow-crowned Elaenia is duller and not found in canopy. **VOICE** Frequently heard call a high-pitched, somewhat sneezy "*tsee tsee TSEW-tsee-TSEW*" occasionally interspersed with a musical, descending, springy phrase: "*TSEE'SEE'see'see'see'sew.*" Also (only in southeast?) a drier, accelerating trill: "*tzi tzi-tzi'tzi'tttttt.*" **Co, E, Br, Bo**

5 FOOTHILL ELAENIA *Myiopagis olallai* 12.5 cm (5 in)

Known only from Cordillera Vilcabamba at 900 m; presumably more widespread, but overlooked. In Ecuador, in canopy of humid lower montane forest at 1000–1500 m, largely above elevational range of very similar Forest Elaenia. Compared to Forest, has a grayer crown (not gray-brown), with pure white (not pale yellowish white), largely concealed crown patch and more well-defined wing bars. Best identified by **VOICE** Calls (song?) a rapid, descending trilled "*t'teerrr,*" and a longer, rising trilled "*t'teerrreeeeeeee.*" Also a rising series, "*tew-tew-tew,*" which may accelerate into a longer, rising trill. **E**

6 FOREST ELAENIA *Myiopagis gaimardii* * 12.5 cm (5 in)

Fairly common to common (by voice), and widespread in Amazonia, to 900 m, locally up to 1300 m; canopy of forest and tall second growth. Singly or in pairs; frequently with mixed-species flocks. Posture relatively upright; sometimes partially cocks tail. Note yellow belly, yellow breast vaguely streaked with olive, and wing bars. Cf. Yellow-crowned and female Gray elaenias. **VOICE** Song a plaintive, rising "*TWEE?,*" "*peeTWEE?,*" or "*PEEchew-TWEE?*" **Co, E, Br, Bo**

GREENISH ELAENIA

PACIFIC ELAENIA

YELLOW-CROWNED ELAENIA

GRAY ELAENIA

♀

♂

FOOTHILL ELAENIA

FOREST ELAENIA

PLATE
191

ELAENIAS (LARGER *ELAENIA*)

Elaenia are mostly frugivorous flycatchers of forest edge and second growth. Drab; most species are crested with semiconcealed white crown patch. Not all individuals can be identified (even in the hand). Important characteristics include voice (although often silent when not breeding), size, overall color, and wing pattern; some are migratory, so also note seasonality and habitat.

1 YELLOW-BELLIED ELAENIA *Elaenia flavogaster* * 15.5–16.5 cm (6–6½ in)
Local along east side of Andes, 450–1500 m. Can be fairly common, especially in dry intermontane valleys and on Pampas del Heath. Found at forest edge, in second growth, and at margins of oxbow lakes. Large, with relatively well-developed, bushy (and often bifurcated) crest, but no distinctive features. Cf. Large, Mottle-backed, and Lesser elaenias. **VOICE** Dawn song a series of burry *"teeotree"* or *"tee-tree"* notes interspersed with an occasional *"wurrTREE."* Day song, often in duet, a long, descending burry note followed by a series of squeaky, burry hiccuping notes: *"BEEER reeTREEP-reeTREEP-reeTREEP..."*; sometimes the introductory note or the hiccuping series is given alone. **Co, E, Br, Bo**

2 LARGE ELAENIA *Elaenia spectabilis* 16.5–18 cm (6½–7 in)
Widespread and common austral migrant (Mar–Oct) to Amazonia, locally to 1450 m. Primarily at forest edge, second growth, and river-edge forest (including on river islands). Large; similar to Yellow-bellied Elaenia, but crest less well developed (often appears uncrested), with less white on crown; also usually a short wing bar on lesser wing coverts (3 wing bars rather than 2), and on average a longer primary extension. Small-billed Elaenia is much smaller and whiter below. Lesser Elaenia is smaller, drabber (browner above, paler below), and underparts are more uniformly colored. Cf. also Mottle-backed and Brownish elaenias, and *Myiarchus* flycatchers. **VOICE** Call a rich, descending *"tchew."* Unlikely to sing in Peru. **Co, E, Br, Bo**

3 SLATY ELAENIA *Elaenia strepera* 15–16 cm (6–6¼ in)
Rare passage migrant (Mar, and Sep–Oct) in Amazonia, where presumably in river-edge forest, forest edge, and other successional habitats. Pale slaty adult male is distinctive (but cf. larger Crowned Slaty-Flycatcher). Adult female similar, but washed with olive; also may have whitish or pale buff wing bars. First-year birds have rufous wing bars; upperparts dull olive, breast olive-brown, and belly deep yellow. **VOICE** Call a dry growl: *"t'grrrrr."* Song (rarely heard in Peru?) a deep, gravelly, accelerating rattle: *"tur tur-tic'tk'tk."* **Co, Bo**

4 MOTTLE-BACKED ELAENIA *Elaenia gigas* 17.5–18.5 cm (7–7¼ in)
Uncommon to fairly common, and widespread along lower eastern slopes of Andes; up to 1800 m and (only when not breeding?) in adjacent lowlands. Found at forest edge, in second growth, river-edge forest, and river islands. Large, with prominent crest, often bifurcated exposing white crown patch. Centers of feathers of upperparts dark (but not appearing particularly "mottled"). Slightly larger than Yellow-bellied and Large elaenias, with breast clouded with olive (rather than light gray), deeper yellow center of belly, and "horned" crest (bushier in Yellow-bellied). **VOICE** Dawn song a deep, burry *"T'CHEE'bjee'djj'jee."* Day song a deep, harsh, rising *"D'JEE."* Call a mewing, rising *"woo'be?"* **Co, E, Bo**

5 BROWNISH ELAENIA *Elaenia pelzelni* 18 cm (7 in)
Uncommon to fairly common on river islands in northern Amazonia; to be looked for on the lower Río Ucayali as well. Found on medium-aged river islands with well-developed stands of *Cecropia*. Apparently resident although may have local movements, presumably following food supplies. Large and drab. Brownish above and on breast. Belly white, lacking yellow tones of Large Elaenia. **VOICE** Calls a deep, gruff *"DJI-drt"* or *"DJI-drt-drt,"* and a rich *"p'chup-urt?"* **Co, Br, Bo**

6 HIGHLAND ELAENIA *Elaenia obscura* * 17–17.5 cm (6¾–7 in)
Fairly common, but local, on east slope of Andes and in Marañón Valley, 1400–2700 m; at edge of humid and semihumid montane forest and scrub, and in second growth. Relatively round-headed, with no crest or crown patch, a relatively short stubby bill, and little or no eyering. Brownish olive above, extensively yellow below. Larger than Sierran Elaenia, and lacks the crest, crown patch, and narrow eyering of that species. **VOICE** Call a burry, rising-falling or descending *"breerr."* Dawn song a deep, burry, musical *"pip pur WUR-TMMweer."* Day song a low, growled *"brrrr"* with an occasional rising, burry *"tch'DJREEE"* and *"pup pup pup"* notes interspersed. **E, Br, Bo**

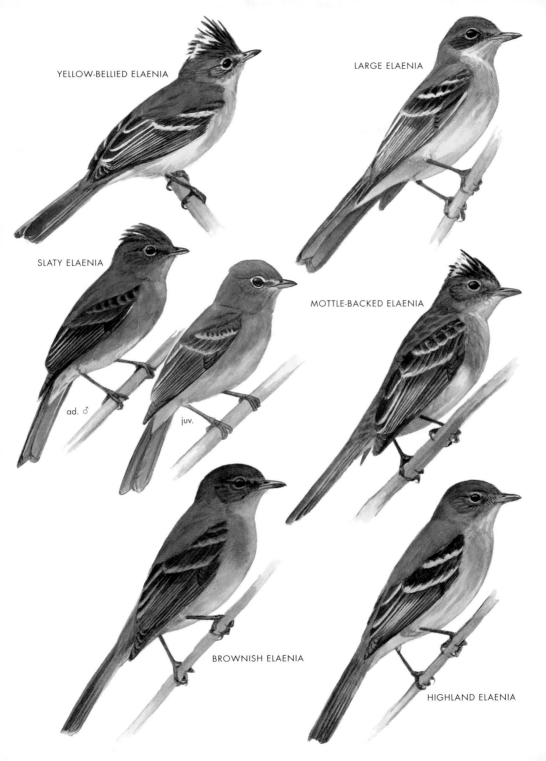

YELLOW-BELLIED ELAENIA

LARGE ELAENIA

SLATY ELAENIA

MOTTLE-BACKED ELAENIA

ad. ♂

juv.

BROWNISH ELAENIA

HIGHLAND ELAENIA

PLATE
192

ELAENIAS (SMALLER *ELAENIA*)

1 SIERRAN ELAENIA *Elaenia pallatangae* * 14–15 cm (5½–6 in)
Common and widespread on east slope of Andes, 1100–3500 m; also in Marañón Valley south to central Cajamarca, and on west slope south at least to Piura. On edge of humid montane forest and in second growth. Note slight crest with white crown patch, relatively obvious yellowish eyering, and pale yellow belly. Yellower on underparts (especially belly) than White-crested or Lesser elaenias; also cf. larger Highland Elaenia. **VOICE** Dawn song a burry "*djee'wee*" interspersed with an occasional sneezy "*tjrr*." Day song a pure rising-falling "*peew*" or rising "*whee?*" Call a low "*djr-djr-djr*." **Co, E, Br, Bo**

2 WHITE-CRESTED ELAENIA *Elaenia albiceps* * 13.5–15 cm (5¼–6 in)
One of the most common and widespread elaenias on coast and in Andes. Several subspecies, some of which are migratory. Resident in Marañón Valley and on Pacific slope (800–3500 m) south to Ancash (*griseigularis, diversa*), and on east slope (1000–3300 m) from Cuzco south (*urubambae, albiceps*). Austral migrant *chilensis* winters (Apr–Oct) on east slope of Andes and in Marañón Valley, 400–2000 m (up to 3200 m during migration). *Modesta* breeds (Nov–Jun) on coast (up to 1600 m in south), but winters (Jun–Dec) on east slope below 1400 m. A small elaenia usually with well-developed white crown patch. Drab, with chest light olive and belly whitish (but flanks and undertail coverts variably washed with pale yellow). Most similar to Lesser Elaenia. *Modesta* has duller wing bars (light olive, never white) and bases of inner remiges are olive or brown (not black). **VOICE** Dawn song (*griseigularis*) a series of deep, burry, falling-rising "*djeewee*" notes interspersed with occasional "*per'brr'djwee*" notes. Calls a low, rich, modulated "*djur*" and a longer, descending "*djeeer*." Call of *modesta* a pure, descending "*peeur*." Dawn song (*albiceps*) a series of burry rising-falling-rising "*djee'awee*" notes interspersed with an occasional "*purt trr'cheewee*." Calls a burry, sneezing "*whi'bur*" and a descending, burry "*wheer*." Calls (*chilensis*) a pure, descending "*weer*," a burry, sneezing "*whi'bur*," and a burry, rising "*chjuree?*"; unlikely to sing in Peru. **Co, E, Br, Bo, Ch**

3 SMALL-BILLED ELAENIA *Elaenia parvirostris* 13–14 cm (5–5½ in)
Fairly common austral migrant (Mar–Nov) to Amazonia, locally up to 1300 m. At forest edge, in second growth, on young river islands, and in river-edge forest. Crest reduced or lacking (head looks rounded), relatively prominent white eyering. Paler and whiter below than most other small elaenias, with greater contrast between throat and auriculars (but some *chilensis* White-crested Elaenias are almost as pale below, although usually have dingier, less contrasting throats). Typically also has short wing bar on lesser wing coverts (3 rather than 2 wing bars). Cf. Lesser and White-crested elaenias. **VOICE** Calls a rich "*tchup*" and a rising-falling "*pee'wur*." Dawn song a stuttering, deep, gravelly "*PEE-jip-p'p'jooee?*" **Co, E, Br, Bo**

4 PLAIN-CRESTED ELAENIA *Elaenia cristata* * 12.5–13.5 cm (5–5¼ in)
Fairly common, but only known from dry middle Urubamba Valley at ca. 1100 m; and on Pampas del Heath, where in forest edge and shrubs on savannah. Crest relatively well developed. Underparts pale yellow. Very similar to Lesser Elaenia, but slightly yellower below; center of crown always lacks white; and primary extension usually shorter. Cf. also Small-billed, Yellow-bellied, and Large elaenias. **VOICE** Call (Venezuela) a rattled "*wee-he-he-he-e*," also a rising-falling "*dsooty-EEo*." Dawn song (Venezuela) a rapid "*CHEE'beer-ip*," the "*beer*" note descending and buzzy. Day song (Venezuela) a low, gravelly, 3-part "*peeu peeu p'pr'pr'pr're'bit pi'pi'pi*." **Co, Br, Bo**

5 LESSER ELAENIA *Elaenia chiriquensis* * 13–14 cm (5–5½ in)
Poorly known. Patchily distributed on east slope of Andes, in shrubs and edges of grasslands; also very local in similar habitats in Amazonia. Small with a modest crest. Usually has a white crown patch (but often semiconcealed; also white reduced or absent in some individuals: primarily juveniles?). Underparts suffused with pale yellow. Very similar to White-crested Elaenia, but pale yellow is more extensive on underparts (center of belly is relatively white in White-crested); wing bars often whiter (wing bars of White-crested more likely to be washed with yellow or olive). Cf. also Small-billed Elaenia. Yellow-bellied Elaenia is larger, with deeper yellow on the belly, and more obvious crest. **VOICE** Dawn song a sharp, burry "*TCHEE'wurr*." Call a clear, squeaky, descending "*whEEW*." **Co, E, Br, Bo**

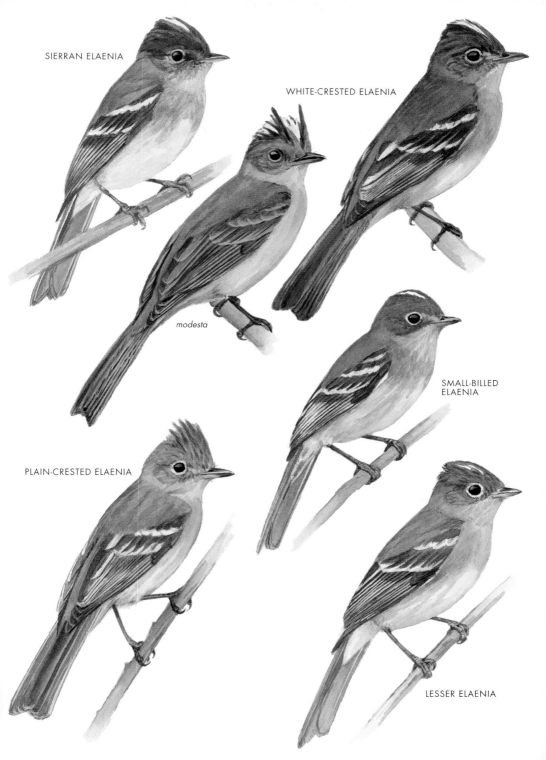

SIERRAN ELAENIA

WHITE-CRESTED ELAENIA

modesta

SMALL-BILLED
ELAENIA

PLAIN-CRESTED ELAENIA

LESSER ELAENIA

PLATE
193

SCRUB-FLYCATCHERS AND TYRANNULETS

Serpophaga are small gray-and-white tyrannulets of water- or river-edge habitats. Scrub-flycatchers (Sublegatus) resemble Elaenia, with drab upperparts, light yellow bellies, and slightly bushy-headed look, but lack white in crown and bill is even shorter, stubbier. The doradito and the wagtail-tyrant also found in wet or river-edge habitats but are mostly yellow and relatively long-tailed.

1 RIVER TYRANNULET *Serpophaga hypoleuca* * 11 cm (4¼ in)

Rare to uncommon. Primarily on islands in larger Amazonian rivers, locally on the mainland; in riparian scrub and other relatively open early successional vegetation. Posture typically horizontal; may hop on ground. Active, found alone or in pairs but typically not with mixed-species flocks. Little or no overlap with Torrent Tyrannulet, which is slightly larger, has black wings and tail, and different habitat. **VOICE** Song a rising trill: *"tsi'rrreeeee."* Call a high, thin *"pit tsip."* **Co, E, Br, Bo**

2 TORRENT TYRANNULET *Serpophaga cinerea* * 11.5 cm (4½ in)

A water sprite. Fairly common along fast flowing, rock-strewn watercourses in and near Andes, where singles or pairs perch on rocks in streams and rivers or on branches hanging very low over water. Often flicks tail upward. On east slope of Andes from 800–3100 m (locally down to 400 m); local on west slope, 800–2800 m. Unmistakable. Little or no overlap with River Tyrannulet. **VOICE** Song a rapid series of twittering chips. Call a high, thin *"ti-tsip."* **Co, E, Bo**

3 SOUTHERN SCRUB-FLYCATCHER *Sublegatus modestus* * 14–15 cm (5½–6 in)

Poorly known. Resident in the semidry portions of Urubamba Valley up to 1500 m. Also a rare austral migrant below 1000 m to southern Amazonia. Probably in edge habitats similar to those occupied by Amazonian Scrub-Flycatcher. Very similar to that species but smaller, belly is deeper yellow, and wing bars are white and more conspicuous. Also cf. Mouse-colored Tyrannulet, which is smaller and more extensively yellow below (lacking gray throat and chest). **VOICE** Song (Argentina) is some short notes followed by a descending, slightly hoarse whistle: *"di-di-di-DZEEE."* Calls (Bolivia) include a quiet, thin, rising-falling *"dzereer"* or falling *"dzeer."* **Co, Br, Bo**

4 AMAZONIAN SCRUB-FLYCATCHER *Sublegatus obscurior* 14–15 cm (5½–6 in)

Poorly known; local (or overlooked?) in Amazonia and Andean foothills below 1000 m. Singles or pairs forage in or near cover at forest edge. Note brownish upperparts, light gray chest, light yellow belly, and dull grayish wing bars. Cf. Southern Scrub-Flycatcher. **VOICE** Song a sweet rising whistle followed by a doubled whistle, descending at the end: *"TWOEE? whi-whiEEE… TWOEE? Whi-whiEEE…."* Call a quiet *"dzeeuree?"* and louder *"whi-wheeeer"* notes, sounding much like the second phrase of the song. Also (Ecuador) gives a descending *"dzeeer!"* and quiet *"du-du-du"* notes. **Co, E, Br, Bo**

5 SUBTROPICAL DORADITO *Pseudocolopteryx acutipennis* 11.5 cm (4½ in)

Poorly known. Apparently breeds locally in Andes, 1400–3200 m, but also a rare austral migrant to southern Amazonia and to Andean foothills below 1000 m. Breeding habitat not well known, but presumably is reedbeds, marshes, and wet pastures and fields; sometimes seen in scrub and urban parks (migrants?). In Amazonia noted in riparian scrub. Small, slender, warblerlike, with black bill; juveniles have pale mandible and buffy (not olive) wing bars. Cf. larger Masked Yellowthroat (no wing bars, has pale mandible and tarsi, and proportionately shorter bill). **VOICE** Largely silent. Song (Argentina), given in aerial display, is 3 thin, dry *"tzik"* notes followed by a dull *"plunk"* produced mechanically. Calls (Argentina) a dry *"tzik"* similar to calls of Wren-like Rushbird, also a series of pumping *"k'slong"* notes in chases. **Co, E, Br, Bo**

6 LESSER WAGTAIL-TYRANT *Stigmatura napensis* * 13 cm (5 in)

Restricted to river islands of northern Amazonia. Found in early successional vegetation, especially even-aged stands of *Tessaria* trees mixed with grass, where can be fairly common. Usually found in pairs, not with mixed-species flocks. Very active, moving frequently with horizontal posture and keeping tail partially cocked. Note very long tail with broad white tips, yellow underparts, and broad white edgings on wing coverts. **VOICE** Song, sometimes in duet, is descending chatter given in rapid series: *"chee'di'di'dew CHEW chee'di'di'dew CHEW…"* or similar series of notes. Call a rich, whistled, rising-falling *"heeu."* **Co, E, Br**

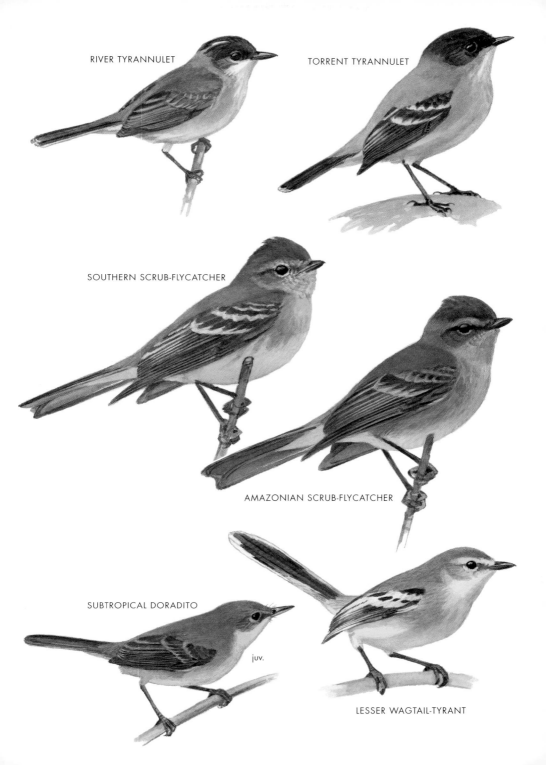

RIVER TYRANNULET

TORRENT TYRANNULET

SOUTHERN SCRUB-FLYCATCHER

AMAZONIAN SCRUB-FLYCATCHER

SUBTROPICAL DORADITO

juv.

LESSER WAGTAIL-TYRANT

PLATE
194

SMALL LOWLAND TYRANNULETS

Small tyrannulets of forest edge, second growth, and scrub at low elevations. Cf. each other, Zimmerius tyrannulets, scrub-flycatchers, and small elaenias.

1 PLAIN TYRANNULET *Inezia inornata* 10 cm (4 in)

Rare austral migrant to southeastern Amazonia, in early successional habitats such as in river-edge scrub. Small, slender; similar to Southern Beardless-Tyrannulet (*bolivianum*), but less bushy-headed; has longer, more slender bill and more well-defined white lores and eyerings. **VOICE** Call a thin, descending trilled "*p'seeeeeeer.*" Unlikely to sing in Peru; song (?) a high, rising-falling trill ending with a sharp note: "*tzreeeer'tsip!*" **Br, Bo**

2 SOUTHERN BEARDLESS-TYRANNULET *Camptostoma obsoletum* * 9.5–10 cm (3¾–4 in)

Small active tyrannulet with short bushy crest. Geographically variable. Gray or brownish-backed birds with dull rufous wing bars are common on coast, and in dry Marañón and Huallaga valleys, up to 2600 m; in dry forest, scrub, and gardens. Similar *bolivianum* an uncommon austral migrant to southern Amazonia. Green-backed *olivaceum*, with yellow underparts and dull white wing bars, uncommon but widespread in northern Amazonia, in river-edge forest and on river islands, also locally in scrub and edge of grassland. **VOICE** Dawn song (gray populations) a series of plaintive, descending whistles: "*pee'per PEER PEER PEE-pee'prt.*" Calls a whining "*eeEEeh*" and "*pi'peee,*" also a faster, squeaky, chattered "*pi'pi'pi*" and "*psi-per,*" often followed by an accelerating series of descending notes: "*pew pew pew-pew'pew.*" Dawn song (*olivaceum*) a descending, slightly accelerating series of piping, plaintive notes: "*PEE pi-pi-pi-pi-peh.*" Calls a rising "*weeEE*" or "*pi'peee,*" and a buzzy "*zz'zz'zrr.*" **Co, E, Br, Bo**

3 GRAY-AND-WHITE TYRANNULET *Pseudelaenia leucospodia* * 12.5 cm (5 in)

Fairly common in arid scrub and dry forests of northwest, below 800 m. Posture may be horizontal when foraging; captures insects with perch- and hover-gleans. Alone or in pairs, usually not with mixed-species flocks. Gray above, largely white below, with ill-defined whitish wing bars. Note shaggy crest with prominent white center. Smaller than elaenias, with more slender bill. **VOICE** Dawn song a squeaky "*pit'i'pew*" or sneezy "*pit'chew*" interspersed with a rising "*weee-wit.*" Call a squeaky, nasal "*tchuEE?*" or "*tchu'bit,*" similar to Necklaced Spinetail. **E**

4 MOUSE-COLORED TYRANNULET *Phaeomyias murina* * 12 cm (4¾ in)

Fairly common in desert scrub and dry forest of coast below 2000 m (*tumbezana, inflava*). Also in similar habitats in dry Marañón Valley (*maranonica*). *Wagae* is widespread but uncommon in Amazonia (below 500 m), at forest edge, in second growth, and locally in savanna. Often associated with mistletoe. All populations have rounded head and indistinct grayish superciliary. Most are drab brown with rufous wing bars; *wagae* has whitish throat, pale yellow belly, and white or buffy wing bars. **VOICE** Calls (*tumbezana, inflava*), often given in duet, various explosive, sneezy, buzzy sounds: "*DZEEK!*" or "*dzz-CHEW!*" and a harsh growl. Dawn song a grating, harsh "*dzzree-dzzree'DJEE.*" Call (*maranonica*) a sharp "*DJZZEE!*" Dawn song a scratchy, sneezy "*dji'dji'dji'dji DJZZEE!*" interspersed with a rising, buzzy "*dzzzrrrEEE?*" Calls (*wagae*) a characteristic "*pew-pew!*" and a popping "*pup'i'lee.*" Dawn song a popping, sneezy "*pi'pi'pi PU'i'chee*" phrase occasionally interspersed with a similar "*pi'pi'pi CHEE'i'chee.*" **Co, E, Br, Bo**

5 WHITE-LORED TYRANNULET *Ornithion inerme* 8.5 cm (3½ in)

Widespread in Amazonia (to 1000 m). Fairly common but inconspicuous except by voice. Canopy of humid forest, especially in vine tangles near edges. Usually solitary, often with mixed-species flocks. Hops along slender vines and branches, perch- and hover-gleaning for insects. Has upright posture when singing. Wing bars made up of discrete white spots on coverts; also note narrow white superciliary. **VOICE** Song a series of thin, rising whistles (usually 3–4): "*weet-weet-weet?*" Call a low chuckle when agitated. **Co, E, Br, Bo**

6 YELLOW-CROWNED TYRANNULET *Tyrannulus elatus* 10.5 cm (4¼ in)

Inconspicuous (except by voice), but common and widespread in Amazonia, to 1050 m. Perches upright, low in second growth or forest edge, but in canopy inside forest. Singly or in pairs, usually not with mixed-species flocks. Hover- and perch-gleans for insects and small fruit. Note small size, stubby bill, strong wing bars, and gray face and crown (with dusky borders); yellow coronal patch often concealed. **VOICE** Song (?) a characteristic, mellow, whistled "*wee-HEW*" or "*we HERE.*" Calls low chatters in aggression and single rising "*treee?*" notes. **Co, E, Br, Bo**

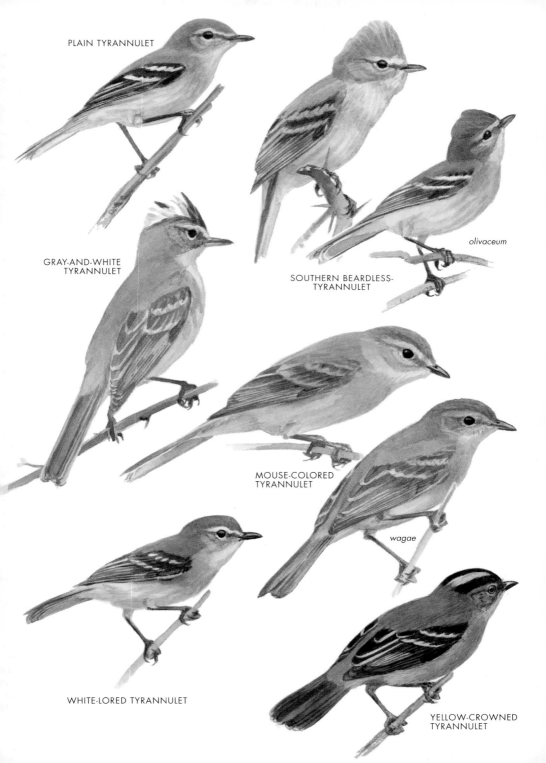

PLAIN TYRANNULET

GRAY-AND-WHITE
TYRANNULET

SOUTHERN BEARDLESS-
TYRANNULET

olivaceum

MOUSE-COLORED
TYRANNULET

wagae

WHITE-LORED TYRANNULET

YELLOW-CROWNED
TYRANNULET

PLATE
195

MECOCERCULUS TYRANNULETS AND RUSH-TYRANT

Mecocerculus are small, active, insectivorous Andean flycatchers. All have wing bars and a superciliary; bases of inner remiges blackish. Regularly follow mixed-species flocks. Most have a horizontal posture (except for White-throated Tyrannulet). Cf. Phylloscartes; *also see plate 188. Very different rush-tyrant occurs in coastal and Andean marshes.*

1 WHITE-BANDED TYRANNULET *Mecocerculus stictopterus* * 12.5 cm (5 in)
Common in humid montane forests and forest edges, on east slope of Andes at 2400–3600 m. Also on west slope south to Cajamarca, again on west slope of Cordillera Blanca, and in Marañón Valley south to La Libertad. Similar to White-tailed Tyrannulet, but at higher elevations; larger, lacks white in the tail, and has broader, white wing bars. **VOICE** Song (?) a rising, wheezy "*rhzeee?*," sometimes followed by a rich "*chew-bit*" or a scratchy, thin, rising-falling chatter. **Co, E, Bo**

2 WHITE-THROATED TYRANNULET *Mecocerculus leucophrys* * 14 cm (5½ in)
Common along east slope of Andes, and on west slope south to northern Lima, 1800–4600 m. Also in Marañón Valley south to La Libertad. Humid montane forest and forest edges, including *Polylepis* woods. Largest *Mecocerculus*. Characteristic white throat (often puffed out) contrasts with olive chest. Wing bars rufous in widespread *brunneomarginatus* (but may be light tawny or whitish in Cuzco or Puno; *leucophrys*, not illustrated). *Pallidior* (Ancash, Lima) duller, with whitish belly. **VOICE** Call a rising-falling, accelerating-decelerating series of dry or metallic notes: "*pit pit-PIT-PIT-PIT-pit-pit-pit.*" Also a series of squeaky "*pew*" notes and a squeaky chatter. Dawn song a quiet series of semimusical notes: "*pi-pi chrr'r'r.*" **Co, E, Br, Bo**

3 SULPHUR-BELLIED TYRANNULET *Mecocerculus minor* 11.5 cm (4½ in)
Uncommon to fairly common on east slope of Andes, 1600–2500 m, in midstory and canopy of humid montane forest and forest edges. Note strongly yellow underparts, short whitish superciliary, and buffy wing bars. Cf. Plumbeous-crowned Tyrannulet (which has white wing bars and dark auricular patch); also bristle-tyrants. **VOICE** Song (?) a descending series of squeaky rising notes: "*dweet dweet duit duit dit.*" Calls a nasal, descending "*dee-dee-di-dunk*" and a liquid "*du'ip.*" Similar to calls of Rufous-winged and Plumbeous-crowned tyrannulets; the latter (or both?) has more staccato pattern. Also similar to White-throated Spadebill, which is squeakier, and in understory. **Co, E**

4 WHITE-TAILED TYRANNULET *Mecocerculus poecilocercus* 11 cm (4¼ in)
Fairly common on east slope of the Andes, 1450–2700 m; also on west slope in Piura. Canopy of humid montane forest. Small, with conspicuous whitish inner webs to rectrices, whitish underparts (pale yellow on belly), and broad buffy wing bars. Rump pale yellow. Cf. larger White-banded Tyrannulet. **VOICE** Day song a descending series of high, rising, sibilant whistles: "*PSEE pswee pswee psweet*," sometimes accompanied with sharper "*pit*" notes. Dawn song a high, lisping "*pseeee-psweet.*" Call a thin, peeping "*pee.*" **Co, E**

5 RUFOUS-WINGED TYRANNULET *Mecocerculus calopterus* 11 cm (4¼ in)
Fairly common on west slope of Andes, 500–1700 m, south to Lambayeque. Also in Marañón Valley and along east slope of Andes south to San Martín, 1100–2400 m. Midstory and canopy of dry, evergreen and humid montane forests. Note gray crown, narrow white superciliary, and prominent rufous wing panel. Inner webs of outer rectrices white (as in smaller White-tailed Tyrannulet). Cf. Rufous-winged Antwren. **VOICE** Call a rising-falling series of squeaky, nasal notes: "*dink-deek*" or "*dink dink-dee-di-dunk.*" Similar to voice of Sulphur-bellied and Plumbeous-crowned tyrannulets, but at least the latter is more staccato in pattern. **E**

6 MANY-COLORED RUSH-TYRANT *Tachuris rubrigastra* * 10.5 cm (4 in)
Small, brightly colored; confined to reedbeds. Widespread on coast, also local on altiplano lakes at 3800–4300 m, rarely to 3100 m. Single birds or family groups forage within or at edge of reeds (but never far from cover), acrobatically gleaning from reeds or on mud or floating vegetation. Adult unmistakable. Juvenile barred brown above and buffy or whitish below, with red of undertail coverts reduced or absent; but retains an indication of the superciliary and has conspicuous white wing patch. **VOICE** Song a quiet, mellow, pleasant series of notes with a short buzz near the start and ending with a loose musical rattle: "*kachup-brrr-kachup'yup'a'trrrrl.*" Calls a loud "*keeYIP*" or "*kaCHOO*" and a quiet, popping "*pip.*" **Br, Bo, Ch**

WHITE-BANDED TYRANNULET

WHITE-THROATED
TYRANNULET

brunneomarginatus

SULPHUR-BELLIED TYRANNULET

pallidior

WHITE-TAILED TYRANNULET

juv.

RUFOUS-WINGED
TYRANNULET

MANY-COLORED
RUSH-TYRANT

ad.

PLATE
196

TIT-TYRANTS

Tit-tyrants (Anairetes) are very small, active, flycatchers of the Andes and the coast. All are crested, and most species are streaked. Often found apart from mixed-species flocks. Unstreaked Tit-Tyrant has a fuller (less wispy) crest, and is more commonly associated with mixed-species flocks.

1 YELLOW-BILLED TIT-TYRANT *Anairetes flavirostris* * 10.5–12 cm (4–4¾ in)
Primarily found in Andes, where fairly common. In far north confined to west side of Marañón Valley, but also on Pacific slope from Ancash south; also in intermontane valleys of eastern Andes from Huánuco to Cuzco. Primarily at 1900–4100 m, but locally lower on west slope of Andes or coastal lomas. Note pale mandible, streaked face and breast, indistinctly streaked brown back, and yellow belly. Cf. Pied-crested and Tufted tit-tyrants. **VOICE** Call a rising-falling, musical trill: "*brrreeeeuu,*" not as ringing as Tufted; also a rising-falling musical chatter: "*tur-tur-TEE'TEE'tee-tee-tchip.*" Dawn song a rising trill with stuttered bursts afterward: "*brreeee brr-br-br.*" **Bo, Ch**

2 TUFTED TIT-TYRANT *Anairetes parulus* * 11–12 cm (4¼–4¾ in)
Fairly common and widespread on east slope of Andes, and in far north on west slope; scarce and local on Pacific slope south of Cajamarca. 1450–4400 m. Overlaps geographically and elevationally with Yellow-bellied Tit-Tyrant, but typically found in more humid situations: occurs in montane scrub, forest edges, and in *Polylepis* woodlands. The smallest tit-tyrant. Note pale iris, black bill, narrow wing bars, wispy recurved crest, unstreaked gray-brown back, and relatively short tail. **VOICE** Call a high, rapid, descending, ringing trill, sometimes ending with a sharp chip: "*teerrrrrr'it!*" Dawn song a rising, sneezy "*wee'whizt?*" or "*t'weee-weet?*" **Co, E, Bo, Ch**

3 BLACK-CRESTED TIT-TYRANT *Anairetes nigrocristatus* 13 cm (5 in)
Uncommon or locally fairly common in *Polylepis* forests and adjacent montane scrub near treeline along west slope of Andes south to Ancash; also on both sides of upper Marañón Valley, and locally (Huánuco) crossing over to the east slope, 2100–4000 m. Makes short, forward sallies to foliage, and also perch-gleans twigs and small leaves. Large, strikingly black-and-white tit-tyrant. Similar to Pied-crested Tit-Tyrant, but larger, with longer crest and more extensive white tips to rectrices. Where both overlap geographically, Pied-crested is found at lower elevations. **VOICE** Calls squeaky sputtered "*trreek! trreek! trreek!,*" a descending, squeaky, chattered "*tee! ti'ti'ti'ti'ter,*" and a rising-falling "*trrreeeer.*" **E**

4 PIED-CRESTED TIT-TYRANT *Anairetes reguloides* * 12 cm (4¾ in)
Uncommon to fairly common, up to 4000 m (but below ca. 2800 m in north, where overlaps geographically with Black-crested Tit-Tyrant). Found in montane scrub, also coastal riparian thickets and hedgerows. Conspicuously streaked black and white; face black; base of mandible yellow. Belly white (widespread *albiventris*) or very pale yellow (from southern Ayacucho south; *reguloides,* not illustrated). Throat and sides of head black (male) or streaked black and white (female; not illustrated). Juvenile mostly buffy brown, with reduced crest. Cf. Black-crested Tit-Tyrant. Yellow-billed Tit-Tyrant is deeper yellow below, and lacks white streaks on back. **VOICE** Call a descending series of squeaky, mewed notes, sometimes with a dry rattle: "*tweek-tweek-twik-tuik-trrr.*" Dawn song a squeaky series of notes and rising churrs: "*teek'teek'trk-trrrk*" or "*tk-tweek! trrrrk.*" **Ch**

5 ASH-BREASTED TIT-TYRANT *Anairetes alpinus* * 13.5 cm (5¼ in)
Very local and uncommon, in small *Polylepis* groves and *Gynoxys* thickets on steep, grassy (often rocky) slopes, 3700–4600 m. Under threat from increasing human demands on *Polylepis* for firewood. Usually in pairs, apart or with mixed-species flocks. The only small, gray flycatcher in its habitat; note white wing and tail markings. **VOICE** Song (?) a rising burry note followed by short, descending notes: "*breee djr-djr-djr.*" Calls a plaintive "*feeet,*" a short soft trill, and "*pip*" or "*peep*" notes. **Bo**

6 UNSTREAKED TIT-TYRANT *Anairetes agraphia* * 13 cm (5 in)
Rare in humid montane forest along east slope of Andes, generally near treeline (2600–3450 m). Especially found near thickets of *Chusquea* bamboo and other forest openings. Often in small groups, typically associated with mixed-species flocks. Black crest lays flat and lacks white center (unlike other tit-tyrants). Note light gray, vaguely streaked face and throat, pale yellow belly, and unmarked brown wings and tail. **VOICE** Song a high, sputtering trill: "*tiii'reeeeeeee.*" Calls high "*ti*" and "*tsee*" notes, and a short, descending trill. **ENDEMIC**

YELLOW-BILLED TIT-TYRANT

TUFTED TIT-TYRANT

BLACK-CRESTED TIT-TYRANT

PIED-CRESTED TIT-TYRANT

ad. ♂
albiventris

juv.

UNSTREAKED
TIT-TYRANT

ASH-BREASTED
TIT-TYRANT

PLATE
197

MYIOBIUS FLYCATCHERS AND PSEUDOTRICCUS PYGMY-TYRANTS

Myiobius *are slender flycatchers with long black tail and pale yellow rump. Forage actively in forest understory, with body tipped forward, tail spread, and wings slightly drooped (much like* Myioborus *redstarts). Regular members of mixed-species flocks. Identification can be difficult; note breast color, and body size and proportions. Pygmy-tyrants (Pseudotriccus) are small, bull-headed, short-tailed flycatchers. Forage solitarily very low in dense understory of humid montane forest. Easily overlooked except by voice and by audible snapping noises made by bill.*

1 BLACK-TAILED FLYCATCHER Myiobius atricaudus * 12.5 cm (5 in)
Fairly common in moist semideciduous forest in Tumbes up to 400 m (where is the only *Myiobius*). Local and poorly known in Amazonia (though can be fairly common), locally up to 1100 m; less widespread than similar Sulphur-rumped Flycatcher (compare), and where the two occur together, usually is the less common. May prefer varzea and drier, semideciduous forests. **VOICE** Song (?) in Amazonia a weak "*tsip*" and "*tsee-too*" notes. Calls weak, high, wheezy chatters. **Co, E, Br**

2 SULPHUR-RUMPED FLYCATCHER Myiobius barbatus * 12.5 cm (5 in)
Most widespread Amazonian *Myiobius*. Uncommon to fairly common, in terra firme below 750 m. Semiconcealed crown patch is golden yellow (male); or reduced and orangey or absent entirely (female). Distinguished from Tawny-breasted by paler green upperparts, olive wash on breast, and more extensively yellow underparts. Very similar to Black-tailed Flycatcher. Distinguished with care by pale olive (not pale brown or pale olive-brown) breast. Also upperparts are slightly paler and greener (less brown); is slightly larger; crown patch is more golden (less sulphur) yellow; tail is more square-tipped; and (in the hand) proportionately shorter tail (tail shorter in length than wing; in Black-tailed, tail is as long as wing). Often one species or the other is present, but locally both overlap at the same site (usually segregating by habitat). **VOICE** Song (?) is a rising, high, sharp note: "*pseet!*" or "*psit!*" Calls include less musical "*tip*" notes. **Co, E, Br, Bo**

3 TAWNY-BREASTED FLYCATCHER Myiobius villosus * 14 cm (5½ in)
Largest *Myiobius*, and easiest to recognize; also is more montane than others. Fairly common in humid montane forest, 650–2000 m, on east slope of Andes and outlying ridges. Note distinctive tawny breast and flanks. Semiconcealed crown patch of male is golden yellow (forecrown sometimes partially orange-rufous); crown patch of female is orange-rufous, and smaller. Black-tailed is smaller, with less extensive, "dirtier" brown breast patch and paler yellow rump. **VOICE** Song (?) is a sharp, slightly descending squeak: "*PSEEuk*." **Co, E, Bo**

4 BRONZE-OLIVE PYGMY-TYRANT Pseudotriccus pelzelni * 11–11.5 cm (4¼–4½ in)
Uncommon to fairly common on east slope of Andes, 1100–2100 m. Notably dull: mostly olive, with yellowish belly and reddish iris. No geographic overlap with Hazel-fronted Pygmy-Tyrant; see juvenile Rufous-headed Pygmy-Tyrant. Also cf. female manakins (especially *Dixiphia, Lepidothrix,* and *Xenopipo*), which are similar in shape but greener, and have different behaviors. **VOICE** Song a high, thin trill followed by a pair of trills that fall, then rise: "*tsee? tseeeeuu-tsuuueeeee?*" **Co, E**

5 HAZEL-FRONTED PYGMY-TYRANT Pseudotriccus simplex 11 cm (4¼ in)
Replaces similar Bronze-olive Pygmy-Tyrant in southern Andes, 1000–2000 m. Adult has dull rufous wash on face and forecrown, breast and flanks are more olive (less "bronzy") than Bronze-olive's, and belly is paler. Rufous of face can be obscure or lacking in first-year birds. **VOICE** Song a high, thin trill followed by a pair of trills that fall, then rise, ending with a hiccup: "*tsee? tseeeeu-tseee'ip.*" Call a rising "*tssuuueee?,*" sometimes stuttered. **Bo**

6 RUFOUS-HEADED PYGMY-TYRANT Pseudotriccus ruficeps * 11 cm (4¼ in)
Fairly common to common on east slope of Andes, 2000–3350 m (higher than other pygmy-tyrants). Adult distinctive. Rufous of face and wings brighter north and west of Marañón (*ruficeps*; not illustrated), and from upper Apurímac Valley south (undescribed subspecies; not illustrated); rufous (especially of wings) duller in *haplopteryx* of central Peru. Juvenile lacks rufous; identified by elevation, greener plumage, and darker (not reddish) iris. **VOICE** Song a deep, descending trill followed abruptly by a rising, higher-pitched trill: "*grrrrrew'REEEEEEE?*" Call a deep, growing trill. Vocalizations similar to some chat-tyrants, which do not regularly snap bill, and do not have the low descending trill. **Co, E, Bo**

SULPHUR-RUMPED FLYCATCHER

BLACK-TAILED FLYCATCHER

♂

♂

TAWNY-BREASTED FLYCATCHER

♂

BRONZE-OLIVE
PYGMY-TYRANT

RUFOUS-HEADED
PYGMY-TYRANT

juv.

HAZEL-FRONTED
PYGMY-TYRANT

ad.

haplopteryx

PLATE
198

MIONECTES AND SMALL ANDEAN
FLYCATCHERS

Mionectes are small frugivorous flycatchers with relatively slender bills and a bull-headed appearance. Found in under- and midstory of humid forest, where often fairly common but quiet and inconspicuous. Single birds forage apart, or may join tanager-dominated mixed-species flocks, especially at fruiting trees. Sometimes "flick" one wing above the back. Ornate and Cinnamon flycatchers are two insectivorous species that forage in the understory and upper strata (respectively) of humid montane forest.

1 OLIVE-STRIPED FLYCATCHER *Mionectes olivaceus* * 13–13.5 cm (5–5¼ in)
Fairly common on lower eastern slopes of Andes and foothills below 1400 m, rarely or locally to 2100 m; also locally into Amazonian lowlands in south. Replaces similar Streak-necked Flycatcher at lower elevations, but the two overlap. Head is olive (not contrastingly gray), underparts are paler, and wing coverts narrowly edged buff. **VOICE** Usually silent. Song a series of extremely high-pitched, thin whistles in rapid succession: "*tseew'tseeet-tseew'tseeet-tseew'tseeet…*"; could be mistaken for a hummingbird. **Co, E, Bo**

2 STREAK-NECKED FLYCATCHER *Mionectes striaticollis* * 13–13.5 cm (5–5¼ in)
Widespread Andean flycatcher, with very broad elevational range (500–3300 m; primarily 1000–2400 m) on east slope; also on west slope south to Cajamarca, 1700–3100 m. In humid montane forest, forest edge, and second growth. Posture upright, but occasionally leans forward and bobs head. Note gray hood with small but conspicuous white spot behind eye, streaked underparts, and lack of wing bars. Cf. Olive-striped Flycatcher. Juvenile (not illustrated) similar in pattern, but paler. **VOICE** Usually silent. Song a melancholy, squeaky, rising-falling note: "*urrEEew.*" **Co, E, Bo**

3 McCONNELL'S FLYCATCHER *Mionectes macconnelli* * 13 cm (5 in)
Very similar to more widespread Ochre-bellied Flycatcher. Local in Andean foothills and in Amazonia in central and southern Peru, where found in terra firme, below 1200 m. Differs from Ochre-bellied by plain wings, lacking rufous tips to tertials or rufous wing bars. In the hand, lining of mouth is black (inside of mouth is yellowish in Ochre-bellied). **VOICE** Song a series of quiet, modulated, yet musical "*trrr*" notes followed by a louder, nasal, querulous "*tequila?*" or "*teeola?*" **E, Br, Bo**

4 OCHRE-BELLIED FLYCATCHER *Mionectes oleagineus* * 13 cm (5 in)
One of the most widespread forest birds of Amazonia, below 1300 m; where it overlaps with McConnell's Flycatcher is more associated with forest edge and with treefalls and other light gaps (rather than forest interior). Also in semideciduous forest in Tumbes, ca. 400 m (*pacificus*). Very drab; note light olive upperparts, cinnamon-tawny breast and belly, and only poorly defined rufous wing bars and tips to tertials. Cf. McConnell's. **VOICE** Not particularly vocal away from communal display grounds (leks). Song (Amazonia) a series of quiet "*prrp*" notes followed by several louder, squeaky, descending "*tseew*" or "*skeew*" notes. Song of *pacificus* similar, but deeper. **Co, E, Br, Bo**

5 ORNATE FLYCATCHER *Myiotriccus ornatus* * 12 cm (4¾ in)
Stunning; one of the most characteristic birds of lower eastern slopes of Andes, 700–2200 m. Usually encountered as singles or pairs, around openings in humid montane forest such as at treefalls, landslides, and stream margins. Perches low, in a somewhat open position (but usually in shade, not in full sun); sallies out to capture insects in flight. Does not join mixed-species flocks and often forages around same site for an extended period. **VOICE** Calls include a sharp, squeaky "*PSEW!*" also quiet "*pip pip pip*" notes in flight. Dawn song a sharp note followed by a chippering trill: "*PSEW! ti'ti'ti'ti'ti.*" **Co, E**

6 CINNAMON FLYCATCHER *Pyrrhomyias cinnamomeus* * 13 cm (5 in)
Fairly common on east slope of Andes (900–3400 m) and outlying ridges, and on west slope south to southern Cajamarca. Fairly common in upper portions of humid montane forest and at forest edge, as singles or pairs that perch on exposed branches and sally to the air for insects. Commonly joins mixed-species flocks, but often remains "on station" after flock has passed. Readily identified by relatively small size, rufous-brown plumage, and broad rufous wing bars. Also has narrow tawny band on uppertail coverts, and yellow semiconcealed crown patch. **VOICE** Song, a frequent sound in montane forests, is a rapid, slightly descending sputter: "*tsi'i'i'i'ew'w'w.*" Calls include thin "*tip*" and "*tchew*" notes. **Co, E, Bo**

OLIVE-STRIPED
FLYCATCHER

STREAK-NECKED FLYCATCHER

OCHRE-BELLIED
FLYCATCHER

McCONNELL'S FLYCATCHER

CINNAMON FLYCATCHER

ORNATE
FLYCATCHER

PLATE
199

MYIORNIS AND *LOPHOTRICCUS* PYGMY-TYRANTS

Myiornis pygmy-tyrants are very small and ridiculously short-tailed insectivorous flycatchers. Solitary or in pairs. Flight mechanical and insectlike. Lophotriccus pygmy-tyrants are small insectivorous flycatchers with long crests, which often are laid flat, giving the small bird a bull-headed look; crest may be raised when excited (producing a mini-"Harpy Eagle" appearance). Usually encountered as singles or in pairs, sometimes briefly joining mixed-species flocks, but often apart. Both genera sit relatively motionless in understory or midstory, capturing prey with abrupt sallies to foliage and then moving to new perch.

1 WHITE-BELLIED PYGMY-TYRANT *Myiornis albiventris* 7 cm (2¾ in)
Fairly common, but local, on east slope of Andes and outlying ridges, 350–1100 m. Midstory and canopy of humid montane forest, especially near vine tangles, forest edges, and light gaps such as treefalls. Extremely small, with lightly streaked white breast and pale sides to face and dark marks on auriculars. Easily overlooked except by **VOICE** Song a mellow, tinkling, rising-falling trill: "*triiiiieww*," sometimes becoming longer, with last few notes stuttered "*trriiiEEEEiiiew'rr'rrl*." Calls a quiet "*trrt*" or "*trrrrl*" and a more slowly trilled "*tree'ee'ee'ew*." **Bo**

2 SHORT-TAILED PYGMY-TYRANT *Myiornis ecaudatus* * 6.5 cm (2½ in)
A tiny ball of feathers, scarcely larger than a large bee. Uncommon but widespread in Amazonia, up to 1000 m. Found in humid forest, especially transitional forest, forest openings, and forest edge. White underparts are unmarked. More readily located by **VOICE** Song a high, insectlike trill, often 2 phrases, the first higher: "*teeeee-tuuuuur*." Calls insectlike, high, rising "*treet*" or "*peet?*" notes, sometimes doubled, often in short series (up to 15 notes). Also a quiet, descending growl or purr. **Co, E, Br, Bo**

3 LONG-CRESTED PYGMY-TYRANT *Lophotriccus eulophotes* 10.5 cm (4 in)
Local in southeastern Amazonia, in floodplain forest, especially near treefalls, forest edge, and tall second growth, and forest with a bamboo understory. Note long, gray-margined crest and relatively plain wings (wing coverts tipped with olive, so wing bars weak or nonexistent). Cf. the more widespread Double-banded Pygmy-Tyrant (no known overlap), which has narrow wing bars and (*congener*) buffy yellow (not gray) margins to crest feathers. **VOICE** Song an accelerating and falling series of ringing notes: "*pip-pit-pit-pit-piteeeeeerrr*." Calls single "*pip*" notes, often in loose series. Also several "*pip*" notes in a rising-falling series, often with the first and final notes highest; resembling White-cheeked Tody-Flycatcher, but drier. **Br, Bo**

4 SCALE-CRESTED PYGMY-TYRANT *Lophotriccus pileatus* * 10 cm (4 in)
Widespread and fairly common on lower east slope of Andes, in understory of humid montane forest, 700–2100 m. Also fairly common in semideciduous forest in Tumbes at 400 m. Unlikely to be confused; note the long crest broadly edged with rufous and the blurry streaks on chest. **VOICE** Primary song a rising trill: "*turreee?*" Aggressive songs like an angry traffic officer blowing a whistle, with ringing, descending buzzy trills: "*dzzeeer-dzeer-dzeer*"; sometimes only one trill given. Calls single "*tik*" notes and quiet rattles. **Co, E, Bo**

5 HELMETED PYGMY-TYRANT *Lophotriccus galeatus* 10 cm (4 in)
Local, in northeastern Amazonia. At some sites, particularly west of the Napo, restricted to white-sand forests, especially with bamboo; but elsewhere it has been found in same habitats as Double-banded Pygmy-Tyrant. Distinguished with care by shorter crest edged with grayish olive (not light gray), and by weak or nonexistent wing bars (wing coverts are only narrowly edged, and with olive, not yellowish green). Also cf. White-eyed Tody-Tyrant, which lacks crest and has yellowish green wing bars. **VOICE** Song (Brazil) a rapid, descending "*brreeew*" interspersed with single "*bik*" notes. Calls (Brazil) a series of "*bik*" notes or a 2-note "*bit-eek*." **Co, Br**

6 DOUBLE-BANDED PYGMY-TYRANT *Lophotriccus vitiosus* * 10 cm (4 in)
Widespread and fairly common in northern and central Amazonia up to 750 m, in humid forest and at forest edge, primarily in terra firme. Note narrow yellowish white wing bars. Crest margined with gray (widespread subspecies) or buffy yellow or buffy olive (*congener*; south of the Amazon and east of the Río Ucayali). Cf. Long-crested Pygmy-Tyrant (no known overlap). **VOICE** Song a descending, harsh, ringing "*djzeeer*." Aggressive song often is more level in pitch and longer. Calls include a quiet, tinkling "*pik*." Song of *congener* similar, but considerably lower-pitched: "*beerrrrrrp*." **Co, E, Br**

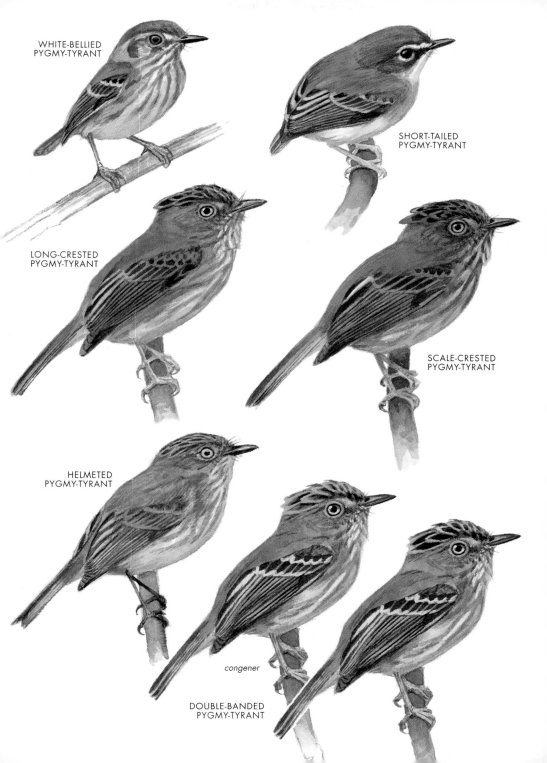

WHITE-BELLIED
PYGMY-TYRANT

SHORT-TAILED
PYGMY-TYRANT

LONG-CRESTED
PYGMY-TYRANT

SCALE-CRESTED
PYGMY-TYRANT

HELMETED
PYGMY-TYRANT

congener

DOUBLE-BANDED
PYGMY-TYRANT

PLATE
200

HEMITRICCUS TODY-TYRANTS I

Hemitriccus *tody-tyrants are small drab flycatchers with long, moderately broad bills; found both in Amazonia and on east slope of Andes. Perch with upright posture, remaining relatively still until sallying to capture insects from adjacent foliage; usually do not follow mixed-species flocks. Identification based on voice, habitat, iris color, and details of pattern of the breast and wings.*

1 WHITE-EYED TODY-TYRANT *Hemitriccus zosterops* * 11 cm (4¼ in)

Locally common in foothills and on outlying ridges, up to 1350 m; less common, or very local, farther east in Amazonia north of the Amazon (but not known east of the Napo). Midstory of terra firme and humid montane forest. Note yellow belly, yellowish green wing bars, and pale iris. Cf. also Double-banded Pygmy-Tyrant and Johannes's Tody-Tyrant. **VOICE** Primary song a short series of 3–5 fairly high, popping, metallic notes: "*pip-ip-ip.*" Aggressive song a longer, rising-falling series of stuttering notes: "*pip'ip'ip-pip'ip'ip'ip'ip.*" Also a higher note followed by a falling, rapid series "*PEEP-ip'ip'ip'ip'ip,*" and a quieter, sputtered rattle. Calls a single "*pip,*" sometimes in a slow series. **Co, E, Br**

2 WHITE-BELLIED TODY-TYRANT *Hemitriccus griseipectus* * 11 cm (4¼ in)

Most common and widespread tody-tyrant of southeastern Amazonia below 900 m; but apparently only local in central and northeastern Peru. Forages in under- and midstory of forest interior. Note whitish belly, pale iris, and dark mandible. Cf. Flammulated Pygmy-Tyrant. In northern Peru, cf. Zimmer's and Snethlage's tody-tyrants, and Double-banded Pygmy-Tyrant. **VOICE** Song a simple chiming pair or trio of notes, the first lower: "*ta-TEEK*" or "*ta-TI'PIP.*" Call a quiet, metallic "*pip.*" **Br, Bo**

[SNETHLAGE'S TODY-TYRANT *Hemitriccus minor*] * 10 cm (4 in)

Known only from sight records on lower Río Yavarí. Understory of varzea; partial to vine tangles, treefalls, and other light gaps. In hand, nostrils are notably large and rounded. Very similar to Zimmer's, White-eyed, and White-bellied tody-tyrants. Differs from all by dull, olive tips to wing coverts (lacks more conspicuous, yellow-green wing bars). Also typically is yellower below than White-bellied. Cf. also Double-banded Pygmy-Tyrant. Best identified by **VOICE** Song a slightly descending, deep, ringing trill: "*beeeerr.*" Similar to song of Double-banded, but note different habitat. Call a rich "*chik.*" **Br, Bo**

3 ZIMMER'S TODY-TYRANT *Hemitriccus minimus* 10 cm (4 in)

Locally fairly common in stunted forests on white-sand soils in northeastern Amazonia, also on ridges in terra firme. Canopy, often near vine tangles; easily overlooked except by voice. Similar to Snethlage's and White-eyed tody-tyrants but has darker, more sharply defined streaks on throat; darker centers to crown feathers; and little or no pale edgings to outermost remiges (contrasting with pale edgings to inner remiges). Further separated from Snethlage's by stronger wing bars (coverts tipped yellowish green, not olive). **VOICE** Song a level or slightly rising-falling, chiming trill: "*treeeeee.*" Similar to song of White-bellied Pygmy-Tyrant, but different habitat, no known overlap. Calls a short, stuttered series of notes with the third and fourth faster and higher: "*tu-tu-TI'TI-tu-tu-tu-tu*"; also a quiet "*tik.*" **Br, Bo**

4 YUNGAS TODY-TYRANT *Hemitriccus spodiops* 11 cm (4¼ in)

Known only from upper Río Inambari drainage, in second growth and at humid montane forest edge; elevational range in Bolivia 800–1600 m. Particularly drab, with dark olive wash on breast and a pale iris. Cf. Flammulated Pygmy-Tyrant, which has dark iris, is browner (less olive), usually occurs at lower elevations, and differs vocally. Cf. also Scale-crested Pygmy-Tyrant. **VOICE** Song a harsh, rapid, descending trill: "*brEEeeeew.*" May also give a level or rising trill of similar quality. Similar to Scale-crested. Calls quiet "*tuk*" or "*bink*" notes. **Bo**

5 FLAMMULATED PYGMY-TYRANT *Hemitriccus flammulatus* * 11 cm (4¼ in)

Uncommon but widespread in southeastern Amazonia below 850 m, where usually in bamboo (especially large thickets of spiny *Guadua*) understory in floodplain forest. Rare away from bamboo, except the isolated northern population in dense understory and second growth of dry forests at 300–600 m. Drab. Similar to White-bellied Tody-Tyrant, but with duller, unmarked wings, dark iris, and pale mandible. **VOICE** Song a popping, slightly descending series of low, stuttered notes: "*pip'ip'ip-pip'ip*" or a shorter series "*pip'ip.*" Calls include "*pip*" notes given singly or in loose series. Wings produce an audible whirr. **Br, Bo**

WHITE-EYED
TODY-TYRANT

WHITE-BELLIED
TODY-TYRANT

SNETHLAGE'S
TODY-TYRANT

ZIMMER'S
TODY-TYRANT

FLAMMULATED
PYGMY-TYRANT

YUNGAS
TODY-TYRANT

PLATE
201

HEMITRICCUS TODY-TYRANTS II

Most species on this plate are restricted geographically or in habitat; two are widespread, one in Amazonia (Johannes's Tody-Tyrant) and another in the Andes (Black-throated Tody-Tyrant).

1 STRIPE-NECKED TODY-TYRANT *Hemitriccus striaticollis* * 11 cm (4¼ in)
Fairly common but local, in dry valleys (Río Mayo, 1000 m; Río Urubamba, 500 m) and on Pampas del Heath (300 m). Found in shrubby growth and forest edge, including shrubs in grassland (Mayo Valley), riparian thickets (Urubamba Valley), and in isolated woodlots in savanna (Pampas). Very similar to Johannes's Tody-Tyrant, but wing coverts are less contrasting (edged olive, not yellow); and lores and narrow eyering white (usually dusky in Johannes's); also throat is whiter and more sharply streaked with dusky. Most easily distinguished by habitat and **VOICE** Song a loud, ringing, phrase with the introductory note highest: *"PEE-ti-ti-ti."* Call a mewing, rising *"pew'ee?"* **Co, Br, Bo**

2 JOHANNES'S TODY-TYRANT *Hemitriccus iohannis* 11 cm (4¼ in)
Widespread in Amazonia but uncommon, inconspicuous, and easily overlooked (except by voice). Below 800 m in under- and midstory of floodplain river- and lake-edge forest, especially in dense vine tangles. Drab; green above with olive breast, yellow belly, inconspicuous yellowish wing bars, and pale iris. Similar to White-eyed Tody-Tyrant, but yellower below with more heavily streaked throat and less obvious wing bars. Also cf. Stripe-necked Tody-Tyrant. Most easily identified by **VOICE** Song an accelerating, rising trilled *"tew-tur'r'r'r'e'e'e'e?"* phrases interspersed with single *"tew"* notes or a slow, rising series of 3–6 *"tew"* notes. Call *"tew"* notes, singly or in pairs. **Co, E, Br, Bo**

3 BUFF-THROATED TODY-TYRANT *Hemitriccus rufigularis* 12 cm (4¼ in)
Uncommon to fairly common, in narrow elevational zone (750 to 1450 m). Primarily on outlying ridges, in midstory of humid montane forest. Locally in canopy of semistunted (10–12 m) forest on ridgetops. May associate with mixed-species flocks, but often forages apart. Usually the only tody-tyrant within its elevational range (but perhaps overlaps with White-bellied Tody-Tyrant at lower elevational limit); readily recognized by buffy throat, white belly, and plain wings. In north, cf. Cinnamon-breasted Tody-Tyrant. **VOICE** Song a slow series of 1–5 rising, mewed, nasal *"dweep"* or *"dwip"* notes. Call a more rapid, rising series of notes: *"dew-dew-dew-DEWP-DEWP?"* **E, Bo**

4 PEARLY-VENTED TODY-TYRANT *Hemitriccus margaritaceiventer* * 10–10.5 cm (4–4¼ in)
Fairly common but local, in isolated populations below 1000 m in the Río Mayo Valley and adjacent portions of the Huallaga Valley; at 600–1600 m in the Chanchamayo Valley; and in the semiarid upper Urubamba Valley at ca. 1000–1100 m. Found in second-growth scrub and shrubby forest edge, perhaps locally also in low dry forest. Note light gray crown and nape and whitish underparts. Does not overlap (geography, habitat) with many other tody-tyrants; cf. Stripe-necked and Flammulated. **VOICE** Dawn song a rising series of rich notes followed by a rapid, descending trill: *"tup tchup tchip ti-teeeeeerrrr."* Calls a musical *"dew dew dew,"* and rich *"tchup"* notes given singly and a short series: *"tup tchip-tchip."* Also a peculiar deep, electrical buzzing sound (vocally): *"brrrrrrrrr."* **Co, Br, Bo**

5 CINNAMON-BREASTED TODY-TYRANT *Hemitriccus cinnamomeipectus* 10 cm (4 in)
Known from a few sites on east slope of northern Andes, both north and south of Río Marañón, at 1700–2200 m. Understory of stunted humid montane forest; locally in taller forest. Rare to uncommon. Note bright tawny breast, dull tawny eyering and auriculars, yellow belly, and plain wings. Buff-throated has paler buffy throat, little or no tawny on the sides of the head, and a whitish belly and is found at lower elevations. Cf. larger Rufous-breasted Flycatcher. **VOICE** Song a tinkling, descending, rapid trill: *"tEEEeeeerrrr."* Call a series of rising, mewed *"weeb"* notes. **E**

6 BLACK-THROATED TODY-TYRANT *Hemitriccus granadensis* * 10.5 cm (4 in)
Uncommon but widespread on east slope of Andes, 1800–3100 m. Found in understory of humid montane forest; partial to forest edges, such as overgrown landslides and dense second growth. Forages as singles or as pairs. Note black throat, pale "mask," and whitish underparts. Lores and eyering are tawny-buff in most of Peru (*pyrrhops*), but grayish white or dull buffy white in Puno (*caesius*). **VOICE** Song a rising-falling, accelerating series of high, peeping notes: *"pup-pip-peep-peep'pip'pip'pip' pip'pip."* Calls a rising or rising-falling, mewed *"weeb"* or *"weeble"* note; also a quiet, rapid, popping trill. Wings produce audible whirr in hovering aerial display. **Co, E, Bo**

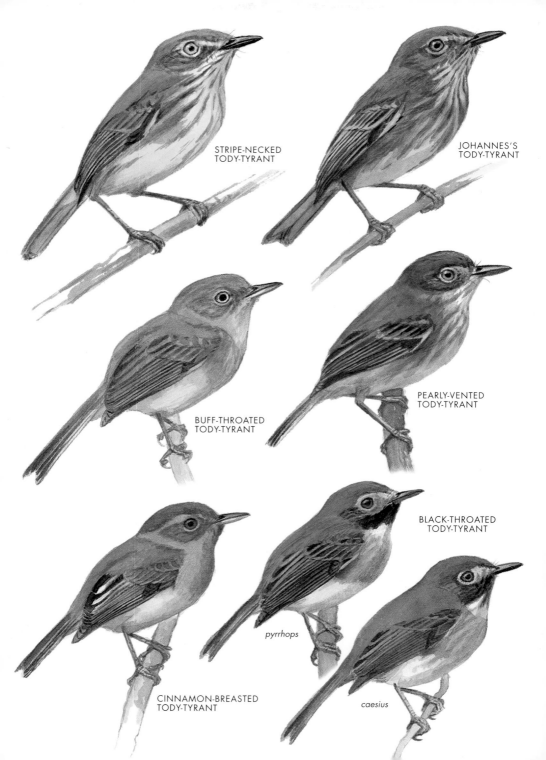

STRIPE-NECKED
TODY-TYRANT

JOHANNES'S
TODY-TYRANT

BUFF-THROATED
TODY-TYRANT

PEARLY-VENTED
TODY-TYRANT

BLACK-THROATED
TODY-TYRANT

CINNAMON-BREASTED
TODY-TYRANT

pyrrhops

caesius

PLATE
202

POECILOTRICCUS TODY-FLYCATCHERS AND TODY-TYRANTS

Poecilotriccus tody-tyrants and tody-flycatchers are small flycatchers of understory of humid forests of the Andes and Amazonia; superficially similar to Todirostrum tody-flycatchers, but the bills are not quite as long or broad. Two species (Black-and-white and White-cheeked tody-tyrants) are sexually dimorphic.

1 OCHRE-FACED TODY-FLYCATCHER *Poecilotriccus plumbeiceps* * 9.5–10 cm (3¾–4 in)

Locally fairly common but known only from southern Andes at 1600–2750 m. Singles or pairs forage low in dense vegetation at edges of humid montane forest, such as in thickets of *Chusquea* bamboo, ferns, and dense shrubbery. Not like any other small flycatcher in southern Peru; recognized by bright tawny-buff face, grayish crown, and buffy wing bars. May overlap with Black-throated Tody-Tyrant, but note different face pattern and white throat. Buff-throated Tody-Tyrant found at lower elevations and has plain, pale cinnamon face, and plain wings. **VOICE** Song a deep, rich sputtered trill: "*tjrrp-tjrrrrrr'rrr'rrp*" or simply "*tjrrrrp*." Call a quiet rich "*tchup*." **Br, Bo**

2 RUSTY-FRONTED TODY-FLYCATCHER *Poecilotriccus latirostris* * 9.5 cm (3¾ in)

Fairly common but secretive. Widely distributed throughout Amazonia, up to 1000 m. Commonly occurs in dense undergrowth of river-edge and river-island forest, also in dense second growth. Forages low, alone or in pairs; rarely associates with mixed-species flocks. Olive above and whitish below; note buffy eyering and tawny margins to wing coverts. Not similar to any other species found in Peru; but cf. *Lophotriccus*, *Hemitriccus*, and Tawny-crowned Pygmy-Tyrant. **VOICE** Song an easily overlooked, insectlike descending trill, low-pitched and rich in quality: "*tchur'r'r'r'r'r*." Calls a deep, rich "*tchup*" and a rising-falling musical rattled "*wrr'ee'e'r'r'r'r'r*." **Co, E, Br, Bo**

3 BLACK-AND-WHITE TODY-TYRANT *Poecilotriccus capitalis* 9.5 cm (3¾ in)

Uncommon. Locally present in northern Amazonia, primarily in tall viny second growth at edge of terra firme and along tangled stream-edge thickets. Also in dense undergrowth at edge of humid montane forest (600–1350 m), with an isolated population in central Peru. Often forages in pairs; may associate with mixed-species flocks. Black-and-white male unmistakable. Female also is distinctive, but cf. other small birds with rufous crowns (female Plain Antvireo, Tawny-crowned Greenlet). **VOICE** Song a deep, churring "*tip-tchurrrrrrrrr*." Also a rising-falling series of rising notes: "*tip'tip-chwee-chwee-chwee-chwee*," and short churred bursts. **Co, E, Br**

4 WHITE-CHEEKED TODY-TYRANT *Poecilotriccus albifacies* 9.5 cm (3¾ in)

Locally uncommon in southeastern Amazonia. Restricted to extensive, tall thickets of spiny bamboo (*Guadua*) in transitional forest, up to 1050 m. Pairs forage in leafy crowns of bamboo thickets, or in immediately adjacent vine tangles, in mid- and understory. Often associate with mixed-species flocks. Forages actively, making frequent, short sallies to foliage; occasionally perch-gleans. Male easily recognized by white cheek patch, rufous crown, and green back. Female very similar to female Black-and-white Tody-Tyrant, but no known overlap; otherwise unique in southern Peru. **VOICE** Song a slightly rising series of rich, deep notes: "*turp-ip-ip-ip ip ip ip*." Calls grinding, rising-falling churrs and a rapid series of rich notes: "*turp-turp'trreeeee*." **Bo**

5 JOHNSON'S (Lulu's) TODY-TYRANT *Poecilotriccus luluae* 9.5 cm (3¾ in)

Replaces Rufous-crowned Tody-Tyrant south of Marañón Valley. Uncommon in understory of humid montane forest at 1850–2900 m in northern Andes; most often in or near bamboo thickets, but also in second growth and forest edge. Often in pairs that rarely associate with mixed-species flocks. Similar to Rufous-crowned, but head is entirely rufous, and belly is more orange-yellow. **VOICE** Song a descending, whinnying chatter: "*djee-djee'trrrrr*." Calls a rising, staccato rattle: "*trr'rr'rr*"; also a quiet, froglike "*prrp*." **ENDEMIC**

6 RUFOUS-CROWNED TODY-TYRANT *Poecilotriccus ruficeps* * 9.5 cm (3¾ in)

Found only on east slope of Andes north of Río Marañón, where uncommon in understory of humid montane forest at 2400–2900. Most often in dense vegetation at forest edges and bamboo thickets. Easily recognized by ornate rufous–and-black head pattern, white throat, and yellow belly. **VOICE** Song a deep, slightly descending, churred "*djrrt*" phrase. Call several deep notes in a series: "*djrt-djrt-djrt*." **Co, E**

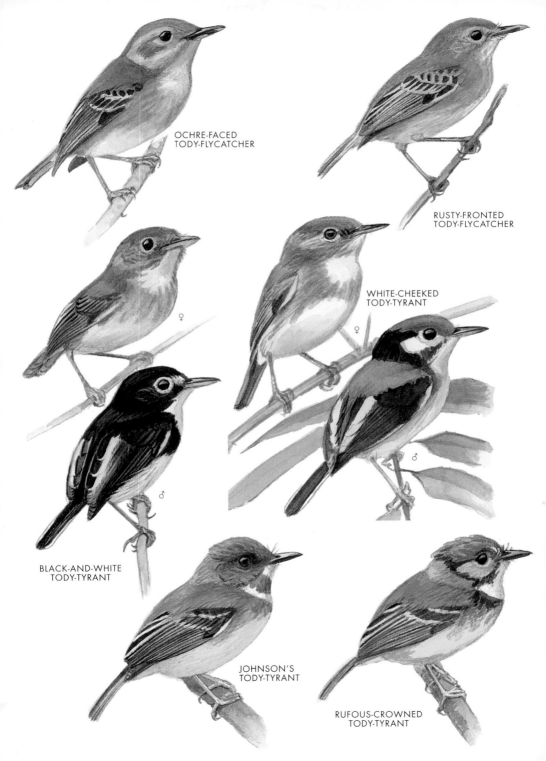

OCHRE-FACED
TODY-FLYCATCHER

RUSTY-FRONTED
TODY-FLYCATCHER

WHITE-CHEEKED
TODY-TYRANT

♀

♀

♂

♂

BLACK-AND-WHITE
TODY-TYRANT

JOHNSON'S
TODY-TYRANT

RUFOUS-CROWNED
TODY-TYRANT

PLATE
203

TAWNY-CROWNED PYGMY-TYRANT AND TODY-FLYCATCHERS

Small insectivorous flycatchers; forage as singles or in pairs, not with mixed-species flocks. Tawny-crowned Pygmy-Tyrant is drab, with relatively narrow bill. Bills of Todirostrum *tody-flycatchers are notably long and relatively broad; these species also often hold the tail partially cocked. The two* Poecilotriccus *are similar to* Todirostrum, *but their bills are narrower and slightly shorter, and they do not cock the tail.*

1 TAWNY-CROWNED PYGMY-TYRANT *Euscarthmus meloryphus* * 10 cm (4 in)
Fairly common in dry forest and scrub of northwest and Marañón Valley, up to 2500 m; also in dry middle Huallaga Valley (*fulviceps*). Forages low, usually in dense cover. Note rufous face and wing bars. Also a rare austral migrant (*meloryphus*) to southern Amazonia, where found in riparian thickets; has partially concealed rufous crown but lacks rufous face, and wing bars may be reduced. **VOICE** Song (*fulviceps*) a series of grinding, musical phrases, the final notes rising: "*pit-pit-pit gri-gree-GREE.*" Calls (both subspecies) a thin series of piping or bubbling notes: "*ptee-pee-pew*" or "*pitter-pittew.*" **Co, E, Br, Bo**

2 YELLOW-BROWED TODY-FLYCATCHER *Todirostrum chrysocrotaphum* * 9 cm (3½ in)
Uncommon and inconspicuous, but widespread in Amazonia (up to 1000 m). In forest and tall second growth, usually in canopy. North of the Amazon, and also south of the Marañón (to Mayo Valley) has small white loral spot and "necklace" of short black streaks on throat and breast (*guttatum*, *chrysocrotaphum*). Elsewhere lacks loral spot and breast unstreaked (*neglectum*). Note broad yellow superciliary, dark iris, and green back. Cf. Common and Spotted tody-flycatchers. Most easily detected by **VOICE** Song an easily overlooked, insectlike high, accelerating chipping series: "*tchit… tchit… tchit tchit tchit tchit-tchit-tchit-tchit-tchit.*" **Co, E, Br, Bo**

3 SPOTTED TODY-FLYCATCHER *Todirostrum maculatum* * 10 cm (4 in)
Widespread in Amazonia. Common, especially in river-edge forest and scrub, also in second growth, even in gardens of riverfront towns. Forages in canopy and midstory. Differs from Yellow-browed Tody-Flycatcher (*guttatum*) by gray crown and sides of face, pale iris, paler yellow underparts, and plainer wings. Cf. also Johannes's Tody-Tyrant. **VOICE** Song, often in duet, a series of high, sweet chips, often becoming couplets (couplets perhaps only by one member of pair?): "*tip tip tip tip-it tip-it tip-it tip-it.*" Notes higher and thinner than similar vocalizations of Common Tody-Flycatcher. Call a more rapid, sputtered trill, often in series: "*tjzr'r'r'r'r'it.*" **Co, E, Br, Bo**

4 COMMON TODY-FLYCATCHER *Todirostrum cinereum* * 9.5 cm (3¾ in)
Fairly common in dry forest and second growth in northwest, up to 1200 m (*sclateri*; not illustrated; throat whitish). Also fairly common on east slope of Andes at 600–2000 m at humid forest edge and second growth; also in dry forest in dry Marañón and Huallaga valleys (*peruanum*). Forages in canopy and midstory. Only tody-flycatcher in northwest; in east cf. Yellow-browed and Golden-winged. **VOICE** Song (*sclateri*), often in duet, a descending, sputtered trill of ringing chips: "*ti'i'i'i'i'i'i'rr.*" Call a slower-paced series of chips. Song (*peruanum*) a slightly accelerating series of sharp chips: "*tchip… tchip tchip tchip-tchip-tchip tchip.*" Also a higher series of short trills: "*ti'i'i'i ti'i'i'i ti'i'i'i,*" higher than similar calls of *sclateri* and Spotted Tody-Flycatcher. **Co, E, Br, Bo**

5 GOLDEN-WINGED TODY-FLYCATCHER *Poecilotriccus calopterus* 9.5 cm (3¾ in)
Uncommon and local, in northern Amazonia and in foothills (up to 600 m; in Ecuador to 1300 m). Found in dense cover at edge of forest and humid montane forest and in second growth. Easily recognized; Common Tody-Flycatcher has a whitish iris, slaty back, and yellow throat and lacks the chestnut and yellow wing patches. No overlap with Black-backed Tody-Flycatcher. **VOICE** Song, often in duet, accompanied by flashing of both wings, a rapid series of descending, rich, sputtered churrs: "*djerr djeer djeer djeer….*" **Co, E**

6 BLACK-BACKED TODY-FLYCATCHER *Poecilotriccus pulchellus* 9.5 cm (3¾ in)
Uncommon in foothills and on lower slopes of the southern Andes, 400–1500 m. Habitat and behavior similar to Golden-winged Tody-Flycatcher. Back is black in male; dark olive in female (not illustrated). Distinguished from Common Tody-Flycatcher by dark iris, blacker upperparts, white throat, and prominent yellow wing patches. **VOICE** Song, often in duet, accompanied by flashing of both wings, is a rapid series of descending, rich, sputtered churrs: "*djerr djeer djeer djeer…*"or bisyllabic "*we'djerr we'djerr we'djerr….*" **ENDEMIC**

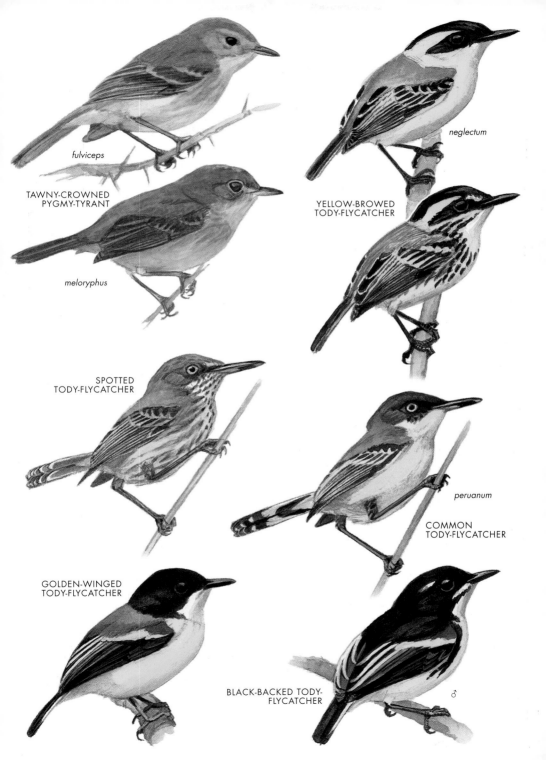

fulviceps

TAWNY-CROWNED
PYGMY-TYRANT

meloryphus

neglectum

YELLOW-BROWED
TODY-FLYCATCHER

SPOTTED
TODY-FLYCATCHER

peruanum

COMMON
TODY-FLYCATCHER

GOLDEN-WINGED
TODY-FLYCATCHER

BLACK-BACKED TODY-
FLYCATCHER

♂

PLATE
204

BROWNISH FLYCATCHER AND FLATBILLS

Broad-billed, medium-sized insectivorous flycatchers; perch upright and sally to vegetation for prey. Brownish Flycatcher distinctively drab. Ramphotrigon flatbills have conspicuous wing bars; bill not as broad or as flattened as in Rhynchocyclus. Nest in holes or tree cavities. Rhynchocyclus build large hanging nests, with entrance low on one side, that hang conspicuously at ends of branches over trails and streams.

1 BROWNISH FLYCATCHER *Cnipodectes subbrunneus* * male 18 cm (7 in); female 15.5 cm (6 in)

Uncommon and patchy in northern and central Amazonia, in dense understory in terra firme. Does not associate with mixed-species flocks. Vocal, but often difficult to see. Iris reddish. Females distinctly smaller than males, with yellower belly. In the hand, shafts of outer primaries of males are thickened, with twisted tips. Also note "shaggy" plumage texture. Cf. Thrush-like Manakin, which has black mandible, darker iris, plainer wings (lacking the narrow rusty margins to wing coverts), and lacks pale loral spot. [An undescribed species of *Cnipodectes* (not illustrated) recently was discovered in southeastern Peru. Local and uncommon in bamboo. Larger and bright rufous, not brownish.] **VOICE** Song usually 3 descending whistled notes, third lower and shorter, often preceded by quiet clicking notes: "*tk tk tk PEW PEW-ew.*" Call a rising, whiny, mewed "*ewwEE?*" or "*ewwIP?*" Wings produce mechanical whirring noises in flight display. **Co, E, Br, Bo**

2 RUFOUS-TAILED FLATBILL *Ramphotrigon ruficauda* 15–16 cm (6–6¼ in)

Uncommon to locally fairly common but widespread in Amazonia below 700 m. Perhaps most common in southeast. In relatively open middle story of terra firme. Rarely follows mixed-species flocks. Breast light olive with blurry pale yellow streaks, belly pale yellow. Readily recognized by extensive rufous of wings and tail. **VOICE** Call a low, rising-falling or slightly quavering, mewing whistle: "*meeooo,*" or with terminal emphasis "*meeooo'OO.*" Dawn song a low, mewing whistle ending with a higher hiccup: "*meeooOOoo'WEEpur!*" **Co, E, Br, Bo**

3 DUSKY-TAILED FLATBILL *Ramphotrigon fuscicauda* 16 cm (6¼ in)

Uncommon in southeastern Amazonia, up to 1050 m. Singly or in pairs in under- and midstory in bamboo thickets (especially *Guadua*) in forest; rarely in viny thickets without bamboo, perhaps especially in swampy forest. May associate with mixed-species flocks but usually apart. Similar to Large-headed Flatbill, but note larger size, narrower superciliary, blurry olive streaks on throat and breast, and dusky tail. Cf. also Rufous-tailed Flatbill. **VOICE** Call a mellow whistle followed by a decelerating, descending musical chatter: "*PEEEWWW trrr'PEER-peer-pur.*" Also a mellow falling-rising whistle: "*PEEer'wee?*" Dawn song a descending mellow whistle followed by a musical hiccup "*PEEWW'wichwee*"; occasionally terminal phrase varies: "*PEEWW'weeher.*" **Co, E, Br, Bo**

4 LARGE-HEADED FLATBILL *Ramphotrigon megacephalum* * 12.5–13 cm (5–5¼ in)

Fairly common in southeastern Amazonia (up to 1200 m), mostly in under- and midstory in large stands of spiny bamboo (*Guadua*) in transitional forest; rare or absent from other bamboos in terra firme. Singly or in pairs; may join passing mixed-species flock. Note short yellowish superciliary and partial eyering, rufous wing bars, and buffy tone to breast. Cf. larger Dusky-tailed Flatbill (often in same bamboo thickets). **VOICE** Calls a 2-note hoot "*HOO-poo*" and a single-noted "*hooo*"; also a quiet, rather antpitta-like 2-note whistle with second note higher: "*hoo-her?*" Twitters softly when disturbed. Dawn song a quiet 2-note hoot; second note lower, followed by a higher warble: "*HOO-poo'chewew.*" **Co, E, Br, Bo**

5 FULVOUS-BREASTED FLATBILL *Rhynchocyclus fulvipectus* 15 cm (6 in)

Uncommon in humid montane forest on east slope of Andes, 1000–2000 m. Note size, sluggish habits, upright posture, tawny breast, rufous wing margins, and broad bill; cf. smaller, more active Rufous-breasted Flycatcher. **VOICE** Call a rising, scratchy "*zreeee'zi'zi'zip.*" **Co, E, Bo**

6 OLIVACEOUS FLATBILL *Rhynchocyclus olivaceus* * 15 cm (6 in)

Uncommon in Amazonia (up to 1100 m), in under- and midstory of humid forest. Singles or pairs regularly associate with mixed-species flocks, but also forage apart. Note very broad bill and unpatterned plumage; much larger than *Tolmomyias*, with plain wings. **VOICE** Song a rising series of high, squeaky whistles, often accelerating into a sharp chatter: "*wee wee WEE WEE-whi'whi'wrrr*" or "*wee wee WEE WEE-whi'whiCHTT.*" Call rapid chatters similar to end of song. Vocalizations similar to those of Wedge-billed Woodcreeper (which has weaker calls, and song does not accelerate into a chatter). **Co, E, Br, Bo**

BROWNISH FLYCATCHER

♂

RUFOUS-TAILED FLATBILL

DUSKY-TAILED FLATBILL

LARGE-HEADED FLATBILL

FULVOUS-BREASTED FLATBILL

OLIVACEOUS
FLATBILL

PLATE
205

TOLMOMYIAS FLYCATCHERS

Confusingly similar small forest flycatchers, with broad bill and wing coverts broadly edged yellow-green. Several species commonly overlap, segregated in part by habitat. Nest a hanging bag with spout-shaped entrance near bottom, similar to nest of Rhynchocyclus, *but less bulky and usually lacks large leaves.*

1 YELLOW-OLIVE FLYCATCHER *Tolmomyias sulphurescens* * 12.5–14 cm (5–5½ in)
Geographically variable (and probably representing several separate species). All populations have gray crown and dark iris, and lack a pale wing speculum; most also have dusky tips to auriculars, forming a dark cheek patch. Fairly common in semideciduous and evergreen forest in northwest, 400–1675 m (*aequatorialis*, not illustrated; cf. Pacific Elaenia). Andean subspecies (northern *peruvianus*; southern *inornatus*, not illustrated, paler with less prominent auricular mark) fairly common in midstory and canopy of humid montane forest along east slope of Andes, 1000–2400 m; cf. smaller-billed Marble-faced Bristle-Tyrant and narrow-billed Slaty-capped Flycatcher. In central Amazonia, local on older river islands and in varzea (*insignis*; not illustrated); margins to tertials olive (not yellow-green). Also in river-edge and floodplain forest in southeast (*pallescens*, not illustrated); paler, with less conspicuous auricular patch. In Amazonia cf. very similar Yellow-margined and Gray-crowned flycatchers. **VOICE** Song (*aequatorialis*) very high, sharp "*ti*" note repeated several times. Song (*peruvianus*) series of high, rising, sharp "*TSREET!*" notes. Day song of *insignis* (central Brazil) a short series of relatively high-pitched, broad amplitude notes, "*chit chit chit chit*"; call a single "*chii.*" Day song of *pallescens* short series of whistles, each note "sweeping" upward in pitch, "*swe swee swee.*" **Co, E, Br, Bo**

2 YELLOW-MARGINED FLYCATCHER *Tolmomyias assimilis* * 13.5 cm (5¼ in)
Widespread and fairly common in Amazonia, up to 1000 m, locally to 1300 m. Found in canopy of terra firme, almost always with mixed-species flocks. Very similar to Yellow-olive Flycatcher, but usually segregated by habitat. Only *Tolmomyias* with a wing speculum (pale bases to outer primaries), although this sometimes indistinct. Iris usually dark, but can be light gray. Always has yellowish margins to tertials (green in *insignis* Yellow-olive of central Amazonia). In the hand, tenth (outermost) primary longer than fourth (reverse is true in Yellow-olive). Cf. also Gray-crowned Flycatcher. **VOICE** Song a raspy, rising series of short, rising or rising-falling whistles: "*zhree zhreee ZHREEE.*" Calls variable single or double "*zhree?*" or "*tueep?*" notes, also quiet trills. Usually can be separated from Gray-crowned by raspy quality of notes. Northern *obscuriceps* (northeastern Amazonia) also gives a "*WEEE'chip!*" **Co, E, Br, Bo**

3 ORANGE-EYED FLYCATCHER *Tolmomyias traylori* 13.5 cm (5¼ in)
Poorly known. In midstory of medium to tall varzea of northern Amazonia; apparently replaces Yellow-olive Flycatcher north of the Amazon. Also (locally?) in similar forest on old river islands. Similar to Gray-crowned Flycatcher but note buffy wash on face and breast, and pale orangey iris; also less of an edge species. Cf. also Yellow-margined Flycatcher of terra firme. **VOICE** Song a rising series of short, rising-falling, raspy whistled notes: "*zreep zreeeep ZREEEP,*" final note often becoming clearer and more squeaky. Call a rising-falling raspy whistle followed by a low chatter: "*ZREEE'-chirr'rr.*" **Co, E**

4 GRAY-CROWNED FLYCATCHER *Tolmomyias poliocephalus* * 12 cm (4¾ in)
Fairly common throughout Amazonia (up to 1000 m, locally to 1400 m). Found in midstory and canopy of river-edge forest and varzea, also at forest edge and tall second growth. Less restricted to mixed-species flocks than are Yellow-olive and Yellow-margined flycatchers. Smaller. Iris usually pale; mandible tipped dusky (uniformly pale in the larger *Tolmomyias*). Lacks wing speculum of Yellow-margined. **VOICE** Song a rising series of clear rising or rising-falling whistles, last notes quavering "*tuee? tuee? TUEE? tuEEuEE? tuEEuEE?*" Call single "*tuee?*" Very similar to calls of Yellow-margined, but usually lacks raspy quality (but beware, begging young can be raspy). **Co, E, Br, Bo**

5 YELLOW-BREASTED FLYCATCHER *Tolmomyias flaviventris* * 12 cm (4¾ in)
Fairly common throughout Amazonia, up to 1100 m, locally to 1500 m. Found in young river-edge forest, second growth, and forest edge. Relatively uniformly colored, with plain wings and olive crown. Cf. Yellow Tyrannulet. **VOICE** Song a rising series of sharp, rising notes: "*tsu tswee tsweet TSWEET! TSWEET! TSWEET.*" Calls single high, sharp, rising "*tsweet!*" notes. Similar to Andean subspecies of Yellow-olive Flycatcher, but lower pitched. **Co, E, Br, Bo**

YELLOW-OLIVE FLYCATCHER

peruvianus

YELLOW-MARGINED FLYCATCHER

ORANGE-EYED FLYCATCHER

GRAY-CROWNED FLYCATCHER

YELLOW-BREASTED FLYCATCHER

PLATE
206

RINGED ANTPIPIT AND SPADEBILLS

Ringed Antpipit is a distinctive terrestrial flycatcher. Spadebills are small flycatchers of forest understory, with notably short tails and broad bills; typically look as if the head is disproportionately large. Usually solitary, apart from mixed-species flocks. Remain relatively motionless, then suddenly sally out to capture insects from nearby vegetation. Plumage dull, but all species have a bright but partially concealed crown patch (may be absent in females in some species).

1 RINGED ANTPIPIT *Corythopis torquatus* * 14 cm (5½ in)
Widespread and fairly common in Amazonia, below 1000 m (locally up to 1500 m). Walks steadily on ground or on fallen logs in forest interior. Makes short sallies to low vegetation for insects. Solitary; does not associate with mixed-species flocks, but will forage at army ant swarms. Breast streaking of juveniles brown (not black). Cf. Banded Antbird. Frequently snaps bill audibly. **VOICE** Song variable for a flycatcher, but typical pattern a rusty rising-falling (sometimes descending or quavering) whistle followed by a longer descending whistle: "*HEE'U-huEEU.*" Short "*pit*" or rattle notes may precede, separate, or follow these whistles. **Co, E, Br, Bo**

2 WHITE-CRESTED SPADEBILL *Platyrinchus platyrhynchos* * 11 cm (4¼ in)
Rare to uncommon in Amazonia below 1100 m. Relatively widespread; not reported east of Río Napo, but may occur (is known from east bank of Napo in adjacent Ecuador). Found in understory of terra firme. Largest spadebill. Readily identified by white throat contrasting with bright buffy breast and belly, and unpatterned gray face and crown. Semiconcealed central crown patch white. **VOICE** Song a rapid, rising-falling musical trill: "*breeEEE-B'RRRrrrewww.*" Calls a loud, descending squeak: "*pew!*" **Co, E, Br, Bo**

3 CINNAMON-CRESTED SPADEBILL *Platyrinchus saturatus* * 9 cm (3½ in)
Poorly known; seemingly rare, found in forests on sandy soils (irapayales and varillales). Dull brown with relatively plain face; rufous crown patch usually concealed. Golden-crowned Spadebill is smaller, more greenish, with bolder head pattern and more obvious, more orange crown patch. More similar to White-throated Spadebill of Andes, but no geographic overlap. White-throated also has bolder face pattern and yellow crown patch. **VOICE** Song an accelerating series of metallic notes: "*tew-ti-tik-tik'tik'tik.*" Call a loud rising squeak: "*week!*" **Co, E, Br**

4 GOLDEN-CROWNED SPADEBILL *Platyrinchus coronatus* * 9 cm (3½ in)
Widespread in Amazonia, but relatively uncommon; inconspicuous and easily overlooked until insectlike song learned. Found in low understory of humid forest. Smallest spadebill. Very greenish. Also note bold face markings: black line separating crown and buff superciliary, black lines framing buffy auriculars. Orange-rufous crown, with golden yellow center in males, more obvious than on other spadebills. **VOICE** Song, easily overlooked, a very high, fast, insectlike falling-rising trill: "*tiiieerrrreeeeeeee?*" **Co, E, Br, Bo**

5 YELLOW-THROATED SPADEBILL *Platyrinchus flavigularis* * 9.5 cm (3¾ in)
Poorly known, apparently rare and local; reported from a few localities on east slope of Andes and on outlying ridges, 1200–2000 m. In Ecuador reported to favor sites with relatively open understory, especially along ridges. Perches motionless for long periods and easily can be overlooked, even when perched in the open. Identified by light rufous crown with semiconcealed white central patch, greenish upperparts, and pale yellow underparts with olive-brown wash on breast. White-throated Spadebill is smaller, browner, and has bold face pattern and yellow crown patch; prefers denser vegetation and perhaps forages closer to the ground. **VOICE** Song a rapid, rising trill ending with a sharp squeak: "*brrrreeEEEE'PEW!*" Call a loud, descending squeak: "*pew!*" **Co, E**

6 WHITE-THROATED SPADEBILL *Platyrinchus mystaceus* * 9.5 cm (3¾ in)
Fairly common low in understory of humid montane forest and forest edge on east slope of Andes at 800–2000 m and on outlying ridges; also present in semideciduous forest in Tumbes at 400 m. The common Andean spadebill. Note brown plumage, whitish lores, whitish auricular spot with dusky borders, and golden yellow crown patch (usually semiconcealed, and smaller or absent in females). Populations in southern Peru (Cuzco and Puno; not illustrated) are buffier below. Cf. much less common Yellow-throated Spadebill. **VOICE** Song a rapid, rising or falling-rising whinny: "*whi'wrr'rr'rr'rr'whee'whee'wheet!*" Call a descending series of squeaky notes: "*dee-dee-dunk.*" Reminiscent of Sulphur-bellied Tyrannulet, but sings from understory. **Co, E, Br, Bo**

RINGED ANTPIPIT

WHITE-CRESTED
SPADEBILL

CINNAMON-CRESTED
SPADEBILL

GOLDEN-
CROWNED
SPADEBILL

YELLOW-THROATED
SPADEBILL

WHITE-THROATED
SPADEBILL

PLATE
207
SMALL RUFOUS AND *MYIOPHOBUS* FLYCATCHERS

Male Myiophobus flycatchers have bright but largely concealed crown patches; crown patch in females reduced or absent. See also plate 208. Ruddy-tailed Flycatcher and the rare Cinnamon Tyrant are two similar small flycatchers of humid forest.

1 CINNAMON TYRANT *Neopipo cinnamomea* * 9.5 cm (3¾ in)

Rare and local in Amazonia, locally up to 700 m. Most often encountered at sites with nutrient-poor soils, such as on sandy soils or outlying ridges. Quiet and inconspicuous, in forest understory; usually solitary, not associated with mixed-species flocks. Behavior like that of very similar Ruddy-tailed Flycatcher, but perhaps more active. Compared to Ruddy-tailed, has darker tarsi (not pink or pale brown), lacks rictal bristles, and tail proportionately shorter; also has semiconcealed yellow or yellow-orange crown patch (rarely visible in the field, and smaller in female). **VOICE** Song a rising, accelerating series of short, ringing notes that then descend and decelerate as notes lengthen: "*peh pi pi PI-PEE-PEE-pee-pee-pew-pu*," sometimes rising portion missing. May be mistaken for song of leaftosser. Call a high, descending "*pseew*" or "*pew*," rather similar to call of Ruddy-tailed. **Co, E, Br, Bo**

2 RUDDY-TAILED FLYCATCHER *Terenotriccus erythrurus* * 10 cm (4 in)

Fairly common and widespread in Amazonia, up to 1300 m. Found in under- and midstory of humid forest. Perches very upright; remains motionless for long periods, then sallies out to capture insect prey from vegetation or from the air. Usually solitary, rarely joining mixed-species flocks. Readily identified by small size, tawny underparts, rufous tail, and "ragged" look to head. **VOICE** Song a high, weak, 2-note, whispering whistle; second note usually higher: "*pew HEE!*" sometimes modulated "*pew hee'e'e.*" Calls single "*psew*" notes, also a lower, descending "*hee-hew.*" **Co, E, Br, Bo**

3 OLIVE-CHESTED FLYCATCHER *Myiophobus cryptoxanthus* 12 cm (4¾ in)

Uncommon to locally fairly common on lower slopes of east side of northern Andes. Inhabits forest edge and secondary woodlands, and shrubby clearings at 900–1750 m. Semiconcealed crown patch yellow (reduced in females); wing bars broad, buffy or whitish. Throat whitish, breast light olive-brown that extends in broad blurry streaks onto pale yellow belly. Similar to more widespread Bran-colored Flycatcher, but yellower below, with blurrier streaks on breast, and duller brown. **VOICE** Song an evenly spaced series of rich "*dewp*" or "*wheep*" notes, sometimes interspersed with chattered phrases: "*dji'dji'dji-wheep dji'dji'dji-wheep dji'dji-wheep....*" Call a rapid, rich, rising "*errr'djidjidjidjidjidji?*" Much faster paced than chatter of Bran-colored. **E**

4 BRAN-COLORED FLYCATCHER *Myiophobus fasciatus* * 12–12.5 cm (4¾–5 in)

Widespread and fairly common. Found in riparian woods, forest edge, and second growth. Streak-breasted *crypterythrus*, with cold brown upperparts and a white breast, is in Marañón and on coast south to southern Cajamarca; unstreaked, largely rufous *rufescens* on coast from Lambayeque south to Tacna. Up to 2700 m. Streak-breasted birds, with rufescent brown upperparts and whitish or pale yellow underparts, occur in Amazonia and foothills of Andes (up to 1800 m), where primarily an austral migrant (but may breed locally, especially near Andes). Usually remains close to cover and perches relatively low. Encountered as singles or pairs, and does not associate with mixed-species flocks. Compare streaked subspecies to larger juvenile and female Vermilion Flycatcher of more open habitats. Also cf. Olive-chested Flycatcher. **VOICE** Song of *crypterythrus* a hesitant, repetitive, series of rich whistles: "*tcheep... wee'bit... chew... tcheep....*" Call a rapid laughing phrase: "*REEH-hi'hi'hi'hi'hi'hi'hi.*" Song in Amazonia a repetitive series of rich notes: "*tchew... weet... tchee'wit... tchew... weet....*" Call a more rapid, rich laughing chatter; more musical than *crypterythrus* and slower, and more falling than Olive-chested: "*errrr-whi'whi'whi'whi'whi.*" **Co, E, Br, Bo, Ch**

5 RORAIMAN FLYCATCHER *Myiophobus roraimae* * 13.5 cm (5¼ in)

Rare and local on east slope of Andes, 900–1800 m. Apparently more prevalent at sites with sandy soil or on outlying ridges. Found in forest understory, as singles or pairs, not associated with mixed-species flocks. Largest *Myiophobus*, and relatively brown. Semiconcealed crown patch (male) orange-rufous. Note well-defined, broad rufous wing bars, olive wash on breast, pale yellow belly, and brown back. **VOICE** Song (Ecuador) a high, sputtering, rising-falling chatter: "*TSEW! TSI pit-pit TSI'TSI'tsi-tew.*" **Co, E, Br**

CINNAMON TYRANT

RUDDY-TAILED FLYCATCHER

OLIVE-CHESTED FLYCATCHER

♂

♂ *rufescens*

BRAN-COLORED
FLYCATCHER

RORAIMAN FLYCATCHER

♂

Amaz.

BRAN-COLORED
FLYCATCHER

crypterythrus

PLATE
208

YELLOWISH OR GREENISH *MYIOPHOBUS* FLYCATCHERS

Largely yellowish or greenish Myiophobus of the Andes (see plate 207).

1 ORANGE-BANDED FLYCATCHER Myiophobus lintoni 13 cm (5 in)

Uncommon and local; in Peru restricted to humid forests on east side of Andes and north of Río Marañón, 2400–2750 m. Usually in small, rapidly moving groups, associated with mixed-species flocks or apart. Forage in crowns of trees, often perching on outer branches and atop leaf clusters. The semiconcealed crown patch (male) is orange or yellow. Larger and longer-tailed than Handsome Flycatcher of lower elevations, with pale iris. No geographic overlap with Ochraceous-breasted Flycatcher. **VOICE** Song a series of evenly spaced, sharp, high, squeaky "*PSEW!*" notes. Call bursts of several "*psew*" and "*pseet*" notes. **E**

2 OCHRACEOUS-BREASTED FLYCATCHER Myiophobus ochraceiventris 13.5–14 cm (5¼–5½ in)

Fairly common on east slope of Andes at 2200–3700 m, in canopy and edge of humid montane forest. Often in small groups, associated with mixed-species flocks. The most widespread *Myiophobus* with yellow underparts. Breast ochraceous buff, belly yellow, and wings have conspicuous wing bars. Upperparts dark olive brown. Crown patch reddish chestnut in females; crown patch of males may be orange (north: Amazonas south to Pasco), reddish orange (south: Cuzco south to Bolivia), or yellow (throughout Peru; juveniles only?). In south cf. Handsome Flycatcher. **VOICE** Song a chip followed by a shrill, short trill: "*tsip… tsip-teeerrr.*" Calls sharp "*tsip*" or "*tip*" notes. **Bo**

3 ORANGE-CRESTED FLYCATCHER Myiophobus phoenicomitra * 11.5 cm (4½ in)

Very local in San Martín; also may occur farther north toward Ecuador. Found in under- and midstory of humid forest; does not associate with mixed-species flocks. Generally at lower elevations (1100–1400 m) than similar Flavescent Flycatcher. Compared to Flavescent, is duller green (more olive, less yellowish), with reduced or no eyering, more well-defined wing bars and pale mandible. Semiconcealed crown patch (male) typically orange-rufous (rarely may be yellow, as in Flavescent). **VOICE** Song (Ecuador) a series of high, sharp notes: "*tsew-TSWEE-tsit!*" **Co, E**

4 FLAVESCENT FLYCATCHER Myiophobus flavicans * 12 cm (4¾ in)

Widespread and fairly common on east slope of Andes, at 1500–2300 m, locally to 3000 m. Found in understory of humid montane forest, as singles or pairs; generally does not associate with mixed-species flocks. Yellowest and most brightly colored of the green *Myiophobus*, with broken yellow eyering and entirely black bill; semiconcealed crown patch of male is yellow (rarely pale orange). Wing coverts tipped and edged with cinnamon-brown (*flavicans*, north of Río Marañón; not illustrated) or plain (widespread *superciliosus*). **VOICE** Song (?) is a rapid, tinny, metallic, sputtering chatter: "*ter-ty'TEERR'it.*" Call an explosive, tinny, sharp "*tsew!*" **Co, E**

5 HANDSOME FLYCATCHER Myiophobus pulcher * 10.5–11 cm (4–4¼ in)

Found at opposite ends of Peru: *bellus* at 2000–2200 m on east slope of Andes, north of the Marañón; and *oblitus* at 1500–2600 m in Cuzco and Puno. Small, short-tailed, brightly colored *Myiophobus* of midstory of humid montane forest and forest edges that often associates with mixed-species flocks. Semiconcealed crown patch (male) orange-rufous; relatively broad wing bars are buffy or cinnamon. Breast of *bellus* washed with ochraceous; cf. Orange-banded Flycatcher. Breast of *oblitus* (not illustrated) pale yellow. Similar to Ochraceous-breasted Flycatcher of higher elevations, but smaller with much stubbier bill and shorter tail, paler yellow-green (not ochre- or tawny-yellow) breast, grayer nape and sides to crown, and more olivaceous (less brown) upperparts. **VOICE** Call of *bellus* a high, thin "*tsew-tsip*" and a descending sputtering trill: "*tsee'tsi'ti'ti'ti'tew.*" Call of *oblitus* a high, descending series of ringing notes: "*TEE-ti-ti-ti.*" **Co, E**

6 UNADORNED FLYCATCHER Myiophobus inornatus 11.5 cm (4½ in)

Uncommon to fairly common on east slope of southern Andes, 1000–2100 m. Largely replaces Flavescent Flycatcher geographically, although in the Apurímac Valley, where sympatric, Unadorned may be more prevalent at lower elevations than Flavescent. Found in under- and midstory of humid montane forest; generally does not follow mixed-species flocks. Similar to Flavescent, also with a semiconcealed yellow crown patch (male), but paler, duller green (more olive, less greenish), wings browner (wing coverts broadly tipped and edged dull cinnamon-brown), and mandible paler (pinkish brown or gray). **VOICE** Call an explosive, thin, sharp "*tsick!*" **Bo**

ORANGE-BANDED
FLYCATCHER

♂

OCHRACEOUS-
BREASTED
FLYCATCHER

♂ n

ORANGE-CRESTED
FLYCATCHER

♂

FLAVESCENT
FLYCATCHER

♂ *superciliosus*

♂

HANDSOME
FLYCATCHER

♂ *bellus*

UNADORNED
FLYCATCHER

PLATE
209
ALDER FLYCATCHER AND SIMILAR-APPEARING SPECIES

Similar small insectivorous flycatchers, with upright posture, and most with noticeable wing bars. Solitary, usually do not associate with mixed-species flocks. Most forage in dense understory, with short sallies to air or to adjacent vegetation, after which usually fly to a new perch. In contrast Olive Flycatcher forages like a pewee (plate 210) with longer sallies to air, often returning to the same perch and quivering tail upon landing.

1 OLIVE FLYCATCHER *Mitrephanes olivaceus* 12 cm (4¾ in)
Fairly common along east slope of Andes, 1400–2300 m, in humid montane forest, especially at openings such as large treefalls and forest borders. Singles or pairs perch in open, at all heights. May associate with mixed-species flocks, but often apart; may forage at same site for extended period. Readily identified by relatively uniform olive color and conspicuous crest. **VOICE** Song a series of high musical chips followed by a loud, high, descending whistle: *"tchi-tchi'SEEEW!"* Calls a rapid series of high, musical chips: *"tchi-tchi-tchi-tchi-tchi."* **Bo**

2 EULER'S FLYCATCHER *Lathrotriccus euleri* * 13 cm (5 in)
Uncommon but widespread resident in humid forest, up to 1600 m (*bolivianus*). Austral migrants (*argentinus, euleri*) occur to north bank of the Amazon (at least May–Oct). Residents brownish olive above, olive and yellow below, with broad buffy wing bars; more deeply colored than Alder Flycatcher, with indistinct pale superciliary. Migrants browner above and paler bellied; cf. Fuscous Flycatcher. Juvenile *bolivianus* very brown above; difficult to distinguish from migrants. **VOICE** Song (*bolivianus*) a repeated, 2-note, buzzy, descending *"DZEER-hur"* (*"hur"* sometimes lacking) interspersed with sneezing *"DZEER-wee'chew"* phrases. Call a buzzy, descending series of 2–7, usually 4, notes *"DZEE-dzee-dzee-dzer"* or *"DZEEW-dzew-dzew-dzeer."* **Co, E, Br, Bo**

3 GRAY-BREASTED FLYCATCHER *Lathrotriccus griseipectus* 13 cm (5 in)
Rare to uncommon in dry forests of northwest coast and in Chinchipe Valley, up to 1200 m. Much grayer, especially on crown, sides of face, and chest, than Alder Flycatcher. Distinguished from Tropical Pewee by white eyering, bolder wing bars, and shorter wings with less primary extension; also differs in foraging behavior. **VOICE** Song a repeated, buzzy *"DZEE-heer… DZEE-dzureet?"*; second note of first phrase variable, may be sputtered or bisyllabic. Call a 2-note phrase of descending raspy notes: *"DZEER-dzee."* **E**

4 ALDER FLYCATCHER *Empidonax alnorum* 14 cm (5½ in)
Fairly common boreal migrant (primarily Sep–Apr) to Amazonia and Marañón Valley; rare on west slope of northwest. Found in edge habitats, such as forest borders, overgrown pastures, young river-island scrub, and open river-edge forest, below 1200 m, occasionally to 3200 m. Often "flicks" tail upward; pewees do not share this behavior. Note white eyering (sometimes reduced or absent), olive-brown upperparts, broad whitish wing bars, and whitish belly. Similar Euler's Flycatcher is in forest interior and is browner above, more olive below, with more rufescent wing bars. Tropical Pewee larger, has longer wings with more primary extension, and different foraging behavior. [**Willow Flycatcher** *Empidonax traillii* * is not reported from Peru but might occur in northernmost Amazonia. Best distinguished from Alder Flycatcher by voice. Song a similar *"FITZ bew"* or *"FRITZ-brew,"* with last note falling. Call a dry *"whit."*] **VOICE** Song (sometimes given on wintering territories) a low, burry *"dzree BEE'it"* or *"free-BEERt"* with last note rising. Call a liquid *"pip,"* similar to some pewees. **Co, E, Br, Bo**

5 FUSCOUS FLYCATCHER *Cnemotriccus fuscatus* * 14 cm (5½ in)
Rare to uncommon, in eastern lowlands; there are two types (species?), which differ in habitat and voice. Both are inconspicuous and share brownish tones and broad wing bars. Widespread *fuscatior*, with dark mandible and relatively prominent pale superciliary, occurs in understory of river-edge forest, on river islands, and in second growth, below 500 m; similar *bimaculatus* of southeast (only an austral migrant?) paler and warmer brown. Cf. Euler's (which has less prominent superciliary and pale mandible). Second type, *duidae* (not illustrated), restricted to forests on sandy or nutrient-poor soil, up to 1350 m, has pale mandible and fainter superciliary. Very similar to Euler's Flycatcher; best distinguished by voice and habitat. **VOICE** Song (?) of *fuscatior* clear, rising, whistled *"whee'ip."* Call deep, harsh chuckling, slightly descending *"djeer-djer-djer-djer."* Also a *"ti'weer-chup."* Calls of *bimaculatus* single *"dzeee'ew"* or *"dzreee?,"* also chatters similar to *fuscatior*. Song of *duidae* a sharp, rising, buzzy *"PIT-rhee?"* Call a descending series of raspy, rising notes: *"ti'RHEE-t'RHEE-t'rhee."* Also a high squeaky *"tseew"* and quiet buzzy squeaks and chatters. **Co, E, Br, Bo**

OLIVE FLYCATCHER

resident

austral migrant

EULER'S FLYCATCHER

GRAY-BREASTED FLYCATCHER

ALDER FLYCATCHER

FUSCOUS FLYCATCHER

fuscatior

bimaculatus

PLATE
210

PEWEES

Pewees are dull colored, with upright posture. Unlike most similar species, pewees characteristically sally to air, after which often return to the same perch; these perches also frequently are relatively conspicuous (cf. Olive Flycatcher). Pewees also have relatively longer wings with greater primary extension, and often appear crested.

1 WESTERN WOOD-PEWEE *Contopus sordidulus* * 14.5 cm (5¾ in)

Uncommon boreal migrant (probably primarily Sep–Apr) to east slopes of Andes, at 600–1800 m. Poorly known, due to confusion with very similar Eastern Wood-Pewee. Found at forest edges and in taller second growth. Wood-pewees are similar to Tropical Pewee but have darker lores; also, little geographic overlap. Wood-pewees also have longer wings, with longer primary extension (especially as compared to resident populations of Tropical; this character less useful for austral migrants). In the hand, tenth (outermost) primary longer than sixth in wood-pewees; tenth shorter than sixth in Tropical. Wood-pewees also similar to Alder Flycatcher but differ in foraging behavior, have duller wing bars, usually lack eyering, are more crested, and have longer wings. See Eastern Wood-Pewee. **VOICE** Call a slightly raspy, rising-falling "*buRREErr*" or rising "*burrEE?*"; also a flat "*chip*." Song, occasionally heard, a descending, raspy "*BEER*" sometimes followed by a quieter, rising, musical "*wurblee?*" **Co, E, Bo**

2 EASTERN WOOD-PEWEE *Contopus virens* 14.5 cm (5¾ in)

Fairly common boreal migrant (Sep–Apr) to east slopes of Andes, below 1400 m and to Amazonia; found at forest edges, in river-edge forest, and in taller second growth. See Western Wood-Pewee account for distinctions from Tropical Pewee and Alder Flycatcher. May overlap very similar Western in Andes; best to rely on voice. Eastern averages paler on breast, has paler mandible, and usually lacks dark centers to undertail coverts. Overlap between the two species extensive in all characters, however, and identification even in the hand is difficult. Juveniles (both species) have buffy wing bars. **VOICE** Call a musical, rising "*p'wee?*"; also a flat "*chip*." Song, occasionally heard, a high, mellow "*peebee-a-wee?… wurblee?… pee-dew*" or parts thereof. **Co, E, Br, Bo**

3 TROPICAL PEWEE *Contopus cinereus* * 14 cm (5½ in)

Fairly common on coastal plain of northwest, continuing south along west slope of Andes and in Marañón Valley up to 2800 m (*punensis*). Also a rare austral migrant to southern Amazonia (subspecies?). See Western Wood-Pewee for distinctions from wood-pewees. In northwest cf. especially Gray-breasted Flycatcher, which has bolder wing bars and an eyering, shorter primary extension, and different behavior and **VOICE** Song (*punensis*) an emphatic, high, 2-note phrase; second note sometimes slightly trilled: "*teew-tee*," "*tee-teew*" or "*tee tee'e'ew*." Calls a single "*tee*" or a quiet chatter. **Co, E, Br, Bo**

4 OLIVE-SIDED FLYCATCHER *Contopus cooperi* 18 cm (7 in)

Uncommon boreal migrant (primarily Oct–Apr) to east slope of Andes, 700–2100 m, occasionally to adjacent lowlands; very rare on west slope. Often perches on exposed snags in canopy of humid forest. Readily recognized by large size, "vested" appearance (olive-gray flanks divided by white central stripe), white patches on either side of lower back (often visible even when wings are closed), and relatively short tail. **VOICE** Call a rich "*pip*" in rapid series, similar to Smoke-colored Pewee. Song, sometimes heard in Peru, a loud, clear cheer: "*whip WE HEAR!*" or "*hip THREE CHEERS!*" **Co, E, Br, Bo**

5 BLACKISH PEWEE *Contopus nigrescens* * 13 cm (5 in)

Rare and local; primarily reported from outlying ridges in northern Peru, 600–1500 m. Usually found in canopy of humid montane forest, especially at forest borders. Dark slaty gray. Much smaller and darker overall than Smoke-colored Pewee, and with less well-developed crest. **VOICE** Call a musical, rich, falling "*pew!*" usually in evenly paced series. Song a slightly burry, rising-falling "*dzree'whew!*" **E, Br**

6 SMOKE-COLORED PEWEE *Contopus fumigatus* * 17 cm (6¾ in)

Fairly common in humid montane forest along east slope of Andes, and on west slope in north, 1000–2800 m. Also in semideciduous forests in Tumbes and Piura, 400–800 m. Usually perches on an exposed site, such as a snag, in forest canopy or at forest border. Large, uniformly dark, crested; mandible may be orange or dark brownish. Juvenile (not illustrated) has cinnamon wing bars, pale scaling on head and back; belly may be pale yellow or buffy. **VOICE** Song, usually at dawn, a mellow, clear whistled series of "*pur-WEER*" or "*WHEER*" notes interspersed with rising "*wur-dee?*" phrases. Call a characteristic "*pip*," usually in pairs or short series. **Co, E, Br**

WESTERN
WOOD-PEWEE

EASTERN
WOOD-PEWEE

TROPICAL PEWEE

OLIVE-SIDED FLYCATCHER

BLACKISH PEWEE

SMOKE-COLORED PEWEE

PLATE
211

BOLDLY-PATTERNED FLYCATCHERS

A disparate collection of distinctive flycatchers; most are restricted to lowlands, but Black Phoebe is widespread in the Andes.

1 VERMILION FLYCATCHER *Pyrocephalus rubinus* * 14.5–15 cm (5¾–6 in)

Widespread, common bird of open country, found in pastures, open woods, and in low river-edge scrub. Resident on west slope (various subspecies) and in Marañón Valley below 2800 m (*ardens*); uncommon to fairly common austral migrant (Apr–Oct or Nov) in Amazonia below 1000 m (*rubinus*). Lower belly of females pinkish on west slope; often more extensively red in *ardens*. Vent of female *rubinus* has only a limited, pale yellow or orange wash. Juveniles, which are scaled light buff above, also have only faint color on vent (usually yellow). Immature male (not illustrated) similar to female, but plumage spotted with red. Either sex may be uniformly sooty on central and southern coast; sooty morphs represent roughly half of population in and near city of Lima but much rarer farther south, and unreported south of southern Arequipa. **VOICE** Song, often in a skylarking display flight, a stuttered, rising series of tinkled notes accelerating into a musical trill: "*pip pip pi'pi'pi'TREEE.*" Call a sharp, squeaky "*peet!*" or "*peep.*" **Co, E, Br, Bo, Ch**

2 WHITE-HEADED MARSH-TYRANT *Arundinicola leucocephala* 13 cm (5 in)

Uncommon along rivers in northeastern Amazonia. Perches conspicuously low over marshes and river-edge vegetation, from which sallies to air to capture prey; only rarely perches on ground (in contrast to water-tyrants). Compare female to Pied Water-Tyrant, which is larger, blackish above (not light grayish brown) with darker crown and nape, and entirely black bill (base of mandible pale in both sexes of marsh-tyrant). **VOICE** Call is a quiet, insectlike, high "*teep*" or "*tip*" note. **Co, E, Br, Bo**

3 BLACK PHOEBE *Sayornis nigricans* * 17.5 cm (6¾ in)

A common sight along fast-flowing, rocky streams and rivers in Andes and foothills, usually in forested areas. Found along west slope commonly to Cajamarca, locally to Ancash; along entire east slope, and on outlying ridges, including Contamana hills. Perches very low near water, often on rocks at water's edge or in midstream. Regularly flicks tail downward; sallies to air. Solitary or in pairs. **VOICE** Song a high, surprisingly loud, series of shrill whistles audible above rush of water: "*swee… pit-seew… swee… pit-seew….*" Call chatters similar to song phrases, also a high "*psi.*" **Co, E, Bo**

4 PIED WATER-TYRANT *Fluvicola pica* * 13 cm (5 in)

Uncommon austral migrant to eastern lowlands. Forages very low along edges of rivers and oxbow lakes, typically perching on ground or on marsh vegetation. Frequently cocks and fans tail. Sexes similar. Strikingly 2-toned, black above with white underparts, forehead, and sides to the face. Cf. paler female of White-headed Marsh-Tyrant. **VOICE** Call a liquid "*pwip.*" **Co, E, Br, Bo**

5 MASKED WATER-TYRANT *Fluvicola nengeta* * 14.5 cm (5¾ in)

Uncommon to fairly common along rivers in lowland northwest. Behavior similar to Pied Water-Tyrant: forages on or near ground on riverbanks and on marsh vegetation. Distinctive black-and-white plumage, with narrow black mask and pale gray back. **VOICE** Song a deep, rasping, froglike "*jibber*" or "*rhub'it*" given in series. Call a loud, somewhat Common Moorhen-like "*kip.*" **E, Br**

6 ROYAL FLYCATCHER *Onychorhynchus coronatus* * *castelnaui* 15 cm (6 in); *occidentalis* 16.5 cm (6½ in)

Notable for long striking crest. Smaller, darker *castelnaui* rare to uncommon, but widespread, in Amazonia. Understory of humid forest, particularly near light gaps. Larger, paler *occidentalis* rare in semideciduous forest in Tumbes below 400 m. Note long bill and tail, brown color, and hammerheaded appearance from long recumbent crest. Crest (primarily red in males, orange in females) rarely seen fully erected in the field; birds in the hand (as when removed from a mistnet) spread crest, open and close bill, and twist or bow head from side to side. Usually encountered as singles or as pairs; does not associate with mixed-species flocks. Nest a very long hanging structure with side entrance, often suspended over stream. **VOICE** Call a loud, plaintive squeak: "*PEE'yuk.*" Similar to some jacamars; perhaps slightly deeper and more punctuated at end. Song (?) a squeaky "*PEE'u*" occasionally followed by a lower, musical "*PEE'u-brrrr.*" In display, *occidentalis* may give a squeaky "*whi-CHEW*" in a series. **Co, E, Br, Bo**

VERMILION FLYCATCHER

♀ coastal

♀ ardens

sooty morph

♂

WHITE-HEADED MARSH-TYRANT

BLACK PHOEBE

♀ rubinus

♀

♂

ROYAL FLYCATCHER

PIED WATER-TYRANT

♀ occidentalis

♂ castelnaui

MASKED
WATER-TYRANT

♂
occidentalis
in spread
crest display

castelnaui
♀

ROYAL FLYCATCHER

PLATE
212
KNIPOLEGUS TYRANTS AND BLACK-TYRANTS

Males of most Knipolegus *are black or dark gray with blue-gray bill. Females brown or gray above with streaked breast and pale wing bars; also often a contrasting rusty patch on rump, and rufous on inner webs of rectrices.*

1 ANDEAN TYRANT *Knipolegus signatus* * 16–16.5 cm (6¼–6½ in)
Rare, at edges of humid montane forest, 1800–2700 m. Male of northern *signatus* uniformly dull black with darker crown. Female has less well-developed rufous rump than female White-winged Black-Tyrant and is browner, much less buffy below with more prominent streaking on breast; also has little buff in the tail. Male *cabanisi* (Cuzco and Puno) uniformly gray; similar in color to Smoke-colored Pewee, but note blue-gray bill. Female similar to female *signatus* but upperparts are more reddish brown, and is paler brownish gray below; also has buff wing bars and rufous inner webs to rectrices. **VOICE** Usually quiet. In display flight, *cabanisi* (Bolivia) produces wing whirr followed by a rich "*tchick!*" Call of *cabanisi* (Argentina) a rapid, low "*chirri'jurriew*," accompanied by bill snaps.
Bo

2 WHITE-WINGED BLACK-TYRANT *Knipolegus aterrimus* * 16–17 cm (6¼–6¾ in)
Uncommon to fairly common in Andes at 1800–3600 m. Found in upper Marañón Valley (*heterogyna*); and in intermontane valleys and, locally, on east side of southern Andes (*anthracinus*). Occurs in drier habitats than other black-tyrants, often in montane scrub or dry forest. Male glossy black with concealed white wing patch, conspicuous in flight. Female (and first-year male) has buff or white wing bars and little or no streaking on breast; cinnamon-buff below with tawny rump (*anthracinus*) or paler below with buffy white rump (*heterogyna*). **VOICE** Usually silent. Song (*anthracinus*), usually performed in a display in which the male jumps vertically, vocalizing on the descent, is a thin, buzzy "*pi-dri'DZEER*." Calls quiet chatters and a single, descending "*dzeew*." **Br, Bo**

3 AMAZONIAN BLACK-TYRANT *Knipolegus poecilocercus* 13.5 cm (5¼ in)
Poorly known. Apparently very local along lower Río Ucayali and adjacent Amazon; perhaps more widespread but overlooked. Found in undergrowth of flooded forest, perhaps especially on blackwater streams and lakes. A small black-tyrant. Male uniformly glossy blue-black. In the hand, note very narrow outer primaries. Distinguished from Riverside Tyrant by size and habitat. Female browner above than female Riverside, with contrasting tawny rump, pale lores, and more obvious wing bars. Cf. also Bran-colored Flycatcher. **VOICE** Occasionally gives several high-pitched, raspy "*tzreet*" notes followed by a jumble. **Co, E, Br**

4 RIVERSIDE TYRANT *Knipolegus orenocensis* * 15 cm (6 in)
Uncommon, primarily in young successional vegetation on islands in larger Amazonian rivers. Male uniformly dull black. Female dull grayish brown above, whitish below with blurry streaks on breast. Cf. Bran-colored Flycatcher and female Vermilion Flycatcher and Amazonian Black-Tyrant. **VOICE** Song is a series of liquid notes that become a hiccup ending on a gravelly note: "*pwip pwip pwip'PI'tjuk*." Calls a liquid "*pwip*" much like dripping water. **Co, E, Br**

5 [HUDSON'S BLACK-TYRANT *Knipolegus hudsoni*] 15 cm (6 in)
Rare austral migrant to southeastern Amazonia; only a few sight records. Reported from low river-edge forest or edges of oxbow lakes. Male (not yet reported from Peru) black with white inner webs to remiges and small white patch, usually concealed, on flanks; in the hand, outermost primaries very narrow. Andean White-winged Black-Tyrant similar but larger and lacks flank spot. Female has rufous rump, rufous inner webs to inner rectrices and buffy breast with blurry dusky streaks. Very similar to female White-winged Black-Tyrant, but smaller and whiter below. Larger than female Amazonian Black-Tyrant, with more rufous rump, whiter wing bars, and dusky tips to rectrices (inner webs entirely rufous in Amazonian). **Br, Bo**

6 RUFOUS-TAILED TYRANT *Knipolegus poecilurus* * 14.5 cm (5¾ in)
Widespread but uncommon at edge of humid forest along east slope of Andes and on outlying ridges, 900–2300 m; also in stunted forest on ridges with sandy or nutrient-poor soils. Iris red in adult (brown in juvenile). Both sexes gray above, very buffy below with gray wash on breast but at best indistinct streaking. Female White-winged Black-Tyrant usually at higher elevations and in drier habitats, is larger, and has prominent rufous rump. **VOICE** Usually silent. Call (?) a dry, buzzy, descending "*dzeer*"; also a series of high peeps and a sharp, rising "*tip*." Display flight includes a vertical, arcing hop with a chiming "*tee-teek*" given at the apex. **Co, E, Br, Bo**

♂ *cabanisi*

WHITE-WINGED
BLACK-TYRANT

♂

♀ *signatus*

ANDEAN TYRANT

♀ *cabanisi*

♀ *signatus*

ANDEAN TYRANT

AMAZONIAN
BLACK-TYRANT

♀ *heterogyna*

WHITE-WINGED
BLACK-TYRANT

♀

anthracinus

♂

♀

♀

♂

RIVERSIDE
TYRANT

♀

HUDSON'S
BLACK-TYRANT

♂

RUFOUS-TAILED
TYRANT

PLATE
213

GROUND-TYRANTS, WATER-TYRANT, AND FIELD-TYRANT

Terrestrial flycatchers of open habitats. Drab Water-Tyrant is found at waters' edge in Amazonia. Short-tailed Field-Tyrant is a bird of low-elevation scrub of the coast and Marañón Valley. Most ground-tyrants (see also plates 214–215) are Andean, but a few occur down to the coast and one is Amazonian. Males of some (perhaps all) have an aerial display flight when breeding. Many are only nonbreeding austral migrants to Peru, however; several species may be found in the same loose flock. At rest have a very erect posture. Forage primarily running in thrush fashion, gleaning small arthropods from ground.

1 LITTLE-GROUND-TYRANT *Muscisaxicola fluviatilis* 13.5 cm (5¼ in)

Small, uncommon ground-tyrant of Amazonia and Andean foothills. Singles or pairs found on muddy river margins, sandbars, and rocky beaches, also locally in human clearings, up to 1500 m. Often perch atop bushes or driftwood. Possibly a partial austral migrant; a few records from austral winter from as far north as the Amazon or as high as Lake Titicaca (3800 m). Note upright posture, small size, buffy breast contrasting with white belly, white margins to rectrices, and ill-defined rufous wing bars. Cf. Drab Water-Tyrant. **Co, E, Br, Bo**

2 DRAB WATER-TYRANT *Ochthornis littoralis* 13.5 cm (5¼ in)

Aptly named: dull-colored flycatcher always found at stream- and river-margins, throughout Amazonia. Singles and pairs perch on low branches and roots overhanging water, less commonly on muddy riverbanks (only rarely on flat open beaches). Often seen in flight low over water, hugging bank. Note small size, dull mouse-brown color, short creamy superciliary and line below eye, and all-dark tail; cf. Little Ground-Tyrant (which is more characteristic of beaches). **VOICE** Song a rapid, excited series of rattling chatters: *"chip-chew treeee-chew treeee-chew treeee-chew treeee-chew."* Similar to flight calls of Collared Plover, but less musical. Call a high, squeaky *"pee'ip"* or *"peep."* **Co, E, Br, Bo**

3 SPOT-BILLED GROUND-TYRANT *Muscisaxicola maculirostris* * 15 cm (6 in)

Widespread and fairly common in Andes (2000–4500 m), also locally in lomas of southern coast. Seasonal status not clear; resident in southwest, but possibly only an austral migrant farther north. Found in open barren areas, often rocky, also in short grass and plowed fields. Small, with pale base to mandible; brown above, with ill-defined rufous wing bars and faint streaking on breast. **VOICE** Song, in display flight, a series of thin, liquid notes followed by a dry rattled sound: *"tew tew tew ti'ti'DZZK."* Also a dry buzzy rattle (mechanically?) in a flight display. Call a high *"pew."* Also a louder sharp *"pit!"* **Co, E, Bo, Ch**

4 SHORT-TAILED FIELD-TYRANT *Muscigralla brevicauda* 12 cm (4¼ in)

Fairly common on coast and in dry Marañón Valley, up to 1200 m. Inconspicuous, in arid scrub and barren fields. Note very long legs and very short tail. Runs along ground, gleaning insects or pursuing them with short flutters; also may perch on low shrubs but remains close to ground. Note yellowish buff rump, chestnut upper tail coverts, whitish lores and superciliary, and prominent wing bars. Both sexes have semiconcealed yellow crown patch. **VOICE** Song, often performed in a display flight, is a series of dry, metallic *"tik"* or *"spit"* notes followed by a buzzy, rising-falling trill: *"tik tik tik tzzZZ-ZZzzew,"* often given in rapid series. Call a metallic, dry *"spit!"* and, when flushed, a sputtering trilled series of *"spit"* and *"trr"* notes. **E, Ch**

5 CINNAMON-BELLIED GROUND-TYRANT *Muscisaxicola capistratus* 18 cm (7 in)

Uncommon austral migrant (Apr–Oct), primarily to Titicaca Basin at 3800–4100 m; very rare vagrant farther north. Found in open grasslands and pastures. Readily identified by distinctive head pattern (black forecrown sharply cut off from rufous crown) and extensively tawny belly. **VOICE** Call a high *"wee tee,"* occasionally with several *"tee"* notes; reminiscent of Spotted Sandpiper. **Bo, Ch**

6 DARK-FACED GROUND-TYRANT *Muscisaxicola maclovianus* * 16 cm (6¼ in)

Uncommon to fairly common austral migrant (Apr–Oct). Frequently found at sea level, although in south also, rarely, up to 4000 m. Found in agricultural fields, on beaches, on lomas, and other bare open habitats. Readily recognized by blackish face, dark chin, dark brown crown, and brownish gray upperparts. **VOICE** Calls a loud, reedy *"cheep,"* sometimes in series; also a low *"tu"* and a combination of the two calls. **E, Ch**

LITTLE GROUND-TYRANT

DRAB WATER-TYRANT

SHORT-TAILED
FIELD-TYRANT

SPOT-BILLED
GROUND-TYRANT

DARK-FACED
GROUND-TYRANT

CINNAMON-BELLIED
GROUND-TYRANT

PLATE
214

NEGRITO AND MEDIUM-SIZED
GROUND-TYRANTS

Andean Negrito is another terrestrial Andean flycatcher, closely associated with water. Ground-Tyrants on this plate are mid-sized, and all are Andean. Similar to one another, but differ in details of the head pattern and overall color tone.

1 ANDEAN NEGRITO *Lessonia oreas* 12.5 cm (5 in)

Locally fairly common on short grasslands of high Andes, 3100–4600 m, almost always at margins of lakes or marshes. Also a very rare vagrant to coast in austral winter. Largely terrestrial. Singles or (more often) pairs pursue insects by running on ground or with short sallies. Inner webs of most remiges are whitish (male) or light sandy brown (female), forming a large pale band in flight (whiter and more prominent from above). Note short tail, long legs, and distinctive black (male) or sooty brown (female) plumage with rufous "saddle." [**Austral Negrito** *Lessonia rufa* (not illustrated) is a possible rare austral migrant to southern coast. Similar to Andean but lacks white in wings and has white edges to outer rectrices; female also is much paler, with rufous wing bars and bases to primaries.] **VOICE** Call a quiet, dry "*djret.*" **Bo, Ch**

2 RUFOUS-NAPED GROUND-TYRANT *Muscisaxicola rufivertex* * 16–17 cm (6¼–6¾ in)

One of most widespread and common Andean ground-tyrants. Resident in Andes at 2700–4200 m, also very locally occurs at 600–1000 m near southern coast. Found in sites with short grassland and rocky outcroppings, often in drier areas than those favored by other ground-tyrants. Very pale gray, readily recognized by uniform pale color and sharply defined patch on rear crown. Crown patch dark rufous in widespread *occipitalis*, but paler, more tawny in southwestern *pallidiceps* (possibly only an austral migrant?). **VOICE** Call a dry, rising-falling chatter: "*rhe'e'e'e'e'er.*" **Bo, Ch**

3 CINEREOUS GROUND-TYRANT *Muscisaxicola cinereus* * 15.5 cm (6 in)

Uncommon austral migrant (Feb–Oct) to Andean grasslands, 4000–4700 m. Prefers relatively dry rocky sites. Larger and grayer than Spot-billed, but smaller than Taczanowski's, Puna, and White-browed ground-tyrants. Pale gray above, with no crown patch; most similar to Taczanowski's Ground-Tyrant but smaller, grayer, and with shorter superciliary that does not extend significantly behind eye. **Bo, Ch**

4 TACZANOWSKI'S GROUND-TYRANT *Muscisaxicola griseus* 16.5–18.5 cm (6½–7½ in)

Fairly common and widespread at 3200–4800 m in open grassland in Andes. Medium-sized and drab (even by ground-tyrant standards), relatively dark grayish brown above with no crown patch. Narrow white superciliary continues past the eye. Very similar austral migrant Cinereous Ground-Tyrant is slightly smaller, and grayer (less brown) above with shorter superciliary. Puna Ground-Tyrant is paler and browner with rufous rear crown. **Bo** [Sight records from north of Río Marañón (2900–3350 m) may refer to **Plain-capped Ground-Tyrant** (*Muscisaxicola alpinus*; not illustrated), which is unconfirmed from Peru; similar to Taczanowski's, but much darker brown above.]

5 PUNA GROUND-TYRANT *Muscisaxicola juninensis* 16 cm (6¼ in)

Fairly common to common at 3800–4800 m in Andes. Most often found in vicinity of bogs and humid puna, also on open grassland with rocky outcroppings. Medium-sized and pale sandy brown above with short white superciliary. Note ill-defined tawny-rufous rear crown patch, which distinguishes it from Taczanowski's and Cinereous ground-tyrants. Also similar to White-browed Ground-Tyrant, but that species has longer, more sharply defined superciliary, is darker above, and has more well-defined rufous crown patch. **Bo, Ch**

6 BLACK-FRONTED GROUND-TYRANT *Muscisaxicola frontalis* 16.5–17 cm (6½–6¾ in)

Rare austral migrant to south (Apr–Sep); most records from southwest (Arequipa, Puno), very rarely farther north. Found in open grasslands at 3750–4300 m, perhaps more frequent near bogs and marshes. Pale gray above, with a large white loral spot but no superciliary. Readily identified by broad black forehead that narrows into black line down center of crown. **VOICE** Calls a soft "*tink*" and "*treet.*" **Bo, Ch**

7 WHITE-BROWED GROUND-TYRANT *Muscisaxicola albilora* 17–17.5 cm (6¾–7 in)

Fairly common austral migrant (Apr–Oct) to Andes, 2900–4200 m. Found in open grasslands and near marshes. Relatively dark grayish brown above, with diffuse rufous rear crown patch, and relatively long and well-defined white superciliary. Much browner than Rufous-naped Ground-Tyrant, with more distinct face pattern but less well-defined crown patch. Similar also to Puna Ground-Tyrant, but darker above, with more well-defined superciliary and more obvious color in crown. Cf. also Taczanowski's and Cinereous ground-tyrants. **VOICE** Call a high "*tseet*" or "*chwip!*" **Co, E, Bo, Ch**

ANDEAN NEGRITO

♀

♂

pallidiceps

occipitalis

RUFOUS-NAPED
GROUND-
TYRANT

TACZANOWSKI'S
GROUND-TYRANT

CINEREOUS
GROUND-TYRANT

PUNA
GROUND-TYRANT

BLACK-FRONTED
GROUND-TYRANT

WHITE-BROWED
GROUND-TYRANT

PLATE
215

LARGE OPEN-HABITAT TYRANTS

Shrike-Tyrants are very large (thrush-sized) flycatchers on open Andean habitats, notable for the heavy bill, often obviously hooked ("shrikelike") at the tip. The two ground-tyrants on this plate are the two largest Muscisaxicola. *Spectacled Tyrant also is an open country, terrestrial flycatcher but is only a vagrant to Peru.*

1 WHITE-TAILED SHRIKE-TYRANT *Agriornis albicauda* * 25 cm (10 in)
Rare in the Andes at 2400–4300 m. Apparently formerly was more common and widespread; now is much less common than Black-billed Shrike-Tyrant. Poorly known; causes for recent decline in abundance are not understood. May have greater preference for semiarid shrub zones (rather than open puna grasslands and pastures occupied by Black-billed). Distinguished, with care, from Black-billed by larger size; much stouter bill, with more pronounced hook; pale brownish mandible, especially at base (but note that immature Black-billed also may show pale base to mandible); more prominent white crescents above and below eye; and purer white throat with broader, blacker streaks. Iris brown (iris of Black-billed often, although perhaps not always, gray or gray-brown). Also typically is browner below, with buffier belly and vent; and has more "bull-headed" shape. **VOICE** Song a haphazard series of loud "*tew*" and "*pew!*" notes. Calls include loud "*pew!*" notes similar to White-capped Tanager, but no habitat overlap, also a metallic "*teck.*" **E, Bo, Ch**

2 GRAY-BELLIED SHRIKE-TYRANT *Agriornis micropterus* * 24 cm (9½ in)
Rare in Andes of southern Peru at 3800–4100 m, where possibly only an austral migrant. Behavior and habitat similar to that of Black-billed Shrike-Tyrant. Differs from other shrike-tyrants by largely dark tail, with only outer web of outer rectrices white. Also browner above and buffier below than Black-billed, with stouter bill with pale mandible. **Bo, Ch**

3 BLACK-BILLED SHRIKE-TYRANT *Agriornis montanus* * 23 cm (9 in)
The most common and widespread shrike-tyrant. Found in open habitats throughout the Andes, 3000–4500 m, locally down to 2200 m. Bill is relatively slender for a shrike-tyrant and typically is entirely black (some, especially immatures, may show pale base to mandible, however). Tail is almost entirely white, other than central pair of rectrices. Upperparts are relatively gray, and breast is washed with gray. **VOICE** Song a loud, musical, whistled, rising-falling "WEEYOO." Calls include a rising "*wee?*" **Co, E, Bo, Ch**

4 [SPECTACLED TYRANT *Hymenops perspicillatus*] * 16 cm (6¼ in)
Very rare austral migrant to southeast. The few records all are sight records of birds in female plumage; most are from Amazonia, with a single record from Andes of Cuzco (3350 m). Found in open areas, especially marshes, also in wet grasslands. Perches conspicuously in bushes or on fence posts, or forages on the ground. Both sexes have yellow fleshy orbital ring, much larger and more conspicuous in male. Black-and-white male distinctive. Female is brown and streaky, similar to a pipit; note whitish iris, eye wattle, rufous primaries, and dark tarsi. **Br, Bo, Ch**

5 OCHRE-NAPED GROUND-TYRANT *Muscisaxicola flavinucha* * 20 cm (7¾ in)
A fairly common austral migrant (Mar–Oct). Found at 3800–4900 m in short or grazed grassland, often at bogs or sites that are relatively moist. Rivaled in size only by White-fronted Ground-Tyrant; like that species has pale margins to coverts and secondaries, and white lores and forehead. Note smaller size and contrasting ochre patch on rear crown. **VOICE** Calls include a high "*tseet*," sometimes in a series. **Bo, Ch**

6 WHITE-FRONTED GROUND-TYRANT *Muscisaxicola albifrons* 24 cm (9½ in)
The largest ground-tyrant. Uncommon to fairly common. Characteristically forages at bogs with cushion plants and matted vegetation, 3700–4900 m. No well-defined crown patch, although rear crown is washed with tawny-rufous. Identified by large size (approaching that of shrike-tyrants), plain crown, and prominent pale edges to wing coverts and inner remiges. Also note whitish lores and forehead. **VOICE** Calls include a soft series of notes "*tip-tip-tip….*" **Bo, Ch**

WHITE-TAILED
SHRIKE-TYRANT

BLACK-BILLED SHRIKE-TYRANT

GRAY-BELLIED
SHRIKE-TYRANT

SPECTACLED TYRANT

♀

♂

OCHRE-NAPED
GROUND-TYRANT

WHITE-
FRONTED
GROUND-
TYRANT

PLATE
216
BUSH-TYRANTS AND CLIFF FLYCATCHER

Large Andean flycatchers. Cnemarchus has a conspicuous white wing patch. Myiotheretes and Polioxolmis bush-tyrants and Cliff Flycatcher show extensive rufous on the wing in flight.

1 RED-RUMPED BUSH-TYRANT *Cnemarchus erythropygius* * 23 cm (9 in)
Rare, on east slope of Andes at 3000–4300 m, usually in shrub zone at treeline or in *Polylepis* groves. Found as singles or pairs; does not associate with mixed-species flocks. Perches in an exposed site, from which it drops to ground for prey. Readily identified by striking rufous, gray, and white plumage. **VOICE** Song (?) a rather unpatterned series of mellow mewed whistles and rich churring notes. Calls include loud, piercing, clear "*TEEER!*," "*PEEP!*," "*pee-ip*," and "*tew*" notes and burrier "*dzeeer*" and "*djip*" notes. **Co, E, Bo**

2 STREAK-THROATED BUSH-TYRANT *Myiotheretes striaticollis* * 23 cm (9 in)
Uncommon but widespread in Andes, 1700–3700 m (rarely in openings down to base of Andes). Usually found in montane scrub and humid montane forest edge, especially at landslides and other natural openings. Forages from exposed perches, often relatively high; sallies to air to capture prey or, less often, drops to ground. Solitary or in pairs; does not join flocks. Large. Extensively tawny-rufous below; throat white, streaked black. Inner webs of remiges extensively cinnamon-rufous, prominent in flight. Cf. Cliff Flycatcher and Rufous-bellied Bush-Tyrant. **VOICE** Fairly quiet. Song a loud, descending whistled "*HEEW*" or "*HEEE'wit*" given periodically, its pitch changed occasionally. Calls a squeaky "*seebit*" and songlike notes. **Co, E, Bo**

3 CLIFF FLYCATCHER *Hirundinea ferruginea* * 18.5 cm (7¼ in)
Locally fairly common along east slope of Andes and outlying ridges; 400–2200 m, locally to 2700 m. Singles, pairs, or family groups perch in open at large openings, such as cliffs, landslides, and road cuts, in humid montane forest. Forages with long aerial sallies, often returning to original perch. Note large size, deep rufous underparts, and extensive rufous in wings. Streak-throated Bush-Tyrant usually found at higher elevations, but locally may overlap; bush-tyrant is even larger, paler brown above, cinnamon tawny below (not deep rufous), and has broad white "bib" (throat and breast) prominently streaked dusky. **VOICE** Call a characteristic, loud, laughing chatter; first note higher and rising: "*REE-chichichichichi!*" Song a rising phrase followed by a descending chatter "*ti'tuee? tchi'ti'ti'ter!*" **Co, E, Br, Bo, Ch**

4 RUFOUS-WEBBED BUSH-TYRANT *Polioxolmis rufipennis* * 21–21.5 cm (8¼–8½ in)
Uncommon but widely distributed in Andes, 3100–4600 m. Often in semiarid sites, in montane scrub or *Polylepis* woodlots. Alone or in pairs, and does not associate with mixed-species flocks. From an exposed perch in a tree, bush, or on a rock or cliff, drops to ground to capture prey; often hovers. Light gray with pale belly and extensive rufous on inner webs of wings and tail. **VOICE** Rather quiet. Song a repeated, high, descending "*seer*" note. Call a descending, quavering "*tee'e'ip.*" **Bo, Ch**

5 RUFOUS-BELLIED BUSH-TYRANT *Myiotheretes fuscorufus* 19 cm (7½ in)
Rare to uncommon in canopy of humid montane forest on east slope of Andes at 2200–3400 m, where overlaps with Smoky Bush-Tyrant; may be present in same flocks. Behavior and habitat similar to Smoky, although perhaps more partial to tall secondary forest, disturbed forest, and forest edge. Much paler than Smoky, with tawny belly and broad rufous wing bars. Cf. also larger Streak-throated Bush-Tyrant. **VOICE** Song a vigorous "*pip-pip-pip pi-DOO*"; the number of introductory "*pip*" notes is variable (2–4), and terminal phrase may be repeated once. Call a rising-falling series of rich "*pip*" notes, similar to Smoke-colored Pewee, but the pewee typically does not vary in pitch. **Bo**

6 SMOKY BUSH-TYRANT *Myiotheretes fumigatus* * 20.5 cm (8 in)
Uncommon in humid montane forest and forest edge along east slope of Andes, 2300–3450 m; also on west slope in northwest. Perches conspicuously in canopy, singly or in small groups. May associate with mixed-species flocks. Sallies for prey, primarily to leaves, epiphytes, and moss-covered branches. Very dark sooty brown (with rufous visible on wings in flight). Cf. Smoke-colored Pewee, which is gray, more crested, and lacks rufous in wings. **VOICE** Song a quiet "*pew*" followed by a louder "*PEE'ew.*" Calls a series of mewing, rich notes "*wip-wip-wip.*" Similar to Smoke-colored Pewee and other bush-tyrants, but not so punctuated. **Co, E**

RED-RUMPED BUSH-TYRANT

STREAK-THROATED BUSH-TYRANT

CLIFF FLYCATCHER

RUFOUS-WEBBED
BUSH-TYRANT

RUFOUS-BELLIED
BUSH-TYRANT

SMOKY BUSH-TYRANT

PLATE
217

FOREST UNDERSTORY CHAT-TYRANTS

Chat-tyrants (Ochthoeca) are small to medium-sized Andean flycatchers. Species on this plate forage low within cover of humid montane forest. They are difficult to see well and are not very vocal. Forage as singles or in pairs and do not associate with mixed-species flocks. See plate 218 for chat-tyrants of more open habitats.

1 YELLOW-BELLIED CHAT-TYRANT *Ochthoeca diadema* * 12.5 cm (5 in)
Similar to Golden-browed Chat-Tyrant in behavior and elevational distribution (2300–3100 m), and replaces that species north and west of the Marañón Valley. Distinguished from other chat-tyrants by yellow-green underparts. Also note yellow superciliary, golden yellow lores, and rufous or tawny-brown wing bars. **VOICE** Dawn song (northwest Ecuador) a high, descending sneeze: "*ts'eew.*" Call a high thin squeaky chatter. **Co, E**

2 CROWNED CHAT-TYRANT *Ochthoeca frontalis* * 12.5–13 cm (5 in)
Fairly common, but quiet and inconspicuous, in humid montane forest along east side of Andes at 2800–3700 m, locally down to 2300 m. Note white superciliary with golden yellow lores, and smoky gray breast. Wings plain (south to La Libertad; *frontalis*) or with rufous wing bars (Huánuco south; *spodionota*); but in some *spodionota*, especially in the Apurímac Valley, wing bars are reduced or absent. No geographic overlap with Jelski's Chat-Tyrant. Cf. Golden-browed Chat-Tyrant, with which there is extensive geographic overlap but which is found at lower elevations. **VOICE** Dawn song (*frontalis*) a descending "*tsew*" sometimes followed by a short, squeaky chatter. Calls squeaky chatters and thin trills. Dawn song (*spodionota*) a high, descending whistle followed by a lower rising note: "*tseeeut... ree?*" sometimes interspersed with a squeaky chatter. Call a long, abruptly rising, then slowly falling, thin, high trill: "*WREEzzeeeeerrrrr.*" Possibly indistinguishable from Golden-browed Chat-Tyrant. Also a rising "*psi-dzreeee?*" **Co, E, Bo**

3 JELSKI'S CHAT-TYRANT *Ochthoeca jelskii* 12.5 cm (5 in)
Uncommon along west slope of Andes and both slopes of upper Marañón Valley, 2300–3200 m. Found in understory of montane forest and in moist shrubby zones. No geographic overlap with Crowned or Golden-browed chat-tyrants, although distributions closely approach one another in eastern Andes, where Jelski's is found on west (Marañón Valley) side of Andes and the two other species on east-facing slopes. Very similar to southern (*spodionota*) Crowned (no overlap), but more rufescent above (especially on rump). Cf. also Piura Chat-Tyrant. **VOICE** Song a high, squeaky "*tseee!*" ending with a "*krrr*" phrase when excited. Calls squeaky chatters and descending high trills. **E**

4 GOLDEN-BROWED CHAT-TYRANT *Ochthoeca pulchella* * 12–13 cm (4¾–5 in)
Similar to Crowned Chat-Tyrant, but Golden-browed is found at lower elevations, 1800–3100 m. Fairly common in understory of humid montane forest. Always has pale yellow superciliary (brightest on lores) and broad rufous wing bars. Northern *similis* (south at least to Pasco) is washed with olive-brown below with buffier belly, and is more rufous-brown above; southern *pulchella* (not illustrated) is purer gray below and darker brown above. Both are distinguished from Crowned by yellower superciliary and by elevation; also note that in northern Peru, Crowned does not have wing bars (although in southern Peru both species do). Cf. also Jelski's (no geographic overlap). **VOICE** Call a long, abruptly rising, then slowly falling, thin, high trill: "*WREEzzeeeeerrrrr,*" also a rising "*dzreeeeeee?*" possibly indistinguishable from Crowned. **Bo**

5 SLATY-BACKED CHAT-TYRANT *Ochthoeca cinnamomeiventris* * 13–13.5 cm (5–5¼ in)
Uncommon in humid montane forest along east slope of Andes, 1800–3300 m, locally down to 1500 m. Almost always close to rushing streams or in humid gullies. Plumage mostly slaty gray with white superciliary. Breast and belly extensively dark reddish brown close to Ecuadorian border (*cinnamomeiventris*); reddish brown color restricted to breast band south and east of Marañón Valley (*angustifasciata, thoracica*), also very locally on west bank of Marañón in southeastern Cajamarca. **VOICE** Song (*cinnamomeiventris*) a high, thin, rising-falling buzzy note: "*drzeeew*" or "*drzeeer.*" Call a high series of thin "*tsi-keet*" notes. Song (*angustifasciata, thoracica*) a high, descending, whistled "*tseeew*" often followed by a squeaky "*tsee-tsip.*" Similar to various fruiteaters, but those usually have higher-pitched voices and lack the terminal phrase. Call a chatter, sometimes given in duet: "*tsee-tsikit tsikit tsikit.*" **Co, E, Bo**

YELLOW-BELLIED
CHAT-TYRANT

CROWNED CHAT-TYRANT

frontalis

spodionota

JELSKI'S CHAT-TYRANT

similis

GOLDEN-BROWED
CHAT-TYRANT

SLATY-BACKED
CHAT-TYRANT

cinnamomeiventris

PLATE
218

SCRUB AND FOREST-EDGE CHAT-TYRANTS
AND TUMBES TYRANT

Chat-tyrants on this plate generally are larger and longer-tailed than species on plate 217. Usually use exposed perches, at forest edge, or in scrub and other open habitats, and typically drop to ground to capture prey. Forage as singles or in pairs, and do not associate with mixed-species flocks. Tumbes Tyrant is similar to chat-tyrants but is restricted to northwest Peru.

1 D'ORBIGNY'S CHAT-TYRANT *Ochthoeca oenanthoides* * 15–15.5 cm (6 in)

Fairly common in montane scrub, forest edge, and *Polylepis* woodlands on west slope and in intermontane valleys, 3400–4600 m, locally down to 3000 m. Generally in drier sites than Brown-backed Chat-Tyrant, but both may occur together or near each other in Cuzco and Puno. Upperparts of d'Orbigny's much duller, grayer; also has plain wings, and superciliary is broad and pure white. Belly deeper buff (more rufous, less cinnamon-buff), throat grayer, and throat and belly colors more sharply defined (rather than gradually merging together as in Brown-backed). **VOICE** Song a weak, squeaky chatter, often in duet of "*tee'per*" phrases. **Bo, Ch**

2 BROWN-BACKED CHAT-TYRANT *Ochthoeca fumicolor* * 15–15.5 cm (6 in)

Fairly common on east side of Andes at 2500–4100 m, also on west slope in northwest. At edge of humid montane forest, in *Polylepis* woodland, and in paramo with scattered shrubs. Superciliary broad and buffy in widespread *brunneifrons*, but narrower and dirty white in eastern Cuzco and Puno (*berlepschi*). Cf. d'Orbigny's Chat-Tyrant (only limited geographic overlap). **VOICE** Song a weak, squeaky chatter, often in duet, of "*tsi'wit*" and "*tee*" notes. Call high squeaky phrase: "*tulee tualee? tulee tualee?....*" Also single "*tew*" notes. **Co, E, Bo**

3 TUMBES TYRANT *Tumbezia salvini* 13.5 cm (5¼ in)

Inconspicuous but locally fairly common in northwest, in dry forest, especially along river courses, and tall arid scrub below 1000 m. Perches relatively low, and usually within cover of vegetation. Solitary or in pairs. **VOICE** Song (?) a quiet, mellow rapid chatter, "*dyer'r'r'r'r*," sometimes ending with a higher note, and occasionally interspersed with a shorter "*DEE'dew*." Calls a more emphatic, squeaky "*PSI'dyer'r'r'r*," and a clear, descending "*pew*." **ENDEMIC**

4 RUFOUS-BREASTED CHAT-TYRANT *Ochthoeca rufipectoralis* * 12.5–13 cm (5 in)

Fairly common and widespread, on both slopes of Andes at 2300–4100 m, at humid montane forest edge and open woodland (such as *Polylepis*) and shrub zones. Rufous breast and throat contrast with white belly. Superciliary strikingly white. Upperparts largely brown and wings with broad rufous wing bars in most of Peru (various subspecies); upperparts grayer and wings plain in eastern Cuzco and Puno (*rufipectoralis*). **VOICE** Dawn song a low, slightly buzzy note followed by a higher whistle given in series: "*djr'tit wiZEEeer?... djr'tit wiZEEeer?....*" Calls (all subspecies), often in duet, a low, buzzy, chattered phrase in a short series: "*bzzter*" or "*bzz'tee*"; call drier, buzzier "*tzzz*" phrases in Urubamba Valley (and elsewhere? *tectricialis*). Song of *rufipectoralis* a high buzzy phrase followed by a buzzy whistle, in series: "*tsi'jit tzee... tsi'jit tzee....*" **Co, E, Bo**

5 PIURA CHAT-TYRANT *Ochthoeca piurae* 12.5 cm (5 in)

Rare and local in northwest, at edge of semihumid forest or in montane scrub at 1400–2850 m. Overlaps locally with similar White-browed Chat-Tyrant but often found at lower elevations. Significantly smaller, is somewhat richer brown above, and has very broad rufous wing bars; White-browed does not show such prominent wing bars (although beware of juvenile White-browed, in which the cinnamon wing bars may be more evident than in adults). **VOICE** Song (?) a thin, high trill similar to Crowned Chat-Tyrant (no overlap). **ENDEMIC**

6 WHITE-BROWED CHAT-TYRANT *Ochthoeca leucophrys* * 15–15.5 cm (6 in)

One of the most common and widespread chat-tyrants of open country. Found in open shrub zones, open woodlands, and cultivated areas with hedgerows or shrubs, often in relatively dry situations at 2400–4200 m; does not occur on more humid east-facing slope of Andes. Also found, locally, in lomas in south. Very gray, with a bold white superciliary. Wings plain, with white edgings to secondaries, and sometimes very narrow cinnamon wing bars; wing bars broader and more rufous in juveniles (not illustrated). **VOICE** Song (?) a squeaky chatter, usually in duet: "*wu-chew'widdu*." Calls a squeaky, rising-falling "*weeo*," and a higher "*weedee?*" **E, Bo, Ch**

D'ORBIGNY'S
CHAT-TYRANT

berlepschi

brunneifrons

BROWN-BACKED CHAT-TYRANT

RUFOUS-BREASTED CHAT-TYRANT

TUMBES TYRANT

rufipectoralis

PIURA CHAT-TYRANT

WHITE-BROWED
CHAT-TYRANT

PLATE
219

LARGE, STREAKED FLYCATCHERS

Large, streaked flycatchers that often perch in relatively exposed sites in canopy. Variegated and Piratic flycatchers are relatively small-billed; Myiodynastes are larger with stouter bills.

1 VARIEGATED FLYCATCHER *Empidonomus varius* * 16.5–17.5 cm (6½–7 in)
Uncommon austral migrant (primarily Mar–Oct) in Amazonia, up to 500 m. Found at forest edge (especially of seasonally flooded forest), in pastures, and in second growth. Apparently primarily a passage migrant in south, but winters from near the Amazon north to Ecuador. Eats fruit, also sallies to air for insects. Not as confined to canopy as Piratic. Cf. also larger, heavier billed Streaked Flycatcher. **VOICE** Generally silent in Peru. Call a thin, shrill "*tzz'ee.*" **Co, E, Br, Bo**

2 PIRATIC FLYCATCHER *Legatus leucophaius* * 15 cm (6 in)
Fairly common and widespread in Amazonia (up to 1400 m), in canopy of humid forest edge, tall second growth, and clearings with scattered tall trees. Heard far more often than seen. Primarily frugivorous. Named after "piratic" behavior: usurps nests of other species (often of caciques or oropendolas). Smaller than Variegated Flycatcher, with stubbier bill that lacks pale base to mandible; lacks rufous in wings and tail; upperparts plain (mottled in Variegated); and has less extensive white margins on wings (although wing coverts and secondaries of both species may be edged pale). **VOICE** Song a loud, high, rising-falling whistle: "*wseeEEEeee,*" often interspersed with a quiet, stuttered "*hee-hee-hee-hee*" or "*pi'pee-pee.*" Call a slower series of "*pee*" notes. **Co, E, Br, Bo**

3 SULPHUR-BELLIED FLYCATCHER *Myiodynastes luteiventris* 21 cm (8¼ in)
Fairly common boreal migrant (Sep–Apr). Distribution not well known; perhaps most common in foothills and adjacent lowlands, 350–1200 m, of central and southern Peru but may winter in small numbers farther north and east. Apparently migrates through most of Amazonian Peru. Canopy of humid forest and at forest edge. Very similar to Streaked Flycatcher, but dusky moustachial streaks are heavier and often converge on chin, superciliary whiter, and belly less streaked and deeper yellow. Also, little or no rufous in wings. **VOICE** Unlikely to sing in Peru. Call a squeaky "*SQUEEaLEEew.*" **Co, E, Br, Bo**

4 STREAKED FLYCATCHER *Myiodynastes maculatus* * 21.5 cm (8½ in); *solitarius* 23 cm (9 in)
Fairly common in Amazonia and northwest. Large, blackish, heavily streaked *solitarius* breeds on east slope of Andes up to 2000 m in southern (and perhaps central) Peru; also a common austral migrant (primarily Mar–Sep) throughout Amazonia, locally up to 1400 m. Juvenile (not illustrated) similar but has narrow rufous edges to wing coverts, remiges, and to crown. Found in canopy of tall humid forest, especially at forest edge, clearings with scattered tall trees (even near houses), and tall second growth. Very different *maculatus* resident in northern Amazonia, where primarily on forested river islands and less commonly in adjacent varzea. Both *maculatus* and similar *chapmani* (dry forest in northwest, up to 1200 m) are smaller and brown with prominent rufous edges to remiges. Cf. Sulphur-bellied Flycatcher. **VOICE** Dawn song (*chapmani*) a rising note followed by a short musical chatter: "*reEET-chewlew'put.*" Calls a dry "*tek*" and excited squeaky chatters. Call (*maculatus*) a flat "*bik.*" Dawn song (*solitarius*) a squeaky: "*reEET tiWICHu'whit.*" Calls a rising, slightly metallic "*whit,*" also an excited chattered series and a quiet puttering. **Co, E, Br, Bo, Ch**

5 BAIRD'S FLYCATCHER *Myiodynastes bairdii* 23 cm (9 in)
Fairly common in northwest in tall arid scrub and dry forests, up to 1200 m. Lacks a dark malar stripe. Note black mask, unstreaked upperparts, and extensive rufous in wings and tail. Breast shows little or no streaking. **VOICE** Dawn song a loud, accelerating series of burry notes, until a final rising chatter: "*rewTCHI! rewTCHI! reTCHIrewTCHIrewTCHI-tip'ti'chip-awee?*" Calls single "*rewTCHI!*" phrases, low "*pew*" notes, and various squeaky phrases in interactions. **E**

6 GOLDEN-CROWNED FLYCATCHER *Myiodynastes chrysocephalus* * 21 cm (8¼ in)
Uncommon along east slope of Andes at 600–2700 m; also on west slope in northern Piura. Humid montane forest and forest edges. Wings plain in widespread *chrysocephalus*, or with more prominent rufous margins to remiges north of Marañón (*minor*; not illustrated), which also has slightly crisper facial pattern. **VOICE** Dawn song (*minor*) a thin, squeaky "*PSEE'chirr'rr.*" Calls loud, squeaky series of "*REE'SQUEE!*" and a descending "*PSEW!*" Dawn song (*chrysocephalus*) a loud "*REE'chewee?*" Call a metallic, slightly squeaky "*rew-TCHI?*" **Co, E, Bo**

VARIEGATED FLYCATCHER

PIRATIC
FLYCATCHER

STREAKED
FLYCATCHER

solitarius

SULPHUR-BELLIED
FLYCATCHER

BAIRD'S FLYCATCHER

GOLDEN-CROWNED
FLYCATCHER

PLATE
220

MEDIUM-SIZED YELLOW-BELLIED
FLYCATCHERS

Medium-sized, yellow-bellied flycatchers, most of which are found in forest canopy; cf. species on plate 221. The two Myiozetetes *have relatively short, stubby bills; bills of Yellow-browed Tyrant and* Conopias *are longer and more slender. Nests of* Conopias *are cups placed in cavities in trees (although nest of Lemon-browed is not known). Nests of* Myiozetetes *are domed, with a side entrance.*

1 DUSKY-CHESTED FLYCATCHER *Myiozetetes luteiventris* * 14.5–15 cm (5¾–6 in)

Small, uncommon *Myiozetetes* of forest canopy in Amazonian lowlands, locally up to 1000 m, found at borders of humid forest, at forest openings such as treefalls, and along smaller rivers and streams (not in varzea). Note unpatterned brown head (with semiconcealed yellow-orange crown patch, reduced in female) and blurry olive streaks on breast. Often cocks tail. Cf. Gray-capped Flycatcher. **VOICE** Calls a mellow, nasal *"dew,"* also low gruff chatters, often in duet: *"dew djrr-djrr-djrr-djrr,"* usually accompanied by wing flapping. Dawn song a loud *"dew DJEEdjrREEdrr!"* **Co, E, Br, Bo**

2 GRAY-CAPPED FLYCATCHER *Myiozetetes granadensis* * 17 cm (6¾ in)

Common and widespread in Amazonia, up to 1400 m, in second growth and at forest edge, especially near water. Forages at all heights, in pairs or in small groups. Head gray with dusky sides, ill-defined whitish superciliary and forehead. Rear crown often looks "ragged" or slightly crested; semiconcealed crown patch reddish orange. Iris often pale gray or gray-brown. Dusky-chested Flycatcher smaller, with blurry streaks on breast. Cf. also Sulphury Flycatcher and Tropical Kingbird, which are larger with heavier bills and do not have whitish forecrown and superciliary. **VOICE** Song (?) a sharp *"dear-DEE'dzzeer!"* Calls nasal *"geer," "dew-dew,"* and a short *"bek,"* often in series. Reminiscent of Dusky-chested, but note different habitats. **Co, E, Br, Bo**

3 YELLOW-BROWED TYRANT *Satrapa icterophrys* 15.5–16 cm (6–7 in)

Rare austral migrant to southeast, occasionally up to 1000 m. Most often encountered as single individuals in low river-edge forest or scrub, or in shrubby second growth. Distinguished from more common Amazonian "stripe-headed" flycatchers (*Myiozetetes, Pitangus,* etc.) by smaller size, yellow (not white) superciliary, and more slender bill. Unlikely to overlap with Lemon-browed Flycatcher of Andes; Lemon-browed also lacks wing bars and has longer, broader superciliary (extending onto nape). **Co, Br, Bo**

4 LEMON-BROWED FLYCATCHER *Conopias cinchoneti* * 15.5–16 cm (6–6¼ in)

Uncommon along east slope of Andes, 800–1950 m. Found in canopy at edge of humid montane forest and at openings such as landslides or agricultural clearings. Typically in pairs or small groups. Readily identified by broad yellow superciliary; cf. Yellow-browed Tyrant (with which overlap is unlikely). Juvenile (not illustrated) has yellowish-buff edging to wing coverts and secondaries, and pale scaling on upperparts and crown. **VOICE** Calls a loud, plaintive laughing *"TI-heeheeheeheeheeer!,"* descending at the very end, or a shorter *"TI heeheer."* Similar to Cinnamon-faced Tyrannulet, but louder, more forceful. Also short *"ti-tew"* notes. **Co, E**

5 THREE-STRIPED FLYCATCHER *Conopias trivirgatus* * 13.5–14 cm (5–5½ in)

Status and distribution very poorly known. Perhaps more regular in Pacaya-Samiria area, but there also are records from scattered sites from northern Loreto south to Madre de Dios. Pairs or small groups in canopy of tall humid forest, usually in river floodplains, and often associated with mixed-species flocks. Smaller than Yellow-throated, with shorter bill; white superciliaries do not meet above bill; crown gray (not black); and back pale olive (contrasting more with dark wings). Also lacks a semiconcealed crown patch. Cf. also Social Flycatcher. More readily located and identified by **VOICE** Call a low, burry *"djer"* and *"djeer-djeer-djeer,"* also an excited *"chiky-chiky-djeer-djeer."* **E, Br, Bo**

6 YELLOW-THROATED FLYCATCHER *Conopias parvus* 15–15.5 cm (6 in)

Locally fairly common in northern Amazonia, in canopy of forest on sandy substrates and on old terraces in terra firme. Usually in pairs or small groups. Superficially similar to Social Flycatcher, but slightly smaller with larger bill and yellow throat; also white stripe on head is broader across forehead and continues in band across nape; crown and sides of head are black (not dusky gray); and semiconcealed crown patch is yellow. Most readily located and identified by **VOICE** Calls a bubbly, liquid, descending laughing *"tewee-hee'hee'hee,"* a louder, excited, more monotone *"TCHREE WEE'HEE WEE'HEE WEE'HEE HEER!"* and a quiet, rising *"tu-ti-tree."* **Co, E, Br, Bo**

DUSKY-CHESTED FLYCATCHER

GRAY-CAPPED FLYCATCHER

YELLOW-BROWED TYRANT

LEMON-BROWED
FLYCATCHER

THREE-STRIPED
FLYCATCHER

YELLOW-THROATED
FLYCATCHER

PLATE
221

LARGE STRIPE-HEADED FLYCATCHERS

Similar yellow-breasted, medium-sized to large flycatchers with bold black-and-white head patterns. Note bill size, details of head pattern, presence or absence of rufous in wings, voice, and habitat.

1 BOAT-BILLED FLYCATCHER *Megarynchus pitangua* * 23–23.5 cm (9–9¼ in)

Fairly common in Amazonia, up to 1200 m, in canopy at forest edge, in river-edge forest, and at lake and stream margins (*pitangua*). Also uncommon in semideciduous forest in Tumbes (*chrysogaster*). Superficially similar to Great Kiskadee, but bill is massively thick and broad, with strongly arched culmen; also wings are largely brown with only a limited amount of cinnamon edgings to remiges. Nest a simple cup. **VOICE** Song (*pitangua*) a falling piercing note followed by a rising thin buzz: "*TCHEE'EERdzuweet?*" Call a characteristic, slow series of rising, buzzy notes, falling at the very end: "*dzwee'zwee'zwee'zwee'zweew.*" Also a loud, piercing "*TCHEE'ee'eer*" or "*TCHWEE'wee'wee'weer,*" often in series or duet. Song of *chrysogaster* perhaps thinner. Call a rapid buzzy "*chzew-chzew-chzew-chzewerrr,*" also piercing notes similar to those of *pitangua*. **Co, E, Br, Bo**

2 LESSER KISKADEE *Pitangus lictor* * 17.5–18 cm (6¾–7 in)

Small, slender-billed kiskadee intimately associated with water; perches low over oxbow lakes and relatively sluggish rivers throughout Amazonia, up to 750 m. Usually in pairs. Much less conspicuous than larger Great Kiskadee, and more closely associated with water. Also has slimmer proportions and more slender bill. Bill much longer than in *Myiozetetes*. Readily identified by distinctive **VOICE** Calls a dry, raspy "*dzrEE-bee*" or "*dzrEE-bee-bee,*" also gives a throaty series of gruff "*daw*" notes. **Co, E, Br, Bo**

3 GREAT KISKADEE *Pitangus sulphuratus* * 21–22 cm (8¼–8¾ in)

Common and conspicuous in Amazonia, up to 1200 m. Found at margins of rivers and oxbow lakes, forest edge, and second growth; frequent in towns and clearings. Usually forages relatively low (midlevels and lower) and often uses a fairly conspicuous perch. Eats a wide variety of foods, including fruit and insects but also small vertebrates. Nest a large globe with side entrance. Note large bill and rufous margins to remiges, wing coverts, and tail. Rictus often pink. *Myiozetetes* are smaller with much stubbier bills. Cf. also Lesser Kiskadee and Boat-billed Flycatcher. **VOICE** Calls, a ubiquitous and familiar sound along rivers and second growth in Amazonia, a loud rising or rising-falling mewed "*weeeeee*" or "*geeeeep*" and a loud "*KEEK-keer'DEER!*" (source of both English and most local names, e.g., "*Bien-te-vi*"), often in duet. Dawn song a loud "*reew REEW'chir'r'r'r'r.*" **Co, E, Br, Bo, Ch**

4 [RUSTY-MARGINED FLYCATCHER] *Myiozetetes cayanensis* * 17 cm (6¾ in)

Locally fairly common, but restricted to far southeast; also should be looked for along lower Río Yavarí. Often close to water, such as at margins of oxbow lakes; also at edges to pastures. Very similar to Social Flycatcher, with which it overlaps. Rusty-margined has more contrasting facial pattern (dark stripes on head blacker; whiter superciliaries; and superciliaries meet over bill); more prominent rufous margins to remiges; and plainer wing coverts (Social has narrow light tips to wing coverts). Juvenile Social has brighter, more rufous edges to remiges but also has more prominent cinnamon tips to wing coverts. Rusty-margined also browner above, less olive, and semiconcealed crown spot is yellower. Also different **VOICE** Calls a high, thin, descending whistle: "*wheeeeeeuu*" (longer than similar call of Dusky-capped Flycatcher), also a rising whistle that becomes a weak chatter similar to that of Social: "*weeeeeeechi-chi-chi-chi*" or "*weeeeeiichiriro-chirio-chirio.*" **Co, E, Br, Bo**

5 SOCIAL FLYCATCHER *Myiozetetes similis* * 17–17.5 cm (6¾ in)

One of most widespread and characteristic birds of second growth and forest edge in Amazonia, up to 1800 m; also in Tumbes. Often in pairs, sometimes found in small groups. Forages at all heights above ground, but typically at midlevels. Noisy and conspicuous. Dark stripes on head sooty gray (not black); also note plain wings and red or reddish orange semiconcealed crown patch. Juvenile (not illustrated) has rufous edges to wing coverts and remiges. Cf. Gray-capped Flycatcher, kiskadees. **VOICE** Call, ubiquitous along rivers and towns in Amazonia, a metallic "*tche-tchetche-tche,*" often introduced by a high, falling "*tsew.*" Also single, metallic "*tchep*" or "*tsep*" notes. Dawn song a metallic note then a high, descending note and a short, low chatter: "*tchep.. tsew-ti'ti'chireh.*" **Co, E, Br, Bo**

BOAT-BILLED FLYCATCHER

LESSER KISKADEE

GREAT KISKADEE

RUSTY-MARGINED FLYCATCHER

SOCIAL FLYCATCHER

PLATE
222

MEDIUM-SIZED GRAY AND BLACK FLYCATCHERS

A diverse set of flycatchers, which are black- or gray-and-white.

1 LONG-TAILED TYRANT *Colonia colonus* * male 25–26.5 cm (9¾–10½ in), female 20–23.5 cm (8–9¼ in)

Characteristic flycatcher of forest edge and clearings in Andean foothills, up to 2300 m. Local also in Amazonia, especially in south in areas with hilly topography; possibly some lowland records may refer to wandering individuals? Often in pairs. Perches in exposed sites such as dead trees or snags; sallies to air for insects. Tail streamers longer in male. Crown whitish or light gray in widespread *niveiceps*; duskier or spotted with dusky in *fuscicapillus* of Amazonas and Loreto. Juvenile uniformly black, lacks tail streamers. **VOICE** Call a rising, squeaky "*weee?*," shorter "*whe*" notes, and a short, musical chatter: "*whi whi whi'wi'her.*" Song a rising note followed by a short chatter: "*weee? tche-chiry.*" **Co, E, Br, Bo**

2 FORK-TAILED FLYCATCHER *Tyrannus savana* * male 38–40 cm (15–15¾ in), female 28–30 cm (11–11¾ in)

Common austral migrant to Amazonia, up to 1000 m; rare vagrant to Andes or coast. Primarily occurs in passage (Feb–Apr, Aug–Oct), when may be found in large flocks, but small numbers also winter (May–Aug) in north. Prefers open or semiopen habitats, but in migration may be found anywhere. Partially insectivorous, but also regularly eats fruit. Juveniles (not illustrated) have shorter tail streamers, are browner above with dusky cap (and no semiconcealed yellow crown spot), and white or buff edgings to wing coverts and remiges. If streamers are missing, may be confused with Eastern Kingbird, which is larger, has square-tipped (not notched) tail with white tip, and is not as distinctly capped. **VOICE** Generally silent in Peru. Calls quiet, deep churring sounds. **Co, E, Br, Bo, Ch**

3 CROWNED SLATY-FLYCATCHER *Empidonomus aurantioatrocristatus* * 16.5–18 cm (6½–7 in)

Uncommon austral migrant (Feb–Nov) to Amazonia, up to 1000 m. Relatively inconspicuous, in canopy at humid forest edge, forest openings, and clearings. Brownish gray above, light gray below with black crown and semiconcealed golden yellow crown patch. Juvenile (not illustrated) duller, with dusky (not black) crown, lacks crown patch, and has narrow white scaling to wing coverts and narrow white edges to secondaries; belly also may be paler, with yellowish wash. Larger than Slaty Elaenia, which lacks dark crown. **VOICE** Generally silent in Peru. Calls thin, high "*tzeer*" and peeping notes. Wings of male may whistle in flight. **Co, E, Br, Bo**

4 EASTERN KINGBIRD *Tyrannus tyrannus* 19–20 cm (7½–8 in)

Common boreal migrant (Sep–Apr) to Amazonia, locally up to 1900 m; rare vagrant to coast. Often in flocks (sometimes very large), in canopy of forest, at forest edge, and in second growth. Communal roosts can number in the hundreds. Largely frugivorous when in tropics, but also sallies for aerial insects. Note 2-toned appearance with white-tipped tail. Juvenile (not illustrated) similar but browner above, with more pronounced white scaling on wing coverts and edges to secondaries. **VOICE** Generally silent in Peru. Call high, thin "*dzee*" notes. **Co, E, Br, Bo, Ch**

5 GRAY MONJITA *Xolmis cinereus* * 21–21.5 cm (8¼–8½ in)

Restricted to Pampas del Heath, where uncommon on grassland with scattered shrubs and woodlots. Perches in relatively exposed sites on tops of shrubs or trees. Pattern recalls a mockingbird (but none present on Heath). Note gray upperparts, black-and-white lines on sides of face, and large white speculum on wing (forms a conspicuous white wing band in flight); tip of tail also usually white or whitish. **VOICE** Song a musical whistled phrase: "*wee huuEEerr.*" Call a single "*wee.*" **Br, Bo**

6 SIRYSTES *Sirystes sibilator* * 18–19 cm (7–7½ in)

Relatively uncommon but widely distributed in Amazonia, up to 700 m, in canopy of forest, especially in varzea and transitional forests, forest edge, and tall second growth. Solitary or in pairs, often with mixed-species flocks. *Myiarchus*-like in proportions, posture, and nest structure. Blackish crown, usually raised in a bushy crest, and dusky wings contrast with pale gray upperparts and white belly; rump white. Wings of first-year birds scaled and edged white and buff. Cf. Eastern Kingbird, tityras, and becards. **VOICE** Song a series of mellow whistles: "*p'weer PEW-pu.*" Call a longer series of "*pew*" notes, the number variable. Also quiet "*kew*" and "*pew*" notes given singly or in haphazard series. **Co, E, Br, Bo**

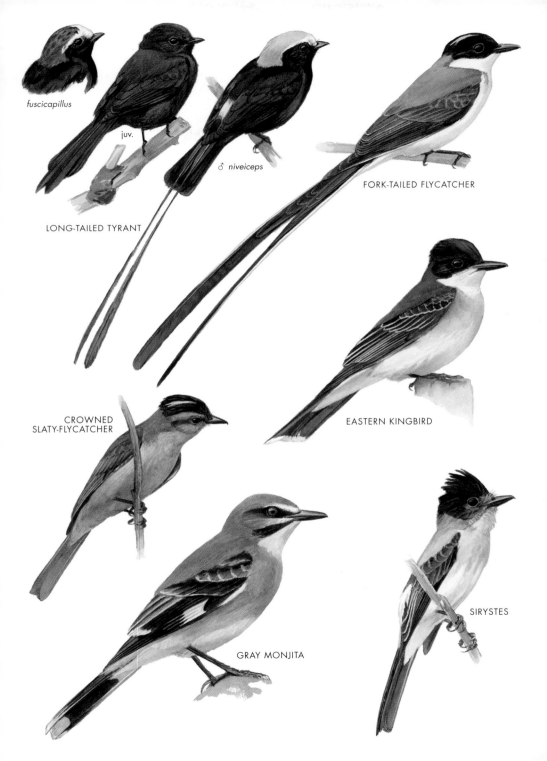

fuscicapillus

juv.

♂ *niveiceps*

LONG-TAILED TYRANT

FORK-TAILED FLYCATCHER

CROWNED
SLATY-FLYCATCHER

EASTERN KINGBIRD

GRAY MONJITA

SIRYSTES

PLATE
223

KINGBIRDS, SULPHURY FLYCATCHER, AND
MYIARCHUS FLYCATCHERS

Kingbirds perch on exposed sites and sally to air for insects; also may eat some fruit. Tropical Kingbird is ubiquitous; learn well as a basis for comparison. Sulphury Flycatcher is an uncommon flycatcher, superficially similar to kingbirds. Also shown here are 2 Myiarchus flycatchers (see plate 224).

1 SULPHURY FLYCATCHER *Tyrannopsis sulphurea* 20 cm (7¾ in)

Rare and local in Amazonia, up to 600 m. Almost always in association with moriche palms (*Mauritia flexuosa*). Usually perches in a relatively high inconspicuous site. Resembles Tropical Kingbird, but bill shorter and deeper; tail square tipped; upperparts browner; and upper breast mottled with olive. Gray-capped Flycatcher smaller, with smaller bill and whitish forecrown. Cf. also much smaller Dusky-chested Flycatcher. **VOICE** Song a shrill, buzzy "*DZEE'E'E djeeh-chew djeeh-chew!*," often in duet. Call a squeaky "*tseee!*" **Co, E, Br, Bo**

2 TROPICAL KINGBIRD *Tyrannus melancholicus* * 22 cm (8½–8¾ in)

One of the most widespread, common, and conspicuous open-country birds of Peru, although absent from high Andes and southwest. Regularly up to 2100 m, locally or seasonally to 3500 m, in cities and towns, in dry scrub and forest, in pastures, along rivers, and at edge of humid forest. Resident, although populations in Amazonia also supplemented in austral winter by southern migrants. Readily recognized by gray head, light gray throat, yellow underparts, and long, notched tail. Juvenile (not illustrated) paler below, with whiter throat and narrow rufous tips to wing coverts. **VOICE** All vocalizations share a characteristic shrill, ringing or tinkling quality. Calls single high, ringing "*tzee*" notes and rising, tinkling phrases: "*tzee-ti'ti?*," "*ti-ti-ti*," or similar phrases. Also excited shrill chatters, often in duet: "*tee-tzee-trr tee-tzee-trrr....*" Dawn song an accelerating, high series of rising phrases: "*ti ti ti ti-ti-ti-TREEE-TREEE?*" **Co, E, Br, Bo, Ch**

3 SNOWY-THROATED KINGBIRD *Tyrannus niveigularis* 18.5–19 cm (7¼–7½ in)

Uncommon seasonal breeder in northwest below 700 m. Typically present Dec–Jun, but may stay longer in strong El Niño years with heavy rains. Found in arid scrub and dry forest. Similar to Tropical Kingbird, but lores and auriculars darker (face more "masked"); paler yellow below with broader white "bib"; grayer upperparts; and tail square tipped. **VOICE** Song an accelerating, rising series of chips followed by musical chatter: "*tup-tip'tchipZZ'DJE'ree?*" Call a thin, metallic "*tip*" and "*peep*," also thin high, squeaky or ringing chatters. **Co, E**

4 WHITE-THROATED KINGBIRD *Tyrannus albogularis* 21 cm (8½ in)

Uncommon austral migrant to eastern Amazonia. Present Mar–Oct. Apparently primarily winters along the Amazon and lower portions of major tributaries, but reported elsewhere during migration, and small numbers may winter south to Madre de Dios. Found in open areas, including in towns and cities. Similar to Tropical Kingbird, but head paler, contrasting more with dusky mask; throat pure white, contrasting more strongly with yellow underparts; and breast has little or no olive wash. **VOICE** Calls (Brazil) very high twittering series and single "*tzip*" notes, similar to Tropical, but thinner, less shrill or metallic. Dawn song not likely to be heard in Peru. **Co, E, Br, Bo**

[GREAT CRESTED FLYCATCHER *Myiarchus crinitus*] 19–20 cm (7½–7¾ in)

Very rare boreal vagrant; single record (tape-recorded) along lower Río Napo. Winters in canopy of humid forest and at forest borders. Colors more saturated than other *Myiarchus*, with deep gray throat and breast contrasting with richer yellow belly. Edges to primaries narrowly rufous, inner webs of inner rectrices broadly rufous (tail appears entirely rufous from below). Bill black, base of mandible paler pink or brownish. Closely resembles, but more richly colored than, Brown-capped Flycatcher. **VOICE** Call a distinctive, loud, rising whistle: "*WHEEEP!*" or "*whee'ip.*" **Co, E**

5 BROWN-CRESTED FLYCATCHER *Myiarchus tyrannulus* * 20 cm (7¾ in)

Locally fairly common resident in dry forest of dry intermontane valleys (Marañón, Huallaga, Pampas, and Urubamba) below 1200 m; also rare to uncommon austral migrant to southeastern lowlands, in canopy of forest and at forest edge. Large *Myiarchus*. Tail largely rufous from below (rufous inner webs to rectrices); no other expected *Myiarchus* in eastern Peru shows such conspicuous rufous in tail. Plumage otherwise relatively pale, with only weak contrast between gray breast and yellow belly. **VOICE** Call a loud, rich "*wick!*," a quiet "*hi-brew*," and low burry rolling rattles and churrs. Dawn song a rich, burry phrase: "*HICK hih-brew!*" **Co, Br, Bo**

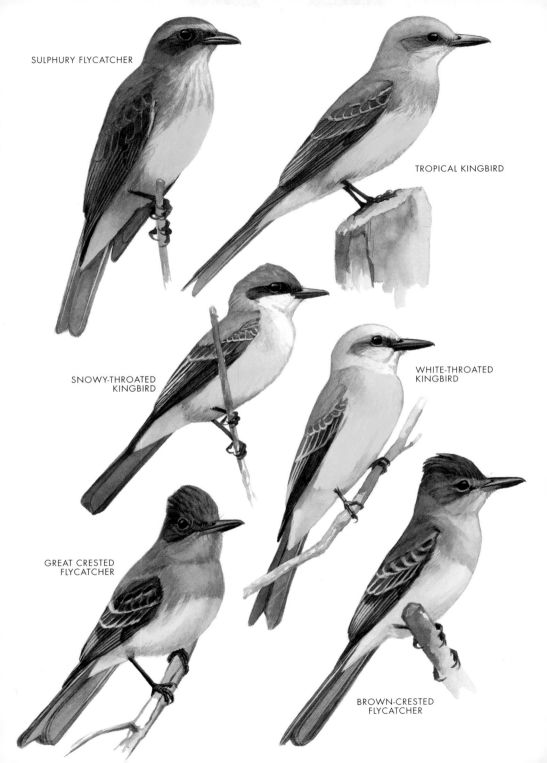

SULPHURY FLYCATCHER

TROPICAL KINGBIRD

SNOWY-THROATED
KINGBIRD

WHITE-THROATED
KINGBIRD

GREAT CRESTED
FLYCATCHER

BROWN-CRESTED
FLYCATCHER

PLATE
224

MYIARCHUS FLYCATCHERS

Myiarchus are slender flycatchers of forest and woods. Often lean forward while perched, raise a bushy crest, and "bob" the head. Primarily forage for insects with hover-gleans; often associate with mixed-species flocks. Nest placed in a tree cavity.

1 SWAINSON'S FLYCATCHER *Myiarchus swainsoni* * 19 cm (7½ in)
Uncommon austral migrant (Mar–Nov) throughout Amazonia, up to 600 m, in canopy of forest and at forest edge. Breeds locally in semideciduous forest in middle Urubamba Valley at ca. 1000 m. Large, drab, with no rufous in wings or tail and a relatively pale yellow belly. Mandible usually conspicuously light pinkish brown; some also show a dusky "mask." Cf. Short-crested Flycatcher, which has dark bill and is darker overall, not "masked," and restricted to edge habitats. **VOICE** Calls variable: a low, descending, whistled "*weeew*," similar to Dusky-capped Flycatcher, but shorter, not rising initially; a rich rising "*whit*," similar to Brown-crested Flycatcher; a hiccupping "*chi'wur*," "*jrrrr*," and rolling trills similar to Pale-edged Flycatcher; and deep, rising-falling whistled "*woOOoo*" notes, a deep, rich "*CHIrrrr*," and rolling series, deeper and richer than any given by other *Myiarchus*. **Co, E, Br, Bo**

2 SHORT-CRESTED FLYCATCHER *Myiarchus ferox* * 18.5–19 cm (7¼–7½ in)
Most common and widely distributed Amazonian *Myiarchus*, in river-edge forest, forest edge, and second growth below 1100 m. Relatively dark olive-brown above and with moderately deep yellow belly. Bill black. Cf. Swainson's Flycatcher. Most similar to less common (in Amazonia) Dusky-capped Flycatcher; Short-crested is slightly larger but best identified by **VOICE** Dawn song and common calls a short, ringing whinny: "*trEE'EE'ew*," similar in quality to a police or referee's whistle. Also a quiet "*kew'it*," an excited burry chatter, and a descending laugh. **Co, E, Br, Bo**

3 PALE-EDGED FLYCATCHER *Myiarchus cephalotes* * 18–19 cm (7–7½ in)
Uncommon but widely distributed along east slope of Andes at 1100–2600 m, in canopy and at edge of humid forest, and in adjacent second growth. Outer web of outer pair of rectrices whitish (although when backlit, outer webs of any species' tail may appear "pale"). Overlaps with *atriceps* Dusky-capped but lacks blackish cap. On lower slopes of Andes could overlap with Short-crested Flycatcher, from which best distinguished by **VOICE** Dawn song and common calls a mellow, descending series of whistles: "*PEE pew-pew-pew-pew*" and a single, loud "*KIP!*"; also a quiet, descending "*du-HEER*" and mellow, rolling chatters. **Co, E, Bo**

4 DUSKY-CAPPED FLYCATCHER *Myiarchus tuberculifer* * 17–18 cm (6¾–7 in)
Fairly common in humid forest and forest borders of both slopes of Andes, 1000–3250 m, and also in semideciduous forest at lower elevations, up to 750 m, in Tumbes and Piura (*atriceps*); and rare to uncommon in Amazonia (up to 1200 m) in second-growth and riparian forest and scrub (*tuberculifer*). Smallest *Myiarchus*, with relatively dusky crown; cap especially dark (blackish) in *atriceps*. Nominate *tuberculifer* very similar to Short-crested Flycatcher; best distinguished by **VOICE** Call (*tuberculifer*) a mellow, rising-falling, whistled "*wheeu*"; similar to call of several other Amazonian species. Also a more excited falling "*WEEU!*," a rough "*djerrt*," "*wur-PEER!*," and a rolling rattle: "*wur-BEER'r'r'r'r*." Calls of *atriceps* generally lower-pitched. **Co, E, Br, Bo**

5 SOOTY-CROWNED FLYCATCHER *Myiarchus phaeocephalus* * 18.5–19.5 cm (7¼–7¾ in)
Uncommon, in dry forests of northwest, up to 1200 m, on west slope (*phaeocephalus*) and in dry Marañón (*interior*); typically in woods that are moister than those inhabited by Rufous Flycatcher but drier than areas where Dusky-capped Flycatcher (*atriceps*) and Pale-edged Flycatcher are found. Forecrown and sides of face washed with light gray; rear crown is dusky, more or less contrasting with back (but much less so than in Dusky-capped). Outer web and tip of outer pair of rectrices light gray, not as whitish as in Pale-edged. **VOICE** Dawn song (*phaeocephalus*) is a musical, whistled "*hurEE hew-hew-hew*." Calls a loud, piping "*hooee!*," a descending "*pew*," and various burry chatters and "*hue-huee-huee-her*" notes in interactions. Dawn song (*interior*) is a rising-falling series of rising whistles with a mechanical snap at the end of each note (bill snaps?): "*huree-hee-hee-hew*." Calls a mellow "*ku-brik*" and a rich, rising "*turee?*" Also an excited burry chatter and a descending laugh. **E**

SWAINSON'S
FLYCATCHER

SHORT-CRESTED
FLYCATCHER

atriceps

DUSKY-CAPPED
FLYCATCHER

PALE-EDGED
FLYCATCHER

tuberculifer

SOOTY-CROWNED
FLYCATCHER

PLATE
225
CASIORNIS, RUFOUS FLYCATCHER, AND
RUFOUS BECARDS

Rufous Casiornis and Rufous Flycatcher are medium-sized, largely rufous flycatchers of Amazonia and arid northwest (respectively). Becards are flycatcher-like birds with relatively large heads (often accentuated by relatively short tails) and broad bills (see also plate 226). Relatively sluggish in behavior, perch- or hover-gleaning to capture prey. Most species are sexually dimorphic in plumage; in the hand, note that in all species the ninth (next to outermost) primary in male is reduced in size (to roughly half the length of outermost primary). Some but not all species associate with mixed-species flocks.

1 RUFOUS CASIORNIS *Casiornis rufus* 17 cm (6¾ in)
Rare austral migrant to southern Amazonia, where forages at low to midlevels in river-edge scrub and second growth at forest edge. Also reported from dry forest along middle Río Huallaga (San Martín) where may be permanent resident. Note slender proportions, relatively long tail, slender bill with pink base to mandible, and rufous plumage (including wings) with yellowish belly. Cf. rufous becards (this plate) and attilas (plate 227); also female White-lined Tanager. **VOICE** Dawn song plaintive and high, a lower note followed by a higher, then mid-pitch note: "*clew CLEE-clee!*" Call a plaintive, even-pitched or descending "*clee.*" **Br, Bo**

2 RUFOUS FLYCATCHER *Myiarchus semirufus* 18–19 cm (7¼–7½ in)
Fairly common in dry forest and tall scrub in northwest, less common farther south (where habitat now largely gone or degraded). Cf. female Slaty and One-colored becards, which have rufous (not dull brown) crowns and backs, and usually are found in moister forest. **VOICE** Call a sharp, high "*pew!*" or "*teep!*," and a quieter "*peeker-peeker,*" as well as quiet, low trills and short, shrill whistles. An excited vocalization, often given as a duet, is a loud, shrill, descending whistle interspersed with softer notes: "*peeker-peekerTCHEEEE! peekerTCHEEE! peekerTCHEEE!*" Dawn song a rasping series of notes: "*CHEE per'chip-errJEER*" interspersed with "*teep*" notes. **ENDEMIC**

3 CRESTED BECARD *Pachyramphus validus* * 17.5–18.5 cm (7–7¼ in)
Rare, restricted to southern Peru. Singles or pairs in forest canopy, usually with mixed-species flocks. Subspecies *audax* apparently an austral migrant to montane forest at 1700–3400 m in Ayacucho and western Cuzco; surprisingly there are no records between there and Bolivian border (so perhaps is local resident, not a migrant?). Also a rare austral migrant (*validus*; not illustrated) to southern Amazonia. Male *audax* are 2-toned, dark gray above with blackish cap and light gray below; paler than Pink-throated Becard and lacks rosy throat band. Male *validus* (not illustrated) grayish buff, not light gray, below. Female of both subspecies similar to female Pink-throated but back is rufous, contrasting with gray crown. **VOICE** Calls (eastern Bolivia) high squeaky notes, for example: "*chew tewww'er'eee?*" **Br, Bo**

4 PINK-THROATED BECARD *Pachyramphus minor* 17–17.5 cm (6¾–7 in)
Uncommon but widely distributed in Amazonia below 1000 m. Found in canopy and subcanopy of forest, primarily terra firme but sometimes also in varzea. Frequently joins mixed-species flocks. Male readily identified by light rosy pink band on lower throat and upper breast. Female tawny-buff below with rufous wings, contrasting with gray crown and upper back. Cf. Crested Becard. **VOICE** Song a thin, wiry, high, rising-falling, whiny "*tewwweeewww*" or a rising "*tueeeet?*" Call a rapid chatter of squeaky whistles and whines and a sharp "*ik.*" **Co, E, Br, Bo**

5 CINEREOUS BECARD *Pachyramphus rufus* * 14 cm (5½ in)
Rare, poorly known. Apparently restricted to edge of varzea and to forested river islands. Male readily identified by black cap, relatively plain wings (lacking strong wing bars), and light gray underparts. Female very similar to more common Chestnut-crowned Becard, but crown entirely rufous. **VOICE** Song (?) a rapid, dry, ringing chatter: "*tee'chi'chi'chi'chi'chi'tchee?*" **Co, E, Br**

6 CHESTNUT-CROWNED BECARD *Pachyramphus castaneus* * 14–14.5 cm (5½–5¾ in)
Uncommon but widely distributed in northern Amazonia; much less common, and more local, in south. Found in the mid- to upper levels of edges of varzea and at forest edge near rivers, locally up to 800 m. Generally does not associate with mixed-species flocks. Sexes similar. Note grayish superciliary that continues as band across nape. **VOICE** Song a musical, melancholy series of descending (occasionally falling-rising) whistles: "*PEE peew pew pew.*" **Co, E, Br, Bo**

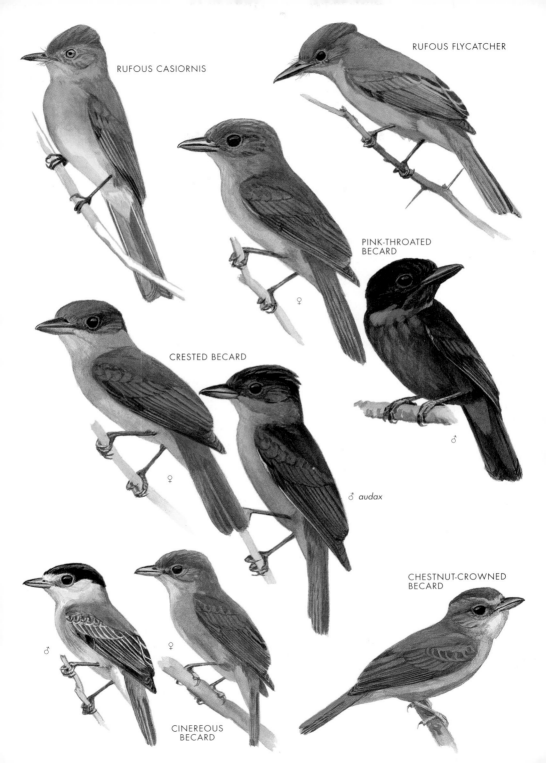

RUFOUS CASIORNIS

RUFOUS FLYCATCHER

PINK-THROATED
BECARD

♀

CRESTED BECARD

♀

♂ *audax*

♂

CHESTNUT-CROWNED
BECARD

♂

♀

CINEREOUS
BECARD

PLATE
226

BECARDS

See notes on becards (plate 225). Usually in midstory and canopy, often with mixed-species flocks.

1 BLACK-AND-WHITE BECARD *Pachyramphus albogriseus* * 14 cm (5½ in)

Uncommon in humid montane forest along east slope of Andes, 1500–3200 m (*salvini*), and in similar habitat on both slopes of western Andes in northwest (*guayaquilensis*). Also uncommon in dry and riparian forests in northwest, down to 150 m. Often joins mixed-species flocks. Similar to Black-capped Becard, but little or no overlap. Black cap of male contrasts with light gray back and pale lores. Female identified by black border to rufous-brown crown, producing a more distinct "capped" appearance. **VOICE** Song (*salvini*) a quiet, musical "*pew-ew-ew-eewee?*" Calls a quiet, descending, rich "*tchew*," sometimes in a long series, also a stuttered series of rich, musical whistles: "*chew chew-chew'ew-chew'ew-chew'ew.*" Song of *guayaquilensis* is an emphatic "*HEW HEW chewy? HEW HEW chewy?*" Calls squeaky chatters and rich "*tchip*" notes. **Co, E**

2 WHITE-WINGED BECARD *Pachyramphus polychopterus* * 14.5–15 cm (5¾–6 in)

One of the most common and widespread Amazonian becards. Found in mid- and upper levels of river-edge forest, second growth, and edges of humid forest up to 1200 m, locally to 1500 m. Sometimes accompanies mixed-species flocks but often forages apart. Resident males (subspecies *tenebrosus, nigriventris*) black with white wing bars and tips to tail. Females have extensive rufous-buff wing bars and edgings, brownish back, and relatively plain head pattern with grayish or brownish crown. Male of *spixii*, an austral migrant to southeast, is sooty gray below; larger and darker than male Black-capped Becard, with dusky lores. Female *spixii* similar to resident females. **VOICE** Song a musical, stuttered series of rich whistles: "*tu-heer tu-tu'tu'tu'tu'tu.*" Call a series of rich "*tchew*" notes, often accelerating slightly. **Co, E, Br, Bo**

3 BLACK-CAPPED BECARD *Pachyramphus marginatus* * 13–13.5 cm (5–5¼ in)

Uncommon but widely distributed in Amazonia, up to 750 m. More typical of forest interior than White-winged Becard; found in terra firme canopy. Male paler below than *spixii* White-winged, with pale lores; distinguished from Black-and-white Becard by black back. Female similar to female White-winged but has a more strongly rufous crown and a grayish olive (not light brown) back. **VOICE** Song a musical "*hew-wiker-wee? hew-wiker-wee?*" Call an accelerating, slightly rising whistles: "*tchew tchew-tchew'tchew'tchewtchew'ti?*" Also quiet squeaky chatters. **Co, E, Br, Bo**

4 SLATY BECARD *Pachyramphus spodiurus* 13.5–14 cm (5¼–5½ in)

Uncommon, in dry forest and forest edge, up to 750 m. Very similar to larger One-colored Becard. Male glossier black above, and gray lores may contrast with black crown; also note narrow white edges to wing coverts and remiges (wings of male One-colored are plainer). Female like larger female One-colored but may show whitish lores. Whenever possible, identify females by accompanying male. **VOICE** Song a rising or rising-falling, accelerating series of squeaky rising whistles: "*ree ree-ree-REE-REE'HEE'HEE'hee'hih'huh.*" Call a rapid, squeaky chatter: "*r'rih'reh'heh'heh-heh-chew.*" **E**

5 BARRED BECARD *Pachyramphus versicolor* * 13 cm (5 in)

Fairly common in humid montane forest, 1500–3000 m, locally down to 1100 m, along east slope of Andes; very local on west slope. Male distinctive; but soft gray barring on underparts sometimes difficult to see in the field. Compare female to Green-backed Becard. **VOICE** Song a tyrannulet-like, rising or rising-falling, accelerating series of thin, high whistles: "*wur wee WEE-WEE'WEE'WEE-WEE.*" Calls thin, squeaky "*wsee*" notes in a chattered series. **Co, E, Bo**

6 ONE-COLORED BECARD *Pachyramphus homochrous* * 16.5–17 cm (6½–6¾ in)

Uncommon to locally fairly common in dry forest in northwest, up to 700 m. Carefully cf. very similar Slaty Becard. **VOICE** Song a thin, wiry, high, rising-falling, whiny "*tswee-ewww.*" Call a squeaky "*ik.*" Also a squeaky, accelerating-decelerating chatter ending with a squeaky whistle: "*peek purr'rr'rr'-rr'hur'hur-teeeew.*" **Co, E**

7 GREEN-BACKED BECARD *Pachyramphus viridis* * 13.5–14.5 cm (5¼–5¾ in)

Uncommon, at edges of humid montane forest and in clearings along east slope of Andes, 500–1500 m; also in dry forest in Marañón Valley. Male distinctive. Compare gray-headed female to female Barred, which is smaller and has more extensively rufous wings and yellow underparts and sides to face. Some female-plumaged Green-backed have green (not rufous) wing coverts. **VOICE** Song a loud, rising series of whistles: "*poor pur-pur-PUR-PUR-PUR-PUR-PEER.*" Calls a falling-rising "*EEwEE?*" and a musical "*whi-whi.*" **E, Br, Bo**

BLACK-AND-
WHITE BECARD
♂

♀

WHITE-
WINGED
BECARD

♂ *spixii*

♀

♂

BLACK-
CAPPED
BECARD
♂

♀

SLATY
BECARD
♂

♀

BARRED
BECARD
♂

♀

ONE-COLORED
BECARD
♂

♀

♀

GREEN-
BACKED
BECARD
♂

PLATE
227 | ATTILAS

Large flycatchers with long, noticeably hooked bills and large rounded heads. Remain motionless for extended periods, then sally for insects; most also eat fruit. Easily overlooked, except for the loud, far-carrying vocalizations. Usually do not associate with mixed-species flocks.

1 CITRON-BELLIED ATTILA *Attila citriniventris* 17.5–18.5 cm (7–7¼ in)

Uncommon, in canopy and midstory of terra firme of northern Amazonia; perhaps most common on sandy soils. Relatively brightly colored, with contrasting light gray crown, nape, and sides to face; throat may be grayish white or tawny, like breast. Smaller than Dull-capped Attila, with more contrast between gray head and rufous body, and has a dark iris. Cf. also smaller, stubby-billed Varzea Schiffornis, which sometimes has gray hood. **VOICE** Song a rising series of rising whistles that usually terminates in a lower note, sounding melancholy: "*wur wer-wer-weer-wee-WEE-WEE-WEE-wur.*" Very similar to Dull-capped, but faster-paced. Call a series of rapid, piping "*pi-pi-pi-pi*" notes. **Co, E, Br, Bo**

2 BRIGHT-RUMPED ATTILA *Attila spadiceus* * 17 cm (6¼ in)

Most common and widespread attila, found throughout Amazonia below 1200 m, although heard far more often than seen. Forages at all heights but most often in the mid- and upper story. Most common in terra firme, less often in transitional forests. Plumage highly variable. Always has rufous wing bars (sometimes ill-defined), bright tawny yellow rump and upper tail coverts (usually concealed when at rest), and streaked appearance on breast and upper belly. Iris usually red or brown, rarely strikingly pale. Upperparts may be rufous-brown or olive-brown; head usually rufous-brown or olive, but may be gray; and underparts may be mostly olive or browner, with center of belly variably white or pale yellow. **VOICE** Song a moderate-paced, rising series of bisyllabic, rising whistles ending with a higher note: "*wur wibber weeber weeber WEEBER WEEBER WEE.*" More enthusiastic and upbeat than songs of Dull-capped and Citron-bellied attilas, which also only rarely give bisyllabic notes. Call a rising, falling series of bisyllabic whistles: "*wibber-WEEBER'weeber'-weeber-weehur,*" also a quiet rattle: "*t'chirr'rr'rr.*" **Co, E, Br, Bo**

3 CINNAMON ATTILA *Attila cinnamomeus* 19.5 cm (7¾ in)

Uncommon to locally fairly common in varzea, lake margins, and forested river islands in northern Amazonia; less common, more local in south. Largely rufous above with dusky primaries; paler, yellower below and on rump and tail. Dull-capped is browner, less rufous above, especially on crown, has pale iris, and bill has a pale mandible. Rufous morph of Bright-rumped is duller above, has rufous wing bars, and usually a pale base to mandible. Cf. also smaller, stubbier-billed Varzea Schiffornis. **VOICE** Song a rising series of pure whistles, sometimes ending with a short, descending, quiet note: "*her heer HEER'chew.*" Call a long, descending whistled "*pur'WHEEER*"; plaintive, raptorlike. **Co, E, Br, Bo**

4 [OCHRACEOUS ATTILA *Attila torridus*] 20–21 cm (8–8¼ in)

Rare to uncommon in semideciduous forest in Tumbes below 800 m. No similar species occurs in this region; cf. Royal Flycatcher. **VOICE** Song a rising series of rising whistles, usually ending on a note lower than the preceding: "*wur wer wheer WHEER WHEER whur.*" Call a loud, rising-falling whistle: "*weeEEeeo*" sometimes ending with a short musical phrase "*weeEEeeo WEE'hur'hee.*" Also a loud "*kyip!*" or "*kip!*" **Co, E**

5 DULL-CAPPED ATTILA *Attila bolivianus* * 20.5–21 cm (8–8¼ in)

Uncommon but widespread in eastern lowlands, mostly if not entirely found south of the Amazon. Found in under- and midstory of varzea and transitional forests and margins of forest streams. Largest, plainest attila. Dull tawny-brown above (not bright rufous as is Cinnamon Attila) with grayer crown; tawny-buff below with wings that are dusky but not blackish. Pale iris usually conspicuous. Rufous morph of Bright-rumped Attila has rufous wing bars, (usually) has a dark iris (but rarely whitish), and usually shows some dark flammulations or streaking on chest and a pale belly that contrasts more with ochraceous breast. **VOICE** Song a slow rising series of rising whistles that usually terminates in a lower note, sounding melancholy: "*wur wer weer wee WEE WEE wurr*"; rarely may give bisyllabic "*weeber*" notes. Similar to Citron-bellied Attila, but slower paced. Call quiet "*pup*" notes and a faster slightly rising series of rising whistles: "*whip-whip-whip-whip-wheep-wheep.*" Also a harsh, somewhat metallic, woodpecker-like chatter: "*TER'terter!*" **Co, Br, Bo**

CITRON-BELLIED ATTILA

rufous morph

BRIGHT-RUMPED ATTILA

OCHRACEOUS ATTILA

DULL-CAPPED ATTILA

CINNAMON ATTILA

PLATE
228
TITYRAS, COTINGAS, AND PURPLETUFT

Tityras are found in the canopy of Amazonian forests. Sluggish; singles or pairs often are seen perched on high snags or other exposed positions at forest edge, in tall second growth, or in clearings. Primarily frugivorous but also eat some insects or small vertebrates. The ninth (next to outermost) primary of males is very short and extremely narrow. Black-faced and Pompadour cotingas are two geographically restricted species. White-browed Purpletuft is a small, widely distributed cotinga.

1 BLACK-TAILED TITYRA *Tityra cayana* * 19.5–21 cm (7¾–8¼ in)

Uncommon but widespread in Amazonia, up to 700 m. Orbital skin and base of bill red in both sexes. Male has black crown and sides of head; similar to male Masked Tityra, but black is more extensive on head (reaching rear crown) and tail entirely black. Female readily recognized by narrow dark streaking on gray back and white breast. **VOICE** Song, often in duet, a deep, croaking "*grrk grr'ik grr'ik grr'ik.*" Call deep-croaked grunting "*grrk*" notes singly or in series. Very difficult to separate from Masked, but generally lower pitched. **Co, E, Br, Bo**

2 MASKED TITYRA *Tityra semifasciata* * 21–22 cm (8¼–8½ in)

Most common and widespread tityra, found up to 1600 m in Andean foothills. Both sexes have red orbital skin and base to bill. Male is the only tityra on which black does not extend onto crown ("masked"); tail gray crossed by broad black band. Head of female dusky gray (not black); tail paler than in male, especially on underside, on which tail band is gray. **VOICE** Song, often in duet, is a deep, buzzy grunting: "*grr'dik grr'dik grr'dik.*" Calls deep, buzzy grunting "*gzzk*" notes singly or in series. Very difficult to distinguish from Black-tailed Tityra, but generally slightly higher pitched. **Co, E, Br, Bo**

3 BLACK-FACED COTINGA *Conioptilon mcilhennyi* 23 cm (9 in)

Uncommon in southeastern Amazonia. Distribution curiously restricted, primarily recorded from sites north of the Río Madre de Dios. Found in canopy of seasonally flooded forest, especially in sites that remain swampy year round. Usually encountered as singles or pairs; does not follow mixed-species flocks but joins other species at fruiting trees. Readily identified by light gray underparts that contrast with black throat, sides of head and crown, and dark upperparts. Sexes alike; immature birds apparently narrowly scaled with white on the upperparts, and remiges margined white. **VOICE** A short, barked "*puh,*" a quiet, descending "*coww,*" and squeaky, rising "*huuEEE?*" (very reminiscent of Smooth-billed Ani). **Br, Bo**

4 BLACK-CROWNED TITYRA *Tityra inquisitor* * 18–18.5 cm (7–7¼ in)

Uncommon but widespread in Amazonia, up to 600 m. Smallest tityra, and only one with no red on face or bill. Crown of male black. Female slightly darker overall with distinctive tawny-brown sides to face. Tail black, with broad, light gray base and narrow white tip, in widespread *albitorques*; tail entirely black north of the Amazon, and perhaps also on south bank of Marañón in Amazonas (*buckleyi*). **VOICE** Vocalizations similar to those of other tityras, but weaker. **Co, E, Br, Bo**

5 POMPADOUR COTINGA *Xipholena punicea* 19.5–20.5 cm (7¾–8 in)

Uncommon and local in northern Amazonia, in forests on nutrient-poor soils, including varillales. Often found in small groups, perching in canopy in manner of blue cotingas (see plate 233). Male wine-red with contrasting white wings; some scapulars are stiff, narrow, and elongated, draping over closed wing. Female a dumpy, relatively short-tailed gray bird with prominent white edges to wing coverts and inner remiges. Also note pale iris. Wings of male produce a hard rattling sound in flight. **VOICE** Call a barked "*PURP*" or "*kirp.*" **Co, E, Br, Bo**

6 WHITE-BROWED PURPLETUFT *Iodopleura isabellae* * 12–12.5 cm (4¾–5 in)

Uncommon but widely distributed in canopy of humid forest, below 850 m; small size, quiet voice, and habit of remaining high overhead make it easy to overlook. Singles or pairs perch upright on high exposed sites, such as snags; sally for insects and fruit. Small and dark with short stubby bill and short tail. Largely dark brown with white spots on lores, behind eye, and on sides of face, and an irregular white stripe down underparts; purple pectoral tufts of male difficult to see in the field. Cf. Swallow-wing (page 266), which is larger and blacker, with dark belly and face. **VOICE** Calls a high, rising "*tuee?*" and a mewing, stuttered "*chee'ee'ee.*" **Co, E, Br, Bo**

BLACK-TAILED TITYRA

♀   ♂

MASKED TITYRA

♀   ♂

ad.   imm.

BLACK-FACED
COTINGA

underside of
tail, *buckleyi*

♀ *albitorques*

♂ *albitorques*

underside
of tail

BLACK-CROWNED TITYRA

POMPADOUR
COTINGA

♂   ♀

♀

♂

WHITE-BROWED PURPLETUFT

PLATE
229
GRAY PIHAS, MOURNERS, AND FRUITCROW

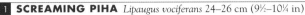

The two mourners are not related to one another, nor to the larger pihas; but all 5 species are superficially similar gray, long-tailed birds of humid forest. Most perch quietly, then sally for fruit or insects. The fruitcrow is a noisy, conspicuous cotinga.

1 SCREAMING PIHA *Lipaugus vociferans* 24–26 cm (9½–10¼ in)

The voice of Amazonia: its far-carrying song is one of the most characteristic sounds of lowland forest. Common and widespread, up to 1150 m, in humid forest, primarily in midstory. Often perches upright, especially when singing; may raise short crest. Note large size and gray color (but cf. Grayish Mourner). Juvenile (not illustrated) has cinnamon-rufous wing coverts and tips to rectrices. **VOICE** Song, in chorus at widely dispersed lek, a rising series of mewing "*ooh-AH*" notes culminating in a very loud, piercing "*SQUEEEE SQUEE-AH!*" Calls loud mewing "*TOWW*" notes, often in a series, and various random piercing squeaks, whistles, and moans. **Co, E, Br, Bo**

2 GRAYISH MOURNER *Rhytipterna simplex* * 20.5–21 cm (8–8¼ in)

Fairly common and widespread in humid forest in eastern lowlands, up to 1400 m. Forages in singles or pairs, apart with mixed-species flocks, in the under- and midstory. Cf. Cinereous Mourner. Similar to Screaming Piha, which is larger, slightly paler gray, lacks pale olive or yellowish wash on belly, and has stouter, broader bill. Iris color of mourner may be reddish brown and of piha gray, although occasionally in either species iris may be dark brown. **VOICE** Call a rising, burry, rapid series ending abruptly with a loud bark: "*wur'ur'ur'ur'ur'ur'ur'ur'DJIRT!*" Dawn song very different, a mellow rising-falling whistle followed by a rising series: "*wee'heer wee'heer wee'heer woo-hoo-her-her-HEER.*" **Co, E, Br, Bo**

3 SCIMITAR-WINGED PIHA *Lipaugus uropygialis* 30 cm (11¾ in)

Rare and local, in humid montane forest at 2100–2400 m. Found in mid- and upper story, often in small groups (3–5), or with mixed-species flocks. Large. Dark gray with rufous-chestnut vent and rump. Most primaries of male are recurved (scimitar-shaped), and outermost primaries also are narrow; primaries of females less strongly modified. **VOICE** Calls, usually in an explosive chorus, loud, squeaky, conversational phrases, for example: "*PEEKsweeA'WEEK!*" Song, performed in a spiraling, falling display flight, a loud, piercing, high "*tseee'e'e'e tsueee?*" with three mechanically produced "*fft*" sounds at the start, middle, and end of the vocal phrase. **Bo**

4 CINEREOUS MOURNER *Laniocera hypopyrra* 20.5–21 cm (8–8¼ in)

Uncommon but widespread in eastern lowlands, up to 900 m. Primarily in terra firme, sometimes also in seasonally flooded or swampy forests. Usually not with mixed-species flocks. Note conspicuous buffy tips to wing coverts and tail. Usually also has yellow or rufous pectoral tufts (sometimes hidden under wing). Grayish Mourner lacks rufous or yellow in plumage and has more angular, less rounded profile to head. **VOICE** Song a tireless, squeaky series of whistles: "*eww EE'eww EE'eww EE'eww....*" Call a descending series of whiny, thin, descending whistles: "*pew peEEeeew peeEEeew peeEEeew.*" **Co, E, Br, Bo**

5 DUSKY PIHA *Lipaugus fuscocinereus* 31–33 cm (12¼–13 in)

Rare and local in humid montane forest canopy along east slope of Andes, north and west of Marañón Valley at 2125–2250 m (1700–2600 m in Ecuador). Encountered singly or with other large-bodied forest birds such as Mountain Cacique, Turquoise Jay, or Hooded Mountain-Tanager. Very large, dull gray; no overlap with Screaming Piha of lowlands. **VOICE** Song a high, piercing, rising-falling-rising-falling whistle; highest pitch reached in last syllable: "*wee'uWEEER.*" Performs a flight display, falling from perch and producing a series of loud, harsh "puffs" with wings. **Co, E**

6 PURPLE-THROATED FRUITCROW *Querula purpurata* male 29–30 cm (11½–11¾ in), female 27.5–28 cm (10¾–11 in)

Fairly common and widespread in eastern lowlands, up to 1000 m. Forages in canopy and midstory in small groups, usually apart from other species. Attracts attention with loud vocalizations. Forages for large insects and fruits, both usually taken in flight. Note blackish plumage and blue-gray bill. Male has purple ruff throat, which can be extended laterally in display. Much smaller than female umbrellabird, and much less likely to be seen flying across rivers and other large openings. **VOICE** Song a mellow, mewing, falling-rising "*COW-uh?*" and a rising "*ohhahhh?*" Call a raspy coughing or "throat-clearing" sound. **Co, E, Br, Bo**

SCREAMING PIHA

GRAYISH MOURNER

SCIMITAR-WINGED
PIHA

CINEREOUS MOURNER

DUSKY PIHA

♂

♀

PURPLE-THROATED
FRUITCROW

PLATE
230
ANDEAN COTINGAS AND PLANTCUTTER

Most species on this plate are cotingas of Andean forests and forest edges. Relatively sluggish, perching upright in an exposed position in the crown of a tree or bush, and often remaining at one perch for extended periods. Largely frugivorous, although some or all may make short sallies for flying insects. The plantcutter is a rare bird of the northwest coastal plain; vocally very similar to some of the Andean cotingas.

1 WHITE-CHEEKED COTINGA *Zaratornis stresemanni* 21 cm (8¼ in)
Rare and local along west slope of Andes, 3800–4400 m. Primarily in *Polylepis* woods; also locally in mixed woods at lower elevations, down to 2700 m, although may be present only seasonally or intermittently at such sites. Mostly feeds on mistletoe berries. Superficially similar to immature Red-crested Cotinga (very local overlap) but has prominent white cheek patch and contrasting black cap, is more broadly streaked, has an unstreaked gray-brown "bib," and lacks white tail band. **VOICE** Song a series of deep, burry accelerating quacks into a rising-calling chatter, slowing at the very end: "*djee-djee-DJEE-DJEE-djee'dje'dje'djer'r'r'r'r'dje'dje.*" Call a deep, burry series of emphatic quacks: "*djee-djee-DJEE-DJEE-DJEEP.*" **ENDEMIC**

2 RED-CRESTED COTINGA *Ampelion rubrocristatus* 20.5–21 cm (8–8¼ in)
Uncommon to fairly common and widespread in humid and semihumid montane forest on east slope of Andes, and on west slope in northwest; an apparently isolated population found as far south as Lima. Primarily at 2400–3700 m in forest edge (including *Polylepis* woods), secondary forest (including hedgerows and degraded woods in agricultural areas), and taller shrubs. Narrow red crest often lays flat on nape (and so is not conspicuous) but may be raised in display. White tail band often visible in flight. Juvenile duller, streaked, but always has white tail band. **VOICE** Song a stuttered series of deep notes ending in a short croak: "*ke-ke-ke-kerrr*" Calls a deep chucking note and a deep, croaking "*crek.*" Also various deep harsh, nasal sounds in interactions. **Co, E, Bo**

3 PERUVIAN PLANTCUTTER *Phytotoma raimondii* 18.5–19 cm (7¼–7½ in)
Very local; can be fairly common where present, but currently is known from only a few, scattered localities on coastal plain (up to 300 m) in northwest. Rarity primarily due to degradation of preferred habitat, open dry forest dominated by *Prosopis* (algarrobo), *Acacia*, and other trees with dense shrubby understory; also in desert scrub and riparian thickets, but absent from much seemingly suitable habitat. Usually in pairs or small groups. Eats buds, shoots, leaves, and some fruit; with a good view (or in the hand), note that stubby bill has fine serrations along cutting edge of maxilla. Often raises a ragged crest. Streaked female vaguely similar to a finch; cf. Streaked Saltator. **VOICE** Song a descending series of rising-falling, annoyed, nasal brays: "*REEEEH reeeh reeeh.*" Call various annoyed nasal whines. **ENDEMIC**

4 CHESTNUT-CRESTED COTINGA *Ampelion rufaxilla* * 20.5–21 cm (8–8¼ in)
Rare, along east slope of Andes at 1700–2800 m. More restricted to continuous humid montane forest than is Red-crested Cotinga; otherwise behavior is similar. Rufous crest fuller than crest of Red-crested Cotinga, and usually more apparent. Note also rufous throat, yellow belly streaked blackish. **VOICE** Song a quiet, deep, nasal croak, often with a stuttered introduction: "*t't'ti'kreeh.*" Calls single nasal croaking notes. **Co, E, Bo**

[CHESTNUT-BELLIED COTINGA *Doliornis remseni* 21 cm (8¼ in)
Not recorded from Peru but is to be expected; reported from southern Ecuador just across border from northeastern Piura. Similar to Bay-vented Cotinga (which it replaces north of Río Marañón), but entire belly is rufous-chestnut (this color is confined to the vent of Bay-vented), and face and throat are darker gray. **Co, E**

5 BAY-VENTED COTINGA *Doliornis sclateri* 21.5 cm (8½ in)
Rare and local in humid montane forest. Primarily at or near treeline, 2600–3800 m, in central Peru. Even more sluggish and inconspicuous than the other Andean cotingas. Note overall dark color, gray sides of head and throat, brown belly, and contrasting rufous-chestnut vent. Male has a black cap. Both sexes have an inconspicuous narrow red crest. **VOICE** Calls (song?) a mewing, rising "*rhee*" or "*rhee-ah,*" louder and scratchier than voice of Red-crested Cotinga. **ENDEMIC**

WHITE-CHEEKED
COTINGA

RED-
CRESTED
COTINGA

juv.

ad.

PERUVIAN
PLANTCUTTER

♂

♀

CHESTNUT-
CRESTED COTINGA

♀

♂

CHESTNUT-BELLIED
COTINGA

♀

♂

BAY-VENTED
COTINGA

PLATE
231
FRUITEATERS AND SHRIKE-LIKE COTINGA

Fruiteaters are heavy-bodied cotingas of humid montane forest. Tail and tarsi are relatively short. Plumage largely green, and sexes differ. Quiet and inconspicuous frugivores; do not join mixed-species flocks, but may congregate at fruiting trees. Bill and (usually) tarsi brightly colored in Pipreola fruiteaters, but not in Scaled Fruiteater (Ampelioides). See also plate 232. Shrike-like Cotinga is superficially similar but not as stocky.

1 BLACK-CHESTED FRUITEATER *Pipreola lubomirskii* 18 cm (7 in)

Uncommon and local. Primarily on east slope of Andes north and west of Río Marañón, 1600–2300 m; also present very locally on west slope (Cajamarca) and in central Amazonas south of Marañón. Distinguished from Green-and-black Fruiteater by pale (yellowish or orange) iris, unmarked tertials, gray tarsi, and brighter green upperparts; male also lacks narrow yellow collar, and center of breast and belly are unmarked. **VOICE** Song a long, very high, thin, rising whistle: "*tseeeeeeeweee.*" Calls short rising or rising-falling whistles: "*tsweet?*" or "*tsee'ik.*" **Co, E**

2 BARRED FRUITEATER *Pipreola arcuata* * 23–23.5 cm (9–9¼ in)

Largest fruiteater, and occupying forests to higher elevations (2100–3500 m) than other species; overlaps at lower end of elevational distribution with Band-tailed and Green-and-black fruiteaters. Primarily found on east slope, but also on west slope in Piura. Note large size, barred underparts, and large pale spots on wing coverts and tertials. Iris color variable, but usually dark in north (*arcuata*); iris pale from Junín south (*viridicauda*). **VOICE** Song a very high, thin, rising whistle, then a descending whistle, often several rising or descending whistles in a loose series. Calls shorter descending, or slightly rising then descending, whistles. Also series of very high "*ti*" or "*tseee*" notes. **Co, E, Bo**

3 BAND-TAILED FRUITEATER *Pipreola intermedia* * 18.5–19.5 cm (7¼–7¾ in)

Fairly common and widespread along east slope of Andes at 2100–3000 m, down to 1500 m in south. Elevational range averages higher than Green-and-black Fruiteater, but there is elevational overlap in La Libertad and Huánuco. Similar to Green-and-black, but slightly larger. Also has black subterminal band on tail (may be faint or missing in female) and white-tipped rectrices. Males also have black scales mixed in with green flank spots. Northern *intermedia* (south to Junín) duller, more heavily marked below than *signata*; cf. Barred. **VOICE** Song a series of very high "*ti*" notes followed by thin, descending whistle: "*ti-ti-ti teeeeeeeew.*" Call a series of high "*ti*" or "*tswee*" notes. **Bo**

4 GREEN-AND-BLACK FRUITEATER *Pipreola riefferii* * 18–18.5 cm (7–7¼ in)

Fairly common and widespread along east slope of Andes at 1700–2900 m, locally down to 1150 m. Note reddish brown iris, red legs, narrow pale tips to tertials, and unmarked tail. Head and chest of male black glossed with green in widespread *chachapoyas*; hood purer black and underparts yellower (less streaked) in *tallmanorum* (Huánuco). Females always have green throat and chest, streaked underparts. Cf. Band-tailed and Black-chested fruiteaters. **VOICE** Song (*chachapoyas*) a series of very high notes followed by thin, descending whistle: "*ti-ti-ti teeeeeeeew.*" Call series of "*ti*" notes. **Co, E**

5 SHRIKE-LIKE COTINGA *Laniisoma elegans* * 17.5–18 cm (6¼–7 in)

Rare and local in humid forest on outlying ridges at 750–1800 m, occasionally in lowlands near Andes. Quiet and inconspicuous. Behavior poorly known, but eats both insects and fruit. Black cap and yellow underparts of male distinctive. Female scaled below with black; cf. fruiteaters. Immatures (not illustrated) have large rufous-chestnut spots on wing coverts; immature males may develop black crown while still retaining rufous wing spots and some ventral scaling. **VOICE** Song a very high series of piercing, falling-rising whistles: "*SEEeeweeEEE SEEeeweeEE SEEeeweeEE....*" Call a squeaky, descending "*ki-ki-ki*" and a squeaky rattle. **Co, E, Br, Bo**

6 SCALED FRUITEATER *Ampelioides tschudii* 20–20.5 cm (7¾–8 in)

Rare to uncommon on east slope of Andes, 700–1800 m. Behaviorally similar to a *Pipreola* fruiteater, but slightly larger than any other fruiteater with which it overlaps in elevation, and even stockier in appearance; posture more hunched over. Note white throat, loral spot and malar (bordered by black lateral throat stripe), and yellowish nuchal collar; also heavily scaled underparts and spotted upperparts. Male blacker above than female, with black crown. Iris color variable; often pale yellow or yellow-green, but may be light brown. **VOICE** Song a raptorlike, loud, rising-falling whistle: "*heeLEEEER!*" Call a falling whistled "*heeer.*" **Co, E, Bo**

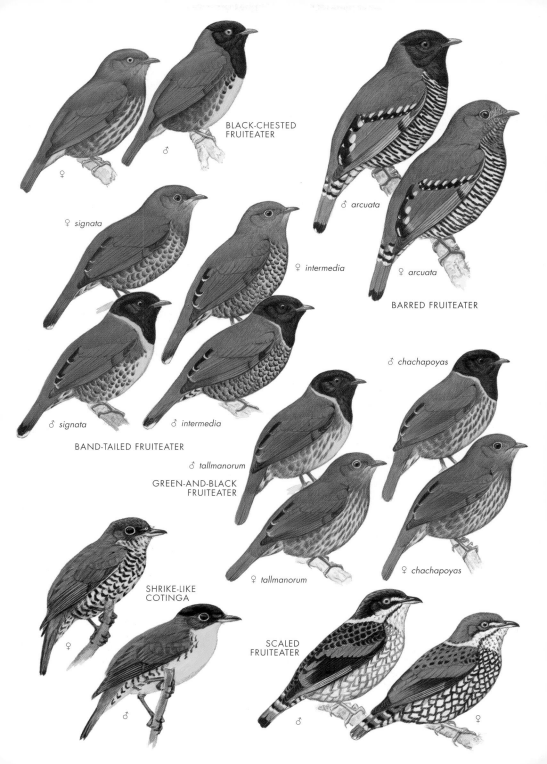

BLACK-CHESTED
FRUITEATER

♀

♂

♀ signata

♀ intermedia

♂ signata

♂ intermedia

BAND-TAILED FRUITEATER

♂ arcuata

♀ arcuata

BARRED FRUITEATER

♂ chachapoyas

♀ chachapoyas

♂ tallmanorum

♀ tallmanorum

GREEN-AND-BLACK
FRUITEATER

SHRIKE-LIKE
COTINGA

♀

♂

SCALED
FRUITEATER

♂

♀

PLATE
232
FRUITEATERS, SHARPBILL, AND GREEN PIHAS

The fruiteaters on this plate all are species of lower-elevation montane forests, and in which the males have bright orange or red areas on the throat or breast. See also plate 231. The Sharpbill is a peculiar flycatcher-like or cotinga-like bird, local in distribution; named for its distinctive, sharply pointed bill. The two species of pihas on this plate are Andean and are mostly green; much more unobtrusive than are the unrelated gray pihas (plate 229).

1 FIERY-THROATED FRUITEATER *Pipreola chlorolepidota* 13 cm (5 in)
The smallest fruiteater, and the least common; 500–1500 m, locally down to 300 m, along east slope of Andes and on outlying ridges. Male has bright red or orange throat that contrasts with unmarked green belly. Female is densely barred below. Both sexes have a relatively short tail and fairly large pale tertial spots. **VOICE** Song a high, thin, descending *"pseeew."* Call a sharp, high *"tsit."* **Co, E**

2 MASKED FRUITEATER *Pipreola pulchra* 18–19 cm (7–7½ in)
Uncommon, at 1600–2400 m along east slope of Andes. Both sexes have pale yellow-green iris and olive tarsi and toes. Male has black face, including upper throat, bordered below by bright orange chest patch. Compared to female Scarlet-breasted Fruiteater, female Masked is entirely streaked (not scaled) yellow and green below, has olive (not pink or red) tarsi and toes, and lacks pale tertial spots. **VOICE** Song a long, very high, thin, rising whistle: *"tseeeeeeeweee."* Calls short rising whistles: *"tsweet?"* **ENDEMIC**

3 SCARLET-BREASTED FRUITEATER *Pipreola frontalis* * 15.5 cm (6 in)
Uncommon along east slope of Andes at 900–2000 m. A relatively small fruiteater with orange or pink tarsi and toes, and small pale tertial spots. Throat and upper breast of male bright red; female densely spotted or scaled below, green on yellow. Male of northern *squamipectus* (south to San Martín) has less red on throat, and flanks are more heavily green; female also lacks yellow marks on face and throat of southern subspecies *frontalis* (Cordillera Azul south). **VOICE** Song (?) of *squamipectus* is a short, rising *"tsweeet."* Call a short, very high *"pseet."* Song of *frontalis* is a rising, high, thin trill that becomes a descending whistle: *"ti'ti'ti'ti'ti'ti'tseeeeeeeeer."* **E, Bo**

4 SHARPBILL *Oxyruncus cristatus* * 17 cm (6¾ in)
Local and uncommon; primarily reported from outlying ridges at 750–1750 m. Easily overlooked except by voice. Singles forage in canopy of humid forest, apart or with mixed-species flocks. Eats both insects and fruit, and can be acrobatic, probing into dead leaf clusters or epiphytes, and hanging upside down near ends of branches. Bill sharply pointed. Upperparts olive. Throat and sides of face pale yellow scaled black; underparts pale yellow speckled with black. Semiconcealed crest red or orange. **VOICE** Song a long, descending, buzzy whistle, often ending with a rising, electric note: *"dzzzzeeeww-chway"* or simply *"dzzzzzeeeewwww."* Usually sings from subcanopy and rarely moves, making it difficult to see. **Co, E, Br, Bo**

5 GRAY-TAILED PIHA *Snowornis subalaris* 23–24 cm (9–9½ in)
Local but can be fairly common, primarily restricted to outlying ridges at 800–1350 m. Found in under- and midstory of interior of humid montane forest. Usually encountered as singles that remain motionless for long periods, then sally to hover-glean for insects; also eats fruit. Olive green with a narrow whitish orbital ring, semiconcealed black crown stripe (often reduced or absent in female), and gray belly and tail. Extent of gray on belly variable; green may be confined to upper breast or may extend to lower belly. Olivaceous Piha is found at higher elevations and has yellow-green belly and olive tail. **VOICE** Song, given with long pauses (often 5–20 min) between, is a loud, ringing, rising *"CUU'EE?"* **Co, E**

6 OLIVACEOUS PIHA *Snowornis cryptolophus* * 23–24 cm (9–9½ in)
Uncommon in interior of humid montane forest along east slope of Andes and locally on outlying ridges, 1350–2300 m. Behavior similar to that of Gray-tailed Piha, which it apparently replaces at higher elevations. Bright olive green, yellower on belly, with semiconcealed black crown stripe (reduced or absent in female). No similar species found in same habitat; see Gray-tailed, also Carmiol's Tanager. **VOICE** Vocalizations not known (surprisingly quiet for a piha? or singing is highly seasonal?). **Co, E**

FIERY-THROATED
FRUITEATER

♀

♂

MASKED FRUITEATER

♀

SCARLET-BREASTED
FRUITEATER

frontalis

squamipectus

♀

♂

♂

♀

SCARLET-BREASTED
FRUITEATER

SHARPBILL

GRAY-TAILED PIHA

OLIVACEOUS PIHA

PLATE
233

UMBRELLABIRD, FRUITCROW, AND AMAZONIAN COTINGAS

Umbrellabird and the fruitcrow are two large, black cotingas of humid forest. Blue cotingas are not very vocal but often perch in exposed sites in canopy. Otherwise singles or pairs visit fruiting trees in canopy or midstory. Shade of blue of male may vary (from cobalt to more turquoise) depending upon angle of the light; cf. smaller Swallow Tanager. Purple-throated Cotinga is behaviorally similar.

1 AMAZONIAN UMBRELLABIRD *Cephalopterus ornatus* male 45–48 cm (17¼–19 in), female 38–42 cm (15–16½ in)

Uncommon in humid montane forest on east slope of Andes, 600–1650 m. Also (locally?) in Amazonia, where apparently confined to floodplains of large rivers and forested river islands; more common in north than in central or southern Amazonia. Forages in canopy. More often seen in flight, crossing rivers and other large openings with deep wingbeats. Easily identified by large size, black plumage, heavy bill, pale eye, and crest (often pulled back in flight). Male also has long feathered wattle on breast. **VOICE** Song, performed with a bowing display, a deep, hollow booming *"ooooooooooo,"* similar to blowing across top of a bottle. **Co, E, Br, Bo**

2 BARE-NECKED FRUITCROW *Gymnoderus foetidus* male 37–39 cm (14½–15¼ in), female 34.5–35 cm (13½–13¾ in)

Fairly common and widespread in Amazonia, up to 600 m. Found in seasonally flooded forests and on forested river islands. Perhaps most often detected in flight across rivers and over canopy, sometimes in small flocks (suggesting regional movements?). Gleans both for large insects and for fruit while hopping along large branches in canopy. Note silvery to blue, bare skin on sides of head and neck; otherwise largely sooty gray (female) or black with gray wing coverts and remiges (male). Deep wingbeats and small-headed appearance lend a distinctive flight profile; gray wings of male also prominent in flight. Juvenile heavily scaled with white, with little bare skin on head. Juvenile like female, but body and wings narrowly scaled white. **VOICE** Usually silent. Song, performed in a display that includes inflating the bare neck, a deep hoot or boom similar to song of Amazonian Umbrellabird. **Co, E, Br, Bo**

3 PURPLE-THROATED COTINGA *Porphyrolaema porphyrolaema* 18–18.5 cm (7–7¼ in)

Uncommon in northern Amazonia; rare and local in central and southern Amazonia. Found in canopy of humid forest, up to 450 m. More often encountered in pairs rather than as solitary individuals. Female superficially similar to female blue cotingas, but barred, not speckled or mottled, below. **VOICE** Song, rarely heard, a loud, raptorlike, descending *"WHEEEEEW."* Call a pure, descending whistle: *"wheew."* Sounds very like Dusky-capped Flycatcher. **Co, E, Br, Bo**

4 SPANGLED COTINGA *Cotinga cayana* 21–21.5 cm (8¼–8½ in)

Uncommon but widespread in Amazonia, below 800 m, locally up to 1350 m. More regular in terra firme than in seasonally flooded forests. Male turquoise, paler than Plum-throated Cotinga, with more extensive, rosier throat patch; black bases to feathers also show through, especially on upperparts (looks "spangled"). Wings largely black (extensively blue in Plum-throated). Female very drab: grayer and more uniform in color than female Plum-throated. Iris brown in both sexes. **VOICE** Usually silent. Song (?) a hollow, descending hoot: *"POOH"* in flight display. **Co, E, Br, Bo**

5 PURPLE-BREASTED COTINGA *Cotinga cotinga* 18 cm (7 in)

Rare and very local; may be restricted to areas in or near nutrient-poor soils (such as on sandy soil), but very poorly known. Male very deep, purplish blue with extensive purple throat and breast. Female narrowly scaled with white or buff above; underparts light buff heavily spotted with dusky brown, vent cinnamon-buff. Smaller, darker above and more heavily spotted below than Plum-throated or Spangled cotingas. Wings produce a rattling sound in flight. **Co, Br**

6 PLUM-THROATED COTINGA *Cotinga maynana* 19.5–20.5 cm (7¾–8 in)

Uncommon but widespread in Amazonia, locally up to 1000 m. More common in seasonally flooded forests than in terra firme. Male unspotted blue, with purple throat and pale iris. Female indistinctly scaled with whitish or buff; underparts lightly mottled, with ochraceous or cinnamon wash (particularly prominent on vent). At least some birds in female plumage have pale iris. Cf. female Spangled Cotinga. **VOICE** Call (?) a quiet, deep, hollow, descending hoot: *"pooh."* In flight display, male's wings produce a sputtering sound. **Co, E, Br, Bo**

AMAZONIAN
UMBRELLABIRD

juv.

♂

♀

BARE-NECKED FRUITCROW

PURPLE-THROATED
COTINGA

♀

♂

SPANGLED COTINGA

♀

♂

PLUM-THROATED
COTINGA

♂

♀

PURPLE-BREASTED
COTINGA

♂

♀

♂

♀

PLATE
234

LARGE COTINGAS, SCHIFFORNIS, AND WING-BARRED MANAKIN

The red-cotinga is a spectacular cotinga of northern Amazonia. Cock-of-the-rock and the fruitcrow are very large Andean cotingas. The two schiffornis are plain, unpatterned birds of forest understory; they have few distinctive features, other than dull plumage and stubby bills. Wing-barred Manakin is a small canopy species, heard more often than seen.

1 ANDEAN COCK-OF-THE-ROCK *Rupicola peruvianus* * 31–33 cm (12¼–13 in)
Emblem of humid montane forests; often proclaimed as Peru's national bird. Widespread along east slope of Andes and on outlying ridges, at 500–2300 m. Nest on ledge on rock face, often near streams or other humid, shaded sites. Male bright orange (*aequatorialis, peruvianus*) or red-orange (*saturatus;* eastern Cuzco south to Bolivia). Female large, orange-brown with pale iris. Immature male (not illustrated) similar to female, but plumage more orange or red-orange, especially on crest; subadult males blotched with orange or red-orange. **VOICE** Male lekking display accompanied by peculiar, loud, hoarse grunts, chuckles, and meows, as well as dramatic bows and jumps. Most commonly a raspy, rising: *"ewREEE?"* Calls (both sexes) hoarse grunts and meows, for example: *"REHHH."* **Co, E, Bo**

2 BLACK-NECKED RED-COTINGA *Phoenicircus nigricollis* male 21.5 cm (8½ in), female 24 cm (9½ in)
Uncommon and local, in midstory and canopy of terra firme in northern Amazonia. Males lek in early morning in midstory, where they call while bowing forward and raising the rump feathers. Black of male replaced by dusky brown in female; otherwise bright red plumage of both sexes unmistakable. **VOICE** Call a loud, squeaky, descending bark, often in chorus: *"KYUNK!"* or *"KYEW!"* Male's wings produce a bell-like, high, tinkling sound in flight. **Co, E, Br**

3 RED-RUFFED FRUITCROW *Pyroderus scutatus* * male 38–40.5 cm (15–16 in), female 35.5–38 cm (14–15 in)
Rare to uncommon to rare along east slope of Andes, 1100–2100 m. Usually encountered as singles in canopy of humid montane forest. Very large, blackish with contrasting orange throat and breast; belly mottled with chestnut. **VOICE** Song, produced as it inflates throat and bows up and down on perch, a "sawing"-patterned series (in time with bowing motion) of deep, booming hoots, similar to blowing across top of a bottle. **Co, E, Br**

4 VARZEA SCHIFFORNIS *Schiffornis major* * 16 cm (6¼ in)
Uncommon but widespread in eastern lowlands, in understory of varzea. Solitary. Largely bright cinnamon-rufous with dusky wings. Extent of gray or grayish brown color on head individually variable; typically gray confined to a broad, dull grayish eyering, but less commonly crown or entire head and throat may be light gray. Cf. Cinnamon Attila; schiffornis is smaller with much smaller, unhooked bill and a different **VOICE** Song slightly variable, generally a loud, clear whistled series: *"HEW chewEE hoo-HUEE'HEE?"* or *"HEW-chewEE HEW-chewEE HEW-chewEE."* Call a musical chatter: *"chew trr'rr'rr'rr."* **Co, E, Br, Bo**

5 THRUSH-LIKE SCHIFFORNIS *Schiffornis turdina* * 15.5–17 cm (6–6¼ in)
Uncommon in humid forest understory in Amazonia and foothills up to 1500 m; also rare in semideciduous forest in Tumbes. Solitary. Often perches on sides of slender vertical stems; sallies to foliage to capture insects. Dull brownish olive with more rufescent wings; throat often washed tawny. Overall browner in Amazonia (*amazona*), more olive in foothills (*aenea, steinbachi*); *rosenbergi* (Tumbes; not illustrated) similar to latter but darker. Identified by drab plumage, large, round-headed appearance, and behavior. Cf. Brownish Flycatcher, which has larger bill with pale mandible, obvious rictal bristles, ragged crown, and different voice and behavior. **VOICE** Song (*rosenbergi*) a high, thin whistled *"teeeeeeew tui-chuEEE?"* Song in foothills a simple *"hew EEuEE TU-hew."* Song of *amazona* a thin high whistled *"teeeeeee tui-ti-TUEE?"* **Co, E, Br, Bo**

6 WING-BARRED MANAKIN *Piprites chloris* * 13 cm (5¼ in)
Uncommon but widespread in Amazonia, up to 1500 m. Singles or pairs forage in canopy of tall forest, almost always with mixed-species flocks. Posture, behavior, and structure recall a small flycatcher or becard. Note yellow forecrown, eyering, and throat that contrast with gray sides of face; bold wing bars; and broad pale tips to tertials. **VOICE** Song a stuttering series of hollow whistles; pace and pattern may vary slightly: *"hoo hoo hoo hoo hooHEE'EE hoo hoo."* Calls quiet, deep *"chew"* and *"chuck"* notes. **Co, E, Br, Bo**

ANDEAN COCK-OF-THE-ROCK

♀

♂

♂ *saturatus*

BLACK-NECKED
RED-COTINGA

♀

♂

THRUSH-LIKE
SCHIFFORNIS

Amaz.

RED-RUFFED
FRUITCROW

Andean

THRUSH-LIKE
SCHIFFORNIS

VARZEA SCHIFFORNIS

WING-BARRED
MANAKIN

PLATE
235

MANAKINS AND TYRANT-MANAKINS

Tyrant-manakins resemble drab tyrant flycatchers. Tyranneutes is very tiny and short-tailed. It is frugivorous, as are the three manakins shown here with brightly colored males. Neopelma are in forest under- and midstory; inconspicuous except by voice. Both species have relatively long tail, pale iris, and yellow coronal patch, often concealed (but may be flared during social interactions). Diet is largely insects. None of the species on this plate associate with mixed-species flocks.

1 STRIPED MANAKIN *Machaeropterus regulus* * 9–9.5 cm (3½ in)
Widespread *striolatus* is uncommon in northern Amazonia and adjacent foothills, in under- and midstory of humid forest. Foothills *aureopectus* (separate species?) restricted to sites at 1000–1350 m in Mayo Valley, and in Cordillera Azul. Females indistinguishable; male *aureopectus* easily recognized by bright yellow breast band. Cf. Fiery-capped Manakin. **VOICE** Call (*striolatus*) a high, sneezy "*cli-CHEW!*" with a quiet hooting overtone concurrent with the "*chew*" note. Song a loud, hollow, popping "*BOOP*" followed by a descending, quavering buzz (mechanically produced?). Calls of *aureopectus* very different, rising, whistled "*chiwee?*" reminiscent of Eastern Wood-Pewee. **Co, E, Br**

2 FIERY-CAPPED MANAKIN *Machaeropterus pyrocephalus* * 9 cm (3½ in)
Widespread but generally uncommon in humid forest of Amazonia and foothills, up to 1100 m, locally to 1500 m. There is local overlap with two different subspecies of Striped Manakin: with *aureopectus* in Mayo Valley, and with *striolatus* in central Peru; in south, Fiery-capped mostly replaces Striped. Male distinctive. Female distinguished from female Striped by olive breast (lacking faint yellow or reddish wash) and yellow-olive belly (not whitish or pale yellow). **VOICE** Call an easily overlooked, bell-like "*ting*" or "*tee*." Male's wings may rattle in flight. Song, performed while male faces female (always perched on vertical branch?) with mouth wide open, is a quiet, descending creak followed by a long chattered buzzy sound (all vocally produced): "*eewwwwdzz'z'z'z'z'z'z'z'z'z'z'-z'z'z'z'z.*" **Br, Bo**

3 SULPHUR-BELLIED TYRANT-MANAKIN *Neopelma sulphureiventer* 13 cm (5 in)
Uncommon and local in Amazonia, below 700 m, locally to 1000 m. Found in seasonally flooded forest, especially near bamboo thickets or vine tangles, especially in southeast; northern population also found in semideciduous scrub and on poor-soil ridges. Drab yellow-green with large sulphur-yellow crown patch. Superficially similar to Greenish Elaenia; but the elaenia has narrow yellow-green margins to remiges, dark iris, and pale gray lores. **VOICE** Calls a squeaky "*dueek*" or "*duet*" in short series, also a scratchy series of "*djurt*" or "*djurit*" notes. **Br, Bo**

4 DWARF TYRANT-MANAKIN *Tyranneutes stolzmanni* 8.5 cm (3¼ in)
Tiny bird with a persistent voice. Fairly common throughout Amazonia, up to 800 m. Rarely noticed other than when vocalizing. Males sing, occasionally changing position, from slender, open perch in upper understory and midstory of humid forest (usually 3–10 m above ground). Forage in canopy or subcanopy. Note very small size, drab color, very short tail, and pale iris. Cf. females of Golden-headed and Round-tailed manakins, which are larger and usually have brown or pinkish (not gray) mandibles; also, iris usually dark (although rarely may be whitish). **VOICE** Song, given incessantly through day, a deep, sneezy "*DJEW'hit.*" Calls a musical, rising "*duit*" or "*dureek,*" often doubled or in series; notes usually longer than similar call of Slender-footed Tyrannulet. **Co, E, Br, Bo**

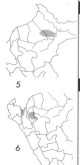

5 SAFFRON-CRESTED TYRANT-MANAKIN *Neopelma chrysocephalum* 13 cm (5 in)
Fairly common, but very local, in northern Amazonia. Restricted to stunted forests on white-sand soils. Drab yellow-green with large, wide golden yellow coronal patch. Does not overlap with Sulphur-bellied Tyrant-Manakin; also, crown is richer, more golden yellow, extends farther onto nape, and is bordered laterally with dusky. **VOICE** Song a loud, nasal, twangy, slightly accelerating series: "*doooWHI dui-dui-dui'urrr.*" Call a rich "*PEW!*" usually in an evenly paced series, of variable speed. **Co, Br**

6 GOLDEN-WINGED MANAKIN *Masius chrysopterus* * 11 cm (4¼ in)
Fairly common along east slope of northern Andes, 1200–2000 m. Inconspicuous, in under- and midstory of humid montane forest. Male black with yellow frontal tuft and forecrown, becoming orange-red on rear crown; inner webs of most remiges and rectrices yellow, largely concealed in closed wing and tail but noticeable in flight. Yellow throat and upper breast of male usually largely concealed. Female yellowish green with relatively long tail and yellowish breast patch. **VOICE** Call a very high, thin, descending "*tsee'ee.*" **Co, E**

STRIPED MANAKIN

♂ *striolatus*

♂ *aureopectus*

FIERY-CAPPED MANAKIN

SULPHUR-BELLIED
TYRANT-MANAKIN

DWARF
TYRANT-MANAKIN

SAFFRON-CRESTED
TYRANT-MANAKIN

GOLDEN-WINGED
MANAKIN

PLATE
236

MANAKINS

Black Manakin is very local in Amazonia. White-crowned Manakin is a small, widespread "classic" manakin, in which males display at leks. Jet and Green manakins are unobtrusive Andean species. The two Heterocercus are large, buffy-bellied manakins with contrasting pale throats and graduated tails.

1 BLACK MANAKIN *Xenopipo atronitens* 12 cm (4¾ in)

Locally fairly common in stunted forest on sandy soil at Jeberos. Also reported from Pampas del Heath and adjacent sites, where status not clear. Male black with contrasting blue-gray bill; no overlap with similar Jet Manakin of Andes. Female drab olive-green; separable from other species of sympatric manakins by dull plumage, dull bluish gray bill, and relatively long, notched tail. **VOICE** Song, given after long silences, a scratchy chatter: "*SKEEE tchew'tchew'tchew'tchtchtch*"; sometimes chatter replaced with a thin, descending, trill. Call a quiet groan or growl. **Co, Br, Bo**

2 WHITE-CROWNED MANAKIN *Dixiphia pipra* * 9–10 cm (3½–4 in)

Fairly common and widespread in northern and central Amazonia; also on east slope of Andes, up to 2000 m. In understory of humid forest, in Amazonia primarily in terra firme. Iris red or reddish. Varies geographically in both voice and plumage. Male black with white crown; generally white crown extends onto nape in Andean populations. Females (and first-year males) geographically variable. Females of Andean populations usually have gray nape or gray crown and sides of head; body bright yellowish green (*coracina*, south to northern San Martín) or olive-green (other Andean subspecies). Amazonian females duller olive-green or grayish green, with light gray nape washed with green (sometimes crown is gray washed with olive, or olive scarcely different from back). **VOICE** Song (?) of *coracina* a hoarse "*pew… WURR'EEO.*" Song in central Andes a rising ringing, burry "*wurrrb'TEE?*"; also a quiet, deep "*tok!*" (mechanical?) as male changes song perches; song in southern Andes (Pasco to Cuzco) apparently unknown. Call a hoarse, descending "*wur.*" Song in Amazonia a descending buzzy "*DZZEW!*" Call a mellow, mewing, descending "*pew*" or "*weeo.*" **Co, E, Br**

3 JET MANAKIN *Xenopipo unicolor* 11.5–12 cm (4½–4¾ in)

Inconspicuous but often fairly common, along east slope of Andes at 900–2200 m; local and less common in south. Singles or (rarely) pairs forage in under- and lower midstory of humid montane forest, or at fruiting trees. Relatively long-tailed, with white underwing coverts. Male otherwise black, glossed with blue. Female very drab olive-brown. Similar in size and shape to Green Manakin of lower elevations, but color much dingier. **VOICE** Call a rising, squeaky "*tueee?*" **E**

4 GREEN MANAKIN *Xenopipo holochlora* * 12 cm (4¾ in)

Uncommon to locally fairly common along east slope of Andes, and on outlying ridges, at 400–1100 m. Solitary, in forest under- and lower midstory, or at fruiting trees. Sexes similar; note relatively bright yellow-green tone, relatively long tail, and dark tarsi. Female *Chiroxiphia* manakins are duller, with pale tarsi; female White-crowned and *Pipra* manakins are smaller, duller, with shorter tails; female Golden-winged Manakin has purplish tarsi and, often, a small forehead tuft. **VOICE** Call a very high, rising "*tueee?*" **Co, E**

5 ORANGE-CROWNED MANAKIN *Heterocercus aurantiivertex* 14 cm (5½ in)

Fairly common, but very local; primarily north of Amazon, but also at a few sites on south bank. Found in under- and lower midstory of varzea, almost always at sites in blackwater drainages. Olive above with grayish cheeks; male has narrow semiconcealed orange coronal patch. Throat white (male) or light gray (female), belly buffy. **VOICE** Song a rising-falling-rising, tinkling chatter: "*TEE'ee'ee'u'u'ee'ee'uu.*" Display includes a rising, spiral flight display high above canopy followed by a rapid drop accompanied by a hissing sound and ending with a "*pop,*" both produced mechanically. A second display occurs low to ground: male hops acrobatically, producing a mechanical "*pop*" during each leap. Call a squeaky chatter. Also produces metallic, vibrating buzzes. **E, Br**

6 [FLAME-CROWNED MANAKIN *Heterocercus linteatus*] 14–15 cm (5½–6 in)

Known only from two sight records near Bolivian border. Also to be looked for at sites along south bank of the Amazon near Brazil. White throat of male contrasts with black head, scarlet crown patch, and rufous-buff breast and belly. Female very similar to female Orange-crowned Manakin; probably not safely identifiable in the field, but is darker, browner olive above and deeper buff below. **Br, Bo**

BLACK MANAKIN

♀   ♂

WHITE-CROWNED
MANAKIN

♂   ♀ Andean

♀ Amaz.

JET MANAKIN

♀   ♂

GREEN MANAKIN

FLAME-CROWNED
MANAKIN

♂   ♀

ORANGE-CROWNED
MANAKIN

♀   ♂

PLATE
237

BLUE MANAKINS AND WHITE-BEARDED MANAKIN

Chiroxiphia are large manakins, in which males have cooperative displays. Lepidothrix are very small understory manakins. Males sing solitarily or in dispersed leks, within a few meters of ground. White-bearded Manakin is notable for the loud whirring and snapping noises produced by the wings of displaying males.

1 YUNGAS MANAKIN *Chiroxiphia boliviana* 12 cm (4¾ in)

Elevationally replaces Blue-backed Manakin at 900–2000 m along east side of southern Andes. Longer-tailed than Blue-backed. Crown of male also darker red (more crimson), and blue of upperparts paler. Females difficult to separate other than by tail length. **VOICE** Song, often in chorus, includes a loud "CHEW'LEW!," "CHEW!," "TCHAW," or "WHEW!" Display call is a quiet, nasal, buzzy "errwahh" repeated several times. Call a rising, ani-like "huLEE?" **Bo**

2 BLUE-BACKED MANAKIN *Chiroxiphia pareola* * 11–11.5 cm (4¼–4½ in)

Relatively widespread in northern Amazonia; very local in central Peru and south. Up to 750 m. Found in under- and midstory of terra firme. Male strikingly black and blue; crown red north of the Amazon and west of Río Ucayali (*napensis*), or yellow south of the Amazon and east of Ucayali (*regina*). Female large, green, with orangey or pinkish brown tarsi. Much larger than female White-bearded Manakin, with more olive belly. Immature males may develop red crown while still largely green. Cf. also Yungas Manakin (found at higher elevations). **VOICE** Song, often in chorus, an explosive, rising, human-like, whistled "WEEO-WEET!" or "HOOWHIT!," also an electric sounding "chir-CHURNG," often doubled. Display vocalization, produced as males cartwheel over one another, a nasal whinny: "errwaah'h'h" repeated several times. **Co, E, Br, Bo**

3 CERULEAN-CAPPED MANAKIN *Lepidothrix coeruleocapilla* 9 cm (3½ in)

Fairly common at 600–1700 m in humid forest understory on east side of Andes in central and southern Peru; replaces Blue-crowned Manakin elevationally. No known overlap with Blue-rumped Manakin. Male black with blue crown and rump. Female extremely similar to female Blue-crowned; underparts duller, paler. **VOICE** Song a burry, frog-like "djew-HAI." Calls a rising, mewed whistle: "weeee?" like Blue-crowned. **ENDEMIC**

4 WHITE-BEARDED MANAKIN *Manacus manacus* * 10–11 cm (4–4¼ in)

Uncommon to locally fairly common in northern Amazonia in understory of humid forest and second growth, primarily in terra firme, below 1000 m; more local in southeast. Also local in semideciduous forest in northwest. Male strikingly black and white; south of the Amazon (*expectatus*) even whiter, with broader nuchal collar and only a little gray on belly. Female largely green with grayish throat; note orange tarsi (but cf. larger *Chiroxiphia*). **VOICE** Song a mechanically produced electric buzz "TRRRT!" followed by a musical "chi'lew" call. Display series of deep electric buzzes and mechanical snapping sounds as male leaps between vertical stems; often gives a loud, mechanical "TOK" as rapidly bounces off an area of bare ground between perches. Call a low, descending, growled "grrrew." Males' wings may rattle in flight. **Co, E, Br, Bo**

5 BLUE-RUMPED MANAKIN *Lepidothrix isidorei* * 8–8.5 cm (3–3¼ in)

Locally fairly common at 1100–1400 m (1000–1700 m in Ecuador) in humid montane forest on east side of northern Andes; replaces similar Blue-crowned elevationally. Male has white crown and nape; rump blue (*isidorei*, north of Marañón) or largely white tinged blue, with blue upper and lower borders (*leucopygia*, south of Marañón). Female very similar to female Blue-crowned; slightly smaller, forecrown tinged yellow. **VOICE** Song a squeaky, rising "wing?" Call a high, rising "sweeee?" **Co, E**

6 BLUE-CROWNED MANAKIN *Lepidothrix coronata* * 9 cm (3½ in)

Fairly common in Amazonia, up to 800 m, locally to 1400 m; more widespread in north, somewhat local in southeast. Male plumage mostly black (glossed with blue) throughout Loreto north of the Amazon, and south, east of Río Ucayali, to northern Ucayali (*coronata, carbonata*). Males from Amazonas south, west of Río Ucayali, to Cuzco, and east to southern Ucayali and Madre de Dios, mostly green with blackish faces (*exquisita, caelestipileata*). Males with intermediate features may be found where two types meet. Females bright green above and on breast, with pale yellow bellies. Smaller and brighter than female *Pipra* or White-crowned manakins, but not readily separable from females of other *Lepidothrix*. **VOICE** Song a thin, rising whistle followed by a froglike croak: "SWEE? tuk'URT." Calls a rising "wee?" and a thin, sputtered, tinkling "ti'i'ir." **Co, E, Br, Bo**

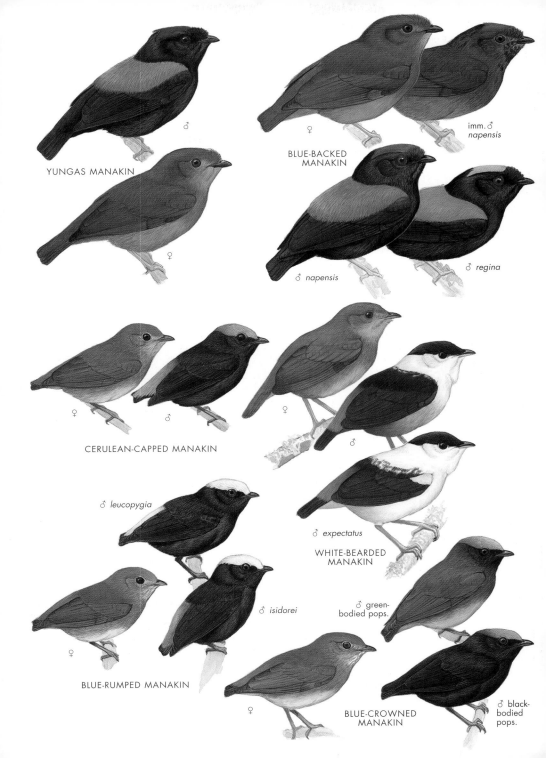

YUNGAS MANAKIN

♂

♀

BLUE-BACKED
MANAKIN

♀

imm.♂
napensis

♂ napensis

♂ regina

CERULEAN-CAPPED MANAKIN

♀

♂

♀

♂

♂ leucopygia

♂ expectatus

WHITE-BEARDED
MANAKIN

♂ isidorei

♀

BLUE-RUMPED MANAKIN

♂ green-
bodied pops.

♀

♂ black-
bodied
pops.

BLUE-CROWNED
MANAKIN

PLATE
238

TYPICAL MANAKINS (*PIPRA*)

Pipra are short-tailed manakins of humid forest under- and midstory. Males engage in stereotyped displays at leks. Otherwise most often seen at fruiting trees. Immature males resemble females, but iris often pale as in adult (except for dark-eyed Red-capped Manakin); also, some females (older individuals?) may have some bright (red or yellow) feathers on crown.

1 WIRE-TAILED MANAKIN *Pipra filicauda* * 11 cm (4¼ in); + tail filaments of 4–4.5 cm (1¾ in) in male, 3 cm (1¼ in) in female

Fairly common and widespread in northern Amazonia, in varzea and seasonally flooded forests. Both sexes have narrow hairlike extensions to rectrices, and white iris. Inner webs of inner remiges of male are white (visible in flight). Male always has yellow throat and breast (cf. Band-tailed Manakin). Female relatively large and brightly colored. Most similar to female Band-tailed, which lacks tail filaments; not known to overlap geographically, but may approach one another (or even meet) in central Peru. **VOICE** Song, often performed in chorus at leks, is descending, nasal, electric "*NEEeeew.*" Call a rising clear whistled "*weee?*" **Co, E, Br**

2 BAND-TAILED MANAKIN *Pipra fasciicauda* * 10–11 cm (4–4¼ in)

Fairly common in Amazonia, below 1000 m. In north only near base of Andes, but more widespread in central and southern Peru (south of range of Wire-tailed Manakin). Understory of varzea and seasonally flooded forests; leks often located in dense understory thickets. Both sexes have white iris. Male always has red crown and largely yellow underparts with red or orangey wash on breast; white band on short tail; and white on inner webs of inner remiges. Male *saturata* (Huallaga drainage) has extensive red wash on breast and upper belly; red of underparts confined to breast in *purusiana* of central Peru; *fasciicauda* of Madre de Dios and Puno has orangey pectoral band and may show complete whitish tail band. Female more yellowish than other sympatric manakins, with distinctly yellow belly; cf. female Wire-tailed. **VOICE** Song, often performed in chorus at leks, is descending, nasal, electric "*NEEeeer,*" also a shorter, bisyllabic "*EE-EW.*" Call a whiny, rising "*weeEEe?*" **Br, Bo**

3 GOLDEN-HEADED MANAKIN *Pipra erythrocephala* * 9–10 cm (3½–4 in)

Fairly common in northern Amazonia; crosses to south bank of Río Marañón, reaching northern Cordillera Azul. Up to 1350 m. Male unmistakable. Female duller and larger than female Blue-crowned Manakin; lacks gray nape of White-crowned. Cf. also female Round-tailed Manakin. Indistinguishable from female Red-headed Manakin. **VOICE** Song bouts include variable high metallic sounds and deep buzzes; a characteristic sound is buzzy "*dzew*" followed by a sputtered "*trr'ee'ee'err*" and a series of rising whistles followed by a low buzz: "*weew weeew WEEW SWEEW'-DZZRT.*" Also high ringing "*TEE'TINK*" notes. Call a loud, emphatic "*pew!*" **Co, E, Br**

4 RED-HEADED MANAKIN *Pipra rubrocapilla* 10.5 cm (4¼ in)

Locally fairly common in eastern Amazonia lowlands. Distribution may approach Golden-headed Manakin on lower Río Huallaga, but no known overlap. Male similar to male Round-tailed Manakin (overlaps in south) but is less crested and has darker iris and white-and-red tibial feathering; also note habitat differences. Female duller than smaller female Blue-crowned Manakin. Differs from female White-crowned by browner iris and by green (not gray) nape; belly also usually greener, less often gray. Cf. female Round-tailed. **VOICE** Song bouts include variable high metallic sounds and deep buzzes, but a characteristic sound is a series of quiet, descending notes followed by a loud, descending thin whistle that ends with a loud buzz: "*tsew tsew-tchew SEEEEEEE'BZZANG!*" Also high "*TSIK*" and "*heeee DJZERT!*" notes. **Br, Bo**

5 ROUND-TAILED MANAKIN *Pipra chloromeros* 10.5–11 cm (4–4¼ in)

Locally fairly common in Andean foothills and in Amazonia, up to 1500 m. Where sympatric with Red-headed Manakin, Round-tailed is more prevalent in seasonally flooded forest (and Red-headed in terra firme); otherwise will occupy terra firme where Red-headed not present. Short tail in both sexes is slightly graduated (not square-tipped). Male often appears crested on nape; note whitish iris and yellow tibial feathering. Cf. Red-headed. Female drab olive, short-tailed; iris may be grayish or whitish. Slightly yellower than female Red- or Golden-headed manakins, but dark-eyed individuals safely distinguishable only by tail shape; also often appears "crested" on nape. **VOICE** Song bouts include variable high metallic sounds, mellow whistles, squeaky chatters, and buzzes; a characteristic sound is a buzzy "*tsuk'ZRRRT*" or "*tsik'DZZRT*" and a high rising-falling laugh. **Br, Bo**

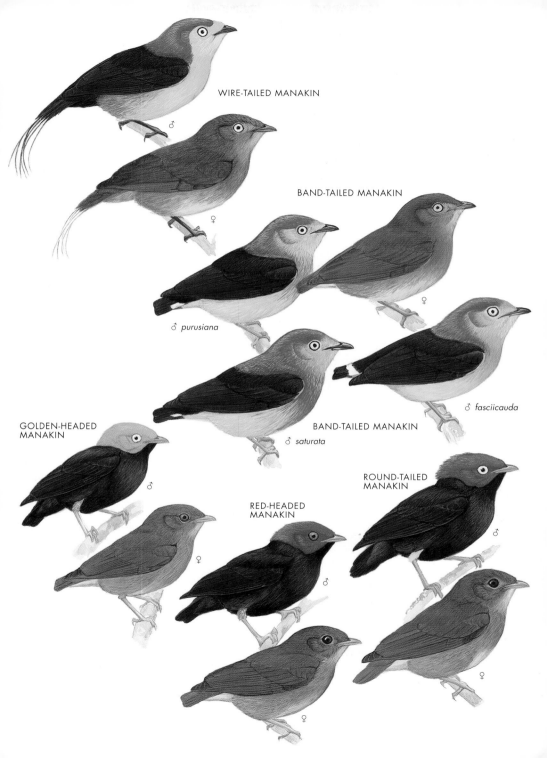

WIRE-TAILED MANAKIN

♂

♀

BAND-TAILED MANAKIN

♂ purusiana

♀

♂ saturata

BAND-TAILED MANAKIN

♂ fasciicauda

GOLDEN-HEADED
MANAKIN

♂

♀

RED-HEADED
MANAKIN

♂

♀

ROUND-TAILED
MANAKIN

♂

♀

PLATE
239

VIREOS, SHRIKE-VIREO, AND PEPPERSHRIKE

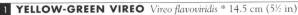

Vireos are plain, mostly insectivorous birds that regularly follow mixed-species flocks. Bill hooked at tip. Shrike-vireo is similar but heavier billed, and plumage is a bit more patterned. Peppershrike has a much deeper bill; more often apart from mixed-species flocks.

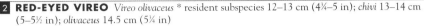

1 YELLOW-GREEN VIREO *Vireo flavoviridis* * 14.5 cm (5½ in)

Locally fairly common boreal migrant (Sep–Mar) to eastern lowlands. Probably winters primarily on or near lower slopes of Andes below 900 m, but in migration may be found well out into Amazonia. Similar to Red-eyed Vireo, but flanks, vent, and sides of breast yellow-green (brighter, more strongly, and extensively yellow than in Red-eyed) and face pattern less distinct (lacks black border to gray crown). **VOICE** Call a raspy, complaining "*hey*" or "*hyaah*"; like Red-eyed. Song sounds like a rapid-paced Red-eyed. **Co, E, Br, Bo**

2 RED-EYED VIREO *Vireo olivaceus* * resident subspecies 12–13 cm (4¾–5 in); *chivi* 13–14 cm
(5–5½ in); *olivaceus* 14.5 cm (5¾ in)

Found in forest canopy of lowlands throughout much of Peru, and locally in montane valleys, in a complicated mixture of resident and migrant populations. Often fairly common. Whitish below, with gray crown, whitish superciliary, and moderately stout bill. Resident birds below 1200 m in semideciduous forests in northwest (*griseobarbatus*; not illustrated), in Marañón Valley (*pectoralis*), and in varzea and second growth along the Amazon and major tributaries (*solimoensis*) are relatively small with yellower upperparts, pale yellow vent, and brown iris. Austral migrant *chivi* (Mar–Sep) winters in Amazonia and on lower slopes of Andes; also breeds in montane valleys in south, locally to 2600 m; has paler yellow vent, narrow black border to crown, duller upperparts, and brown iris. Also boreal migrant (*olivaceus*; Sep–Mar) to northwest and to eastern Peru, mostly below 1000 m, occasionally to 1900 m. Very similar to *chivi*, but usually longer winged (longer primary extension), and adult has red iris. *Chivi* and *olivaceus* replace one another seasonally in Amazonia and overlap with resident forms in north. **VOICE** Song of most populations a leisurely series of musical warbled phrases, with a fair amount of repetition of phrases: "*chew-lee chee-lew wee-chee chew-lee….*" Song of *solimoensis* is somewhat less musical, more rapid. Call (all forms) a raspy, complaining "*hey*" or "*hyaah*." **Co, E, Br, Bo, Ch**

3 SLATY-CAPPED SHRIKE-VIREO *Vireolanius leucotis* * 14 cm (5½ in)

Widespread but uncommon in canopy of terra firme, up to 1400 m; often more common in foothills than in lowlands. Heard far more often than seen. Easily identified by yellow underparts and gray-and-yellow face pattern. Some, especially in north, also may show white stripe on side of face (along lower edge of auriculars). **VOICE** Song a long (often seemingly endless) series of a single, descending whistled note: "*heer… heer… heer…,*" with a note approximately every 2 sec. **Co, E, Br, Bo**

4 BROWN-CAPPED VIREO *Vireo leucophrys* * 12.5 cm (5 in)

Fairly common along east side of Andes, and on outlying ridges, at 1100–2600 m; also in similar habitats on west slope in northwest. In canopy of humid montane forest and forest edge. Note pale yellow underparts, white superciliary, dull brown crown, and lack of wing markings. **VOICE** Song a hesitating, pleasant warble of variable pattern, yet fairly easy to identify: "*wurzle-wee-wee wurzle-weezle-wee wurzle-wee.*" Call a wheezing, descending "*zreeEEEEw.*" **Co, E, Bo**

5 RUFOUS-BROWED PEPPERSHRIKE *Cyclarhis gujanensis* * 15 cm (6 in)

Fairly common in northwest (400–3100 m), in dry Marañón Valley, and along east side of Andes (900–2900 m), in dry forest, edge of humid montane forest, and second growth. Also locally in Amazonia, especially in river-edge forest and (on Pampas del Heath) in woodlots on savanna. More easily heard than seen. Chunky, with stout bill and rufous eyebrow. In Amazonia, and along Andes from Pasco south, crown and sides of head mostly gray (*gujanensis*). Head largely green, with rufous eyebrow, in northwest (*virenticeps*); or crown mixed green and rufous, with rufous eyebrow and green cheeks, in Marañón Valley and on east side of northern Andes (*contrerasi; saturata*, not illustrated). **VOICE** Song a variable, rich warbling, multisyllabic phrase, usually repeated; similar to Slate-colored Grosbeak, but with more syllables, for example: "*chewWEE-cheelu-cheWEEO.*" Call variable, typically a series of clear rising whistles: "*CUI Cui cui cui*"; series sometimes descending (not rising) or decelerating. **Co, E, Br, Bo**

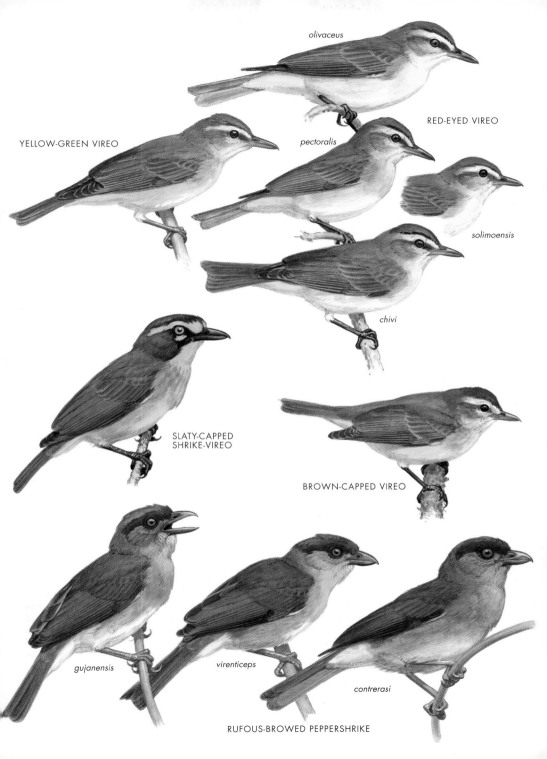

olivaceus

RED-EYED VIREO

YELLOW-GREEN VIREO

pectoralis

solimoensis

chivi

SLATY-CAPPED
SHRIKE-VIREO

BROWN-CAPPED VIREO

gujanensis

virenticeps

contrerasi

RUFOUS-BROWED PEPPERSHRIKE

PLATE
240

GREENLETS

Greenlets are small, active vireos. Often cling upside down to leaf clusters while foraging. Cf. some conebills (*Conirostrum*) and antwrens (*Terenura*).

1 **LESSER GREENLET** *Hylophilus decurtatus* * 10 cm (4 in)

Locally fairly common but restricted to semideciduous and humid forests in Tumbes at 400 m. Forages in canopy and midstory with mixed-species flocks. Only greenlet in northwest. Small, short-tailed, and 2-toned: yellow-green above and white below, with yellow wash on sides of breast and flanks. **VOICE** Song a fairly simple, ringing, warbled phrase given repeatedly, for example: "*key-chain*." Similar to a single, repeated phrase of a Red-eyed Vireo song but without introducing new phrases. Calls a dry, descending series "*djeer-djeer-djeer…*" and a dry chatter "*trr-ee-ee-er*." **Co, E**

2 **TAWNY-CROWNED GREENLET** *Hylophilus ochraceiceps* * 11.5 cm (4½ in)

Widespread and locally fairly common in Amazonia, up to 1200 m. Found in understory of humid forest, especially in terra firme. Regular member of understory mixed-species flocks. Olive above with contrasting tawny crown and pale iris; pale yellow-green below, slightly brighter on breast. On lower slopes of Andes, cf. female Plain Antvireo. **VOICE** Song a clear, descending (or occasionally ascending) whistle: "*heeeeeeeeu*," similar to song of Collared and Half-collared gnatwrens. Call a low, mewing, churring chatter with each note rising: "*djreeee djree-djree-djree*." **Co, E, Br, Bo**

3 **OLIVACEOUS GREENLET** *Hylophilus olivaceus* 12 cm (4¾ in)

Fairly common, but local, along east side of Andes at 1000–1700 m, locally down to 750 m. Singles or pairs forage at forest edge, in tall second growth, and at openings in forest. Often remains within cover; heard much more often than seen. Generally not with mixed-species flocks. Drab above and dull yellow-green below, with pale iris. **VOICE** Song a single note repeated in a series, for example: "*wee wee wee wee wee wee wee*." **E**

4 **DUSKY-CAPPED GREENLET** *Hylophilus hypoxanthus* * 11.5 cm (4½ in)

Widespread and fairly common in Amazonia, up to 1100 m. Forages in canopy and midstory, usually with mixed-species flocks. Drab yellow-green above, grayer on crown, with pale yellow underparts and contrasting white throat. Superficially similar to female *Terenura* antwren, which may occur in same flocks, but antwren is smaller, even more active and has wing bars and a graduated tail. **VOICE** Song a pleasant, often repeated multisyllabic phrase, for example: "*ti-weecho-WEEo*," and other variations. Call a wheezy "*dee-dee*." **Co, E, Br, Bo**

5 **GRAY-CHESTED GREENLET** *Hylophilus semicinereus* * 12 cm (4¾ in)

Local in river-edge thickets along Amazon and major tributaries in north. Often remains concealed within dense vegetation. Very drab, with dingy-colored breast and ill-defined gray wash on nape. Iris usually pale. Much drabber than Lemon-chested Greenlet. **VOICE** Song (Brazil) a series of rising notes: "*wee wee wee wee wee wee*." **Co, Br, Bo**

6 **LEMON-CHESTED GREENLET** *Hylophilus thoracicus* * 12 cm (4¾ in)

Uncommon and local in Amazonia, locally up to 850 m. Forages in canopy and subcanopy of humid forest; may be more common, and forage lower, in river-edge thickets. Note small size, whitish underparts with yellow breast, pinkish bill, and gray nape. Iris usually white or straw colored. **VOICE** Song a series of a single repeated note or phrase, for example: "*chew-ew chew-ew chew-ew chew-ew*." Occasionally gives song more similar to that of Ashy-headed Greenlet: "*REE trr'r'r'r'r'r*." Call a rich, whistled "*wur'it?*," sometimes doubled. **Co, E, Br, Bo**

7 **ASHY-HEADED GREENLET** *Hylophilus pectoralis* 12 cm (4¾ in)

Restricted to dry rain-shadow region of middle Huallaga Valley; fairly common on dry hilltops and forest edge, mostly below 500 m. Very similar to Lemon-chested Greenlet, but iris brown, and entire crown and sides of head gray or gray-brown. Both occur in Mayo Valley, but not known to occur together; presumably are separated by habitat. Juvenile Lemon-chested may have gray-brown forecrown and lores (thus more closely resembling Ashy-headed); but has dusky (not pink) bill and retains faint yellow wash on auriculars. **VOICE** Song a short introductory note followed by a musical trill: "*REE trr'r'r'r'r'r'r*." Call a harsh scold note, often in a series: "*djzshh djzshh….*" **Br, Bo**

LESSER GREENLET

TAWNY-CROWNED
GREENLET

OLIVACEOUS GREENLET

DUSKY-CAPPED
GREENLET

GRAY-CHESTED
GREENLET

LEMON-CHESTED
GREENLET

ASHY-HEADED
GREENLET

PLATE
241   JAYS

Jays are large, noisy, gregarious birds of forest and woods. Bills stout, pointed, with a tuft of stiffened feathers covering nostrils. Sexes similar. Jays are usually encountered in small flocks, which may be family units; these groups may forage on their own or in association with other species of large flocking birds, such as oropendolas, caciques, and mountain-tanagers (Buthraupis). Omnivorous.

1 PURPLISH JAY *Cyanocorax cyanomelas* 36–37 cm (14–14½ in)
Locally fairly common, but largely restricted to floodplain of Río Madre de Dios and tributaries in southeastern Amazonia up to 1000 m. Overlaps with Violaceous Jay, but less likely to be found away from river-edge habitats. Much dingier overall and lacks contrasting paler nape. Juvenile (not illustrated) even duller: largely dusky gray except for blue margins to remiges and rectrices. **VOICE** Fairly small repertoire for a jay. Most frequent call a low, rough "*DJEW*" or "*DJOW*." Also may give a low note as a couplet or series: "*djeh-djeh*." Voice is lower and more growling than Violaceous. **Br, Bo**

2 VIOLACEOUS JAY *Cyanocorax violaceus* * 36–37 cm (14–14½ in)
Uncommon but widespread in Amazonia, up to 900 m, locally to 1400 m. Primarily in varzea and along margins of rivers, streams and lakes, where found in canopy and midstory; also in second growth. Very large. Light purplish blue with black face and throat, contrasting with paler nape. Only jay in most of Amazonia; in southeast cf. Purplish Jay. **VOICE** Fairly small repertoire for a jay. Most frequent call a loud, garrulous, and rough "*JEER*" with ringing quality, often in pairs or series of notes. Also a squeakier "*CHO*," higher and more ringing than Purplish. **Co, E, Br, Bo**

3 WHITE-TAILED JAY *Cyanocorax mystacalis* 32–33 cm (12½–13 in)
Fairly common in dry forest and desert scrub in northwest, up to 1800 m. A spectacular bird, easily recognized by blue, black, and white plumage. Iris of juvenile dark. **VOICE** Fairly small repertoire for a jay. Most frequent call is a hollow "*cleh-cleh*," sometimes becoming a longer series, particularly in alarm. **E**

4 GREEN JAY *Cyanocorax yncas* * 30–33 cm (11¾–13 in)
Fairly common and widespread in humid montane forest along east side of Andes, and on outlying ridges, at 1100–2400 m (*yncas*). Also at 450–2000 m in dry Marañón and Huallaga valleys (*longirostris*), in dry forest and wooded scrub. Forages primarily in midstory and canopy. Green and yellow plumage, with pale crown and black throat, are unmistakable; *longirostris* averages paler. Iris pale yellow in adult, but typically dark in juvenile. **VOICE** Large and varied repertoire. Common calls a raucous "*shook-shook-shook*" or "*djeh-djeh-djeh-djeh*," also a more querulous "*kyen kyen*" (hence the widespread local name "*Quien-quien*"). Also produces dry rattles (often on two pitches: "*tre'e'e'-e'e'r'r'r'r'r'r'r*") and various squeaks, whines, chatters, and other noises. **Co, E, Bo**

5 TURQUOISE JAY *Cyanolyca turcosa* 30–32 cm (11¾–12½ in)
Replaces similar White-collared Jay in humid montane forest at 2400–3000 m north and west of Marañón Valley. Paler and bluer than White-collared, especially on throat. Throat also bordered below with dusky, lacking narrow white "collar." **VOICE** Large and varied repertoire. Common call is a static or electric note, "*SHEEW*," often as couplets or series. Also produces many squeaks, popping noises, electric or static sounds, and other noises. **Co, E**

6 WHITE-COLLARED JAY *Cyanolyca viridicyanus* * 30–32 cm (11¾–12½ in)
Widespread and fairly common in humid montane forest along east slope of Andes, 2200–3500 m, occasionally as low as 1800 m, south of Marañón. Forages primarily in midstory and canopy. Blue with a white forehead, dusky cheeks, and a blue or black throat outlined below with narrow white line (the white "collar"). Northern *jolyaea* (Amazonas south to Junín) cobalt blue overall, including on throat, and has reduced white forecrown and narrower white collar. Southern *cyanolaema* (Ayacucho to Puno) bluer overall, with purplish blue throat and broad white forecrown. In easternmost Puno *viridicyanus* similar but throat blackish blue. **VOICE** Large and varied repertoire. Calls loud, electric or static sounds, popping noises, and high whistled phrases. Also a wheezy whistled series: "*chew chew chew*." Song (?) a very quiet, but remarkably varied, series of whistles, warbles, electric crackles, static, and other sounds. **Bo**

510

PURPLISH JAY

VIOLACEOUS JAY

WHITE-TAILED JAY

GREEN JAY

yncas

longirostris

TURQUOISE JAY

jolyaea

cyanolaema

viridicyanus

WHITE-COLLARED JAY

PLATE
242

MARTINS

Swallows have very short, broad bills, very short tarsi, and long wings; forage entirely by capturing small insects in flight. Superficially similar to swifts, but wings broader, wingbeats less "twinkling." Often perch on snags, wires or other surfaces; swifts only cling to vertical surfaces. Often in small flocks, which may include several species of swallows and sometimes also swifts. Martins are large, broad-winged swallows; most species are sexually dimorphic.

1 BROWN-CHESTED MARTIN *Progne tapera* * *tapera* 16.5–17 cm (6½–6¼ in); *fusca* 17–18 cm (6¼–7 in)

Uncommon resident in Amazonia, below 600 m, along rivers and at lake margins (*tapera*); also locally near rivers and reservoirs in northwest. Status and distribution of *fusca*, austral migrant to Amazonia, not well-known. Usually in pairs or small groups. Characteristically glides with bowed wings and drooping tail. Brown above. Breast of *tapera* light gray-brown, merging into grayish white throat but contrasting more strongly with white belly. Cf. much smaller Southern Rough-winged Swallow. Larger *fusca* is purer white below with darker, more well-defined breast band; also has series of brown spots down center of breast, just below breast band. Superficially similar to much smaller Bank Swallow, from which readily distinguished by size, shape, and flight style. **VOICE** Song a series of liquid, rolling, descending trills, for example: "*trr-tee-tuk-TEEERRR trr-tee-tuk-TEEERRR….*" Calls a dry, buzzy "*djzeut*" and a more musical "*dureet*" similar to calls of other martins. **Co, E, Br, Bo, Ch**

2 GRAY-BREASTED MARTIN *Progne chalybea* * 17–18 cm (6¼–7 in)

Uncommon to fairly common in Amazonian lowlands and in northwest, locally up to 1000 m. Found along rivers, in second growth, and over towns and cities. Nests in small colonies. Male (Amazonia) glossy blue above (extending below eye); dusky gray throat and breast (with blue semicollar) contrast strongly with white belly. Female (Amazonia) similar but duller above, with paler face and breast, and no blue semicollar on sides of breast. In northwest both sexes similar to Amazonian female but even duller above with paler gray-brown throats and cheeks. Contrasting white belly separates it immediately from Southern Martin. **VOICE** Call rich, musical churrs, similar to tapping on a taut cable: "*churr*" or "*chu-ler.*" Also various similar musical, electric warbles and churrs. **Co, E, Br, Bo**

3 PERUVIAN MARTIN *Progne murphyi* 16.5–17 cm (6½–6¼ in)

Small, rare martin of coast, below 100 m. Very few breeding sites known, in small colonies on seaside cliffs or offshore islands in northern Peru (Piura and La Libertad). Records farther south may be of nonbreeding migrants, or might suggest undiscovered breeding sites. Male glossy blue; similar to male Purple Martin (rare vagrant to coast), but smaller and with shallower notch to the tail. Female distinctive: ashy gray, with blue across center of back and onto wings. **Ch**

PURPLE MARTIN *Progne subis* * 18–19.5 cm (7–7¼ in)

Boreal migrant. Status not clear, due to confusion with other martins. Reported from the Iquitos area, where may be rare but regular migrant, at least in Aug or Sep. Also reported from central coast, where perhaps regular in small numbers. Male glossy blue; probably not safely distinguishable in field from male Southern Martin, but tail sometimes is slightly less deeply notched (notch 1.5 cm rather than 2 cm). First-year males similar to female, but variably blotched with blue. Females duller blue above with light grayish forehead and nuchal collar. Throat gray, belly white more or less narrowly streaked dusky; variable, some individuals much darker than others. Similar to Gray-breasted Martin, which always has dark forehead and lacks gray collar. Female Southern much darker below, with little or no lightness on face or collar. See also Peruvian Martin. **VOICE** Call a rich "*chu,*" similar to tapping on a taut cable; also a slightly buzzy "*dee-chuwi*" and rich gurgling notes. **Co, E, Br, Bo**

4 SOUTHERN MARTIN *Progne elegans* 18.5–19.5 cm (7¼–7¼ in)

Austral migrant. Primarily known from eastern Loreto, where winters in large numbers along Amazon near Iquitos; less commonly reported during migration (Mar–May, Aug–Sep) farther south. Male glossy blue with deeply notched tail. Female very dark, vaguely scaled; lacks pale belly and vent of Gray-breasted and female Purple martins. **VOICE** Calls a deep, dry, trilled "*drrr*" and chattered "*djk-djk-djk*" notes. Very unlike other martins, more similar to Bank Swallow. **Co, E, Br, Bo, Ch**

BROWN-CHESTED
MARTIN

tapera

tapera

fusca

BROWN-CHESTED
MARTIN

tapera

fusca

GRAY-BREASTED
MARTIN

Amaz.

Amaz.

Amaz.

nw

Amaz. ♂

♀

GRAY-BREASTED
MARTIN

PERUVIAN
MARTIN

♀

♀

♂

PERUVIAN MARTIN

♀

ad. ♂

PURPLE
MARTIN

♀

1st year ♂

PURPLE
MARTIN

light ♀

♀

dark ♀

♀

♂

SOUTHERN
MARTIN

♀

SOUTHERN
MARTIN

PLATE
243

SWALLOWS I

Swallows on this plate are variable in appearance, but all are small to medium-sized. See also plates 244–245.

1 ANDEAN SWALLOW *Haplochelidon andecola* * 14 cm (5½ in)
Common but restricted to high open habitats in Andes, 3500–4600 m. Forages over puna grassland and bogs. May be found in towns and villages; nests in spaces under roofs of buildings or in holes in banks and roadcuts. Stocky, drab swallow with relatively blunt tail and gray-brown throat. Generally appears dark with paler rump and belly. Juvenile (not illustrated) brown above with light cinnamon-buff rump; superficially similar to Cliff Swallow but much drabber. **VOICE** Call a dry, rising "*dzree*" and a descending, slightly more musical "*chleep.*" **Bo, Ch**

2 BLUE-AND-WHITE SWALLOW *Pygochelidon cyanoleuca* * 11–12 cm (4¼–4¼ in); *patagonica* 12–13.5 cm (4¼–5¼ in)
A widespread, familiar swallow; frequently seen in cities and towns, over agricultural areas, as well as over broken forest. Common resident along coast (*peruviana*; not illustrated) and on both slopes of Andes, including foothills extending into Amazonia (*cyanoleuca*), up to at least 4300 m. Larger *patagonica* an austral migrant (Apr–Oct) to east slope of Andes and to Amazonia. Adult white below, with black vent and undertail coverts, or white vent (with black undertail coverts) in *patagonica*. Underwing coverts dusky (*cyanoleuca*) or light gray (*peruviana, patagonica*). Juveniles duller; less crisply marked and washed with buff on underparts, especially breast. *Patagonica* usually in worn plumage or molting when in Peru, while residents are in fresher plumage. **VOICE** Call a shrill, yet somewhat liquid "*tew.*" Characteristic call (song?) a gravelly warble that ends with a piercing note: "*cheet-djshhhhhhhhTEW.*" **Co, E, Br, Bo, Ch**

3 PALE-FOOTED SWALLOW *Notiochelidon flavipes* 11.5 cm (4½ in)
Locally common in humid montane forest along east slope of Andes, 2000–3500 m. Typically flies rapidly and low over or through forest canopy in small flocks. May associate with similar Blue-and-white Swallow, but Blue-and-white often flies higher and prefers more open habitats. Pale-footed also is smaller, has blackish sides and a faster, more direct flight. Look for cinnamon throat (difficult to see in the field, however). **VOICE** Call a rising, mellow yet buzzy trill: "*drzee*" or "*djurree.*" Song a series of buzzy, yet musical, trills and thin warbles. Voice is rather unlike that of any other high elevation swallow; individuals in mixed flocks can be detected easily by call. **Co, E, Bo**

4 WHITE-THIGHED SWALLOW *Neochelidon tibialis* * 10.5–11.5 cm (4¼–4½ in)
Uncommon and local in eastern Peru, below 1250 m. Most records are from foothills, but there are scattered records well into Amazonia, especially north of Amazon. Found at edge of humid forest or in forest openings. Usually in small groups, flying low over or through the forest. Small and dark, with paler rump, deeply notched tail, and white tibial tufts (usually hidden). Often with Southern Rough-winged Swallow, which is larger, relatively shorter tailed, with rufous throat and yellowish belly. **VOICE** Call a sweet, slightly descending "*tchew*" or "*tseew.*" **Co, E, Br, Bo**

5 BROWN-BELLIED SWALLOW *Notiochelidon murina* * 13.5 cm (5¼ in)
Fairly common on both slopes of Andes, 2200–4300 m (but absent from southwest). Forages over open grasslands and scrub, nearly always above treeline, usually in relatively moist situations. Very dark. Glossy bluish green above in most of Peru (*murina*); purer blue in *cyanodorsalis* (not illustrated) of easternmost Puno. Juvenile browner above; may be paler below, especially on throat and belly. **VOICE** Call deep, buzzy "*tchjet.*" Sometimes followed by a gravelly sound, ending with a musical lower note: "*tchjet-djshhhhEW*"; lower, drier, less musical than Blue-and-white Swallow. **Co, E, Bo**

6 TUMBES SWALLOW *Tachycineta stolzmanni* 12 cm (4¼ in)
Locally fairly common in lowlands of northwest, over dry scrub and agricultural fields. Small. Only white-rumped swallow in northwest. Rump and underparts very narrowly streaked dusky. **VOICE** Call a dry, rising "*zhreet?*" **E**

7 WHITE-BANDED SWALLOW *Atticora fasciata* 14.5 cm (5¼ in)
Common and widespread in Amazonia, up to 800 m (locally to 1000 m). Usually in small groups, foraging over forested rivers. Perches on snags protruding from water or on low bare branches that overhang rivers. Juvenile similar, but more frosted below and tail is shorter. **VOICE** Call a pleasant, tinkling, twittered phrase: "*ti-ti-tur.*" Also a buzzier call when alarmed or interacting: "*dzi-dzi-dzi.*" **Co, E, Br, Bo**

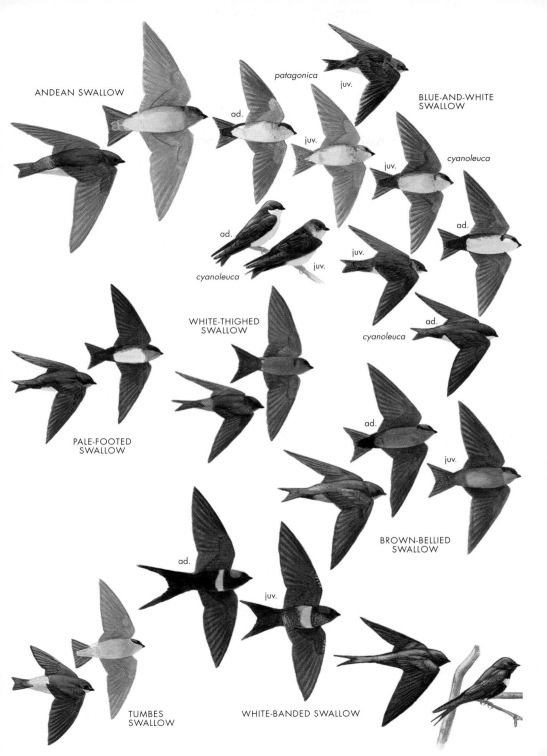

ANDEAN SWALLOW

patagonica

ad.

juv.

juv.

BLUE-AND-WHITE
SWALLOW

cyanoleuca

juv.

ad.

cyanoleuca

ad.

juv.

cyanoleuca

WHITE-THIGHED
SWALLOW

ad.

PALE-FOOTED
SWALLOW

ad.

juv.

BROWN-BELLIED
SWALLOW

ad.

juv.

TUMBES
SWALLOW

WHITE-BANDED SWALLOW

PLATE
244

SWALLOWS II

Small to medium-sized swallows, several of which also have tawny or chestnut throats. See also plates 242, 243, and 245.

1 BANK SWALLOW *Riparia riparia* * 12 cm (4¼ in)

Uncommon boreal migrant (Aug–Apr). Primarily occurs below 500 m, but rarely to 4500 m. Seasonal patterns not well understood. Usually seen in small numbers during migration (Mar–Apr, Sep–Nov) but large flocks have been seen in north (Lambayeque; and, more frequently, along Amazon and lower Río Napo) during Jan–Feb. Forages over rivers, marshes, and fields. Small; rapid, batlike flight with wings often half-closed. Brown above with partial white collar; white below with narrow brown breast band. Cf. juvenile Blue-and-white Swallow, also much larger Brown-chested Martin. **VOICE** Call a very deep, gravelly "*dzzee-dzzee-dzzee*" or "*djit-djit*." **Co, E, Br, Bo, Ch**

2 BARN SWALLOW *Hirundo rustica* * 14–16.5 cm (5½–6½ in)

Common boreal migrant, primarily present Sep–Apr, but a few may linger at least until June. Found in open habitats, primarily in lowlands, but recorded up to at least 4000 m. Flight graceful; usually includes short glides with wings half-closed. Adults in fresh plumage steely blue above with long deeply forked tail (shorter in female); throat chestnut; belly tawny, light buff or almost white. First-year birds duller and paler below with shorter tail. Most complete a molt into fresh plumage shortly before departing in March; prior to molt, become very worn, with duller colors and shorter tail streamers. **VOICE** Call a reedy "*vit*," sometimes in series; also a higher "*pit-seet*," often in alarm. Song (?), usually given from perch, an excited series of pleasant, electric warbles and short trills. **Co, E, Br, Bo, Ch**

3 TAWNY-HEADED SWALLOW *Alopochelidon fucata* 12 cm (4¼ in)

Apparently rare austral migrant to southeast (few confirmed records). Usually over open habitats. Brown above, white below, with square tail and tawny head and upper breast. Distinguished with care from much more common, widespread Southern Rough-winged Swallow by more extensive tawny color on head and breast, white (not yellowish) belly, and rump concolor with back. Also has distinctive shape, with shorter, broader wings and stockier build. **VOICE** Call a high chirping series. **Co, Br, Bo, Ch**

4 SOUTHERN ROUGH-WINGED SWALLOW *Stelgidopteryx ruficollis* * 13 cm (5 in)

Fairly common and widespread in eastern lowlands (*ruficollis*), up to 1500 m. Also locally in lowlands of northwest (*uropygialis*). Nests in small colonies in holes in banks or in roadcuts. Often forages along rivers or over open areas near roads. Rump usually pale, contrasting with darker brown back and blackish tail; rump averages particularly pale (often whitish) in *uropygialis*. Throat tawny, contrasting with grayish brown breast; belly light yellow. Juveniles have pale (sometimes tawny) tips to tertials, wing coverts, and lower back; breast paler, may be washed with tawny. Populations in Amazonia may be supplemented by austral migrants. **VOICE** Call a musical, rising: "*zwee*." Also a buzzier, more even-pitched "*pjzee*." **Co, E, Br, Bo**

5 [CLIFF SWALLOW *Petrochelidon pyrrhonota*] * 13–13.5 cm (5–5¼ in)

Rare boreal migrant; apparently annual, but known only from sight records. Usually encountered as singles or small numbers with other swallow species over open habitats during southbound passage (Aug–Oct), up to at least 4000 m. Few records of northbound migrants (Mar–Apr), all from northeastern Amazonia. Note square tail and prominent tawny rump; stockier, heavier-bodied than Barn Swallow. Adult glossy blue above, with inconspicuous whitish stripes on back, buffy forehead and nuchal collar; chestnut throat and sides of face contrast with buffy gray belly. Juveniles much duller, with mottled throat; face pattern less distinct. **VOICE** Calls a descending, reedy "*pew*" and a creaking "*grrreeee*." **Co, E, Br, Bo, Ch**

6 CHESTNUT-COLLARED SWALLOW *Petrochelidon rufocollaris* * 12–12.5 (4¼–5 in)

Locally common along coast, below 1000 m. Forages over agricultural fields. Breeds in colonies; enclosed mud nests, ball-shaped with a side entrance, placed under eaves of buildings or on cliffs. Bluish above with rufous-chestnut nuchal collar and rump, and dark brown forecrown. Throat and belly white, with rufous breast band, flanks, and vent. Cf. Cliff (which is obviously larger, when both species seen together) and Bank swallows. Juvenile (not illustrated) duller than adult, and forecrown may be paler. **VOICE** Calls quiet "*chit*" notes, sometimes in series. Also a creaking "*grrreeee*." **E**

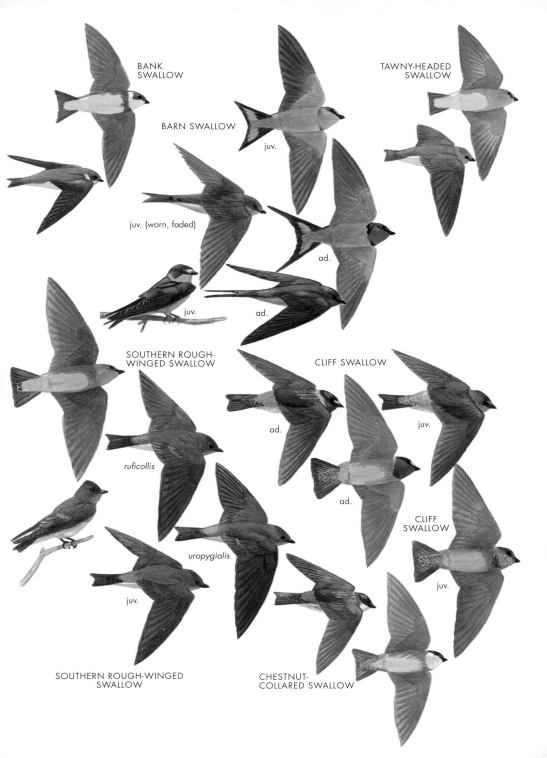

BANK
SWALLOW

TAWNY-HEADED
SWALLOW

BARN SWALLOW

juv.

juv. (worn, faded)

ad.

juv.

ad.

SOUTHERN ROUGH-
WINGED SWALLOW

CLIFF SWALLOW

ad.

juv.

ruficollis

ad.

CLIFF
SWALLOW

uropygialis

juv.

juv.

SOUTHERN ROUGH-WINGED
SWALLOW

CHESTNUT-
COLLARED SWALLOW

PLATE
245

WHITE-RUMPED SWALLOWS AND PIPITS

Only one of these three white-rumped swallows is common. Pipits are small, terrestrial, streaked birds of grasslands and fields. Note thin bill (which distinguishes pipits from finches), pale outer rectrices, and elongated claw on hind toe. Song usually given in skylarking flight, but sometimes from ground.

1 WHITE-RUMPED SWALLOW *Tachycineta leucorrhoa* 13.5 cm (5¼ in)
Rare austral migrant; perhaps regular, but only a few records. Bluish green above, with white rump and underparts, and narrow white loral line; little or no white on upper surface of wing. White below, with white wing linings. Cf. White-winged Swallow. **Br, Bo**

2 WHITE-WINGED SWALLOW *Tachycineta albiventer* 13.5 cm (5¼ in)
Common and widespread in Amazonia, below 600 m, along large open rivers, on lakes, and in adjacent open areas (but always near water). Frequently perches on snags and driftwood over water; forages low over water's surface. Juvenile similar to adult, but grayer above. **VOICE** Call a rising, buzzy "*dzree.*" **Co, E, Br, Bo**

[CHILEAN SWALLOW *Tachycineta meyeni*] 12–13.5 cm (4¾–5¼ in)
Status not clear; possibly a very rare austral vagrant, but known only from a few undocumented sight records from southwest. Very easily confused with White-rumped Swallow, but is bluer (less green) above, lacks the small white loral spot, and underwing coverts are light gray (not white). **VOICE** Call a harsh, nasal, buzzy "*dzzk.*" **Br, Bo, Ch**

3 CORRENDERA PIPIT *Anthus correndera* * 14.5–15 cm (5¾–6 in)
Fairly common but apparently local in dry puna grassland, 3800–4600 m. Relatively large; only pipit with prominent pale longitudinal streaks on upperparts. Overall color tone light buff. Breast and flanks boldly streaked. Superciliary relatively bold. Outer two rectrices largely white. Overlaps with Short-billed, which is more scaled above and more sparsely streaked below. **VOICE** Song a variable, rich series of gurgling, warbling, and trilling phrases. Call is a rising, buzzy "*tjzee?*" **Br, Bo, Ch**

4 SHORT-BILLED PIPIT *Anthus furcatus* * 14 cm (5½ in)
Fairly common in dry puna grassland, 3500–4100 m. Breast light ochre, streaked dusky; throat, belly, and flanks whiter, with few or no streaks. Other pipits more uniformly colored below. Also note narrow dusky malar stripe. Outer two rectrices largely white. Cf. Correndera Pipit. **VOICE** Song (Bolivia) a series of reedy introductory notes followed by a musical gurgling trill: "*chi-chi eewww-wwwwCHEWCHEWCHEW.*" Call a flat "*clep.*" **Br, Bo**

5 YELLOWISH PIPIT *Anthus lutescens* * 13 cm (5 in)
Fairly common along coast, up to 450 m, in coastal marshes, pastures, and agricultural fields. Uncommon on savannas of Pampas del Heath. Small pipit, and only pipit in lowlands. Underparts dirty white (coastal *peruvianus*) or pale yellow (Amazonian *lutescens*; not illustrated). **VOICE** Song (*peruvianus*) one or several introductory notes followed by descending sizzle: "*tik tik SIZZZZZZZZ-ZZZZZ.*" Call a dry "*chit-it.*" Song of *lutescens* very different, slightly more musical descending buzz: "*titi DJEEEEEEEUU.*" Call a very different "*chu-ee.*" **Co, Br, Bo, Ch**

6 HELLMAYR'S PIPIT *Anthus hellmayri* * 14 cm (5½ in)
Restricted to east slope of Andes in Puno, in humid grassland near treeline, 2450–3350 m. Few distinctive features. Sides of face plain, with only a weak superciliary and no dusky malar. Only outer rectrix is pale, and usually light brown or buffy, not white. Only overlaps with very different Paramo Pipit. **VOICE** Song (Bolivia) a rather musical series of clear notes interspersed with buzzes: "*chew swee-tusweepit-shhh swee-tusweepit-shhhh swee-tusweepit-shhhhh....*" Calls (Bolivia) a piercing "*chew!*" and thinner, buzzy "*tizik.*" **Br, Bo, Ch**

7 PARAMO PIPIT *Anthus bogotensis* * 15 cm (6 in)
Fairly common at 2950–4400 m in humid grassland near treeline along east side of Andes, and on west slope south to Ancash; less common, and local, in drier grassland on puna. Buffy below, with only a few streaks on breast. Tail pattern similar to Hellmayr's: only outer rectrix is pale, and is light brown or buffy, not white. **VOICE** Song a fairly musical, though scratchy, warble (pattern seems remarkably variable) usually with a buzzy phrase inserted. Calls (Ecuador) a musical, descending "*treeleelee,*" a high "*tsip,*" and a rising "*chewee?*" **Co, E, Bo**

WHITE-RUMPED SWALLOW

WHITE-WINGED SWALLOW

juv.

ad.

ad.

CHILEAN SWALLOW

ad.

juv.

WHITE-WINGED SWALLOW

CORRENDERA PIPIT

YELLOWISH PIPIT

SHORT-BILLED PIPIT

HELLMAYR'S PIPIT

PARAMO PIPIT

PLATE
246

LARGE WRENS (*CAMPYLORHYNCHUS*) AND WOOD-WRENS

Wrens are small to medium-sized insectivores with drab plumage, but they call attention to themselves with loud songs, some of which are among the loveliest bird songs of the world. Many species characteristically carry the tail cocked upright. Wrens often travel in pairs (or, in some species, in what may be family groups). Nests are domed, ball-shaped structures or are placed in cavities. The two Campylorhynchus *are large (thrush-sized). Wood-wrens are small with notably short, stubby tails. Forage on or near ground in pairs or, less frequently, as solitary individuals; do not associate with mixed-species flocks.*

1 THRUSH-LIKE WREN *Campylorhynchus turdinus* * 18.5–19 cm (7¼–7½ in)
Fairly common and widespread in Amazonia, up to 1500 m, in midstory and canopy at forest edge, in adjacent second growth, and at gaps in forest interior. Usually in small (family?) groups that noisily investigate viny tangles and other thickets. Drab gray-brown above, indistinctly spotted dusky. Off-white below, spotted dusky. Unmistakable (and not particularly thrushlike). **VOICE** Song, nearly always in duet or chorus, a surprisingly loud, rollicking series of rhythmic, hollow electric sounds (pattern variable): "*tik-TOO-TI-TOO-cuh*"; can be longer, with more repetitive phrases. Characteristic sound of Amazonian riverine forest. Common call, often in series, a loud, pumping, bisyllabic phrase: "*kung-PAH.*" Also occasionally gives quiet, dry "*tchik*" notes or rough churrs. **Co, E, Br, Bo**

2 FASCIATED WREN *Campylorhynchus fasciatus* * 20 cm (8 in)
Common and conspicuous in dry forest, arid scrub and gardens in northwest, up to 1500 m; in dry Marañón Valley, 500–2200 m; and upper Huallaga Valley, 1800– 2100 m. Usually encountered in groups that forage at all heights. Juveniles (not illustrated) banded dusky and light buff, with brown crown and buffy superciliary, and have reduced spotting on breast. Cf. Long-tailed Mockingbird. **VOICE** Song, nearly always in duet or chorus, a rather unpleasant, nasal rasping series, pattern variable: "*kek-kek-kek-kadik-KWOW-reh-KUHDEK KWOW-reh-KADEK KWOW-reh-KADEK….*" Calls nasal rasps "*raah,*" sometimes in series, also a raspy chattering: "*kek-kek-kek.*" **E**

3 BAR-WINGED WOOD-WREN *Henicorhina leucoptera* 11 cm (4¼ in)
Very local. Primarily on outlying ridges, especially at sites with stunted forest such as on nutrient-poor sandy soils, at 1350–2600 m. Elevational range overlaps that of Gray-breasted Wood-Wren, which usually is found nearby at sites with taller forest. Bar-winged has white tips to wing coverts (especially greater wing coverts; also some tips to median coverts), is dingier brown above and whiter below (with gray mottling at the sides of the breast), and has a longer bill; sides of breast usually streaked (streaking often extending across center of breast as well). **VOICE** Song, extremely variable, is a mellow, whistled warbling phrase, usually less complex than Gray-breasted Wood-Wren (but more so than White-breasted), and never (?) with high introductory notes. For example: "*WEEwer-wurdleWEE?*" Songs can be given in antiphonal duet. Call a dry "*tchut,*" sometimes given in a chattered series, not as rich as call of Gray-breasted. Also a squeaky "*wink.*" **E**

4 GRAY-BREASTED WOOD-WREN *Henicorhina leucophrys* * 11 cm (4¼ in)
One of most characteristic birds of humid montane forest, where found along east side of Andes at 1100–2850 m. Also present at 750 m in semideciduous forests in Tumbes. Readily identified by small size, gray breast, chestnut upperparts, and short stubby tail. **VOICE** Song, extremely variable, usually a mellow, whistled warbling phrase of varying complexity, usually preceded by very high introductory notes, for example: "*see-see-see WEEchewWEEchew-wur.*" Songs can be given in antiphonal duet. Call a rich "*tcht*" or "*tuk,*" often given in a chattered series, not as dry as call of Bar-winged Wood-Wren. **Co, E, Bo**

5 WHITE-BREASTED WOOD-WREN *Henicorhina leucosticta* * 10 cm (4 in)
Locally common but patchily distributed in terra firme in north central Amazonia, becoming more widespread in Andean foothills, 600–1400 m, south at least to Huánuco. Russet brown above with blackish crown, white superciliary, striped cheeks, and white underparts. Cf. Gray-breasted Wood-Wren, which replaces White-breasted at higher elevations. **VOICE** Song, extremely variable, pleasant; often a ringing whistled trill preceded by high, rising introductory notes, for example: "*see-seeee tree'e'e'e'e'e'e'e.*" Overall structure generally simpler than songs of Gray-breasted and Bar-winged wood-wrens. Call a dry chatter: "*trr'r'r'r'r.*" **Co, E, Br**

THRUSH-LIKE WREN

FASCIATED WREN

BAR-WINGED
WOOD-WREN

GRAY-BREASTED
WOOD-WREN

WHITE-BREASTED
WOOD-WREN

PLATE
247

MUSICAL WRENS AND GRAY-MANTLED WREN

Most species on this plate are terrestrial; can be difficult to see, but have notably complex and beautiful songs. Gray-mantled Wren is a small, slender wren of the canopy of humid montane forest.

1 CHESTNUT-BREASTED WREN *Cyphorhinus thoracicus* * 13.5–14.5 cm (5¼–5¾ in)
Uncommon but widespread along east slope of Andes, 1200–2700 m, locally down to 800 m. Pairs forage on ground in dense cover in humid montane forest, rummaging through leaf litter; typically do not associate with mixed-species flocks. Base of bill has a high narrow "keel." Very dark overall, with rich rufous throat, breast, and sides of neck; little geographic variation in plumage, but dramatic variation in **VOICE** Song north of Marañón (*dichrous*) a haunting series of 2 or 3 melancholy whistled phrases repeated several times. Song south of Marañón (*thoracicus*) quite different, with varied song phrases that include trills, squeaks, purrs, and musical whistles. Call a fussing, mechanical, hollow "*jrr*," often in short, chattered series. **Co, E, Bo**

2 MUSICIAN WREN *Cyphorhinus arada* * 13–13.5 cm (5¼ in)
Uncommon but widespread in Amazonia below 500 m, locally to 1000 m. Pairs forage on ground in dense cover in interior of humid forest. Generally does not associate with other species, but occasionally may attend army ant swarms. Dark, with a tawny-rufous breast, forecrown, and sides of the neck. Cf. female Salvin's Antbird or leaftossers. **VOICE** Song a remarkable series of pure whistled notes and rapidly changing pitches, interspersed with mechanical purred sounds; overall effect is very musical and pleasing, if rather unbirdlike. Call a deep, mechanical, rather unbirdlike "*tchr*" or "*tuk*," often in chattered series. Also a mechanical purring interspersed with whistled or squeaked notes. **Co, E, Br, Bo**

3 WING-BANDED WREN *Microcerculus bambla* * 10.5–11 cm (4–4¼ in)
Very poorly known; distribution curiously patchy. Reported from upper Río Tigre in north, and scattered sites in south-central Peru, below 1000 m. Similar to Scaly-breasted Wren, but light gray below (not white) and with broad white tips to greater wing coverts, forming prominent white wing bar. Also cf. Banded Antbird. **VOICE** Song (Ecuador) a series of varied, loud, ringing whistled series either ascending or descending in pitch with single notes interspersed. Probably not safely distinguished from that of southern Amazonian song of Scaly-breasted. Call a quiet, hoarse "*zweh*." **E, Br**

4 SCALY-BREASTED WREN *Microcerculus marginatus* * 10.5–11 cm (4–4¼ in)
Heard far more often than seen, but fairly common and widespread in humid forest in Amazonia, up to 1200 m. Frequently teeters rear end of body while walking. Solitary. Small and dark, with long bill and very short tail. Throat and breast of adult are white, lightly scaled with dusky; immatures darker below, more heavily scaled with dusky. No geographic variation in plumage. **VOICE** Song north of the Amazon and west of Río Ucayali a loud series of pure, ringing whistles, decelerating and descending in pitch (almost on a musical scale) with each note after an introductory crescendo: "*tsiiTI TI… TEE…. TEE….. TEE…… TEE……*"; a complete song may last 2 min or more. South of Amazon and east of the Ucayali, song rather different in pattern: usually begins with the crescendo, then gives a short series of notes, followed by a pause, then a different series of notes. Each series may be even in pace and pitch, accelerate, decelerate, or change pitch (usually rising). For example: "*tsiiTI… tur-tur-tur-TUR-TUR-TUR-TUR-TUR-TUR… TEE TEE TEE TEE… taytaytaytaytayTAYTAYTAY….*" Call a low, rich "*tchk*," usually given singly. **Co, E, Br, Bo**

5 GRAY-MANTLED WREN *Odontorchilus branickii* * 12 cm (4¾ in)
Uncommon along east slope of Andes, 750–1800 m. Single individuals and pairs forage in subcanopy and canopy of humid montane forest, almost always with mixed-species flocks. Often carries long thin tail cocked upward. Hops along horizontal limbs, probing into moss clusters and leaning over to peer at underside of branches. No similar species has a barred tail; in northern Andes, cf. Equatorial Graytail. **VOICE** Songs, variable, are high pitched and repetitive, including wiry trills and long, slowly quavering whistled series. **Co, E, Bo**

CHESTNUT-BREASTED WREN

MUSICIAN WREN

WING-BANDED WREN

imm.

ad.

SCALY-BREASTED WREN

GRAY-MANTLED WREN

PLATE
248

WRENS (*THRYOTHORUS*)

Thryothorus wrens forage in pairs or family groups in understory, usually at forest edge and other disturbed or successional habitats. All duet antiphonally, with coordinated songs between members of the pair.

1 CORAYA WREN *Thryothorus coraya* * 14–16 cm (5½–6¼ in)
Common in northern and western Amazonia, below 2000 m, but in central Peru reported only from Andean slopes (replaced by Moustached Wren at lower elevations?). Malar broad, black; auriculars black or dark gray. North of Amazon, auriculars often narrowly streaked white and breast grayer (*griseipectus*). In Pacoya-Samiria similar, but malar narrow; resemble Moustached, but breast grayer (another zone of intergradation?). Populations in and near Andean foothills, from Huallaga Valley south, have black auriculars, sometimes with a narrow white superciliary; often brownish buff below. **VOICE** Probably not safely distinguished by voice from Moustached. **Co, E, Br**

2 MOUSTACHED WREN *Thryothorus genibarbis* * 14–15.5 cm (5½–6¼ in)
Common in eastern Amazonia, below 1500 m. Replaces Coraya Wren south of Amazon and east of Río Ucayali, but may cross to west bank of middle Ucayali. Distinguished from Coraya by gray, white-streaked auriculars and narrow black moustachial stripe; underparts also usually buffier (little or no gray on breast). Birds on west bank of Ucayali (not illustrated) show some Coraya features, suggesting intergradation. Juvenile (not illustrated) lacks moustache and facial streaking, and has light gray breast. **VOICE** Song a varied, rich, warbled series of whistles and hoots, often interspersed with a growling "*DJEER DJEER.*" Call "*DJEER DJEER,*" also a dry chatter. Probably not safely distinguished by voice from Coraya. **Br, Bo**

3 PLAIN-TAILED WREN *Thryothorus euophrys* * 16–16.5 cm (6¼–6½ in)
Uncommon along east slope of Andes, 2200–3200 m, both north (*atriceps*) and south (*schulenbergi*; not illustrated) of Río Marañón; also an undescribed population in Junín (not illustrated). Inhabits *Chusquea* bamboo. Rufous-brown or (*schulenbergi*) light brown above with gray crown and white superciliary; underparts with little or no spotting. Tail unmarked or (Junín) lightly barred. Juveniles (not illustrated) may be largely buffy on head and underparts; cf. *Cinnycerthia* wrens. **VOICE** Song (*atriceps*) a rich warbled series of whistled phrases; *schulenbergi* has deeper, almost hooting, phrases; song of Junín population like *atriceps*, but higher pitched. Call a dry "*ter-TICK,*" sometimes in chattered series. **Co, E**

4 INCA WREN *Thryothorus eisenmanni* 14.5–15.5 cm (5¾–6 in)
Locally common on east side of southern Andes, 1700–3350 m. Often in *Chusquea* bamboo. Note rufous upperparts, streaked underparts; streaking reaches belly in males but may be confined to breast in most females and immatures. Tail may be lightly barred. Juvenile (not illustrated) duller above with brown crown, and unmarked light grayish brown underparts (resembles Plain-tailed Wren). **VOICE** Song a rich, varied, warbled series of whistled phrases, similar to *atriceps* Plain-tailed, but higher pitched. Call a rich "*tchp*" or "*tchp-er,*" sometimes in chattered series. **ENDEMIC**

5 SUPERCILIATED WREN *Thryothorus superciliaris* * 15 cm (6 in)
Common in dry scrub and dry forest in northwest below 1000 m; usually found in more arid habitats than is Speckle-breasted Wren. Note particularly long bill and very white superciliary, sides of face, and throat. **VOICE** Song, often an antiphonal duet, an explosive, loud series of ringing whistled or trilled phrases. Calls a dry rattle, "*chit*" notes, and a rich, ringing, songlike "*TCHEW'R.*" **E**

6 SPECKLE-BREASTED WREN *Thryothorus sclateri* * 14.5–15.5 cm (5¾–6 in)
Fairly common in dry and semideciduous forests at 400–2000 m in northwest (*paucimaculatus*) and in dry Marañón Valley (*sclateri*). Underparts barred (*sclateri*) or spotted (*paucimaculatus*). **VOICE** Song a fairly simple but musical liquid series of whistles, for example: "*HEEU tu-seeWHIT*" answered by a "*whip SEE-terWHEEO.*" Call a musical trill that rises: "*tri'i'i'i'i'i'i?*" **Co, E**

7 BUFF-BREASTED WREN *Thryothorus leucotis* * 12.5–13.5 cm (5–5¼ in)
Locally common in Amazonia below 500 m; largely confined to river-edge forest, and similar habitats on river islands. Brown, with buffy underparts. Coraya and Moustached wrens have stronger, black-and-white face patterns and lack barring on wings. Buff-breasted also has relatively shorter tail, and crown concolor with back. **VOICE** Song a strident, yet musical, series of sharp whistled phrases, usually interspersed with a characteristic doubled couplet: "*TU-TU TU-TU.*" Not as rich and fluty as songs of Coraya or Moustached. Calls a quiet series of liquid "*tip*" notes, a harsher chatter, also a deep "*k'lunk.*" **Co, E, Br, Bo**

Andean

Andean

griseipectus

MOUSTACHED WREN

CORAYA WREN

INCA WREN

atriceps

PLAIN-TAILED WREN

SUPERCILIATED WREN

sclateri

SPECKLE-BREASTED
WREN

paucimaculatus

BUFF-BREASTED
WREN

PLATE
249

ANDEAN WRENS (*CINNYCERTHIA, CISTOTHORUS*)

Cinnycerthia are large wrens of understory of humid montane forest. Usually are encountered in small flocks, presumably family units, that may be associated with mixed-species flocks. Often detected by beautiful songs given by several birds at once. Sedge Wren is a small, usually solitary wren of Andean grasslands.

1 RUFOUS WREN *Cinnycerthia unirufa* * 16.5 cm (6½ in)

Locally fairly common, but restricted to areas north and west of Marañón Valley, in humid montane forest at 2200–3200 m. Found in dense undergrowth, especially in thickets of *Chusquea* bamboo. One of the few montane forest birds that responds vigorously to "pishing" or squeaking. Large and uniformly dark chestnut-brown with dusky lores. Remiges and rectrices very indistinctly barred dusky. Cf. Sharpe's Wren. Also cf. smaller-bodied, longer-tailed Rufous Spinetail. Juveniles duller, with grayish heads and paler bills. **VOICE** Song, often in chorus, a varied, musical series of trills, whistles, and warbling notes. Alarm call, usually in chorus, is a chatter, somewhat richer, more musical, than that of Sharpe's: "*tchrr.*" **Co, E**

2 SHARPE'S WREN *Cinnycerthia olivascens* * 15.5 cm (6 in)

Locally fairly common, but geographically restricted, in northern Andes. North and west of Río Marañón overlaps with Rufous Wren, although generally found at lower elevations (2000–2450 m); south and east of Marañón reaches 3300 m. Very similar to Rufous, but browner (less rufous); wings and tail are more strongly barred; and lores less dusky. Also overlaps very locally with Peruvian Wren south of Marañón in Amazonas and San Martín, where usually is found at higher elevations than Peruvian. Slightly larger than Peruvian, and plain-faced, with no pale superciliary. **VOICE** Song, often in chorus, is a varied, musical series of trills, whistles, and warbling notes. Alarm call, usually in chorus, is a chatter, somewhat drier than that of Rufous. **Co, E.**

3 FULVOUS WREN *Cinnycerthia fulva* * 14–14.5 cm (5½–5¾ in)

Uncommon and local in southern Peru, at 1700–3000 m, where geographically replaces Peruvian Wren. May be found in smaller flocks than other *Cinnycerthia*, and perhaps less attracted to mixed-species flocks. Smallest *Cinnycerthia*. Paler below than Peruvian, especially on throat. Crown and sides of head darker brown, framing a more well-defined long buffy superciliary. **VOICE** Song, often in chorus, is a varied, musical series of trills, whistles, and warbling notes. Alarm call, often in chorus, a rapid, dry chattering. **Bo**

4 PERUVIAN WREN *Cinnycerthia peruana* 14–14.5 cm (5½–5¾ in)

Fairly common in humid montane forest of central Peru at 2400–3350 m. Brown with paler, tawny superciliary and barred wings and tail. Head pattern quite variable. Some adults have white eyerings; faces or even whole head and upper throat may be white; significance of this variation unknown. Juveniles have broader, light gray superciliary and pale bill. In Amazonas and San Martín cf. Sharpe's Wren; otherwise no overlap with other *Cinnycerthia*. **VOICE** Song, often in chorus, a varied, musical series of trills, whistles, and warbling notes. Alarm call, often in chorus, a rapid, dry chattering, similar to congeners. **ENDEMIC**

5 SEDGE WREN *Cistothorus platensis* * 12–12.5 cm (4¾–5 in)

Fairly common but local. Widespread along east side of Andes at 3200–4600 m, locally down to 2300 m; also patchily distributed at similar elevations on both slopes of upper Marañón Valley, and very locally on west slope in Piura. Not yet reported, but may occur, on Pampas del Heath. Usually in dense, damp grasslands; very rarely reported from reedbeds bordering lakes. Typically keeps well under cover except when singing. Small and buffy, with streaked crown and back and barred wings and tail. Tail often held cocked up perpendicular to back or even folded forward of perpendicular. No similar wren in its grassland habitat; grassland canasteros are larger, longer-tailed and do not have barred wings. **VOICE** Song, often in duet, a complex, variable, and musical series of notes. Usually, 1 bird gives a 2- or 3-part song phrase: "*chee-tewee'e'e'e' TEE'E'E'E'E.*" A second individual (female?) usually responds with a simpler series of notes, either a harsh "*jer-jer-jer-jer…*" or a slightly more musical, trilled "*je'e'ew-je'e'ew-je'e'ew…*" or similar notes. These latter vocalizations are also the most commonly given calls. **Co, E, Br, Bo, Ch**

juv.

SHARPE'S WREN

ad.

RUFOUS WREN

FULVOUS WREN

ad.

juv.

ad. white-headed

PERUVIAN WREN

SEDGE WREN

PLATE
250

WRENS (*TROGLODYTES*), MOCKINGBIRDS, AND DONACOBIUS

Mountain and House wrens are two small, particularly spritely wrens; Mountain Wren is restricted to humid montane forest, whereas House Wren is widespread in open habitats. Mockingbirds are superficially thrushlike; slender, long-tailed, usually conspicuous birds. The donacobius is a peculiar slender, long-tailed bird of Amazonian marshes.

1 MOUNTAIN WREN *Troglodytes solstitialis* * 10–11 cm (4–4¼ in)

Replaces House Wren in humid montane forest on east slope of Andes, 2000–3600 m; also found on west slope of Andes in northern Piura. Found in humid montane forest; comes to forest edges but does not venture out into second growth. Singles or pairs forage from subcanopy down to near ground, often with mixed-species flocks; frequently seen creeping along trunks and larger branches, probing moss and epiphytes. Readily recognized by small size, tawny color, and well-defined buffy superciliary. In south cf. larger Fulvous Wren. **VOICE** Song a very high, thin, wiry series of tinkling notes, rather variable in pattern. Call a descending trill: "*dze'e'e'e'e'eer-trr*" or "*ti'i'i'i'i'i'i'i*." **Co, E, Bo**

2 HOUSE WREN *Troglodytes aedon* * 12–12.5 cm (4¾–5 in)

Widespread and common virtually throughout Peru, up to 4600 m, although often very local in Amazonia and on humid slopes of Andes. Found in open habitats with scattered low bushes and shrubs, such as forest edge and young second growth, montane scrub, and agricultural areas; frequently a conspicuous presence in gardens and other areas near human habitation. Usually solitary. Small, brown, with expressive tail that frequently is carried cocked; otherwise rather plain, but note barred wings and tail. Color, especially of underparts, somewhat variable. Birds on the coast from La Libertad south to northern Ica, and in central highlands from Amazonas south to Bolivia, tend to be the deepest buff below; but there is considerable individual variation as well. **VOICE** Song, familiar in most open habitats and sung nearly all year, a musical gurgle followed by a rapid, liquid, chattering warble. Although variable in pattern, the overall quality is distinctive. Calls a mewing wheezed "*rhee*," and a deep, gruff "*grrt*." **Co, E, Br, Bo, Ch**

3 LONG-TAILED MOCKINGBIRD *Mimus longicaudatus* * 29–30 cm (11½–11¾ in)

Common and widespread along coast (although rare and local south of Ica) and in Marañón Valley, up to 2600 m. Found in desert scrub, light woodlands, agricultural areas, and gardens. Often perches conspicuously in crown of bush or tree. Also frequently feeds on ground, running with tail carried cocked upward. Outer tail feathers broadly tipped white. Unmistakable; note unique shape and harlequin face pattern. Juvenile duller, with dark iris (iris light olive-yellow in adult), and spotted or streaked on underparts. **VOICE** Song a fairly slow-paced series of variable rich whistled notes, churrs, rattles, squawks, and other noises, often with phrases repeated; there appears to be little or no mimicry involved. Calls a throaty "*gar!*" and rasping "*gaawrrr*." Begging call of fledgling is a ringing, high, even "*teeee*." **E**

4 BLACK-CAPPED DONACOBIUS *Donacobius atricapilla* * 22–23 cm (8½–9 in)

Fairly common in marshy vegetation at edge of oxbow lakes and other backwater areas in eastern lowlands; occasionally in wet meadows away from open water. Pairs or small groups perch conspicuously in low bushes or on clumps of grass; they also are very vocal. Note pale yellow iris (gray in juvenile). Broad white tips to tail feathers and narrow white bases to inner webs of primaries are conspicuous in flight. Juvenile has narrow white superciliary. **VOICE** Song, nearly always in duet (while wagging the flared tails laterally, white outer rectrices easily visible, and inflating small orange bare-skinned neck sacs), a loud series of musical bubbling notes or wheezy rasps, for example: "*wooEE wooEE wooEE wooEE wooEE*." Call a musical, churred "*jee'e'e'e'rr*." **Co, E, Br, Bo**

[WHITE-BANDED MOCKINGBIRD *Mimus triurus*] 23 cm (9 in)

Very rare austral migrant to Peru; known only from a single sight record (Dec) from Lake Titicaca. Slender, long-tailed bird with white outer rectrices, extensive white on wing coverts and secondaries, and rufous-brown rump contrasting with gray-brown back. Cf. Bar-winged Cinclodes. **Br, Bo, Ch**

MOUNTAIN WREN

HOUSE WREN

ad.

juv.

LONG-TAILED
MOCKINGBIRD

BLACK-CAPPED
DONACOBIUS

BLACK-CAPPED
DONACOBIUS

juv.

ad.

WHITE-BANDED MOCKINGBIRD

PLATE
251

GNATCATCHERS AND GNATWRENS

Gnatcatchers are small, slender, long-tailed arboreal birds. Microbates gnatwrens are small, long-billed birds that forage, often in pairs, very near the ground in terra firme understory. Short tail often held cocked, and often join mixed-species flocks. Long-billed Gnatwren is similar, but longer-tailed, and forages higher, usually in viny tangles.

1 IQUITOS GNATCATCHER *Polioptila clementsi* 11 cm (4¼ in)
Very local in northern Amazonian Peru. Recorded only in the Zona Reservada Allpahuayo-Mishana southwest of Iquitos, where rare in canopy of forest growing on poorly drained sandy soils. Note specialized habitat and very localized distribution. Additionally distinguished from Tropical Gnatcatcher by light gray throat and breast, with white on underparts confined to belly; also note narrow white crescents above and below the eye. **VOICE** Song a high, loose trill, similar to *Terenura* antwrens (but with a differing pattern): "*see see see ti'i'i'i'i'i'i'i.*" **ENDEMIC**

2 TROPICAL GNATCATCHER *Polioptila plumbea* * 10.5–11 cm (4¼ in); *maior* 12–12.5 cm (4¼ in)
Three subspecies (different species?) occupy different regions of Peru. *Bilineata* fairly common in dry forest and scrub up to 700 m in northwest. Male has black cap, which begins above eye (with very narrow dark line below eye); female similar but crown is gray. Larger *maior* is common in similar habitats in Marañón Valley at 200–2700 m. Darker gray above, and both sexes have black cap. In male the cap extends down to eye; female is similar to male *bilineata* with white lores and short superciliary. Amazonian *parvirostris* locally is found in varzea and secondary forest locally up to 1000 m. Male similar to male *maior*, with black cap to eye, but back paler; female shares this pattern but cap is gray. **VOICE** Song of *bilineata* a series of rising, sweet whistles: "*swee-swee-swee-swee-swee.*" Call a wheezing "*zwhee.*" Song of *maior* is more complex, involving various mewing whistles, whines, and wheezing notes. Call a descending wheeze: "*zheew.*" Song of *parvirostris* variable, a series of simple notes, for example: "*chee-chee-chee-chee-chee.*" **Co, E, Br, Bo**

3 COLLARED GNATWREN *Microbates collaris* * 10–10.5 cm (4 in)
Local and uncommon in northeastern Amazonia, north of the Amazon and east of Río Napo. Note long bill and white underparts with a black crescent on chest. Also has distinctive facial pattern, with white superciliary and auriculars separated by dusky line extending back from eye, and a black malar streak. **VOICE** Song (?) a descending, pure whistle: "*teeeoo*"; resembles Tawny-crowned Greenlet. Call a rapid chatter similar to Half-collared Gnatwren, but weaker, thinner, less musical. **Co, E, Br**

4 HALF-COLLARED GNATWREN *Microbates cinereiventris* * 10.5 cm (4 in)
Uncommon, patchily distributed. Local in northern Amazonia, west of Río Napo; also on outlying ridges and locally on east slope of Andes, 450–1000 m. Note long bill and striking tawny-rufous patch on sides of head and neck. Throat white, more or less bordered below with black or dark gray streaks (the "half collar"). **VOICE** Song (?) a descending, pure whistle: "*heeeoo*"; resembles Tawny-crowned Greenlet. Call a descending, wheezy, mewing "*eew!*" and a rapid chatter, sometimes ending with a mewed note: "*trr-ch'ch'ch'ch'ch'ch-eerw.*" **Co, E, Bo**

5 LONG-BILLED GNATWREN *Ramphocaenus melanurus* * 11.5–12.5 cm (4½–4¾ in)
Uncommon and somewhat local in Amazonia, up to 800 m. Found in under- and midstory of humid forest. Prefers edges, such as around treefalls and interface of forest and second growth. Also fairly common in semideciduous forest in Tumbes, at 750 m (*rufiventris*). Forages actively as singles or in pairs, often in vine tangles, generally apart from mixed-species flocks. Note very long bill, tail that often is cocked, and drab plumage. Amazonian birds are plain, with brown upperparts and light buff flanks; tail dark in most populations but *obscurus* (not illustrated) has white tail spots (dry central Huallaga Valley, also in southern Ucayali and Madre de Dios, where may be more prevalent in bamboo). *Rufiventris* more colorful, with tawnier sides of face and flanks, and white tail spots. **VOICE** Typical song (Amazonia, Tumbes) a fairly level or slightly rising, musical, ringing trill, lasting about 2.5 sec: "*trr'r'r'r'r'r'r'r'r'r'r'r'r.*" Calls a "*kip,*" a rising-falling trill, and a quiet, rich "*tchup.*" Song of *obscurus* different, variable, with 2 or 3 parts: "*tch tch tch trr'r'r'r-CHURT-CHURT-CHURT-CHURT*"; recalls Dusky-cheeked Foliage-Gleaner, but quieter, less carrying. **Co, E, Br, Bo**

IQUITOS
GNATCATCHER

♀ *parvirostris*

♂ *parvirostris*

♂ *maior*

♀ *bilineata*

TROPICAL
GNATCATCHER

♀ *maior*

TROPICAL GNATCATCHER

♂ *bilineata*

COLLARED GNATWREN

HALF-COLLARED GNATWREN

Amaz.

rufiventris

LONG-BILLED GNATWREN

PLATE
252

SOLITAIRES, THRUSHES, AND BARE-EYED ROBIN

"Typical" thrushes are large and long-legged. Adults usually drab; juveniles paler, spotted on breast and often streaked on upperparts. May retain pale-tipped, juvenile greater wing coverts for first calendar year. Underwing coverts, other than in species where male is black or gray, usually rufous or tawny. Some species frequently feed on ground. Solitaires are shorter-legged, strictly arboreal thrushes.

1 RUFOUS-BROWN SOLITAIRE *Cichlopsis leucogenys* * 20.5 cm (8 in)
Very poorly known. Reported from a few sites on outlying ridges, 900–1100 m. Behavior probably similar to Andean Solitaire's. Dull brown with brighter tawny throat and vent; also note bicolored bill. **VOICE** Voice of Peruvian subspecies unknown. Songs of other populations contain strident whistles and trills. Call a high, descending, slightly trilled "*tseeeeu*" (western Ecuador) or a high, sibilant "*tsueeee*" (eastern Brazil). **Co, E, Br**

2 ANDEAN SOLITAIRE *Myadestes ralloides* * 18 cm (7 in)
A characteristic bird of humid montane forest, more frequently heard than seen. Fairly common along east slope of Andes at 1200–2900 m, locally down to 600 m. Perches very upright and remains still for long periods. Note white outer rectrices and white band at base of remiges (visible in flight). Mandible orange north of Marañón (*venezuelensis*), black south of Marañón (*ralloides*; not illustrated). Juvenile mostly brown, heavily spotted with buff, but with adult wing and tail pattern. **VOICE** Song usually heard from vegetation along running water or along steep cliffs. Song of *venezuelensis* remarkably similar to Red-eyed Vireo, but more deliberate, a little thinner and more ringing in quality. Song of *ralloides* a rusty, squeaky series of thin whistled phrases, often descending. In aggressive interactions, both subspecies may give a quiet, but remarkably varied and musical, song with many trills and liquid ethereal phrases. Call a low, harsh rasp (*venezuelensis*) and a high, ringing, rising "*tzee*" (*ralloides*). **Co, E, Bo**

3 MARAÑON THRUSH *Turdus maranonicus* 22.5–23 cm (8¾–9 in)
Fairly common but restricted to dry middle and upper Marañón Valley and tributaries, in dry forest and riparian growth, 400–2000 m. Very retiring in nonbreeding season. Underparts heavily scalloped and spotted with dusky brown. Superficially similar to juvenile of other *Turdus*, but ventral spotting much heavier, and upperparts plain brown (no pale streaks); also overlaps with few other *Turdus*. **VOICE** Song a slow caroling similar to that of other *Turdus*, particularly Black-billed Thrush, but does not seem to repeat phrases as does Black-billed. Calls a rising "*rzeet rzeet*," a ringing "*tseet*," and a mellow "*wurk*." **E**

4 WHITE-EARED SOLITAIRE *Entomodestes leucotis* 23 cm (9 in)
Fairly common along east slope of Andes, 1200–2900 m. Found in humid montane forest and forest edges. Black and rufous plumage, with prominent white side to face, unmistakable. Sexes similar, but crown of female dusky brown (usually black in male). Underwing coverts and axillars also white; broad white bases to inner webs of primaries visible in flight. First-year birds duller, browner below with rufous crown. **VOICE** Song a single, ringing, even note, repeated approximately once every 10–20 sec. North of Cordillera Vilcabamba, song tends to be a little more musical, although sounds "rusty." From central Cuzco south, flatter, buzzier, and more nasal: "*zzzeeee*." Call a quiet "*dzz*" and a high, ringing "*tseee*." In alarm, a low growl. **Bo**

5 [PALE-VENTED THRUSH *Turdus obsoletus*] * 23 cm (9 in)
Known only from sight records from semideciduous forest in Tumbes at 400–800 m, where apparently uncommon or rare. Dull brown thrush of forest interior. Lacks an eyering, and bill is dark. Vent and lower belly white, rather sharply set off from brown breast and flanks; throat only weakly streaked. Cf. more common Bare-eyed Robin, which has orange-yellow eyering, a yellower bill, more conspicuous streaking on throat, and less contrast between belly and vent. **VOICE** Song a rich, slow caroling. Calls a low "*werk*" and an upslurred "*tu-ree?*," sometimes doubled. **Co, E**

6 BARE-EYED ROBIN *Turdus nudigenis* * 23 cm (9 in)
Fairly common but restricted to semideciduous and humid forests in Tumbes at 400 to 750 m. A light brown thrush with an orange-yellow eyering and an olive-yellow bill. **VOICE** Song a rich, moderate to slow-paced caroling, more mewing and slurred than the song of other west-slope *Turdus*. Call a characteristic rising mew: "*rrreeeww?*" **Co, E, Br**

ANDEAN SOLITAIRE

juv.

RUFOUS-BROWN
SOLITAIRE

ad.

imm.

WHITE-EARED SOLITAIRE

♂

MARAÑON THRUSH

PALE-VENTED THRUSH

BARE-EYED ROBIN

PLATE
253

NIGHTINGALE-THRUSHES AND SMALL
MIGRANT THRUSHES

Catharus are relatively small, long-legged thrushes; primarily forage on or near the ground but may ascend higher at fruiting trees. Catharus *thrushes may retain juvenile, pale-tipped greater wing coverts for all of their first calendar year.*

1 SLATY-BACKED NIGHTINGALE-THRUSH *Catharus fuscater* * 17 cm (6¾ in)

Uncommon along east slope of Andes at 1500–2900 m, locally to 3300 m and on Pacific slope in northwestern Peru from 1200–1700 m. Shy and retiring, in the undergrowth of humid montane forest (particularly along streams). Dark with a contrasting blackish cap and gray, unspotted breast. Also note red or orange bill, orbital ring, and tarsi; iris often is grayish brown or even grayish white. Spotted Nightingale-Thrush has a spotted breast and is generally at lower elevations. Male Slaty Thrush is larger and paler with striped throat and yellow bill and tarsi. **VOICE** Song a fairly simple series of ringing, rolled whistles, each phrase starting at a different pitch with the second note higher and louder than the first: *"tur-teeEE err-CHAY taa-TAY."* Calls a whistled descending *"whew"* and a mewed or raspy, rising-falling *"greee."* **Co, E, Bo**

2 SPOTTED NIGHTINGALE-THRUSH *Catharus dryas* * 17.5 cm (6¾ in)

Uncommon along east slope of Andes and on outlying ridges, at 700–1800 m, where found in understory of humid montane forest. Also found in semideciduous forest in Tumbes at 400 m. Like Slaty-backed Nightingale-Thrush, usually remains well concealed in vegetation. Bill, orbital ring, and tarsi orange. Note the spotted breast and deeply "peach yellow" underparts. **VOICE** Song a series of various musical trills interspersed with more whistled phrases, for example: *"zeee... che'e'e... tur'r'r... tooHEEuur... tre'e'e...."* Call a quiet, rising, mewed *"rhee?"* **Co, E, Bo**

3 GRAY-CHEEKED THRUSH *Catharus minimus* * 18 cm (7 in)

Rare boreal migrant to northern Amazonia, largely present Oct–Apr. At least some remain through the northern winter, but possibly is more common as a passage migrant. Also possibly occurs farther south in Peru. Dull grayish brown above, with plain face. Underparts whitish, usually with light buffy wash on breast; breast with blackish spots. Swainson's Thrush has prominent buffy "spectacles" (buffy eyering and loral streak), and a stronger buffy wash on the breast. **VOICE** Call a slightly hoarse rising-falling *"quee-ah!"* May sing quietly on wintering grounds (particularly before migration); song an ethereal series of fluty notes ending on a downwardly inflected note: *"dze-dze vree-vree veer-VEER."* **Co, E, Br**

4 SWAINSON'S THRUSH *Catharus ustulatus* * 18 cm (7 in)

Common boreal migrant to Peru, present Sep–Apr. Found throughout most of eastern Peru, up to 3500 m, but particularly common on lower slopes of Andes and in foothills between 600–2000 m. Also regular in northwest; rare vagrant farther south along coast (as far as Arequipa). Found in humid forest, including forest edge and second growth. Note buffy eyering and loral streak ("spectacles"), buffy breast heavily spotted with dusky, and brownish olive flanks. **VOICE** Calls a liquid *"wick,"* very like the sound of dripping water; also a rising, pure, whistled *"eee?"* May sing quietly on wintering grounds (particularly before migration); song an ethereal, rising series of fluty, warbled notes: *"wurzel werzel weezel ezee zee?"* **Co, E, Br, Bo**

5 [VEERY *Catharus fuscescens*] * 18 cm (7 in)

Rare boreal migrant; status in Peru not clear. Known from a single sight record (Nov) from Madre de Dios, but has been found several times (Oct) on the Brazilian side of the lower Río Yavarí, suggesting that it may be a rare but regular migrant to extreme northeastern Peru (at least in southbound passage). Usually light reddish brown above, with plain face. Upper breast has a few small spots and a buffy wash. Flanks light gray. Carefully cf. Gray-cheeked Thrush (usually grayer brown above, whiter below, and more heavily spotted) and Swainson's Thrush (has buffy "spectacles", brown flanks, and is more heavily spotted). **VOICE** Calls a rich, wheezy, descending, mewed *"EEW"* or a falling-rising *"veer-y?"* Probably does not sing in Peru; song an ethereal descending series of fluty notes: *"VEER-EER veer-eer."* **Co, Br, Bo, Ch**

SPOTTED
NIGHTINGALE-THRUSH

SLATY-BACKED
NIGHTINGALE-THRUSH

GRAY-CHEEKED THRUSH

SWAINSON'S THRUSH

VEERY

PLATE
254

DARK ANDEAN THRUSHES

Four Andean thrushes in which the plumage is particularly dark. Chiguanco and Great thrushes are found at forest edge and other open habitats, often feeding on ground whereas Glossy-black and Pale-eyed are more associated with humid montane forest and are more arboreal. See also plate 255.

1 CHIGUANCO THRUSH *Turdus chiguanco* * 25–27.5 cm (10–10¾ in)

One of the most common and widespread thrushes of Andes above 1600 m on west slope and from 2400–4300 m on east slope; also locally down to near sea level in west and down to 1300 m on eastern Andes. Inhabits forest edge, agricultural areas with hedgerows or scattered trees, and towns and gardens; locally overlaps with Great Thrush but prefers more arid environments. Dull gray-brown; similar to Great in appearance and behavior, but smaller and paler than widespread *gigantodes* (much paler than *ockendeni* subspecies of southeast); does not have pale orbital ring of male Great. **VOICE** Calls a short series of "*chup*" notes, a rusty "*sweet*" often given in alarm and flight, and a high "*seeee.*" Song, usually given predawn, is a rich and pleasant caroling series of "typical thrush" song phrases with a somewhat echoing quality. Song probably indistinguishable from Great; some also sound like Glossy-black Thrush (note habitat). **E, Bo, Ch**

2 GREAT THRUSH *Turdus fuscater* * 30–33 cm (11¾–13 in)

The largest thrush, and a characteristic bird of the humid high Andes. Common and widespread along east slope, 2400–4200 m, throughout Marañón Valley, and on west slope south to Lima, where occurs down to 1600 m. Found at edges of humid montane forest, in humid secondary forests and hedgerows, and in *Polylepis* woods. Frequently feeds on ground. Dark, with orange bill and tarsus, and (in male) a narrow yellow or orange orbital ring. Widespread *gigantodes* is grayish brown. Male *ockendeni* (eastern Cuzco south to Bolivia) blacker; female *ockendeni* paler than male, similar to *gigantodes* but browner. All females lack orbital ring; are more similar to Chiguanco Thrush but are larger, darker, and grayer (less sandy brown), and also have gray underwing coverts (usually tawny-rufous in Chiguanco). **VOICE** Calls a short series of "*chup*" notes, a higher "*chee-chee-chee…,*" a loud, rusty "*sweet*" often given in alarm and flight, and a high "*seeee.*" Song, usually given predawn, is a rich and pleasant caroling series of "typical thrush" song phrases with a somewhat echoing quality. Voice probably indistinguishable from Chiguanco. **Co, E, Bo**

3 GLOSSY-BLACK THRUSH *Turdus serranus* * 24–25 cm (9½–10 in)

Fairly common in humid montane forest along east slope of Andes, 1800–3000 m, locally down to 1400 m and up to 3450 m; uncommon in similar habitat on west slope in northwest from 1200 to 2900 m. Found in interior of humid montane forest, less commonly at edge, but does not feed in the open. Male a medium-sized glossy black thrush with orange bill, tarsi, and narrow orbital ring, and a dark iris. Female uniformly dark reddish brown, with moderately long tail, narrow orbital ring, and a dull bill (usually dusky, sometimes mixed yellow and dusky); cf. female Pale-eyed Thrush. **VOICE** Song a characteristic series of high, melancholy phrases, each ending with a thin, quiet trill or squeak, for example: "*hur-HEER tzee-it… hur-HEER too-cheet… hur-HEER chit-cup….*" Usually recognizable within its forested habitat. Calls a low "*chuk*" or "*chup,*" often in series, and a loud, ringing, harsh chatter in alarm. **Co, E, Bo**

4 PALE-EYED THRUSH *Turdus leucops* 20.5–21 cm (8–8¼ in)

Uncommon along east slope of Andes and on outlying ridges, 850–2000 m, locally to 2600 m. Found in canopy of humid montane forest. Male readily recognized by black plumage and white iris (with no orbital ring). Female a confusingly drab brown, mid-sized thrush. Compared to female Glossy-black Thrush, has shorter tail and bill (so looks stockier), lacks orbital ring, is more olive (less rufescent brown), and is paler on center of belly and vent (Glossy-black more uniformly colored; also, has brown, not rufous, underwing coverts). Throat of female Slaty Thrush whiter, more heavily streaked. **VOICE** Song a varied series of high-pitched, ringing phrases, some musical and warbled, others buzzing or lisping, including some mimicry of other birds, insects, and frogs. Calls a high, ringing "*ti-seee,*" a descending "*seeee,*" and a rising "*pit-tsee'e'e.*" **Co, E, Br, Bo**

CHIGUANCO THRUSH

juv.

ad.

GREAT THRUSH

♂ *gigantodes*

♂ *ockendeni*

juv.

GLOSSY-BLACK THRUSH

♀

♂

GLOSSY-BLACK THRUSH

♂

♀

PALE-EYED THRUSH

PLATE
255

ANDEAN AND ARBOREAL THRUSHES

Largely arboreal "typical" thrushes. See also plates 254, 256.

1 LAWRENCE'S THRUSH *Turdus lawrencii* 21–23 cm (8¼–9 in)

A dull-colored thrush with a remarkable song. Found in the interior of humid forest up to 700 m. Male is rich dark brown with distinctive yellow bill and bold yellow eyering; female (not illustrated) is similar, but eyering narrower or absent and bill dusky. Hauxwell's Thrush is more rufescent, less olive, and lacks eyering. Female Slaty (only limited overlap with Lawrence's) often is gray-brown above, with a gray rump; also underwing coverts usually dull brown (not extensively orange-brown as in Lawrence's). **VOICE** Song a varied series of mimicked environmental sounds (other birds, insects, frogs, human machines, etc.); few if any song phrases are not mimicry. Whereas some accomplished individuals can imitate up to 70 other sounds with remarkable fidelity, others have a far less impressive repertoire. Normal pattern is a single imitated phrase, a pause, a different phrase, a pause, etc., usually with little repetition within 10 phrases or so. Some phrases may be a fusion of the mimicked sounds of two different sources. Calls include a musical crescendo that sounds somewhat like splintering glass: "*tutilee-teeHEE?*"; also gives a "*kuk*" or "*wurk*," sometimes doubled or in a rising series, similar to that of other *Turdus*. Another call is a hoarse, rising, whistled series: "*chree'ee'ee'-ee'ee'ee?*" **Co, E, Br, Bo**

2 WHITE-NECKED THRUSH *Turdus albicollis* * 20–21 cm (8–8¼ in)

Uncommon to fairly common in the interior of humid Amazonian forest, up to 1300 m. Forages on the ground or in understory. Smallest Amazonian *Turdus*. Readily recognized by contrast between dark brown upperparts and light gray flanks and breast, white crescent across upper chest, and heavily streaked throat. Has a narrow orange eyering and dark bill. **VOICE** Song a slow, low-pitched, rich caroling with relatively little within-song variation: "*reewur-CHEE wuur-CHEE reewur-CHEE djeer wuur-CHEE....*" Calls a low "*kirk*" and a rising "*rheer*," sometimes followed by rising notes: "*rheer-ree-ree?*" **Co, E, Br, Bo**

3 PLUMBEOUS-BACKED THRUSH *Turdus reevei* 22.5–23 cm (8¼–9 in)

Fairly common in northwestern Peru, up to 1500 m. Found in dry and semideciduous forest, especially along river courses. Two-toned: blue-gray above and light buff below. Also note bluish white iris. **VOICE** Song a pleasant, mellow caroling, similar to other *Turdus*, particularly Black-billed Thrush. Call a ringing "*tseeet.*" Also gives a descending "*seeer*" and a wheezy, rising "*rheet.*" **E**

4 SLATY THRUSH *Turdus nigriceps* * 19–20 cm (7½–8 in)

Uncommon austral migrant (May–Oct) to east slope of Andes, 700–1800 m, occasionally during migration to 2650 m. Also an uncommon and local breeder at 1500–1850 m on Pacific slope in Piura and Lambayeque, where present Nov–Feb but apparently departs following breeding (presumably crosses to east side of Andes). Found in humid forest and forest edges. Male readily recognized by gray upperparts and breast contrasting with white throat streaks (but in northwest cf. Plumbeous-backed Thrush). Female is a drab brown or gray-brown thrush with striped brown-and-white throat and gray belly; most similar to female Pale-eyed and Lawrence's thrushes. **VOICE** Song a strident caroling with several high notes, similar to song of Pale-eyed, but generally lower in pitch and lacking the mimicry. Calls a characteristic, squeaky, ringing "*tchee-eh*" or "*tcheeEElu,*" also a high "*seeee.*" **E, Br, Bo**

5 CHESTNUT-BELLIED THRUSH *Turdus fulviventris* 23–24 cm (9–9½ in)

Uncommon; restricted to east side of Andes north and west of Marañón Valley, at 1800–2350 m. Found in humid montane forest and forest edges, where it may be seen foraging on the ground. Sexes similar, but head of female is dusky (not black). Unmistakable; note contrasting black head and bright rusty belly. **VOICE** Song a variable caroling with some phrase repeating. Calls a rapid series of hollow, popping "*perp*" notes that are not particularly thrushlike, some versions becoming a somewhat harsh "*pjer,*" also a ringing "*tzee.*" **Co, E**

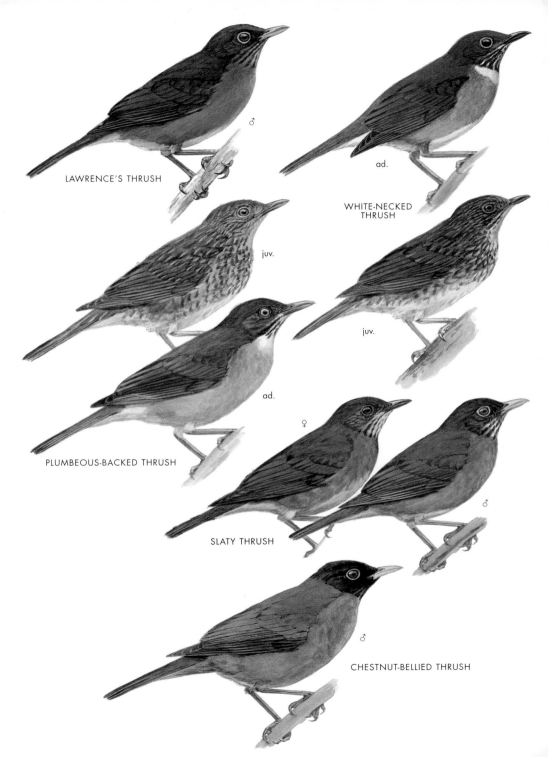

LAWRENCE'S THRUSH

♂

ad.

WHITE-NECKED
THRUSH

juv.

juv.

ad.

PLUMBEOUS-BACKED THRUSH

♀

SLATY THRUSH

♂

♂

CHESTNUT-BELLIED THRUSH

PLATE
256

AMAZONIAN THRUSHES AND DIPPER

Four particularly dull-colored "typical" thrushes; see also plate 254 (but no overlap with Andean species on plate 253). The dipper somewhat resembles a short-tailed thrush; restricted to edge of Andean rivers and streams.

1 CREAMY-BELLIED THRUSH *Turdus amaurochalinus* 23 cm (9 in)
Uncommon austral migrant (May–Oct) to southeastern lowlands. Found at forest edge, clearings, and river-edge forest; rarely found in forest interior, although sometimes present at forest openings. Characteristically wags tail vertically. Drab, with light gray-brown upperparts, blackish lores, heavily streaked throat bordered below by white crescent, and light buffy brown breast. Bill yellow or yellowish brown (yellow may be reduced in female); underwing coverts pale fulvous. Cf. resident Black-billed Thrush, which has entirely dark bill, is grayer below, has less contrasting lores, and has pale brown or brownish white underwing coverts; also lacks regular tail movements. **VOICE** Song (probably not likely to be heard in Peru) is a slow caroling similar to that of Black-billed. Call a rising, mewed "*rheedee?*" **Br, Bo, Ch**

2 BLACK-BILLED THRUSH *Turdus ignobilis* * 21.5–22 cm (8½–8¾ in)
The widespread thrush of forest edge in Amazonia, up to 1200 m. Fairly common at forest edge, in clearings, and in river-edge forest; avoids forest interior. Drab, with few distinctive features. Note black bill, light grayish brown breast, and only weakly streaked white throat; often shows a narrow white band on lower throat or upper chest. **VOICE** Song a pleasant and musical caroling, often with a particular phrase given twice. Calls a low "*kirk*" or "*wurk*," a liquid "*kwip*" or "*quit-quit*," and a rising "*week*." **Co, E, Br, Bo**

3 PALE-BREASTED THRUSH *Turdus leucomelas* * 23 cm (9 in)
Uncommon and geographically restricted; found in Mayo Valley (in dry forest and forest edge, 800–1400 m) and Pampas del Heath (gallery forest and woodlots scattered across savanna). Warm brown above with contrasting light gray crown and sides to head; breast and belly light buffy brown; orbital ring orange; bill dark olive or gray. Cf. Black-billed and Creamy-bellied thrushes (which have duller, more uniformly colored upperparts). **VOICE** Song a rich caroling, similar to Hauxwell's Thrush, but slightly faster paced. Call a harsh "*djer-djer-djer*," a more musical "*djeer-REE-REE-REE*," a descending series "*DJEER-jeer-jur*," a ringing "*tlee*," and a "*kuk*." **Co, Br, Bo**

4 HAUXWELL'S THRUSH *Turdus hauxwelli* 22–23 cm (8¾–9 in)
Uncommon but widespread thrush of humid forest interior (primarily transitional or varzea) in Amazonia, up to 800 m, and locally to 1200 m. Primarily forages on ground, but may attend fruiting midstory trees. Widespread "standard" morph (throughout Amazonia) uniformly rufescent brown with white lower belly, white vent (sometimes spotted with brown), and dark bill. Recognizable by color tone and lack of strong plumage pattern or eyering. Less well-known "gray-tailed" morph (probably a separate species) reported from lower Río Napo south to northern Ucayali, and west to San Martín; differs by being duller brown, with gray-brown tail, more prominent throat streaking, yellow-green bill, and narrow yellow-orange eyering. Superficially similar to female Lawrence's Thrush, which is darker brown and has a dusky bill. **VOICE** Song a rich, slow caroling, similar to that of Pale-breasted Thrush, but even slower-paced, and has a regular repetition of phrases. Calls a musical "*hurLEW-tijet-tijet*," sometimes without the second 2 notes, also a low "*kirk*." Songs and calls of gray-tailed morph very like those of Bare-eyed Robin. **Co, E, Br, Bo**

5 WHITE-CAPPED DIPPER *Cinclus leucocephalus* * 15–16 cm (6–6¼ in)
An aquatic passerine; always found along swiftly moving rivers and streams, in forest and open country, 1500–3100 m, locally down to 900 m and up to 4200 m. Stands on rocks in midstream or along bank. Forages by diving or by gleaning from rocks while standing partly immersed in water. Flight very low over water, with buzzy wingbeats. Easily recognized by habitat, rotund shape, and white cap and breast. Present throughout on east slope of Andes but only locally on west slope. Widespread *leucocephalus* has dark back and belly. In far north (south to central Amazonas and San Martín) has white on back and a white belly (*leuconotus*). **VOICE** Song a loud, varied warbling with some harsh phrases; remarkably audible over the rushing sound of water. Call, most often given in flight, a ringing, nasal "*djit*." **Co, E, Bo**

CREAMY-BELLIED THRUSH

BLACK-BILLED THRUSH

gray-tailed morph

PALE-BREASTED THRUSH

HAUXWELL'S THRUSH

leuconotus

leucocephalus

WHITE-CAPPED DIPPER

PLATE
257
LARGE LOWLAND TANAGERS

Ramphocelus are ubiquitous at forest edge, in second growth, and in gardens; notable for swollen base to the mandible, which also is silvery blue (especially in adult males). Black-faced and Magpie tanagers are birds of forest edge or open habitats. Black-and-white Tanager has an unusual east-west migration across the Andes. Red-billed Pied Tanager is an uncommon forest interior species.

1 BLACK-BELLIED TANAGER *Ramphocelus melanogaster* * 16–18 cm (6¼–7 in)
Restricted to Mayo and upper Huallaga valleys, 500–1800 m, where mostly replaces Silver-beaked Tanager, but the two closely approach one another or locally overlap, and have hybridized. Male distinguished by red rump and flanks; cf. Masked Crimson Tanager. Female very similar to female Silver-beaked, and usually not identifiable with certainty; averages darker on upperparts and throat, with brighter red rump, redder tone to underparts, and greater contrast between dark throat and red breast and belly. **VOICE** Probably indistinguishable from Silver-beaked. **ENDEMIC**

2 SILVER-BEAKED TANAGER *Ramphocelus carbo* * 18 cm (7 in)
Widespread and common in second growth and forest edge throughout Amazonia, up to 1800 m (but see Black-bellied Tanager in Huallaga Valley). Throat of male crimson; but in poor light bird may appear all dark with white bill. Dull brown female distinguished (except from other *Ramphocelus*) by silvery mandible. **VOICE** Song a quiet, wheezy, repetitive series of short phrases, for example: "*chi-chi churee-chew chi-chi churee-chew….*" Calls a thin, rising wheezy "*zweet*," and a frequently heard metallic "*chep*," similar to call of Magpie Tanager, but not quite as loud or metallic. **Co, E, Br, Bo**

3 MASKED CRIMSON TANAGER *Ramphocelus nigrogularis* 18–19 cm (7–7½ in)
Fairly common and widespread in Amazonia, largely below 600 m, locally to 1100 m. Closely associated with water: usually at margins of oxbow lakes, but found in second growth near rivers and streams. Forages in flocks, sometimes with Silver-beaked Tanager. Female similar but duller, with dusky (not black) belly. **VOICE** Song a deliberate series of simple notes: "*chup whip weehur… chup whip weehur….*" Calls a high, squeaky "*tip*" and a metallic "*tink*." **Co, E, Br, Bo**

4 BLACK-FACED TANAGER *Schistochlamys melanopis* * 17.5–19 cm (7–7½ in)
Uncommon and local along east slope of Andes, 900–1800 m, also locally in lowlands; at forest edge, and in grasslands with scattered shrubs, savanna, and pastures. Adult unmistakable. Compare yellow-green, long-tailed immature to female Black-and-white Tanager (which is shorter-tailed, has more patterned face, and breast flammulated or streaked). Also see female *Piranga* tanagers. **VOICE** Song a rich, pleasing warble similar to a *Pheucticus* or saltator, but shorter, simpler in structure, e.g. "*weeo wurchick weeo wurchick twee-twee-twee*." Calls a dry "*tchep*," "*spit*," and "*spit-churt*." **Co, E, Br, Bo**

5 MAGPIE TANAGER *Cissopis leverianus* * 27 cm (10½ in)
Fairly common. Singles, pairs, or small groups are conspicuous in midstory and canopy at forest edge, in second growth, and in river-edge forest, up to 1600 m. Often apart from mixed-species flocks. Distinctive. Immature (not illustrated) has dark iris, and black of plumage is less glossy. **VOICE** Song a varied series of loud, wiry notes, trills, and rattles, usually interspersed with call notes. Calls a rising, high "*tsee*" and a hard, metallic "*tchip!*," similar to, but louder and more metallic than, Silver-beaked Tanager. **Co, E, Br, Bo**

6 BLACK-AND-WHITE TANAGER *Conothraupis speculigera* 16–16.5 cm (6¼–6½ in)
Rare to uncommon seasonal breeder in dry forest of northwest, up to 1500 m; primarily present Feb–May but may linger much later during wetter years. Migrates to Amazonia, where found at forest edge, in second growth, and in river-edge forest, below 700 m; recorded Jun–Sep but probably present longer. Compare male to Black-and-white Seedeater. Females and immatures significantly larger, and greener, than female seedeaters, with less conical bill; cf. also other greenish tanagers. **VOICE** Song a loud, repetitive, liquid phrase: "*chi-DONG chi-DONG chi-DONG….*" Call a high, descending "*tee*." **E, Br, Bo**

7 RED-BILLED PIED TANAGER *Lamprospiza melanoleuca* 18 cm (7 in)
Rare to uncommon tanager of terra firme canopy south of Amazon, below 600 m. Usually in small noisy groups, with mixed-species flocks. Only black-and-white tanager of forest interior; note red bill. Cf. Magpie Tanager. **VOICE** Calls, loud and attention-grabbing, a sharp, descending "*TEW*" and a higher, plaintive "*ti-chee*" or "*ti-ti-ter*." Song a rapid, squeaky warbled series; an expanded version of the "*ti-ti-ter*" call. **Br, Bo**

SILVER-BEAKED
TANAGER

MASKED CRIMSON TANAGER

BLACK-BELLIED TANAGER

BLACK-FACED TANAGER

ad.

imm.

MAGPIE TANAGER

BLACK-AND-WHITE TANAGER

imm. ♂

♀

RED-BILLED PIED TANAGER

♂

♀

♂

PLATE
258

ANDEAN TANAGERS (*CREURGOPS,*
HEMISPINGUS)

Slaty and Rufous-crested tanagers are two geographically replacing species of Andean tanager; mostly insectivorous. Almost always forage in the canopy of humid montane forest with mixed-species flocks. Hemispingus (Hemispingus) are a diverse group of small, largely insectivorous Andean tanagers. Most species forage in small groups that often join mixed-species flocks; see also plate 259.

1 SLATY TANAGER *Creurgops dentatus* 14–15 cm (5½–6 in)
Replaces the behaviorally similar Rufous-crested Tanager in southern Peru. Uncommon in the canopy of montane humid forest, 1200–2500 m. Male is unlike any other Peruvian species (but cf. *canigenis* subspecies of Slaty Brush-Finch). Female is superficially similar to other tanagers with rufous or chestnut in the plumage, but note details of plumage pattern. In particular cf. Black-eared Hemispingus. **VOICE** Song a high, wheedling series of notes. Call a thin "*tchip*." **Bo**

2 RUFOUS-CRESTED TANAGER *Creurgops verticalis* 14 cm (5½ in)
Uncommon in humid montane forest along east slope of Andes, 1100–2400 m. Singles and pairs forage in canopy of humid montane forest in association with mixed-species flocks. Hops out on slender limbs to the outer branches, gleaning insects from foliage. A slender, long-tailed 2-toned tanager, gray above and buff below; male with rufous crown patch. Other Andean tanagers that are tawny or rufous below are blue above or have black on face. **VOICE** Calls a high "*tsit*" and "*tchew*." **Co, E**

3 BLACK-HEADED HEMISPINGUS *Hemispingus verticalis* 14–14.5 cm (5½–5¾ in)
Fairly common and conspicuous member of canopy mixed-species flocks in humid montane and elfin forests, north of Río Marañón, 2700–2950 m. Small groups accompany mixed-species canopy flocks. Similar in behavior to Drab Hemispingus, which it replaces geographically. Unmistakable. Young birds have a pale throat and may show white over eyes. **VOICE** Song a rapid series of "*tchip*" notes that accelerate into a jumble of squeaky warbles. Calls a high "*tseet*" and "*tip*." **Co, E**

4 DRAB HEMISPINGUS *Hemispingus xanthophthalmus* 14 cm (5½ in)
Fairly common near treeline in canopy of humid montane forest along east slope of Andes, 2200–3350 m. Walks and hops across crowns of small-leaved trees and bushes, often perching on leaves and gleaning their upper surfaces. Small groups regularly associate with mixed-species flocks. A small, very slender gray–and-white tanager. Note the pale eye and plain face. **VOICE** Song a rapid series of "*tchip*" notes that accelerate into a jumble of squeaky warbles. Calls include a high "*tsit*." **Bo**

5 RUFOUS-BROWED HEMISPINGUS *Hemispingus rufosuperciliaris* 16 cm (6¼ in)
Rare and local in elfin forest on east slope of Andes, 2550–3500 m. Found in dense undergrowth, especially in thickets of bamboo. Forages as singles, pairs, or small groups, apart or in association with mixed-species flocks. Forages very close to the ground, and is rather deliberate in actions. A striking tanager, black and gray above and rufous below, with very broad rufous superciliary. Unmistakable. **VOICE** Song a loud series of jerky, wiry squeaks and chips. Call a dry "*tik*" or "*tsip*." **ENDEMIC**

6 THREE-STRIPED HEMISPINGUS *Hemispingus trifasciatus* 13.5–14 cm (5¼–5½ in)
Uncommon in mixed-species flocks in canopy of elfin forest or treeline of humid montane forest, 3000–3650 m. Regularly associates with mixed-species flocks in forest canopy, in groups of 4 or 5 individuals; occasionally also apart from mixed-species flocks. Gleans leaves at or near the ends of limbs. A small, brown–and-buff tanager with black sides to face and a prominent whitish superciliary. **VOICE** Song a buzzy chattered phrase; also gives a single note repeated in a long series, from an exposed perch over canopy. Calls a high "*tzzp*" or lisping "*tssp*." **Bo**

SLATY TANAGER

♂

♀

RUFOUS-CRESTED
TANAGER

♂

♀

imm.

BLACK-HEADED
HEMISPINGUS

ad.

DRAB HEMISPINGUS

RUFOUS-BROWED
HEMISPINGUS

THREE-STRIPED
HEMISPINGUS

PLATE
259

ANDEAN TANAGERS (*HEMISPINGUS*)

Hemispingus (Hemispingus) *are a diverse group of small, largely insectivorous Andean tanagers. Most species forage in small groups that often join mixed-species flocks; see also plate 258. The yellow-green* Hemispingus *are larger and heavier billed than are* Basileuterus *warblers (plate 294).*

1 OLEAGINOUS HEMISPINGUS *Hemispingus frontalis* * 14.5 cm (5¾ in)
Uncommon to locally fairly common in humid montane forest on east slope of Andes, 1500–2600 m. Forages in understory, often in thickets and tangles. Dull-colored, medium-sized tanager, olive above and yellow below with indistinct yellowish superciliary. Often flicks or twitches tail. Superficially similar to *Basileuterus* warblers, which are smaller, have broader, more well-defined superciliaries, are brighter yellow, and have all-black bills. **VOICE** Song an accelerating series of nasal "*enk*" notes and chips that can become a chatter of musical chippering notes: "*enk enk-enkenk-paCHEER pa-CHEER pa-CHEER.*" Similar to songs of Black-eared Hemispingus, but lower pitched and more musical. Call a metallic "*tip*." **Co, E**

2 BLACK-EARED HEMISPINGUS *Hemispingus melanotis* * 13.5–14.5 cm (5¼–5¾ in)
Locally fairly common in humid montane forest along east slope of Andes, 1100–2200 m; also fairly common on both slopes of western cordillera in northwest, 1200–3050 m. Forages in small groups or pairs in understory, especially in bamboo thickets. A small tanager with black face, rufous or tawny breast, and gray or brown upperparts. Geographically variable. Populations along east slope of Andes north of Marañón (*melanotis*) and from south of Marañón to western Cuzco (*berlepschi*) have tawny breasts and no superciliary. From eastern Cuzco to Bolivia (*castaneicollis*), chin is black and there is weak white superciliary (often reduced or lacking). Most divergent birds are in western Andes (*piurae, macrophrys*), with black crown and broad white superciliary. **VOICE** Song (*berlepschi*), often given in duet, a rapid mechanical chatter of metallic notes. Call a rising "*tsee*" and nasal "*enk*." **Co, E, Bo**

3 PARODI'S HEMISPINGUS *Hemispingus parodii* 15.5 cm (6 in)
Locally fairly common, but patchily distributed in elfin forest on east slope of southern Andes, 2600–3500 m. Small yellow-green tanager, with "dingy" face and short greenish superciliary. Citrine Warbler (which may flock with the tanager) has a more slender, solid black bill; blacker lores but a more olive crown; and a shorter, yellower (less greenish) superciliary. **VOICE** Song a series of notes, most buzzy: "*tzzew tzeee titititi,*" repeated incessantly. Call a high, lisping, descending "*tseew*" and sharp "*ti*." **ENDEMIC**

4 SUPERCILIARED HEMISPINGUS *Hemispingus superciliaris* * 14 cm (5½ in); *urubambae* 12.5–13 cm (5–5¼ in)
Fairly common in humid montane forest along east slope of Andes, 2200–3450 m, and on west slope south to southern Cajamarca, 2200 to 2900 m. Almost always forages with mixed-species flocks, usually as pairs or singles. Usually in canopy but may range lower at forest edge. A small, warblerlike tanager, geographically variable: populations north and west of Marañón Valley (*maculifrons*) and from Vilcabamba south (*urubambae*) are green above and yellow below with a short white superciliary. Populations in central Peru (*insignis, leucogastrus*) have similar pattern but lack yellow; instead are gray above and dull white below. Cf. *Basileuterus* warblers (superficially similar to the yellow and olive populations), which forage in understory. **VOICE** Song a rapid, dry, chippering chatter. Call a high "*ti*." **Co, E, Bo**

5 ORANGE-BROWED HEMISPINGUS *Hemispingus calophrys* 16 cm (6¼ in)
Only in humid montane forests on east side of Andes near Bolivian border, 3000 m. A southern replacement to Black-capped Hemispingus, and behaviorally similar; often forages low near ground in *Chusquea* bamboo. Note rather broad orange-ochraceous superciliary. **VOICE** Calls various high chips and rapid twittering chatters. **Bo**

6 BLACK-CAPPED HEMISPINGUS *Hemispingus atropileus* * 15–17 cm (6–6¼ in)
Fairly common in understory of humid montane forest and elfin forest along east slope of Andes, 2600–3700 m, locally down to 2300 m; often forages in thickets of *Chusquea* bamboo. Superficially similar to *Basileuterus* warblers but larger; readily identified by long white superciliary interrupting black of crown and sides of face. **VOICE** Calls a high, sibilant "*tseet*" and a thin "*tip*." Also a songlike excited series of high chippering and single notes. Dawn song a simple, almost hummingbird-like "*swee chew swee chew swee chew….*" **Co, E**

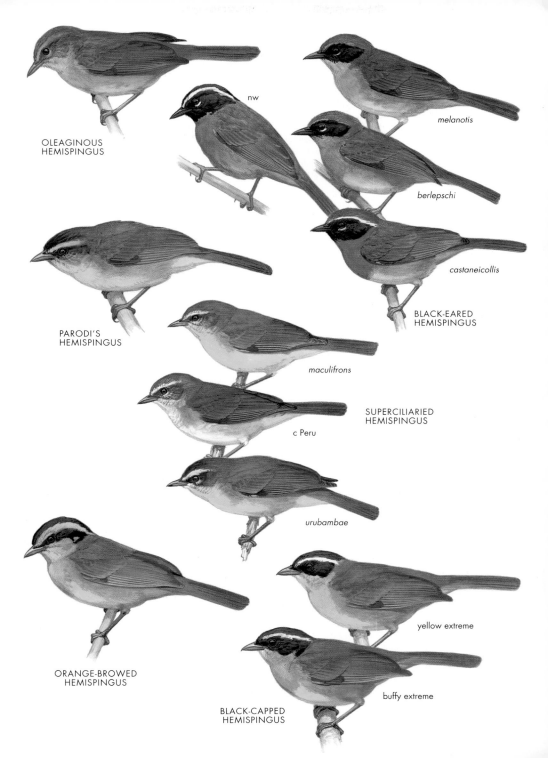

OLEAGINOUS
HEMISPINGUS

nw

melanotis

berlepschi

castaneicollis

BLACK-EARED
HEMISPINGUS

PARODI'S
HEMISPINGUS

maculifrons

c Peru

SUPERCILIARIED
HEMISPINGUS

urubambae

ORANGE-BROWED
HEMISPINGUS

yellow extreme

buffy extreme

BLACK-CAPPED
HEMISPINGUS

PLATE
260

SMALL TANAGERS (*HEMITHRAUPIS, THLYPOPSIS*)

Hemithraupis are two similar species of small tanagers, with relatively slender, warblerlike bills. Pairs regularly associate with canopy mixed-species flocks in humid forest. Acrobatically search foliage, especially leaf clusters near the ends of branches, for arthropods; also consume fruit. *Thlypopsis* are small, largely insectivorous tanagers with slender bills. Most species are Andean and forage low in dense shrubs, but may ascend into the canopy. Active and warblerlike. The five Peruvian species replace one another geographically or elevationally with only limited overlap.

1 GUIRA TANAGER *Hemithraupis guira* * 13 cm (5 in)
Widely distributed in Amazonia, locally up to 1500 m, but typically uncommon; apparently more common in northern Peru than in southern. Also in mangrove forest in Tumbes. Ornate male distinctive. Female very similar to female Yellow-backed Tanager but has brighter yellow sides to face and more uniformly patterned yellow-green wings (coverts and remiges of Yellow-backed have brighter, more contrasting, yellow edges); also often has yellow lores and eyering (lores olive, eyering lacking in Yellow-backed). **VOICE** Song an accelerating series of high chips ending with some "*sew*" notes. Calls a "*tsik*" and a nasal "*enk*." **Co, E, Br, Bo**

2 YELLOW-BACKED TANAGER *Hemithraupis flavicollis* * 13–14 cm (5–5½ in)
Uncommon but widely distributed in Amazonia, below 750 m, locally up to 1350 m. Males geographically variable. *Peruana*, found north of the Amazon and the Marañón, has yellow lesser upper wing coverts; these feathers are black in all populations in central and southern Peru (*sororia, centralis*). Compare female to female Guira Tanager. **VOICE** Calls a rich "*chew*," and a higher "*tsew*" and "*seew*." **Co, E, Br, Bo**

3 RUFOUS-CHESTED TANAGER *Thlypopsis ornata* * 13–13.5 cm (5–5¼ in)
Fairly common on both slopes of western Andes in northwestern Peru; uncommon along east slope of Andes, 1600–3300 m, locally to 3800 m. Found in under- and midstory at forest edge, in dense montane shrubbery, and bamboo thickets; sometimes also in *Polylepis* woods. Forages in pairs or small groups, apart from or with mixed-species flocks. Gray back contrasts with orange-rufous head, breast, and flanks. Immature duller and yellower. In central Peru overlaps very locally with Brown-flanked Tanager. **VOICE** Song a simple series of high "*swee*" notes. Calls high "*tsit*" and "*tip*" notes. **Co, E**

4 BROWN-FLANKED TANAGER *Thlypopsis pectoralis* 13–13.5 cm (5–5¼ in)
Uncommon in central Peru; primarily found in intermontane valleys (on western side of eastern cordillera) at 2500–3200 m. In montane shrubbery, at forest edge or bordering cultivated areas. Often forage in pairs, apart from mixed-species flocks; but sometimes joins flocks, including those containing Rufous-chested Tanager. Similar to that species, but flanks are dull brown. **ENDEMIC**

5 ORANGE-HEADED TANAGER *Thlypopsis sordida* * 13.5–15 cm (5¼–6 in)
Uncommon but widespread in Amazonia, below 1000 m; rarest in southeast. Primarily found in river-edge successional habitats, such as shrubbery on river islands and in river-edge second growth. Forages in under- and midstory in pairs and small groups. A small gray-and-white tanager with sharply contrasting, ochre-and-yellow head and throat. The yellowish immature is less distinctive; cf. the smaller Yellow Warbler and immature Bicolored Conebill. **VOICE** Call an unobtrusive, chattered series of thin "*tseer*" notes. **Co, E, Br, Bo**

6 BUFF-BELLIED TANAGER *Thlypopsis inornata* 13.5–14 cm (5¼–5½ in)
Uncommon in shrubby and forest edge in the semiarid middle Marañón Valley, 450–2000 m. Behavior similar to other *Thlypopsis* tanagers; forages in under- and midstory in small groups. Gray above and buff below with rufous crown. Locally overlaps geographically with Rufous-chested Tanager, but generally occurs at lower elevations and in more arid habitats; also differs in uniformly buff underparts and sides of face. **VOICE** Call an unobtrusive, chattered series of thin "*tseer*" notes; similar to call of Orange-headed Tanager. **ENDEMIC**

7 RUST-AND-YELLOW TANAGER *Thlypopsis ruficeps* 12.5–14 cm (5–5½ in)
Fairly common along east slope of Andes at 1500–3700 m, in montane shrubbery, at forest edge, and in bamboo thickets; locally also in *Polylepis* woods. Forages in under- and midstory in small groups, often with mixed-species flocks. Numbers may be supplemented by austral migrants; apparent vagrant north to Huánuco. Adult unmistakable. Yellow immature is less distinctive; cf. *Basileuterus* warblers, which are slightly larger and have more contrasting superciliaries and eyelines. **VOICE** Song a thin, high, wheedling phrase. Call a thin "*tip*" or "*tink*." **Bo**

♀

♂ *peruana*

YELLOW-BACKED
TANAGER

GUIRA TANAGER

♂

♀

♂

RUFOUS-CHESTED
TANAGER

imm.

ad.

imm.

ad.

BROWN-FLANKED
TANAGER

imm.

ad.

ORANGE-HEADED TANAGER

imm.

ad.

BUFF-BELLIED TANAGER

imm.

ad.

RUST-AND-YELLOW TANAGER

PLATE
261

LARGELY BLACK TANAGERS (*TACHYPHONUS*)

Tachyphonus tanagers are a diverse group of medium-sized tanagers found in forest and at forest edge. Most species are frequent members of mixed-species flocks. Males are largely black, often with a narrow crest; females are olive or brown in color, and some are superficially similar to foliage-gleaners (Philydor, Furnariidae). Most species probably omnivorous.

1 FULVOUS-CRESTED TANAGER *Tachyphonus surinamus* * 15.5–16.5 cm (6–6½ in)
Uncommon but widespread in northern and central Amazonia, below 750 m. Perhaps more prevalent in forests on sandy and weathered soils. Singles and pairs forage in mid- and understory of forest and at forest edge, often but not always in association with mixed-species flocks. Males geographically variable: crest and rump are buffy north of the Amazon (*brevipes*), tawny south of the Amazon and in southern Peru (*napensis*), and variably intermediate south of the Marañón/west of the Ucayali. White pectoral tufts often visible at edge of closed wing. Female is strongly 2-toned, olive above with tawny throat. **VOICE** Song a series of high hummingbird-like screeches interspersed with rich "*chip*" notes: "*soo-see-soo-see'chip'chip soo-see-soo-see'chip....*" Calls high "*tseet*" notes and a rapid, rich chatter. **Co, E, Br**

2 FLAME-CRESTED TANAGER *Tachyphonus cristatus* * 16–17 cm (6¼–6¾ in)
Fairly common in midstory and canopy of forest interior, up to 900 m; primarily in pairs in terra firme. Seen from below, male often appears as slender black bird with narrow buff throat patch (although buff throat sometimes is reduced or lacking). Crest brilliant orange in north, but scarlet in southeast Amazonia (*madeirae*). Compare duller, buffy brown female to yellower female shrike-tanagers and to canopy foliage-gleaners. **VOICE** Calls (Brazil) a high "*tswee*" and a dull "*unk.*" **Co, E, Br, Bo**

3 RED-SHOULDERED TANAGER *Tachyphonus phoenicius* 15.5–16 cm (6–6¼ in)
Fairly common, but very local in Peru; known only from dry portions of Río Mayo Valley at 1000–1350 m and from white-sand areas between the Marañón and lower Huallaga rivers. Forages as singles and pairs in shrubs at forest edge and on savannas and in open woods. Male is similar to, but much smaller than, White-lined Tanager, with which it may occur in Río Mayo area; red lesser wing coverts often not visible in the field. Female is very gray, with distinctive dark mask; immatures are similarly dull, but variably streaked below. **VOICE** Calls a wheezy "*tew*" and a nasal, almost thrushlike "*perk.*" **Co, Br, Bo**

4 YELLOW-CRESTED TANAGER *Tachyphonus rufiventer* 15–16 cm (6–6¼ in)
Fairly common and widespread in Amazonia south of the Amazon, up to 1250 m (but largely confined to foothills in southernmost Peru, where replaced in lowlands by Flame-crested Tanager). Behavior similar to that of Flame-crested. Male easily recognized. Female similar to female White-shouldered Tanager but is larger, more ochraceous below, and has a buffier throat. Cf. also Gray-headed Tanager. **VOICE** Song/calls (?) include high "*tswee*" and buzzier "*dzz dzz dzz*" notes. **Br, Bo**

5 WHITE-LINED TANAGER *Tachyphonus rufus* 19 cm (7½ in)
Locally fairly common but patchily distributed in eastern Peru, up to 1800 m. A tanager of forest edge and second growth, especially in less humid areas or (locally) at sites with sandy soil. Usually encountered as singles or pairs, not in association with mixed-species flocks. The association of the black male and uniformly rufous female often is a clue to identification. Compare male to smaller and more local Red-shouldered Tanager, and female to various furnariids (such as Buff-fronted Foliage-gleaner). **VOICE** Song (Ecuador) a musical, but repetitive, "*chip chirp weep chirp chip chirp weep....*" Calls a rising "*sweet*" similar to flight call of some hermits, also a quiet "*enk.*" **Co, E, Br, Bo**

6 WHITE-SHOULDERED TANAGER *Tachyphonus luctuosus* * 13.5–14 cm (5¼–5½ in)
Fairly common and widespread in Amazonia below 1000 m, although scarce or very local in northeastern Amazonian Peru. Pairs are frequent members of mixed-species flocks in midstory of humid forest; may prefer dense vegetation such as at forest edge or treefalls in forest interior. Female is similar to female Yellow-crested Tanager but is smaller and brighter yellow below, with whiter throat. Cf. also much larger Gray-headed Tanager. **VOICE** Song a repetitive, musical note given about 2 notes/sec: "*tchert tchert tchert tchert...,*" interspersed with "*tseet*" notes. Calls a rising "*swee*" and a low "*chep.*" **Co, E, Br, Bo**

FULVOUS-CRESTED TANAGER

♂ *napensis*

♂ *brevipes*

♀

♂ *madeirae*

FLAME-CRESTED TANAGER

♂

♀

RED-SHOULDERED TANAGER

♀

imm.

♂

YELLOW-CRESTED TANAGER

♂

♀

WHITE-LINED TANAGER

♂

♀

WHITE-SHOULDERED TANAGER

♀

♂

PLATE
262

SHRIKE-TANAGERS AND TANAGERS

A disparate group of tanagers of humid forests. Most typically forage with mixed-species flocks, other than the mostly frugivorous Fawn-breasted Tanager. Shrike-tanagers perch with relatively upright posture, sally to capture prey (usually arthropods flushed by other members of flock).

1 FULVOUS SHRIKE-TANAGER *Lanio fulvus* * 17–17.5 cm (6¾–7 in)

Uncommon but widespread in terra firme, up to 1350 m; mostly north of the Amazon, but crosses Marañón to San Martín. No known overlap with White-winged Shrike-Tanager, although these may approach each other between lower Huallaga and Ucayali rivers. Drab female superficially similar to female Flame-crested Tanager but differs in behavior; also is more deeply colored (light olive and tawny on underparts, rather than buff). **VOICE** Calls a piercing "TCHEW," also a light chatter. Song a lisping, rising series of high, thin whistles interspersed with call notes: "*wsss-tew wsss-tew wsss-tew... TCHEW.*" **Co, E, Br**

2 WHITE-WINGED SHRIKE-TANAGER *Lanio versicolor* * 16–17 (6¼–6¾ in)

Uncommon but widespread in Amazonia south of Amazon up to 1200 m; crosses to west bank of Ucayali but not known west of lower Huallaga. Other than by behavior, drab female can be confusing. Cf. female Flame-crested Tanager (which is much buffier, less yellow, below). **VOICE** Call a piercing "*t'SEER*" or "*TSEW!*" Song a pleasant musical series, for example "*tur-ree-tur pe'chew,*" reminiscent of Dusky-capped Greenlet; sometimes embellished with various high, wiry notes, squeaks, and warbles. **Br, Bo**

3 BLACK-GOGGLED TANAGER *Trichothraupis melanops* 16.5 cm (6½ in)

Uncommon and local in humid montane forest and at forest edge along east slope of Andes, 900–1800 m; few records north of Huánuco. Pairs forage actively in understory; sallies to air and foliage for insects, also consumes some fruit. Medium-sized, dull-colored, with contrast between dark wings and tawny underparts; white band across bases to inner webs of remiges conspicuous in flight. Male has prominent black "mask" and semiconcealed yellow crest. **VOICE** Song (eastern Brazil) a weak, mewing series of high warbled phrases. Calls dry, warblerlike "*tchik*" and quiet warbled phrases. **Br, Bo**

4 FAWN-BREASTED TANAGER *Pipraeidea melanonota* * 14 cm (5½ in)

Rare but widespread along west slope south to southern Cajamarca, sparingly south to Lima; and on east slope of western Andes in Marañón Valley. Also along east slope of Andes, 1100–2900 m. Scattered records in southern Amazonia below 600 m may represent austral migrants or dispersing individuals. Singles or pairs forage in midstory and canopy at edge of forest; rarely associate with mixed-species flocks but may join congregations of other species at fruiting trees. Female duller than male, but always shows some blue on upperparts, especially on crown and rump. Cf. larger Chestnut-bellied Mountain-Tanager. **VOICE** Song a thin, high, wiry series of rising notes: "*swee swee swee swee swee.*" **Co, E, Br, Bo**

5 GRAY-HEADED TANAGER *Eucometis penicillata* * 17.5–18.5 mm (7–7¼ in)

Uncommon but widespread in northern and central Amazonia (*penicillata*); rare in southeast (presumably *albicollis*). Typically found near water. Singles or pairs forage in under- and midstory of varzea; often very low near ground, in dense understory. Consumes both insects and fruit. Green and yellow with contrasting light gray hood and "shaggy" crest. Immature has reduced crest and is largely yellow-green. Albicollis (not illustrated) has browner head; reduced crest with no white in crown; and paler bill. **VOICE** Song a loud, strident series of jerky, ringing notes interspersed with high sibilant sounds, seeps, and chips. Calls a low "*tchup*" and a high, sibilant, descending series "*swee-swee-swee-swee.*" **Co, E, Br, Bo**

6 CARMIOL'S TANAGER *Chlorothraupis carmioli* * 17 cm (6¾ in)

Locally fairly common in humid montane forest along east slope of Andes in central and southern Peru, 400–1350 m; perhaps most common on outlying ridges. Also uncommon and local on outlying ridges in north-central Peru. Appears to favor dark, wet valleys and lush stream edges. Travels in small groups in under- and midstory. Consumes both arthropods and fruit. Note stout black bill, stout body, and relatively short tail, also loud **VOICE** Song, usually only at dawn, a very loud series of variable liquid whistled phrases, often with a phrase repeated several times before continuing to the next, for example: "*tew tew tew tew WOIT WOIT WOIT wah-CHEER wah-CHEER wah-CHEER....*" Call a deep, descending, growled "*gree'e'e'r,*" often in series. **Co, E, Bo**

FULVOUS SHRIKE-TANAGER

♂

♀

WHITE-WINGED SHRIKE-TANAGER

♂

♀

♀

BLACK-GOGGLED TANAGER

♂

♂

FAWN-BREASTED
TANAGER

♀

ad.

GRAY-HEADED TANAGER

imm.

CARMIOL'S TANAGER

PLATE
263

TYPICAL TANAGERS (*THRAUPIS*, *WETMORETHRAUPIS*)

Thraupis are medium-sized tanagers of forest edge and second growth. Omnivorous; usually forage in pairs or small groups. Most species often are apart from mixed-species flocks, although may join other species at fruiting trees. Orange-throated Tanager is restricted to foothills near Ecuador border.

1 BLUE-CAPPED TANAGER *Thraupis cyanocephala* * 18 cm (7 in)
Fairly common in humid montane forest and forest edge along east side of Andes, 1500–3100 m, and on west slope south to southern Cajamarca. Pairs and small flocks forage in the mid- and upper levels; regularly with mixed-species flocks. Blue crown and nape contrasts with olive upperparts and bluish gray underparts; note blackish mask, and yellow tibial feathering and underwing tufts. Female Blue-and-yellow Tanager superficially similar but yellow-ochre (not bluish gray) below, and drabber overall. **VOICE** Song a high accelerating and decelerating series of thin notes. Calls high, thin "*tseet*" and "*ti*" notes. **Co, E, Bo**

2 BLUE-AND-YELLOW TANAGER *Thraupis bonariensis* * 17–18 cm (6¼–7 in)
Fairly common and widespread in Andes, at 2000–4200 m in dry montane scrub, forest edge, and agricultural areas; locally descends to coast in central Peru, and to 800 m on east slope of Andes. Common in intermontane valleys but typically replaced on humid east-facing slopes by Blue-capped Tanager. Forages at all heights. Adults distinctive; note contrasting yellow rump. Drab juveniles and immatures more confusing but usually have at least a little blue-gray on head and wings; also note bill shape and behavior. **VOICE** Song a repetitive 2- or 3-syllable series of notes, occasionally very loud and wiry in quality, for example: "*chew see-wee chew see-wee chew see-wee….*" Calls a high "*tip*" note and screechy chatters. **E, Br, Bo, Ch**

3 ORANGE-THROATED TANAGER *Wetmorethraupis sterrhopteron* 17–18 cm (6¼–7 in)
Uncommon and local; reported from lower Río Cenepa Basin, and from areas south of Río Marañón opposite mouth of the Cenepa, 400–800 m. Pairs or small flocks forage in canopy of terra firme and humid montane forest, often in association with mixed-species flocks. Omnivorous. Not easily confused with other tanagers; cf. Gilded Barbet. **VOICE** Song a loud, jerky series of wiry whistled notes. Calls a loud, ringing "*tchee*," also a hesitant "*ptee-chee-tew*." **E**

4 PALM TANAGER *Thraupis palmarum* * 17–19 cm (6¼–7½ in)
Widespread and common in Amazonia, up to 1600 m. Often found in or near palms. Color of body can vary from olive to purplish depending upon light; at all times, 2-toned appearance of wings usually is conspicuous. **VOICE** Song a series of slurred, screechy notes that accelerate into a warbling chatter. Calls single rising or falling screeched notes. Voice similar to Blue-gray Tanager. **Co, E, Br, Bo**

[SAYACA TANAGER *Thraupis sayaca*] * 16–17.5 cm (6¼–7 in)
Status in Peru uncertain. A few undocumented sight records from Madre de Dios, but great similarity to juvenile Blue-gray Tanager calls for extreme care in identification (difficult to distinguish even with the bird in the hand). Generally grayer, with a lighter, greener shade to blue of wings and tail. Compared to first-year Blue-gray Tanager, adult Sayaca paler on throat and breast, and almost white on vent and undertail coverts. These are very subtle differences, however, and difficult to evaluate in the field. **VOICE** Song similar to that of Blue-gray, but squeakier, less screechy. **Br, Bo**

5 BLUE-GRAY TANAGER *Thraupis episcopus* * 16–18 cm (6¼–7 in)
Common and widespread in lowland Peru, locally up to 2000 m. Geographically variable, but all populations are bluish gray; bluer on wings. Usually forages in midstory and canopy. Blue-shouldered *quaesita* is uncommon in northwest. White-shouldered subspecies are common in Amazonia and Marañón Valley. Juveniles and immatures of all subspecies are much duller and lack white wing markings (so are similar to adult *quaesita*); also, edges of remiges are greener (more turquoise) blue. A feral population is fairly common in and near the city of Lima, where both blue- and white-shouldered birds are found. **VOICE** Song a series of slurred, screechy notes that accelerate into a warbling chatter. Calls are single rising or falling screeched notes. Voice similar to Palm Tanager, but has a more electric, screechy quality. **Co, E, Br, Bo**

BLUE-CAPPED TANAGER

♀

juv.

♂

BLUE-AND-YELLOW TANAGER

ORANGE-THROATED TANAGER

PALM TANAGER

BLUE-GRAY TANAGER

nw

Amaz.

juv.

SAYACA TANAGER

BLUE-GRAY TANAGER

PLATE
264

BUSH-TANAGERS AND ANT-TANAGER

Bands of bush-tanagers (Chlorospingus) often are seen in humid montane forests in the Andes. They travel as pairs or, more commonly, in small groups that may travel apart, but often are with mixed-species flocks. Restlessly forage for fruit and arthropods in the under- and midstory of forest and forest edge. Gray-hooded Bush-Tanager similar but is more of a canopy species. The ant-tanager is very different, a larger, drab tanager of lowland forest understory.

1 SHORT-BILLED BUSH-TANAGER *Chlorospingus parvirostris* * 14.5 cm (5¾ in)
Locally fairly common along east slope of Andes, 1100–2750 m. Iris pale, whitish or light gray. Sides of throat usually brighter than center, and yellow in most of Peru; sides of throat have orangey tint in northern *huallagae* (south to San Martín). Cf. Yellow-throated Bush-Tanager. **VOICE** Call a modulated, high "*tsrrree.*" **Co, E, Bo**

2 YELLOW-THROATED BUSH-TANAGER *Chlorospingus flavigularis* * 15 cm (6 in)
Fairly common along east slope of Andes and on outlying ridges, 750–1800 m. Less often with mixed-species flocks than other bush-tanagers. Superficially similar to southern subspecies of Short-billed Bush-Tanager, which it replaces at lower elevations, but has darker iris (light brown or pinkish brown, not grayish or whitish), gray lores, is brighter green above, and is slightly larger. Also differs in **VOICE** Calls a buzzy "*tzz*" and "*tk,*" each sometimes given in stuttered chatter. Crepuscular song a monotonous series of two high, ringing notes: "*swee tew swee tew swee tew….*" **Co, E**

3 ASHY-THROATED BUSH-TANAGER *Chlorospingus canigularis* * 13.5 cm (5¼ in)
Locally fairly common, but very patchily distributed, along east slope of Andes, 1000–1800 m (*signatus*). Usually found at lower elevations than larger Common Bush-Tanager. Further differs by dark iris and short white superciliary; also, in northern and central Peru Common Bush-Tanager has dull breast band or lacks breast band entirely. Rather different *paulus* is fairly common in semideciduous forest in Tumbes at 750 m (where it is the only bush-tanager). **VOICE** Song (*signatus*) an accelerating series of high chipping notes that falls, then rises in pitch. Call a dry, metallic "*tik,*" usually given in a stuttered series. **Co, E**

4 COMMON BUSH-TANAGER *Chlorospingus ophthalmicus* * 14–14.5 cm (5½–5¾ in)
Fairly common along east slope of Andes, 1100–2650 m. Geographically variable. All populations have a grayish crown and sides of head, and grayish white iris. Breast band dull yellow in north (south to Huánuco), and bright yellow in *peruvianus* (eastern Cuzco south to Bolivia); but breast band lacking in *cinereocephalus* (Pasco to western Cuzco). **VOICE** Crepuscular song a series of rich "*tchew*" notes, sometimes doubled, usually accelerating into a loose trill and occasionally terminated with a dry rattle. Calls a high "*ti,*" "*tip,*" a dry chatter, and a rising "*sweet.*" **Co, E, Bo**

5 RED-CROWNED ANT-TANAGER *Habia rubica* * 17–17.5 cm (6¼–7 in)
Fairly common and widespread in Amazonia, up to 1100 m, locally to 1500 m. Found in interior of humid forest, primarily in terra firme but also in low-lying forests. Forages in pairs in understory and often associates with mixed-species flocks. Largely insectivorous but consumes some small fruit. Drab female superficially similar to a foliage-gleaner, but note stouter (more tanager-like) bill. Cf. female Silver-beaked Tanager (which does not enter forest interior). **VOICE** Song a mellow, rich series of whistled phrases that rise, pattern somewhat variable, for example: "*hur-HEEdur chur-HEER.*" Calls are a characteristic series of deep, fussing "*chjit*" notes interspersed with a descending whistled "*hur*" note, the latter sometimes in series. **Co, E, Br, Bo**

6 GRAY-HOODED BUSH-TANAGER *Cnemoscopus rubrirostris* * *rubrirostris* 16.5–17 cm (6½–6¾ in); *chrysogaster* 15.5–16 cm (6–6¼ in)
Fairly common in humid montane forest along east slope of Andes, 2000–3100 m. Pairs or small groups accompany mixed-species flocks. Forages in midstory and canopy; creeps along limbs, from interior of a tree toward outside, gleaning insects. Frequently dips or wags tail. Gray hood, sharply contrasting with green back and yellow belly, is distinctive. Nominate subspecies north and west of Marañón Valley is larger with pink bill; more widespread *chrysogaster* has black or gray bill. **VOICE** Song of *rubrirostris* a squeaky series of lisping warbles, with repetitive phrases. Song of *chrysogaster* is similar but may lack the repetitive quality. Calls a high, metallic "*tsip,*" "*titip,*" and a rich "*tchp.*" **Co, E**

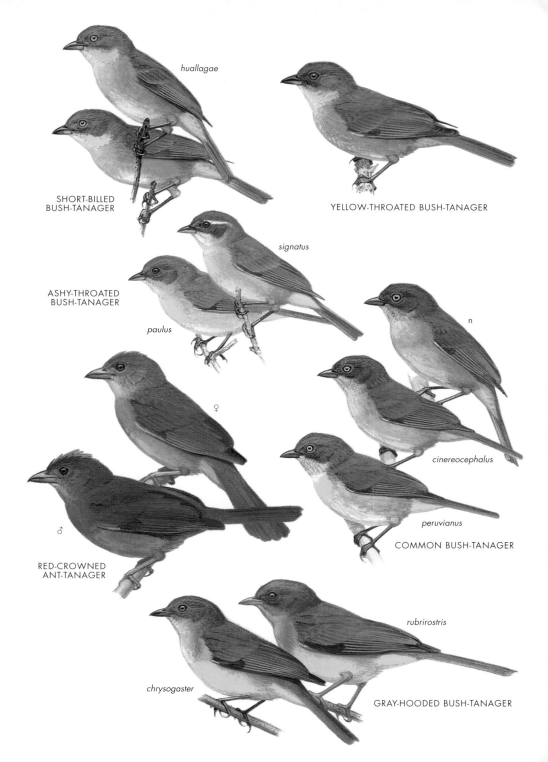

SHORT-BILLED
BUSH-TANAGER

huallagae

YELLOW-THROATED BUSH-TANAGER

ASHY-THROATED
BUSH-TANAGER

signatus

paulus

n

♀

♂

cinereocephalus

RED-CROWNED
ANT-TANAGER

peruvianus

COMMON BUSH-TANAGER

rubrirostris

chrysogaster

GRAY-HOODED BUSH-TANAGER

PLATE
265

MOUNTAIN-TANAGERS

Medium-sized to large tanagers of high-elevation montane humid forest. Typically in small groups, often with mixed-species flocks, but also encountered apart from flocks.

1 BLACK-CHESTED MOUNTAIN-TANAGER *Buthraupis eximia* * 21 cm (8¼ in)
Uncommon in elfin forest on east slope of Andes, north and west of Marañón Valley, 2850–3300 m (rarely to 2745 m). Largely replaces Hooded Mountain-Tanager at higher elevations. Behavior similar to Hooded, but remains more concealed within dense cover. Note blue crown and green (not blue) upperparts. **VOICE** Song a monotonous series of low, musical notes: "*t'seeit chewer t'seeit chewer t'seeit chewer….*" Calls high "*ti*" notes. **Co, E**

2 HOODED MOUNTAIN-TANAGER *Buthraupis montana* * 23–24 cm (9–9½ in)
Fairly common in humid montane forest along east slope of Andes, 2200–3500 m, but limited to below 2900 m north and west of the Marañón Valley. Small groups forage in the mid- and upper stories of forest; often in mixed-species flocks containing Mountain Cacique. Often very conspicuous as they fly long distances over the forest. Hops along limbs, peering at clumps of moss and epiphytes. Cobalt blue back, black "mask" (face and throat), and red iris distinctive; cf. smaller Lacrimose and Buff-breasted mountain-tanagers. **VOICE** Song, most often delivered at dusk while circling high over a forest slope, is a series of high, lisping, rising "*TSEET*" notes given in an excited manner. Calls rising "*tseet*" and "*tsueet*" notes, also a lower "*chew*," usually given in series. **Co, E, Bo**

3 MASKED MOUNTAIN-TANAGER *Buthraupis wetmorei* 21.5 cm (8½ in)
Rare and perhaps local, in elfin forest on east slope of Andes, 2900 m, north and west of Marañón Valley. Inconspicuous. Sometimes found in mixed-species flocks that include Black-chested Mountain-Tanager. Largely olive green and dull yellow; black is limited to face (where bordered by dull yellow), and blue restricted to wing coverts. **VOICE** Song a series of high notes, often decelerating "*tsi-tsi-tsee tsee tsee.*" Calls include a series of high, sibilant "*tsi*" notes. **Co, E**

4 GOLDEN-BACKED MOUNTAIN-TANAGER *Buthraupis aureodorsalis* 23 cm (9 in)
Uncommon to fairly common in treeline elfin forest at 3000–3700 m, on east slope of Andes. Forages at all heights but most often at midstory. Spectacular; readily identified by yellow back and rump, and by prominent chestnut streaking on yellow breast and flanks. **VOICE** Song a long series of loud squeaky notes, a particular phrase repeated several times before proceeding to the next phrase. **ENDEMIC**

5 BUFF-BREASTED MOUNTAIN-TANAGER *Dubusia taeniata* * 19 cm (7½ in)
Uncommon in humid montane forest, 1900–3500 m. Primarily remains within dense undergrowth, especially bamboo, although also visits fruiting trees. Northern *taeniata* occurs on both slopes of Andes, north and west of Marañón Valley; *stictocephala* (with bluer crown) is in similar habitats along east slope of Andes, south of Marañón. Always recognizable by blue superciliary contrasting with black face, and buff band on breast separating black throat from yellow belly. Cf. larger Hooded and Black-chested mountain-tanagers. **VOICE** Song of *taeniata* is 2 or 3 notes, high and melancholy, falling in pitch overall, for example: "*teee-tuuuuu,*" the first note sometimes doubled. Calls include a rising "*tsee.*" **Co, E**

6 CHESTNUT-BELLIED MOUNTAIN-TANAGER *Delothraupis castaneoventris* 17 cm (6¾ in)
Uncommon in humid montane forest along east slope of Andes, 2000–3500 m. Singles or pairs forage in canopy. Hops slowly along limbs and deliberately probes mosses and bromeliads for insects; also consumes fruit. Two-toned, blue above and chestnut below with a narrow black mask. Cf. the smaller, paler Fawn-breasted Tanager (usually found at lower elevations). **VOICE** Song high and melancholy, usually 2 notes, the first rising and the second falling in pitch: "*tsee-tseeuu,*" sometimes expanded to 3 falling notes. Call a thin "*seeip.*" **Bo**

7 GRASS-GREEN TANAGER *Chlorornis riefferii* * 20.5 cm (8 in)
Fairly common in humid montane forest along east slope of Andes, 2000–3500 m. Singles, pairs, or small groups occur in forest and at forest edge, but only rarely venture into second growth. Forages for fruit and insects at all heights. A large, chunky, brilliant green tanager with contrasting rufous face, and salmon-red bill and tarsi. **VOICE** Song a nasal, mechanical series of notes, variable in pattern, for example: "*chu chu-ENK'r-ENK'r.*" Calls include nasal "*enk*" and "*chi*" notes, sometimes in series. **Co, E, Bo**

BLACK-CHESTED
MOUNTAIN-TANAGER

HOODED MOUNTAIN-TANAGER

MASKED MOUNTAIN-TANAGER

GOLDEN-BACKED MOUNTAIN-TANAGER

taeniata

stictocephala

BUFF-BREASTED
MOUNTAIN-TANAGER

CHESTNUT-BELLIED MOUNTAIN-TANAGER

GRASS-GREEN TANAGER

PLATE
266

ANDEAN TANAGERS (*ANISOGNATHUS,*
IRIDOSORNIS)

Anisognathus and Iridisornis *are common, brightly colored Andean tanagers. All probably are primarily frugivorous but also consume some insects. Forage in pairs or small groups that often associate with mixed-species flocks, but also travel apart.*

1 BLUE-WINGED MOUNTAIN-TANAGER *Anisognathus somptuosus* * 18 cm (7 in)
Fairly common in humid montane forest and forest edge along east slope of Andes, 1000–2200 m. Primarily forages in midstory and canopy. Geographically variable, but all populations have yellow nape and underparts, contrasting with black back and sides of face. Rump olive in northern *somptuosus* (south to the Urubamba Valley) or blue in *flavinuchus* (eastern Cuzco south to Bolivia). **VOICE** Song of *somptuosus* is a high, weak wheedling "*si-titi si-titi tsu-ti-tsu-ti-tsu-ti-tsu-ti*"; calls "*teep*" and "*tsip*." Song of *flavinuchus* very different; louder and more musical, a rising series of wiry, quavering notes: "*tchu-tchu-twEE-aWEE twEE-aWEE WEE-WEE WEE-WEE.*" **Co, E, Bo**

2 SCARLET-BELLIED MOUNTAIN-TANAGER *Anisognathus igniventris* * 18.5 cm (7¼ in)
Fairly common along east slope of Andes, 2400–3500 m; also rare and local in woodlots on both sides of upper Marañón Valley. This spectacular tanager is emblematic of upper montane forest; especially prevalent in elfin forest, at forest edge and in forest openings, but also found in continuous forest. Forages at all heights. Geographically variable. Subspecies *erythrotus* is found north and west of Marañón Valley; *ignicrissa* occurs south of the Marañón to Junín, where it intergrades with *igniventris*, which continues south to Bolivia. Immatures (not illustrated) of all subspecies are duller, with burnt orange bellies. **VOICE** Song geographically variable but always a squeaky, nasal, mechanical-sounding warbling with much repetition of phrases (recalling song of Grass-green Tanager). Calls include a high "*ti.*" **Co, E, Bo**

3 LACRIMOSE MOUNTAIN-TANAGER *Anisognathus lacrymosus* * 18 cm (7 in)
Fairly common and widespread along east slope of Andes, 1800–3500 m; also found along both slopes of western Andes, south to southern Cajamarca. Found in humid montane forest and at forest edge, and in adjacent second growth. Forages at all heights. In most of Peru head largely blue with a small yellow spot ("tear drop") just below eye (*lacrymosus*); north and west of the Marañón has an additional yellow spot on side of neck (*caerulescens*). **VOICE** Song a high, squeaky, mechanical-sounding phrase repeated several times. Calls include various high "*tsi*" and "*tsit*" notes, sometimes in chattered phrases. **Co, E**

4 GOLDEN-COLLARED TANAGER *Iridosornis jelskii* * 15 cm (6 in)
Uncommon in elfin forest and humid forest edge along east slope of Andes (but apparently absent from Apurímac Valley), 2900–3700 m, locally down to 2500 m. Found in under- and midstory of shrubs and trees in treeline forest, or in isolated woodlots in grassland near treeline. Note the golden band extending from sides of head across crown, and extensive dull chestnut-brown belly. Cf. Yellow-scarfed Tanager. **VOICE** Song a high, wheedling series of weak, thin notes. Calls include a high "*tsik.*" **Bo**

5 YELLOW-THROATED TANAGER *Iridosornis analis* 16 cm (6¼ in)
Uncommon to fairly common in humid montane forest along east slope of Andes, and on outlying ridges, 1000–2350 m. Typically found in or near dense undergrowth, but will range into canopy. Mostly dull bluish green, with conspicuous yellow throat; crown also deep blue. **VOICE** Characteristic vocalization a descending, piercing "*tsi'tsiEEEUU*" or simply "*tsiEEUU.*" **Co, E**

6 GOLDEN-CROWNED TANAGER *Iridosornis rufivertex* * 16.5 cm (6½ in)
Fairly common in humid montane and elfin forests along east side of Andes, north and west of Marañón Valley, 2400–3000 m; replaced south of Marañón Valley by Yellow-scarfed Tanager. Usually at forest edge and in isolated stands of trees and shrubs in grassland near treeline. Tends to stay concealed within dense vegetation. Deep blue, with black head and golden-yellow crown; also, undertail coverts are chestnut. **VOICE** Song (?) is a rising high buzz: "*tzzt.*" Calls include high, thin "*tst*" and "*tseet*" notes, as well as a sharper "*ti'tit.*" **Co, E**

7 YELLOW-SCARFED TANAGER *Iridosornis reinhardti* 16.5 cm (6½ in)
Fairly common in humid montane and elfin forests along east slope of Andes, 2000–3700 m. Forages at all heights in humid forest and forest edge. Superficially similar to Golden-collared Tanager but much bluer (especially on underparts) with a more restricted yellow band across crown. **VOICE** Song (?) is a clear "*tsee tsee-dee.*" Calls include a high "*tzi-zi,*" "*tip,*" and "*ti.*" **ENDEMIC**

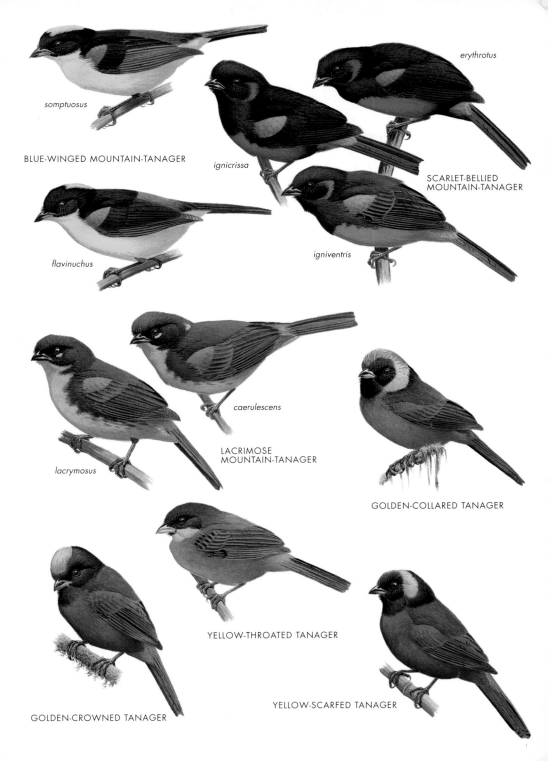

somptuosus

BLUE-WINGED MOUNTAIN-TANAGER

flavinuchus

ignicrissa

erythrotus

igniventris

SCARLET-BELLIED
MOUNTAIN-TANAGER

caerulescens

LACRIMOSE
MOUNTAIN-TANAGER

lacrymosus

GOLDEN-COLLARED TANAGER

YELLOW-THROATED TANAGER

GOLDEN-CROWNED TANAGER

YELLOW-SCARFED TANAGER

PLATE
267

MONTANE *TANGARA* TANAGERS

Most Tangara *are regular members, often as pairs or small groups, of mixed-species flocks in humid forests; such flocks may contain up to a half dozen species of* Tangara. *These tanagers also may congregate with other species at fruiting trees.* Tangara *tanagers also consume arthropods; species often differ in their arthropod-searching foraging behavior. Many species are brightly colored; in some, the plumage is partly opalescent, and the appearance may vary as the light changes. Juveniles, however, can be largely gray and quite drab. Species on this plate are Andean or (Silver-throated) in the northwest. See also plates 268, 269, 270.*

1 **GREEN-THROATED TANAGER** *Tangara argyrofenges* * 13 cm (5 in)
Uncommon; relatively widespread along east slope of Andes in north, with a few records from Pasco and Junín in central Peru, 1100–2200 m. Forage in canopy of humid montane forest and at forest edge. Both sexes have opalescent green throat. Male otherwise largely black, with opalescent buff back and flanks. Female mostly yellowish green, with dusky crown. Cf. Silver-backed Tanager, with which it overlaps locally in northern Peru. **VOICE** Song a high, wheezy series of lisping notes and a long, even, chlorophonia-like "*weee.*" Calls a high, descending "*tsew*" and a dry "*tip.*" **E, Bo**

2 **SILVER-BACKED TANAGER** *Tangara viridicollis* * 13 cm (5 in)
Fairly common. Found on both slopes of western Andes in northwestern Peru, and along east slope of Andes, 1200–2600 m, locally down to 800 m and up to 2900 m. Found at edge of forest, in forest fragments and second growth; rarely encountered far inside continuous forest, and seems most common in less humid habitats. Throat color may vary from coppery brown to light bronze (depending upon lighting conditions). Male otherwise largely black, with opalescent bluish green back and flanks; female mostly green with a dusky crown. **VOICE** Song a series of rapidly given falling notes. Calls a high wheezy, descending "*tseer*" and a thin "*pit.*" **E, Bo**

3 **SIRA TANAGER** *Tangara phillipsi* 13 cm (5 in)
Distribution extremely limited: known only from northern end of Cerros del Sira, 1300–1600 m. Fairly common. Usually in pairs or small groups, rarely in flocks of up to 20 individuals. Black crown, side of neck, and breast of male contrast with opalescent green throat; back and flanks opalescent bluish green. Female mostly green with dusky crown and opalescent green throat. Cf. Silver-backed Tanager, which also occurs in the Sira; throat of Silver-backed is coppery brown, not green.
ENDEMIC

4 **FLAME-FACED TANAGER** *Tangara parzudakii* * 14–14.5 cm (5½–5¾ in)
Fairly common in humid montane forest along east slope of Andes, 1100–2500 m, and on outlying ridges. Usually found in upper levels of forest. Forages for arthropods by hopping along mossy branches and leaning down to inspect the undersides; only rarely takes prey from leaves. A relatively large *Tangara*, readily identified by bright red face and forecrown, and golden yellow crown, nape, and sides to neck. Larger, more opalescent below and blacker above than Saffron-crowned Tanager. **VOICE** Calls include a high "*ti,*" sometimes in series (especially in flight), "*tsi,*" and a deep harsh chatter: "*di-dj'dj'dj'dj.*" **Co, E**

5 **[SILVER-THROATED TANAGER** *Tangara icterocephala*] * 13.5 cm (5¼ in)
Known only from a sight record from humid forest in eastern Tumbes, on the border with Ecuador, 800–900 m. Not known if this represents a small resident population or a vagrant from Ecuador. Accompanies canopy mixed-species flocks. Unlikely to be confused within range. **VOICE** Calls include a high, buzzy "*dzee*" or "*dzrt.*" **Co, E**

6 **GOLDEN TANAGER** *Tangara arthus* * 13.5–14 cm (5¼–5½ in)
Fairly common in humid montane forest along east slope of Andes, 600–2000 m. Primarily found in forest interior, less commonly in adjacent second growth. Forages in mid- and upper levels of forest. Hops along mossy branches while foraging for arthropods, leaning down to examine undersides of limbs. Shows modest geographic variation. North and west of Marañón Valley has a tawny-rufous wash on throat and breast (*aequatorialis*; not illustrated). Breast more solidly tawny-rufous in *pulchra* (Amazonas to Junín) and in *sophiae* (Cuzco to Bolivia). **VOICE** Calls include a high "*tip,*" "*tsee,*" and thin "*sweep.*" **Co, E, Bo**

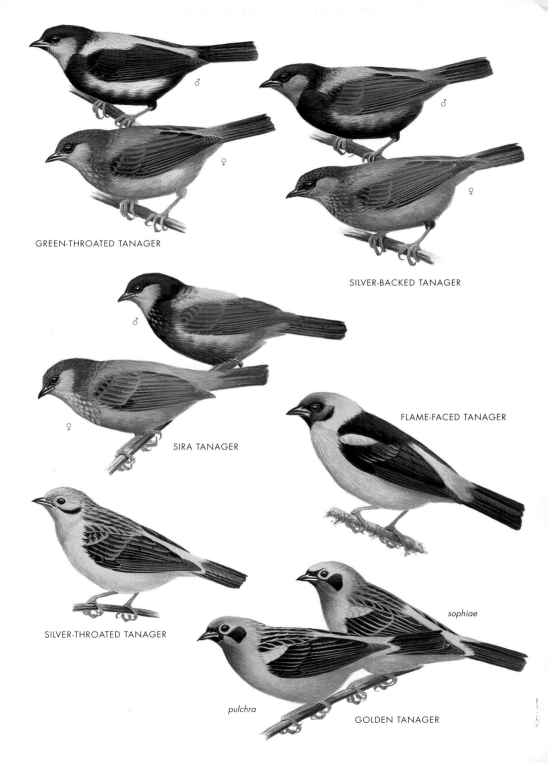

GREEN-THROATED TANAGER

♂

♀

SILVER-BACKED TANAGER

♂

♀

SIRA TANAGER

♂

♀

FLAME-FACED TANAGER

SILVER-THROATED TANAGER

sophiae

pulchra

GOLDEN TANAGER

PLATE
268

ANDEAN *TANGARA* TANAGERS

Andean Tangara; *see also plates 267, 269, and 270. All species associate with mixed-species flocks in canopy of humid montane forest.*

1 BLUE-AND-BLACK TANAGER *Tangara vassorii* * 13 cm (5 in)

The highest-ranging *Tangara*, found in humid montane forest, elfin forest, and adjacent second growth at 1900–3500 m; but most common above 2500 m. Gleans arthropods by hopping along limbs and leaning down. Entirely blue and black *vassorii* is uncommon to fairly common on both slopes of western Andes in northwest. Silvery-crowned *branickii* is common from central Amazonas south to La Libertad; replaced farther south by *atrocaerulea*. Female *vassorii* similar to male but duller; females of other subspecies closer in color to male. **VOICE** Calls a high, thin "*psst*" and "*tsit*" notes. **Co, E, Bo**

2 BERYL-SPANGLED TANAGER *Tangara nigroviridis* * 13.5 cm (5¼ in)

Fairly common in humid montane forest and second growth along east slope of Andes, 1500–2900 m; one of the most common *Tangara* species in these upper montane forests. Forages in mid- and upper stories. Searches for arthropods by hopping along slender bare branches and leaning down to search undersides. Breast and belly largely black, but heavily spotted with opalescent green. Plumage may appear bronzy in some lights. **VOICE** Calls include a high, thin "*psst*" and slightly descending "*tsew*." **Co, E, Bo**

3 GOLDEN-NAPED TANAGER *Tangara ruficervix* * 13 cm (5 in)

Uncommon to fairly common in humid montane forest and adjacent second growth along east slope of Andes, 1000–2400 m. Forage in mid- and upper stories. Blue, with a yellowish buff band across crown and a white belly. Northern *amabilis* (south to Huánuco) is lighter blue with a broader, paler crown patch, replaced in south by *inca*; the two may intergrade in central Peru. **VOICE** Calls include a high "*tsip*" and "*ti*" notes, sometimes as chattered phrases. **Co, E, Bo**

4 SAFFRON-CROWNED TANAGER *Tangara xanthocephala* * 13.5 cm (5¼ in)

Fairly common in humid montane forest along east slope of Andes, 1000–2300 m. Forages in small groups in humid montane forest, at forest edge and in tall second growth. Forages for arthropods by hopping along slender branches, often moss-covered, and leaning down to inspect underside. Yellow-crowned *venusta* south to northern Pasco; orangey-crowned *lamprotis* occurs from Ayacucho south to Bolivia; and central Peru (southern Pasco and Junín) occupied by intermediate *xanthocephala* (not illustrated). **VOICE** Song (?) is a short wheezy, warbled phrase. Calls a high descending "*tsew*" and a thin "*tsit*," sometimes in series. **Co, E, Bo**

5 BLUE-BROWED TANAGER *Tangara cyanotis* * 12 cm (4¾ in)

Uncommon in humid montane forest along east slope of Andes, 900–1950 m. Forages in canopy of forest, and at forest edge and in second growth; searches for arthropods by hopping along relatively bare branches and leaning down to inspect the underside. Mostly light opalescent blue, with prominent superciliary that contrasts with black crown, sides to face, back, and wings. **VOICE** Calls a high "*tip*" and a hoarse, wheezy chatter. **Co, E, Bo**

6 METALLIC-GREEN TANAGER *Tangara labradorides* * 13 cm (5 in)

Uncommon in humid montane forest along east slope of Andes in northern Peru, 1350–2200 m. Forages primarily in midstory and canopy, especially at forest edge and in second-growth. Gleans arthropods from leaves, especially near tips of branches. Mostly opalescent green, with narrow black crown and black scapulars. Cf. more widespread Blue-browed Tanager; Metallic-green is greener (less blue), with broad greenish blue forehead and center to the back. In some lights head may appear golden; cf. Golden-eared Tanager. **VOICE** Calls a rising "*sick*" and "*tip*" and a descending, nasal "*nyah*." **Co, E**

7 GOLDEN-EARED TANAGER *Tangara chrysotis* 14 cm (5½ in)

Uncommon, and restricted to a relatively narrow elevational band along east slope of Andes, 850–1600 m. Forages in midstory and canopy of humid montane forest. Typically gleans arthropods from upper surface of slender branches; less commonly searches leaves or underside of branches. Largely light bluish green with streaked back and tawny-rufous belly and vent; also note coppery sides to face and light bluish green superciliary. Cf. Metallic-green Tanager. **VOICE** Calls include a rich "*chup*." **Co, E, Bo**

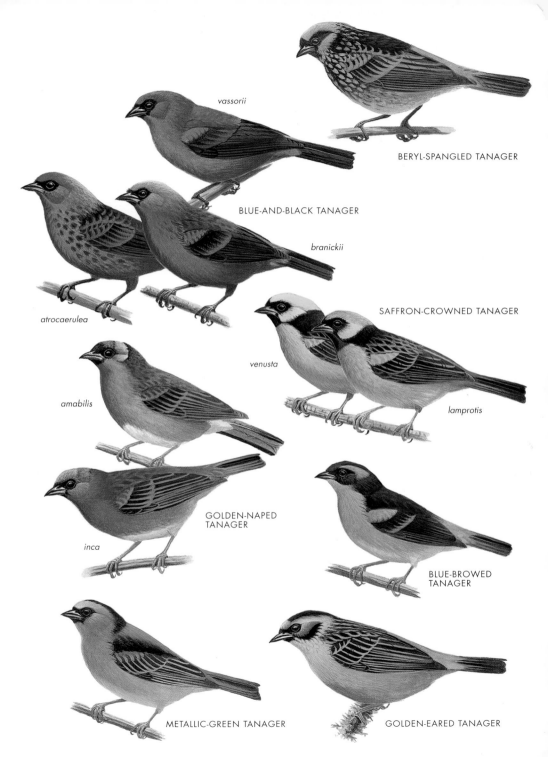

vassorii

BERYL-SPANGLED TANAGER

BLUE-AND-BLACK TANAGER

branickii

atrocaerulea

SAFFRON-CROWNED TANAGER

venusta

amabilis

lamprotis

inca

GOLDEN-NAPED
TANAGER

BLUE-BROWED
TANAGER

METALLIC-GREEN TANAGER

GOLDEN-EARED TANAGER

PLATE
269

AMAZONIAN AND FOOTHILLS *TANGARA* TANAGERS

A *mix of* Tangara *of Amazonia and of the lower slopes of the Andes; see also plates 267, 268, and 270.*

1 BLUE-NECKED TANAGER *Tangara cyanicollis* * 13 cm (5 in)
Fairly common along east slope of Andes; primarily 800–2000 m, sometimes as low as 350 m (especially in south). Forages in canopy at forest edge and in second growth; much less common inside unbroken forest. Gleans arthropods from relatively bare branches or from leaves. Mostly black with a contrasting light blue hood (and narrow black mask) and coppery yellow wing coverts. Northern *caeruleocephala* is found south at least to southern San Martín; *cyanicollis* is known from Huánuco south. **VOICE** Calls a high "*tsit*," rich "*tchup*," and "*ti*." **Co, E, Br, Bo**

2 MASKED TANAGER *Tangara nigrocincta* 13 cm (5 in)
Fairly common in Amazonia, up to 1350 m. Forage in canopy of humid forest and at forest edge. Mostly black with light lavender blue hood, greenish blue wing coverts, and white belly. Immatures (not illustrated) may lack black below but usually have at least a suggestion of black along lower edge of hood. **VOICE** Song a characteristic high "*tseeew-tseeew*," similar to song of Pectoral Sparrow, but less lisping, lacking the introductory "*tik*." Calls rich "*tsip*" and rising, high "*sick*" notes, also a low chatter. **Co, E, Br, Bo**

3 SPOTTED TANAGER *Tangara punctata* * 13 cm (5 in)
Fairly common in humid montane forest and forest edge along east slope of Andes, 600–2000 m. Forages in forest canopy. Searches leaves for arthropods; gleans from both upper- and undersurfaces of leaves, sometimes while walking or hopping over leaves at ends of limbs. Has whiter underparts that are more heavily spotted than Yellow-bellied Tanager. **VOICE** Calls a smacking "*tsew*" and higher "*tsick*." **E, Br, Bo**

4 BAY-HEADED TANAGER *Tangara gyrola* * 13.5 cm (5¼ in)
Fairly common in humid montane forest along east slope of Andes, up to 1700 m. Less common in Amazonia, where primarily found in terra firme. Also fairly common in semideciduous forest in Tumbes. Searches for arthropods almost exclusively on bare branches, largely by leaning over to glean from underside. Chestnut head contrasts with green upperparts and light blue underparts; also note narrow yellow nuchal band. Females and immatures (not illustrated) duller than male; can appear mostly green, but readily recognized by dull rufous wash to head; cf. female Blue Dacnis. **VOICE** Song (?) a high, wiry series, the final 2 notes descending: "*tsip ti tsew-tsew*." Calls a descending, loud "*tseeu!*" and a rising "*tsui*." **Co, E, Br, Bo**

5 YELLOW-BELLIED TANAGER *Tangara xanthogastra* * 12 cm (4¾ in)
Uncommon but widely distributed in Amazonia, up to 1500 m. Forages in forest canopy, at forest edge and in second growth. Searches for arthropods by gleaning from leaves and slender branches. A small *Tangara*, mostly green, lightly spotted with black, with bright yellow belly and vent. Superficially similar to Green-and-gold Tanager, but smaller, with plainer face and black-spotted throat and breast. Spotted Tanager is much whiter below and is confined to Andes. **VOICE** Song (?) a high, buzzy "*tik tik-tik dzheeweew*." Calls high "*ti*" and "*tchew*" notes. **Co, E, Br, Bo**

6 DOTTED TANAGER *Tangara varia* 11.5 cm (4½ in)
Uncommon, and restricted to outlying ridges (especially ridgetops with stunted vegetation) in San Martín and in the Cordillera Azul, 400–1100 m. Small groups forage in canopy of humid forest. A small tanager, largely bright green with dark lores; wings and back of male are bluish (greener in females), and males also may have dark speckles on throat and breast. May be confused (especially duller female) with female Blue Dacnis, or with immatures of other *Tangara*, such as Green-and-gold, Bay-headed, and Yellow-bellied tanagers; no overlap with Spotted Tanager. **VOICE** Song a characteristic high, hissing series of descending, melancholy notes: "*tsip... tsee-tsee-tsee-tsee-tsee*." Call a high "*tsip*." **Br**

7 GREEN-AND-GOLD TANAGER *Tangara schrankii* * 13.5 cm (5¼ in)
Fairly common and widespread in Amazonia, up to 1600 m. Found in humid forest and adjacent second growth. Pairs and small groups forage primarily in subcanopy and canopy. Forages for arthropods by gleaning slender branches and leaves. Sexes similar, but female duller and lacks yellow crown of male. **VOICE** Calls thin, high "*tsi*" and "*psew*" notes, often given in chattered phrases. **Co, E, Br, Bo**

BLUE-NECKED TANAGER

caeruleocephala

cyanicollis

MASKED TANAGER

SPOTTED TANAGER

YELLOW-BELLIED
TANAGER

♂

BAY-HEADED TANAGER

♀

♂

DOTTED TANAGER

♂

GREEN-AND-GOLD TANAGER

PLATE
270

TANGARA TANAGERS AND SWALLOW TANAGER

Most Tangara on this plate occur in the eastern lowlands, but Green-capped Tanager is Andean. Swallow Tanager is brightly colored, like a Tangara, but has different behavior.

1 TURQUOISE TANAGER *Tangara mexicana* * 13.5 cm (5¼ in)
Fairly common and widespread at forest edge, in second growth, and in forest (especially varzea) in Amazonia, up to 1000 m. Often forages apart from mixed-species flocks. Searches for arthropods on bare branches in canopy. **VOICE** Calls a very high, thin "*ti*" and slightly lower "*tew*." **Co, E, Br, Bo**

2 PARADISE TANAGER *Tangara chilensis* * 14 cm (5½ in)
The quintessentially gaudy tropical bird; one of the most widespread and common tanagers in Amazonia, up to 1300 m, locally to 1600 m. Found in canopy of humid forest and adjacent second growth. Searches for arthropods by hopping along limbs, leaning down to glean undersides of slender branches and vines. Rump red in widespread *chilensis*, but red and yellow in upper Huallaga Valley (*chlorocorys*). **VOICE** Calls a rich "*tchip*," a high, lisping "*tseet*," and a rising "*swee?*;" these calls are common sounds from canopy tanager flocks in Amazonia. Dawn song a regularly spaced series of "*swee? tchip*" phrases. **Co, E, Br, Bo**

3 OPAL-RUMPED TANAGER *Tangara velia* * 14.5 cm (5¾ in)
Uncommon but widely distributed in Amazonia, below 750 m. Forages in canopy of humid forest and forest edge. Searches for arthropods by hopping along bare branches and leaning over to inspect underside. Opal-rumped and Opal-crowned tanagers have longer, thinner bills than other *Tangara* tanagers. Note the chestnut belly (a useful distinction from Opal-crowned when birds are viewed from below). **VOICE** Song (?) is a rising-falling chattered series of high, wiry squeaks: "*psi-psi-PSI-PSI-psi-psi*." Calls very high "*pseet*" and quiet, rich "*tchip*" notes. **Co, E, Br, Bo**

4 OPAL-CROWNED TANAGER *Tangara callophrys* 14.5 cm (5¾ in)
Uncommon but widely distributed in Amazonia; primarily below 600 m but to 1000 m in south. Behavior similar to Opal-rumped Tanager's. Dark blue, with black lower belly, opalescent straw forecrown and rump, and black nape and back. **VOICE** Like Opal-rumped Tanager, but slightly lower-pitched. **Co, E, Br, Bo**

5 BURNISHED-BUFF TANAGER *Tangara cayana* * 14 cm (5½ in)
Fairly common but very local. Found in second growth and woodland edge in Río Mayo Valley at 1000–1150 m, and in isolated woodlots on savanna and at forest edge on Pampas del Heath. Rarely with mixed-species flocks. Both sexes mostly dull buff with light blue wings and tail, and with a dull rufous crown; breast of male also is dull blue. **VOICE** Calls a descending "*pseew*" and thin "*tchip*." **Co, Br, Bo**

6 GREEN-CAPPED TANAGER *Tangara meyerdeschauenseei* 14 cm (5½ in)
Fairly common but geographically restricted: known from the upper Inambari drainage. Found at forest edge and in gardens; probably originally restricted to semiarid intermontane valleys but may be spreading due to deforestation. Usually encountered as pairs or in groups of 3 or 4. Similar to Burnished-buff Tanager, but found at higher elevations (1450–2200 m); also distinguished by the greenish buff (not rufous) crown, greenish turquoise (not blackish) auriculars, and bluer (male) or greener (female) back. In life appears largely buff with greenish wings and tail; the opalescent green of the cap rarely visible in the field. **Bo**

7 SWALLOW TANAGER *Tersina viridis* * 15–15.5 cm (6 in)
Fairly common and widespread in Amazonia, up to 1500 m. Presence and abundance at many sites variable, suggesting migration or nomadic movements. Easiest to see (and more common?) at edge of humid forest and of second growth, but also in forest interior. Usually in small groups, apart from other species, that perch in canopy, often at a high exposed site. Largely frugivorous, taking fruit with gleans or sallies. Captures arthropods with short sallies. Nests in a cavity, typically a burrow in a dirt bank. Patterned and colored somewhat like a *Tangara* tanager, but note the characteristic upright posture and broad bill. Male takes several years to reach definitive plumage; younger males are variably blotched green and blue, and black face mask is duller. Cf. larger cotingas (*Cotinga*). **VOICE** Call a distinctive, rising, crystalline "*t'see?*" Song, rarely heard, is a slurred, jerky series of high squeaks and warbled phrases, often interspersed with calls. **Co, E, Br, Bo**

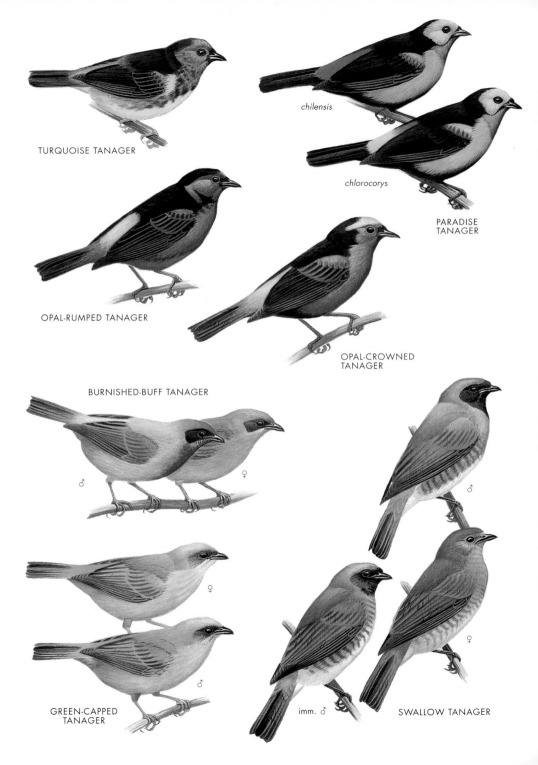

TURQUOISE TANAGER

chilensis

chlorocorys

PARADISE
TANAGER

OPAL-RUMPED TANAGER

OPAL-CROWNED
TANAGER

BURNISHED-BUFF TANAGER

♂   ♀

♂

♀

GREEN-CAPPED
TANAGER

imm. ♂   SWALLOW TANAGER

PLATE
271

TANAGERS, HONEYCREEPERS, AND CONEBILLS

White-capped Tanager is a large Andean species that resembles a jay more than other tanagers. Orange-eared Tanager is like a slender-billed Tangara. Honeycreepers are small, brightly colored tanagers with slender, slightly curved bills. Conebills, with sharply pointed bills, resemble small warblers.

1 WHITE-CAPPED TANAGER *Sericossypha albocristata* 24–26 cm (9½–10¼ in)
Uncommon in humid montane forest along east slope of Andes, 1700–2800 m. A large, black tanager with snowy white crown. Found in small flocks in forest midstory and canopy, apart from other species or in association with White-collared Jays or caciques. Throat bright crimson in male, dark crimson in female, and black in first-year birds. **VOICE** Calls, very loud, piercing, and almost jay-like, include a descending: "*PSEEU!*," "*PEW!*," and a "*tew-tew-tew-tew…*" series. Carry long distances and often announce the birds' presence before they are seen. Often calls in flight and mobs intruders like a jay. **Co, E**

2 GREEN HONEYCREEPER *Chlorophanes spiza* * 14 cm (5½ in)
Fairly common and widespread in Amazonia, up to 1600 m. Pairs or small groups are found in canopy of humid forests and at forest edge, often with mixed-species flocks, but sometimes apart. Omnivorous. Plumage of male can appear greener or bluer depending upon light conditions. Note yellow or yellowish mandible of both sexes. Compare female to female Blue Dacnis and to immatures of some *Tangara*. **VOICE** Calls a rich, descending "*tchup*" and a higher "*tseet.*" **Co, E, Br, Bo**

3 ORANGE-EARED TANAGER *Chlorochrysa calliparaea* * 12.5 cm (5 in)
Fairly common in humid montane forest and adjacent second growth along the east slope of the Andes, 1000–2200 m. Singles or pairs regularly associate with mixed-species flocks in mid- and upper stories of forest. Gleans arthropods while hopping along mossy limbs; active and acrobatic, sometimes hanging from leaves while reaching out to glean. Largely insectivorous, but also eats some fruit. Female slightly duller, or may appear all-green. Geographically variable: *bourcieri* is found south to Huánuco; *calliparaea* from Pasco to western Cuzco; and *fulgentissima* from eastern Cuzco to Bolivia. **VOICE** Song a complex, long series of high, wiry warbles, with certain phrases repeated many times. Calls include a high "*tsit.*" **Co, E, Bo**

4 GOLDEN-COLLARED HONEYCREEPER *Iridophanes pulcherrimus* * 11.5 cm (4½ in)
Uncommon in humid montane forest and forest edge along east slope of Andes, 1100–2000 m. Behavior and general appearance similar to a *Tangara* tanager, but note more slender, slightly longer bill with yellow base. Pairs and small groups regularly associate with mixed-species flocks in mid- and upper levels of forest. Consumes both fruit and arthropods. Male distinctive. Duller female may be more confusing; note overall yellowish tones, bill shape, narrow nuchal collar, and brighter margins to wings. **VOICE** Call a high, lisping "*psee*," given by both sexes, that may be elongated and rise, then fall in pitch. **Co, E**

5 TAMARUGO CONEBILL *Conirostrum tamarugense* 11–12 cm (4¼–4¾ in)
Locally fairly common, but geographically restricted. An austral migrant (Mar–Sep) to montane scrub, primarily open *Polylepis* scrub, on west slope of Andes, 3400–4100 m. May flock with Cinereous Conebill. Adult readily recognized by rufous superciliary, throat, and vent; also is darker gray than sympatric *littorale* subspecies of Cinereous. Immatures are duller but show enough rufous or buff on face and vent to be identifiable. **VOICE** Song a rapid jumble of squeaks. Call a high "*tsee.*" **Ch**

6 CINEREOUS CONEBILL *Conirostrum cinereum* * 11–12 cm (4¼–4¾ in)
Common and widespread, from coast up to 4200 m in western Andes and intermontane valleys; locally to as low as 2150 m on east slope of Andes. Found as singles, pairs, or small groups in gardens, open woodland, hedgerows, and shrubs in agricultural areas, montane scrub, and forest edge. In eastern cordillera of Andes, more prevalent in intermontane valleys than on more humid, east-facing slopes. Small and largely gray, with pale superciliary, prominent white speculum, and white or buffy tips to greater wing coverts. *Littorale* is found on coast and in western Andes, reaching eastern cordillera in northern Peru; *cinereum*, of the eastern cordillera from central Peru south to Bolivia, averages grayer (but plumages are variable). Immatures of both subspecies are yellower than adults. **VOICE** Song a rapid jumble of high squeaks. Call a high, thin "*tseep.*" **Co, E, Bo, Ch**

imm.

WHITE-CAPPED TANAGER

GREEN HONEYCREEPER

♂

♀

♀

♂ *bourcieri*

♂ *calliparaea*

♂ *fulgentissima*

ORANGE-EARED
TANAGER

♂

♀

GOLDEN-COLLARED
HONEYCREEPER

ad. *littorale*

imm.

TAMARUGO
CONEBILL

♀ ad.

CINEREOUS
CONEBILL

imm.

ad. *cinereum*

PLATE
272

DACNIS AND *CYANERPES* HONEYCREEPERS

Dacnis (Dacnis) and honeycreepers (Cyanerpes) are small, active tanagers of canopy of Amazonian forest. All have slender bills (strongly decurved in honeycreepers); honeycreepers also have brightly colored tarsi and are notably short-tailed. Both genera are sexually dimorphic; within each genus, females can be confusingly similar. All typically are encountered in pairs or small groups, and often associate with mixed-species flocks. They consume small fruits, arthropods, and (especially honeycreepers) at least some nectar.

1 YELLOW-BELLIED DACNIS *Dacnis flaviventer* 11.5–12 cm (4½–4¾ in)

Uncommon to fairly common but widespread in Amazonia, up to 600 m, locally to 1000 m. Primarily found at forest edge and in second growth of river-plain forest, less commonly in forest interior. Less tightly associated with mixed-species flocks than are other *Dacnis*. Iris red or reddish brown. Male distinctive. Female is lightly mottled below, olive-brown and pale yellow; similar to female Black-faced Dacnis, which is more uniformly colored and is more olive green (less brown). Female Yellow-bellied also more strongly yellow on center of belly and vent, has a reddish (not yellow) iris, and a heavier bill. **VOICE** Calls a high "*see*," and a lower "*tcheew*." **Co, E, Br, Bo**

2 BLACK-FACED DACNIS *Dacnis lineata* * 11–11.5 cm (4¼–4½ in)

Fairly common and widespread in Amazonia, extending up to 1400 m on lower slopes of Andes. Found in humid forest, at forest edge and in second growth, in mid- and upper levels. Male distinctive. Female is nondescript; note olive tone to plumage, bill shape, and pale yellow iris. **VOICE** Call a modulated, high "*trree*" note; fairly distinctive. **Co, E, Br, Bo**

3 BLUE DACNIS *Dacnis cayana* * 12 cm (4¾ in)

Fairly common and widespread in Amazonia, up to 1500 m on lower slopes of Andes. Found in canopy of humid forests, at forest edge, and in second growth. Gleans arthropods from leaf surfaces, often focusing on surfaces with obvious leaf damage. Note female's small size, blue crown and bill shape; cf. female Green Honeycreeper (often found in same flocks). **VOICE** Song a wheezy series of thin, high notes, somewhat variable in pattern, for example: "*wee-tee tsee-tew wee-tee tsee-tew wee-tee*," interspersed with call notes. Calls a thin, high, descending, lisped "*tsew*" and high "*tsee*." **Co, E, Br, Bo**

4 WHITE-BELLIED DACNIS *Dacnis albiventris* 11 cm (4¼ in)

Rare, poorly known. Relatively widely distributed in northeastern Amazonia; reported also from south, where status is uncertain. Probably primarily found in areas with nutrient-poor substrates, such as well-weathered terraces in terra firme. Iris bright yellow. Male distinctive. Female is very similar to female Black-faced Dacnis, but is greener (less olive) above and yellower below; bill is slightly shorter and stubbier. **VOICE** Song, rather characteristic, a high, lisping "*seee-suleee*" interspersed with a trilled "*tip-tu'tee'e'e'e*" and various call notes. Calls a high, descending "*tseew*" and rising "*tee?*," also a thin "*ti*" often given in series. **Co, E, Br**

5 RED-LEGGED HONEYCREEPER *Cyanerpes cyaneus* * 12–13 cm (4¾–5 in)

Status and distribution unclear. Widely distributed, and locally fairly common, especially at sites with nutrient-poor substrates, but absent or very rare at many sites (especially in south), where recorded only occasionally (suggesting seasonal movements). The largest *Cyanerpes* honeycreeper, with red tarsi, yellow underwings, and moderately long tail. Female has narrow pale superciliary and whitish throat. Nonbreeding males (not illustrated) like female but with black wings and tail. **VOICE** Calls a lisping, rising, trilled "*dzrrreet*" and a high, descending "*tseew*." **Co, E, Br, Bo**

6 SHORT-BILLED HONEYCREEPER *Cyanerpes nitidus* 9.5–10 cm (3¾–4 in)

Uncommon to locally fairly common in northern and central Amazonia, below 1000 m. The smallest honeycreeper, with the shortest bill. More closely associated with mixed-species flocks than are other *Cyanerpes* honeycreepers. Note pink tarsi. Female further distinguished from more widespread Purple Honeycreeper by plainer throat, dusky (not buff) lores, and green sides of head (lacking narrow buff streaks on auriculars). **VOICE** Call a short, high, rising "*tsee?*" **Co, E, Br, Bo**

7 PURPLE HONEYCREEPER *Cyanerpes caeruleus* * 10.5–11 cm (4–4¼ in)

The most common and widespread *Cyanerpes* honeycreeper. Fairly common throughout Amazonia, up to 1400 m. Readily recognized by yellow tarsi, long slender bill, and, in female, buff throat and lores. **VOICE** Call a short, high, lisping "*psit*." **Co, E, Br, Bo**

YELLOW-BELLIED DACNIS

♂

♀

BLACK-FACED DACNIS

♂

♀

BLUE DACNIS

♂

♀

WHITE-BELLIED DACNIS

♂

♀

RED-LEGGED HONEYCREEPER

♀

SHORT-BILLED
HONEYCREEPER

♀

♂

PURPLE HONEYCREEPER

♂

♀

PLATE
273
CONEBILLS AND HOODED TANAGER

Conebills (Conirostrum) are small birds with slender, pointed bills. They occupy a wide variety of forest types and scrubby habitats throughout Peru. Warblerlike and largely insectivorous. Pairs of the Andean species regularly accompany mixed-species flocks. Hooded Tanager is an Amazonian species.

1 BICOLORED CONEBILL *Conirostrum bicolor* * 11.5 cm (4½ in)

Fairly common, but confined to islands in larger rivers of northeastern Amazonia. Less specialized than is Pearly-breasted Conebill; found both in stands of *Cecropia* and other trees and in shorter scrub (*Tessaria*). Adult is bluish gray above, dirty buff below, with pinkish tarsi and reddish orange iris. Cf. the larger female Hooded Tanager. Immature is very yellowish; cf. immature Orange-headed Tanager (which is larger, with heavier bill, and less uniformly yellow below), also female Yellow Warbler. **VOICE** Song (north Venezuela) is a hesitant series of high, ringing notes, for example: "*psi-tsi psi-tew psi-tew-tsi....*" **Co, E, Br**

2 HOODED TANAGER *Nemosia pileata* * 13 cm (5 in)

Fairly common in northern and central Amazonia; much rarer and more local in southeast. Associated with large river courses, where found in second growth and riparian forest, especially on *Cecropia*-dominated river islands. Singles or pairs forage in midstory and crowns of trees. Female similar to Bicolored and Pearly-breasted conebills, which are much smaller and lack white lores and buff throat. **VOICE** Song descending, musical series of notes: "*tchee-tchee-tchew-tchew-tchew,*" very similar to song of Golden-bellied Warbler (no overlap). Calls high "*tsee,*" "*ti,*" a dry chatter, and a nasal "*enk.*" **Co, Br, Bo**

3 PEARLY-BREASTED CONEBILL *Conirostrum margaritae* 11.5 cm (4½ in)

Rare. Restricted to islands in larger rivers of northern Amazonia. Forages in canopy of even-aged stands of *Cecropia* woods on medium-aged islands; unlike Bicolored Conebill, does not use adjacent scrubby vegetation. Pale, pearly gray below, with no buff tones. Immature (not illustrated) is yellowish below, olive above; very similar to immature Bicolored (identify by accompanying adults). **VOICE** Song a variable, rapid, high jumble of squeaky warbles and sharp chips. Calls a high "*teep*" and "*ti-ti-ti.*" **Br, Bo**

4 CHESTNUT-VENTED CONEBILL *Conirostrum speciosum* * 10–11 cm (4–4¼ in)

Uncommon to fairly common in central and southern Peru below 600 m, locally to 900 m. Largely confined to riverine habitats; where found pairs or small groups forage in varzea forest and at forest edge. Male readily recognized. Female more confusing, but note bluish crown and slender bill. **VOICE** Song, usually given at dawn, is a variable repetitive phrase of high, squeaky notes, for example: "*tsip'er-TSEE tsip'er-TSEE tsip'er-TSEE....*" Hummingbird-like in pattern and quality. Calls a high "*tip*" and "*tseep*" notes, also a rapid squeaky chatter. **Co, E, Br, Bo**

5 BLUE-BACKED CONEBILL *Conirostrum sitticolor* * 12.5–13 cm (5 in)

Fairly common in humid montane and elfin forest, 2300–3600 m. Northern subspecies *sitticolor* is found on both slopes of western Andes, and on eastern slope of Andes south at least to Amazonas. Blue-browed *cyaneum* occurs along east side of Andes from San Martín (where intergrades with northern *sitticolor*) south to Bolivia. **VOICE** Song a high, rapid and repetitive series of strident wheedling phrases. Calls a high "*tsi*" and "*sew.*" **Co, E, Bo**

6 CAPPED CONEBILL *Conirostrum albifrons* * 13–13.5 cm (5–5¼ in)

Fairly common along east slope of Andes, 1500–3000 m; also locally on western side of Andes in Piura. Forages in canopy of humid montane forest and at forest edge. Active; frequently wags the relatively long tail. Male often appears entirely black in the field. Northern *atrocyaneum* is found in western cordillera, and in eastern Andes south to Amazonas; replaced farther south by *sordidum*. **VOICE** Song variable, but usually is a high, wiry, repetitive series of notes, sometimes with different terminal notes: "*ti-teeteetee tzeew-tzeew.*" Calls a rich "*tchew*" and high "*sick.*" **Co, E, Bo**

7 WHITE-BROWED CONEBILL *Conirostrum ferrugineiventre* 12 cm (4¾ in)

Fairly common in humid montane forest and elfin forest along east slope of Andes, 2600–4100 m. Especially prevalent at forest edge and in isolated woodlots and shrubs in paramo grassland near treeline, also locally in humid *Polylepis* woodland. Forages deliberately in crowns of trees and shrubs, searching and gleaning upper and lower leaf surfaces and twigs. May associate with Cinereous and Blue-backed conebills. **VOICE** Song a high, wiry jumble of notes. Call a thin "*tsit.*" **Bo**

BICOLORED CONEBILL

imm.

ad.

HOODED TANAGER

♂

♀

PEARLY-BREASTED
CONEBILL

CHESTNUT-VENTED
CONEBILL

♀

♂

sitticolor

BLUE-BACKED CONEBILL

cyaneum

♀ *atrocyaneum*

CAPPED CONEBILL

♂ *atrocyaneum*

WHITE-BROWED CONEBILL

♀ *sordidum*

♂ *sordidum*

PLATE
274

RED TANAGERS

Piranga *tanagers forage in the forest canopy. Most species often are apart from mixed-species flocks. Largely insectivorous but also consume some fruit. Vermilion Tanager is a superficially similar Andean species.*

1 SUMMER TANAGER *Piranga rubra* * 18 cm (7 in)

Uncommon boreal migrant; present primarily Sep–Mar. Found in Amazonia and on lower slopes of Andes, up to 1400 m, occasionally to 2200 m; very rarely reaches coast. Primarily in second growth and at forest edge. Similar to Hepatic Tanager, but lacks dusky lores, has paler and slightly less stout bill, and generally brighter plumage. Male also is rosier red. Female is brighter, yellower green; some are washed with orange below and may even have a few scattered red feathers. Immature males (primarily those in first alternate plumage) may be heavily blotched red and green. **VOICE** Call a staccato "*pit-i-tuck*" or "*pit-i-tuck-i-tuck*." Flight call a rich, whining "*rheeaweh*." May sing on wintering grounds (particularly before migration). Song a rich, *Turdus*-like caroling, a little higher and thinner than song of Hepatic. **Co, E, Br, Bo, Ch**

2 HEPATIC TANAGER *Piranga flava* * 18 cm (7 in)

Fairly common and widespread in montane scrub, in semideciduous and humid forests, and at forest edges. Occurs along west slope of Andes (locally down to near coast) in northwest, on both sides of Marañón Valley, and along east slope of Andes and on outlying ridges, 400–2700 m. Cf. Summer Tanager. Adult male dull red, female yellow-green. Occasionally females are more orangey, less yellow, below, but this variant less frequent than in Summer. Some males (in molt? or a distinct first-year plumage?) strikingly blotched red and green. **VOICE** Call a rich "*chuck*" or "*chup*." Song a rich, warbled caroling, similar to a *Pheucticus* grosbeak, but usually faster paced, not so sweet, and less slurred. **Co, E, Br, Bo**

3 RED-HOODED TANAGER *Piranga rubriceps* 18.5 cm (7¼ in)

Rare to uncommon, in humid montane forest along east slope of Andes, 1800–3000 m. Frequently perch on exposed sites in canopy. Sexes similar, but female typically has less extensive red hood. **VOICE** Calls a characteristic triplet of rising notes: "*tseet-tseet-tseet*," and a descending tinkled laugh "*tee-hee'hee'hee'hee*." Song a quiet series of liquid whistles, short warbles, and buzzy notes interspersed with call notes. **Co, E**

4 SCARLET TANAGER *Piranga olivacea* 17 cm (6¾ in)

Uncommon boreal migrant (Sep–Mar) to Amazonia and lower slopes of Andes, up to 1500 m; very rarely reaches coast. Visits forest edge, but more associated with canopy of forest than is Summer Tanager. Male arrives largely in basic plumage, but acquires alternate plumage before departing; molting males are blotched red and green. Gray wings of female contrast with green body. Cf. Summer; also, Scarlet has smaller, paler bill and comparatively shorter tail that is gray, not green, below. First-year male (not illustrated) similar, but black wing coverts contrast with duller remiges; these are retained into first alternate plumage. **VOICE** Calls a sharp "*TCHP*" or "*TCHP-err*." Flight call is a wheezy "*hewee?*" May sing on wintering grounds (particularly before migration); song a rich, but hoarse, caroling, somewhat reminiscent of a *Turdus* thrush or a raspy Hepatic Tanager. **Co, E, Br, Bo**

5 VERMILION TANAGER *Calochaetes coccineus* 17–18 cm (6¾–7 in)

Uncommon, in humid montane forest along east slope of Andes, 1100–2100 m. Pairs or small groups accompany mixed-species flocks in midstory and canopy of forest. Gleans insects while hopping along branches, or consumes *Cecropia* catkins or other fruits. Cf. males of White-winged and Scarlet tanagers. Female (not illustrated) duller, can be orangey. **VOICE** Calls a high, descending "*tsee*" and a short "*tip*." Song a quiet series of slurred high "*tseet*" notes and short warbled phrases. **Co, E**

6 WHITE-WINGED TANAGER *Piranga leucoptera* * 14 cm (5½ in)

Fairly common in humid montane forest along east slope of Andes and on outlying ridges, 900–1800 m. More often with mixed-species flocks than other *Piranga*. Smaller than other *Piranga*, or than Vermilion Tanager, with two bold white wing bars. **VOICE** Calls a characteristic "*pit-cheweet*," the second note often doubled; also a tinkling, monotone laugh "*tee-hee-hee*." Song a quiet series of liquid squeaks, short warbles, and buzzy chattered notes interspersed with call notes. **Co, E, Br, Bo**

♀

♂ 1st alt.

HEPATIC TANAGER

♀

♂

♂, 1st alt.?

SUMMER TANAGER

♂

♀

♂ molting

SCARLET TANAGER

♀

♂ alt.

♂ basic

RED-HOODED
TANAGER

♂

WHITE-WINGED
TANAGER

♀

VERMILION TANAGER

♂

PLATE
275

BLUE FLOWERPIERCERS AND ODD ANDEAN TANAGERS

The blue flowerpiercers forage for fruit and insects (flowerpiercers of plate 276 are more nectarivorous), and regularly join mixed-species flocks. Giant Conebill is restricted to Polylepis woods. Pardusco, Tit-like Dacnis, and Plushcap are disparate Andean tanagers.

1 BLUISH FLOWERPIERCER *Diglossa caerulescens* * 13.5 cm (5¼ in)

Uncommon to locally fairly common, but widespread, along east slope of Andes, and on outlying ridges, 1300–3100 m. Found at forest edge and in scrubby forest; may prefer sites with nutrient-poor substrates, such as along ridgecrests and on sandy soil. Dull blue-gray, with a less prominently hooked bill than other flowerpiercers. Iris red or dull red. **VOICE** Song a variable, high, lisping, melancholy warble, descending in overall pitch. Call a high, rusty "*seek.*" **Co, E, Bo**

2 MASKED FLOWERPIERCER *Diglossa cyanea* * 14.5 cm (5¼ in)

One of the most frequent members of mixed-species flocks in high-elevation, humid montane forests of Andes, 1500–3600 m. Occurs along east slope of Andes, and on west slope of western Andes south to southern Cajamarca. Forage in upper levels of the forest. Immature duller, with brown iris and pale base to bill. **VOICE** Song a variable, high, lisping, melancholy warble. Similar to songs of Deep-blue and Bluish flowerpiercers, but usually more melodic and complex. Calls a high "*tsit*" and "*ti.*" **Co, E, Bo**

3 GIANT CONEBILL *Oreomanes fraseri* 15 cm (6 in)

Locally fairly common, but restricted to *Polylepis* woods, 3500–4600 m. Present in both eastern and western cordilleras of Andes, although occurs farther north in western Andes. Singles or pairs hitch along *Polylepis* trunks and limbs, where noisily flakes off bark in search of arthropods. **VOICE** Song a high, squeaky, jerky warble. Dawn song (?) a highly repetitive, 2-note series interspersed with a higher note: "*tew-tuSEEtu tew-tuSEEtu tsee? tew-tuSEEtu....*" Call a high "*ti.*" **Co, E, Bo, Ch**

4 DEEP-BLUE FLOWERPIERCER *Diglossa glauca* * 12 cm (4¼ in)

Fairly common in humid montane forest and forest edge along east slope of Andes, 1000–2300 m. Forages in mid- and upper levels of forest. Iris striking golden-yellow. Female slightly duller than male. **VOICE** Song variable, very high and wheedling with a melancholy quality. Less musical than song of Masked Flowerpiercer, more varied in note structure than Bluish. Call a sharp "*psew.*" **Co, E, Bo**

5 TIT-LIKE DACNIS *Xenodacnis parina* * *petersi* 14.5–15 cm (5½–6 in); *parina* 12–12.5 cm (4¼–5 in)

Fairly common but local, in shrubbery at or above edge of humid forest and in *Polylepis* woods (especially where *Gynoxys* shrub is present), 3200–4600 m. Feeds largely on aphidlike insects and their sugary secretions gleaned from undersides of *Gynoxys* leaves; also gleans from leaves of other trees and shrubs. Note the short stubby bill. Geographically variable. Larger, darker in eastern cordillera of north (*bella*) and in western cordillera (*petersi*); smaller, brighter *parina* in the eastern cordillera and in associated river valleys in south-central Peru. **VOICE** Song a surprisingly loud, rising series of bubbling whistles ending in more rasping phrases, with some variation, for example: "*quik-quik-quik-wi-wi-wi-tzz-tzz-tzz.*" Calls low, scratchy, warbled notes. **E**

6 PARDUSCO *Nephelornis oneilli* 13.5 cm (5¼ in)

Fairly common but restricted to elfin forest edge and humid grassland with scattered shrubs on east slope of northern Andes, 3000–3800 m. Forages actively, gleaning foliage in flocks of 5–15 individuals, often with mixed-species flocks. Has few "field marks"; note the restricted distribution, habitat, and social behavior. Some juvenile flowerpiercers are dull brown and are about the same size but have a distinctively shaped hooked bill. **VOICE** Song (?) a series of weak, high, jerky, warbled phrases. Calls thin, high "*tsip*" and "*ti*" notes. **ENDEMIC**

7 PLUSHCAP *Catamblyrhynchus diadema* * 14 cm (5½ in)

Uncommon to locally fairly common in humid montane forests, 2000–3450 m. Primarily occurs along east slope of eastern Andes, but present on west slope south at least to Lambayeque. Singles or pairs accompany mixed-species flocks, in dense understory of forest and at forest edge, especially in and near thickets of *Chusquea* bamboo. Primarily forages by actively hopping up bamboo stems or acrobatically clinging as it presses the bill into the internodes. Adult distinctive. Immatures much drabber, but note the short conical bill and behavior. **VOICE** Song a jerky, disjointed series of high, squeaky notes: "*tseep-tseu-teep-ti-tsip-tseep....*" Calls a high "*pseep*" and "*ti-ti-ti*" notes. **Co, E, Bo**

BLUISH FLOWERPIERCER

ad.

imm.

MASKED FLOWERPIERCER

DEEP-BLUE
FLOWERPIERCER

GIANT CONEBILL

♂ bella/petersi

♀ bella/petersi

TIT-LIKE DACNIS

TIT-LIKE DACNIS

♂ parina

♀ parina

PARDUSCO

ad.

PLUSHCAP

imm.

PLATE
276

FLOWERPIERCERS

Flowerpiercers (Diglossa) *have relatively long, slender bills with a distinct hook at tip, usually with a sharply upturned tip to the mandible. Species on this plate use the hooked bill to puncture flower bases, from which they extract nectar ("robbing" the nectar, without pollinating the flower); also eat small arthropods. Typically do not associate with mixed-species flocks.*

1 RUSTY FLOWERPIERCER *Diglossa sittoides* * 11.5 cm (4½ in)

Uncommon but widespread. Found on west slope of Andes south to Lima, and on both slopes of upper Marañón Valley; also along east slope of Andes, 1200–3500 m. Occasionally wanders to coast. Occurs in montane scrub and at forest edge. Subordinate to larger flowerpiercers and even to hummingbirds at flowering shrubs. Male distinctive. Female identified by bill shape, small size, relatively olive color, and lack of white flank plumes. **VOICE** Song a high, metallic trill or chatter, variable in pace. Calls a descending, high "*tsip*" or a sharp "*tip*." **Co, E, Bo**

2 MOUSTACHED FLOWERPIERCER *Diglossa mystacalis* * 14.5 cm (5¾ in)

Fairly common along east slope of Andes, 2400–3700 m; locally also in Marañón Valley on west slope of eastern cordillera. Found in humid montane forest and elfin forest, at forest edge, and in shrubs in paramo grassland near treeline. Note prominent white moustachial streak and tawny-rufous vent, but geographically variable in breast pattern: *unicincta* occurs from Amazonas south to central Huánuco (west and north of Río Huallaga); *pectoralis* from central Huánuco to Junín; and *albilinea* from Ayacucho south to Bolivia. Immatures (not illustrated) are similar to adults but duller, with a pale mandible; juveniles streaked with buff below. **VOICE** Song a strident, loud, musical warbling of wiry, quavering notes. Somewhat similar to song of *striaticeps* Citrine Warbler, but more quavering quality. Call a high "*ti*." **Bo**

3 GLOSSY FLOWERPIERCER *Diglossa lafresnayii* 14.5 cm (5¾ in)

Fairly common at edge of humid montane forest and elfin forest, and in shrubs in paramo grassland near treeline, 2000–3250 m, along east slope of Andes north and west of Marañón Valley. Juvenile (not illustrated) similar to adult, but mandible is pale. Little overlap with similar Black Flowerpiercer (which primarily is found at less humid sites); Black also smaller, duller (less glossy) black, and lacks bluish gray "shoulders." **VOICE** Song a strident, loud, musical warbling of wiry, quavering notes; similar to song of Moustached Flowerpiercer. Call a hard "*bint*." **Co, E**

4 BLACK-THROATED FLOWERPIERCER *Diglossa brunneiventris* * 14 cm (5½ in)

Almost ubiquitous at forest edge and treeline, at 2400–4300 m along east slope of Andes, and in many intermontane valleys; locally fairly common as well on west slope of Andes, from central Cajamarca south to Chile, although uncommon and local south of Lima. Found at forest edge, in hedgerows in agricultural areas, and in *Polylepis* woods. Adult distinctive. Juvenile much drabber, streaked below with a whitish or grayish malar stripe. Intermediate plumages are frequent, similar to juvenile but with underparts spotted with brick red. **VOICE** Song a rapid, jumbled series of musical warbles. Call a high "*ti*." **Co, Bo, Ch**

5 BLACK FLOWERPIERCER *Diglossa humeralis* * 13.5 cm (5¼ in)

Fairly common on both slopes of western cordillera at 1850–3300 m, south to central Cajamarca. Narrowly overlaps, and hybridizes with, Black-throated Flowerpiercer. Found at forest edge, in hedgerows in agricultural areas, and in *Polylepis* woods. Adult uniformly dull black; cf. Glossy Flowerpiercer. Juvenile is dark gray-brown, obscurely streaked dusky on breast. Cf. female Rusty and White-sided flowerpiercers. **VOICE** Song a rapid, jumbled series of musical warbles. **Co, E**

6 WHITE-SIDED FLOWERPIERCER *Diglossa albilatera* * 12 cm (4¾ in)

Fairly common at 1650–3000 m on east slope of Andes in northern Peru and in middle Marañón Valley; less common and local on west slope of western cordillera in Piura. Also uncommon and local on east slope of Andes in south-central Peru at 2100–3300 m. Found at forest edge. A small flowerpiercer with conspicuous white tufts on sides of body. Juvenile female (not illustrated) is similar to adult female but may be slightly streaked below. Juvenile male is very dark; similar to juvenile Black Flowerpiercer but smaller, more olivaceous (less gray-brown) and with white pectoral tufts. **VOICE** Song a high, dry, rattled trill; song of birds south of Marañón more musical. Call a high "*ti*." **Co, E**

RUSTY FLOWERPIERCER

♀
♂

unicincta

juv.

pectoralis

albilinea

MOUSTACHED
FLOWERPIERCER

GLOSSY FLOWERPIERCER

juv.

ad.

BLACK FLOWERPIERCER

BLACK-THROATED FLOWERPIERCER

juv.

ad.

♀
♂

WHITE-SIDED
FLOWERPIERCER

juv. ♂

PLATE
277
SPARROWS AND GRASSLAND FINCHES

Finches and sparrows are primarily granivorous, foraging on or near the ground, and have relatively conical bills. Most species on this plate are geographically restricted; in contrast, Yellow-browed Sparrow is widely distributed and very common in the eastern lowlands.

1 WEDGE-TAILED GRASS-FINCH *Emberizoides herbicola* * 18–20 cm (7–8 in)

Locally uncommon to fairly common, but very patchily distributed: locally in the Marañón Valley and adjacent upper Río Mayo Valley in northern Peru at 800–1450 m, and also on the Pampas del Heath in southeastern Peru. Found in tall grasslands, with scattered shrubs or woodlots. Readily recognized by very long tail and largely orange bill (but cf. female Bobolink). **VOICE** Song a series of somewhat variable musical warbled phrases with pauses between each phrase. Call a dry "*pit.*" **Co, Br, Bo**

2 YELLOW-BROWED SPARROW *Ammodramus aurifrons* * 13 cm (5 in)

Common and widespread in Amazonia, up to 1800 m. Found along rivers, in pastures, town squares, and gardens, along road edges, and in other open grassy areas. Hops and runs quickly along the ground but may sing from an open, elevated perch. Note small size, flat-headed look, and relatively short tail; amount of yellow on face variable, but tends to "bleed" outside of superciliary (unlike Grassland Sparrow). Juvenile even drabber, with little or no yellow on the face and a narrowly streaked breast. **VOICE** Song a high, thin, buzzy "*tic tic'ZEEEEEE-tic'ZEEEEEE*" or "*zreeee-zreeee.*" Calls thin sputters and a high "*tik.*" **Co, E, Br, Bo**

3 BLACK-MASKED FINCH *Coryphaspiza melanotis* * 13.5 cm (5¼ in)

Restricted to the Pampas del Heath, where uncommon in tall savanna grasslands with scattered shrubs. Forages on the ground within cover, but perches higher when singing. Male readily recognized by striking black-and-white face pattern; also note white-tipped rectrices. Female (not illustrated) is similar in pattern but duller; black of face is replaced by gray, and there is less white in tail. Juvenile even duller, lacking white superciliary and is streaked below; note pale mandible. **VOICE** Song a repetitive series of high, ringing notes: "*tsee-tsee tsee-tip... tsee-tsee tsee-tip....*" Calls high "*tsip*" notes. **Br, Bo**

4 GRASSLAND SPARROW *Ammodramus humeralis* * 13 cm (5 in)

Locally fairly common in savanna grassland on the Pampas del Heath. Also found near Puerto Maldonado, where recently has colonized pastures and other newly cleared areas. Typically prefers areas with moderate grass cover, within which it forages on the ground for seeds and small arthropods. Cf. widespread Yellow-browed Sparrow, Grassland is grayer and darker, with very little yellow on face (only a small well-defined loral spot), has narrow white eyering and brighter, more rufous margins to secondaries. **VOICE** Song variable; is a pleasing, weakly delivered, series of thin, wheezy notes, often introduced with little clicks, for example: "*tic'seet eee-eee-errrr tic'SEEE SEEET.*" **Co, Br, Bo**

5 [BLACK-STRIPED SPARROW *Arremonops conirostris*] * 16.5 cm (6½ in)

Known only from a sight record from edge of evergreen forest in Tumbes, 600 m (*striaticeps*). Found in understory of forest edge, second growth, and relatively open forest. Forages on the ground under dense cover, as singles or in pairs; does not associate with mixed-species flocks. Cf. Orange-billed and Black-capped sparrows. Also reported from eastern Ecuador, in understory of wooded islands in the Río Pastaza; not known from adjacent Peruvian portions of the Pastaza, but should be looked for in this area. **VOICE** Song a slow series of deep, rich, hesitating whistles with a slightly buzzy quality, for example: "*djay... hew... churee....*" This may lead into an accelerating series of low, rich "*chew*" notes. Call (Colombia) a deep, sharp "*tchup*" note given in series. **Co, E, Br**

6 TUMBES SPARROW *Aimophila stolzmanni* 14.5 cm (5¼ in)

Fairly common in northwestern Peru, up to 1000 m. Found in dry scrub and dry forest. Singles or pairs forage on or near ground, near cover. Juvenile is similar to adult but duller, with narrow streaks across breast. Unlikely to be confused within range. **VOICE** Song variable, a thin, sweet, 2 or 3-part phrase, for example: "*toosoo-toosoo*" and "*tuswee-CHI'I'I'I'I.*" Call a sweet, metallic "*tink,*" often given in an excited series. **E**

WEDGE-TAILED GRASS-FINCH

YELLOW-BROWED SPARROW

ad.

juv.

ad.

BLACK-MASKED FINCH

juv.

GRASSLAND SPARROW

Pastaza

ad.

TUMBES SPARROW

striaticeps

BLACK-STRIPED SPARROW

juv.

PLATE
278

INCA-FINCHES AND SIERRA-FINCHES

Inca-finches share white outer tail feathers, a pointed yellowish bill, and generally gray-and-rufous plumage; juveniles duller, with a streaked breast. Found in arid scrub, especially where cactus and terrestrial bromeliads are prevalent. Forage on ground under dense cover, and tend not to flock with other species; can be difficult to observe when not singing. Species mostly replace one another geographically or elevationally. Cf. Band-tailed Sierra-Finch (which has different tail pattern and a streaked back, and lacks rufous wing coverts and a black throat). The two sierra-finches are geographically replacing species of high Andes.

1 GRAY-WINGED INCA-FINCH *Incaspiza ortizi* 16.5 cm (6½ in)
Uncommon on west bank of central Marañón Valley and tributaries, 1800–2300 m; also known from a single site on west slope of Andes in Cajamarca. Not known to contact Rufous-backed Inca-Finch, although it is possible that their ranges may abut; note that Gray-winged occurs at lower elevations. A large, dull inca-finch; mostly lacks rufous in plumage, and back is obscurely streaked. Locally overlaps with the smaller, more patterned Buff-bridled Inca-Finch. **VOICE** Song a series of weak, quavering, high whistles: "*seeew sweeee? seeee? seeew sueeesu....*" **ENDEMIC**

2 GREAT INCA-FINCH *Incaspiza pulchra* 16.5 cm (6½ in)
Uncommon, on west slope of Andes, 1000–2700 m, mostly above 1500 m. Overlaps locally with slightly larger Rufous-backed Inca-Finch in central Ancash, but is the only inca-finch in southern Ancash and Lima. Compared to Rufous-backed, Great has less black on face above the bill, black throat patch is larger, and breast and sides of face often are purer gray (less washed with light brown). Also, center of back is brown, contrasting more with rufous of scapulars and wings (center of the back rufous in adult Rufous-backed; but immature Rufous-backed also may have a dull brown back). **VOICE** Song a series of high, thin whistles: "*tsew tswee? tsew tswee?....*" Calls a short, descending, quavering high note: "*tsee'le'le'le'le'le'le*"; also a single "*tsew*" or "*tsee.*" **ENDEMIC**

3 LITTLE INCA-FINCH *Incaspiza watkinsi* 13 cm (5 in)
The smallest inca-finch. Restricted to arid scrub at 350–900 m in lower portion of dry Marañón Valley, where it is the only inca-finch present. Relatively dull-colored above, with some streaking on back. **VOICE** Song a high, thin "*tsee-TSEW! swee?*" Call high "*tseet*" notes. **ENDEMIC**

4 RUFOUS-BACKED INCA-FINCH *Incaspiza personata* 17–18 cm (6¾–7 in)
Uncommon, in north-central Peru, 2300–4000 m. Found on both slopes of upper Marañón Valley. Also on west slope of Andes, where it overlaps geographically with Great Inca-Finch; but where they overlap Rufous-backed is found at higher elevations (largely above 3000 m), so contact between the two species is limited. **VOICE** Song a weak, high "*tisew-ti'TSWEE?*" **ENDEMIC**

5 BUFF-BRIDLED INCA-FINCH *Incaspiza laeta* 14.5 cm (5¾ in)
A medium-sized inca-finch of the middle and upper Marañón Valley, 1000–2750 m; overlaps geographically with Gray-winged and Rufous-backed inca-finches, although usually found at lower elevations; also is slightly smaller than both and readily recognized by broad buffy stripe on either side of throat. **VOICE** Call a high "*tsee.*" **ENDEMIC**

6 BLACK-HOODED SIERRA-FINCH *Phrygilus atriceps* 15.5–16 cm (6–6¼ in)
Fairly common but restricted to west slope of Andes in south, 3150–4150 m, where largely replaces Peruvian Sierra-Finch; extent of overlap of the 2 species (especially when breeding) not entirely understood. Found in dry montane scrub, especially open *Polylepis* woods. Forages in small flocks on the ground near cover. Similar to Peruvian, but hood is darker and blacker (dull black in male, sooty gray in female), lacking the blue-gray tones of Peruvian; and back and (to a lesser extent) breast are tawnier (less olive). Juveniles are more similar, although even at this age Black-hooded is tawnier above. **VOICE** Song (Bolivia) a repetitive series of short warbles, with some variations: "*djee-chew djee-chew djee-chew djee.*" Calls a high "*tsi*" and a rich "*tchip.*" **Bo, Ch**

7 PERUVIAN SIERRA-FINCH *Phrygilus punensis* * 15.5–16 cm (6–6¼ in)
Common and widespread in Andes, except in far southwest where replaced by Black-hooded Sierra-Finch; 2800–4700 m, locally down to 2400 m. Found in open habitats with scattered shrubs, including montane scrub, *Polylepis* woods, agricultural fields and associated hedgerows, and villages. Forages on the ground in small groups, often in association with other species. **VOICE** Song a repetitive series of short warbles, with some variations: "*cheedew cheedew cheedew churee churee.*" Calls include a high "*tchip.*" **Bo**

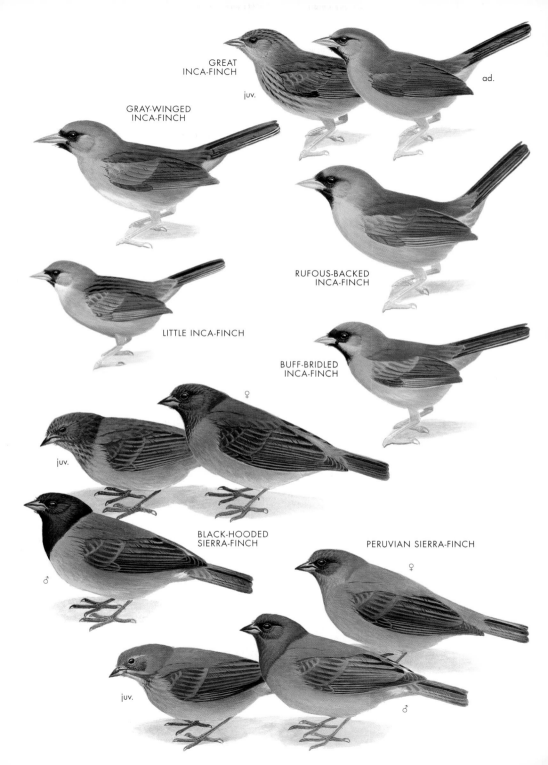

GREAT
INCA-FINCH

juv.

ad.

GRAY-WINGED
INCA-FINCH

RUFOUS-BACKED
INCA-FINCH

LITTLE INCA-FINCH

BUFF-BRIDLED
INCA-FINCH

♀

juv.

BLACK-HOODED
SIERRA-FINCH

PERUVIAN SIERRA-FINCH

♀

♂

juv.

♂

PLATE
279

SIERRA-FINCHES, SHORT-TAILED FINCH,
AND DIUCA-FINCH

Sierra-finches are a diverse group of finches, most of which are found in open and scrubby habitats in the high Andes. Short-tailed Finch and the diuca-finch are superficially similar to sierra-finches; Short-tailed is uncommon and very local, but the diuca-finch is fairly common and widely distributed.

1 MOURNING SIERRA-FINCH *Phrygilus fruticeti* * 17–18 cm (6¾–7 in)
Fairly common and widespread in the Andes, 2300–4200 m. Found in dry montane scrub; overlaps with Black-hooded or Peruvian sierra-finches, but has greater tolerance for more arid habitats. Male with black bib unlikely to be confused with other species, but cf. male of much smaller Band-tailed Sierra-Finch. Female readily recognized by large size and by the tawny auriculars and sides of face. Often encountered in pairs or small groups; occasionally joins mixed-species flocks. Forages on the ground near shrubby cover; tends to fly long distance when disturbed, giving distinctive call. **VOICE** Song a fairly unmusical buzz followed by a short, squeaky note: "*bjzzzz-tcheeLEEuu.*" Call a distinctive, nasal, raspy "*rheeeah.*" **Bo, Ch**

2 ASH-BREASTED SIERRA-FINCH *Phrygilus plebejus* * 12–13 cm (4¾–5 in)
Common and widespread in open habitats of high Andes, 2400–4700 m (*plebejus*; also *ocularis*, north of Marañón Valley). Occurs in montane scrub, fields, and puna grassland. Tolerant of relatively arid conditions, and of habitat degradation; often found on well-grazed grasslands. Also fairly common in desert scrub below 1000 m in coastal northwestern Peru, and at 1400–3300 m in the semiarid central Marañón Valley (*ocularis*). Small and pale, adults (both sexes) with whitish gray underparts. Immatures are browner and streaked. Females of desert population also streaked but are buffier below. Feeds on the ground in open country, in flocks, often with other finches. Cf. larger, darker Plumbeous Sierra-Finch, which shows little or no pale superciliary. **VOICE** Song (*plebejus*) a metallic buzzy trill followed by some chipping notes. Song of *ocularis* appears to lack additional chip notes added after the trill. Similar to song of Plumbeous, but shorter, "looser." Calls high "*ti*" and "*tip*" notes. **E, Bo, Ch**

3 PLUMBEOUS SIERRA-FINCH *Phrygilus unicolor* * 14–15 cm (5½–6 in)
Fairly common and widespread in the Andes, 3000–4700 m. Found in a variety of open grassy habitats in puna and paramo; more partial, however, to moister paramo grasslands than is Ash-breasted Sierra-Finch. Pairs and small groups forage on the ground. Male uniformly slate gray with short conical bill. Females of widespread subspecies *inca* (most of Peru) are very similar but may show some obscure streaking on back and crown; prominence of dorsal streaking possibly greater in southern Peru. Females in northern Piura and Cajamarca (*geospizopsis*), and immatures of all populations, are heavily streaked. **VOICE** Song a long, slightly descending buzz: "*djeeeer.*" Calls include high "*tew*" and short raspy notes. **Co, E, Bo, Ch**

4 SHORT-TAILED FINCH *Idiopsar brachyurus* 18.5–19.5 cm (7¼–7¾ in)
Very local near east slope of Andes in south, 3900–4600 m. Found on talus slopes. Forages on the ground near boulders, and investigates lichen-encrusted boulders and perches atop them, sentinel-like; also enters edges of *Polylepis* woods. Superficially similar to the more common and widespread Plumbeous Sierra-Finch; but Short-tailed is significantly larger, not as blue-gray, and has a much larger and longer bill. **VOICE** Song a simple, repeated series of high notes: "*tseet tsu tsree tseet tsu tsree…*" with occasional high chattered notes interspersed. Call a high rising "*tseep*" note. **Bo**

5 WHITE-THROATED SIERRA-FINCH *Phrygilus erythronotus* 18–18.5 cm (7–7¼ in)
Rare to uncommon, and only in high Andes of southwest, 4200–4600 m. Found in puna grassland and at edges of bogs and lakes. Forages on the ground in small groups. Cf. the similar but more widespread White-winged Diuca-Finch, which has extensive white at bases of outer primaries, larger white spot below eye, and narrow white margin to outer rectrices. **VOICE** Call a high "*chee.*" **Bo, Ch**

6 WHITE-WINGED DIUCA-FINCH *Diuca speculigera* * 18–19 cm (7–7½ in)
Locally fairly common, although apparently scarce or absent from some areas with seemingly suitable habitat in central and southwestern Peru. Found in puna grasslands, especially near bogs with cushion plants, 3950–4800 m. Forages on the ground in small groups, often with sierra-finches (in southwest, cf. White-throated Sierra-Finch). **VOICE** Call a sharp, rising "*tswee?*" **Bo, Ch**

♀ desert form

ASH-BREASTED SIERRA-FINCH

imm.

ad.

MOURNING
SIERRA-FINCH

♂

♀

♂

♀ inca

♀ geospizopsis

PLUMBEOUS SIERRA-FINCH

SHORT-TAILED FINCH

WHITE-WINGED DIUCA-FINCH

WHITE-THROATED
SIERRA-FINCH

PLATE
280

GRAY SEEDEATERS AND FINCHES

Catamenia are small, high-elevation seedeaters found in open habitats, often in small flocks. Rufous vent on largely gray males diagnostic. Streaky, pale-billed females resemble some species of sierra-finches, especially smaller species such as Band-tailed and Ash-breasted. Slender-billed and Cinereous finches are two mostly gray, pale-billed finches of the coast.

1 PLAIN-COLORED SEEDEATER *Catamenia inornata* * 13.5 cm (5¼ in)

Uncommon to fairly common, in the Andes at 2600–4400 m. Found in montane scrub, agricultural fields and associated hedgerows, low open woods (including *Polylepis*), and grassland. In eastern cordillera, more common in drier intermontane valleys but locally found on more humid east-facing slope as well. Often occurs with Band-tailed Seedeater, sometimes in mixed-species finch flocks. Male is much paler gray than male Paramo Seedeater; cf. also female Paramo Seedeater. **VOICE** Song a series of long, off-key buzzy whistles of variable order: "*dzzzzz djeeeeee durrrrr.*" Calls a high, descending "*tsee*" and a buzzy "*dzeer.*" **Co, E, Bo, Ch**

2 BAND-TAILED SEEDEATER *Catamenia analis* * 12.5 cm (5 in)

Fairly common in the Andes, up to 4000 m; also descending to coastal plain in central Peru. Found in montane scrub and agricultural fields and associated hedgerows; in eastern cordillera of Andes, found in drier intermontane valleys but not below 3000 m on more humid east-facing slope. Usually in pairs or small groups, often joining mixed-species finch flocks. All plumages have white band on inner web of most rectrices, forming a broad white tail band visible from below or in flight. Cf. larger Band-tailed Sierra-Finch. **VOICE** Song a dry, quavering buzz, with a somewhat electric quality to it: "*DJZZZ.*" Call a high, buzzy "*tzi.*" **Co, E, Bo, Ch**

3 PARAMO SEEDEATER *Catamenia homochroa* * 13.5 cm (5¼ in)

Rare. Found at edge of humid montane or elfin forests and in shrubby paramo grasslands along east slope of Andes, 2350–3500 m. Preferred habitat is much more humid than sites occupied by other *Catamenia*. All plumages darker than corresponding plumages of Plain-colored Seedeater. Blackish face of male Paramo Seedeater accentuates pale bill (which is more pointed, and even paler and whiter, than bill of Plain-colored). **VOICE** Song a series of long, melancholy buzzy whistles: "*dseeeeeeee DJUUUUU-DJUUUU-DJUUUU.*" Call a high "*ti.*" **Co, E, Br, Bo**

4 BAND-TAILED SIERRA-FINCH *Phrygilus alaudinus* * 14–14.5 cm (5½–5¾ in)

Uncommon to locally fairly common in montane scrub, borders to agricultural fields, and, locally, dry scrub. Local near coast in northern Peru; more commonly found at lower elevations in central and southern Peru, also up to 4100 m in the Andes. Geographically variable in size: smallest are populations in coastal deserts of north and in semiarid upper Huallaga Valley. All plumages have white band in tail (most visible from below and in flight). Cf. smaller Band-tailed Seedeater, which has rufous vent, dark legs, and stubbier bill; in north, also cf. inca-finches. **VOICE** Song a high, slightly electric-sounding "*tszz-zzew zz-zzew zz-zzew*"; occasionally more complex in skylarking flight display. Call a high "*ti.*" **E, Bo, Ch**

5 SLENDER-BILLED FINCH *Xenospingus concolor* 15 cm (6 in)

Locally fairly common in riparian thickets; primarily on or near coastal plain but locally up to 1600 m. Found in dense shrubbery along streams and rivers, also patchily in thickets away from water, even in isolated patches of shrubs in otherwise bare sand dunes. Usually forages for arthropods and seeds low and within cover of vegetation. Formerly occurred north to city of Lima, and populations elsewhere subject to habitat loss or degradation. Note the long slender pale bill. Sexes alike. Juvenile is brown and buff, lightly streaked below; note habitat and bill shape. **VOICE** Song a series of short chips and squeaky whistled phrases. Calls a sharp "*tchip,*" "*ti,*" a low "*churt,*" and a descending, chattering churr. **Ch**

6 CINEREOUS FINCH *Piezorhina cinerea* 16.5 cm (6½ in)

Fairly common in desert scrub in northwest, below 200 m. Usually encountered as singles or pairs. Often on or near ground, but will perch in tops of bushes when singing or disturbed. Adult unmistakable. Juvenile is much drabber with pinkish brown (not yellow) bill; but shares adult's chunky shape, relatively stout pale bill, and is unstreaked. **VOICE** Song a jerky series of short, rich, squeaky phrases. Calls loud chips, "*teep*" and "*tee-too*" notes, as well as a dry "*tik-tik-tik.*" **ENDEMIC**

PLAIN-COLORED
SEEDEATER

juv.

♂

♀

BAND-TAILED SEEDEATER

♂

♀

juv.

PARAMO
SEEDEATER

♂

♀

♀

♂

BAND-TAILED SIERRA-FINCH

juv.

ad.

SLENDER-BILLED FINCH

ad.

juv.

CINEREOUS FINCH

PLATE
281

WARBLING-FINCHES AND YELLOW-FINCHES

Warbling-finches are small, mostly arboreal finches of the coast and western Andes. Mountain-finch is similar in color pattern, but mostly forages on the ground. Sicalis finches are mostly yellow or yellow-green in color (except for Sulphur-throated Finch), and also forage mostly on the ground, sometimes in large flocks. See also plate 282.

1 PLAIN-TAILED WARBLING-FINCH *Poospiza alticola* 16 cm (6¼ in)
Uncommon, in montane scrub on both sides of western Andes of northern Peru, 3100–4600 m. Primarily occurs in *Polylepis-Gynoxys* woods, but locally found in other scrubby forests (especially where *Gynoxys* is present). Singles, pairs, or small groups forage in shrubs and trees, usually in association with mixed-species flocks. Gleans arthropods from leaves; also may feed on sugary secretions from *Gynoxys* leaves. **VOICE** Song a rich warble: *"chew tew-tuueee?"* Calls a slightly buzzy, rising *"zree"* note, often given rapidly in series; also a sharp *"tip."* **ENDEMIC**

2 COLLARED WARBLING-FINCH *Poospiza hispaniolensis* 13.5 cm (5¼ in)
Fairly common on the coast and lower slopes of western Andes, up to 2900 m, although scarce and local in Arequipa. Occurs in dry scrub, dry forest, riparian forest, and hedgerows bordering fields. Often arboreal, but also forages on the ground near cover. In northwest compare male to Black-capped Sparrow (which is found in the undergrowth of dry forest). Female similar in pattern to male, but the breast collar is reduced to a grayish brown wash streaked with black, the upperparts are brown, and female lacks the small rufous patch on the vent. Both sexes have white inner webs to outer rectrices (especially visible from below). **VOICE** Song a variable rich warble. Call a low, gruff *"djer djer."* **E**

3 RUFOUS-BREASTED WARBLING-FINCH *Poospiza rubecula* 16.5 cm (6½ in)
Rare and poorly known. Reported from only a few localities, in Marañón Valley in Cajamarca and La Libertad, and on Pacific slope in Ancash and Lima, 2500–3800 m; nowhere common, even at known localities. Found in montane scrub and woods, including edge of *Polylepis* woods. There are no obvious reasons for its scarcity; presumably it is more sensitive than other finches to habitat degradation. Behavior probably similar to that of Plain-tailed Warbling-Finch: singles or pairs forage within shrubs and trees, sometimes with mixed-species flocks. Adult distinctive. Immature (not illustrated) gray above (lacking superciliary), white-and-rufous below, streaked dark gray on breast and flanks. **VOICE** Song a slightly accelerating, variable, rich, emphatic warble with a squeaky component, sometimes ending on a buzzy note. **ENDEMIC**

4 CHESTNUT-BREASTED MOUNTAIN-FINCH *Poospiza caesar* 18.5 cm (7¼ in)
Uncommon in montane scrub of interior valleys in the Andes of south-central Peru, 3000–3800 m. Much larger than other *Poospiza* and, unlike smaller species, primarily forages on the ground (but near shrubby cover); sometimes associates with other finches, but also forages as singles or pairs apart from other species. **VOICE** Song a variable rich warble with a squeaky component. Similar to song of Golden-billed Saltator, but more complex, often with some buzzy notes. Calls a thin *"tsee?"* and *"tuee?"* **ENDEMIC**

5 STRIPE-TAILED YELLOW-FINCH *Sicalis citrina* * 12 cm (4¾ in)
The smallest, and most geographically restricted, yellow-finch in Peru. Known from a few sites in northern Puno, ca. 2100 m, where not known to overlap with any other yellow-finch. Has been found in small flocks at edges of agricultural fields in semiarid intermontane valleys. Inner webs of outer rectrices broadly tipped white (visible largely from below); note that occasionally Grassland Yellow-Finch may show a white spot near tip of outermost rectrix, but does not show as much white as in Stripe-tailed. Otherwise most similar to Grassland, but male Stripe-tailed has yellower crown and plainer face (lacks contrasting yellow eyering). **VOICE** Song (Bolivia) a very distinctive series of long, musical, buzzy whistles punctuated with short squeaks or chips, for example: *"sweeeeeeee-T'chewwwwwww'eet."* **Co, Br, Bo**

6 SULPHUR-THROATED FINCH *Sicalis taczanowskii* 12 cm (4¾ in)
Common in northwest, below 300 m in desert scrub. Often forms large flocks when not breeding. Very plain, but distinctively shaped, with stout heavy bill and relatively short tail; consequently looks bull-headed. Adult has pale yellow throat, but this may be difficult to notice at a distance (and is lacking in immatures). **VOICE** Calls a thin *"tzzz,"* *"tur,"* and scratchy warbled phrases. **E**

PLAIN-TAILED WARBLING-FINCH

COLLARED
WARBLING-FINCH

♂ ♀

RUFOUS-BREASTED
WARBLING-FINCH

CHESTNUT-BREASTED
MOUNTAIN-FINCH

♀ ♂

SULPHUR-THROATED FINCH

ad.

STRIPE-TAILED YELLOW-FINCH

imm.

PLATE
282

YELLOW-FINCHES AND SAFFRON FINCH

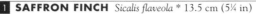

Sicalis finches are yellow or yellow-green in color and forage mostly on the ground. Saffron Finch usually is in pairs, but other species often form large flocks. See also plate 281. Some species can be difficult to identify unless seen well.

1 SAFFRON FINCH *Sicalis flaveola* * 13.5 cm (5¼ in)

Fairly common in northwest, on coast and in lower portion of semiarid Marañón Valley, up to 2200 m. Frequent in towns and gardens, otherwise occurs in desert scrub. Often in pairs or small flocks. Commonly kept in captivity. Escaped cage birds can be encountered in towns and cities away from original range; established in Lima and perhaps Puerto Maldonado, and reported from other towns as well. **VOICE** Song an accelerating, stuttered, loose musical series of metallic chips: "*tsip tip ti-tchip ti-chip-tew-tew.*" Call a metallic "*tink.*" **Co, E, Br, Bo**

2 GREENISH YELLOW-FINCH *Sicalis olivascens* * 14 cm (5½ in)

Fairly common and widespread in Andes, 1650–4200 m. Found in montane scrub and in agricultural fields and pastures; does not occur on puna grassland. Drab olive-gray. Male in fresh plumage has light gray wash on nape and back, but no streaks; males in worn plumage often are much duller, with little or no gray visible, and weakly streaked. Female is washed with brown on crown and back, weakly streaked. Immatures very drab, largely light brown with yellow center to belly and yellowish rump. **VOICE** Song variable, with rich buzzy warbling, churrs, and trills. Calls a dry "*djrt*" or series of gruff "*djurr*" notes, also a more musical "*wur-wurt.*" **Bo, Ch**

3 RAIMONDI'S YELLOW-FINCH *Sicalis raimondii* 12.5 cm (4¼ in)

Drab yellow-finch of the west slope of Andes, 200–2500 m. Similar to, and broadly sympatric with, Grassland Yellow-Finch; but Raimondi's occurs on arid rocky hills, Grassland in pastures and marshes. Raimondi's is grayer, less tawny, than Grassland, and usually is less prominently streaked; note gray-brown upperparts, gray (not tawny or yellow-green) auriculars, reduced amount of yellow on face, and narrow gray (not yellow-green) margins to remiges. **VOICE** Song a dry chatter or reedy rattle: "*tchitchitchitchitchi.*" Calls a dry "*djer-djer-djer*" and a rising "*kewee?*" **ENDEMIC**

4 GRASSLAND YELLOW-FINCH *Sicalis luteola* * 12–13 cm (4¼–5 in)

Fairly common but local; occurs on both sides of Marañón Valley (and very locally on Pacific slope) in north, in intermontane valleys near east side of Andes in central and southern Peru, 1700–3900 m, and locally on or near coast. In Andes primarily found in fields, but on coast usually in or near marshes. Small, drab; the most widespread streaked yellow-finch (but cf. Raimondi's Yellow-Finch). Male has yellow eyering offset by darker auriculars; sometimes (but not always) has narrow malar stripe. Female like male, but duller. Immatures even drabber; breast washed with brown and obscurely streaked. **VOICE** Song a pleasing series of thin, somewhat dry warbles and trills, reminiscent of familiar domestic Canary (*Serinus canaria*). Flight call a thin, strident "*tsee-tsik.*" **Co, E, Br, Bo, Ch**

5 PUNA YELLOW-FINCH *Sicalis lutea* 13.5 cm (5¼ in)

Locally common in south, 3800–4500 m. Found in open, often bare, grasslands and open scrub. Forages in small flocks, usually apart from other species. Very yellow and rather uniformly colored. Female very similar to male but slightly duller (more olive, less yellow). Most similar to Greenish Yellow-Finch, which is more greenish (especially above) and in particular has duller, greener margins to wing coverts and remiges. **VOICE** Calls (Bolivia) a rich "*tchew*" and mewing "*meluu.*" **Bo**

6 BRIGHT-RUMPED YELLOW-FINCH *Sicalis uropygialis* * 14 cm (5½ in)

The most common and widespread yellow-finch of the altiplano at 3300–4700 m. Found in puna grasslands and pastures; also enters villages and towns. Sometimes forages with other finches. Males readily identified by gray back (contrasting in flight with yellow rump) and largely yellow head with gray auriculars. Widespread subspecies *sharpei* entirely yellow below; southern *uropygialis* (north at least to Cuzco and Arequipa) has gray flanks. Females similar, but brown not gray, and crown is washed with brown. **VOICE** Song (Bolivia) a series of scratchy phrases, each repeated several times before proceeding with the next; may also give a more *Carduelis*-like song of jumbled trills, warbles, and churrs. Call a musical, low, warbled "*whitleew.*" **Bo, Ch**

SAFFRON FINCH

imm.

ad.

GREENISH
YELLOW-FINCH

♂ fresh plumage

imm.

♂ worn plumage

GRASSLAND
YELLOW-FINCH

♀

♂

imm.

RAIMONDI'S YELLOW-FINCH

♀

♂

PUNA YELLOW-FINCH

♀ sharpei

♂ sharpei

BRIGHT-RUMPED
YELLOW-FINCH

♂ uropygialis

PLATE
283

SEEDEATERS (*SPOROPHILA*), GRASSQUITS, AND SLATY FINCH

Seedeaters and grassquits often forage in small flocks on ground in open grassy areas. Species on this plate are present on the west slope (although some also are found in eastern lowlands). See also the general comments on seedeaters, plate 284. Slaty Finch is a nomadic Andean finch.

1 CHESTNUT-THROATED SEEDEATER *Sporophila telasco* 10.5 cm (4¼ in)
Fairly common on coast and in Marañón Valley, up to 700 m. Small. Throat of male always looks dark (although chestnut color sometimes difficult to see); also note narrow white rump band. Female is only streak-backed *Sporophila*; cf. female Blue-black Grassquit (which has a more pointed, darker-colored bill and heavily streaked underparts). **VOICE** Song, rather variable, a rapid, jerky series of warbled, snappy, and squeaky phrases, some buzzy. Calls a dull "*thck*," a rich "*tchip*," and a *Carduelis*-like "*dcher*." **Co, E, Ch**

2 BLUE-BLACK GRASSQUIT *Volatinia jacarina* * 10.5–11 cm (4–4¼ in)
Common and widespread throughout lowlands (up to 2400 m); particularly common on coast and in Marañón Valley, widespread but less common in Amazonia. Often in gardens, also fields, pastures, and other open grassy habitats. Small, with conical bill and slightly rounded tail. Male has white underwing coverts. Coastal *peruviensis* rarely if ever completely blue-black; remiges dusky brown, body usually narrowly scaled rusty or grayish brown. Female has narrowly streaked breast; also note rather pointed bill. **VOICE** Song a dry, sizzling "*tsi-SZZZEW*," usually falling in pitch at end, sometimes preceded by a series of very high "*ti*" notes. Often given just after apex of an upward leap during which wings produce 2 or 3 dry snaps (audible at close range) as they are struck together over back. Call a high "*ti*." **Co, E, Br, Bo, Ch**

3 DRAB SEEDEATER *Sporophila simplex* 11–11.5 cm (4¼–4½ in)
Uncommon, on coast and in dry Marañón Valley. Primarily at 500–2500 m in north, but to sea level in central Peru. Plain. Male in alternate plumage gray or dull grayish brown above, with white underparts and wing speculum, and bright yellow to pinkish pale bill; upper throat variably black. Male in basic plumage (not illustrated) similar but duller. Female buffy brown (no gray) with two wing bars. Cf. female Parrot-billed Seedeater. **VOICE** Song a variable, rich, rapid jumble of warbled phrases and buzzes; reminiscent of Parrot-billed, but normally has more notes per phrase. Calls a squeaky, rising "*zwee?*" and "*du*." **E**

4 PARROT-BILLED SEEDEATER *Sporophila peruviana* * devronis 10.5 cm (4¼ in); *peruviana* 12–12.5 cm (4¼–5 in)
Fairly common in west, below 600 m, south regularly to Ica; recently reported from northern Arequipa, where status (rare resident or nonbreeding visitor) not clear. Bill very deep, rounded, pale. Northern *devronis* (south to Lambayeque; not illustrated) smaller than southern *peruviana*, but plumage similar. **VOICE** Song a short series of musical, deep, buzzy notes, usually introduced with series of rising "*djzureet?*" notes. In flight, may give a more varied series of rattles, trills, and buzzy notes. Calls a descending, wheezy "*chew*" and "*chut*." **E**

5 DULL-COLORED GRASSQUIT *Tiaris obscurus* * 11–11.5 cm (4¼–4½ in)
Uncommon along coast and west slope of Andes, and in dry Marañón and Huallaga valleys; rare but widespread along east slope of Andes, 350–2100 m. Found in gardens, fields, dry scrub, and forest edge. Very plain; mostly brown, with more or less a grayish tone to breast and flanks. Superficially similar to female *Sporophila*, but note more pointed, bicolored bill. **VOICE** Song similar to Blue-black Grassquit, but usually longer, more complex, and more musical. Call a high "*ti*." **Co, E, Bo**

6 SLATY FINCH *Haplospiza rustica* * 12.5 cm (5 in)
Widespread along east slope of Andes, 1400–3100 m, occasionally down to 950 m and up to 3600 m; also local on west slope south at least to Piura. Abundance highly variable, apparently at least partially nomadic; often most common near seeding bamboo. Otherwise in understory of humid montane forest or forest edge. Note rather long, slender bill. Male superficially similar to Plumbeous Sierra-Finch but much smaller; also note different habitats. Female very dull, often obscurely streaked; also note short tail, pointed bill. **VOICE** Song a very high, sizzling of variable pattern, for example: "*tititi zeeeSIIIzeee-djzzz*." Males perform extended songs in a flight display. Call a high, lisping "*tseep*." **Co, E, Bo**

♀ fresh
plumage

♂ coastal

BLUE-BLACK GRASSQUIT

♂

imm. ♂

♀

♂ Amaz.

♀ worn
plumage

♂

PARROT-BILLED SEEDEATER

CHESTNUT-THROATED SEEDEATER

peruviana

♀

♂

♀

DRAB SEEDEATER

SLATY FINCH

♂ alt.

DULL-COLORED
GRASSQUIT

♀

PLATE
284

SEEDEATERS (*SPOROPHILA*) I

Some (most?) Sporophila *may take several years to reach adult male plumage, but plumage sequences are not well known. Females and immatures often difficult or impossible to identify (even in the hand); unfortunately, such birds often predominate in feeding flocks. See also plates 283, 285.*

1 LESSON'S SEEDEATER *Sporophila bouvronides* * 10.5–11 cm (4–4¼ in)
Uncommon intratropical migrant to eastern lowlands; reported Oct–Jul, but probably primarily present Oct–Apr or May. Male a small black-and-white seedeater with black crown, prominent white malars, and narrow white rump band; cf. Lined Seedeater. Females of both (not illustrated) pale olive brown above, pale tawny below with whiter belly and pale bills; indistinguishable from each other, and very similar to female Yellow-bellied, Double-collared, and Black-and-white seedeaters (all of which usually, but perhaps not always, have dusky bills). **VOICE** Perhaps not separable from Lined. **Co, E, Br, Bo**

2 LINED SEEDEATER *Sporophila lineola* 10.5–11 cm (4–4¼ in)
Uncommon migrant (intratropical?) to eastern lowlands below 1300 m, Oct–May. Male very similar to Lesson's Seedeater, but has white crown stripe, and underparts are purer white (no light gray mottling on sides of breast and flanks). Female (not illustrated) indistinguishable from female Lesson's. **VOICE** Song a stuttering series of musical warbles, often changing between two phrases, for example: "*chee-dee chee-dee chew, chur'r'r'r chur'r'r-tew*"; may insert other, more complex phrases. Call a descending "*tchew.*" **Co, E, Br, Bo**

3 CAQUETA SEEDEATER *Sporophila murallae* 12–12.5 cm (4¾–5 in)
Fairly common in northern and central Amazonia; status in south not clear. Male only black-and-white Amazonian seedeater with white throat and neck collar. Female perhaps not safely identifiable, but bill relatively large; drabber (less tawny) brown than Chestnut-bellied; and less olive than female of Double-collared, Yellow-bellied, and Black-and-white seedeaters. **VOICE** Song (Ecuador) a variable warbling series that rises and falls in pitch and often repeats phrases, for example: "*wee-chee wee-chew wee-chew wee-chee wee chew….*" **Co, E, Br**

4 VARIABLE SEEDEATER *Sporophila corvina* * 11–11.5 cm (4¼–4½ in)
Locally fairly common in northwest, up to 700 m. No geographic overlap with Caqueta Seedeater. Male easily distinguished from Black-and-white Seedeater by white throat and collar and white rump. Female yellower than other west slope seedeaters. **VOICE** Song (Ecuador) a rapid series of warbles and short buzzes and trills. Call a descending "*tew.*" **Co, E**

5 PLUMBEOUS SEEDEATER *Sporophila plumbea* * 11–11.5 cm (4¼–4½ in)
Uncommon. Restricted to Pampas del Heath, where may be resident or only a nonbreeding visitor. Male only gray seedeater with blackish bill. Buffy brown female larger, paler (especially on belly) than female Chestnut-bellied Seedeater; larger and larger-billed than female Dark-throated and Tawny-bellied seedeaters, and wings mostly unmarked. **VOICE** Song (eastern Bolivia) a pleasant warbling somewhat like that of Chestnut-bellied. Calls a variety of *Carduelis*-like notes, including a rising "*rhee?*" and descending "*chew.*" **Co, Br, Bo**

6 DOUBLE-COLLARED SEEDEATER *Sporophila caerulescens* * 11 cm (4¼ in)
Fairly common austral migrant (May–Nov), north at least to central Peru, up to 1000 m, but perhaps is regular north to the Amazon. Male gray with pale bill and a distinctive black-and-white throat pattern; has gray rump and lacks white wing speculum. Female is more olive, less tawny than female Lesson's and Lined seedeaters, with yellower belly; bills of female Black-and-white and Yellow-bellied usually are more uniformly dark, unlike usually paler mandible of female Double-collared. **VOICE** Song (Bolivia, Brazil) a rich, rapid jumble of warbled phrases, highly variable in pattern. Calls slurred "*churee?*," "*chew,*" and sharp, ringing "*chi*" notes. **Co, E, Br, Bo**

7 SLATE-COLORED SEEDEATER *Sporophila schistacea* * 11–11.5 cm (4¼–4½ in)
Rare and local in Amazonia and east slope of Andes, up to 1700 m; more common in southeast, but reported north to northern Loreto. Only forest-based seedeater; often in bamboo. Male mostly gray with pale bill; some (older individuals?) are darker, with white spot on side of throat. Other males (subadult?) olive-gray with reduced white speculum and browner bill; may sing (and breed?) in this plumage. Brown, black-billed female very similar to several other species, especially Yellow-bellied and Black-and-white seedeaters. **VOICE** Song a variable high, insectlike series of rapid, sizzling trills, buzzes, and screeches, for example: "*dzzz ti'i'i-tur-tzz-tzz-tzz-tzz.*" Also an infrequently given, more elaborate song with more musical trills and warbles. Call a musical "*psew.*" **Co, E, Br, Bo**

LESSON'S SEEDEATER ♂

LINED SEEDEATER ♂

CAQUETA SEEDEATER ♂

♀

VARIABLE SEEDEATER ♂ ♀

DOUBLE-COLLARED SEEDEATER ♂ ♀

PLUMBEOUS SEEDEATER ♂ ♀

♂ gray

♂ gray

♀

♂ olive

SLATE-COLORED SEEDEATER

PLATE
285

SEEDEATERS (*SPOROPHILA*) II

See general comments on Sporophila *seedeaters (plate 284). Yellow-bellied and Black-and-white seedeaters may breed in the Andes, but disperse to lower elevations for part of the year. Chestnut-bellied Seedeater is widespread and common in Amazonia. White-bellied, Dark-throated, and Tawny-bellied seedeaters are very rare, nonbreeding visitors.*

1 YELLOW-BELLIED SEEDEATER *Sporophila nigricollis* * 11–11.5 cm (4¼–4½ in)
Fairly common along east slope of Andes and immediately adjacent lowlands, and in Marañón Valley, 600–2600 m; also local on Pacific slope, south to southern Cajamarca. The overall brown or olive color of the male, combined with black throat, pale belly, and lack of white in wing, are distinctive. Female very similar to females of several other seedeaters, in particular Black-and-white and Double-collared. **VOICE** Song (western Ecuador) a pleasant, thin series of buzzy trills and warbles. Calls *Carduelis*-like "*zjee-wee*" and "*du*" notes. **Co, E, Br, Bo**

2 BLACK-AND-WHITE SEEDEATER *Sporophila luctuosa* 11 cm (4¼ in)
Fairly common in northwest, in Marañón Valley, and along east slope of Andes; primarily 1400–3200 m (especially in western Peru) but locally down to 450 m. Some descend to Amazonia when not breeding, Sep–Mar. Black "hood" of alternate-plumaged male (Dec–Aug) is distinctive; but cf. also male Yellow-bellied Seedeater and male Black-and-white Tanager. Basic-plumaged males (Jul–Dec) are dull brown with scattered black, prominent white speculum, and white belly. Female is olive-brown above and yellowish below, with black or dusky bill; very similar to the females of several other species, such as Yellow-bellied and Double-collared seedeaters. **VOICE** Song includes a characteristic, telephone-ring-like rattled "*brrr-dur'r'r-HEER*" and other trills. A whispered song may be given (mostly outside breeding season?), and this includes more warbled *Carduelis*-like phrases. Call a wheezy "*djew*." **Co, E, Br, Bo**

[WHITE-BELLIED SEEDEATER *Sporophila leucoptera*] * 12–12.5 cm (4¼–5 in)
Very rare austral migrant; known from a sight record from Madre de Dios. A large seedeater. Black-and-white male is most similar to Lesson's and Lined seedeaters, both of which are smaller, have small dark bills, and have prominent white malar patches and black throats. Female's large size, large pale bill, and buffy underparts may be identification aids; female Plumbeous Seedeater is very similar, but is slightly smaller and is warmer brown above, with dark bill. **VOICE** Song (Bolivia) a highly variable slow series of clear, melancholy whistles, rising or falling in pitch. Quite distinctive for a seedeater. **Br, Bo**

3 CHESTNUT-BELLIED SEEDEATER *Sporophila castaneiventris* 10.5–11 cm (4–4¼ in)
The most common and widespread seedeater in Amazonia. A familiar sight in towns, along roads, in grassy clearings, and in other open habitats with grass (including young river islands), up to 1400 m. Male is the only widespread gray and chestnut seedeater in Peru. Female similar to several other species of Amazonian seedeaters; it is buffier, less brown, than female Caqueta Seedeater, and buffier, less olive than female Black-and-white, Yellow-bellied, and Double-collared seedeaters. **VOICE** Song a slow series of musical, descending "*tew*" notes on various pitches, short warbles, and wheezy notes. Fairly different from other seedeater songs. Call a descending "*tseeu*." **Co, E, Br, Bo**

4 [DARK-THROATED SEEDEATER *Sporophila ruficollis*] 10.5–11 cm (4–4¼ in)
Rare austral visitor to Pampas del Heath; status poorly known, perhaps does not occur annually. Small. Male similar to Tawny-bellied Seedeater (and associates with that species) but has black throat (which may be obscured in fresh plumage by pale feather tips), and tawny of belly often deeper in color. Female is small and tawny; very similar to female Tawny-bellied. Plumage differences between the 2 species not well understood; possibly female Dark-throated is generally grayer brown above and deeper tawny below. **VOICE** Calls various *Carduelis*-like notes such as "*tew*," "*tee*," and "*eelew*." **Br, Bo**

5 [TAWNY-BELLIED SEEDEATER *Sporophila hypoxantha*] 10.5–11 cm (4–4¼ in)
Rare austral visitor to Pampas del Heath; possibly does not occur annually in Peru, but status not well known. Small. Rufous rump and underparts of male are distinctive; associates with similar Dark-throated Seedeater (compare). Female (not illustrated) is small and buffy; wing markings are more prominent than in female Chestnut-bellied Seedeater, but probably not safely distinguished from female Dark-throated. **VOICE** Song (Bolivia) is similar to that of Chestnut-throated. **Br, Bo**

♀

♂ alt.

♂ basic

♀

BLACK-AND-WHITE
SEEDEATER

♂

YELLOW-BELLIED
SEEDEATER

♂

♀

♂

CHESTNUT-BELLIED SEEDEATER

WHITE-BELLIED
SEEDEATER

♂

DARK-THROATED
SEEDEATER

TAWNY-BELLIED
SEEDEATER

imm. ♂

♂

PLATE
286
SEED-FINCHES, BLUE SEEDEATER, FINCHES, AND CARDINAL

Seed-finches resemble large, heavy-billed Sporophila *seedeaters; but do not flock. Other species on this plate are rather different from each other, and from other finches.*

1 BLUE SEEDEATER *Amaurospiza concolor* * 12.5 cm (5 in)
Rare and local on the west slope of Andes, 1700–2000 m. Found in understory of humid montane forest. Usually remains in dense cover, including bamboo (where bamboo is present). Not known to flock with other species. Male is blue-black but may appear black in dim light of forest understory; cf. male Blue-black Grassquit. Female is the only montane, fairly tawny-brown finch in northwest. **VOICE** Song a pleasant reedy warble. **Co, E**

2 CHESTNUT-BELLIED SEED-FINCH *Oryzoborus angolensis* * 12.5 cm (5 in)
Fairly common and widespread in Amazonia, up to 1500 m. Found at forest edge and in clearings; sometimes in stunted forest on ridges. Remains in or near cover when foraging, but male sings from an exposed, elevated perch. Female superficially similar to female *Sporophila*, but larger and darker with much heavier bill. Cf. also female Silver-beaked Tanager and female Blue-black Grosbeak (which is a bird of forest interior, not of forest edge). **VOICE** Song a variable, though nevertheless distinctive, series of musical warbles that often ends in quiet gurgles and rattles. Usually includes a characteristic series of introductory notes given in pairs, for example: "*teetlew swee-swee chew-chew....*" Calls a musical "*deedle,*" "*ti,*" or "*tew.*" **Co, E, Br, Bo**

3 LARGE-BILLED SEED-FINCH *Oryzoborus crassirostris* 13.5 cm (5¼ in)
Poorly known, found only in northern Amazonia and apparently rare and local. Presumably found in grassy sites such as marshes at edge of oxbow lakes or in grassy pastures. Male easily recognized by combination of black plumage and large, pale bill; cf. male Black-billed Seed-Finch. Female is significantly smaller than female Black-billed, with a smaller bill; plumage is paler and buffier. Larger and buffier than female Chestnut-bellied Seed-Finch. **VOICE** Song (Ecuador) a rich warbling that may include mimicry; deeper than song of Chestnut-bellied Seed-Finch. **Co, E, Br**

4 BLACK-BILLED SEED-FINCH *Oryzoborus atrirostris* * 15–16.5 cm (6–6½ in)
Rare and local. Most records are from sites near base of Andes up to 1050 m, but also very locally east of Río Ucayali. Found in grassy marshes bordering oxbow lakes. Larger than Large-billed Seed-Finch with an even heavier bill. Male also has a black bill and shows little or no white wing speculum. Female is darker, more olive-brown than female Large-billed. Female Chestnut-bellied Seed-Finch is much smaller, and is more rufescent on belly. **VOICE** Song is a variable rich warbling; similar to but deeper than song of Chestnut-bellied Seed-Finch. Sometimes includes short buzzy trills between warbled phrases as if is "inhaling." Calls a gruff, descending "*djert*" and a liquid "*dewp.*" **Co, E, Bo**

5 RED-CRESTED FINCH *Coryphospingus cucullatus* * 13.5 cm (5¼ in)
Fairly common, but patchily distributed. Found in dry scrub in lower portion of dry Marañón Valley, 400–700 m, and in similar habitats in dry middle Urubamba Valley at 700–2200 m. Male's crest is rarely raised. **VOICE** Song a musical 2- or 3-note series: "*chidut-WEET chidut-WEET chidut-WEET....*" Call (Bolivia) a high "*spit.*" **Br, Bo**

6 CRIMSON FINCH *Rhodospingus cruentus* 11 cm (4¼ in)
Rare to uncommon in northwest, below 750 m. Found in understory of dry forest and in desert scrub. Usually found as singles or pairs; often associates with *Sporophila* flocks when not breeding. Small, with short tail and long slender bill. Male unmistakable. Female identifiable by size, shape, and overall buffy plumage. **VOICE** Song (Ecuador) a rather uninspired, high, lisping hiss: "*tssrrrssss,*" similar to song of Blue-black Grassquit, but rising in pitch and with no suggestion of 2 distinct notes. Calls a sharp "*tchip*" and a descending "*tseer.*" **E**

7 RED-CAPPED CARDINAL *Paroaria gularis* * 16.5 cm (6½ in)
A familiar sight at edges of oxbow lakes and rivers in Amazonia, below 600 m. Forages as singles or pairs, almost always perching on snags or shrubs low over water. Immature similar in pattern to adult, but cap is rusty brown. **VOICE** Song a hesitating, repetitive series of warbled notes: "*cheeber wee? cheeber wee? cheeber.*" Calls a wheezy "*rhee?*" and "*chew*" and a rapid chatter in flight. **Co, E, Br, Bo**

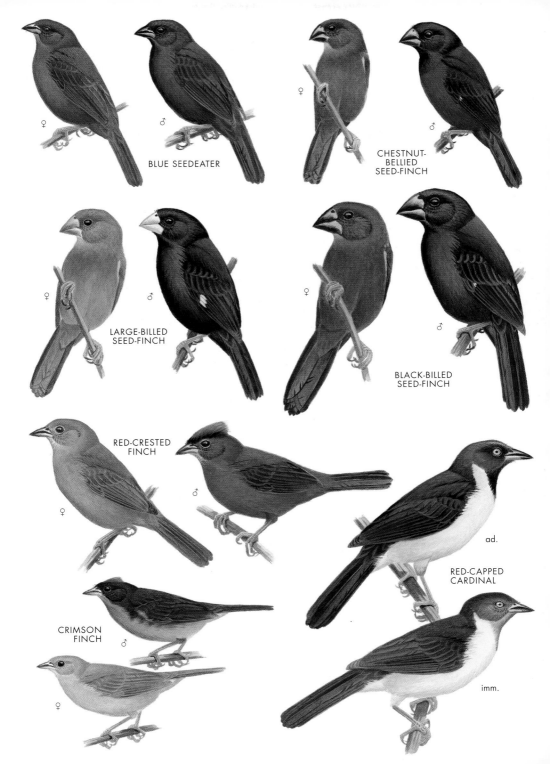

BLUE SEEDEATER

♀ ♂

CHESTNUT-
BELLIED
SEED-FINCH

♀ ♂

LARGE-BILLED
SEED-FINCH

♀ ♂

BLACK-BILLED
SEED-FINCH

♀ ♂

RED-CRESTED
FINCH

♀ ♂

RED-CAPPED
CARDINAL

ad.

imm.

CRIMSON
FINCH

♂

♀

PLATE
287

GREEN-BACKED SPARROWS AND
BRUSH-FINCHES

Arremon sparrows (lowlands) and Buarremon brush-finches (mostly Andean) both forage on or near ground in forest interior; singles or pairs stay in dense cover, typically not with mixed-species flocks. Buarremon brush-finches characteristically hop along the forest floor, flicking leaves aside with the bill. When excited, species raise the crown feathers, forming a triangular crest, and puff out conspicuous white throats. Olive Finch is an uncommon, terrestrial Andean finch.

1 ORANGE-BILLED SPARROW *Arremon aurantiirostris* * 14–14.5 cm (5½–5¾ in)
Uncommon in northern Andean foothills and locally in adjacent Amazonia, 300–1100 m, where found in undergrowth of humid forest and forest edge (*spectabilis*). Also uncommon in evergreen forest in Tumbes (*santarosae*; not illustrated). Sexes similar, but females may show a buffy gray wash on flanks and across breast below black band. Bill bright orange (but may be dark in juvenile). Lesser wing coverts orange in *spectabilis*, yellow in *santarosae*. **VOICE** Song (southeast Ecuador) similar to that of Pectoral Sparrow, a high, lisping "*tik tseeeew-tseew-tsee*," the final note rising. Calls a high, metallic "*tik*." Song of *santarosae* very different: more musical tinkling phrases with jerky pattern. **Co, E**

2 PECTORAL SPARROW *Arremon taciturnus* * 15 cm (6 in)
Uncommon, in understory of humid forest interior of southern Amazonia, up to 1000 m. Center of crown in male is gray, and underparts are white with narrow partial black breast band; female buffier below, with buffy gray coronal stripe and little or no breast band. **VOICE** Song a high, lisping "*tik-tseeeeeu tseeeeeu*"; reminiscent of song of Masked Tanager. Call a high "*tik*." **Co, Br, Bo**

3 BLACK-CAPPED SPARROW *Arremon abeillei* * 15 cm (6 in)
Fairly common in dry and riparian forests, up to 1800 m. Black crown often raised as bushy crest. Back gray (west slope of Andes; *abeillei*) or green (Marañón Valley; *nigriceps*). Some *abeillei* (females only?) may have white wing bars; otherwise sexes alike in both subspecies. **VOICE** Song (both subspecies) a variable high series of thin, buzzy whistles and loose trills, for example: "*tsew tsew tsi-tetetetete*." Calls a high, dry "*ti*" or "*tik*" and a sibilant "*swee*." **E**

4 STRIPE-HEADED BRUSH-FINCH *Buarremon torquatus* * 19–20 cm (7½–7¾ in)
Fairly common in humid montane forest along east slope of Andes; replaces Chestnut-capped Brush-Finch at higher elevations, 2000–3500 m. Also in similar habitats on west slope of Andes from 1200 to 3100 m, south to southern Cajamarca; and at 400–750 m in semideciduous and evergreen forests in Tumbes. Geographically variable. Birds on Pacific slope (*nigrifrons*) and on east slope south to La Libertad (*assimilis*) have gray superciliary but no black breast band; *poliophrys* from Huánuco south to Puno has gray superciliary and black breast band; *torquatus* of easternmost Puno is similar but with white superciliary. Juveniles are olive with dusky cheeks; also may have a weakly defined, pale olive superciliary. **VOICE** Song a high, sibilant series of thin whistles with a characteristic conversational tone, with short spaces between different phrases (usually 3), for example: "*weseer-twee tewsee? sewtsee? weseer-twee tweswee? sewtsee?....*" Calls high "*ti*" and "*tseer*" notes. **Co, E, Bo**

5 OLIVE FINCH *Lysurus castaneiceps* 15.5–16.5 cm (6–6½ in)
Rare and local (but also overlooked?) in understory of humid lower montane forest along east slope of Andes, 750–1800 m. Poorly known. Found in very dense undergrowth, usually near streams. **VOICE** Song similar to that of Chestnut-capped Brush-Finch, but song (typically?) more continuous, lasting unbroken for over 10 sec. Also similar to song of Ecuadorian Piedtail, but latter is more shrill and lisping in quality. Call a high, descending "*tsew*." **Co, E**

6 CHESTNUT-CAPPED BRUSH-FINCH *Buarremon brunneinucha* * 19–20 cm (7½–7¾ in)
Fairly common and widespread in humid montane forest along east slope of Andes and on outlying slopes, 1300–2200 m, locally to 3100 m. White throat often is the most visible feature when foraging on the ground in dense understory; also note chestnut cap. Juveniles are largely olive with dusky cheeks and a dull chestnut superciliary. **VOICE** Song a high, sibilant series of thin whistles, usually with short (about 2–3 sec) song phrases that are repeated incessantly, for example: "*see-swee-sew-see-swee-SEER*." Aggressive song usually consists of longer phrases with chipping between. Cf. song of Stripe-headed Brush-Finch. Call a very high "*ti*." **Co, E**

ORANGE-BILLED
SPARROW

♀

♂

♀

♂

PECTORAL SPARROW

nigriceps

BLACK-CAPPED
SPARROW

abeillei

ad. *poliophrys*

ad. *torquatus*

STRIPE-HEADED
BRUSH-FINCH

ad. *assimilis / nigrifrons*

juv.

OLIVE FINCH

juv.

ad.

CHESTNUT-CAPPED
BRUSH-FINCH

PLATE
288

HUMID MONTANE FOREST BRUSH-FINCHES

Atlapetes is a large genus of Andean brush-finches that primarily are birds of forest edge and montane scrub. Often travel in small flocks (family groups?) that may associate with other species. Forage low in shrubby vegetation or on the ground near cover; less commonly ascending higher. The taxonomy of the genus is uncertain. Some populations that traditionally have been recognized only as subspecies probably will be shown to represent different species (especially within the Rufous-naped and Slaty brush-finch complexes). Species on this plate are found at edge of humid montane forests.

1 RUFOUS-NAPED BRUSH-FINCH *Atlapetes rufinucha* * 17 cm (6¾ in)
Fairly common in humid montane forest in Andes at 1900–3450 m, locally down to 1200 m. Geographically highly variable. Populations in northern and central Peru all have yellow throat, but otherwise differ in crown color and the presence or absence of a white wing speculum: *comptus* (Pacific slope of Piura) has a rufous crown and no speculum; *latinuchus* (east slope of Andes) has rufous crown and large white wing speculum; *chugurensis* (not illustrated) and *baroni* (both sides of upper Marañón Valley, and locally on Pacific slope in Cajamarca) have buffy crown with whitish nape, and no speculum. There also is minor variation in the presence or absence of a yellow loral spot and of black malars. Collectively, *comptus, latinuchus, chugurensis,* and *baroni* are the "Yellow-breasted" (or "Cloud-Forest") Brush-Finch group. *Terborghi* (Cordillera Vilcabamba; "Vilcabamba" Brush-Finch) has a yellow throat and belly but a greenish breast. Most distinctive is *melanolaemus* of southern Peru ("Black-faced" Brush-Finch), with throat and breast heavily mottled with black. **VOICE** Song of *latinuchus* is variable, usually a pleasant, musical series of notes given in 2 or 3 parts that usually alternates between 2 song phrases in a typical song bout. Pair excitement duet includes a low, trilled churr, high screeches, and descending "*tew tew tew*" notes. Call a high, buzzy, rising "*tzee?*" Song of *melanolaemus* a pleasing, simple series of whistled phrases, somewhat variable, for example: "*twee-twee*" and "*chew-seelip.*" Pair excitement duet includes a series of wiry whistles and chatters, often ending in a rattling trill. Call a high "*ti.*" **Co, E, Bo**

2 SLATY BRUSH-FINCH *Atlapetes schistaceus* * 18 cm (7 in)
Fairly common in humid montane forest and forest edge on east slope of Andes, 2450–3700 m. Occurs in 2 disjunct populations. Northern *taczanowskii* has blackish sides to face and white throat; southern *canigenis* ("Cuzco" Brush-Finch) is more uniformly sooty gray. **VOICE** Song of *taczanowskii* a variable, pleasant series of rich introductory notes followed by a different trill or series of notes, for example: "*chew-chew-chew ZEEEE.*" Pair excitement duet includes a mellow "*dee-du-dew-dew*" interspersed with high screeches and twittering. Call of *canigenis* high "*tip*" notes. **Co, E**

3 PALE-NAPED BRUSH-FINCH *Atlapetes pallidinucha* * 18 cm (7 in)
Fairly common and conspicuous, but limited to humid east slope of Andes north and west of Río Marañón, 2500–3200 m. Found low near the ground in dense shrubbery and low trees at edge of humid montane and elfin forests; also found in interior of humid forest where it has a preference for bamboo thickets. Note whitish rear crown. **VOICE** Song, variable, is 1 or 2 high notes followed by a musical series of notes or chatter. Pair excitement duet is a rapid, strident chattered series with a falling-rising "*pee-sueet*" interspersed. Call a rising "*tsweet.*" **Co, E**

4 TRICOLORED BRUSH-FINCH *Atlapetes tricolor* * 18 cm (7 in)
Uncommon to fairly common along east slope of Andes, and on outlying ridges, of central Peru at 1750–3050 m. Occurs at edge of humid montane forest and in second growth. No overlap with Pale-naped Brush-Finch. Cf. also Rufous-naped Brush-Finch (only limited or no overlap). **VOICE** Song pleasant, 2 or 3 parts usually with 2 long, descending introductory notes followed by a more rapid series of notes. Pair excitement duet includes a long chattered phrase: "*pi tuee-chi tu-tu-tu zzz TEW TEW TEW TEW.*" Call a high "*ti.*" **Co, E**

latinuchus

comptus

baroni

terborghi

RUFOUS-NAPED BRUSH-FINCH

melanolaemus

canigenis

SLATY BRUSH-FINCH

taczanowskii

TRICOLORED BRUSH-FINCH

PALE-NAPED BRUSH-FINCH

PLATE
289
MONTANE SCRUB BRUSH-FINCHES

See general notes on Atlapetes on plate 288. Species on this plate are found in scrub, either in the western cordillera or in intermontane valleys.

1 BAY-CROWNED BRUSH-FINCH *Atlapetes seebohmi* * 16.5 cm (6½ in)
Found in montane scrub along west slope of western Andes, 1150–2800 m. Relatively uncommon in north, but fairly common in La Libertad and Ancash. Much larger than White-winged Brush-Finch with darker crown; also lacks the prominent white wing speculum. Does not show white speckling on face (as do many individuals of White-winged). Replaced farther south by Rusty-bellied Brush-Finch. **VOICE** Song (Ecuador) a variable, pleasant, tinkling warbled series, usually ending with a series of rising or falling slurred whistles. Calls (Ecuador) a rising "*tsuee?*," also a thin "*ti.*" **E**

2 WHITE-WINGED BRUSH-FINCH *Atlapetes leucopterus* * 15.5 cm (6 in)
Subspecies *dresseri* is fairly common in dry forest and forest edge on Pacific slope in northwestern Peru, 400–2000 m. A small gray and white brush-finch. Always shows a rufous rear-crown and nape. Forecrown typically is black; highly individually variable, however, with many birds showing white spotting on face (and rarely almost entire face can appear white (cf. White-headed Brush-Finch). Subspecies *paynteri* is rare to locally fairly common on east slope of Andes in northernmost Peru, 1700–2200 m, where found at edge of humid montane forest. Rear crown and nape of *paynteri* pale cream. **VOICE** Song (*dresseri*; Ecuador) a high, 2-part series of thin notes; relatively few warbled phrases compared to sympatric brush-finches. Call a high, descending "*tseeu.*" Song of *paynteri* a pleasant, musical "*chew-chew tee-tee*" or "*chee-chee tewr tewr.*" Call a high "*ti.*" **E**

3 RUSTY-BELLIED BRUSH-FINCH *Atlapetes nationi* * 17 cm (6¼ in)
Found in montane scrub along west slope of western Andes in central Peru, 2100–4000 m; fairly common in central Peru but becoming more uncommon farther south. All populations differ from Bay-crowned Brush-Finch by having very dull crowns and extensively buffy bellies. Northern *nationi* (department of Lima) is particularly dark; southern *brunneiceps* (southern Lima to Arequipa; not illustrated) has paler crown, and sides of crown often are randomly spotted with white. **VOICE** Calls (*nationi*) a hard, rich "*tchip,*" less metallic than that of Rufous-collared Sparrow, also a high "*ti.*" **ENDEMIC**

4 WHITE-HEADED BRUSH-FINCH *Atlapetes albiceps* 16 cm (6¼ in)
Fairly common in dry and riparian forests on Pacific slope of northwestern Peru, up to 1400 m. Larger than White-winged Brush-Finch, and usually found at lower elevations (although the two locally overlap). Forecrown always white, rear-crown always black. **VOICE** Song a series of squeaky whistled notes, for example: "*PEE-ti-ti SEW-tew'tew'tew see-see.*" Pair excitement duet a liquid descending chatter with some high screeches and twitters. Calls a high rising-falling "*tseeEEee,*" high "*ti,*" and "*tseeip*" notes. **E**

5 BLACK-SPECTACLED BRUSH-FINCH *Atlapetes melanopsis* 19 cm (7½ in)
Poorly known; on east slope of Andes in central Peru at 2500–3400 m. Found in montane scrub and edge of forest in upper Mantaro Valley. Similar to southern subspecies (*forbesi*) of Rufous-eared Brush-Finch, but has more extensive black on face, completely enclosing eye, upperparts are blacker, and crown is paler rufous. Juvenile may be greenish above and yellowish below. **VOICE** Pair excitement duet includes a characteristic "*swee tititi chew chew tsew-tsew.*" Call a lisping "*wees?*" **ENDEMIC**

6 RUFOUS-EARED BRUSH-FINCH *Atlapetes rufigenis* * 19 cm (7½ in)
Fairly common in montane scrub and *Polylepis* woods at 2700–4600 m. All populations are pale gray above with rufous crown and nape. Northern *rufigenis* is found on both slopes of upper Marañón Valley, and locally on Pacific slope in Cordillera Blanca. Southern *forbesi* ("Apurimac" Brush-Finch) of intermontane valleys of south-central Peru is similar but has a variable amount of black on face and prominent white lores. **VOICE** Song of *forbesi* a hesitant series of thin whistles and slow trills, for example: "*tchip TSEEW! tchi pi-pi.*" Pair excitement duet of *rufigenis* consists mostly of low chatters and some high, lisping notes. Calls include a high "*ti*" or "*tsi*" (*rufigenis*) and high "*pi*" notes (*forbesi*). **ENDEMIC**

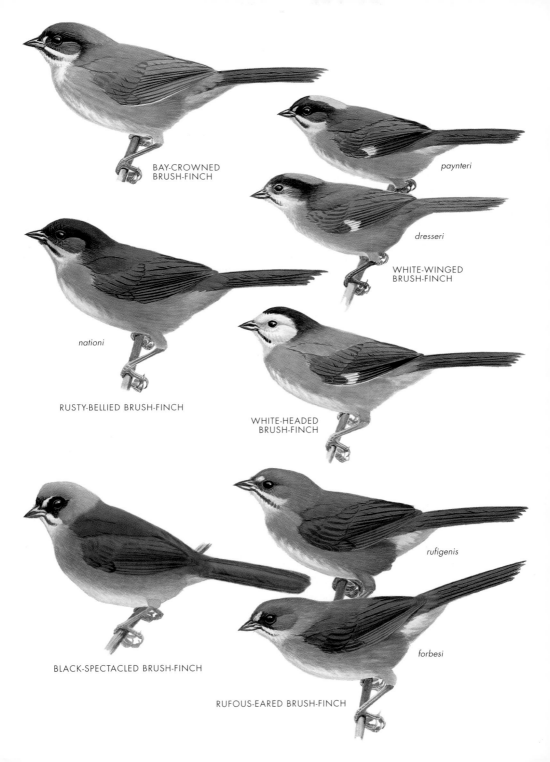

BAY-CROWNED
BRUSH-FINCH

paynteri

dresseri

WHITE-WINGED
BRUSH-FINCH

nationi

RUSTY-BELLIED BRUSH-FINCH

WHITE-HEADED
BRUSH-FINCH

rufigenis

BLACK-SPECTACLED BRUSH-FINCH

forbesi

RUFOUS-EARED BRUSH-FINCH

PLATE
290

GROSBEAKS AND RUFOUS-COLLARED SPARROW

Grosbeaks are large, heavy-billed finches that primarily are frugivorous (but eat some insects as well); they are birds of forest, forest edge, or scrub; most are arboreal. Rufous-collared Sparrow is one of the most familiar birds of the coast and Andes, a common sight throughout in towns, fields, and gardens.

1 YELLOW-SHOULDERED GROSBEAK *Parkerthraustes humeralis* 16 cm (6¼ in)

Rare but widespread in interior of humid forest in Amazonia, below 750 m. Singles or pairs are found in canopy, usually with mixed-species flocks. Gleans insects from leaf surfaces, but also consumes some plant material. **VOICE** Call a distinctive, high, lisping "*tsuit-wsst.*" Song, rarely heard, is a repetitive high, lisping "*seet tseer-tseer.*" **Co, E, Br, Bo**

2 GOLDEN-BELLIED GROSBEAK *Pheucticus chrysogaster* * 21 cm (8¼ in)

Fairly common in dry forest in northwest and in Marañón Valley. Uncommon farther south along coast and on west slope of Andes; rare to uncommon in eastern cordillera, primarily in intermontane valleys but less commonly on humid east slope as well. To 3500 m. Found in open woodlands or at forest edge. **VOICE** Song a pleasant, rich caroling, similar to song of Hepatic Tanager, but slightly sweeter, shorter phrases with more slurred notes. Call a sharp, squeaky "*pink.*" **Co, E**

ROSE-BREASTED GROSBEAK *Pheucticus ludovicianus* 18.5 cm (7¼ in)

Very rare boreal migrant. Very few records, all of females or immature males, on east slope of Andes south to Cuzco, below 2500 m. Male has rosy lower throat and upper breast; cf. male Purple-throated Cotinga of Amazonia. Note large size, heavy bill, and striped head of female. **VOICE** Call, very similar to other *Pheucticus* grosbeaks, a squeaky, sharp "*eek.*" Flight call a slightly wheezy "*ffew*" or "*tew.*" May sing on wintering grounds (particularly before migration); song a rich warbling, very similar to other *Pheucticus* grosbeaks. **Co, E**

3 BLACK-BACKED GROSBEAK *Pheucticus aureoventris* * *terminalis* 22.5–23.5 cm (8¼–9¼ in); *aureoventris* 20.5–21.5 cm (8–8½ in)

Rare to locally fairly common, and found only in eastern cordillera, mainly 1200–3200 m. More prevalent than Golden-bellied Grosbeak on east slope of Andes, at edge of humid montane forest; also locally in drier intermontane valleys. Resident south to Cuzco and Apurímac (*terminalis*); rump yellow, and upper tail coverts have large white spots. The rump of the smaller *aureoventris* is dark (black or olive), with no spots on the upper tail coverts; presumably breeds in southern Andes (north at least in Puno) but also may be an austral migrant further north. This species also is a very rare visitor to southern Amazonia (presumed austral migrants). **VOICE** Song a pleasant, rich caroling, similar to Golden-bellied, but thinner. Call a squeaky "*pik.*" **Co, E, Br, Bo**

4 BLUE-BLACK GROSBEAK *Cyanocompsa cyanoides* * 16 cm (6¼ in)

Uncommon but widespread in humid forest in Amazonia, up to 1400 m (*rothschildii*). Also uncommon in evergreen forest in Tumbes at 700 m (*cyanoides*). Usually remains concealed within dense cover in forest understory or at forest edge and adjacent second growth. Found as singles or pairs, which generally do not associate with mixed-species flocks. **VOICE** Song (*rothschildii*) a variable, pleasant, weak series of chiming notes that normally ends off-key: "*pee tee-tu-tu-ti-pee'chee.*" Call a harsh, dry "*tchit.*" Song (*cyanoides*) slightly more complex, usually dying away toward the end in a rapid series of notes. **Co, E, Br, Bo**

5 RUFOUS-COLLARED SPARROW *Zonotrichia capensis* * 14 cm (5½ in)

Common and widespread on coast and Andes, from sea level up to 4500 m; also locally found down to 350 m on east slope in Mayo and central Huallaga valleys. Found in gardens, agricultural fields, and other open habitats. In Andes, much more common on west slope and in intermontane valleys than on east-facing slopes. Largely granivorous; forages on ground, usually near shrubby cover. May form large flocks when not breeding, often flocking with other species. Juvenile streakier overall but has rufous collar and same shape as adult. **VOICE** Song very variable, with noticeable regional dialects, but readily recognizable by pattern and quality, with loud, sweet notes and sometimes trills. For example: "*swee TEW-CHEW.*" A commonly heard song year-round in most towns and cities. Call a metallic "*tink*" (coastal) or a softer "*chink*" (Andes); also churring growls in aggressive interactions. **Co, E, Br, Bo, Ch**

YELLOW-SHOULDERED
GROSBEAK

♀

♂

♂

GOLDEN-BELLIED GROSBEAK

♀

♀

ROSE-BREASTED
GROSBEAK

ad. ♂ basic

imm. ♂

♂ *terminalis*

BLACK-BACKED
GROSBEAK

♂ *aureoventris*

BLACK-BACKED GROSBEAK

♀ *terminalis*

♀ *aureoventris*

juv.

♂

♀

ad.

RUFOUS-COLLARED
SPARROW

BLUE-BLACK GROSBEAK

PLATE
291

SALTATORS AND SLATE-COLORED GROSBEAK

Saltators are large, long-tailed, heavy-billed finches; most species are primarily arboreal.

1 GRAYISH SALTATOR *Saltator coerulescens* * 21 cm (8¼ in)

Fairly common and widespread in Amazonia, up to 1200 m, at forest edge, in second growth, and in river-edge forest. Juvenile (not illustrated) duskier on throat, and breast washed with buff and with blurry olive streaks; much darker overall than Streaked Saltator (little overlap). **VOICE** Song a variable series of rich slurred whistles, with characteristic, slurred, rising or falling terminal note. Typical song phrases include *"chu-chu-chu-chu HOOooowr"* or *"huw chu-chu HEEEU."* Another vocalization (song?), often given in duet, is a rapid squeaky warble, also usually ending with a slurred terminal note. Calls a squeaky, descending *"tsin"* and lower *"chin."* **Co, E, Br, Bo**

2 BUFF-THROATED SALTATOR *Saltator maximus* * 20.5–21 cm (8–8¼ in)

Fairly common and widespread in Amazonia and east slope of Andes, up to 1750 m, in subcanopy and canopy of humid forest (especially at forest openings and fruiting trees), forest edge, and taller second growth. Also uncommon in evergreen forest in Tumbes. Singles or pairs may associate with mixed-species flocks. **VOICE** Song a mellow caroling (*Turdus*-like, but more mellow, less variable); each song phrase a little different than the previous until ending in a querying phrase, then repeats: *"will-cheeloo will-cheelo will-cheeloo wee-alee? will-cheeloo...."* Call a high squeak followed by a warble: *"tseet! cheeolee-cheelow."* Also a metallic *"tick,"* a high *"seek,"* and a mewing *"CHEEluloo."* **Co, E, Br, Bo**

3 BLACK-COWLED SALTATOR *Saltator nigriceps* 22 cm (8½ in)

Uncommon, in humid montane forest and forest edges on west slope of northern Andes, 1200–2500 m. Largely arboreal. Not known to overlap with Golden-billed Saltator. **VOICE** Song a variable, abbreviated, high, almost screeching phrase: *"peet PEECHEW-EEZ."* Call a metallic ringing *"chee!"* and high *"tsee."* **E**

4 GOLDEN-BILLED SALTATOR *Saltator aurantiirostris* * 19–20.5 cm (7½–8 in)

Fairly common. Occurs on west slope of Andes in Ancash and Lima (sparingly south to Arequipa), on both slopes of Marañón Valley, and in intermontane valleys of eastern cordillera of Andes, 2100–4000 m. Found in montane scrub, forest borders, and hedgerows in agricultural fields; not found in more humid habitats. **VOICE** Song variable, a loud, strident, musical whistled phrase, for example: *"twi CHEW tew-SWEE?"* Calls a metallic *"tchip"* and a low gravelly churr. **Br, Bo, Ch**

5 SLATE-COLORED GROSBEAK *Saltator grossus* * 20 cm (7¼ in)

Fairly common in Amazonia, up to 1100 m, locally to 1800 m. Found in subcanopy and canopy of humid forest. Inconspicuous, often remaining concealed within vegetation. Singles or pairs may join mixed-species flocks but more often encountered apart. Female (not illustrated) is paler brownish gray below and lacks black border to throat. **VOICE** Song a variable, mellow warble, usually the same phrase repeated monotonously, for example: *"chewee chewee-whew."* Similar to song of Rufous-browed Peppershrike, but shorter and simpler in pattern. Calls a descending, mewing *"reeeehr"* and a metallic *"tchip."* **Co, E, Br, Bo**

6 MASKED SALTATOR *Saltator cinctus* 21.5 cm (8½ in)

Poorly known. Rare and perhaps local in humid montane forest along east slope of Andes, 1700–3000 m. Singles may join mixed-species flocks, but probably more often apart. Consumes fruit of *Podocarpus* trees. **VOICE** Song (Ecuador) a rich, mellow whistled phrase: *"tu-chew-chew-chew-wuri?"* Calls high *"ti"* and lower *"cup"* notes. **Co, E**

7 STREAKED SALTATOR *Saltator striatipectus* * 19–20.5 cm (7½–8 in)

Fairly common. Found in dry forests and scrub, hedgerows and gardens along coast and the Marañón Valley. Most common below 1200 m, but in south up to 2500 m. *Flavidicollis* (Tumbes and northern Piura) green above with pale eyebrow, yellow wash on underparts, and variable streaking. Underparts white farther south on coast, superciliary reduced, and upperparts grayer (*immaculatus*). Heavily streaked in Marañón, with green upperparts and little or no superciliary (*peruvianus*). Bill often tipped yellow, especially in *peruvianus*. **VOICE** Song (*peruvianus*) variable; similar to song of Grayish Saltator, but song has more contrasting pitches, usually ending with 1 or 2 down-slurred whistles (which may be buzzy), for example: *"wur HEE woe HEER CHEW-CHEW."* Calls a high *"tsi"* and a low, nasal *"chew,"* often in a short series. Songs on coast similar, but usually lack down-slurred terminal notes. Calls a sharp, ringing *"tip,"* descending *"jer,"* and whistled *"heer."* **Co, E**

GRAYISH SALTATOR

BUFF-THROATED
SALTATOR

SLATE-COLORED
GROSBEAK

♂

BLACK-COWLED
SALTATOR

GOLDEN-BILLED
SALTATOR

flavidicollis

peruvianus

STREAKED SALTATOR

MASKED SALTATOR

immaculatus

PLATE
292 | MIGRANT WARBLERS AND TROPICAL PARULA

Wood-warblers are small, very active, insectivorous birds. Capture arthropods primarily by gleaning vegetation but also with short sallies. All species on this plate are frequent members of mixed-species flocks. Tropical Parula is a common resident; other species on this plate are migrants from North America, some of which have been reported on only a few occasions. Note that all Dendroica (see also plate 293) species have white or (Yellow Warbler) yellow spots on underside of tail.

1 CERULEAN WARBLER *Dendroica cerulea* 12 cm (4¾ in)
Rare to uncommon boreal migrant (Sep–Mar) to east slope of Andes, 700–1500 m. Forages in the mid- and upper levels of tall humid montane forest. Blue-and-white adult male, with black "necklace" on breast, distinctive year-round. Females and immatures duller, but always have prominent pale superciliary, unstreaked back, blue or blue-green tone to upperparts, and relatively short tail. Cf. immature Blackburnian Warbler. **VOICE** Call a buzzy "*zit.*" Song a burry 3-part series, each part slightly higher-pitched than the previous: "*zeer-zeer-zi'zi'zi zeeee.*" **Co, E, Br, Bo**

2 TROPICAL PARULA *Parula pitiayumi* * 11 cm (4¼ in)
Fairly common in dry forests in northwest and Marañón Valley at 200–2400 m, and in humid montane forest along lower east slope of Andes and on outlying ridges, 700–1900 m. Singles or pairs forage in the mid- and upper levels of forest. Sexes similar; female duller, with reduced black mask and smaller and paler orangey wash on throat and breast. **VOICE** Song variable, but generally recognizable by its rising and falling buzzy quality, for example: "*tip zeer-zeer-ti'i'i'i'i'i'i-ZEER.*" Parula song buzzier, less metallic than song of Three-striped Warbler, lacking such a crescendo effect. Call a metallic "*tchip.*" **Co, E, Br, Bo**

[GOLDEN-WINGED WARBLER] *Vermivora chrysoptera* 12 cm (4¾ in)
Vagrant boreal migrant; known from a single undocumented sight record from edge of humid montane forest in Cuzco at 2700 m. Confirmation of its occurrence highly desirable. Face and throat pattern distinctive (although lighter gray, less blackish, in first-year birds); also note broad yellow margins to wing coverts, and small size. **VOICE** Flight call a wheezy "*zheet.*" **Co, E**

3 BLACKBURNIAN WARBLER *Dendroica fusca* 12.5 cm (5 in)
Fairly common boreal migrant (Sep–Apr) to humid montane forest on east slope of Andes and on outlying ridges, 950–3000 m; uncommon (but probably regular) south to Puno. Also occurs in similar habitats on west slope of Andes south at least to Piura. Vagrant to Tumbes and Lima. Forages in upper levels of humid forest. In all plumages note dark cheeks surrounded by orange or yellow, and pale streaks on back. Face and throat color variable; can be intensely orange in alternate plumage (especially in males), paler and orangey yellow in females and males in basic plumage; may be only pale yellow in immatures. **VOICE** Call a buzzy "*zit.*" Song is a very high, thin, rising series of lisping notes. **Co, E, Br, Bo**

BLACK-AND-WHITE WARBLER *Mniotilta varia* 12.5 cm (5 in)
Vagrant or rare boreal migrant; a few records (Nov, Dec) from both Amazonia and northern Andes, up to 2200 m. Forages primarily in mid- and upper stories of forest and woods. Foraging behavior distinctive: creeps along trunks and larger branches, gleaning arthropods from bark. Cf. streaked antwrens and alternate-plumaged male Blackpoll Warbler. Adult male has black auriculars and throat (throat may be partially or entirely white in basic plumage, and in males in first alternate plumage). Auriculars and throat of females mostly white; flanks light buff, with weaker streaking. First basic male like female, but with more distinct flank streaking on white background. **VOICE** Call a wheezy "*zheep.*" **Co, E**

4 BLACKPOLL WARBLER *Dendroica striata* 13 cm (5 in)
Uncommon boreal migrant (Sep–Apr) to northern Amazonia. Found in canopy of humid forest and at forest edge. Forages with mixed-species flocks or apart. Basic plumage washed with yellow (especially immatures). Cf. Andean *Dendroica* (but with which there is little or no geographic overlap). Male Blackpoll acquires distinctive alternate plumage only shortly before departing Peru. Female in alternate plumage much duller; note tail spots, wing bars, and whitish underparts. **VOICE** Call a buzzy "*zit.*" Song is a very high series of thin "*seep*" notes; pace variable. **Co, E, Br, Ch**

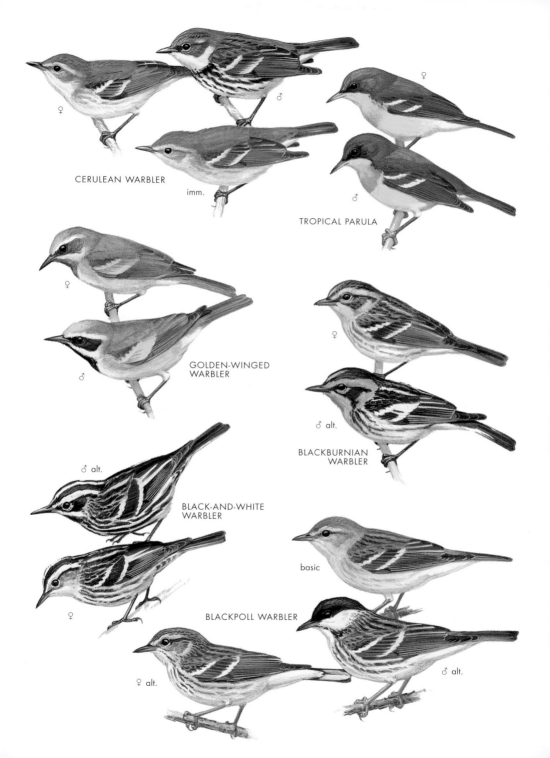

CERULEAN WARBLER

♀

imm.

♂

TROPICAL PARULA

♀

♂

GOLDEN-WINGED
WARBLER

♀

♂

BLACKBURNIAN
WARBLER

♀

♂ alt.

BLACK-AND-WHITE
WARBLER

♂ alt.

♀

BLACKPOLL WARBLER

basic

♀ alt.

♂ alt.

PLATE
293

MIGRANT WARBLERS, REDSTARTS, AND BANANAQUIT

Myioborus *redstarts have prominent white outer tail rectrices (source of alternate name, "whitestarts"). Very active, frequently spreading tail and drooping wings while foraging; often capture prey with short sallies. Other warblers on plate are boreal migrants, but Yellow Warbler also has a resident population. Bananaquit is a warblerlike bird with a distinctly curved bill.*

1 CANADA WARBLER *Wilsonia canadensis* 13 cm (5 in)
Fairly common boreal migrant (Sep–Apr) to east slope of Andes, 650–1600 m. Vagrant or rare migrant to northwest and Amazonia near base of Andes. Found in understory, usually with mixed-species flocks, at edge of humid forest, and in second growth. Note bold yellow eyering and dark "necklace" (less distinct in female and immature). **VOICE** Song (may be heard just before migration) a variable, strident series of rich notes, for example: *"cherkee-sideler-tiddleedum."* Call a rich *"chep."* Flight call a hard *"chet."* **Co, E, Br, Bo**

2 SLATE-THROATED REDSTART *Myioborus miniatus* * 13.5 cm (5¼ in)
Common and widespread in humid montane forest and at forest edge, 700–2600 m, along east slope of Andes, outlying ridges, in Marañón Valley and on west slope in northwest; also in evergreen forests in Tumbes and northern Piura. Singles or pairs often with mixed-species flocks but also forages apart, at all heights but primarily in mid- and upper stories. Upper breast yellow or (regularly from central Peru south, occasionally farther north) ochraceous. **VOICE** Song a variable, fairly short series of ringing notes, for example: *"teechit-teechit tooslee tooslee."* Call a metallic *"teep"* or *"tip."* **Co, E, Br, Bo**

3 YELLOW WARBLER *Dendroica petechia* * 12.5 cm (5 in)
Fairly common resident in mangroves in Tumbes (*peruviana*). Also rare boreal migrant to northern Amazonia (*aestiva* group), rarely south to Junín; reported Nov–Apr (but probably arrives by Sep?). Migrants found in riparian scrub, gardens, second growth, and forest edge. Male has chestnut streaks on yellow underparts; *peruviana* also has chestnut cap. In Amazonia duller females and immatures distinguished from immatures of Orange-headed Tanager and Bicolored Conebill by yellower color (especially under tail), yellow wing bars and tail spots, and (from tanager) by smaller size. **VOICE** Song (*peruviana*) a short, musical warbled phrase, for example: *"chew-sit-tseetsee-WEEhew."* Call (boreal migrants) a rich *"tchip"*; flight call is a buzzy *"zit."* **Co, E, Br, Bo**

4 SPECTACLED REDSTART *Myioborus melanocephalus* * 13.5 cm (5¼ in)
Common and widespread in humid montane forest and forest edges; mostly replaces Slate-throated Redstart at higher elevations. Brown-crowned *griseonuchus* found on both slopes of Andes north and west of Marañón Valley; black-crowned populations along east slope of Andes from south of Marañón to Bolivia, 1800–3450 m. **VOICE** Song a musical, high warbled phrase, rapidly repeated and swelling in volume, for up to 10 sec or more. Sometimes answered by a simple series of *"ti!"* notes (female only?). Call metallic *"tik"* notes. **Co, E, Bo**

AMERICAN REDSTART *Setophaga ruticilla* 12.5 cm (5 in)
Rare boreal migrant; primarily Oct–Apr but also reported Jun and mid-Aug. Most records are of females or immatures (including males in black-speckled first alternate plumage) on west slope, up to 3000 m; also a few records from the Andes and Amazonia near base of Andes. Very active: often droops wings and fans tail (like a Myioborus redstart), and frequently captures prey with short sallies. **VOICE** Call a rich, smacking *"chew"*; flight note a rising *"tuee."* **Co, E, Br, Ch**

5 BANANAQUIT *Coereba flaveola* * 9.5–11 cm (3¾–4¼ in); *magnirostris* 12.5 cm (5 in)
Common in northwest and in Marañón Valley, up to 1600 m, locally to 2800 m in dry scrub and forest, forest edge, and gardens. Less common and local on east slope of Andes and in Amazonia below 1500 m, where mostly at forest edge. Nectarivorous; not with mixed-species flocks but joins other species at flowering trees or shrubs. Rump yellowish. Geographically variable. *Pacifica* and *intermedia* (northwest and northern Amazonia; also a feral population common in Lima) have white wing speculum. *Magnirostris* (Marañón) similar but larger, bill and tail longer. Lacks speculum in central and southern Peru (*dispar, chloropygia*). Juvenile (not illustrated) duller; throat white or pale yellow. **VOICE** Song a variable series of high, thin, sizzling phrases, for example: *"szzzzewy-szewy-szewy szzz."* Calls high, thin *"tsit"* and *"tseep"* notes. **Co, E, Br, Bo**

CANADA WARBLER

SLATE-THROATED
REDSTART

s

n

YELLOW WARBLER

♂ *peruviana*

YELLOW WARBLER

♀ *peruviana*

♂ *aestiva*

♀ *aestiva*

griseonuchus

SPECTACLED REDSTART

♂

imm. ♂

♀

AMERICAN REDSTART

magnirostris

pacifica/intermedia

BANANAQUIT   *dispar/chloropygia*

PLATE
294

WARBLERS (*BASILEUTERUS*)

Basileuterus inhabit forest understory; forage in pairs or small groups with mixed-species flocks. Species replace one another elevationally in the Andes, usually with significant overlap.

1 PALE-LEGGED WARBLER *Basileuterus signatus* * 13.5 cm (5¼ in)

Fairly common on east slope of Andes of central and southern Peru, 1700–2900 m; but scarce or absent from Apurímac Valley. Found in understory of humid montane forest, especially in thickets of *Chusquea* bamboo, and at forest edge and in second growth. Northern *signatus* (Pasco, Junín) averages duller below and with shorter superciliary than southern *flavovirens*. Similar to larger Citrine Warbler, although primarily occurs at lower elevations. Superciliary of Pale-legged is shorter and narrower, lores dusky (not blackish), and forecrown with little or no black; also has more noticeable yellow crescents below eye and smaller bill. **VOICE** Song an accelerating series of ringing notes that rises and falls before ending with a more rapid flourish. Lower, more musical than song of *euophrys* Citrine Warbler. Call a low "*djitit*", sometimes in a chatter. **Co, Bo**

2 CITRINE WARBLER *Basileuterus luteoviridis* * 14 cm (5½ in)

Most common and widespread high elevation *Basileuterus* (but uncommon north and west of Marañón Valley). Found in understory of humid montane and elfin forests along east slope of Andes, 2500–3700 m, locally down to 2100 m. Superciliary particularly short and narrow in *luteoviridis* (north of Marañón Valley); superciliary relatively broad and lores blackish, in widespread *striaticeps*; superciliary broadest, contrasting with black forecrown and blackish borders to crown, in *euophrys* (Marcapata Valley south to Bolivia). **VOICE** Song (*luteoviridis*) a high, rapid, weak, chippering series. Call a high "*ti*," sometimes given as a chatter. Song of *striaticeps* different, a long (5–12 sec) series of rich, jerky, ringing warbles, starting softly and building until quite loud before ending abruptly. May be answered by a stuttered, metallic chatter. Call a rich "*tchit*." Song (*euophrys*) more an accelerating series of high, twittery chips that rises and falls, ending in a rapid high, metallic warble. Call a fast "*tititi*." **Co, E, Bo**

3 TWO-BANDED WARBLER *Basileuterus bivittatus* * 13.5–14 cm (5¼–5½ in)

Fairly common in southern Andes, in understory of humid forest and at forest edge, 750–1500 m, where may be associated with bamboo. Strikingly similar to more widespread Golden-bellied Warbler, but has yellow-green lores and broken yellow-green eyering; typically shows little or no yellow on superciliary, while dark stripes bordering crown are blacker. Where the two overlap, Two-banded has a higher elevational range; also differs in **VOICE** Song a deep, rich, accelerating warble, often in antiphonal duet, with some variation: "*churt-churt-churt-SEE-djidjidjidjew*" answered by "*ti-ti-ti-chip-djerditew*." Call a deep, rich "*djurt*," often in rapid stuttering chatter. **Br, Bo**

4 GOLDEN-BELLIED WARBLER *Basileuterus chrysogaster* * 13 cm (5 in)

Uncommon in understory of humid montane forest along east slope of Andes, 300–2000 m (but only up to 1250 m in south). In central Peru apparently is restricted to outlying ridges. In south, cf. Two-banded Warbler. Best distinguished by **VOICE** Song a series of loud, ringing, descending notes: "*tee tee chew chew CHEW CHEW CHEW*," reminiscent of song of Buff-rumped Warbler but quieter. Call a low, chattering "*tchep*," usually in rapid stuttered series. **Co, E, Bo**

5 BLACK-CRESTED WARBLER *Basileuterus nigrocristatus* 13.5 cm (5¼ in)

Fairly common in humid montane forest, *Chusquea* bamboo thickets, forest borders, and hedgerows in northwest, 1800–3300 m. Found along west slope of western Andes south to southern Cajamarca, and on both slopes of Marañón Valley. Some juvenile females (not illustrated) are green crowned; resemble Citrine Warbler (especially *luteoviridis* subspecies), but the two are not reported to overlap; also, juvenile Black-crested has greener, less distinct supercilaries and paler lores. **VOICE** Song a loud, accelerating, falling then rising series of musical notes ending on a louder note, for example: "*tik tik ter ter-ter-ti-ti-ti-TEW*." Call a dry "*tik*" or "*thk*." **Co, E**

6 GRAY-AND-GOLD WARBLER *Basileuterus fraseri* * 14 cm (5½ in)

Common in understory of dry forests on west slope of Andes in northwest, 400–1800 m. Only *Basileuterus* that is gray above. **VOICE** Song a melancholy series of ringing whistles, similar to song of Russet-crowned Warbler, for example: "*tu ti tu ti tur-JZEE-JZEEOO*." Calls a short "*tp*," a more musical "*cheet*," and a deep "*djrt*." **E**

signatus

PALE-LEGGED WARBLER

flavovirens

luteoviridis

striaticeps

euophrys

CITRINE WARBLER

TWO-BANDED
WARBLER

GOLDEN-BELLIED WARBLER

BLACK-CRESTED
WARBLER

GRAY-AND-GOLD
WARBLER

PLATE
295

WARBLERS, YELLOWTHROAT, AND WATERTHRUSH

Three-striped, Russet-crowned, and Three-banded are warblers of Andean forest understory. Masked Yellowthroat is found in scrub and forest edge. Northern Waterthrush and Connecticut Warbler are very rare boreal migrants. Buff-rumped Warbler is a mostly terrestrial warbler of Amazonian stream margins.

1 THREE-BANDED WARBLER *Basileuterus trifasciatus* * 12.5 cm (5 in)

Fairly common in understory of dry and humid forests, and forest edge, on west slope of Andes in northwest, 650–3000 m. Locally overlaps with gray-bellied subspecies of Russet-crowned Warbler; no overlap with Three-striped Warbler. **VOICE** Song very similar to song of Three-striped, but perhaps a little weaker, less strident. Calls a metallic "*twit*," a high "*ti*" and a buzzy "*dzr*," sometimes given as a chatter. **E**

2 THREE-STRIPED WARBLER *Basileuterus tristriatus* * 13 cm (5 in)

This active, excitable warbler is common and widespread in understory of humid montane forest along east slope of Andes, 1050–2200 m. Widespread, yellow-bellied subspecies *tristriatus* is replaced in Puno by paler *inconspicuus*. **VOICE** Song loud, high, ringing, rising crescendo of chipping notes, usually with weaker terminal notes. Sometimes in duet, the second bird (female only?) gives a more jerky series of high, ringing chips in a random pattern. Call a high series of "*ti*" notes, often in an accelerated series when excited. **Co, E, Bo**

3 RUSSET-CROWNED WARBLER *Basileuterus coronatus* * 14 cm (5½ in)

Common and widespread in understory of humid montane forest in Andes, 1500–2900 m, locally down to 1100 m and up to 3150 m. Note gray head with rufous crown, and black stripes bordering crown and through the eyes. Color of underparts geographically variable: light gray (both slopes of Andes, north and west of Marañón Valley) or yellow (east slope of Andes, south of Marañón to Bolivia). **VOICE** Song (all northern populations, including both gray- and yellow-bellied subspecies), often given in antiphonal duet, a loud, strong, melancholy series of slightly burry, ringing whistles that normally rise at the end. Call deep growled "*grr*" or "*djrt*" notes, often in rapid series. Song (Cuzco south; *notius*), also often in antiphonal duet, a thinner, higher series of soft notes ending in a long ringing note: "*tee-lee-teeZJEEEE.*" Call a higher, thinner "*djit.*" **Co, E, Bo**

4 MASKED YELLOWTHROAT *Geothlypis aequinoctialis* * 13–14 cm (5–5½ in)

Fairly common in northwest; continues, less commonly, south along coast to Ica (*auricularis*) and into middle and upper Marañón Valley up to 2700 m (*peruviana*); also in southern Amazonia and in intermontane valleys locally up to 2200 m (*velata*), where may be only an austral migrant. Found low in grassy undergrowth at forest edge and (Amazonia) in river-edge scrub. Male has gray crown and black mask (mask more extensive in *velata*). Duller female largely yellow; cf. smaller Subtropical Doradito. **VOICE** Primary song a variable rich, lilting warbled series that accelerates and descends in pitch, for example: "*dree chree-chee-chee'chi'chur'di.*" Aggressive song a high, descending, chippering whinny. Calls include a wheezy "*rhee?*" and a trisyllabic, wheezy "*dew-djee'ew.*" **Co, E, Br, Bo**

NORTHERN WATERTHRUSH *Seiurus noveboracensis* 14 cm (5½ in)

Rare boreal migrant. One record from Lima; reported also from northern Amazonia, where possibly regular in small numbers. Solitary. Walks on the ground under cover, almost always near water (streams, lake margins or swamps). Posture horizontal, and frequently teeters the body up and down. Cf. Ringed Antpipit. **VOICE** Call a metallic "*chink*"; flight call a buzzy "*zeep.*" **Co, E, Br**

CONNECTICUT WARBLER *Oporornis agilis* 14 cm (5½ in)

Rare boreal migrant to eastern Amazonia; probably only as passage migrant (the few records all are from Nov). Solitary. Walks on or near the ground in dense cover. Note hooded appearance and distinct white eyering. **VOICE** Call a sharp, squeaky "*wheep!*" Flight call a high "*tsit.*" **Co, E, Br, Bo**

5 BUFF-RUMPED WARBLER *Phaeothlypis fulvicauda* * 13.5 cm (5¼ in)

Fairly common and widespread in Amazonia, up to 1200 m. Singles or pairs forage along the margins of streams and rivers in forested areas; does not venture far into the open. Hops on the ground at or near water's edge, frequently with tail fanned. **VOICE** Song a loud, musical, ringing series that grows louder towards the end: "*tee tee pit-it-chewchewCHEWCHEWCHEW!*" Call a metallic "*chink.*" **Co, E, Br, Bo**

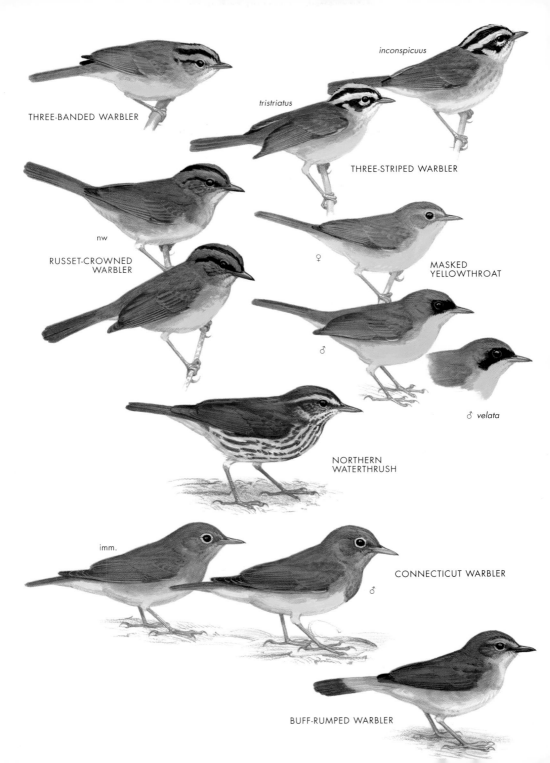

THREE-BANDED WARBLER

inconspicuus

tristriatus

THREE-STRIPED WARBLER

nw

RUSSET-CROWNED
WARBLER

♀

MASKED
YELLOWTHROAT

♂

♂ *velata*

NORTHERN
WATERTHRUSH

imm.

♂

CONNECTICUT WARBLER

BUFF-RUMPED WARBLER

PLATE
296

OROPENDOLAS

Oropendolas are large blackbirds that breed colonially; clusters of long, pendant oropendola nests hanging from a large tree are a common sight in Amazonia. Often forage in flocks, of single species or with other oropendolas, caciques and jays, in the mid- and upper levels of the forest and at forest edge. Larger species fly with deep, steady wingbeats. Males significantly larger than females. See also plate 297.

1 DUSKY-GREEN OROPENDOLA *Psarocolius atrovirens* male 41–43 cm (16–17 in), female 33 cm (13 in)

Fairly common on east slope of central and southern Andes, at 800–2600 m, in humid montane forest, especially at forest edge. Similar to Andean subspecies (*alfredi*) of Russet-backed Oropendola, but slightly smaller, more olive, and more even-colored; also, usually lacks a yellow forecrown (although present in some adults and all juveniles). **VOICE** Song a gurgled phrase that is often repetitive or stuttering and contains a harsh quality, variable, for example: "*hu-DJAW-DJAW hu-DJAW-DJAW*" or "*cu-cu-dzz-dzz-CAW-zzCAW*." Usually falls forward on perch while singing, raising wings and flaring crest. Calls a squeaky "*chik*" or "*chuk*" and a rising "*chew-y?*" **Bo**

2 RUSSET-BACKED OROPENDOLA *Psarocolius angustifrons* * male 44–48 cm (17¼–19 in), female 34.5–38 cm (13½–15 in)

One of most common, widespread oropendolas. Fairly common throughout Amazonia (although perhaps scarcer on immediate south bank of Amazon) and on east slopes of Andes, up to 2000 m. Mostly dull brown with rufescent rump, and olive tone to head. In northern lowlands is browner overall and bill black (*angustifrons*). Greener, pale-billed *alfredi* of Andes also extends into southern Amazonia, north at least to northern Ucayali. **VOICE** Song a gurgle followed by a liquid trill, variable, for example: "*gluglu-TZZZ'CHUI.*" Usually falls forward on perch while singing, raising wings and flaring crest. Calls a hollow "*C'LAK,*" "*cak,*" and mewing "*eww.*" **Co, E, Br, Bo**

3 CASQUED OROPENDOLA *Clypicterus oseryi* male 36–38 cm (14–15 in), female 28–29.5 cm (11–11½ in)

Uncommon to locally fairly common in humid forest up to 1000 m. Typically in forest interior, not foraging at forest edge or in second growth as do most other oropendolas. Note relatively small size, contrast between russet brown upperparts and olive throat and breast, and relatively short bill with noticeably swollen casque. **VOICE** Song a descending loud, electric, buzzing "*tok'DJZZEEEEEEROP.*" Calls a reedy "*dzeer,*" querulous "*chewy,*" and a low "*chup.*" **Co, E, Br, Bo**

4 GREEN OROPENDOLA *Psarocolius viridis* male 46–49 cm (18–19¼ in), female 37–38 cm (14½–15 in)

Rare to locally fairly common in northern Amazonia; also local in central Peru, near base of Andes. Much more olive than Russet-backed, with pale (not black) bill. Similar to larger Olive Oropendola, but note mostly pale (not mostly dark) bill, and feathered cheeks. **VOICE** Song a variable, accelerating series of liquid bubbling, sometimes ending in a quavering, liquid hooting phrase, for example: "*glug-ug-ug'ug'ug'OP'wuubawuub.*" Some songs possibly indistinguishable from song of Crested Oropendola. Call a harsh "*chu'uk.*" **Co, E, Br, Bo**

5 CRESTED OROPENDOLA *Psarocolius decumanus* * male 46–47.5 cm (18–18¾ in), female 36–37 cm (14¼–14½ in)

Fairly common and widespread in Amazonia, up to 1200 m, primarily in river-edge forest and second growth. Less often in flocks than other oropendolas. Very dark, with contrasting pale bill and iris. South of Amazon may show a few pale yellow feathers scattered through plumage (*maculosus*); some individuals all but lack such yellow spotting, as does northern *decumanus*. **VOICE** Song a variable, descending, rattling gurgle, usually ending in a quavering liquid hooting phrase, then sometimes some rustling sounds (from wings?), for example: "*glug'te'e'e'e'e'er'OP wuubuubuub.*" Usually falls forward on perch while singing, raising wings and flaring crest. Call a hard "*chuk.*" **Co, E, Br, Bo**

6 OLIVE OROPENDOLA *Psarocolius bifasciatus* * male 47.5–52 cm (18¾–20½ in), female 41–43 cm (16–17 in)

Largest oropendola. Fairly common and widespread in Amazonia, below 1000 m. Olive and russet, with dark, bicolored bill and large bare patch of exposed pink skin on side of face. **VOICE** Song a long series of descending, gurgling, bubbling notes ending in a loud, quavering note, like someone pouring water from a jug: "*gr-r-r-r-r-GWO'WOH.*" Usually falls forward on perch while singing, raising wings and flaring crest. Call a harsh "*chuk.*" **Co, E, Br, Bo**

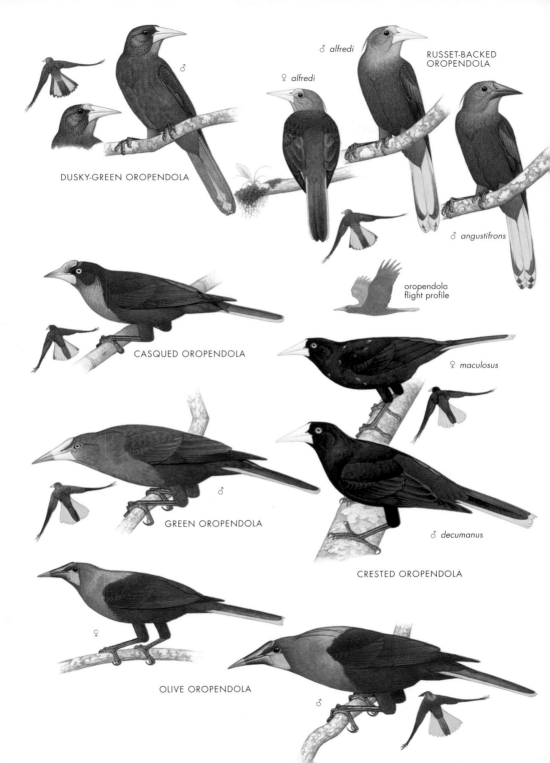

DUSKY-GREEN OROPENDOLA

♂

♀ alfredi

♂ alfredi

RUSSET-BACKED OROPENDOLA

♂ angustifrons

CASQUED OROPENDOLA

oropendola flight profile

♀ maculosus

GREEN OROPENDOLA

♂

♂ decumanus

CRESTED OROPENDOLA

OLIVE OROPENDOLA

♀

♂

PLATE
297

BAND-TAILED OROPENDOLA AND CACIQUES

Band-tailed is a small oropendola. Caciques resemble small oropendolas. Most have large hanging nests, but nest of Yellow-billed Cacique only a cup. Most caciques forage in midstory and canopy.

1 BAND-TAILED OROPENDOLA *Ocyalus latirostris* male 32.5–33.5 cm (12¾–13¼ in), female 25–26 cm (9¾–10¼ in)

Uncommon, in varzea of northern Amazonia. Tail less strongly graduated than that of other oropendolas. Small; almost size of Yellow-rumped Cacique, but lacks yellow in wings and on rump. Central two pairs of rectrices black, others yellow, tipped black; tail appears mostly yellow from below. Bill color variable (seasonally?). **VOICE** Song a fairly short twanging "*ka'CHAWWW*" or "*CHOOO*" interspersed with higher rusty squeaks. Little or no accompanying display. Calls rich, throaty "*g'luck*," "*rhaw*," and "*chaw*" notes. **Co, E, Br**

2 YELLOW-RUMPED CACIQUE *Cacicus cela* * male 27–29 cm (10½–11¼ in), female 23–25 cm (9–9¾ in)

One of most characteristic Amazonian birds (*cela*); up to 1300 m, in forest, at forest edge, in clearings and towns. Also rare in evergreen forest in Tumbes (*flavicrissus*; not illustrated) below 750 m; shows less yellow at base of tail and on wing coverts, and bill is darker. **VOICE** Song (*cela*) a series of toots, whistles, and gravelly sounds mixed with mimicry (of birds, frogs, insects, and human-made sounds). Frequent phrase a querulous mewing "*dJEERu dJEERu-wer*." Varied calls include a grinding "*juRIK*," and a harsh "*chack!*" Song (*flavicrissus*) a series of honking whistles and squeaks, for example: "*HEUU clunka-cloo*"; may be repeated many times. Not known to mimic. Call a "*chleck*." **Co, E, Br, Bo**

3 YELLOW-BILLED CACIQUE *Amblycercus holosericeus* * male 23.5 cm (9¼ in), female 22 cm (8½ in)

Fairly common in humid montane forest along east slope of Andes, 2100–3350 m. Also uncommon in semideciduous forest in Tumbes below 750 m. Forages as singles or pairs in dense forest understory; in Andes often in *Chusquea* bamboo. May join mixed-species flocks. **VOICE** Song a variable, loud rich whistling, for example: "*HEE-HOO HEE-HOO HEE-HOO*." Call a quiet, throaty chucking sound, sometimes in short chattered series. **Co, E, Bo**

4 SELVA CACIQUE *Cacicus koepckeae* 23 cm (9 in)

Rare, poorly known. Similar in behavior to Ecuadorian Cacique, which it replaces geographically in southeastern Peru. Small, black with yellow rump. Most common in river-edge or varzea forest, where forages as singles, pairs or small groups in the canopy. No overlap with larger Mountain Cacique of Andes. **VOICE** Call repetitive series of notes, for example: "*tchi-CHIRP tchi-CHIRP tchi-CHIRP....*" May be lengthened, often in duet, into a "*CHEEP-CHEEP ur-chewchew CHEEP-CHEEP ur-chewchew …*"; reminiscent of Troupial, but less musical, more metallic, louder. **ENDEMIC**

5 MOUNTAIN CACIQUE *Cacicus chrysonotus* * male 29.5–30.5 cm (11½–12 in), female 24–25 cm (9½–9¾ in)

Fairly common in humid montane forest along east slope of Andes, 1800–3450 m. Black with yellow rump. Wing coverts extensively yellow in north; may hybridize with black-winged, southern *chrysonotus* in Junín. **VOICE** Song variable, includes squeaky honking, similar to Dusky-green Oropendola, but quieter, and often interspersed with calls, also grating sounds. Varied calls include a reedy "*wek-wek-wek-wek*," "*eewer-kee-kee-kee-kee*," and a squeaky, honking "*UBEE keek-KEYR*." **Co, E, Bo**

6 SCARLET-RUMPED CACIQUE *Cacicus uropygialis* * male 28–30.5 cm (11–12 in), female 25–25.5 cm (9¾–10 in)

Uncommon in humid montane forest along east slope of Andes and on outlying ridges, 900–1900 m. Forages in mid- and upper story of forest interior. Cf. Red-rumped Cacique of Amazonia. **VOICE** Song a series of loud screeches and ringing gurgles. Varied calls include a musical "*churLEEur*," a reedy "*weee-wee-wee*," and a short "*er*." **Co, E**

7 RED-RUMPED CACIQUE *Cacicus haemorrhous* * male 27.5–28.5 cm (10¾–11¼ in), female 22.5–23.5 cm (8¾–9 in)

Uncommon, local, in Amazonia, below 1000 m. Forages in varzea, and at margins of oxbow lakes and in river-edge forest. Red rump conspicuous in flight but may be concealed at rest; cf. Solitary Black Cacique. Little or no overlap with Scarlet-rumped Cacique; also, has more extensive red on rump and lower back, base of bill often swollen, and tail has slight notch at tip. **VOICE** Song like that of *cela* Yellow-rumped Cacique, but softer and without mimicry. Call a harsh "*chack*." **Co, E, Br, Bo**

BAND-TAILED
OROPENDOLA

♂

dark-billed
variant

♀

YELLOW-RUMPED
CACIQUE

♀

♂

YELLOW-BILLED CACIQUE

MOUNTAIN CACIQUE

n

SELVA CACIQUE

chrysonotus

RED-RUMPED CACIQUE

SCARLET-RUMPED CACIQUE

PLATE
298

COWBIRDS, GRACKLE, AND BLACK
BLACKBIRDS

A varied set of blackbirds, with little in common except for entirely black plumage (at least in males). Cowbirds are brood parasites; females lay eggs in nests of other species. Giant Cowbird parasitizes caciques and oropendolas; Shiny Cowbird parasitizes a wide range of passerines.

1 GIANT COWBIRD Molothrus oryzivorus * male 34–35 cm (13¼–13¾ in); female 30 cm (12 in)

Fairly common in Amazonia, up to 900 m, locally up to 1200 m; also uncommon in Tumbes below 400 m. Found at forest edge, and along rivers and lakes. Forages both in trees and on ground; often seen on sandbars and at river margins. Very large, but female smaller and duller, and lacks male's neck ruff. Iris usually pale, but may be red or brown. Solitary or in small groups. Undulates in flight with wings folded between bouts of flapping. **VOICE** Song series of high-pitched rusty screeches and creaks, like unoiled hinges. Call a dull "chuck." **Co, E, Br, Bo**

2 SHINY COWBIRD Molothrus bonariensis * 19–21 cm (7½–8¼ in)

Common in open areas (agricultural fields, forest edges) on coast, mostly below 700 m, but to 2900 m in Marañón Valley (occidentalis); formerly absent in southwest but now invading that region. Often in flocks. Rare to uncommon in Amazonia (riparius), primarily along rivers, mostly below 500 m. Compare male to Scrub Blackbird. Female riparius similar to male but duller. Female occidentalis drab gray, lightly streaked; juvenile similar, but more olive, more heavily streaked. **VOICE** Song, often delivered in flight, a musical series of thin whistles followed by high tinkling and liquid warbles. Call of female a reedy chatter. **Co, E, Br, Bo, Ch**

3 CHOPI BLACKBIRD Gnorimopsar chopi * 23–24 cm (9–9½ in)

Only on Pampas del Heath. Small flocks forage in savanna with scattered woodlots. Grooves on base of mandible not evident in field. Larger than Shiny Cowbird, with longer bill; also lacks glossy blue sheen of male cowbird. **VOICE** Song, incessant, a loud series of rich slurred whistles and short buzzy notes. Calls whistled "hee," "hew," and low "chuck" notes. **Br, Bo**

4 SCRUB BLACKBIRD Dives warszewiczi * warszewiczi 22 cm (9 in); kalinowskii male 30–31 cm (11¼–12¼ in), female 27–29 cm (10¾–11½ in)

Fairly common in dry scrub, fields, and gardens west of Andes, up to 2400 m, locally to 3600 m; also local in dry intermontane valleys. Forages in small groups, on ground. Larger, duller (less glossy) than male Shiny Cowbird, with longer bill and legs, and different vocalizations. Northern warszewiczi (south to northern La Libertad) smaller than more widespread kalinowskii. **VOICE** Song variable, usually in duet, an explosive series of loud liquid notes, some with harsher quality, for example: "hooEE triZEER chee-t't't't't." Usually fluffs up plumage, sky-points with bill, and bows as sings. Calls a rising "ree?," also a piercing, descending "teee." **Co, E**

5 ECUADORIAN CACIQUE Cacicus slateri male 23–23.5 cm (9–9¼ in), female 19.5–20 cm (7¾–8 in)

Rare to locally fairly common in northern Amazonia, south at least to south bank of the Marañón (Pacaya-Samiria). Relatively inconspicuous; singles or pairs forage in canopy of varzea or at forest edge. Cf. Solitary Black and Red-rumped caciques. **VOICE** Song a short, musical gurgle: "wu wu CHILEEONG." Calls a metallic "ching," a lower "chik," and a repetitive "cur-chik cur-chik…." **Co, E**

6 VELVET-FRONTED GRACKLE Lampropsar tanagrinus * male 21.5–22 cm (8½–8¾ in), female 19–19.5 cm (7½–7¾ in)

Uncommon in varzea in northern and central Amazonia. Forages in small flocks in canopy. Cf. Red-rumped, Ecuadorian, and Solitary Black caciques. **VOICE** Song a short, rapid nasal bubbling series, for example: "tootuCHEW," sometimes with more introductory notes. Calls low, harsh "chuck" and "tchk" notes. **Co, E, Br, Bo**

7 SOLITARY BLACK CACIQUE Cacicus solitarius male 27 cm (10¾ in), female 23 cm (9 in)

Uncommon but widespread in Amazonia, up to 900 m, locally to 1300 m. Dense understory of varzea, margins of oxbow lakes. Not colonial; singles or pairs remain low within dense cover. Note dark iris (pale in other caciques). **VOICE** Song variable, contains liquid whistles, churrs, squeaks, trills, squawks, and other cries, usually starting with quiet liquid hooting, for example: "hoop-hoop-hoop TZEE-ONG!" Phrases usually repeated several times. Call a characteristic wheezy "bwah!" **Co, E, Br, Bo**

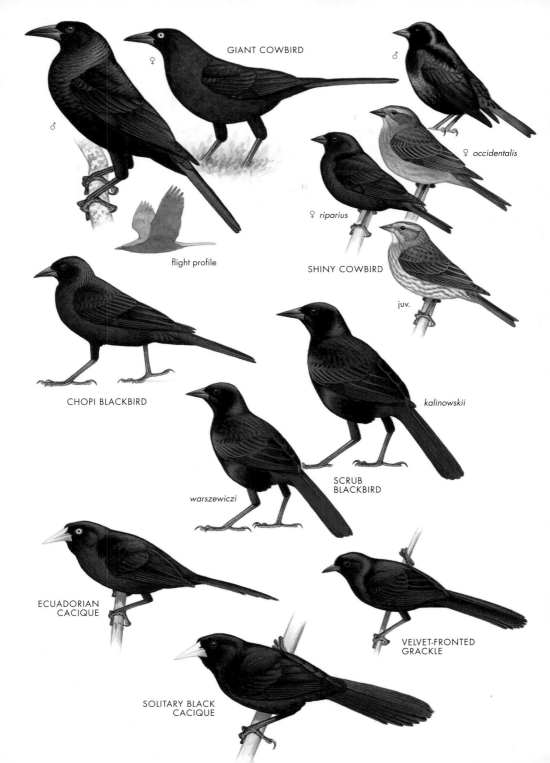

GIANT COWBIRD

♂

♀

♂

♀ *occidentalis*

♀ *riparius*

flight profile

SHINY COWBIRD

juv.

CHOPI BLACKBIRD

kalinowskii

SCRUB
BLACKBIRD

warszewiczi

ECUADORIAN
CACIQUE

VELVET-FRONTED
GRACKLE

SOLITARY BLACK
CACIQUE

PLATE
299

ORIOLES, TROUPIAL, GRACKLE, AND
ORIOLE BLACKBIRD

Orioles (including Troupial) are slender, long-tailed arboreal blackbirds. Great-tailed Grackle is a very long-tailed blackbird, found only in mangroves in the far northwest. Oriole Blackbird is a distinctive bird associated with water in eastern lowlands.

1 WHITE-EDGED ORIOLE *Icterus graceannae* 20.5–21 cm (8–8¼ in)

Fairly common in northwest, locally up to 1800 m, where is the most common oriole. Found in dry forest and in tall desert scrub. Shorter-tailed than Yellow-tailed Oriole; also readily distinguished by the white inner remiges, clearly separated from the yellow "wedge" on wing coverts, and by white-margined outer rectrices. Juvenile duller, lacking yellow wing coverts; older immatures (not illustrated) more similar to adults, but underparts paler yellow, back olive. **VOICE** Song a peculiar, repeated series of nasal, throaty warbles interspersed with calls. Calls a rhythmic, loud "*chiwer-chup chiwer-chup chiwer-chup…*," also a ringing "*blink*" and musical "*chewer.*" **E**

2 MORICHE ORIOLE *Icterus chrysocephalus* 20.5–21 cm (8–8¼ in)

Fairly common in northern Amazonia, up to 1500 m. Largely replaces Epaulet Oriole geographically, but the two locally overlap between the middle Huallaga and Ucayali rivers, and north of Amazon near Iquitos. Singles or pairs forage in canopy at forest edge and along rivers, often in palm fronds. Joins mixed-species flocks but often forages apart. **VOICE** Probably indistinguishable from Epaulet Oriole. Also beware of similarity to some euphonias. **Co, E, Br**

3 EPAULET ORIOLE *Icterus cayanensis* * 20.5–21 cm (8–8¼ in)

Fairly common and widespread in Amazonia, up to 1200 m. Found in canopy at forest edge, and at the edge of oxbow lakes and along rivers. Mostly occurs south of the Amazon, but local on north bank near Iquitos. Very slender and long-tailed. Usually forages as singles or as pairs, apart or sometimes with mixed-species flocks. **VOICE** Song, usually given from an exposed perch, a disjointed series of whistles, chips, growls, and trills; extremely variable, often a repeated series of euphonia-like whistles and short chips and other notes, for example: "*wheet chip-er… wheet chip-er….*" May include some mimicry. Calls a slightly metallic "*chep*," a low "*chu-chuk.*" **Br, Bo**

4 YELLOW-TAILED ORIOLE *Icterus mesomelas* * 21.5–22 cm (8½–8¾ in)

Uncommon in dry forest and scrub in northwest below 1700 m; also in Marañón Valley, where perhaps more common. Juvenile duller, with little or no black on throat or yellow on wing coverts. Older immatures (not illustrated) similar to adults, but central rectrices olive, back olive, or olive mixed with black. Cf. White-edged Oriole. **VOICE** Song, often a synchronized duet, a variable, rhythmic series of rich, deep whistles, for example: "*cup-cu-HEERAY cup-cu-HEERAY cup-cu-HEERAY….*" Call a rich "*chirp.*" **Co, E**

5 TROUPIAL *Icterus icterus* * 23–23.5 cm (9–9¼ in)

Unmistakable in Amazonia, where fairly common and widespread, below 1100 m. Found in river-edge forest, forest edge, and in second growth (especially near rivers). Seen singly or in pairs; does not associate with mixed-species flocks. Appropriates the nest of other species, often of Yellow-rumped Cacique. **VOICE** Song a variable, lazy series of 2 or 3 mellow whistles that usually follow a repetitive pattern, for example: "*too HUUEET? ti… too HUUEET? ti….*" Call a rich, musical "*turp.*" **Co, E, Br, Bo**

6 GREAT-TAILED GRACKLE *Quiscalus mexicanus* * male 43–46 cm (17–18 in), female 32–34 cm (12½–13½ in)

Fairly common but restricted to mangrove thickets. Noisy and bold. Often in flocks, feeding on the ground on mudflats. Note pale eye, and long tail and legs. **VOICE** Song a loud series of rising whistles, squeals, chatters, dry scratching sounds, and quavering electric sounds. Call a loud "*chuck.*" Begging young give a reedy "*rheep*" or "*jheep.*" **Co, E**

7 ORIOLE BLACKBIRD *Gymnomystax mexicanus* male 30.5 cm (12 in), female 26.5 cm (10½ in)

Fairly common in northern Amazonia. Found in open habitats near rivers, such as low grassy growth on river islands and riverbanks, marshes, and pastures (especially damp pastures or near water), locally up to 1000 m. Forages on or near the ground, often in small groups; also perches high in snags. Juvenile has black cap. **VOICE** Song, often in chorus, a harsh, nasal, repeated "*djzzzarh,*" sometimes followed by a more musical "*clu-clu,*" and interspersed with calls. Calls a loud, descending, whistled "*cheeeru,*" a quiet "*cluck,*" and a metallic "*chink.*" **Co, E, Br**

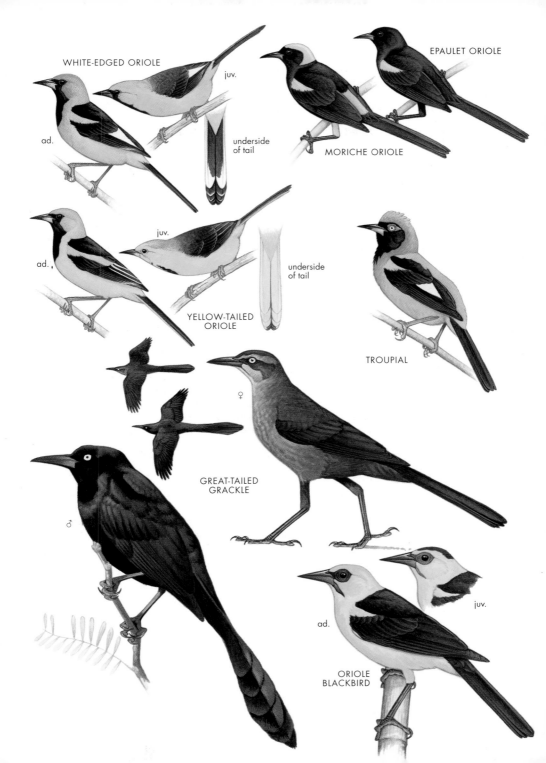

WHITE-EDGED ORIOLE

juv.

ad.

underside
of tail

EPAULET ORIOLE

MORICHE ORIOLE

ad.,

juv.

underside
of tail

YELLOW-TAILED
ORIOLE

TROUPIAL

♀

GREAT-TAILED
GRACKLE

♂

ad.

juv.

ORIOLE
BLACKBIRD

PLATE
300

BOBOLINK, MARSH BLACKBIRDS, AND MEADOWLARKS

Bobolink is a short-billed blackbird. Marsh blackbirds (Chrysomus, Agelasticus) are medium-sized, slender blackbirds of aquatic habitats. Meadowlarks (Sturnella) forage on the ground in fields and pastures. When not breeding, may travel in single species flocks. In most species on this plate (with possible exception of Pale-eyed Blackbird), feathers of male in fresh plumage tipped with buff or greenish buff; plumage becomes darker as pale tips wear off.

1 BOBOLINK *Dolichonyx oryzivorus* 17–18 cm (6¾–7 in)
Boreal migrant in grasslands and open second growth. Uncommon in Amazonia, rare on coast; mostly in lowlands, but recorded to 3450 m. Present Sep–Apr; probably primarily a passage migrant (Oct–Nov, Mar–Apr) but small numbers overwinter north at least to Lima and Junín. Note short pink bill, short spiky tail, and pointed wingtips. Streaked, sparrowlike plumage of female, male (basic plumage), and immature similar, although immature is more richly colored. Male in Mar–Apr may show black-and-white alternate plumage, heavily scaled with buff feather tips, and a duskier bill. **VOICE** Call, often given in flight, a wheezy rising *"fink."* **Co, E, Br, Bo, Ch**

2 YELLOW-HOODED BLACKBIRD *Chrysomus icterocephalus* * 17–18 cm (6¾–7 in)
Uncommon to locally fairly common; in small flocks in marshes bordering lakes and rivers in northern Amazonia. Also a feral population in some coastal marshes in Lima. Immature male similar to female, but throat brighter yellow; wings blacker; and may have scattered black on underparts. **VOICE** Song a series of slurred rasps, rusty squeaks, and thin, descending buzzes interspersed with occasional series of descending, musical notes: *"chee-chee-chee."* Call a reedy *"chimp."* **Co, Br**

3 PALE-EYED BLACKBIRD *Agelasticus xanthophthalmus* 20.5 cm (8 in)
Rare and local, in marshes and grassy margins of oxbow lakes; apparently prefers sites with floating marsh grasses, and shrubs that protrude above grasses. Does not flock; singles or pairs remain close to cover. Sexes alike. Juveniles (not illustrated) largely brown above, streaked brown and buff below. **VOICE** Song a short series of sweet rising or descending whistles, *"tew tew tew,"* or a more rapid rattled series of liquid chips: *"ti'ti'ti'ti'ti'ti."* Calls a dry *"chep"* and a reedy *"chirh,"* sometimes in series. **E**

4 YELLOW-WINGED BLACKBIRD *Agelasticus thilius* * 18–18.5 cm (7–7¼ in)
Fairly common to common in marshes bordering Andean lakes in south, 3300–4200 m. Also may feed in adjacent pastures. Yellow shoulder of male may be concealed at rest. Immature male similar to female, but blacker; also may have conspicuous superciliary. **VOICE** Song a variable series of loud wheezy mews, slurred whistles, and trills, for example *"whew chee- ZZEEW,"* or a series of descending clear whistles *"tew-tew-tew-tew."* Call a reedy *"chimp."* **Br, Bo, Ch**

5 RED-BREASTED BLACKBIRD *Sturnella militaris* 19 cm (7½ in)
Fairly common but local in Amazonia; distribution expanding as more forest is converted to open habitats. Compare streaked female to Bobolink (female). Cf. White-browed Blackbird. **VOICE** Song a variable series of high, rusty screeches and buzzes, for example: *"chew-TEEK'bzzzzzzzzzz."* Calls a quiet, wheezy *"rhe"*; also a sputtered series of ringing notes in flight (female only?): *"pee-ti'ti'ti'ti."* **Co, E, Br, Bo**

6 WHITE-BROWED BLACKBIRD *Sturnella superciliaris* 18 cm (7 in)
Rare austral migrant to southeast, up to 700 m. Much like Red-breasted Blackbird; use great care to distinguish the 2 species. Male White-browed always shows a prominent, well-defined superciliary. Male Red-breasted, in fresh plumage, also may show a superciliary, although it is less contrasty, grayer (not buff or white), and usually has internal dusky flecks. Bill of White-browed averages slightly shorter, stouter; but extremely similar females probably are not safely distinguishable in the field. **VOICE** Probably indistinguishable from Red-breasted. **Br, Bo, Ch**

7 PERUVIAN MEADOWLARK *Sturnella bellicosa* * 20.5 cm (8 in)
Fairly common to common along coast, and in Marañón and upper Huallaga valleys, up to 2800 m. No known overlap with Red-breasted or White-browed blackbirds, which also are smaller, have shorter bills, and dark (not white) underwing coverts; males of both also lack red lores and have black (not brown) wings. **VOICE** Song, variable in pattern, a pleasant series of high, thin whistles and buzzy notes, for example: *"heeu deer-tu-DZZZZZZZ."* Song longer, more elaborate in skylarking song flight. Calls a buzzy *"dzzt,"* a low *"chup,"* and *"chep."* **E, Ch**

♂ fresh alt.

BOBOLINK

♀

YELLOW-HOODED
BLACKBIRD

♀

♂

imm. ♂

PALE-EYED BLACKBIRD

♀

♂

YELLOW-WINGED
BLACKBIRD

imm. ♂

♂ worn plumage

♀

RED-BREASTED
BLACKBIRD

♂ fresh plumage

♂

WHITE-BROWED
BLACKBIRD

♀

PERUVIAN
MEADOWLARK

♂ worn
plumage

♂ fresh plumage

♀

PLATE
301

SISKINS

Siskins are small finches of montane scrub, parks and gardens, forest edge, and other open habitats. Often in flocks, usually of a single species but of sometimes of mixed siskin species. Songs similar across the genus; songs of some (and possibly all) also incorporate mimicked phrases. Frequently call in flight.

1 THICK-BILLED SISKIN *Carduelis crassirostris* * 14 cm (5½ in)

Rare to uncommon. Most frequent in *Polylepis* woods and scrub at 3600–4600 m, occasionally in other montane scrub. A large siskin with thick bill (showing more extensive silvery at base than Hooded Siskin), restricted amount of yellow in tail, and narrow but elongate yellow speculum on outer primaries (comparable speculum is broader, and somewhat shorter, in Hooded). Also note whitish belly and grayish flanks of adult male. Larger duller *amadoni* occurs from Cuzco and Arequipa south; a smaller, more brightly colored undescribed subspecies occurs from Ancash south to Ayacucho. Female is mostly gray, with yellow restricted to wing; hood may be dark gray (*amadoni*), accented by pale sides to neck, or scarcely apparent. Immature male similar to female but has duskier hood. **VOICE** Calls a wheezy "*hew-li?*," a mewing "*rhee?*," and a low chatter. **Bo, Ch**

2 YELLOW-RUMPED SISKIN *Carduelis uropygialis* 13–14 cm (5–5½ in)

Rare, in montane scrub at 3200–4200 m in western Andes and in southern Titicaca Basin. Sexes similar; note large size and contrast between dusky olive back and yellow rump. Reportedly may hybridize locally with other species (Hooded Siskin?), but this has not been studied in detail. **VOICE** Calls a rising "*rhee.*" **Bo, Ch**

3 HOODED SISKIN *Carduelis magellanica* * 10.5–12 cm (4¼–4¾ in)

The most widespread and common siskin, sea level up to 4200 m. Common on coast (although local in north), west slope of Andes, and in intermontane valleys; uncommon on humid east-facing slope of Andes; rarely below 2000 m on east slope of northern Andes but in south descends to 400 m. A medium-sized to small siskin with yellow obvious in base of tail and a short but broad yellow primary patch. Size variable; birds in the northwest are small, the largest populations may be those in Cuzco and Puno. Hooded Siskin should be learned well as a basis for comparison to other species. Unfortunately, plumages confusingly variable; patterns of variation (geographic, seasonal, or individual) not well known, and perhaps are complicated by nomadic or seasonal movements of some populations. Male varies in overall color tone. In particular, color of back ranges from bright yellow-green to dull olive; rump usually yellow or yellowish green, but on some individuals rump shows little or no contrast to back. Back usually mottled with dusky, but mottling can be faint. Male always has yellow belly, and white edges to tertials. Females apparently occur in 2 morphs, gray and yellow. **VOICE** Song a rich, rapid jumble of wheezy notes and warbles. Calls a wheezy descending "*rheer*," rising "*see-lu?*," and low chatter. **Co, E, Br, Bo, Ch**

4 SAFFRON SISKIN *Carduelis siemiradzkii* 10 cm (4 in)

Uncommon. Restricted to semideciduous and evergreen forests and forest edge in Tumbes below 750 m. Very similar to the slightly larger Hooded Siskin; difficult to identify, even in the hand (but there is no documented overlap of the 2 species). Male yellower above, bright brownish yellow rather than olive or yellow-green; generally lacks dark mottling (but subtle mottling may be present, and mottling of Hooded sometimes difficult to see). Underparts and rump may average deeper yellow (but this subtle color difference rarely apparent in the field). Female similar to yellow-morph female Hooded; perhaps not identifiable in the field by plumage characters. **VOICE** Calls a descending "*p'seer*," also low chatters. **E**

5 OLIVACEOUS SISKIN *Carduelis olivacea* 10–11 cm (4–4¼ in)

Uncommon along east slope of Andes, 1100–2500 m; more associated with humid montane forest and forest edge than is similar Hooded Siskin. Underparts of both sexes light olive or strongly washed with olive. Tertials also have no pale margins, or have narrow gray margins; margins of the tertials of Hooded typically are broad and are whiter (but beware of Hoodeds with severely worn remiges, on which the white margins may be narrow, or even completely worn away). **VOICE** Calls a wheezy "*rhee?*," a sharp descending "*see*," and a low chatter. **Co, E, Bo**

imm. ♂ *amadoni*

♂ undescribed subsp.

THICK-BILLED SISKIN

THICK-BILLED SISKIN

♂ *amadoni*

♀ undescribed subsp.

♀ *amadoni*

♀ yellow morph

subad. ♂

YELLOW-RUMPED SISKIN

♂

♀ gray morph

HOODED SISKIN

SAFFRON SISKIN

♀

OLIVACEOUS SISKIN

♂

♂

♀

PLATE
302
BLACK-BACKED SISKINS, GOLDFINCH, AND CHLOROPHONIAS

The two siskins on this plate are the blackest species; Yellow-bellied Siskin is very restricted geographically, whereas Black Siskin is widespread in high Andes. See also plate 301. Lesser Goldfinch similar to siskins, but usually in singles or pairs (not in flocks). Euphonias (plates 303, 304) and chlorophonias are small, short-tailed finches of forest canopy and edge. Highly frugivorous, specializing on mistletoe berries. Often in pairs or small groups, sometimes with mixed-species flocks. Nest domed, with side entrance.

1 YELLOW-BELLIED SISKIN *Carduelis xanthogastra* * 10.5–11.5 cm (4¼–4½ in)

Very local. Rare to uncommon at edge of humid montane forest on east slope of Andes in south at 2000 m (*stejnegeri*). Also reported from evergreen forest edge in Tumbes at 750–950 m (*xanthogastra*). Males black with yellow lower breast and belly and yellow wing and tail markings. Other blackish siskins (Yellow-rumped, Black) found only at higher elevations. Female *stejnegeri* similar to male but duller. Female *xanthogastra* (not illustrated) similar to a pale, yellow female Hooded Siskin, but lacks yellow on greater wing coverts and often has greater contrast between olive breast and yellow belly. **VOICE** Song (*xanthogastra*) rapid; also may have more mimicry than other siskins. Call a series of reedy, descending "*chew*" notes. Song (*stejnegeri*) slower, perhaps richer, than other siskins, but similar in quality. Calls a descending "*seer*" and rising "*pee-wee?*," also a low chatter. **Co, E, Bo**

2 BLACK SISKIN *Carduelis atrata* 12–12.5 cm (4¾–5 in)

Uncommon to fairly common in montane scrub and puna, 3500–4700 m. Largely black (male) or sooty (female), with relatively little yellow on belly (some individuals have more extensive yellow bellies than do others) and little or no yellow on wing coverts, but a broad yellow band across base of remiges. **VOICE** Song like other siskins. Calls, particularly given in flight, include a descending "*tew*," "*chew*," and a "*hew-li?*" **Bo, Ch**

3 LESSER GOLDFINCH *Carduelis psaltria* * 11 cm (4¼ in)

Uncommon in dry forest and forest edge in north; primarily 1200–2800 m, but locally (or seasonally?) lower. Compare bicolored male to Thick-billed Euphonia (male). Some males (subadults? not illustrated) have green upperparts contrasting with black crown and wings. Female similar to female Hooded Siskin but lacks yellow in wing and tail. **VOICE** Song (North America) similar to siskins, but has many minor notes, creating a melancholy quality. Calls a descending "*p'seew*," a melancholy "*hear-r*," a rolling "*hew-lili*," and a low chatter. **Co, E**

4 CHESTNUT-BREASTED CHLOROPHONIA *Chlorophonia pyrrhophrys* 11.5 cm (4½ in)

Rare to locally uncommon, in humid montane forest along east slope of Andes; 1700–2450 m. Usually found at higher elevations than Blue-naped Chlorophonia but otherwise similar in behavior. Ornate male is distinctive. Female superficially similar to female Blue-naped but has blue crown bordered by a narrow black line and lacks the blue eyering. Cf. also female Golden-rumped Euphonia (which has more uniform underparts and a narrow ochraceous forecrown). **VOICE** Call a unique series of nasal notes: "*bee bee...*" or "*CHEE bee-bee-bee.*" Also a high, thin whistled "*seeee.*" Song a mechanical series of squeaks, liquid notes, and whistles, often with a characteristic nasal note inserted. **Co, E**

5 BLUE-NAPED CHLOROPHONIA *Chlorophonia cyanea* * 10.5–11.5 cm (4¼–4½ in)

Fairly common in canopy of humid montane forest along east slope of Andes and on outlying ridges, 900–2100 m. In southern Peru also occurs locally in Amazonia, near base of Andes. Quiet and unobtrusive; often remains concealed within canopy vegetation, moving relatively little for long periods of time. Readily recognized by contrast between green hood and yellow or yellowish belly, green crown, and narrow blue eyering. **VOICE** Call a descending, whistled "*heu*" or "*seeu*" and a nasal, mechanical "*enk*" and "*dit.*" Song a choppy series of call notes mixed with liquid whistles, short warbles, and piercing notes. Very euphonia-like overall. **Co, E, Br, Bo**

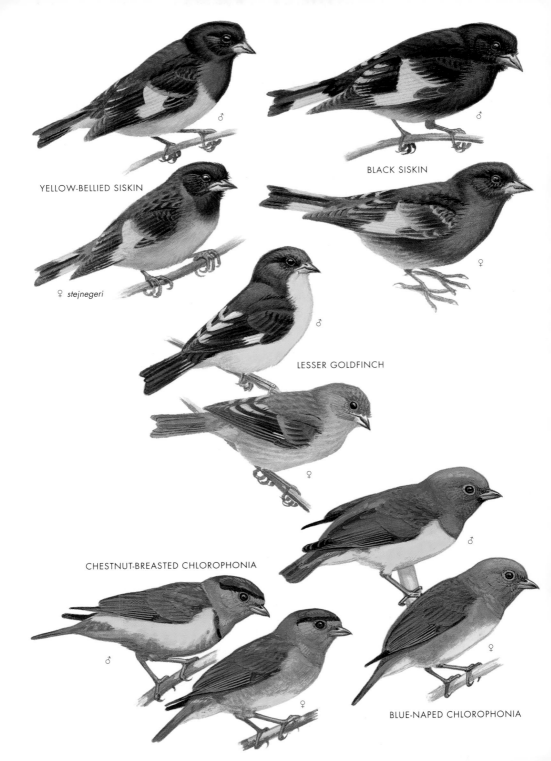

YELLOW-BELLIED SISKIN

♂

♀ *stejnegeri*

BLACK SISKIN

♂

♀

LESSER GOLDFINCH

♂

♀

CHESTNUT-BREASTED CHLOROPHONIA

♂

♂

♀

BLUE-NAPED CHLOROPHONIA

♀

PLATE
303

TYPICAL BLUE-BACKED EUPHONIAS

Males of species on this plate are glossy blue-black above, and most also have a blue-black throat contrasting with yellow or yellow-orange breast and belly. See also plate 304.

1 RUFOUS-BELLIED EUPHONIA *Euphonia rufiventris* * 11–11.5 cm (4¼–4½ in)
Fairly common in humid forest and forest borders, up to 1000 m. Male distinctive. Female usually has noticeably tawny undertail coverts (this color sometimes reduced, however). Otherwise cf. similar female Golden-bellied and Orange-bellied euphonias. **VOICE** Calls include a rapid, deep, ringing chatter: "*tcheetcheetcheetcheetchee*" and a liquid "*whit*," similar to calls of Slender-footed Tyrannulet, Dwarf Tyrant-Manakin, and Golden-bellied Euphonia. Song includes a disjointed, mechanical series of pure whistles, quiet liquid sounds, and short warbles, with various phrases given before any is repeated. **Co, E, Br, Bo**

2 THICK-BILLED EUPHONIA *Euphonia laniirostris* * 11–11.5 cm (4¼–4½ in)
Fairly common. In dry and semideciduous forest in northwest (*hypoxantha*), and in Amazonia in river-edge forest. Up to 1200 m. Large, relatively large-billed. Only euphonia in which male has yellow throat. Immature male similar to female but has blue-black "mask" and yellow throat. Male *hypoxantha* brighter yellow, with white inner webs to outer rectrices; tail spots small in males of southern Amazonia (*zopholega*; not illustrated) or lacking (*melanura*: south to Pasco). Females unpatterned yellow-green with gray lores; cf. male Golden-bellied Euphonia. **VOICE** Calls a single "*seee*," a pair of rising whistles "*see-see*," and a short liquid "*duit*." Song, highly variable, a choppy series of call notes mixed with whistles, warbles, and piercing notes. Similar to other euphonias and Moriche and Epaulet orioles. Second, rarer song very rapid; reminiscent of siskin song, even including mimicry. **Co, E, Br, Bo**

3 ORANGE-BELLIED EUPHONIA *Euphonia xanthogaster* * 11 cm (4¼ in)
Most common, widespread euphonia. Humid montane and lowland forests, up to 2450 m on east slope of Andes and in Amazonia; also rare in humid forest in Tumbes, below 750 m. Crown of male yellower west of Andes and in north, more ochraceous in south (*brunneifrons*). Cf. Purple-throated and Orange-crowned euphonias. On female note distinct gray nape, yellow wash on forecrown, gray breast and buffy center to belly; cf. female Rufous-bellied Euphonia. **VOICE** Call usually a descending note, often doubled: "*dew dew*." Song highly variable, a choppy series of whistles, pops, warbles, and other notes; similar to songs of other euphonias. A second song-type consists of quiet, thin, high, warbles and electric sounds. **Co, E, Br, Bo**

4 PURPLE-THROATED EUPHONIA *Euphonia chlorotica* * 10–10.5 cm (4–4¼ in)
Common below 1400 m in dry forest of intermontane valleys, especially in Marañón. Also locally common in river-edge forest and second growth in Amazonia, and at edges of savanna on Pampas del Heath. Male brighter, purer yellow than similar male Orange-bellied; note smaller crown patch. Female yellow below with white belly; cf. female Golden-bellied. **VOICE** Call a pure whistle, given 1–3 (usually 2) times, even or rising in pitch: "*wee? wee?*" Song a rapid, jerky series of warbles with occasional squeaks and electric notes. Second song type very similar to Golden-rumped, but lacking long wheezy notes. **Co, E, Br, Bo**

5 ORANGE-CROWNED EUPHONIA *Euphonia saturata* 9.5 cm (3¾ in)
Rare; semideciduous forest and edge in Tumbes, below 800 m. Male more ochraceous below than similar male Orange-bellied Euphonia, and tail entirely dark (inner webs of outer rectrices of Orange-bellied largely white, visible from below). Female similar to female Thick-billed Euphonia but slightly smaller with more slender bill; best identified by accompanying male. **VOICE** Calls a ringing series of pure notes: "*tree-tree-tree*" and a sharp "*peet!*" Song a series of ringing, metallic notes, "*tre-tre-tre-tre*," interspersed with whistles and other notes. **Co, E**

6 WHITE-VENTED EUPHONIA *Euphonia minuta* * 9–10 cm (3½–4 in)
Uncommon, in humid forest or forest edge, up to 1500 m. Small. Male brighter yellow than Orange-bellied Euphonia; also note white vent and lower belly, and more restricted forecrown patch. Female has yellow-green breast band, separating light gray throat from whitish belly. **VOICE** Call a rising "*tree-tree*." Song, very similar to Golden-bellied Euphonia (not safely separable?), a variable, short phrase with whistles, pops, and wheezes. **Co, E, Br, Bo**

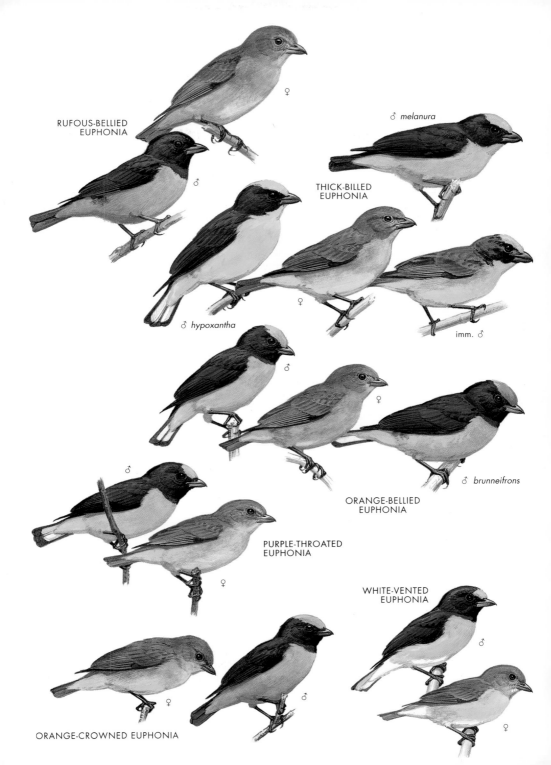

RUFOUS-BELLIED
EUPHONIA

♀

♂

♂ *melanura*

THICK-BILLED
EUPHONIA

♂ *hypoxantha*

♀

imm. ♂

♂

♀

♂ *brunneifrons*

ORANGE-BELLIED
EUPHONIA

♂

PURPLE-THROATED
EUPHONIA

♀

WHITE-VENTED
EUPHONIA

♂

♂

♀

♀

ORANGE-CROWNED EUPHONIA

PLATE
304

EUPHONIAS AND HOUSE SPARROW

Golden-rumped is an attractive but uncommon Andean euphonia, and is another species in which the male is mostly glossy blue-black (see plate 303). The other species of euphonia on this plate are mostly yellow or yellow-green in both sexes. House Sparrow is a native of the Old World; introduced and widely distributed in Peru, especially in urban areas.

1 GOLDEN-RUMPED EUPHONIA *Euphonia cyanocephala* * 11–11.5 cm (4¼–4½ in)

Uncommon, at borders of humid and semideciduous forest in Marañón Valley, also on west slope of Andes in Piura and locally on east slope. Primarily 1300–2600 m, but occasionally wanders (only in austral winter?) to lowlands of southern Amazonia. Both sexes readily recognized by light blue nape (but see also female Chestnut-breasted Chlorophonia). Also note large yellow rump patch of male. **VOICE** Calls include a descending whistle: "*heu*." Song a long, rapid series of liquid warbles with occasional squeaks and electric notes punctuated by longer wheezy notes that rise or fall. **Co, E, Br, Bo**

2 GOLDEN-BELLIED EUPHONIA *Euphonia chrysopasta* * 11 cm (4¼ in)

Fairly common in humid forest and forest edge, especially in floodplain forest, up to 1200 m. Both sexes have large white loral spot and gray nape; male also has narrow white chin. Often switches tail from side to side, especially when singing. Compare male to female Thick-billed Euphonia; compare female to similar females of Rufous-bellied and Orange-bellied euphonias. **VOICE** Call a rising, liquid "*wick*," similar to calls of Slender-footed Tyrannulet or Dwarf Tyrant-Manakin, but louder, more forceful. Song a staccato, repeated phrase containing various liquid whistles, pops, and electric wheezes, for example: "*tee-tick-tokzzzzWHEE?*" Very short compared to other euphonias. A second song-type is a choppy series of whistles and short chip notes that is similar to song of Thick-billed Euphonia or Moriche or Epaulet orioles. **Co, E, Br, Bo**

3 BRONZE-GREEN EUPHONIA *Euphonia mesochrysa* * 10.5 cm (4¼ in)

Uncommon in humid montane forest along east slope of Andes and on outlying ridges, 1000–2000 m, locally down to 450 m in Puno. Elevational range higher than most other species (apart from Golden-rumped and Orange-bellied euphonias). Drab. Male readily recognized by the small but bright yellow forecrown (cf. immature male Thick-billed Euphonia). Female superficially similar to female Orange-bellied, but has greenish yellow throat and a whitish belly. **VOICE** Song variable, but usually a whistled note followed by one or more ringing rattles, for example: "*peew brrrrrrr brr brr*." Calls include similar ringing rattles as in song. **Co, E, Bo**

[PLUMBEOUS EUPHONIA *Euphonia plumbea*] 8.5–9 cm (3½–3¾ in)

Known only from a few sight records; apparently very local in scrubby or low-stature forest on sandy soils in the Mayo Valley (San Martín) and perhaps northern Loreto. Tiny. Male only euphonia that is gray (not "blue" or green) above; not particularly similar to any other species, but cf. male Rufous-vented Euphonia (which is only other euphonia with entirely dark crown and dark throat contrasting with paler belly). Female similar in pattern to male but duller; lacks white lores of female Golden-bellied Euphonia and underparts are more extensively yellow. Cf. also female White-vented Euphonia. **VOICE** Song (Brazil) a short phrase containing a jerky series of liquid warbles with occasional squeaks and electric notes. Call (San Martín) a pair of rising whistles: "*wee-wee?*," very similar to call of Purple-throated Euphonia. **Co, Br**

4 HOUSE SPARROW *Passer domesticus* * 14–15 cm (5½–6 in)

Not native, and a human commensal: present, and often common, in towns and villages and adjacent fields, but rarely encountered far from human habitations. Widespread along coast, up to 750 m; also present very locally in Andes, primarily along Central Highway, and at Pucallpa. Forages primarily on the ground, often in flocks. A stocky sparrow. Male readily recognized by black throat, gray crown, and rufous nape. Female and immatures quite drab, but note broad pale superciliary, plain face, streaked back, and plain breast. **VOICE** Various chirps, quiet rattles, and twittering sounds. Song, often given by several males from 1 bush, is an excited cacophony of chirping. **Co, E, Br, Bo, Ch**

GOLDEN-RUMPED EUPHONIA

GOLDEN-BELLIED
EUPHONIA

BRONZE-GREEN EUPHONIA

PLUMBEOUS EUPHONIA

HOUSE SPARROW

VOCAL CREDITS

José Alvarez A.: Gray-legged Tinamou *Crypturellus duidae*; Allpahauyo Antbird *Percnostola arenarum*, calls; Zimmer's Antbird *Myrmeciza castanea*, calls, in part; Spotted Antpitta *Hylopezus macularius*, song; Cinnamon-crested Spadebill *Platyrinchus saturatus*

John Arvin: Sungrebe *Heliornis fulica*, calls (in part)

Eustace Barnes: Red-billed Ground-Cuckoo *Neomorphus pucheranii*, song

Alfredo Begazo: Royal Flycatcher *Onychorhynchus coronatus occidentalis*, song; Yellow Warbler *Dendroica petechia peruviana*, song; Red-crested Finch *Coryphospingus cucullatus*, song; Plain-tailed Warbling-Finch *Poospiza alticola*, song; Raimondi's Yellow-Finch *Sicalis raimondii*, song

Dan Christian: Bamboo Antshrike *Cymbilaimus sanctaemariae*, call (in part)

Benjamin Clock: Black Rail *Laterallus jamaicensis*

Mario Cohn-Haft: Rufous Potoo *Nyctibius bracteatus*; Snethlage's Tody-Tyrant *Hemitriccus minor*, song

Paul Coopmans: Cocha Antshrike *Thamnophilus praecox*, calls; Ochre-striped Antpitta *Grallaria dignissima*, call; Amazonian Scrub-Flycatcher *Sublegatus obscurior*, calls (in part); Bicolored Conebill *Conirostrum bicolor*

Paul Donahue: White-chinned Woodcreeper *Dendrocincla merula*, song

A. Bennett Hennessey: Wattled Curassow *Crax globulosa*

Charles Hesse: Rufous-breasted Warbling-Finch *Poospiza rubecula*

Phyllis Isler and Mort Isler: Spot-backed Antbird *Hylophylax naevius*, comments on geographic variation in song; Bay Antpitta *Grallaria capitalis*, call; Red-rumped Bush-Tyrant *Cnemarchus erythropygius*; Pardusco *Nephelornis oneilli*, song; Rufous-browed Hemispingus *Hemispingus rufosuperciliaris*, song and call

Alvaro Jaramillo: Black-necked Stilt *Himantopus mexicanus melanurus*

Niels Krabbe: Ornate Tinamou *Nothoprocta ornata*, call when flushed; Rufous-chested Dotterel *Charadrius modestus*; Stripe-headed Antpitta *Grallaria andicolus*, calls (in part); Correndera Pipit *Anthus correndera*; Pardusco *Nephelornis oneilli*, calls; Rufous-browed Hemispingus *Hemispingus rufosuperciliaris*, call; Rufous-eared Brush-Finch *Atlapetes rufigenis forbesi*, song; Raimondi's Yellow-Finch *Sicalis raimondii*, call; Great Inca-Finch *Incaspiza pulchra*, call

Huw Lloyd: Great Horned Owl *Bubo virginianus*; Great Spinetail *Siptornopsis hypochondriacus*, calls (in part); Elusive Antpitta *Grallaria eludens*, call; Spectacled Bristle-Tyrant *Phylloscartes orbitalis*, song; Rufous-webbed Bush-Tyrant *Polioxolmis rufipennis*, song; Cerulean-capped Manakin *Lepidothrix coeruleocapilla*, call; Giant Conebill *Oreomanes fraseri*, dawn song; Guira Tanager *Hemithraupis guira*, song; Black-masked Finch *Coryphaspiza melanotis*, song; Rufous-eared Brush-Finch *Atlapetes rufigenis rufigenis*, call; Short-tailed Finch *Idiopsar brachyurus*, song and call; Plain-tailed Warbling-Finch *Poospiza alticola*, call

Curtis Marantz: Snethlage's Tody-Tyrant *Hemitriccus minor*

Todd Mark: Pale-billed Antpitta *Grallaria carrikeri*, call; White-crowned Tapaculo, *Scytalopus atratus*, song north of the Río Marañón; Wedge-tailed Grass-Finch *Emberizoides herbicola*, call; White-winged Brush-Finch *Atlapetes leucopterus paynteri*, song and call

Sjoerd Mayer: Taczanowski's Tinamou *Nothoprocta taczanowskii*; Line-fronted Canastero *Asthenes urubambensis*, call;

White-crested Elaenia *Elaenia albiceps albiceps*, song and calls; Andean Tyrant *Knipolegus signatus cabanisi*, flight display

John Moore: Bar-bellied Woodcreeper *Hylexetastes stresemanni*, call

Jonas Nilsson: Taczanowski's Tinamou *Nothoprocta taczanowskii*; Cloud-forest Screech-Owl *Megascops marshalli*; Ruddy Spinetail *Synallaxis rutilans*, call; Large-footed Tapaculo *Scytalopus macropus*, Junín vocalization; Green-throated Tanager *Tangara argyrofenges*

Patrick O'Donnell: Gray-bellied Hawk *Accipiter poliogaster*

John Rowlett: Brown Tinamou *Crypturellus obsoletus*, San Martín (*Crypturellus obsoletus* [*castaneus?*])

Thomas Valqui: Band-winged Nightjar *Caprimulgus longirostris decussatus*; Plumbeous Euphonia *Euphonia plumbea*, call

Mark Van Beirs: Orange-browed Hemispingus *Hemispingus calophrys*

Barry Walker: Stripe-faced Wood-Quail *Odontophorus balliviani*, call; Rufous-necked Wood-Rail *Aramides axillaris*; Rufous-bellied Seedsnipe *Attagis gayi*, call (in part); Red-rumped Woodpecker *Veniliornis kirkii*, call; Grayish Miner *Geositta maritima*, song; Dark-winged Miner *Geositta saxicolina*; White-bellied Cinclodes *Cinclodes palliatus*; Streak-backed Canastero *Asthenes wyatti*; Puna Canastero *Asthenes sclateri*; Junin Canastero *Asthenes virgata*; Cordilleran Canastero *Asthenes modesta*, song; Cactus Canastero *Asthenes cactorum*; Streak-throated Canastero *Asthenes humilis*, song; Great Inca-Finch *Incaspiza pulchra*, call; Rufous-backed Inca-Finch *Incaspiza personata*, call; Little Inca-Finch *Incaspiza watkinsi*

Bret Whitney: Napo Sabrewing *Campylopterus villaviscensio*, call; Brown Violetear *Colibri delphinae*, call; Sapphire-spangled Emerald *Amazilia lactea*, song; Green-and-rufous Kingfisher *Chloroceryle inda*, song; Rusty-breasted Nunlet *Nonnula rubecula*; White-chinned Woodcreeper *Dendrocincla merula*, song; Zimmer's Woodcreeper *Xiphorhynchus kienerii*; Ocellated Woodcreeper *Xiphorhynchus ocellatus perplexus*; Bluish-slate Antshrike *Thamnomanes schistogynus*, comments on song; Rio Suno Antwren *Myrmotherula sunensis*, call (in part); Black Bushbird *Neoctantes niger*, call (in part); Spot-backed Antbird *Hylophylax naevius*, comments on geographic variation in song; Black-faced Antthrush *Formicarius analis*, comments on song; Spotted Antpitta *Hylopezus macularius*, call; Spectacled Bristle-Tyrant *Phylloscartes orbitalis*, song; Southern Scrub-Flycatcher *Sublegatus modestus*, song; Andean Tyrant *Knipolegus signatus cabanisi*, call; Crested Becard *Pachyramphus validus*; Black-and-white Becard *Pachyramphus albogriseus guayaquilensis*; Dusky Piha *Lipaugus fuscocinereus*; White-crowned Manakin *Dixiphia pipra coracina*, song; Chilean Swallow *Tachycineta meyeni*; Iquitos Gnatcatcher *Polioptila clementsi*; Wing-banded Wren *Microcerculus bambla*, call; Short-tailed Finch *Idiopsar brachyurus*, call; Yellow-shouldered Grosbeak *Parkerthraustes humeralis*, song; Purple-throated Euphonia *Euphonia chlorotica*, second song type; Golden-bellied Euphonia *Euphonia chrysopasta*, notes on song

Kevin Zimmer: Pavonine Quetzal *Pharomachrus pavoninus*, call (in part); Green-and-rufous Kingfisher *Chloroceryle inda*, song; Red-rumped Woodpecker *Veniliornis kirkii*, calls (in part); Golden-green Woodpecker *Piculus chrysochloros*, calls (in part); Rusty-backed Spinetail *Cranioleuca vulpina*; Pearly Antshrike *Megastictus margaritatus*, call (in part); Black-tailed Antbird *Myrmoborus melanurus*, call; Yellow-olive Flycatcher *Tolmomyias sulphurescens insignis*

VOCAL REFERENCES

Coopmans, P., J. V. Moore, N. Krabbe, O. Jahn, K. S. Berg, M. Lysinger, L. Navarrete, and R. S. Ridgely. 2004. The birds of southwest Ecuador (CD). San Jose, CA: John V. Moore Nature Recordings.

Evans, W. R., and M. O'Brien. 2002. Flight calls of migratory birds: eastern North American landbirds (CD-ROM). Old Bird Inc.

Hardy, J. W., B. B. Coffey, and G. B. Reynard (revised by T. Taylor). 1999. Voices of the New World owls (cassette). Gainesville, FL: ARA Records.

Hardy, J. W., G. B. Reynard, and B. B. Coffey. 1989. Voices of the New World pigeons and doves (cassette). Gainesville, FL: ARA Records.

Hardy, J. W., G. B. Reynard, and T. Taylor. 1996. Voices of the New World rails (cassette). Gainesville, Florida: ARA Records.

Hardy, J. W., J. Vielliard, and R. Straneck. 1993. Voices of the tinamous (cassette). Gainesville, FL: ARA Records.

Isler, P. R., and B. M. Whitney. 2002. Songs of the antbirds (CD). Ithaca, NY: Cornell Laboratory of Ornithology.

Jahn, O., J. V. Moore, P. Mena Valenzuela, N. Krabbe, P. Coopmans, M. Lysinger, and R. S. Ridgely. 2002. The birds of northwest Ecuador, vol. 2 (CD). San Jose, CA: John V. Moore Nature Recordings.

Krabbe, N., J. V. Moore, P. Coopmans, M. Lysinger, and R. S. Ridgely. 2001. Birds of the Ecuadorian highlands (CD). San Jose, CA: John V. Moore Nature Recordings.

Krabbe, N., and J. Nilsson. 2003. Birds of Ecuador (DVD). Westernieland, Netherlands: Bird Songs International.

Lysinger, M., J. V. Moore, N. Krabbe, P. Coopmans, D. F. Lane, L. Navarrete, J. Nilsson, and R. S. Ridgely. 2005. The birds of eastern Ecuador: the foothills and lower subtropics (CD). San Jose, CA: John V. Moore Nature Recordings.

Maccormick, A., and R. MacLeod. nd. Birds of the Bolivian Yungas: a sound guide to Carrasco National Park, Bolivia (CD). Glasgow, Scotland: Bolivian Yungas Project, Glasgow University.

Mayer, S. 1999. Birds of Bolivia (CD). Westernieland, Netherlands: Bird Songs International.

———. Unpublished. Birds of Peru, Bolivia, and Paraguay (DVD). Westernieland, Netherlands: Bird Songs International.

Moore, J. V. 1994. Ecuador: more bird vocalizations from the lowland rainforest, vol. 1 (cassette). San Jose, CA: John V. Moore Nature Recordings.

———. 1996. Ecuador: more bird vocalizations from the lowland rainforest, vol. 2 (cassette). San Jose, CA: John V. Moore Nature Recordings.

———. 1997. Ecuador: more bird vocalizations from the lowland rainforest, vol. 3 (cassette). San Jose, CA: John V. Moore Nature Recordings.

Moore, J. V., P. Coopmans, R. S. Ridgely, and M. Lysinger. 1999. The birds of northwest Ecuador, vol. 1 (CD). San Jose, CA: John V. Moore Nature Recordings.

Moore, J. V., and M. Lysinger. 1997. The birds of Cabanas San Isidro (cassette). San Jose, CA: John V. Moore Nature Recordings.

Schulenberg, T. S. 2000a. Voices of Andean birds, vol. 1: Birds of the hill forest of southern Peru and Bolivia (CD). Ithaca, NY: Cornell Laboratory of Ornithology.

———. 2000b. Voices of Andean birds, vol. 2: Birds of the cloud forest of southern Peru and Bolivia (CD). Ithaca, NY: Cornell Laboratory of Ornithology.

Schulenberg, T. S., C. A. Marantz, and P. H. English. 2000a. Voices of Amazonian birds. Birds of the rainforest of southern Peru and northern Bolivia, vol. 1: Tinamous (Tinamidae) through barbets (Capitonidae) (CD). Ithaca, NY: Cornell Laboratory of Ornithology.

———. 2000b. Voices of Amazonian birds. Birds of the rainforest of southern Peru and northern Bolivia, vol. 2: Toucans (Ramphastidae) through antbirds (Thamnophilidae) (CD). Ithaca, NY: Cornell Laboratory of Ornithology.

———. 2000c. Voices of Amazonian birds. Birds of the rainforest of southern Peru and northern Bolivia, vol. 3: Ground antbirds (Formicariidae) through jays (Corvidae) (CD). Ithaca, NY: Cornell Laboratory of Ornithology.

Stouffer, P. C., L. N. Naka, M. Cohn-Haft, C. A. Marantz, and R. O. Bierregaard, Jr. Unpublished. Voices of the Brazilian Amazon (CD).

Whitney, B. M., T. A. Parker, III, G. F. Budney, C. A. Munn, and J. W. Bradbury. 2002. Voices of the New World parrots (CD). Ithaca, NY: Cornell Laboratory of Ornithology.

ARTISTS' CREDITS

David Beadle: Plate 8 (Ruddy Duck, two figures resting on water); Plate 16 (except Southern Fulmar, Peruvian Diving-Petrel); Plate 17 (except Cape Petrel); Plate 21 (Red-tailed Tropicbird); Plate 63 (Sooty Tern; Black Tern, basic plumage)

F. P. Bennett: Plate 91 (hummingbirds); Plates 92–111

Peter S. Burke: Plate 5 (Lesser Rhea); Plate 12 (Pied-billed, White-tufted, and Great grebes); Plates 13–15; Plate 16 (Southern Fulmar, Peruvian Diving-Petrel); Plate 17 (Cape Petrel); Plates 18–19; Plate 21 (Humboldt Penguin); Plate 60 (except Herring Gull); Plate 61 (except Gray-hooded and Laughing gulls, and Kittiwake); Plate 62 (Sandwich, Elegant, and Peruvian terns, and skimmer); Plate 63 (South American, Common, Arctic, and Snowy-crowned terns); Plates 296–300

Hilary Burn: Plate 68 (Red-fan Parrot); Plates 69–76

Dale Dyer: Plates 1–4 (tinamous); Plates 6–7; Plate 8 (except Ruddy Duck, two figures resting on water; and except for Sungrebe); Plate 9 (wood-quail); Plate 12 (Least, Titicaca, Silvery and Junin grebes); Plate 45 (trumpeters, Sunbittern); Plate 51 (seedsnipes); Plate 60 (Herring Gull); Plate 61 (Gray-hooded and Laughing gulls, and kittiwake); Plate 62 (Large-billed, Royal, Yellow-billed and Least terns); Plate 63 (Gull-billed Tern; Black Tern, alternate plumage); Plate 239–240; Plates 257–261; Plate 262 (except Fawn-breasted Tanager); Plate 263 (except Orange-throated Tanager); Plate 264; Plate 271 (Green Honeycreeper, conebills); Plates 272–276; Plate 280 (seedeaters); Plate 283 (except Slaty Finch); Plates 284–285; Plates 292–295; Plate 302 (chlorophonias); Plate 303; Plate 304 (except House Sparrow)

Daniel F. Lane: Plate 8 (Sungrebe); Plate 9 (chachalacas); Plates 10–11; Plate 45 (wood-rails); Plates 46–49; Plate 50 (Wattled Jacana); Plate 79 (Hoatzin); Plates 80–90; Plate 91 (swifts); Plate 137 (Scale-throated Earthcreeper, in part); Plate 156 (Pale-billed Hornero, in part); Plate 191 (Slaty Elaenia, juvenile); Plates 193–202; Plate 203 (Tawny-crowned Pygmy-Tyrant); Plates 242–244; Plate 245 (swallows); Plate 252 (Pale-vented Thrush)

Lawrence B. McQueen: Plate 59; Plates 64–67; Plate 68 (quail-doves); Plates 77–78; Plate 79 (except Hoatzin); Plates 112–121; Plates 125–190; Plate 191 (except Slaty Elaenia, juvenile); Plates 192–202; Plate 203 (except Tawny-crowned Pygmy-Tyrant); Plates 204–227; Plate 228 (except Black-faced and Pompadour cotingas); Plate 229 (except Purple-throated Fruitcrow); Plate 231 (Shrike-like Cotinga); Plate 234 (schiffornis); Plates 246–251; Plate 252 (except Pale-vented Thrush); Plates 253–256

John P. O'Neill: Plates 122–124; Plate 241; Plate 245 (pipits); Plate 262 (Fawn-breasted Tanager); Plate 263 (Orange-throated Tanager); Plates 265–270; Plate 271 (tanagers, Golden-collared Honeycreeper); Plates 277–279; Plate 280 (seed-finch, finches); Plates 281–282; Plate 283 (Slaty Finch); Plates 286–291; Plate 301; Plate 302 (except chlorophonias); Plate 304 (House Sparrow)

Diane Pierce: Plate 5 (except Lesser Rhea); Plates 23–26

H. Douglas Pratt: Plate 20; Plate 21 (except Humboldt Penguin, Red-tailed Tropicbird); Plate 22

N. John Schmitt: Plates 27–44

Barry Van Dusen: Plate 50 (except Wattled Jacana); Plate 51 (except seedsnipes); Plates 52–58

Sophie Webb: Plate 228 (Black-faced and Pompadour cotingas); Plate 229 (Purple-throated Fruitcrow); Plate 230; Plate 231 (except Shrike-like Cotinga); Plates 232–233; Plate 234 (except schiffornis); Plates 235–238

INDEX

English names are printed in roman type; scientific names are in *italics*.

INDEX